BY LEONARD BAKER

THE JOHNSON ECLIPSE:
A President's Vice Presidency

BACK TO BACK:
The Duel Between FDR and the Supreme Court

THE GUARANTEED SOCIETY

ROOSEVELT AND PEARL HARBOR

BRAHMIN IN REVOLT

John Marshall

A LIFE IN LAW

WE

MUST NEVER

FORGET

THAT IT IS

A

CONSTITUTION

WE ARE

EXPOUNDING

JOHN MARSHALL

1819

JOHN MARSHALL

A LIFE
IN LAW

Leonard Baker

Macmillan Publishing Co., Inc.
NEW YORK

Collier Macmillan Publishers
LONDON

COPYRIGHT © 1974 BY LEONARD BAKER

ALL RIGHTS RESERVED. No part of this book may be reproduced or transmitted in any form or by any means, electronic or mechanical, including photocopying, recording or by any information storage and retrieval system, without permission in writing from the Publisher.

Macmillan Publishing Co., Inc.
866 Third Avenue, New York, N.Y. 10022
Collier-Macmillan Canada Ltd.

FIRST PRINTING 1974

PRINTED IN THE UNITED STATES OF AMERICA

Library of Congress Cataloging in Publication Data
Baker, Leonard.
  John Marshall: a life in law.
  Bibliography: p.
  1. Marshall, John, 1755-1835.   I. Title.
KF8745.M3B3   347'.73'2634 [B]   73-2751
ISBN 0-02-506360-X

) *To LIVA* (

Acknowledgments

THE STORY OF JOHN MARSHALL is the story of one man's devotion to law and his efforts to persuade his country of the wisdom of such a devotion. It is an interesting story from a historical viewpoint. It is an essential story from the viewpoint of a modern society in which violence is a way of life and men and nations share in their disregard for the law.

For me the story began in 1958 when I first sat in the press section of the United States Supreme Court. I am indebted to the Justices of that Court, the lawyers who argued before it, and the individuals who sought the Court as their medium of recourse and complaint. They demonstrate the value of a life in law.

At the College of William and Mary in Williamsburg, Virginia, the Marshall papers are being edited in preparation for publication, a project of the Institute of Early American History; and the staff there was most generous to me. The National Historical Publications Commission made available to me the thousands of documents found in its fifteen-year search for Marshall papers in the National Archives.

The staffs of the manuscript depositories listed in the bibliography to this book were invariably kind to me and my wife when we visited them in person or sought their assistance through the mails.

I have taken advantage of the recent studies of this period and of the studies of John Marshall. I wish to express my admiration for the work of these scholars.

My thanks to the descendants of John Marshall and to their families—Dr. H. Norton Mason and Mrs. Mary Douthat Higgins of Richmond, Virginia; Mrs. Katherine Marshall Williams of Alexandria, Virginia; Richard C. Marshall of Washington, D.C.; Robert Morris Marshall, Sr., of Laurel, Maryland; Mrs. Richard T. Ewing of Rockville, Maryland; and Mr. and Mrs. James Marshall Plaskitt, Mrs. James Green, and Mrs. John D. McCarty, all of Fauquier County, Virginia. They not only filled me with their family lore but demonstrated to me the graciousness and courtesy that was so much a way of life for John Marshall and his family.

I was also assisted by John Eisenhard, Mr. and Mrs. Paul B. Sullivan, Paul Wells, and Mr. and Mrs. Michael Hudoba of Fauquier County; Dr. Glenn H. Pratt of the Monumental Church in Richmond, Virginia; Kenneth C. Judd and Mrs. Bernice Usdane of Washington, D.C.; Judy Sharff and the Rev. Neil J. Twombly, S.J., of Georgetown University; Edwin C. Hutten of Buffalo, New York; and Harley P. Holden, curator of the Harvard University Archives.

The Macmillan Company exhibited great faith in me and this project, and I wish to extend my appreciation to that organization and to my editors there, first Peter V. Ritner and then Ray A. Roberts, and to my copy editor, Miss Carole Freddo.

Contents

Illustrations

ILLUSTRATIONS

ILLUSTRATIONS

Book One:

SOLDIER

I

WEDNESDAY April 19, 1775, dawned clear and cold, shedding slowly its light on the fifty men standing in uneven ranks on the Lexington village green. Those men with muskets held them casually, tucked under their arms or by the barrels with the butts resting on the ground. Several rubbed sleep from their eyes with grimy hands or scratched beard stubble on their chins. They shuffled their feet, looking from Captain Jonas Parker, standing in front of them, to the British Redcoats, smoothly forming into ranks three men deep one hundred yards away, the morning sun dancing down the line of their bayonets.

"Stand your ground," Jonas Parker ordered the Americans. "Don't fire unless fired upon. But if they mean to have a war, let it begin here."

As if in answer, a British officer's command boomed out to them: "Lay down your arms, you damned rebels, and disperse."

Again: "Damn you! Why don't you disperse!"

The Americans did not disperse. The British did not relent. Within a few moments eight Americans lay dead and the British were marching to Concord, to the second bloodletting of the American Revolution.

Horsemen carried the news of the battles to every village in the thirteen American colonies. British and Americans actually had fired upon each other! The war had begun! And—as they had done at Lexington—the farmers and shopkeepers, professional men and artisans came together in their muster fields, some in linen and boots with silver buckles, others in homespun cloth and shoes with buckles of dull brass. They brought their long muskets, or flaring-mouthed blunderbusses, and some even, short fowling pieces. Often with bravado but sometimes with evident nervousness they practiced what they thought was the manual of arms and sighted along the barrels of their weapons; rarely did they fire—powder and ball were too scarce to waste on practice shots.

One such company of militiamen met a few weeks after

the battles of Lexington and Concord at the muster field twenty miles from the Fauquier County Courthouse in western Virginia. The members had heard little detail of what had happened, and they had come to learn the news and, if necessary, to assume the responsibilities they understood to be theirs every time they lined up on that field with muskets in their hands.

The captain who had called them together did not appear that day but the second-in-command, nineteen-year-old John Marshall, did. John was the eldest son of Thomas Marshall, who himself had once drilled this troop and was one of the most prominent men in the county as well as in the Virginia colony. His son was well known to these militiamen. So they crowded around young John. What had happened? they wanted to know What was going to happen?

Although only nineteen, John Marshall had the appearance and physique of a man. He was six feet tall, straight and slender. The face was round, "nearly a circle," with "an upright forehead, rather low . . . terminated in a horizontal line by a mass of raven-black hair of unusual thickness and strength." He was dark, sun-browned, and dressed as a frontiersman, in pale-blue hunting shirt and trousers of the same color fringed with white, and with a round black hat, a buck's tail hanging from it for a cockade.

Years later it was said of him that his most striking feature that day—as it would be when he was a politician fighting for the adoption of the Constitution, when he was an articulate spokesman for the United States in the diplomatic councils of Europe, and finally when he was Chief Justice of the United States—was his eyes, "dark to blackness, strong and penetrating, beaming with intelligence and good nature."[1]

But in one respect John Marshall was little different that day from many of the young men answering calls on the muster fields of the thirteen colonies. The glamor and excitement of military action caught him as it did them. The fife and drum summoned to romantic adventure. "The controversy between Great Britain and her colonies had assumed so serious an aspect as almost to monopolize the attention of the old and the young," John Marshall said. "I engaged in it with all the zeal and enthusiasm which belonged to my age."[2]

As the members of the militia company crowded around him that spring day in 1775, Marshall took his first step in a career of public service that was to last for the next sixty years. That career was to make him a leading participant in man's greatest adventure—the adventure of law. Always before government had been imposed upon man; now man would willingly accept only a government of his own choosing. Previously man bowed to physical prowess; now he bowed only to reasoned justice. Previously man had settled his disputes by the sword; now he would settle them by the law. As well as man's greatest adventure, this was his greatest challenge: to live under the rule of law. And it was John Marshall's struggle to establish the rule of law.

He told the other militiamen that the captain would not be present, and that he had been appointed lieutenant "instead of a better." He came to meet them, he said, as fellow soldiers who were likely to be called on to defend their country, and their own rights and liberties. The Americans and British had fired on each other in Massachusetts, he reported, and the Americans were victorious—a description that would have surprised the Americans who had actually been present at the battle scenes. Marshall then said that more fighting was anticipated, "that soldiers were called for," and that it was time to brighten their firearms and learn to use them in the field. If they all would fall into a single line, he would demonstrate the new manual of arms. Just for that reason, he said, he had brought his musket with him.

He went through the drill with each word and motion "deliberately pronounced and performed" before asking the men to follow his command. A participant recalled years later that Marshall then "proceeded to exercise them, with the most perfect temper. Never did man possess a temper more happy, or if otherwise, more subdued or better disciplined." When the manual exercises were finished, Marshall asked the men to form a circle around him and he spoke to them for approximately an hour. Said one witness:

> I remember, for I was near him, that he spoke at the close of his speech of the Minute Battalion, about to be raised, and said he was going into it, and expected to be joined by many of his hearers. He then challenged an acquaintance to a game of quoits, and then closed the day with foot races, and other athletic exercises, at which there was no betting.[3]

John Marshall had walked the ten miles to the muster field from his father's house at Oak Hill. That night he walked back, reaching the frame cottage a little after sunset.

The Americans in the late 1700s had obscure origins. One who knew John Marshall wrote that Marshall's grandfather "was a native of Wales [who] settled in Westmoreland County, Virginia, about the year 1730 when he married Elizabeth Markham, a native of England."[4] Other accounts record the Marshall ancestor arriving earlier in Virginia; still others, that he was born there. Record-keeping in the 1600s and early 1700s was not the most accurate, and the exodus of people from England to the New World too great then to successfully trace the origins of John Marshall's grandfather. Undoubtedly the first of that family to come to America was one without prospects in his native land who risked an ocean voyage in a stubby wooden boat, as so many did, because of the promise of fifty acres free for himself and every member of his family. In doing this, the unknown Marshall ancestor was helping to establish a tradition that has ever since been a part of America: the search for a better life.

In the first half of the eighteenth century, however, the Marshall family had become sufficiently established to be traced. By 1728 John Marshall's grandfather, also named John Marshall, had acquired two hundred acres of second-rate land in Westmoreland County that John Washington and Thomas Pope had patented but failed to use. As with all men of the time who lived in undeveloped wooded regions, this Marshall was known as "of the Forest," and so "John of the Forest"—whatever his origins— is the first male Marshall ancestor history can positively identify.

This John of the Forest was industrious and successful in the breeding of slaves, as were many of his contemporaries. When he died, according to George Washington's biographer Douglas Southall Freeman, he possessed seventeen Negroes, liquor and herb stills, a fiddle, and a variety of other items with a total value of 730 pounds. He also had a son, Thomas, who was two years older than his neighbor George Washington, and who became for the young George someone to look up to.[5]

This early relationship between George Washington and Thomas Marshall, John's father, lasted throughout the two men's lives and had as much impact on the young John Marshall as it did upon his father. George Washington was his hero, model, and, finally, benefactor.

When John of the Forest died in 1752, he divided his seventeen slaves among his wife, five daughters, and four sons. Thomas, the eldest son, received two slaves and also the two-hundred-acre estate in Westmoreland County.[6]

Thomas realized the land would not be productive and determined to move to western Virginia. For him this meant a settlement in Prince William County known as Germantown. There he married the daughter of a minister of the Church of England, Mary Randolph Keith. She was the great-granddaughter of William Randolph and Mary Isham, a family that could trace its ancestry back several hundred years and also trace its numerous progeny in succeeding generations of American history through such names—in addition to that of John Marshall—as Thomas Jefferson, Edmund Randolph, and the Lees of Virginia.

Thomas Marshall and his young bride rented the iron-worker's cottage and settled down. John, their first child, was born September 24, 1755.

One writer of this period commented about family life in colonial Virginia that "children increase and thrive so well there that they themselves will sufficiently supply the defect of servants, and in small time become a nation of themselves sufficient to people the country."[7] To this nation Thomas and Mary Marshall contributed handsomely. John was the first of fifteen children they had. It is a mark of their diligence as parents and of the healthfulness of frontier life that all fifteen children grew to adulthood.

At Germantown, Thomas Marshall was the American agent for Lord Fairfax, the Britisher who owned much of northern Virginia, and he also did some farming. About ten years after his first child had been born, he moved further west, leasing 350 acres from the Lee family and building a log house for himself called the Hollow.

In one way Thomas Marshall was different from his contemporaries. Although he saw land as a site for a relatively small farm, or as an investment for later generations of Marshalls, he never visualized it as the self-contained center of his world as George Washington visualized Mount Vernon, or as the cultural achievement of his career as Thomas Jefferson did Monticello. He never developed a Montpelier to support his son as the father of James Madison did. Thomas Marshall was a wanderer, restlessly moving on; and his son John felt about the land as his father did. In later years he owned farms in western Virginia and often returned to enjoy the beauty of the country. He was also a land speculator on a grand scale, seeing investment as a means of guaranteeing the comfort of his family for generations. But home for him was not a pretentious estate; it was never more than a simple brick building in Richmond or a plain farmhouse.

Thomas Marshall was a prominent member of his community. In 1759 Fauquier County split off from Prince William, and he was appointed surveyor by "the President and Masters of the College of William and Mary." The second item recorded in the county deed book is a bond for 500 pounds placed by Thomas Marshall, his brother-in-law James Keith, and Cuthbert Bullitt as a financial guarantee that Marshall would "truly and faithfully to the best of his knowledge and honor" fulfill his responsibilities.[8]

His job as surveyor was to divide Fauquier into districts

and then list the residents of each district for tax collection purposes (taxes were collected then on a per capita basis rather than on the amount of property owned). He also was assigned the task of collecting taxes in the first district after it was formed "below the Mountain Church to the county line."[9]

In 1767 Thomas Marshall was appointed Fauquier County sheriff, a fee-collecting office, and he apparently received a percentage of the fees collected as his income. For this post he had to put up a bond of 1,000 pounds. He pledged the money along with three other men.[10] Again he was obviously successful. About this time, for example, he won a suit against a man named John Ariss for 500 pounds, no small sum when most commerce was conducted by the barter system.[11]

During these years in Fauquier Thomas Marshall continued his relationship with George Washington. Family tradition says that he fought alongside Washington in the French and Indian Wars, but there is no documentation to support it. The two men did remain close, however. Both were surveyors of the Virginia land owned by Lord Fairfax. In 1764 they were two of five men appointed by the Virginia legislature "to examine, state, and settle the accounts of such pay, provisions, arms, and necessaries for the militia of the counties for which they are appointed commissioners respectively."[12] Washington's diary records that Thomas Marshall often dined at Mount Vernon in the years before the Revolutionary War.[13]

In contrast to the high social life of the plantations, the center for the frontier families was the church and the vestry, which controlled it. The vestry, which had come into existence when the Church of England was established as the state church in Virginia, was the lay body designed to supervise the ecclesiastical affairs of the parish. Twelve men were selected to be members of this governing body. In the 1600s these men had been appointed, but in the 1700s they were elected by the members of the church. The vestry, then, was the smallest governmental unit in Virginia; originally created to run the affairs of the church, it became the governing body of the parish. As one commentator points out:

> The vestry publicly published all laws pertaining to servants, slaves, morals, and vital statistics; it posted notices about lost property, stray animals, runaway servants, and the docking of entails; it announced all the governor's proclamations. Of first importance to everyone was the power of the vestry to apportion among the freeholders their shares of the tithes, or taxes, for the support of the church as well as the county and colony levies. The

care of the parish poor also devolved upon this body of gentlemen, who were authorized to lay taxes for their support.[14]

In 1769 the parish of Hamilton became too large for a single vestry and was divided in two, with the upper parish being known as Leeds. Thomas Marshall was a member of the first vestry of Leeds.[15] His great-grandson recalled many years later that Thomas built a small church at the north end of Little Cobbler Mountain on a one-acre site. It was for the use of all Protestant denominations, a liberal gesture at a time when the state recognized only one denomination. "No bishop ever consecrated it—that I ever heard of," the great-grandson recalled, "but no cathedral on earth ever contained a more Godly set of worshippers than those who from Sunday to Sunday met there —whether convened to listen to the Methodist circuit-rider, the Baptist preacher, or the Episcopal minister."[16]

Religious liberalism was not easy on the Virginia frontier during the years before the Revolution. A brother of Thomas Marshall, William, had in his youth been known, in the phrase of the time, "for his devotion to the fashionable amusements." William, however, saw the light, and it was so blinding that he became a Baptist minister. He was a good one—"One of the most remarkable seasons of ingathering which Virginia has ever known resulted from his labours." The anti-Baptists, not taking kindly to William's success, seized and attempted to imprison him and were balked only by the interference of Thomas Marshall. The freed William then stayed in Fauquier, continuing as a minister "with unabated zeal and success."[17]

When John Marshall was growing up, the church and the vestry were the sinews of his society, the establishment upon which it stood. He always remained a regular churchgoer, believing in God in an accepted Protestant fashion. If he could never formally affiliate with any congregation because of the corruption of the established church which became so apparent at the end of the eighteenth and the beginning of the nineteenth century, he could not reject the church as an institution worth preserving and perfecting; it was too much a part of his youth.

As a responsible and prominent member of his community, Thomas Marshall was appointed a justice of the peace, a position he held most of the years from 1759 until the American Revolution. He sat with the other leading men of the community, acting as a governing official and a magistrate.[18] Law was crucial to his community. The men had come to a wilderness to establish estates for themselves and their families. Their own hard work and courage transformed that wilderness into the homes they desired, but it was the law that assured their continued ownership, that protected their holdings for their children and their children's children. Without law, their land was at the mercy of any aggressor willing to use his musket to take what was not his. In this environment, at this local level, the Americans first understood that law, written and administered fairly, was necessary for them to live together in peace. And it was in Fauquier County, at the magistrate's court, that the Marshall family's deep involvement with the law began, an involvement that played such a role in the life of Thomas Marshall's eldest son John.

Depending as much as they did upon the law and the judges, Americans soon developed an appreciation for an independent judiciary. That had been the standard in England since 1701 when Parliament enacted a statute guaranteeing judges lifetime tenure. The American colonies attempted to gain such rights for themselves, but were constantly balked by the government in England. The home government recognized that if an independent colonial judiciary were established to protect people against abuse, it may very well end up protecting them against the English Crown.

John Marshall had a deep affection for his father. Many years later his friend Joseph Story recalled that he often heard Marshall speak of his father "in terms of the deepest affection and reverence." The father's character was a subject on which the son "broke out with a spontaneous eloquence." Story quoted Marshall as saying: "My father was a far abler man than any of his sons. To him I owe the solid foundation of all my own success in life."[19]

Although Marshall rarely spoke of his mother, he obviously was very fond of her. A descendant reported years later that she "was a woman of great force of character and strong religious faith. She was pleasing in mind, person and manners, and her son loved her with that chivalrous, tender devotion which made him gentle with all women throughout his life." Every night of his life Marshall repeated the prayer that begins "Now I lay me down to sleep"—a habit learned from his mother.[20]

Marshall always retained an abiding respect for women. Harriet Martineau, a leading feminist in the first half of the 1800s, met him when he was an aged man and was struck by his "reverence for women as rare in its kind as in its degree . . . he brought not only the love and pity which they excite in the minds of the pure, but a steady conviction of their intellectual equality with men, and with this a deep sense of their social injuries."[21]

The Marshall family, as it moved about western Virginia, was never a wealthy one; neither was it poor. There was the subsistence that the family gained from farming the land—food, clothing, and handmade utensils. And then there was extra money which Thomas Marshall earned either as the agent for Lord Fairfax or through his duties as surveyor, sheriff, and justice of the peace. The work was hard, but there were ample rewards. John grew into a tall and healthy young man, and his good health served him well throughout his life. That was one result of frontier life. Another was that the Marshall family looked westward. The west was important to the frontier families, for they had large families, and were confident that when their children were grown, they could migrate westward to the untouched lands beyond the mountains. Development of the west always was an interest of Marshall's.

Another fact of frontier life distinguished it from life on the eastern plantations. Residing mainly on small farms and in towns, the frontiersmen looked on themselves as part of an interdependent community of neighbors who would come to the rescue when Indians attacked, who would help rebuild barns when fire struck, and who were equal in worldly goods. On the plantations there was no such egalitarianism. The plantations were independent communities; huge isolated tracts of land controlled by owner-sovereigns apart from other men.

The final difference, perhaps, between the frontier and the plantations was slavery. Virginia was a slave society. Thomas Marshall—and John Marshall after him—owned slaves. In the year 1782, when Thomas was at the height of his wealth, he owned 20 slaves. This made him one of the largest slaveowners in Fauquier. Of the 672 slaveowners in the county, only 88 owned more than 15 slaves.[22] In contrast to Thomas Marshall's 20 slaves, Thomas Jefferson, on the death of his father-in-law in 1773, came into possession of 135 slaves.[23] At Montpelier the Madison family had 118 slaves by 1782.[24] The difference was more than numbers. The plantations depended upon slavery for their existence. The slaves worked the fields at cheaper rates than paid laborers commanded. They could be bred and sold for a substantial profit (Jefferson's father-in-law had made much of his fortune that way and the industry ultimately became one of Virginia's largest). Loans were raised with slaves as security. Jefferson, Madison, and Washington all cursed slavery but, at the same time, they lived by it. The Marshalls never depended so heavily on slavery. The few slaves they owned held the status of house servants and hired field hands almost. Not until the closing decades of John Marshall's life was there any indication that he regretted slavery for what it did to the blacks; in this, however, he was not alone—no one seemed to understand that aspect of it in early Virginia. But because slavery was not a mainstay of his existence, he could see it with some detachment, coming to realize it degraded the South at the same time it threatened to split the young nation. Three decades before the Civil War forced the end of slavery, John Marshall's own son would lead a struggle, unsuccessful then, to end slavery in Virginia.

Life on the frontier was hard. Farming was done for subsistence rather than for trade. The Marshalls produced their own food, made almost all of their clothing, and manufactured their own tools. Money was not of importance to the frontier farm, other than the amount needed for taxes. But subsistence farming required hard work from every member of the family. Marshall obviously gained some benefits that other children of the time did not. Because his father was one of the leaders in the county, he enjoyed a respect and a courtesy above that shown to other young men not yet twenty—and it is a mark of his own character that he did nothing to disabuse his contemporaries from extending that respect and courtesy. There is no record that John ever traveled far or often from Fauquier County prior to the Revolution, but his father certainly did and John's horizons expanded as he heard stories of the small village on the James River known as Richmond and of the elegant capital of the state, Williamsburg.

But the most important difference between the youth of John Marshall and that of his contemporaries was that he received a formal education. "The young men within my reach," he later reported of his youth, "were entirely uncultivated; and the time I passed with them was devoted to hardy athletic exercises."[25] But Thomas Marshall had determined that his son would be well educated. In this he was carrying on the tradition that the first Marshall ancestor to come to the colonies had begun: the passion to improve the life of his children. That first Marshall had realized then that what was needed was land, an economic base on which to build. Thomas understood that what his children needed was education, the equipment with which to lead their fellow Americans. In this passion, the Marshall family was typical of many of the families who came to America before them and for generations after them.

The father worked hard with the son. "My father possessed scarcely any fortune," wrote Marshall, "and had received a very limited education; but was a man to whom nature had been bountiful, and who had assiduously improved her gifts. He superintended my education, and gave me an early taste for history and poetry. At the age of twelve I had transcribed Pope's *Essay on Man*, with some of his moral essays."[26] Thomas, being a surveyor, had a rudimentary understanding of mathematics and astronomy. He also gradually acquired a library of history and literature. All of this he shared with his son.

There were, of course, no formal schools on the frontier and Marshall's education at first was entirely in his own home, tutored by his father and mother, until he reached the age of fourteen. Then he was given an opportunity rare for a frontier youth. His father was able to afford to send him "about one hundred miles from home, to be placed under the tuition of Mr. Campbell, a clergyman of great respectability."[27] John stayed there one year. A classmate at the school was a young man from Westmoreland County, James Monroe. They remained friends for many years, during the excitement of the American Revolution and the turbulence of the following years under the Articles of Confederation. Their friendship cooled in the first years after the United States Constitution was adopted, as Monroe became a follower of the Jeffersonian Republicans, adamant opponents of John Marshall's federalism. Then again in their later years, when age had mellowed animosities and given them the perspective to choose what they could enjoy, their friendship was rekindled.

When John Marshall returned home, his father, still unsatisfied with his education, wrote a friend in Edinburgh, Scotland, requesting a tutor for his children, specifically a college graduate well versed in Greek and Latin, an Episcopalian, and—most important—a gentleman. The man sent over was the Reverend James Thomson,* who had just been ordained a deacon. He stayed with the Marshall family one year, living with them, teaching the children, and ministering to the Leeds parish. At the end of the year he returned to England to be ordained a priest in the Episcopal Church. This was in the late 1760s and he was the only professional minister of the Episcopal faith the parish had until 1816. When Thomson left the Marshall household John Marshall was reading Horace and Livy in Latin.[28] These two years of instruction, the one at Campbell's school and the one under Thomson's tutelage, plus a few weeks at William and Mary College later in his life, were the only formal instruction that John Marshall—the future Chief Justice of the United States —ever received.

Marshall's education, far better than that of many of his contemporaries, was exceptional to his environment rather than

---

* The name is sometimes spelled incorrectly as Thompson.

to his time. James Madison and Thomas Jefferson had superior formal educations, Madison at the College of New Jersey (later Princeton) and Jefferson at William and Mary. They spent years reading philosophical works, jousting with their fellows over such things as the theoretical objections against the doctrine of moral liberty.[29] Marshall never engaged in such arguments, but his reasoning powers developed better than most men's. His reading was extensive, and his later writings in the form of Supreme Court decisions indicate a breadth of knowledge. But he was a practical man. His formal education was a tool given him by a father who wished to offer his son an opportunity to use his ability. And Marshall used that tool for specific tasks. He did not articulate a philosophy of government. He applied it.

Marshall, then, grew up with the advantages of two worlds. From the frontier he inherited good health, self-reliance, and a fellowship that served him well all his life. From the educational discipline insisted upon by his father and welcomed by his own natural intelligence he developed an intellect that made him a major participant in the formation of the American concept of government. While he had the best of two worlds, he ultimately passed from one to the other, from the frontier to the sophisticated world of politics and decision-making, and never could he be content as the farmer or the frontiersman his father had been. And in this also the Marshall family was typical of the families coming to the New World: the son taking a step beyond the limits reached by the father.

John Marshall himself reports that before the Revolution he was reading Blackstone's *Commentaries on the Laws of England*.[30] * His father, by the time John was approaching twenty, had been a justice of the peace for more than a decade and a member of the Virginia House of Burgesses. He had great respect for the law and undoubtedly wished to persuade his son to choose the law as a career. In addition, the four-volume work was popular in Virginia and readily available. On the front page of the *Virginia Gazette* of November 25, 1775, for example, is an advertisement that the Blackstone *Commentaries* were for sale "at a very low Advance, for ready Money."[31] Anticipating a more modern spirit of advertising, the notice did not specify how much "ready Money" was required.

Thomas Marshall frequently was chosen to represent his neighbors in the House of Burgesses which met in Williamsburg by the grace of the appointed governor and the King of England.

---

* Some Marshall scholars consider this statement merely figurative, but I see no reason to doubt it.

This governing body, not surprisingly, was controlled by the rich tobacco farmers and plantation owners who had developed their aristocratic way of life in tidewater Virginia. More than fine suits, silk stockings, patent leather pumps, and frilled lace at the neck set these men apart. Already the plantation was developing its unique economic-social characteristic: supported by slave labor, the plantations allowed the Tidewater aristocrats to devote their lives to intellectual and cultural pursuits. Gathering, intellectually at least, around Thomas Jefferson, they were drawn together by the breadth of their knowledge, the sophistication of their philosophy, and the understanding that they had the time and the ability to achieve what they set out to do.

Despite his dusty boots and his homespun linen, Thomas Marshall was welcome when he came to Williamsburg as the delegate from the western county of Fauquier. He was married to a distant relative of a prominent Virginian, Thomas Jefferson (distant or not, family ties were important in Virginia) and he was an old friend of George Washington, already a leader among his fellow Virginians. If Thomas Marshall did not have the elegance or education of Thomas Jefferson, he did represent the small landed farmer that Jefferson so much admired. ("I know no condition happier than that of a Virginia farmer might be," Jefferson had once rhapsodized.[32]) And, of course, there were always men like Patrick Henry among the Burgesses, easy to admire and clever enough himself to admire others.

Like the Virginians he met in Williamsburg, like his fellows from all the thirteen colonies, Thomas Marshall was a reluctant revolutionary.

A dozen years earlier, when the French and Indian Wars at last had come to an end, the Americans considered themselves tied to England. "At no period of time," said John Marshall, "was the attachment of the colonies to the mother country more strong, or more general. . . ."[33] That attachment is understandable. The French had been driven from the continent. The Indians had been subjugated. A wilderness lay before the Americans, ready for them to develop.

The Americans were British subjects, and for them there was no prouder boast. This was the British Empire on which it would be said that the sun never set. It had demonstrated itself to be not only the most powerful military empire and the wealthiest land, but also the most democratic government of the time. Fighting alongside their fellow Englishmen, the Americans had brought the wars splitting the continent to an end. Now they were all brothers.

England destroyed that relationship in only twelve years.

Not that everything she did was wrong, but everything she did was characterized by arrogance. The lesson had been taught before and would be taught again. Power is not sacrosanct. Institutions are not eternal. If those members of institutions who are entrusted with power abuse it, they, along with their institutions, will be overthrown. The American colonies taught that lesson to England.

The movement toward rebellion, however, developed slowly.

"While the excellence of the English constitution was a rich theme of declamation in America," said Marshall, "every man believed himself entitled to a large share of its advantages; nor could he admit that, by crossing the Atlantic, his ancestors had relinquished the essential rights of British subjects."[34] It was just those rights that were denied to them.

The first time this was made bluntly plain to the Americans was October 7, 1763, when King George issued a proclamation which had the result of shutting off westward expansion. By royal decree the Appalachian Mountains became the western wall for the Americans. The ostensible purpose was to prevent a clash between the American colonists and the Indian tribes living beyond the mountains, and this may well have been a valid reason. The Americans, however, discerned other causes and other problems. While fighting, they had understood that one of the purposes of the French and Indian Wars was to open up these very lands to settlement. Land was their riches. Land was their sons' wealth. Land was what they struggled for. Now it was abruptly and arbitrarily denied them. To prevent a war with the Indians? Perhaps. Perhaps, also, to keep the thirteen colonies economically stagnant and so forever at the mercy of British merchants.

The effect of the proclamation was to force Americans to violate the law. One of the largest land investors in the colonies wrote from his home in Virginia to a friend on the western frontier asking him "to secure some of the most valuable lands in the King's part." The land speculator acknowledged the existence of the King's proclamation but he could not think of it as anything but "a temporary expedient to quiet the minds of the Indians and must fall of course in a few years. . . ."[35] The writer was George Washington. When he wrote that letter four years after the King's order shutting off the west to the Americans had been issued, he was not a rebel. Rather, he was one of the most respected of the Virginia plantation owners; Mount Vernon, his estate, already was a model for other plantations. He had proven his courage and his loyalty to the King by marching with the

British in the earlier wars. He had much to gain by the preservation of the established order—the more wealth one has, the more one must abhor anarchy. Yet he moved to acquire land in the west against the King's order. This made him a lawbreaker. He was not alone. The King's order made many Americans lawbreakers.

Perhaps the Americans might have respected their King's command if they had any power to influence the policy of the government that sought to control them. But they were given no voice in the councils of the royal government. There was no American representative in England with standing in Parliament or in the court of George III. America had her friends in London; some of whom were listened to on occasion, some of whom exerted influence—also on occasion. The Americans did not consider this representation adequate for free men.

In 1766 George III had opened Parliament with a speech urging "Such sound and prudent resolutions, as might tend at once to preserve the constitutional rights of the British legislature over the colonies."[36] That was the important point to the British government: that its power be preserved as it was. The establishment had come to see itself as an end rather than a means.

The land restriction was only the beginning. The end of the wars with the French brought the prospect of an enormous economic expansion for the American colonies, a prospect eagerly sought by the Americans. But this England could not permit. For her, the colonies were outposts existing to provide raw materials which England used to amass her wealth. This was the system known as mercantilism. The colonies produced the raw materials, shipped them to England, where they were transformed into finished goods which were then sold back to the Americans. The colonies could sell their raw materials only to England; they could purchase finished products only from England. At all times they were dealing with rigged prices. They could never earn enough from sales to cover purchases. Mercantilism, rather than being dictated by the traditional laws of economics, was a result of England's determination to enjoy all the economic benefits of colonialism while assuming none of the responsibilities. One of Jefferson's modern biographers reports that the great irritant was credit, not trade, and he then quotes Jefferson as explaining:

> The advantages made by the British merchants, on the tobacco consigned to them, were so enormous, that they spared no means of increasing those consignments. A powerful engine for this purpose was the giving of good

prices and credit to the planter, till they got him more immersed in debt than he could pay, without selling his lands and slaves. They then reduced the price given for the tobacco, so that let his shipments be ever so great, and his demand of necessaries ever so economical, they never permitted him to clear off his debt. These debts had become hereditary from father to son, for many generations, so that the planters were a species of property, annexed to certain mercantile houses in London.[37]

It was the mercantile system that allowed the British merchants to use credit as such a weapon against the Americans. As long as Britain controlled America's economy, as long as the mercantile system existed, the only prospect for the colonies was long-term debt and penury.*

There were advantages for the Americans—the protection of the British army and navy, assured markets for their products. But these could not outweigh the fact that the Americans were denied access to the major European markets both as buyers and sellers. One English historian has described the British commercial policies as "the great check to industrial growth. . . . The colonies had their place allotted to them in the system. They were to help swell the stream."[38]

The Americans did not take kindly to being allotted their place. But they were given no choice. Again, as with the closing of the western lands, they had no voice in their affairs. The established government they had wished to embrace rejected their advances.

The more the established order spurned the Americans' desire for a voice in their own affairs, the closer the Americans moved toward open revolt. "We must be blind to that malice, inveteracy and insatiable revenge which actuate our enemies, public and private, abroad and in our bosom, to hope that we shall end this controversy without the sharpest of conflicts . . ." shouted Josiah Quincy, Jr., to his fellow Bostonians at the Old South Meeting House.[39]

---

* I. S. Harrell reported in *William and Mary Quarterly*, July 1926, pp. 168–69, that the Marshall family was in debt to British merchants and took advantage of a Virginia law allowing them to pay the debts in depreciated currency. He cited the *Auditor's Cash Book*, 1778–1780, at the Virginia State Library as his source. A thorough study of all the pertinent record books at the Virginia State Library made in 1971, however, shows no listing for the Marshall family and indicates that its members were not in debt to British merchants. That is not surprising, considering that Thomas Marshall was neither a merchant nor the owner of a large plantation.

Sam Adams, another Bostonian who came into his own as a firebrand in the early 1770s, wrote his friends: "But what else could have been expected from a Parliament too long under the dictates and controul of an Administration which seems to be totally lost to all sense and feeling of morality, and governed by passion, cruelty and revenge? For us to reason against such an Act would be idleness. Our business is to find means to evade its malignant design."[40]

England insisted on her right to quarter troops among the racalcitrant Americans. She also insisted on the right to tax the Americans—not only because of the revenue that would be produced but also because she wished to assert that right. The Americans were unwilling to pay taxes to the British, for the same reason—because they wished to assert the right to be taxed only with their own consent. George Washington summed it up. "I think the Parliament of Great Britain," he wrote to an English friend in 1774, "hath no more right to put their hands into my pocket, without my consent, than I have to put my hands into yours for money; and this being already urged to them in a firm, but decent manner, by all the colonies, what reason is there to expect any thing from their justice?"[41]

To Washington, as to most Americans, "those from whom we have a right to seek protection are endeavouring by every piece of art and despotism to fix the shackles of slavery upon us."[42]

The British, of course, had a different perspective.

A twentieth-century historian of the traditional British persuasion has asked if the colonies did not anticipate that the British fleet would protect them if a French force moved toward New York. The counter to the cry of taxation without representation, he claimed, should have been "no defence without contribution." The historian, Sir John Fortescue, editor of King George's correspondence, claimed the Crown and the ministers "wished to conciliate the American colonies. . . . Their difficulty was that they had to do not with reasonable men labouring under a legislative grievance, but with revolutionaries. . . . The real causes of American discontent—stagnation of business—they were powerless to remove."[43]

The arguments do not stand up. The Americans did not object to contributing to their own defense. They had done so with their money, their lives, and their property in the French and Indian Wars. They did object, rather, to making such a contribution without opportunity to influence the determination of the size or the manner of that contribution. And, because England denied the Americans free access to markets, she could not avoid responsibility for the "stagnation of business."

The real problem was that England saw the colonies in the New World as she saw all her other colonies, that is, as parts of a dominion over which she had absolute power. The Americans, in contrast, saw themselves not as colonial servants but as Englishmen living abroad.

Years later, in 1797, an American diplomat in London, Rufus King, had a long talk with a Mr. West, who claimed to know George III very well and to be acquainted with George's most intimate thoughts. West told King that George was "step by step led into the American war," that he was persuaded that most of the Americans were against the war and that a few British regiments "and a firm language would chase away the agitators" and restore peace between the mother country and her colonies. That is the traditional story of great powers when they make the mistake of believing that their military power can resolve the problems their political leaders have created. Only a few regiments were needed; when these proved insufficient, George III was told "that a small additional force would be sufficient," that if a firm stance were taken, "peace and order would return." When peace and order did not return, George III was told that it was because George Washington intended to make himself the sovereign of the New World. "Can I doubt my friends," asked George III, "ought I not to protect them?"[44] By his friends, he meant the Americans loyal to him. By protecting them, he meant saving them from George Washington. The King made the mistake common to those with power who wish to hold on to it. He listened only to those who told him what he wanted to hear and believed only what did not discolor the picture he had of himself as a ruler whose righteousness could never be questioned.

Parliamentary politics and economic pressures conspired to subjugate the Americans while in London men struggled for power and for sterling. But there was no resistance to these politics and pressures from George III; rather he welcomed them as a means of keeping the world he knew—with his throne as its center—intact. Historians generally have accepted that, as Winston Churchill wrote, George's "responsibility for the final breach is a high one."[45] The American historian Samuel Eliot Morison stated that "It is quite clear that the King's aversion to give up his system of personal government was the real reason for prolonging the war."[46] Other historians have been even less kind to George, describing him as stupid, with a closed mind, and even insane. Said J. H. Plumb, the English historian: "Had he [George] been born in different circumstances it is unlikely that he could have earned a living except as an unskilled manual laborer."[47] All these interpretations have been challenged; in some cases successfully; in others, not so.

No one, however, has ever suggested that the King was not motivated basically by a compulsion to preserve the empire as he had found it, with the position of Parliament and the Crown, in relation to the English people both at home and abroad, unchanged. "George, be King," his mother had enjoined him,[48] and George III, King of Great Britain and Ireland, obeyed. "Any criticism of monarchial powers, any suggestion of reform or change," said Plumb, "he regarded as a personal affront."[49]

George III correctly predicted in 1774 that "The dye is now cast, the colonies must either submit or triumph." Three months later he protested of the colonies: "I do not want to drive them to despair but to submission."[50]

In his disdain for the Americans he was not alone. In 1773 when Parliament voted on the requirement that only tea from the East India Company could be sold in the American colonies, the intent was to rescue the financially harassed tea company; neither the reaction of the Americans nor their welfare was seriously considered. "There was some debate," Lord North, the Prime Minister, reported from Downing Street the evening of April 26 to the King, "but the question pass'd without a division at half an hour after six o'clock."[51] Perhaps more than any other single act by the British government, the action giving a tea monopoly to the East India Company precipitated the Revolution, yet it was enacted only after "some" debate and without a record vote.

Nor was there much respect among the British military for the Americans' fighting ability. In 1774 one of George III's generals, Thomas Gage, had told him, as the King recounted it, that the Americans "will be Lyons, whilst we are Lambs but if we take the resolute part they will undoubtedly prove very meek."[52]

The Americans proved nothing of the kind. Rather than have a monopoly forced upon them, they dumped the tea into Boston harbor. "A most daring spirit of resistance and disobedience" George III called it, and he vowed his intention "to withstand every attempt to weaken or impair the supreme authority of this legislature over all dominions of the crown."[53] The Americans were equally determined to preserve for themselves the right to determine the course of their lives.

"I could wish, I own," said George Washington to a friend, "that the dispute had been left to posterity to determine, but the crisis is arrived when we must assert our rights, or submit to every imposition, that can be heaped upon us, till custom and use shall make us as tame and abject slaves, as the blacks we rule over with such arbitrary sway."[54]

Thomas Jefferson also was deeply involved in what history has described as the American Revolution. In words plaintive, succinct, and devastating in their impact, he cried the basic American complaint against the British. "For us," he said, "not for them, has government been instituted here."[55]

What was not understood was that by the 1770s the American Revolution had virtually ended, except for the fighting that was the result of British obstinacy and arrogance. The original settlers, such as John Marshall's unknown ancestor, had come as Englishmen hoping to re-create a life style they envied in their homeland. But the American continent worked its will on the settlers. It taught them that men did not have to inherit wealth to be wealthy; wealth waited for men strong enough, brave enough, and intelligent enough to wrest it from the earth. It taught them that no man was better than another; they battled Indians, cleared fields, starved, froze, married, raised children, built homes where before there had been a wilderness. From the beginning they understood their independence. John Marshall reported that beginning:

> In the year 1692, immediately after the receipt of their new charter, the legislature of Massachusetts had passed an act, denying most explicitly the right of any authority, other than that of the general court, to impose on the colony any tax whatever; and also asserting those principles of national liberty, which are found in Magna Charta. Not long afterwards, the legislature of New York, probably with a view only to the authority claimed by the governor, and not to that of the mother country, passed an act similar to that of Massachusetts, in which its own supremacy, not only in matters of taxation, but of general legislation is expressly asserted.[56]

Marshall wrote further, however, that the English Parliament declared such laws void. This declaration had taken place almost one hundred years before the war between the British and the Americans. It was a reaction to the American Revolution. The question of independence was a philosophical one, and Americans would enjoy trading philosophers back and forth, seeking justification for the acts they would undertake. It also was a very practical one. It was the Americans, after all, who must pay the taxes imposed upon them by someone else. It was the Americans who saw their economy straitjacketed by a power they could not influence. It was the Americans whose horizons were limited by the Proclamation of 1763 closing the lands west of the Appalachians to development. The system of representative government that ultimately emerged from the American revolutionary process was not the result of esoteric discussions nor of the advancing sophistication of philosophical thought. Rather, it was the result of the very practical experiences the Americans underwent. They understood that when a people cannot have an impact on their government legitimately, they will have an impact illegitimately. So they determined that the government they fashioned would permit its citizens to make an impact by legitimate means. Marshall and the others had learned the folly of despotism to preserve an ancient order. They themselves proved that no establishment need be permanent.

In England some understood the folly of the government's ways. On Monday, April 10, in the year 1775, King George was visited at the Court of St. James's by the Lord Mayor of London, the aldermen, the sheriffs, and a committee of the Livery of the City of London. One of the delegation stepped forward to read from the paper in his hands.

"We, your Majesty's dutiful and loyal Subjects, the Lord Mayor, Aldermen, and Livery, of the City of London, beg leave to approach the Throne," he began, "and to declare our abhorrence of the measures which have been pursued, and are now pursuing, to the oppression of our fellow subjects in America. These measures are big with all the consequences which can alarm a free and commercial people."

The speaker then listed the dangers: damage to commerce, the ruin of England's growing manufacturing industry, the decrease in the revenues and the consequent increase in taxes as well as "the blood of your Majesty's subjects." And the group, insisted the speaker, agreed with the Americans "that no part of the Dominion can be taxed without being represented," and he pointed out to George that "dutiful petitions for redress of these grievances from all Your Majesty's American subjects have been fruitless."

George's reaction was in keeping with the understanding of monarchy he had shown since ascending the throne in 1760. "It is with the utmost astonishment," he answered, "that I find any of my subjects capable of encouraging the rebellious disposition which unhappily exists in some of my colonies in North America. Having entire confidence in the wisdom of my Parliament, the Great Council of the Nation, I will steadily pursue those measures which they have recommended for the support of the constitutional rights of Great Britain, and the protection of the commercial interests of my kingdom."[57]

There would be no compromise, and one week later the British appeared at Lexington green and shortly from all over the thirteen colonies the young men came to their muster fields, as John Marshall had come to the one near the Fauquier County Courthouse, to do what they recognized must be done.

John Marshall and his family could not have avoided the conflict that engulfed the North American continent. Thomas Marshall was first elected to the House of Burgesses in 1761, just two years before the proclamation shutting off the western lands. He served until 1767 when he became sheriff to Fauquier County. In 1769 he was returned to the governing body and served intermittently until the war began.[58] He was with the Americans in their resistance to England. He met with Washington, Jefferson, Patrick Henry, and others at the Raleigh Tavern in Williamsburg, May 18, 1769, and May 27, 1774, and also in August of that year when they agreed to retaliate against England by refusing to import or purchase goods manufactured in England.[59] He voted in the Burgesses to express opposition to the British act closing the port of Boston—as punishment for the Americans' dumping of the East India Company tea into Boston harbor. That resolution approved by the House of Burgesses reads:

> This House, being deeply impressed with Apprehension of the great Dangers to be derived to British America, from the hostile Invasion of the City of Boston . . . deem it highly necessary that the said first day of June be set apart by Members of this House as a Day of Fasting, Humiliation, and Prayer, devoutely to implore the divine Interposition for averting the heavy Calamity, which threatened Destruction to our civil Rights, and the Evils of civil war. . . .[60]

John Marshall later said the purpose of that day of prayer was "to give one heart and one mind to the people, firmly to oppose every invasion of their liberties." He reported that "Similar resolutions were adopted almost everywhere, and the first of June became throughout the old colonies a day of fasting, humiliation, and prayer, in the course of which, sermons were universally preached to the people, well calculated to inspire them with the utmost horror against the authors of the unjust suffering of their fellow subjects in Boston."[61] The British order closing the port of Boston had accomplished what 150 years of history in the New World could only prepare for: it turned the members of the various colonies into Americans with "one heart and one mind."

That resolution passed in May of 1774 spoke of praying for divine assistance to sway the British Parliament. In March of the next year Patrick Henry stood before the Burgesses and spoke not of divine acts but of those by men. It was the speech that history remembers as ending: "Give me liberty or give me death!" Historians since have questioned the accounts of that speech,[62] but none have challenged its impact. Patrick Henry was the greatest orator of the time. "The Virginians boast of an orator . . . and he is the only orator of whom they do boast," said one writer of Henry.[63] Henry cultivated the appearance of a farmer or back-country planter. His dress was drab, his demeanor belittling of himself. As he began to speak, the members of his audience relaxed, feeling they were listening to one of their good neighbors. "But," said an account of his oratorical skill, "by and by, when it was little expected, he would take a flight so high, and blaze with a splendour so heavenly as filled them a kind of religious awe, and gave him the force and authority of a prophet."[64]

And that is what he did with his speech in March of 1775 exhorting his fellow Virginians to action—"Why stand we here idle? What is it that gentlemen wish? What would they have?"

The questions would be asked by Americans over and over again for the next several years. One of Patrick Henry's listeners wrote of his contemporaries, those who sat with him listening to Henry's exhortations, that "All of them had at stake, fortunes, which were affluent or competent, and families, which were dear to them: neither of these blessings would have been jeopardized upon a political speculation, in which their souls were not deeply engaged. If some misguided historian should at a future day, revive the exploded calumny of evil motives which agitated this convention, let these names be adduced as monuments of absolute refutation."[65] Among the names listed by this writer as refuting the charge of evil motives were those of George Washington, Henry, and Thomas Marshall.

Returning to Fauquier County, Thomas Marshall reported to nineteen-year-old John that Patrick Henry had made "one of the most bold, vehement, and animated pieces of eloquence that had ever been delivered."

And when Patrick Henry's speech was done, the father continued, Richard H. Lee rose to calculate the American odds in a battle with Britain. Lee said that Britain could bring greater force than the Americans could muster and had far greater resources. But, after conceding these odds, he concluded:

We are assured in holy writ that the race is not to the swift, nor the battle to the strong; and if the language of genius may be added to inspiration, I will say with our immortal bard

"Thrice is he armed, who hath his quarrel just!
And he but naked, though locked up in steel,
Where Conscience with injustice is oppress'd!"[66]

It was a romantic time they lived in. A lone man still mounted his horse and rode off to claim his fortune and establish his honor. Words still moved men to a daring and courage they did not know they possessed. Leaders emerged to articulate powerful ideas. No wonder that John Marshall and so many other young Americans came marching to the sound of the fife and drum.

A few months after John Marshall had offered instruction in the manual of arms to the militiamen on the muster field near Fauquier County Courthouse, Colonel Patrick Henry took command of the Virginia militia and called for men to join his command. He had no trouble finding volunteers. As was true of all the gatherings of men who were to be called the American army, they "came together in various uniforms, or without uniforms, and mostly armed with their own fowling pieces."[67]

John Marshall was part of a group organized in neighboring Culpeper County. The battalion, he recalled many years later, "was ordered to assemble on the first of September 1775 at Culpeper court house. In about ten days or a fortnight we were ordered to Williamsburg."[68] According to an account written by one of Marshall's fellow soldiers, when Patrick Henry called for volunteers, "One hundred and fifty men from Culpeper, one hundred from Orange, and one hundred from Fauquier, rendezvoused here, and encamped in a field the property of the late Honorable John S. Barbour, half a mile west of the village of Fairfax. An old oak marked the spot. These were the first Minute Men raised in Virginia."[69]

Lawrence Taliaferro of Orange County was chosen their colonel; Edward Stevens of Culpeper, lieutenant colonel; and John Marshall's father, major. Not only was the leadership representative of the best men in the area, it was also representative of the area itself—each county had a man in the upper ranks.

The Culpeper Minutemen's flag featured a picture of a coiled rattlesnake about to strike, and on the other side were the words "Liberty or Death" and "Don't Tread on Me." The men wore hunting shirts, some emblazoned with the "Liberty or Death" slogan. The group, like most groups, had its humorists, and one suggested that liberty or death offered too severe an alternative; he would stay, he said, if it were cut back to liberty or be crippled.[70]

The men wore bucktails in their hats and carried tomahawks and scalping knives in their belts. And as they moved through the Virginia hills and valleys, crossing the estates of those who already were developing into the colony's aristocracy, marching through the communities where the residents had not been concerned about Indians for years, their warlike appearance frightened a good many of their countrymen. Said one of Marshall's fellow soldiers: "The people hearing we came from the backwoods, and seeing our savage looking equipments, seemed as much afraid of us as if we had been Indians." The soldier added: "We took pride in demeaning ourselves as patriots and gentlemen, and the people soon treated us with respect and great kindness."[71]

In this manner John Marshall, just turned twenty years old, marched off to war.

War never again was the same.

These men who elected their officers, volunteered for duty, brought their own weapons, and wore a variety of uniforms were introducing a new concept into warfare: the citizen soldier. Prior to the American Revolution wars were fought by men compelled to serve, beaten by the whip into obedience. Thousands responded to a single command as if they were one; in contrast, the independent life of the American frontier had taught the colonists to respond in their own good time. But there was another difference, and it would be all-controlling and result in the citizen soldier in the American Revolution and in every war that followed becoming the most feared warrior of all. The professional soldier charged because he feared punishment by his commanding officer if he did not. The citizen soldier charged because he wished to be beside his commanding officer.

The first battle that John Marshall, citizen soldier, marched to, along with his father and the other men of Fauquier, Orange, and Culpeper counties, was the first major battle fought in Virginia. It is known as the Battle of Great Bridge.

The morning of December 9, 1775, dawned for the American forces at Great Bridge as had many other mornings—with the sound of British muskets and cannon. "As the enemy had paid us this compliment several times before," said one of the American soldiers, "we at first concluded [the firing] . . . to be nothing but a morning salute." In another moment, however, the Americans knew it was something more.

"Boys," cried Adjutant Blackburn, "stand to your arms!"[72]

So began the Battle of Great Bridge, and John Marshall's first taste of military combat. Over Great Bridge, then a small town in southern Virginia of not more than three dozen homes and one church, would hang the future of the American revolutionary effort in Virginia and perhaps also in the other colonies. "This was a second Bunker's Hill affair, in miniature," said the American commander, Colonel William Woodford, a few hours after the battle, "with this difference, that we kept our post. . . ."[73]

That rattlesnake on the flag beneath which John Marshall had marched had twelve rattles. The head, about to strike, represented Virginia and the rattles represented the other colonies. The Virginians were not presumptuous in considering their colony the head of the thirteen. It was the center of much of the Americans' commercial and intellectual strength. More important, however, was its location. The colonies were strung out along the eastern coast of North America. Virginia was the central colony. If she fell to the British, the colonies would be split geographically and the end of the American Revolution would be dated from that moment. The British could take Boston, New York City, and Philadelphia—as they did—without dividing America into two sections and destroying their cause, but the colonists could not afford to lose Virginia.

The British governor-general of Virginia, the Right Honorable John Earl of Dunmore, had determined that Virginia must fall to the British.

In the spring of 1775 Lord Dunmore had been chased from Williamsburg by the colonists because he had stolen the Americans' gunpowder and damaged their muskets, which had been stored in a building under his control. John Marshall later reported: "These circumstances excited so great a ferment, that the governor thought proper privately to withdraw from the place, and go on board the *Fowey* man of war, then lying at Yorktown, twelve miles below Williamsburg."[74] Safe aboard the British ship, Dunmore engaged in a letter-writing contest with the Americans in the House of Burgesses. The Americans wanted him to return to Williamsburg. Dunmore, realizing the depth of their anger, insisted they meet with him on the *Fowey*—where he was assured of his safety. The House of Burgesses finally dissolved itself and its members were largely returned to a state convention about to meet at Richmond. The Burgesses were the creation of the British government; the Richmond convention was the creation only of the Americans. John Marshall caught the significance of the change. "Thus," he wrote, "terminated forever the royal government in Virginia."[75]

As the weeks dragged on to the confrontation that would take place December 9, Dunmore was busy. Enlisting what few loyalists he could find in the colonies, he retreated to a small fleet of British ships in Chesapeake Bay from which he marauded the Virginia coast. More so than most colonies, Virginia was vulnerable to such attacks; it is streaked by broad rivers, which made perfect avenues for Dunmore's ships. The Virginians feared they would be unable to repel such attacks. They also were concerned about possible slave uprisings. Southerners then did not pretend their slaves were happy. Two weeks before the Battle of Great Bridge, for example, two southerners visited John Adams, the influential Bostonian who was attending the Continental Congress in Philadelphia. They told him that if the British were to land in the South with enough guns and supplies "and proclaim freedom to all the negroes who would join [the British] camp, twenty thousand negroes would join it. . . ."[76] Well aware of this sentiment, Lord Dunmore declared free on November 25, 1775, "all indentured servants, Negroes, or others, appertaining to rebels . . . that are able and willing to bear arms, that joining his Majesty's troops, as soon as may be. . . ."[77]

Dunmore was interested neither in emancipation nor in increasing his forces with freed slaves. The purpose of the declaration, rather, was to persuade landed Virginians to return to their estates instead of taking up arms against the British, in order to prevent their slaves from running away.

That plan, however, did not work. The Virginians stayed at their posts. John Marshall reported that Dunmore "collected such a force of the disaffected and negroes, as gave him an entire ascendancy in that part of the colony. A body of militia who assembled to oppose him, were easily dispersed, and he flattered himself that he would soon bring the lower country to submit to the royal authority."[78]

This perhaps was the first time Marshall realized that slavery, so much a part of the Virginia life he knew, could be more a hindrance than a help.

The key spot in Dunmore's strategy was Great Bridge. Located about a dozen miles from Norfolk, the port city Dunmore was using as his headquarters, the "great bridge" was a contraption of wooden planks hanging over the southern branch of the Elizabeth River. It was part of the major route from the south to Norfolk, and those loyalists who wished to join the British would have to cross it. Actually the bridge was part of a 160-yard causeway connecting two spits of land which were surrounded by marshland. Who controlled the bridge, controlled the land access to Norfolk.

In the fall the British had built a small wooden fort on the north side of the bridge. Armed with cannon, they believed themselves impregnable. To attack the fort, the Americans would have to advance across the causeway, exposing themselves directly to British cannon fire. Perhaps Dunmore considered the Americans foolish enough to try such an attack; John Marshall believed that the British governor probably went along with "that contempt for the Americans which had been so freely expressed in the House of Commons."[79]

The Americans made their headquarters in a small church at Great Bridge and constructed breastworks between two houses at the southern end of the causeway to effectively block the street.[80] They had no cannon. They could neither attack the British fort nor destroy its walls. It seemed a long wait for John and Thomas Marshall and the other Americans. And this waiting showed them that the American Revolution would be marked by those qualities by which all wars are known to fighting men: dirt, loneliness, and hunger.

While they waited, there was much skirmishing—"we killed sixteen negroes, and five white men, the first day we got to this place," reported one American in a letter to a friend. This American, a colonel, continued in his letter:

> Last night was the first of my pulling off my clothes for twelve nights past. We are surrounded with enemies; I do verily believe that nine-tenths of the people are Tories, who are the poorest, miserable wretches I ever beheld. Believe me, I do not think there is as much provision within ten miles round as would serve us one day. I am very sorry that I have it not in my power to write to you oftener, but I assure it is not my fault. You may be assured, my good friend, I never was so fatigued with duty in my whole life. I make not the least doubt, if we do not get into some kind of winter quarters soon, that it will cost me my life, which I set but little value on, in comparison. A gun is just fired; I must stop. . . .[81]

That letter was written December 4. That night John Marshall participated in a brief skirmish with the British, his first time under fire. After dark Colonel Stevens led the Culpeper Minutemen across the causeway toward the British fort. The intent was to stage a hit-and-run raid, in retaliation for the British burning of some shacks. The Americans crept silently along the road and about midnight reached the sentinel post in front of the fort, where they were discovered. When they did not answer the British sentry's cry, he fired. The Americans fired back at the sentry, who had been joined by about thirty British soldiers. The fracas lasted fifteen minutes before the Americans retreated in good order. They estimated they had killed one British soldier and they had captured two Negroes who had joined Dunmore's forces.[82]

During the following days there was sporadic firing between the British fort and the Americans behind the breastworks at the other end of the causeway. Both had contributed to the burning of the few houses that lay between them so that neither side could use them to cover an advance. The British fired their cannon at the American breastworks, and the American marksmen tried to pick off any British soldier who showed his red coat above the walls of the fort.

During that week a Negro slave owned by Thomas Marshall deserted the American forces one night to join the British. He informed them that the Americans at Great Bridge numbered no more than three hundred "shirtmen"—the name given to the Minutemen because of their fringed hunting shirts. More Americans from North Carolina were expected, however, the Negro reported.[83]

When the British heard this, an immediate attack against the Americans was ordered—to strike before the North Carolinians arrived. According to one report, a group of dissident Negroes was to circle behind the Americans, attack them, and drive them toward the British cannon. But, according to this report, the Negroes became lost and were never able to attack the Americans.[84] That story may be true, or it may simply be that Dunmore was led to foolishly attack on the morning of December 9 because he could no longer allow himself to be blocked by the Americans. Their patrols along the Elizabeth River were slowing the loyalist tide to Norfolk. Especially if the Americans secured more troops, they could seal off the river, blocking all loyalists from crossing.

Early on the morning of Saturday, December 9, 1775, the British moved out of their fort. Quietly they replaced the planks in the bridge which had been removed to prevent any large body of Americans from crossing the bridge. The American commander, Colonel Woodford, had directed that all sentries withdraw to the breastworks at night to protect themselves against being picked off one by one by British guns, so the Americans were not aware of the work by the British on the bridge in the early hours of Saturday morning.

The Americans were lucky. Repairing the bridge took longer than the British had expected. They were unable to cross, Colonel Woodford later reported, until "just after our reveille had beat; and lucky time for us, and, you will say, rather an improper season for them to make their push, when, of course, all our men must be under arms."[85]

This was the moment when Adjutant Blackburn cried to the American soldiers to stand to their arms.

Contrary to Woodford's account, at the moment of attack there were not more than sixty Americans at the breastworks; the others were, however, ready to move, and came running. The attack was a breathtaking sight to John Marshall and the other Minutemen. Across the causeway marched more than one hundred British soldiers, only six abreast on the narrow road, their bayonets fixed—the prelude to the deadly British charge. Over the heads of the advancing Redcoats, British cannon roared grapeshot at the American breastworks and at the soldiers racing with their muskets from the church where they were quartered. "As is the practice with raw troops," Marshall reported, "the bravest of Americans rushed to the works."[86]

The American officer in charge at the breastworks was a Lieutenant Travis. His men were armed with muskets which, with the best of luck and also of skill, had an effective range of fifty yards. He apparently understood the British technique of battle, which was to advance in a close-order, steady march and provoke the enemy into firing. Once the enemy's singleshot, muzzle-loading muskets had been fired, the British then charged, usually managing to reach the enemy fortifications before the enemy could reload. The British bayonet charge was the terror of the eighteenth-century battlefield. No group of untrained, inexperienced soldiers—such as the Americans at Great Bridge—could stand up before such an attack.

The American soldiers were anxious to fire. But Lieutenant Travis ordered them to hold until the British were within effective musket range. At the right moment, he gave the order, and not before. The result was a slaughter. Captain Woodford reported that "perhaps a hotter fire never happened, or a greater carnage, for the number of troops."[87] Most of the American forces had now reached the breastworks and were able to keep up a steady stream of firing at the British. Colonel Stevens took his Culpeper Minutemen out to the left, exposing them to British cannon fire. From this flank, the Minutemen sent a withering crossfire at the British attackers.

The British troops were led by Captain Fordyce of the Grenadiers. As his men fell behind him, he exhorted the remaining British soldiers to continue forward. He shouted to them of the ancient glories of the British fighting man. He waved his hat over his head and ran toward the American position, pulling his troops with him by the sheer force of his personality. He fell dead within fifteen steps of the American position, his body riddled with a dozen wounds. Said an American who witnessed his death: "His wounds were many, and his death would have been that of a hero, had he met it in a better cause."[88]

Fordyce's death ended the British attack. Unable to use their bayonets, the Redcoats broke and retreated across the causeway, protected from pursuit by the cannons in their fort. In less than thirty minutes the Battle of Great Bridge was ended, except for one more act. The Americans slipped from behind the protective breastworks, exposing themselves to the fire from the British cannons, to rescue wounded British soldiers. The Redcoats had been well indoctrinated. "For God's sake," the wounded cried, "do not murder us."[89] But the Americans helped the wounded British soldiers back to the breastworks and out of the fire of the British cannons, which killed indiscriminate of uniform.

When the British commander at the fort, Captain Leslie, saw the Americans' actions, he climbed to a platform on top of the fort, where he could be seen by the Americans, and bowed to them as a mark of his gratitude for their treatment of the British wounded.

In the wake of their defeat the British evacuated the fort at Great Bridge. Colonel Woodford was able to report to the Virginia Convention: "I have the pleasure to inform you that the victory was complete, and that most of the dead and wounded, with two pieces of cannon, were carried off under cover of their guns from the fort. We buried twelve besides the Captain [Fordyce], him with all the military honors due to his rank, and have prisoners Lieutenant Batut and sixteen privates, and three officers' fusils, powder, ball, and cartridges, with sundry things, have likewise fallen into our hands."[90]

The Americans never knew exactly how many of the British were killed or wounded because the Redcoats carried away many bodies as they retreated across the causeway. But the toll obviously was high. "In this ill-judged attack," John Marshall wrote, "every grenadier is said to have been killed or wounded."[91] Miraculously, the only American casualty was a soldier who suffered a slight wound in the hand.

For Virginia and for John Marshall, the Battle of Great Bridge was their first blood. It had taught them something. They knew now that with some intelligence and luck they could defeat the British. They knew that what they had begun was a carnage —"perhaps a hotter fire never happened," Woodford had said. Perhaps. But hotter fires were frequent in the coming years.

They learned other things also. They learned of their own courage, and by helping to rescue the British wounded they learned something of graciousness in victory, which is much more difficult than graciousness in defeat. They learned they could both admire the bravery and regret the death of the enemy; if only Captain Fordyce had met his end in a better cause, lamented the Americans, not because they were his enemy but because they were his fellow human beings.

One final thing they learned. This was something that all the speeches of Patrick Henry could never convince them of, something that none of the pamphlets so popular at the time could persuade them of. This was something that no one can believe until he personally hears the grapeshot exploding toward him, until he wipes from his own body the blood of a wounded man, until he follows his commanding officer knowing that there is no longer any protection from the enemy's bullets except God's grace.

They learned they were at war.

2

AFTER THE Battle of Great Bridge John Marshall marched with his fellow militiamen to Norfolk. They looked out at the harbor where Lord Dunmore sulked aboard his ship with his men. Angry at being beaten by what he considered no more than a mob, Dunmore sent a detachment of British soldiers ashore with orders to burn the town. If the British could not use the port, no one would. Marshall resolved a controversy over whether the Americans also contributed to the burning of the town by saying that he was present when the Redcoats first set the town afire and "afterwards when the remaining houses were burnt by orders from the American committee of safety."[1]

The burning of Norfolk marked the end of the British occupation of Virginia. The colony no longer was at war. The immediate danger had ended. John Marshall and the other soldiers went home.

The Americans had not sought independence but, rather, the rights they understood to be theirs by virtue of being born Englishmen. After the battles at Lexington, Concord, and Bunker Hill, the Continental Congress had declared: "Our cause is just. Our union is perfect," but the Americans assured any who would listen "that we mean not to dissolve that union which has so long and so happily subsisted between us, and which we sincerely wish to see restored." Their object, they said, was "reconciliation on reasonable terms . . . thereby to relieve the empire from the calamities of civil war."[2] Two days later the Americans sent the "Olive Branch" petition to George III. "Attached to your Majesty's person, family and government, with all devotion that principle and affection can inspire; connected with Great Britain by the strongest ties that can unite societies," it read. It asked for an end to bloodshed and that "such statutes as more immediately distress any of your Majesty's Colonies may be repealed. . . ."[3]

It was a challenge to statesmanship by men who were meeting that challenge themselves, offering to resolve the mutual problems and arrive at reasonable solutions. It would have been, of course, difficult to do otherwise. Despite the British attacks at Lexington and Concord, there was little spirit for independence. The Pennsylvania Assembly, for example, directed its four representatives to the Continental Congress to "dissent from and utterly reject any propositions . . . that may cause or lead to a separation from our mother country. . . ."[4]

Elbridge Gerry, a Massachusetts delegate to the Congress, received a letter from a friend in the South, saying that, as certainly expected, "The Tories dread a declaration of independence and a course of conduct on that plan more than death." The friend continued, however, that the Tories believed that "the Southern colonies will not accede to it. They say they never will. . . ."[5]

But in England the King believed that military might could accomplish what political decisions had failed in: maintaining the allegiance of the Americans to the British throne. On August 23, 1775, George III issued a royal proclamation declaring the Americans to be in a state of rebellion and calling on all British officers, both civilian and military, "to exert their utmost endeavours to suppress such rebellion, and to bring the traitors to justice." All British subjects were obliged "to disclose and make known all traitorous conspiracies and attempts against us, our crown and dignity."[6]

John Marshall no longer was a student of political affairs by the fact of his father's involvement in the House of Burgesses. He had risked his life at Great Bridge as a soldier. He had come to that battle as the son of Thomas Marshall and emerged from it an adult in his own right. No longer did his father explain to him; John Marshall understood for himself.

He knew that the war in the months following the opening battles and even after Great Bridge was not being fought for independence. "The utmost horror . . . had been expressed" at such a prospect, he said, and the desire of continuing the union with England "was openly and generally declared." But the Americans could not retain their desire for a continuing relationship while the British continued to think and act in terms of war. "However sincere the wish to retain a political connexion with Great Britain might have been at the commencement of the conflict," said Marshall, "the operation of hostilities on that sentiment was infallible." The Americans had begun the war as reluctant revolutionaries, hoping not to destroy their relationship with England but to improve it for themselves. To attempt to maintain ties with England "whilst every possible effort was making, by arms, to repel the attempt, was an absurdity too great not to be felt," said Marshall. The revolutionaries were no longer reluctant. "The human mind, when it receives a vast momentum, does not, like projectiles," said Marshall, "stop at the point to which the force originally applied may have been calculated to carry it. . . ."[7] That was something the established power had not understood—only it could reduce the momentum, but it chose not to exercise that option. And its defeat is not dated by the last gunshot but by the decision to use force when reasonableness would have prevailed.

Few men, certainly not one with the perception of John Marshall, could live through that time and misunderstand its meaning. The use of force, as England learned, is itself a defeat. The rule of law—the rule that England had declined to extend to the colonies—is a victory when men understand it is to their advantage.

And so the Americans, in John Adams' words, were "in the very midst of a revolution the most complete, unexpected and remarkable of any in the history of nations."[8] To formalize this revolt they issued a declaration of independence. The document is interesting for what it says of the Americans—more specifically for what it says of the representatives they sent to the Continental Congress in Philadelphia who directed that a declaration be drafted, then endorsed it without a dissenting vote, and, pledging "to each other our Lives, our Fortunes and our sacred Honor," signed the document.

They met in the State House in Philadelphia the summer of 1776. They sat at small desks in a first-floor room, these members of the Continental Congress, where they could look out of the tall windows onto busy Market Street, and wonder what impact the document they approved on July 2 would have on the apparently peaceable people who went about their business quietly. For none of them was it an easy decision. These fifty-six men were not

wastrels willing to sacrifice other men's possessions for their
own ideals. They were, in fact, risking their all. John Hancock
was a wealthy merchant in Massachusetts. Thomas Jefferson, to
whom goes most of the credit for the words in that declaration,
already was an established landowner in Virginia. Robert Morris
of Pennsylvania and Charles Carroll of Maryland were on their
way to wealth. John Adams of Massachusetts and George Wythe
of Virginia were among the leading lawyers of America; Adams'
defense of the British soldiers accused in the Boston Massacre a
few years earlier represents a triumph of law over mob violence
and Wythe's lectures on the law at William and Mary would later
inspire Virginia's leading lawyers.

Still, they were revolutionaries and the document they
wrote is an appeal to the conscience of mankind to understand
why they were breaking the law. However one judges these lawbreakers, one must agree they produced a brilliant brief to lay
before the world. They began their presentation by claiming that
government's purpose is to secure for all men life, liberty, and the
pursuit of happiness. Then they made the bold claim that when a
government fails to do this, "it is the Right of the People to alter
or abolish it." Man, they were saying, has the right to break the
law on some occasions. They acknowledged this should not be
done for frivolous reasons, and then maintained that they were
acting only after "patient sufferance." To demonstrate this, the
Americans submitted a long list of grievances "to a candid
world." Then follow twenty-seven specific complaints against
George III. They read like a history of the colonies: quartering of
troops, dissolution of colonial governments, controlling judges,
taxation without consent, cutting off trade, blocking migration.
The list in its cumulative effect is devastating, leading to the
Americans' conclusion that "A prince, whose character is thus
marked by every act which may define a Tyrant, is unfit to be
the ruler of a free People." At the end of their paper they asserted
that they were "appealing to the Supreme Judge of the world for
the rectitude of our intentions."

History generally has looked kindly upon the Americans'
revolution and their declaration, not because the law was broken
but because of what the Americans created from their law-
breaking. In criticizing George III they were stating they could
do a better job themselves of securing "Life, Liberty and the pursuit of Happiness." They redeemed themselves from the onus of
lawbreakers by ultimately developing order rather than anarchy,
an order that most men could subscribe to, influence, and benefit
from. This was not an accidental development. From the very
beginning of their complaints against England they had not

sought privilege but legal rights, and it was natural that they would extend those legal rights once they came into power. Also, they were willing to take upon themselves whatever cost and sacrifice the new government would demand.

The declaration was formally signed on July 4, 1776, and read to the people gathered in the Old State House yard in Philadelphia on July 8 by John Nixon. The reaction was in the eyes of the beholder. One witness, for example, Charles Biddle, thought there were "very few respectable people" among the crowd and many of the Whigs present who would be expected to support a declaration "were much opposed to it."[9] But John Adams reported: "Three cheers rended the welkin. The battalions paraded on the Common, and gave us the *feu de joie*, notwithstanding the scarcity of powder. The bells rang all day and almost all night."[10]

The Declaration of Independence was the formal severing by the Americans of their ties with England and the throne of George III, a severing that would be confirmed in blood during the next five years. But it was much more than an announcement of a separation. It was an attack on the traditional role of government. No longer, insisted the Americans, will the role of government as protector of the power and property of the few be acceptable. No longer will the mass of people be supine before such arrogance by the few. They now were willing to risk all that they possessed because of their belief that the role of government is to establish certain "self-evident" truths—"that all men are created equal, that they are endowed by their Creator with certain unalienable Rights, that among these are Life, Liberty and the pursuit of Happiness."

No man who lived through that experience could be untouched by it, as few men in later generations can be unmoved by it. The Declaration of Independence was both an acknowledgment that government can fail and an affirmation that government, when its purpose is to serve the people over whom it holds sway, is worth preserving. It is a plea for a sense of law, for justice.

John Marshall was greatly influenced by the Declaration of Independence, the environment that produced it, and the environment it produced. In his later years he would speak of an ordered liberty. What he meant was a political system responsive to its members and a code of laws based on ultimate fairness rather than upon whim. This is what the authors of the Declaration had cried that they lacked.

But the immediate impact upon Marshall was that he returned to the army. In July of 1776, after the signing of the

Declaration, he joined the Third Virginia Regiment of the Continental Line as a lieutenant. He was no longer a Virginia militiaman, but a member of the army of the thirteen colonies from Virginia. He was no longer a fighter for a colony, but an advocate of a nation.

This army he now became a part of and in which he would spend four demanding, exciting, and influential years was an interesting institution, almost charming in its youthful vigor and ineffectiveness. The Continental Congress, which had authorized it, declined to take the actions necessary to support it. Its commander, George Washington, lacked for nothing in zeal but lacked for a great deal, in the beginning at least, in ability to command a large land army. The soldiers themselves were somewhat quixotic. They were willing to serve their country, except when they had to return to their plowing. They were willing to obey orders, if given by a man whom they knew well, respected, and usually had elected to his position of command. They did not understand the rules of warfare that prevailed then. They figured that if they showed up when they were supposed to and aimed their muskets as they always had done, they should be able to get themselves some Redcoats as they used to get themselves some wild turkeys.

And yet there was something about this American army that held it together from the months after the battles of Lexington and Concord to the months after the Battle of Yorktown six years later. And in the end these novices at war outgeneraled, outfought, and outpoliticked the professional British army. The essential ingredient of their ultimate success was the democratization of war. They were not fighting for land, although land would be one of their rewards. They were not fighting for glory, although few of the participants would lack for glory at the end. Nor were they fighting for rank, although they would recall with pride at a later time the rank they had achieved. Basically they were fighting for what they considered to be right. Before their war was done, approximately one hundred thousand of the Americans had participated in it as soldiers, a not insignificant figure considering that the total population of all the colonies was barely more than three million. The battles swept from Massachusetts in the North to Georgia in the South, leaving few communities unscathed. The war, then, touched all Americans, not only those who chose to be professional soldiers, and it taught them that they were dependent upon one another, that they were Americans rather than citizens of separate colonies. When the original settlers had crossed the ocean they were seeking a better life. When the colonists fought in their Revolution, they were making the ultimate commitment—the risk of their lives—to preserve and enhance what their fathers had found. When men fight in such a cause, they can be destroyed by a massive military juggernaut but they can never be defeated.

Marshall apparently spent a year in the service without seeing action. In the winter of 1776–1777 he marched north but spent several months in Philadelphia to escape the smallpox that constantly harassed and decimated the American forces. Later that year he fought in his first battle since Great Bridge, almost two years earlier. This was the skirmish at Iron Hill.[11]

Iron Hill was the first battle in the campaign around Philadelphia in the fall of 1777 which led, in December, to the American army's retreat to Valley Forge. In August Washington had led the Americans in a formal march through the city of Philadelphia with the intention of impressing the Tories there with the power of the American forces. Sixteen thousand Americans marching twelve abreast required nearly two hours to pass any given point along Front or Chestnut streets. They were impressive, well armed, handsome even with their disarrayed uniforms, seemingly well disciplined. But there were some skeptics. John Adams, present for the meetings of the Continental Congress, had his doubts. To him the Americans just missed the ingredient essential to be successful soldiers. "They don't step exactly in time," he said. "They don't hold up their heads quite erect, nor turn out their toes exactly as they ought. They don't all of them cock their hats, and such as do, don't all wear them the same way."[12]

Adams' skepticism was undoubtedly a minority view that summer day, as John Marshall and the other American soldiers marched past him. Unfortunately, however, Adams' viewpoint was the correct one.

Marshall commanded a company that varied in size from thirty to sixty men, depending upon how many were sick, on furlough, or back home plowing. In addition to himself there was one other commissioned officer—another lieutenant—three sergeants, two corporals, one drummer, and the remainder were privates.[13] The company was part of a regiment of riflemen commanded by Colonel Daniel Morgan. They were formed into a corps of light infantrymen with nine officers, eight sergeants, and a hundred rank and file soldiers and then placed under the command of Brigadier General William Maxwell of New Jersey. They encountered the British the morning of September 3. Generals Howe and Cornwallis, having landed at the Head of the Elk River south of Philadelphia, were marching along a narrow road with forest pressing close upon them. It was not a pleasant spot for British regulars accustomed to fighting on open terrain. In the van were the Hessians. The Americans had observed the British preparations and Washington had ordered Maxwell to station a detachment of men along the road to block the British forces. According to Marshall, "the column under Lord Cornwallis fell in with, and attacked Maxwell, who made a short resistance, and then retreated over White-clay creek, with the loss of about forty killed and wounded."[14]

Apparently the Americans had opened fire from the protection of the trees, and the British forces responded smartly. Although they were not used to fighting in woods, this would not be another Braddock's defeat for them. They managed to beat off the Americans. Sir William Howe, Marshall reported, claimed only three British were killed and nineteen wounded in the heavy if brief firing. Marshall did not agree that the Americans had done that poorly. "The opinion of the Americans," he said some years later, "corroborated by accounts from the country people, ascribed to their arms in this skirmish much more effect."[15]

The next battle in which Marshall participated was fought only a few days later at Brandywine Creek. This battle and another at Germantown, early in October, must be understood as one unit. The landing by Howe at the Head of Elk River early in September was the first step in what the British believed would be the destruction of the American army. They had chased the Americans through the North. Now they intended to bag them. At Brandywine they came close to achieving their goal, but at Germantown the Americans were able to retain their status as a fighting body. The Battle of Germantown was significant not because the Americans won, but because it was not the followup, definitive victory the British had anticipated.

The Battle of Brandywine took place the morning of September 11. Maxwell's infantrymen, the group to which Marshall belonged, had been sent out early in the morning to scout the British and to delay their advance if possible. Maxwell's men moved south to a meeting house at Kennett Square, and a small detachment of men was sent further ahead. This small group stopped at a tavern and, while standing at the bar, suddenly saw British soldiers moving toward them. The Americans escaped through the rear door, leaving their horses—and apparently their drinks—for the British. The Redcoats chased the detachment toward the meeting house where they were surprised, after their easy victory at the tavern, to meet stiff resistance. Using what was then the standard American fighting technique, the Americans fired from behind trees and walls, retreated, then halted behind another shield, and fired again. It was a deadly business both for the British, who were being attacked by an enemy they could not see, and for the Americans, who had to keep calm and orderly under circumstances fraught with the utmost danger.

Maxwell's troops finally reached a ford at Brandywine Creek where they were joined by other Virginians. They held the British for a while, were pushed across the creek, returned, were pushed back again. Both sides brought in reinforcements. Before the day was done the Americans had suffered a major defeat.

This battle, like the one at Great Bridge, was a family affair for the Marshalls. John's father was present also, and his heroism on the battlefield was attested to by several persons. Unlike his son, Thomas Marshall never left the army after Great Bridge. He had been appointed a major in the state's third regiment by the state convention looking after Virginia's defenses. That was on January 13, 1776, a few weeks after Great Bridge.[16] On March 23 Thomas Marshall "subscribed the Articles of War" and was given his commission in the Continental army,[17] almost four months before his son joined him in becoming an American soldier rather than only a Virginia defender. Thomas also had moved north with Washington and was successively promoted to lieutenant colonel and then to full colonel.[18] He was a respected and well-liked commander. "Fresh intelligence," reports one of his men in the summer of 1777. "Col. Marshall has just come from Head-Quarters where he has dined with the finest ladies in Jersey, feasting his eyes and his stomach. His eyes sparkle at the thought of it."[19]

At Brandywine Thomas Marshall was a daring commander willing to risk himself—the gunfire came close enough to wound his horse twice—and led his regiment in an equally brave performance. One soldier at the battle, except for overestimating the "drubbing" the Americans gave the British, presented an accurate description of the sense of battle and of Thomas Marshall's heroism. In a letter to a friend a few days after the battle, he wrote:

> . . . we had very nigh given the enemy a severe drubbing. The action commenced about 8 o'clock in the morning, and with several intermissions, continued till night. About 5 o'clock it resembled an earthquake, far exceeding the loudest thunder. . . . Col. Marshall, of the 3rd regiment, attacked the enemy's left column with his single regiment, and at first repulsed them; but, overpowered by numbers, was obliged to retire, which he did in good order. In this contest, which continued violent for three quarters

of an hour, this brave regiment left four officers on the spot, amongst them a brave young Gentleman, Lieutenant Peyton, and Captain Chilton, who, brave as Wolfe, imitated his manner in death, inquiring about the success of the day as he expired. . . .[20]

George Washington thought highly of his old friend's performance under fire. When Thomas Marshall wished to transfer from the infantry to an artillery unit being formed in Virginia, Washington wrote to Governor Patrick Henry of Virginia asking that the appointment be made. Thomas Marshall's "mathematical abilities are sufficiently known in Virginia," said Washington of the man who once did surveying with him. Marshall also is a man, Washington attested, "of indubitable Bravery, of which he has given proofs upon every occasion." The appointment of Thomas Marshall as a colonel in the artillery was made shortly thereafter.[21]

The British victory at Brandywine appeared greater than it was. Once again, the British could report the Americans had suffered a major defeat, as they had on Long Island the year before. The way was open for the British to Philadelphia, the capital of the rebellious colonies, and they quickly occupied that city. Now they had both New York and Philadelphia. But the members of the Continental Congress simply moved themselves from Philadelphia to York and set up a new capital city. Washington's army was intact. Despite another in a long series of major defeats, the American army continued to exist, and that fact outshone both the defeat and the occupation of Philadelphia. John and Thomas Marshall and the other thousands of Americans from the colonies had survived and stayed. Now Washington turned around and used them as they had always hoped to be used. His orders: Attack.

The major British encampment was at Germantown, outside Philadelphia. It was here that Washington planned to attack. The American army, divided into four groups, would move against the British troops aided by the element of surprise. One historian has described Washington's plan as a classical one, saying it was similar to that devised by Hannibal to win the battle of Cannae, and by Scipio Africanus, whose outnumbered Roman soldiers defeated seventy-four thousand Carthaginians at Ilipa.[22] In design it may have had illustrious forebears. In practice it did not work as well. Marshall explained why. A point had come, he said, when victory seemed close. The Americans had attacked with great spirit and several units of the American forces had penetrated into Germantown, and:

there was the utmost probability that the two wings of the British army would be separated from each other, and that they would be entirely routed. Had [Washington's] troops possessed the advantages given by experience, had every division performed precisely the part allotted to it; there is yet much reason to believe that his most sanguine hopes would have been realized. But, the face of the country, and the darkness of the morning, cooperating with the want of discipline in the army, blasted all the flattering appearances of the moment, and defeated an enterprise which, in its commencement, promised the most happy and brilliant results.[23]

As Marshall also pointed out, there was a heavy fog that morning making visibility almost nonexistent. The terrain was broken by walls and other enclosures that so often before had helped the Americans as they retreated but this time assisted the British who were doing the falling back. "The brigades were soon thrown into disorder," reported Marshall, who witnessed the confusion. "Some of the regiments pursuing with vivacity while others endeavoured to proceed more circumspectly, they were entirely separated from each other." The major failure of the Americans was taking hold: they were not an army. They were a potentially powerful mass of men, but they could not act in a military fashion. They could not synchronize their movements, communicate with each other, respond to each other's calls for help. "These embarrassments, arising entirely from circumstances which would have been overcome by experienced troops," Marshall wrote, "gave the British time to recover from the consternation into which they had at first been thrown."[24]

Technically the Americans had lost another battle. But great causes are not won or lost on technicalities. "This was the first time we had retreated from the Americans," said a British officer, "and it was with great difficulty we could get men to obey our orders."[25] And an American officer realized how close Washington's army had come to victory. "We are in high spirits," he wrote when the battle was done. "Every action [gives] our troops fresh vigor and a greater opinion of their own strength." He added a line that was the most significant point about Germantown, about a battle in which the inexperienced, poorly trained, and undisciplined American army had attacked the British in their stronghold: "Another bout or two must make their [the British] situation very disagreeable."[26]

That was the lesson of Germantown; the Americans were marching closer and closer to victory.

They still had a long way to go, however—far in time, far

in energy, and a very great distance in personal sacrifice that could not be anticipated even as the casualties of the Philadelphia campaign were being counted. They still must go to Valley Forge.

The American soldiers came to Valley Forge not as an army but as the remnant of one. Apparently defeated by the British, forgotten—or so it seemed—by their fellow Americans (the members of the Continental Congress had returned to their homes from York the month before and the colonies were not sending supplies), spurned so far by those European nations that might have become their allies, the Americans came to the plateau formed by the meeting of the Schuylkill River and the Valley Creek in eastern Pennsylvania ready to dissolve as an organized military force. "At no period of the war," said John Marshall, who was one of the eleven thousand soldiers who came to Valley Forge with Washington, "had the American army been reduced to a situation of greater peril than during the winter at Valley Forge."[27]

They came to Valley Forge in December of 1777 when the war was more than two years old and their prospects of victory, despite the near success at Germantown, even more distant. The British were warm and well fed, armed and healthy. The Americans, in contrast, were none of these things. "We were ordered to march over the river," recorded one soldier in his diary on December 12. "It snows—I'm sick—eat nothing—no whiskey—no forage—Lord—Lord—Lord. . . ."[28]

That was only the beginning. Two days later that same soldier wrote that he was sick, discontented, "and out of humour." He could not be blamed as he explained: "Poor food—hard lodging—cold weather—fatigue—nasty clothes—nasty cookery—vomit half my time—smoaked out of my senses—the Devil's in't—I can't endure it—There comes a bowl of beef soup, full of burnt leaves and dirt, sickish enough to make a Hector spue. . . ."

Many soldiers died at Valley Forge—some three thousand, according to most estimates—not from British gunfire but from starvation, sickness, and freezing. Many deserted. More stayed. The holding together of the American army in the winter of 1777–1778 is one of the great stories of human endurance. "I shall soon be no more!" cried a soldier. "And all the reward I shall get will be: 'Poor Will is dead.' "[29]

The soldiers at Valley Forge were no longer young men caught up, as Marshall had been, by the "zeal and enthusiasm" of their age. Those who had survived were battle-hardened veterans. Marshall was twenty-two years old, had fought his first battle at Great Bridge two years earlier, had survived other battles, had witnessed the producing of the Declaration of Independence, and now he would live through another of the great adventures of his life. As his frontier upbringing and the Declaration of Independence had emphasized the absolute necessity for a fair system of law that would do justice for all men, so the Valley Forge experience impressed upon him the need for a strong federal government. He came to believe that the United States must have a central authority with power to enforce the system of law that men democratically arrive at. What happened at Valley Forge was not untypical of the soldiers' situation during the entire war—those at home rarely volunteered to make the sacrifices necessary to support those who had left home to fight. Valley Forge epitomized the problems of the loosely knit colonies, and most men who survived that severe experience held the belief that a strong central government was a necessity. Each soldier, as he hungered and froze, knew that the colonies did not lack food, clothing, or ammunition. But the Continental Congress had authority only to request such supplies for the army, no authority to commandeer them. So the Americans at home, with but few exceptions, kept their supplies for themselves or sold them to the British for gold rather than making them available to their fellow Americans in exchange for some vague promise of payment at a later time.

George Washington begged for help. In a letter written two days before Christmas to the Congress, he sounded an appeal that was typical of many others to follow:

> . . . unless some great and capital change suddenly takes place in that line, this Army must inevitably be reduced to one or other of these three things. Starve, dissolve, or disperse, in order to obtain subsistence in the best manner they can; rest assured Sir this is not an exaggerated picture . . .

Perhaps realizing that help would not be forthcoming, he continued: "What then is to become of the Army this Winter?" There was no answer, except what he had projected himself.[30]

With the restraint that marked much of his writing, John Marshall commented that the situation of the American army being unable to perform any of its duties because of an "absolute want of food" is "one of those extraordinary facts, which cannot fail to excite some degree of attention. . . ." To Marshall the surprising development was "that the great body of the army bore without a murmur, a circumstance so irritating, and, to them, so unaccountable."[31]

The Americans, of course, stayed because they believed in their cause, because many were young and believed their youth would carry them through any adversity, and because many of them led the others to new heights of self-sacrifice. Marshall was one of the last. The testimony of those with him at Valley Forge shows a man doing what was expected of him and then considerably more. In later years the soldiers who were with Marshall described him as the best-tempered man they knew at Valley Forge. He did not complain, either about the lack of bread or about the lack of meat. When his fellow officers showed their discouragement, Marshall worked to cheer them up. "He was an excellent companion," goes this account of John Marshall at Valley Forge, "and idolized by the soldiers and his brother officers, whose gloomy hours were enlivened by his inexhaustible fund of anecdote."[32]

That rosy account fails to indicate one important, and rare, quality John Marshall possessed: he could deal with diverse and disgruntled people and encourage them not always to agree but at least to respect and understand one another, to accept their situation, to deal with it and improve upon it. This ability to work with a small group of people and to elicit from them the best they have to offer first surfaced during the ordeal of Valley Forge, and it would show again a quarter of a century later when as the Chief Justice of the United States he presided over the Supreme Court and brought it not always to unanimity, but at least to reasonableness and toward the end of justice.

At Valley Forge the men passed their time in athletics. They threw quoits (round stone discs) for distance and accuracy. Marshall was skilled at the game and enjoyed it all his life. They had running and jumping contests—and Marshall excelled at these sports. He was the only man, according to several contemporary accounts, who could with a running jump clear a stick laid over the heads of two men as tall as himself. As a runner he was known as "Silverheels." There are several versions of the origin of the name. According to one, the men raced in their stocking feet and Marshall's stockings had silver heels sewn in by his mother.[33] But an account by a contemporary offers a somewhat different story. Marshall, so this version goes, had the only pair of silk stockings in the regiment. The night before the Battle of Brandywine, he wore his silk hose when, dressed in his finest, he went to a party in the country. He returned late that night and slept on a bed of leaves with his silk stockings resting beside him. At midnight alarm guns were fired; the men leaped up and quickly began to dress. Marshall could not find his hose and did not want to leave the pair behind. Angry and in a hurry, he struck his flint to make a light—and quickly set fire to his bed of leaves and to his silk stockings. When he finally put the fire out and thrust his feet into his stockings, his toes pushed out through the holes that the fire had burned. To his own amusement and that of his fellow soldiers, he went off that way—"Silverheels."[34]

The few occasions of merriment the soldiers salvaged at Valley Forge do not obscure how dreadful an experience it was. The Americans arrived at Valley Forge the same time winter did, and the cold and snow were more at home than they were. Washington directed that they build small huts made of logs with a mortar of mud to fill the cracks. A dozen men lived in each hut, bunks stacked one on top of the other. Years later, when Marshall wrote about Valley Forge, he still would not complain. The huts, "after being dried with fires," he said, "formed comfortable habitations, and gave content to men long unused to the conveniences of life."[35] By all standards his description is generous. But he did concede that "A warm blanket was a luxury in which very few participated."[36]

That was not an exaggeration. "[I]t is certain that half the army are half naked, and almost the whole army go barefoot," said one officer.[37] John Marshall's friend from Culpeper, Philip Slaughter, a captain in the same regiment and a messmate, had one shirt that winter. When it was being washed, he wrapped himself in a blanket. To be fully dressed for parade, he had the breast pocket of his shirt torn off and made into wristbands and a collar so his uniform appeared complete.[38] The men had a great deal of pride and were embarrassed when Washington invited them to dinner at the small stone house that was his headquarters. Washington, or so it seemed, was attempting to feed all the officers of the American army from his own resources, against the promise of reimbursement at a later time, if at all. But the officers would not attend his dinners unless properly dressed. This meant considerable borrowing among them so the invited officer could appear in a decent uniform.

The three thousand Americans who died at Valley Forge from hunger, cold, and sickness represented approximately one out of every four men there. "Their food was not adapted to their habits," explained Marshall, "nor to the climate . . . a sufficient quantity of salted provisions was not mingled with the rations delivered to them. The supply of vinegar was insufficient." In the hospitals, "a dreadful mortality still continued to prevail in those miserable receptacles of the sick, where death was often found by those who entered them in quest of health." If a soldier did return pronounced fit for duty, he still was so wretchedly dressed and in such poor health that he was not expected to be a fighting soldier.[39]

But the men scratched some subsistence from the soil, searched the nearby farms and found some grain the farmers were hiding, traveled far and wide to find an animal to slaughter. Then early in February the commissaries announced that the country was exhausted. The army could not be supplied beyond the end of the month. The American army and the cause for which it fought had reached their lowest point after two and one-half years of battle. The British had beaten the Americans in battle and the winter at Valley Forge had destroyed them both as a fighting force and as individuals.

On February 12 an American officer wrote from Valley Forge:

> The situation of the camp is such that in all human probability the army must soon dissolve. Many of the troops are destitute of meat, and are several days in arrear. The horses are dying for want of forage. There cannot be a moral certainty of bettering our circumstances while we continue here. . . .[40]

The Virginia soldiers had their huts on a small sloping hill near the parade ground. The snow was deep, too deep it seemed to trudge to another detachment, to talk, to seek out nonexistent food, to find a bare spot for a military drill which no one was interested in leading. The deaths mounted at a faster pace, and the dead soldiers were buried in unmarked graves. In the cold and the damp and among the dying and the dead, it seemed that the American cause also was dead. Perhaps all men were not created equal, or at least perhaps another occasion was needed before the theme of democracy could be established. It seemed the young soldier who had cried when he came to Valley Forge that all the reward he would get is the acknowledgment that "Poor Will is dead" had written the epitaph for the entire American army as well as the colonies' claim to the right of self-government.

On January 13, 1778, Sam Adams in Boston wrote to his friend Elbridge Gerry, who was with the Continental Congress, a letter of introduction for a big, gruff man who had been recommended by Benjamin Franklin in Paris as a strong military personage. The bearer of the letter was, supposedly, a Prussian general and Adams took him "to be a gentleman of real Merit, from whose knowledge and experience . . . great advantages may be derived to our army."[41] No matter that the Prussian, known as Baron von Steuben, could not speak English. The Americans would take anything they could get, and taking Steuben was their first piece of luck that winter of 1778. He was a drillmaster. He came to Valley Forge and lined up a few Americans on the parade ground. With his big, guttural sounds he persuaded them to understand what he meant. Those few soldiers learned to march like soldiers, to turn, to wheel, to charge, to halt, to aim, and to fire like soldiers. And then those few soldiers returned to their own units and taught them what they had learned from the man who swore at them with words they could not understand. And the farmers, and the shopkeepers, the artisans, and the schoolmasters, the young men and their fathers, learned to move together as an army moves. They acted like soldiers. They looked like soldiers. They responded like soldiers. They felt like soldiers. At last they *were* soldiers. John Marshall later recalled von Steuben as being of "real service" by establishing one system of maneuvers "and by his skill and persevering industry, effected during the continuance of the troops at Valley Forge, a most decisive and important improvement through all ranks of the army."[42] The Americans had first come together as a loosely tied group of men from different colonies who were willing to fight alongside each other at times of their own choosing. The obdurate stand by the British had forced them to suppress their loyalties to individual colonies and to begin thinking of themselves as Americans. Now von Steuben was teaching them how to act together as an American army.

The next month, February, the Americans experienced additional good fortune. Martha Washington, wife of the commander-in-chief, arrived at Valley Forge. She was a charming and attractive woman who immediately began working to cheer up the demoralized American army. The other officers' wives joined her daily to sew and mend clothing for the soldiers. She led the other women to the hospital huts and to the soldiers' encampments carrying baskets of food, tending the sick. But she contributed more to the cause of the Americans at Valley Forge than a few pieces of food and a cooling hand upon a fevered forehead. Her real contribution was to bring vivaciousness to the bleak winter camp. Every evening officers came to the Washington house to drink coffee, laugh, talk with the attractive ladies whom Martha had gathered. Now again there was spirit and laughter in the Valley Forge encampment. Alexander Hamilton, a young man from New York of whom George Washington was extremely fond, was often present and was much admired for his quick wit and charm. James Monroe, John Marshall's old friend from the Campbell school, was frequently present as was John Marshall himself.

Because of his own abilities as a leader as well as his father's relationship with George Washington, it was natural that Marshall became part of Washington's command group. On November 20, 1777, he was appointed a deputy judge advocate and served on several courts-martial during the coming months.[43] Originally the judge advocate in the American army was to attend all general courts-martial, but as the army increased in size this became impossible. Local commanders, down to the brigade level, then were authorized to convene the trials and deputy judge advocates officiated in the sense that they received documents and generally watched over the procedures of the trials. Marshall did not preside as a judge would nor did he operate as either a defense or prosecution lawyer. Still, these courts-martial were his first participation in legal proceedings. And he was active. According to the muster rolls he acted as deputy judge advocate in February, March, April, July, and August of 1778, and in September of 1779.[44]

In moving into Washington's command group Marshall strengthened old relationships and developed new ones that were part of his life in the decades that followed. He continued as Washington's protégé. He became Hamilton's agent—certainly at least his source of information regarding Virginia politics—in future years. His relationship with Monroe continued. Five decades later they would, as old men and by then former political enemies, join together to welcome to Virginia another comrade-in-arms in the American Revolution—the Marquis de Lafayette.

The third piece of luck for the Americans at Valley Forge was the appointment of Nathanael Greene as quartermaster general. A brilliant and industrious military man, Greene did not welcome the assignment, but once he accepted it, he determined to do as good a job as possible. Scouring the countryside, he, "from the necessity of the case, foraged as in the enemy's country and seized every animal fit to slaughter," said Marshall. His men delved into the woods and swamps and found horses and cattle that had been hidden by farmers who preferred British gold to American paper. Quite suddenly the Americans, who had been close to starving, now found great quantities of supplies and "the principal difficulty experienced," Marshall said, "was in obtaining wagons to convey it to camp."[45] Then when spring broke the winter cold, nature also helped. "Shad's running!" cried a soldier summoning his comrades to the Schuylkill River, and they raced to its banks to haul in the fresh fish by the cask.

The American army had survived Valley Forge.

This survivability had not gone unnoticed in the capitals of the world. By the spring of 1778 militarily powerful England had been at war with her colonies for three years and, although winning battle after battle, still had not conquered them. And in some few instances the Americans had shown real ability on the battlefield, as in northern New York, when General Burgoyne had surrendered his army to them.

France, England's traditional enemy, had watched events in the colonies with interest and in the spring of 1778 joined with the American colonies in making war against England. The news reached Valley Forge on May 5 and the next day, May Day, was a time of celebration. The Americans now had a powerful ally.

The entry of France into the war was the turning point. From then on England could not give the attention to the rebellion in the colonies she once had, and the colonies had military and other supplies streaming in as well as a naval force to rely on. Much, properly, has been made of France's assistance to the young United States, but the enormity of her aid should not obscure the fact that her motives were not purely altruistic— France expected to reap many benefits from the defeat of England—and that the step was taken cautiously and only after the Americans had demonstrated their ability to persevere in their struggle against England.

The American army that emerged from Valley Forge was a far different organization than that which had arrived there in so pitiful a condition six months earlier. Under von Steuben's tutelage the soldiers had been trained as an army. The supplies Nathanael Greene had produced for them had made them healthy, well fed, and well armed. The men themselves now numbered thirteen thousand and many of them were, like John Marshall, veterans. Experienced in warfare, highly motivated to fight for their rights as human beings, and buoyed by the news of France joining their cause, they were ready to meet the British in battle. They would not have to wait too long.

The British, forced to reduce their effort in North America because of the potential threat from the French in Europe, decided to retreat from Philadelphia and consolidate their forces in New York. This land march of thousands of soldiers and wagon supplies strung out across most of New Jersey was an ideal target for a commander of an opposing army. Washington, apparently still unsure of the military power of the army under his command, delayed giving orders for the attack for almost a month, until the end of June 1778.

The conflict began on the morning of June 28 in the vicinity of the Monmouth courthouse. And all those who were associated with George Washington that day, as John Marshall was, became his admirers for life. For whatever mistakes Washington had made previously, he made up for them gloriously by his conduct at the Battle of Monmouth.

The battle began with the news that the British were evacuating their encampment near the Monmouth courthouse. Washington ordered Major General Charles Lee to attack the Redcoats. Lee had been reluctant to engage the British in battle but was the senior American officer under George Washington, was believed competent, and there seemed no reason to deny him the command. Later in the morning, after the battle was underway, Washington and a small group of officers rode past the courthouse confident that up ahead the American forces under Lee were routing the British. First they were surprised to meet an American fifer coming toward them. Obviously, if the Americans were advancing, the fifer should have been marching in the other direction. Washington ordered the young man to identify himself, and when the fifer reported he was an American soldier and that the Americans were retreating, the commander-in-chief refused to believe the story. If the young soldier talked such nonsense anymore, Washington promised, he would be whipped.

Washington and his men rode about fifty yards further. They met three more American soldiers who identified themselves and said all the American troops were retreating. Again Washington refused to accept the accounts. He knew the American army was ready for battle and was at least the equal, if not the superior, of the British. Also, except for a few cannon shots, he had heard no sounds of battle. What had gone wrong?

A young officer offered to ride ahead and find out. He returned shortly with the news that the entire American army was being routed and that the British were only fifteen minutes away from the very spot where Washington himself now stood. General Lee had ordered a retreat. The retreating soldiers, reported Marshall, "neither understood the motives which had governed General Lee, nor his present design; and could give no other information than that, by his orders, they had fled without fighting."

Washington found Lee and the two men exchanged harsh words; the exact phrases are in dispute but not the tone. Washington "spoke in terms of some warmth, implying disapprobation of [Lee's] conduct," said Marshall.[46] More important, Washington immediately took command. He ordered two regimental commanders to organize their men to check the British advance. The two regiments managed to slow the enemy and even Lee, placed in command of the troops at a second line, acquitted himself well.

The moments gained were sufficient to reorganize the American army in a line to stand against the British as soldiers should. Through the long hot afternoon the two armies surged back and forth at each other. The British army, the best-trained military force in the world, no longer could repel the Americans. The Americans turned, aimed, fired, stood their ground against the best that Europe could offer. More was engaged on that field than two armies. The American army did well that day because the cause for which it fought had attracted the best men in the colonies—men like George Washington to lead and John Marshall and his comrades from Fauquier County to fight. The British cause, in contrast, was defended by what had been England's scum—convicts, drunkards, paupers, idlers from the streets who had been cajoled, duped, bribed, and kidnapped into the army. Quicktime marches under a hot sun, bellowing sergeants, and the threat of the lash had transformed them into disciplined fighters. What was at stake was the ability of men in power to force men to die for their country. A lesson of the American Revolution, summed up that day at Monmouth when the Americans achieved the proficiency they had long struggled for, was that ultimate victories must go to those men motivated by a cause to give their all. The professional soldier was inadequate. He was no match for the citizen soldier when the citizen soldier was highly trained and well led, as he was that June 28 when Washington finally assumed personal command.

And Washington that day was without equal. A tall man and a superb horseman, he rode up and down the line on his white horse, his cape billowing about him, exhorting his men to stand firm. He shouted, waved, frequently exposed himself to the Red-coats' firing, personally rallied the American army until late that night he dropped exhausted to sleep with his men on the Monmouth battleground. The Americans knew they had a leader that day. When in the coming turbulent years Washington again emerged as the leader the Americans needed, the men he had led in battle rallied to him because he had been tested and had proven himself able. The success of the Americans in their Revolution was due to many causes but no single element had the impact of George Washington's leadership. A quarter of a century after the Revolution John Marshall summed up Washington's role in what is still the best summation of Washington as a military leader:

> Had Washington not often checked his natural disposition, had he not tempered his ardour with caution, the war he conducted would probably have been of short dura-

tion, and the United States would still have been colonies. At the head of troops most of whom were perpetually raw because they were perpetually changing; who were neither well fed, paid, clothed, nor armed; and who were generally inferior, even in numbers, to the enemy; he derives no small title to glory from the consideration, that he never despaired of the public safety; that he was able at all times to preserve the appearance of an army; and that, in the most desperate situation of American affairs, he did not, for an instant, cease to be formidable.[47]

Who "won" the Battle of Monmouth is often a matter of dispute. Washington personally stopped the defeat of his army. But he did not destroy the British army, and so most historians consider it a draw. Who won or lost that particular battle, however, is not as important as that the Americans had proven themselves an army. With this demonstration, the assistance of the French, and the growing disenchantment of England with what had become an insignificant part of a war almost worldwide, the outcome of the American Revolution no longer was in doubt. There were other campaigns and other battles, more deaths and pillage, but the end was inevitable following the Battle of Monmouth.

Monmouth was the last battle of the Revolution in which Marshall personally participated.* He stayed on in the army for another year, serving often as a deputy judge advocate, the position to which he had been appointed shortly before he arrived at Valley Forge; usually in this period he was stationed with Washington's headquarters unit. In September of 1778 he was promoted to captain, and his full pay went from 11 pounds to 18.[48]

In addition to John Marshall and his father, his younger brother, James Markham Marshall (born in 1764), also was in the war. James joined the artillery company commanded by his father in 1779, when he was only fifteen years old. He stayed in the army, seeing action in the South, until after the siege of

---

* Beveridge said Marshall was "one of those selected" for the subsequent assault on Stony Point (vol. I, p. 139), but in a footnote two pages later added: "The fort was captured so quickly that the detachment to which Marshall was assigned had no opportunity to advance." Rhodes also said Marshall was involved in the storming of Stony Point (vol. I, p. 14), citing Marshall's pension application of January 26, 1833. This is obviously an error as the application does not mention Stony Point. (See JM's file, S5731, National Archives.) Marshall himself answers the question in an undated letter in the Revolutionary War Pension File of Churchill Gibbs (S46002, National Archives): "I was not myself engaged in storming Stony Point," he wrote, "but was in the fort the morning after its capture."

Yorktown. With so many of the men away at war for years, the Marshall family suffered economically. Money was in short supply; the landholdings were withering. Late in 1778 John Marshall went on a lengthy furlough to visit his family in Fauquier County and was distressed at the suffering he saw there. He had brought with him some of his fellow American officers and some young Frenchmen he had met in the army. "When supper time arrived," his sister's account goes, "mother had the meal prepared for them, and had made into bread a little flour, the last she had, which had been saved for such an occasion. The little ones cried for some." At that point Marshall realized the poverty his family had been subjected to. "He would eat no more of the bread which could not be shared with us," his sister said. "He was greatly distressed at the straits to which 'the fortunes of war' had reduced us, and mother had not intended him to know our condition."[49]

This experience also would have an impact on Marshall. In future years the obligation he felt to obtain economic security for his family was a consuming passion. Repeatedly he would reject requests to enter public service because he was unwilling to sacrifice his family's financial well-being.

And there was yet another impact. War is itself a concession that a civilized rule of law has failed, and traditionally war meant unrestricted barbarism. The British fought this way. "The savage barbarities, which had been perpetrated by the Indians belonging to the army of Burgoyne, as well as to that of St. Leger, excited still more resentment than terror," Marshall wrote. "As the prospect of revenge began to open, the effect of those barbarities became the more apparent; and their influence on the royal cause was the more sensibly felt, because they were indiscriminate."

One act in particular excited the colonists. Indians attached to General Burgoyne's army captured a young woman named Jane McCrea, who was attractive, a British sympathizer, and actually engaged to a Tory serving as a British officer. She was shot, scalped, and her body stripped of its clothing. The Indians then brought her scalp to the British camp where a young officer recognized it; he was Jane McCrea's fiancé. The story was widely told in the colonies, embellished, as Marshall said, "by the hand of more than one master" and "excited everywhere a peculiar degree of sensibility."[50]

The Americans tried not to fight that way. In Marshall's first battle, that of Great Bridge, they helped the wounded British to protection. They buried the slain British officer, Fordyce, with full military honors. Of the Battle of Stony Point, which the

Americans won only after undergoing "a tremendous fire of musketry and grape shot," Marshall proudly wrote: "The humanity displayed by the conquerors was not less conspicuous, nor less honourable, than their courage. Not a single individual suffered after resistance had ceased."[51]

The Americans were trying to maintain whatever decency can exist in a time of war because basically they were decent people. For almost two hundred years they had lived in an uncivilized wilderness, and they had learned that one must count on one's neighbors for help against the attacks of Indians and the ravages of nature. They had learned they were part of a community and that they must maintain certain standards of conduct if that community was to survive. They were ambitious and independent people, but civil also in the sense that their actions befitted citizens. And this would be one of their legacies to future generations—a combination of ambition, independence, and a sense of decency in their attitudes toward their fellow men.

In late 1779 Marshall was, in effect, discharged from the army. The Virginia soldiers' enlistment periods had expired, and the officers were directed to return home to wait for the calling up of new units, but the units were never called up.[52] Marshall's family was at Yorktown, and he went there. He was twenty-four years old and apparently up to this point had had no romantic involvements. With his military service now behind him and his career ahead of him, he was ready for romance. And romance was waiting for him at Yorktown.

Whatever else the Revolutionary War did for the belles of Yorktown, it had certainly spiced their social life. Handsome American officers frequently moved through the town, as did many young Frenchmen. Few of the Frenchmen spoke English but their continental charm quite intrigued the young American girls, who were not used to such attention. One young lady, perhaps more prudish than the others or maybe only envious, had this to say of her feminine friends' conduct in the presence of so many dashing soldiers:

> Appearance and effect is everything, and really between ourselves [she confided to a friend], it would seem as if ever solid virtue was sacrificed to these; but I will not be censorious, fain would I cast a veil over their frivolities, but really their late conduct has been so extraordinary, that all eyes are fixed upon them.[53]

Of all the soldiers, American or French, who intrigued the young ladies of Yorktown, none was preceded by the reputation earned by John Marshall. "Our expectations were raised to the highest pitch," reported sixteen-year-old Eliza (Betsy) Ambler, "and the little circle of York were on tiptoes on his arrival."

For the Ambler family that winter of 1779–1780 already knew John Marshall. His father was in charge of the garrison at Yorktown. Colonel Marshall lived next door to the Amblers and took a protective interest in the four Ambler daughters while their own father, Jacquelin Ambler, spent considerable time in Williamsburg. Thomas Marshall, immensely proud of his eldest son, often spoke of him to the Ambler girls, telling them of his bravery and his amiability. He even read them his son's letters, and did not suggest restraint when his younger children spoke of their older brother whom they worshipped. "We had been accustomed to hear him spoken of by all as a very paragon," Betsy Ambler recalled some years later. "We had often seen letters from him fraught with filial and fraternal affection . . . devoted from his earliest years to his younger brothers and sisters he was almost idolized by them, and every line received from him, was read with rapture."[54]

When the senior Marshall announced that his son would at last visit Yorktown, all the young ladies of that Virginia city faced a perplexing social problem. Which of them should be first introduced? John Marshall obviously was an outstanding catch, or at least sounded like one, and who should have the first opportunity to meet him? Then what Betsy Ambler called a "remarkable" thing happened. Her younger sister—Mary Willis Ambler, but called Polly—was then only fourteen, had never been to a dancing class, and, according to Betsy, was "diffident beyond all others." But she had listened carefully to the stories of the dashing John Marshall, and they had created for her a vision of him as the man for her. To her sisters and their friends, the young Polly Ambler announced that they were worrying themselves for nothing; *she* would go to the ball where John Marshall was expected to make his first social appearance. Although it would be her first ball, she announced, she intended "to set her cap" for John Marshall. The rest of the Yorktown belles could just forget about him, she made clear, and concern themselves about some other young officer.

And with that determined announcement by a fourteen-year-old girl, yet to take her first formal dance step, began one of the great love stories of American history. Spanning more than five decades, the romance of John and Polly Marshall was played against the backdrop of a society that considered marriage a relationship of economic convenience in which faithfulness was almost an eccentricity. For John and Polly, however, it was a relationship of love.

When John Marshall first arrived in Yorktown, Betsy Ambler was glad to surrender her interest to her younger sister Polly. Betsy had been expecting an Adonis, she recalled, and "lost all desire of becoming agreeable in his eyes when I beheld his awkward figure, unpolished manners, and total negligence of person."

Marshall's appearance always would be deceptive. He was a frontiersman, born and raised in the western part of Virginia. He wore the buckskin of the hunter rather than the soft velvet and white lace of the plantation owner. His grace was that of the woodsman who moves stealthily through the woods in search of game, not that of the urbanite whose skill is in the minuet. But Betsy Ambler was not alone in being deceived by Marshall's appearance. In the course of a long public career as lawyer, politician, legislator, diplomat, and finally for thirty-four years as Chief Justice of the United States, many who gave too great a weight to the appearance of sophistication would be deceived by John Marshall.

Fourteen-year-old Polly Ambler was not. Her older sister Betsy reports that Polly's "superior discernment and solidity of character has made me feel my own insignificance; she with a glance developed his character and understood how to appreciate it." And what did Polly see in John Marshall? "Under the slouched hat," her sister Betsy wrote, "there beamed an eye that penetrated at one glance the inmost recesses of the human character; and beneath the slovenly garb there dwelt a heart replete with every virtue."

The courtship was typical for Virginia in the 1780s. Marshall often read to the Ambler girls "from the best authors, particularly the poets with so much taste and pathos." For a frontiersman who had personally experienced the agony of war, Marshall had an unusual interest in poetry, one that lasted all his life. The beauty of the words, the rhythm of the lines, the meaning of the phrases touched a part of him that the bloodshed of war and, later, the intrigues of politics never could dull. "He was enamoured," a friend said many years later, "of the classical writers of the old English school of Milton and Shakespeare, Dryden and Pope."[55]

And, of course, there were many balls. At Williamsburg Betsy and Polly stayed with friends when a dance was given in their honor at the governor's palace. For the young girls the evening was quite a moment. "[F]or the brilliancy of the company too much cannot be said," Betsy reported. "It consisted of more beauty and elegance than I had ever witnessed before." Betsy was not fond of her escort—"I cannot for my life treat the poor fellow . . . with common good manners"—but she enjoyed the opportunity to be the belle of the ball "and playing off a thousand airs." Polly, however, had no such concerns. John Marshall was her escort, and that was quite satisfactory. "Marshall," said Betsy, "was devoted to my sister."

This Polly to whom John Marshall quickly and forevermore became devoted was the daughter of Thomas Jefferson's first love, Rebecca Burwell. Jefferson wrote of her as "Belinda" and danced with her in the Apollo Room at the Raleigh Tavern in Williamsburg when he was a twenty-year-old law student and she was a beautiful young lady of sixteen. He loved her, so he swore to his friends, but he could not bring himself to specifically and directly propose marriage; there was too much he wanted to do before he tried that! But Rebecca Burwell would not wait for a marriage proposal that might never come. She had been orphaned at age thirteen. A lonely child, she often climbed to the attic of her home and there prayed at a little altar she had built. Her friends criticized her as being overly enthusiastic about her religion, but she ignored the comments, finding in religion her only respite from loneliness. Early in her life, perhaps even in these years before her marriage, the illness began that according to her daughter Betsy "laid the foundation as years increased for sufferings and sorrows beyond the power of description." This "nervous malady," apparently a combination of extreme nervousness and anemia, also afflicted Polly, many years after her marriage.

And so lonely, attractive, nervous, wanting companionship, Rebecca Burwell married another suitor, Jacquelin Ambler. An educated and wealthy Virginia businessman, he was twenty-four years old when he and Rebecca were married in May 1764. Betsy was born the following March and Polly in March of 1766. Two other daughters, Ann and Lucy, were born later.

Jacquelin Ambler was a devoted father. When his wife became ill, he took over the education of his daughters. He was collector of the King's Customs at Yorktown when his daughters were growing up, but he took time from that consuming position to fill the void created by Rebecca's illness. At a time when the education of women was at best superficial, Ambler devoted considerable attention to educating Betsy and Polly and their younger sisters. "Such attentions as we experienced were without parallel," Betsy recalled. She remembered her father with great admiration and said he was a deeply religious man who usually began and ended each day in prayer.

The war destroyed the Amblers' prosperity, involving them "in poverty and perplexity of every kind," said Betsy. For a period the Amblers lived in Winchester, Virginia, with relatives who were unable to care for both an ill mother and four young children while the father was away. Polly by this time was twelve, and Betsy fourteen, but it was Polly who apparently showed the maturity the situation required. "But for the remarkable discretion of my sister who was only twelve years of age," conceded Betsy, "my cousin and myself would have been perpetually involved in difficulties."

Then the family moved to Yorktown where young Polly met John Marshall in his slouch hat, and their romance began. His intentions apparently were serious from the very beginning. But in addition to waiting for the fourteen-year-old Polly to grow older, Marshall was in no position to marry and raise a family. True, when the war ended with the American victory that seemed more certain every day, he would be eligible for the generous land grants promised by both the Continental Congress and the Virginia colony. But this was not enough means to support a young woman such as Polly Ambler, who had been brought up to be a fine lady. There still was the law, however. John Marshall would become a lawyer. His experience on the western frontier had taught him the need for a just system of law among men, and the Revolutionary War and the Declaration of Independence had taught him the need for a similar system among nations. Now he would go to school to acquire the formal education necessary for him to translate that need into action. He turned to the College of William and Mary at Williamsburg.

The formal study of law in the young American nation at the closing of the eighteenth century was, at best, a casual affair. Most potential lawyers apprenticed in a law office for a period of time, then announced that they were ready to practice by themselves, and sought admission to the bar. The procedure was eminently sound for the time. A Philadelphia lawyer, speaking for his own colony but using words that described Virginia as well, said that there was not one volume of reports on American decisions and only about fifty volumes from England. "We had not yet fairly passed from the feudal into the commercial existence," he wrote. "The rules of evidence were much less attended to; and if a man understood a few Acts of Assembly, and knew Dalton's Justice of the Peace, he had all the legal education which any one could teach, and almost all that any could attain."[56]

In deciding to go to William and Mary, John Marshall was probably as much motivated by its proximity to the young Polly as he was by any desire for a formal education. At the time he still apparently was considering returning to Fauquier County to practice, and an education at William and Mary was superfluous to the kind of law practice he envisioned for himself there.

Actually he only stayed at the college for a few weeks, enough time to make some valuable acquaintances. A classmate was Bushrod Washington, a nephew of George Washington. The law professor at William and Mary was George Wythe, who was a major Virginia figure for years not only because of his political leadership and his legal knowledge, but also because of the strength of his character which influenced those fortunate enough to be his students.

Prior to the Revolution most wealthy young men went to England to school, whether to study for the legal profession, medicine, or the clergy. Once the hostilities began, however, that path to knowledge was closed to young Americans and they turned instead to Harvard in Cambridge and to the College of New Jersey, which later became known as Princeton. William and Mary, founded in the late 1600s, had slowly been building a reputation as a solid school but still it was one that only attracted young southern gentlemen who could not make it to one of the better schools in the North. Many Maryland youths crossed the colonial line to Virginia to attend William and Mary, and this, according to one social historian, accounts for the many marital alliances between Maryland and Virginia families in the 1700s,[57] indicating that at least the social atmosphere in Williamsburg was satisfactory.

Shortly before Marshall matriculated, the divinity professorship was abolished. It had been established to produce clergymen for the Church of England, "but it is now thought that Establishments in Favor of any particular Sect are incompatible with ye Freedom of a Republic," explained the president of the school on August 27, 1780, approximately the time Marshall was at the school. The comment was part of a letter to the president of Yale, which also includes this description of how the school operated:

> The Doors of ye University are open to all, nor is even a knowledge in ye ant. Languages a previous Requisite for Entrance. The Students have ye Liberty of attending whom they please, and in what order they please, or all of ye diffr. Lectures in a term if they think proper. The time of taking Degrees was formerly ye same as in Cambridge, but now depends upon ye qualifications of ye candidate. He has a certain course pointed out for his first Degree, and also for ye rest. When Master of Either, ye Degree is conferred.[58]

Such a liberal atmosphere could not help but have an impact on any student, even one who remained there only a few weeks. The school itself was not attractive, at least according to Jefferson, a student in the 1760s, who described the buildings as "rude, mis-shapen piles, which but that they have roofs, would be taken for brick-kilns."[59] The professors were paid eight hogsheads of tobacco a year, and tuition varied, depending upon the number of lectures the student attended. For one thousand pounds of tobacco, he could attend any two of the professors' lectures, and for fifteen hundred pounds, he could attend any three. "The students have to procure a steward, with whom they are to board at whatever rate can be agreed on," wrote a student at the time. "They are to pay rent for their rooms, provide every other necessary. . . ."[60]

And then there was George Wythe, professor of law. Born poor and raised in poverty, Wythe had overcome that handicap by sheer fortitude. He learned Greek at home as a child by studying the Bible in Greek while his mother held an English copy and guided him. After his mother died, he continued his education at William and Mary, probably at the grammar school, then studied law under a prominent Prince George County attorney. By 1779 he had served in the Virginia House of Burgesses, the Continental Congress (he was a signer of the Declaration of Independence), the Virginia House of Delegates, and as a judge of the Virginia High Court of Chancery. He also had been law tutor to Thomas Jefferson, and when on December 4, 1779, the board of visitors of William and Mary—of which Governor Jefferson of Virginia was a member—established the "Professorship of Law and Police," the first chair of law in an American college, Wythe was appointed to it. During the twelve years he held the chair he earned a reputation as the foremost professor of law in America. He also was a classical scholar who imparted to his students the beauty of the classics as well as the majesty of the law; Jefferson is perhaps the finest example of his success.[61]

His students found his course hard work. One, a young man named John Brown, wrote to a relative on February 15, 1780, a few months before John Marshall attended, that the study of law was "a more difficult science than I expected." But John Brown hoped with Wythe's assistance "to make some proficiency in it." This young man had talent; he later became one of the first United States Senators from Kentucky. Of those who finished the law courses in a few months, he said that they "either have strong natural parts, or else they know little about it."[62]

In addition to lecturing his students on law, Wythe organized moot courts. At least once a month the class moved to the former capitol building in Williamsburg where, in the chamber once used by the Virginia General Court, they pleaded the causes assigned to them by Wythe before the professors of the school, who acted as judges, and "the most respectable of the citizens," who made up the audience. Wythe also organized a mock legislative body which met every Saturday. Acting as speaker of the house (only two years before Wythe had been Speaker of the Virginia House of Delegates), he instructed the students in parliamentary procedures. "We meet every Saturday," reported John Brown, "and take under our consideration those bills drawn up by the Committee appointed to revise the laws, then we debate and alter—I will not say amend—with the greatest freedom."[63]

For Wythe, one of the most important parts of a legal education—as it would in fact turn out to be for John Brown, John Marshall, and many of his other students—was to prepare men to be leaders as well as lawyers. His goal, he once said, was "to form such characters as may be fit to succeed those which have been ornamental and useful in the national councils of America."[64]

One of the great strengths of the United States is that it was founded primarily by lawyers. Men like Thomas Jefferson, James Madison, John Adams, Alexander Hamilton, and John Marshall had an affinity for the law, an understanding of the need for order and for a system designed to make the law operable. They argued among themselves, and their arguments were the seeds of political struggles in the United States long after they died; but their disputes were over peripheral matters— economics, the strengths of the federal government versus the state and local governments, the support to be given foreign nations. They never disputed the need for solving these problems through what each understood the law to be. None ever advocated the replacement of a legal system with a system of physical strength and violence. And it was due to the genius of men like George Wythe, who encouraged the development of lawyers into men concerned about government, that such men were forthcoming when the young nation needed them.

At William and Mary Marshall was apparently a popular and earnest student. With some of his classmates he inscribed his name in the plaster of a wall in the college building. It was a juvenile prank for a man who was only a few months shy of twenty-five. But then he had been away soldiering for more than four years and had lost many of the normal opportunities for juvenile mischief and can be excused for trying to catch up.[65] He also was invited to join Phi Beta Kappa, a fraternity organized at the school in 1776 and devoted to intellectual pursuits. The list of members includes persons who would be among Virginia's most illustrious in later years—Spencer Roane, John Page, Stevens Thomson Mason, William Cabell, Bushrod Washington, as well as Marshall, who was listed as the fortieth member of the fraternity. He was inducted into the group May 18, 1780. At the group's next meeting, Saturday, May 21, members debated the pros and cons of the execution of Charles I. Several of the members, Marshall among them, were then assigned the topic "Whether any form of government is more favourable to public virtue than a Commonwealth?" for debate. There is no record of Marshall's argument on this subject, which took place June 3, but it was probably not very effective. The topic called for a theoretical discussion, and this was not and never would be his strong point. He would prove himself with specifics. Then he would produce his arguments in such a logical and persuasive manner that few could stand against him.[66]

Marshall's notes from his college days survive. They cover almost 200 manuscript pages (238 actual pages but 44 are blank), and include a compilation of notations of legal subjects arranged alphabetically from Abatement to Limitation of Actions. These were not notes taken at a college professor's lectures. As William F. Swindler has pointed out, they were intended as a summary of the common law as it was practiced in Virginia at the time.[67] This common law was a mixture of the traditional and the haphazard. It was traditional in that the Americans brought with them to the New World the law as practiced in the courts of the Old. It was haphazard in that the Americans jettisoned that which they believed was inapplicable to their environment and modified that which needed change. In colonial days the Americans had been ingenious in developing their local law within the framework of the English common law, knowing that the decisions of their courts ultimately could come under review by the Privy Council in England, if not the Parliament and the Crown.

Marshall's notes are taken from the third edition of Matthew Bacon's *New Abridgement of the Law*, the *Acts of the Assembly Now in Force in the Colony of Virginia*, and Blackstone's *Commentaries*. His project was ambitious; he was trying to do as a student what the Virginia bar had not accomplished: to compile the laws that a Virginia lawyer must know to practice. The project indicates his eagerness to work hard at something that interested him—the notebook was done in a relatively brief period of time, no more than two months—and also shows his tendency for orderly procedures when involved with the law—the alphabetical arrangement of the topics and then the careful arrangement of the applicable principles beneath each topic.

Though Marshall applied himself, his thoughts occasionally wandered, for he was a young man and he was in love. Across the top of the first page of his notebook, above "Abatement," he had written "Ambler" and then underlined it. Throughout the notebook he occasionally scrawled "Polly Ambler," only "Polly," or "Miss Maria Ambler," or "Miss M. Ambler." He was a diligent student, but even the most diligent student surrenders to love on occasion.[68]

Sometime in July 1780 Marshall's formal legal education ended. At the most he had spent between two and three months in school. By modern standards such brief schooling is unacceptable, but it was not unusual for the period. Bushrod Washington, who was at William and Mary with Marshall, spent only three months there before going to Philadelphia to "read" in the office of a lawyer. John Adams, although he had a complete undergraduate education at Harvard, learned his law entirely by reading in a lawyer's office.

Marshall had in addition to his formal schooling a habit of study and an ability to learn quickly. From his father in the years before the war he had learned something of law as the sinew that holds society together. In the army as deputy judge advocate he had learned how to apply the law in dealings between soldiers. And finally at William and Mary he had learned what printed material was available to him—to pore over, to learn, and to use. And, of course, in the few brief weeks he was there he had made contact with men who would be among the most prominent in Virginia in coming decades. As a soldier he had won many friends who gave him a strong political base in future years. As a student he made many influential acquaintances that also would be valuable to him. There was little lacking in his education for the time.

In the summer of 1780 he was ready to enter the bar, begin his career as a lawyer, and perhaps then claim his beloved Polly. But she was still in her early teens and, in fact, had moved to Richmond with her family. Young John Marshall obviously believed he should return to Fauquier County where his roots were and there begin his career. Accordingly, on August 28, 1780, he presented himself at the county courthouse and produced a license signed by Governor Thomas Jefferson allowing him to practice law and was thereby admitted to the bar of Fauquier County. That his legal career received its formal start with the signature of Jefferson is not without irony considering the enmity that later developed between the two men.[69] Family tradition has Marshall working in a lawyer's office for a time in Fauquier, but there is no evidence to support that tradition.

In the fall Marshall went to Philadelphia to be inoculated against smallpox. The disease was the greatest ravager of the time and probably was responsible for more deaths in the American army during the Revolution than were the British. As a soldier, Marshall had seen the deadly impact of the disease and this prompted him to be inoculated, which was perhaps the most daring thing he did in a long life that was often marked by adventure. Inoculations against smallpox were so dangerous at the time that Virginia did not even permit them. Controlling the disease when given in the inoculation process was so difficult that only persons in supremely good health were accepted for inoculation and only under the best of all possible circumstances. Marshall certainly fit the description of being in perfect health. He made the journey to Philadelphia from Fauquier on foot, walking between thirty and thirty-five miles a day. That didn't faze him. He always enjoyed walking and took long walks almost every day of his life. But it played havoc with his appearance. In later years he enjoyed telling of his arrival in Philadelphia—a war hero and a lawyer—and being denied a room in a hotel there because of his shabby clothing, long beard, and unkempt hair.[70]

Marshall had been away from the army for almost a year, and civilian life obviously was pleasant. But the war continued in the North and then returned to Virginia. After the Battle of Great Bridge and the subsequent burning of Norfolk the colony had largely been spared the ravages of war, but early in 1781 the people of the city of Richmond were thrown into a panic when news reached them that British forces, under the leadership of the American traitor Benedict Arnold, had landed downriver on the James and were marching toward the city. "What an alarming crisis this is," cried Betsy Ambler. Her father, a prominent member of the colonial government, was a sure target for the British soldiers, so the Amblers decided they must flee the city. Jacquelin disguised himself in an old coat and left first, usually traveling alone, attended by a single slave, a man named Sam. His wife and children fled after him, staying with friends and begging lodgings along the road. One night, after watching their father start down the road, the Ambler girls and their mother crowded into a "miserable little hovel" to eat their supper when they heard the sound of horses on the road. Their immediate fear was the British, but it was only some Virginia militiamen warning them that British soldiers were on the way. The Ambler women held their council and determined that "we should be off in a moment." Their destination was the Virginia mountains, far away from the rivers that the British used so easily for traveling. They rode all night in their carriage, over bumpy back roads to avoid any British patrols until just at sunrise they reached the plantation of a friend. Curiously, the house was empty, but the Ambler women were too tired to question this. They stretched out blankets to sleep on when the owner of the plantation charged into the house. British soldiers had passed him on the road, headed toward Charlottesville. That cut off the escape route for the Amblers; but more important to them, Jacquelin Ambler was ahead of them on the road to Charlottesville. The British would surely capture him.

Fortunately, Jacquelin was able to evade the British. He successfully hid from them, doubled back on his trail, found his family, and led them back to the spot they had left the previous night. "Thus were we one whole night, and a greater part of the next day, accomplishing a journey," said Betsy Ambler, "that placed us precisely in the same situation we were in before." It had been two days' hard traveling, hiding like animals, always fearful of imminent capture by the British. Polly was not yet fifteen years of age. Certainly the experience contributed to the nervousness that afflicted her in later years.

There was another escape from the British that spring that also affected John Marshall's life, or at least the attitudes he held in later years. Thomas Jefferson's term as governor ended on June 2, a Saturday. The state legislature, not meeting on Saturday, postponed a vote for a new governor. That Monday morning a horseman came dashing up to Monticello, Jefferson's hilltop home in Charlottesville, to inform him that the British were near. Jefferson saw to the escape of his guests and his family and then himself—and came close to being captured. To the public at the time, however, the picture was of the governor of the colony ignominiously fleeing the British. Betsy Ambler, for example, described as "laughable" the picture of Jefferson, "who they say took neither rest nor food, for man or horse, till he reached Carter's Mountain." The Virginia legislature later investigated Jefferson's conduct and found nothing about it to formally criticize.[71]

After the war Thomas Jefferson was never very popular with John Marshall and the other young Virginians who had spent years away from their homes risking their lives and sacrificing their fortunes for the cause Jefferson espoused so nobly. Perhaps they were unfair, but human emotions are not always fair. Jefferson did not make the same sacrifices they did, and then when danger threatened that June, he had appeared to flee in a "laughable" manner. If that were not sufficient, during the war, according to Jefferson's most recent friendly biographer, Merrill D. Peterson:

> The hospitality enjoyed by the English and German officers—who were technically prisoners—at the seats of Virginia gentlemen suggests a kind of international community among men of rank and breeding that even the hatreds of war could not abate. Jefferson despised royalty and its trappings, but he was charmed by Phillips, Riedesel, and their like. He opened his doors to them, and entertained them, loaned them books, tried to make them comfortable in the strange and primitive country they inhabited.[72]

To the young Virginians who were being shot at by Phillips, Riedesel, and their like, an international community that included the enemy was not acceptable. To the veterans of the Revolution, Thomas Jefferson was never a hero.

The British invasion of Virginia in 1781 was a traumatic experience for the Americans there. Arnold reached Richmond and ravaged the city before leaving it. The militiamen were called up again and John Marshall returned to the army. He was with a group of officers who were to lead a detachment to join the American army farther south. But the immediate threat from Arnold's forces subsided as the regular American army challenged him, and Marshall resigned; his second tour in the military had been brief and uneventful.[73]

Later in 1781 another military event produced a worldwide trauma. At about noon on October 19 the British forces under Lord Cornwallis at Yorktown surrendered to the combined American-French forces. For the British, who had entered the war certain of their military power and ultimate victory, the day represented disaster. The British troops made plain their distaste at participating in an event they had never anticipated. "We are not to be surprised," said an American officer, "that the pride of the British officers is humbled on this occasion, as they have always entertained an exalted opinion of their own military prowess, and affected to view the Americans as a contemptible, undisciplined rabble."[74]

No one felt this distress more than Cornwallis. Not having the courage to lead his men in their defeat as he would certainly have led them in victory, he dispatched an aide to handle the actual surrender. Cornwallis wrote the next day to Sir Henry Clinton: "I have the mortification to inform your Excellency, that I have been forced to give up the Posts of York and Gloucester, and to surrender the Troops under my Command, by Capitulation. . . ."[75]

The Americans had won their revolution. To George III who, three months to the day before the surrender, had vowed that "I will never put my hand to any other conclusion of this business" except the return of the American colonies to English rule,[76] Cornwallis's mortification was a political and personal blow. His Prime Minister, Lord North, who had created the policy of suppressing the colonies and was identified with the war, took the news of the Cornwallis surrender, according to a description of the time, "as he would have taken a bullet through his breast" and shouted "Oh God! It is all over."[77] He was right. His policies had failed and he was out of power. The King was forced to come to terms with the opposition and his power, and the power of the English throne, which he had struggled to regain, was never again as great as it had been prior to that surrender.

George never forgot that he not only lost a war but had also destroyed the concept of kingly power he had dedicated his life to preserving. And what he could not forget he could not forgive. His bitterness toward the Americans lasted the rest of his life. In 1783 he agreed to the sailing of 150 English convicts to Virginia and Maryland, saying he would give the Americans no favor "but the permitting them to obtain Men unworthy to remain in this Island I shall certainly consent to."[78] His bitterness focused on George Washington. Nineteen years after the Cornwallis surrender, on February 28, 1800, London heard of Washington's death. The news was treated with the respect that the death of a great leader deserves by all persons in that city, except the King. George III deliberately took no notice of it. On three occasions the American minister in London, Rufus King, while "in full mourning" met with George III but George refused in any way to acknowledge the death of Washington. At the meetings others present expressed their formal condolences to King, but George III remained silent.[79]

And well might Cornwallis have been mortified and George III bitter over the American victory. That victory meant that the many had grasped power from the few, the silent had succeeded in making themselves heard, democracy had displaced despotism. Never again would the world be the same. The resistance of the many to the inherited power of the few spread from the New World to the Old and then to Asia and Africa, becoming a universal cry for decency and justice and the opportunity to determine one's own fate. What was created in the United States was the ambition, if not always the model, for a worldwide

revolution, and a responsibility for the United States to demonstrate that a revolution could produce the results its participants
sought and need not inevitably lead to another despotism. That
responsibility would rest upon all Americans for all time, but
some would bear a greater share, and one of these was John
Marshall.

But an understanding of such a role was not yet evident in
the twenty-six-year-old Marshall. He was much more concerned
in the early 1780s with the practical side of his life: Where
should he earn a living and should be marry Polly? She was
growing out of her early teens; sixteen was a marriageable age
in colonial Virginia. Frail in body, lovely in appearance to John
Marshall, a foot less than his six feet, she continued to be his true
love although he now lived in Fauquier and she was in Richmond
with her family.

Then Marshall moved to Richmond. He said it was because
he wanted to practice law in the state's superior courts, which
met there. These were the General Court, the High Court of
Chancery, and the Court of Admiralty.[80] From the standpoint
of his future career, the decision was a wise one. Not only did he
ultimately develop a thriving practice before the high state courts
and then before the federal courts in Richmond, but he also
mixed with the other young lawyers of the colony. He met the
budding politicians, heard the gossip of the community leaders,
and ultimately was drawn into this group of leaders himself. It
was a stimulating society. The Virginia bar at the end of the
eighteenth and the beginning of the nineteenth century, with its
center in Richmond, was perhaps one of the most brilliant as-
semblages of legal talent ever gathered together. Patrick Henry
was one of its members. Another was John Wickham, later a
defense lawyer in the Aaron Burr treason trial. There was
Spencer Roane, who became a brilliant exponent on the Virginia
bench of Jefferson's philosophy of limited government. Still
another was William Wirt, whose arguments before the United
States Supreme Court became classics. And there was John
Marshall. With his convivial spirit and brilliant mind, he became
a member of this inner circle of leaders.

He may have been aware of this potential when he made
the move, but probably the prospect of being near Polly was more
influential in determining his action. There were two significant
criteria in Virginia for choosing a wife. One was the woman's
ability to become the gracious mistress of the house. The task
demanded impeccable manners, dignity, modesty, and the ability
to preside at entertainments with the same skill she applied to
her work in the kitchen and at the spinning wheel. Besides rais-

ing children of whom her husband would be proud, the Virginia wife was supposed to be deeply religious and not very knowledgeable about affairs of the world.

The second criterion for a proper wife was that she have money. The ideal marriage of the time was of a poor but hardworking and honorable man to a wealthy woman. This was not the dishonorable alliance that later generations would think. Fathers of young women anticipated buying husbands for their daughters. "'[I]t was not in my power to pay him all the money this year that I intended to give my daughters," wrote one father of the bride to a father of the bridegroom, ". . . but [I will] give him five hundred pounds next spring, and five hundred pounds more as soon as I can raise or get the money. . . ."

The ideal woman for such a marriage of financial convenience was the wealthy widow, of whom there were many in the Virginia of Revolutionary times. Husbands often died at an early age, leaving their wives with large landholdings and usually little experience in managing such affairs. It was considered proper for the widow to marry as quickly as possible—so quickly that in at least one instance the meats prepared for the funeral meal also were served at the marriage celebration. Often a husband, suspecting he was about to die, arranged for a single man to become his wife's second husband. Such second husbands were taken care of by the first, usually by being made the executor of the first husband's estate.[81]

Such an alliance could have been made by John Marshall, as it was by George Washington and Thomas Jefferson. In his mid-twenties, tall and handsome, Marshall was a war hero and an attractive personality. If he lacked the sophistication of the cultured city dweller, he had a great deal of natural charm. But rather than seek a rich and attractive widow, he continued his suit of young Polly Ambler. She was assumed to possess all the genteel qualities required to be gracious mistress of the house, but she could not fulfill the second requirement. The war had depleted her father's financial resources, and he was starting again in Richmond as a businessman and political figure. But this did not deter John Marshall. He loved Polly. For him that was the requirement that overrode all others.

Marshall had competition for Polly's hand. Major Richard Anderson, also a war hero—who was called "Major Dick"—was an ardent suitor. And there were the inevitable disagreements and misunderstandings that are part of young people's courtships. This was due to Polly more than to Marshall. His mind was made up; he would marry this young girl who had set her cap for him almost two years earlier. But Polly was not yet certain she wished to marry. Marshall family tradition has it that John proposed to her in direct terms, and Polly refused him. He then strode out of her house and mounted his horse to ride off toward Fauquier County—toward an oblivion from which perhaps the nation might never have recovered.

Polly watched him go, and then when he had turned the corner, she began to cry hysterically. Nothing would quiet her. The uncertainty of youth had led her to say "no" when she meant "yes." A cousin, John Ambler, put his arm around her to console her. Without Polly's being aware, he cut off a lock of her hair. He then excused himself, raced after John Marshall, and presented the lock to the disappointed suitor. "My father," said John and Polly's youngest child many years later, "supposing she had sent it, renewed his suit and they were married."

Polly placed the thin snip of light-brown hair that had brought John Marshall racing back to her in a locket and wore it all her life. And when she died, he wore it.[82]

The wedding ceremony took place in the Hanover County home of John Ambler on January 3, 1783. Christmas greens probably still decorated the parlor. Polly, two months shy of seventeen, looked lovely in a dress of white brocade in an off-the-shoulder style popular at the time, with shirred sleeves. A short train flared from the back of the dress.

At his wedding John Marshall was twenty-seven years old. He was a member of the bar, had a lovely wife, a gift from his father of three horses and a Negro slave named Robin, and—so family tradition insists—exactly one guinea to his name. He now must earn a living.[83]

Book Two:

LAWYER
AND POLITICIAN

I

A N ELDERLY GENTLEMAN from the country arrived in Richmond one morning in the 1780s on serious business. His case was being argued before the appeals court, and he needed a lawyer. Not knowing many people in the city, the country gentleman asked his landlord, the owner of the Eagle Hotel, who was the best advocate in the city. The answer was quick in coming: John Marshall. But when the prospective client saw Marshall, he immediately decided against hiring him. What he saw was not inspiring. Marshall did not appear the lawyer type, not at all. He was a man of about thirty, wearing a plain linen roundabout hanging out over his knee breeches and had his hair tied in an unkempt queue at the back of his head. Even more ludicrous, he was eating cherries from a straw hat he carried under his arm!

No, this John Marshall, no matter how highly recommended by the owner of the Eagle Hotel, was not a fit lawyer for the country gentleman. The man then went to the courthouse where he struck up a conversation with the clerk of the court. Explaining his circumstances, the country gentleman asked the clerk to recommend a lawyer for hire. The clerk was happy to oblige. The best young advocate, he said, was John Marshall. The country gentleman had been through that once. No, John Marshall was not the lawyer for him. He wanted a sophisticated city lawyer, not a country bumpkin.

At that moment, his obvious choice entered: an elderly lawyer wearing a dark coat and a powdered wig. His appearance said he was an advocate of rare ability, and the country gentleman hired him immediately. He had brought $100 for a lawyer's fee, and he gave $95 to the man with the powdered wig.

While waiting for his own case to come up, the country gentleman sat in the courtroom listening to the other cases being argued. The first was between John Marshall and the lawyer in the powdered wig. Immediately, the man from the country realized he had made a serious mistake. Marshall was vastly superior to the man to whom he had given his $95. When the first case was over, the country gentleman approached Marshall, explained the events of the day, and asked if he would take his case for the remaining $5. Marshall agreed. He accepted the $5 and joked about the power of a powdered wig and a black coat.[1]

That story is one of the more famous about John Marshall as a young lawyer. It reveals much about him. There is the casual attitude he had toward his appearance, the reputation he had built early as an outstanding lawyer, and, finally, his own ability to be amused by a situation in which he received a fee of only $5.

Richmond was an excellent place for a young lawyer to establish his practice. The state's highest trial courts met there —the General Court, the High Court of Chancery, and the Court of Admiralty as well as the appeals court—which meant there was more than enough business for a bright young lawyer. And John Marshall certainly was that. He was also a veteran. "My extensive acquaintance in the army was of great service to me," he recalled in later years. "My numerous military friends, who were dispersed over the state, took great interest in my favour, and I was more successful than I had reason to expect."[2]

He had served, on and off, for four years in the Virginia militia and the American army. He had served well, impressed his comrades, and earned the respect of all who came across him. They knew, these ex-soldiers, that John Marshall understood them and would look after their legal problems with both sympathy and courage. The issues were not insignificant. Virginia and the Continental Congress decided to reward soldiers with large tracts of land. To be eligible, veterans had to prove their military service and then make certain that their land warrants were used to claim land in the West in such a manner that their titles could not be challenged. This meant they must turn to a lawyer, and the lawyer many of them turned to was John Marshall.

"They knew," he said, "that I felt their wrongs and sympathized in their sufferings, and had partaken of their labors, and that I vindicated their claims upon their country with a warm and constant earnestness."[3]

Joseph Story, his friend and fellow Justice on the Supreme Court in later years, affirmed how Marshall had been "spoken of by some of these veterans in terms of the warmest praise. In an especial manner the Revolutionary officers of the Virginia line— now 'few and faint, but fearless still'—appeared almost to idolize him, as an old friend and companion in arms, enjoying their unqualified confidence."[4]

The first pension legislation for American soldiers was enacted by the Continental Congress on August 26, 1776. It offered half-pay for disabled soldiers for as long as their disability

lasted. Two years later, on May 15, 1778, the Congress authorized half-pay to military officers for seven years after the war if
they stayed in the service until the end of the war. On October
21, 1780, that law was changed to offer half-pay for life, but on
March 22, 1783, it again was changed, to half-pay for only five
years. The Congress also offered land as a bounty for veterans. A
lieutenant was eligible for two hundred acres, and other officers
could receive up to five hundred acres. The separate colonies also
were generous, actually much more so than the Continental Congress, in distributing unclaimed lands, primarily in the West, to
their young men returning from the wars.

Many young soldiers who did not understand the law
turned to John Marshall, assuming he would make certain they
received all the back pay and all the land to which they were
entitled. For John Harris, Marshall secured 103 pounds, 7 shillings, and 4 pence. For Simon Hill, he managed to get 24 pounds.
For William Hoge, he was able to obtain 59 pounds, 11 shillings,
and 10 pence. And there were many others who enjoyed the
largesse of a grateful nation, secured for them through the
watchful eye of John Marshall, so that they could begin new lives
on their own land where they could farm, hunt, and raise
families.[5]

Such cases were superficially simple. The various pension
laws offered certain benefits, those eligible applied for those
benefits and received them. But there was another point that
must soon be apparent to one intimately involved in those laws.
They were not capricious nor were the men who implemented
them frivolous. Eligibility was not determined arbitrarily. Much
of the legal work in the American courts for the next forty years
stemmed from conflicting claims of ownership of land, and as a
private person, a lawyer, and then as a judge, Marshall insisted
on a strict interpretation of the law. As one who had seen how
that law had benefited young veterans he could not do otherwise.
Men formed together in a society and law was their tool to
resolve their differences; it was not a response to the most impassioned plea.

Marshall himself was eligible for a considerable amount of
land as well as for the half-pay benefits, and he took advantage of
that eligibility. On July 4, 1782, he picked up a certificate worth
116 pounds, 15 shillings, and 4 pence as the back pay owed him.
Later he picked up 119 pounds, 16 shillings, 4 pence for his
father.[6] But that money was only the beginning of the benefits
he secured because of his veteran's status. Starting with what
was owed him because of his military service, Marshall became
one of the largest land speculators of his time, a time when men

gambled on the future of land even more readily than they chanced their money on the popular horse races or cock fights.

On November 30, 1782, slightly more than one month before his marriage, Marshall was issued a warrant for 4,000 acres of land because of his three years' service as an officer. The next year, on July 10, 1783, his father Thomas received a land warrant for 6,666⅔ acres.[7] The warrants meant that they could go to the western Virginia lands, called Kentucky, locate desirable land, patent it, and exchange their warrants for it. Thomas Marshall, with his experience as a surveyor, was the ideal choice to travel to the Kentucky lands, identify the choice sites, and patent them for his family. That is exactly what he did.

There was another means to acquire land. At the end of the war Virginia called in her depreciated currency and exchanged it for untitled lands in Kentucky, a move that sparked a great land rush in which the Marshalls eagerly participated. Thomas Jefferson recalled in 1809 that after the war, "There were considerable quantities of good lands being granted," but at the time he was writing, Jefferson conceded, "there is probably none cultivable ungranted,"[8] the land rush had so consumed the vacant acreage. John Marshall's participation in this land rush, although it was perhaps not much greater than that of other Virginians, staggers the modern mind. On July 12, 1783, for example, he received a warrant, for which he paid $64,000 in the depreciated and almost worthless Continental money, for forty thousand acres of land. The land was chosen and surveyed, apparently by his father, in 1785, and was formally conveyed to Marshall in 1787 by Governor Edmund Randolph. There also were land warrants for his father and for his brothers who had been in the war, particularly James Markham Marshall. Before the Marshall family was finished, it owned land in the Kentucky region of Virginia in the tens of thousands of acres.[9]

That the Marshalls and other Virginians invested so heavily in land is not surprising considering how worthless paper money had turned out to be. There was no national currency. Each state printed its own money, which other states either did or did not honor, as they chose. Individuals and organizations were forced to rely on the barter system. In the 1780s Virginia passed an act proclaiming that tobacco, hemp, flour, grains, and skins could be accepted by the government as payment for taxes.[10]

Only land retained its value and promised to increase in value. A growing demand was inevitable. Families had many children who needed new land to develop their own farms. To John Marshall, who had seen his family impoverished by the war and who always felt strongly the need to provide economic security, the possession of land was the means to riches, if not for himself, at least for his children and their children.

For a young man beginning a family and establishing a career, Richmond was an attractive city to live in. The town had been laid out in 1737 and was incorporated five years later. In 1751 it became the site of the Henrico County courthouse. At that century midpoint the population was between 250 and 300 persons. But even then the town showed promise. With its location on the James River and its proximity to the thriving communities of Williamsburg, Yorktown, and Norfolk, it could be the funnel through which the raw goods produced by the western settlers passed to the merchants on the eastern shore and then to the European markets. In 1779 the city became the state capital. Burned by the British under Benedict Arnold two years later, it was rebuilt into a more attractive city. When Marshall moved there, it was a bustling market and political town of perhaps two thousand people and three hundred houses.

Main Street, the only street where the buildings were "not few and far between," was an unpaved streak of dust and mud, with only occasional sidewalks. The houses themselves were of wood and one or two stories high. There was a market house at Main and Seventeenth Streets, in reality an open shed supported by long posts, where the men more often than the women came to do the daily shopping. A green pasture sloped from it to Shockoe Creek. There the laundresses did their washing and then laid the clothes out on the pasture to dry in the sun. A narrow bridge crossed the creek. While it was ample for pedestrians, horseback riders and wagons had to ford the creek. After heavy rains one season, however, the planks in the bridge were removed and a ferry boat was installed.[11]

The town had one newspaper, issued twice weekly, and according to one observer, "inferior in every respect to the sorriest of the Philadelphia sheets."[12] But the city was growing. By the mid-1780s its population probably was close to four thousand. There were numerous stores, and European ships brought finished goods to trade with these merchants for tobacco. In the newspapers the sellers boasted of their wares, calling the residents to "the green painted store near the Capitol," to "Lewis Ganot's Store, the west side of the Bridge," to "William Waddell, Goldsmith & Jeweler at the Sign of the Thirteen Stars opposite Mr. Anderson's Tavern." The shops offered a variety of wares: shoe buckles, watches, hair devices; Jamaica spirits, sugar, coffee, gin in bottles; coats and capes . . . scarlet, crimson, black, and drab-cloth; jellies, chocolate, oil in flasks, and on and on.

Richmond was becoming a wealthy city. Planters in the

nearby lands came there to do their selling and their shopping. They also came to Richmond for their amusements, the horse races in the spring and fall, the fancy balls, the theater, and even, after 1785, a library.[13] For a young man from the country, as John Marshall was, Richmond was a sophisticated community. He enjoyed it, and it was his home for the next five decades of his life.

There was only one church, St. John's on Church Hill. For the Virginians to return to the practice of regular church attendance and of support of an established church would take some years. To most of them, established church meant the Church of England, which was too closely associated with the British Crown. They did not object to its theology, only to its politics. This aversion was particularly aggravated after the war when followers of the Church of England attempted to regain for it the privileged position it had held in Virginia prior to the Revolution. Marshall, however, because of his father's association with the vestry in Leeds in the years before the war, could never be completely hostile to an established church, and shortly this would bring him into his first major political conflict with Thomas Jefferson and Jefferson's protégé, James Madison.

The people of Richmond had much to occupy themselves. There were many taverns and grog shops. Drinking was considered a sign of masculinity and most Virginia gentlemen, including Marshall, drank liberally. There was gambling on horses, cards, and on most other events in which the outcome was in the slightest doubt. Ladies were not permitted to join in most of these diversions, although many of them enjoyed cards —including a game called loo, which was played for high stakes. But they occupied themselves constructing social orders which they adhered to strictly. The statement of equality in the Declaration of Independence not only did not extend to blacks; it also did not extend to the female social circles.[14]

With prosperity and sophistication came the beginning of the debilitation of the Virginians. They had their food and drink, slaves to do the menial labors that so annoyed the genteel, land in the West to pass on to their children, and very little else to worry about, or so it seemed. Within several decades the debilitation would become obvious, a large concern of such senior statesmen then as John Marshall, and even more obvious to and admitted by his grandchildren. But in the late 1780s and early 1790s the Virginians did not realize they were becoming the victims of their own sloth. In later years Marshall's enemies, and occasionally some of his friends, charged him with having succumbed too much to the pleasures of a thriving Richmond. And it is true that he relished life and lived it heartily. But there is no record, nor any indication, that his pursuit of any of these social activities was excessive or in any way embarrassed himself, his friends, or his family. The respect he gained in the city of Richmond demonstrates that.

Marshall's rise to prominence as a lawyer was helped by his family connections. His father-in-law, Jacquelin Ambler, was beginning the slow climb back to wealth and prominence, and his political connections were of value to his son-in-law. In 1782 Ambler became a Richmond alderman. That year he also won a contest for state treasurer. "Empty as the strong box is, I am told there was a warm contest for this office," Edmund Pendleton reported to James Madison. Pendleton, a prominent Virginian, was satisfied at the result, that Ambler beat a man named Foster Webb—"a clever youth in business, but too young for the dignity and importance of that office."[15] Pendleton believed that age added a great deal to a person's qualifications. He would shortly make similar remarks about John Marshall.

Marshall's father was also an asset to his son's career. Thomas Marshall had moved to Kentucky permanently and established a western link for the family that was a large source of legal business for John Marshall. The father's move west was prompted by a situation typical of many Revolutionary soldiers: he was short of money. As the war was ending, Thomas Marshall appeared to be a wealthy man. In Fauquier County he owned about two thousand acres of land, twenty-two slaves, horses, and cattle. But the men had not been home for years to work the land; prices and taxes were high. Thomas asked his old friend George Washington to help him out by buying some of his land, but Washington was in the same position as Marshall. His tenure as commander-in-chief had practically ruined him financially. Mount Vernon had been neglected and most of his other resources had gone to keep the army together. He could not help his friend. Finally, Marshall was able to sell a large tract of land to Thomas Massey. The one thousand acres sold for 30,000 pounds and was part of a seventeen-hundred-acre tract Thomas Marshall had purchased seven years earlier for 912 pounds. The escalation of the price was not a sign that the land had increased in value but that paper currency had so depreciated.[16]

Thomas Marshall was appointed surveyor for Fayette County in the Kentucky region, and began a career of prominence in Kentucky affairs as well as a career as a land developer built on the land warrants he and his family had earned on the basis of their involvement in the Revolution.[17] He was, of course, one of the best-known men in Virginia, because of his service in the House of Burgesses prior to the war and also because of his military service. Naturally, the Virginia government gave him assignments in the Kentucky territory. He was appointed a commissioner to settle disputed land claims. In May 1783 the Virginia Assembly named him a trustee of the Transylvania Seminary, a school the trustees were to establish. Eight thousand acres were turned over to them, "as a free donation from this commonwealth," to provide the proposed school with a financial start. Later in the 1780s Thomas Marshall was appointed receiver for Kentucky, a tax-collecting position.[18]

Thomas Marshall had grown up on the frontier and had been a soldier. Still, like the other Virginians in the Kentucky wilderness, he was not unruffled by the threat from the Indians. A report filed in Richmond in 1788 indicates that the threat was not an idle one. "The delegates from Kentucky, D. Boone, T. Marshall, and J. Fowler, Jr.," it said, "inform the Executive that the number of militia necessary to defend the frontier of that District will depend upon the vigor with which the savages may carry on the war. They therefore recommend that the matter be left to a meeting of the Field Officers of the District, to be called by the County Lieutenant. Most of the cavalry in that country were volunteers; had selected their own officers subject to the general militia law, and they therefore decline to recommend any." The report concluded: "The arms sent out in the Spring of 1787 were generally unfit for service, and not a single scabbord, belt, cartrid'e box or sling came with them."[19]

John Marshall had a favorite story about his father's adventures in Kentucky, one that he retold for many years afterwards. The common method of traveling to the Kentucky territory was by flatboat down the Ohio River. The marauding Indians, who had no boats equal to the currents in the wide and swift-flowing Ohio, hid on shore and attempted to trick the boats into landing. In the early 1780s Thomas Marshall was the leader of a group taking three boats down the river with cattle, horses, and other supplies. The trip was uneventful until, at about ten o'clock one night, they passed the mouth of the Kanawha River and were hailed from the shore by a man who spoke good English. He identified himself as James Girty, brother of Simon Girty, a notorious white renegade who had lived with the Indians. James shouted to the men on the boat that he was posted there, by order of his brother Simon, to warn all boats against being decoyed ashore. The Indians apparently had lost their respect for Simon Girty, who now was an outcast from both worlds. In hope of regaining a position in the white man's world, Simon and

James were taking upon themselves the responsibility for warning against the Indians' tricks.

"Every effort would be made to draw passengers ashore. White men would appear on the bank, and children would be heard to supplicate for mercy. But," continued James Girty, "do you keep the middle of the river, and steel your heart against every mournful application which you may receive."

Thomas Marshall thanked Girty and the three flatboats continued on their way, the men more alert. Other boats, however, had missed the warning. And the Indians managed to capture one with a crew headed by a man named Johnston. That was prize enough until the Indians on shore saw Marshall's three boats coming downriver laden with a rich haul. The Marshall boats were about a mile upstream when first seen by the Indians. Immediately the Indians pulled out the captured boat and ordered their white prisoners, headed by Johnston, to begin rowing. The chase was on.

The three Marshall boats floated down the river rapidly, a hundred yards apart. Thomas Marshall was manning the steering oar on the last boat, readily visible as he stood at the stern, a red bandana wrapped around his head. The three boats were in midstream, moving quickly in the current. The Indians, moving out from shore toward the middle of the river, were going against the current and moved slowly. They were unable to head off the three Marshall boats, but they came up rapidly enough behind them to come within rifle range. Once in the middle of the river they moved faster and drove their white captives to work the oars harder. They soon must overtake their target.

Thomas Marshall's boat was in the most danger. He had only one pair of oars and simply could not compete with the Indian boats, which had double oars and also men armed with rifles—which they used. The deck of Tom Marshall's boat was swept with rifle fire from the pursuing Indians. Marshall was a brave man. Despite the Indians' fire, he stood straight and tall at the steering oar. He managed to keep his boat in the midstream current where it could move faster, while the Indians' boat slipped out of the current and slowed. The chase lasted for the next hour and Marshall's skill as an oarsman kept his boat ahead of the Indians. But the attackers were coming closer, and the chase obviously soon would be over.

The only possible escape was to buy off the Indians. The second of Marshall's three boats slowed down until the flatboat commanded by Marshall reached it. Then Marshall and his crew jumped aboard the second boat, leaving the third for the Indians.

They did the same with the first boat, leaving the Indians two boats laden with supplies. At this point the Indians stopped their pursuit. On the deserted boats they found several horses, flour, sugar, chocolate, and a keg of whiskey. Thomas Marshall and his men escaped.[20]

Thomas Marshall kept up his friendship with George Washington. Although it is probable that the two men never saw each other again after the Revolution, they often wrote, and Thomas became an agent for Washington in the Kentucky region. This also helped keep John Marshall's name before George Washington, whose importance within the United States was continually rising.[21]

Thomas Marshall managed to secure a large amount of legal business for his son because of the disputed land claims. Land was claimed by veterans under Treasury warrants issued by the Continental Congress and also by veterans under state warrants issued in Richmond. The granting of land in the years before the war, the laws enacted by the Americans to destroy the British titles to the land, the vague boundaries drawn, all combined to totally confuse title to land. In 1788 a group of veterans agreed to take their problems to the High Court of Appeals with the understanding that the decision handed down by the Richmond court would be used by the Supreme Court of the Kentucky district to settle future claims. Thomas Marshall wrote to the Virginia governor that if the Treasury warrants were given precedence over the state claims, he hoped other land would then be found to satisfy the state claimants. "For further information on this head," he told the governor, "I beg leave to refer you to my son John who will be engaged on the part of the officers and will have a full statement of the matter sent down to him."[22] (Later, when Kentucky sought statehood, John Marshall became the agent for the territory in the Virginia Assembly; a later generation would have described him as a lobbyist.)

By the middle and late 1780s, then, John Marshall was a successful member of the Richmond bar. He had become noted for his ability to handle cases on appeal and became a lawyer's lawyer, one called on by other lawyers to argue their cases before the high courts. According to one account of Marshall as an advocate in that period of his life, he was not "unskilled in the use of those keen and glittering weapons of the law logic, which, like the sword of Saladin, are formidable mainly from the dexterity with which they are wielded." But Marshall, it was said, preferred "the ponderous battle-axe to the Turkish scimitar." And while he could "apply with admirable felicity . . . he never delighted in discussing a mere technical principle," but "if he did, it was with him technical in the best and highest sense of the term . . . not a mere verbal distinction or quibble of logic."[23] Although that description may be worth preserving more for its colorful language than for its accuracy, it does suggest one of Marshall's qualities as Chief Justice in the next century. As an interpreter of the United States Constitution his great ability was to cut through to the heart of an issue without being distracted or diverted by false issues. He had what Edward S. Corwin described as "a discerning eye for fundamental issues,"[24] and he always understood it was a *Constitution* he was expounding.

In a period when orators like Patrick Henry could move men to war, Marshall was not considered a great orator. "He was admired rather as a profound reasoner . . . his manner was unstudied, and on common occasions frequently careless, but he constantly rose with his subject," said an account of Marshall written while he was still alive. "Without the appearance of formal divisions his arguments fell naturally into the most luminous and happy arrangement." His style was said to be simple and clear' and he possessed "a quickness of perception that enabled him at once to lay hold on the strong points of his own cause and the weak ones of his adversaries."[25]

He made influential and useful friends. When Edmund Randolph was elected governor of Virginia in 1786 he ran a notice in the Richmond newspaper saying that because being governor was incompatible with practicing law, "I beg leave to inform my clients that John Marshall, Esq., will succeed to my business in general."[26] He also apparently was a generous man, willing to help others. Albert Gallatin, in later years a prominent politician and political enemy of Marshall's, much later recalled having spent the years between 1783 and 1789 in Richmond where he was treated "with that old proverbial Virginia hospitality, to which I know no parallel." Everyone befriended him, he wrote sixty years later, but two persons impressed him particularly. One was Patrick Henry and the other was John Marshall, "who, though but a young lawyer in 1783, was almost at the head of the bar in 1786, offered to take me into his office without a fee, and assured me that I would become a distinguished lawyer."[27]

Still, Marshall retained his casual attitudes. His carelessness in dress was a sign of other careless habits. To one client he wrote in 1785: "I had drawn the ejectment some time past and meant to have brought it up with me, but when I searched I found I had left it behind me. I will send it to the sheriff as soon as possible from Richmond."[28] Two years later he had a more serious problem with a client named John Alexander in

London. When in Richmond, Alexander had talked to Marshall about his suit against a man named Belfield. But Marshall forgot what was said. That became embarrassing when Belfield asked Marshall to represent him in the same case, offering "very high fees indeed." Marshall wrote to Alexander: "I have refused [Belfield] till I see or hear from you because no consideration would tempt me to engage for him if I had promised to appear for you. I do not recollect or believe that I did, but I wish to be certain on the subject."[29]

This casualness, however, did not deter prominent Virginians from using him as their attorney. In 1789 George Washington asked Marshall to recover a debt from the estate of William Armstead and "as a compensation for your trouble therewith I will allow you ten per cent upon whatever you may obtain. . . ." But as Washington thought about the matter, he had misgivings. A month later he again wrote to Marshall, saying: "I have been lately informed that Mr. Armstead's sons are dead and have left their families not in very good circumstances. If this is the case—and the payment of the debt due to me would distress them, I must beg that you will not proceed any further in the matter, for however pressing my want of money is at present I had much rather lose the debt than the widow and fatherless should suffer by my recovering it." Washington also called on Marshall in more significant matters. In 1788 he had followed one lawyer's advice but then feared it "may involve me in a more litigious and expensive prosecution, or defense of it," and asked for Marshall's opinion.[30] Marshall wrote a lengthy answer, advising Washington that he could proceed as he had planned. "The dismission of the caveat," concluded Marshall, "can in no sort impair your title. As your patent is the eldest and comprehends within its lines the land caveated, the junior patentee can only establish a claim against you by a suit in chancery. To this he may resort should the caveat be determined in your favor."[31]

His distant cousin, Thomas Jefferson, also called on him for legal assistance. A provision in the treaty of peace formally ending the American Revolution called for the Americans to pay their debts to British merchants. The various state legislatures were not certain they should acquiesce in this agreement. Many Americans believed strongly that the war had been fought to abrogate those debts. Others did not believe Americans should pay their debts until the British made restitution for the slaves lured from the colonies or released the northwestern posts, or whatever else the legislatures could contrive as an excuse. The law was most confused. Jefferson's problem was the debts of his father-in-law's estate. Jefferson had sold some of the lands his wife had inherited from her father to pay the debts, but the British merchants declined to accept the notes with which Jefferson had been paid. (There was no valid currency at the time. Men paid their own IOUs with IOUs they received from other men.) After consultation with Marshall, Jefferson concluded that all lands inherited by his wife from her father's debt-ridden estate were liable for the father's debts.[32]

Marshall also did legal work for his old school and wartime comrade James Monroe. In the 1780s, at least, that seemed to amount largely to dealing with Monroe's creditors. Marshall wrote him in 1784 that he wished it were possible to assist Monroe, who was then at Annapolis, but "the exertions of the Treasurer and of your other friends here have been ineffectual. There is not one shilling in the Treasury and the keeper of it could not borrow one on the faith of government." Bad weather apparently had made collecting taxes difficult and Monroe could not anticipate exchanging his warrants for cash at the Treasury for another five or six weeks. Marshall continued that he was "pressed warmly" by two of Monroe's creditors, including Monroe's former landlady who "begins now to be a little clamorous." Marshall then said it might be necessary to sell some of the warrants at a discount to pay some of Monroe's bills.

But once that business was done, he brought his friend up to date on the news of their mutual acquaintances. "This excessive cold weather has operated like magic on our youth," gossiped Marshall, who was not yet twenty-nine. "They feel the necessity of artificial heat, and quite wearied with lying alone, are all treading the broad road to matrimony. Little Stewart—could you believe it?—will be married on Thursday to Kitty Hair and Mr. Dunn will bear off your old acquaintance Miss Shera." Marshall, like Monroe, did not lack appreciation of feminine charm. "Tabby Eppes," he wrote, "has grown quite fat and buxom, her charms are renovated and to see her and to love her are now synonymous terms. She has within these six weeks seen in her train at least a score of military and civil characters. Carrington, young Selden, Wright (a merchant) and Foster Webb have alternately bowed before her and been discarded. Carrington tis said has drawn off his forces in order to refresh them and has marched up to Cumberland [where] he will in all human probability be reinforced with the dignified character of legislator. Webb has returned to the charge and the many think from this similitude of manners and appetite that they were certainly designed for each other." Marshall also reported on the "other

Tabby," who was "high spirited" and who "firmly believes her time will come next. She looks quite spruce and speaks of matrimony as of a good which she yet means to experience."[33]

Because of his interest in the law, his father's experiences as a community leader and in the Virginia Assembly, and his own large circle of friends in Virginia, it was natural that John Marshall enter politics. Though politics in the Virginia of the 1700s was an obligation for members of the upper economic and well-educated groups, candidates had to vie with one another for popular favor in democratic elections, and victory often went to the one who supplied the greatest quantities of rum. Marshall ran first for the House of Delegates in the General Assembly in 1782 as the candidate from Fauquier County. A family tradition has it that he received every vote except one, and his father, "taking the delinquent to task inflicted upon him a good whipping."[34]

When the Assembly met in Richmond in November of 1782 the members elected Marshall to the Privy Council. The Council was the governor's advisory body and positions on it generally went to more experienced persons, so Marshall's election was not universally well received. Edmund Pendleton, a Virginian who was not respectful of youth, thought Marshall clever "but I think too young for that department." He believed Marshall "should rather have earned as a retirement and reward [the privy council position] by ten or twelve years hard service in the Assembly."[35] The oath Marshall took as a member of the Privy Council was administered by Jacquelin Ambler, who had just become an alderman and would soon become his father-in-law.[36]

As a Council member, Marshall had a closer glimpse into the workings of government than generally available. To whom should appointments as tobacco inspectors go? Should militia officers in the western country have discretionary powers to call on neighboring counties for help when Indians attacked? Was a certain convicted felon "a proper object of mercy"? There was one case that gives an indication of how Marshall's mind was developing in relationship to the judiciary. On February 20, 1783, the governor laid before the Privy Council a formal petition from the county of New Kent concerning a magistrate named John Price Posey, who, according to the petition, "had been guilty of diverse gross misdemeanors, disgraceful to the character which should be preserved by a justice of the peace, and praying that the Executive would give their opinion and advise whether the said John Price Posey is worthy to be continued in the office of Magistrate and whether for the malpractices aforesaid he ought not to be displaced and removed from the said office."

At the time Virginia law permitted the executive branch of the commonwealth to inquire into the conduct of magistrates to determine whether they were guilty of improper acts. But the Privy Council recommended against the executive exercising its specific right. To do so, said the Council, is, despite any specific legal mandate, "contrary to the fundamental principles of our constitution and directly opposite to the general tenor of our laws."[37] The report was signed by Samuel Hardy, Beverley Randolph, and John Marshall. Already Marshall was defending an independent judiciary, one that could not be attacked by another branch of the government. One cause of the American Revolution had been King George III's arbitrary treatment of judges—"He has made Judges dependent on his Will alone, for the tenure of their offices, and the amount and payment of their salaries," said the Declaration of Independence. Pre-Revolutionary judges had not been able to protect the Americans from the King's tyranny and Marshall and other thoughtful Americans were determined not to permit the same kind of tyranny to develop under their new system of government. Judges could be tried in courts for illegal acts, but they were not to be victimized capriciously by the executive branch of government. For the remainder of his life Marshall was an advocate of an independent judiciary.

The first Assembly which Marshall attended as a delegate from Fauquier County scheduled its opening session for Monday, October 21, 1782. But there were insufficient members to hold a formal session. Nor did an adequate number of delegates show up in the next two days. Finally the sergeant at arms was ordered to "take into custody" a long list of members who had not yet appeared. Marshall was not on the list, but Thomas Jefferson was. The Assembly could not get down to real work until Saturday, November 9, when enough members finally arrived. Marshall then was appointed to a committee to examine the state of the laws in Virginia, "what laws have expired since the last session and inspect such temporary laws as will expire with the end of this session or are near expiring, and report the same to the House, with their opinions, which of them are fit to be revived and continued." Marshall served on a similar committee during most of his years in the Virginia Assembly, and that committee work, as well as his own law practice, gave him a deep familiarity with the established law. In later years he could quote precedents in great detail when he needed to, often with a precision bordering on the mathematical. He also was on a committee "to form a plan of national defence against invasions." His first vote was for the relief of one John M'Lean. He voted to assist M'Lean, and the bill passed 63–17.[38]

In 1783, in his second year as a member of the Assembly, he grew discouraged with the legislative process. In December he wrote to a friend the news of the session. "Never could there have been less to give," Marshall lamented in his letter. He wrote of the few bills of significance, of the politicking. He was particularly distressed by the way members were playing with legislation to achieve their personal objectives, and he closed the letter with a complaint voiced by many legislators before and since: "It is surprising that gentlemen of character cannot dismiss their private animosities, but will bring them in the Assembly."[39]

He revealed even greater disillusionment to another friend: "The grand object of the people is still as it has ever been, to oppose successfully our British enemies and to establish on the firm base of certainty the independence of America." But, complained Marshall, to achieve this objective there was such a "contrariety of measures that tis sometimes difficult to determine whether some other end is not nearer the hearts of those who guide our counsels." He continued that the recruiting bill had been passed and produced a considerable sum of money, but "We have not yet recruited in the course of the winter three hundred men." He then went on about how much money Virginia had paid and agreed to pay in the future to the Continental Congress. Other states were paying more and boasting of it, but Marshall believed that if accounts could be settled fairly (something he doubted), "the Continent could have no demands on Virginia." Similar comments probably were being made at the same time by members of other state assemblies.

In the same letter Marshall also gave a glimpse of the social life available in Richmond to a young lawyer of growing political importance who had an attractive wife. "Am I not uncommonly dull?" Marshall asked his friend. "I'll give you reason for it. I have been sitting up all night at an assembly. We have them in Richmond regularly once a fortnight. The last was a brilliant one; twas on the Generals birthnight. Never did I see such a collection of handsome ladies. I do not believe that Versailles or Saint James's ever displayed so much beauty. I wish you had been present—the Virginia ladies would have retained their high place in your opinion. . . ."[40]

Patrick Henry was an influential member of the Assembly, and Marshall was impressed by his skill. In one instance the issue was a bill establishing citizenship in Virginia. When the author of one of the various bills spoke "with his usual sound sense and solid reason," Marshall reported, Henry rose to oppose him. "The speaker replied with some degree of acrimony," said Marshall, "and Henry retorted with a good deal of tactness but with much temper." Then Marshall pointed out a debating quality of Henry's which was one of the keys to his success. "Tis his peculiar excellence," Marshall explained, "when he altercates to appear to be drawn unwillingly into the contest and to throw in the eyes of others the whole blame on his adversary."[41]

As his first term in the Assembly drew to a close, Marshall was uncertain whether he should seek reelection. He determined that he must definitely resign from the Privy Council. Being a counsellor and being a lawyer were not compatible because of, he told James Monroe, "the opinion of the Judges with regard to a counsellor standing at the bar." Apparently the judges had misgivings about their independence in deciding a case in which one of the lawyers was a close and formal advisor to the governor. Marshall made a trip to Fauquier "to enquire into the probability of my being chosen by the people should I offer as a candidate at the next election."[42] The result was not negative; his popularity among his home folks never abated. But he was not certain of what he should do. In a long letter to a friend, Arthur Lee, he wrote of going to Kentucky to live. He already was involved in its politics and he then assumed that the western lands "in all probability will be ultimately my place of residence too." Lee had mentioned he might move there, and Marshall expressed pleasure that they might continue their friendship in the "New World." Then Marshall indicated, indirectly, a frustration with the political situation in Virginia:

> Surely, Sir, no people on earth possess a fairer prospect of political happiness than do the inhabitants of Kentucky. The Constitution of the thirteen United States having been formed by persons whose political ideas grew entirely under a monarchy is not matter of surprise if they have in some instances introduced principles unnecessary and perhaps improper in a Republic by guarding against the influence of the crown where no crown exists.
>
> The constitution of a new state may be formed with more experience and less prejudice. Happy will they be if on their separation from Virginia they can draw from this and the neighboring states a few of the wise and virtuous. I receive the most flattering accounts of that country from Mr. Daniel. Their commerce and their society have improved beyond the hopes of the most sanguine. The uncertainty of, together with the disagreeable circumstances attending publick office, have induced me to resign my seat in the Executive. . . .[43]

The "Constitution of the thirteen United States" referred to by Marshall was the Articles of Confederation, and the weaknesses of that document already were beginning to show. They were caused, as he said, by guarding against a crown when no crown existed—by refusing to create a powerful enough central government. His desire for a strong central government was a continuation of a belief impressed upon him during his years in the American army, particularly by his experiences at Valley Forge.

Despite his disenchantment with the development of the young nation, however, Marshall did not go to Kentucky, as strong as was the family pull and as "flattering" as were the accounts he heard of the land. Instead, he was reelected to the Assembly as the delegate from Fauquier County, and he continued the political career that ultimately led to his becoming an eloquent spokesman for a strong central government.

The Assembly began slowly. "We made a House on Wednesday," Marshall wrote to Monroe, adding with an almost resigned tone that "Nothing has yet been done. . . ."[44] Again Marshall's familiarity with the law was utilized well. He and another young lawyer—Spencer Roane—were appointed to a committee to prepare a bill establishing a county court system. Roane and Marshall lived near each other and frequently came into contact during these early years. Later they would be enemies, and not friendly ones.[45]

Marshall was not a man characterized by prejudice. With Patrick Henry, for example, he supported a bill encouraging marriages between white Virginians and Indians, as a principal means of solving racial difficulties between the two groups. Such a bill, Marshall believed, would have been "advantageous to this country." But he understood why it failed: "Our prejudices, however, oppose themselves to our interests, and operate too powerfully for them."[46]

As tolerant and unprejudiced as he was, Marshall was unable to go along with the movement led by Thomas Jefferson and James Madison for complete religious freedom in Virginia. Jefferson hated the established church—any established church. It was not that he was personally irreligious; he was as devout a believer in the principles of Christianity as any man in early America, perhaps much more so than most. But the established church in Virginia in the years before the American Revolution was not an organization entitled to much respect. The members of the clergy, far from the watchful eyes of their superiors, slipped into unfortunate habits. They were noted more for their drinking, gambling, and general carousing than for any inclination to walk in what was understood to be God's way.

Clergymen of the established church were supported by levies collected by the government and paid to them without question. Thus their corruption was protected. Jefferson had fought this for years. In 1779, supported by the ministers of the other faiths and their flocks, he had succeeded in disestablishing the Anglican Church. But specific support for the Anglican Church was replaced by general support for all Protestant faiths —all taxpayers had to pay under a general assessment and the funds would be distributed to all the Protestant sects. Jefferson also opposed the general support, but the backing he had had from the other Protestant faiths was quickly withdrawn.

The general assessment movement was led by Patrick Henry and had the support of many prominent Virginians, including John Marshall. The son of a member of the Leeds vestry was unable to join in dealing what many considered a deathblow to organized religion. Growing up in the western and primitive Virginia lands, Marshall had seen the church hold the community together, governing it when there was little else to govern with, and had seen its leaders—including his father—set an example of propriety and decency that he believed all men should emulate. This man could not support a move that would deny to the organized churches in Virginia what seemed like nothing more than an opportunity to have the government collect dues for them. In their separate views on this issue, as on others, John Marshall and Thomas Jefferson were products of their unique experiences.

The issue came to a head in the Assembly the day before Christmas in 1784. The question was whether teachers of the Christian religion would be provided for. Henry was the sponsor of a bill establishing an annual assessment to support the Christian faith. It was understood that the assistance would go to all Protestant denominations in Virginia. Jefferson at this time was abroad, and Madison was carrying on the fight for him in the Assembly. Realizing that they probably would lose in 1784, Madison bargained for a one-year postponement of the vote. Supporters of the general assessment knew Madison would use that year to build support for his own position and opposed him; John Marshall was among the thirty-eight members voting "no." But Madison was a shrewd politician. In seeking supporters he agreed to vote for a bill incorporating the Episcopal Church, and the "yes" votes for postponement totaled forty-eight.

Given a year to turn the tide against state support of religion, Madison and his friends were active. In the western regions where the tradition of an established church was weak, supporters of Madison's position were elected. The various religious denominations took another look at the bill and doubts developed. No matter what the bill said about not favoring one Protestant sect over another, all but the Anglicans had once been victims of an organized and heated prejudice; they suspected it could rise again. Even some followers of the Episcopal faith had their doubts. Did they really want their clergy to be too independent? When the climactic vote finally came at the end of 1785, not only was the bill to support Protestantism defeated but the old Jefferson proposal calling for complete religious freedom was passed. For Madison and Jefferson both, that act of the Assembly was one of the great moments of their lives.

And well it might have been. They were establishing more than a principle of toleration. They were establishing the principle of independent thought, of man's right to be free spiritually as well as physically. After this, when men turned to the church it was with intelligence and genuine emotion rather than by command. The result was that religion took strong root in the new land, because of this fundamental principle of the separation of church and state gloriously spoken for by Thomas Jefferson and brilliantly politicked for by James Madison. It was unfortunate that prominent men in Virginia, such as Patrick Henry, the Lees, George Washington, and John Marshall, on this issue at least, remained trapped by their earlier experiences. They missed the opportunity to participate in what was one of the great contributions of America to the modern world—the principle of religious freedom.[47]

Actually Marshall never had the opportunity to vote directly on the Jefferson proposal and his position rests on his vote against the postponement a year earlier. He did not seek reelection to the Assembly in 1785 as the delegate from Fauquier. Perhaps his disenchantment with the Assembly had grown too strong. But what is more probable, he considered himself by this time a full-time resident of Richmond, as his coming involvement in politics there demonstrated. In 1786 he did make an effort for statewide office. A year earlier Patrick Henry had been elected governor (this was a political coup by Madison to keep Henry, the strongest advocate of the state's support of religion, out of the Assembly). By November 1786 Henry was ready to step down, and the contest for the governorship was between Richard Henry

Lee and Attorney General Edmund Randolph. Randolph won that election, leaving the office of attorney general open and John Marshall sought it. But Marshall was still a young man, only thirty-one; his opponent was popular; and Marshall lost. But Marshall did gain "a handsome vote," according to Madison.[48]

Marshall retained his standing among the members of the Assembly; they continued to respect him and often assigned him important tasks, some bordering on a judicial role. In October of 1786, for example, he and five other men were appointed as trustees, in effect, to handle the claims of the owners of tobacco that had been stored in Byrd's warehouse in Richmond when the warehouse had been destroyed by fire. Their job was to find out how much tobacco was destroyed—more or less than the owners of the crop said they had stored there—and they were authorized to hold hearings and swear in witnesses.[49]

Two months later he was involved in a more interesting situation. A man named Simon Nathan had purchased bills of exchange, drawn on the Virginia Commonwealth, and claimed he was to be paid in specie. The commonwealth wanted to pay him in paper currency, so depreciated as to be almost worthless. The conflict was assigned by the Assembly to Marshall and another prominent lawyer, Cyrus Griffin, for examination and recommendation for action. Marshall was in good company in being attached to Griffin. Griffin had been one of the Virginia delegates to the First Continental Congress in 1774. Later, after this case with Marshall, he was elected president of the Continental Congress and was the last man to hold that office. He also had been the presiding judge when John Marshall was admitted to law practice. And many years later, that same Cyrus Griffin would sit side by side with Chief Justice John Marshall through one of the most agonizing of American criminal trials, that of Aaron Burr for treason.

On the question of who was right, Nathan or Virginia, Marshall and Griffin agreed that Nathan was right. Their opinion is an interesting one for the inkling it gives of Marshall's later thoughts about the law of contracts. The two men said they had examined the documents given to them by both Nathan and the lawyers for Virginia. They concluded "First that there is no convincing testimony that the Bills in question were drawn for depreciated money" and "secondly that there are considerable proofs that the bills in question were purchased by Mr. Nathan as bills drawn for specie value." Marshall and Griffin then said that only "evidence of fraud" could discharge Virginia from its debt to Nathan and "No such evidence of fraud has been adduced in the proofs before us." Therefore, they determined, the commonwealth "both in law and equity" should not only pay Nathan what was owed him but also the "legal interest arising thereon."[50]

The decision said, simply, that when two parties make an agreement, one cannot arbitrarily break it. Parties to a contract depend on the other parties' fulfilling their obligations—and commerce and arrangements between people cannot survive without such an understanding of contracts. As obvious as the thought was, contracts would be one of the great legal battles in the early years of the United States. On the Supreme Court, Marshall would be the umpire settling these battles, and he would always take the same position he had taken in 1786 in the dispute between Simon Nathan and the Commonwealth of Virginia: that when two parties make an agreement, one cannot arbitrarily change it.

In July 1785 Marshall ran for the office of alderman for Richmond. In the election on July 5 there were seventy-six candidates for sixteen positions, and Marshall had the second-highest number of votes. These aldermen, in turn, elected the city's mayor and recorder. On July 17 they chose John Marshall as recorder for the city of Richmond. He kept records for the city, signed various orders, and served on the Hustings Court, which was somewhat comparable to a justice of the peace court. It was presided over by the mayor and included the recorder and varying numbers of aldermen, with at least four officials sitting on the court. This was Marshall's first formal judicial role, and he served on the court for three years. The court met generally once a month and was concerned primarily with personal debt cases. This would be not only the first but also the only formal experience John Marshall had as a judge prior to his appointment to the Supreme Court in 1801.[51]

His personal life with Polly was happy and their love for each other carried them through many difficulties. One was Polly's developing illness, the nervousness combined with an anemia that often left her weak—apparently inherited from her mother. Polly's sister Betsy wrote to a friend in 1786 of "my poor Mother whose complaints are in a degree similar to yours . . . her extreme nervous debility and excessive timidity leave her often a prey to the most overwhelming despondency."[52] Polly also did not suffer childbirth well. After her second child was born, months passed before she regained her health. John and Polly had ten children, the last one born in 1805 when Polly was almost forty. Of those ten, four died in childhood, and two of those four

—John James Marshall and Mary Ann Marshall—died within a few weeks of each other in the summer of 1792.*

As the second of these two children, little Mary Ann, lay dying, John Marshall persuaded his frail wife to come away from the death bed. "We soon afterwards heard a voice in the room which we considered as indicating the death of the infant," he said. Marshall believed the child to be dead but when he returned to the room, he found her still breathing. Certain that she must die, he persuaded his wife to go to her mother's. The infant lived two days and, said Marshall, "I was agonized with its condition and with the occasional hope, though the case was desperate, that I might enrapture" Polly with the news that the child had survived. But the child died, and Polly could not bear to return home.

To bring his wife back, John Marshall wrote her a letter in verse "in which our mutual loss was deplored, our lost children spoken of with the parental feeling which belonged to the occasion, her affection for those who survived appealed to, and her religious confidence in the wisdom and goodness of Providence excited. The letter closed with a pressing invitation to return to me and her children." The verses succeeded in cutting through Polly's grief and persuading her to return to her family.[53]

That experience, coming after the ravages of the war years and in addition to her own inherited physical problems, made her less and less a companion for the robust man who was her husband. But never did his love for her falter.

Marshall assumed the leadership of his own family as well as Polly's. His younger brother William became a clerk of the court, a position won obviously because of John's influence and position. When in the late 1790s Major George Keith Taylor paid court to John's sister Jane—and Jane responded—John Marshall was the one concerned. "This affair embarrasses me a good deal," he said. "I believe Taylor is a young gentleman of talents and integrity for whom I profess and feel a real friendship." But there were other considerations. "Major Taylor possesses but little if any fortune and is encumbered with a family and does

---

* According to the Marshall family Bible, Rebecca, the Marshalls' second child, was born June 19, 1786, and died the next day; Mary Ann Marshall, the fourth child, was born November 24, 1789, and died August 1, 1792; John James Marshall, the fifth child, was born February 13, 1792, and died June 10, 1792; and Charles William Marshall, the ninth child, was born February 11, 1803, and died in October of that year. After Mary Ann and John James died, the Marshalls named two other children Mary and John.

not like his profession." John Marshall was twenty-four years older than his sister Jane and, in the absence of their father and mother in Kentucky, naturally had a paternal feeling toward her. "Had I conjectured that Major Taylor was contemplated in the character of a lover," he said, "I should certainly have made to her all the proper communications."[54] Whether or not he was right to be concerned, Jane did marry her major.

When members of the family required assistance, they found they could rely on him. His sister-in-law Betsy had married at age twenty, and then her husband had died suddenly six weeks after the ceremony. Marshall came to offer her solace and to escort her back to Richmond. "My good brother" is how Betsy referred to her sister's husband.[55]

And, as always, John Marshall was an amiable and respected person. Following the custom of the time, he did much of the marketing. He sauntered down to the wooden shed near Shockoe Creek, his coat often slung over his shoulders on the hot summer days, talking with the other men, nodding to the women, joking with the young gallants, usually bowing to the blacks whether they were slaves or not. While he apparently did not express it, he had some sympathy for the position of the blacks in a slave society. He always was remembered by the Virginia blacks who met him as a man who treated them with complete courtesy.

And the Marshalls, both John and Polly, were willing to speak out for what they believed was the cause of justice even if it meant taking an unpopular side or one that could cause them embarrassment. There was the case of Robert Minns, for example, who had been indicted and convicted of keeping a disorderly house. His punishment was a fine of 60 pounds. Minns operated a billiard table at which John Marshall and several other men played. According to the custom of the time, the players purchased drinks from Minns. Also according to the practice of the time, Minns did not have a liquor license although, strictly speaking, he should have. He petitioned to have the fine of 60 pounds waived, and Marshall was one of six men willing to state publicly that "they had frequently been at the billiard table of the petitioner and had never seen anything to warrant the charge made against him."[56]

There were more serious cases. In one Marshall passed on to the governor a petition for clemency for a man convicted as a result of a shooting. Marshall added his personal note—on a point omitted by the petitioners—that the convicted felon had not sought the gun but it was "rather forced upon the prisoner at a time when his mind seems to have been in a state of listless torpor, rather fitted to be moved by the impulse of others than to act from any formal design of his own." In another instance Marshall joined with other men asking that mercy be shown to a man named Ralph Anderson, who had been convicted of murder. Their petition claimed that Anderson had been subjected to fits of insanity "which proceeding from the will of the Almighty, it hath not been in his power to avert."[57]

Perhaps the most serious case that Marshall became involved in as an interested citizen concerned a free black woman named Angelica Barnet, who was sentenced to death for murder. A white man had broken into her house, assaulted her before her family, and she had killed him by striking him with an adze. None of this could be presented at her trial, however, because it would have meant a black presenting evidence against a white, which was not permitted in the Virginia courts. To aggravate matters, after Angelica Barnet was imprisoned she became pregnant by a jailed debtor who apparently had raped her. A group of thirty-six white women in Richmond, Polly Marshall among them, pleaded with the courts to show mercy to the woman. A few months later a group of Richmond men also sought mercy for the woman, declaring that "She was possessed of many of the rights of a free citizen, and among [these was] the great right of personal immunity in her own house. This unquestionably was invaded by the person who was unfortunately killed." The men pointed out that this could have been proven "if her associates were not incompetent by law to give testimony against a white person." Also, the men said, "from what they have heard, that the venire might have conceived prejudice against the prisoner. . . ." John Marshall was asked to sign this petition, but he declined because he knew none of the facts of the case. However, "having heard a favorable character of the prisoner," probably from Polly, he joined as a "petitioner for mercy."[58] And she was in fact pardoned.

Being a prominent lawyer, an active politician, as well as a gregarious person, Marshall joined many of the social organizations developing in Richmond. He was a member of the Sons of Cincinnati, a group organized by Revolutionary War officers. Jefferson came to believe that this was a cabal determined ultimately to make George Washington king of the United States, but it appears to have been nothing more than a group of ex-soldiers who enjoyed maintaining a relationship with one another. He was also a member of a group which apparently had even more fun. This was the society of St. Taminy, as Marshall spelled it. Once a year the members dressed up as Indians, apparently drank too much whiskey, and generally had a high time.

He was an active Mason. In later years, when Masonry fell into disrepute, he denied this affiliation, but the record is strong. In 1785, when he was Richmond recorder, he was a member of a committee that arranged for a lottery to build the first Mason's hall in the city. (Lotteries were a common form of fund-raising at the time; most churches, schools, canals, roads, and public buildings were financed through them.) Marshall apparently considered his responsibility more than merely pro forma. According to Richmond tradition, "It was largely through the efforts of John Marshall . . . that this building was completed."[59] He became a member of the lodge, eventually rising to deputy grandmaster and then grandmaster. Upon completion of his term as grandmaster, the lodge presented him with "an elegant Past Master's jewel."[60]

But the group he seemed most to enjoy and with which he was associated for almost the remainder of his life was a small group known first as the Quoit Club and later, and more enduringly, as the Barbecue Club. Begun in 1788 by a group of professional and business men in Richmond,* the group's only rule apparently was that neither business nor religion could be discussed at the meetings. Every Saturday afternoon the members set out to Buchanan's Spring, a small resort area a mile outside of Richmond. There, under the shade of broad oak trees, they ate well, drank heartily, joshed with each other, and played quoits.

The club had only thirty members, and the governor of the state was always included. Each member could bring one guest, but it was understood that the guest was to be a prominent visitor to the area. Other than the clergymen John Buchanan and John Blair there were no honorary members. It became an honor to be invited to join the club, and its members soon included bank presidents, the more successful merchants, the leading politicians, as well as the prominent members of the Virginia bar. The meetings were managed by Jasper Crouch, a mulatto cook, who officiated at the dinners and indulged so heavily that he acquired gout and "the rotundity of an alderman." One account of this club gives its "exercise and recreation, bodily and mental, at the close of the week's labours" high marks for being "grateful and

---

* John Marshall was an original member of the club. The basic source on the club's origins is the *American Turf Register* of 1829, reprinted in the *Southern Literary Messenger*, February 1836, pp. 188– 89, which described him in 1829 as the only original member surviving. Questions have been raised about this in recent years, which is why I am stressing the point.

invigorating." Guests at the Saturday meetings could see "Liberty, Equality and Fraternity without licentiousness, presumption of demagoguism," as well as "Pure Republicanism, represented by some of the distinguished men, who aided in forming the Republic."[61]

They also could watch a group of successful men having a very good time, as indicated by a first-person account of a meeting when John Marshall was responsible for the catering. He was host that day with John Wickham, another prominent Richmond lawyer. Marshall sat at the head of the table and Wickham at the foot, and between them "a better dinner of the substantials of life was rarely seen." According to the eyewitness, the "only dessert" indulged in was "a steaming, juicy mutton chop, cooked to a turn, and 'deviled ham,' highly seasoned with mustard, cayenne pepper, and a slight flavoring of Worcester sauce."

After the "dessert" was out of the way, the members got down to the serious business of the meeting. Marshall noted with pleasure the presence of the two honorary members, the Reverends Blair and Buchanan. Parson Blair had written a rhymed response to the invitation which Marshall read aloud. "This was received with marked approbation," goes the report, "each member taking the cue from Mr. Wickham and striking the table with the handle of his knife in three successive rounds." The pleasantries over, Marshall's voice then became grave. Now there was really serious business before the club. He began, his face somber:

> It was known to the club that two of the members at the last meeting, had contrary to the constitution, introduced the subject of politics, which ought to be tabooed here, and though warned to desist, had continued the discussion. The consequence was that, by unanimous vote, they had been fined a basket of champagne for the benefit of the Club. They had submitted to the imposition like worthy members.

At that point Marshall's voice lost its gravity and he produced the champagne as "a warning to evildoers." Champagne was an unusual treat for the Barbecue Club. The members, lacking the proper glasses, had to drink it from large tumblers, but no one objected. Wickham raised his glass for a toast to Parsons Buchanan and Blair. Buchanan responded that he had no qualms about a little wine for—he was certain they would understand— "his many infirmities." And he added the hope that those who drank the champagne from tumblers would not "prove to be tumblers under the table." Parson Blair then looked around the table and praised his companions for their oratorical powers and eloquence and said he was certain none "would ever sink into bathos," which he seemed to define as sinking under the table.

After the meal several members adjourned for a game of quoits. Marshall challenged Blair, another skilled player. Most of the players had smooth, highly polished brass quoits, but Marshall had a set of the largest, roughest quoits made of iron. He was perhaps the only man at the club who could throw those discs with any accuracy. Here we see at work John Marshall, quoit player without equal:

> Mr. Marshall, with his long arms hanging loosely by his side, a quoit in each hand, leaning slightly to the right, carried his right hand and right foot to the rear; then, as he gave the quoit the impetus of his full strength, brought his leg up, throwing the force of the body upon it, struck the meg near the ground, driving it in at the bottom, so as to incline its head forward, his quoit being forced back two or three inches by the recoil.

The club members were perfectly silent now as they stared at the quoit on the ground, a few inches away from its target, to the second quoit in Marshall's hand. Could he do better a second time?

> Without changing his position, [Marshall] shifted the remaining quoit to his right hand, and fixing the impression of the meg on the optic nerve by his keen look, again threw, striking his first quoit and gliding his last directly over the head of the meg. There arose a shout of exulting merriment.

But Parson Blair still had his turn. Among the club members the tension was almost unbearable as the parson, "his body square to the front," brought the quoit up to eye level, "aimed it as if sighting a gun," and then threw it with only a shoulder motion. The quoit, flying like "an Indian arrow at the edge of a cent, performed the same exploit as Mr. Marshall, ringing the meg on top of his quoit." This feat was received with "uproarious applause." Then, of course, Marshall and Blair had the inevitable argument, in mock seriousness, over who was the winner. Finally it was determined that the club members should be the jury. Marshall by this time of his life had argued many legal causes but perhaps none ever produced such impassioned pleading as this one did.

Since both quoits were tied, he said to the Barbecue Club, the question of the winner was not one of measurement but of the rules of the game. Blair's responsibility, Marshall insisted, was to knock off the first quoit "and then to take its position." Marshall contended that "This is the skill of the game, and unless he can rise to this pitch of perfection he cannot be decreed to be the winner." Marshall now turned to Blair. "My friend, the worthy Parson," he said with that air of condescension lawyers enjoy using on persons they know to be guilty, "deserves to rise higher and higher in esteem, and I am sure he will be in that higher firmament to which we all aspire at some future day; but if he expects to reach Elysium by riding on my back, I fear, from my many back slidings and deficiencies, he may be sadly disappointed."

Marshall then invoked an old legal maxim. His quoit was the first occupant and his right therefore extended from the ground "up to the vault of heaven, and no one had a right to become a squatter" on his back. If Blair had an adversary claim, Marshall insisted, he must obtain a writ of ejectment or drive Marshall from his position by force of arms.

Parson Blair, not being a lawyer, had John Wickham argue his cause. Wickham began by praising Marshall for fairly submitting the question "and ingeniously [stating] his view of the rule." Wickham then told the jury: "We intend to meet him squarely, and deny his rule, his law, and his inference." This was indeed a legal challenge. But Wickham seemed to make the stronger point. "It is well known to the club," he argued, "that our friend Marshall's quoit is twice as large as any other. . . . It is an iron quoit, unpolished, jagged, and of enormous weight." Then Wickham jumped to his major premise. "It is impossible for an ordinary light quoit to move it from its position. No rule requires an impossibility. He is not entitled to such an advantage."

After thus disposing of the issue of whether Blair's quoit could be expected to dislodge Marshall's, Wickham turned to what seemed the more formidable argument, that Marshall retained legal position "to the vault of heaven." Wickham conceded that "is the very question at issue." Using a tactic that Marshall was considered to excel at, Wickham turned the question around. "The first squatter on Parson Buchanan's land is not better than the second," he insisted. As to Marshall's claim that Blair should drive him off by force of arms, Wickham declared that men of the cloth are men of peace and do not struggle with their enemies by force of arms.

The jury of club members agreed that they had rarely heard two more forceful legal arguments. They then proceeded to vote. The voting was public and seemed designed more to keep up the suspense than to settle the argument according to the rules of law. Finally after a period in which first Marshall led, then Blair, then the two men tied, then took turns leading again, the final verdict of the jury was that the two men had been tied. The case was closed.[62]

So this was John Marshall's life as he entered his middle years. He had demonstrated his courage in the Revolution, established a thriving law practice, begun a family. He had influential friends and his future in Richmond seemed serene and secure. But events were overtaking him, and his life would never again be so predictable as it seemed on those carefree Saturday afternoons when he was surrounded by his good friends. In Philadelphia men were writing the Constitution that John Marshall later would be called upon to interpret.

2

AFTER THE Revolution the problems that beset the United States were caused, as Marshall had said, because the framers of the government had feared the crown when there was no crown to fear. The Articles of Confederation rested essentially on the principle of voluntarism. As a result, there were difficulties with trade and taxes that threatened the continued existence of the young nation.

The dangers were apparent from the very beginning. In 1783 the Continental Congress was besieged by American soldiers demanding overdue pay. The Congress was meeting in Philadelphia at the time and sought physical protection from the Pennsylvania government, but the state would not voluntarily comply with such a request, and the government of the United States had to slink away to Princeton, New Jersey, to carry on its business.[1]

Trade, an essential activity for the young nation, was proving impossible to maintain. Tenche Cox, a prominent Pennsylvanian, reported to several of his Virginia friends that the states were discriminating against one another more severely than against England. Duties imposed by states on cargoes carried on ships built out of state were equal, in some cases higher, than duties on cargoes carried on foreign-built ships.[2] Marshall reported that the Continental Congress was considering a uniform system for regulating commerce. To protect the state authority, the central government would collect the duties "under the authority, and secure to the use of state in which the same should be made payable." But the resolution was not agreed to. There was fear that the separate states would lose their powers to the central government, and the different sections of the country were uncertain whether their interests coincided. New England and the South, the former with its small farms and growing industry and the latter with its large plantations and dependence upon foreign industry, already were suspicious of each other.

But the issue was more than philosophical. England was a nation of traders. The young United States, with its thirteen members and its thirteen different sets of trade regulations, would be at the mercy of sophisticated British trade practices. "The several states," said Marshall, "acting without concert, would be no match for Britain in a war of commercial regulation." The prospect was that the victories gained on the battlefield would be lost in the trading houses.[3]

The demise of trade precipitated an acute shortage of funds. The central government could raise funds only by requisitioning money from the states. "As to the Continental revenues," remarked one New Englander, "we find at present no motives in the several States sufficiently strong to induce them to furnish the means necessary to discharge the contracts made by Congress."[4] Marshall reported that from November 1, 1784, to January 1, 1786, the Continental Congress was able to raise only half a million dollars. In Europe John Adams managed to borrow some money for the treasury with which part of the interest on the foreign debt was paid, but that was running out. Not only were there no funds for the interest but payments on the principal soon must be made. The United States was faced—in Marshall's words—with "the humiliating circumstance . . . of a total failure to comply with [its] most solemn engagements." As one who had seen at Valley Forge the difficulties when the separate states refused to submit voluntarily to the will of the central government, Marshall, and many like him in the 1780s, had little hope that there would be any change in the fortunes of the young country without a radical change in its government. As Marshall expressed it:

A government authorized to declare war, but relying on independent states for the means of prosecuting it; capable of contracting debts, and of pledging the public faith for their payment, but depending on thirteen distinct sovereignties for the preservation of that faith; could only be rescued from ignominy and contempt, by finding those sovereignties administered by men exempt from the passions incident to human nature.[5]

The movement for change was broad-based. The merchants along the coast saw a stronger government as a means of regulating, and making more profitable, their trade with Europe. The large plantation owners in the South, particularly those like Washington who had fought in the war, realized that only a stronger government offered them hope of a stable commerce. They had to sell their products to Europe, and they did not want to be at the mercy of the English merchants solely; that supine position had contributed to their decision to begin the Revolution. Suspicion of a strong central government existed among the small farmers in the western lands. Isolated from their fellow colonists, they were autonomous on their farms without much awareness of or concern for the problems of their fellows in the other states. Trade was important to them also, but their route was through the Mississippi Valley, not overland to the Atlantic, and they doubted that a central government would watch over their interests properly—a doubt that was justified. But while support in the West was not as strong for a new government as it was in other parts of the nation, still it existed. It grew stronger every time the people in the western lands, threatened by Indians or Spaniards, sought military protection.

This widespread support began to show itself. "[T]he wise and thinking part of the community, who could trace their evils to their source," Marshall reported, "laboured unceasingly to inculcate opinions favourable to the incorporation of some principles into the political system, which might correct the obvious vices, without endangering the free spirit of the existing institutions."[6]

"Resolved," said the General Court of Massachusetts on July 1, 1785, "That it is the opinion of this Court that it is highly expedient, if not indispensably necessary, that there should be a Convention of Delegates from all the States in the Union at some convenient place, as soon as may be, for the sole purpose of revising the Confederation. . . ."[7]

In North Carolina a grand jury for the district of Edenton called for a new constitution, saying the consequences of the Articles of Confederation had been "our public debts unpaid, the treaty of peace unfulfilled on both sides, our commerce at the very verge of ruin, and all private industry at a stand. . . . Quotas demanded which we can never pay, and Congress preserving merely the shadow of authority, without possessing one substantial property of power."[8]

Some later historians have doubted this picture of the United States under the Articles of Confederation as a nation floundering toward disintegration. Charles A. Beard, the leader of this school, charged that the history of the period was written largely by Federalists, who believed in strong central government, and that they had distorted the facts. "Great care," he wrote, "should be taken in accepting without reserve, the gloomy pictures of the social conditions prevailing under the Articles of Confederation. . . ."[9] With all proper care taken, however, it continues difficult to find other than gloomy accounts of the prospects for the United States under the Articles.

That the United States was moving rapidly toward disintegration was demonstrated in 1786 by what has since become known as Shays' Rebellion. The small farmers in the western part of Massachusetts, in effect, revolted against the government. "The inferior courts in the counties of Hampshire, Worcester and Middlesex in Massachusetts have within this three weeks been prevented by armed men from transacting their official business," reported a citizen in neighboring New Hampshire. "Previous to the meeting of the Court in Middlesex, the governor of that Commonwealth, with advice of his council, issued his orders directing a portion of the militia to assemble at Concord in the County of Middlesex to protect the county courts and suppress the daring insurrection. But on examining the laws he had no authority and before the militia assembled he rescinded his orders. Two hundred and fifty insurgents met and forcibly prevented the Court from proceeding to business."[10] The farmers moved against the courts because the courts were collecting debts the farmers did not want to pay. Marshall believed the rebellion was caused by "the restlessness produced by the uneasy situation of individuals, connected with lax notions concerning public and private faith, and erroneous opinions which confound liberty with an exemption from legal control."[11] Marshall would always be disturbed by those who confounded liberty with an exemption from the law. Such a definition might be appropriate for one man living alone, but it could not be appropriate for a society of men. And Marshall realized that the problem was to make the law and government instruments for all men.

George Washington expressed this thought accurately at the time of Shays' Rebellion. "For God's sake tell me," he cried to a friend, "what is the cause of all these commotions?" If they proceeded from licentiousness or British influence, he asked, why were they not put down immediately? If they proceeded from "real grievances which admit of redress . . . why was the redress delayed until the public mind had become so much agitated?"[12]

There could be no redress because there was no government capable of providing it. There was no government that could foster growth in trade, development of industry; no government that could assure an equitable distribution of the tax burden, that could provide the embattled farmers with an outlet for their complaints. It was ironic that the Americans, who had rebelled against the British because the British had not permitted them a voice in their own government, were now rebelling a second time because, in reality, they had no government. Washington, who had given so much of himself and his fortune to the American cause, spoke for many Americans when he said after Shays' Rebellion: "Let us have a *government*, by which our lives, liberties, and properties will be secured; or let us know the worst at once."[13]

There was also a grave danger that the reaction to disorders would be so great that the democratic ideals enunciated in the Declaration of Independence would be abandoned in the name of law and order. Many discounted that high or unfair taxes had produced the disturbances. "That they are the real cause is as far remote from truth, as light is from darkness," commented Henry Knox, one of the brilliant Revolutionary generals. He argued that the insurgents had never been struck too hard by taxes, but "they see the weakness of government. They feel at once their own poverty compared with the opulent, and their own force; and they are determined to make use of the latter in order to remedy the former."[14]

The natural extension of Knox's remarks is that an exceedingly strong central government is needed to counter the force of the poor and to crush it; perhaps a return to a monarchy. The feeling had always existed as an undercurrent in American politics, both during and after the Revolution, that monarchy itself had not been the problem, only the particular British monarchy. After the war many of Washington's officers, having closely observed and admired him, believed he should have been crowned monarch of the United States, a belief he did not share. As the shambles of the Articles of Confederation became more obvious, however, the possibility of a return to monarchy increased. "Indeed the present system neither has nor deserves advocates," lamented James Madison, "and if some very strong props are not applied will quickly tumble to the ground." Recalling Shays' Rebellion a few months earlier, Madison said: "A propensity towards monarchy is said to have been produced by it in some leading minds." And if not a monarchy, Madison continued, then the United States might split "into three more practicable and energetic governments."[15]

The problem the Americans faced in the late 1780s was to construct a new government that would keep the nation together, allow it to prosper, permit all its citizens to share in its opportunities, without restricting the freedoms for which they had fought and to which they were entitled.

George Washington, perhaps more than any individual, understood the difficulties of a weak central government. In June of 1783 he had written to the governors of the states, saying that after the victory on the battlefield, "There is an option still left to the United States . . . whether they will be respectable and prosperous, or contemptible and miserable as a nation." He continued:

> This is the time of their political probation; this is the moment when the eyes of the whole world are turned upon them; this is the moment to establish or ruin their national character forever; this is the favourable moment to give such a tone to our federal government, as will enable it to answer the ends of its institution, or this may be the ill-fated moment for relaxing the powers of the union, annihilating the cement of the confederation, and exposing us to become the sport of European politics. . . . For according to the system of policy the states shall adopt at this moment, they will stand or fall; and by their confirmation or lapse, it is yet to be decided, whether the revolution must ultimately be considered as a blessing or a curse . . . a blessing or a curse not to the present age alone, for with our fate will the destiny of unborn millions be involved.

Washington wrote that four elements were essential to the success of the United States. They were "a sacred regard to public justice," "a proper peace establishment," a feeling of unity among Americans "which will induce them to forget their local prejudices and politics," and "an indissoluble union of the states under one federal head."[16]

But the United States ignored his advice and did not form an indissoluble union under a strong leader. As a result there was little regard for justice, no feeling of security, and local prejudices were aggravated rather than eliminated. "We have probably had too good an opinion of human nature in forming our confederation," Washington said in 1786. "Experience has taught us that men will not adopt and carry into execution measures the best calculated for their own good, without the intervention of a coercive power."[17] This was, of course, the lesson of the Articles of Confederation: men must agree to be governed.

John Marshall, living in Richmond in the 1780s, was an intimate witness to the shambles the country he had fought for was falling into. As a member of the state legislature he recognized the difficulty the central government had in raising funds. He had discussed with the Richmond merchants their problems in dealing with the British. He had seen the value of currency fluctuate rapidly because there was no means of controlling it. And his sense of orderly liberty had been disturbed by Shays' Rebellion, increasing his discouragement at the confusion of licentiousness with liberty. "I fear," he wrote to an acquaintance, "and there is no opinion more degrading to the dignity of man, that those have truth on their side who say that man is incapable of governing himself. I fear we may live to see another revolution."[18] A few weeks later Marshall was pleased to learn that some of the leaders of the rebellion in Massachusetts had been captured. "I congratulate you on the prospect of re-establishing order and good government in Massachusetts," he wrote to a friend. "I think their government will now stand more firmly than before the insurrection, provided some examples are made in order to impress on the minds of the people a conviction that punishment will surely follow an attempt to subvert the laws and government of the Commonwealth."[19]

Why was revolution acceptable in 1776 but not in 1786?

There may be no definitive answer to the question. Or it may be that revolution is not the point. The real point is that government must provide a process of acknowledging and correcting, when proper to do so, the grievances of citizens. By 1776 it had been demonstrated that the British monarchy provided no such process; this was the justification the Americans used for their Revolution, for their violation of the laws. There was no such demonstration in 1786, however. Whatever grievances the Massachusetts farmers had, they had taken up arms as their first recourse rather than as their last.

The result of all this ferment was the convention in Philadelphia in 1787 which produced the Constitution of the United States. The delegates arrived in the city with a feeling of uncertainty. George Mason, one of the Virginians, had been in Philadelphia several days when he wrote to a friend that he had found so few other delegates in the city that "I am unable to form any certain opinion on the subject of our mission." But the most prevalent idea, he found, was "a total change of the federal system." It would be replaced by "A great national council or parliament upon the principles of equal, proportionate representation . . . and [making] the state legislatures subordinate to the national. . . ."[20]

When sufficient delegates did arrive, they gathered behind closed doors to draft the document. They kept their vow to work in secret. As the weeks went by, the suspense grew among Americans not privy to the Convention proceedings. James Madison, another Virginia delegate, received this letter from a relative in Williamsburg:

> We are here, and I believe everywhere, all impatience to know something of your conventional deliberations. If you cannot tell us what you are doing, you might at least give us some information of what you are not doing. This would afford a clue for political conjecture, and perhaps be sufficient to satisfy present impatience.[21]

The purpose of the secrecy had been to allow the document to stand or fall on its overall merits, rather than on any particular section of it. This was a wise decision because the American Constitution is an intricately balanced creation. Its provision for a President, for example, cannot be considered alone. It must be considered in relationship to the provisions for a Congress and a Supreme Court.

This balancing of power is the essential ingredient in the Constitution. Its philosophical origins can be traced to Aristotle, to the Old Testament, and to the French philosophers who so inspired the Americans. Winston Churchill, with a charming touch of chauvinism, insisted much later that the American Constitution is a "reaffirmation" of the principles developed by the English peoples over centuries.[22] All of these descriptions are true. The American Constitution is both a historical and a philosophical evolvement, drawing upon the great thinkers and the experiences of all nations. Yet it is also a uniquely American creation. The various arms of the government, as well as their relationships to one another, had been tested in the American colonies for years. The need which produced the document had been vividly demonstrated for the prior ten years. The men who authorized it understood that need. They also recognized that they must justify the document to their fellow countrymen; they could rely on neither time nor history to defend them. The American Constitution drew richly from the past but it was basically a result of its time and place.

The writing of the Constitution in Philadelphia had been

the first step. Ratification by the states would be the second. The Constitution would take effect when nine of the thirteen states had approved it. All men well understood, however, that there could be no United States under the Constitution without the ratification of Virginia. The geographic center of the thirteen colonies, Virginia was an intellectual and commercial center. It also was the home of George Washington, Thomas Jefferson, and James Madison, three men without whom there probably could be no United States. During the Revolution the British could capture Boston and New York, as they did, without defeating the Americans, but the capture of Virginia would have had a more severe impact. And so with the adoption of the Constitution; ratification by Virginia was imperative. In this struggle John Marshall, the prominent lawyer, astute, if not significant, local politician, and charming young man, would reveal himself to be considerably more than the sum total of those attributes.

The state legislatures were expected to call special conventions to consider the ratification question. As simple as that seemed, it was not easily done. In Pennsylvania, for example, a motion was made on September 28, 1787, that a special convention be held. The vote was scheduled for the next day, but it could not be taken because nineteen members who opposed the Constitution refused to attend the session of the House, and there was no quorum.

The sergeant at arms was sent to find the absent members, and he reported that he had found them but they would not attend the legislature. According to the journals of the House, two members—James McCalmont and James Miley—did appear and there was a quorum. One witness to the events, Charles Biddle, told a somewhat different story. "The fact is," he reported, "some gentlemen went to Boyd's, where most of the absent members lodged, and there found McCalmont and Miley, and finding they could not persuade them, forced them to the House, by which means they had a quorum, and the resolution calling a Convention was adopted."[23]

In Virginia there was similar doubt about whether a convention would be called. Before the Virginia Assembly convened, James Monroe predicted there would be no opposition to a convention.[24] But it was not quite as smooth as Monroe anticipated. The object of the opponents of the Constitution was to insist upon amendments. If each of the thirteen states ratified the Constitution with the provision that certain amendments be adopted, then another Constitutional Convention would be necessary to incorporate the amendments from all thirteen states into the document. The ratification process could be dragged on indefinitely through this strategy. When the motion to call for a special convention to consider the Constitution was presented to the Virginia legislature, it met with quick opposition from Patrick Henry, the leading foe of the Constitution in the state, on the grounds that he could not support any procedure which did not specifically permit amendments. His position was endorsed by George Mason, a delegate from Virginia to the Constitutional Convention in Philadelphia who had refused to sign the finished document. On the surface their position seemed reasonable, but it was really an attempt to prevent ratification by opening the Constitution to proliferating amendments. Marshall, after a two-year hiatus, had returned to the legislature, this time as a delegate from Henrico County, which included the city of Richmond. He compromised the situation by offering a substitute for the Henry proposal. Rather than dealing specifically with amendments, it authorized a special convention "with full free investigation and discussion." It passed.[25]

While the Marshall motion made the special convention possible, it did not remove the threat that ratification would be made contingent on the adoption of certain amendments. This would still be the strategy at the convention. The supporters of the Constitution were aware of what they were up against. Washington pointed out that even those Virginians who wanted amendments could not agree among themselves on what specific amendments they wanted, and then said: "If the opponents in the *same* State cannot agree in *their* principles, what prospect is there of a coalescence with the advocates of the measure when the different views, and jarring interests of so wide and extended an Empire are to be brought forward and combated?"[26] There was, of course, little prospect. As James Madison reported to Thomas Jefferson, if the movement for previous amendments carried, the result would be either a conditional ratification or a proposal for a new Constitution. "In either event," Madison remarked, "I think the Constitution and the Union will be both endangered."[27]

In retrospect, it is easy to criticize Patrick Henry, George Mason, and the other opponents of the Constitution in Virginia, but it must be remembered that these were not idle men. They had given much of themselves to the American cause, and they believed there was ample reason to oppose the Constitution. They had reached their maturity and led their adult lives as Virginians and their loyalty was to their state. It was not that they were disloyal to the United States, but rather that they did not understand the concept of the United States. They understood Virginia. That was their nation. They believed they had good cause to be suspicious of an unproved national authority asserting power over the state. Part of that cause was the debts Virginians owed the British merchants. These were holdovers from the time before the Revolution, and the Virginians believed they had been the unfair victims of a system which had weighted all the advantages on the side of the British and all the disadvantages on the side of the Virginians—and they were not far from wrong. Their debts to the British amounted to millions of dollars, and there was little doubt in their minds that a strong central government would insist upon payment of the debts to assure the new country's standing in the economic councils of the European world. For many Virginians this meant economic ruin, or at least they believed it did. After the Constitution was adopted, for example, one Virginia gentleman wrote to his stepsons that since the recovery of the British debts could not be avoided, "There now seems to be a moral certainty that your patrimony will all go to satisfy the unjust debt from your papa to the Hanburys. The consequence, my dear boys, must be obvious to you. Your sole dependence must be on your own personal abilities and exertions."[28] Such fears were only somewhat exaggerated. Also, Patrick Henry was concerned both about what the North would do about slavery in the South and what the eastern powers would do about the western settlements which were so dependent upon the Mississippi River.

Virginia was one of the few states that had prospered under the Articles of Confederation. Her ports were usable year-round. Her roads cut from the port cities to the hinterlands. Her farm products made profitable cargoes to carry back to Europe. Virginia had her own custom houses, her own marine hospitals, and her own revenue cutters. Because the ships entering her ports were many, she was able to keep her import duties light— which meant that more ships came to her ports, making her merchants even more prosperous. A Virginia historian reported that the net amount coming into the commonwealth treasury from customs for only the nine months ending May 31, 1788, was 60,000 pounds.[29]

After the adoption of Marshall's substitute motion at the end of October 1787, the suspense over how the question of the future government would be answered continued to grow. The prospects were favorable for passage of the new Constitution. The common opinion is summed up in the words of a man named John Wendell to Elbridge Gerry of Massachusetts in December 1787. Gerry, like George Mason, was one of the five delegates to the Constitutional Convention who had refused to sign the finished document. Wendell argued that the nation could not continue under the chaos of the Articles of Confederation and then insisted that "Necessity, fatal necessity, obliges me to determine in [the Constitution's] favor if it was only to obtain the institution of a revenue to support public credit or we are undone."[30] The problem was not to persuade the people to favor the document but to prevent its opponents, including some of the shrewdest politicians in the nation, from defeating it.

In some cases the arguments went beyond discussion. In Orange County, North Carolina, the dispute over a federal constitution became heated between a man named Hooper and one named McCauley. Hooper "came off second best, with his eyes blacked," according to a contemporary account.[31]

But in most cases the disputes would be settled in a more or less gentlemanly fashion in a convention hall. This was particularly true in Virginia, with its long tradition of representative government. The leader for the pro-Constitution forces was George Washington. He had been a delegate to the Constitutional Convention from Virginia, then the president of the Convention, and indirectly the individual perhaps most responsible for that gathering's approval of the final document. (The members heeded Washington because all assumed he would be elected President of the United States.) But back in Mount Vernon, his home on the broad Potomac River, Washington realized the struggle was only beginning. It had always been his plan to lead in promoting a change of government for the young nation he had helped father and he was quick to assume a commanding position in the political battle.

Once the Virginia legislature had decided to hold a special convention, Washington naturally was pleased. But he was concerned about the tenor of the feeling in the state and wrote long letters to his friends asking them for information. "Is this your opinion," he asked, "from what you have seen, heard and understood?" And where there was opposition he quickly sent copies of *The Federalist Papers*, a series of newspaper articles signed by "Publius" (the name used by authors James Madison, John Jay, and Alexander Hamilton) defending the Constitution. "If there is a printer in Richmond who is really well disposed to support the New Constitution," said Washington, "he would do well to give them a place in his paper."[32]

The prestige of Washington in the state was so great that his advocacy of the Constitution obviously would swing much support to it, particularly among the men who had followed him in the American Revolution. But the situation was so questionable in Virginia that even Washington's entrance into politics could not guarantee the outcome. The Virginia convention would not be held until June of 1788, and Washington predicted that if several of the other states had approved the Constitution by that time, Virginia would be carried by the momentum and probably follow suit. But, Washington continued, "If some of them should reject it, it is very probable that the opposers of it here will exert themselves to add this State to the number."[33]

That actually had been the purpose of scheduling the Virginia convention so late, to see first what the other states did. If they showed themselves unable to agree on a Constitution, then Virginia—so James Monroe reported—"might mediate between contending parties and lead the way to an union more palatable to all."[4]

A key to the success or failure of the Constitution in Virginia appeared likely to be the caliber of the delegates elected to the special convention. "So small, in many instances, was the majority in its favour," Marshall said, "as to afford strong ground for the opinion that had the influence of character been removed, the intrinsic merits of the instrument would not have secured its adoption."[35] In this instance George Washington and James Madison showed what extraordinary politicians they were. They urged candidates of such high reputations to run for the special convention that the opponents had little chance. And only later did the opponents realize they had been outclassed. Patrick Henry, for example, was convinced that 80 percent of the people of his state opposed the Constitution, and in southern Virginia the percentage might even have reached 90. "And yet," he said, obviously puzzled, "strange as it may seem, the numbers in the convention appear equal on both sides, so that the majority, which way soever it goes, will be small." He believed that the supporters of the Constitution had "wiggled themselves into the choice of the people."[36] Wiggling had not been all. The way the convention was set up under Marshall's resolution, each county had the same representation. This meant that the eastern counties, which supported the Constitution, had the same power in the convention as the western counties, which opposed it, although the western counties had larger populations.

Marshall was nominated as a candidate for delegate from Henrico County. He was immensely popular in Richmond, which was the county center, but still he appeared to be in trouble as the March election neared. The opposition to the Constitution was strong in the county; Edmund Randolph, governor of the state, also was running as a delegate and anticipated being elected only because he had refused to sign the finished document in Philadelphia. To worsen matters for Marshall, he was approached and told that all opposition to his election as a delegate to the special convention would evaporate if he would sign a pledge to vote against adoption of the Constitution. He refused to sign such a pledge. Feelings ran high, but John Marshall had lived in Richmond for half a dozen years. He had been the city's recorder, a member of its Hustings Court, and its representative in the legislature. Every voter knew him, liked him, trusted him, and respected him. He was elected.[37]

Some years later when Marshall was explaining why he supported the Constitution he attributed it "at least as much to casual circumstances as to judgment." He had grown up, he explained, at a time when love of country and opposition to England were inseparable, "and I had imbibed these sentiments so thoroughly that they constituted a part of my being." And then in the army, he continued, he had met men from all the states who had risked their lives in the cause of country. His interest in the Union continued when he returned to civilian life, particularly when he entered the legislature and discovered "that no safe and permanent remedy could be found but in a more efficient and better organized general government." The part of the Constitution which imposed restriction on the states most appealed to him because he had come to realize that without such a central power, there was "no safe anchorage ground" and so he became a "determined advocate" for adoption of the Constitution. He explained his election amid the general anti-Constitution attitude in the county by his personal popularity and also because the parties had not yet "become so bitter as to extinguish the private affections."[38]

Marshall's account of the reasons for his support of the Constitution is, in effect, an analysis of the politics which had made adoption of the Constitution a necessity. The account, written four decades later, reveals him as a man who grasped the needs of his time and understood how those needs must be translated into political action.

Washington himself did not seek to be a delegate to the special convention, believing he should not because of his involvement at the Philadelphia Convention and also because of the obvious possibility of his becoming President if the Constitution was adopted. But he worked behind the scenes, and the principal object of his efforts was Patrick Henry. Other than Washington, and perhaps Jefferson, who was out of the country, Henry was the most influential politician in the state. His leading of the opposition meant the question of ratification was in serious doubt.

From the very beginning, Washington aimed at Henry. Immediately after returning to Mount Vernon from Philadelphia, Washington had sent a copy of the Constitution to Henry. "I accompany it with no observations; your own judgment will at once discover the good." Henry quickly answered that he had to "lament that I cannot bring my mind to accord with the proposed Constitution."[39]

Henry could not be influenced by Washington; he had to be challenged at the convention. Taking on Patrick Henry would be a formidable task for any experienced politician; it obviously would be more so for a younger man without Henry's oratorical prowess and reputation in the state. In the end it would be John Marshall who stood up to Patrick Henry on the floor of the convention hall to challenge him in debate, and who bested him at backstage politicking in the corridors of the hall.

Marshall opposed Henry in the backstage politicking because of his role as a lobbyist for Kentucky in Richmond. There were two issues for the Kentuckians. One was cutting loose from Virginia to become a separate state, and the other was the threat that the Mississippi River would be closed as an avenue for commerce. Kentucky wanted statehood because it was too far away from Richmond to rely on Richmond for governance. Marshall, because of his own landholdings in Kentucky, his relatives living there, and his sympathy with the people there, became the advocate for Kentucky statehood before the Virginia legislature. Historians of the region have described Marshall as "the political agent for the district of Kentucky" who "sincerely sympathized in the movement for a new State organization."[40] By 1788, partly because of the plain logic of the Kentuckians' case and partly because of John Marshall's painstaking work, Virginia was about ready to cede Kentucky its independence and the Continental Congress was about ready to recognize it as a separate state. Then the problem of the Mississippi River arose. The river was controlled by Spain and, as the Virginians understood it, John Jay, the American minister in Madrid, was agreeing to the closing off of the Mississippi to the Americans for a period of twenty-five years. The westerners seethed. To them the closing of the river was only a device to sacrifice the West for the benefit of the East. Without the Mississippi to carry their freight, the westerners then would be forced to cart their goods overland to the eastern merchants. Marshall agreed, at the time at least, that the proposal was—in his words—"so dishonourable and injurious to America, so destructive of the natural rights of the western world."[41]

The motivation behind the proposal was not completely venal. Many Americans, including George Washington, believed the United States would be better off if the western lands became more closely tied to the East. In 1785, after touring western Virginia, he had written to a friend that the Mississippi should be closed to American commerce. If, instead of using the Mississippi, the westerners had to deal with the East, reaching it by way of a network of canals across Virginia, the prospect was that the parts of the nation would grow closer—or so Washington believed. "There is nothing which binds one county or one State to another, but interest," Washington wrote. "Without this cement the western inhabitants, who more than probably will be composed in a great degree of foreigners, can have no predilection for us, and a commercial connexion is the only tie we can have upon them."[42] Also, it is probably true that John Jay, coming from New York, did not understand the emphasis the westerners placed on navigation of the Mississippi; Jay undoubtedly thought he was assisting them by purchasing for them some degree of peace with Spain.

But the westerners did not see it that way, and the fourteen delegates from the Kentucky territory came to Richmond ready to vote against the new Constitution; the proposed Jay Treaty was to them an example of how badly they would be treated by a strong federal government. Rumors spread. According to one, supposedly emanating from James Monroe and traveling fast to Patrick Henry, the Jay Treaty was the first step in a northern plot to debilitate the South and then to separate from it. Henry's inclinations against a strong federal union then were reinforced by his sympathies for the West. He was heard to say that he would rather part with the United States than relinquish the navigation of the Mississippi.[43] And, of course, he was quick to communicate to the Kentucky delegates his fears that their interests would be ignored by any strong federal government. "No pain is spared to inculcate a belief that the Government proposed will without scruple or delay, barter away the right of navigation to the river Mississippi," complained Washington.[44]

The threat was a real one for the Kentuckians. And the fourteen delegates had to choose between what seemed their strong local interests and the blandishments of John Marshall, whom they knew and trusted. In the end Marshall persuaded three of them, including his cousin Humphrey Marshall, to support the Constitution, and the vote was so close that those three votes were almost decisive.

Marshall also would be the one to challenge Patrick Henry within the Convention Hall itself because Henry's chief target for attack was the judicial system established by the Constitution, and John Marshall, as a prominent attorney, was a logical choice to answer Henry's arguments. For Marshall the debates with Henry not only brought him to the forefront of Virginia politics as well as to national prominence, but they also gave him the opportunity to codify and articulate the philosophy of law he had been developing ever since, as a young man, he had watched his father preside as a justice of the peace.

Sunday, June 1, 1788, was a bright and warm day, one of the last days of a drought that had ravaged the Virginia tobacco crops and covered the roads with dust. A good thing too, the townspeople said, realizing that a rainstorm would have made the roads impassable and prevented the delegates from gathering the next day for the opening of the special convention to ratify or reject the Constitution that had been signed eight months earlier in Philadelphia.

The people of Richmond could not disguise their excitement. They watched Patrick Henry, tall and, so the descriptions of him at the time went, "capable of enduring fatigue," come up from the south, driving a plain and topless stick gig. He was covered with dust and his body was bent forward, but no one who watched him move slowly through the streets of Richmond doubted that here was a brilliant man. Those who had not personally heard his oratory ignite the resistance that became the American Revolution were nevertheless aware of his reputation. Coming to fight for the Constitution was his political opponent of more than twenty years, Edmund Pendleton. As if to accentuate their differences, as Henry came to the city from the south, Pendleton arrived from the north, driving a fancy covered carriage known as a phaeton. But it moved very slowly. Pendleton was a cripple who could barely move without assistance. These two men were about to engage in what most understood could be their last battle. Considering the stakes, it promised to be a good show.[45]

Seven states were known to have ratified the Constitution by the time of the Virginia meeting. South Carolina was believed also to have done so, but official word was still lacking. The New York convention was scheduled to meet June 17 in Poughkeepsie, and the New Hampshire convention in Concord on June 18. James Madison in Virginia and Alexander Hamilton in New York established a special express between Richmond and Concord with a stop at Poughkeepsie. The intention was to use the first ratification by one of those states to influence the others. As George Washington commented, "The plot thickens fast."[46]

Perhaps never before had a document been submitted to public approval with such publicity. The newspaper articles, which in their book-published form are known as *The Federalist Papers*, were only one of the many facets of the debate in the months following the meeting in Philadelphia. Politicking was done by pamphlet and the opposition statements of George Mason, Edmund Randolph, and others were printed by the hundreds and distributed throughout the state. In every community men had public discussions, many of them heated. At one meeting in Prince Edward County where Patrick Henry had been particularly critical of the Constitution, his opponent in the debate wheeled toward him and asked why he had not gone to Philadelphia and helped write a better document. "I smelt a rat," Henry answered. In Danville, Kentucky, the "Political Club" met every Saturday night and examined the Constitution line by line, disputing almost every word. John Marshall recalled later that "The press teemed with the productions of temperate reason, of genius, and of passion; and it was apparent that by each party, power, sovereignty, liberty, peace, and security; things most dear to the human heart, were believed to be staked on the question depending before the public."[47] The delegates coming to Richmond and the voters who had sent them understood what was to be debated.

On Monday, June 2, the convention opened in the building known as the Old Capitol. It was about fifty feet square and three stories high, and had been the temporary home of the Virginia legislature when the capital of the state was moved from Williamsburg to Richmond. But the Old Capitol was not large enough for this gathering. So great were the crowds of delegates and spectators that on the second day the convention was moved to the New Academy on Shockoe Hill, the largest assembly room in the city.

The first decision the delegates faced was the election of a president. There were two men who were held in such high repute, whose passion for fairness was so intense, who so much held the affection of their fellow Virginians that they were the obvious candidates. One was Edmund Pendleton, the cripple who only a few years earlier had scoffed at the young men who rose so quickly to political prominence in Virginia, and the other was George Wythe, who had been the mentor at William and Mary of many of the men who now were delegates. Both favored ratification of the Constitution. Pendleton's name was offered for the presidency, and, when Wythe did not oppose him, he was elected unanimously.

The next organizational step was the naming of a committee of privileges and elections. It included the prominent men of Virginia—George Mason, Governor Randolph, Patrick Henry, James Monroe, George Wythe, and John Marshall.[48]

James Madison arrived in Richmond that Monday night. Although he was obviously pleased at Pendleton's election, he still was not certain of the outcome. "There is reason to believe," he wrote to Rufus King, " . . . that the majority will be but small and may possibly be yet defeated."[49]

George Wythe was elected chairman of the committee of the whole, and presided over most of the convention's proceedings. Wythe did not make formal speeches and did not involve himself in the intricate political dealings of the next few weeks, but his very presence and the influence he had over many of his former students obviously helped the cause.

And the cause needed all the help it could get. Henry was winning the support of George Mason, a man whom he had opposed during most of his political career but with whom he was willing to join on the issue of opposition to the Constitution. Since both men opposed the Constitution, who supported whom within the New Academy is an academic question, but outside it was obvious that Patrick Henry was supporting George Mason. They were seen coming out of the Swan Tavern, Mason needing all the support he could get from Henry's arm. One convention member some years later told Patrick Henry's son how impressed he was by Mason, who was "remarkable for the urbanity and dignity with which he received and returned the courtesies of those who passed him."[50]

The debates formally began on Wednesday, June 4, and two developments happened that day to make the prospects brighter for ratification. The first was the arrival of news that South Carolina had ratified; this made it more probable that Virginia would be almost alone if she refused to ratify. The second was the declaration by the Virginia governor, Edmund Randolph, that he had switched from opposing the Constitution—he was one of those who had refused to sign it at Philadelphia—to favoring it. The sudden reversal, if that is what it was, by Randolph was as startling a development as any political act can be. At the Philadelphia Convention he not only had joined with George Mason in refusing to sign the finished document, but he also had broadcast his refusal widely. In the March election for delegates to the special ratification convention, he had only been chosen because he was believed to be an opponent. As governor of the state, he obviously was an influential figure and his position would bring several votes with him.

The reversal, however, should not really have been that surprising. At the Philadelphia Convention he had said that his refusal to sign should not be interpreted to mean that he opposed the document without amendments—"the Constitution without doors," as he described it. Rather, he explained, he feared that the required nine states might fail to ratify, meaning new action would be needed and he wanted to be free to act then as he thought best. When he sent a copy of the Constitution to the Virginia legislature after the Philadelphia Convention, he again asserted that his refusal to sign should not be taken as meaning he was opposed to its adoption. He specifically stated, in fact, that he had become persuaded "that the confederation was destitute of every energy which a constitution of the United States ought to possess. . . ." He then restated his desire to be free to support amendments. This statement of Randolph's, in the form of a letter to the speaker of the Virginia House of Delegates, was circulated in the state and led to the widespread conclusion that Randolph would vote against ratification. A careful reading, however, reveals that those who so believed were indulging in wishful thinking, for nowhere did Randolph predict what he would do; he only explained what he had done.[51]

In the months that followed the Philadelphia Convention Randolph came to the conclusion that this Constitution, even without amendments, was better than none at all. Washington and Madison had been urging this position on him, and by April there were signs they were making their point. Randolph, Madison wrote to Thomas Jefferson then, "is so temperate in his opposition, and goes so far with the friends of the Constitution, that he cannot properly be classed with its enemies."[52] The surprise of Henry and the other opponents was due to their taking Randolph for granted.

When Randolph began speaking to the convention on June 4, they still did not doubt him. He said he planned to continue as he had begun, "to repeat my earnest endeavors for a firm, energetic government, to enforce my objections to the Constitution, and to concur in any practical scheme of amendments." Such words, of course, would have soothed the opponents; the words sounded as if Randolph were still with them. Then came the sentence that shocked them. "But I never will," declared Randolph, "assent to any scheme that will operate a dissolution of the Union, or any measure which may lead to it." He then explained that the postponement of the Virginia session had extinguished the possibility of amendments prior to ratification. His opinion was that the question before the Virginia convention was the simple one of take it or leave it, and leaving it meant "inevitable ruin to the Union." "The Union," he asserted, "is the anchor of our political salvation." Raising his arm dramatically he cried: "I will assent to the lopping of this limb before I assent to the dissolution of the Union."[53] It was an effective performance.

The opponents met to discuss the two events—South Carolina's ratification and Randolph's announcement of support. "[T]hough we are alarmed we do not despair," said one, adding, "The district of Kentucky is with us, and if we can get over the four counties which lie on the Ohio between the Pennsylvania line and Big Sandy Creek, the day is our own."[54]

The two almost simultaneous developments meant that the debate must be that much sharper; the opponents must give no quarter. It was against this background that George Mason rose to attack the proposed Union. "These two concurring powers cannot exist long together," he insisted, "the one will destroy the other: the general government being paramount to, and in every respect more powerful than, the state governments, the latter must give way to the former." He was appealing to those men who looked upon Virginia as their nation to reject the concept of a Union spoken for so dramatically by Randolph. Said Mason:

> Is it to be supposed that one national government will suit so extensive a country, embracing so very different in manners, habits, and customs? It is ascertained by history, that there never was a government, over a very extensive country, without destroying the liberties of the people: history also, supported by the opinions of the best writers, shows us, that monarchy may suit a large territory, and despotic governments ever so extensive a country; but that popular governments can only exist in small territories. Is there a single example, on the face of the earth, to support a contrary opinion?[55]

His historical analysis basically was correct. Democracy and representative government had not proven viable in large territories containing people of varied backgrounds and interests. Mason's mistake—and it would be the same mistake that others with similar doubts in later years would make—was in believing that what had not been could never be. Mason's analysis was not a reason for rejecting the Constitution, as he thought it was, but a challenge to those who would live under the Constitution. That challenge can never be considered at an end.

The next day Patrick Henry rose. A strong Union, he charged, is an opponent of freedom. "You will find this state more particularly interested to support American liberty, and not bind our prosperity by an improvident relinquishment of our rights." He was answered by Randolph, who acknowledged the problems of two political bodies joining together when their "situation and construction of government are dissimilar." Randolph insisted that the crucial question was whether Virginia could exist outside the Union. "A hard question, perhaps after what has been said. I will venture, however, to say she cannot. . . ."[56]

At the end of the first week the situation did not appear bleak for the supporters of the Constitution in Virginia. Washington at Mount Vernon was receiving complete reports of the events in Richmond. "I can't avoid hoping and believing," he commented on Sunday, June 8, "that Virginia will make the ninth column in the federal temple."[57]

In the second week the debate appeared somewhat disorganized. On Monday Henry Lee spoke on the question of loyalty to the Union versus loyalty to one's state:

> One would have thought that the love of an American was in some degree criminal, as being incompatible with a proper degree of affection for a Virginian. The people of America, sir, are one people. I love the people of the north, not because they have adopted the Constitution, but because I fought with them as my countrymen, and because I consider them as such. Does it follow from hence that I have forgotten my attachment to my native state? In all local matters I shall be a Virginian: in those of a general nature, I shall not forget that I am an American.[58]

The same day Patrick Henry took up the question of the Mississippi River. Although he spoke to the entire convention, he was in reality addressing himself only to the fourteen delegates from the Kentucky district; he needed all their votes. He said:

> There is a dispute between us and the Spaniards about the right of navigating the Mississippi. This dispute has sprung from the federal government. . . . This new government, I conceive, will enable those states who have already discovered their inclination that way, to give away this river.[59]

John Marshall had not yet spoken to the convention, but he was an interested participant. Sometimes, however, listening with interest was difficult. During one of the sessions in the second week he scribbled this piece of doggerel:

> *The State's determined Resolution*
> *Was to discuss the Constitution*
> *For this the members came together*
> *Melting with zeal and sultry weather.*
> *And here to their eternal excuse*
> *To find its history spared three days.*
> *The next three days they nobly roam*

Through every region far from home
Call in the German, Swiss, Italian,
The Roman robber, Dutch Rapscallion,
Fellows who freedom never knew
To tell us what we ought to do.
The next three days they kindkli dip yea
Deep in the river Mississippi—[60]

That was probably as accurate a description of the convention's first nine days as could be crowded into fourteen lines.

The Richmond convention was a *tour de force* for Patrick Henry. "I fear that overwhelming torrent, Patrick Henry," Henry Knox said, and both the emotion and the description were justified.[61] Of the twenty-three days the convention met, Henry spoke on eighteen. Several days he made more than one speech; often three, one day five, on another eight. For one speech he is reported to have held the floor for seven hours.[62] Henry could be both subtle and obvious. James Madison spoke of how at this convention he would make "a most conclusive argument" in favor of the Constitution, only to have Henry effectively counter it with "a pause, a shake of the head, or a striking gesture, before he uttered a word."[63] But sometimes Henry went too far. During a speech on slavery he predicted disastrous consequences for the black and white populations in Virginia if a centralized government were adopted. As his rhetoric soared, his body crouched lower and he suddenly exclaimed: "They'll free your niggers!" For a brief moment the convention delegates were locked in fear and then suddenly they burst into laughter.[64]

This was the orator against whom John Marshall was speaking when in the second week, on Tuesday, he first addressed the convention. Marshall on this day was less than four months shy of being thirty-four years old. He was not considered an accomplished orator, and properly not. His voice was dry and, at the time, no match for the oratorical prowess of Henry. Marshall was a handsome man, however, almost a commanding figure. He was tall with long dark hair tied at the back of his neck, and those who saw him that day remarked about his "piercing eyes," as witnesses to John Marshall's career remarked of him throughout his long public life. But he was casually dressed as always, lacking the elegance of the plantation owners. Many in that room had played billiards with him or drunk wine with him, and they knew him to be a convivial person. Many also had watched him in court or in the Assembly and recognized him as a persuasive lawyer and a constructive politician. But none knew him as a man destined for greatness. When the convention ended, however, they knew differently.[65]

With his very first sentence Marshall demonstrated his ability to cut to the heart of an argument. "Mr. Chairman," he began, "I conceive that the object of the discussion now before us, is, whether democracy, or despotism, be most eligible." Quickly he defended the framers of the Constitution and those who supported it as intending "the establishment and security" of democracy. "The supporters of the Constitution," he said, "claim the title of being firm friends of liberty and the rights of mankind. They say, that they consider it as the best means of protecting liberty." He was, of course, responding to the charges of Henry and Mason that the Constitution would eliminate liberty by giving too much power to a central government. Marshall's answer, coming at the beginning of his talk, showed he would not be apologetic about his defense. "We, sir," he insisted, "idolize democracy." He and the other supporters of the Constitution, Marshall said, preferred it to a monarchy "because we are convinced that it has a greater tendency to secure liberty and promote our happiness. We admire it, because we think it a well regulated democracy." There again was the concept that dominated his thinking—a well-regulated democracy. Whether he was criticizing those who confused liberty with licentiousness, or speaking favorably of an "ordered liberty," Marshall always advocated a system of fairness and decency for all men, not only those strong enough to claim their right to liberty.

Now he turned to answer specifically the arguments of Patrick Henry, the man who had been governor of Virginia when John Marshall had fought in the Battle of Great Bridge as a twenty-year-old soldier. Henry had called for the observance of certain maxims. Marshall said he agreed. "What are the favourite maxims of democracy?" he asked. Answering himself, he said: "A strict observance of justice and public faith, and a steady adherence to virtue. These, sire, are the principles of a good government." He only wished—"Would to Heaven" is how he phrased it—that those principles had been observed under the Articles of Confederation.

Henry had argued against giving the power of taxation to Congress. Taxation, of course, was a prime instrument of power. Henry's objection was that of the older Virginians who had grown up with the belief that their colony was their homeland. Each man is shaped by his environment and Patrick Henry had lived most of his life in the environs of Virginia before there ever was a United States of America. Those men who rallied around him, in most cases, were likewise older men who understood Virginia but were skeptical of the United States. When John Marshall rose to speak on the taxation question, he spoke

from a different background, across the gap between generations. Here was speaking the young soldier who had starved and
frozen at Valley Forge. Here was speaking the young soldier who
had been a friend of George Washington's during the testing
years of the Revolution when the American army always was
short of what the colonies seemed to possess in abundance. Here
was speaking the legislator who had personally witnessed the
refusal of the states to respond to requests from the Continental
Congress for funds. Here was speaking the young man who
learned that men must agree to be governed.

For a central government, he said, the power to tax is
"essentially necessary" if that government is to be efficient. "We
have had," he reminded the delegates, "a sufficient demonstration
of the vanity of depending on requisitions." Again in a sentence
he cut to the heart of the dispute. "Why then hesitate to trust the
general government: The object of our inquiry is—Is this power
necessary, or is it guarded?" For Marshall those two questions
would always be the test of power. Was it necessary to bestow a
power? And could that power be so restricted that it was not
abused? Thirty-one years later, in the case of *McCulloch v.
Maryland*, Chief Justice John Marshall restated that theme to
make it the law of the land. "Let the end be legitimate," he said
in 1819, "let it be within the scope of the constitution, and all
means which are appropriate, which are plainly adapted to that
end, which are not prohibited, but consist with the letter and the
spirit of the constitution, are Constitutional."

Henry had argued that the central government would
more easily give away navigation rights to the Mississippi. Marshall, who knew the Kentucky delegates well and who knew that
they trusted him, challenged Henry's thesis. "To the debility of
the confederation alone," said Marshall, "may justly be imputed
every cause of the complaint on this subject." Marshall was turning Henry's own arguments against him. Henry had asked if
the new Constitution would pay Virginia's debts. Marshall
answered that the Constitution "will compel the states to pay
their quotas. Without this, Virginia will be unable to pay."

Marshall's speech covers nine pages of closely printed type
in the official record of the debates. It is a well-organized, persuasive argument. It is also more a lawyer's brief than an
impassioned political plea, but that was probably the better
approach before an audience that included some of the most distinguished lawyers in Virginia. In the last paragraph of this first
speech, however, Marshall abandoned the arguments of the lawyer to enunciate a primary article of the democratic faith. Henry

had argued that the men who led a government under the Constitution would seek to destroy liberty. Marshall answered with a passionate denial:

> Will our most virtuous and able citizens wantonly attempt to destroy the liberty of the people? Will the most virtuous act the most wickedly? I differ in opinion from the worthy gentleman. I think the virtue and talents of the members of the general government will tend to the security, instead of the destruction of our liberty.[66]

This too was part of Marshall's faith in democracy. Along with justice, public faith, and virtue was the belief that good men would enter government to secure liberty for their brethren. He believed in people.

The next week, on Monday the 16th, Marshall spoke again. William Grayson had argued that the Constitution required the states to surrender control of their militias. Marshall challenged this. He insisted that the states still retained power over their militias "as they had not given it away . . . [and] does not a power remain till it is given away?" He acknowledged that the federal government would have the power to call up the militia in time of emergency, but Marshall turned this to a defense of the Constitution rather than an attack. "On this government," he said, "thus depending on ourselves for its existence, I will rest my safety, notwithstanding the danger depicted by the honorable gentleman. I cannot help being surprised that the worthy member thought this power so dangerous. What government is able to protect you in time of war? Will any state depend on its own exertions? The consequence of such dependence and withholding this power from Congress will be, that state will fall after state, and be a sacrifice to the want of power in the general government." Marshall was right, of course. Individually the states were helpless against any other nation; together they were invincible. Moved by this thought, Marshall cried to the delegates: "United we are strong, divided we fall."[67]

Marshall's third speech, and his last major address to the convention, occurred at the end of the third week, on Friday, June 20. At that point the vote count of the delegates was uncertain. According to one of the opponents of ratification, his side had ten of the fourteen Kentucky delegates "but we wanted the whole," and the four upper counties were in doubt with "both sides . . . contending for [them] by every means in their power." All in all, the opponents then were counting eighty votes "which are inflexible" plus eight votes undecided. The debate on the judiciary powers would yield the opponents two additional votes "if the point is conducted in an able and masterly manner."[68] The opponents then believed they counted between eighty and ninety votes against the Constitution. Eighty-five was a majority.

It was late in the afternoon of the second day of the debate on the judiciary when Marshall rose to speak. Those who heard him that hot afternoon could not have guessed that in less than two decades he would again enunciate those same principles he spoke that day.

The role of the judiciary was considered the most important item because of the role this department was assigned as an umpire between the legislative and the executive, between the central government and the states. If the judiciary could indeed act as umpire, it was the most powerful arm of the proposed federal government. Because of its importance, the supporters of the Constitution assigned the opening speech on the subject of the judiciary to Edmund Pendleton, the crippled and much respected statesman who had been elected president of the convention.

Friends helped the wrecked man to stand on his crutches and then moved away from him as he began his defense of the proposed federal court system. He envisioned the courts as the guardian of the people against the executive. Since it was necessary, he said, the judiciary must be coequal with the executive and legislative; otherwise it could not fulfill its role.[69]

Patrick Henry and George Mason both answered Pendleton. Mason's comments include a criticism of the courts that would follow the federal judiciary system for more than a century, beginning after John Marshall became Chief Justice. Mason argued that the judiciary would be the means to slowly take from the states their power. "There are many gentlemen in the United States who think it right, that we should have one great national consolidated government," he said, "and that it was better to bring it about slowly and imperceptibly, rather than all at once." Those who so believed, he charged, would support a strong judiciary.[70]

Then it was Marshall's turn.

The delegates were tired, hot, perhaps even bored with what seemed an endless debate. Perhaps sensing this, Marshall began speaking slowly. Again, he was the lawyer making a case, appealing to the intellects of the men in the room rather than pleading for their emotional allegiance.

"This part of the plan before us," he began, "is a great improvement on that system which we are now departing." There would be courts, he argued, to settle controversies "which were before, either not at all, or improperly provided for." The next two sentences underline Marshall's thesis that men must support law as the means of civilization. "That many benefits will result from this to the members of the collective society," he said, "every one confesses. Unless its organization be defective, and so constructed as to injure, instead of accommodating the conveniences of the people, it merits our approbation."

As to the contention that federal courts will not offer fair trials—"no foundation" was his answer. And then he challenged the complaint about the Congress being allowed to establish a number of lower federal courts. This, Marshall declared, was necessary to the system's success so that citizens would not have to travel to the office of the central government to have a case argued. Then he turned to the major arguments made against the Constitution.

The first was that the federal government being paramount, ultimately all state laws would be wiped out. "Has the government of the United States power to make laws on every subject?" answered Marshall. "Does he [Mason] understand it so? Can they make laws affecting the mode of transferring property, or contracts, or claims between citizens of the same state? Can they go beyond the delegated powers? If they were to make a law not warranted by any of the powers enumerated, it would be considered by the judges as an infringement of the constitution which they are to guard. They would declare it void." That is exactly what John Marshall did a quarter of a century later in the case of *Marbury v. Madison*. Not only was an act of the government declared invalid, but the principle of judicial review—described here in Richmond on a late Friday afternoon in 1788—was firmly established as the bulwark of the American system of law.

The second major argument was that the federal court system would destroy the state and local courts. One can almost hear the mocking tone of disbelief in Marshall's words. "Does not every gentleman here know, that the causes in our courts are more numerous than they can decide, according to their present construction? Look at the dockets. You will find them crowded with suits, which the life of man will not see determined. If some of these suits be carried to other courts, will it be wrong?" Marshall insisted the state courts "will still have business enough." He argued that there was no danger that the loss of "particular subjects, small in proportion," to a federal system would render the state courts "useless and of no effect." He then asked: "Does the gentleman imagine this to be the case? Will any gentleman believe it? Are not controversies respecting lands

claimed under the grants of different states, the only controversies between citizens of the same state, which the federal
government can take cognizance of?"

One hundred and fifty-three years after this moment, in 1941,
Robert H. Jackson, then the Attorney General of the United States
and later an Associate Justice of the Supreme Court, wrote:
"Struggles over power that in Europe call out regiments of
troops, in America call out battalions of lawyers."[71] Perhaps
better than anything else that explains the stability of the
American government. No government of another major power
has lasted so long, has been so much the product of rationality
rather than violence. With no other government in a major
nation has civilized democracy succeeded quite so well. And this
was the key, that the combatants came into the courts with their
lawbooks rather than onto the battlefield with their guns. And in
that hot assembly room in the New Academy on Shockoe Hill,
John Marshall promised that such was the purpose of the federal
judiciary as outlined in the Constitution. He declared:

> Is it not necessary that the federal courts should have
> cognizance of cases arising under the constitution, and
> the laws of the United States? What is the service or pur-
> pose of a judiciary, but to execute the laws in a peace-
> able, orderly manner, without shedding blood, or creating
> a contest, or availing yourselves of force? If this be the
> case, where can its jurisdiction be more necessary than
> here? To what quarter will you look for protection from an
> infringement on the constitution, if you will not give the
> power to the judiciary?

He told the delegates, and the statement has not been effectively challenged since, that "There is no other body that can
afford such a protection."

No other man would influence the development of the
Supreme Court into the body where struggles of power were
settled peaceably as did John Marshall. And his question that
day to the delegates—where else can such a settlement take
place?—was the plea of all men who seek a high level of
civilization, a peak where life is sacred, where force gives way
to reason and power to justice.

The other complaints against the Constitution that day had
to do with the rights of citizens of one state to sue another state
or to sue citizens of another state. To men like George Mason and
Patrick Henry, Virginians before they were Americans, the prospect of a suit by a non-Virginian was like the prospect of a suit
by an alien. On whether a state could be sued by a citizen of

another state, Marshall's interpretation would be superseded by facts. "I hope no gentleman will think that a state will be called at the bar of the federal court," he said. He argued that there existed then many cases in which the legislature of Virginia was a party "and yet the state is not sued." This, he argued, would not happen under the Constitution as it had not happened under the Articles of Confederation. As for the wording in the Constitution that the power of the federal judiciary shall extend to cases arising "between a state and citizens of another state," Marshall argued that the intention was to allow the states to recover against individuals rather than individuals against states, as Mason had said. "I contend this construction is warranted by the words," Marshall said. He argued that contemplating George Mason's interpretation was unnecessary because, "If an individual has a just claim against any particular state, is it to be presumed, that on application to its legislature, he will not obtain satisfaction?" Of course, George Mason's predictions of individuals suing states did come to pass. But that June day the delegates were more prone to accept John Marshall's predictions. After all, they were—many of them—either present, past, or hopefully, future members of the Virginia legislature and to deny his interpretation was to impugn their own integrity.

Marshall then spoke of the right of citizens of one state to sue citizens in another state. He conceded that it might not be "absolutely necessary. . . . But are not the objections to it carried too far?" Every so often, he said, such a suit might be necessary, and "What is the evil which this can produce? Will he get more justice there? The independence of the judges forbids it. What has he to get? Justice. Shall we object to this? . . ."[72]

This was Marshall's last major address to the convention. It covered almost eight pages of closely printed type and is a brilliant defense of the federal judiciary system. Marshall gave an equally brilliant performance as a speaker when compared to George Mason, and, particularly, to Patrick Henry. When Marshall had stood up, he was an engaging young man with, perhaps, potential for greatness. When he sat down that Friday afternoon, there was no question that potential had been realized. James Madison, who was leading the fight for ratification at the convention, later remarked that his young lieutenant had shown "a great deal of ability" in the debates.[73] It was a remark that all who had heard John Marshall that day would have agreed with.

As the vote neared, no one was making firm predictions. Madison did not believe the attack on the judiciary had been as effective as the opponents had hoped and that his side had not lost as many votes as he had once feared. He considered the vote of the Kentuckians as being decisive and "there is perhaps more to fear than to hope from that quarter." He estimated that the Constitution would win by three to six votes but conceded that his tally could be off.[74]

The morning of Wednesday, June 25, the hall was filled; the 168 delegates had arrived even before ten o'clock, the hour for starting; spectators also crowded into the room. Word had gone out that a vote was to be taken this day, and no one wanted to miss the excitement. The first vote was on the Henry tactic of insisting on a bill of rights. As the voting began, each man who cast a "nay" vote understood that he might later be criticized for voting against a bill of rights. But each man knew that to insist on amendments at this time meant destroying the Constitution, as every state would then insist on amendments and the Constitution would never be ratified.

The vote on the amendments question was eighty votes for requiring amendments and eighty-eight against. The Constitution had passed its test in the Virginia ratification convention. There was a second vote, this one on the straight question of ratification. But there was no suspense remaining as everyone realized the issue had been settled with the first vote. The Constitution then was ratified by a vote of eighty-nine to seventy-nine. John Marshall had voted "no" the first time, against insisting on amendments, and "yes" the second time, for ratification. Of the fourteen delegates from Kentucky, three—Humphrey Marshall, John's first cousin, and two delegates from Jefferson —also supported the Constitution. Humphrey said the three lost a considerable amount of political support in Kentucky because of their vote and suffered much criticism. But, he said, they voted "under a conviction, that *previous* amendments, amidst the divided, agitated, and conflicting opinions, and views of the popular leaders throughout the continents, were impracticable."[75] In supporting the Constitution, the three Kentuckians were betting that their statehood and the opening of the Mississippi would be obtained under a strong central government. The bets shortly paid off. John Marshall's old friend Alexander Hamilton was chairman of a special committee in Congress to deal with John Jay's report on the future of the Mississippi. On September 15, 1788, that committee issued a report demanding the "clear and essential right" of the United States to free navigation on the Mississippi. The report was in Hamilton's handwriting. Hamilton also withdrew his opposition to statehood for Kentucky and the Continental Congress recommended to the new government to be formed under the now-ratified Constitution that Kentucky be admitted as a state.[76]

The victors in Virginia were careful to show restraint in victory. "There was no bonfire illumination, etc.," James Monroe said.[77] And James Madison described the closing of the convention as being with "due decorum and solemnity."[78] The victors not only were being restrained, they were being careful. Throughout the entire convention there had been the fear that if Henry lost, he would lead his followers in seceding from the state or perhaps into some violent act of rebellion. He was, after all, the orator who had ignited the resistance movement in Virginia before the Revolution and he held the power to do so again. "Some apprehend a secession," Madison had conceded as the vote had neared. He personally did not believe it would happen but he could not be certain.[79]

In one authoritative account of the convention it was stated that "the fierce tone of Henry in the debate" suggested that if the Constitution were ratified by the Virginia convention, he might lead his supporters in a walkout. "The secession of so large a number of the most able and most popular men in the Commonwealth," said this account, "would in every aspect be fatal to the Constitution."[80] It was against this background that Patrick Henry rose to speak at the end of the convention. His defeat was certain. His future actions were in doubt.

"I beg pardon of this house for having taken up more time than came to my share," he began, "and I thank them for the patience and polite attention with which I have been heard." No indication yet of Henry's plans. "If I shall be in the minority," he continued, his voice perhaps growing stronger and bolder, "I shall have those painful sensations which arise from a conviction of being overpowered in a good cause." He could not concede he was wrong. At this point, his course of action could go either way: secession and possibly violence or obeisance to a system he abhorred and had fought so valiantly to defeat. Then the answer came. "Yet," he announced, "I will be a peaceable citizen. My head, my hand, and my heart, shall be at liberty to retrieve the loss of liberty, and remove the defects of that system in a constitutional way."[81] And with that last eleven-word promise Patrick Henry assured that the Constitution would indeed become the law of the land. If the most ardent and respected foe was willing to accept his defeat with dignity and respect for the law, even the law he so opposed, then all foes of the Constitution must accept it. Henry made clear that he still opposed the new system of government—"I shall therefore patiently wait in expectation of seeing that government changed"—but, he said, "I wish not to go to violence."[82]

Henry's closing paragraph moved all those who heard it or of it. "Mr. Henry has given exemplary proofs of his greatness," wrote one Virginian, "and in the opinion of many, of his virtue."[83] George Washington was particularly pleased. "There is every reason to expect a perfect acquiescence therein by the minority" because of Henry's statement that his future opposition to the new government would be limited to those constitutional means within his power. Washington was certain that Henry "both by precept and example" will influence others also to acknowledge the authority of the Constitution.[84]

That, of course, was one result of the movement to produce and ratify a new system of government for the young United States, that men would learn how to accept defeat. No longer would the defeat of a man send him to the countryside to rally his supporters for battle. Now men bowed to a cause greater than themselves. Now men understood that on some occasions it was necessary to surrender their own ambitions and their own views of righteousness to a decision arrived at by democratic means. If the concept of statesmanship has meaning, Patrick Henry demonstrated it that June day in Richmond when he rose above himself.

That was only one result of the process that took place in the United States between 1787 and 1788. Another result was articulated a few days after the Virginia vote by a Connecticut orator named Simeon Baldwin. Speaking on the twelfth anniversary of the signing of the Declaration of Independence, Baldwin said of the Constitution: "Revolutions in government have in general been the tumultuous exchange of one tyrant for another, or the elevation of a few aspiring nobles upon the ruins of a better system. Never before has the collected wisdom of any nation been permitted quietly to deliberate and determine upon the form of government best adapted to the genius, views and circumstances of the citizens. Never before have the people of any nation been permitted, candidly to examine and then deliberately adopt or reject the Constitution proposed."[85] That process demonstrated that government can be arrived at without violence and without coercion, that reasonable men can meet together and produce a result that all—both the George Washingtons and the Patrick Henrys—can agree to honor. That demonstration was the second result of the process of adopting the Constitution.

The third result was summed up in a line by Joseph Story more than thirty years later when Story had served on the

Supreme Court for almost a decade. "I will say no more about the rich and the poor," he said. "There is no parallel to be run between them, founded on permanent constitutional distinctions."[86] And that was the third great result, that the distinction between rich and poor, which was a permanent part of the European society from which these Americans had come, no longer was blessed by law. At a later time Charles Beard charged that the Constitution was an economic document written by people who had a substantial interest in its being adopted to protect their own holdings.[87] This was true. It also was true that the Constitution was produced by people representing various geographical backgrounds and various political factions without any one of these powers controlling the writing and the ratification process. Of course property was protected. The people involved in writing the Constitution understood that the protection of property is a legitimate aim of government because a man is motivated by the desire for security for himself and his children. The genius of the system devised was that—with the exception of the slaves, an omission for which the Americans would pay dearly—opportunity was denied to no one. The system, rather, protected an individual's opportunity, all individuals' opportunities. No longer was government a tool of the rich. That had been the role of government in the Old World. In the New power had been transferred to the people.

This, then, was part of the experience of John Marshall, the awareness that the American government demanded statesmanship, established a new standard for reasonableness and nonviolence, and excluded no man from its benefits. Like what he had learned at Valley Forge about the need for a strong government, this experience gained in 1787 and 1788 would be part of his future.

3

THE NIGHT of Monday, October 1, in the year 1792, a carriage carrying Richard Randolph, his wife Judith (who was a distant cousin of her husband and whose maiden name also was Randolph), and Judith's younger—and more attractive—sister Nancy arrived at the Virginia estate Glenlyvar in southern Virginia, the home of a cousin named Randolph Harrison.

By this time Virginia already had its first families, and the Randolph clan with its many uncles, aunts, and cousins was perhaps the first of these. The Randolphs owned large estates and numerous slaves. They were active in state politics, were members of the legislature. Little happened in Virginia without a Randolph—or one of their distant cousins, such as Thomas Jefferson or John Marshall—being involved.

They were not a family of murderers and criminals, these Randolphs, yet within a few weeks after that October night when Richard Randolph, his wife, and her sister arrived at Glenlyvar in Cumberland County, most responsible persons believed that at least two of them were murderers. And before the story was done, a story in which John Marshall and Patrick Henry were major characters as lawyers for the defense, the Randolph scandal drew a stain across the pages of Virginia society, a stain not removed in almost two centuries.

Richard Randolph, the husband who led the visitors to Glenlyvar, was twenty-three years old that October. He had been educated in the law, but he saw no reason to practice as an attorney. "What inducement," he once said, "have I to leave a happy and comfortable home to search for bustle, fatigue and disappointment? I have a comfortable subsistence, which is enough to make me happy." His "subsistence" was largely his estate "Bizarre" where hundreds of slaves toiled on the thousands of acres he had inherited so he would not be bothered by any inducement to work. He was considered indolent, passionate when he wanted something, and weak-willed when he met resistance. He had married his cousin Judith when he was nineteen and she was sixteen. Judith's mother believed her daughter too young for marriage, feared she was not yet ready to make a wise choice of a husband. Perhaps neither was Richard yet ready to make a wise choice of a wife. Judith was a drab young lady, lacking both the physical attractiveness and the spirit to be mistress of an estate like Bizarre.

Then there was Nancy, the younger sister. She was seventeen that October night in 1792, beautiful, charming, and with a wild spirit of adventure. Some time earlier she had a dispute with her mother and father, and had come to live with her sister and brother-in-law. She apparently was welcomed by them both. An uncle, Carter Page, later commented that he had frequently seen Richard Randolph and his sister-in-law Nancy together. They had been kissing and seemed fond of each other. Randolph Harrison, who was their host this October night, acknowledged having observed "imprudent familiarities" between Richard and Nancy. But he said he had too high an opinion of them both to attach anything improper to the scene. And Archibald Randolph, another cousin as well as Nancy's suitor, said that some eighteen months earlier he had believed that Richard and Nancy were "too fond of each other," but he had entirely dismissed such suspicions.

All of this would be recalled after the night of October 1st.

When the carriage stopped in front of Glenlyvar, Randolph Harrison was waiting to greet his guests. He helped Nancy step down from the carriage, noting that she wore a coat closely buttoned around her. His observation was the first major piece of evidence used by John Marshall and Patrick Henry for the defense.

Nancy complained of not feeling well. That in itself was not unusual. A carriage ride over the ribbons of mud, bumps, and dust that were then Virginia roads was not very comfortable for a genteel young lady. Also, and this was something about which little was said among the Randolphs, Nancy—or so the story went —was recovering from a broken heart. She supposedly had been in love with Richard Randolph's younger brother, Theodorick, who had died almost eight months earlier. Since Theodorick's death, his name was not to be mentioned in Nancy's presence. A third brother, the youngest one, John, mentioned Theodorick's name to Nancy, or so he testified later, and she burst into tears. Why John Randolph did so, he never explained. But now, and in later years when he was one of the young nation's most influential politicians, he often did and said many things that hurt others.

It was an interesting trio that had come to Glenlyvar: the husband, the wife, and the sister. The husband was unpredictable. The wife was unattractive. The sister was beautiful and supposedly recovering from the loss of the man she loved. And the sister and the husband were good friends . . .

Nancy went to bed shortly after dinner. She was known to suffer from "colic," a label used then to describe any internal upset. Mrs. Harrison, her hostess, sympathized with her and brought her some essence of peppermint. The seventeen-year-old Nancy looked unwell.

The visiting Randolphs were staying on the second floor of the unfinished Glenlyvar mansion. At the top of the stairs there was one door leading to a bedroom where Richard and Judith Randolph slept. On the other side of the room was a second door leading to a smaller bedroom where Nancy slept. It was necessary to walk through the husband and wife's room to enter the sister's room.

Everyone retired early. Long carriage rides in the afternoon and candlelight at night did not encourage late hours. The Harrisons slept in a bedroom on the first floor, directly beneath that of their guests. They were never sure at what hour they heard the screams above them, except that it was a late one. Soon a black servant came scurrying into their room. Miss Nancy was sick! Could Mrs. Harrison bring some laudanum?

Laudanum was an opiate used for most ailments at the time. Taking a lighted candle to guide her, Mrs. Harrison brought some of the medicine. First she had to pass through Richard and Judith's room. Judith was sitting up in bed; Richard was not there. Judith said that she did not know what was the matter with her sister. She suggested that Nancy must be suffering from "an attack of the hysterics" because the colic "could hardly make her scream so."

Mrs. Harrison hurried to the second door, the one leading to Nancy's room. It had been fastened from the inside by a bolt. At first Mrs. Harrison considered that unusual, but then decided it was not. The spring catch on the door was broken, Mrs. Harrison noted, and the door could only be kept shut by a bolt. She knocked. Richard Randolph was in the room with his wife's sister. He opened the door immediately.

He stopped her from bringing a candle into the room. Nancy, he explained, was in great pain and could not bear the light on her eyes. From her bed Nancy confirmed that. Mrs. Harrison placed the candle outside the doorway and entered the room. Besides Richard and the ailing Nancy, she could see in the dark shadows two slaves, a girl about fifteen years of age and another about seven. Standing in the dark, beside the bed, Mrs. Harrison talked to Nancy for a few moments, waiting until the girl began to calm down, and then left. In her own bedroom downstairs Mrs. Harrison tried to sleep. But sleep did not come for either her or her husband. Later they were certain they heard footsteps on the stairs, coming down and then returning to the second-floor bedrooms some minutes later. It must be Richard Randolph, they thought, sending for a doctor.

The next day Nancy stayed in her room. Randolph Harrison, her host, went into her room to fix a fire for her. She was in bed, the covers drawn closely to her; her face was very pale. Still, he noticed nothing except what one would see in the room of a woman who had been ill with something termed colic or hysteria the previous night. His wife was more observant.

She saw bloodstains on the stairs. There were more stains on the pillow case. The bed had neither sheets nor quilt this morning. The previous evening it had both. Later when Mrs. Harrison examined the bed more carefully, it appeared to her that an effort had been made to wash it. Obviously Mrs. Harrison should have been suspicious, but Judith, the wife, eliminated all suspicion. Her only concern seemed to be for her younger sister's health.

The three Randolphs left Glenlyvar at the end of the week. Nancy still seemed pale but was obviously much better. About three weeks later Randolph Harrison visited Bizarre and found the relationship between the three Randolphs—the husband, the wife, and the sister—as pleasant as he had remembered it. Nancy seemed her former self. She shone with good health and was doing considerable horseback riding, her favorite sport. The night of October 1st might have passed forgotten, except that it could not.

The Negro slaves spread the story. Nancy Randolph, they said, had given birth to a baby that night. And Richard Randolph had killed it. One slave even claimed to know the exact spot among some old shingles behind Glenlyvar where Randolph had deposited the dead child. The slave led Randolph Harrison to that spot. Although this was some weeks after the night of October 1st, Randolph Harrison could see bloodstains on the shingles. Richard Randolph, everyone assumed, was the baby's father. Talk spread rapidly throughout southern Virginia. As other plantation owners heard the story, they enjoyed retelling it. It was good for the Randolphs to get their comeuppance.

There was another reason the scandal was interesting. Even then there was a social code for the Virginia white man. When he dallied romantically, he did so with a Negro slave girl; he did not have sexual relations with a white woman outside of marriage. As long as that code was honored, the easy relationship existing then between the sexes continued. The young ladies played the coquette and the men were the ardent wooers, because both knew there were limits beyond which they would not go. But now Richard Randolph and Nancy Randolph, his wife's sister, had gone beyond those limits. Of that, most of the leading families in Virginia were certain.

As the story was retold, it was embellished. Everyone, it seemed, remembered witnessing some romantic incident between Richard and his Nancy. Sympathy built up for Judith, apparently the deceived wife. The honor of the Randolph family became a matter for jest. Richard Randolph, always impetuous, could endure no more of it. He went for advice to his stepfather, Henry St. George Tucker. Tucker was a prominent lawyer. He told his stepson the only way to stop the ugly stories was to prove them false in a court of law. There was no one against whom a libel action could be brought, which would have been one way to bring the issue before a court. And it did not appear that Richard Randolph would be arrested for the crime of murdering Nancy's unnamed baby; after all, no body had been found.

Tucker then suggested that Randolph demand arrest, that he insist those who believed he had murdered a baby prove their case in court. Accepting his stepfather's advice, Richard Randolph announced he would present himself at the Cumberland County Courthouse on April 29, 1793, and insist on being charged with the crime of murder and on being tried for that crime. Considering the widespread belief that he and Nancy had been lovers, had conceived a child, and that Richard had killed it, he seemed to be taking undue risk by placing himself in the hands of the law. But he had two things going for him. One was John Marshall and the other was Patrick Henry.

Whatever Marshall's personal reaction to the case, he could not turn down an appeal from his distant kinfolk, particularly when one of them was the stepson of St. George Tucker, a close friend of Marshall's in Richmond. Marshall would bring to the defense his analytical mind, which had produced so many persuasive arguments in the many civil cases he had handled. But in a criminal case, especially one that had caused as much scandalous talk as the Randolph affair, more than analysis was needed.

No one complemented Marshall's analytical approach as did Patrick Henry, who had the ability to give a jury all the histrionics its members expected. Marshall and Henry had been on opposite sides in the fight over Virginia's ratification of the Constitution five years earlier, but they had never permitted their conflicting theories of government to prevent them from enjoying a personal relationship based on mutual respect. Marshall had no objection to Henry's joining him for the defense.

Henry's initial reaction, however, was to refuse. Few Virginia lawyers had had his experiences: wartime governor, legislator, loyal leader of the opposition. Now he was tired and ill, not too many years from death; although he was only fifty-seven years old at this time, in the 1790s he simply wanted to live on his estate in ease. Or that was what he professed when a messenger arrived from Richard Randolph offering Henry a fee of 250 guineas to join the defense. Although that was an extraordinary fee, Henry declined, saying he was not well enough to make the trip to the Cumberland Courthouse. A few days later the messenger returned. Richard Randolph would double the fee.

Henry asked his wife's advice. "Mr. Randolph seems very anxious that I should appear for him, and 500 guineas is a large sum. Don't you think I could make the trip in the carriage?" Apparently realizing her husband was eagerly sniffing at the drama of the trial arena, she consented and Patrick Henry agreed to appear for the defense.

A murder trial that involved a Virginia family as prominent as the Randolphs was the social event of the season. Men came on their horses and in their carriages from miles around to crowd into the Cumberland County Courthouse to head the lurid details and watch the Randolphs squirm. It took place before a jury made up of sixteen of what were called then "gentlemen justices." These sixteen were supposed to be men of the highest standing in the county, and they were. All landed gentry, each of the sixteen was respected for his honesty and good judgment. Several of them, however, were known to be on bad terms with the Randolph family, and particularly with Richard Randolph. No one was certain why. Family feuds in early Virginia had ways of widening without anyone understanding them.

As the trial opened, there were several points assisting the defense. First, neither Richard nor Nancy Randolph could be compelled to testify against themselves. Also, Virginia law did not permit slaves to testify against white citizens. The Negroes, the fifteen-year-old and seven-year-old girls who had been in Nancy's bedroom that night, would not be allowed to tell the court what they had seen. Also, there was the testimony of Richard's wife Judith Randolph. She claimed that she had been awake all that night, that no child could have been born or disposed of without her being aware of it, and that she was certain it had not happened. However, her testimony would be largely dismissed, or so the defense lawyers feared, as the story of a woman loyal to her errant husband and protective of her younger sister.

As John Marshall mapped the defense, he saw five points against his clients that he and Henry must counter. The first was the apparent fondness of Richard and Nancy for each other. There was much testimony by relatives and friends of intimacies between the husband and his wife's younger sister. The second point was testimony by several persons that Nancy appeared to be pregnant. The third point was that Nancy Randolph had the means to effect an abortion. About a month before the alleged infant murder took place, Nancy and Richard Randolph were talking with a cousin, Mrs. Martha Randolph, about colic. Mrs. Randolph (who was Thomas Jefferson's daughter) recommended gum guiacum as an "excellent medicine" for colic. She quickly added that one should be careful of using it because it could produce an abortion. Nancy, she remembered, said nothing at the time, but later she sent for some of the medicine. The fourth point against the defendants was the suspicious appearances that

Monday night at Glenlyvar. Although it was true there could be other explanations for the events of that night, even the one offered at the time, it was also true that the most logical appeared to be those associated with the basic charges: that an illegitimate child had been born, then murdered, and its body hidden.

The fifth point was the testimony of Mrs. Carter Page, the aunt of the Randolph sisters. She had visited the Bizarre estate on several occasions in the months before the night of October 1st. She suspected an improper relationship had developed between Richard and Nancy about the end of March or the first of April—at least that is when she first believed they were fonder of each other than Mrs. Page considered a husband and his sister-in-law should be. And Mrs. Page and her husband had noticed an alteration in Nancy's figure about May. Nancy also seemed very melancholy. On several occasions Mrs. Page attempted to be present when Nancy was undressing for bed, but Nancy did not permit her. This, of course, had only increased Mrs. Page's suspicions. One night she was passing Nancy's bedroom and overheard the young girl and her maid talking. The door was locked, but Mrs. Page could see through a crack. Nancy was undressed and appeared to Mrs. Page to be pregnant. Mrs. Page heard her ask the maid whether she thought she was smaller; the maid replied she thought her larger.

There seemed no end to Mrs. Page's meddling. After the October 1st visit the Glenlyvar and the rumors of that night's occurrences began to circulate, she approached her niece Nancy and asked for proof that the stories were not true; Mrs. Page said she wished to contradict them publicly. Nancy angrily replied that if her own denials were not adequate, she should give no further satisfaction. Mrs. Page also testified that she once saw Nancy stare down at her waist and then look up in a heavenly direction—as if either regretting her situation or imploring divine assistance.

As Marshall examined the evidence of the various witnesses, he realized there could be little dispute with what those witnesses presented the facts to be. Either one believed Nancy looked pregnant or one did not. Either there had been a discussion of an abortion-producing agent or there had not. Either Richard and Nancy had engaged in intimacies or they had not. It would not be a question of disputing facts. Rather, it would be a problem of interpreting them.

First, it was important to demonstrate to the sixteen gentlemen justices that most of the testimony against Richard Randolph and Nancy was, in fact, nothing more than the worst kind of gossip. This Patrick Henry did. It was when Mrs. Carter

Page was on the stand, responding to his questions. Breathlessly she told her story, of the lurid intimacies she had observed between Richard and Nancy, of the change in Nancy's size. And she spoke of wanting to confirm her suspicions by seeing Nancy undressed and of Nancy's refusal to permit that. Finally, Mrs. Page told of passing the locked door of Nancy's bedroom and staring through a crack to observe whether the young girl was pregnant.

Mrs. Page was the daughter of Archibald Cary, an old political foe of Henry's. In the Virginia legislature one time he had vowed to plant his dagger in Patrick Henry's heart. Although Cary never attempted to carry out his threat, Henry remembered being the object of his venom and enjoyed what he was about to do. He bided his time as Mrs. Page told her story until she finished the part about observing Nancy through the crack in the door and of overhearing her discussing her size with her maid.

Henry waited just long enough for the import of her comment to be absorbed in the courtroom. Then he turned toward her, his tall figure bending over her. He paused one moment.

"Which eye," he finally demanded, "did you peep with?"

The courtroom exploded with laughter as Mrs. Page flushed with embarrassment. When the room had quieted, Henry's voice boomed out to the justices: "Great God, deliver us from eavesdroppers!"

In his summation John Marshall assumed the responsibility for offering a rational explanation for the testimony that had been given, for presenting a story that the justices could believe, that would allow them to reject the testimony of peeping toms and eavesdroppers with a clear conscience.

"Let us," said Marshall to the court of the points against Richard Randolph and Nancy, "examine them without favor or prejudice."

The first point was the apparent fondness between Richard and Nancy. "I believe there is no man in whose house a young lady lives," said Marshall, "who does not occasionally pay her attentions and use fondnesses, which a person prone to suspicion may consider as denoting guilt." He said this would be particularly true with the young sister of a man's wife. Marshall added that there were additional reasons for Richard to show Nancy added tokens of tenderness. She had left her parents' house because of a dispute with them, then she had suffered more when the man she loved—this, said Marshall, was the younger brother of Richard Randolph, Theodorick—had died. "Is it," he asked the court, "any wonder that the attentions of Mr. Randolph should be somewhat particular?"

Then he bore in, to prove that what appeared to be evidence against the pair was, in reality, evidence in their favor. "Had they been conscious of guilt," he said, "they would have suppressed any public fondness" and would have avoided all public demonstrations of affection. His point that the two had not acted in a guilty fashion was. well taken. Certainly if they had been engaged in improper conduct, they never would have been so blatant about it.

The next point was Nancy's appearance of pregnancy. He conceded her figure had changed. But was the cause a pregnancy? "Let us then look into the testimony for truth," he said. Marshall recalled that Mr. and Mrs. Carter Page had told of noticing an alteration in Nancy's shape in May and of then believing her pregnant. But if this were true, Marshall continued, "she must have then been advanced three or four months," meaning that by the first of October she would have been eight or nine months pregnant "and must have been of the size of a woman about to be delivered." He asked the court: "Was this so?" He reminded the justices that Mrs. Martha Randolph—Thomas Jefferson's daughter—had seen her in September and did not report any increase in her size. To clinch this argument, he pointed out that when the Randolph carriage arrived at Glenlyvar the night of the alleged crime, Randolph Harrison had met his guests and helped Nancy out of the carriage. She had been wearing her coat buttoned tightly around her, Randolph Harrison had said, and did not appear pregnant. Marshall's conclusion was inescapable and seemingly irrefutable: any change in Nancy's figure the previous May must be ascribed to a cause other than pregnancy.

The third point against Richard Randolph and Nancy was the sending to Martha Randolph for gum guiacum. Marshall conceded it was an abortion-producing agent but he also pointed out that it was used for regular medicinal purposes. "It might then be designed for the one purpose," he said, "as well as the other." He had little trouble convincing the court that the purpose had been a legitimate medical one. "If she was near a delivery," he said of Nancy, "it would have been unnecessary to take this medicine to procure an untimely one." He also asserted that if she were interested in using the medicine for an abortion, "she would have taken it at home, where the event would have been concealed, and not abroad where discovery was inevitable." Again the logic of his argument seemed to have won out.

The fourth point was the events at Glenlyvar. Marshall dismissed them as not being contradictory to the story told by the Randolphs at the time. Nor did he give credit to the stories told by the slaves about an infant being born, suggesting the stories were the product of overactive imaginations. "Let it be remembered," he said, "that suspicions had been propagated, and had probably reached the servants." But what of the stained shingles in the rear of Glenlyvar where the body was supposedly deposited? That, said Marshall, has no significance. "Had the fact been as supposed," he insisted, "no person on earth would have deposited the birth on a pile of shingles." He did not have to say that if Richard Randolph had been creeping down the stairs to dispose of a baby's body when the Harrisons heard his footsteps, he would have buried it deeply in the ground.

The fifth point was Nancy's refusal to be inspected by her aunt, Mrs. Page, while undressed. "If that unfortunate young lady be innocent," Marshall declared, "she had abundant cause to regret her refusal." But, he continued, "the most innocent person on earth might have acted in the same manner. We all know that the heart conscious of its own purity resents suspicion; the resentment is still stronger when we are suspected by a friend." Marshall argued that Nancy could not have known then how important it would be to have a witness to her not being pregnant, "and the pride of conscious innocence was sufficient to produce the refusal." Instead of Nancy's refusal being a sign of her guilt, it was a demonstration of her pride in her innocence.

There was little disagreement in the courthouse as Marshall concluded that while "the friends of Miss Randolph cannot deny that there is some foundation on which suspicion may build," it also cannot be denied "by her enemies but that every circumstance may be accounted for, without imputing guilt to her. In this situation candor will not condemn or exclude from society a person who may be only unfortunate."

The verdict was in Richard Randolph's favor, and the court and the community which had largely been hostile to him cheered the result. Most Virginians took the position that Thomas Jefferson did when he advised his daughter Martha and her husband to continue their friendship with Nancy Randolph, whom he described as "the pitiable victim." He told Martha and her husband that for Nancy "it is the moment of trying the affection of her friends, when their commiseration and comfort became value to her wounds." He continued: "I hope you will deal them out to her in full measure, regardless of what the trifling malignant may think or say."

The story should have ended there with the honor of the young people confirmed. But the gossip never ceased, fed primarily by the stories told by the slaves from one generation to another. More recently they have become accepted as historical fact. "The facts [of the charge] were unquestionably correct," says a 1966 account. This was preceded by a fictionalized account in the mid-1950s and a magazine article in the early 1960s, both accepting as true the charges that an illegitimate child fathered by Richard Randolph was born and destroyed.

There is, however, another version. This one, told some years later by Nancy herself, contradicts both the accepted historical account and the version included in John Marshall's summation for the defense. A major participant in this account is John Randolph, the younger brother of Richard and Theodorick. He had been extremely fond of both his brothers, and had been hurt, first, by Theodorick's death in 1792 and, then, by Richard's in 1795, only two years after the trial in which he had been exonerated.

John Randolph had apparently loved Nancy himself, but it was a love that ultimately turned to hate. Not only did she not return his affections, but he would have been unable to claim her if she had. A youthful illness had left him impotent. John Randolph later became a prominent member of Congress and the chief agent in the House of Representatives for Thomas Jefferson when Jefferson was President. His hatred showed in his politics as it showed in his personal life. Dumas Malone, in his authoritative biography of Jefferson, wrote that "Randolph's excesses of arrogant belligerency may perhaps be explained, in terms of modern psychology, as over-compensation for his lack of virility." Belligerent is a modest word to describe his later attacks against Nancy.

Nancy was without an estate of her own and so was compelled to live with Richard Randolph's family after his death in 1795. She never was treated particularly well by them. In 1809, however, she met Gouverneur Morris, an elderly and single New York politician, who hired her as his housekeeper. Late that year, on December 2, he wrote to his old friend John Marshall, explaining that Nancy had joined his household "and has the care of my family."

> I hear that the World [he wrote], that is to say the Gossips, male and female of New York, circulate sundry reports respecting this unfortunate young Lady, founded on Events which happened while I was in Europe. I presume that no particular malevolence is directed at her, but if she can be depicted in black color, it may serve as a foundation for calumny against me. It will be argued that I would not treat with respect a person so undeserving, unless there existed between us an illicit connection. . . .

Morris insisted to John Marshall that he was not concerned about such calumnies because of his own reputation but because he feared that the situation would be used as an attack on the Federalist party, of which he was a prominent member. Then Morris asked if he might "lay a small tax on your goodness." Would Marshall tell him "frankly the reputation Miss Randolph left in Virginia, and the standing she held in society. . . ."

Although Morris did not spell it out, marriage to Nancy Randolph obviously was his intention, and Marshall replied that he was pleased that Morris had decided "to extend your protection to that unfortunate young lady." In his answer, written December 12, Marshall shows himself a true gentleman. Was any indiscretion ascribed to Nancy? "The suspicion has never reached my ears." He recalled that the infanticide charge "was very public and excited much attention." But, he continued, "Some circumstances adduced in support of it were ambiguous, and rumor, with her usual industry, spread a thousand others which were probably invented by the malignant, or magnified by those who love to supply any defects in the story they relate."

John Marshall recalled that Judith, the wife and sister, "who had the fairest means of judging of the transaction and who was most injured by the fact if true," not only provided Nancy with a home while Richard Randolph lived but for many years after his death.

Marshall conceded that opinion was divided back in 1792 and 1793. "Many believed the accusations brought against Miss Randolph to be true, while others attached no criminality to her conduct and believed her to be the victim of a concurrence of unfortunate circumstances." Marshall stressed that "Among the latter class of persons were those ladies with whom I am connected." Although Nancy had ceased to appear in public, Marshall concluded, she still was received in the homes of many families "who felt for her situation and were not disposed to condemn because the world had pronounced an unfavorable sentence."

Marshall's letter reached Morris on December 23. The next morning he made his proposal and the following day, Christmas, he and Nancy Randolph were married. John Marshall's letter defending her reputation had been the deciding factor. Morris made this clear in a letter to Marshall dated December 28. He explained that he had been impressed by Nancy's good sense, good temper, and cleanliness. He was skeptical about her housekeeping abilities, but he believed she was learning. He said he had no interest in beauty, "but, if I did, she has her share." Nor was he interested in marrying for money; he had enough and she had none. "The only point, therefore, worth a rush," he said, "was her reputation."

Gouverneur Morris and his wife Nancy had a child and were very happy. Nancy Randolph, now in her late thirties, seemed at last to have acquired the happiness that never before had been hers.

Then John Randolph struck.

For reasons never explained, but probably because Nancy was at last happy, he set out to destroy her marriage. In a lengthy letter to Gouverneur Morris, which he also distributed in Virginia, Randolph recalled the night so many years before at Glenlyvar and the trial in Cumberland. Then he charged the verdict was in error. He claimed Nancy had had a child that night, and that the child had been murdered. He went on, the venom in his sick body overcoming any sense of rationality he might have possessed. He charged that while Gouverneur Morris considered her an ideal wife she actually was being unfaithful to him, with a Negro. That last was the strongest charge that could be made about a Virginia woman from a well-established family.

It was an incredible letter. Nancy Randolph, now Mrs. Gouverneur Morris, determined that she must respond to it effectively, in such a way as to end all slanders on her reputation. In her answer, dated January 16, 1815, and addressed to John Randolph, she denied deceiving her husband. And then she proceeded to reveal what had really happened at the Randolph estate Bizarre and then at Glenlyvar in 1792, twenty-three years earlier. She made several copies of the letter and sent them to prominent Virginians, to be certain that her story was widely circulated.

A child had been born—dead—at Glenlyvar, she wrote, but Theodorick, not Richard, was the child's father. She had been engaged to marry Theodorick, she wrote in the letter addressed to John Randolph, but "Your property, as well as that of your brothers, was hampered by a British debt. My father, therefore, preferred for my husband a person of clear and considerable estate. The sentiment of my heart did not accord with his intentions. Under these circumstances, I was left at Bizarre, a girl, not seventeen, with the man she loved. I was betrothed to him and considered him as my husband in the presence of that God whose name you presume to invoke. . . . We should have been married, if Death had not snatched him away a few days after the scene which began the history of my sorrows."

Nancy said that Richard Randolph knew what had happened but had never told, even when he was the object of the community's opprobrium. "He," she declared, "was a man of honor."

One can choose which story to believe, but Nancy's account in her 1815 letter seems believable. It offers the most complete explanation of the events of that October night in 1792. It is most in keeping with the character of the Randolphs and their relationships with one another, and the respect with which people like Thomas Jefferson and Patrick Henry as well as John Marshall held them. Also, there simply is no proof to suggest it is not true. Finally, the strongest point in Nancy's favor was the attitude of her husband, Gouverneur Morris, toward her after John Randolph made his charges and her reply was well publicized. Morris by this time was an old man but not a fool. He had been a distinguished politician and diplomat. Apparently he was not stupid about women. When he was the American minister in Paris, he was famous for his romantic exploits. After this incident with John Randolph the relationship between Gouverneur Morris and Nancy became all the stronger. Their happiness together was not impaired. Apparently he believed what she had written and was sympathetic to her situation.

As for Marshall? When Nancy's letter was widely distributed, he had been Chief Justice of the United States for fourteen years and he apparently did not speak of her letter or of the case. But there was no reason for him to have done so. When he was involved in the case, his role had not been that of judge. Rather his role had been to force the state to prove his client guilty beyond a doubt or else to free that client. That is the proper role of a defense attorney, and Marshall had demonstrated himself a brilliant one. Without evidence to refute the charges against his client, he had successfully destroyed the case against Richard Randolph by using the prosecution's evidence. While he had no other case so lurid during his career, he may not have had any other case that required quite as adroit and persuasive an interpretation of the known facts. However one considers such an ability to persuade, Marshall possessed it to an extraordinary degree. Perhaps no other lawyer or judge could marshall facts into a common cause as well. Indeed, some people found this ability of his frightening. Thomas Jefferson is reported to have remarked once:

When conversing with Marshall, I never admit anything. So sure as you admit any position to be good, no matter how remote from the conclusion he seeks to establish, you are gone. So great is his sophistry, you must never give him an affirmative answer, or you will be forced to grant his conclusion. Why, if he were to ask me whether it was daylight or not, I'd reply, "Sir, I don't know. I can't tell."[1]

Another equally famous, if not as lurid, case involving Marshall during this period concerned the Reverend John Bracken and William and Mary College. Chartered in 1693, the college was a Virginia institution in the best sense of the term. Most prominent Virginians had been students there, or had children there, or anticipated sending children there. As a result, anything that happened at the Williamsburg campus was of interest and concern to the Virginians. In addition, there was the practical matter that the school was chartered by the state and the Board of Visitors, the school's governing body, was appointed by the General Assembly; the school was, in effect, a state agency.

The night of December 4, 1779, the governing board of the school voted to make certain changes in the structure of the college, one being the discontinuance of the grammar school. Reverend Bracken was the grammar master at the school, and the reorganization would put him out of a job. He sought a writ of mandamus directing the school to reinstate him.

When the case finally reached the state Court of Appeals in 1790, Marshall was the lawyer for the school and a young Virginian named John Taylor represented Bracken. Taylor and Marshall crossed paths for the next several decades, and the issue that separated them always was enunciated in the case of *Bracken v. William and Mary:* Marshall's belief that government can expand to fulfill its responsibilities versus the Jeffersonian concept of a restricted government.

To win his client a writ of mandamus Taylor had to demonstrate that firing Bracken was illegal. He argued that the governing board had only limited power, that it could do nothing except what was expressly allowed it by the original charter. The charter, he said, "is the constitution of the college, and like all other constitutions, ought to be preserved inviolate." The original charter, Taylor argued, had allowed for both a board and the masters. The position of master had been created not by the board but by the charter, and therefore the board could not abolish any position of master—"that which cannot create, cannot destroy," he said. There were other arguments involved—the board had dropped the directive to teach ancient languages and, instead, was teaching modern languages; no longer was the support of a religion a purpose of the school.

Marshall began in typical lawyer fashion, using every

weapon at his disposal. His first argument was that a writ of mandamus could not be issued against the school under any circumstances because William and Mary is "a mere eleemosynary institution." He then cited a dozen references bearing out his claim that a writ cannot be issued against a charitable institution. At this point the court stopped him and assured him that its members also knew their law. If William and Mary was an eleemosynary institution, the judges agreed, a writ could not be granted.

"This is an eleemosynary institution," Marshall insisted. Using a few citations for the source of his definition, he then argued that "It is founded on charity. That the donations proceeded from the King and from the government, is perfectly immaterial, as Visitors are appointed. Colleges are considered as mere Eleemosynary institutions, as entirely as hospitals."

Then he quickly shifted his arguments. If by any chance, he said, the court does believe it possesses jurisdiction, it should not exercise it because the governing board members "have not exceeded the powers given them in the charter." First he explained that the charter established the offices of president and of masters for divinity, philosophy, languages, and other good arts. But the charter did not specify, he continued, that a grammar master be part of the system. He said:

> The Visitors or Governors have power to make such laws for the government of the College, from time to time, according to their various occasion and circumstances, as to them should seem most fit and expedient. The restraining clause annexed, serves to show the extent of the grant: "Provided that the said laws, etc. be no way contrary to our prerogative royal, etc." Their power of legislation, then, extended to the modification of the schools, in any manner they should deem proper, provided they did not depart from the great outlines marked in the charter; which are divinity, philosophy, and the languages. It was proper, that this discretion should be given to the Visitors, because a particular branch of science, which at one period of time would be deemed all important, might at another, be thought not worth acquiring. In institutions, therefore, which are to be durable, only great and general principles, ought to be immutable.

Marshall concluded that if the board had acted properly in eliminating the grammar school, as he had maintained, "it is not for this Court to enquire, whether they have legislated wisely, or not, and if the change should even be considered as not being for the better, still it is a change; still the grammar school is lawfully put down."

Marshall had made two points in his arguments that would become a part of the judicial fabric he later wove into American constitutional law. The first was his argument that the Visitors had the power to make such laws as they considered necessary as long as they did not step outside "the great outlines" marked in their charter. In arguing that "only great and general principles ought to be immutable" he was saying that a constitution or a charter is a document to be used, to be permitted to grow, to expand when necessary "in institutions . . . which are to be durable." The system of law used by people, he said, must not prevent them from meeting their obligations, from meeting new problems with new solutions. In the field of education, as Marshall pointed out, a branch of science considered important at one time would, at another, "be thought not worth acquiring." And so it would be with all fields. The great challenge, he was saying then as he would reiterate in the *McCulloch v. Maryland* decision twenty-nine years later, is not to freeze an institution through a limited interpretation of its basic document into the mold of its yesterdays. Rather, the great challenge was to allow a people to grow without diminishing the principles they hold important. With William and Mary, in that 1790 case, those principles were the teaching of divinity, philosophy, and language. With the United States, the great principles were the political freedoms that men had fought for in the American Revolution after enunciating them in the Declaration of Independence, and the system of governance incorporated into the Constitution. Marshall's attitude toward the United States Constitution was identical to his attitude toward the charter governing William and Mary: it was a set of rules by which an organization could govern itself within certain confines; it was not a set of rules preventing that organization from governing itself.

The second point Marshall made in that argument was in articulating a philosophy of judicial restraint that is a model for all jurists. Once the court determined that the board had the power to dissolve the grammar school, the court itself was without authority to ask whether the decision was a wise one or not. Even if the court was convinced that the change was an improper one, still it must not challenge the act so long as the act was legal. That is judicial restraint. In the thirty-four years that Marshall served on the Supreme Court, he presided over, and largely caused, an expansion of judicial power, perhaps the greatest expansion of power ever achieved without military arms. But this expansion was of *judicial* power. It was not the extension of judicial authority into other areas. He understood the role of a federal judge and he never shrank from that understanding. But he did not abuse it.

The court decided unanimously in favor of Marshall's client. And just as Marshall began here a career of insisting that the nation accept the doctrine of an expanding constitution, his opponent in that case, John Taylor, began a career of arguing for a restricted document. One of the judges of that five-man court was Spencer Roane, who in later years would renounce the principle of an expanding constitution he had supported in this decision, to become with Taylor and Thomas Jefferson one of John Marshall's most severe critics and serious opponents.[2]

If the case of *Bracken v. William and Mary* was the more significant because of its indicators for the future, another case involving Marshall was considerably more important for the "here and now" of the Virginians. This one involved their pocketbooks and is known as *Ware v. Hylton.* It is the only case in which Marshall argued as a lawyer before the United States Supreme Court. He lost.

The debts the Americans owed the British were one cause of the Revolution; the Americans realized that as long as the British continued the mercantile system they could never be free, for the British controlled their incomes, their credit, and their futures. In fighting to disentangle themselves from this system in the future, the Americans were avoiding the disturbing question of how to deal with the debts incurred prior to the Revolution. During the Revolution this problem, understandably, was not given sympathetic consideration by the Americans. In January 1778, for example, the Virginia legislature enacted a law virtually giving the colony control over the estates of those Virginians who had sided with England. Another provision allowed the Americans to pay off their debts to the British by paying Virginia paper money into a state fund which, theoretically at least, would be used to satisfy British creditors at the war's end. The law was pure hokum. The Americans had borrowed money from the British when the money had value and, under the law, were paying it back with Virginia currency which had depreciated to the point where it had almost no value. But the Americans had been the victims before the war of a system which benefited the English, so it was difficult to draw definitive lines between villains and heroes.

The law had originally been proposed by the Virginia governor, then Thomas Jefferson. He did not consider it unjust. Virginians were required to accept their colony's paper currency as payment of debts, and he could see no reason why the British should not be expected to do the same. In later years, however, he may have had second thoughts. He paid off his own British creditors in full value rather than with the depreciated Virginia money that the law he had sponsored made legitimate.[3]

When the war ended, the Treaty of 1783 called for the payment of the debt to the British in full. The effect of the treaty was to overturn the Virginia law. But enforcement of that treaty provision could not take place under the Articles of Confederation because the states at that time chose which laws of the central government they would or would not obey. With the ratification of the Constitution and the promise of a strong central government, the possibility of collecting the debts turned into a probability for the English. A British creditor went into the Virginia courts seeking payment of a debt contracted by a Virginian prior to the American Revolution. He was represented by a number of distinguished Richmond lawyers, led by John Wickham. The Virginian countered that he had paid the amount into the state loan office, as allowed under the law of 1778 which Jefferson had sponsored, and therefore was freed of his obligation to his creditor, freed sufficiently to prevent his being forced by a court to pay a second time. The Virginian was also represented by a distinguished group of Virginia lawyers, led by John Marshall.

The case involved a debt of 2,976 pounds, 11 shillings, and 6 pence incurred on July 7, 1774, by Daniel Hylton and Company and Francis Eppes of Virginia. They owed the money to the English merchants Farrel and Jones.[4] The case became known as the *Great British Debt Case* because on its outcome hinged the question of whether all Virginians must pay the debts claimed by the British merchants. The debts were enormous. The British claimed that 3 million pounds sterling were owed to the merchants. But this included almost two decades' worth of interest. When the interest claims were deducted, the debt, for Virginia at least, was down to 275,000 pounds, about one-half the total owed by all the states. This was a tremendous sum and represented the amount paid by the Virginians into the government of the colony after passage of Jefferson's law in 1778. If Marshall won, then payment into the state office made during the war would be considered sufficient. If Marshall lost, then the Virginians would be liable in the American courts to produce 275,000 pounds. The adjective "Great" was well suited.

There were other complications. The British had agreed in the Treaty of 1783 to vacate the western outposts once the debts owed by the Americans were paid. As they considered the debts outstanding, however, the British remained in the outposts. The action was understandable; staying in the western forts, and thus blocking development of the western fur trade by the American explorers, was the only power the British retained. They had a friend in court, however. This was John Jay, who was both Chief Justice of the United States and the American minister to the Court of St. James's in the 1790s. Jay understood the plight of the British merchants and some British officials believed he supported their position in holding on to the western outposts and would be sympathetic when the issue was argued in the federal courts in Virginia, where he would be sitting as one of the presiding justices. But in 1793 when the case was argued, Chief Justice Jay was ill and was unable to ride circuit (as the Supreme Court Justices then did). The case would be argued without his being on the bench.[5]

James Iredell, an Associate Justice who heard the case in Richmond in 1793, was impressed with the arguments. "The discussion was one of the most brilliant exhibitions ever witnessed at the Bar of Virginia," according to contemporary accounts. The counselor who attracted the most attention and the one upon whom the brunt of the argument fell in the Circuit Court was Patrick Henry, who had once again allied himself with John Marshall. Henry spoke for three days in defense of the Virginians. Judge Iredell was a North Carolinian and had heard that Patrick Henry was a demagogue, so he came expecting to dislike Henry. But "I never was more agreeably disappointed than in my acquaintance with him," said the judge. "I have been much in his company, and his manners are very pleasing, and his mind, I am persuaded, highly liberal." Iredell regretted that "violent party prejudice" had built up a false image of Henry. The judge made these comments in a letter to his wife. In addition to what they say of Henry they are also significant for what they say of the relationship in that era between a judge and a lawyer arguing a case before him. "I have been much in his company," said Iredell of Henry. Ten years later Chief Justice John Marshall would be in the company of a lawyer arguing a case before him, and the result would be one of the few damaging incidents in his career.

Iredell was so impressed with the oratorical skill displayed not only by Henry but also by Marshall and the lawyers for the British creditors that, in announcing his decision, he could not avoid complimenting the lawyers. "The cause has been spoken to," he said, "at the bar with a degree of ability equal to any occasion. However painfully I may reflect at any time on the inadequacy of my own talents, I shall as long as I live, remember with pleasure and respect the arguments which I have heard in this case. They have discovered an ingenuity, a depth of investigation, and a power of reasoning fully equal to any thing I have ever witnessed, and some of them have been adorned with a splendor of eloquence surpassing what I have ever felt before. Fatigue has given way under its influence, and the heart has been warmed, while understanding has been instructed."[6] Then Iredell decided for the Virginians. They would not have to pay the British the 275,000 pounds.

Marshall's role was considerable. "I have just returned from Richmond where I have been listening to a very lengthy and able argument on the subject of the British debts," reported one observer. "The bar all acquitted themselves well, but most of all our friend Marshall, it was acknowledged on all hands, excelled himself in *sound sense* and *argument*, which you know is saying an immensity. . . ."[7]

A case of this importance, however, had to go to the Supreme Court of the United States, then meeting in Philadelphia. Arguments were first scheduled for the 1795 term, but then were delayed a year. At least it was on Monday, February 2, 1795, that John Marshall appeared before that Court, raised his right hand, and said:

> I John Marshall do solemnly swear that I will demean myself as an Attorney and counsellor of this court, uprightly, and according to law, and that I will support the Constitution of the United States.[8]

Dozens of lawyers had taken that oath before him. Thousands would after him. As many times as it is repeated, it never ceases to produce a touch of awe. For the nation it means that a group of men has assumed the mantle of justice and vowed to struggle for its perpetuation and the perpetuation of the United States with the talents of their intellects. These men are the modern soldiers who have relegated the weapons of the battlefield to the past and adopted the nonviolent tools of their minds and their hearts as the devices of the present and as the hope of the future. For the men themselves it means that in the area they have chosen to test their competence, that of the law, they are now entering the highest arena and facing their greatest professional challenge. There they may know a victory greater than that available to those who will not test their abilities to the fullest.

John Marshall unquestionably was excited to be arguing before the Supreme Court. His reputation as a Federalist, a supporter of President Washington, had preceded him to Philadelphia and a number of people there were ready to be his friends. "I thus became acquainted with Mr. Cabot, Mr. Ames, Mr. Dexter, and Mr. Sedgwick of Massachusetts, Mr. Wadsworth of Connecticut, and Mr. King of New York," said Marshall, reeling off a list of names which, unknown to him then, would become a roster of the leading Federalist politicians in the United States within a few years. "I was particularly delighted with these gentlemen," he remarked. "The particular subject [the British treaty] which introduced me to their notice, was at that time so interesting, and a Virginian, who supported with any sort of reputation, the measures of the government, was such a *rara avis*, that I was received by them all with such a degree of kindness which I had not anticipated."[9]

Most likely the Federalists in Philadelphia were catering to Marshall's vanity somewhat. He was a follower of President Washington at a time when many Virginians were beginning to identify themselves as Jeffersonian Republicans, so it is not surprising that when Marshall came to Philadelphia the Federalists courted him. Undoubtedly they believed he deserved their attentions, but also undoubtedly they felt he might be useful to them in Virginia at a later time.

A young lawyer named William Wirt, later an Attorney General of the United States and always an admirer of John Marshall, was in Philadelphia that February of 1796 when the British debt case was finally argued, and wrote of it many years later. "Marshall spoke, as he always does, to the judgment merely, and for the simple purpose of convincing," said Wirt of Marshall's presentation before the Supreme Court. He continued: "Marshall was justly pronounced one of the greatest men of the country; he was followed by crowds, looked upon, and courted with every evidence of admiration and respect for the great powers of his mind. . . . Marshall's maxim seems always to have been, 'aim exclusively at strength.' "[10]

The case on which so many Virginians' fortunes hung opened before the Court at ten o'clock the morning of Saturday, February 6, 1796. It was argued before a five-man Court, presided over by Associate Justice William Cushing (the position of Chief Justice then was vacant). The arguments continued for one week, ending Friday, February 12. For John Marshall the case was personally a difficult one. He was arguing the cause of the debtors against the laws of the federal government. He had been an advocate of the supremacy of the federal government, he believed in a strong central government, and yet he was expected to represent those who would challenge the federal government. Either the federal treaties and laws demanding that the debts be paid or the state law enacted during the Revolution was supreme. One or the other; they both could not be. In this case, however, Marshall took the position that both were supreme. What little remnants of his argument are available indicate his position was that there was no conflict between the federal and state authorities here. Acknowledging that federal law was supreme over state law, he then insisted that the Virginia law was supreme in this specific instance because at the time it was enacted, there was no federal law with which it could have been in conflict. The Treaty of 1783 and the federal Constitution making that treaty binding upon the states had come after the passage of the state law. While they would supersede any local law passed after they had become fact, they did not supersede local law existing before they came into being.[11]

"It has been conceded," he told the Court, "that independent nations have, in general, the right of confiscation, and that Virginia, at the time of passing her law in 1778, was an independent nation." The opposing argument was that the citizens of each colony "having been members of the same government, the general rights of confiscation did not apply, and ought not to be exercised." Marshall insisted that his clients did not have to refute that argument because "it is incumbent on those, who wish to impair the sovereignty of Virginia" to justify it. He asserted that if England had won, she would have confiscated the property of Virginians, and then asked: "Why should the confiscation of British property be deemed less just in the event of the American triumph?"

The report of his argument runs slightly more than four pages and harps on the point that Virginia had independent status in 1778 and her legislative acts were not affected by the treaty with England. It is an interesting argument, demonstrating Marshall's adroitness as a lawyer searching out a device that satisfies the law as he understands it while still presenting a case for his clients. There is a second intriguing side to it. If the Supreme Court was of a mind to assist the Virginians and the other colonists who owed debts to the British, John Marshall was giving them an out. He provided a device the Justices could use to retain federal sovereignty while upholding the Virginia law.

But the Supreme Court chose to meet the issue directly. Justice Samuel Chase answered Marshall's argument: "[B]y the modern law and practice of European nations, Virginia was not justified in confiscating debts from her citizens to subjects of Great Britain; that is, private debts. . . ." He seemed sympathetic to the Virginians' plight, but insisted that "A treaty cannot be the supreme law of the land, that is of all the United States, if any act of a state legislature can stand in its way. . . ." Justice

William Cushing said the Virginia act was alleged to work "a discharge and a bar, to the payer. If such payment [to the state of Virginia during the Revolution with the greatly depreciated paper money] is to be considered as a discharge, or a bar, so long as the act had force, the question occurs—was there a power, by the treaty, supposing it contained proper words, entirely to remove this law, and this bar, out of the creditor's way?" Did the treaty and the Constitution, Cushing was asking, knock down the state law? "This power seems not to have been contended against by the defendant's counsel," he said, answering his own question, "and indeed, it cannot be denied; the treaty having been sanctioned, in all its parts, by the constitution of the United States, as the supreme law of the land."[12]

There were other reasons why it was proper that John Marshall's only case before the Supreme Court ended in defeat for him. The Virginia act had the effect of negating the debts owed by the Americans to the British, and it would have been poor law to declare that one governmental unit could wipe out or greatly reduce the debts its citizens owed to the citizens of another governmental unit. Such a precedent would mean that no trade or other kinds of commerce could be carried on across political boundaries. A second reason why the United States was better off as a result of Marshall's defeat had to do with its standing in the councils of nations. The United States under its Constitution was less than a decade old in 1796 and still had to prove itself, demonstrate its respectability. If it renounced its debts before it had an opportunity to incur new ones, it would never have had such an opportunity. (Even this decision did not settle the debt question; it only settled that the debts must be paid. The settlement came several years later under the leadership of Secretary of State John Marshall, who masterminded a new treaty with England that included a commission to resolve the debt question finally.)

This case was not Marshall's only defeat as a lawyer, but the most significant one for the nation. It also, along with the Randolph scandal and the *William and Mary* case, was one of the spectacular cases he handled in the 1790s. Most of the others he handled were routine, involving collecting of debts and settlement of land disputes. Financially he did well. In 1784, his account book indicates, he was involved in about a hundred cases, most of them paying just several pounds; one, involving a will, paid him 10 pounds, a grandiose sum. His income from his law practice that year, as recorded in the account book, amounted to 498 pounds. By the next year this amount had almost doubled, to 848 pounds. Two years later, in 1787, Marshall's income from his law practice reached 1,000 pounds for the first time. By then also he was doing a substantial amount of his work in the Court of Appeals. Marshall in the late 1780s and 1790s became distinguished as an appeals court lawyer, who often was hired for a case only when it moved that high.

Sometimes, though, there were severe money problems. Marshall did some work for John Breckinridge: "The certiorari is obtained. . . . Mention to Mr. Harris the necessity of sending some money." Sometimes the payments were quixotic. "If I failed I was to receive nothing," said Marshall of one case. "If I succeeded I was to have a Negro or fifty pounds." In another instance: "I would take a stout able young plough horse for my claim."[13]

His correspondence of the time is most revealing about his law practice. To one client, who had been informed that an action was coming before a land commissioner while Marshall had not been informed, Marshall said angrily: "You had notice when the report was made up and ought to have attended to the business." Major Cadwallader Jones was badgered about a note he had signed promising a large amount of tobacco payable to a Mr. Gratz, and, said Marshall, "which is returned unpaid [and] had been in my hands upwards of twelve months and Mr. Gratz is now anxious about payment." Marshall added: "I wrote to you on the subject but had not the pleasure of receiving your answer." In another case Marshall sought the advice of Bushrod Washington, his old friend from their law studies together at William and Mary and now also a Richmond lawyer, who agreed with Marshall that an agreement was "very carelessly and incautiously drawn." To another client Marshall offered assurances that "Your appeal shall be particularly attended to. Perhaps it may come this spring." For another client Marshall was selling half-pay certificates and land warrants: "I have sold them to Mr. John Hopkins, the certificate for 4/6 in the pound, the interest warrant issued in 88 at 17/ in the pound and that issued in 89 for 15/ in the pound. I had hoped to have sold the warrants on better terms but I could not."[14]

Young men entered his office to study, before going on to practice law themselves. One such was Robert Barraud Taylor, who before coming to Marshall's office in the early 1790s had been wounded in a duel with John Randolph, and after leaving Marshall went to Norfolk where he became a prominent lawyer. And Marshall had contact with the important men of the state. He had been associated with Patrick Henry in both the Randolph scandal case and in the *British Debt Case* and also in other cases. Other prominent Virginians came to him for advice. In answer to a question from the rising young lawyer Albert Gallatin, Marshall wrote a long letter explaining the development of separate courts of common law and chancery. ". . . There was an apparent absurdity in seeing the same men revise in the characters of chancellors the judgments they had themselves rendered as common law judges," Marshall wrote.[15]

Marshall was associated at times with another young lawyer named William Branch Giles. "I think, tho I am not perfectly master of the subject," wrote Marshall to Giles, "that this case is in our favor—at any rate we have a good chance for it. . . ." And another time: "Write our client Jones," Marshall directed Giles, "that he must come immediately to execute an appeal bond." And finally when Giles went to Congress, Marshall wrote an introductory letter for him to James Madison. "I should not presume so far on the degree of your acquaintance with which I have been honored as to introduce gentlemen to your attention if I did not persuade myself that you will never regret or change any favorable opinion you may form of him," Marshall wrote in that letter.[16] Helped by friends such as Marshall, Giles went on to become a prominent politician and ultimately governor of Virginia. In later years he sided with Madison and the other Jeffersonians in the struggle over the independence of the judiciary, and Giles' implacable foe on this issue for almost three decades was John Marshall.

Marshall also was the lawyer in Richmond for Robert Morris, the Philadelphia financier who had raised much of the money with which the colonies financed their Revolution and who was quickly becoming one of America's great land speculators. And true to that type, Morris was having trouble raising ready cash. "I have postponed acknowledging the receipt of your letter of the 23d November week after week," Morris wrote apologetically to Marshall, "in the expectation of getting so far ahead of my pecuniary necessities as to enable me to remit the remaining $1,500 of the sum directed by your brother to be so remitted." But Morris never seemed to get ahead of his "pecuniary necessities." "Nothing in this city," he explained to Marshall, "ever equalled the scenes of general distress occasioned by the demand for and want of money."[17] Marshall, however, was not prone to press Morris. His brother, James Markham Marshall, had married Morris' daughter, and by the mid-1790s Marshall himself was a business partner of Morris.

In 1796, when Marshall had been practicing law in Richmond for a decade and a half, he had a reputation for being one of "the most eminent lawyers of our state."[18] A distinguished French observer, François La Rochefoucauld-Liancourt, toured the United States, spending considerable time in Richmond where he found Marshall "the most esteemed and the most renowned of all [the lawyers] in that city. . . . [Marshall] is without doubt one of the men of Richmond whom public opinion most honors." La Rochefoucauld-Liancourt continued:

> He is what is called a federalist, perhaps sometimes a little fervent, but never beyond the limit a spirit as good, as wise, as enlightened as his can go beyond; he is considered as a distinguished personage in the United States. The enemies of his opinions accord him great talents, but they accuse him of ambition. I do not know if that is well founded, if his ambition will push him beyond the limits of his principles, but I am disposed not to think so. He has refused several places in the general government, instead he prefers the revenue, as well as the moderate manner of living which his work produces, and in addition to a tranquil life, in the middle of his family, in his own city.

The Frenchman noted how Marshall and the other Richmond men he had met had a variety of opinions, but, said La Rochefoucauld-Liancourt of these men, "There exists between them a society with a tone of gentlemanliness and distinction which is hidden from strangers who do not perceive it unless they are informed in advance."

Marshall had a reputation, even among his friends, La Rochefoucauld-Liancourt reported, "of being a little lazy, and there may be some basis for that, but that does not prevent him from being a most superior person when he sets down to his work." By this time Marshall was earning approximately $4,000 to $5,000 a year—a respectable sum then—from his law practice. After citing that figure, La Rochefoucauld-Liancourt reported that a mainstay of American legal practice may have had its beginnings in the experience of Marshall and his contemporaries. "The lawyers in general in Virginia," he wrote, "take care to be paid for their work in advance."[19]

As La Rochefoucauld-Liancourt had reported, Marshall consistently turned down public positions after the adoption of the Constitution. As Marshall himself explained it: "I felt that those great principles of public policy which I considered as essential to the general happiness were secured by this measure and I willingly relinquished public life to devote myself to my profession." Another factor he acknowledged was the party strife already developing in Virginia. "Indeed the county was so thoroughly antifederal, and the parties had become so exasperated," he said, "that my election [to the Virginia legislature] would have been doubtful." He insisted, however, that his primary reason for not seeking another term in the legislature was that his law practice had broadened and he could not spare time from it.

He also had been asked in 1789 to become a candidate for the first federal Congress and here his chances would have been much better. "Though the district was unequivocally antifederal I could have been elected because the party was almost equally divided between two candidates who were equally obstinate and much embittered against each other." Faced with the choice of being in the First Congress and involved in the organization of the new government in 1789 or of staying in Richmond to work at his law practice, Marshall chose the "victory of prudence." The Federalist candidate, Samuel Griffin, won with a plurality of "rather more than one-third of the votes in the district."[20]

Marshall's reluctance to jeopardize his career is understandable in the context of his background. He probably never forgot the experience of returning on leave from the Revolution to find his family destitute. He felt strongly his financial responsibility to his children—there were three living children by 1790 —and he would not be the first father to emerge from poverty and give his own children too much. He also understood that public life required sacrifice. He was familiar with the experiences of George Washington, whose estates had deteriorated while he was away. A few years later, writing of the resignation of Alexander Hamilton as Secretary of Treasury in George Washington's cabinet, Marshall made a comment that has held true in American government ever since. "The penurious provision," he wrote, "made for those who filled the high executive departments in the American government, excluded from a long continuance in office all those whose fortunes were moderate, and whose professional talents placed a decent independence within their reach."[21]

However, Marshall's abilities and his reputation were such that his reluctance to involve himself in public life had to be constantly restated. When Samuel Griffin arrived in New York where the Congress was meeting, he suggested to President George Washington that Marshall be appointed United States Attorney for the Virginia District. Griffin may have been moved as much by Marshall's ability as by his desire to repay Marshall for having stepped aside so Griffin could be elected. Also Griffin believed Marshall wanted the post. Washington was receptive to the idea; he knew John Marshall personally as a Federalist politician, a good lawyer, and a friend. The appointment was made, confirmed by the Senate, and announced formally September 26, 1789.[22] Because of the delays in communications, Washington had not personally checked the nomination with Marshall. He was somewhat chagrined to receive a rejection: "I thank you, sir, very sincerely for the honor which I feel is done me by an appointment flowing from your choice, and I beg leave to declare that it is with real regret I decline accepting an office which has to me been render'd highly valuable by the hand which bestow'd it." Marshall then explained that he could not practice as a private lawyer before the Virginia superior courts and as United States Attorney before the federal courts, because they met at the same time but in different cities and "attendance on the one becomes incompatible with the duties of an attorney in the other." Some thirty-five years later, writing about that offer, Marshall gave the same reason, and then added: "Before the inconvenience was removed, the office was conferred on another gentleman."[23]

Washington, however, did not forget his young friend in Richmond. As the years went by, Marshall's fame as a lawyer and his loyalty to the Federalist cause at a time when many Virginians were rallying to the anti-Federalist banner of Thomas Jefferson were well reported in the seat of national government, which had moved to Philadelphia. In 1795 Washington asked him to become Attorney General of the United States. The position was not considered as important a post as the other cabinet offices. The secretaries of War, Navy, State, and Treasury each led a department, of varying sizes, and each had his own constituency. The Attorney General, in contrast, was considered then as the President's lawyer and had no department. By this time Washington was well aware of Marshall's financial considerations and advised him that not only would there be a salary of $1,500 a year but also the position carried with it "the prospect of a lucrative practice in this city." Uncertain of Marshall's reaction, Washington asked that, if Marshall refused it, "it might be as well to say nothing of this offer." Marshall did turn down the offer—"the business I have undertaken to complete in Richmond forbids me to change my situation tho for one infinitely more eligible." He also assured Washington that he would not speak of it publicly—"I respect too highly the offices of the present government of the United States to permit it to be suspected that I have declined one of them."[24]

Washington continued to think well of Marshall, relying on his advice in the search for an Attorney General. After Marshall turned down the position, Washington wanted to offer it to Patrick Henry if Henry no longer opposed the Constitution and if

"his opinion of the government was friendly." Washington asked
Edward Carrington to make the offer to Henry after first discussing it with Marshall, of whose "honor, prudence and judgment" Washington said he had "a high opinion." Carrington did
not believe the offer should go to Henry but bowed to Marshall's
opinion, and the offer was tendered. Henry, now old and sick,
turned it down. The position finally went to Charles Lee. In other
appointments also Washington relied on Marshall's and Carrington's advice, an indication of how Marshall's reputation was
gradually spreading among the leaders of the Federalist party.[25]

The next year Washington again turned to Marshall. The
American minister to France, James Monroe, had been recalled,
and the situation between the two countries was rapidly deterio-
rating. Washington explained to Marshall that it was "indispensably necessary . . . to send [a new minister] who will explain
faithfully the views of this government and ascertain those of
France." To Washington, "nothing would be more pleasing" than
Marshall's taking over the post. But knowing Marshall's position,
Washington sent him two letters. The first offered Marshall the
post. If Marshall turned it down, he was to pass the second letter
on to Charles Cotesworth Pinckney of South Carolina, who was
Washington's second choice for the post. Marshall refused the
ministerial position because of "the present crisis of my affairs."
When Pinckney received the second letter, offering him the post,
he accepted. Marshall then wrote to Washington expressing his
gratification "as a citizen of the United States that a gentleman
of General Pinckney's character will represent our government at
the court of France."[26]

Washington accepted Marshall's refusal with a resigned
shrug. "It is difficult to fill some offices with characters which
would fit them in respects," he conceded to Marshall. As a case
in point, Washington then spoke of the position of Surveyor
General. One man had turned it down. Others had been recommended but more for their general characters than for their
abilities as surveyors. There were several persons in Virginia
who were considered, and Washington favored one of them
because he knew the Kentucky region where much of the work
would be done. "But how he is in other respects," Washington
said, "and what may be the course of his politicks, I know
nothing; and but *little* of the other three." The emphasis in
Washington's letter to Marshall showed that the President was
giving added weight to party regularity. He then asked Marshall
to examine the records of the candidates and to supply the
results "confidentially" to him.[27] Marshall, obviously, by this time
was a leading Federalist in Virginia.

On one other occasion George Washington would ask John Marshall to accept public office, and on that occasion Washington would not accept a negative answer.

Although Marshall was adamant about not accepting federal service, he easily was persuaded to seek reelection to the state legislature. He had no trouble being elected when the city of Richmond became entitled to its own delegate; the city itself was Federalist, and he was well liked. "I yielded to the general wish partly because a man changes his inclination after retiring from public life, partly because I found the hostility to the government so strong in the legislature as to require from its friends all the support they could give it, and partly because the capitol was then completed [in Richmond], and the courts and the legislature sat in the same building, so that I could without much inconvenience leave the bar to take part in any debate in which I felt a particular interest."[28]

But the state legislature was not an exciting enough arena for John Marshall. "We have as yet done nothing finally," he lamented in a letter to James Monroe, who still was his friend although Monroe had opposed Virginia's ratification of the Constitution. "Not a bill of public importance in which an individual was not particularly interested has passed." The most consequential bill voted, Marshall reported, was one giving exclusive rights to build and navigate a boat.[29]

He was on a number of committees having to do with the law, the most important being one for the revision of the laws of Virginia. The eight-man committee was to examine English statutes to determine which should be incorporated into Virginia's laws, to study the Virginia laws to determine if they could be simplified—"ought from their multiplicity to be reduced into single acts," which should be dropped, to index the state laws, and "to instruct the clerk of the House of Delegates as far as it may be in their power, how to obtain for the use of his office, copies of those laws, the rolls whereof are lost."[30] He was on the committee which drew up the bill ceding land in northern Virginia for a national capital city and undoubtedly voted for the bill (no record vote was reported). That same day, November 28, 1789, Marshall's father-in-law, Jacquelin Ambler, was elected treasurer of the state.[31] "After the session of 1791," Marshall said, "I again withdrew from the assembly, determined to bid a final adieu to political life."[32] He was then thirty-six years old.

Although not in public office, Marshall could not escape the obligations of his ability and his prominence. He was frequently called upon to serve in semi-public roles. Along with other prominent lawyers in Richmond, he was appointed to committees to examine the mental capacities of persons charged with crimes. So Marshall and two others reported to Governor Edmund Randolph of James Goss that "tho the unhappy object is ignorant and stupid to a great degree, yet we are perfectly convinced he does not come under the terms of Idiotum or insanity, but is a competent Judge of Right from Wrong." And of Catherine Crull, that she appeared to be "almost in a state of entire ideotcy. Her mind seems so much disordered that we think her totally incapable of distinguishing right from wrong, or even of knowing what is said to her."[33]

By 1795 John Marshall was acting as attorney general for the state in the absence of the regular attorney general. Some of the advisory opinions he offered in that capacity are interesting for the glimpses they give into the formation of his judicial mind. In one case a tax-collecting agent had acquired a tract of land in lieu of back taxes. The agent then sold the land for a substantial profit, "and it is inquired," Marshall wrote, "whether the surplus is a gain to the Commonwealth, or ought to be credited to the sheriff." The law was not explicit, and there were points substantiating either interpretation. Marshall then was faced with a situation he frequently would confront as Chief Justice of a nation with a developing law: he had to render a decision that was convincing as law but for which he could find no definitive statute and no guiding precedents. He began by pointing out that the "object of the Commonwealth is not to speculate, but to secure the collection of debts due to itself." The agent's acquisition of the land was a medium of collection, and he then had the right to sell the land either for money, land certificates, or whatever else was negotiable in Virginia then. Marshall said this indicated that the agent was to be directed to sell the land in a manner "most advantageous for the Commonwealth" and "the produce of the sale was not to be credited to the sheriff." Marshall's own father had been a sheriff, and Marshall understood that these men made their living by receiving a percentage of the taxes they and their agents collected. It could be a precarious financial position, particularly, as Marshall pointed out, "if the Sheriff should be credited with the profits of the sale, he ought to be debited with the loss." Marshall concluded that the agent should credit the profit of the sale to the Commonwealth. If the sheriff challenged that ruling and won his case in court, "the Commonwealth will be assured on losing the profit of this sale, that she is secure against loss on a future occasion when the property may sell for less than the sum given by the agent." In other words, if the sheriff insisted on the profit rather than merely the normal percentage, he must understand that in the future he also would be obligated for any loss. The decision was a commonsense one, enforceable, practical, and just.

In another case the question was whether persons who failed to fulfill their militia obligations were liable to the fine imposed by the federal Congress and also to a fine imposed by the state. "I rather incline to the opinion that only the fine imposed by the Act of Congress ought to be collected," said Marshall. "The words of our Act of Assembly are general, and I have no doubt of the power of the legislature to give additional penalties for the breach of any law of the Union, but I rather suppose the act of the Virginia Assembly would be construed to apply to cases to which the Congressional Act could not comply." The line is a neat differentiation between the federal and the state powers.

In still another case a man named White was commissioned as sheriff on August 13, 1794, and was to begin his duties on November 6, provided he posted the required bond within two months. But White did not post the bond until after the two-month period had passed. The question presented to Marshall was whether the court should have received the bond late or the governor should have appointed someone else. Marshall found that the law "seems to leave no discretion with the Executive to judge of those circumstances which shall dispense with a compliance with the law." The law "positively requires" the posting of a bond within a certain time or "directs a new commission to issue." Over and over again in later years Marshall would return to this theme that the law is what its words say it to be, and all men must obey the law—all laws, not only some of them.[34]

In 1795 he and his old law teacher George Wythe, along with John Brown, Bushrod Washington, and John Wickham— five of the leading lawyers in Richmond—were directed by the state legislature to collect all the property laws of Virginia. This was the most ambitious project yet, covering "all the laws and clauses of laws, whether public or private, relating to lands, tenements, or hereditaments, within this Commonwealth, at any time passed since the first settlement of Virginia." The collection, which resulted in the publication of Hening's *Statutes*, a collation of laws, was needed because of the growing confusion over land holdings. This kind of experience strengthened Marshall's grasp of precedents.[35]

Virginia was having border difficulties with Maryland and Kentucky, and Marshall was involved in settling them both. In the Kentucky matter, commissioners had been appointed to work out an adjustment and Marshall served on a committee to review their work. Although he approved the commission's plan, appar-

.ently their recommendations were not satisfactory to Virginia because there was talk of appointing new commissioners. Marshall and three other members of the review committee wrote a sharp note to Governor James Wood on December 12, 1796, expressing "our strong approbation of the measures pursued by those Commissioners, and our opinions that it is an object of great importance to procure their aid in the prosecution of their business." They argued that any new commissioners appointed could not be as qualified for the job as those already appointed. Marshall also was named along with Thomas Jefferson, Edmund Randolph, Robert Brooke, and Ludwell Lee to a committee to examine all documents relating to the boundary line with Maryland and to meet with the corresponding commissioners from that state.[36]

There were other signs of the prominence which John Marshall had achieved in Richmond. When the Bank of Richmond was established in 1792, he was one of the men supervising the opening of subscriptions for stock. And then, he never could escape local politics. In the spring of 1795 elections were being held in Richmond for the state legislature. Marshall, true to his announced intention of not returning to public life, had not sought election. The day of the voting he appeared at the polls to vote for one of the two candidates, who also happened to be a close friend. Voting then was a simple procedure. There was a long table located at a central place within the community, usually the town square. Each candidate had his men sitting at the table, and the voters approached the representative of their choice to announce their vote. There was no secret ballot. When Marshall appeared that morning to vote for his friend, someone in the crowd suggested that Marshall himself be a candidate. It was much more than a casual remark. Since Marshall had chosen in 1791 not to seek reelection, the Federalists in Richmond had divided among themselves. His candidacy would unite them. Marshall politely refused, saying he was supporting his friend. He cast his vote and then walked over to the courthouse. After he had left, some of his friends decided a Marshall candidacy was a good idea and they established a Marshall representative at the polling table. By evening John Marshall, the non-candidate, was the elected delegate of the people of Richmond to the state Assembly.[37]

An activity in Richmond which occupied much of Marshall's time during the 1790s was the generalship of the Virginia militia. He now was finishing his fourth decade of life and beginning his fifth; he was an experienced soldier, and was well liked by his fellow Virginians, despite any political differences. This meant that he was a proper choice for a military leader; men would follow him. That was important because being general of the Virginia militia in the 1790s was more than an honorary position. It was a job requiring a great deal of time, organizational ability, and, at times, the willingness to face danger.

The duties were varied. He was sent out to the sloop *Phoenix* lying off Manchester to determine if she should be quarantined. Marshall investigated, returning with a report on a medical examination of two persons on board the ship. He added: "Altho every person on board seems healthy she still appears to come under the description of those vessels which ought to perform quarantine. . . ." Marshall also had closely questioned the ship's captain who "appeared very uneasy" and did some other sleuthing, all of which led him to recommend a quarantine.[38]

In 1794 the Virginia government heard that a man named Captain Sinclair in Smithfield in the county of Isle of Wight was outfitting a ship as a privateer. Worse, the county militia did not appear anxious to take any action. Marshall was then sent to Smithfield at the head of a militia troop with orders to enforce the laws against privateering. When he arrived the morning of July 22 between six and seven o'clock, he found that news of his coming had preceded him, and the county militia had stirred itself to take possession of the ship *Unicorn*. "Every idea of resisting with violence the execution of the laws," Marshall reported, "seems to have been abandoned."

Prior to Marshall's arrival, Sinclair was contemplating—at least this was the suspicion—trying to recover his ship. His house overlooked the small inlet which was Smithfield's access to the James River and the *Unicorn*, commanded by the county militia, would have to pass beneath it. "The situation of the house," Marshall noted, "is such as completely to command the deck of the vessel. I do not think that one hundred men placed in the vessel could have protected her ten minutes from fifteen placed in the house, and at this time . . . only a guard of six or seven badly armed men had been raised." The night after the county militia had seized the ship, "persons were heard for a considerable time loading fire arms in the house of Captain Sinclair," said Marshall, adding: "The drawing of iron ramrods, and ramming down the charge were distinctly heard."

Whatever plot to recover the *Unicorn* that may have existed was abandoned when Marshall appeared at the head of the state militia. Captain Sinclair allowed the militiamen to search his house and thirteen pieces of cannon with ball, grapeshot, and powder were found as well as fifteen muskets—"These were found all charged," Marshall said. Sinclair, who had cooperated in allowing the search to be made, told Marshall that the only resistance contemplated was against a possible search of his house without a warrant. Marshall did not believe him, being aware that Sinclair knew a search warrant had been applied for. "This circumstance," Marshall said, "added to the evidence that the vessel had been designed for a privateer," impressed him to the point where he wanted to increase the guard.

Although the confrontation ended peacefully, it still was a matter of concern to Marshall. While he was in Smithfield he talked with residents of Isle of Wight County. "So far as I can judge of their sentiments from their expressions," he said, "I am persuaded that they feel no inconsiderable degree of mortification that a necessity should exist for calling militia from a distance to their neighborhood, to protect from violence the laws of our common country, and I am persuaded too that this sentiment will so affect the commanding officers as to secure more activity from them on any future occasion than has been exhibited on this." To Marshall, who believed that the law was an essential ingredient of society, the reluctance to enforce it by the people of the Isle of Wight was a mystery. What kind of society would they have? How would they live together without honoring the law? And the particularly disturbing element in the *Unicorn* incident was that the leaders of the county—who had an even greater responsibility than the average citizen simply because they were the leaders—were reluctant to enforce the law. "They seem not to have been sufficiently impressed with the importance of maintaining the sovereignty of the law," Marshall declared. "They seem not to have thought it a duty of strong and universal obligation to effect this object." He added that he did believe "a more proper mode of thinking is beginning to prevail."

John Marshall was generous in his optimism. What he described as a belief probably was more a hope that the law would prevail with the people of the Isle of Wight, with all Virginians, all Americans, and with all men.[39]

But incidents like that involving the *Unicorn* were the exceptions. Primarily the Virginia militia in the 1790s served the purpose of protecting the Virginians from the blacks held in bondage. Winthrop D. Jordan's study *White Over Black* documents how the attitudes of the whites toward blacks developed throughout history and in the early years of the United States. It is not a story in which one can find reason for pride. By the second half of the 1700s the blacks well understood the nature of the treatment they were receiving, and they were responding in the only way apparently available to them—open revolt.

Since the slavery era a picture has developed of a benevolent society in which kind white masters took care of a black population which was content in its labor and with its meager rewards. That society never existed. Rather it was created after the Civil War in Southern fiction and folklore in an attempt to justify an evil which could never be justified. Jordan, for example, reports this account from the June 22, 1781, diary entry of a Pennsylvania soldier. The soldier was having dinner at a Virginia plantation at which Negro boys served:

> I am surprised this does not hurt the feelings of this fair Sex to see these young boys of about Fourteen and Fifteen years Old to Attend them. Their whole nakedness Expos'd and I can assure you It would Surprize a person to see these d—d black boys how well they are hung.[40]

But the "whole nakedness" of the young blacks did not embarrass the white women because they did not see them. They did not see them as human beings entitled to respect and decency. The blacks were allowed no more consideration than the animals that pulled the plows. There may not have been a more decent man in Virginia during this period than George Washington. His kindliness, his courtesy, his natural graciousness are legendary. Yet the slaves he owned at Mount Vernon were treated in the usual manner, without regard for their humanity. A Polish nobleman visited Mount Vernon in 1798. This is his description of slave life there:

> We entered one of the huts of the Blacks, for one can not call them by the names of houses. They are more miserable than the most miserable of the cottages of our peasants. The husband and wife sleep on a mean pallet, the children on the ground; a very bad fireplace, some utensils for cooking, but in the middle of this poverty some cups and a teapot. A boy of fifteen was lying on the ground, sick, and in terrible convulsions. The Gl. had sent to Alexandria to fetch a doctor. A very small garden planted with vegetables was close by, with five or six hens, each one leading ten to fifteen chickens. It is the only comfort that is permitted them; for they may not keep either ducks, geese, or pigs. They sell the poultry in Alexandria and procure for themselves a few amenities. They allot them each one pack [peck], one gallon of maize per week; this makes one quart a day, and half as

much for the children, with twenty herrings each per month. At harvest time those who work in the fields have salt meat; in addition, a jacket and a pair of homespun breeches per year. Not counting women and children the Gl. has three hundred Negroes of whom a large number belong to Mrs. Washington. Mr. Anderson told me that there are only a hundred who work in the fields. They work all week, not having a single day for themselves except for holidays. One sees by that that the condition of our peasants is infinitely happier. The mulattoes are ordinarily chosen for servants. According to the laws of Virginia the child follows the condition of the mother; the son or daughter of a mulatto woman and a white is a slave and the issue through the daughter, although white, are still slaves. Gl. Washington treats his slaves far more humanely than do his fellow citizens of Virginia. Most of these gentlemen give to the Blacks only bread, water and blows.

The visitor found that the blacks appeared gay "either from habit or from natural humor." In this, however, the visitor was not so perceptive. Within a few years, after George Washington had died, John Marshall, then Chief Justice of the United States, and Bushrod Washington, an Associate Justice of the Supreme Court and the nephew of George Washington, had to gallop from Washington to Mount Vernon to rescue the general's widow from a threatened slave uprising.

A few days after making the above entries in his diary the Polish nobleman had a talk with a local doctor named Stuart, who told him: "No one knows better than the Virginians the cruelty, inconvenience and the little advantage of having Blacks. Their support costs a great deal; their work is worth little if they are not whipped; the Surveyor costs a great deal and steals into the bargain. We would all agree to free these people; but how to do it with such a great number? They have tried to rent them a piece of land; except for a small number they want neither to work nor to pay their rent. Moreover this unfortunate black color has made such a sharp distinction between the two races. It will always make them a separate caste, which in spite of all the enlightenment of philosophy, will always be regarded as an inferior class which will never mix in the society of Whites."

The Polish nobleman, Julian Ursyn Niemcewicz, recognized the doctor's allegation for the sophistry it was. Slavery existed in the South because it was to the South's economic advantage. "The real cause, or so it appears to me," wrote Niemcewicz, "for the necessity and existence of Negroes in the United States is the excessive extent of the individual properties, and the small number of Whites that there are in view of the size of the country. The owners, not being able either to cultivate their lands themselves or to find white cultivators to lease them, find it necessary to keep this large number of Negroes. It is the greed of the Liverpool merchants who before the Revolution peopled this country with Blacks. This greed, in spite of all the remonstrances of the Legislatures then, served only to make this infamous traffic grow daily. The cultivation of tobacco and of cotton is again one of the reasons why the Southern States still have slaves; while those of the East, where properties are more divided and where they do not cultivate this sort of produce, do not have them."[41]

Even as enlightened a man as Thomas Jefferson was part of the greed and the sophistry. He benefited from slave labor, traded in slaves, and made no real effort to end the evil. Merrill D. Peterson, Jefferson's more recent and certainly friendly biographer, concedes that while Jefferson "continued to favor the plan of gradual emancipation, first published in the *Notes on Virginia* in 1785, neither he nor any other prominent Virginian was ever willing to risk friends, position, and influence to fight for it." When Jefferson was writing the Declaration of Independence, he had included a phrase criticizing George III for allowing trafficking in slaves. Jefferson said the line was deleted in Congress at the request of South Carolina and Georgia, which wanted to continue the trade. Peterson comments, however, that "Congress had other reasons as well for removing this bombast. True, as Jefferson knew from Virginia's experience, the Crown had suppressed legislative attempts to stop the importation of slaves. But the Virginians had been motivated perhaps less by humanitarian than by selfish considerations, such as protecting the value of their property in slaves and securing their communities from the dangers of an ever-increasing slave population. It ill became the Americans, north and south, who had profited from this infernal traffic to lay the blame on George III."[42]

Living in this environment the southern whites always realized they were in danger from their blacks. During the American Revolution the British often tried to threaten the southerners by appealing to the slaves.[43] In the years following the Revolution the situation worsened. John Marshall's mother-in-law, always a nervous woman, never went to bed at night without first having her personal servant (a Negro slave) look under the bed, so frightened was she. And also according to the Marshall family tradition, Polly herself lived in constant fear of slave assaults.[44] The problem not only existed in cities like Richmond, but was rampant among the plantations. At night, for example, plantation owners felt compelled to patrol around their homes with dogs because they feared attack. Slavery had imprisoned the whites.

For Marshall, as a brigadier general in the militia, the problem was an official as well as a personal one. On September 24, 1793, he received a letter from a Robert Mitchell, warning of a possible slave uprising in Powhatan County, just northwest of Richmond. Slaves from various plantations were congregating at a schoolhouse when they were surprised by some whites who captured and whipped them. The slaves then confessed that three hundred of them were to meet at the schoolhouse. One slave was seen in the neighborhood with a sword. "Taking all matters into consideration," said Mitchell, "I can't help thinking that the intended rising is true." Marshall immediately sent the letter on to the governor and asked that the militia be furnished with extra cartridges.[45]

That was not an isolated scare. From Northampton: "Sir: By the inclosed letter you will perceive that the people of this County are very much alarmed with the apprehension of an Insurrection of the Slaves. . . ."[46] From Charles City County in 1792 came a report of armed fugitive slaves killing an armed overseer, and the fugitives' ultimate capture after being chased by a band of whites using dogs to track them.[47] During the 1790s there was a wave of incendiarism throughout the United States, in both the North and the South. The cause of the fires was never proven, but the popular belief was that they were set by slaves. A white man imprisoned in the Richmond jail in 1800 met a number of jailed blacks there and reported that "It has come out that the fire in Richmond within these two years was the work of negroes."[48]

Fear of a black insurrection became stronger after 1791 because of what happened that year in Santo Domingo. The United States did much trading at that port, and the news from that city was quickly carried back to the American mainland where it had eager listeners. There seemed to be an analogy between the situations in the two areas in that both had white populations which were the masters and black populations which were the slaves. This is Marshall's account of what happened:

> Instead of proceeding in the correction of any abuses
> which might exist, by those slow and cautious steps which
> gradually introduce reform without ruin, which may pre-
> pare and fit society for that better state of things designed
> for them; and which by not attempting impossibilities,
> may enlarge the circle of happiness, the revolutionaries of
> France formed the mad and wicked project of spreading
> their doctrines of equality among persons, between whom

there exist distinctions and prejudices to be subdued only by the grave. The rage excited by the pursuit of this visionary and baneful theory, after many threatening symptoms, burst forth on the 23d day of August 1791, with a fury alike destructive and general. In one night a preconcerted insurrection of the blacks took place throughout the colony of St. Domingo, and the white inhabitants of the country, while sleeping in their beds, were involved in one indiscriminate massacre, from which neither age nor sex could afford an exemption. Only a few females, reserved for a fate more cruel than death, were intentionally spared; and not many were fortunate enough to escape into the fortified cities. The insurgents then assembled in vast numbers, and a bloody war commenced between them and the whites inhabiting the towns. The whole French part of the island was in imminent danger of being totally lost to the mother country.[49]

The same kind of catastrophe nearly happened in Richmond one hot night at the end of August in 1800. The details are not exact, having been mutilated somewhat by hyperbole over the years. But apparently a slave calling himself General Gabriel did organize an insurrection and plan an attack on the city of Richmond. His purpose was to take the town and then rouse the other blacks in the state to revolt. How many slaves were actually with him at the beginning is a matter of dispute, with estimates ranging anywhere from fifty to five thousand. But undoubtedly there was a sufficient number of blacks armed with scythes, swords, guns, and whatever other weapons they could gather to threaten the city. The city was saved from attack only because a torrential downpour made all roads and bridges impassable and because at least one and possibly two slaves alerted the whites to the plot. The city quickly armed itself, and the insurrection ended before it had really begun. The accounts say that thirty or forty slaves were hanged for their roles in the revolt, including Gabriel.[50]

In this environment of hostility, guarding the safety of Richmond was a constant concern. From the governor to Marshall in 1793: "You will be pleased to take the necessary measures for calling into immediate and actual service, an ensign, Sergeant, Corporal and twenty privates of your militia. They are to be employed as a Guard over the public arms in this city . . . besides guarding the Public Arms, you direct them to perform such duty as you may think conducive to the public safety of the city." A few weeks later Marshall told the governor that if the guard was to be continued, some means would be necessary to supply its members with rations. He wanted the members of the militia to be given arms. He also was dealing with butchers to provide meat for his men, arranging to have shelters built for the cannon, and counting out the dollars that the state government provided him to finance the militia exercises.[51] It was at all times arduous and time consuming, as well as being a task of importance, considering the threat faced by the people of Richmond.

Marshall approached all men and women with respect and courtesy, and there are no records or suggestions that he ever abused any black person, slave or free, in any manner. As he grew older, he became increasingly aware that slavery was the issue threatening the Union he had labored for so long and he was to fear the Union would not survive, a fear that almost was realized. He also was to recognize in his later years that slavery was debasing the whites and was as much a threat to them as it was a shackle to the blacks.

While Marshall was developing in his profession and growing in reputation in his community, the city of Richmond was also growing. From a few hundred wooden buildings in the 1780s, it was becoming a thriving and cosmopolitan city. The buildings now were of brick. Commerce was lively. Country products were purchased in Richmond, then shipped on small vessels down to Norfolk where they were resold and loaded on oceangoing vessels bound for the European markets. The James River was the main highway leading to the city, but all roads in the state led to Richmond; it was the one community to which all men aspired —whether they sought profit, culture, or a good time. "The brick row on lower Main Street was not then opulent enough to call forth the scorn of the country folk who could find hospitable treatment and comfortable lodging at the Bird in the Hand, the City Tavern, or the Union Hotel," says a contemporary account. "Meanwhile they could enjoy a concert of the Musical Society at Tanbark Hall, witness a play at the theater, invest their savings in lottery tickets, or read the columns of the Enquirer and the Gazette."

Another account of the time describes the markets as being stocked with "all kinds of meat, vegetables, and fish. Good water is found through all the country above the falls of the rivers." This account was written by a Unitarian minister who had come from England to scout the area as a living site. Jobs, he said, were available in farming, brickmaking, building, carpentry, shoemaking, "and in the country in weaving for private families. Employment for literary men would be chiefly as instructors of youth. Richmond alone would not afford employ for a musical professor."

This reporter found that the common fly was troublesome but there were only a few mosquitoes. While "apples, peaches, grapes, etc., are in plenty," the Virginians did not pay "a proper attention" to growing them. As for illnesses, "bilious and intermitting complaints are the most prevailing diseases. Children are sometimes afflicted with a dysentery. Colds are not so common as in England." The clergyman also found that "Those European prejudices are not known which insulate the man of rank and property and make him solitary in the midst of society. The man who made such pretensions to superiority would be despised." His account of the Virginia government, in which John Marshall took such an active part, is revealing of the caliber of the men in that government:

> Popular assemblies are convened only in the state to elect the members of the legislature. Business is conducted in them with regularity and propriety. There are no symptoms of aristocratic influence. There is a prevailing jealousy of property. The candidates sometimes canvass, but the established reputation of those who have not canvassed has often been sufficient to counterbalance the activity of the canvassing candidate. The elections are not attended with disorders, or at most very rarely. No expenses attend them, except to those who give a barbecue, or an entertainment in the woods, and then they seldom amount to a hundred pounds or a hundred and fifty pounds Virginia currency. Both houses are elected in the same manner, only a senator is for three years, the other house for only one year.
> Corruption in the legislature is unknown.

The minister also was impressed by the manner in which the people of Virginia cared for their poor. He wrote:

> Every county has certain respectable persons appointed, who are called overseers of the poor, who in their different wards ascertain who are objects of charity and at a yearly meeting assess all the free males and slaves, for what will be sufficient, and put the poor into decent, comfortable families, who receive a stipend for their care. A few beggars occasionally appear about towns. After travelling two months about this country I have met with one only. . . .
> There are no instances of oppression from the great. There are no instances of tumult among the multitude.[52]

On July 7, 1789, Marshall purchased lot 786 in Richmond for 150 pounds, and the next year the Marshalls moved into their new home. Although the house was built on what was then Richmond's outskirts, it was only a few minutes' walk from the courthouses, making the Shockoe Hill area where it was located a popular place for lawyers to live. The Marshalls soon had as neighbors John Wickham, Spencer Roane, and other prominent lawyers.* John Marshall drew the general design of the house himself. He avoided both the carefully constructed elegance of Jefferson's Monticello and the studied efficiency of Mount Vernon. Instead, he built a simple but commodious house, forty-five feet square, for himself and Polly and their children. Two and one-half stories high, the house is symmetrical, with doors centrally located in the exterior walls and each flanked by a window on its sides. The style of architecture is Federalist, which was prominent then. Actually the Federalist Style was a copy of an English style popular in the 1700s (and the English were imitating the Romans). Records indicate that the main house was surrounded by a number of smaller buildings, for the kitchen, the slaves' quarters, and also for John Marshall's law office.

Inside the house there is a parlor and a dining room. On the second floor is the master bedroom and two other bedrooms. Although the Marshalls ultimately had ten children, six of whom lived to maturity, the house with its three bedrooms was ample. The children doubled up in beds or slept in trundle beds; the custom of each child having a separate room was not then popular.

The house was a comfortable one and soon began to acquire signs that an active and prominent man lived there. The serving bowl on the dining room sideboard first belonged to Patrick Henry. The china was acquired almost thirty years after the house was built. Marshall's old school friend, James Monroe, was President of the United States then, and ordered the china in France, but a parsimonious Congress refused to appropriate the funds to pay for it. Marshall saved Monroe from embarrassment by purchasing the china himself. On the parlor shelves were Marshall's books, the histories, law books, and popular novels of the day. He read much and enjoyed it. In later years, when Polly was almost a total invalid and most of the time was confined to the bedroom, Marshall would sit with her, resting in a wingback chair and reading aloud to her.

---

* The Marshall house still stands in Richmond at the corner of what is now Ninth and Marshall streets. Owned by the city of Rich- mond, it is operated as a tourist attraction by the Association for the Preservation of Virginia Antiquities.

But that was in the future. In the 1790s he began what became known as his "lawyers' dinners." Around the large dining room table would be thirty of the most prominent Virginians. The table was covered with a damask cloth and laden with huge platters of beef, joints of mutton, poultry of all kinds, vegetables, pickles, potato pudding, blanc manges for dessert, and much wine. No women came to these dinners; Polly usually spent these evenings with her parents. But the men's talk was not ribald. For these were thinking men who enjoyed the challenge and exchange of ideas. Good food and good wine relaxed and mellowed them, made them comfortable for the exercise of their minds. Intellectually convivial, they discussed the growing enmity between the Washington faction and the Jefferson faction (faction was the word used originally to refer to what a later time described as a political party), the troubles with France (in the 1790s), and then with England (in the 1800s).

The dinners lasted usually from midafternoon until late evening. Beginning with the first held in the 1790s until the last held in the early 1830s, an invitation to one of Marshall's dinners was among the most coveted in the city.[53]

With his success as a lawyer and his prominence in the city, Marshall's personal wealth also increased. In 1787, according to the city tax records, he owned five adult blacks, two horses, and no carriages. Four years later, he owned ten adult blacks, still had two horses, and six "carriage wheels." He also received 40 pounds in rentals from a lot he owned. By 1797 he owned eight adult blacks, two horses, and four carriages with wheels, and was collecting 150 pounds in rentals.[54]

He invested in stocks and bonds, but not heavily. As an investor he was always more interested in land speculation than in buying paper. The records show he was somewhat casual about his money, as he was casual about most of his personal things, picking up dividends sometimes months late. Marshall, however, not only purchased stocks for himself, but he also acted occasionally as a broker. On September 30, 1791, he subscribed for certificates in the debt of Virginia worth 1,861 pounds, 11 shillings, and 2 pence. He then proceeded to sell the certificates; his father purchased the bulk of them—1,119 pounds, 16 shillings, and 4 pence. The next year he subscribed for certificates worth 2,012 pounds, 16 shillings, and 8 pence, and also resold them, including 300 pounds' worth to Thomas Marshall. But even with all this speculation, Marshall did not earn much income from stock dividends. Sometimes his dividends were $7.50, other times, $59.35. Because there is no certainty that all the records have survived, one cannot be positive of his total stock income.

All appearances, however, suggest it never was more than several hundred dollars a year.[55]

It was a full life John Marshall led. By 1795, when he was forty years old, he could derive more satisfaction from his years than most men who had lived twice as long. He had proved his courage in battle, his ability in the courtrooms in Virginia, and his devotion to his country in the state legislature and in the special session that ratified the Constitution. His family was growing. His friends were legion. A reasonable estimate of his life at this point—which, it turns out, was the midpoint of his years—would say that his fame was behind him, that he would spend his remaining years growing old and rich in the comfort of his family.

But America does not permit its citizens such luxuries. In 1787 Thomas Jefferson had written to William Smith that "The tree of liberty must be refreshed from time to time, with the blood of patriots and tyrants. It is its natural manure." When Jefferson said those words violence and physical action were uppermost in men's minds; his context was armed revolt. But the words could apply as well, at a later time, to the need for men to devote their energies, their intelligence, and their fortunes to their country. The Constitution had not created America, but rather the promise of America, and the fulfillment of that promise would require the talented to come forth when they were needed to refresh the tree of liberty with the blood of their efforts and of those they vanquished. And so it would be for John Marshall. His serene and comfortable existence would become a luxury, pleasantly recalled but rarely enjoyed again.

The brilliance of the American system of government was not that it established an absolute, but rather that it established several absolutes. Dumas Malone, in his account of Thomas Jefferson's first term as President, has said of the struggles between absolutes then that "there is no denying that this situation was serious." He then adds: "Statesmanship had failed in permitting it to become so."[56] Perhaps. Perhaps, however, statesmanship had succeeded in permitting it to become so. Perhaps the men who formed the American government realized there were no answers they could provide at that moment for all future moments. So what they did, instead, was to establish a system in which advocates of one or another absolute—whether it be nationalism versus states' rights, order versus democracy, private property versus civil rights—could struggle with each other until one side or the other had so established its moral cause as to convince the nation which way it must lean. Perhaps this is what James Madison really meant when he said at the Virginia rati-

fication convention that the federal government then proposed
"is of a mixed nature. . . . In some respects, it is a government of
a federal nature; in others it is of a consolidated nature . . . this
government is not completely consolidated,—nor is it entirely
federal."[57]

Marshall would become an advocate of an absolute; Jefferson, also. From the clash of these two men—not from either
one, but from both of them together; from the clash of their
philosophies—not from the philosophy of either one—would
emerge the concept of the United States of America.

Almost from the adoption of the Constitution John Marshall
had been aware that problems remained unsolved, and he was
concerned by them. The news in 1790 that Canadian troops had
occupied Presque Isle, supposedly an American possession, made
Marshall feel that "we must bid adieu to all hope of peace and
prepare for serious war." By 1794 he was lamenting that "there
appears to me every day to be more folly, envy, malice and
damned rascality in the world than there was the day before."[58]
These were only partly the modest ravings of a middle-aged man
who was growing slightly stuffy. More it was concern at the
apparent unfulfillment of the American promise. A few years
later, in his biography of Washington, Marshall wrote this explanation of what was happening in the 1790s:

> It has been already stated that the continent was di-
> vided into two great political parties, the one of which
> contemplated America as a nation, and laboured inces-
> santly to invest the federal head with powers competent
> to the preservation of the union. The other attached itself
> to the state authorities, viewed all the powers of congress
> with jealousy; and assented reluctantly to measures which
> would enable the head to act, in any respect, independently
> of the members. Men of enlarged and liberal minds who,
> in the imbecility of a general government, by which alone
> the capacities of the nation could be efficaciously exerted,
> could discern the imbecility of the nation itself; who, view-
> ing the situation of the world, could perceive the dangers
> to which these young republics were exposed, if not held
> together by a cement capable of preserving a beneficial
> connexion; who felt the full value of national honour, and
> the full obligation of national faith; and who were per-
> suaded of the insecurity of both, if resting for their pres-
> ervation on the concurrence of thirteen distinct sovereign-
> ties; arranged themselves generally in the first party. The
> officers of the army, whose local prejudices had been
> weakened by associating with each other, and whose ex-

perience had furnished lessons on the inefficacy of requisitions which were not soon to be forgotten, threw their weight almost universally into the same scale.[59]

What was actually happening was the development of a political structure in which the philosophical dispute could be handled. The need quickly became evident. In 1791 Congress had enacted an excise tax on whiskey. The tax was suspect at first among the followers of Jefferson because its foremost advocate was Alexander Hamilton. Jefferson and Hamilton already were squaring off in their conflict over the powers of the central government. The trouble escalated when some western Pennsylvanians refused to pay the tax, and the federal government was obliged to send troops to blunt what seemed to be developing into open rebellion. Although the taxation-without-representation issue that had sparked the American Revolution was not an issue in the Whiskey Rebellion, some persons were critical of the show of force by President Washington, comparing it to George III sending troops to quell the American rebellion.

Washington particularly was saddened by what had happened. "The protection they receive," he said to a friend of the westerners who had revolted, "and the unwearied endeavours of the General government to accomplish—by repeated and ardent remonstrances—what they seem to have most at heart, viz., the navigation of the Mississippi, obtain no credit with them, or what is full as likely, may be concealed from them or misrepresented by those Societies who under specious colourings are spreading mischief far and wide either from *real* ignorance of the measures pursuing by the government, or from a wish to bring it, as much as they are able, into discredit; for what purposes, every man is left to his own conjectures."[60]

The "Societies" he referred to were the Democratic clubs organizing throughout the United States in support of Jefferson and his principle of decentralized government; at least, many of these societies were taking Jeffersonianism as their theme. Believing that these societies were fomenting revolt "for what purposes every man is left to his own conjectures," it was not difficult for Washington and the other Federalists to believe that Jefferson himself was the man responsible. In turn, Jefferson was suspicious of the Society of Cincinnati formed after the Revolution by American officers. It was a not uncommon belief then that power lay with men who had both arms and the discipline to use them. The Society of Cincinnati seemed to Jefferson to be a quiescent army, waiting to fall in and march into battle

—an army of Federalists waiting to make Washington monarch.[61]

In Richmond John Marshall, who advocated liberty without license, saw in the Whiskey Rebellion license without liberty. In writing about this period Marshall later described George Washington, upon whom the responsibility fell for quieting the outbreak, as "a real republican." In defining that phrase in relation to Washington, Marshall also defined it in relation to himself. The President, Marshall wrote, was "devoted to the constitution of his country, and to that system of equal political rights on which it is founded. But between a balanced republic and a democracy, the difference is like that between order and chaos. Real liberty, he believed, was to be preserved, only by preserving the authority of the laws, and maintaining the energy of the government. Scarcely did society present two characters which, in his opinion, less resembled each other, than a patriot and a demagogue."[62]

The domestic situation was aggravated by the foreign situation. France, catching a spark from the American revolt, had its own. But rather than a system of disciplined democracy, the French experience produced violence, corruption, and a total lack of responsible leadership. Still, there were many Americans who believed that the cry of "Liberty, Equality and Fraternity" had not been totally obliterated in France and that it should be supported so that the best that was in the revolt would have a chance to survive the worst. Across the United States there were debates over the extent of the support that the United States should give France. President Washington was adamantly opposed to aiding France. The Jeffersonians were more amenable. On August 17, 1793, Marshall and some others presented a public meeting with resolutions lauding Washington's policy of nonsupport of the French government. When these resolutions were approved and others similar to them were approved in other Virginia communities, Madison believed a "Philadelphia cabal" was responsible. Members of this cabal, by Madison's definition, were the merchants in Philadelphia who were rallying behind Alexander Hamilton; they opposed aid to France because of their own commercial dealings with England, the hereditary enemy of France.[63] For Madison and Jefferson it was an easy step to conclude that Marshall, the most articulate supporter of Washington in Virginia, was closely tied to the Philadelphia cabal. Marshall's brother, James Markham Marshall, was, after all, married to the daughter of Robert Morris, a prominent Philadelphia businessman. John and James Markham Marshall and others were entering into a large land purchase in northern Virginia which required extensive financing. Also, Hamilton liked Marshall. Jefferson heard that Alexander Hamilton had declared that Marshall, more than any other Virginian, should be in the federal Congress, and Marshall had been interested in going. "Hence I conclude," said Jefferson, "that Hamilton has played him well with flattery and solicitation." Jefferson then closed that note with what, from his point of view, may have been the worst estimate he ever made. Speaking of Marshall, he said: "I think nothing better could be done than to make him a judge."[64]

In 1796, as Washington was nearing the end of his second term as President and it was known he did not intend to succeed himself, a motion was made in the General Assembly of Virginia praising him. His enemies worked hard to tone down the praise so as to leave only a declaration without the warmth that should go out to a fellow Virginian who had served his country well. Marshall, in the Assembly this term, led the fight to rewrite the declaration on Washington, to make it more fitting. However, he lost.[65]

And so that was how the service of one man appeared ended, without the thanks due him from his closest brethren. But it was not the end of the story, only one part of it. And because the part had ended badly for Washington, a new story must begin for Marshall—and George Washington shortly would tell him that in no uncertain terms. John Marshall would become an advocate of an absolute and would do battle for his cause as the authors of the Constitution intended, in the politics and courts of the country. The issues would not seem to be great ones, but rather ones more concerned with personalities and details. Behind the controversy and the detail, however, lay the great struggle with which the United States must always contend— how it can, at the same time, offer both order and liberty.

Before John Marshall could assume this new role he had one additional journey in his long career. It would be a journey to another land. From it he would learn, become hardened, and emerge with a nobility that would always be part of his nation's history.

Book Three:

DIPLOMAT

I

THE REVOLUTION which began in America, and which succeeded there with the assistance of France, never ceased, but spread ultimately to the entire world. The next country it engulfed was France itself. But France did not possess a Washington, Jefferson, Hamilton, Madison, or Marshall. And the French Revolution became not a beginning for men but rather an end, the destruction of a society in blood, chaos, and anarchy. Still, it had its supporters in the United States. Americans remembered the line of French ships hemming in the port at Yorktown to force Cornwallis to surrender. They remembered the young Frenchmen who had come to the American shores begging for the opportunity to share in the glory of America's struggle for independence. Their hearts were stirred by the French cry of "Liberty, Equality and Fraternity," not realizing that the French were turning it into a demagogic slogan rather than a democratic banner.

In 1793 when Louis XVI was guillotined and France declared war against England and Spain, there were a considerable number of sympathizers in the United States for the French cause. This concerned George Washington, who was just beginning his second term as President. He had been appalled by the executions and other excesses of the French revolutionists. More than that, however, his concern was based on the knowledge that the United States—less than a half-dozen years after the adoption of its Constitution—needed to avoid a war, particularly a European war. England and France at that time were hereditary, traditional, and constant enemies. To become involved in their wars meant to enter on to a path leading to physical, economic, and emotional exhaustion. In April Washington issued a proclamation stating, in effect, that the United States was at peace with both England and France and that Americans should not engage in hostile acts against either nation. His Secretary of the Treasury, Alexander Hamilton, was particularly pleased by the announcement. He strongly believed that the United States needed to develop an active commerce with England, a commerce that would be threatened if the United States aided

France. The New England merchants agreed with him. Washington's Secretary of State, Thomas Jefferson, was not so comfortable with the proclamation. He had been American minister to France, felt sympathy for the announced causes of the Revolution there—if not its excesses. He also wondered if the United States, in exchange for making a few dollars at trade, was not sacrificing morality in refusing to return the assistance France had once rendered Americans. Many of the southern farmers agreed with him. But Jefferson was a faithful member of the Washington administration, and, whatever his personal predilections, he did not abuse the trust placed in him.

The question of whether the United States should assist France perhaps would have divided the nation even more than it did except for the arrival in the United States early in 1793 of Citizen Genêt, the new French minister to the United States. He solved all the Americans' problems for them by his arrogance and presumptuousness. Traveling through the southern United States from Charleston, South Carolina, where he had landed, to Philadelphia, where the American government sat, he traded on the sympathy of the small farmers for France. Not even yet formally received by the American government, he appeared to be seeking support behind the backs of the elected American leaders. He did, in fact, commission ships in American ports to attack British ships.

Charles Biddle, who met Genêt in Philadelphia, described him as "a handsome, agreeable man, but, like most of his countrymen, of a hasty disposition." Biddle also described a scene which was typical of those that led Genêt to believe he could do as he wished in the United States. "The first of June a dinner was given to Mr. Genêt at Oeller's Hotel," Biddle reported. "It was attended by men of all parties, for at that time many who detested the proceedings of the French, did not wish to see them subdued, not knowing what would be the consequence of this country. . . ." Then Biddle listed a number of prominent Philadelphians who showed up at the dinner to honor Genêt. "Many toasts were given expressive of our love for our *sister Republic*," Biddle continued, adding the emphasis. "The *bonnet rouge* was passed from head to head round the table, and many patriotic songs, made to celebrate the day, were sung, some of them truly ridiculous; they served, however, to increase our mirth. The Marseilles Hymn was sung by Mr. Genêt, and we had several other French songs."[1] No wonder Genêt believed it might be possible to appeal to the people against the wishes of President Washington.

"Never in my opinion, was so calamitous an appointment

made," said Thomas Jefferson to James Madison, "as that of the present minister of France here." He then described Genêt as "hotheaded, all imagination, no judgment, passionate, disrespectful and even indecent towards the President in his written as well as verbal communications, talking of appeals from him to Congress, from them to the people, urging the most unreasonable and groundless propositions, and in the most dictatorial style." If ever the public or the Congress learned of Genêt's communications to the American government, the result would be, Jefferson predicted, "universal indignation." For Thomas Jefferson, who sincerely wished to help France, the situation was intolerable:

> He renders my position immensely difficult. He does me justice personally, and, giving him time to vent himself and then cool, I am on a footing to advise him freely, and he respects it, but he breaks out again on the very first occasion, so as to show that he is incapable of correcting himself. To complete our misfortune we have no channel of our own through which we can correct the irritating representations he may make.[2]

Genêt's attitudes toward the American government soon became generally known and the earlier favor he had found began to fade. His position with his own government became precarious as another faction took control in France and sought his arrest. The Genêt affair ended for him with the indignity of his having to accept the protection of George Washington, whom he had so derided; Genêt spent the remainder of his years in the United States after the American President refused to allow his extradition to France.

But for others, the Genêt affair continued for many years. It had drawn sharp lines between the Hamilton faction of merchants and businessmen and the democratic societies organizing across the nation, made up of small farmers and loyal to Jefferson. Coming shortly before the Whiskey Rebellion, the incident encouraged Washington to look on these societies with skepticism and distrust. Washington speculated that Genêt's real purpose had been either to involve the United States in a war "or having become the dupe and tool of a Party formed on various principles, but to effect local purposes, is the only solution that can be given of his conduct. . . ."[3]

Jefferson decided then that he should leave the Washington administration. Over his name had been the shadow of a sympathy for France too great for a man in his position. Ten years later John Marshall, by this time a confirmed Federalist and bitter opponent of Jefferson, wrote of Jefferson's departure, saying Jefferson's "fixed opposition" to Hamilton's economic plans, which Washington had accepted, "his ardent and undisguised attachment to the revolutionary party in France," and his animosity toward Great Britain had attracted a large following to him. "To the opposite party," Marshall said, "he had, of course, become particularly unacceptable." There is nothing, however, in the Marshall comments suggesting any impropriety on Jefferson's part. Then Marshall took up the Jefferson-Genêt relationship. Publication of letters between the two men, Marshall said, "dissipated much of the prejudice which had been excited" against Jefferson. In that correspondence, Marshall reported, Jefferson had "maintained with great ability the opinions embraced by the federalists. . . ." Whatever "partiality for France" Jefferson had shown was no greater, Marshall said, than "the partialities for that republic" felt also by Federalists. Marshall believed that Jefferson's position in regard to Genêt had actually increased the respect in which he was held by Federalists.[4]

For John Marshall also, the Genêt affair did not end with the Frenchman gratefully accepting Washington's protection. Genêt had begun a series of debates across the United States about the direction the United States would take, debates in which John Marshall was compelled, by virtue of his standing in the Richmond community, his intelligence and ability, and his devotion to George Washington and the Federalist cause, to take a leading role.

Although political parties were a new development in the 1790s, their organizers did not lack knowledge of techniques for building support. The Federalists sponsored a number of meetings around the country. One such was held in Richmond on Saturday, August 17, 1793. Presided over by George Wythe, by this time the elder statesman of the commonwealth, but apparently organized and run by Marshall, this meeting approved three resolutions which were written by a six-man committee headed by Marshall. One advocated American neutrality in the conflict between France and England. The second praised Washington. The third criticized the actions of Genêt. The meeting was a public one, and the vote was unanimous.[5] Although such an accusation is not found in connection with this meeting, in connection with later meetings John Marshall was charged with filling meeting halls with Federalists so all votes would be "unanimous."

The resolutions were printed in the *Richmond Gazette and General Advertiser* September 11, along with George Washington's answer. In addition to the anticipated expressions of thanks, the letter contained Washington's rationale for his policy.

"It will always be a source of consolation and encouragement, that the calamities of war, if at any time they shall be experienced, have been unsought and unprovoked," Washington wrote, adding: "Every good citizen will then meet events with the firmness and perseverance which naturally accompany the conscience of a good cause, the conviction that there is no ground for self-reproach."[6]

The Jeffersonians realized they were being outclassed by such tactics. The August 17 meeting in Richmond was only one of many held around the country, all of which were equally well planned to attract support for Washington. A major political propaganda technique then was the newspaper essay, and it was well used in Richmond, where a series of articles was written against the President's policy. The antagonist who signed his name "Agricola" was James Monroe, Marshall's old school friend and then opponent at the Virginia ratification convention. Monroe's series, in turn, produced essays in support of Washington under two names, "Gracchus" and "Aristedes." Whether Marshall was one or both is unknown, although he undoubtedly was intimately involved in their preparation. And the two "Gracchus" letters sound as if they could be his.[7]

Monroe, writing as "Agricola," began his first essay by accusing the supporters of the neutrality policy of being "enemies to the French revolution" as well as being "likewise notoriously the partisans for Monarchy." That charge developed into a major one used by the Jeffersonians against the Federalists: that they planned to institute a monarchy in place of the republic. The fear had always existed, and Washington perhaps could have been proclaimed king after the Revolution if he had so chosen. But he had not so chosen and by the 1790s the charge was so without substantiation that one wonders how reasonable men could even voice it.

Monroe realized he could not justify the behavior of Genêt; no one seriously was arguing that a foreign minister had the right to bypass the President and appeal directly to the American people. Instead, he criticized "the management, by which this incident had been brought before the public," and said it "deserves to be more particularly noticed, because its object must be deemed unfriendly to the best interests of our country." He then charged that "there exists among us a powerful faction, who are opposed to the great principles of the French revolution, and who are likewise much more attached to the constitution of England, than to that of their own country."[8]

Monroe's final charge is interesting because its thesis—that a domestic political party was more loyal to a foreign power than to the United States—has been used more in history against Monroe's party than against the party of Washington, where Monroe had directed it.

Monroe's first letter appeared September 3. It produced an answer September 11, signed "Aristedes." In its direct attacks on both Monroe, in his guise as "Agricola," and on the Jeffersonians, this paper does not ring true as having been written by Marshall. "Is there a man among us who has so buried the love of country under a zeal for party or affection for a foreign nation," it asks, "that he could stoop to be dictated to by the minister of that nation. . . ." As for the charge that the Federalists sought to establish a monarchy, "Aristedes" bluntly replied: "If this be the idea of Agricola, the calumny grows not out of the fact." "Aristedes" then charged that the democratic societies backing Jefferson—"an active, but I trust not a numerous party" —were "incessant in their efforts to disgust America with the government of her choice."[9]

On October 9 Monroe produced a second letter signed by "Agricola." "Should America and France be parted," this one began, "what other friend or ally remains for either nation upon the face of the globe?" He traced the relationship of the two nations from the American Revolution to the French Revolution, and said that to America "the people of France looked for countenance." The letter then charged that the administration of George Washington deliberately had sought to antagonize France.[10]

This drew an answer in the October 16 issue of the newspaper signed by "Gracchus," which does have the ring of John Marshall's mode of reasoning, his philosophy, and his syntax. It began:

If in the political, as in the natural body, much real misery may flow from imagined ills, he can be no friend to the public happiness, who plays upon the public mind, and seeks without cause, to dissatisfy the people with that government to which their dearest interests have been willingly entrusted. In a republic, which united America is, and I trust will ever be, the people, who are, and ought to be, the source of all power, chuse from among themselves the men who fill all the high departments of government. In the exercise of this important right, they can have no motive to balance against general good, and it is therefore to be presumed that they will endeavour to select those who are distinguished from their virtues and their talents. No human institution can be free from error, nor can human decisions be uniformly right; but a government thus constituted, affords the fairest prospect for general felicity, and the probability must ever be more in favor of, than against, the patriotism of his measures.

That was a statement of Marshall's faith in the people, "the source of all power," that they would act only for the general good and that a government they selected would most likely act for the general good, and should at least be allowed that semblance of respect.

If Marshall seems naive in that passage as he expresses hope for the integrity of self-government, he quickly became the sophisticated needler when he suggested that "It is as possible that those who are disgusted at not guiding the councils of their country may be mistaken in the opinions they give as that those to whom this high trust has been confided shall sacrifice the public interest to private or unworthy objects." While arguing that the neutrality policy was not wrong simply because it was being criticized, Marshall also conceded that "Neither is a blind approbation of every governmental act to be countenanced." He continued: "The public happiness may be alike affected by approving what is wrong, or condemning what is right."

Then Marshall argued that the duty of a "wise and virtuous" people was to view the acts of government "with a scrutinizing but not a hostile eye." He asked that the people not condemn because an accusation is made. "But let us look temporarily into the charge," he continued, "and exercise the best judgment upon it." He then proceeded to deny at length that Washington was seeking to harm France rather than only to steer a neutral course.[11]

On November 13 both "Agricola" and "Gracchus" had letters in the Richmond paper. Monroe continued his attack on the administration: "[F]rom the adoption of the government to the present day [the administration's] uniform course has been marked by a disposition unfriendly to France." The "Gracchus" essay apparently was written by Marshall who was again defending the administration against charges of being too friendly toward England. "The charge then of humiliating and pusillanimous conduct towards Britain," "Gracchus" wrote, "is as ill supported as that of enmity to France." He closed his letter by discussing an issue which was a major cause of concern to the Federalists. The paragraph read:

Altho' every just and honorable means of avoiding war should be used, it is more than possible that we may yet be engaged in one with Britain. Should the event take place, it is not by disgusting the people with their government, it is not empty declamations to excite suspicions against that government, nor is it by a change in the executive that we are to be carried happily through it. The previous measures ought to be such as firmly to unite the people by convincing them that the war was not sought for by us, but was inevitable, and when engaged in it, those who conduct it must have our confidence, or the wisest plans will prove unsuccessful.[12]

There was one final exchange in the Richmond papers, one essay by "Aristedes" on November 20 and one by "Agricola" on December 4. This essay by "Aristedes," as does the first signed with that name, lacks the careful construction which characterized Marshall's arguments and also drives home too personal an attack on "Agricola" for it to be accepted as having been written by Marshall. The most likely explanation is that Marshall and another Richmond Federalist had divided between them the responsibility for defending the administration in the newspaper. Two weeks later, on December 4, when the last essay by "Agricola" appeared, it had a repetitious ring to it, as the author again criticized the administration for being overly friendly toward England. The essays probably ended at the right time.[13]

The essays served not merely as political polemics. They staked out the arguments used by members of the rapidly developing political parties then and by historians since. For the Federalists, the responsibility was to avoid war if possible so as to allow the nation to develop; this meant keeping on reasonably good terms with England, which was the chief trading partner of the United States. For the Jeffersonians the issue was whether the United States should not support what appeared to be a genuine democratic revolution in a nation which had helped the Americans. The arguments about monarchy, subservience to one foreign nation or another, the questions of loyalty, and the possibilities of war, all were political arguments being used at the time to sell a point, and all have been used later to justify or dispute one side or the other.

This political dispute, when joined with geographical, economic, and cultural differences between areas of the young nation, threatened its continued existence. In the spring of 1794, for example, a Virginia Senator, John Taylor, was approached by Rufus King, a Federalist Senator, who asked to speak privately to him. Once alone in a committee room, King declared that continuation of the Union was utterly impossible. The southern and eastern peoples, he continued, were in constant disagreement and would not yield to each other. At this point in the conversation, they were joined by Oliver Ellsworth, another Federalist. His entry appeared to be an accidental one, but Taylor was beginning to be suspicious; he believed Ellsworth's arrival planned. With Rufus King still doing the major part of the talking, the Federalists made the point that a planned separation would be better than an accidental one. John Taylor answered that, as far as he could see, the major issue dividing the two parties was the matter of the debts to the British. The Jeffersonians were suspected of refusing to want the debt paid while the Federalists were suspected of trying to use the debt issue to destroy the Jeffersonian party.

"Suppose, therefore," said John Taylor, "the two parties were to act in such a manner as to remove these mutual suspicions, might it not give new vigor to the union?" Taylor then listed a number of measures he considered as possible devices to raise revenue to pay off the debts to the satisfaction of all. Rufus King did not respond to this suggestion, saying that there were more problems than the debt. Taylor then asked the two Federalists whether some alternative could not be found which would be preferable to dissolving the Union. But neither King nor Ellsworth offered any answer.

Taylor later sent an account of this meeting to James Madison, saying he was "thoroughly convinced that the design to break the union is contemplated."[14] More likely, King and Ellsworth, aware that anything communicated to Taylor would quickly go back to Madison and then probably to Jefferson, were using Taylor as a means of persuading Jefferson to become as conciliatory as possible. Still, Taylor's attitude, fearful of separation, indicates how strongly that possibility existed within the United States.

The issue came to a climax with the Jay Treaty, signed in London in November 1794. "Much . . . you are sensible depends on Great Britain," Harrison Gray Otis wrote, before the treaty provisions were known. "The moderate and respectable part of the community wait with patience and anxiety the result of Mr. Jay's mission; but should justice be denied to our claims, I think a very general sentiment of indignation and spirit of resentment will prevail here among all classes of people and produce a rupture between the countries."[15] This treaty made faction an absolute fact of American life. It caused a serious challenge to President George Washington's leadership from his native state. The treaty also catapulted John Marshall from a leading Virginia

Federalist to a leading Federalist in the nation. "As this subject was one in which every man who mingled with public affairs was compelled to take part," said Marshall, "I determined to make myself master of it."[16]

Ever since the treaty between England and the United States ending the American Revolution had been signed in 1783, many of its provisions had been ignored. The British continued to hold military outposts in the Northwest Territories; the United States was not paying its debts to the British. American ships were being hounded by the British in defiance of the tradition that neutral ships carry neutral cargoes. British ports in the Indies were closed to the Americans. Obviously, a new settlement had to be reached.

In Philadelphia, the center then of America's commerce, the merchants wanted Alexander Hamilton to go to London to negotiate a treaty. But he was ruled out by his known propensity for seeking a satisfactory commercial solution to the elimination of practically all other points. He did, however, suggest John Jay, then Chief Justice of the United States, and Washington named Jay. The appointment was a poor one. No matter how favorable a treaty Jay negotiated, many Americans would not accept it because of his reputation for being pro-English. In the western lands he still was remembered with disfavor as the man who had wanted to bargain away the navigation rights to the Mississippi River. In the new treaty with England it seemed as if he had not produced much of value to the United States. The British agreed to evacuate the posts in the Northwest Territories, as they had promised to in 1783, but not until 1796. The principle of repaying the debts to the British was restated. The neutrality of American trading vessels was not recognized. There was no provision for repayment to the Americans of property appropriated by the British during the Revolution.

The Americans did receive some trading rights in the Indies and a solution to the northern boundaries was agreed on. More important, however, the treaty established the principle for the United States of settling international disputes by arbitration, a principle that proved itself more in later years perhaps than it did at the moment. The best thing that could be said at the time for the treaty was that the United States was weak militarily and could not expect anything better from England, except war. The treaty, in other words, bought peace for a time at the price of internal dissension, of alienating France, a former ally, and of the surrender of a certain amount of honor. John Jay realized this. In a letter to Washington the day the treaty was signed, Jay justified the document by saying that "to do more was impossible." He also expressed the hope that "it may have a fair trial."[17]

Washington did not like the treaty either. But he believed the United States had no choice. "In time," he said, "when passion shall have yielded to sober reason, the current may possibly turn; but, in the mean while, this government in relation to France and England, may be compared to a ship between Scylla and Charybdis. If the treaty is ratified, the partisans of the French— or rather of war and confusion—will excite them to hostile measures, or at least to unfriendly sentiments . . . if it is not, there is no foreseeing all the consequences that may follow as it respects Great Britain."[18] There can be no question of Washington's personal bravery nor of his willingness to sacrifice all that he possessed for the American cause; he had done that in the American Revolution. Whatever one's reaction to Jay's Treaty, whether one believes the United States sold too cheaply or that the nation secured the best bargain possible, one must admire Washington's courage. He was willing to risk personal criticism and his place in history to secure the peace he considered necessary for the nation he had fathered to grow and prosper.

The furor caused by the treaty spread throughout the United States. Effigies of John Jay were burned or guillotined in major cities. Alexander Hamilton, who was particularly pleased by the treaty, was stoned in New York. Essays again appeared in newspapers. Mass meetings were held, and generally the point of all of them was opposition to the treaty and animosity toward Washington. The first battleground was the Senate.

"The fate of the treaty is not yet known," Abigail Adams, wife of the Vice President, wrote to her sister. "It is, however, the general opinion that it will be ratified. I say the outdoor opinion, for the Senate are secret and silent. It had been discussed with much calmness, coolness, and deliberation, and considered in all its various lights and operations."[19]

There was another factor in the discussions, of which Abigail Adams and most other Washingtonians were unaware. The French obviously were extremely interested in the treaty. England was their enemy, and anything that was to England's benefit was to their disadvantage. The French minister, Joseph Fauchet, had many close conversations with politicians in Philadelphia whom he considered friendly to the French cause. In the spring of 1795 his replacement, Pierre Auguste Adet, had arrived in the United States, and the two of them became angry at the possibility of the treaty being ratified. Fauchet wrote a memoir detailing the actions he took. It reads:

For some it was a question of fear since it was represented to them that England would consider it an insult if [Congress] refused to ratify the treaty and war with England might be the result. Other arts were used to influence those with whom this kind of argument might prevail. [Henry] Tazewell, who had replaced M. Monroe in the Senate, had already had several conversations with me on the treaty since the opening session of the Senate and had talked as a sincere friend of [French] interests. On the 20th of June, four days before the decision of the Senate, he came to see me and informed me of his fears concerning the outcome; only ten members could be counted upon to vote against the treaty and eleven would be needed to defeat ratification. He did not attempt to conceal that the fear of a rupture with England and a subsequent failure of France to come to the country's aid if that happened, was causing several timid Senators to waver who did not dare expose their constituents to such gross chances nor to assume themselves such a heavy responsibility.

Fauchet then wrote of Tazewell:

He indicated to me two members whom it would be possible to buy with pecuniary advances.* All that I could do in these respects which were of such high importance was to conduct M. Tazewell to my successor [Adet]. I had reason to think that he took decisive action; he wrote me the same evening that things were arranged and that we could count on full success.

In fact, at the meeting the next day, oscillations were apparent for which the source was clear to knowledgable men. M. Randolph went into action, the English minister who had retired to the country to display his neutrality was called in haste to open negotiations which soon bore fruit. On the 23rd the votes resumed their original division and the 24th the treaty was definitely ratified.[20]

For many members of the Senate the vote was a difficult and a dangerous one. Humphrey Marshall, a Senator from Kentucky and a cousin of John Marshall's, voted for ratification and came close to paying for the vote with the loss, at least, of his dignity. After he had returned home, a mob surrounded his house, seized him, and was on the brink of throwing him into a

---

* Il m'indiqua deux membres qu'il étoit possible d'avoir par quelques avances pécuniaires.

nearby pond. But Marshalls were not easily played with. Humphrey Marshall told his captors he understood that persons about to be baptized were allowed to relate their experiences, and he hoped for the same opportunity. He began speaking, explaining his position in relationship to the treaty, and talked for "half an hour with so much wit and pleasantry that they huzz'd him—omitted the rude ceremony—and conducted him to his house with every mark of respect that such a rabble was capable of manifesting to him."[21]

But the Senate vote was not the end. "The commotion began at Boston and seemed to rush through the Union with a rapidity and violence which set human reason and common sense at defiance," said Marshall.[22] In Marshall's account of what happened next there is a disappointment with democracy. John Marshall always supported democracy, but he did not hesitate to criticize the reality of it when he believed that democratic government had failed to live up to its promise. The Jay Treaty, he argued, required "a patient and laborious investigation" before an individual could judge it. "But an immense party in America," he continued, "not in the habit of considering national compacts, without examining the circumstances under which that with Britain had been formed, or weighing the reasons which induced it; without understanding the instrument, and in many instances without reading it, rushed impetuously to its condemnation, and seemed to expect that public opinion would be surprised by the suddenness, or stormed by the fury of the assault; and that the executive would be compelled to yield to its violence." Even worse to Marshall was that "many intelligent men . . . stood aloof, while the most intemperate assumed, as usual, the name of the people [and] pronounced a definitive and unqualified condemnation of every article in the treaty."[23]

Marshall's reaction to the treaty opponents was too strong, but then so was their opposition. The crucial question was one of stability. Washington and the Federalists were willing to accept what little Britain gave them, to avoid war and to give the young nation a chance to prosper. The Jeffersonian Republicans believed the treaty was a sellout of American honor for the dribs and drabs of British trade.

Perhaps the Federalists made the choice they did because they now were twenty years older than they had been when the shots at Lexington and Concord were heard. John Marshall was an adventurous lad of nineteen with no responsibilities when he went to war. When he defended the Jay Treaty he was a man of thirty-nine with a family, a career, and strong stakes in the future of his community. He certainly was wealthier, with more to lose by the prospect of war. One provision of the Jay Treaty stabilized ownership of the British land grants in the hands of the British citizens with titles to them. And at this time Marshall was involved in the purchase of one of these land tracts, the Fairfax estates, a purchase that could not be consummated without ratification of the treaty. But perhaps also the Federalists recalled that the meaning of the American Revolution was not the battlefield victory but the society that could be constructed after that victory, and perhaps they did not wish to risk that society by becoming involved in a war that could benefit only Europe.

Whatever reason or combination of reasons motivated Marshall, he was not one of those who stood aloof. His activities in the Genêt affair in arousing the people of Virginia against the French minister were well known. "The resentments of the great political party which led Virginia had been directed towards me for some time," Marshall later recalled, "but this measure [the opposition to Genêt] brought it into active operation. I was attacked with great virulence in the papers and was so far honoured in Virginia as to be associated with Alexander Hamilton, at least so far as to be termed his instrument." He continued to defend in Richmond the foreign policies of George Washington. "The public and frequent altercations in which I was unavoidably engaged weakened my decision never again to go into the legislature. . . ." It was at this point, in 1795, that Marshall was drafted by his fellow citizens into becoming again a member of the legislature, and thus he returned to public life.

The Jay Treaty came up for discussion shortly after the state legislature opened on November 10. The state's two Senators, Henry Tazewell and Stevens Thomson Mason, had voted against the treaty, and the Assembly had before it a motion praising them for their vote. Marshall was part of a group countering that the Assembly members should express no opinion. That lost 52–98. The original measure, praising the two United States Senators for voting against the treaty, then passed, 100–50. Marshall was among the fifty dissenters.

The next day a motion praising Washington was offered. It read: "Resolved, That the motives which influenced the President of the United States, to ratify the treaty lately negociated with Great Britain, meet the entire approbation of this House; and that the President of the United States for his great abilities, wisdom, and integrity, merits and possesses the undiminished confidence of his country." That was passed only after an amendment was added to it, praising, for the second time, the two

Senators for their negative vote on the treaty. Marshall opposed the amendment.[25]

The debate, which lasted only two days, is not reported in the *Journal* for the House of Delegates, which is unfortunate because it apparently included one of Marshall's better speeches. The issue discussed was the constitutional one of whether the executive branch could negotiate a commercial treaty, or whether such a treaty was an infringement of the power given to Congress to regulate commerce. "The objectors believed themselves to be invulnerable," Marshall reported.

Several of Marshall's friends advised him to stay out of the debate, because he would be totally destroyed politically and might not even be allowed to finish his arguments. Marshall, however, took the position that "a politician even in times of violent party spirit maintains his respectability by showing his strength; and is most safe when he encounters prejudice most fearlessly."

When the question of the treaty was brought up in the Assembly, "the constitutional objections were brought forward most triumphantly." But to John Marshall there was no question "susceptible of more complete demonstration, and I was fully prepared not only on the words of the constitution and the universal practice of nations, but to show . . . that Mr. Jefferson, and the whole delegation from Virginia in Congress, as well as all our leading men in the convention on both sides of the question, had manifested unequivocally the opinion that a commercial treaty was constitutional." He did succeed in destroying the argument that such a treaty was unconstitutional.[26]

A Supreme Court Justice, James Iredell, was in Richmond at the time and was impressed by Marshall's speech. "I am told there were few members who were not convinced by Mr. Marshall's arguments as to its being constitutional, which few members thought it was before the debate began," he wrote, "and some of the speakers on the other side had the candor to acknowledge their conviction, though not in the House."[27]

It was that defense of the Jay Treaty in the state Assembly which made Marshall such a hero to the Federalists across the nation, and particularly welcome in Philadelphia when he argued the case of *Ware v. Hylton* before the Supreme Court there a few months later. Jefferson fumed at Marshall's action. "Though Marshall will be able to embarrass the republican party in the assembly a good deal," said Jefferson a few days after the debate, "yet upon the whole, his having gone into it will be of service." Jefferson believed that Marshall had done more damage to the Republicans "acting under the mask of Republicanism than he

will be able to do after throwing it plainly off." Jefferson believed
that Marshall's "lax lounging manners have made him popular
with the bulk of the people of Richmond" and also that Marshall
was respected by "many thinking men of our country." These
men, Jefferson was certain, would desert Marshall after having
seen him "come forth in the plentitude of his English principles."[28] Marshall, of course, had not suddenly dropped a
Republican mask. Rather, he had emerged as a Federalist leader
for the first time, and from that time on was a factor to be considered by Jefferson.

The opponents of the treaty were not done. The fight would
continue and so would Marshall's role. Fauchet, the outgoing
French minister, believed that France could persuade the American House of Representatives to decline to appropriate funds to
put the treaty into effect, thus nullifying it. On his return to
France, Fauchet recommended avoiding divisive techniques such
as Genêt had used. He also suggested that France cooperate with
her friends in the United States so as not to embarrass them, as
Jefferson had been embarrassed by Genêt. Fauchet advised the
Directory to work for the replacement of Washington as President with Jefferson.[29]

When the Congress convened early in 1796 William
Branch Giles—the man Marshall had recommended to Madison
and who had become a leading exponent of Jeffersonian Republicanism in Congress—started right off with the position that the
House could veto the actions of the President and the Senate,
which had approved the treaty, by refusing to appropriate funds
to carry it into effect.[30] As Marshall explained the position of
Giles and the other opponents in the House, the Representatives
"were at full liberty to make or to withhold such appropriation,
or other law, without incurring the imputation of violating any
existing obligation, or of breaking the faith of the nation." This
became the formal position of the House, and this placed President Washington in a "peculiarly delicate" situation, Marshall
reported. He continued:

> In an elective government, the difficulty of resisting the
> popular branch of the legislature is at all times of serious
> magnitude, but is particularly so when the passions of the
> public have been strongly and generally excited by exer-
> tions which have pervaded the whole society . . . and fur-
> nished motives, not lightly to be overruled. . . .

But there were other motives, "though less operative with
men who fear to deserve the public favour by hazarding its loss,"
said Marshall, but which do "possess an irresistible influence over

a mind resolved to pursue steadily the path of duty, however it may abound with thorns." Washington was concerned, Marshall wrote, that future diplomatic transactions of the United States would be jeopardized if he gave in to the House on this occasion. Also, Washington was concerned about the presidency losing power by gradual encroachment. Therefore he refused to acknowledge the correctness of the House position.[31] Actually even the Jeffersonian Republicans did not seriously believe the position they had succeeded in persuading the House to adopt was correct. One of their leaders was John Taylor, who believed the House should have gone along with the treaty "with groans and execrations" and then tried to amend the Constitution.[32]

Washington's position put the President and the House of Representatives on a collision course. One of them had to yield. The House seemed to have public opinion behind it, but the Federalists determined to create some public opinion of their own. Again, as with Washington's Neutrality Proclamation three years earlier, public meetings were organized across the country. The business interests had the most to gain by preserving economic stability and were willing to sponsor and populate these sessions. Marshall arranged one in Richmond for April 25, 1796. It was held at the state capitol and attracted between three hundred and four hundred persons, an extremely large turnout. One of James Madison's friends was at the meeting and reported to Madison that "a large proportion" of those present "were British merchants, some of whom pay for the British purchases of horses—their clerks—officers, who have held posts under the President at his will—stockholders—expectants of office—and many without the shadow of a freehold." But the Republicans still were well represented—"tho' inferior, [they] were inferior in a small degree only." The writer continued that "Marshall's argument was inconsistent, and shifting; concluding every third sentence with the horrors of war."[33]

Apparently, however, the letter writer had more than a little bias himself. That night after the meeting Marshall wrote a long report to Alexander Hamilton on the session. He first said he had been reluctant to call a meeting—"We could not venture an expression of the public mind under the violent prejudices with which it has been impressed"—as long as there was hope the House would not try to block the treaty. But when that hope died, "it was deemed advisable to make the experiment, however hazardous it might be." Marshall then said the meeting was called and the crowd "was more numerous than I have ever seen at this place." The "very ardent and zealous discussion . . . consumed the day." And at the end, "a decided majority declared in favor of a resolution that the welfare and honor of the nation requires us to give full effect to the treaty negotiated with Britain." The "experiment" of presenting the case for the treaty to the public despite that public's "violent prejudice" had produced a victory at that meeting for Jay's Treaty, for the Federalists, for George Washington, and for John Marshall.

Marshall continued that the intention was to send the resolution and a petition along the same lines to Congress. He conceded that "The subject will probably be taken up in every county in the State, or at any rate in very many of them. It is probable that a majority of the counties will avow sentiments opposed to ours, but the division of the State will appear to be much more considerable than has been stated. In some of the districts there will certainly be a majority who will concur with us, and that perhaps may have some effect. As man is a gregarious animal, we shall certainly derive much from declarations in support of the constitution and of appropriations, if such can be obtained from our sister states." The position taken by Marshall and the other Federalists, he wrote, was to admit "the discretionary constitutional power of the representatives on the subject of appropriations, but contend that the treaty is as completely a valid and obligatory contract when negotiated by the President and ratified by him, with the assent and advice of the Senate, as if sanctioned by the House of Representatives."[34] The House may have the right to refuse appropriations, Marshall was arguing, but not without bearing the onus of being responsible for violating a valid agreement. The position of Giles and the other Jeffersonian Republicans was that withholding the funds could be done without the House assuming such a responsibility.

The general outlines of Marshall's account, that the meeting was well attended and that a majority supported the implementation of the treaty, was supported by a newspaper account. (That account did end, however, with the lament that "a PEOPLE so enlightened, possessing such fair prospects of unequalled happiness, under the best Constitution ever yet invented, should be so divided among themselves, the consequences of which may tend to disunion, and at length loss of liberty."[35])

Marshall's letter to Hamilton was directed to him via Rufus King. "I take the liberty to avail myself of your aid for forwarding to Mr. Hamilton the enclosed letter," Marshall said. He wrote briefly to King of the meeting and of the expected reaction to it: "The ruling party of Virginia are extremely irritated at the vote of today and will spare no exertion to obtain a majority in other counties." He continued of the Jeffersonian Republicans:

Even here they will affect to have the greater number of freeholders and have set about counter Resolutions to which they have the signatures of many respectable persons, but of still a greater number of mere boys; and altho' some caution has been used by us in excluding those who might not be considered authorized to vote, they will not fail to charge us with having collected a number of names belonging to foreigners and to persons having no property in the place.

Marshall assured King that "The charge is as far untrue as has perhaps ever happened on any occasion of the sort." To demonstrate how untrue, Marshall said that "We could, by resorting to that measure, have doubled our list of petitioners." He closed his letter by saying he was trying to set up similar meetings and petitions from other parts of the state. "*Exitus in dubio est*," he concluded.[36]

But the issue was not in as much doubt as he feared. His argument that the treaty was a valid document and that the House must honor it or bear the opprobrium of reneging on America's international agreements was a valid one which the public, and ultimately the House, accepted. In the confrontation between George Washington and the Jeffersonian Republicans over the Jay Treaty, Washington had won—with the assistance of Marshall.

Shortly after the April meeting on the Jay Treaty Hamilton again called on Marshall for assistance. The year 1796 was the last of Washington's second term, and he would not seek a third. The problem was to find a strong Federalist who would run, could be elected, and would be compatible with Hamilton—at least that was how Hamilton saw it. A major strategy would be to divide, if possible, the Virginia Democrats. One way of doing so was to enlist Patrick Henry on the presidential ticket, as a Federalist. Although still immensely popular in Virginia, his opposition to a central form of government which he had expressed so eloquently at the Virginia ratification convention of 1788 had mellowed. He would be safe in a Federalist government—as Vice President. Also George Washington and the other Federalists remembered well Henry's eloquent vow to abide by the law when he lost in that convention, a vow that, more than anything else, established in the new nation the concept that the defeated would decline to oppose the victorious by violent means.

Marshall was a particularly good friend of Henry's; they often met at the various courthouses where they practiced and they had been co-counsel in both the Randolph scandal case and the *Ware v. Hylton* arguments before the Supreme Court. Marshall then was asked by Hamilton, via Rufus King, to sound out Henry on the possibility of his seeking the presidency. Under the Constitution at the time, all candidacies were for the presidency —the candidate with the most votes became President, the one with the second highest number of votes became Vice President. The expectation probably was that Vice President John Adams would be elected President and that Henry would win sufficient votes from Virginia and other southern states to become Vice President, or at least enough to deny that office to Thomas Jefferson.

But Henry would not go along with the plan. "Mr. Henry has at length been sounded on the subject you committed to my charge," Marshall reported. "Genl. [Henry] Lee and myself have each conversed with him on it, tho' without informing him particularly of the persons who authorized the communication. He is unwilling to embark in the business. His unwillingness, I think, proceeds from an apprehension of the difficulties to be encountered by those who shall fill high executive offices."[37] Sixty years old in 1796, ill and tired, Patrick Henry's fighting days were behind him, and he knew it better than most.

One result of Henry's refusal to enter national politics was the election of John Adams, the Federalist, as the nation's second President, and of Thomas Jefferson, the Republican, as its second Vice President. James Iredell witnessed the inauguration and was heartened by it. "There is every appearance of harmony between the President and Vice President, who lodge together, and appear on very friendly terms," he said, adding: "God grant it may continue, and serve to allay that vile party-spirit which does so much injury to our country."[38]

It did not last, of course, as it could not. There could not be unanimity about how the United States should be governed, for great men have different, often conflicting, ideas, and John Adams and Thomas Jefferson were both great men. John Marshall would be part of their dispute, and the role he played took him halfway round the world to France, forcing him to leave his family for more than a year, and finally gave his fellow Americans a sense of national pride desperately needed.

2

THE DIFFICULTIES between France and the United States, which were to involve John Marshall, worsened. Partly this was caused by French hostility growing out of the Jay Treaty, but even more important was the general disdain that European nations had for the United States. It was a young nation that had yet to prove itself the equal of the European powers. In the councils of Europe the Treaty of 1783 between the United States and England ending the American Revolution was considered a triumph of French foreign aid. America remained a wilderness to be manipulated and abused. Europe dictated to the United States. The British haughtily announced they would not evacuate the Northwest forts despite any promises to the contrary in any treaty. Spain proclaimed the conditions under which the Americans might be able to use the Mississippi River; she did not negotiate them. The Barbary Pirates expected their tribute from the United States, which, lacking a navy, was even less capable of refusing than was any European nation. When France played the game of international tough guy, then, the United States seemed an easy victim.

In the United States fear exacerbated the situation. All Americans, even the Jeffersonian Republicans who were friendlier to France, feared the excesses of her Revolution and feared what might happen if those excesses spread to other countries. That possibility did not seem remote. Vice President John Adams received a letter from his son, John Quincy Adams, written from The Hague, raising this possibility. Dated August 13, 1796, the letter warned: "It is proper, however, that you should be aware that to all appearance they have seriously resumed the plan of revolutionizing *the whole world*, so openly professed by the Brissotine party in 1792, though at present they think proper totally to deny such a design."[1] The emphasis is John Quincy Adams'. Although he was exaggerating, and his exaggerations probably stemmed more from his Federalist concern regarding Thomas Jefferson than from any French actions, he was accurately reflecting the Americans' fear of a revolution in their own land modeled after the French Revolution.

The Americans also were concerned by what they considered French interference with the election of 1796. Fauchet had recommended such interference, but there is no proof that it actually took place. Still, the possibility worried the Americans. John Quincy Adams reported from The Hague that the French planned to use the start of a new administration to appeal again directly to the people, as Genêt had done, in hopes of persuading the Americans to sever the ties being formed with England, as represented by the Jay Treaty. "[T]his patronage of France will give such weight to the efforts of faction that they will be no longer resistible, and the system of neutrality will necessarily be overturned," he wrote.[2]

Also, the French were attacking American ships. No nation can stand such abuse, but it was particularly harmful to the young United States which was just beginning to develop its trade patterns. The Americans naturally wanted to live by the principle that free ships made free cargoes, for such a principle would allow them to sell to both England and France, which were at war with each other. On July 2, 1796, however, France had announced that she would treat neutral ships "by the manner in which they should suffer the English to treat them." In the European cities French consuls then authorized the capture and condemnation of American ships destined for a British port. "But its fullest effect," summed up Secretary of State Timothy Pickering, "has been produced in the West Indies, whose seas swarm with privateers and gun-boats, which have been called forth by the latitude allowed to their depredations, by the indefinite terms of the decree, and the exploratory orders of the agents of the directory at Guadeloupe and St. Domingo."[3]

Charles Cotesworth Pinckney, named in 1796 to serve as the American minister to France, was a native of South Carolina who had traveled widely and been educated in Europe. A hero of the American Revolution, he had been at the battles of Brandywine and Germantown but had not met John Marshall there. Although a prominent Federalist—he had been a member of the Constitutional Convention and George Washington long had sought to enlist him in public service—he was not antagonistic toward France, although he was not as friendly as James Monroe, his predecessor, had been. He came to his position as an intelligent man seriously interested in making a rapprochement with France.

But the Directory had misgivings about the Federalists, misgivings fed by their agents in the United States. "You know that their protestations of friendship are false," reported one agent to the Directory in October of 1796, "and that their caresses are faithless. You will recall that in our misfortunes they have insulted and betrayed us and that, if today they pay the Republic a too just tribute of admiration, if they appear to share as friends its success and triumphs, fear alone dictates a language that their hearts deny."[4] France refused to receive Pinckney. She also demanded that Pinckney leave the country or face arrest. Only when the United States acceded to French demands to turn against England would an American minister be received. It was an incredible act of diplomatic discourtesy which shocked the United States.

From The Hague John Quincy Adams wrote to his mother that the discourtesy was a result of France's being "mortified and provoked" at her inability to block a Federalist, John Adams, from being elected President. In Richmond Marshall believed the French guilty of "haughty determination." The next move was up to John Adams, who in March of 1797 had become the second President of the United States.[5]

On May 16, 1797, Adams reported to Congress in a message John Marshall believed was "well adapted to the occasion." It was by all standards brilliant, and it marked the outlines for John Marshall's conduct in the coming year. Adams made clear that he and the United States were aware of the insult. "The refusal on the part of France to receive our minister, is then the denial of a right," he said, "but the refusal to receive him until we have acceded to their demands without the discussion and without investigation, is to treat us neither as allies, nor as friends, nor as a sovereign state."

The President of a nation only eight years under its form of government cannot permit another country to treat it as less than a sovereign state. Listing the French abuses, Adams then told the Congress and the American people that "such attempts ought to be repelled with a decision which shall convince France and the world that we are not a degraded people humiliated under a colonial spirit of fear and sense of inferiority, fitted to be the miserable instruments of foreign influence, and regardless of national honor, character, and interest. . . ." If Adams had ended his speech at this point, the only choices available to the American people would have been either to reject their President or to follow his apparent lead and make war against France. War was the device nations used, and use, to demonstrate they are not "a degraded people" without "national honor, character, and interest." But Adams was a statesman. He then read this paragraph:

> It is my sincere desire, however, that the dispute may be healed. It is my desire, and in this I presume I concur with you and with our constituents, to preserve peace and friendship with all nations; and believing that neither the

honor nor the interest of the United States absolutely forbids the repetition of advances for securing these desirable objects with France, I shall institute a fresh attempt at negotiation, and shall not fail to promote and accelerate an accommodation on terms compatible with the rights, duties, interests, and honor of the nation. If we have committed errors, and these can be demonstrated, we shall be willing to correct them. If we have done injuries, we shall be willing, on conviction, to redress them; and equal measures of justice we have a right to expect from France and every other nation.[6]

If possible, John Adams would solve America's problems by peaceful means. His turn to negotiations, toward a conciliatory approach, did not win him support. He was telling the American people that they were part of a great nation that must not allow itself to be insulted but which would not redress insults by force of arms. The United States would be firm, and strong, and civilized. To an America that lived by the musket his position was not a popular one, and Adams' insistence on peace if at all possible destroyed him politically; he did not win reelection to the presidency and his reputation was tarnished for many years. Still, if he lost a moment's glory, he gained the satisfaction of knowing that no lands were ravaged by his command, no families destroyed, no young men killed to solve a problem that was solvable by other means. And also if he lost the adulation of the majority at that time, he gained a position in history as one who demonstrated—for those courageous enough to see beyond the pressures of the time—that the peacemakers are indeed blessed.

The new attempt at negotiating with France had to be politically acceptable. There was no single person, given the political split in the country, who would be acceptable as a new minister to France. Realizing this, Adams named three persons "to be jointly and severally envoys extraordinary and ministers plenipotentiary to the French Republic." He was remarkably candid in explaining to the Senate why he had selected three. He considered it important, he said, "to engage the confidence of the great portions of the Union" and therefore "thought it expedient to nominate persons of talents and integrity, long known and intrusted in the three great divisions of the Union."[7] He renominated Pinckney to represent the South (Pinckney had remained at The Hague following France's refusal to receive him). From the New England states, he nominated Francis Dana, chief justice of the state of Massachusetts. And from the middle states, Adams nominated John Marshall of Virginia.

The three men were brilliant political choices. Although considered a Federalist, Pinckney had the trust of the Deep South. Dana was not considered a Federalist, although he was popular in a center of Federalism. And Marshall was a highly respected person in Virginia, even though his Federalism was at variance with the political beliefs of most of the people in the state. By bringing a Federalist from the South, a non-Federalist from the North, and Marshall from the Middle States, John Adams seemingly avoided all criticism while weighting the group in favor of the Federalists.

Still, criticism came. The President's wife, Abigail Adams, said the appointments "will be censured by those who make a point of abusing every thing." Marshall, she wrote, was "said to be a very fair and Honorable man, and truly American, a lawyer by profession, against whom no objection is offered, but that he is not Frenchman enough for those who would have sent Jefferson or Madison." Jefferson was concerned about the naming of the man who had been so instrumental in developing the impression that Virginia favored George Washington in the question of the Neutrality Proclamation, and then in the handling of the Genêt matter. "Charles Lee consulted a member from Virginia to know whether Marshall would be agreeable," Jefferson reported to Madison from Philadelphia. "[The member] named you, as more likely to give satisfaction. The answer was, 'Nobody of Mr. Madison's way of thinking will be appointed.' "[8]

Until this time Marshall had refused all appointments to public service that might interfere with his career and the development of a strong financial base for his growing family. Now forty-one years old, this consideration still weighed heavily with him. His first inclination, upon learning that he had been named a minister to France, was to reject the appointment as he had turned down George Washington's appeals to enter public service.

He hesitated, however—"It was the first time in my life that I had ever hesitated concerning the acceptance of office," he recalled years later. He felt "a very deep interest" in the French situation; he had been involved in it actively since 1793 and he had helped create it by his vociferous defense of George Washington. He believed John Adams sincerely wanted to adjust the differences with France peacefully, and that he himself could contribute to that adjustment: "I felt some confidence in the good dispositions which I should carry with me into the negotiation, and in the temperate firmness with which I should aid in the investigations which would be made."

There was another factor, interesting because it expresses

a facet of Marshall's personality which rarely showed. "I will confess," he said, "that the *eclat* which would attend a successful termination of the differences between the two countries had no small influence over a mind in which ambition, though subjected to controul, was not absolutely extinguished."

The determining point, he said later, was that the appointment would be a temporary one, or so he believed: "I should return after a short absence, to my profession, with no diminution of character, and I trusted, with no diminution of practice. My clients would know immediately that I should soon return and I could make arrangements with the gentlemen of the bar which would prevent my business from suffering in the meantime."[9] To Polly, from whom he had never been separated for any lengthy period of time since their marriage fourteen years earlier, he talked of returning home in six or seven months. He could not know that more than a year would pass before he again saw Polly, his children, and the Richmond community.

Perhaps there was another factor. John Marshall was by now an educated, even a cultivated man. He had seen the American communities along the eastern seaboard and traveled far west into the Kentucky region in his youth. But never had he been to Europe. Never had he experienced that cosmopolitan aura of Paris, and perhaps he believed it was time to correct that oversight. Marshall accepted the appointment.

John Adams was particularly pleased at Marshall's acceptance. "Mr. Marshall is a plain man," said the President, "very sensible, cautious, guarded, and learned in the law of nations. I think you will be pleased with him." This was a general opinion. An early biographer of Jefferson, St. George Tucker, wrote of the appointment that "General Marshall of Virginia [was] a gentleman of the federal party, in the first rank at the bar of his native state, and as much loved for his private virtues and unostentatious simplicity of manners, as he was admired for his unrivalled powers of argument."[10]

Francis Dana rejected his appointment. Dana did not enjoy sea travel and was concerned about his ill mother. Adams then asked his "dear friend" Elbridge Gerry to accept the post. Adams said he had expected that Dana would decline the appointment "and should have nominated you at first, if I had not been overruled by the opinions of many gentlemen, that Mr. Dana's experience in this line, and especially his title of chief justice [of Massachusetts] would be great advantages in France, as well as among our people in America."[11] Originally Adams had wanted Gerry on the mission but had decided against it after discussing it with his cabinet members.

[218]

"Gentlemen," he had asked them, "what think you of Mr. Gerry for the mission?"

After waiting a few moments to see if anyone else answered, Secretary of War James McHenry spoke up. "I have served in the Old Congress with Mr. Gerry. If, sir, it was a desirable thing to distract the mission, a fitter person could not perhaps be found," he said. "It is ten to one against his agreeing with his colleagues."

"Mr. Gerry was an honest and firm man," replied the President, "on whom French acts could have no effect."[12]

McHenry proved the more correct.

Gerry was incorruptible personally, an active politician, one of the few delegates to the Constitutional Convention to oppose the finished document, definitely not a Federalist, and a firm friend of France. He may very well have been appointed because of that last characteristic; a shrewd politician such as John Adams must have been aware that criticism was developing of his appointments for there was not one identifiable friend of France among the three ministers. Gerry was so identifiable a friend of France that the Senate almost rejected his nomination. "It is doubtful whether the aristocratic party in [the] Senate will appoint him," said Albert Gallatin. But the Senate did confirm Gerry's appointment on June 22, with six votes against him. "The real reason of the opposition," said Gallatin the next day, "was that Gerry is a doubtful character, not British enough; but the ostensible pretence was that he was so obstinate that he would not make sufficient concessions. . . ."[13]

The appointment of Gerry was particularly pleasing to Thomas Jefferson; at least France would have one firm friend among the three ministers! He and Gerry had known each other for at least thirty years. In 1766, when Jefferson had just finished college, he spent some time in New York City, lodging in the same building with Gerry, then four years out of Harvard. They knew each other in Philadelphia when the young nation was meeting under the Articles of Confederation. In 1784, before Jefferson went to Paris as American minister, he traveled through the various states to familiarize himself with local problems. He was treated particularly well in Boston because of letters of introduction written for him by Gerry.[14]

The day after Gerry's appointment Jefferson sat down and wrote him a letter. This message from the Vice President strongly influenced Gerry's future conduct, and, as a result, the fate of the mission. Jefferson described Gerry's appointment as assuring "a preponderance in the mission sincerely disposed to be at peace with the French government." He continued:

Peace is undoubtedly at present the first object of our
nation. Interest and honor are also national considerations. But interest, duly weighed, is in favor of peace even
at the expense of spoliations past and future; and honor
cannot now be an object. The insults and injuries committed on us by both the belligerent parties, from the beginning of 1793 to this day, and still continuing, cannot
now be wiped off by engaging in war with one of them.
. . . Our countrymen have divided themselves by such
strong affections, to the French and the English, that
nothing will secure us internally but a divorce from both
nations; and this must be the object of every real American, and its attainment is practicable without much self-
denial. But for this, peace is necessary. Be assured of
this, my dear Sir, that if we engage in a war during our
present passions, and our present weakness in some quarters, that our Union runs the greatest risk of not coming
out of that war in the shape in which it enters it. My reliance for our preservation is in your acceptance of this
mission. I know the tender circumstances which will oppose themselves to it. But its duration will be short, and
its reward long. You have it in your power, by accepting
and determining the character of the mission, to secure
the present peace and eternal union of your country.[15]

That was a heavy charge that Jefferson placed on Gerry:
upon him of the three depended the future of the United States.
A few days later John Adams also wrote to Gerry, and also
placed a responsibility upon him: "There is the utmost necessity
of harmony, complaisance, and condescension among the three
envoys, and unanimity is of great importance." Adams conceded
there was division among the American people over France but
did not consider it as significant as did the Vice President. "All
nations are divided," he said. "France is divided; so are Holland,
England, Italy, and Germany. There will ever be parties and
divisions in all nations." He insisted, however, that "our people
will support their government, and so will the French theirs. Not
to expect divisions in a free country would be an absurdity."
And as for peace: "It is my sincere desire that an accommodation may take place, but our national faith, and the honor of our
government, cannot be sacrificed."[16]

In any negotiation between nations there is always danger.
The successful diplomat is the one who understands how much
risk to allow, and the three ministers would split on how much
risk they could and should allow. It would become Pinckney and
Marshall against Gerry as Gerry responded more to Jefferson's

message of peace at any price rather than to that of Adams of peace without sacrificing faith and honor.

Because of Marshall's association with a hard-line approach in Paris, a tradition has grown that Adams did not really wish to conciliate France and appointed Marshall because of his aversion to conciliation. This would be one of the many unfounded charges that developed out of the Marshall trip to Paris; some still hang over his memory. John Marshall left Richmond and the United States with no ill will toward France and with hope for peace. St. George Tucker, later a friendly biographer of Jefferson, was a witness. "In Richmond," he wrote, ". . . I did not hear a single denunciation against the Executive directory of France though I dined with at least fifty Anglo-American patriots at the Eagle on the occasion of Marshal's [sic] intended departure." Tucker, of course, knew Marshall very well and had a long private conversation with him. He was pleased to report "that of all the to'ther side men that I know he appears to me to preserve the best disposition to conciliate and to preserve our pacific relations with France." Tucker was confident that by the time Marshall received his instructions, the political situation would have cooled down. "Like the natural atmosphere of last Saturday," he said, "it had risen above blood heat."[17]

On his way to Philadelphia Marshall stopped at Mount Vernon to visit George Washington. Marshall, as visitors before and since, considered the former President's estate "certainly one of the most delightful places in our country." The two men talked of common problems such as farming. Marshall confirmed the reports that Washington had heard of a new threshing machine. Naturally, they considered the French situation. Washington wrote a letter of introduction for Marshall to Pinckney, still then at The Hague. "You will find [Marshall] well worthy of your friendship and confidence. His is a firm friend, upon true principles to his country, sensible and discreet," the letter said.

From Mount Vernon Marshall went to Alexandria, arriving there on the afternoon of June 24. Polly apparently had been concerned about his traveling, but he wrote her that "All your other fears will be as foundationless as this," and he added: ". . . I shall soon see you again to be the two happiest persons on earth." Polly also had been distressed about seeing him ride off on the beginning of a journey that would take him across the ocean to a foreign land. "Let me hear from you by the time I have been two days at Philadelphia," he wrote her, "and do tell me and tell me truly that the bitterness of parting is over and your mind at rest—that you think of me only to contemplate the pleasure of our meeting and that you will permit nothing to distress you while I am gone."

He told her of the pain he felt at reflecting that "every step I take carries me further and further from what is to me most valuable in this world." He would suppress such sensations, he told his wife, "if I can only be certain that you are so." In the years that followed John Marshall would endure many separations from his wife, particularly after he joined the Supreme Court and had to spend months each year in Washington while his wife, becoming more and more invalid, was restricted to Richmond. He was a romantic, and when he was away from his wife, he poured out his heart to her in long letters that began "My dearest Polly" and show a man forever deeply in love.[18]

Marshall had always been casual in his personal habits, and did not change merely because he had been appointed an American minister. Shortly after arriving in Philadelphia he received a letter from a friend that some papers had slipped out of his pocket and been found and were being held for him in New Castle, and what would he like done with them? Somewhat embarrassed, Marshall sent for the papers. A few days later he wrote Polly directing her to look immediately in his desk for a bundle of deeds which must be filed, immediately, with the clerk of the General Court. He was always losing or misplacing important papers, just as his dress always looked slightly unkempt; casualness was a way of life with him, and he never corrected it.[19]

Marshall had come to Philadelphia from Baltimore by boat, then found himself waiting in the capital city to sail for Europe. Ocean crossings were erratic at the time, and one had to be available when the ship's captain decided to sail. The time passed pleasantly in Philadelphia. He dined one night alone with President Adams and found him "a sensible, plain, candid, good tempered man and was consequently much pleased with him." He passed another evening with Robert Morris and his family. Morris was the investor—a later generation would have called him "wheeler-dealer"—who helped finance the American Revolution. After the war Morris had become a land speculator in the grand fashion, owning unmanageable tracts. At one time he owned more land than any other single individual in the United States. Marshall was connected to him in two ways. There was the marriage of his brother James Markham to Morris' daughter Hestor, called Hetty, and the involvement of the two Marshalls with Morris in purchasing the Fairfax land tract. But Morris had overextended himself and was entering a period of financial difficulties. The Morris house, thought Marshall, "seems to preserve in a great degree its vivacity but it must be discernible that a heavy gloom hangs around them which only their good sense restrains them from showing," although the Morris family was trying to live as elegantly as it always had. Marshall came away from that dinner hopeful that the Morris family could retrieve its affairs. But it never did, and ultimately Robert Morris, whose financial cunning had provided the necessary oil to make the wheels of the American Revolution turn, was sent to a debtors' prison. He was released in 1801, after more than three years in jail, because of passage of a federal law barring the imprisonment of debtors—a law that was passed with the active support of John Marshall when he was a member of the House of Representatives.[20]

On July 4, still waiting for his sailing arrangements to be completed, Marshall dined with a group of Senators and Representatives who were celebrating the anniversary of the signing of the Declaration of Independence. "The company was really a most respectable one and I experienced from them the most flattering attention. I have much reason to be satisfied and pleased with the manner in which I am received here but something is wanting to make me happy," he wrote Polly, continuing: "Had I my dearest wife with me I should be delighted indeed."[21]

The wait became more protracted but was relieved somewhat when he got news from Polly. "I thank heaven that your health is better," he wrote her after receiving her letter. "To know that it is so, will take off one half from the unpleasantness of a voyage over the Atlantic. In your next I promise myself the delight of receiving assurance that your mind has become tranquil and as sprightly as usual." He begged her not to succumb to her melancholy. She apparently had written him that she believed she was pregnant, and he told her: "Remember that if your situation should be as suspected, melancholy may inflict punishment on an innocent for whose sake you ought to preserve a serene and composed mind."[22] Her situation was as she suspected. A son named John Marshall was born on January 13, 1798.

Marshall was becoming irritated at the delay. "The life I lead here does not suit me. I am weary of it," he lamented. "I dine out everyday and am now engaged longer than I hope I shall stay. This dissipated life does not long suit my temper. I like it very well for a day or two but begin to require a frugal repast with good cool water." He preferred being home in Richmond, dining on cold meat, with his daughter Mary "running backwards and forwards over the floor playing the sweet little tricks she is full of" and his sons sitting beside him.[23] He was lonely and impatient.

Three days later, on July 14, he wrote Polly that his ship, the *Grace*, was sailing from Philadelphia the next day, although he himself would travel by land to New Castle and board her there rather than trouble himself with the uncomfortable river and bay passage. He assured Polly that the ship was safe and said he expected to land in Europe six weeks later, at the end of August. "My utmost endeavors will be used to get back by Christmas," he wrote her. "If that should be practicable you will see me; if it should be impracticable, you must not permit your fears in any situation to subdue you." And he added: "If you will only give me this assurance I shall be happy."[24]

He left Philadelphia three days later for New Castle and finally came aboard the *Grace* the morning of July 18. He found his accommodations pleasant: a neat and clean cabin, a berth large enough for his six-foot frame with plenty of sheets. He had no concerns about sleeping, finding that he slept soundly even though on water. The ship was well stocked with cattle and poultry; he had brought along his own porter, wine, and brandy.* He discovered some agreeable fellow passengers and anticipated a pleasant journey. As the *Grace* was in Delaware Bay, he wrote a few last lines to Polly and gave the letter to the ship's pilot to mail. He advised her not to be concerned if news of his arrival in Europe were delayed because "At this season of the year there are such frequent calms as to create fear of a lengthy passage." And he closed by begging her to write him often. "Some of your letters may miscarry," he said, "but some will reach me and my heart can feel until my return no pleasure comparable to what will be given it by a line from you telling me that all remains well."[25]

The letter was done, the pilot was gone, the *Grace* slipped out of the bay into the Atlantic Ocean, and John Marshall was turned toward Europe. Waiting for him in Europe was Charles Cotesworth Pinckney: educated in Europe, widely traveled, urbane, sophisticated. Coming on another ship was Elbridge Gerry: Harvard graduate, officeholder, shrewd politician. In contrast, Marshall's formal education was less than two months at William and Mary, and cosmopolitan would have been an inappropriate description of him. Waiting for these three in Europe was a year of intrigue and adventure. The wiliest and the most venal of men, the most experienced diplomats that Europe had

---

* Marshall's liquor list is interesting. Porter was a modest alcoholic drink, comparable or perhaps even weaker than modern beer. The inclusion of wine and brandy suggests a person who enjoyed libations with his meals, while the absence of harder liquor suggests a person who did not drink excessively.

to offer, would challenge them to a duel of wits, daring, and honor. And it is a tribute to the three Americans that they would emerge the victors, and it is a tribute to their country that ultimately they would be well honored. Gerry became Vice President of the United States. Pinckney was twice the Federalist candidate for President. Marshall, after this point in his career, could never again return to the serenity of private life.

There was a reason for the success these men would have in Europe, a reason that was particularly American. "For us, not for them, has government been instituted here," said Thomas Jefferson at the beginning of the American Revolution. This was not only a demand for a change in the form of government, but a cry that men reach for something beyond themselves, that they serve not only to enrich themselves but also to assist others. This was the theme of the young America, its message to the world: that man finally must honor his God and understand that his purpose is to contribute rather than to take. And when men organize together into a society that theme is implemented through that society's government, meaning that government must be devised to contribute to the well-being of all its citizens and not as a mechanism to take from the many and give to the few. Many criticisms can be made of the American government that was established in the first two decades after the Revolution, but one fact is irrefutable. That government did make possible the well-being of most men. For the first time, when a man earned something, when he earned it fairly, when he earned it in a manner that respected the rights of others, it was his and no one could take it away from him. This was the story of America that other nations in coming years tried to repeat. No matter that many failed, no matter even that America often fails. The example had been set and never again can be erased. Selflessness was the highest political morality. And that quality the three Americans who would rendezvous in Paris had. Among themselves they disagreed, and their accounts of what happened in Paris were in dispute. But it cannot be said of these three men that in the year they spent in France they were concerned with themselves. And that was why they succeeded. For the idea that it is a man's obligation to assist others, and that the purpose of government is to assure the well-being of all men, was the rising tide of the future. Pinckney, Gerry, and Marshall were part of that tide, and it was sweeping them, if not to total victory, at least to personal honor and glory.

The crossing was uneventful, lasting one month and nine days. The wind was gentle and Marshall was rarely seasick, spending most of his time reading. The morning of August 29 the *Grace* arrived at the mouth of the Texel Gat but was stopped from entering the channel leading to the Zuider Zee by a British fleet which had blocked entry for four months. The British ordered the *Grace* to halt and she was boarded by officers from a British frigate. "The Captain of which," Marshall reported, "on learning that a minister from the United States was on board, immediately discharged her, and accompanied the discharge with a very polite tender of any service it might be in his power to render us."[26]

The *Grace* continued on her way. Once in the Texel they saw the Dutch fleet, consisting of more than thirty ships—all ready to sail. The rumor was that with the first favorable wind the Dutch planned to sail out to engage the British. There had been no ships blockading Delaware Bay when Marshall left the United States and no American navy ready to sail out to join battle. The difference between Europe and America was quickly evident.

Marshall was in Amsterdam the night of August 30 and learned that Pinckney was at The Hague. While waiting for traveling accommodations to join Pinckney, he inquired about the political situation in Paris, and what he learned was discomforting. French politics were in a turmoil, with the army threatening to intervene and the French legislature attempting to pass laws blocking military intervention. Whether France intended to continue the war with England also was unknown. The members of the Directory, who held the executive power, wished to continue and expand the war. The legislature, being more representative of the people, wished 'it to end. There was one item of information that had a positive tone to it. Orders had been sent to the different French seaports to expedite overland passage of any American minister, avoiding usual delays. Perhaps if Marshall had understood then what lay in store for him in Paris, he would not have found that news so encouraging.[27]

He arrived at The Hague the evening of September 3 and joined Pinckney. The two men struck up a close friendship immediately, one that lasted for many years. While they waited there for the arrival of Gerry, they heard news of a *coup d'état* in Paris. "The majority of the Directory by one bold decisive stroke has probably prostrated the opposition," Marshall reported in a letter to Secretary of State Pickering. Marshall advised that the coup would have little impact on France's foreign affairs—"The internal commotions of France produce no external weakness, no diminution of exertion against her enemies. Parties ready to devour each other unite in fighting the battles of their country.

In this they display real patriotism." Marshall was surprised that the coup had produced no sense of shock among the diplomatic community at The Hague. "Such are the political tenets of the Republicans of Europe," he wrote, not hiding his sarcasm, "that a seizure by a military force of two members of the executive and of many leading members of the legislature is spoken of as the masterly execution of a well digested plan by which the royalist party is suppressed and unanimity restored to the counsels of France."

Marshall was concerned about the French people, and his concern reveals his humanitarianism; it also challenges the charge that he was anti-French. "The course of this wonderful people sets at defiance all human calculation," he wrote. "Any other nation which could practice and quietly submit to, such a total subversion of principles, would be considered as prepared for and on the eve of experiencing a military despotism. For the sake of human happiness I hope this will not be the lot of France."[28]

A few days later Marshall sent another report. Those members of the Directory and of the legislature arrested had been banished "unheard" without any court trial. "The same violence . . . is practiced . . . on several citizens whose only offence was that they had printed free comments on the conduct of the Directory and of the armies." The military now was ruling Paris, Marshall continued, and "it requires no political knowledge to perceive that while the name of a republic may be preserved its very essence is destroyed." Marshall assured Pickering that he would make no public comment about the coup, realizing that would be undiplomatic. "It is not, however, to be concealed that our differences appear to increase," he said. "All power is now in the undivided possession of those who have directed against us those hostile meaures of which we so justly complain."[29]

That same day Marshall wrote a long letter to George Washington. He described his trip and his arrival, and his meeting with Pinckney. Then he talked of the impact of the European war and the blockade of Holland. Although that country still seemed prosperous, "its decline is visible," he wrote. More than two-thirds of Amsterdam's shipping lay idle in port. In addition, the Dutch people were paying France huge indemnities—"It is supposed that France has by various means drawn from Holland about 60,000,000 of dollars. This has been paid, in addition to the national expenditures, by a population of less than 2,000,-000." Marshall added that "Not even peace can place Holland in her former situation." Marshall always would be with the Federalists in opposing war if it were possible to avoid it. More so than most, he understood why it must be avoided; he had seen the economic destruction of Holland.

Marshall then began recounting the details of the recent coup in Paris. As he had done in his reports to Pickering, he stressed the efforts to still free speech. "The journalists who have ventured to censure the proceedings of a majority of the directory are seized and against about forty of them, a sentence of transportation is pronounced. The press is placed under the superintendence of a police appointed by a dependent on the executive," he wrote. In the United States there shortly would be an effort to silence the press—the Alien and Sedition Laws enacted by Marshall's own party. On that occasion John Marshall opposed his party and attracted the enmity of many of its principal members. His experiences in Paris led him to understand that attacking the press is the first step toward the destruction of free government.

He then wrote of the arrests made in France since the coup. One of those charged was not tried because the military power in France was reluctant to bring him before any judicial body, even one the military believed it could intimidate. So the man was punished without a trial. Troops were stationed where the constitution forbade their presence. The Directory ordered opposition members of the legislature arrested, again contrary to the constitution. Many members of the legislature were seized in their beds despite procedural safeguards that said a man could be arrested only during the day and that his home could not be entered at night.

"Indeed, Sir," Marshall concluded to Washington, "the Constitution has been violated in so many instances that it would require a pamphlet to detail them. The detail would be unnecessary for the great principle seems to be introduced that the government is to be administered according to the will of the armies and not according to the will of the nation."[30] What Marshall was witnessing was the fragility of democracy. The French constitution was being destroyed by people claiming to save it. The law had been made impotent by the gun. And when the destruction was over, few seemed to realize it had happened and fewer seemed to care. The French experience was one of John Marshall's most important teachers. Democracy must be protected, but not with a gun. The use of force to impose a way of life is a contradiction of the word "democracy." Rather, democracy must be protected by law, a law which offers all men the opportunity to solve their problems in a fair and just manner, which offers all men the knowledge that they are protected by a force stronger than the gun. He had experienced that lesson on the Virginia frontier when his father was a justice of the peace. It was reinforced in Europe. As Chief Justice of the United States, he would obey that lesson.

Marshall and Pinckney originally had determined to leave immediately for Paris, but they received information that Elbridge Gerry was on his way and wished them to wait for him at The Hague. "You cannot conceive—yes, you can conceive—how these delays perplex and mortify me," John Marshall wrote to Polly. He spent much time taking long walks, enjoying the city. There was a theater near his lodgings and he frequently attended to watch a French company. "Though I do not understand the language, I am much amused by it." The Hague was a diplomatic center, but he did not find the ministers from other nations friendly. He blamed their hostility on the difficulties between France and the United States—representatives of other nations did not want to get caught in the diplomatic crossfire. It was particularly sad for the Pinckneys, he wrote, because they had a young daughter with them and she had made no friends since the family arrived in The Hague at the beginning of the year.

He told Polly about the coup, that the "moderate men and friends of peace" had been arrested. He said there was some conjecture that this might mean the immediate end of his mission and his quick return home. "A speedy return is my most ardent wish," he told her, "but to have my return expedited by the means I have spoken of is a circumstance so calamitous that I deprecate it as the greatest of evils." In this letter he also told Polly that he probably would not be able to return until the spring, and that he was regretting he had consented to cross the Atlantic. Marshall was a few days shy of his forty-second birthday when he wrote that letter to Polly. The words have a sincere ring to them. John's love for his dearest Polly seemed strong enough to withstand the parting of thousands of miles and of more than a year. Like everything else about the man, this, too, would be tested in Paris.[31]

Pinckney and Marshall anticipated Gerry's ship, the *Union*, would dock at Rotterdam and that he would quickly join them. But they heard from the ship's agent that the *Union* instead was arriving at Le Havre in northern France. They then decided to go on to Paris and meet Gerry there.[32] Passing through Antwerp, Marshall stopped to write another report on the political situation. "We understand that all is now quiet," he wrote on September 22, eighteen days after the coup in Paris. The impact of France's internal chaos was evident in Antwerp. "Today, being the anniversary of the foundation of the republic, was celebrated with great pomp by the military at this place [but] very few indeed of the inhabitants attended the celebration. . . . Since the late revolution a proclamation has been published forbidding any priest to officiate who has not taken the oath preserved by a late order. No priest at Antwerp has taken it and yesterday commenced the suspension of their worship. All the external marks of their religion too with which their streets abound are to be taken down. The distress of the people at this calamity is almost as great as if the town was to be given up to pillage."[33]

That day, September 22, Elbridge Gerry arrived, not at Le Havre, but at The Hague where he was met by William Vans Murray, the American minister there. Vans Murray traveled to Amsterdam with Gerry to bring him up to date and saw him off for Paris on September 24. Vans Murray, by this time experienced in the ways of European diplomacy, anticipated that the three Americans would receive a friendly reception in Paris. Such friendliness, he believed, would be a calculated device to divide the Americans and also to divide the reaction at home. "If they mean to be honest and fair, which God grant, we ought to know it soon; if not, the discovery ought to be made while the spirits and expectations of the people are not fatigued," he wrote to John Quincy Adams.[34]

Pinckney and Marshall arrived in Paris on September 27, and informally notified the Minister of Foreign Affairs the next day that they were in Paris. They suggested that their formal reception be delayed until Gerry joined them. They received an answer, equally informal, that the delay was acceptable. There seemed to be no problems, and protocol had not been violated. Gerry arrived the night of October 4. Immediately the Americans notified the Minister that all three of them now were present in Paris and would like the opportunity of officially so informing him. Following the Minister's directions, an aide from the American ministry appeared at the Foreign Minister's office at noon, October 6, with a letter officially announcing the arrival of the three Americans. The Americans formally requested an audience with the Foreign Minister to present their letters of credence, which identified them as emissaries of the United States. "This move is deemed more respectful than to transmit a copy of the letters of credence," Marshall explained. The Americans assumed they would be received promptly and were therefore surprised to learn from the aide that they would not be received at the Foreign Ministry until October 8, at one o'clock.[35]

The mandate the Americans had from their government was not simple. In his instructions to the three Americans Secretary of State Pickering listed the complaints of the United States against France. He cited aspersions against the American government by French ministers, the refusal to accept Pinckney as the American minister earlier in the year, the various decrees issued by the French Directory against American shipping and property, and the attacks on American commerce and the seizure of American possessions: ". . . and for all these wrongs you will seek redress. . . ." He reminded them, however, that one of their "great" objects was to correct any mistakes the United States might have made. This undoubtedly could have led to trade arrangements with France, giving her benefits similar to those gained by the British in Jay's Treaty. Pickering warned them on their style of behavior. If the French government was determined to frustrate the negotiations, he pointed out, "warmth and harshness" on the part of the three Americans could be made the pretext. He advised them to "unite" as much as possible, calm dignity with simplicity, force of sentiment with mildness of language, and . . . impress an idea of inflexible perseverance, rather than distrust. . . ."[36]

How well the three would do their job was of interest to many nations other than the United States. France was poised between continuing on the path of European conquest or negotiating for peace with her neighbors. Diplomats watched the unfolding relationship with the three Americans to learn if France were serious about negotiating. Robert Liston, the British minister to the United States, was careful to do nothing to disrupt the negotiations in Paris. He had been tempted at first to write a formal letter to the President expressing the hope that the United States and France would enter into no agreement harmful to England. But he was afraid such a letter would be printed in an American newspaper "as an additional evidence of what is asserted with equal insolence and perseverance in the opposition newspapers of every day—that neither the Secretary of State nor the President ever do anything without the previous opinion and advice of the British Minister, [and] I determined to content myself with the verbal representations I had already made."[37]

In France, also, there was considerable speculation about the upcoming negotiations. The French people, like most peoples, did not want war. Their merchants realized, for example, that the United States was developing into one of the great commercial nations of the time. She had forty thousand sailors and more than half a million tonnage of shipping. Her ships docked at almost every port in the world. But the United States— the French merchants ruefully pointed out—barely purchased French goods, while she spent millions of dollars in England. Rather than war or continued difficulties between the two nations, the merchants wanted the difficulties conciliated, a prominent Frenchman sent to the United States as minister to encourage trade, and the depredations by French ships against American commerce ended. Other Frenchmen understood that to embitter the United States was to drive that country to England's assistance, against whom France was then fighting. "To ruin the American commerce," cried one, "is that not to increase the strength of Great Britain?"[38]

An astute Frenchman, Louis-Guillaume Otto, who had spent much time in the United States, wrote in July 1797 a long report to the Directory, "Considerations on the Conduct of the Government of the United States Toward France, 1789–1797," in which he advocated conciliation. He pointed out that the United States could be a dangerous enemy. The French government was advised not to pay too much attention to the fact that the United States appeared to lack a navy. The Americans, he said, are the greatest navigators in the world. They could become pirates, the scourge of French commerce and the means of destroying it. He also advised the French government against believing that the followers of Thomas Jefferson were so pro-French as to sacrifice their own nation to the will of France. "Our agents wished to see only two political parties in the United States, the French party and the English party," he continued, "but there is a middle party, much larger, composed of the most estimable men of the other parties. This party, whose existence we have not even suspected, is the American party which loves its country above all. . . ."[39]

The French knew then that peace and conciliation was the only intelligent and reasonable path for them to follow. Even the letters of credence which the Americans carried to Paris, signed by the President of the United States, spoke of the United States being "desirous of terminating all differences between the United States of America and the French Republic" and assured the French government "of the sincerity of our wishes for the welfare of the French Republic."[40]

The French government at that moment had a rare opportunity for peace and good will. Its people wanted peace and the expansion of their economy. The United States wished peace, and although believing herself grossly insulted, was willing to negotiate and compromise. The other European nations also were interested in the outcome and were doing nothing to ruin the negotiations. What was needed in France, of course, were selfless men who would reject the temptation to achieve personal glory through war and direct their energies to the betterment of their people, selfless men on the order of President John Adams and Vice President Thomas Jefferson of the United States. What was needed were selfless men like Charles Cotesworth Pinckney, John Marshall, and Elbridge Gerry to come to the negotiations with no thought of profit for self.

France, however, did not offer such men.

3

THE FOREIGN MINISTER whom the Americans were to meet the afternoon of October 8 was Monsieur Charles-Maurice de Talleyrand-Périgord. Then beginning a diplomatic career that was to last a half-century, Talleyrand had an uncanny ability to succeed, largely at bettering or saving the fortunes of Talleyrand. He was a defrocked priest who considered politics and diplomacy a means of personal aggrandizement. He was perhaps the most skillful diplomat his nation ever produced, perhaps the most skillful diplomat the world ever knew. And that was his tragedy, that the enormous talent was wasted, used for destruction, when it could have contributed to such benefit for the world. "He was without a code," said one of his biographers. But this was not true. He did have a code, a way of life by which he measured everything he did, including always selling to the highest bidder: his code was Talleyrand.

Talleyrand had been lamed as a child, neglected by his family at birth, thrust into the clergy against his will, and had grown into a man whose ugliness was "colossal." Whether this background had caused his lust for power and his lack of regard for people or institutions, or whether there was some other mysterious motive which made one of the world's most capable men also one of its most corrupt, is unknown. But whatever the cause, it produced a man whose deep gray eyes displayed no emotion, whose face never indicated what went on in his cunning mind—which was almost always the improvement of the fortunes of Monsieur de Talleyrand.[1]

His venality was not unique to his time and place. To secure his position as Minister of Foreign Affairs, he had sought the help of Madame de Staël, a woman with intimate links to the powers in the French Revolutionary government. According to one account, Talleyrand approached her, pleaded for her assistance in getting the ministerial post, and claimed he would kill himself if it were not given him, he was so financially destitute at the time. "If you do not find me the means of securing a remunerative post," he threatened, "I must blow my brains out. . . ." Emotionally stirred, Madame de Staël rushed to her influential friends who held the power of appointment, and cried of Talleyrand: "[I]t is possible that at this moment he no longer exists." Assisted by such drama, Talleyrand won the appointment.[2] Madame de Staël had been willing to help Talleyrand, but kindness had not been her motive. The government was holding two million francs which had once belonged to her father. With Talleyrand's help, once he was appointed, she believed she could persuade the government to give her the money. Talleyrand used the post profitably for himself. He early recognized Napoleon Bonaparte as a great military leader with the potential to rule France and Europe, and he began a systematic program of flattery so that as Napoleon's fortunes rose, he would not forget his old friend Talleyrand. As Foreign Minister, Talleyrand also began his policy of extortion. He expected people to buy him, as the three Americans soon learned, and he expected to buy other people; believing firmly in the corruption of men, he could expect nothing less. And once he came close to money, he could never do without it. He gambled, dabbled in stocks, responded to any proposition that would make him money no matter how much it compromised his official position. "He loves little presents —*douceurs*, as he terms them—and he himself admits to us that in the course of his diplomatic career he has received sixty millions from foreign powers," said one of his biographers toward the end of Talleyrand's life.[3]

That Talleyrand's venality was only in keeping with the level of political morality in Europe at the time perhaps explains why Europe was entering into more than a century of chaos, war, and revolution; a time when Europeans sought to leave their homelands for the New World.

Talleyrand himself had been to the United States, in the early 1790s when he had been in political exile for a short period. His perception even then was great. Some years later a French lady met him at a Paris ball. "You have not forgotten, Prince, the ball you and I were at together in Philadelphia?" she asked him. "Ah, no!" Talleyrand replied. There was a slight shrug to his shoulders, highlighting the sneer on his face, as he continued: "The Americans are a hospitable people, and are destined to be a great nation—*mais leur luxe est affreux!*"[4]

Such was the Foreign Minister the Americans were to see at one o'clock the afternoon of October 8.

They arrived at the proper time, but Talleyrand was not waiting for them. The Americans were informed that the Foreign Minister was at the Directory and wished them to return at three. The Americans did so. They were then informed that Talleyrand was with the Portuguese minister and would they be so kind as to wait a few moments. They waited.

Finally, at ten minutes past three they were ushered into the office of Talleyrand. If there had been any effort to offend or condescend by delaying the meeting, it did not show in Talleyrand's manner, which Marshall considered "polite and easy." The Americans spoke in English, and Talleyrand spoke in French, although his English was excellent when he chose to use it. The meeting began with Pinckney presenting Talleyrand with copies of the letters of credence given to the three Americans by their President. Talleyrand accepted them, and said that the Directory required a report from him on the relations existing then between France and the United States. When the report was done, "in two or three days," the Americans would be given further information about their future in France.

The Americans asked for cards of hospitality, and Talleyrand immediately called in his secretary and directed him to make them out. "The residue of the conversation which continued about fifteen minutes," said Marshall, "was perfectly unimportant." The Americans were quite pleased with the first session, particularly because they had been led to believe that Talleyrand was grossly anti-American. "Mr. Talleyrand, the minister, has been most misrepresented in the United States, his conduct having been very different from what was stated," Elbridge Gerry wrote to his wife the next day. "He sent us this day cards of hospitality and is to inform us in a few days what steps are next to be taken."

So disarming had Talleyrand been that apparently not one of the three Americans noticed that he had made no firm offer to present them to the Directory, the first step necessary in their opening negotiations with France. Charles Cotesworth Pinckney's wife Mary wrote in a letter home that "no day is yet appointed for [the three Americans] to be received by the directory." The tone of the letter indicated that her husband believed it would be only a matter of time. It would be a matter of a great deal of time.[5]

Three days after the Americans had met with Talleyrand an American named Church stopped by to see Elbridge Gerry. Not finding Gerry in, Church chatted with John Marshall. Church presented himself as a former American consul in Lisbon, as one desirous of seeing the difficulties between France and the United States at an end, and then said he had heard something of importance from someone in a position to have such knowledge authoritatively.

The visit of Church began a series of confrontations between the Americans on one side and people who knew someone in a position to know something on the other. These may have been the most bizarre negotiations in the history of diplomacy, a dance in which the two sides never moved from their original positions but in which intermediaries, often without names, moved between them.

Church said he had just talked with a "Mr. Payne," who was putting forth a general plan which, if the Directory adopted it, would be extremely advantageous to the United States. This "Mr. Payne" was Tom Paine whose pamphlets had given voice to much of the American passion in the Revolution but who had since fallen into disgrace among the Federalists for his radical politics. Church then advised the Americans not to press their own case too hard at that particular moment, while the Paine plan was before the Directory. The present is a most unfavorable moment, Church told Marshall, and if you advance hastily, all will probably be lost. What is Paine's plan? asked Marshall. Church declined to answer, saying he was not at liberty to communicate the details of the plan. Be assured, Church insisted, your true policy is to wait for events. Marshall answered that he, Pinckney, and Gerry had brought with them hopes for a reconciliation with France, that he recognized that the Directory could not be hurried to consider the Paine plan or to do anything else, but that the Americans also were concerned about the critical situation of American commerce and could not be casual about it.

Later that night, after Church had left, the three Americans received a letter from Paine describing his plan. Basically it called for an unarmed neutrality. The three Americans each reacted differently, and this first breach indicated how they would split in the coming months. John Marshall's origins were of the frontier where a man does not take insult lightly, and he considered the Paine letter an insult. He believed it had been sent with the knowledge of the Directory and that any response by the Americans would also go to the French government. He argued with Gerry and Pinckney that nothing could be worse than to lead the French government to believe that the United States would risk her future on an unarmed neutrality with France. To commence on such a path, Marshall continued, would only produce more irritation on the part of the French when they realized that the United States in the end would not accept an unarmed neutrality. Also, the Paine letter included some negative remarks about the United States which, said Marshall, "ought to be received in a manner which would mark our dis-approbation of them."

Elbridge Gerry was of a contrary opinion. He pointed out that Paine was in favor with the Directory, and that by dealing with him the three Americans might find out what the Directory intended as far as the United States was concerned. Gerry also said he was worried that by refusing to deal with Paine, the Americans might be giving France the opportunity to accuse the United States of being hostile to France, and then declare war. Gerry was, of course, remembering his letter from Jefferson and its plea for peace at almost any price.

Pinckney had been designated the leader of the diplomatic trio, and he performed that role. Cutting away from both the emotional outbursts of Marshall and the overcautiousness of Gerry, he produced a polite reply that satisfied both men. Marshall wanted to make one additional alteration in the reply, to change "thankful for" to "properly attentive to." This was only a minor change but one suggesting a more aloof tone. Gerry would not agree to it, however, and Marshall did not force the issue.[6]

By Saturday, October 14, six days had elapsed since the Americans had met with Talleyrand, and still they had heard nothing from him. But that day they did receive a curious communication, again from someone in a position to know something. This was Monsieur Osmond, the private and confidential secretary to Talleyrand. He met with Major Mountflorence, a member of the American ministry. According to Osmond, the Directory was "greatly exasperated" at the speech of John Adams in May, in which Adams had spoken sharply of French insults to the United States and then had said he hoped to settle the matter by negotiations. The Directory, again according to Osmond, wanted an explanation from the three American ministers. The particular parts which had so disturbed the Directory were not listed. The two men met again the same day and Osmond had more tidbits. The Americans could not expect the Directory to receive them formally until after the negotiations were finished. According to Osmond, some person would be appointed to deal with the Americans, and he would report to Osmond, who would be in charge of the negotiations. The intention of such a procedure was obvious. The Americans were being asked to buy formal acceptance with negotiations most favorable to the French; they would not be dealt with as equals. Mountflorence conveyed the information to Pinckney, and the three American ministers held a conference together that night. The three assumed that Talleyrand was the original source of the information, that Osmond obviously had been carrying out orders. But since the information had come to them in a manner not requiring an answer, they decided to do nothing about it.[7]

The Americans were becoming increasingly concerned about the silence with which they were being received. While they were sitting in Paris, they knew, French ships continued to attack American commerce. On Sunday, October 15, Marshall urged that within a few days the Americans send a message to Talleyrand asking that all further proceedings against American vessels be suspended. "In this I would not be precipitate," Marshall told the other two men, "but we have already permitted much time to pass away [that] we could not now be charged with precipitation. . . . France would be content that we should remain silent, so long as the season for privateering lasts. The existing state of things is to France the most beneficial and the most desirable, but to America it is ruinous." Again, Elbridge Gerry disagreed with Marshall. He was concerned about irritating the French government and giving it an excuse to declare war against the United States.

"But in the address I propose," Marshall answered, "I would say nothing which could give umbrage, and if, as it is to be feared, France is determined to be offended, she may quarrel with our answer to any proposition she may make or even with our silence."

Pinckney this time apparently agreed with Marshall, but neither he nor Marshall felt they wanted to act without Gerry. "We are restrained by a high respect for his opinions," Marshall wrote in his diary that night, "and by a wish to preserve unanimity in every thing."[8]

So far the French had merely been softening up the Americans, treating them disdainfully in hopes of making them nervous and fearful, feeling them out with suggestions of actions to take or not to take. Now, after the Americans had been in Paris two weeks, the French were ready to get down to what a later generation would call the nitty-gritty. France was for sale by its government. That government wanted to know whether or not the United States was buying.

The morning of Wednesday, October 18, a man Pinckney knew came by and said that in Paris was a Mr. Hottinguer, who wished to meet with Pinckney. Hottinguer was reputed to be a man of considerable credit and reputation, Pinckney's acquaintance said, and the Americans could rely on him.

That evening Hottinguer came to see Pinckney. The two men chatted for a few minutes, and then Hottinguer leaned forward to whisper. He had, he said, a message from Talleyrand to deliver at Pinckney's convenience. Pinckney immediately rose and led Hottinguer into another room where they were alone. Hottinguer began slowly, explaining that he was charged with a business at which he was a novice. He knew Talleyrand, he said, and was certain that the Foreign Minister had a high regard for the United States and its citizens and very much wished a reconciliation. Talleyrand had a plan, Hottinguer continued, which it was hoped would bring about such a reconciliation.

Pinckney said he would be happy to hear it. This was the American's first mistake: agreeing to talk with intermediaries rather than insisting on talking only to Talleyrand.

Hottinguer then referred to President Adams' speech, and said that at least two members of the Directory were irritated by it and wanted amends made before the Americans would be formally received. Then came an even more crucial point. A sum of money was required, Hottinguer said, for the pockets of the Directory members and the Ministers which would be distributed by Talleyrand. Also, a loan from the United States to France was required. If the Americans acceded to these terms, Hottinguer continued, then Talleyrand had no doubt that the differences between the two nations would be accommodated.

Pinckney said nothing at that moment of his reactions. Rather, he probed Hottinguer further. But no, Hottinguer said, he did not know which passages had so offended the Directory. And no, he could not say with any specificity how much of a loan was needed. But the *douceur*—the sweetener, the bribe—must be about 50,000 pounds sterling.

Pinckney held his temper. Since he and his fellow ministers had arrived in Paris, he told Hottinguer, they had been insulted and treated with disrespect. The three of them earnestly wished for peace and reconciliation with France, and they had the power to achieve those ends, on honorable terms. As for this communication Hottinguer had just given him, Pinckney said there would be no response without discussion between him and his colleagues despite Pinckney's own strong personal reaction.

The three Americans considered it that night, after Hottinguer had left, and again the next morning. Marshall was aghast at the proposition. No mention had been made of the American property that the French had confiscated, except the possibility that part of the loan made by the United States might be used to satisfy its own citizens. Acquiescing to these demands, said Marshall, meant the "absolute surrender of the independence of the United States." Apparently unspoken in the discussion was the realization that England, still at war with France, would consider a substantial United States loan to France as an act of war against England. Marshall also insisted that countenancing the terms presented by Hottinguer would encourage the French to make even more impossible demands and destroy any opportunity for a settlement on legitimate lines. "I therefore thought we ought so soon as we could obtain the whole information to treat the terms as inadmissible." Pinckney agreed with Marshall that the terms could not be considered as the basis for negotiation, but did not express himself as strongly. Gerry continued to be concerned about the possibility of war and insisted that a reply along the lines of those suggested by Marshall would lead to war. He argued that it was impossible to understand exactly what the terms were on the basis of the oral communication. The final decision was that Pinckney would see Hottinguer again to gather fuller details and also to request that Hottinguer meet all three of them together.

Pinckney sought out Hottinguer, and the agreement was that Hottinguer would come at six o'clock that evening with the details of the proposition on paper. The paper Hottinguer left with the Americans that night began with an offer that "a person who possesses the confidence of the Directory" would give his services to help effect a reconciliation between the United States and France; the Americans understood this person to be Talleyrand. In return, the President's speech to Congress would be given "a softening turn." The difficulties caused by charges that France was attacking and confiscating American property would be solved by a group of commissioners, chosen by both nations. Any payments the French were to make, as decided by these commissioners, "are to be advanced by the American government itself." Also, the French government wanted a loan from the United States but was agreeable to the loan being given in a manner so that it "should not give any jealousy to the English government, nor hurt the neutrality of the United States." The loan then would be "masked" by the United States' agreement to advance payments for debts contracted by agents of the French with American citizens.

"There shall also be first taken from this loan," the Hottinguer paper said, "certain sums for the purpose of making the customary distributions in diplomatic affairs."

Hottinguer was still vague about details. He did not know which sections of Adams' speech were objected to. Nor could he specify the amount of the loan, although at least one day had elapsed since Pinckney had first directed these questions to him. The amount of the *douceur* held firm at 50,000 pounds sterling, however. The next step was for Hottinguer to find the answers to those questions and report to the three Americans. But the following day, the morning of October 20, Hottinguer came by to say that his source of information now was willing to meet the Americans face to face and would like to come by that evening. He explained that his source was a Mr. Bellamy, a resident of Hamburg, Germany, now visiting in Paris, who was a close friend of Talleyrand's.

That day the three Americans again discussed the mess they found themselves in. Marshall said the propositions were totally unacceptable and again argued that even to consider them meant cutting off any hope of serious negotiations along lines more acceptable to the United States. Pinckney agreed. But Gerry again argued against what he termed precipitous action, saying that they could not completely understand the scope and object of the propositions. He suggested that rather than rejecting them, they lay the terms before the government in Philadelphia.

At this point the differences between the three ministers had solidified; they were repeating themselves. Gerry would do nothing that might give the French an opportunity to claim that the Americans had broken off the negotiations, despite any pleas from Marshall and Pinckney. Marshall and Pinckney would do nothing that they considered debased the integrity and independence of the United States. They did not want war, but their country would emerge from the negotiations with honor.

Hottinguer arrived at seven o'clock that night with Bellamy, whom he introduced as a confidant of Talleyrand's. As Hottinguer had done, Bellamy began by stating that Talleyrand had warm feelings for the United States stemming from the many kindnesses he had been shown when he was there. Talleyrand wished to repay those kindnesses but was blocked, Bellamy said, because the Directory, irritated at President Adams' speech, refused to receive the Americans and instructed Talleyrand also not to have any formal communication with them. This was the second notice that they would not be formally received. Talleyrand, however, had authorized Bellamy to lay before the Americans certain propositions and to receive the Americans' answer. If the Americans would consider them as the basis of the proposed negotiation, Bellamy continued, Talleyrand would intercede with the Directory to persuade that body to recognize the Americans. Bellamy added that he, Bellamy, was visiting them without any official capacity and only as a favor to Talleyrand and as a friend to the United States.

Bellamy then produced a French translation of President Adams' speech with the parts marked which the Directory considered objectionable. Bellamy spent much time talking about the resentment the speech had produced among the members of the Directory, and then he brought out a list of demands. Basically these added up to the three American ministers disavowing the President's speech and claiming that the French had done nothing to offend the United States. The Americans were to say that the comments about French depredations in Adams' speech did not refer to actions by the French government or by agents of that government. Not only was this objectionable but it was impossible; ministers appointed by the President of the United States can hardly declare him wrong publicly—particularly when they believe him right.

Also, France and the United States were to enter a new commercial relationship which would place France on the same footing as England; this provision the Americans probably would have been willing to agree to. Another provision was a secret loan, the amount still to be determined, and "it would be endeavoured to consult the convenience of the United States with respect to the best method of preventing its publicity." Bellamy then again referred to the insult felt by the members of the Directory at the President's speech and said there must be satisfaction.

"But, gentlemen," he said, "I will not disguise from you, that this satisfaction being made, the essential part of the treaty remains to be adjusted: *Il faut de l'argent—il faut beaucoup d'argent.*" The three Americans understood the meaning of his words perfectly: "You must pay money. You must pay a great deal of money." But they understood the reference to be to the loan, not the *douceur* or bribe. Of that little was said. "That being completely understood, on all sides, to be required for the officers of government, and therefore needing no further explanation," according to the official report of the three Americans. The meeting ended at nine-thirty.

After Hottinguer and Bellamy had left, the three Americans again discussed their future course of conduct. Marshall maintained his original position, that the procedure was totally improper and carrying on a clandestine dialogue with persons who had no evidence that they were in reality authorized to negotiate harmed the interests of the United States. Here he touched a vital point. The Americans could not know whether Hottinguer and Bellamy were a couple of international confidence men attempting to hoodwink them and obtain some money from them or whether, in fact, they did speak for Talleyrand. French society then was so corrupt that either explanation was possible.

Pinckney again agreed with Marshall, but Gerry, Marshall recorded in his diary, "was quite of a contrary opinion and the old beaten ground about precipitation, etc., was trodden once again." They had scheduled a meeting the next morning, October 21, at nine o'clock with Hottinguer and Bellamy, and before the three Americans retired that night, they tentatively agreed to end the secret talks abruptly the next morning.[9]

But the next morning the Americans were led on again. Hottinguer arrived at the appointed time, but Bellamy did not bustle in until ten, explaining that he had spent the morning with Talleyrand. Again he talked of the Directory's anger at the President's speech which must be appeased unless, he continued, the Americans could find some other way of salving the wounds of the members of the Directory. The Americans let that pass for a few moments, then returned to it. What did Bellamy mean by some other way?

The Americans had come to Paris with open minds and open hearts. They anticipated skillful and hard negotiations, but they had not anticipated what they were experiencing. Their second mistake was in not realizing they were being victimized. Whether Talleyrand was part of the scheme could not then be known because the type of arrangement being offered is never written on paper and the perpetrators always expect to be disavowed, as the participants in this scheme were later disavowed by Talleyrand. But it was a classic confidence game, with or without Talleyrand's involvement, and the object was to bilk money from the United States.

Bellamy told the Americans that he had no authorization to state any other ways to salve the hurt feelings of the Directory members. You, he said to the Americans, must search for them and propose them yourselves.

Being novices at this kind of dealing, the Americans apparently did not pick up Bellamy's intention quickly enough for he hurried on. If, however, he continued, the Americans were to ask his private opinion, he would make a suggestion.

What was it?

"Money," he told the Americans.

If the Americans wanted him to say how much, he would be happy to do that. They told him to proceed. The deal would be, Bellamy explained, that the United States would advance to France 32 million Dutch florins. Once the war was over, Holland might be persuaded to repay the United States the money, so that the United States would ultimately lose nothing.

The Americans knew this new figure was in addition to the as yet unspecified loan, but was it also, they asked, in addition to the 50,000-pound *douceur*? Bellamy answered affirmatively.

The three Americans withdrew. Away from Hottinguer and Bellamy, they resumed their argument over what formal reaction they should have. Gerry wanted the Americans to say that they would take the propositions under consideration. Marshall exploded. "I improperly interrupted him," is how Marshall himself phrased it. Marshall said he would not consent to any such proposition. As far as he was concerned, the matter was ended and "I would not permit it to be supposed longer that we could deliberate on such propositions as were made to us." Pinckney agreed with Marshall, but Gerry continued to haggle. Finally, to achieve unanimity and to placate Gerry, Marshall agreed that he would return to the United States to inquire of the government whether a loan to France could be negotiated. The condition Marshall insisted on, however, was that all depredations by the French on American commerce should cease while he was away. Gerry agreed to this, and Marshall wrote a memorandum. Gerry then considered Marshall's memorandum too strong and himself wrote the one that was used. One can imagine the tone of Marshall's, as Gerry's memorandum cannot be described as obsequious. It reads:

> Our powers respecting a treaty are ample: but the proposition of a loan in the form of Dutch inscriptions, or in any other form, is not within the limits of our instructions; upon this point therefore the government must be consulted: one of the American ministers will, for the purpose, forthwith embark for America: provided the Directory will suspend all further captures on American vessels, and will suspend proceedings on those already captured, as well where they have been already condemned, as where the decisions have not yet been rendered: and that where the sales have been made, but the money not yet received by the captors, it shall not be paid until the preliminary questions, proposed to the ministers of the United States, be discussed and decided.

The Gerry memorandum was read to Bellamy and he was told he could copy it if he chose. He refused to. The Americans did not understand, he said. They treated the money proposition —the loan in the form of the Dutch florins—as coming from the Directory. Actually, he insisted, it had come neither from the Directory nor from Talleyrand but was only his own personal suggestion. The Americans informed Bellamy that they did not believe him. "We had believed [Hottinguer and Bellamy] when they said they were from the minister, and had conversed with them in like manner, as if we were conversing with M. Talleyrand himself; and that we could not consider any suggestion [Bellamy] had made, as not having been previously approved of" is the Americans' account of their reply.

They argued for a few moments and Bellamy blurted out that if the Americans would not come up with the 32 million florins, the Directory would insist on the formal apologies. The Americans replied that they could not be responsible for the Directory's action, "it was for the Directory to determine what course its own honour and the interests of France required it to pursue." The Americans also said that it was for them "to guard the interests and honour of our country."

Bellamy then returned to the possibilities of a disavowal of President Adams' speech. The answer was that it could not be done and that the Americans did not consider that the French really expected the disavowals to be forthcoming but had only suggested them as openers for the real negotiations.

Bellamy told the Americans they would never be received, and the Americans saw him shudder at what he considered the consequences. The Americans replied that their country had made every possible effort to remain on friendly terms with France, and was still trying. If France did not respond to these overtures, but made war on the United States, they said, "nothing remained for us, but to regret the unavoidable necessity of defending ourselves." No confidence game can succeed unless the object of the game, the people to be fleeced, can be frightened. This confidence game did not succeed because Charles Cotesworth Pinckney, John Marshall, and Elbridge Gerry did not frighten.

Hottinguer and Bellamy left. All five men expressed their mutual respect, and the Americans agreed to protect Hottinguer and Bellamy by not identifying them in their dispatches. Hottinguer then became "X" and Bellamy became "Y."[10]

It seemed that the game had been played out. Marshall wrote to William Vans Murray that he anticipated being ordered out of France shortly and asked Vans Murray to stop his subscription to the Leyden *Gazette*.[11] Marshall also wrote to Washington, and in his letter is a resigned note of despair at his failure: "The captures of our vessels seem to be only limited by the ability of capture [and] that ability is increasing. . . ." Marshall had promised Washington to write out his observations and he did so in this lengthy letter, dated October 24, 1797. He obviously was traveling through the countryside and noted that the farms were productive despite the war. "The whole earth appears to be in cultivation and the harvests of the present year appear to be as productive as the fields which yield them are extensive," he wrote. The manufacturing resources of France had not fared as well—"War has been made upon the great manufacturing towns and they are in a considerable degree destroyed." He noted that English manufactured goods still were flowing into France despite the war between the two nations. Once the war ended, he said, France would have to import a considerable number of goods. Marshall thought that France "can take from America tobacco and raw cotton [and] she can supply us with wines, brandies, and silks"—if peace comes.

Because of his own background, Marshall was particularly interested in what was happening to property in France. He had been a member of a frontier family which realized that property —land—was the means of gaining security and passing it on to one's children, and that law was the means of protecting that property. In France much land had been nationalized. "It is true," Marshall wrote George Washington, "that much of this property formerly belonged to the church but it is also true that much of it belonged to those who have fallen under the guillotine or have been termed emigrants. Among the emigrants are many whose attachments to their country has never been shaken and what is remarkable, among them are many who were never out of France." Being a lawyer, Marshall was interested in how the law deprived these persons of their land.

"Any two persons," he wrote, "no matter what their reputation, may, to some authority, I believe the municipality of the district, write and subscribe against any person whatever a charge, that such person is an emigrant, on receipt of which the person so charged is without further investigation inscribed on the list of emigrants." This meant his land could be confiscated. The law did not appear to provide any defense. "If the person so inscribed be afterwards apprehended while his name remains on the list," Marshall continued, "the trial, as I understand, is not of the fact of emigration but of the identity of the person, and if his identity be established, he is instantly fusilleered." Marshall also learned that the law is "either rigidly executed or permitted to be relaxed, as the occasion or temper of the times may direct." To John Marshall, a man of the law, such arbitrary procedures were incredible. Again the fragility of democracy was manifesting itself. In later years he would become the staunch defender of property. On the frontier and then in France he had learned why it must be defended.

Marshall did not conclude his letter to Washington on a

very hopeful note. "At present," he said, "[the French govern-ment] seems to me to be radically hostile to our country." He wished it were otherwise, "but to do so I must shut my eyes on every object which presents itself to them, and fabricate in my own mind nonexisting things, to be substituted for realities, and to form the basis of my creed." In Marshall's opinion, "the Atlantic only can save us, and that no consideration will be sufficiently powerful to check the extremities to which the tem-per of this government will carry it, but an apprehension that we may be thrown into the arms of Britain."[12]

Although Marshall believed the diplomatic game France had been playing with them was done, actually it was not. The evening of October 26 in Paris peace was announced between France and Austria, on terms strengthening the militarists in the French government. The next day about noon, "X"—Hottin-guer—visited the Americans. The Directory had been waiting for an answer to the proposition made earlier "and would take a decided course with regard to America if we could not soften them." Pinckney replied that the Americans had already given their answer. Hottinguer then mentioned the peace with Austria, the implication being that France was now much stronger. Pinckney replied that this made no difference. Hottinguer stopped implying. He came right out and said that because of the peace with Austria, the Directory had determined that all nations either would help France or be considered France's enemies. There would be no neutrals. Pinckney responded that there still would be no change.

Gerry reminded Hottinguer that the American ministers had no power to negotiate a loan and for them to arrange a loan would be without meaning "and would only deceive France and expose ourselves."

Hottinguer again mentioned the military power of France and spoke of war, but the Americans were not to be moved by threats. Pinckney then said that America's present situation was worse than a war; unprotected American ships were being plundered. Then he added that if war was declared, the United States would seek to protect her ships. Hottinguer caught the significance of the remark immediately, saying he hoped the United States would not seek a military alliance with England. Pinckney's answer indicated how well he had learned diplomacy. He said he hoped also that the United States would not join with England. He pointed out that he, Marshall, and Gerry had fought in the American Revolution against England and still did not consider England a friend. But "if France should attack us,"

Pinckney said, "we must seek the best means of self defense." France could not ignore the possibility of an Anglo-American alliance.

Hottinguer became desperate. "Gentlemen," he said, "you do not speak to the point. It is money—it is expected that you will offer money."

Pinckney replied that the three Americans had spoken very explicitly to that point.

"No," Hottinguer insisted, "you have not. What is your answer?"

"It is no," said Pinckney. "No. Not a sixpence."

Hottinguer again spoke of the danger of war between France and the United States. Marshall asked if there were not some person within the French government to whom they could appeal. Hottinguer scoffed at the suggestion. The men in power in France, he said, disregarded the Americans' claims and considered themselves invulnerable to criticism from the Americans.

The conduct of the French government, the Americans replied, was such "as to leave us much reason to fear that should we give the money it would effect no good purpose and would not produce a just mode of thinking with respect to us."

The emissary pushed harder. The Americans, he said, should compare the payment to money given to a lawyer to argue a case. The lawyer takes the money but does not guarantee success. This time it was the Americans' turn to scoff. A lawyer is paid, they said, for his efforts, not for his judgments—because he cannot render judgments, but the Directory can. "It had only to order that no more American vessels should be seized and to direct those now in custody to be restored," the Americans said.

Hottinguer then explained why he believed this would not happen. Some members of the Directory, he said, were not interested in ending the French attacks on American shipping; one Directory member, no matter how much the Americans paid, for example, would accept no American money, he said. Pinckney replied that he understood that particular member was bribed by the men who owned the privateers. Hottinguer nodded his head in agreement.

Then he raised a point which has been raised about these negotiations since. You Americans, he said, pay money to Algeria and to the American Indians in order to assure peace. Why not to France? Pinckney and Gerry joined in explaining to him that in those treaties the question of money was an integral part of the treaty. It was known. It was open. It was aboveboard. Hottinguer was shocked that the Americans had not realized that money would be involved in dealing with France. He declared there was not an American in Paris who could not have provided them with the correct information.

Hamburg and other European states purchased peace from France, Hottinguer continued, and it was equally in the interest of the United States to do so. Again he referred to France's military power. The Americans acknowledged that they could not deny France's superior military power nor could they deny their own concern at the prospects of war. But, while they wished the two nations to be friends, it was more important that the United States maintain its independence. The United States, they said, had taken a neutral position, as it had a right to. To lend money to France was, in effect, to surrender that neutrality and to participate in the war. To lend the money under "the lash and coercion" of France was "to relinquish the government of ourselves and to submit to a foreign government imposed upon us by force."

The Americans knew, of course, that if they acceded to France on this occasion, their country would become the victim of any nation that coveted part of the North American continent or wanted to raise money by molesting American ships. Peace at any price would not buy security. They vowed to Hottinguer that they and their fellow Americans would make "at least one manly struggle" before they would permit that to happen.

Nor did the Americans accept comparison with European states which had agreed to pay France for peace. The European nations could not maintain their independence, being so close geographically to the superior power of France. In contrast, argued the Americans, the United States was a great and a powerful nation distant from Europe. She was able to preserve her independence. If she were not willing to do so, said the Americans, then she deserved to lose it.

The accounts of this meeting, the formal report by the American ministers and John Marshall's private diary, which is almost identical to the formal report, do not even suggest the drama of this moment. Three middle-aged Americans, practically alone in Paris, were being threatened by the most powerful nation in the world. Their country might be destroyed. They might be destroyed. Still, they stood strong, unbending. Much was involved for them: their reputations, their honor, their own sense of integrity. But if these were all that mattered that day in Paris, the Americans would have done better to have agreed to spending dollars for peace. They were, however, making their stand for something much more valuable. This was the opportunity for the people of the United States to live their lives as they wished without having to pay obeisance to the mistakes of Europe, to the travesties of justice that the Americans had already witnessed in Europe, to the tradition of power to the few, to the habit of war. They said as much to Hottinguer. France and Britain had been at war for fifty years of the past one hundred and probably would be at war for fifty years of the next hundred, they continued, and added that America had neither the desire nor the intent to waste herself in those wars. If she did not make her stand at this point, they said, the United States could not anticipate being allowed to remain a neutral in any future European war.

Hottinguer tried another approach, and this also is one that has since been raised in historical critiques of this affair. France had loaned the American colonies money in their war, he said, why should not the United States return the courtesy? Gerry replied that the situations were not comparable. The American colonies, he said, had sought a loan but France was at liberty to grant or refuse it. In contrast, he continued, France was demanding that this loan be granted.

Pinckney and Marshall then joined in. They pointed out that France had loaned the money to America for France's own national interests. The purpose of that money had been to harm England, France's ancient and bitter enemy. A loan by the United States would not serve any American purpose, they said, but would only allow France to extend her conquests.

The meeting had gone on for two hours, with Hottinguer pressing the matter of money in every way he could think of. Finally, realizing that the Americans were as adamant as they sounded, he gave up. He even conceded that he did not blame them for the position they took and promised to pass along their answers to either Mr. Bellamy or directly to Talleyrand. At the end he told the Americans that while he acknowledged their position was proper, he believed that they would be forced to change it.[13]

The same day of that meeting, a Monsieur Hauteval had also visited Gerry. Hauteval had seen Talleyrand and reported Talleyrand's surprise that the Americans had not come to see him in their private capacities even though they could not meet on a diplomatic level. Hauteval returned the next day and met with the three Americans, apparently making a strong impression. In his journal Marshall wrote that Hauteval "is sincerely solicitous of preserving peace."[14] This was one of the few judgments about individuals he made that events proved wrong. Prior to the French Revolution, when nobility still ruled, Hauteval was known as "Monsieur le Comte d'Hauteval." Came the Revolution and

Hauteval was quick to dissociate himself from the nobility. John Quincy Adams is a witness. "I was present at the performance of Mass after the head of Louis XVI was cut off," he wrote, "at which the said Hauteval thundered out the 'Dominie salvum fac regem' with as much devotion and enthusiasm, as if he had been ready to suffer martyrdom for the cause." The next Quincy Adams heard of Hauteval was in 1796 when Hauteval was trying to get appointed as French minister to the United States but could not raise sufficient funds to buy the position. He was as venal a man as Talleyrand.[15] He became the "Z" in this affair.

In response to Hauteval's news that Talleyrand wished to meet the Americans informally, Pinckney and Marshall said the situation had deteriorated to such a point that they did not believe they could visit Talleyrand with propriety unless he specifically requested them to come. Elbridge Gerry, however, had previously known Talleyrand—only slightly—in Boston, and believed that acquaintanceship allowed him to call on the minister. Gerry still remembered Jefferson's admonition to him that peace must be secured at almost any price.

The next day Gerry and Hauteval paid a call on Talleyrand. He was meeting with the Directory and made a formal appointment for Gerry on October 28 at six-thirty.

Gerry was there at six-thirty but was not ushered into Talleyrand's presence for another hour. The French minister came directly to the point. The Directory had passed a decree demanding explanations for President Adams' speech and also reparations. Talleyrand said that the talked-about loan could block the decree—the enforcement of such an order by the Directory could result in either the arrest of the three Americans or their exposure to physical danger. During this meeting Gerry had been speaking in English which Hauteval translated into French for Talleyrand, and Talleyrand spoke in French which Hauteval translated into English for Gerry. But now Gerry was angry. He turned directly to Talleyrand and spoke in English, knowing full well that Talleyrand understood the language. Bluntly he told Talleyrand that the envoys had no such power to effect a loan. Nor did they have the desire or authority to apologize for their President. He pointed out that French officials had made disparaging remarks about the United States but that the Americans were not seeking redress. His anger growing, he told Talleyrand that he believed him sufficiently familiar with the American Constitution to understand that when the Americans said they lacked power to negotiate specific issues or to apologize for their President, they were telling the truth. Gerry continued that he and his fellow envoys had all the authority necessary to settle the real differences between the two nations and were prepared to do so at any moment. As for the money, he reminded Talleyrand of the Americans' previous offer to send Marshall back to the United States for further instructions, provided France stopped attacking American shipping.

Talleyrand replied that there could be no delay about the money, and that he would send the decree to the Americans after one week. The implication was clear: the Americans must come up with the loan by that time. Hauteval and Gerry returned together and informed Marshall and Pinckney of the meeting. They said they knew of no reason for Talleyrand to delay the decree "unless its injustice and impolicy could stop it." They asked Hauteval to return to Talleyrand and say that unless the Directory itself could be "prevailed on by reason" to alter its plan, the Americans did not wish it delayed for a moment. "We were ready to receive it now," Marshall wrote in his journal, "as we should be eight days hence."[16]

Actually at this point the Americans had won, although they did not know it. France would not make war with the United States; she could not risk the danger of fighting a combined Anglo-American alliance. Nor could France allow one nation, the United States in this case, to escape without paying for peace. If the United States so escaped, then no nation would be willing to bow to France's military might. The problem was no longer the Americans'; their firmness had successfully solved it for them. The problem now belonged to France. The Americans, of course, did not know this. Gerry wrote to a friend about this time of what an "unpleasant situation" he, Pinckney, and Marshall were in. He said they expected "every moment a formal hint to depart . . . what the result of this business will be I know not."[17]

An inkling of the French position came the morning after Gerry's visit with Talleyrand. Hottinguer bustled in, the "X" of the three intriguers. He had a deal. If the Americans at least would pay the *douceur*, then the Directory would allow two of them to stay in Paris while the third returned to the United States to secure authorization to negotiate a loan. Would France stop the marauding of American commerce while this was happening? the Americans wanted to know. The answer was that it would not. For the Americans this meant paying 50,000 pounds so that two of them might remain in Paris, "which could only give us the benefit of seeing the plays and operas of Paris for the winter."[18] The deal was unacceptable.

Hottinguer became alarmed and sent Bellamy to speak with the Americans. Their conversation, which took place the next morning at breakfast, was a repetition of everything that had been said in the past several weeks, with two additions—both made by the Americans. They pointed out to Bellamy that under the present treaty existing between France and the United States, French ships could seek protection in American coastal ports from British warships, a protection that could be lost if that treaty were destroyed. They also said that France was staking too much on the supposed "French party" in the United States and reports that members of that party would support France in a dispute with the United States. The three Americans—northerner, southerner, man from the middle states; two Federalists and one Jeffersonian Republican—stated their belief that the "extreme injustice" committed by France against the United States would unite every American against France.[19]

The Americans decided on November 1 that they would carry on no more secret negotiations with underlings, a decision they had made once before.[20] Two days later Hottinguer arrived in the afternoon holding a paper which he claimed had been prepared by Talleyrand. It contained the previously offered proposals. Then Hottinguer tried a new approach. Intelligence received from the United States, he said, indicated there would have been an entirely different result if Aaron Burr and James Madison had been named ministers instead of the three who were, and that Talleyrand was preparing a letter to be sent to the United States complaining about the three American ministers. The intimation here was, as it had been throughout many of the conversations, that a large number of Americans were prepared to support France in this dispute. This poor attempt to frighten the three Americans with the possibility of embarrassment for them at home did not succeed.[21]

Marshall by this time well understood what was happening. As he wrote that day to Charles Lee, the American Attorney-General in Philadelphia, "France wishes to retain America in her present situation until her negotiations with Britain, which it is believed is about to recommence, shall have been terminated. A present absolute rupture with America might encourage England to continue the war, and peace with England pending [France's] differences with us will put us more in her power." Marshall was concerned by the "remarkable [French] sentiment" that if the ministers believed they could unite America by claiming that France was hostile, they were mistaken, "that we ought to know the diplomatic skill of France and her means in our country sufficiently to be convinced that the French party in America would throw all the blame of rupture on the Federalists as we styled ourselves, on the British party as they style us."[22]

Still the Americans did not feel they could leave Paris. They had been charged by Secretary of State Pickering to do nothing that would give France the opportunity to claim that the United States had terminated the talks without cause. On November 11 they sent a letter to the Directory asking to be received, and then waited for an answer. They would be kept waiting a long time.

Meanwhile, what was happening in Paris was of interest throughout all of Europe and caused various reactions. John Quincy Adams, the American minister in Berlin, was ready for war. He believed France could do no worse injury to the United States than it was already doing, nor did he consider the French formidable enemies. "It is not the fury of the tusks," he wrote, "but the venom of the sting that we have to dread from them." To Elbridge Gerry, Quincy Adams wrote sympathetically of the "painful and uncomfortable situation" the American ministers must find themselves in. But perhaps, he suggested, good would come if, as a result, the American people understood the French efforts to split the American Union between the supporters of England and of France.[23]

In London, however, Rufus King, the American minister, had different ideas about an American war with France. King, a Federalist, wrote to the three American envoys in Paris:

> No one detests more than I do the conduct of France towards our country, still I earnestly desire that we may remain in peace. War would retard our progress; which with all the disadvantages to which we are exposed, brings daily additions of wealth and strength; and to the economical and moral motives which should influence nations to cultivate peace, we may add the danger to be apprehended from the division of our people.

He then included some news about European politics, and the reaction of the countries there to the threat of France ("Spain is alarmed and Portugal trembles") and generally painted a bleak picture. He also included the information that Portugal did give money as a "preliminary" before France opened negotiations with her, and that the final treaty did include a secret provision stipulating a loan from Portugal to France. It was money from that loan, King wrote, which allowed the Directory to accomplish the *coup d'état* of September 4 which solidified the militarists in power. King assured the three American ministers in Paris that, although he could not identify his sources, "I am not deceived."[24]

By the end of November the American envoys, tired and discouraged, could report no progress. Their letter earlier in the month was unanswered and France seemed as unfriendly as ever. They continued to confront persons trying to persuade them to deal with the Directory on the Directory's terms. They reported to Secretary of State Pickering that they no longer were engaging in such dealings and "we have very little prospect of succeeding in our mission."[25]

Despite the frustrations of their mission, they were in Paris. And they could not escape her charms. For John Marshall, the young man who had grown up on the western frontier, it was a world he had never known in Richmond or Philadelphia. Of St. Cloud, the former royal palace, he said of its beauty that if he were the owner of it, he should fear it would attach him too much to life.

"Paris presents an incessant round of amusement and dissipation," he reported after having been in the city two months. "Every day you may see something new, magnificent and beautiful, every night you may see a spectacle which astonishes and enchants the imagination. The most lively fancy aided by the strongest description cannot equal the reality of the opera. All that you can conceive and a great deal more than you can conceive in the line of amusement is to be found in this gay metropolis. . . ." Still, the city had its drawbacks for Marshall. "I suspect it would not be easy to find a friend," he said. "I would not live in Paris to be among the wealthiest of its citizens."

He wrote that in a letter in November to his dearest Polly, a letter in which he poured out how much he missed her. He had not received one letter from her since his departure from the United States in July. But he would not consider that it was because she had not written. It must, he told her, be because of the difficulty of mail getting through. He also told her that his arrival home was being continually delayed. When he had left the United States, he had hoped to be home by Christmas. After arriving in Paris, he had written her that it might be March. "I now apprehend that it will not be in my power to reach America til April or May," he told her in this letter. And he closed. "Let me see you once more and I can venture to assert that no consideration can induce me ever again to consent to place the Atlantic between us." He signed off the letter with "Adieu my dearest Polly. Preserve your health and be as happy as possible till the return of him who is ever yours."

In that same letter he mentioned that he had changed his lodgings. He had been living, he said, in a house "where I kept my own apartments perfectly in the style of a miserable old bachelor without any mixture of female society." But now he had taken rooms, he wrote, "in the house of a very accomplished, a very sensible, and I believe a very amiable lady whose temper, very contrary to the general character of her country women, is domestic and who generally sits with us two or three hours in the afternoon." He explained that "This renders my situation less unpleasant than it has been but," he assured Polly, "nothing can make it eligible."[26]

Marshall and Gerry had been living in the same house with the Pinckneys. "We are in Fauxbourg St. Germains, Rue de La Fontaine Grenelle," Mary Pinckney reported. "The three commissioners have the house among them, except a few apartments on the third story reserved for the proprietor of the building." She found it a pleasant building "entre cour et jardin—the latter is about the size of ours in Charleston, and the view from the windows on that side command half a dozen gardens."[27]

But the house was unsatisfactory for Marshall and Gerry. Gerry explained why in a letter to his wife: "Six weeks . . . with only a bedroom and parlour for myself, and [an] antechamber for my servants. General Marshall had just such a suite of apartments, and both his . . . were badly furnished." Gerry did not have a carpet on the floor and his chimneys were stuffed. There also was a stable beneath his rooms with "a constant noise, as of persons breaking through the wall." Added to this, Gerry felt compelled to keep a pair of pistols beneath his pillow, making sleep difficult. He asked Americans he knew in Paris if they could find a better place for him. The result was that Gerry and Marshall took lodgings in the home of the "very amiable lady," as Marshall described her, who was Madame Villette.

Madame Villette was the adopted daughter of Voltaire. In 1776, when she was Reine Philiberte de Varicourt, a girl in her early teens of a noble but poor family, Voltaire became entranced by her and rescued her from a convent. Eventually he married her to the Marquis de Villette. Gerry's description of her in his letter to his wife is perhaps one of the best of the woman who would so enchant him and Marshall. "Madame Villette is a widow lady of about thirty-five years old," he wrote, "her husband died about four years ago at the age of fifty-five and left her a daughter who is now about twelve and a son about four years old." He explained that Madame Villette would continue staying in the house through the winter. He described her as "one of the finest women in Paris; on account of the goodness of her heart, her excellent morals, and the richness of her mind."

Her history, as Gerry described it, was somewhat romantic. Voltaire, Gerry said, mentioned her often in his writings as the Belle et bonne "by which name she is distinguished here." Her family was in the military and most of them lost their lives, leaving her in difficult financial straits. And this caused her to rent out rooms because, Gerry reported, "She cannot do too much, she says, for her petite enfants." She spoke only French, and "She is not handsome," Gerry assured his wife, "but such a woman as you would like."

The rent was only twelve and one-half guineas a month, five guineas less than he and Marshall had paid for their other apartments. Gerry had four "large, elegant rooms" on the second floor while Marshall "has only three on the ground floor."[28]

For John Marshall, Madame Villette was another of the excitements of Paris. He was tall and handsome and, if not smoothly sophisticated in a continental way, conveyed an innate sense of decency and charm which women found attractive. If not, as Gerry assured his wife, a handsome woman, Madame Villette was a mature woman of the world who understood the elegance and charm of gracious living certainly better than any other woman John Marshall knew. They spent considerable time together, riding in a carriage, sitting together in her salon, enjoying the theater.

The indications are that the two resisted romance, or at least avoided any incident which their very strict society would have considered improper. Mary Pinckney was entertained at the Villette house and entertained Madame Villette, and also treated her with respect. Mary joked about the arrangement, commenting in a letter to a relative that Madame Villette "is an agreeable pleasing woman, about 32 years of age. She always dines with the two *batchelors*"—Mrs. Pinckney underlined the reference to Marshall and Gerry—"and renders their situation very agreeable." In that same letter she told of Madame Villette inviting her to a party at her house. She planned to go herself and regretted that she could not bring her teen-aged daughter because the young girl was ill. This was not the attitude Mary Pinckney would have displayed had she believed Madame Villette was having a romantic liaison with either Gerry or Marshall.[29]

About a week after moving into Madame Villette's house, on the evening of December 2, Gerry attended a dinner with Talleyrand. Afterward he returned to Madame Villette's and told Marshall what had happened. Marshall scribbled the following note in his journal:

> Mr. Gerry dined with Mr. Talleyrand. Mr. Bellamy and
> Mr. Hottinguer were both of the party. After dinner Mr.
> Hottinguer again asked Mr. Gerry in direct terms whether
> he would now give the douceur which had been before
> mentioned. Mr. Gerry answered positively in the negative
> and the conversation dropped.[30]

That dinner and Marshall's account of what he understood Gerry had told him of it became crucial points in the months to come. For the dinner, as Marshall understood what had taken place, was the only direct link between Talleyrand and the request for the *douceur*. Otherwise, the demands for the *douceur* could be construed as only an independent confidence game being played without Talleyrand's knowledge.

The dispute over the dinner became significant also because of the growing separation between Elbridge Gerry on one side and John Marshall and Charles Pinckney on the other. The three Americans obviously were under intense pressure; the international situation was constantly perilous. On December 9 Rufus King in London sent them a confidential message to the effect that French port officers were being instructed to delay as long as possible "without open force" departing American vessels because orders to appropriate American property were anticipated at any moment.[31] If the American envoys made a wrong move, their country might be at war with France and they would be blamed for it; and there did not seem to be any right move, at least it appeared that way to them. It is not surprising then that differences between the three were magnified. Gerry, knowing the other two envoys were Federalists and believing them to be anti-French, felt that he alone might succeed in securing peace through negotiation. This meant he must be as open, friendly, and responsive to the French as possible. "I was always fond, you well know, of the manners of the French," Gerry wrote his daughter from Paris the day before Christmas 1797. "They are so hearty, sprightly and generous as that it is impossible for me not to love their society."[32]

In Paris there was an American colony, and its members were particularly responsive to the interests of France and angered at what they considered the errors of their own government. Gerry became a part of this colony. As Mary Pinckney described these Americans, "They are amazingly fearful of hurting the feelings of this government, but are ready enough to find fault with their own—if an indecent paragraph against this government appears in our papers, where the press is free, they snort with anger and fear, but they can read the most violent tirades against us in the French papers without any emotion." She summed it up: "In short they would have their own government and its ministers to consider what effect their fortune in France and to act accordingly."[33]

Gerry was very responsive to the overtures of these Americans and of their French hangers-on. To a friend he wrote of how handsomely the American envoys were being treated in Paris and of how optimistic he was of ultimate success. William Vans Murray heard of this letter and complained that Gerry "has mistaken the lamps of Paris for an illumination on his arrival, and the salutations of the fishwomen for a procession of chaste matrons hailing the great Pacificator."[34]

Samuel Eliot Morison has written that Gerry "was encouraged in an ultra-conciliatory course by the American colony in Paris, speculators whose property would have been seized at the first open breach."[35] Whether the attentions, flattery, and arguments of these Americans so moved Gerry, whether he was primarily motivated by the mandate given him by Jefferson, or whether his aversion to war was so great as to command him to seek peace at any cost, that is what he did—and, in fact, it did not turn out to be an ignominious role that he played.

The discussion of loans and bribes continued. The three emissaries from Talleyrand continued to flit around the Americans, hoping for some break in their position. And there were other overtures. On December 20, Pinckney reported, "a lady who is well acquainted with M. Talleyrand" approached him and again suggested the loan, saying that if the Americans stayed in Paris another six months, "you would not advance a single step further in your negotiations, without a loan."

"If that is the case," Pinckney replied, "we may as well go away now."

The lady was shocked. "Why that possibly might lead to a rupture, which you had better avoid," she said, "for we know we have a very considerable party in America, who are strongly in our interest."[36] The French had convinced themselves that their supporters in the United States would ignore the interests of their own nation to support France, and nothing could persuade them otherwise. At almost the same time Pinckney was being so threatened, George Washington at Mount Vernon was writing to that same point. He had received a letter from Marshall written three months earlier, and in his answer Washington said: "If the French Directory proceed on the supposition that the parties in these United States are nearly equal, and that one of them would advocate their measures in the dernier resort, they will greatly deceive themselves; for the *mass* of our citizens require no more than to understand a question, to decide it properly. . . ."[37]

There was another overture to the Americans that same month. Beaumarchais, a prominent Frenchman in Paris, had a suit against the state of Virginia for payment for supplies he had provided; Marshall was his lawyer in Virginia. Bellamy—the Y of the XYZ trio—approached Marshall and said that Beaumarchais had agreed to allow 50,000 pounds of his settlement,

provided he won his case, to be used as the "private gratification."
The Americans turned this down also. But the French now were
selling very cheap. They were willing to have one of their own
citizens, Beaumarchais, pay the *douceur* as well as have the loan
taken care of by juggling Dutch debts. They were playing the
game now in name only, trying to retain their pose as the superior military power to which all other nations must bend.[38] The
pose was necessary to sustain the corrupt level to which the
French government had descended. In this month, for example,
the Directory, through Talleyrand's office, informed England that
peace between the two governments was available for a price of
a million pounds, divided among the Ministers; Talleyrand's
department would divide among its members 100,000 pounds. It
was for this that Frenchmen were dying.[39]

Why did the three Americans stay in Paris? "We have
remained this long in Paris without being accredited ministers,"
Marshall wrote Rufus King, "because we would really submit to
any situation however irksome while a hope remained that such
submission could produce good and because too we deem it necessary to satisfy our country and our government as well as ourselves that we have made every effort for accommodation which
is compatible with the independence of our nation." But the frustrations of the position were increasing. "Submission has its
limits," Marshall continued, "and if we have not actually passed
we are certainly approaching them." Marshall, who had hoped to
return to Richmond with "no diminution of character," was concerned that the course he and his fellow envoys were on would be
sharply criticized at its end. "We regret the impossibility of consulting our government or of those in whom we can confide," he
told King. "We must act upon our own judgments and our opinion
is that we ought not to remain much longer." He continued then
as if a decision had been made to seek an immediate reply or
demand passports, but apparently Gerry worked his will somewhat on the other two. Marshall later added to the letter that "the
resolution mentioned of demanding a passport in January is not
so positively taken as I had supposed it to be. There is now some
hesitation concerning it."[40]

That same day the three Americans sent another report to
Secretary of State Pickering explaining their plans. First they
said they had not yet received any formal response to their letter
of November 11. If no answer was forthcoming by January 10,
they said, the Americans would send another letter to Talleyrand.
The three Americans still were concerned about setting off a war
between their own nation and France. All were agreed that it

might happen, but not one of them wished it to result from precipitous action.[41]

The sense of isolation about which Marshall had written to King—"We regret the impossibility of consulting our government"—was very much a reality rather than only a mood. The normal time for correspondence to travel from Paris to Philadelphia was three months, if the letters arrived at all. That meant a half-year was required to send a message and receive an answer. The Americans were indeed on their own in a hostile city, well aware that their country's future, the lives of its young men, as well as their own safety and reputations, were at stake in the outcome of their efforts.

"The mind of Congress as well as of the rest of the world seems suspended as to the measures our nation should adopt in relation to France," wrote one member of Congress from Philadelphia as the year ended, "upon the expectation of intelligence to be received from our commissioners which will enable us to act with decision."[42] Reports, letters, summations of what had happened were then on their way to the United States so that the minds of all could be taken out of suspension. But the information carried no more specific data than what the three Americans in Paris knew, and what they knew with assurance was only that nothing had been settled. On the last day of the year John Marshall wrote in his journal that "we had another meeting in my room at which it was again determined that we could give no money and that Mr. Gerry should make this determination known to those who should apply to him."[43] As far as they could tell, they had made no progress since their arrival in Paris three months earlier, none since John Marshall had left the United States six months earlier with his mind divided by regret for leaving his Polly and excitement at his forthcoming adventure.

4

As with all venal men, the French ultimately allowed their venality to destroy their discretion. When William Vans Murray at The Hague heard that France was demanding payment, he wrote to John Quincy Adams, almost with glee, that "We are not used to tribute, however disguised. This piece of intelligence I *believe* may be relied upon. It will work well in the United States." From Berlin, Quincy Adams answered: "I dare say those of our own people, who instruct them in the measures to take with us, have advised them to keep it out of sight."[1] Vans Murray and Adams, both Federalists, believed that the French were in league with the Jeffersonian Republicans, and they recognized that the revelation of French demands for tribute would unite the American people and perhaps even destroy Jefferson's developing political organization.

In Paris Marshall, Pinckney, and Gerry had other concerns. One was the American seamen captured by French ships and detained in prison. They received a report from the American consul in Brest that Americans captured aboard British vessels could be freed, at a cost of 24 livres a man. The envoys were willing to pay the money but wanted special care taken that all sailors so freed would embark for their own country. "We wish all proper measures to be taken to restore our fellow citizens to their friends, their families and their liberty," the envoys said, "but we can make no advance for those who would still continue in Europe."[2]

On January 5 still another problem arose for the Americans. The Directory called upon the nation's legislature, the Council of Five Hundred, to enact a law challenging the traditional concept that the flag of the ship covered the property. What this meant was that the French would feel free to attack any American ship carrying goods produced in England or in English territories. In the past they had been attacking only ships carrying goods to and from England. Also, any American ship that touched at an English port would find all French ports closed to it. The law was passed unanimously by the Council, and French ships virtually were on a complete war footing with American commerce. The attacks no longer were limited to stings.[3]

These acts were part of the pressures to force the United States and the three American ministers to surrender to the French demands for money. It was a typical French ploy to exert force to produce an end that could not be achieved by diplomacy. The application of force, however, often produces an equally forceful response. The British had learned that in the American Revolution. The French would also learn it from the United States.

While these pressures were building, Marshall was drafting the second letter the American envoys planned to send to Talleyrand. On January 2 the three men met in Marshall's rooms at Madame Villette's, and Marshall read what he had written so far. They agreed that Gerry should go over it first and then Pinckney; all were to be in agreement when the letter was sent. The second part of the letter was done by January 10, and the same procedure was followed: first Gerry would check it and then Pinckney.[4]

This presented problems, as Gerry by this time was very much in disagreement with his colleagues. He took a long time going over the draft, and on January 20 he and Marshall had an argument about it. "I had so repeatedly pressed Mr. Gerry on the subject of our letter prepared for the Minister of Exterior Relations," Marshall reported that day, "and manifested such solicitude for its being so completed as to enable us to send it, that I had obviously offended." Apparently he did not believe that hurrying Gerry's deliberations was worth dividing the delegation, for he wrote: "Today I have urged that subject and for the last time."[5]

Vans Murray at The Hague received an extract of the letter and considered it "mild and affecting, and admirable for the nerves of America." He guessed the whole was "excellent." His correct assumption was that Marshall had written the letter. He was not familiar with Gerry's or Pinckney's writing style, but he said he considered Marshall, whom he had met in Philadelphia when Marshall was arguing the British Debts Case, "as one of the most powerful reasoners I ever met with either in public or in print." Vans Murray considered this quality important because he assumed that what was now being done was for domestic consumption in the United States. "Reasoning in such cases will have a fine effect in America," he said, "but to depend upon it in Europe is really to place Quixote with Gines de Passamonte and among the men of the world whom he reasoned with, and so sublimely, on their way to the galleys. They answer him you know with stones and blows, though the knight is an *armed* as well as an eloquent knight."[6] The United States might not be able to escape the stones and blows of Europe but at least it would maintain its self-respect.

Gerry finished his study of the letter on January 22. Additional work was required on it, then it was translated, and, finally on January 31, was ready for delivery. It was turned over to an American officer at the ministry for delivery to Talleyrand, who was trying to delay dealing with the American ministers as long as possible. Although by now he realized they would not yield to him, he didn't want them to break off the talks as long as France's war with England continued. The Americans' letter was not actually delivered to Talleyrand until February 7, so successful was he in dodging it.[7]

The "letter" is a statement of approximately twenty thousand words. It states clearly and concisely, once again, the American complaints against the French, and it is an equally clear and concise indictment of the French treatment of the United States on the seas and of her envoys in Paris. This was an important point because Marshall, as had King, understood he was writing more for American domestic consumption than for the French government. Of himself and his two colleagues, Marshall wrote: "Bringing with them the temper of their government and country, searching only for the means of effecting the object of their mission, they have permitted no personal considerations to influence their conduct, but have waited under circumstances beyond measure embarrassing and unpleasant, with that respect which the American government has so uniformly paid to that of France, for permission to lay before you, citizen minister, these important communications with which they have been charged."

Realizing that they would not be allowed to begin negotiations, Marshall continued, the ministers considered it a proper course to review the events leading up to this moment. The letter maintained a reasonable tone, saying that the three Americans "pray that it may be received in the temper with which it is written, and considered as an additional effort . . . to cultivate and restore, if it be possible, harmony between the two republicks." If there was any chance whatsoever, Marshall's letter read, to achieve that harmony, the Americans "still solicit and will still respectfully attend the development of those means." Marshall's letter closed with:

> If on the contrary no such hope remains, they have only to pray that their return to their own country may be facilitated; and they will leave France with the most deep-felt regret that neither the real and sincere friendship which the government of the United States has so uniformly and unequivocally displayed for this great Republick, nor its continued efforts to demonstrate the purity of its conduct and intentions, can protect its citizens, or preserve them from the calamities which they have sought by a just and upright conduct to avert.[8]

The Americans had placed it squarely before the French government. They would return to the United States and make the case that the government of France was to blame for the failure of the negotiations. France still hoped it might be able to persuade the Americans to come up with a loan, but the hope was fading fast.

Pinckney now could not be more adamant. "I beg leave to repeat that I adhere to the opinion," he told Gerry and Marshall, "that a prompt immediate and decisive negative should be given to any proposition that may be made on insinuation given to obtain money from us in any shape or under any pretence."[9]

But the "insinuations" continued to come, from friends and merchants. Du Pont de Nemours visited Pinckney on February 1 to ask if there had been any dispatches from the United States; he had gone directly to Pinckney's from a meeting with Talleyrand. Beaumarchais arrived the next day. The French government, he said, still wanted the Americans to produce some money. A few days later an American businessman named Nathaniel Cutting, who had lived in Paris many years, wrote the three ministers a letter. He argued that the Americans must have "ample" powers, wide enough to propose a loan, because he could not believe that the United States government "would send three gentlemen of your respectability" on such a mission "and tie you up to future orders" which were dependent upon a six-month oceangoing correspondence. He recommended that the three ministers not only, in effect, excuse the French from compensating for their attacks on American commerce and property, but that "a loan of effective money should be made to France, under guarantee of our government."[10]

Talleyrand, however, was not content now with only indirect approaches. He correctly understood that Elbridge Gerry was the American who would be most responsive to him and singled him out for special treatment. They had had several meetings together—without, of course, Gerry being received formally as an American minister. But these had been marked by Talleyrand's discourtesy. Gerry would arrive at the appointed time, but Talleyrand would not be there and would not apologize for his absence. This now changed. On February 3 a secretary of Talleyrand's called on Gerry and offered profuse apologies for Talleyrand's not having been available as promised. The secretary assured Gerry that Talleyrand had arrived within moments after Gerry's last departure and regretted having missed him.

Gerry then met the next day with Talleyrand. After the meeting he returned to Madame Villette's house and told Marshall that Talleyrand had made certain "communications and propositions" to him which he was not at liberty to discuss either with Marshall or Pinckney. He did say there were some changes from what had been suggested previously. He added that he must give an answer within one or two days and, obviously impressed with his importance, he said that upon his answer "probably depended peace or war."

This was the first time any one of the three had not been completely open with the others, and this too would become a matter of controversy in later years as Elbridge Gerry denied the account Marshall recorded at the time in his journal.

Alone, Marshall gave serious thought to this new development. He was intrigued that the French were unwilling "to part with us or to profess the war which is in fact made upon us." The three Americans had been poorly treated, threatened with expulsion, with menacing decrees. "From our first arrival there has been a continuing effort to operate on our fears," he realized. He believed it all stemmed from the French war with England. If France quickly ended that war, then it would turn on the United States unless the United States bought peace. If the war did not end quickly, however, France did not wish to drive the United States into an alliance with England. Marshall suspected that a recent messenger from the United States to the French government had brought information that France might lose the support of what she considered her party in the United States unless she became more tractable.

Maintaining her political support in the United States was important to France, Marshall reasoned. To this end France would, he assumed, try to throw the blame for the failure of the negotiations on Pinckney and himself. If by any chance the negotiations were to succeed, then France would want Gerry alone credited.

"I am led irresistibly by this train of thought to the opinion that the communication made to Mr. Gerry in secret is a proposition to furnish passports to General Pinckney and myself and to retain him [Gerry] for the purpose of negotiating the differences between the two Republics," Marshall wrote. This would allow "the partizans of France this fruitful seed," that Marshall and Pinckney could be blamed for the difficulties in the negotiations. Certainly if Marshall and Pinckney returned to the United States and Gerry concluded the negotiations apparently successfully, that argument could be made effectively.

The next day Marshall discussed his suspicions with Pinckney. They agreed they would not object to Gerry acting as he considered proper. Marshall wrote in his journal following the meeting:

> We shall both be happy if by remaining without us, Mr. Gerry can negotiate a treaty which shall preserve the peace without sacrificing the independence of our country. We will most readily offer up all personal considerations as a sacrifice to appease the haughtiness of this Republic.[11]

Marshall's journal was a private document, and there is no reason to doubt the sincerity of what he wrote in it.

Gerry met with Talleyrand on February 7. Again he would not discuss the specifics with Marshall and Pinckney and repeated that peace or war would be the outcome of his decision. He also said that he had rejected one proposition from Talleyrand and was considering another which Talleyrand had modified as a result of suggestions made by Gerry. He described all the propositions as "perfectly new." Marshall countered to Gerry with his own fears that France would offer nothing consistent with American independence. He also said he believed that Talleyrand was only attempting to continue the negotiations until the war with England was settled. Gerry, however, was unconvinced.

Two days later Marshall and Gerry attended the theater in the evening together. When they returned to Madame Villette's, Gerry revealed to Marshall that he had had "a very extraordinary conversation" that day with Monsieur Dutrimond, a clerk of Talleyrand's. But he could not communicate the substance of it. Marshall had become a little impatient with Gerry's growing aura of self-importance and said he had no desire to hear of it; he then turned toward his rooms. Gerry quickly added that he was "at liberty" to discuss with Pinckney and Marshall money for France.

Marshall turned back. It was "perfectly unnecessary" to consult about that, he answered, as the Americans had given their answer many times. Gerry agreed that was so and insisted he had said the same thing to both Dutrimond and Talleyrand. But, and this was the point he wished to emphasize, his last answer had been withheld from the Directory by Talleyrand in order to allow further time for consideration—or so Dutrimond reported. And the added element was that the three Americans would be ordered out of France in twenty-four hours unless they changed their position.

John Marshall did not believe this. There had been so many decrees, orders, threats, hints of expulsion—all of which had come to nothing. He told Gerry that the purpose of the Dutrimond conversation was "only to amuse us still longer and to prevent our taking those measures which would produce unequivocal explanations on the part of France." Gerry obviously was not pleased at being told he was being duped. He said Marshall could not make such judgments because he was unaware of the propositions that had been made to Gerry.

That was true, Marshall replied. But, he continued, he did know something of the general aims of the government and of the attitude of every man in it respecting the United States.

Marshall said that he had no doubt that whatever the propositions were, "they must comport with these objects." Marshall wrote in his journal that "Mr. Gerry was a little warm and the conversation was rather unpleasant." Marshall discontinued the conversation at that point, believing any additional words would only exacerbate an already disturbing situation.[12]

But the break between the three ministers could not be repaired. Early in February Marshall had prepared a letter to Talleyrand demanding passports; the Americans would go home. The draft was given to Gerry on February 6 and he returned it eight days later with some changes. This letter was the basis of another disagreement among the three ministers. In his journal Marshall reported that he signed the letter and offered it to Gerry to sign but Gerry declined. The official copy which was returned to the American State Department has Pinckney's and Marshall's signatures and carries the notation: "but which Mr. Gerry, after promising, finally refused to sign." Sixteen months later Gerry wrote to John Adams explaining why he had not signed the letter:

> . . . On the evening preceding the 22nd of February when General Marshall and myself had agreed to visit Madame Villette at her country seat, he informed me that the letter to M. Talleyrand, demanding our passports, was ready, and proposed that we should sign it, and leave it with General Pinckney. I answered, that this was an unexpected proposition, that he knew we had engaged to go the next day to Villette, 30 or 40 miles distant, that on delivery of that letter to M. Talleyrand, our passports would probably be sent to us, with an order to depart immediately, that my baggage was unpacked, and my bills were unpaid, that a day or two, at least, would be requisite for these matters, but that I would send an apology to Madame Villette, would prepare immediately to leave the City and would sign the letter. This he declined, and preferred a postponement of the signature till our return. Soon after this the proposition of a loan was made, to take place at the peace.

Marshall reported the incident as happening on February 18 and does not mention Madame Villette in his journal. He wrote:

> It was not our object to send it under three or four days until we should have enquired for an answer to our former letter, but I was desirous of having it completed so as to send it whenever we should chuse.[13]

It was then Marshall reported that Gerry "declined" to sign it, as opposed to Gerry's later explanation that he only preferred to delay his signature. Considering Gerry's greater willingness to bargain at the price of any discourtesy, it is probable that Gerry's later explanation was manufactured.

On February 25 there was another appeal for a loan, this from Dutrimond to Gerry. The Frenchman had suggested that the Americans agree to a loan to be paid at the end of the French-English war. Pinckney saw little value in the idea. If the United States agreed to a loan, he said, France could raise money on the promise of ultimately receiving the American loan. The effect would be the same as if the United States had loaned money to France for use in the war. Marshall wrote that "Mr. Gerry supported the proposition very decidedly." Gerry argued that an agreement could be made under which France would not make any use of the money until after the war. He said he did not understand how Marshall and Pinckney could "incur the expenses and dangers of a dreadful war with the most formidable power on earth."

John Marshall snapped back that if the real question was one only of money, he would agree to the loan. But a loan under present circumstances, he insisted, meant the United States surrendered its independence. He also argued that Dutrimond's proposal, like every other one the Americans had received, was not intended seriously. On four occasions, he said, they had been told to offer money or be forced to leave; they had never offered the money and the threats all went unenforced. The whole purpose, Marshall said, was to keep the Americans in Paris until the war with England was settled. He argued that France would make war against the United States whenever it pleased her no matter what the three American ministers did or did not agree to, and that the only way to prevent such a war "was a firm and moderate conduct on our part."

Gerry considered the argument of America's retaining or losing her independence exaggerated. Nothing France did, he said, would be acceptable to Marshall. One cannot give himself up entirely to suspicion, he said, and the person who was governed by suspicion in great national concerns would often find himself mistaken.

Marshall charged Gerry with misrepresenting what he had said. The best guide for the future the Americans could take, he said, was the past. And the past conduct of France indicated she was not willing to enter into any negotiations from which the United States could emerge with its independence.

"Mr. Gerry remained inflexible in his opinion that the loan

was proper, that peace or war depended on it, and that on granting the loan we secured all the objects of our mission, the whole of which would infallibly be lost if we refused it," Marshall wrote in his journal. Gerry also argued that France did not really care about the money, "but that it was the proudest as well as the most unjust government on the face of the earth, that it was so elevated by its victories as to hold in perfect contempt all the rights of others and that with this disposition it would certainly make war" on the United States if the loan were refused.

Marshall accepted that the loan was unimportant to France. When France makes a proposition unimportant to herself but distressing to the nation to which it is made, in this case the United States, and then declares that war will result unless that nation accedes to the proposition, he argued, "there was much reason to doubt the sincerity of the proposition."

The argument between the two men grew hotter. Marshall accused Gerry of completely misunderstanding and totally misstating his (Marshall's) arguments and "that indeed he could not answer the argument but by misstating it . . . and if he would permit me I would point out his mistake." Gerry answered that he preferred that Marshall not mingle his statements with observations which would entangle them. The debate continued without resolution and finally, the three Americans agreed to meet again the next evening.

The next evening it was more of the same, with Gerry, so Marshall wrote, still insisting upon the loan. At one point, Marshall wrote in his journal: "Mr. Gerry showed some resentment and considered me as having charged him with an intention to trick us into measures we were opposed to." Marshall answered that talking in such a manner was not worthwhile, and insisted he had said and meant nothing personal. The result of the evening was that, at Marshall's suggestion, the three ministers would seek to meet with Talleyrand to inform him they could not negotiate a loan, but that if Talleyrand suggested a loan at the end of the war, they would say it could be considered. A note was sent to Talleyrand requesting the meeting.[14]

Throughout this entire discussion is the stated fact of Gerry's insistence upon a loan to France. Sixteen months later, when it became a public issue, Gerry denied ever supporting the loan. In a letter to John Adams he wrote that "General Marshall in his journal has stated that I advocated a loan generally." Gerry continued:

> . . . but I cannot think he meant this, as there was not the least pretext for such an assertion. It would be such a

flagrant violation of truth so directly contrary to all the documents of the embassy, and to my well known conduct in France, as to induce me to suppose he never intended to make such an impression. It would indeed be repugnant to his own conviction and to common sense for he knew that in regard to the war between France and Great Britain, I considered the United States in many respects as being embarked with the latter, that I conceived the overthrow of her government as involving that of our own. . . .[15]

Whatever Gerry intended, there was no doubt at the time that he impressed Pinckney and Marshall with his determination in favor of the loan to France.

Gerry had never told Marshall and Pinckney any of the secret details upon which depended the peace or war he talked of so much. But Talleyrand had told another party that the plan was for Marshall and Pinckney to leave and for Gerry to remain and negotiate a treaty. This party told it to Pinckney, confirming Marshall's suspicions. On March 1 Pinckney told this to Marshall and also said it had come in a circuitous manner but was meant to reach the Americans. Marshall was particularly concerned. He was "entirely of the opinion" that Gerry had originated the idea of the loan payable at the end of the war, and Marshall considered it "a contribution for the purpose of conquering Britain and the world for the purpose of subjugating ourselves."[16] The break between Gerry on the one side and Pinckney and Marshall on the other was complete.

The three Americans met with Talleyrand, at their request, the afternoon of March 2. Both sides began with protestations of friendship. Then Talleyrand revived the old arguments the Americans had been hearing since their arrival in Paris. But now not only was the Directory angered at Adams' speech of last May, its members also were upset by a speech of General Washington prior to his leaving the presidency. The Americans were surprised at this new element, and Pinckney observed that the reference to the Washington speech was a new complaint but Talleyrand shrugged it off.

Talleyrand said he was hurt that they had not visited him. The Americans pointed out that they were waiting to be recognized formally, but Talleyrand insisted they could have met and talked with him on an informal, private basis. In that session and another one in the evening, he continued to insist that there must be some form of assistance from the United States to France "to prove our friendship." Gerry brought up the idea of a loan payable after the war, attributing its origin to Dutrimond,

Talleyrand's clerk. Talleyrand replied that was one technique of making the loan to be considered.

Talleyrand's tactic was obvious. The Americans must agree to the loan before being formally recognized by the Directory. The loan, in fact, was the price of recognition. Just before the Americans left, Marshall told Talleyrand that he and his colleagues had no interest in seeing the Directory, "that we were perfectly indifferent with regard to it," but that the Americans would negotiate nothing unless they were treated as ministers and recognized as representatives of the United States. If France wanted something from the United States, Marshall was saying, France would have to extend formal diplomatic courtesy to the three Americans.[17]

After leaving Talleyrand the three Americans discussed the meeting, but only to the extent of rearguing their old opinions. The next morning, March 3, Gerry came to Marshall's rooms. Gerry indicated he believed the loan still might be agreed to. "I told him," Marshall said, "that my judgment was not more perfectly convinced that the floor was wood, or that I stood on my feet and not on my head, than that our instructions would not permit us to make the loan required." Gerry's only alternatives, Marshall said, were to negotiate the loan himself or return to the United States for consultations. The two men agreed that they both would return to the United States to seek new instructions, leaving Pinckney in Paris.[18]

This suggestion was made March 6 by the three Americans at another meeting with Talleyrand. He made no response, but seemed interested in knowing when or if new instructions would be coming from the United States. Marshall replied that the ministers had sent their first dispatches from Amsterdam November 28 and that Talleyrand could guess as well as they when an answer might be anticipated. Gerry made another appeal for "a treaty on liberal principles" which he said would be "infinitely more advantageous to France than the trifling advantages she could derive from a loan." Gerry spoke of the friendship between the two nations which could be created, but again Talleyrand made no reply.

As the Americans left Talleyrand that afternoon they told him again that Marshall and Gerry were willing to return to the United States to receive any new instructions regarding a loan that the American government wished to give. That, in effect, was the best they would do in response to the French demand for money. If it was not acceptable to the Directory, they said, they would wait to receive their instructions. The implication was that "instructions" meant expulsion.[19]

The dispatches the ministers had sent November 28 via Amsterdam had been a long time reaching Philadelphia, the winter ocean being extremely difficult for crossings. Meanwhile in the United States the suspense had increased. While there was no word from Paris, the insults by the French escalated. A French ship had attacked a British ship in the harbor of Charleston, South Carolina, and plundered and burned it without regard to the fact that Charleston harbor was part of a neutral's territory.

President Adams told the Congress that the incident dramatized the "propriety and necessity of enabling the executive authority of government to take measures for protecting the citizens of the United States, and such foreigners as have a right to enjoy their peace and the protection of their laws within their limits. . . ." The French excesses were pushing a reluctant Adams toward a war he did not want.

Most Americans conceded the issue was being decided in Paris. "Upon the whole," said Albert Gallatin in Philadelphia, "we remain in suspense in relation to the most important subject that can attract our attention, the success of our negotiation with France, and till we know its fate we will not, I believe, enter into any business with much spirit."[20]

Not everyone was so restrained, however. "Are our commissioners guillotined?" demanded George Washington, "or what else is the occasion of their silence?" Thomas Jefferson wasn't certain that the silence was so ominous. He figured that if war were close, the American ministers would have discovered some way to put the United States on her guard. "No news, therefore," the Vice President said, "is good news."[21]

But the news finally arrived in Philadelphia on March 4, and it was not good news. Abigail Adams, the President's wife, was as closely attuned to his political reactions as anyone. "I fear we shall be driven to war," she said. And as Adams read the dispatches, with the accounts of Talleyrand's condescension, the Directory's offensiveness, the intrigues of X, Y, and Z, he agreed that war seemed the only possible choice. He regretted the "pedantical, timorous" behavior of his three ministers, believing they should have spoken with no one until received by the Directory. But that could not be helped now. He sat down to write a message to Congress and all his anger erupted. He was angry not only with France but with "those Americans who had so fantastically espoused the cause of France without understanding what they were about." The message, however, never was sent. He did not believe he could make the dispatches public while his three ministers were in Paris because he feared for their lives. This meant the public and the Congress could not know what he had learned about the dealings in Paris. Also, Adams, like Jefferson, understood that war was something the United States should try to avoid, and one did not avoid it by writing in anger.[22]

Despite Adams' secrecy word quickly spread in Philadelphia that the dispatches had arrived, that they were filled with offensive material, and that war might come. One Congressman, Robert Goodloe Harper, a Federalist from South Carolina, echoed the sentiments of many of his party when he wrote to a constituent: "Are we my dear sir to submit; or shall we rouse once more the spirit of '75. . . . At only fifteen years old, I took up arms to resist the English, and I then resolved to live free or die. At thirty-three my resolution is not altered. . . . I have my life, which belongs to my country; and I promise my friends that in the hour of danger they shall find me by their sides."[23] It was with this sentiment from members of his own party that John Adams must deal.

In a message to Congress on March 19 Adams—still without divulging the content of the dispatches—said there was no expectation that the Americans would be able to reach any agreement with France "on terms compatible with the safety, honour, or the essential interests of the nation." He blamed the French for the impasse and again asked Congress to approve recommendations he had made earlier for improving American defenses. Also, he removed the order which forbade American merchant ships from sailing armed; that order had been an effort by President George Washington to demonstrate the American desire for neutrality. No longer would American ships be undefended marks for the French.[24]

Adams' speech actually was a moderate one, considering the circumstances. The United States had been grossly insulted, and at the time such insults were answered by war declarations. Still, Adams was holding back, calling for defensive measures but not going all the way. Jefferson, the Vice President, however, considered the Federalists "the war party" and said the French actions had made them "inveterate" and "more firm in their purpose" but "without adding to their numbers."* Jefferson made those comments in a letter to James Monroe and predicted that

---

* Jefferson, of course was not "Adams' Vice President." Under the system for electing the President and Vice President then, the two men had no tie politically. The system, in fact, practically ensured the two would be political opponents, and it is not surprising that Jefferson was so critical of Adams.

the Federalists' opponents in Congress would demand to see the dispatches, "for if Congress are to act on the question of war, they have a right to information."[25]

In April Congress voted a demand to see the dispatches from the three American ministers. Not all of the Republicans were enthusiastic about the move. And they were right to be suspicious. Adams immediately, and perhaps with some pleasure, made the documents available. The papers were widely circulated; newspapers published them in full; and the American people were able to read about the offensiveness of the Directory in demanding that the three ministers apologize for their President, about the intrigues of X, Y, and Z, of Pinckney's answer of "It is no. No. Not a sixpence."

"The Jacobins in Senate and House were struck dumb," Abigail Adams wrote her sister, "and opened not their mouths."[26] Vans Murray's prediction that the news would "work well" in the United States had proved correct. John Adams could have had a war declaration then for the asking, if he wished it.

Not only did Adams not wish a war, he actually directed Secretary of State Pickering to write the three ministers telling them to continue the negotiations if there was any chance of concluding them, despite the past offensiveness of the French government. "If you are in treaty," Pickering said, "with persons duly authorized by the Directory, on the subjects of your mission, then you are to remain and expedite the completion of the treaty. . . ." Pickering insisted, however, that "In no event is a treaty to be purchased with money, by loan or otherwise," adding: "There can be no safety in a treaty so obtained."[27]

In Paris the American envoys had no knowledge of the reaction in the United States to their dispatches, nor of any new instructions which might then be on the way to them. They had given up any idea of having their passports returned to them so they could leave when they chose. Instead, they anticipated being ordered out of France now that the Directory was becoming convinced there would be no loan. Marshall reported that in a letter to George Washington and said members of the French government needed only money to do everything they wished to do. They had the army and most of Europe obeying their commands. "Yet," said Marshall, "there is a difficulty in procuring funds to work this vast machine." He wrote of how the war machine necessitated huge tax levies to fuel itself. Owners found their estates yielded them nothing. Few were volunteering funds. France, as a result, was looking around at her neighbors in hopes of extorting more money from them to feed her voracious war machine and to feed the men who speculated on its success and stole from it. Marshall was learning that war destroys; it destroys even the side that wins.[28]

The American ministers were, in fact, only biding their time in Paris until their departures were arranged. Beaumarchais visited Marshall one evening. The intention of the French government, Beaumarchais said, is to give passports to Pinckney and Marshall, directing them to leave, while retaining Gerry in Paris. There was some discussion of money, all of it repetitious. Beaumarchais then explained that Pinckney and Marshall were considered by the Directory "as being sold to the English," and that Marshall was believed to be the leader of the two in this respect. The Directory believed Marshall's opposition to the loan, Beaumarchais reported, was the result of his devotion to England.

"I felt some little resentment," Marshall recorded in his journal, "and answered that the French government thought no such thing; that neither the government nor any man in France thought me English, but they knew I was not French. They knew I would not sacrifice my duty and the interests of my own country to any nation on earth, and therefore I was not a proper man to stay." Marshall believed the "epithet of being English" was only an excuse invented by the French. "The [French] government knew very well I loved my own country exclusively," Marshall continued, "and it was impossible to suppose any man, who loved America, fool enough to wish to engage her in a war with France, if that war was avoidable."

Before Beaumarchais left, "he hinted very plainly at what he had before observed, that means would be employed to irritate the people of the United States against me and that those means would be successful." Marshall recorded that he answered the threat by declaring he relied on his conduct itself to justify him. He told Beaumarchais that he had no fears for his own reputation, "that in public life considerations of that sort never had and never would in any degree influence me." Marshall kept careful notes of the conversation because he believed that Talleyrand had initiated it and that Marshall's comments would be reported to him.

The next day Marshall mentioned to Gerry that the plan was to order Pinckney and Marshall back and to retain Gerry. Gerry then insisted he would not stay. Marshall reported, however: "I find I shall not succeed in my efforts to procure a serious demand of passports for Mr. Gerry and myself." Whatever Gerry wanted to do, the Directory wanted him to stay.[29]

Much later Gerry explained his version of why the French wanted him to remain. The resentment directed at Marshall and Pinckney, Gerry maintained, was not because of their role as ministers but because of anti-French statements they had made in their correspondence which the French had intercepted. Gerry claimed he refrained from such comments because making them would have been "an evil practice." The suggestion that he was willing to "surrender the honor, the interest, or the independence" of his country, Gerry stoutly maintained, was "injurious, unjust, [and] contrary to well known facts." A friendly and contemporary biographer of Gerry cited a letter of Talleyrand's which makes the same point. "The advantages that I prized in him," wrote Talleyrand of Gerry, "are common to all Americans who have not manifested a predilection for England. Can it be believed that a man who should profess a hatred or contempt of the French republic, or should manifest himself the advocate for royalty, can inspire the directory with a favourable opinion of the government of the United States?"[30] Perhaps what the protestations really mean is that the French believed Gerry could be more easily persuaded to agree to some kind of financial settlement.

On March 20 Gerry produced a letter from Talleyrand suggesting that two of the American ministers return home while a third remain in Paris. The one to remain was not specified, but the obvious implication was that it should be Gerry. At a meeting the next day of the three Americans Gerry refused to stay and negotiate alone. Pinckney stated that Gerry should not remain alone, and Gerry seemed to agree. He also told his colleagues that he had previously maintained the same position in private discussions with Talleyrand. The decision was that Marshall should answer the letter, stating that none of the ministers could consent to remain and that none of the three felt himself free to leave unless ordered to do so by their own country.

Talleyrand's clerk, Dutrimond, visited Marshall on March 23. Unless, he said, one of the Americans agreed to stay, all three would be quickly ordered out of the country and the probable result would be war. When Gerry returned to Madame Villette's that afternoon Marshall told him of the conversation. Gerry now said that a letter agreeing that one of the Americans stay should be written immediately. Marshall declared such a course impossible. But Gerry replied that he would, despite his previous reluctance, remain in Paris "to prevent a war." "I made no observation on this declaration of Mr. Gerry," Marshall wrote.[31]

Marshall was anxious to return to the United States. He had been away much too long. First he had hoped to be home by Christmas, then by spring, now he could not be home before summer. In Richmond he was much missed. Polly's father had died, and Polly "fell into a deep melancholy"; with her husband in Paris, "the malady increased."[32]

In Paris the only details left undecided was how the Americans should leave. Beaumarchais, who apparently had replaced Hottinguer, Bellamy, and Hauteval as the conduit between Talleyrand and the Americans, approached Marshall and asked how he planned to return to the United States. Marshall said he probably would go by way of England. Beaumarchais advised strongly against touching England. Such a move, he said, would greatly offend France, which was still at war with England, and might harm Marshall back in the United States. Marshall did not like the implication of the remark. He also believed, as he told Beaumarchais, that he did not trust the French to allow him to return to the United States safely. He had heard rumors that instructions were going out from the Directory to the captains of privateers to capture the American ministers and take them to the West Indies where the climate would probably kill them. Marshall said he would accept a letter of safe conduct as protection, but there had been no sign of one.

Beaumarchais was shocked at the suggestion that his government would be guilty of such a scheme as Marshall had outlined. Marshall said he was "well assured" that he would be subject to seizure on the high seas. He certainly had no reason to trust the French.

Beaumarchais met with Talleyrand and then bustled back to see Marshall. Talleyrand advised strongly against Marshall's stopping in England, Beaumarchais reported, and threatened that if he did the French government would charge he went there "to receive the wages" he had earned by blocking an agreement between the United States and France. Marshall called the accusation "too contemptible" to be considered seriously and made it clear again that a letter of safe conduct, to which he believed he was entitled, would make a stop in England unnecessary.[33]

It was the end of March, and John Marshall was still waiting.

By this time Pinckney and Marshall no longer made even a pretense at friendliness with Gerry. In one heated argument Pinckney accused Gerry of acting in a manner "calculated to embarrass our government" and to increase the danger of war. Gerry countered that Pinckney and Marshall had turned against him and had not been honest with him. "It is false, sir," shot back Pinckney. In this conversation, on the evening of April 2, Elbridge Gerry again repeated his firm conviction that he must stay in Paris to avert a war. By this time there was little dispute that Elbridge Gerry would stay in France to attempt to make peace, and Pinckney and Marshall would leave.[34]

How long the Directory would toy with them was unknown. Pinckney wanted to go to the south of France where his ailing daughter could regain her strength, and the only question was when Marshall would receive his passport. On April 9 he still was uncertain. There had been no information on when he could leave and from which port, although he had received some assurances of getting a letter of safe conduct.[35]

The next day Marshall called on Beaumarchais. Intimations he had received, Marshall said, indicated he should be ready to leave momentarily—"I could not even lay in a moderate stock of wine or send my foul linen to be washed." But there was nothing definite. Marshall insisted he had a right to expect better treatment. Also, he said, within a few days no vessels bound for the United States would remain in France.

Beaumarchais then went to Talleyrand with Marshall's complaint, and Talleyrand said that Marshall was not considered a minister and could apply for a passport like an ordinary citizen. Beaumarchais met with Talleyrand twice that day, vigorously advocating Marshall's position to the Foreign Minister. Talleyrand argued back to Beaumarchais that John Marshall was responsible for the breakdown in negotiations, that he belonged to the English political faction in the United States and only sought to cause a rupture with France. Once Marshall left, Talleyrand insisted, the negotiations could proceed.[36]

Talleyrand made no commitment about a passport that day, but he apparently soon realized that if he meant what he said about negotiations getting under way once Marshall left, he might as well send Marshall on his way. Marshall received his passport and left Paris on April 15. Pinckney stayed in Paris, preparing to go to the south of France with his daughter. Elbridge Gerry stayed in Paris to continue alone the negotiations that the three men had been unable to consummate. Pinckney was bitter at Gerry's actions. "I never met with a man of less candour and so much duplicity as Mr. Gerry," he said, adding that "General Marshall is a man of extensive ability, of manly candour, and an honest heart. . . ."[37]

Marshall arrived at Bordeaux on April 21, six days after leaving Paris. It was an uneventful trip "since as usual," he wrote Pinckney, "two wheels broke down on the road." Ready to sail was the *Alexander Hamilton*, and Marshall was vastly amused at the prospect of leaving France and arriving in the United States aboard a ship named for a man who was such a *bête noire* to the French. "A very excellent vessel," he called it, "except for the sin of the name which makes my return in her almost as criminal as if I had taken England in my way." Assuming his baggage caught up with him, Marshall continued, he would take a boat out to the *Alexander Hamilton* and bid "I believe an eternal adieu to Europe."

But no one can come to Europe, especially Paris, and not enjoy its gaiety, its vibrancy, its aura of a cultured and accomplished society. Marshall had tasted all of these pleasures. And so he was not only bidding good-by to Europe, but "I wish to add . . . to its crimes—Mark I only mean its political crimes," he wrote Pinckney, "for those of a private nature are really some of them so civilized that it requires men of as much virtue and less good temper than you and myself to hate them."[38]

That same day Marshall wrote another note, this one to a man named Fulmer Skipworth, also in Paris. He sent along some papers he had planned to give Skipworth, told him of his projected sailing, and then at the end, almost casually, added: "Present me to my friends in Paris and have the goodness to say to Madame Villette in my name and in the handsomest manner, everything which respectful friendship can dictate. When you have done that you will have rendered not quite half justice to my sentiments."[39] With those few lines that phase of John Marshall's life ended—a friendship, brief and warm, ceased. There is no evidence that he and Madame Villette ever communicated with each other again.

Marshall's luggage arrived two days later, on April 23. He boarded his ship and sailed for New York on April 24.[40]

Elbridge Gerry came under, and would continue to come under, increasing criticism from the Federalists for staying in Paris. "I can see nothing but mischief to proceed from such a measure," said John Quincy Adams. The French wished Gerry to stay alone, Adams charged, because they believed him willing to incur dishonor, disgrace, "and vile indignity rather than risk a rupture with France; they believed him malleable; they can toy with him and can make him consent to terms which would only increase political divisions in the United States."[41]

Gerry always insisted he was motivated by hopes of peace. Talleyrand "informed me that a rupture would be the consequence of my leaving France," he wrote at this time to his wife to explain his staying. In a later letter to Secretary of State Pickering, Gerry elaborated on that thought, saying: "To have left France under such circumstances was a measure which I could not justify." He insisted that to have left would have caused a war, and he did not feel that he had the power to declare war. He also argued that Talleyrand, in the end, did want peace—perhaps, Gerry said, because of his commercial and land holdings in the United States. For whatever reason, Gerry insisted, Talleyrand's "professions, conduct, and interest . . . all concurred to prove that he ardently wished for peace."[42]

Gerry was, of course, correct. France did not want war. She much preferred attacking unarmed American ships without worrying whether the United States might join England's war against France. "I have operated on the principle that the Directory did not wish to carry things to extremities," Talleyrand explained, "and that it would be impossible even with a declaration of war to avenge ourselves on the American government more than we have done."[43]

Gerry's continued stay in Paris was only one of the reasons he brought upon himself the censure of his countrymen. When the XYZ papers were published in the United States early in April, it was only a matter of time until the American newspapers crossed the Atlantic and the news of the scheme spread throughout France. By the end of May the people of Paris knew the story as well as did the American public, and they were equally shocked. All assumed that Talleyrand had been the force acting behind the three men known as X, Y, and Z, and that he had directed the demand for a *douceur*.

In the tradition of such activities, however, Talleyrand played the innocent, saying he knew nothing of the affair and certainly nothing of any *douceur*. Madame de Staël, who had been responsible for Talleyrand's appointment, rushed to him and asked him to stop the rumors and scandal connecting him with the XYZ Affair, since she was afraid he might be ousted from his job. Talleyrand listened to the woman for a while, then finally—bored—left the room and did not return. To a friend Tallyrand described the scene and remarked, "Madame de Staël has only one fault: she is insufferable."[44]

In the United States Talleyrand's behavior was termed "scarcely credible" by James Madison, who could not understand how the Frenchman could have been so stupid. Speaking of the demand for a bribe, Madison told Thomas Jefferson: "I do not allude to its depravity, which however heinous, is not without examples. Its unparalleled stupidity is what fills one with astonishment." Madison did not understand how a man "of sagacity . . . could have committed both his character and safety, by such a proposition."[45] Although he was astonished, Madison did not disbelieve the report.

In Paris Talleyrand had to go through the motions of protesting that he knew nothing of the matter. On May 30 he sent to Elbridge Gerry a copy of the *London Gazette* in which the

XYZ dispatches were printed, identifying Hottinguer, Bellamy, and Hauteval only by letter and not by name. "I pray you to make known to me immediately the names," said Talleyrand. Gerry refused at first but ultimately complied. When John Marshall learned of this, he believed that Gerry had unnecessarily played into Talleyrand's hands. Marshall still remembered the dinner in December at which the emissaries had been present as well as Gerry and Talleyrand. At this dinner, as Marshall understood it, the *douceur* had been acknowledged. Gerry had erred by allowing the pretense that Talleyrand did not know the names of the three emissaries, or so Marshall believed. In doing so, Gerry also was attacking the position of Marshall and Pinckney, since their credibility depended on the supposition that Talleyrand had been responsible for the abuse they and their nation had suffered.[46]

But that was for the future. When John Marshall arrived in New York aboard the *Alexander Hamilton* on June 17, he did not know what sort of reception he would receive. He and his two colleagues, after all, had not negotiated a settlement. They had dealt with intermediaries without insisting upon being recognized. They had, perhaps, stayed too long in Paris. When he had left Richmond a year earlier, it was in hopes that he could bring about a successful settlement without harming his own position. He knew he had solved nothing, and he did not know what his own position would be.

Marshall, however, had accomplished something which perhaps even he did not understand. When he had left Richmond a year earlier, the United States was looked on with disdain by the European powers as a nation to be abused and pushed. It was a nation without power, a pawn. True, the American ministers had solved nothing, but they had not surrendered either. Nations on the European continent were accustomed to bowing in fear to the demands of France, to paying for their peace, and to seeing their emissaries slink away from the negotiating table hoping they would not be troubled again too soon. John Marshall, Charles Cotesworth Pinckney, and Elbridge Gerry, however, had refused to purchase peace. They had refused to surrender their nation's independence to a military power. And they could not be accused of acting precipitously. They had stayed in Paris through insult after insult. They could not be accused of causing any rupture. Gerry even was willing to risk his personal reputation by staying on to try again for a peace of which men would not be ashamed. They had demonstrated that their nation was made up of men of courage and of honor, not men who sought war but men who realized that war is not avoided by cowardice but by bravery, great patience, and intelligence. They had shown this to the European nations and to their own people as well. John Marshall came home a hero.

He took a carriage from New York to Philadelphia, where he expected to report to President Adams and Secretary of State Pickering. As his carriage was passing the Jolly Post Tavern it was met by three troops of the Light Horse Cavalry, about 150 mounted soldiers, plus about 50 mounted citizens "making a very long cavalcade," according to one witness. A newspaper report describes Marshall's approach from the outskirts to the center of the city: "the streets, the windows, and even the tops of the houses in many instances, were crowded with people, whose voices seemed to vie with the joyful peal from the steeple of Christ Church in giving him a sincere and hearty welcome." Editorializing a little, the friendly account continued that the reception was "not the shout of a giddy populace, responsive to the flattering cant of a hypocritical demagogue." Rather, "it was the voice of respect, affection and gratitude, towards a man who, at the hazard of his life, had displayed the most eminent talents and fortitude in support of the interest and honour of his country."

Obviously surprised and pleased at the reception, Marshall showed himself "a very modest man" who "seemed to be rather disconcerted" at the reception. A European who witnessed the events described the man who came to Philadelphia a hero as "a man of more than forty years, quite handsome and one could recognize in his bearings that he had breathed the air of Paris."[47]

Before Marshall left Philadelphia the members of the government insisted upon honoring him. There were resolutions, toasts, and dinners. The largest was held Saturday night, June 23, at O'Eller's Hotel. Arranged by members of Congress, the dinner was attended by more than 120 prominent persons—congressional leaders, members of the executive branch, army officers, state officials, as well as prominent Philadelphians. Vice President Thomas Jefferson, of course, was invited.

He was suspicious of Marshall's return. "No doubt he there [in New York] received more than hints from Hamilton as to the tone required to be assumed," Jefferson said. As for Marshall's reception in Philadelphia, Jefferson believed it had been staged by the Federalists "to secure him [Marshall] to their views." The Federalists' game, so Jefferson believed, was to stir up a war with France. Marshall was saying France did not really want a war; that was the rationale for the strong position he and Pinckney had taken. But since Marshall's arrival in Philadelphia, Jefferson charged, the Federalists "are disseminating through the town things, as from [Marshall] diametrically opposite to what he said. . . ."[48] Jefferson's comments, made in a letter to James Madison, are inconsistent. First, he accused Marshall of following the lead of Hamilton, the Federalist political leader, and then he conceded that Marshall was advocating a position diametrically opposite to that of the Federalists.

On Saturday, June 23, the morning of the planned party, Jefferson twice called on John Marshall at O'Eller's, where Marshall was staying. Marshall was in neither time, and Jefferson left a note for him, presenting his compliments and writing originally that he "was so lucky as to find that he was out on both occasions." But Jefferson adjusted that line so that it read "was so *un*lucky as to find. . . ." Jefferson, writing of himself in the third person, continued: "He wished to have expressed in person his regret that a preengagement for today which could not be dispensed with would prevent him the satisfaction of dining in company with General Marshall, and therefore begs leave to place here the expressions of that respect which in common with his fellow citizens he bears him." According to a family tradition, which has never been verified, John Marshall believed that Jefferson had written "*un*lucky" to be deliberately offensive. However, Marshall answered the note politely the next day. Explaining that he was leaving for Winchester on Monday, he said he "would with pleasure charge himself with any commands from Mr. Jefferson to that part of Virginia. . . ."[49]

At the dinner Saturday night there were two noted omissions. One was Jefferson. The other was that no toasts were drunk to Elbridge Gerry. And there were many toasts, to everyone and everything, or so it seemed. They were to the United States, to her people, to President John Adams, to former President George Washington, to Charles Cotesworth Pinckney, to the army and navy and militia, to the youth; and the more toasts that were drunk, the more excuses for toasts were sought. After John Marshall had retired, there was a toast to him—"General Marshall, the man whom his country delights to honor." And there was another, which made its way into every American history book. Robert Goodloe Harper, a Federalist member of Congress from South Carolina, well remembered fellow South Carolinian Pinckney's answer to the French attempts at extortion. "Millions for defence," Harper cried, "but not a cent for tribute." Jingoist slogan or not, the toast meant then, and still means, that America will be preserved, the national character as well as the physical nation.[50]

On Monday morning John Marshall left Philadelphia for Winchester, Virginia, for a reunion with his beloved Polly and to meet his new son John.[51] Polly was still recuperating from the birth—births were never easy for her—and the shock of her father's death. Marshall waited for the public coach, and, seeing that every inside seat was taken, he climbed up and sat next to the driver.

The European who had witnessed Marshall's arrival in Philadelphia as a conquering hero was equally impressed with his exit. He was the Polish nobleman Julian Ursyn Niemcewicz who kept a detailed journal of his American travels. "No incident . . . better paints a picture of the government, the attitudes and habits of this country," he wrote. "The height of office, the applause of the populace, great favor with all, never erases from the American mind the idea of equality and simplicity." Europeans would always be impressed by this ability of individual Americans to move from ordinary citizen to hero and back.[52]

The XYZ Affair had many repercussions. An immediate one was the attack on Elbridge Gerry. Marshall delivered to President Adams and Secretary of State Pickering a letter from Gerry explaining his position—that he must stay in Paris to prevent a war. The President and Pickering responded by sending Gerry a letter June 25 which he was instructed to consider as a letter of recall. Gerry's protestations about the threat of war and the necessity for him to stay in Paris to secure peace were no longer listened to. Apparently from some things that John Marshall himself said when he stopped in New York and Philadelphia, the picture of Gerry allowing himself "to be wheedled in Paris" was widely discussed.[53]

Weeks later, when the Americans learned of Talleyrand's request to Gerry to identify X, Y, and Z, and of Gerry's acquiescence, Gerry's reputation seemed to be destroyed. "This is the finishing stroke to his conduct in France," fumed Pickering, "by which he has dishonoured and injured his country, and sealed his own indelible disgrace." Pickering and Marshall then carried on a lengthy correspondence in which Marshall lamented that the three Americans had appeared to bow to Talleyrand's demands. Marshall also told of the December dinner in which, as he had recorded it in his journal, Talleyrand had been present with Hottinguer, Bellamy, and Hauteval when the proposed money transactions were discussed. Gerry, when he returned to the United States, denied Marshall's account of that dinner, declaring that it was not a private dinner, that fifteen or sixteen persons other than X, Y, and Z were present, and that the financial proposition spoken of—which may or may not have been heard by Talleyrand —was only the loan and not the *douceur*. On November 12 Marshall wrote Gerry that the denial is "to me still more wonderful than the fact itself." Marshall then insisted that the dinner was a private one, that only X, Y, and Z were referred to as having been guests, and "If the application was confined to the loan you misinformed General Pinckney and myself. You stated it to us as a repetition of the money propositions which had been rejected, and you expressed a good deal of indignation that such a time should have been chosen for the purpose, and you spoke in strong terms of the unblushing front with which the application was made." Gerry's contemporary and friendly biographer recorded the Gerry version, writing: "The dinner at Talleyrand's was what is called a private dinner, in opposition to those dinners called public, in which the ministers of the directory were accustomed to receive the public functionaries. It was in fact as public as forty or fifty guests of different classes, countries and sexes would permit. At such a private dinner was the money concerns of the American embassy supposed to be brought into discussion, and in such privacy was it that the American envoy was plotting treason against the rights of his country!"[54]

Gerry long suffered under the charge of having surrendered his nation's honor, of having dealt secretly with Talleyrand, and of being dishonest in his accounts of the affair. He wrote President Adams and, later, Thomas Jefferson protesting the charges and claiming innocence of any dishonorable action. He claimed much of his trouble was due to the "war party faithfully reward[ing] the other envoys for declaring explicitly in favor of war." This was not true. Marshall consistently refrained from advocating war with France and assiduously worked to prevent war to the extent of using duplicity with members of his own party in the next year. As late at least as 1810, when he was a candidate for governor of Massachusetts, Gerry campaigned against the "war party"—"A party devoted to Great Britain were determined at that time to involve this country in a war with France" read his campaign literature then defending his own role in the XYZ Affair. Apparently the strategy was successful. Gerry twice was elected to two-year gubernatorial terms and then was elected Vice President of the United States on a ticket headed by James Madison.[55]

Another repercussion of the XYZ Affair was the cementing of party lines. From this time on, there was never any hope of reconciliation between the Federalists and the Jeffersonian Republicans. Both factions tried to capitalize on the affair for political reasons. The Federalists quickly printed up large numbers of the three ministers' reports for distribution throughout the country. Pickering, the Secretary of State, sent Marshall half a dozen copies of all the papers "in a compact form" for distribution to Marshall's friends. And Pickering added that he intended to send an additional eighteen hundred for distribution in Virginia. Certainly this would anger the Republicans, who more and more found themselves under attack for being too closely aligned with the French. All the references in the negotiations to a "French party" in the United States were understood to be references to Jefferson's followers. The nation's leading Federalist, George Washington, was angered equally on the other side. "The Demos," as he called the Jeffersonians, "oppose the government in all its measures" and were challenging those who wanted peace as being "Monarchists, Aristocrats, and infractors of the Constitution."[56]

But these repercussions—the strengthening of political factions and the threat to an individual's reputation—are insignificant compared to the major question before the nation. Would there be a full-fledged war with France? The prospects were strong. Robert Liston, the British minister in the United States, reported home that the Adams administration considered "a rupture with France as an event almost unavoidable." Although Adams did not want war, Liston continued, war was not dreaded and the members of the administration "are convinced the trade of the United States will not suffer more after the commencement of hostilities than it does at the present moment:—that they expect the ultimate and hearty support of the people of the country in the struggle into which they may be forced:—that they have a very favourable idea of their public resources and that they look forward to an eventual concern and cooperation with Great Britain."[57]

Liston had considerable reason to believe that war between the United States and France was inevitable. "I will never send another minister to France," John Adams declared, "without assurances, that he will be received, respected and honoured, as the representative of a great, free, powerful, and independent nation." That was on June 21, shortly after Marshall's return. Four days later the President's wife, Abigail, wrote to her sister that she expected Congress would declare war "before they rise." The public was receptive, Talleyrand was burned in effigy. "A military spirit has spread with rapidity through the United States," one newspaper proclaimed. Young men were volunteering for service. All over the United States newspapers were dropping their advertisements to devote pages to printing the dispatches of the American ministers. America would take on the most powerful nation in Europe. Once again the drums would beat. Once again the young men would march onto the battlefield, only some of them to return.[58]

Adams was prepared to seek a declaration of war from

Congress, until he spoke with John Marshall. Marshall was against it.

Of John Marshall's personal courage there can be no question. It had been tested and proven in the Revolutionary War and in Paris. But he had seen Valley Forge and had personally known many of the three thousand men who had died there for lack of food, clothing, and medicine. He also had seen what the French depredations had done to Holland and to the French people themselves. And he firmly believed that France did not want a war with the United States. Because the United States had not been intimidated, he argued when he had stopped in Philadelphia on his way home, perhaps now France would be more willing to negotiate a settlement. Adams was a man of great intellect and even more courage. He discerned the wisdom of Marshall's reasoning and accepted it although his own party members were anxious for war. In standing firm against the popular tide, John Adams brought about his own political downfall. His standing with his own party declined so rapidly that he was ripe for political attack by dissident Federalists headed by Alexander Hamilton when he sought reelection to the presidency. Adams lost the game but won a place in history as a man with sufficient courage to avoid an unnecessary devastation of his country by war.[59]

John Marshall joined Adams in resisting a war declaration. The Constitution gives Congress the right to declare war, and the Federalists in Philadelphia were inclined to exercise that right no matter what Adams did. Marshall, who was a hero to the Federalists, argued with them that they should wait for France to declare war, that it would be advantageous to the United States to appear as the nation attacked rather than as the attacker. But would France declare war? He answered with certainty that France would as soon as the XYZ dispatches were published in Paris. Marshall quite obviously was telling John Adams one thing and the Federalists in Congress another. He did not want war, did not believe war was necessary, and was too much of a statesman to allow it to come if he could prevent it. "This opinion of Mr. Marshall [that France would declare war] damped the ardor of some, furnished excuses to others and satisfied a few of the best men that as it would be advantageous to us that France should take the odium and that she would do it, therefore we ought to forbear," lamented a Federalist named George Cabot. This delaying tactic by Marshall succeeded in dissipating some of the momentum of the war movement.[60]

Was Marshall right that war could be avoided? It was a dangerous game. If he were wrong, the United States would sink into dishonor. In Europe the predictions were mixed. In Berlin

John Quincy Adams had one opinion and then another, but finally concluded that the French "do not wish an open rupture now." At The Hague William Vans Murray, an equally astute American minister, had a different opinion. He wrote that France had been hurt by the publication of the XYZ papers, held up to ridicule, and "her efforts of revenge will merit all our attention. The tiger is wounded while he devours his prey. Her exertions will be strong. . . ." In England, where diplomacy had been elevated to a science, Lord Grenville, the Foreign Secretary, was writing at the same time that France and the United States would engage in hostile acts "which must ultimately lead to a state of general and open war."[61]

But Marshall won his gamble. There was no war. He had been correct in believing that Talleyrand was wise enough not to push the United States into joining forces with England against France. Also, he assumed that France did not want to lose American trade. Only England could gain from such a development. Talleyrand, however, needed more than his own beliefs to persuade the members of the Directory that they should abandon their lucrative practices—many were being paid either directly or indirectly by the French privateers that were raiding American ships. Talleyrand received what he needed in the form of a message from a man named Victor Du Pont. Du Pont was sent as consul general to the United States in the spring of 1798. President Adams refused to see him, but Du Pont did have a long talk with Thomas Jefferson. Because of Jefferson's supposed friendship with France, his advice had to be taken seriously. It was simple: make peace. One explanation for Jefferson's motivation was that a war with France would have destroyed his political organization. More likely, he realized that the United States could not be intimidated, and that if France did not step back, war would be the result. Jefferson also encouraged a friend of his, Doctor George Logan, a Philadelphia Quaker, to travel to Paris in a private capacity but as a known confidant of Jefferson's. With letters of introduction from Jefferson, Logan was feted in Paris as an envoy of those factions in the United States solicitous of France's interests. In Paris he found that the French had become friendly to the United States. Believing he had accomplished a great deal, Logan returned to the United States and never could understand why he was not well received in official government circles.[62]

France's intention to seek peace assumed tangible forms. The attacks on American commerce stopped. American sailors were released. Talleyrand also sought out indirect means by which to resume negotiations with the United States. William

Short, an American in Paris, reported to Elbridge Gerry that "I am more and more confirmed in the belief that this Government is at present sincere—have had their eyes opened as to the errors committed in their conduct towards the U.S. . . ."[63] Late that year President Adams reported to Congress that "the French government appears solicitous to impress the opinion, that it is averse to a rupture with this country, and that it has, in a qualified manner, declared itself willing to receive a minister from the United States. . . ." Earlier that year Adams had vowed never to deal with France again unless he was certain a minister would be properly received. He now had that certainty. He had won his point; there would be no war.

There would be in the years ahead what was called a quasi-war, with French and American ships occasionally firing at each other on the high seas. More diplomacy would be required before this would be settled, and before true amicability between the two nations was established. But a full-fledged war had been avoided. "It is peace that we have uniformly and perseveringly cultivated," Adams told Congress, and it was peace that the United States had achieved.[64]

In the months and years that followed, friends of Jefferson argued that greater efforts by Marshall, Pinckney, and Gerry at the very beginning would have achieved a reconciliation earlier. "I see several ways in which the US might have avoided a great deal of insult and injury," William Short reported to Jefferson. Joel Barlow, another American in Paris and later a devoted follower of Jefferson, reportedly wrote to George Washington that the Directory would have negotiated with the three Americans except "for some unfortunate circumstances." Perhaps. But all evidence indicates that France intended to treat the United States as it treated European nations at that time: make a semi-war, demand payment, promise peace, and then start the process all over again.[65]

For John Marshall there was no question but that France's object had been an intentional offensiveness. "History," he wrote a few years later, "will scarcely furnish the example of a nation, not absolutely degraded, which has experienced from a foreign power such open contumely, and undisguised insult, as were on this occasion suffered by the United States in the persons of their ministers."[66]

In later years Marshall, because he felt so strongly about the XYZ Affair, became increasingly bitter over the slurs made against his conduct by Thomas Jefferson and by Jefferson's biographers, and he became, in turn, more personal in his comments about the XYZ Affair. In 1832, for example, thirty-four years after the event, "the most interesting communication which I recollect," said Marshall, was the comment by the French that they had sufficient influence in the United States "that we should find our country men ready to take part against us." That was a slap at the Jeffersonian Republicans. Marshall then also charged that Logan had gone to Paris to "assure the Directory that they had gone too far and that their party in this country would be ruined" unless the Directory changed its policy.[67]

The XYZ Affair was a great event in the history of the United States, but in few great events does any participant emerge a complete hero. It can be said of John Marshall that he exercised in Paris courage, intelligence, and restraint—and continued to exercise those qualities when he returned to the United States although there were pressures on him. It can also be said that the policies he enunciated—refusing to cower and then seeking peace—were successful. That should be sufficient to say of any man's endeavor.

There was one other result of XYZ, a negative one that has dogged the history of John Marshall since. It began with a piece of gossip by Thomas Jefferson, was picked up by Marshall's biographers, and has been repeated until it has become an accepted fact, although there is nothing to support it. About two years after Marshall returned from Paris Jefferson—whose comments on Marshall and XYZ should be considered suspect—said: "Mr. John Marshall has said here that had he not been appointed minister to France he was desperate in his affairs, and must have sold his estate and that immediately. That the appointment was the greatest Godsend that could ever have befallen a man." Jefferson's source? "I have this from J. Brown and St. T. Mason," he said. John Brown, United States Senator from Kentucky, and Stevens Thomson Mason, Senator from Virginia, were two of Jefferson's staunchest supporters, and their remarks about Marshall would have been received with considerable suspicion by anyone except Jefferson. A Marshall biographer, however, picked up this gossip, accepted it, repeated it, and embellished it, stating that Marshall had accepted the ministerial post because he needed funds for the Fairfax land purchase in which he was involved, and then stating that Marshall "received in the sorely needed cash, over and above his expenses, three times the amount of his annual earnings at the bar." This has been repeated since, and has grown to where it is now written that Marshall "was impelled to accept the ministry to France in 1797 by the possibility of a generous award from a grateful Congress."[68]

When Marshall accepted the post there was no prospect of any "generous award." Ministers' salaries were set. A minister received $9,000 for his "outfit," which was to cover his expenses, an allowance of $1,350 a year for a secretary, plus a salary of $9,000 a year. When James Monroe was minister to France prior to the XYZ Affair, he was paid on that basis. He did not emerge from the position a wealthy man nor did anyone else who assumed governmental responsibilities at that time. Pinckney received a total of $28,875.93. This included $9,000 for his outfit, $14,669.17 for his salary from September 2, 1796, "the day on which I sailed from South Carolina to enter upon my mission," to April 19, 1798, "the day I quitted Paris," plus $2,250, "the sum allowed by law for returning to the United States equal to three months salary." The remainder was taken up by office expenses. Elbridge Gerry received a total of $20,451.70. This included $9,000 for his outfit, $8,728.76 as salary from August 17, 1797, "the day on which I embarked for France to the 26th of July the day on which I left Paris to return to the U.States, both days included," and $2,250 allowance for returning to the United States, equal to three months' salary plus some individual expenses.[69]

John Marshall received a total of $19,963.97. This included $9,000 for his outfit and $9,591.78 for "my salary from the 20th of June 1797, to the 14th of July 1798 comprehending three months after I received my passport in Paris to return to the United States, being 1 year & 24 days at 9,000 dollars per annum." It also included $1,372.19 for the salary of his secretary. Of this amount, Marshall received $3,500 from Secretary of State Pickering before sailing for France, $8,222 while in Europe (from a Dutch banking firm which handled the American accounts), and $2,000 more from Pickering on June 23, 1798, when he returned to Philadelphia from Paris. The balance of $6,241.97 was paid by Pickering in October.[70] If Marshall showed any "profit" out of the XYZ Affair, it was this $6,241 paid four months after his return. Considering that his law practice which paid him approximately that much annually had been neglected for well over a year and that it was necessary for his family to have funds for living expenses while he was in Europe, and considering that the amount was the usual amount paid to ministers and not in any manner a special reward, it cannot be construed as excessive or even as the object of his endeavors. There is no basis to the claim that financial considerations persuaded Marshall to become one of the three envoys to Paris.

A legitimate question does exist as to why Marshall, after so many years of refusing any public service that would take him away from Richmond, finally did accept the post. There is a family tradition that John and James Markham Marshall rescued a younger brother, Louis (*né* Lewis), who was a prisoner in a Paris jail. According to this tradition, Louis was a medical student in Edinburgh and, caught up in the romance of the French Revolution, had traveled to Paris where he was imprisoned after being involved in the storming of the Bastille and other student endeavors. In a 1941 master's thesis at Washington and Lee, William Buchanan effectively demonstrated that Louis Marshall could not have been in Paris when that tradition places him there.[71] Also, in all of the John Marshall correspondence while he was in Paris, there is no reference to any brother, and it is difficult to accept that he could see his brother Louis after a separation lasting years and rescue him from prison without mentioning it in a letter. Also the timing of James Markham's correspondence indicates he left Europe in 1797 without ever having had the opportunity of traveling to Paris and joining John.

Why, then, did John Marshall go to Paris? Perhaps it was simply as he said, that he believed he could make a contribution to a cause which greatly concerned him. Perhaps he only wished to travel to Paris once in his lifetime, a not unusual ambition. Or also perhaps, contrary to the general belief that he went to Europe to help raise funds for the Fairfax land purchase, the financial problems of that transaction had already been solved and he was free to assume projects without having to worry about money.

The Fairfax land purchase was a central point of Marshall's life from his childhood through his old age and also produced litigation long after his death. In the 1600s large sections of North America were given away by the English throne to friendly nobles as rewards for service and loyalty. The land seemed endless, and the presents were in reality cheap ones. To the recipient, the land—a barren wilderness—was more a promise of wealth for his future family than for himself. In some instances the actual size of the grant never could be accurately gauged—the gift lines were rather vague. It was difficult to appreciate the size of the North American continent from a throne room in London. One of the largest land grants was called the northern neck of Virginia. It encompassed hundreds of thousands of acres and eventually became known as the Fairfax lands. In the years before the American Revolution George Washington and Thomas Marshall had surveyed these lands for Lord Fairfax, probably with Thomas' young son John coming along on the surveying trips occasionally. Thomas Marshall at this time also was the agent in western Virginia for Lord Fairfax.

During the Revolution the Virginia legislature enacted legislation denying all British subjects the right to own land in the commonwealth. But Lord Fairfax, apparently a well-liked landlord, was considered an American citizen by the legislature and his lands specifically were exempted from any such legislation. Fairfax died in 1781 and left the lands to his nephew, the Reverend Denny Martin, with the provision that his nephew assume the family name Fairfax. The nephew did so and in the mid-1780s came to Virginia to claim his land holdings. He met troubles. While his uncle may have been considered an American citizen by the Virginia legislature, Denny Martin Fairfax was, without question, an English citizen. Was he prohibited from holding American land? The Virginia legislature had said he could not have title to any lands held prior to the Revolution. Even this was vague, however, for the Fairfax lands were characterized in two ways—manor lands for which specific claims had been made, and ungranted lands which were still wilderness. The act denying English citizens title spoke of both lands, but the legislature seemed interested only in implementing the sections having to do with ungranted lands.

Also to be considered was the Treaty of 1783 which appeared to restore all British possessions to their owners. It was on the basis of that treaty that Denny Martin Fairfax came to Virginia to claim his fortune. Because of the earlier association between his uncle, Lord Fairfax, and the Marshall family, he hired John Marshall as his lawyer. Marshall advised him to claim both the manor lands and the ungranted sections. And so began one of the great legal struggles in Virginia's history. The state had granted in 1789 a total of 788 acres of Fairfax's ungranted land to a man named David Hunter. Denny Fairfax challenged this grant, arguing that the Treaty of 1783 had assured his ownership of these lands. In the Virginia ratification convention of 1788 the question of the Fairfax lands specifically had been brought up, and Marshall had answered it in this manner:

> If Fairfax has this right, and comes to Virginia, what laws will his claims be determined by? By those of this state. By what tribunals will they be determined? By our state courts. Would not the poor man, who was oppressed by an unjust prosecution, be abundantly protected and satisfied by the temper of his neighbors, and would he not find ample justice?

David Hunter presented his case to the temper of his neighbors in the District Court at Winchester in 1791, and lost. He then carried it to the Court of Appeals, and then in 1796 to the Supreme Court in Philadelphia. The ultimate verdict could be a crucial one, not only for John and James Markham Marshall who by this time were actively engaged in purchasing the Fairfax land grant, but for many Americans whose titles to land holdings were mired in vague boundaries, confusing and conflicting state and federal laws, as well as treaty obligations. Shortly before the case was to be argued, however, David Hunter sent the Court a letter, dated July 29, 1796, explaining that his lawyer, Alexander Campbell, had died in Richmond, and requesting that arguments be delayed. In effect, Hunter was seeking an indefinite post-ponement. The Court granted his request, but one Justice had a reservation. Samuel Chase said that in a similar case, a Mary-land court had decided against the tenant (who would be Hunter in the Fairfax tangle). "It is a matter, however, of great moment," said Chase, "and ought to be deliberately and finally settled." Chase may have been more prescient than the other Justices, because Hunter did not seek to push his case again until 1809.[72]

Exactly when John Marshall decided to purchase the Fair-fax land grant is unknown. Probably in the late 1780s, as he realized that title to the land, and profit from it once title was won, would require decades to complete. This made the land an ideal investment for a man like himself who wanted to secure the financial independence of his family in later years. It also made the land a poor investment for a man, as Denny Fairfax apparently was, who was interested in a quicker profit. To pur-chase the land, Marshall needed first to be certain that the title was secure, and then he needed funds.

Securing title, as far as the Virginia Commonwealth was concerned, was not difficult. Marshall worked out an arrange-ment, which he submitted to Governor Robert Brooke, in March of 1795. The Fairfax purchasers would surrender rights to the ungranted lands if Virginia would allow them clear title to the manor lands. These amounted to 160,000 acres. His offer was turned down at first because of the expectation that the courts would soon settle the matter. But the courts did not appear ready to reach a solution in the case, and the settlers in the western territories were becoming concerned at the delays. They wanted to use the land but did not feel they could until its title was set-tled. By late 1796 three western counties, Hampshire, Hardy, and Shenandoah, had petitioned the state legislature to settle the matter once and for all. As a result an act was passed December 10, 1796, dividing the land along the compromise suggested by John Marshall. He formally acquiesced to the compromise in a letter dated November 24, 1796, identifying himself as "one of the purchasers of the lands of Mr. Fairfax."[73]

Raising the money was a more serious problem. He organized a syndicate with his brother James Markham Marshall, James' father-in-law Robert Morris, John's own brother-in-law Rawleigh Colston, and Henry Lee. Lee apparently dropped out and Morris went bankrupt. An agreement of intention was signed on May 17, 1793, and the purchase price contemplated was 20,000 pounds. (The exact amount is listed variously between 14,000 and 22,000 pounds. Apparently some of the land was bought by the three men as individuals as well as an organized group. But the syndicate paid 20,000 pounds.) The money did not seem excessive for the men to raise. John Marshall in the early 1790s was a prominent lawyer. James Markham Marshall was in Europe as the agent of Robert Morris and as the commercial agent for the cities of Charleston, New York, and Boston. Colston had made a large amount of money in the West Indies. But they did have troubles. In 1793 Marshall, for example, was lamenting that "my brother Mr. James Marshall is now in London with full powers to bind some other gentlemen with myself to the immediate payment of a sum of money which I cannot command." In Europe James Marshall devoted much of two years, between 1795 and 1797, to trying to raise funds for the purchase. The letters to him from Robert Morris in Philadelphia tell an intriguing story of eighteenth-century international financiers at work. "Should a general Peace in Europe take place this winter —I think you will find money grows plenty," Robert Morris advised James Markham in the middle of 1795. When the case of *Hunter v. Fairfax* was postponed indefinitely by the Supreme Court in July 1796, Morris reported the bad news to James Markham, that a final court decision on the ownership of the lands had been postponed. Morris feared "that real disadvantage will result to your concern thereby."[74]

But later that year prospects brightened for the entrepreneurs. James Markham Marshall reported that he was going to Holland in hopes of making the loan. "I hope you may do so," Morris told him, "for it would afford sensible relief at this time." In Holland, however, James Markham Marshall first met with disappointment. Robert Morris wrote to John Marshall that James had left Amsterdam for London "on the invitation of some capitalists with whom he was negotiating for a loan of $400,000" but this had fallen through. "Mr. Hottenguer, who first put the thing in motion," Morris continued, "says it will come on again and he thinks it will be carried into effect, if so your brother will of course be ready for Mr. Fairfax and he was trying to raise money from other sources lest that should fail. . . ." John Marshall in Richmond was keenly interested in how the European negotiations were working out, and traveled to Philadelphia in

February of 1797 to learn what the prospects were. At that point they were dreadful. Morris had received only bad news from James Markham in Europe and had no money of his own. The Fairfax land purchase was in trouble.

But the situation brightened. In April Morris heard from Europe that a loan had been arranged. "The accomplishment of the loan you mention," he wrote to James Markham, "altho' but small in comparison of the wants, is very pleasing, as it enables you to take the first steps with Lord Fairfax for securing your bargain and I am in hopes that the Events which have since taken place in England may have enabled you to obtain as much more money as may be necessary to compleat that business."[75]

The timing of the letters is significant. By April of 1797, two months before John Marshall was asked to go to France as minister, the immediate financial problems of the Fairfax land purchase had been settled, and this was known in the United States. Contrary to the Jefferson charge that he accepted the ministerial post because the Fairfax land purchase was hanging over his head, a charge repeated endlessly since, Marshall felt free to go to Europe because the immediate problem of the Fairfax land purchase in fact had been solved. This was apparent in the timing of the negotiations between James Markham in London and Denny Martin Fairfax. After weeks of negotiations James Markham wrote Fairfax a letter, dated September 6, 1797, in the city of London, making a formal offer of 20,000 pounds "in sterling money of England" for the land. The only condition was that the remaining details about the Fairfax title be settled. The letter is dated a few days after John Marshall had arrived in Holland to begin the XYZ mission. The time required then to travel across the Atlantic means that James Markham could not have known his brother John was coming, and also that he must have felt secure about the funds for the Fairfax land purchases long before John's arrival in Europe.

The syndicate actually paid about 7,000 pounds then, and the remainder in 1806 to Denny Martin Fairfax's heir. And beginning in 1800 the Marshalls again concerned themselves with raising funds to meet that 1806 deadline. The three remaining members of the syndicate divided up approximately 220,000 acres of land in northern Virginia—the 160,000 acres they had purchased jointly plus the land they had purchased as individuals. John Marshall ended with almost 100,000 acres; James Markham, 80,000 acres; and Rawleigh Colston, 40,000 acres.[76]

The deal was an immense one, but not terribly unique for the time. (Robert Morris engaged in larger transactions but turned out to be not as adroit a businessman as the Marshall brothers, in that he overextended himself.) Nor was it in any way improper. A fair price was paid for land with potential for development. Excluding Thomas Jefferson's gossip—which in the light of evidence seems less and less justified—there is no suggestion whatsoever that John Marshall's participation in the XYZ mission was motivated by the Fairfax land grant transactions.

5

WHEN JOHN MARSHALL returned to Richmond he was anxious to settle down again, resume his law practice, and reacquaint himself with his family. Such luxuries, however, were not to be his. The elections for the Sixth Congress were coming up in April of 1799. The Federalists' strategy was to line up strong candidates as early as possible to assure a majority when the Congress finally met late in 1799. At first it seemed that the XYZ Affair would keep the Federalists in power permanently. But they had made the mistake of enacting the Alien and Sedition Acts. These caused them a great deal of trouble, and ultimately destroyed their party.

The Representative in Congress from the Richmond district was a man named John Clopton, who was a firm supporter of Thomas Jefferson. He was a Revolutionary War veteran, had served in the state legislature, and had first been elected to the Congress in 1795. He was considered a strong, almost an unbeatable candidate. The Virginia Federalists knew that one man in Richmond was popular enough to defeat Clopton, but John Marshall had said he was done with public life. He found that his law practice had not suffered because of his absence, and to pleas that he run he gave a peremptory refusal, "and I did not believe," he later said, "it possible that my determination could be shaken. I was however mistaken."[1]

One man could persuade Marshall to become an active candidate, and George Washington was willing to try. At Mount Vernon, the former President's pique at Thomas Jefferson and his Republican faction was growing. He believed Jefferson had actually embraced the French cause. Traitorous was perhaps too strong a word for Washington's description of Jefferson, but not very. As a result in 1798 and 1799 Washington—as John Marshall later described it—exerted his influence "to induce men whose talents he respected, but who had declined political life, to enter into the national and state legislatures." Two such men

George Washington immediately started working on were Bushrod Washington, his nephew and a prominent Virginia lawyer in his own right, and John Marshall. He wrote to his nephew in August of 1798, asking both men to visit him, saying: "The crisis is important. The temper of the people of this State in many, at least in some, places, are so violent and outrageous, that I wish to converse with General Marshall and yourself on the elections which must come soon."[2]

On their way to Mount Vernon the two men stopped their horses for a few minutes to rest them, and John Marshall realized his knee breeches were badly torn. He reached into his saddlebags for a replacement, but found no clothes at all. That morning he apparently had taken another man's saddlebags, from the tavern where he had stopped overnight. Greatly embarrassed, Marshall entered Mount Vernon in torn pants. George Washington was vastly amused and offered him a pair of his own.[3]

John Marshall and Bushrod Washington arrived at Mount Vernon on September 3 and stayed until the morning of September 6, leaving before breakfast. During this visit Marshall and George Washington walked along the porch, and Washington spoke of the seriousness of the political crisis and said that every man who could contribute to the "success of sound opinions" was required to take up public service. Washington's plan was that Marshall should run for Congress from Richmond and Bushrod Washington should run from Westmoreland County. Marshall refused. He explained that he had made "large pecuniary engagements" which required building up his law practice.

Washington refused to accept his answer, and finally he did something which was uncharacteristic of him. He used himself as an example. Few people knew as well as Marshall the extent of Washington's personal sacrifices for public service; the years that Mount Vernon was wasted while Washington commanded the American forces, the personal resources that Washington had given to the Revolutionary cause to keep it aflame, and then the years as President in which he had been subject to personal abuse as vindictive as it was uncalled for. Washington did not have to repeat this. He did not point out that once again he had agreed to accept public office. (Washington was commander of the army being raised to counter the French threat. The army, like the threat, turned out to be unreal, but no one could have been certain of that in the fall of 1798, just three months after John Marshall had returned from Paris.)

"My resolution yielded to this representation," Marshall recalled some years later. "After remarking that the obligation which had controlled Washington's course was essentially different from that which bound me, that no other man could fill the place to which his country had called him, whereas my services could weigh but little in the political balance, I consented to become a candidate. . . ."[4]

Marshall knew what he was in for. "The conflict of parties in this state is extremely ardent," he wrote in a letter to a friend, then said a few days later that he was a candidate "as a punishment for some unknown sins." With all the strength of the Jeffersonian Republicans turned against him, he had a fight on his hands. A few days later he had an opportunity to pull out. James Wilson, an Associate Justice on the Supreme Court, had died, and John Adams wanted to fill the position from Virginia—"It is true that some regard to States ought to be always remembered," he said, "but Pennsylvania has always had a judge. Virginia has had none since the resignation of Mr. Blair. . . ." And particularly Adams wanted John Marshall. "Of the three envoys," he said, "the conduct of Marshall alone has been entirely satisfactory, and ought to be marked by the most decided approbation of the public." But Marshall by this time had committed himself to the congressional race and would not retreat from it. The offer then went to Bushrod Washington, who accepted.[5]

The major issue of the campaign was the Alien and Sedition Laws, enacted by the Congress and signed by President Adams in the dramatic glow following the publication of the XYZ papers. The Alien Law permitted the President to expel from the United States or imprison any alien he considered dangerous. The Sedition Law extended the authority of the federal courts to seditious libel, and much more. In effect, this law made a public statement critical of the President a cause for arrest, prosecution, and conviction. Passage of the two laws was a bold move by the Federalists to strike at their political opposition. They acted with what they considered justification.

The Federalists believed they faced a conspiracy to destroy the government. To the Federalist way of thinking, the Whiskey Rebellion in the early 1790s was not an outburst of indignation by some westerners but part of a much wider movement. The westerners had been encouraged to believe that they could violate the tax law because, Marshall later wrote, "the measure was censured on the floor of Congress as unnecessary and tyrannical; that resistance to its execution was treated as probable; that a powerful, influential, and active party, pervading the union, arraigned with extreme acrimony the whole system of finance as being hostile to liberty." The Federalist view, then, was that much lawlessness was the result of the opposition's agitation, and that if the opposition could be silenced, law and order would return.

The Federalists believed that for the opposition, again in Marshall's words, "The victory of the party becomes the great object, and, too often, every thing is deemed right or wrong as it tends to promote or impede it. The attainment of the end is considered as the supreme good, and the detestable doctrine is adopted that the end will justify the means. The mind, habituated to the extenuation of acts of moral turpitude, becomes gradually contaminated, and loses much of its horror for vice, and of its respect for virtue."[6]

The whiskey tax inflamed the western frontier for most of the 1790s. In western Pennsylvania there was a brief and unsuccessful movement toward armed revolt. Throughout western Kentucky the tax collectors feared for their lives, or else did not attempt to enforce the law. John Marshall was particularly conscious of this lawlessness; one of the endangered collectors was his father. Thomas Marshall had certain responsibilities to the federal government and he would fulfill those as he had always fulfilled his responsibilities. "There may be some persons who may pretend a want of knowledge" about the tax, he said, but "all spirits found in possession of any such person . . . will be seized. . . ." The people of Kentucky then proceeded to burn Thomas Marshall in effigy and to assault his deputies. When John Marshall spoke of the "multiplied outrages committed on the persons and property of the revenue officers," he was speaking from personal knowledge of the danger to his own family. He believed that the Whiskey Rebellion had begun with the encouragement of the Jeffersonian Republicans, but had reached a point where those who had encouraged it "now trembled at the extent of the conflagration. It had passed the limits they had assigned to it, and was no longer subject to their control."[7]

This picture of a conspiracy was added to by the XYZ papers with their insinuations that there was "a French party" in the United States which would obey the commands of the Directory in Paris rather than those of the American government in Philadelphia. If there was a war with France, some Federalists said they feared they would be murdered in their beds by their neighbors acting at the instigation of a politician who sat across from them in the halls of Congress.

Out of this fear grew the Federalist determination to repress dissent and opposition, to defeat enemies not through the political system or by appeal to the electorate's reason, but by using the power of government to crush them. The Federalists controlled the government, and they would use it for their own ends. Defenders of the Federalists may find solace in the fact that their successors were not immune to similar temptations. When

Thomas Jefferson was President he believed that "a few prosecutions of the most prominent offenders would have a wholesome effect in restoring the integrity of the presses—not a general prosecution, for that would look like persecution, but a selected one."⁸ His conduct concerning the Aaron Burr trial was government tyranny at its worst. Abraham Lincoln suspended the writ of habeas corpus during the Civil War, and examples continue into recent times. But these subsequent events cannot mitigate the fact that the Federalists were perverting American principles, and the success of the United States may very well have hinged upon the defeat of the Federalists and the erasure of their Alien and Sedition Laws.

John Adams, the President who had performed gloriously in keeping the United States out of a war with France, failed in not blocking the acts. And once they were law, he did not concern himself with their enforcement, which was another failure. But his appointees—Secretary of State Pickering, the federal marshals and attorneys—worked diligently at seeking out newspaper editors critical of the administration. Approximately two dozen persons were arrested under the Sedition Law, and perhaps half were tried and convicted. The arrests were aimed primarily at the major Republican newspapers which were vehicles of the opposition propaganda. Criticism was described as seditious libel, and the intent was to destroy the Republican party.⁹

The public reaction to the Alien and Sedition Laws, particularly the latter, was quick in coming. Petitions were circulated in most communities to collect signatures against the laws. At William and Mary the students on July 4, 1798, their graduation day, paraded through the Williamsburg streets with a figure representing John Adams crowned as king receiving a royal address from a subservient Congress. Even John Marshall, as popular as he was in Virginia after his return from the XYZ mission, was not immune from attack. At a theater in Fredericksburg he was insulted by an angry mob for his association with the Federalist party and threatened with physical harm.¹⁰

On the other side, Thomas Jefferson was quite certain, as were many of his followers, that the Alien and Sedition Laws were only the first step toward other acts, leading ultimately to the establishment of an American monarchy with George Washington as king. "That these things are in contemplation, I have no doubt," Jefferson charged.

Marshall never forgave Thomas Jefferson these attacks on Washington. Many years later he charged that "a great portion of the calumny" hurled at the Federalists was based "on the fact that they supported their own government against the aggressions and insults of France." Marshall, his anger having increased over the years, said that Jefferson had accused the Federalists, instead, of a "hostility to republicanism and a desire to introduce a monarchy on the British model. That his opinion was fallacious, that he was wrong and the federalists right on this subject of the French revolution was surely demonstrated long before his death."[11]

As for the Alien and Sedition Laws, Marshall had mixed feelings. In August of 1798, before he became a congressional candidate, he wrote to Timothy Pickering, the Secretary of State who was zealously pushing their enforcement, that the laws would be the basis for attacks upon the administration. "I am extremely sorry to observe that here [Richmond] . . . those two laws, especially the sedition bill, are viewed by a great many well meaning men, as unwarranted by the Constitution." But, he continued, he was "entirely persuaded" that many of these critics had an "implacable" hatred for the government, and that if the Alien and Sedition Laws did not exist, "some clamor would be made by them on some other account." Marshall, however, did feel compelled to add that "There are also many who are guided by very different motives and who tho less noisy in their complaints are seriously uneasy on the subject."[12]

Already John Marshall was beginning to move away from the extremist position adopted by the Federalist party. His ultimate course was one of opposing the laws without dissociating himself from his party or offending George Washington, who had come to believe that opposition to the Alien and Sedition Laws was nothing more than partisan ravings by the Jeffersonians. Like all compromises, Marshall's did not work entirely, primarily because the Federalists became more and more convinced that either one was with them entirely or against them entirely. They did not believe John Marshall could have it both ways.

Once he became a congressional candidate Marshall had to map out a specific position that would get him elected in Virginia where the Alien and Sedition Laws were not very popular but still keep him welcome among his fellow Federalists. On September 12, just a few days after he had agreed to become a congressional candidate, a letter appeared in the Virginia newspapers, signed "A Freeholder," and asking Marshall five questions, including his position on the Alien and Sedition Laws. The tone of the letter, its phrasing, as well as its timing, suggest that Marshall either wrote it himself or superintended its writing as a device that would permit him to publicize his position. A Virginia newspaper that printed the questions and then Marshall's answers conceded that Marshall probably had instigated the questions for electioneering purposes but insisted that was "immaterial," the important point being what he had to say. The letter to Marshall first appeared September 12 and his answer appeared September 20.

The first question asked whether "in heart, and sentiment, [you] profess yourself an American. . . ." Marshall's answer: "In heart and sentiment, as well as by birth and interest, I am an American." He went on to say he believed in the Constitution "as the rock of our political salvation." In the second question "Freeholder" began to move away from rhetoric to concrete issues. Did Marshall believe that America's true interests were "dependent upon an alliance with any foreign nation?" Marshall was firm in his opposition to an "alliance with any foreign nation." In the third question "Freeholder" became more specific. Did Marshall favor any kind of alliance with Great Britain? This question, of course, referred to the Federalist party's supposed connections with England. In his answer Marshall insisted that he opposed any alliance with England and any "closer connexion with that nation than already exists." He added, however, that "Should France continue to wage an unprovoked war against us, while she is also at war with Britain, it would be madness and folly not to endeavour to make such temporary arrangements as would give us the aid of the British fleets to prevent our being invaded; but I would not, even to obtain so obvious a good, make such a sacrifice as I think we should make, by forming a permanent political connexion with that, or any other nation on earth." In the fourth question Marshall was asked if he agreed with the administration's policies toward France. Naturally he agreed with those policies; he had been so much a part of them. The United States, he argued, had no other choice "unless we would have relinquished the rights of self government and have become the colony of France."

When the fifth question was propounded, it was apparent that everything else had been only background for this query. It read: "Are you an advocate for the Alien and Sedition Bills? Or, in the event of your election, will you use your influence to obtain a repeal of these laws?"

"I am not," began John Marshall's answer, "an advocate for the Alien and Sedition Bills." At a time when his political party had made the Alien and Sedition Laws its *raison d'être*, at a time when the Alien and Sedition Laws were the major—almost the only—political issue, those eleven words of John Marshall's required courage. "Had I been in Congress when they passed, I should, unless my judgment could have been changed, certainly have opposed them." Marshall, however, still a Federalist, still the admirer of George Washington, could not completely disown the handiwork of Washington and his own party. "I do not think them fraught with all those mischiefs which many gentlemen ascribe to them," he said. His opposition, he continued, would have been based on his belief that the bills, rather, were useless and because they "are calculated to create unnecessary discontents and jealousies at a time when our very existence, as a nation, may depend on our union." He then added that if the bills, when originally proposed, had been fought on that basis by someone "not suspected of intending to destroy the government, or being hostile to it"—meaning a prominent Federalist such as himself—they never would have been enacted. As for opposing them if he were elected, Marshall said he believed the issue would be settled before he could take his seat. In the event of any doubts, however, he added: "I shall indisputably oppose their revival."[13]

The arguments regarding the Alien and Sedition Laws encompassed the question of whether English common law existed in the United States. Although federal law might without question authorize the punishment of persons who attacked the country, did it also authorize punishment of persons who might encourage such attacks through libelous statements in the press? The Federalists answered that it did, that that was part of the common law which had been absorbed by federal law. Therefore to prosecute under the Alien and Sedition Acts was not to violate the First Amendment's guarantee of press freedoms, but only to follow the traditions of common law. The Jeffersonian Republicans opposed the concept that the common law held sway in the federal courts. If it did, the federal courts were then all-powerful because the common law was all-encompassing.

Marshall at this time did not publicly speak to the issue of the common law. Two years later, however, he did make clear his belief that the common law had not been incorporated into the federal law. The states indeed did have the common law. "Our ancestors brought with them the laws of England both statute and common law as existing at the settlement of each colony, so far as they were applicable to our situation," he said. The American Revolution did not change the law in each state, Marshall continued, although state laws could be altered or nullified by specific federal acts or by treaties. He believed "That on adopting the existing constitution of the United States the common and statute law of each state remained as before and that the principles of the common law of the state would apply themselves to the magistrates of the general as well as to magistrates of the particular government. . . ." His argument here, like most of his arguments, was one of logic. When the United States was formed under the Constitution, the states had legal systems which had to be left intact as long as they did not interfere with federal law. To have done otherwise would have wiped out existing legal traditions without cause and without assurance of being able to replace them with anything better. But organizing the federal government was a different situation. The federal Union replaced nothing. It was created out of dreams, ambitions, and needs and not from an existing political entity. To say that the common law was absorbed into the powers of the federal government was virtually to say that this new political organization had the power to do whatever it liked and was not limited by the Constitution. As for the Alien and Sedition Laws, Marshall said in 1800 that the Federalists "contended, not that the common law gave the courts jurisdiction in cases of sedition but that the constitution gave it." In fact, a constitutional defense of the Alien and Sedition Laws was offered toward the end of 1798, and it was a persuasive one; so persuasive that its unknown author is believed to have been John Marshall.[14]

Marshall's answers to "A Freeholder," disavowing the Alien and Sedition Laws, aroused a storm of protest from his fellow Federalists. In New England Harrison Gray Otis "condemns him *ore rotundo*," reported Fisher Ames, himself charging that "no correct man—no incorrect man even, whose affections and feelings are wedded to the government—would give his name to the base opposers of law." Secretary of State Pickering, Marshall's friend and supporter, conceded that "I have not met with one good federalist who does not regret [Marshall's] answer to the Freeholder." These men controlled Marshall's political party and perhaps even his political future. He had angered them, defied them, and if he were elected to Congress, they would be his enemies.[15]

In addition to angering his fellow Federalists, Marshall's answer on the Alien and Sedition Laws also angered the Jeffersonians who believed him guilty of the worst duplicity. A typical attack against him at this time came in a series of letters, written for publication in the Virginia newspapers, signed "Curtius." "Curtius" was John J. Thompson of Petersburg, Virginia, who was not yet twenty-one years of age. The level of the public debate can be seen from Thompson's opening. In the first letter addressed to Marshall, he begins:

> Many events have combined, to render you a very important character in this country. You have long been regarded as the leader of that party in this state who arrogate to themselves the exclusive name of Federalists, while they demonstrate their federalism, by a servile attachment to the administration, by a rancourous perse-

cution of every enlightened republican, and by audacious
efforts to erect a monarchy or aristocracy upon the ruins
of our free constitution. . . .

Thompson then charged that Marshall's position on the
Alien and Sedition Laws was motivated purely by political expediency and posed no political dangers for Marshall. The Federalists' "gratitude for your past services and their sanguine expectations from your future exertions will readily induce them to
forgive a momentary affection of the good principles which they
abhor," Thompson charged. He pointed out in the third letter,
and quite correctly, that Marshall's answer to "A Freeholder"
did not discuss the constitutionality of the laws. "It is hardly possible to believe," Thompson wrote, "that you can be seriously of
opinion that these flagrant usurpations are constitutional laws."
Near his conclusion, Thompson wrote: "I defy all the powers of
your mind, I defy the collected wisdom . . . to justify your conduct
in concealing your opinions upon a momentous constitutional
question. Your silence is a confession of guilt. . . ."[16]

If the major impact of the Alien and Sedition Laws in Virginia had been the attacks on John Marshall, they would not have
been significant factors in his life, nor in the lives of most Virginians, nor of most Americans—except as a historical example
of the excesses to which governments are sometimes prone. But
they had a much more lasting impact when they produced the
Virginia and Kentucky Resolutions. Largely written by Jefferson,
with assistance from Madison, the resolutions were a reaffirmation of the powers of the states. Merrill Peterson, Jefferson's
recent biographer, has conceded that "In the final analysis it is
impossible to say precisely what Jefferson's theory was in the
Resolutions of '98. They were not conceived in the oracular realm
of constitutional law but in a desperate struggle for political
survival."[17]

To Jefferson, not yet President himself, the power of the
central government was the danger facing the United States,
while powerful state governments would save democracy. So the
resolutions declared that the states had the right to nullify federal acts which they considered unconstitutional. In effect, that
meant that the political bodies that made up the United States
could decide which of the federal laws they would allow to be
enforced within their borders. The theory became in later years a
defense for slavery, and still later, a defense for maintaining
segregationist practices in violation of federal laws.

In 1798, however, the immediate problem was to answer
the Virginia and Kentucky Resolutions. A minority of the mem-

bers of the Virginia legislature drew up an answer, which is believed to have been the handiwork of John Marshall. There is no evidence that Marshall actually wrote the paper at the request of the Federalist minority in the state legislature, except that persons familiar with his work believed it probable that he had, and historians since then have gone along with the assumption.[18]

Parts of the Federalist response do read as if Marshall wrote them—the careful analytical approach that, seemingly without effort, builds argument upon argument until the wall hemming in the opposition cannot be scaled. Also the theory of a federal government allowed by an expanding Constitution to do what necessity required unless specifically forbidden, which was expressed in that minority report, became one of the themes of John Marshall's decisions as Chief Justice of the United States.

In arguing that the Constitution does not prohibit the Alien Law, the minority report asserted that while the federal government "is indubitably limited as to its objects," the means of obtaining those objects are not subject to such limitations. "It is necessary, in pursuing this enquiry," the report said, "to bear in mind that we are investigating a constitution which must unavoidably be restricted in various points to general expressions, making the great outlines of a subject, and not a law which is capable of descending to every minute detail." The report argued that if the Constitution were to be examined for specific justification for "every minute detail," then "the power of fortifying our ports and harbours might well be questioned." It continued that the Constitution must be examined liberally. This sounds like John Marshall defending the role of a powerful federal government.

The minority report then argued that the federal government not only has the power to repel attacks against the United States but also to protect each state against invasion. "To protect against an evil," concluded the section dealing with the Alien Law, "includes the right of taking proper and necessary steps, the government possessed of the power must judge. To cause to depart from our territory the individuals of a nation from whom invasion was apprehended, is most obviously a measure of precaution dictated by prudence and warranted by justice. . . ."

Defending the Sedition Law, the minority report argued that "To contend that there does not exist a power to punish writings coming within the description of this law, would be to assert the inability of our nation to preserve its own peace, and to protect themselves from the attempt of wicked citizens, who incapable of quiet themselves, are incessantly employed in devising means to disturb the public repose. . . . Government cannot be secured if, by falsehood and malicious slander, it is to be deprived of the confidence and affection of the people." Here the report was on shaky ground. There was not then, and there has not been since, a politician in office who does not feel that some of the campaign attacks against him are "falsehood and malicious slander." Actually, contrary to what the minority report said, the American government has grown more secure by permitting the "public repose" to be disturbed, for public officials who know they are subject to public scrutiny and comment must be able to justify their conduct. This section of the minority report still could have been written by John Marshall—though he never conceded authorship and none of it has ever been positively tied to him. But one can understand his responding to the appeals of his fellow Virginia Federalists to produce for them a constitutional brief on behalf of the Alien and Sedition Laws anonymously, which would not embarrass him because of his earlier comments to "A Freeholder" saying he did not support the laws.

It is the last part of the minority report, however, that is difficult to square with what is known of John Marshall. This part searches for a common law defense of the Alien and Sedition Laws, something which John Marshall two years later disavowed. In this section the minority report does seem to suggest the kind of dangers that Jefferson and the Republicans feared when they contemplated the federal government absorbing all of common law. "That rule is the common or unwritten law which pervades all America," it said, "and which declaring libels against government to be a punishable offence, applies itself impartially and protects any government which the will of the people may establish." To substantiate that the Constitution did contemplate the absorption of common law, the minority report offered an ingenious justification. The First Amendment to the Constitution forbids an infringement upon the freedom of the press. "It would have been certainly unnecessary thus to have modified the legislative powers of Congress concerning the press," said the report, "if the power itself does not exist." The protection of the press was being used against the press. Opposing the concept of the absorption of the common law into federal law as Marshall said he did, it is difficult to accept that he wrote that part of the report.

There is another factor which casts doubt on whether John Marshall was the sole author of the minority report, as was generally believed. In France he had seen the destruction of government by irresponsible men, and he had understood that the press is always the first element of society attacked by despots. He respected the Federalist party and he revered George Washington, but he was fortunate in having been out of the country during the emotional times which led to passage of the Alien and Sedition Laws and thus could look at them with some objectivity. His experience in France had taught him such laws were destructive, and this knowledge had led him to publicly oppose them. Perhaps he was able to write a constitutional defense, as it is assumed he did, but certainly it is questionable that he wrote the entire report.[19]

George Washington sympathized with his young friend and understood that Marshall's opposition to the laws was not an easy position for the congressional candidate. From Mount Vernon Washington sent Marshall a written defense of the laws. "Whether any new lights are cast upon them by [the author's] charge, you will be better able to decide when you have read it," said Washington, who obviously did not want to force the issue with Marshall. Washington continued that the opposition, i.e., Thomas Jefferson and his followers, "have points to carry, from which nothing will divert them in the prosecution" and if they didn't have the Alien and Sedition Acts to oppose, they would find something else. Washington again expressed his best wishes for Marshall's success in the coming April election, "and if it should fail—of which I hope there is not the least danger—I shall not easily forgive myself for being urged with you to take a Poll."

Marshall wrote a long reply in which he described the defense of the Alien and Sedition Laws sent by Washington as "certainly well written" and said he wished it could be more widely read. But he would not retreat from his opposition to the acts, and again repeated his "regret" at their passage. He did state, repeating Washington's own belief, that the Alien and Sedition Laws were not the cause of the political tempest. "Its cause lies much deeper and is not easily to be removed," Marshall wrote. Had the Alien and Sedition Acts never been passed, "other measures would have been selected which would have been attacked with equal virulence." Marshall's next sentence seems carefully contrived as a criticism without offense. "The misfortune," he wrote, "is that an act operating on the press in any manner, affords to its opposers arguments which so captivate the public ear, which so mislead the public mind that the efforts of reason to correct false impressions will often fail of success." As for the election and his own chances, Marshall told Washington:

> I am by no means certain who will be elected for this district. Whatever the issue of the election may be, I shall neither reproach my self nor those at whose instance I have become a candidate, for the step I have taken. I

feel with increased force the objections of duty to make sacrifices and exertions for the preservation of American union and independence, as I am more convinced of the reality of the danger which threatens them. The exertions made against me by particular characters through the state and even from other states have an activity and a malignancy which no personal considerations would excite. If I fail I shall regret the failure more on account of the evidence it will afford of the prevalence of a temper hostile to our government and indiscriminately so to all who will not join in that hostility, than of the personal mortification which would be sustained.[20]

It appeared that Marshall would have the opportunity to regret that failure. In the beginning of 1799 his prospects for election to the United States Congress were dim. Previously, when he chose to run for the state Assembly as the Richmond candidate, he was so popular in that city and its immediate environs that he never had to fear defeat. But the congressional district included not only Henrico County (with Richmond in its center) but also the counties of Hanover, New Kent, Charles City, and James City, and was Republican by a large majority. To add to his difficulties, word began to spread within the district that Patrick Henry favored Clopton, Marshall's opponent. Henry, now feeble, was revered by his fellow Virginians. He had been out of politics long enough for any animosities to have disappeared to the point where he was remembered as a statesman who had been a Revolutionary leader, then a fighter for the rights of Virginians against the developing federal monolith. Although Henry and John Marshall had been associated in legal cases, for Henry to oppose Marshall in the election would have been natural. Patrick Henry had always opposed a strong central government and Marshall was running for Congress as a defender of the advocates of such a government.

Aware of this, Patrick Henry wrote a letter to Archibald Blair, a prominent citizen who, Henry knew, would disseminate the letter widely. Henry began by praising John Marshall's conduct in France and said: "Can it be thought that, with these sentiments, I should utter anything to prejudice General Marshall's election? Very far from it indeed." Being out of politics, Henry could afford the luxury of changing his mind. With this letter he demonstrated he had become a Federalist. "His temper and disposition were always pleasant," Henry continued regarding the man who had defeated him at the Virginia ratification convention eleven years earlier, "his talents and integrity unquestioned. These things are sufficient to place that gentleman far above any competitor in the district for Congress. But when you add the particular information and insight which he has gained, and is able to communicate to our public councils, it is really astonishing, that even blindness itself should hesitate in the choice." Considering Henry's previous political opposition to Marshall, this description can be taken as a fair assessment of Marshall's qualities at this time.

Henry then charged that France was behind the Marshall opposition, trying "to blacken the characters most eminently distinguished for virtue, talents, and public confidence." The French intention, so Henry charged, was to pave "the way to conquest." He ridiculed the campaign charges being made against Marshall. "The story of the Scotch merchants and old torys voting for him is too stale, childish, and foolish, and is a French *finesse;* an appeal to prejudice, not reason and good sense," said Henry. And Henry directed Blair: "Tell Marshall I love him, because he felt and acted as a republican, as an American." The letter was widely circulated, as Henry intended it should be, and is believed to have made a substantial impact on the outcome of the election.[21]

The campaign was typical of the time, robust and friendly. According to James Callender, a bitter enemy of Marshall's, Marshall sought votes by telling Republicans there was not much difference between his positions on public issues and those of his opponent, by dancing around bonfires at public meetings with the voters, and by spending "five or six thousand dollars upon barbecues. . . ." Callender intended his comments to be scathing. He referred to Marshall as "the paymaster of strong liquors, the barbecue representative of Richmond."[22]

While Callender's estimate of how much money Marshall spent is obviously high, his description of Marshall's campaign techniques is most likely reasonably accurate. John Clopton, believing the congressional seat was safe for him and his party, did very little campaigning. Marshall, in contrast, worked very hard at demonstrating to the voters that his political tenets were not such as to be objectionable to them and that he personally was the type of man they could enjoy and feel comfortable with as their elected Representative. Undoubtedly Marshall purchased some liquor for the gatherings at which he appeared during his campaign. That was a standard practice in Virginia politics at the time, one in which George Washington had engaged when he ran for local office prior to the American Revolution and in which even "the best gentlemen" were expected to engage when they were campaigning.[23] Although Callender made an issue over Marshall's campaign style, it appears Marshall merely worked harder than his opponent.

Personal attacks were also made against John Marshall in this campaign, and the later stories circulating of his having too great a thirst for liquor probably originated at this time, established upon what was a healthy but controlled habit. Another campaign charge, saved for posterity in an 1802 book, accused Marshall and Pinckney, while in Paris, of being responsible for an "unhappy female of a respectable family in Paris" losing her reputation by gaining an illegitimate child. The charge continued that the two men spurned her in Paris and caused her to be arrested in Charleston when she came with her child seeking help. Although absolutely disproving this story is impossible, a fair man would tend to discount the charge, which is without other substantiation. Also Marshall's character was such that if he had fathered an illegitimate child while in Paris and away from his family for a year, he would have lived up to his responsibilities and supported it.[24]

As election day neared, Marshall was uncertain of the outcome. "The means used to defeat [me] are despicable in the extreme and yet they succeed," he wrote to his brother James Markham Marshall. "Nothing I believe more debases or pollutes the human mind than faction."

There were no precinct elections then. All the voters came to a central site, presented themselves before the voting bench, and publicly announced for whom they were voting. The candidates themselves, Marshall and Clopton, were present, and whenever one received a vote, he thanked the voter. The procedure had a festive air about it. Each party provided a barrel of whiskey and the voters enjoyed testing both barrels before deciding for whom to vote. The party leaders searched throughout the district for voters they believed they could rely on. A story told about Marshall's election has the Federalists searching out Parsons Blair and Buchanan; these were the two favorites of the people of Richmond and mainstays of the Barbecue Club. While both were inclined toward federalism, they had tried to avoid the election because they did not wish to lose their middle position in the community by choosing between Marshall and Clopton. But they were sought out and coaxed, almost forced, to the polls. The story continues:

> There were shoutings and hurrahs perfectly deafening. Men were shaking fists at each other, rolling up their sleeves, cursing and swearing with angry and furious denunciations. Some became wild with agitation. Then came Mr. Thomas Rutherfoord and voted for Marshall, and there was again a tie. One fellow growled out an imprecation, and another replied, "You, sir, ought to have your

mouth smashed for your impudence." The crowd rolled to
and fro like a surging wave. Parson Blair came forward.
A swaggering fellow, just above him said, "Here comes
two preachers, dead shot for Marshall." Both candidates
knew them intimately and rose from their seats, and the
shout was terrific.

"Mr. Blair," said the sheriff, "who do you vote for?"
"John Marshall," said he. Mr. Marshall replied, "Your vote
is appreciated, Mr. Blair." Another fellow cried out, "Bring
out the Darby town boys. The Darbys have another shot in
the locker. I see you, old Thom, you are the devil to plump
the Parson," and old Thom came pushing and elbowing
with a howl; but Parson Buchanan was at the sheriff's
elbow.

The whole Federal party, and the Democrats too, thought
this vote was certain, beyond the possibility of a doubt,
for Marshall. "Who do you vote for, Mr. Buchanan?" "For
John Clopton," said the good man. Mr. Clopton said, "Mr.
Buchanan, I shall treasure that vote in my memory. It
will be regarded as a feather in my cap forever." The astonishment expressed in Mr. Marshall's face, in Parson
Blair's countenance, by the friends of Mr. Buchanan generally, can only be imagined. . . .

When our friends entered the carriage on their return
home, Parson Buchanan said, "Brother Blair, we might as
well have staid at home. When I was forced against my
will to go, I simply determined to balance your vote, and
now we shall hear no complaints of the clergy interfering
in elections."[25]

Marshall won the election by a scant majority of 108 votes.
"For the honor of the District I wish the majority had been
greater," Washington told him, "but let us be content. . . ."

Marshall's coming to Congress had been watched with
great interest. If his opposition to the Alien and Sedition Laws
meant he would oppose Federalist policies generally, then, said
Theodore Sedgwick, "it would have been better that his insignificant predecessor should have been re-elected." But Marshall also,
Sedgwick conceded, "may and probably will give a tone to the
federal politics south of the Susquehannah." Because of that,
Sedgwick continued, "There never was an instance where the
commencement of a political career was so important as is that
of General Marshall."[26]

George Cabot, a leading Federalist in Congress, had never
believed that Marshall should be ostracized by the party for his
stand against the Alien and Sedition Laws. Marshall had the
potential to become "a very useful man," Cabot argued to his
skeptical Federalist friends. "Some allowance too should be made

for the influence of the atmosphere of Virginia which doubtless makes every one who breathes it visionary and, upon the subject of free government, incredibly credulous," Cabot continued. "But it is certain that Marshall at Philadelphia would become a most powerful auxiliary to the cause of order and good government, and therefore we ought not to diminish his fame which would ultimately be a loss to ourselves."[27]

Cabot's point was well taken, and John Marshall did turn out to be, as predicted, a very useful man.

On Monday, December 2, 1799, Marshall presented himself at the opening of the First Session of the Sixth Congress of the United States. Presenting his credentials, he took his seat along with ten other Virginians—the other Virginians would straggle in during the coming weeks—and seventy-four other Representatives from the fourteen states. The first order of business was the election of a Speaker, and Marshall undoubtedly voted with the other Federalists for Theodore Sedgwick, who won the post on the second ballot. Marshall and two other members were appointed to officially inform the President, as the Constitution requires, that the House was in session. Marshall returned to the House a few moments later to announce that the constitutional duty had been fulfilled and that the President had said he would return the courtesy the next day at noon when he anticipated meeting both the House and Senate in the House chamber.[28]

John Adams' speech, his State of the Union address, was a defense of his policies and, in effect, a plea for support of those policies from Congress. The Senate Federalists did not feel obliged to be enthusiastic in their message of response, being more inclined to support the Hamiltonian wing of their party. But the House was different. John Marshall and four others were appointed to draft a reply, and it is believed that Marshall did most of the actual writing. Adams found the Marshall reply "so full and unqualified" a praise of his measures that he was very pleased. The Marshall answer, naturally, was laudatory of Adams' policies toward France: "Experience, the parent of wisdom, and the great instructor of nations, has established the truth of your position, that, remotely as we are placed from the belligerent nations, and desirous as we are, by doing justice to all, to avoid offence to any, yet nothing short of the power of repelling aggressions will secure to our country a rational prospect of escaping the calamities of war or national degradation."[29]

Marshall's influence with his fellow southerners was the most significant point about him, or so it was believed at the beginning of the session. Although not a Jeffersonian Republican, he was respected by many of them. "A number of distinguished men appear from the southward," commented one Federalist leader, "who are not pledged by any act to support the system of the last Congress; these men will pay great respect to the opinions of General Marshall." This particular leader in John Adams cabinet, Oliver Wolcott, suspected that with all Marshall's virtues, "he will think much of the State of Virginia, and he is too much disposed to govern the world according to rules of logic; he will read and expound the Constitution, as if it were a penal statute, and will sometimes be embarrassed with doubts, of which his friends will not perceive the importance." Wolcott's comments were written after Marshall had been in Congress almost a month and should be accepted, therefore, as an accurate picture of how the Federalists were assaying Marshall's legislative performance to that point. The picture emerges of a politician paying careful attention to the desires of his constituents and unwilling to embrace the extremism of his own party. The comment about Marshall's tendency to interpret the Constitution narrowly is interesting in the context of Marshall's later role in interpreting the Constitution from the Supreme Court.

But Marshall did win over the Federalist leaders. Partly this was because a leadership vacuum had been created since Harrison Gray Otis, the Federalist leader in the House, was not as interested in playing that role as he had been. "He and [Robert Goodloe] Harper as majority leaders were quietly superseded by a man greatly their superior, John Marshall, who brought judicial moderation and statesmanlike qualities of the very highest order to the service of Federalism," wrote Otis's biographer, Samuel Eliot Morison. Even Sedgwick was coming around, won over as much by Marshall's good fellowship as by his political ability. "I have been much in company with General Marshall since we arrived in this city," said Sedgwick when the session was a month old. "He possesses great powers and has much dexterity in the application of them." Marshall was proving himself particularly valuable in the role of liaison between the northern Federalists and the southerners, the role the Federalist leaders had mapped out for him. "In short," conceded Sedgwick, "we can do nothing without him." Sedgwick then proceeded to praise Marshall as a man of "perfectly honorable" intentions, but lamented, if only "his education [had] been on the other side of the Delaware."

By the time the session was less than two months old, however, all the Federalists were acknowledging John Marshall as a leader. He still thought more of his home state than one fellow Federalist liked and insisted on applying logic to governance.

This particular Federalist, George Cabot, expressed the hope that Marshall ultimately would overcome such "errors" because he "seems calculated to act a great part."[30]

Congress began, as all Congresses do, slowly. "The material business of the session is preparing in the committees," explained Marshall at the end of the first month. The event that month which caused the most agitation in the House was the death of George Washington. He had been taken ill suddenly and died unexpectedly. A passenger in a stagecoach first brought the news to Philadelphia, and it quickly reached the House of Representatives. "The utmost dismay and affliction was displayed for a few minutes," Marshall reported. He was asked to move for an adjournment, and did so, according to the *Annals of Congress*, "in a voice that bespoke the anguish of his mind, and a countenance expressive of the deepest regret."

"After receiving the information of this national calamity," Marshall told the House, "so heavy and so afflicting, the House of Representatives can be but ill fitted for public business." The House adjourned until the next morning. "Never was mourning more universal or so generally sincere," said Marshall of the congressional reaction to the news. When the House returned, Marshall offered the resolutions that include the description of Washington as "first in war, first in peace, and first in the hearts of his countrymen." The line is perhaps the most famous ever uttered about George Washington, and it is traditionally associated with Marshall. Marshall was embarrassed by this, for he did not write the line, Henry Lee did, and he always made a point of ascribing the authorship to Lee. In the mammoth biography of George Washington which Marshall wrote in the early 1800s the authorship is credited to Lee "who happening not to be in his place when the melancholy intelligence was received and first mentioned in the House, placed them in the hands of the member who moved them." The "member" was, of course, Marshall himself, but he never identified himself by name in that work. Despite this disclaimer, in the last years of his life Marshall was still explaining that he was not the author of the line.[31]

The first substantive piece of legislation that came before the House in that session concerned slavery. The problem could be solved in only one way, by ending slavery, but the Congress was loath to try. The debate began when Robert Waln of Philadelphia presented a petition by some free blacks of that city "praying for a revision of the laws of the United States relative to the slave trade; of the act relative to fugitives from justice; and for the adoption of such measures as shall in due course emancipate the whole of their brethren from their present situation." The reference to the "fugitive from justice" act was to the law requiring the return of escaped slaves across state lines; many blacks in the north charged that the law was used to kidnap innocent and free blacks and transport them into slavery. The authors of the petition said there were then 700,000 black slaves in the United States, and their intention was not immediate emancipation of all of them, "knowing that their degraded state and want of education would render that measure improper, but they ask an amelioration of their hard situation."

The first opponent to speak was John Rutledge, Jr., of South Carolina. He began by expressing a hope for what could never be, that the motion be voted down "with a view never to be called up hereafter." The debate proceeded in the same vein for two days as both southerners and northerners joined in denouncing it. Harrison Gray Otis of Massachusetts, for example, allowed to his fellow House members that he had "never seen a petition presented under a more dangerous and unpleasant aspect." And Samuel W. Dana of Connecticut thought the whole thing was "nothing but a farago of the French metaphysics of liberty and equality." If his fellow House members did not watch out, he warned, they would witness "some of the dreadful scenes of St. Domingo."

Not only did the motion ultimately voted reject the petition, but it also charged that such petitions have "a tendency to create disquiet and jealousy, and ought therefore to receive no encouragement or countenance from this House." Only one person voted against that motion, George Thatcher of Massachusetts, who believed the House was being somewhat silly in its attitude and was willing to appear against that motion "even though no other gentleman should think fit to vote with him." He had his wish. Even Robert Waln, who had sponsored the original petition, supported the motion condemning it. So did John Marshall. He was not yet impressed enough with the inherent evil of slavery either to speak on the subject—he did not enter into the two-day debate—or to work to end it.[32]

Certainly his silence at the beginning of January on the slavery question was not due to any of the bashfulness sometimes associated with a freshman member of Congress. A few weeks later he not only entered into a major debate, but was the principal speaker for the Federalists. This debate was on the case of a seaman named Thomas Nash, and its political and legal ramifications were many. It was Marshall's role in this debate that led Albert Gallatin, a Jeffersonian Republican, to say that of the "many clever" Federalists he had met in Congress, he had known "but two superior men," one of whom was John Marshall. Marshall "took an active part in the debates only two or three times," Gallatin recalled, "but always with great effect."[33]

Nash was a British seaman, or believed to be, who had murdered a man aboard a British frigate. He was held by the American courts in South Carolina until President Adams, in the words of the proposed congressional resolution condemning him, wrote to the court that he, Adams,

> considered an offence committed on board a public ship of war on the high seas to have been committed within the jurisdiction of the nation to whom the ship belongs; and, in consequence of such opinion and instruction, did advise and request the said Judge to deliver up the person so claimed to the agent of Great Britain, who should appear to receive him, provided only that the stipulated evidence of his criminality should be produced.[34]

The prisoner was so delivered after the President's order was received, and then the controversy began. President Adams believed he had no other choice under Article 27 of the treaty between the United States and Great Britain negotiated by John Jay. But any sign of good will toward Great Britain was considered by the Jeffersonians as an unnecessary bow in the direction of monarchial England and a snub at democratic France. Also, after Nash had been imprisoned in South Carolina for a time, he claimed to be not an Englishman but an American named Jonathan Robbins who had been impressed into British service and had only committed murder in an effort to escape impressment. If this story were true, then the United States would not be obligated to release him to Great Britain. Rather, the United States would be morally obligated to defend him from Great Britain. It was against this background that Adams had ordered Nash/Robbins released to the British. Not only was the fate of the sailor involved but there was also criticism of Adams for interfering with the courts. Since 1800 was a presidential election year, the political debate on this case obviously was destined to be a serious one. In this instance Marshall's role went far beyond influencing some wavering southerners. His speech on the House floor defending the part played by President Adams was long remembered as both a forensic *tour de force* and a brilliant legal analysis.

The debate began about the middle of February and lasted until March 7, a Friday. That was the day John Marshall spoke against the motion condemning John Adams. Marshall, almost from the beginning, had been concerned that the attacks were more political than legal. The Adams forces had placed documents in the House records on Friday, February 7, apparently disproving that Nash was an American. The opponents of the President, however, rather than abandoning their move to censure Adams, pressed it more vigorously. One tactic they hoped to use was to press for a lengthy delay in the debate, ostensibly to allow other documentation to come up from Charleston. Marshall argued against the postponement on February 17 because of "how much time must be employed in procuring those papers." The documents were not significant to the censure motion, in Marshall's opinion, and his point was that by the time the papers arrived, the House either would have adjourned or would be ready to adjourn. The result would be to delay a vote on the censure motion until the next session. This, Marshall explained to his brother James, "would impress the public mind that we really believed [the censure] resolution maintainable." Marshall did not say but understood that such an impression could last until the presidential election. "The debate took a turn as if we were precipitating a decision without enquiry and without evidence," he wrote to James.[35]

Marshall's March 7 speech was the major Federalist argument against the censure motion. He began by saying that he "most seriously" believed "that in a Government constituted like that of the United States, much of the public happiness depended, not only on its being rightly administered, but on the measures of Administration being rightly understood." That was a typical beginning for him—a general statement with which no one could argue and which no one was certain had anything to do with the subject at hand. As John Marshall always did, he quickly demonstrated that his beginnings were not wasted oratory.

His first point was that the Nash case "was completely within the 27th Article of the Treaty of Amity, Commerce, and Navigation." The article was quite specific about requiring the United States to give up a British citizen charged with committing a crime while under British jurisdiction. The question was, did the British jurisdiction extend to the high seas? In arguing that it did, Marshall displayed a broad knowledge of international law and of the precedents making up that body of law. Commentators on Marshall's career often have enjoyed criticizing his legal background, charging that he was unfamiliar with precedents. But through the process of self-education, the traditional process for a lawyer then, he had become well acquainted with the established law of the time and could recall specifics when he needed to. "The principle is," he said, "that the jurisdiction of a nation extends to the whole of its territory, and to its own citizens in every part of the world. The laws of a nation are rightfully obligatory on its own citizens in every situation where those laws are really extended to them. This principle is founded on the nature of civil union. It is supported every where by public opinion, and recognized by writers on the laws of nations. *Rutherforth*, in his second volume, page 180, says: 'The jurisdiction which a civil society has over the persons of its members, affects them immediately, whether they are within its territories or not.' " The reference was to Thomas Rutherforth's *Grotius De Jure Belli et Pacis*, first printed in 1754 under the title *Institutes of Natural Law* and reprinted in Philadelphia in 1799.

Marshall then argued that that general principle "is especially true, and is particularly recognized, with respect to the fleets of a nation on the high seas." Punishing for offenses committed on their fleet ships was a universal practice of nations, Marshall said and again cited Rutherforth (vol. II, p. 491) that "there can be no doubt about the jurisdiction of a nation over the persons which compose its fleets, when they are out at sea, whether they are sailing upon it or are stationed in any particular part of it."

Marshall's belief in that principle of law was not a matter of political expediency. Sixteen years earlier he had taken a similar position as a member of the Virginia legislature. The proposal he had then supported authorized delivery of any Virginian wanted for a crime in another nation "for which, in the judgment of the United States in Congress assembled, the law of nations, or any treaty between the United States and a foreign nation requires him to be surrendered to the offended nation."

Marshall's second attack was against the proposition that President Adams had acted improperly because the Nash case was a matter for judicial action rather than executive action. In this section Marshall presented an analysis of the judicial function which continues as a masterful explanation. The resolution attacking Adams had stated that the Constitution gave power to the judiciary in all *questions* in law and equity arising under the Constitution, laws, and treaties of the United States. But Marshall countered that the Constitution gave power to the judicial branch not in all questions but in all *cases*. A play on words? Marshall insisted it was not. "If the judicial power extended to every question under the Constitution," he told the House, "it would involve almost every subject proper for Legislative discussion and decision; if, to every question under the laws and treaties of the United States, it would involve almost every subject on which the Executive could act." Marshall opposed such swallowing up of the legislative and executive branches by the judicial branch. He then continued:

> By extending the Judicial power to all cases in law and equity, the Constitution had never been understood to confer on that department any political power whatever. To come within this description, a question must assume a legal form for forensic litigation and judicial decision. There must be parties to come into court, who can be reached by its process, and bound by its power; whose rights admit of ultimate decision by a tribunal to which they are bound to submit.

The courts could become involved in the implementation of a treaty if the rights of an individual are to be defended in court, Marshall said, continuing: "But the Judicial power cannot extend to political compacts; as the establishment of the boundary line between the American and British dominions; the case of the late guarantee in our Treaty with France, or the case of the delivery of a murderer under the twenty-seventh article of our present Treaty with Britain."

Marshall continued that President Adams could not be charged with infringing upon the power of the judiciary because "The case was in its nature a national demand made upon the nation. The parties were the two nations. They cannot come into court to litigate their claims, nor can a court decide on them." There seemed little possibility of disputing his statement that "Of consequence, the demand is not a case for judicial cognizance."

Marshall's argument in the Nash/Robbins case covers twenty-two columns of closely-packed type in the *Annals of Congress*. He spoke to every argument raised during the weeks of debate, defending the President's role with knowledge and authority. The speech was widely reprinted in newspapers and in pamphlet form and probably was the most significant factor in destroying the case as a political issue against Adams. When Marshall sat down that Friday afternoon, the Republicans were desperate. They rushed to Albert Gallatin, one of their members who had been leading the fight against Adams on this issue, and urged him to answer Marshall's speech immediately, but Gallatin reportedly replied: "Gentlemen, answer it yourself; for my part I think it unanswerable."[36]

A vote was taken the next day and the motion to censure President Adams was defeated 61–35. Marshall not only had presented a brilliant argument, he had done what few members of

Congress ever have been able to do: he had won over some of the opposition. His work was appreciated. Secretary of State Pickering considered the speech "a very luminous argument." It has since been described by commentators as "a perfect model of argumentative eloquence" and as one which "deserves to be ranked among the most dignified displays of human intellect." As for John Marshall himself, he remarked a few days later of the case that "The debate was for the purpose principally of affecting the next election of President, but I believe it has completely failed of its object."[37]

One legislative proposal that particularly interested John Marshall was the uniform bankruptcy bill. The states still clung to the archaic practice of imprisoning a man for debt, thereby making it impossible for him to earn any funds to pay off his debts. Marshall was particularly incensed by the practice because his good friend Robert Morris was languishing in debtors' prison. Morris, like Marshall, had invested heavily in undeveloped lands. But unlike Marshall, he invested not for the benefit of future generations of his family, but rather in the hope of making a quick profit. Land was rising in value, but slowly. As a result Morris could not sell his land fast enough and at a high enough profit to pay his taxes and the interest on his debts. He was forced to declare bankruptcy when John Marshall had passed through Philadelphia on his way to Paris in 1797. Morris then went to jail, and ultimately the man who had lost most of his personal fortune by investing it in the American Revolution spent three and a half years in debtors' prison.

The uniform bankruptcy bill before Congress would establish a law that would be pervasive throughout the entire Union. Also, under the proposed law, imprisonment could not be used as a punishment for debt. In the House the fight for passage was particularly difficult. "For some days past we have been labouring very hard to carry thro the House our bankrupt bill," reported one member, James A. Bayard, on February 1. One reason for the opposition, he said, was that "The antis have discovered that it will add strength to the federal compact, and they make every exertion to defeat it."[38]

One "exertion" was to add weakening amendments to the bill, one of which would have completely eradicated any help the bill might have been to Robert Morris. This was an amendment to eliminate its retroactive feature. According to the *Annals of Congress*, this motion "was opposed by Messrs. Bayard and Marshall, and finally negatived, only twenty-four members voting in the affirmative."[39]

The House Speaker, Theodore Sedgwick, testified to Mar-

shall's skill as a politician. Writing at the end of the session to
Rufus King, Sedgwick complained that "none, almost, of my
hopes have been realized." About the only measure of value enacted, he continued, was the Bankruptcy Law. While this bill
was important, the final act was not very close to what Sedgwick
had wanted. He particularly objected to the provision requiring
trial by jury on the question of whether a person was bankrupt
or not. This, he said, would be "inconvenient, embarrassing, and
dilatory." His next comments indicate how strong a position
John Marshall held in that Congress although he was only a
freshman member. "This mischief [trial by jury]," said Sedgwick,
"was occasioned by Virginia theory. It was the whim of General
Marshall; with him *sine qua non* of assent to the measure, and
without him the bill must have been lost, for it passed the
House by my casting vote."

What Sedgwick was describing was John Marshall at work
as an astute politician. Marshall had brought in the necessary
southern votes by insisting upon the trial by jury provision, and
although Sedgwick believed the provision was too costly, it was
not costly from the standpoint of votes. On controversial measures the good legislative leader wins by only one vote because
for every vote above one he has bargained away part of the bill
that could have been retained.[40]

John Marshall can be accused of inconsistency in the bankruptcy bill. In *Ware v. Hylton* in 1796 he had argued that the
treaty provision insisting upon the repayment of debts was not
retroactive. With the Bankruptcy Law, he was insisting that the
federal assumption of power must be retroactive. In the first, he
had found what he had hoped the Supreme Court would
consider an extenuating circumstance—the claim that Virginia
was an independent nation in 1788. The two incidents demonstrate how the legal mind must sometimes somersault to accomplish its ends. In *Ware v. Hylton* he was trying to save his fellow
Virginians from paying millions of dollars in what undoubtedly
were unfair debts to the British merchants. In the Bankruptcy
Act he was trying to release Robert Morris and other debtors
from jail. Although he failed in the first, he succeeded in the
second. The Bankruptcy Act passed the House on Friday, February 21, by a 49–48 vote after Speaker Sedgwick cast the determining vote.[41] The Senate later acted and on August 26, 1801,
Robert Morris was released from jail after having served three
years, six months, and ten days.

Because of his experience in France, John Marshall
believed in a military force strong enough to defend the United
States. Among the few speeches he made in the session are two

calling for a sufficient defense because of the resumption of French belligerency. He was even willing to see the nation go into debt—a controversial position in 1800—in order to pay for the arming. In justifying the debt, he argued: "The system of defence which has rendered this measure necessary was not only essential to our character as an independent nation but it has actually saved more money to the body of the people than has been expended and has very probably prevented either open war or such national degradation as would make up the object of general contempt and injury. . . . It has been so plainly proved to us that French aggression has been greatly increased, and that their contemptuous refusal even to treat with us as an independent nation has been entirely occasioned by a belief that we would not resist them."

Marshall undoubtedly was sincere in his belief that a strong national defense was necessary to prevent a war, but the question of which is the greater evil, an attack that some political leaders fear or the preparations against such an attack, was raised even then. Marshall's position on a strong defense was widely known, and a critique of his position, signed by "Manlius," was widely distributed. "A great and free people upon emergencies can perform wonderful things—but we ought to pause and solemnly consider whether those great emergencies do now exist," read this critique, and it continued: "Does war ravage our country? Are there strong assurances of invasion? . . . No. We have only the apprehensions of invasion." Although the "Manlius" position was certainly a political tract which might never have been written if Marshall had pointed out the dangers of the English rather than of the French, it raised disturbing points—points which continue to disturb Americans about the position Marshall advocated then and which has continued as a basic American stance. By erecting a military organization "to avert a contemplated evil from abroad," charged "Manlius," "we shall certainly bring on an increased dissatisfaction against the general government, and increased national debt, and probably an effusion of human blood, more fatal to our internal repose, than the combined warfare of Europe against us. . . ."[42]

Marshall had hoped that when he came to Congress he could avoid having to take a position on the Alien and Sedition Laws. He had said in his campaign that he opposed them, without, however, taking a position on their constitutionality. The laws were due to expire and probably, or so he reasoned, would not be extended while he was in Congress and so he had seen no reason to proceed further in his opposition. On Thursday, January 23, Nathaniel Macon of Georgia on the House floor called for the repeal of the Sedition Law, and also to allow "The defendant to give in evidence, in his defence, the truth of the matter charged as a libel." This could be construed as nothing less than a rebuff to the Federalists. Faced with this blunt choice between his party and his conscience, John Marshall chose his conscience. He voted to repeal the Sedition Law, and joined a group that included almost all the Federalist opponents. His vote was the key one. The count was 50–48 to repeal. If Marshall had voted with the Federalists, the result would have been a tie and Speaker Sedgwick could have cast the deciding vote against repeal. Marshall also supported the second section of the Macon proposal, allowing truth as a defense in libel (after it had been amended slightly) and it also passed 51–47.[43]

The First Session of the Sixth Congress ended on May 14, a Wednesday, with Speaker Sedgwick "taking an affectionate farewell of the members, and expressing his wish for their safe return and happiness, during the recess." When the House returned on the third Monday in November, it was to move from its temporary home in Philadelphia to its new and permanent home in the District of Columbia, the new community created to house the young government.[44]

Sedgwick, the leader of the Federalists in the House as well as the Speaker, did not feel as affectionate in private as he did in public. As he had indicated in his letter to Rufus King, he considered the session a failure except for the Bankruptcy Law. Much of Sedgwick's evaluation of the session revolved around John Marshall. "Marshall was looked up to as the man whose great and commanding genius was to enlighten and direct the national councils," Sedgwick wrote. "This was the general sentiment." Sedgwick acknowledged that Marshall's campaign position on the Alien and Sedition Laws had created some doubts about him. Some "thought him temporizing, while others deemed him feeble," said Sedgwick. "None had in my opinion justly appreciated his character. As his character has stamped itself on the measures of the present session, I am desirous of letting you know how I view it."

Sedgwick's analysis of John Marshall—bearing in mind that he did not consider Marshall an extreme enough Federalist—is probably as accurate a picture of John Marshall at age forty-four as one can have. "He is a man of very affectionate disposition," Sedgwick began, "of great simplicity of manners and honest and honorable in all his conduct. He is attached to pleasures, with convivial habits strongly fixed. He is indolent, therefore, and indisposed to take part in the common business of the house. He has a strong attachment to popularity but indisposed to sacrifice to it his integrity; hence it is that he is disposed on all popular subjects to feel the public pulse and hence results indecision and *an expression* of doubt." This last concerned Sedgwick because Marshall's expression of doubt created doubts "in more feeble minds [and] which are irremovable." Sedgwick believed that Marshall expressed too much respect for the people and tended "to quote their opinions as an evidence of truth." Sedgwick, the Federalist, added that relying too heavily on public opinion "is of all things the most destructive of personal independence and of that weight of character which a great man ought to possess." He believed that John Marshall, "when aroused, has strong reasoning powers; they are indeed almost unequalled." But often Marshall required so much time to become "aroused" that when he finally did, it was too late for him to have any impact.[45]

What emerges from that description of John Marshall is a picture of a man with the ability to be a strong leader, but sometimes reluctant to use that ability. Marshall also is depicted as a democrat in the sense of being responsive to the public's demands. There is another side which Sedgwick's comments suggest but which Sedgwick himself apparently was unable to see. The Speaker had accused Marshall of having "convivial habits strongly fixed" and of being "indolent" to the point where he did not take part in the "common" business of the House. But when Marshall was not taking part in the common business of the House, he was convivially taking part in the uncommon business of searching out the southern votes that the Federalists needed to push through such legislation as the bankruptcy bill. A failing of some of Marshall's contemporaries and of some of those who later commented on his life was to underrate him. Marshall, who had grown up on the western frontier, had not adopted the appearances of a more urbane easterner, and, as a result, he was often mistaken for a country bumpkin. That was a serious mistake. In his middle years he was an adroit and sophisticated man. As a lawyer, he had proven his competence among the members of the Virginia bar, a first-rate group of lawyers. As a political philosopher, he had demonstrated his depth in the Virginia convention which ratified the Constitution. As a diplomat matching wits with Talleyrand in Paris, he had shown himself as a man of skill and strength. Even as a businessman, he demonstrated he was the superior of such contemporary financiers as his friend Robert Morris; Morris went bankrupt but John Marshall prospered. And finally, Marshall was a talented politician who was elected to Congress when his party was being heavily criticized for the Alien and Sedition Laws. Once in Congress, he proved himself as an able legislator, bridging the gap between the moderate Federalists and the moderate Jeffersonian Republicans. Years earlier, as a young lawyer, Marshall used to walk through the streets of Richmond with his coat slung over his shoulder, eating cherries from his hat, and that appearance put off some clients who wanted a more lawyerly-looking lawyer. John Marshall's appearance always disarmed people; they learned only afterwards that they had met more than their equal.

Polly Marshall could have told them that her husband's appearance was deceiving. She had realized that when she first glimpsed him in Yorktown, in 1779, more than twenty years earlier. The other young ladies had been disappointed, but not Polly. She had looked beneath that slouch hat he wore and recognized that here was a man who was more than the sum of his rough manners and casual dress. Now in 1800 she was the wife of a well-liked and famous man, one of the leaders of the community of Richmond, who was also a tender and loving husband.

When John Marshall went to Congress, Polly went with him to Philadelphia, for she wanted to be with her husband to avoid the anguish they had known when they were separated by the XYZ Affair. Her eighth child, James Keith Marshall, was born in that city February 13, 1800. (Of those eight children, three had died in infancy. Polly would have two more children—Charles William Marshall, born February 11, 1803, who died in October of that year; and Edward Carrington Marshall, born January 13, 1805.[46]) According to a family tradition, John and Polly, while in Philadelphia, paid a courtesy call on Vice President Jefferson, who refused to repay the call because of his political differences with Marshall. This supposedly exacerbated the relations between the two men.[47]

For John Marshall, having his wife near him was important because the family relationship was always important to him. One of his disappointments at this time was the separation from his father, Thomas Marshall, who was making his permanent home in Kentucky. When Thomas Marshall had moved to Kentucky, he had given much of the Virginia land he owned to John Marshall "for and in consideration of the sum of five shillings"[48] because he was the kind of father who looked after his children, as John Marshall would so look after his own children. In Kentucky Thomas had begun a new life, helped, of course, by his acquaintances from the old. It was his friend and former military comrade George Washington, who, as President of the United States, had appointed him collector of the whiskey taxes for a salary of $450 a year plus 1 percent of all he collected.[49]

For many years Thomas Marshall acted as Washington's land agent in Kentucky. In writing once to Robert Morris, Washington referred to some lands he owned "on the opposite side of the little Miami . . . [and] they were obtained for me under the auspices of Colonel Thomas Marshall of Kentucky." On one occasion Washington asked Marshall to handle some tax requirements on land he owned in Kentucky. The two men continued as friends. "I was glad to hear . . . that you continued to enjoy tolerable good health, perfect health at our time of life is not to be expected," George Washington wrote him in 1795. "The natural decline of men, after they have entered into, or passed their grand climacteric, will make its appearance in a variety of ways. . . ."[50]

In the 1790s Thomas Marshall was in his sixties, a long life for that time. He was particularly proud of John. When George Washington was under attack because of his attitudes toward the French, Thomas wrote his son congratulating him for defending Washington: "[T]he part you take in the present storm gives me much pleasure, indeed you never seriously disobliged me in your life." John had hoped to visit his aging father in 1796 but was deterred by the Citizen Genêt affair and by his own involvement in the Fairfax land purchase. In 1797 and 1798 he was in Paris and then in 1798 he ran for Congress at George Washington's request. Family tradition has him visiting his father in 1799, between his election in April and the time Congress convened. This apparently was the last time he saw his father alive.[51]

Thomas Marshall is, of course, more famous for his son than for his own accomplishments, yet these were not inconsiderable. He was a man who had cut his own home out of the forest, raised his children to be honest people with a sense of duty and a love of the law, and had served his country well. He had been a justice of the peace, a sheriff, a legislator, a soldier, and finally a tax collector in Kentucky under conditions of personal danger. That he was not unique, that many others did as much, is not a comment on his inferiority but rather on the high caliber of the men who sacrificed and worked to build a nation for themselves and their children.

The older Thomas Marshall became, the more difficult it was for him to fulfill the responsibilities of tax collector, and in 1797 he resigned the post in a letter to President John Adams. The letter reveals much of the man's character. After announcing his intention to resign, Thomas Marshall continued:

> It may possibly be a subject of inquiry, why, after holding the office during the most critical and troublesome times I should now resign it, when I am no longer in-

sulted and abused, for endeavouring to execute the laws of my country—when those laws appear to be more than formerly respected—when the probability is, that in [the] future they may be carried into effect with but little difficulty? In truth this very change among other considerations, furnishes a reason for the decision I have made. For having once engaged in the business of revenue I presently found myself of sufficient importance with the enemies of the government here to be made an object of their malevolence—and while this was the case, I was determined not to be driven from my post. At this time, advanced in years and declining in health, I find myself unfit for the cares and active duties of the office, and therefore cheerfully resign a situation which I at first accepted, and afterwards held, more from an attachment to the government than from any pecuniary consideration, to be filled by some more active officer as still more conducive to the public service.

To the late president I had the honor of being known, and combined with respect and veneration for his public character, the more social and ardent affections of the man and of the friend.

You, sir, I have not the honor to know personally but you have filled too many important stations in the services of your country; and fame has been too busy with your name to permit me to remain ignorant of your character; for which in all its public relations permit me to say, I feel the most entire respect and esteem. Nor is it to me among the smallest motives for my rejoicing that you are the president, and of my attachment to your administration to know that you have ever been on terms of friendship with the late president—that you have approved his administration—and that you propose to yourself his conduct as an example for your imitation.

On this occasion I may say without vanity that I have formerly and not infrequently, given ample testimony of my attachment to Republican government, to the peace, liberty and happiness of my country, and that it is not now to be supposed that I have changed my principles— or can esteem those who possess different ones.

And altho I am too old, and infirm for active service— for which I pray our country may not face a call—yet my voice shall ever be excited in opposition to foreign influence—from whence the greatest danger seems to threaten, as well as against internal foes—and in support of a manly, firm, and independent exercise of those constitutional rights, which belong to the president and government of the United States.[52]

There would be many occasions in the future when the men and women of America would be called for active service, not as soldiers perhaps but in other capacities. John Marshall, whatever his intentions when he first ran for Congress, was one of these. He never returned to private life.

Adams had grown increasingly dissatisfied with some of his cabinet members, believing them too closely aligned with Alexander Hamilton in New York and not sufficiently loyal to him. This was well known in Philadelphia among the members of Congress, but there had been little hint that Adams would take action. On May 7, a few days before the session ended, John Marshall stopped by the War Department to inquire about land patents for some of his military friends. He was leaving Philadelphia a few days before the session ended because he wanted to be in Richmond when the courts opened, and he wanted to clear up the patent business. At the department's office he was "a good deal struck with a strange sort of mysterious coldness which I soon observed in the countenance of Mr. McHenry, the secretary of war." This surprised Marshall because he considered McHenry a good friend. He continued uncertain of what was happening until one of the clerks offered congratulations. "I did not understand him," Marshall recalled, "and was really surprized at hearing that I had been nominated to the Senate as secretary of war."

The nomination was sent to the Senate May 7 and confirmed on May 9. Marshall, however, did not believe himself qualified for the post and did not want to surrender his hopes of returning to the bar as an active lawyer. Attendance in Congress required only a few months a year, while a cabinet post was a full-time job. Marshall wrote a letter to President Adams, asking that the nomination be withdrawn. Adams did not honor his request and Marshall did hold the title of Secretary of War although he never performed any official duties.[53]

Adams' disputes with his cabinet members were not over. After McHenry, the next to go was Timothy Pickering. On May 12, three days after the Senate had confirmed Marshall as Secretary of War, it received a message nominating him to be Secretary of State. The same message nominated Samuel Dexter of Massachusetts to be Secretary of War, replacing Marshall. The Senate confirmed the Marshall appointment the next day, May 13, and John Adams then issued a proclamation announcing the appointment of Marshall as Secretary of State. Marshall was by this time in Richmond getting ready for the opening of the courts and was totally oblivious of events in Philadelphia. He did not know he had been Secretary of War, briefly, or that he had been nominated and confirmed as Secretary of State. Charles Lee, who was acting as Secretary of State, wrote him a letter, enclosing the commission to the office, and asking whether or not Marshall would accept.[54]

Marshall was in a quandary. "I never felt more doubt than on the question of accepting or declining this office," he said. He wanted to return to his law practice, but much of that practice had dissipated over the last few months as he had campaigned for Congress and then left Richmond for Philadelphia. There was some question about whether he could rebuild it, or at least rebuild it to the point it had reached before he entered Congress. He also was not certain he wanted to retire from Congress. "The press teemed with so much falsehood, with such continued and irritating abuse of me that I could not bring myself to yield to it," Marshall said, adding that he could not "conquer a stubbornness of temper which determines a man to make head against and struggle with injustice." These objections are the same as had existed a few days earlier when he announced he did not want to be Secretary of War.

However, while Marshall was not interested in being Secretary of War and did not believe he was particularly qualified for the position, that of Secretary of State was another matter. "The office," he said, "was precisely that which I wished, and for which I had vanity enough to think myself fitted." He realized the position was not permanent, but if there was a change in parties in the presidency, Marshall could always return to his law practice, certainly no worse off than if he had turned the position down. "I determined to accept the office," he said.[55]

As Secretary of State John Marshall received an annual salary of $5,000 and had a staff of nine, meaning the entire department consisted of ten persons with a combined total in salaries of $11,500. Shortly after taking office, Marshall and his nine assistants moved to Washington, and he spent almost all of the remainder of the year in the new city with its muddy streets and tropical climate. Some of Marshall's work was caused by this move. He and Benjamin Stoddert had the responsibility of watching over the building of the President's House, which was nearing completion, on Pennsylvania Avenue about a mile from the Capitol. They were urging the commissioners of the District of Columbia to "put as many workmen as can work in it on that House for one week." Later when Adams had moved in, Marshall and Stoddert complained to the commissioners that so many people are "constantly passing thro' all the rooms of the President's House, that it is impossible for him to have the furniture set out, or the room put in order." They requested that some "decent person" be placed at the entrance of the House to prevent unauthorized people from roaming around inside.[56]

But these represented the minor problems Marshall had to deal with. He had many major ones. The great powers then in the world were England, France, Spain, and the Barbary "pirates," and America had diplomatic problems with all of them. The Barbary powers were an old problem and would continue to be one long after John Marshall left the State Department. These Mediterranean countries controlled that sea and simply refused to allow the ships of any other nation to sail there unless a bounty was paid. All the commercial nations paid it; it was a formal part of their treaties with the Barbary powers, and the United States was not exempt. Marshall's responsibilities in this area dealt largely with making certain that the payments were made on time and dealing with those who objected to the payments.

John Adams spent the summer in Quincy, Massachusetts, while Marshall was in Washington, and this geographical split has led many people to believe that Marshall was, in effect, running the government until Adams' return in October. Actually the correspondence between Adams and Marshall at that time reveals that Marshall was faithfully reporting to the President and carrying out the President's orders. In the summer there was some question over a payment of jewels to the Barbary pirates, and Marshall wrote Adams for instructions. Adams recalled that the question had come up with Pickering and he believed "it was best to make the present rather than hazard a rupture. After the expenditure of such great sums, I thought with him that it would be imprudent to hazard an interruption of the peace on account of these jewels. . . ."

After receiving that letter from Adams, Marshall wrote to William Eaton, the American representative, of the President's wishes. While Marshall's letter has a stronger tone than Adams' comments, it does not go beyond anything in Adams' instructions. Some of Marshall's phrases are identical with those of Adams:

> The President [Marshall wrote] has but with very much reluctance consented to direct the purchase of the jewels. The exorbitant and unwarrantable demands of the Barbary powers sit very uneasy on us and are submitted to with difficulty. For the jewels merely we are unwilling to go to war, and thus lose the benefit of the heavy expenses already incurred. But this system of heavy exaction must not be continued. You must persevere in your endeavours so long as you may safely do so to avoid entirely or diminish this demand.[57]

On many occasions there had been talk of forming an international force to sail into the Mediterranean and subdue the Barbary powers; Jefferson when he had been minister to France had toyed with the idea. It was revived again in Berlin when representatives of the governments of Sweden and Denmark approached the American minister to suggest that the three nations organize a Mediterranean fleet to keep watch on the Barbary pirates. The minister reported this to the Secretary of State. Since this minister was John Quincy Adams, the son of the President, one could expect his advice to carry great weight. But when Marshall reported the offer to President Adams in Quincy, the response was negative. "There is no part of the administration of our government which has given me so much discontent as the negotiations in the Mediterranean," Adams said. The President continued:

> As, however, the promises of the United States, although made to their hurt, ought to be fulfilled with good faith, I know not how far we can acceed to the proposition of uniting with Sweden and Denmark in appointing with them and others convoys for their and our trade. Convoys for our own trade I suppose we may appoint at any time and . . . to protect our commerce, according to our treaties and the law of nations. If, indeed, the Barbary powers, or any of them should break their treaties with us and recommence hostilities in our trade, we may then be at liberty to make any reasonable arrangements with Sweden and Denmark.

This position, that the United States must live up to its treaty with the Barbary powers, is the one Marshall enunciated in his reply to John Quincy Adams. "[The President] is far from being pleased with the state of our affairs with the Barbary powers," Marshall explained to John Quincy Adams, "but he conceives that the engagements of the United States, tho' unreasonably burthensome, ought to be performed." Marshall added that while the United States and France continued to have "difficulties," stationing American ships in the Mediterranean would be stretching America's infant navy beyond realistic bounds.

The extent of the American purchase of peace from the Barbary powers is seen in a letter to a Congressman from Marshall, dated January 15, 1801, explaining why so large an appropriation was needed. The amount was $288,886.51, a significant sum for the time. Marshall explained that the annuity to the Regency in Algiers was $80,000 and was two years in arrears. For these two years and the current year, then, $240,000 was needed. The next item was $10,000, because "it is usual to make a biennial present." Finally, the United States owed a commercial house in Algiers the total of $38,886.51. "I am not sure that good policy requires absolute punctuality with Algiers," Marshall conceded, "but I believe the annuities ought not to accumulate too considerably."[58]

While the problems with the Barbary powers were primarily financial, those with the European nations were of greater seriousness. France and England were still at war, and France again considered the United States her enemy. John Adams had succeeded in avoiding open hostilities with France, but a conflict at sea between American and French ships had begun. Spain considered herself an ally of France and believed the United States was ripe for the picking. On September 8, 1800, Secretary of State Marshall wrote to the American minister in Madrid, David Humphreys, about American policy toward Spain. "From the commencement of the present war, which has raged so long and with so much violence in Europe," Marshall began, "the efforts of the United States to maintain a fair and an honest neutrality have been unremitted." The United States had tried to keep for itself the rights of a neutral, Marshall said, "by avoiding strict political connection with any nation, by performing with scrupulous good faith its engagements to all, and by affording equally to all, where uncontrouled by express stipulations, those benefits and advantages, which the laws and usages of nations permit, and which friendship and social intercourse enjoin."

He then said that the United States particularly had followed such a course with Spain. "With this fair and upright conduct on our part," Marshall continued, "we had a right to expect, and we have now a right to require, some attention on the part of Spain, to those duties towards the United States, which her own particular engagements, as well as the laws and usages of nations, bind her to perform." Marshall then included a long list of grievances—attacks on American ships by Spanish ships and the selling of cargoes had occurred with such "frequency and notoriety . . . [as to] render unnecessary the recital of particular cases." He then directed that Humphreys demand that the Spanish government cease such practices. "These demands on our part," Marshall insisted, "are rendered indispensable by the high duties of every government to itself, and to that people whose interests it superintends. His Catholic Majesty is urged to accede to them by his sacred regard for that honor, justice and good faith, which have so long influenced the conduct of the Spanish Government."[59]

Marshall's instructions to Humphreys are important not for

the results they accomplished—problems with Spain would not be settled for another two decades—but rather because they reveal the position the United States was taking. Without the military power to back him up, Secretary of State Marshall still refused to permit any foreign power to believe that the United States would allow itself to be attacked. His letter to Humphreys was a cornerstone of American foreign policy for years to come: the United States would stay out of European troubles, but the European nations, likewise, must leave the United States alone.

Marshall had more success with France than with Spain. Before his own ministry to Paris, the troubles between the two nations had seesawed between a troublesome status quo and calamity. But after the XYZ Affair—and certainly partly because of it—Talleyrand had come to the conclusion that peace must be made with the United States. A new commission was sent to Paris, after Talleyrand had agreed to receive it, and when Marshall assumed leadership of the State Department it was still questionable whether the commission would report back with a treaty acceptable to the United States. The prospects did not look bright. "Our last dispatches from Paris do not come later than the 20th of May," Marshall reported to the President. "From their contents no conclusion can be drawn with any sort of certainty respecting the fate of the embassy."

Although all of Marshall's statements and instructions while he was in diplomatic service have a tone of strength about them, a determination that the United States will be tampered with only at the offender's peril, he genuinely sought peace for the young nation. This had been his position in Paris, that by exerting the proper amount of resistance the United States would be able to maintain its independent and peaceful status. The choice of peace or war was forced on him again when he was dealing with France as Secretary of State. Although the Jeffersonian Republicans were accusing the Federalist leaders such as President Adams, Hamilton, and Marshall of being anti-French and pro-English, those three actually were trying to avoid a full-fledged war with France, the single act that would most benefit England.

Marshall felt strongly about maintaining the peace. In September when the United States still had not heard from its ministers in Paris, he had to consider the possibility that no treaty would be forthcoming and ponder how the United States should react to such a stalemate. Even if there were no treaty, he believed, the United States should not act hastily despite the clamor for expanding the quasi-war into a full-fledged shooting war. "It will very much depend on the intelligence and assurances [the ministers] bring," he said, "what course sound policy will direct the United States to pursue."

Marshall argued that the French government in 1800 was "much inclined" to correct the faults of the government in 1797 and 1798. "Of these," he said, "perhaps, none were more conspicuous, or more injurious to the French nation, than their haughty and hostile conduct to neutrals." France already had begun correcting herself in that respect, Marshall said, and the expectation was that the process would continue. "Should this expectation not be disappointed," Marshall urged, "there will be security, at least a reasonable prospect of it, for the future, and there will exist no cause of war, but to obtain compensation for past injuries." Marshall said he did not believe that obtaining compensation for what had happened in the past was sufficient reason to go to war.

The American ministers returned in October with a treaty. From the American point of view, the treaty was inadequate. Although Marshall had had no part in drawing it up and could have urged its rejection without any injury to his own reputation, he pushed for its acceptance. To have rejected the treaty, he realized, meant war, and he did not want war. His views were persuasive and the treaty was signed and then ratified by the Senate. Marshall was sufficiently wise to realize that there were limits on the power of the United States, limits that prudently could not be overstepped. Between the jingoists who put their fists up at the slightest affront and those who cowered before any enemy, John Marshall had walked a careful line, to victory for his country, honor for himself, and peace.[60]

But the difficulties with Spain and France were minor compared to those with England. These revolved around impressed seamen, captured ships and confiscated cargoes, and the old question of the debts the Americans owed to the British. The English policy of impressing American seamen was of most concern because it was so brutal. The extent of the problem is seen in one quarterly report in 1800 by David Lenox, the American agent in England who was trying to obtain the release of Americans impressed into the British naval service. In the three-months period there had been 109 new applications for release of Americans and 3 applications renewed which, with 61 cases pending from the previous quarter, made a total of 173. Lenox reported that he had secured the release of 22 Americans and that 33 others were about to be released. Twenty-nine were detained in the British navy because they had no documentation to prove their American citizenship. Twelve had enlisted in the British navy. Six were held by the British because their British citizenship had been proven. The remainder either could not be located, did not wish to leave the British service, or their cases remained unanswered. In another report, an abstract for the year 1800 based on reports from the Collectors of Customs from America's port cities, the total number of American seamen impressed during the twelve-month period was put at 3,390, and the next year the figure was 6,917.

John Marshall's responsibility was, once he received the name of an American impressed into the British service, to find proof of the American's citizenship and send that proof along to Lenox, in hopes he could secure the man's release. This meant amassing lists of names of impressed seamen from each port, sending the name to the Collector of Customs at that port, and asking him to locate the necessary documents. Many of these requests for documentation are written in John Marshall's own hand, as were his directives to Lenox. "I enclose documents proving that the men, whose names are noted below," goes one letter from Marshall to Lenox, "are citizens of the United States, and detained on board British ships of war, where they came by impressment. Mrs. Hopkin, the mother of Hercule Whitney, requests that his case may not be considered as a common one: and therefore if I did not know your uniform and punctual attention to every case, I should request your particular notice of it."[61]

Marshall's duties in dealing with the British attacks on American ships and cargo confiscations were much the same. He amassed the proof and sent it to the American ministry in hopes that they could effect a judgment for the Americans in the British courts. The United States had no other course, being without a navy with which to fight the British. Even granted that condition, though, Marshall's insistence on the courts settling the disputes had the ring of sincere preference. "The most effectual restraint is an upright judiciary," he insisted in a letter to Rufus King. If the practice of the courts deciding impartially between the captured and the captor was "not honestly and rigidly observed" then "there will exist no restraint on the captors." The assaults on the American ships could be stopped "only by infusing a spirit of justice and respect for law into the courts of Vice Admiralty," he believed, but conceded the difficulty of this because the courts were controlled by the British government. "It is not to be supposed that judges circumstanced as are those of the courts of Vice Admiralty, would dare to pursue openly and invariably this vicious system, if it was known to be offensive to their Government," he concluded.[62] Within a very few years John Marshall would lead the struggle to keep the judiciary in the United States independent so that it could be, unlike the British admiralty courts, honest. It became a cause with him, one he could not resist.

For many Americans, working through the British courts was insufficient. "If, Sir! our property is thus to be sported with by the piratical conduct of the British courts of vice admiralty," thundered one merchant whose ship had been stolen from him, "a total annihilation of the American commerce must follow." But the United States had no choice then except to use the court system for redress. War would have been destructive, certainly of American commerce and perhaps of its land. Ultimately war would be the device used to settle the disputes over impressment and confiscation, but when it came, the Americans at least could say they had tried to prevent it.[63]

These problems were peripheral to the main problem existing between England and the United States. This was the question of British debts. Until that problem was settled, the United States could not hope to develop an active commerce. The debts were to be paid, the Americans had agreed to that, and as long as they were not paid, the Americans could anticipate no efforts by the British to treat them with respect. John Marshall was well acquainted with the problem. Although his family was not personally involved, many Virginians he knew did owe large sums of money to the British merchants, debts which the Virginians and other Americans believed had been exacted from them unfairly. Marshall certainly knew that the inequity of the mercantile system which had produced those debts was one of the reasons he had been fighting in the American Revolution. He also well understood that no one in the United States could avoid paying them —the case of *Ware v. Hylton*, in which he had been on the losing side before the Supreme Court, had demonstrated that.

By treaty with England the debts problem was to be settled by a commission of two Americans, two Englishmen, and a fifth member chosen by lot. This fifth position went to an Englishman, and the British-dominated commission had produced a number of requirements which the Americans could not—or would not— agree to. The commission broke up, with the problem unsettled.

President Adams and Secretary of State Marshall took the position that the fault lay with the British side for making demands at the commission meetings far beyond those allowed by the treaty. The American government, Marshall wrote on August 23, 1800, to Rufus King, the American minister in England, "is, as it has ever been, sincerely desirous of executing, with perfect and scrupulous good faith, all its engagements with foreign nations. . . ." This desire, Marshall continued, should have been demonstrated by the American commissioners' efforts "to proceed and decide on particular cases, instead of laying down abstract principles believed to be untrue in themselves." Understanding that his letter to King would be used by that minister as the basis of the American position in future negotiations, Marshall argued the resolutions demanded by the British-controlled commission were "such as the government of the United States can never submit to. They are considered, not as constructive of an existing treaty, but as imposing new and injurious burthens, unwarranted by compact, and to which if in the first instance plainly and intelligibly stated, this government never could and never would have assented." After making certain that King understood that he was to argue that the breakup was England's fault entirely, although it had been the American ministers who had walked out, Marshall then told King he had *carte blanche* to work for a new settlement. This was not unusual for the time. The travel distance and the hazard of the journeys made communication almost impossible. Nations had to trust in their ministers. After giving King leeway to do as he believed appropriate, however, Marshall then suggested that the best way to settle the whole business was to agree upon a lump sum which the American government could pay to the British government "in full compensation of all claims made or to be made on this government."

In another letter to Rufus King the next month Marshall expressed the hope that once negotiations resumed on the debt that the issues of impressment of American sailors and confiscation of American property could be resolved. Again, Marshall believed that the United States should not cower before any European nation. England obviously was pleased by the quasi-war between America and France; the American ships then attacking French ships were, in effect, England's allies. But Marshall wanted England to know that for the United States there was no choice between England and France. "It has been the object of the American government from the commencement of the present war [between France and England] to preserve between the belligerent powers, an exact neutrality. Separated far from Europe, we mean not to mingle in their quarrels. This determination was early declared, and has never been changed. In pursuance of it we have avoided, and we shall continue to avoid, any political connections which might engage us further than is compatible with the neutrality we profess. . . ." He continued:

> The aggressions, sometimes of one, and sometimes of another belligerent power have forced us to contemplate and to prepare for war, as a probable event. We have repelled, and we will continue to repel, injuries not doubt-

ful in their nature, and hostility not to be misunderstood. But this is a situation of necessity, not of choice. It is one in which we are placed, not by our own acts, but by the acts of others, and which we change so soon as the conduct of others will permit us to change it.

Twelve years later the United States and Britain would go to war because Britain did not heed that warning that the United States intended to maintain her own interests and not another power's.

King eventually did negotiate an agreement by which the United States would pay 600,000 pounds in three annual installments. By the time it was completed, John Adams had left Washington and Thomas Jefferson was President. The new administration praised the agreement, praise which John Marshall found hollow. Were a Federalist in office then, he wrote Rufus King in 1801, "a very different reception I still believe, would have been given to the same measure . . . [it] would then have been pronounced by those who now take merit to themselves for it, as humiliating national degradation, an abandonment of national interests."

The negotiations begun by King under the leadership of Adams and Marshall had led to the successful conclusion of the debt question which had vexed relations between England and the United States for decades, and the successful conclusions of those negotiations can only be construed as a diplomatic coup. It was natural that the administration in power in 1801, that of Thomas Jefferson, attempt to take credit for them. Certainly Jefferson does deserve some credit, for not stifling negotiations begun by his Federalist predecessors and carried on by King, a prominent Federalist.[64]

John Marshall served as Secretary of State for approximately ten months. When he completed his term, he found that in his accounts "there appears to be $242.38 in my hands, which I am desirous of paying into the Treasury" and which he returned to the government. He also left a detailed memorandum for his successor (this would be James Madison) about the problems he would face. "The state of our affairs with the Barbary powers generally and with Tripoli in particular requires immediate attention," Marshall wrote. He said "some mischief from Tripoli" can be expected. He also cautioned his successor about "our affairs with Spain [which] will command the very serious attention of this department." He said that increasing complaints from American merchants will be made about British depredations, and Marshall indicated that he might have taken a stronger position regarding the British "had it not been proper to avoid any step" which might have locked in the Jefferson administration. The memorandum also advised about the discussions with Britain over the American debts.[65]

The memorandum indicates that the problems Marshall was leaving were similar to those he had found, but that generalization underrates his service. He had been instrumental in avoiding a war with France. He had helped shape the negotiations that would bring the British debts question to a settlement. More than that, in his letters of instructions to both King and Humphreys, he had articulated what would be America's foreign policy for a century. Simply put, John Marshall told the European nations: Don't bother us, and we won't bother you. It was this policy, once its firmness had been demonstrated by the War of 1812 and the Monroe Doctrine, that allowed the United States to expand across the North American continent, to grow strong, to become the home for Europe's homeless, and to attempt to solve its own problems. It was the appropriate policy for its time.

Marshall's tenure as Secretary of State ended in March 1801, when John Adams, who had failed to be reelected, was succeeded by Thomas Jefferson. This election has sometimes been described as the true American Revolution—as have some subsequent presidential elections—because it brought to an end the twelve-year rule of the Federalists and introduced a new party, the Jeffersonian Republicans, to the presidency. The election did represent a significant transfer of power, and the question was whether a young nation with little experience in self-government and controlled by passionate and ambitious men could experience a nonviolent change of power. This election was a test of the Americans' devotion to the legal system of government they had devised.

That the election would be an emotionally charged one was seen very early. Shortly after John Marshall had come to Philadelphia as a freshman House member in December of 1799, he realized that John Adams would have trouble being reelected because the eastern Federalists had turned against him. "They are strongly disposed to desert him and to push some other candidate," Marshall wrote. Presidents and Vice Presidents were elected by state electors who then were chosen in a variety of ways within the separate states, with the candidate receiving the highest number of votes becoming President and the one receiving the second highest Vice President. It was this system which had elected John Adams and Thomas Jefferson, political and philosophical opponents, to the presidency and vice presidency for the term that began in 1797. John Marshall, in that 1799 letter to his brother, pointed out the danger of the eastern Federalists dropping their support of Adams in the next election—Jefferson then would have the highest number of votes and become President. "I think not improbable that they will vote generally for Adams and Pinckney so as to give the latter gentleman the best chance, if he gets the southern vote, to be President," Marshall predicted accurately. But he was concerned that the scheme of pushing Charles Cotesworth Pinckney into the presidency would not work because of the growing debt. The United States then still required a strong defensive posture and this was costing a great deal of money. "I am apprehensive that our people would receive with very ill temper a system which should keep up an army of observation at the expence of the annual addition of five million to our debt. The effect of it would most probably be that the hands which hold the reins would be entirely changed."[66]

Partisanship developed rapidly during the next year. The election of 1800 would be the first one in which political parties played an important role; power was not merely being passed from wise man to wise man but, rather, was being contested for by politicians. "Party spirit is too prevalent," lamented a Jefferson follower. "The only hope for a good Republican must be in the firm belief that God reigns and let the people rejoice." The Federalists had some similar thoughts. "Danton, Marat and Robespierre were angels compared with this man from slave-holding Virginia," ran a comment on Thomas Jefferson by some New Englanders. Jefferson was denounced as a "French system monger" and as an apostle of "atheism, bloodshed and plunder." All in all it was typical of later presidential elections.[67]

It was not, however, typical of presidential elections to that point in America's history, and few people concerned for their country could be calm about the depths to which political discussion was then leading. Perhaps they should have been more sophisticated, but that is a quality that comes with experience and political rancor was not something the Americans had experienced before on a national scale. John Marshall was particularly aware of the political animosity. He was replaced in the House, after he became Secretary of State, by "one of the most decided democrats in the union" who was elected by "an immense majority." Marshall also was aware of movements against the Federalists in New Jersey and Maryland. "There is a tide in the affairs of nations, of parties, and of individuals," he lamented. "I fear that of real Americanism is on the ebb." But this despair, and the fear that America would die without a strong Federalist as its President, were atypical of him. A little later, for example, he was writing that "However the election may terminate, good men ought still to continue their endeavour for the public happiness." As for himself, Marshall said: "I pray devoutly—which is no very common practice with me—that the future administration may do as little harm as the present and the past."[68]

Marshall believed in participating in events, in helping to shape them. He was a constant meddler in politics and always would be, although, at the same time, he insisted he had no part in politics. His involvement is seen in his letters to Charles Pinckney in South Carolina. Pinckney was the Federalist choice for Vice President as Marshall had predicted a year earlier he would be, but more and more the contest was shaping up as one between Thomas Jefferson and Aaron Burr of New York, who originally were to be the Republican candidates for President and Vice President. This was because Alexander Hamilton, perhaps the nation's most influential Federalist, was working to defeat John Adams, around whom the party should have solidified, and all else was being sacrificed to that design.

In November 1800 Marshall wrote Pinckney a letter explaining how the presidential election looked to him. Maryland was divided. "The New England vote except Rhode Island will be indisputably right . . . the Senate of Pennsylvania will maintain their ground." But South Carolina, Pinckney's home state, was crucial. "It is now rendered an absolute certainty," Marshall said, "that any success in your state elects [Jefferson]." He repeated that warning in another letter the following month: "Should South Carolina vote for Mr. Jefferson he will be the President according to present appearances. Our last letters from your state were unfavorable and of consequence we are a good deal alarmed. We expect, however, every day to receive a line from some of our federal friends which may dispel the doubts with which the election is at present overcast."

On December 18 the situation changed. Burr and Jefferson had tied for the presidency with seventy-three electoral votes each, and the House of Representatives was to choose the next President. Marshall wrote Pinckney, "It is extremely uncertain on whom the choice will fall. Having myself no voice in the election, and in fact scarcely any wish concerning it, I do not intermeddle with it." Marshall's protestations of unconcern are charming, particularly as he then advised Pinckney that "Once more I suspect the contest—should one be made—will be decided by South Carolina. So far as I am enabled to conjecture I think the person for whom your state votes will be President. . . ." If Pinckney did not understand from those warnings that he must exert himself politically in his state to ward off a Jefferson victory, then nothing could so alert him.

In that December letter John Marshall also included, casually, some other Washington news—"Mr. Ellsworth has resigned his seat as chief justice and Mr. Jay has been nominated in his place. Should he, as is most probable, decline the office I fear the President will nominate the senior Judge to that office." Marshall also spoke of his own future plans. "I shall return to Richmond on the 3rd of March to recommence practice as a lawyer," he declared. "If my present wish can succeed so far as respects myself I shall never again fill any political station whatever."[69]

Still protesting his lack of interest in the presidential election, Marshall wrote a letter to Polly's brother-in-law, Edward Carrington, on December 28, saying that "I take no part and feel no interest in the decision. I consider it as a choice of evils and I really am uncertain which would be the greatest." He guessed that Burr seemed to have a better chance than Jefferson. "It is not believed that he would weaken the vital parts of the Constitution, nor is it believed that he has any undue foreign attachments"—statements which are indicative of Marshall's fears of Jefferson. Marshall also made clear his intention of returning to Richmond. He hoped to be there by February, but certainly no later than "the 3rd of March at this place."[70]

By this time Marshall's hostility toward Jefferson was such that he could not visualize the man as President. There were some personal disputes involved, but the major difference between the two men went much deeper than merely personal pique. They were political enemies. More than that, Jefferson had attacked George Washington, or at least the Federalists believed he had been referring to Washington as among those who had been seduced by England (this comment was made in what is known as the Mazzei letter), and Marshall could never tolerate that kind of insult against the American he most revered. Marshall was also inclined to be distrustful of Jefferson. As a former Virginia soldier in the Revolution, he never forgot that Thomas Jefferson had stayed home, entertaining captured Hessians, and then apparently fled ignominiously when the British approached Monticello. Marshall's attitude toward Jefferson was revealed even more bitingly in a letter a few days later to Alexander Hamilton.

Hamilton for personal and political reasons had destroyed John Adams' chances for reelection, and in so doing had written a finish to the Federalist party. Never again would it have the opportunity to prove in the presidency that it was capable of rising above the Alien and Sedition Laws of the Adams term. Now faced with the choice of either Aaron Burr or Thomas Jefferson as President, Hamilton decided that Jefferson must be the next President. He wrote a series of remarkable letters to members of Congress and prominent officials in Washington asking them to support Jefferson over Burr. He described Aaron Burr as an immoral man with predilections to despotism. The attack on Burr runs on for several pages in these letters, growing more and more strident, until finally the letters conclude with an appeal: "For heaven's sake, my dear sir, exert yourself to the utmost to save our country from so great a calamity." The difficulties between Hamilton and Burr were many, political as well as personal, and would ultimately be settled on the dueling grounds at Weehawken, New Jersey. Still, Hamilton's animosity toward Burr in December 1800—considering that Burr was a member of Hamilton's own party and that the alternative to Burr was the *bête noire* of the Federalist party—can only be described as extreme.

Hamilton wrote one of these letters to Marshall on December 26, and Marshall received it on New Year's Day. The letter obviously was a cause of concern for Marshall. He had once been Alexander Hamilton's agent in Richmond, taking the Federalist position in a state controlled by Jeffersonian Republicans. He had a good deal of respect for Hamilton. He also knew Hamilton's support for Federalism and his devotion to the memory of George Washington. Now here was Hamilton urging that Jefferson be elected President. Did Hamilton really want elected the man who would do most to destroy Federalism, the man who was a harsh critic of George Washington? Apparently he did.

Marshall began his answer by acknowledging that there was little question now but that Jefferson and Burr would have to fight out the election in the House of Representatives. "The returns have been all received," he said, "and this is the general opinion." He continued that "Being no longer in the House of Representatives, and consequently compelled by no duty to decide between them, my own mind had scarcely determined to which of these gentlemen the preference was due."

He then proceeded with an analysis of Thomas Jefferson that is obviously his complete estimate of the man at this point. "To Mr. Jefferson," he began, "whose political character is better known than that of Mr. Burr, I have felt almost insuperable objections. His foreign prejudices seem to me totally to unfit him for the chief magistracy of a nation which cannot indulge those prejudices without sustaining deep and permanent injury. In addition to this solid and immovable objection, Mr. Jefferson appears to me to be a man who will embody himself with the House of Representatives. By weakening the office of President, he will increase his personal power. He will diminish his responsibility, sap the fundamental principles of the government, and become the leader of that party which is about to constitute the majority of the legislature. The morals of the author of the letter to Mazzei cannot be pure."

For John Marshall those were the three sins to be avoided: too great a fondness for a foreign power, a weakening of the presidency, and personal attacks against Washington. "With these impressions concerning Mr. Jefferson," he continued, "I was in some degree disposed to view with less apprehension any other characters, and to consider the alternative now offered as a circumstance not to be entirely neglected." Marshall then conceded that Hamilton's description of Burr, "with whom I am totally unacquainted," indicated that electing Burr would be a greater mistake than electing Jefferson.

So far he had told Alexander Hamilton nothing that he did not already know. In writing to Marshall, Hamilton obviously was hoping to persuade the Secretary of State to use his immense influence with the Federalists for Jefferson's election. This Marshall could not do. "Believing that you know [Burr] well," he wrote to Hamilton, "and are impartial, my preference would certainly not be for him; but I can take no part in this business. I cannot bring myself to aid Mr. Jefferson."

He then added that another reason he believed he should stay out of the dispute was that he might be criticized for angling for a reappointment as Secretary of State. "Although no consideration could induce me to be the Secretary of State while there was a President whose political system I believe to be at variance with my own, yet this cannot be so well known to others," he explained, "and it might be suspected that a desire to be well with the successful candidate had, in some degree, governed my conduct."[71]

Although Marshall had insisted in his letter to Hamilton that he would take no part in the election proceedings before the House, rumors were abundant in Washington that he was part of a cabal to take over the government. Thomas Jefferson told a friend on the last day of 1800 that the Federalists were planning, somehow, to prevent Congress from electing a President and "to transfer the government by an act to the C.J. or Secretary of State or to let it devolve on the President pro tem of the Senate till next December, which gives them another year's predominance." If Jefferson sounded paranoid, and almost all the major figures of his political party were equally fearful of the Federalists, it was because they simply did not believe that the party in power would surrender that power without a struggle. Albert Gallatin reported to his wife the same fears. The Federalists, he said, "would vest the Presidential power in the hands of some man of their property." He did concede, however, that the leading Federalists "have openly declared against the project and recommend an acquiescence in Mr. Jefferson's election." The rumors spread to Richmond through the newspapers. A series of letters signed "Lucius" and appearing in the *Richmond Examiner* charged that Marshall had determined that if the House of Representatives divided evenly between Jefferson and Burr, the full Congress could determine who would become President, apparently from among candidates other than Jefferson and Burr. "You are accused of advancing opinions dangerous to liberty," "Lucius" charged in his first letter. "Unless you will publicly disclaim the charge, not even the eminence of your station shall protect you. I will unveil your motives. I will expose you uncovered to the sight of the people—your depravity shall excite their odium—and you shall experience the resentment even of those, who once loved, admired, and adored you." There were two additional letters in which the author challenged the constitutionality of Marshall's alleged opinion, and then accused Marshall of being willing to destroy the nation to preserve the dominion of the Federalists. Marshall, of course, had no such opinion. He remained at all times an interested observer, but outside of the few letters he wrote to his friends urging them to work through the electoral system for the defeat of Jefferson, he took no part in the election.[72]

Fact could not outpace rumor, however, particularly when ears were receptive to the rumor. James Monroe, then governor of Virginia, first took the attitude that there was nothing to the scheme of the Federalists blocking Jefferson from becoming President. "I cannot believe any such project is seriously entertained," he wrote Jefferson, "because it would argue a degree of boldness as well as wickedness in that party which I do not think it possessed of." Less than two weeks after he wrote that letter, however, he sent off another to Jefferson in which he wrote: "It is said here that Marshall has given an opinion . . . that in case nine states should not unite in favor of one of the persons chosen, the legislature may appoint a President till another election is made, and that intrigues are carrying on to place us in that situation." Monroe said he had heard that report from one of the Virginia members of the House of Representatives in Washington and that it "has excited the utmost indignation in the legislature." A few days later he again wrote to Jefferson assuring him that the Virginia Assembly had adjourned "in confidence [that] should any plan of usurpation be attempted at the federal town, the Executive would convene it without delay; a confidence which was not misplaced."[73]

These letters almost have the tenor of an armed conflict in the making, or at least a challenge between the "federal town" and the Virginia capital. This never happened, and it never really was in the offing. The Federalists had handled the election stupidly. Alexander Hamilton had used the party to indulge his own personal biases, first against Adams and then against Burr. And he succeeded ultimately in contributing to the election of Thomas Jefferson, which meant the demise of the Federalist party. But despite this, the election of 1800 still has a glory about it. Power had been transferred peacefully. There were no coups, no armed force. Jefferson finally became President because some members of the House believed they should be statesmen and elect a President rather than be obstinate party members and destroy their nation—a precedent that often has been imitated in subsequent years. Jefferson came to the most powerful office in the nation—and he would use it powerfully, despite John Marshall's fears—without military power. Representative democracy had succeeded.

Before this occurred, however, there was an event that was to control John Marshall's life for the next thirty-four years and that was to have an irreversible impact on the country he loved and had struggled so long for.

The Chief Justice of the United States in 1800 was Oliver Ellsworth, the third man to have held that position. He was ill, however, and resigned from the Supreme Court. John Adams received the resignation in December. The question of who should be nominated to the Chief Justiceship had, until this time, been more a philosophical one than a practical one. George Washington, when he became President in 1789, had been impressed with the conviction that he must name good men to the Justiceships. "I have considered the first arrangement of the judicial department as essential to the happiness of our Country, and to the stability of its political system," he said, "hence the selection of the fittest characters to expound the laws, and dispense justice, has been an invariable object of my anxious concern." Washington chose John Jay as the first Chief Justice of the United States, and when he said to Jay that "It is with singular pleasure that I address you as Chief Justice of the Supreme Court of the United States," he may have been the first person to refer to the holder of that office incorrectly.[74]

Jay was a New York Federalist, certainly a safe appointment from Washington's point of view. When Jay resigned, the President was faced for the first time with the question of whether to choose a successor from among the five Associate Justices or from outside the Court. Washington selected John Rutledge, from outside the Court. Jefferson at the time remarked to James Monroe that the naming of Rutledge "seems to have been intended merely to establish a precedent against the descent of that office by seniority, and to keep five mouths always gaping for one sugar plum."[75] Rutledge served one term as Chief Justice and then the Senate refused to confirm him. The next appointment went to Oliver Ellsworth, and when President Adams received his letter of resignation in December 1800, he was faced, as Washington had been, with making one of the most significant decisions a President can make.

Perhaps more than anything else a President does, the appointment of a Justice to the Supreme Court can extend that President's philosophy to succeeding generations. The Justice's tenure is controlled only by his health and inclinations and not by the electorate. His decisions are influenced only by his own integrity and intellect and not by fear of a political act ousting him from office. The impact of his philosophy is limited only by his ability to enunciate it in relation to the specific problems that come before the Court and not by any restriction placed by any other organization or political body. A Justice of the Supreme Court is as independent a man as any responsible official in a democracy can be, and when a President selects a Justice who is in agreement with his understanding of what government should accomplish, then, as much as possible, that President has ensured that understanding will be espoused in one branch of the government long after the President himself has left office. Some deride this situation as "politics," but the derision is undeserved. The situation exemplifies the nobility of politics, that men who come to office by legal means seek out legal courses in which to extend their understanding of government.

Thoughts of this kind were in John Adams' mind as he pondered the significance of his replacement of Ellsworth. This was in December and Adams knew he himself would not have another term in office; Jefferson most likely would be the next President. The Federalists also were in trouble in Congress. Only the appointment of a strong Federalist to the Chief Justiceship offered the prospect of securing the remaining branch of government to the Federalists. Adams considered elevating an Associate Justice to the position, and then naming another Federalist to the Associate Justiceship that would thereby be vacated. That would have created a problem. Justice William Cushing was the senior of the five Associate Justices, but he would be sixty-nine on March 1 and Adams considered him too old to provide a vigorous advocacy of Federalist principles over what Adams believed would be several presidential administrations of Jeffersonian Republicans. Adams was more inclined toward naming Associate Justice William Paterson, who had turned fifty-five in December. Marshall, then Secretary of State and one of Adams' close advisers, had recommended Paterson—or "Patteson" as Marshall spelled it. (Paterson, incidentally, died in 1806 at the age of sixty; Cushing died in 1810 at the age of seventy-eight.) The general expectation was that the appointment would go to Paterson. Timothy Pickering, the ousted Secretary of State, watched the Adams administration in Washington from a perch in Philadelphia and predicted the Paterson appointment.[76] But Adams had two problems with Paterson. First, he feared offending Cushing by passing over the senior Associate Justice. Also, Adams believed that Paterson had been too close to Hamilton in the recent party split that had resulted in Adams being denied a second term.

The alternative was to go outside of the circle of five Associate Justices. Adams chose that alternative and reappointed John Jay as Chief Justice. Jay had resigned from the Court in 1795, and then had been governor of New York. He was a Federalist and had not been aligned with the Hamiltonian faction of the party that had worked against the reelection of Adams. Because he remained outside internal party squabbles and had himself been George Washington's choice as Chief Justice, Jay's selection could cause little dispute. Adams' letter to Jay informing him of the appointment reveals exactly how the President viewed his opportunity of filling the position of Chief Justice. He wrote:

> Mr. Ellsworth, afflicted with the gravel and the gout, and intending to pass the winter in the south of France, after a few weeks in England, has resigned his office of Chief Justice, and I have nominated you to your old station. This is as independent of the inconstancy of the people, as it is the will of a President. In the future administration of our country, the firmest security we can have against the effects of visionary schemes or fluctuating theories, will be in a solid judiciary and nothing will cheer the hopes of the best men so much as your acceptance of this appointment. You have now a great opportunity to render a most signal service to your country. I therefore pray you most earnestly to consider of it seriously, and accept it. . . . I had no permission from you to take this

step, but it appeared to me that Providence had thrown in my way an opportunity, not only of marking to the public the spot where, in my opinion, the greatest mass of worth remained collected in one individual, but of furnishing my country with the best security its inhabitants afforded against the increasing dissolution of morals.

The President sent the nomination to the Senate on December 18, and the next day the Senate confirmed the appointment. As was the practice then, these actions were taken without Jay's being informed of them and without his having had the opportunity to indicate his interest in the appointment. Communication then was such a problem that Presidents had to act on the assumption that appointees would not refuse. In this case the assumption was incorrect. In a letter received by Adams early in January 1801 John Jay refused reappointment as Chief Justice. His letter reveals his understanding of the Court's position in American government:

> I left the bench perfectly convinced that under a system so defective it would not obtain the energy, weight, and dignity which was essential to its affording due support to the national government; nor acquire the public confidence and respect which, as the last resort of the justice of the nation, it should possess. Hence I am induced to doubt both the propriety and the expediency of my returning to the bench under the present system. Independently of these considerations, the state of my health removes every doubt.[77]

With Jay eliminated, Adams began to scurry around for another candidate. Time was beginning to work against him. On March 4 a new President would take office, most likely Jefferson who certainly would not appoint a Federalist to the position of Chief Justice if it were still open. Also, Congress was considering a new law making changes in the judicial system. One change was to reduce the work of the Justices by eliminating the requirement that they preside at Circuit Courts. Another proposed change was to reduce the size of the Supreme Court from six to five at the next vacancy. Before the law was passed, Adams could appoint a Chief Justice who would be the sixth member of the Court. If he waited until after the law was passed, he would have to choose a Chief Justice from among the five Associate Justices because the law, once it became effective, would restrict the total Court to five members. He had to hurry.

He wanted a person of strong Federalist persuasion, a man

who had been loyal to him, a man who knew the law, a man of comparative youth; more important, a man with a brilliant mind who could turn the Supreme Court into an effective counter-weight against the executive and legislative branches of the government. Adams had one such man in his administration.

When John Marshall had first suggested that William Paterson be named Chief Justice, the President had countered with the possibility of offending Cushing. Adams did not then discuss with Marshall any resentment he might have felt because of Paterson's relationship with Alexander Hamilton. "I never heard him assign any other objection to Judge Patteson," Marshall later remarked. It was only after Paterson had been rejected that Adams made the offer to John Jay, which Jay subsequently refused—contrary to the general belief that the order of consideration was Jay first and Paterson second.

The letter including Jay's refusal came to Secretary of State John Marshall who delivered it to the President.

"Who shall I nominate now?" John Adams wondered aloud.

Marshall answered that he had no other ideas since he assumed that Adams' objections to Paterson still existed.

"I shall not nominate him," said Adams in what Marshall later recalled as "a decided tone."

Adams paused for a moment and then said to Marshall: "I believe I must nominate you."

Marshall was surprised. His name had never figured in the speculation. But he was pleased, and he bowed silently as a sign of his acquiescence.[78]

In a letter at the time Adams explained his selection. The letter was to a friend who had written suggesting that Adams work some kind of arrangement so that Adams himself could be Chief Justice. While Adams said he considered the proposal "very flattering," he believed that "The office of Chief Justice is too important for any man to hold of sixty-five years of age, who has wholly neglected the study of the law for six and twenty years." Then Adams wrote that he had already excluded himself, "by the nomination of a gentleman in the full vigor of middle age, in the full habits of business, and whose reading in the science is fresh in his head, to this office."[79]

John Marshall, when nominated to be Chief Justice of the United States, was forty-five years old and in excellent health. Although his standing as a lawyer in 1801 has been questioned by some historians,[80] the fact is that he was a brilliant attorney whose expertise extended to both domestic and international law. His standing among his peers in Richmond and his speech in the House of Representatives on the Robbins case—really a legal brief—and his record as Secretary of State demonstrate that. Even discounting the personal loyalty he had shown to John Adams and his obvious Federalist persuasions, he was an ideal choice for the position. Few men have come to the Supreme Court with the experience in law, legislative work, and politics that John Marshall possessed. Some years later John Adams referred to this appointment of Marshall as "the pride of my life." Even at the time there seemed little grounds to dispute such an estimate.[81]

The Marshall appointment was sent to the Senate on January 20. It met with opposition, not because Marshall was appointed but because William Paterson was not. Paterson had many friends in the Senate who believed that he was entitled to the position. "Painful as it would be for the Senate to reject a man of such respectable talents and standing as Mr. Marshall unquestionably is," wrote Senator Jonathan Dayton to Paterson on the day of the appointment, "I am convinced nevertheless that they would do it, if they could be assured that thereby *you* would be called to fill it, and *he* brought upon the bench as a Junior Judge." But, Dayton lamented, if Marshall were blocked, the prospect was for another nomination "more improper and more disgusting." Dayton, however, promised he would consult with some of the other Senators "upon the propriety of making a stand here."

Paterson had no feelings of animosity, however, and held out no hopes for himself. On January 26, after Marshall had been nominated but before he had been confirmed, Paterson wrote him a letter of congratulations. Marshall responded in the same vein: "For your polite and friendly sentiments on the appointment with which I have been lately honored I pray you to accept my warm and sincere acknowledgements."

On January 27 Marshall's nomination was confirmed by the Senate unanimously. Senator Dayton, who had led the opposition, explained in a letter to Paterson the next day why there were no negative votes:

> The delay which has taken place was upon my motion for postponement, and was intended to afford an opportunity for ascertaining whether the President could be induced under any circumstances whatever to nominate you. If we could have been satisfied of this, we should have taken measures to prevail on Mr. Marshall to have himself declined the *highest* for a *lower* seat, upon the bench, or in case of his refusal, have negatived him. This would have been a course of proceeding, painful indeed to the Federalists on account of their esteem for that gentleman and their respect for his talents, and to

which nothing could have brought them, but their very strong attachment to you, and their very high sense of your superior title and pretensions. It must be gratifying to you to learn that all voices, with the exception of one only were united in favor of conferring of this appointment upon you. The President alone was inflexible, and declared that he would never nominate you. Under these circumstances we thought it advisable to confirm Mr. Marshall, lest another not so well qualified, and more disgusting to the Bench, should be substituted, and because it appeared that this gentleman was not privy to his own nomination, but had previously exerted his influence with the President in your behalf.[82]

The Dayton letter stressed three points about Marshall's nomination. First is that Adams was adamant in his opposition to Paterson, a position which gives some credence to the speculation at the time and later that he was disturbed because of Paterson's involvement with Alexander Hamilton. Second is that the opposition to Marshall existed only because of a greater preference in the Senate for Paterson and not because of any dissatisfaction with Marshall. And third is that Marshall's earlier support of Paterson and his refusal to work for his own nomination worked well for him when the supporters of Paterson had to determine if they wanted to support him after all.

On the morning of Wednesday, February 4, John Marshall received his commission as Chief Justice. He immediately sat down and wrote his formal acceptance to the President: "I pray you to accept my grateful acknowledgments for the honor conferred on me in appointing me Chief Justice of the United States. This additional and flattering mark of your good opinion has made an impression on my mind which time will not efface." Adams replied with a request that Marshall, in addition to his new position as Chief Justice, continue as Secretary of State until the end of his administration.

In his letter of acceptance Marshall had said he would assume his new duties immediately. The session of the Court had opened on February 2, a Monday. But only William Cushing had shown up, and the Court therefore adjourned until Tuesday. On Tuesday the situation was the same, and the Court adjourned again. But on Wednesday, February 4, 1801, John Marshall, armed with his commission as Chief Justice of the United States, attended and for the first time took his seat on the tribunal which he would lead for the next thirty-four years.[83]

The room where the Court met that day was a small one in the Capitol, twenty-four feet wide, thirty feet long, and with one wall curved. It was on what was then the first floor of the building. The Court was lucky to have that. When the government had moved from Philadelphia to the new federal city the previous June, the President had the President's House and the Congress had the Capitol, neither one finished but both usable. The Court, however, had no permanent home, and while there was talk of one ultimately, there were no plans to build one. On January 20, just a few days before the Court was to meet, the city commissioners petitioned Congress to allow the Court to meet in one of the rooms in the Capitol. The Senate gave its permission the next day, and the House followed suit on January 23.[84]

The city in which the Supreme Court met was almost as unsuitable for the seat of government as was the Court's meeting room. The District of Columbia was created as the home for the federal government, and it included the Georgetown community on the west (on the northern side of the Potomac River) and Alexandria on the east (on the southern side of the Potomac). In between, where the great government edifices were to rise, there was little. The President's House had yet to take on the classical appearance that the later version, known as the White House, would have. The Capitol, a mile further up Pennsylvania Avenue, was so far only a low structure; this was the North Wing of the projected building and there would not be a South Wing nor a center for years. There were no roads, except for some lanes wide enough for the coaches that made the round trip from Georgetown to the Capitol and back in three hours. The main business of the community—the only business in fact—was caring for the members of the government. For the Congressmen, this meant being provided with lodgings. James A. Bayard, a member of Congress in 1801, told what it was like then in the new city. "I have no lodgings yet," he wrote in January 1801 after having just arrived in the city, "and am in no manner arranged. The city I have seen only from the window of the Capitol. The prospect furnishes a view of a few scattered houses and a great deal of dreary rough country." A few days later his situation had changed but he was not pleased. "I am now lodged at Stelle's Hotel, with about thirty members of Congress. The fare is indifferent and the expence immoderate; for self and servant I pay twenty dollars a week. We have the name of a city but nothing else. The wing of the Capitol which is finished is a beautiful building. The President's House is also extremely elegant. Besides these objects you have nothing to admire, but the beauties of nature. There is a great want of society especially female. An invitation to dinner costs you a ride of six or eight miles and the state of the roads obliging you to return before night, you have just time to swallow your meat."[85]

But from the Capitol and the few boardinghouses nearby there was a beautiful view of the surrounding woods, which sloped down the hills to the Potomac and Tiber Creek. The trees and plants grew wild—poplars, magnolias, azaleas, wild roses. It was beautiful country if one could stand the winter cold and damp and the summer tropical heat. There were only several thousand people in the entire District, including Georgetown and Alexandria. All in all, the city, like the government it housed, had its attractions as well as its problems.

The casualness that typified the new city's development also typified the inaugural of Thomas Jefferson as the third President of the United States. On March 4, 1801, at a few moments before noon, Jefferson emerged from Conrad's, the boardinghouse on Capitol Hill where he lived as Vice President, and walked to the Capitol not more than two hundred feet away. His Republican simplicity was characterized by his wearing only everyday clothes. He was escorted by some militiamen and a few government officials. In the Senate chamber he was greeted by Vice President Aaron Burr, who had been sworn into office a few moments earlier. They came to the podium and Burr sat on Jefferson's right and Chief Justice John Marshall sat on his left. "After a short pause," according to the Senate records, "the President of the United States rose, and addressed the audience as follows." This was the inaugural in which Jefferson described Americans as united: "We are all Republicans; we are all Federalists."[86]

By any standard this was one of America's finest moments, one of man's great achievements. Twenty-six years earlier at Lexington and Concord the Americans had begun a war in the hope that they could establish the rule of law, a rule under which power would surrender to law, a rule under which power would be passed peacefully when the law commanded it. What later generations considered commonplace was in 1801 not only unique but uncertain. For months before the inaugural men had said they were concerned that the rule of law would be thwarted. What really worried them was that the American experiment might perhaps have failed, that men had not been sincere when they talked about a cause greater than themselves, that they had not really sacrificed for anything more than themselves. But in the end they remembered they had pledged themselves to the rule of a universal and just law, and it succeeded in its first test.

One witness to the scene caught this significance. "I have

this morning witnessed one of the most interesting scenes a free people can ever witness," wrote Margaret Bayard Smith. "The changes of administration, which in every government and in every age have most generally been epochs of confusion, villainy and bloodshed, in this our happy country take place without any species of distraction, or disorder."[87]

The "happy country" was not the result of party dissensions suddenly disappearing. That could not happen. John Marshall's concern continued real. A few days before the inaugural he had written to Rufus King predicting that it was Jefferson's intention to "strengthen the state governments at the expense of that of the Union and to transfer as much as possible the powers remaining with the general government to the floor of the House of Representatives." As for the possibilities of war, Marshall was not so certain. "Among the men who have supported [Jefferson]," he pointed out, "are men who on this subject differ widely from each other. The most intelligent among them are in my opinion desirous of preserving peace with Britain but there is a mass of violence and passion in [Jefferson's] party which seems to me disposed to press on to war." Marshall's own guess was that the Jefferson administration would push its anti-English attitudes to the brink of war but no farther.[88]

Nor were the Jeffersonian Republicans without their animosities. They were angry at the Federalists for, as James Monroe expressed it, retiring "into the judiciary in a strong body where [the Federalist Party] lives on the treasury and therefore cannot be starved out." The Jeffersonians were angry not only at the appointment of Marshall but also at the creation of new judgeships and the filling of them with Federalists by President Adams in the last days of his administration. There was little doubt that the Federalist takeover of the judiciary branch had as its intention the preservation of one branch of the government to the Federalists. ". . . Conservation of Federalist principles was assured by the appointment of John Marshall as Chief Justice," reported Samuel Eliot Morison in his biography of Harrison Gray Otis.[89]

Certainly Thomas Jefferson realized this. His own choice for the Chief Justiceship probably was Spencer Roane, a Virginia lawyer also but one more attuned to Jefferson's viewpoint than Marshall. For the remainder of his long life Jefferson always understood that his great political enemy, John Marshall, had achieved his position of power only because Oliver Ellsworth could not wait a few months longer before resigning.

But for the inaugural there was courtesy between the two men. Jefferson wrote to Marshall on March 2, two days before the event, asking him to administer the presidential oath. "I presume a precise punctuality to it will be expected from me," wrote Jefferson. Marshall replied later that day that he would be pleased to administer the oath "and I shall make a point of being punctual." Jefferson also asked Marshall to hold the position of Secretary of State until James Madison arrived to assume the responsibility, and Marshall agreed, serving for one day as Secretary of State in the Jefferson administration. And so the two men came to the inauguration on March 4, if not as friends and not as political cohorts, at least as men who understood that they must oppose each other through the political and legal process and as men who respected each other.[90] *

Marshall had his concerns as he went to that inaugural to swear in Jefferson as President. Before leaving his lodgings he had written a few words to Charles Pinckney in Charleston. First Marshall made clear that he intended to use his position on the Supreme Court to preserve Federalism. "Of the importance of the judiciary at all times but more especially the present I am very fully impressed and I shall endeavor in the new office to which I am called not to disappoint my friends. . . ."

Marshall then reflected in this letter on the meaning of the change. "Today the new political year commences," he wrote, "the new order of things begins. Mr. Adams I believe left the city at four o'clock in the morning and Mr. Jefferson will be inaugurated at twelve. There are some appearances which surprise me. I wish however more than I hope that the public prosperity and happiness may sustain no diminution under democratic guidance. The democrats are divided into speculative theorists and absolute terrorists. With the latter I am not disposed to class Mr. Jefferson. If he arranges himself with them it is not difficult to foresee that much calamity is in store for our country—if he does not they will soon become his enemies and his calumniators." Marshall stopped writing then and proceeded to the inauguration.

Marshall obviously was impressed by the conciliatory tone of Jefferson's inaugural. Not only did the line "We are all Republicans: we are all Federalists" indicate that Jefferson was appeal-

---

* Four years later, at Jefferson's 1805 inaugural, a reporter for the Republican newspaper the *Aurora* claimed that at the 1801 inaugural John Marshall had deliberately turned his back on Jefferson while administering the oath to him. There is no other evidence of such an act of blatant discourtesy. Also I find it in conflict with Marshall's attitudes toward that first inaugural and his whole sense of propriety. I therefore credit the act not to John Marshall but to the habit of some newspapermen of suddenly remembering events which support their prejudices. See Warren, vol. I, p. 183 (*n*).

ing to a national loyalty above faction, he also made it clear he believed in the firm rule of law. He described the United States government as "the only one where every man, at the call of the law, would fly to the standard of the law, and would meet invasions of the public order as his own personal concern." The speech was a promise of intelligence and reasonableness in the coming administration, an appeal for support, and, at the end, an appeal to that "Infinite Power which rules the destinies of the universe" to lead the Americans "to what is best, and give them a favorable issue for your peace and prosperity."

When Jefferson finished his inaugural speech Marshall rose and administered the presidential oath to him. Then Jefferson left the chamber and the Senate adjourned until the next day, Thursday.

Back at his boardinghouse Marshall continued his letter to Pinckney. "I have administered the oath to the President," he wrote. "You will before this reaches you see his inauguration speech. It is in the general well judged and conciliatory. It is in direct terms giving the lie to the violent party declamation which has elected him, but it is strongly characteristic of the general cast of his political theory."[91]

And this was the achievement of America. These two men, so opposed to each other for political and philosophical and personal reasons, could meet on that platform in the Senate chamber of the United States Capitol and agree to try to conciliate their differences. Of course, they never could. And during the next several decades the history of the United States would largely be the story of John Marshall against either Thomas Jefferson or the apostles of Thomas Jefferson.

The three areas in which the conflict took place were the role of the judiciary, the strength of the federal government, and the sanctity of contracts. For John Marshall who had come to maturity during the movement to establish the rule of law over the sword of violence, the coming years would be a testing such as few men have ever endured.

Book Four:

JUDGE

Part I

The Struggle for an Independent Judiciary

I

POLITICS IN 1801 succeeded in accomplishing what procedure
and pronouncements had been unable to do—establish the
federal judiciary as a significant institution. President John
Adams, leaving the President's House involuntarily and fearing
the death of his Federalist party, had sought to perpetuate it in
the court system. The appointment of John Marshall as Chief
Justice of the United States was one part of this perpetuation
process. The Judiciary Act of 1801 was another part. This law,
passed in the waning days of the Adams administration, relieved
the Supreme Court Justices of the onerous task (for men of advanced age) of riding circuit and holding court in communities
far from their homes. It also, however, created a number of circuit judgeships, which would be filled by Federalists. The Marshall appointment and the Judiciary Act made the courts the
great political battleground. There is where the enemy was. That
was where the Jeffersonian Democrats had to attack. And that is
what they did.

As the head of the federal judiciary system, the Supreme
Court was the principal target of attack. In 1801 this was curious. The Court was not then considered a significant institution
and very little attention was paid to it. John Jay, while he was
Chief Justice, had felt the duties of that office to be so light as to
allow him to be American minister to the Court of St. James's
and then to campaign successfully for governor of New York.
From his own experience on the Court, he did not consider a
second appointment as Chief Justice worthwhile. Oliver Ellsworth also believed being Chief Justice allowed time for outside
activities: he was minister to France in 1800 while still holding
the title of Chief Justice. And no one thought it unusual for John
Marshall to continue as Secretary of State in the Adams administration for one month after receiving his commission as Chief
Justice. (Marshall did not accept a salary as Secretary after
becoming entitled to the salary of Chief Justice.)

Nor had the Court demonstrated itself as a powerful organ
of government. Even the *British Debts Case*, the case which

Marshall lost when he made his only appearance as a lawyer before the Court, presented an issue which was only solved later by action of the executive branch of the government, with John Marshall as Secretary of State and Rufus King as minister to the Court of St. James's. In some years the Court had met without cases to hear. Its decisions, when they came, were neither forceful—six men offering six opinions about one subject cannot present a forceful appearance—nor articulate. After the one occasion when the Court sought to exert power, in the case of *Chisholm v. Georgia*,[1] by accepting the right of a citizen of one state to sue another state for breach of contract, the states and the federal legislature enacted the Eleventh Amendment to the Constitution prohibiting such suits. The Supreme Court existed. It officiated. But it was without power.

The first year in which John Marshall served as Chief Justice produced cases that seemed to emphasize the innocuousness of the Court he headed. No decisions were handed down in the February term when he first took his seat, only one in the August term, and two major and two minor cases in the December term. Two involved disputes over ships captured as prizes on the high seas and a third involved title to a tract of western lands. These were the problems which had been badgering Americans for decades—land titles and the fruits of plunder on the high seas. There was nothing of a sensational nature in any of the three cases, nothing on which to establish a precedent that would set a path for American law in decades to come. And yet, before John Marshall was finished, he had pulled from these three cases principles which he was using to build an independent judiciary. From the very beginning of his tenure as Chief Justice he had resolved to strengthen the judiciary, to strengthen the system of using the law to solve the political problems that must be solved if the United States was not to be torn apart.

The first case in which Marshall delivered an opinion was in August 1801, a month when Washington is at its most tropical and unpleasant. Since there was only the one case at this session, Marshall presumably was able shortly to hurry off to the Virginia hills where he had begun to spend his summers. The case is formally known as *Talbot v. Seeman* and involves the merchant ship *Amelia*.[2] The ship was owned by a Hamburg merchant, a neutral, and was captured by the French. The French then armed her and sailed her. The *Amelia* was recaptured by an American ship and the American captain, Silas Talbot, wanted salvage from her owner in Hamburg before returning her to him. A law of 1799 allowed salvage to the extent of half the ship's value, if the ship was taken from the enemy, which was Talbot's claim.

The owner of the ship in Hamburg, in turn, claimed he was a neutral and that no salvage was allowed for neutral ships seized.

In this decision Marshall displayed the logical sequence for which his decisions later became distinguished. The first question was, did the American ship under Captain Talbot have the right to attack the *Amelia*? Marshall argued that the right existed because the *Amelia* was wearing the colors of France and was armed, and because the United States and France then were in a partial state of war. This meant that American ships could expect to be attacked by French ships, so an American ship therefore had the right to attack and seize a French ship, such as the *Amelia* appeared to be.

Having attacked and seized the *Amelia*, did the Americans then have the right to salvage? Yes, said Marshall, relying more on common sense than upon any congressional authorizations. The Chief Justice argued that the right to salvage was contingent upon services rendered. "We cannot presume this service to have been unacceptable to the Hamburger," Marshall said, "because it has bettered his condition." But the recapture was accomplished without the owner's authorization. "[A] recapture must always be made without consulting the recaptured," Marshall answered.

Marshall continued with a discussion of a contract which is interesting in that the definition of contract would become one of the most important achievements of his tenure on the bench. "To give a right to salvage, it is said," he explained, "there must be a contract, either express or implied. . . . If a contract be necessary, from what circumstances would the law, in that state of things, imply it? Clearly, from the benefit received, and the risk incurred. If, in the actual state of things, there was also benefit and risk, then the same circumstances concur, and they warrant the same result. . . ." He pointed out that the ship's danger was "real and imminent." The service rendered the *Amelia* "was an essential service, and the court is, therefore, of opinion, that the recaptor is entitled to salvage."

Marshall had established that the Americans had the right to seize the *Amelia*, that an implied contract must have existed between the ship's owner and her rescuer, and that the terms of that contract had been fulfilled by the Americans taking risks themselves and then offering benefits to the owner by returning the ship. It was a step-by-step argument which Marshall offered in his decision, one that a critic would have difficulty challenging successfully.

But Marshall was not done. After giving the points to the American, he had something left for the Hamburg owner. Captain Talbot had wanted salvage up to 50 percent of the ship's value, under the provisions of the 1799 law. The Court under Marshall, however, would not accept that 1799 law as applicable. That law referred to vessels taken from the enemy. And Marshall asked, the enemy of whom? He concluded that the concept could not refer to ships, such as the *Amelia*, which were the property of neutrals. "By this construction," said John Marshall in his decision, "the act of congress will never violate those principles which we believe, and which it is our duty to believe, the legislature of the United States will always hold sacred." The Court then allowed Talbot salvage equal to one-sixth of the ship's value.

What Marshall had done was allow salvage, not because the congressional act authorized it but because an implied contract made it reasonable. And he then allowed what seemed a fair amount. As for the federal law enacted by the Congress, Marshall and his fellow Justices had taken it upon themselves to interpret what the Congress had meant. The Congress didn't mean to penalize equally the enemy owners and the neutral owners of a ship. At least, that's what the Court said.

In the second case in which he handed down a decision, Marshall worked even harder at strengthening the Supreme Court. This case, *Wilson v. Mason*,[3] came in the December term and involved disputes over landholdings. John Marshall, of course, was particularly concerned about the confusion hanging over land titles then. He himself, as well as other members of his family, was a big investor in real estate. His plan was to buy large tracts of uninhabited land cheaply and then sell the land in parcels at a profit. But the identity and often the legal rights of the original owners were obscure, something Marshall had learned from his involvement in the Fairfax purchase. Also land boundaries were vague. Often the written descriptions of a tract's borders referred to physical landmarks that perhaps only half a dozen men had seen. Land wars were common in the West. The western lands, to put it mildly, were a mess.

John Marshall's reaction to this situation was a strict adherence to the law. The point of such adherence was that anyone who owned land or who aspired to own land would understand that ownership no longer would be decided on a hit-or-miss basis. A land title was good or it was not. The law protected people who held a good title or it did not.

The case that came before the Court in 1801 involved large tracts of land in what had been part of Virginia but later became the state of Kentucky. Ownership of the disputed lands was claimed by George Mason, and then, after his death, by his heir, Richard Mason. The James Madison family was involved with the Masons in this land deal. Mason's title came into dispute because it was apparently described inaccurately in the surveyed papers. A man named George Wilson realized this and applied for the same land. The lower courts ruled in Mason's favor, and Wilson then appealed to the Supreme Court. His case was argued by Joe H. Daviess, who two years after appearing as Wilson's counsel before Marshall married Marshall's sister Nancy—a point that critics of Marshall's ultimate decision have made much of.[4]

Marshall decided the case in favor of Wilson, and the other Justices supported him unanimously. In a decision which runs fifteen pages Marshall outlined the entire history of the laws governing the land in question, pointed up the deficiencies in the Mason claim to ownership, and defended Wilson's right to seek redress in court. The decision is a complicated one, as was the case, and is interesting in that it reveals Marshall's exhaustive knowledge of the Virginia property laws. It is also known for two other points. The first is the suggestion, implicit in some Madison biographies, that Marshall was influenced to read the law in an overly narrow way in this decision because one of the lawyers for Wilson was a future brother-in-law and also perhaps because by this time Marshall was a political opponent of Madison and the Masons.[5] A careful reading of the decision, however, suggests a second point. This is that the federal courts were serving notice that in dealing with land titles—an issue of tremendous significance to the Americans then who had much of their fortunes tied up in land—the law must be strictly adhered to.

There was another aspect to that case, one even more significant than whom the decision was for or against. This arose over the claim by the lawyers for Mason that the Supreme Court had no right to hear such an appeal, because Virginia and Kentucky, where the case had been argued back and forth for years, had agreed in a compact between them that such cases were not appealable beyond the local district courts. Marshall took up that point before he got to the crux of the case. He wrote:

> To maintain this proposition [the lawyer for Mason] relies on an act of the legislature of Virginia, making the judgments of the district courts of the state final in cases of caveat; and on the compact between Virginia and Kentucky, which stipulates that rights acquired under the commonwealth of Virginia shall be decided according to the then existing laws.
> This argument would not appear to be well founded had Virginia and Kentucky even been for every purpose in-

dependent nations; because the compact must be considered as providing for the preservation of titles, not of the tribunals which should decide on those titles. But when their situation in regard to the United States is contemplated, the court cannot perceive how a doubt could have existed respecting this point. The constitution of the United States, to which the parties to this compact had assented, gave jurisdiction to the federal courts in controversies between citizens of different states. The same constitution vested in this court an appellate jurisdiction in all cases where original jurisdiction was given to the inferior courts, with only "such exceptions and under such regulations as the congress shall make." Congress, in pursuance to the constitution, has passed a law on the subject, in which the appellate jurisdiction of this court is described in general terms so as to comprehend this case, nor is there in that law any exception or regulation which would exclude the case of a caveat from its general provisions. If then the compact between Virginia and Kentucky was even susceptible of the construction contended for, that construction could only be maintained on the principle that the legislature of any two states might, by agreement between themselves, annul the constitution of the United States.

Marshall had spoken to two principles in that overly long response to the counsel's challenge. The first was in the sentence that the intention of the compact was to preserve land titles and not to preserve the tribunals which must judge the validity of those titles. This represented a theme running through his life. Government must operate to serve, not to be served. Institutions must be tools of the people; people are not to be tools of the institution. As a very young man John Marshall had seen how the English Crown had refused to serve its constituency but, rather, had expected that constituency to serve it; and he had witnessed the Revolution that had followed. He had seen the devastation in France following her Revolution in which the people were plundered by institutions originally established to serve them. He had been a participant in the American struggle to devise operable institutions to serve the people. And so the belief that government must be responsive to the people had been deeply ingrained.

The second principle came at the end of the response. John Marshall was the guardian of the Court, which he understood to be the interpreter of the Constitution. And he was not going to allow any members of the federal Union to take on themselves the power to destroy the Constitution. He had written to his friend Charles Pinckney the day of Thomas Jefferson's inauguration that he intended not to disappoint his Federalist friends while on the Court. He had meant this in more than a political way. He had meant it in connection with the struggle for the supremacy of the federal Union. This case had been the first test for him, and Marshall had seized the test and passed it. "The jurisdiction of the court being perfectly clear," he said, and his meaning went beyond *Wilson v. Mason* to any attempt to weaken the power of the Supreme Court, its jurisdiction, and the federal Union it must protect.

The third major case decided by the Supreme Court in that year involved another prize case, somewhat similar to the *Amelia*. The case is known as *United States v. Schooner Peggy*.[6] The *Peggy*, apparently French, had been seized and returned to the United States where it was sold. Under the 1799 law, the captors were eligible for half of the proceeds, and the United States government, the other half. The Circuit Court in Connecticut so ruled on September 23, 1800. Seven days later, however, the United States and France signed a peace treaty ending their quasi-war. The treaty stipulated that "Property captured, and not yet definitively condemned . . . shall be mutually restored."

Thomas Jefferson, who had become President in 1801, took the position that the ship had not been definitively condemned by the Circuit Court's action and ordered that the entire proceeds of the ship's sale be returned to the French under the terms of the treaty. The money was being held in Connecticut and officials there refused to pay the money to the French. The issue came before the Supreme Court. In the decision Marshall agreed with Jefferson. "The last decree of an inferior court is final in relation to the power of that court," he said, "but not in relation to the property itself, unless it be acquiesced under. The terms used in the treaty seem to apply to the actual condition of the property and to direct a restoration of that which is still in controversy between the parties. On any other construction the word definitive would be rendered useless and inoperative. Vessels are seldom if ever condemned but by a final sentence."

But the assertion had been made that the Court had no right to inquire beyond the action of the inferior court. If that court had acted properly at the time, then the Supreme Court could not reverse its decision no matter what laws may have come into effect after the inferior court's action. On September 23, 1800, when the Circuit Court had ruled that the proceeds of the sale of the *Peggy* should be split, that was a perfectly proper decision; no one questioned that. Marshall, however, re-

fused to accept the assertion. In his refusal, he again strengthened the federal government and the power of the executive to
enforce the federal law. "The constitution of the United States
declares a treaty to be the supreme law of the land," Marshall
said. "Of consequence its obligation on the courts of the United
States must be admitted. It is certainly true that the execution
of a contract between nations is to be demanded from, and, in
the general, superintended by the executive of each nation, and
therefore, whatever the decision of this court may be relative to
the rights of parties litigating before it, the claim upon the
nation if unsatisfied, may still be asserted. But yet where a treaty
is the law of the land, and as such affects the rights of parties
litigating in court, that treaty as much binds those rights and is
as much to be regarded by the court as an act of congress; and
although restoration may be an executive, when viewed as a
substantive, act independent of, and unconnected with, other
circumstances, yet to condemn a vessel, the restoration of which
is directed by a law of the land, would be a direct infraction of
that law, and of consequence, improper." Marshall concluded
that if a law intervenes after the lower court has acted, and "If
the law be constitutional [in this case the treaty], and of that
no doubt in the present case has been expressed, I know of no
court which can contest its obligation."

In that case Marshall upheld the constitutional mandate
that a treaty is the supreme law of the land and added to it the
contention that the President is responsible for enforcing it. That
decision and the other two made for an interesting year. In the
Amelia case the Court had declared its right to interpret congressional intentions, and in *Mason v. Wilson* the Court had said
it would not allow its authority to be weakened. For an opening
year, it was not a bad record.

Five men sat on the Supreme Court when John Marshall
joined it in 1801. And while they were quiet that first year, their
backgrounds and abilities indicate that they were not silent when
the Justices held their private meetings to plan their decisions.
All five had been appointed by Federalist Presidents, were of that
political persuasion, but had shown on the Court allegiance to
no persons or philosophies except themselves and their consciences.

The senior Associate Justice was William Cushing of
Massachusetts, who was the first man to be appointed by George
Washington as an Associate Justice. He had been a judge in his
home state, one known for his taciturnity. During Shays' Rebellion, when the insurgents attempted to halt the courts, Cushing
is reported to have faced down the rioters armed with nothing

except his reputation and a firm step that carried him through the mob without harm; his court continued in operation. Cushing was the last American jurist to wear a wig as do the British judges. The other American judges were content to rely on their full-length judicial robes as the only trappings of judicial dignity.

Next in seniority was William Paterson of New Jersey. He had been appointed to the Court in 1793 after having been governor of his state. At the Constitutional Convention of 1787 Paterson was responsible for the compromise that gave the large-population states control of the House of Representatives and all the states equal representation in the Senate, a compromise that was one of the important breakthroughs leading to the adoption of the Constitution. The universal respect in which he was held by the Federalists was evidenced by their attempt to have him appointed Chief Justice instead of Marshall.

Samuel Chase of Maryland was appointed to the Court in 1796. He was described as a "firebrand" of the Revolutionary movement. As a state legislator before the war he opposed the royal governor and had been denounced for being a leader in the Sons of Liberty movement. During the Revolution he had been a member of the Continental Congress and had resisted the intrigues there against George Washington. Perhaps Washington remembered that when in 1796 he had a vacancy on the Court to fill and named Chase. Chase is generally considered the only Justice prior to Marshall whose opinions could be described as brilliant. In *Ware v. Hylton* he had articulated the supremacy of treaties over state law and in *Hylton v. the United States* he laid down a definition of a direct tax that was accepted for the next one hundred years.[7] But he was a mercurial person, given sometimes to excess, and that tendency shortly would place the Supreme Court in jeopardy.

Alfred Moore and Bushrod Washington were appointed to the Court in 1799. Moore of North Carolina had been a soldier and a brilliant lawyer but never made any impact as a jurist. He would resign in 1804, citing ill health, after having written only one decision while on the Court. Bushrod Washington, however, would have a distinguished career on the Court. The nephew of George Washington, Bushrod and John Marshall had been friends since their student days together at William and Mary. Their friendship was reinforced by their association together as Virginia lawyers. The attachment between John Marshall and Bushrod Washington is, at first glance, odd. Where Marshall was tall and robust, Washington was short and seemingly frail. Marshall was masculine in his enjoyment of hearty company, good food and drink, and his eager participation in athletics—even in his old age he walked several miles each day. Washington was feminine in appearance, with a finely chiseled face and an almost beardless chin. Where Marshall became widely read in the classics as well as the popular writings of his time, Washington, it was said, had such little interest in reading "that it was questionable whether he even knew who was the author of Macbeth."

And yet these two men were drawn close together, becoming fast friends, eminent jurists of similar persuasions, and collaborators in writing a biography of George Washington. Both had wives who were becoming increasingly invalid. Both venerated George Washington. But more than that, both men understood the roles they were to perform during the next decades. "Before Judge Washington," said one commentator of the time, "no just cause could fail; no artifice succeed, whatever might be the talent of its advocates. The judge had no partialities, no prejudices, no sectional or party bias. The proudest man was awed, and the humblest man was sustained before him. . . ."[8]

These were the men John Marshall was leading, but they would not have the luxury of only struggling with their intellects in the courtroom and in conferences behind closed doors. For the first time in American history one political party had ousted another one, and there were rewards to be reaped. This led to the struggle over the judiciary which began in Thomas Jefferson's first year as both a political and a philosophical struggle and continued to escalate in bitterness in the ensuing years.

Thomas Jefferson, when he was sworn in as President on March 4, 1801, was particularly concerned by the judicial branch. All its members were Federalists. A Jefferson biographer, Dumas Malone, writes that Jefferson never was hostile to the judiciary as such but wished it to become representative of the people and responsive to them, apparently by placing some Jeffersonian Republicans among the judges.[9] Since the time of Thomas Jefferson, Americans have developed a more sophisticated attitude toward their courts. Judges are not expected to be representative or responsive to the people—those roles are left to the President and the Congress. Rather, judges are expected to be representative of the law as they understand it and responsive only to it. In practice this can never be achieved entirely, but the value of having one branch of the government free of public pressures and clamor has been demonstrated many times.

Still, Jefferson's concern with the judiciary was not without basis. The Judiciary Act of 1801 had been enacted in the closing days of the Adams administration, and President Adams had in the final hours of his administration filled the newly created positions with loyal party members. "The judiciary bill has been crammed down our throats without a word or letter being suffered to be altered," complained Stevens Thomson Mason. "It creates eighteen new judges at $2,000 salary each for sixteen of them and $1,500 for the other two." Mason, a Senator from Virginia, believed the bill's purpose was to assure the Federalists a permanent position in the government, a position that the voters had denied them in the recent elections. Jefferson had no doubts in his own mind as to what the course should be for his administration. In April, about one month after becoming President, he was at Monticello making arrangements for moving to Washington and the President's House. "You know that the last Congress established a western judiciary district in Virginia, comprehending chiefly the western counties," he wrote to a friend. "Mr. Adams, who continued filling all the offices till nine o'clock of the night, at twelve of which he was to go out of office himself, took care to appoint for this district also." Then Jefferson added: "The Judge, of course, stands till the law shall be repealed, which we trust will be at the next Congress."[10]

Jefferson also was concerned about the actions of two of the new Federalist judges for the Circuit Court for the District of Columbia. They had ordered a libel suit against the editor of a newspaper which had published a letter criticizing the federal courts. One of these judges was William Cranch, who shortly became the reporter for the Supreme Court. The other was James Markham Marshall, John's brother.[11]

Jefferson, however, did not plan a wholesale bloodletting. He had come to the presidency as a moderate, an approach which he had expressed in his inauguration speech and which John Marshall had understood. Within his party there were extremists. One was William Branch Giles, a legislative leader for the Jeffersonians and the man who had first come to the national government a decade earlier with a letter of introduction from John Marshall. A few days after Jefferson's inaugural Giles had written Jefferson that "a pretty general purgation of office has been one of the benefits expected by the friends of the new order of things." While this would not mean ouster of all Federalists, Giles continued, it would mean that "the obnoxious men will be ousted." He continued: "It appears to me that the only check upon the judiciary system as it is now organized and filled, is the removal of all its executive officers indiscriminately. The judges have been the most unblushing violators of the constitutional restrictions and their officers have been the humble echoes of all their vicious schemes." Jefferson resisted such extreme actions, and Giles and the other extremists began to take a more strident position. From only seeking the removal of the "obnoxious," by

June Giles wanted "an absolute repeal of the whole judiciary system, terminating the present officers and creating an entirely new system, defining the common law doctrine, and restraining to the proper constitutional extent the jurisdiction of the courts."[12]

The dialogue made clear the federal courts would be attacked. The first assault was on the Judiciary Act of 1801.

The Constitution gives the Congress the power to establish certain rules and procedures for the operation of the federal courts. This the Congress did when it first met in 1789. That Act of 1789 established a three-tiered system of federal courts—the District, Circuit, and Supreme courts. The Supreme Court Justices, in addition to their duties on that Court, also joined with locally placed justices to hold the Circuit Courts. John Marshall's Circuit Court duties had him presiding at court in Richmond and at Raleigh, North Carolina. The Justices of the Supreme Court objected to this circuit-riding. When John Jay was Chief Justice he wrote a letter explaining his objections which was also signed by Associate Justices William Cushing, James Wilson, John Blair, James Iredell, and Thomas Johnson. The first objection was that the traveling was too arduous because "some of the present judges do not enjoy health and strength of body sufficient to enable them to undergo the toilsome journies through different climates and seasons." Jay added that no set of judges, "however robust," would be able to withstand the rigors of frequent travel across the United States in the late 1700s and early 1800s. He also made another point, one perhaps even more valid. The Supreme Court was an appellate court and heard appeals from the Circuit Courts, meaning that the Justices while on the Supreme Court would hear appeals from cases they had helped to decide while on the Circuit Courts. "Appointing the same men finally to correct in one capacity, the errors which they themselves may have committed in another," said Jay, "is a distinction unfriendly to impartial justice, and to that confidence in the Supreme Court, which it is so essential to the public interest should be reposed in it." In the letter Jay also argued that the system of riding circuit was supposed to be only temporary when written into the 1789 act, and he hoped that Congress soon would take action to change it.[13] Jay may have been correct, but in the early 1790s, when he was Chief Justice, the Supreme Court simply did not have sufficient business to convince anyone that the problem was serious.

Another part of the 1789 act caused more concern among Americans. This was Section 25, which expressly gave claimants the right to appeal adverse decisions of the highest courts in the states to the Supreme Court if some constitutional issue could be found. The effect of this section was to assure the supremacy of the federal over the state law. To the Jeffersonian Republicans with their strong beliefs in states' rights, this section was anathema. John Jay realized this. In 1793, when writing to Rufus King seeking his support for eliminating the circuit-riding, Jay said: "The federal courts have enemies in all who fear their influence on state objects. It is to be wished that [the courts'] defects should be corrected quietly. If these defects were all exposed to public view in striking colors, more enemies would arise and the difficulty of mending them be increased."[14]

John Jay's prediction proved correct.

In the late 1790s the Federalists began considering a new judiciary act. One intention of the new act was to relieve the Supreme Court Justices of having to ride circuit. This meant more Circuit Court judgeships would have to be created, opening up positions for Federalist appointments. The second intention was to broaden the power of the Supreme Court. Section 25 of the 1789 act had given the Supreme Court review power over certain state court decisions; the new proposal would expand that power. There was no secret about the rationale behind this second intention. The land squabble which Chief Justice John Marshall faced in *Mason v. Wilson* was typical of western land disputes. The westerners did not want these questions to be determined by federal judges from outside the area—"foreigners," such judges were called. They wanted these questions decided by local people. In moving for a strengthened court system, the Federalists were moving toward land disputes being determined by these "foreigners." Because many of the Federalists, including John Marshall, were large and absentee landholders, it became easy to interpret the new Judiciary Act as merely a device to protect their holdings. Certainly that had to be part of it. Also, however, there had been many land transactions over the years, sales to citizens all over the United States who purchased their property in the belief the transactions were honest. The Federalists believed these people had a right to have their disputes settled before impartial judges who were above local prejudices and passions.[15]

When the Federalists pushed the Judiciary Act through early in 1801, finishing action just a month before Jefferson's inaugural, politics was very much in their minds. Although the act had originated prior to the election of 1800 and the Federalists' rout from both the presidency and the Congress, it was passed after that election and the Federalists knew the judgeships would provide positions in government for them. They also tried a trick which was a direct slap at Jefferson. They added a section to the bill reducing the number of Supreme Court Justices from six to five at the next vacancy. This meant that Thomas Jefferson as President would probably be denied the opportunity of making an appointment. (This had been one of the factors persuading Adams to appoint Marshall as Chief Justice. If Adams apppointed an Associate Justice to head the bench, he would not have the opportunity of naming another Justice; that is, of placing another Federalist on the Court.)

John Marshall as John Adams' Secretary of State and then as the new Chief Justice was, of course, very much aware of the political struggles over the judiciary. In September of 1800 Adams had written him from Quincy, Massachusetts, asking Marshall to draft some ideas for Adams' upcoming State of the Union message. Marshall is believed to have written the speech in its entirety. It includes this section on the judiciary:

> It is in every point of view of such primary importance to carry the laws into prompt and faithful execution, and to render that part of the administration of justice which the Constitution and laws devolve on the federal courts, as convenient to the people as may consist with their present circumstances, that I cannot omit once more to recommend to your serious consideration the judiciary system of the United States. No subject is more interesting than this to the public happiness, and to none can those improvements which may have been suggested by experience, be more beneficially applied.[16]

Whatever the motivations of the bill's sponsors, to John Marshall the principal feature was the separation of the Circuit Court and the Supreme Court duties. Two days prior to his appointment to the Chief Justiceship, Secretary of State Marshall wrote Rufus King, the American minister in London, a long letter regarding the diplomatic situation. Then at the end, Marshall added that "The Congress are probably about to pass a bill reorganizing our judicial system. The principal feature in the new bill is the separation of the supreme from the circuit courts." A few days later, writing to Associate Justice Paterson, he said the Senate was expected to take up the judiciary bill shortly and it was expected to pass. "Its most essential feature is the separation of the judges of the supreme from those of the circuit courts," Marshall said, "and the establishment of the latter on a system capable of an extension commensurate with the necessities of the nation."[17] If John Marshall saw the bill as a means of guaranteeing his landholdings or as a blow against states' rights, his private comments at the time to his Federalist friends did not so indicate.

This Judiciary Act of 1801 was the bill Jefferson planned to have repealed, as he indicated shortly after his inaugural. And what the Jeffersonians planned in Washington, they pretty much could do, being in control of both the presidency and the Congress. The repeal took place in March 1802. James A. Bayard, a Federalist member of Congress, wrote of the final congressional action: "This day the constitution has numbered thirteen years and in my opinion has received a mortal wound." Alexander Hamilton did not consider the repeal a deathblow, only as "a vital blow to the Constitution." Marshall, who had been Chief Justice for a year now, was not quite so pessimistic. He hoped the feature in which he was most interested would be resurrected—the separation of the Circuit Court and the Supreme Court responsibilities. He himself was a logical man and he saw no logical reason for any opposition to the separation. "There are some essential defects in the system which will I presume be remedied as they involve no part of political questions," he wrote to a friend, "but relate only to the mode of carrying causes from the circuit to the supreme court. They had been attended to in the bill lately repealed and I make no doubt will be again." Marshall here perhaps was being naïve in believing the Jeffersonians would do anything to assist the court system. But he was not underestimating their power to accomplish whatever they determined was their end. "The power which could pass that act," he said, referring to the repeal, "can fail in nothing."[18]

His optimism was misplaced. The new bill drawn up by the Jeffersonians continued the former practice of the Justices riding circuit. It also eliminated the Court's summer sessions. This served to relieve the Justices of one trip to Washington a year, at the worst time of year. The nation's capital then was little more than a swamp from which most persons fled in the summer. Students of John Marshall's career speculate that his life was prolonged many years because of the elimination of the summer sessions of the Supreme Court.

Whatever the intention in eliminating the summer session, a result was that the Justices of the Supreme Court would not have an opportunity to meet before they were next scheduled to hold Circuit Court. The point was that if they intended to disobey the new law and refuse to hold Circuit Court, they would not have the opportunity to plan that strategy together. Nor would they have the opportunity to declare the act unconstitutional prior to individually facing the choice of whether or not to preside at their Circuit Courts.

Marshall sought to remedy this by writing letters to the Associate Justices. He himself said he doubted the constitutionality of this new act which directed him to preside over Circuit Courts without his being commissioned as a Circuit Court judge. "I am not of opinion that we can under our present appointments hold circuit courts," he wrote, "but I presume a contrary opinion is held by the court and, if so, I shall conform to it. I am endeavoring to collect the opinion of the Judges and will, when I shall have done so, communicate the result. . . ." In another letter Marshall explained why he now was opposed to something, holding Circuit Court, which had been the practice since the Judiciary Act of 1789. He said he would have gone along with the Circuit Court responsibilities "if the late discussion had not unavoidably produced an investigation of the subject which from me it would not otherwise have received." The result of his study, prompted by the congressional debate, was that the Constitution required separate appointments for Circuit and Supreme Court judges. "It is, however, my duty and my inclination in this as in all other cases," Marshall continued, "to be bound by the opinion of the majority of the judges. . . ." Marshall conceded that he was raising a difficult issue for the Justices, the possibility of their refusing to obey a law. "The consequences of refusing to carry the law into effect may be very serious," he said. "For myself personally I disregard them, and so I am persuaded does every other gentleman on the bench when put in competition with what he thinks his duty." He cautioned, however, that "the conviction of duty ought to be very strong before the measure is resolved on"; civil disobedience, he was saying, is not to be taken up casually. Marshall was anxious for replies, he explained, because the Justices had to reach a decision before the first of them held Circuit Court. The public would not support the other Justices for refusing to hold Circuit Court if one of them did, he believed.

There is speculation that writing this letter had been suggested to Marshall by Federalist politicians who hoped to use him and the Court to produce a confrontation with the Jeffersonians. There is no proof of this, however, and Marshall's letters indicate he was acting on his own. Not only did the tone of the letters suggest this, but also he equivocated on the issue. Two weeks after saying that he personally disregarded the consequences of refusing to obey the law, he was writing that he had "no doubt myself but that policy dictates" that the Justices obey the law. Bushrod Washington had written him that the question of whether the Justices should ride circuit was a settled one. They had; they should again; and that was that. "I own I shall be privately gratified if such should be the opinion of the majority and I shall with much pleasure acquiesce in it," Marshall said after reading Washington's letter. From apparent opposition to the law, Marshall had quickly moved to willingness to obey it. Undoubtedly his move was influenced partially by the position taken by Bushrod Washington for whom Marshall had great respect. More likely, Marshall did not relish a fight with the Jeffersonians on an issue he was not certain he could win.

The only one of the six Justices willing to fight was Samuel Chase. His lengthy letter to Marshall explaining his position is a plea for judicial independence and an example of what Marshall could have written, or perhaps should have written. Saying that he felt "every desire to yield my opinion to my brethren," Chase continued that "my conscience must be satisfied, although my ruin should be the certain consequence." Chase argued that the repealing act could not abolish the Circuit Court judgeships which the Federalists had created and filled because the Constitution said that a judge can be removed only by impeachment. The government may be able to strip the judges of their duties but not of their offices. Chase's point is an extremely important one. If Congress has the right to strip judges of their positions, then the judges are at the mercy of the political process. The intention of the Constitution was to free them from this pressure:

> I admit that Congress may, in their discretion, increase the number of Judges in any of the Courts established; they may also lessen the number of Judges in *such* Courts, on the death of any of them; they may diminish, or enlarge the jurisdiction of any of the Courts; they may enlarge or contract the extent of the Districts, or Circuits; and they may require *additional judicial* duties of any of the judges, agreeably to the provisions of the Constitution: But still the Judges, and their offices must remain independent of the Legislature. If Congress should require of the Judges duties that are *impracticable*; or if Congress should impose duties on them that are *unreasonable, and* for the *manifest* purpose of compelling them to resign their offices; such cases—if they should ever happen—will suggest their own remedy. It cannot be questioned, that the Judges of the inferior courts were intended by the Constitution to be as independent as the Judges of the Supreme Court.

Chase continued that "It has been the uniform opinion— until very lately—that the Supreme Court possess the power, and that they are bound in duty, to declare acts of Congress, or any of the States, contrary to the Constitution, *void*: If the Supreme Court possess this power, the inferior Courts must also have the same power; and of course ought to be as independent of Congress as the Supreme Court; but the Judges of *both* Courts will not be independent of but dependent on the Legislature, if they be not entitled to hold their offices during good behavior.".

Chase said he would refuse to hold his Circuit Court unless the other Justices persuaded him that he should. He also suggested that the Justices meet in Washington in August to discuss their reactions and their strategy. There was no favorable response from the other Justices.[19]

Why did not Marshall seize this opportunity to make a bold stroke for an independent judiciary? In his defense, it can be said that John Marshall chose his areas of battle carefully, and he rarely lost. He probably believed that he should not publicly call unconstitutional a practice that had been in use for a dozen years and had been acquiesced in by leading Federalists. Also perhaps he was not yet sure of the powers of the Chief Justice and the Supreme Court outside of the courtroom. Whatever the reason, his defense of judicial independence would come at a later time.

The end of the story of the repeal of the Judiciary Act of 1801 came in the February 1803 term. In the case known as *Stuart v. Laird*[20] the Court was faced with a direct constitutional challenge to the repeal and a new bill, passed April 29, 1802, restoring the Supreme Court Justices to circuit-riding. A man named John Laird had won a judgment against Hugh Stuart in the Fourth Circuit Court in Virginia's eastern district. He then obtained in the Fifth Circuit Court a judgment against Stuart's bond, using the first judgment as the basis for his claim. Stuart challenged the second judgment, saying that a judgment could not be issued by one court (the Fifth Circuit) on the basis of an action by another court (the Fourth Circuit) and, also, that Supreme Court Justices could not sit as Circuit Court justices— John Marshall had sat on the Circuit Court hearing the case in November of 1802.

William Paterson gave the Court's decision and disposed of both issues along lines indicated by Marshall's November ruling. "Congress have constitutional authority to establish from time to time such inferior tribunals as they may think proper; and to transfer a cause from one such tribunal to another," he said. "In this last particular, there are no words in the constitution to prohibit or restrain the exercise of legislative power." To the objection that Supreme Court Justices cannot sit on Circuit Courts without specific commissions to do so—the point that Chase considered unconstitutional—Paterson was equally certain in his answer. "To this objection, which is of recent date, it is sufficient to observe, that practice and acquiescence under it for a period of several years, commencing with the organization of the judicial system, affords an irresistible answer, and has indeed fixed the construction," he said, concluding his decision with: "Of course, the question is at rest, and ought not now to be disturbed."

A point about the Paterson decision is that it assumed the right of the Supreme Court to determine the constitutionality of legislative acts. The Congress had done certain things in that April 1802 act—it had created courts and transferred causes between them and it had directed the Supreme Court Justices to specific responsibilities—and the Supreme Court said the congressional action was proper. There was no question at the time about the propriety of the Supreme Court making such a judgment, that it had the right to judicially review acts of the legislative branch. Nor has there been much controversy since on this issue as exercised in *Stuart v. Laird*. That is because history paid more attention to a more forceful and articulate pronouncement on judicial review handed down by John Marshall several days earlier in *Marbury v. Madison*.

Judicial review is the substitution of a court of law for the battlefield to determine the correctness of a governmental act. As such, the development of judicial review is almost synonymous with the development of a civilized state.

The practice of courts declaring acts of state legislatures null and void was common prior to the decision in *Marbury v. Madison*,[21] in which Chief Justice John Marshall enunciated the doctrine of judicial review at a federal level. In at least nine states legislative acts had been set aside by judges who had no hesitation in asserting the power of courts over legislatures. One of these judges in the states, in fact, was John Marshall himself. He spoke of the rights of the courts to declare acts of the legislature unconstitutional while sitting on the Circuit Court in North Carolina only months before the *Marbury v. Madison* decision was handed down.

The principle of judicial review had been brought to America by settlers from England, where the courts had been at war with Parliament and the Crown. Sir Edward Coke, almost two hundred years prior to *Marbury v. Madison*, had stated it: ". . . And it appears in our books, that in many cases, the common law will controul acts of parliament, and sometimes adjudge them to be utterly void, for when an act of parliament is against common right and reason, or repugnant, or impossible to be performed, the common law will controul it, and adjudge such act to be void. . . ."[22] One distinguished historian has described Coke's career as a judge in the early seventeenth century as a struggle between himself and King James I over whether the Crown was subject to the law or above it.[23]

The colonists had no doubt that they did retain the courts' protection when they came to the New World. In some instances —265 between 1680 and 1780 by one count—the Americans used the British Crown's Privy Council as a court of last resort. This Council had no difficulty in declaring acts by the colonial legislatures null and void.[24] In one case involving an inheritance in Connecticut, brought under an act by the local legislature authorizing the division of an inheritance, the Council declared "that the said act for the Settlement of Intestates' Estates should be declared null and void, being contrary to the laws of England, in regard it makes land of inheritance distributable as personal estates, and is not warranted by the charter of that colony."[25]

The jump from having English courts declare legislative acts void to having local courts do the same thing was not a great one. The colonists understood that judicial review was a powerful weapon, and they were not afraid to use it—even against the parent government in England. In 1738 and 1739, for example, the Superior Court of Judicature of Massachusetts Bay, refused to enforce a royal order because "they have no authority by any law of this province, or usage of this Court to order such an execution."[26]

Massachusetts was, of course, a hotbed of dissidence and challenge. Witness the cry of James Otis in 1761 when the British authorities in Boston wanted a general order to search the homes of Americans for smuggled goods. "As to Acts of Parliament," Otis said, "an Act against the Constitution is void: an Act against natural Equity is void: and if an Act of Parliament should be made, in the very Words of this Petition, it would be void. The Executive Courts must pass such Acts into disuse."[27]

Virginia was not far behind in using the power of judicial review as a weapon against the Crown. When the government of George III passed the Stamp Act, requiring a tax stamp on public documents, the county court in Northampton, Virginia, simply declared the law null and void: ". . . The Court unanimously declared it to be their opinion that the said act did not bind, affect or concern the inhabitants of this Colony, in as much as they conceive the same to be unconstitutional, and that the said several officers may proceed to the execution of their respective offices, without incurring any penalties by means thereof. . . ."[28]

But judicial review in the young America was primarily a

matter of settling constitutional disputes rather than a means of revolt. This right of the courts to be the final arbiter was not always readily accepted by the American public. The case of *Rutgers v. Waddington*[29] in New York City in 1784 is an example. During the American Revolution a British citizen named Joshua Waddington occupied "a brew-house and malt-house" owned by Elizabeth Rutgers. The Rutgers property had been taken over by the British and assigned to Waddington by the commissary-general. When the war ended, however, the New York legislature passed a law, on March 17, 1783, allowing a person such as Miss Rutgers to bring action for damages against anyone who had destroyed her property. The case was important. If the Mayor's Court decided for the plaintiff, a number of New Yorkers could collect from British citizens. If the court decided for the defendant, then the anxious New Yorkers had no legal means of collecting for damages.

In the specific case the court split the decision, saying that Miss Rutgers could collect for part of the time the house was occupied by Waddington but not for the entire time. However, the court specifically ruled the Act of 1783 invalid, thus destroying the hopes of those New Yorkers who had plans to collect large amounts of money. How the court dealt with the issue of judicial review is interesting. First, it denied exercising the power. The decision reads:

> The supremacy of the legislature need not be called into question; If they think fit positively to enact a law, there is no power which can control them. When the main object of such a law is clearly expressed, and the intention is manifest, the judges are not at liberty, although it appears to them to be unreasonable, to reject it; for this were to set the judicial above the legislative, which would be subversive of all government.

Then the court explained:

> But when a law is expressed in general words, and some collateral matter, which happens to arise from those general words, is unreasonable, there the judges are in decency to conclude, that the consequences were not foreseen by the legislatures; and therefore they are at liberty to expound the statute by equity, and only *quoad hoc* to disregard it.
> When the judicial make these distinctions, they do not control the legislature; they endeavor to give their intention its proper effect.[30]

The court then determined that any persons who would be exempted from the legislative act by the law of nations or the Treaty of 1783, "this court must take it for granted, could never have been intended to be comprehended within it by the legislature. . . ."[31]

Whatever the court believed it was or was not doing regarding the doctrine of judicial review, there was no question that the people of the city understood what was happening, and they didn't like it. A meeting was held and an address "To the People of the States" was published on November 4, 1784, condemning the decision. "From what has been said we think that no one can doubt of the meaning of the law," said the address. "It remains to inquire whether a court of judicature can consistently, without Constitution and laws, adjudge contrary to the plain and obvious meaning of a statute. That the Mayor's Courts have done so in this case we think is manifest from the aforegoing remarks. That there should be a power vested in courts of judicature whereby they might control the supreme legislative power, we think is absurd in itself."[32]

That protest was the exception, however, to a growing acceptance of the doctrine of judicial review, an acceptance based on the logic of the doctrine as well as on its espousal by the more prominent and respected lawyers of the time. An example of the first was in New Jersey in 1780 when David Brearly, chief justice of the state's Supreme Court, ruled invalid an act by the state legislature allowing a trial by only six men. The law, passed in 1778, authorized the seizure of contraband if a six-man jury found the owner guilty of trading with the British. A militia major named Elisha Walton seized goods worth perhaps $70,000 from two men named John Holmes and Solomon Ketcham. When the case was tried the next year before a justice of the peace and a six-man jury, Walton won. The lawyers for Holmes and Ketcham challenged this lower court decision claiming that the laws of the land mandated a twelve-man jury.

The mandate was vague. The right of trial by a twelve-man jury had become traditional; it was a fundamental expectation of a man charged with a crime in New Jersey. The state constitution included the phrase that the "inestimable right of trial by jury shall remain confirmed as part of the law of this colony, without repeal forever." Apparently the phrase "trial by jury" only assumed a twelve-man jury; at least the number wasn't mentioned. The state constitution also included the directive that the members of the legislature never alter or weaken that right. The lawyers for Holmes and Ketcham insisted that reducing the size of the jury from twelve to six was a dilution of the right to a trial by jury as guaranteed by the constitution and, therefore, was unconstitutional. Chief Justice Brearly upheld their contention and reversed the lower court's verdict on the basis that the six-man jury was contrary to the state constitution.[33]

Several years later when New Jersey sent delegates to Philadelphia to write what became the federal Constitution, those delegates included Brearly himself and William Paterson. Paterson had been attorney general of the state at the time of the decision, obviously was familiar with it, and later as an Associate Justice of the Supreme Court himself abided by the same imperative, that the courts can judge the validity of legislative acts, in both the *Marbury v. Madison* case, in which he did not dissent from Marshall's opinion, and in *Stuart v. Laird*.[34]

Brearly's decision in *Holmes v. Walton* has been lost; probably it was an oral opinion, never written down. If it had been saved, it might have earned as much recognition as that which went to George Wythe for his decision two years later in the case of *Commonwealth v. Caton* in Virginia. Caton and two other men were convicted of treason and sentenced to die. The three of them asked the state legislature for a pardon. The House of Delegates approved the pardon and sent the bill to the state Senate, which rejected it. The day the three men were to be executed, the sheriff was presented with a copy of the House action and was told it was a pardon and that the prisoners should be set free. Uncertain of what action to take, the sheriff delayed the execution but held the three men in jail. The case eventually worked its way up to the state Court of Appeals which was presented with three questions. Could the lower court send the case to the higher court? Could the Court of Appeals rule an act of the legislature unconstitutional? And could the House of Delegates pardon persons convicted of treason? The presiding justice was Edmund Pendleton, who has been accused of dodging the issue of judicial review in this instance. He said that in searching precedents for judicial review in other nations there had been little guidance, with "Lord Coke asserting at one time the omnipotence of Parliament, who may even change the Constitution, and another exalting the Judiciary above them, giving Courts power of declaring Acts of Parliament void because they are impertinent or contrary to right and Reason. . . ."

Then turning to the Virginia constitution, Pendleton said the question of how far the state courts can go in voiding a legislative act "without exercising the power of legislation, from which they are restrained by the same Constitution, is a deep, important, and, I will add, an awful question." He insisted that from that question "I will not shrink—if ever it shall become my duty to decide it." He then argued that this was not the time for such responsibility because "the treason act, in fixing the power of pardon for that offence in the General Assembly, does not counter the Constitution."[35]

Another member of the court, however, had exactly the opposite point of view. The law was violated because the pardon was not concurred in by the Senate, George Wythe believed. As a chancery judge, Wythe served as a member of the appeals court. Disturbed by an apparent usurpation of power, he said:

> I have heard of an English chancellor who said, and it was nobly said, that it was his duty to protect the rights of the subject against the encroachment of the crown; and that he would do it, at every hazard. But if it was his duty to protect a solitary individual against the rapacity of the sovereign, surely it is equally mine to protect one branch of the legislature, and, consequently, the whole community, against the usurpations of the other and, whenever the proper occasion occurs, I shall feel the duty and fearlessly perform it. Whenever traitors shall be fairly convicted, by the verdict of their peers, before the competent tribunal, if one branch of the legislature, without the concurrence of the other, shall attempt to rescue the offenders from the sentence of the law, I shall not hesitate, sitting in this place, to say to the general court, *Fiat justitia, ruat coelum;* and to the usurping branch of the legislature, you attempt worse than a vain thing; for, although you cannot succeed, you set an example which may convulse society to its center.

Wythe then added:

> Nay more, if the whole legislature, an event to be deprecated, should attempt to overleap its bounds, prescribed to them by the people, I, in administering the public justice of this tribunal will meet their united powers; and, pointing to the constitution, will say, to them, here is the limit of your authority: and hither, shall you go, but no further.[36]

Wythe's statement, particularly the last section, was the most forceful exposition not only of the right of judicial review but also of the obligation of the judiciary to review the acts of the other branches of government. In 1782, when he wrote those words, Wythe was one of the most—if not the most—significant member of the Virginia bar. He is the outstanding example of respected members of the legal community adopting the doctrine of judicial review. Never mind that his words were dicta, his pupils had included Thomas Jefferson, Spencer Roane, and John Marshall, and although Wythe's opinion apparently was not printed until well into the 1800s, it is inconceivable that his decision was not widely discussed, understood, and that it did not make an impression upon the young lawyers in Virginia. It is not necessary to search out concrete links between Wythe in 1782 and Marshall in 1803 handing down his decision in *Marbury v. Madison*. They exist. John Marshall was a member of the legal community which had developed with the understanding that judicial review was not only a right of the courts but also an obligation.

Over the next several years acceptance of judicial review grew even more common in the American colonies. In 1785 in Connecticut the courts struck down an act of the Assembly establishing dividing lines between several communities because the lines "operated to restrict and limit the western extent of the jurisdiction of the town of Symsbury, but could not legally operate to curtail the land before granted to the proprietors of the town of Symsbury," without their consent.[37]

A lawyer in North Carolina named James Iredell, within a few years as an Associate Justice of the United States Supreme Court, said in 1787 that the judicial department's duty "in all cases is to decide according to the laws of the State. It will not be denied, I suppose, that the constitution is a law of the State, as well as an act of Assembly, with this difference only, that it is the *fundamental* law, and unalterable by the legislature, which derives all its power from it." He continued: "The judges, therefore, must take care at their peril, that every act of Assembly they presume to enforce is warranted by the constitution, since if it is not, they act without lawful authority." Iredell then insisted that the decision of the courts is final.[38]

It was against this background of state acceptance of judicial review that the authors of the federal Constitution met in Philadelphia in 1787. These men were skilled in the law, the law as it was practiced in their states, and they understood that practice included judicial review. As Edward S. Corwin has pointed out, not only did the majority of those who spoke on the issue favor it, but among those supporters were the convention leaders, the men who drew up the document, the convention's "statesmen and articulate members."[39]

The interesting quality of the debate over judicial review at the Constitutional Convention is that it was so bland. "The judiciary was subjected to much less critical working over than the other departments of government," Julius Goebel, Jr., has observed. "Indeed," he continued, "it is difficult to divest oneself of the impression that, to some delegates, provision for a national judiciary was a matter of theoretical compulsion rather than of practical necessity."[40] The remarks of the delegates indicate they assumed that judicial review would be part of the governing process they were creating. On June 4, for example, Elbridge Gerry was speaking on the question of whether the judiciary should be part of a council advising the President. He was opposed to including the judiciary in any such council, as the judges will have "a sufficient check against encroachments on their own department by their exposition of the laws, which involved a power of deciding on their constitutionality." He added that "In some states the judges had set aside laws as being against the constitution. This was done too with general approbation." Later that same day Rufus King, speaking to the same point, said that "the judicial ought not to join in the negative of a law, because the Judges will have the expounding of those laws when they come before them; and they will no doubt stop the operation of such as shall appear repugnant to the constitution."

Benjamin Franklin and James Madison followed with comments about the advisability of placing the Justices in a special advisory council, but neither these two, nor anyone else, questioned King's point that the Justices will "no doubt stop" laws they considered unconstitutional in the normal course of their duties.[41]

Several times during the lengthy debates the same point arose, and usually it was treated with the same lack of interest. In a discussion of a proposal to allow the federal Congress to overrule the act of a state legislature, Gouverneur Morris took a negative position. He argued that "The proposal of it would disgust all the States. A law that ought to be negatived will be set aside in the judiciary department and if that security should fail; may be repealed by a national law. . . ." Luther Martin of Maryland argued at the Convention that no special negativing power was needed, for "as to the constitutionality of laws, that point will come before the judges in their proper official character." He added: "In this character they have a negative on the laws." George Mason spoke to Martin's point, saying that Martin was only allowing judges to weigh the constitutionality of acts, not whether they were "unjust, oppressive, or pernicious." Again, the concept of the courts weighing the constitutionality of acts went unchallenged.[42]

There was minor disagreement with the concept of judicial review during the debates. At one point, for example, John Francis Mercer of Maryland said he opposed the judges having the right to review the constitutionality of acts and the power to declare them void. He believed "laws ought to be well and cautiously made, and then be uncontroulable." Mercer's point was accepted by John Dickenson of Pennsylvania. But while Dickenson was against any such power of review for the judges, he admittedly was at a loss to suggest an alternative. "The Justiciary of Aragon," he observed, "became by degrees the lawgiver." Gouverneur Morris suggested as a possible solution that the executive have an absolute veto over legislative acts. Still, he added: "He could not agree that the Judiciary which was part of the Executive, should be bound to say that a direct violation of the Constitution was law." But this kind of discussion challenging the propriety or legitimacy of judicial review was rare. In most instances when the question came up, the right to judicial review was assumed.[43]

This was true in the state conventions over whether to approve or reject the new federal Constitution. At the Connecticut convention, on January 7, 1788, Oliver Ellsworth—later Chief Justice of the United States—described the Constitution as defining the powers of the proposed government. What protection did the people have against abuses by that government? Ellsworth answered: "If the general legislature should at any time overleap their limits, the judicial power is a constitutional check. If the United States go beyond their powers, if they make a law which the Constitution does not authorize, it is void; and the judicial power, the national judges, who to secure their impartiality, are to be made independent, will declare it to be void. On the other hand, if the states go beyond their limits, if they make a law which is a usurpation upon the general government, the law is void; and upright independent judges will declare it to be so." And it was at the Virginia ratification convention in 1788 that John Marshall first espoused the theory of judicial review. "To what quarter will you look for protection from an infringement on the Constitution," he asked the other delegates, "if you will not give the power to the judiciary: There is no other body that can afford such protection."[44]

In *The Federalist Papers* Hamilton, Jay, and Madison argued for the acceptance of the Constitution and explained judicial review as being an integral part of the proposed government: ". . . the courts were designed to be an intermediate body between the people and the legislature in order, among other things, to keep the latter within the limits assigned to their authority. The interpretation of the law is the proper and peculiar province of the courts. A constitution is, in fact, and must be regarded by the judges as, a fundamental law. It therefore belongs to them to ascertain its meaning as well as the meaning of any particular act proceeding from the legislative body. If there should happen to be an irreconcilable variance between the two, that which has the superior obligation and validity ought, of course, to be preferred; or, in other words, the Constitution ought to be preferred to the statute, the intention of the people to the intention of their agents." That was by Alexander Hamilton in the *Federalist* paper number 78. This theme was stressed several times in *The Federalist Papers*, and considering the circulation these had at the time, there can be no question but that they were widely read and understood. Judicial review was an accepted political fact in the young country.[45]

Thomas Jefferson, perhaps the greatest political philosopher of the time, had been an admirer of the concept of judges being a check on the other branches of government. In 1776 he had written to George Wythe that "the judicial power ought to be distinct from both the legislative and executive, and independent upon both, that so it may be a check upon both, as both should be checks upon that." When the Constitution was written, Jefferson was in Paris but kept abreast of the developments through his correspondence with James Madison. "In the arguments in favor of a declaration of rights," Jefferson wrote, "you omit one which has great weight with me, the legal check which it puts into the hands of the judiciary."[46]

Once the new government was established, there again was no question over the right of judicial review. The House of Representatives in June 1789 held a lengthy debate on the President's right to fire a cabinet member. The Congressmen felt they should not legislate but let the Supreme Court determine the issue. Such phrases as "the judges are the constitutional umpires on such occasion" and "the judiciary may disagree with us, and undo what all our efforts have labored to accomplish" were typical of the tenor of the debate. The right of judicial review was not questioned.[47]

The Supreme Court from its earliest days understood that it possessed this right. In 1792 the Congress enacted legislation directing the circuit judges (including the Supreme Court Justices then sitting on the Circuit Courts) to act as pension commissioners. When this came before the Circuit Court in New York, with Chief Justice John Jay presiding, Jay rejected the congressional act, saying that Congress was without right under the Constitution to direct judges to participate in nonjudicial activities. In the Pennsylvania Circuit Court Associate Justice James Wilson of the Supreme Court said flatly that the law was not operable. Before the issue could reach the Supreme Court for decision, Congress had changed the procedure for handling pension claims, so the question ceased to exist. The Supreme Court then did not have the opportunity to rule an act of Congress invalid, although there was no question that the Justices were willing to do so.[48]

The first instance of the Supreme Court reviewing the constitutionality of an act of Congress was in 1795, the case of *Hylton v. the United States.*[49] Alexander Hamilton, when Secretary of the Treasury, had recommended a tax on pleasure carriages. The Congress approved it, over the objections of James Madison, who claimed the tax was a direct tax, then prohibited by the Constitution. Hamilton argued the constitutionality of the tax before the Court, and his position was upheld. The Supreme Court had reviewed the legislative branch and found its work constitutionally acceptable. To everyone concerned the question was the constitutionality of the congressional act, never the Supreme Court's power to determine that constitutionality.

This judicial review power already was recognized as important. A friend of Hamilton's, writing to him a few months after the *Hylton* case was argued, lamented that Hamilton was not interested in becoming the new Chief Justice. Jay had just resigned and the position was vacant. "I am afraid that department," wrote the friend to Hamilton, "as it relates neither to war, finance nor negotiation, has no charms for you: and yet when one considers how important it is, where [the Justices] have the power of paralyzing the measures of the government by declaring a law unconstitutional, it is not to be trusted to men who are to be scared by popular clamor." The friend was William Bradford of Pennsylvania, who then was Attorney General of the United States. His purpose in writing the letter was clearly stated. "I wish to heaven," he said, "you would permit me to name you."[50]

The judicial review issue arose again in 1799 after the Virginia and Kentucky legislatures passed the resolutions written by Jefferson and Madison declaring that the states had the power to review acts of the federal Congress. In effect, the state resolutions were taking the power of review from the judiciary and giving it to the separate states. This would have allowed a single state to declare unacceptable a law that every other state was willing to accept. This position was answered by Chief Justice Francis Dana of Massachusetts in a case involving two men named Adams charged under the Alien and Sedition Laws. Dana described as a "monstrous position" that within the United States there are "as many supreme, independent, disconnected *judicial* authorities as there are States in the Union."[51]

In 1802, when Congress was considering repeal of the

Judiciary Act of 1801, the question of judicial review figured in the debates briefly. Senator John Breckinridge of Kentucky, who feared the federal courts deciding issues which he believed were of specific concern to the people of Kentucky, rose late in the afternoon of Wednesday, February 3, and began: "I did not expect, sir, to find the doctrine of the power of the courts to annul the laws of the Congress as unconstitutional, so seriously insisted on." To the argument that the courts are to be checks on the legislature, he answered: "I would ask where they got that power, and who checks the courts when they violate the Constitution?" He denied that such power existed and demanded to be shown where it was spelled out.

The answer came from Gouverneur Morris of New York. "I answer," Morris said, "they [the judges] derived that power from authority higher than this Constitution. They derive it from the constitution of man, from the nature of things, from the necessary progress of human affairs. When you have enacted a law, when process thereon has been issued, and suit brought, it becomes eventually necessary that the judges decide on the case before them, and declare what the law is. They must, of course, determine whether that which is produced and relied on, has indeed the binding force of law. The decision of the Supreme Court is, and, of necessity, must be final." Morris argued that was better than giving the final authority to some other element in the national government.

Senator James Jackson of Georgia did not wish to let that go by. One did not have to appeal to authority beyond the Constitution, he said, and charged that Morris, in doing so, was raising "an alarm without foundation." The Court, he insisted, had the right to hear appeals, and he cited the section of the Constitution giving the Court original jurisdiction in cases affecting ambassadors, other public ministers, and consuls, and cases in which a state shall be a party, and giving the Court appellate jurisdiction "in all other cases . . . both as to law and fact."

When Jackson ended his citation at that point, Jonathan Dayton of New Jersey rose to say there was a foundation for alarm and that Jackson's argument "reminds me of the story of a man who boldly denied the existence of a Deity, and undertook to prove it from Scripture. He opened the sacred volume, and read therein the words, 'there is no God.' A bystander, who was not disposed to take such things upon trust, took up the book and recited the whole phrase: 'The fool hath said in his heart there is no God,' and the position of this daring infidel vanished into air." Dayton then pointed out that the Constitution gives the Court

appellate jurisdiction "both as to law and fact, with such exceptions and under such regulations as the Congress shall make."[52]

This debate, however, was a minor part of the repeal discussions, and there was no attempt made to eliminate this power
which had been developing for so many years. Judicial review
was an issue debated but not voted on, and never rejected.

While judicial review was developing at the federal level,
it continued strong at the state level. In 1793 when the Pennsylvania Supreme Court could not declare a legislative act unconstitutional, it was obviously disappointed. A case was brought under
an act dated August 4, 1784, and the court said it would have
"no difficulty in declaring . . . [it] unconstitutional." The court
pointed out, however, that the law had been repealed by the
legislature the next year so the court did not have to face the
constitutional question.[53] In 1801 the Kentucky Court of Appeals
struck down a law authorizing courts to assess property values
when the state constitutional procedure appeared to direct that
such assessment be made only by a jury.[54] The next year, in
the Maryland General Court, the judges also felt free to determine not only that "an act of assembly repugnant to the constitution is void," but that "The court have a right to determine an act
of assembly void which is repugnant to the constitution."[55]

There was a similar case in December of that year before
the Circuit Court in North Carolina. The state legislature had
passed a number of laws in the eighteenth century dealing with
estates and creditors' claims upon them. In 1799 the legislature
enacted a law which had as its purpose interpreting the intent of
two of these earlier laws, one passed in 1715 and one passed in
1789 apparently replacing it. When the 1799 law was challenged before the Circuit Court, the judge was John Marshall,
Chief Justice of the United States. He said in his decision:

> The act of 1799 declares that the act of 1715 hath con-
> tinued, and shall continue to be in force. I will not say at
> this time that a retrospective law may not be made; but if
> its retrospective view be not clearly expressed, construc-
> tion ought not to aid it: that however is not the objection
> to this act. The bill of rights of this state, which is de-
> clared to be part of the constitution, says in the fourth
> section, "That the legislative, executive and supreme ju-
> dicial powers of government, ought to be forever separate
> and distinct from each other.["] The separation of these
> powers has been deemed by the people of almost all of
> the states, as essential to liberty. And the question here
> is, does it belong to the judiciary to decide upon laws

when made, and the extent and operation of them or to the legislature? If it belongs to the judiciary, then the matter decided by this act, namely, whether the act of 1789 be a repeal of the 9th section of 1715, is a judicial matter, and not a legislative one. The determination is made by a branch of government, not authorised by the constitution to make it; and is therefore in my judgment, void. It seems also to be void for another reason; the 10th section of the first article of the federal constitution, prohibits the states to pass any law impairing the obligation of contracts. Now will it not impair this obligation, if a contract, which at the time of passing the act of 1789, might be recovered on by the creditor, shall by the operation of the act of 1799, be entirely deprived of this remedy?[56]

Three months later John Marshall took the same approach in *Marbury v. Madison*. That decision is rightly considered one of the great papers in American history, and one of the most significant—if not the most significant—in the history of the United States Supreme Court.

2

AFTER THE CONGRESS had passed the Judiciary Act of 1801 in the closing weeks of the Adams administration, John Adams had rushed to fill the new judgeships so as to be certain that the positions went only to loyal Federalists. The task of sending out the commissions fell on John Marshall, who had continued as Secretary of State and who was late getting the commissions out. Marshall did not believe there would be any problems caused by the commissions being delayed, actually withheld until the next Secretary of State could deliver them. The withholding was an act of which "I entertained no suspicion." Still he would have sent them out before the Adams administration left office "but for the extreme hurry of the time and the absence of Mr. Wagner [clerk to the Secretary of State] who had been called on by the President to act as his private secretary."[1]

Jefferson, however, believed that the appointment process was not completed until the commissions had been delivered, meaning that as far as he was concerned the Federalists did not hold the new judgeships if they did not have their commissions in hand. Jefferson definitely wanted to oust some of the Federalists from the judicial branch. In addition to believing that the government would be more representative if that branch were not so stacked with members of one party, he also was under considerable pressure from his own party to oust men of the opposing faction. And certainly Jefferson was angry at Adams for acting in what he considered an unfair manner by filling the posts just prior to leaving office. On March 2, for example, Adams sent to the Senate for confirmation the names of forty-two persons to be justices of the peace for the District of Columbia. The Senate immediately confirmed them. It was the commissions for these appointments that Thomas Jefferson instructed his Secretary of State, James Madison, not to deliver. Some of these men actually were appointed later to the same posts by Jefferson; he was not seeking one hundred percent Jeffersonian purity, even if the Federalists believed that he was—"Mr. Jefferson in direct contradiction of his inaugural speech is pretty generally displacing the federalists," Robert Troup reported that summer to Rufus King.[2]

One of those justices whose commission was not delivered was William Marbury. Later that year he went to the Supreme Court asking "for a rule that [Secretary of State Madison] show cause why a mandamus should not be issued commanding you to deliver to me a commission of justice of peace." That was on December 16, 1801. Two days later, on December 18, the Court directed Secretary of State Madison to appear and show cause why such a mandamus should not be issued.[3]

Marbury was one of four appointees who brought action for a writ against James Madison. Why they waited almost ten months after Jefferson's inauguration is unknown. Perhaps they hoped that Jefferson would reappoint them as he was doing with the majority of the Adams appointees to justice of the peace positions in the District. Perhaps there were personal causes for the delay, difficulty in appearing before a judge, or perhaps they decided to wait until the Supreme Court actually was sitting in Washington. There has been speculation that Federalist politicians persuaded Marbury to take the action in hopes of embarrassing the Jefferson administration, or at least of securing a few more justices for Federalist party members. This last may be true—Charles Lee, a Federalist Attorney General, argued Marbury's case before the Court.

The December 18 order to the Secretary of State was a bold stroke. Because of the political backgrounds of the Chief Justice and the President, little that they did could be considered outside the political context. No matter what motivations existed for Jefferson's attack on the judiciary through the repeal of the Judiciary Act of 1801, for his refusal to deliver the commissions, and the subsequent writing of a new Judiciary Act in 1802, one purpose at least was to strike a blow at the Federalist party. And on the other side, from the Court's action the possible motive of preserving the Federalists and attacking the Jeffersonians could not be eliminated. The order to Madison, a prominent member of the Jefferson administration, was considered an attack upon the President through his Secretary of State. Did, indeed, the Court have the right to command such an appearance from the President or from his servants?

While the movement for repeal of the Judiciary Act of 1801 had been begun by the Jeffersonians long before the *Marbury* case began, the case certainly gave impetus to the final votes which came in 1802. It also gave impetus to the writing of the new Judiciary Act which the Federalists interpreted as an attack on the only branch of government they still controlled.

The next session of the Supreme Court after the order had been sent to the Secretary of State was not until February 1803, more than a year later. When the Court opened on Monday, February 7, John Marshall was not present. He often missed the opening day of the Court term; apparently traveling conditions were such that one could never be certain of arriving when one anticipated. But he was present the second day. It made little difference as there was no business ready for the Court until Wednesday, February 9. The case of *William Marbury v. James Madison, Secretary of State*, was argued the next two days, Thursday and Friday.

In his presentation Charles Lee called two witnesses, Jacob Wagner and Daniel Brent, who had been clerks in the office of Secretary of State. But they were uncertain, they said, whether Marbury's commission actually had been signed.

Jefferson's Attorney General, Levi Lincoln, appeared before the Court, but only reluctantly. "Having been summoned" is how the record explained his appearance. The record said he also objected to answering any questions. It continued: "He requested that the questions might be put in writing, and that he might afterwards have time to determine whether he would answer. On the one hand he respected the jurisdiction of this court, and on the other he felt himself bound to maintain the right of the executive"—a conflict that often troubles members of the government. Lincoln was involved in the case because he had been acting as Jefferson's Secretary of State for the period when the commissions were not sent.

Lincoln's request for written questions was honored. But,

after studying them, he still refused to answer, saying that he was not bound to speak about his official duties while he was acting as Secretary of State, and also that he should not be obliged to say anything that might incriminate him. Charles Lee answered with his argument that the Secretary of State has a dual function: one as a servant to the President, for which he cannot be questioned; and the other as a public servant, for which he is accountable. The delivery of the commissions falls into the second category, Lee argued.

The Court made clear to Lincoln that it expected the questions to be answered and gave him overnight to consider. The next morning he came in and said he had no objection to answering the questions. His answers were that he did not know whether the commissions had ever come into James Madison's possession, or whether there was, in fact, a commission for Marbury or for the others bringing the suit.

Lee then countered with an affidavit signed by James Markham Marshall. James Marshall had been appointed a circuit judge for the District of Columbia at the beginning of March 1801, only several days before Adams left the presidency, and he held the position until November 16, 1803.

In the affidavit read that day James Marshall said that on March 4, 1801, he was in Washington when he learned that a riot was anticipated in Alexandria that night, and he believed he should hurry back there. His home was in Alexandria at the time, and he held Circuit Court there. He called at the Secretary of State's office to pick up the commissions for the justices of the peace; he apparently was going to distribute them to those appointees living in the Alexandria area. He picked up a number of the commissions, probably at least a dozen, and he signed a receipt for them. But after signing the receipt, he realized he could not carry the bulky package and returned some of them, making a mark on the receipt against the names of those he was returning. "This affiant saith that to the best of his knowledge and belief amongst the commissions delivered to him there was one for Robt. T. Hooe and also one for William Harper," two of the men bringing suit with Marbury.

All this testimony had been preliminary, its point being to establish that the commissions did exist. The Court and everyone else was aware that they did, but the fact had to be demonstrated as a matter of law. The important question was taken up by Lee next. It was whether the Court can order a member of the executive branch to fulfill a responsibility which his President tells him to refuse.

Lee's arguments indicate he was taking a conservative

approach. This, he seemed to be saying, is a matter of law and not of politics. To the question of whether the President was under attack, Lee volunteered this answer:

> Can a mandamus go to a secretary of state in any case? It certainly cannot in *all* cases; nor to the President in *any* case. It may not be proper to mention this position; but I am compelled to do it. An idea has gone forth, that a mandamus to a secretary of state is equivalent to a mandamus to the President of the United States. I declare it to be my opinion, grounded on a comprehensive view of the subject, that the President is not amenable to any court of judicature for the exercise of his high functions, but is responsible only in the mode pointed out in the constitution.*

Then Lee restated his argument that the Secretary of State has two roles, one as a servant to the President for which he cannot be questioned and one as a servant to the public for which he can. Lee's denial that he was attacking Thomas Jefferson through his Secretary of State was an attempt to tell the Court that it could act without risking a political counterattack. Despite all the talk during the previous year about the Court seeking to attack Jefferson through this case and the order against Madison, Lee was insisting it was not true.

As to whether the Court had power to issue such an order to the Secretary of State, Charles Lee argued that it did, "for the act of congress expressly gives the power to award it, 'in cases warranted by the principles and usages of law, to any persons holding offices under the authority of the United States.'"

The arguments were finished on February 10, and on February 24 Chief Justice John Marshall delivered the opinion of the Supreme Court.

Marshall at this time was forty-seven years of age. In appearance he was not impressive: "Tall, meagre, emaciated; his muscles relaxed, and his joints so loosely connected, as not only to disqualify him, apparently, for any vigorous exertion of body, but to destroy everything like elegance and harmony in his air and movements" is how a contemporary described him. This description continued that in Marshall's "whole appearance, and demeanour; dress, attitudes, gesture: sitting, standing or walking; he is as far removed from the idolized graces of Lord Chesterfield as any other gentleman on earth. To continue the portrait:

---

* This view of the sanctity of the presidential office would be challenged in the Aaron Burr trial.

his head and face are small in proportion to his height; his complexion swarthy; the muscles of his face, being relaxed, give him the appearance of a man of fifty years of age, nor can he be much younger."

Marshall's appearance then was one of good humor, and this observer—William Wirt, a lawyer who frequently practiced before Marshall's Court—noted the physical characteristic that so intrigued so many reporters on Marshall. This was Marshall's "black eyes, that unerring index, [which] possess an irradiating spirit, which proclaims the imperial powers of the mind that sits enthroned within."

Wirt, who wrote this description a few months after the *Marbury v. Madison* decision was handed down, described John Marshall "as one of the most eloquent men in the world . . ." although his "voice is dry, and hard; his attitude, in his most effective orations, was often extremely awkward." What then was the source of Marshall's eloquence?

> All his eloquence [Wirt wrote] consists in the apparently deep self conviction and emphatick earnestness of his manner; the correspondent simplicity and energy of his style; the close and logical connexion of his thoughts; and the easy gradations by which he opens his lights on the attentive minds of his hearers.
>
> The audience are never permitted to pause for a moment. There is no stopping to weave garlands of flowers, to hang in festoons, around a favourite argument. On the contrary, every sentence is progressive; every idea sheds new light on the subject; the listener is kept perpetually in that sweetly pleasurable vibration, with which the mind of man always receives new truths; the dawn advances in easy but unremitting pace; the subject opens gradually on the view; until, rising, in high relief, in all its native colours and proportions, the argument is consummated, by the conviction of the delighted hearer. . . .

This was the man who began reading the *Marbury v. Madison* decision on February 24, a decision that more than any other act by the Supreme Court in its long history, perhaps more than any single act by a government official or branch, affected the history of the United States. Marshall began simply, almost perfunctorily. "At the last term on the affidavits then read and filed with the clerk," reads his opening sentence, "a rule was granted in this case, requiring the secretary of state to shew cause why a mandamus should not issue, directing him to deliver to William Marbury his commission as a justice of the peace for the county of Washington, in the district of Columbia."

Marshall then pointed out that the Secretary of State had not responded, "and the present motion is for a mandamus." He then announced that he was aware of the controversy the case had aroused during the previous year, that it was looked upon as an attack on President Jefferson, and that political factions were involved. "The peculiar delicacy of this case," Marshall said, "the novelty of some of its circumstances, and the real difficulty attending the points which occur in it, require a complete exposition of the principles, on which the opinion to be given by the court, is founded." For the Supreme Court the response would be "a complete exposition" without any attempt to dodge anything.

After congratulating Charles Lee for his able arguments—this was among the courtesies the Court then extended to lawyers appearing before it—Marshall said the case revolved around three questions. Did Marbury have a right to the commission? If he had such a right which had been violated, did he have a remedy under law? And, finally, if the laws did afford him a remedy, "is it a *mandamus* issuing from this court?"

Those questions appear to be in reverse. Logically, one would consider whether a court has a right to hear a case, whether the law is applicable, and then determine whether a person has had his rights violated; if so, the decision must be in his favor. But that is not how John Marshall visualized the opportunity the decision had given him. Much more was at stake than William Marbury's commission.

Marshall then entered into a long discussion of the appointment and commissioning process. "The last act to be done by the President is the signature on the commission" after the Senate has approved the nomination. This, Marshall said, had been done with the Marbury appointment. Next Marshall came to the basis of the Jefferson refusal, that the process was not finished until the appointment had been actually delivered. Marshall denied this was so. "Some point of time must be taken when the power of the executive over an officer, not removeable at his will, must cease," Marshall declared. "That point of time must be when the constitutional power of appointment has been exercised. And this power has been exercised when the last act, required from the person possessing the power, has been performed." So there would be no confusion, Marshall then said: "This last act is the signature of the commission."

He then traced the law which had transformed the Department of Foreign Affairs into the Department of State and which gave to the Secretary the seal of the United States. The law stipulated that the seal was not to be affixed to a commission until after the President had signed it. "The signature is a warrant for affixing the great seal to the commission," Marshall continued, "and the great seal is only to be affixed to an instrument which is complete. It attests, by an act supposed to be of public notoriety, the verity of the Presidential signature."

At this point John Marshall revealed what was the first purpose of his decision. That was to lecture the President of the United States and the Secretary of State on what the law was. The next four paragraphs often have been read as a political diatribe against the leader of the opposition party; and such a motive may well have existed. Those same paragraphs can be read as the act of a petty man seeking to embarrass a foe against whom he has had objections and complaints for years; and this too may have been true. But those four paragraphs can also be read as a demand that all men obey the law, even the President of the United States and the Secretary of State, that all men understand that the law is not capricious, that it may not be bent to suit one person's biases or political fortunes. The Americans had fought a war to demonstrate the maxim that the law must be justly and fairly administered. John Marshall had been part of that war and then had struggled for years afterwards for the success of that principle. At this point in his life, at this point in the life of his country, he was not going to allow that principle to go by default.

> The commission being signed, [he said] the subsequent duty of the secretary of state is prescribed by law, and not to be guided by the will of the President. He is to affix the seal of the United States to the commission, and is to record it.
>
> This is not a proceeding which may be varied, if the judgment of the executive shall suggest one more eligible; but it is a precise course accurately marked out by law, and is to be strictly pursued. It is the duty of the secretary of state to conform to the law, and in this he is an officer of the United States, bound to obey the laws. He acts, in this respect, as has been very properly stated at the bar, under the authority of law, and not by the instructions of the President. It is a ministerial act which the law enjoins on a particular officer for a particular purpose.
>
> If it should be supposed, that the solemnity of affixing the seal, is necessary not only to the validity of the commission, but even to the completion of the appointment, still when the seal is affixed the appointment is made, and the commission is valid. No other solemnity is required by law; no other act is to be performed on the part of government. All that the executive can do to invest the person with his office, is done. . . .

> After searching anxiously for the principles on which a contrary opinion may be supported, none have been found which appear of sufficient force to maintain the opposite doctrine.

Marshall acknowledged, of course, that when a person is appointed to serve subject to the will of the President, he can be removed at any time. But when he is appointed for a fixed term, as Marbury was, "the appointment is not revocable and cannot be annulled." Anyone who assumes public responsibility can read Marshall's words with value and keep them as a constant reminder that it is the duty of the public servant to conform to the law and he is bound to obey the law.

The first question Marshall had raised—did Marbury have a right to the commission?—had been answered then emphatically. "To withhold his commission," said Marshall concluding the first section of his decision, "therefore, is an act deemed by the court not warranted by law, but violative of a vested legal right."

Marshall then moved to his second question. If a wrong has been committed, does a remedy exist? His answer demonstrated his intellectual agility. "The very essence of civil liberty certainly consists in the right of every individual to claim the protection of the laws, whenever he receives an injury," he began. "One of the first duties of government is to afford that protection."

Marshall then cited two references in Blackstone to support that point. "The government of the United States has been emphatically termed a government of laws, and not of men," Marshall continued. "It will certainly cease to deserve this high appellation, if the laws furnish no remedy for the violation of a vested legal right."

To find whether there might be anything in the *Marbury* case to "exempt it from legal investigation," Marshall said the first question was whether it should be considered a loss without an injury. He dismissed that quickly, explaining that the justice of peace position was created by Congress and was to give its holder security for his appointment which was to run five years. So Marbury did suffer an injury.

Then Marshall asked, since there was an injury, if there were any special circumstances in the "nature of the transaction"? In other words, was the withholding of the commission a political act for which the executive branch could not be questioned? In the first part of his decision Marshall had determined that Marbury had a right to receive the commission; now Marshall was questioning whether Jefferson and Madison had a right to refuse to deliver it. Marshall's answer shows him at his best in developing an answer that appears irrefutable.

He cited a 1794 law directing the Secretary of War to place the names of wounded veterans on a pension list. "If he should refuse to do so, would the wounded veteran be without remedy?" Marshall asked. "Is it to be contended that where the law in precise terms, directs the performance of an act, in which an individual is interested, the law is incapable of securing obedience to its mandate? Is it on account of the character of the person against whom the complaint is made? Is it to be contended that the heads of departments are not amenable to the laws of their country?"

Marshall answered that such a possibility can "never be maintained." Neither legislative act nor common law allowed it.

He then cited another example: a 1796 law directing the President to grant land patents in certain cases and the Secretary of State to issue them. If the Secretary refused to issue the patent, Marshall asked, "can it be imagined that the law furnishes to the injured person no remedy? It is not believed that any person whatever would attempt to maintain such a proposition."

Marshall concluded that some acts of a department head could be examined by the courts, and "there must be some rule of law to guide the court in the exercise of its jurisdiction." For his answer Marshall relied on the differentiation that Charles Lee described in his arguments before the Court, that where the President or his aides act in a political manner they are responsible to the voters; "But when the legislature proceeds to impose on that officer other duties," when he is directed to perform certain acts, when individual rights are dependent upon his performing those acts, "he is so far the officer of the law; is amenable to the laws for his conduct; and cannot at his discretion sport away the vested rights of others," said Marshall, repeating the point he had made in the first part of his decision. Whether Marshall accidentally repeated himself or took the occasion to re-stress a point he considered important is unknown; probably the latter. That the law is above any officeholder was such an important principle to him that he probably felt the need to state it often and emphatically.

In his decision thus far Marshall had established that Marbury was entitled to his commission and that he had a remedy under law for its being withheld. He now came to the third point. Was that remedy a mandamus issued by the Supreme Court?

Before answering that question Marshall addressed the political issue. He acknowledged that the question of whether to issue a mandamus to a member of the President's cabinet is a task "peculiarly irksome, as well as delicate" and raised some doubts as to the propriety of considering such an action. He continued: "Impressions are often received without much reflection or examination, and it is not wonderful that in such a case as this, the assertion by an individual, or his legal claims in a court of justice; to which claims it is the duty of that court to attend; should at first view be considered by some, as an attempt to intrude into the cabinet, and to intermeddle with the prerogatives of the executive."

John Marshall, of course, would never do anything like intrude or intermeddle with the President—as he quickly assured everyone. "It is scarcely necessary for the court to disclaim all pretensions to such a jurisdiction," he said. "An extravagance, so absurd and excessive, could not have been entertained for a moment. The province of the court is, solely, to decide on the rights of individuals, not to enquire how the executive, or executive officers, perform duties in which they have a discretion. Questions, in their nature political, or which are, by the constitution and laws, submitted to the executive, can never be made in this court."

This definition of judicial restraint was no less sincere because it was offered to meet political criticism. Marshall always believed in using the powers of the Court to their utmost, but he did not believe in using powers that did not belong to the Court.

Returning to the issue, Marshall said that the act establishing the court system authorized the Supreme Court to issue writs of mandamus. The facts so far in the case seemed to bring it under this authorization, Marshall said. He then made this point: "If this court is not authorized to issue a writ of mandamus to [the Secretary of State], it must be because the law is unconstitutional. . . ."

This was a totally new and unexpected point. It had not been discussed in the proceedings. That the Court had the power to issue a mandamus had been accepted. But to Marshall the point was essential. As his decision so far had made clear, he did not believe one could trust the members of the executive branch to adhere to laws with which they disagreed. Only the judiciary could be entrusted to insist that the law be adhered to. This meant that the judiciary must say what the law is. This is the power of judicial review. This is the power that had been developing in the colonies almost since the first Englishmen left their homes for the New World. This is the power that the framers of the Constitution accepted as a fact of their society when they wrote the Constitution. This is the power that the state courts had been wielding without hesitation against their state legislatures. This is the power to make the act of a political body subject to the dispassionate review of a body which can be free of all political pressures. This is the feature of the American political process that is unique and perhaps on which its greatness rests. In other nations a person who considers himself wronged by the executive or legislative must seek his ultimate remedy on the battlefield. In the United States such a person seeks his ultimate remedy in the courtroom.

This power never before had been used by the Supreme Court to overrule a legislative act. John Marshall now was about to do just that.

The constitutional question arose over the right of Congress to assign original jurisdiction in cases such as Marbury's, where an individual seeks a writ of mandamus against a federal officeholder, to the Supreme Court. The Constitution gives the Court original jurisdiction "in all cases affecting ambassadors, other public ministers and consuls, and those in which a state shall be a party. In all other cases, the Supreme Court shall have appellate jurisdiction."

In the arguments Charles Lee had addressed this point, to establish for the record that the Court had the power to issue a mandamus. He said that the Supreme Court "must have the superintendence of the inferior tribunals and officers, whether judicial or ministerial. In this respect there is no difference between a judicial and a ministerial officer . . . [and] the term 'appellate jurisdiction' is to be taken in its largest sense, and implies in its nature the right of superintending the inferior tribunals." And if every wrong has a remedy, he had argued, "Where are we to look for it but in that court which the constitution and laws have made supreme, and to which they have given appellate jurisdiction?" His arguments on that point had been perfunctory because the question had not been seriously challenged previously.

Marshall did not accept Lee's argument. "If it had been intended to leave it in the discretion of the legislature to apportion the judicial power between the supreme and inferior courts according to the will of that body, it would certainly have been useless to have proceeded further than to have defined the judicial power, and the tribunals in which it should be vested," he said. "The subsequent part of the section is mere surplussage, is entirely without meaning, if such is to be the construction. If Congress remains at liberty to give this court appellate jurisdiction, where the constitution has declared their jurisdiction shall be original; and original jurisdiction where the constitution has declared it shall be appellate; the distribution of jurisdiction, made in the Constitution, is form without substance." And for John Marshall the Constitution could never be form without substance.

Since the Constitution did not include issuing the mandamus among its grants of original powers, issuing the mandamus "must be shewn to be an exercise of appellate jurisdiction" before the Court can act. In responding to this necessity, Marshall laid down a definition of appellate jurisdiction, that "it revises and corrects the proceedings in a cause already instituted, and does not create that cause." Issuing a writ under the *Marbury* circumstances, Marshall then said, "is in effect the same as to sustain an original action for that paper, and therefore seems not to belong to appellate, but to original, jurisdiction." The congressional act authorizing the Supreme Court to issue the writs, declared Marshall, "appears not to be warranted by the Constitution; and it becomes necessary to enquire whether a jurisdiction so conferred, can be exercised."

Marshall then proceeded to lecture the American people on the sacredness of their Constitution. "The question," he said, "whether an act, repugnant to the Constitution, can become the law of the land, is a question deeply interesting to the United States; but, happily, not of an intricacy proportioned to its interest. It seems only necessary to recognize certain principles, supposed to have been long and well established, to decide it. That the people have an original right to establish, for their future government, such principles as, in their opinion, shall most conduce to their own happiness, is the basis, on which the whole American fabric has been erected. The exercise of this original right is a very great exertion; nor can it, nor ought it to be frequently repeated. The principles, therefore, so established, are deemed fundamental. And as the authority, from which they proceed, is supreme, and can seldom act, they are designed to be permanent."

After reminding the American people that their Constitution was too important to be trifled with, Marshall then said that the government had limited the powers of the three branches. "The powers of the legislature are defined and limited; and that those limits may not be mistaken, or forgotten, the constitution is written. To what purpose are powers limited," he argued, "and to what purpose is that limitation committed to writing, if these limits may, at any time, be passed by those intended to be restrained?" And then he came to his point: "It is a proposition too plain to be contested, that the constitution controls any legislative act repugnant to it."

In the next several paragraphs Marshall embedded judicial review into American life so deeply that it could never be removed:

> Between these alternatives there is no middle ground. The Constitution is either a superior, paramount law, unchangeable by ordinary means, or it is on a level with ordinary legislative acts, and like other acts, is alterable when the legislature shall please to alter it.
>
> If the former part of the alternative be true, then a legislative act contrary to the Constitution is not law: if the latter part be true, then written Constitutions are absurd attempts, on the part of the people, to limit a power, in its own nature illimitable.
>
> Certainly all those who have framed written constitutions contemplate them as forming the fundamental and paramount law of the nation, and consequently the theory of every such government must be, that an act of the legislature, repugnant to the Constitution, is void. . . .
>
> If an act of the legislature, repugnant to the Constitution, is void, does it, notwithstanding its invalidity, bind the courts, and oblige them to give it effect? Or, in other words, though it be not law, does it constitute a rule as operative as if it was a law? This would be to overthrow in fact what was established in theory; and would seem, at first view, an absurdity too gross to be insisted on. . . .
>
> It is emphatically the province and duty of the judicial department to say what the law is. Those who apply the rule to particular cases, must of necessity expound and interpret that rule. If two laws conflict with each other, the courts must decide on the operation of each.
>
> So if a law be in opposition to the Constitution; if both the law and the Constitution apply to a particular case, so that the Court must either decide that case conformably to the law, disregarding the Constitution; or conformably to the Constitution, disregarding the law; the Court must determine which of these conflicting rules governs the case. This is of the very essence of judicial duty.
>
> If then the courts are to regard the Constitution; and the Constitution is superior to any ordinary act of the legislature; the Constitution, and not such ordinary act, must govern the case to which they both apply.

To those who claimed that the law enacted by the legislature had supremacy over the Constitution, Marshall answered that such a position "reduces to nothing what we have deemed the greatest improvement on political institutions—a written constitution." He continued:

The judicial power of the United States is extended to all cases arising under the Constitution.

Could it be the intention of those who gave this power, to say that, in using it, the Constitution should not be looked into? That a case arising under the Constitution should be decided without examining the instrument under which it arises?

This is too extravagant to be maintained.

In some cases then, the Constitution must be looked into by the judges. And if they can open it at all, what part of it are they forbidden to read, or to obey?

Whatever the politics of the moment, Marshall's decision went far beyond them. And he considered it important that the people understand this. He asked what would happen if a suit came before the Supreme Court challenging a duty on the export of articles from a state enacted in direct violation of the Constitution? "Ought judgment to be rendered in such a case? ought the judges to close their eyes on the Constitution, and only see the law?" He asked if the Court should condemn to death those persons convicted under an ex post facto law enacted in direct violation of the constitutional prohibition against such laws. If the Congress says that a person may be convicted of treason on the testimony of one witness when the Constitution demands two witnesses, "must the constitutional principle yield to the legislative act?" Marshall's answer obviously was "no." The courts must not tolerate a legislative act that is in violation of the Constitution. He concluded:

> It is also not entirely unworthy of observation, that in declaring what shall be the *supreme* law of the land, the Constitution itself is first mentioned; and not the laws of the United States generally, but those only which shall be made in pursuance of the Constitution, have that rank.
>
> Thus, the particular phraseology of the Constitution of the United States confirms and strengthens the principle, supposed to be essential to all written constitutions, that a law repugnant to the constitution is void; and that *courts*, as well as other departments, are bound by that instrument.
>
> The rule must be discharged.[4]

The Marshall opinion denying Marbury his commission covers seventeen pages in the official reports of the Supreme Court. But its breadth cannot be measured in pages. It must be admired for its assertion that all men, even Presidents, must adhere to the law. It must be admired for its definition of the role of civil liberties and the role of government in implementing that definition. It must be admired for both its restraint in not going beyond the powers of the judiciary and its daring in using those powers to their utmost. It must be admired primarily, however, for establishing a rule of law, a procedure for settling disputes without the sword. One definition of civilization, surely, is a state in which men are able to live with their fellow men so that they settle their conflicts fairly and without force of arms. According to that definition then, John Marshall's decision in *Marbury v. Madison* was one of civilization's finest hours, one of mankind's greatest achievements.

The decision caused immediate and widespread comment throughout the nation. Newspapers in the cities of Philadelphia, New York, Boston, Richmond, Baltimore, Washington, Charleston, and Savannah printed either news items or the full text of the decision, often with lengthy editorial comments that in some cases must be described as brilliant analyses.[5] These newspapers were the chief means of political communication in that period —the full texts of legislative proceedings, court reports, and diplomatic exchanges were commonplace newspaper items—as well as of political propaganda. They were widely read by the populace and passed from one city to another. The papers were known for their political allegiances and thrived on the charges of partisanship. In these newspapers the Marshall decision in *Marbury v. Madison* was attacked and defended to the point where no one with any public conscience could fail to be aware of it.

Politics was the charge leveled by the *Independent Chronicle*, a Boston newspaper and the leading Republican journal in New England, which began with an attack on the concept of judicial review. "The efforts of *federalism* to exalt the Judiciary over the Executive and Legislature, and to give that favorite department a political character & influence, may operate for a time to come, as it has already, to the promotion of one party and the depression of the other, but will probably terminate in degradation and the disgrace of the Judiciary. Politics are more improper and dangerous in a Court of justice, if possible, than in the pulpit. Political charges, prosecutions, and similar modes of official influence, ought never to have been resorted to by any party. The foundations of justice should be unpolluted by party passions and prejudices. The *attempt* of the Supreme Court of the United States, by a mandamus, to control the Executive functions, is a new experiment. It seems to be no less than a commencement of war between the constituted departments. The

Court must be defeated and retreat from the attack; or march on, till they incur an impeachment and removal from office."[6]

In addition to the charges of politics there also were strong critiques of the decision from the standpoint of law. One of the most impressive was a series of letters, signed by "Littleton" and printed in the Virginia *Argus* and then reprinted in the *Aurora* in Philadelphia. Addressed to Chief Justice Marshall, the letters called upon him "to rescue your fame from the hungry jaws of obloquy, by disowning the child of which you are the chief putative parent," i.e., the *Marbury v. Madison* decision. "Littleton's" major point was that "Three questions are reported to have been decided. The last decision was that the court had no jurisdiction to decide the other two, which they nevertheless had decided." He argued that the third question should have been decided first, making unnecessary the answering of the other two questions, a criticism which has continued to follow the decision. "Littleton's" answer is as brilliant a piece of writing as is Marshall's decision. He takes up each point made by Marshall, considers it from every angle, and attacks it. Although he does not convince, he makes an impressive case.[7]

Judicial review was attacked directly in another series of letters, these signed in false modesty by "An Unlearned Layman." Whatever the author was, he was not "unlearned," as his letters make clear. Curiously these were published in the *Washington Federalist*, a newspaper considered to be both pro-Federalist and a Marshall mouthpiece. The paper introduced the series back-handedly enough. The "Unlearned Layman" sentiments are surprising, the paper said, because "We had thought the subject almost too clear for controversy," particularly "when elucidated by the able opinion of the Supreme Court, scepticism itself could no longer doubt."

The letters were directed to Charles Lee, who had argued the case before the Supreme Court for Marbury. The author asserted that if the Court could "suspend or dispense with a solemn act" of the legislature, then that power "has erected an ephoral power in the judges *above* the legislature, fatal to its own independence." Nor did he accept that judicial review had not been mentioned in the Constitution because it was an accepted part of the judicial process. "If it had been intended to confer this pre-eminent power on the judiciary," he continued, "would not those great and wise men, who composed the convention, have given it by *marked* expression, as they have given to the President, the *limited* veto, and not left them to assume, as they now do from *inference*, the *unlimited*?" And he answered his own question with "No sir!"

As for the Court's power to review all cases arising under the Constitution claimed by Marshall, the "Unlearned Layman" was an unbeliever. "Such an interpretation, not only corrupts the text, but destroys the compact," he charged. "There is enough to satisfy these words without resorting to this broad construction. The clause must refer, solely, to questions *properly judiciary*, and not to those, which impinge upon legislative jurisdiction—Cases in law may arise, which do not arise from statutory provisions: for instance, all cases of libels, all at common law adapted to our situation; and all cases in which the state legislatures shall pass acts in contravention to the Constitution and laws of the land, and, pervade and extend over the legislative jurisdiction of each and every state in the union." The author acknowledged, somewhat grudgingly, that Congress, not intentionally but perhaps accidentally, might enact a law that was in conflict with the Constitution. This is his answer to such an occurrence:

> The interference of the Judiciary here would not surely be necessary; if, on the contrary, it be a cardinal law, and they pass it, knowingly, in violation of their oath; when it comes to this, what do they propose? to break the compact and subvert the government—do you think then that the civil determination of the judges will aught avail? No Sir, when it comes to this, other tribunals than five judges must be resorted to. A people who deserve liberty and have it ought to know how to preserve it; if they do not and willingly bend their neck to the yoke, they ought to lose it—But the people here have the most peaceable mode, even in the extreme case above stated, to right themselves—"discontinuance in office"—Should they continue such violators of their trust, it only shews, that they are ripe for a revolution, and willing instruments of their own destruction.

To Marshall's assertion that the Constitution controls the acts of the legislature, the "Unlearned Layman" replied that he agreed, but defined the obligation this way: "That the Constitution—not the judges—ought to control the legislature."[8] It is a tribute to the "Unlearned Layman" that the critics of judicial review since *Marbury v. Madison* have not improved upon him. None of the arguments against judicial review have ever resolved the problem of who would be the arbiter if the Supreme Court were not. Felix Frankfurter, an Associate Justice of the Supreme Court in the 1940s and 1950s, defined judicial review as "a deliberate check upon democracy through an organ of government not subject to popular control." Robert H. Jackson, an Associate

Justice at approximately the same time as Frankfurter, argued that "Some arbiter is almost indispensable when power is distributed among many states and the nation and is also balanced between the different branches, as the legislative and executive, and when written and fundamental limitations on all governmental agencies, such as the Bill of Rights, are set up for the protection of the citizen. Each unit cannot be left to judge the limits of its own power."[9] Whether one accepts the Frankfurter view of judicial review as a restraining force or the Jackson view of it as an arbitrating force, there is no substitute for a peaceable, reasonable, and lawful force. Even "An Unlearned Layman" acknowledged this tacitly when he spoke of revolution—"A people who deserve liberty and have it ought to know how to preserve it"—and when he assumed that the majority would oust from office those who violate the Constitution, which is confusing the will of the majority with the guarantee of civil liberties to all men, whether belonging to the majority or to the minority, promised in the Constitution.

Such were the public arguments made against John Marshall's decision. They were not the idle rantings of political foes. They were learned examinations and caustic rebuttals to him. The people of the United States knew what was happening, and so did Thomas Jefferson.

Actually Jefferson had no argument with judicial review, as he understood it, nor did most lawyers. Alexander J. Dallas, an avid Jefferson follower, argued before the Supreme Court one year after *Marbury v. Madison* that "The constitution is the supreme law of the land, and not only this court, but every court in the union is bound to decide the question of constitutionality." His only restriction was that "the act and the constitution [be] in plain conflict with each other."[10]

Jefferson's understanding of judicial review, however, was similar to that of the "Unlearned Layman": that the courts had authority over what was judicial but not over acts of the executive and legislative branch. He stated this in 1804 in a letter to Abigail Adams, wife of his predecessor. "Nothing in the Constitution has given [the judges] a right to decide for the Executive, more than to the Executive to decide for them," he wrote. ". . . The opinion which gives to the judges the right to decide what laws are constitutional, and what not, not only for themselves in their own sphere of action, but for the legislature and executive also, in their spheres, would make the judiciary a despotic branch."[11] He would take the same position during the trial of Aaron Burr when the Circuit Court in Richmond, John Marshall presiding, subpoenaed certain presidential records. Jefferson did not then deny the court's right to subpoena him; he assumed the court would not deny his right to refuse to respond.

Jefferson apparently never understood the true significance of *Marbury v. Madison*, that Marshall had established the Supreme Court as the ultimate arbiter of those disputes which could be framed in legal questions. Twenty years after the decision, in 1823, Jefferson wrote to an Associate Justice named William Johnson, who was Jefferson's first appointment to the Court, replacing Alfred Moore who had resigned in 1804. In that letter Jefferson revealed his animosities toward *Marbury v. Madison*. He wrote:

> The practice of Judge Marshall, of travelling out of his case to prescribe what the law would be in a moot case not before the court, is very irregular and very censurable. I recollect another instance, and the more particularly, perhaps, because it in some measure bore on myself. Among the midnight appointments of Mr. Adams, were commissions to some federal justices of the peace for Alexandria. These were signed and sealed by him, but not delivered. I found them on the table of the department of State, on my entrance into office, and I forbade their delivery. Marbury, named in one of them, applied to the Supreme Court for a mandamus to the Secretary of State, Mr. Madison, to deliver the commission intended for him. The court determined at once, that being an original process, they had not cognizance of it; and therefore the question before them was ended. But the Chief Justice went on to lay down what the law would be, had they jurisdiction of the case, to wit: that they should command the delivery. The object was clearly to instruct any other court having the jurisdiction, what they should do if Marbury should apply to them. Besides the impropriety of this gratuitous interference, could anything exceed the perversion of law? For if there is any principle of law never yet contradicted, it is that delivery is one of the essentials to the validity of the deed. Although signed and sealed, yet as long as it remains in the hands of the party himself, it is in *fieri* only, it is not a deed, and can be made so only by its delivery. In the hands of a third person it may be made an escrow. But whatever is in the executive offices is certainly deemed to be in the hands of the President; and in this case, was actually in my hands, because, when I countermanded them, there was as yet no Secretary of State. Yet this case of Marbury and Madison is continually cited by bench and bar, as if it were settled law, without any animadversion on its being merely an obiter dissertation of the Chief Justice.[12]

Jefferson's comments show he did not understand that John Marshall had given to the Supreme Court as strong a tool as that body could have. It was in the 1820s that Jefferson's criticisms of the federal judiciary became the most strident, but that tone was caused by the series of decisions after 1810 giving the federal government supremacy over the states and not by *Marbury v. Madison*. His comments in that letter to Johnson, however, do show that Jefferson was aware that Marshall was not afraid to go beyond the specific case before him to enunciate general principles that he intended to be controlling in future generations— "travelling out of his case" is how Jefferson described it. Considering that the Court believed itself without power to issue the mandamus, the discussion of whether Marbury was entitled to his appointment, and the lecture to Thomas Jefferson and to all future Presidents about the need to adhere to the law, was unnecessary. It was dicta. Marshall was a master at dicta. He saw the Supreme Court, as he had promised Charles Cotesworth Pinckney he would see it in his letter of March 4, 1801, as a platform for the espousal of certain principles of law which he believed necessary for the development of the United States. His genius was that he could develop these principles in such a coherent way, make them appear to be so much a part of the case as he did in *Marbury*, that they seemed irrefutable—at least to future generations of judges. Edward S. Corwin quoted John Randolph crying in despair at a Marshall decision: "All wrong, all wrong, but no man in the United States can tell why or wherein."[13]

Another technique of power assumed by Marshall was the practice of having one judge, usually the Chief Justice, render a single decision for the whole court. Prior to Marshall's joining the Supreme Court, the Justices gave their decisions individually. Each member of the Court had his say, and anyone who cared could discover what each judge believed about the issue before the Court. Marshall changed that. In *Marbury v. Madison* six men did not speak individually about an issue. Rather, the Supreme Court spoke. It spoke as an institution, and in so doing it sought and achieved a moral force as great as that obtained by the presidency and the Congress. Rather than six men going in six directions, the Marshall practice of having a single opinion meant that one institution was attempting to lead the nation in the direction it believed proper.

How Marshall developed the concept of a single opinion is not known definitively. But reasonable speculation provides some clues. He was an admirer of Lord Mansfield, Chief Justice of the King's Bench in England from 1756 to 1788. Mansfield had developed the tactic with effective results. "Mansfield's decisions had the full weight of the authority of the court of King's Bench," one account reports, "and, since his colleagues were all lawyers of great learning, the influence of his decisions was much increased."[14]

When Edmund Pendleton became the chief justice of the Virginia Court of Appeals, he instituted the same system, and John Marshall was familiar with that system from his experience in arguing before that court. It was obvious to him that a court rendering a single decision was a more effective body than one rendering many decisions, even if all of them came to the same point in the end.

How much this new development was a product of Marshall's urging can be understood from an examination of the 1805 term. Marshall disqualified himself from two cases that year, *Lambert's Lessee v. Paine* and *Marine Insurance Co. of Alexandria v. Wilson*, and in both the Court reverted to seriatim decisions.[15]

Some years later Jefferson realized what had happened; apparently he was one of the first to do so. "Another most condemnable practice of the Supreme Court to be corrected," he complained to a friend in 1821, "is that of cooking up a decision in caucus and delivering it by one of their members as the opinion of the court, without the possibility of our knowing how many, who, and for what reasons each member concurred." Jefferson argued that this prevented any possible impeachment proceedings "by smothering evidence." He believed the Justices should give their opinions seriatim and "publicly endeavor to justify themselves to the world by explaining the reasons which led to their opinion. . . ." Jefferson repeated the same complaint the next year to Associate Justice William Johnson.[16]

Johnson, who had been appointed to the Supreme Court in 1804, replied to Jefferson in a revealing letter demonstrating the difficulty of being a lone dissenter. The eighteen years he had served on the Court, he said, had been "no bed of roses," and he had constantly wished for assistance or advice but believed there was no one on the Court to whom he could completely unburden himself. Johnson said he did agree with Marshall that the dignity of the Court should be preserved, but not to the extent of letting "private or party feeling run counter to the great interests of the United States." While on the state court, Johnson had given decisions seriatim and was, therefore, surprised to find on the United States Supreme Court that Marshall delivered all opinions in cases in which he participated, "even in some instances when contrary to his own judgment and vote."

Johnson said he "remonstrated in vain; the answer was he

is willing to take the trouble and it is a mark of respect to him."
Johnson said the real cause soon became apparent. "Cushing was
incompetent," he wrote. "Chase could not be got to think or write
—Paterson was a slow man and willingly declined the trouble,
and the other two judges [Marshall and Bushrod Washington]
you know are commonly estimated as one judge." Johnson then
wrote of the struggle he had in the ensuing years to establish
some independence for himself and other judges:

> Some case soon occurred in which I differed from my
> brethren, and I thought it a thing of course to deliver my
> opinion. But, during the rest of the session I heard nothing
> but lectures on the indecency of judges cutting at each
> other, and the loss of reputation which the Virginia ap-
> pellate court had sustained by pursuing such a course. At
> length I found that I must either submit to circumstances
> or become such a cypher in our consultations as to effect
> no good at all. I therefore bent to the current, and per-
> severed until I got them to adopt the course they now pur-
> sue, which is to appoint someone to deliver the opinion of
> the majority, but leave it to the discretion of the rest of
> the judges to record their opinions or not ad libitum.[17]

Some of Johnson's acerbity must be ascribed to partisanship. Whatever their difficulties, Cushing, Chase, and Paterson
were not men to be manipulated easily. Paterson, not Johnson,
was the first Justice to dissent from a Marshall opinion; this was
in *Simms v. Slocum* in 1805.[18] If the Justices acquiesced in
Marshall's plan for concurring opinions, part of that acquiescence
must be attributed to a sincere belief that Marshall was right to
so strengthen the Supreme Court. Also, after 1812 when Joseph
Story joined the Court, there was a strong Justice with an independent frame of mind on the bench. Johnson's comments are
still fascinating, however, for the glimpse they give of the inner
workings of the Supreme Court even if they cannot be accepted
in their entirety.

Both Johnson and Jefferson realized what was happening
to the Supreme Court, although neither expressed it in so many
words. They knew it was becoming Marshall's Court. He was the
fourth man to sit as Chief Justice but the first man with whom
an era of the Court would be identified, and he made it so. He
became "practically the sole mouthpiece," at least until the
arrival of Story. The Court in this manner began to develop an
aura. One contemporary account rhapsodized on this point. "How
dignified is such a judicial deportment—how gratifying and
encouraging to the advocate—how impressive upon all the

beholders and encouraging to the advocate. . . . The world may talk of the dignity and majesty of the Court of King's Bench, but we hazard nothing in saying, that no judicial tribunal at home or abroad, ancient or modern, has ever surpassed, in these respects, the Supreme Court of the United States."[19] That rhapsody indicates that the Court was developing majesty. The Court would be attacked in the future, as it had been attacked by the Jeffersonians with the repeal of the Judiciary Act of 1801, but the Supreme Court would never be defeated, clothed as it is in the mystery and majesty that began surrounding it in those early years of John Marshall's tenure.

But its invincibility was a matter for the future, a quality still to be proven. The first test would soon be coming.

3

THE *Marbury v. Madison* decision had proven that the repeal of the Judiciary Act of 1801 and the subsequent enactment of a new Judiciary Act the next year, while eliminating some judgeships, was not sufficient to defeat a judiciary so filled with Federalists. "A total change in the judiciary system is undoubtedly intended," reported Manasseh Cutler of Connecticut, a Federalist House member. When the Judiciary Act of 1801 was being repealed, Cutler believed that the Jeffersonians objected not to the system "but to its independence."[1]

In retrospect, considering subsequent events, a case can be made that Cutler was correct—the ravings of William Branch Giles indicated that he was. Certainly the Federalists believed the attack was on. The question was whether it was the work of a few Jeffersonian Republicans in Congress or an organized attempt by Thomas Jefferson and his party.

On May 13, 1803, only a few weeks after the *Marbury v. Madison* decision, Thomas Jefferson wrote to a friendly Congressman from Maryland that "I have no doubt that the agitation of the public mind on the continuance of tories in office is excited in some degree by those who want to get in themselves." There may have been some prophecy in that comment to Representative Joseph H. Nicholson, who would three years later be appointed an associate justice of the Court of Appeals. Jefferson in that same letter at first sounds almost as if he were trying to dampen the ardor for an assault on the judiciary. He explained that sixteen justices had been removed "for political principles, that is to say, to make room for some participation for the republicans." But then at the very end, he added:

You must have heard of the extraordinary charge of Chace [sic] to the Grand Jury at Baltimore. Ought this seditious and official attack on the principles of our Constitution, and on the proceedings of a State, to go unpunished? and to whom so pointedly as yourself will the public look for the necessary measures? I ask these questions for your consideration, for myself it is better that I should not interfere.[2]

Samuel Chase was a good target for an opening attack on the Court. He long had confused his duties as an Associate Justice of the Supreme Court with his duties as a partisan of the Federalist cause. He had campaigned for John Adams after he was appointed to the Court. He openly had advocated the passage of the Alien and Sedition Laws, and he had not hesitated to use the judge's bench as a political stump. In presiding over the trials of James Thomson Callender and John Fries, two ardent Jefferson supporters, Chase exhibited bias. The particular charge Jefferson had referred to happened before a Baltimore jury. Contrary to custom and judicial fairness, Chase at the beginning of the trial explained the law as he intended to charge the jury at the end of the trial. In this commentary Chase, who was still smarting from the repeal of the Judiciary Act of 1801, made a vicious attack on the Jeffersonians. He was sitting with a local judge named Richard Peters. Peters was familiar with the Philadelphia lawyers and warned Chase that the "bar would certainly take the stud" if the attack was delivered. But Chase did not hesitate. He was a violent man by nature, given to oratorical excesses.[3]

Also, the time seemed appropriate for an assault on the Supreme Court. The Jeffersonians were still smouldering from the Marshall lecture to the President embodied in the *Marbury v. Madison* decision. More important, an actual impeachment proceeding against a federal judge had begun and seemed to be succeeding. John Pickering, a federal District Court judge in New Hampshire, was believed to be insane and seemed incompetent to perform his duties. Ill health, whether mental or physical, is not grounds under the Constitution for removal of a federal judge; only "high crimes and misdemeanors" are. The House of Representatives, however, indicted John Pickering, and the Senate, early in 1804, found him guilty.

The situation revolving around John Pickering presented the United States with a real problem. Thomas Jefferson, writing later, best summed up one side: ". . . We have gone beyond the English caution by requiring a vote of two thirds in one of the Houses for removing a judge: a vote so impossible where any defence is made, before men of ordinary prejudices and passions, that our judges are effectually independent of the nation. But this ought not to be." He then added in a footnote: "In the impeachment of Judge Pickering of New Hampshire, a habitual and maniac drunkard, no defence was made. Had there been, the party vote of more than one-third of the Senate would have acquitted him."[4]

Where Jefferson complained of how difficult ousting an incompetent judge was, a Federalist Senator from New Hampshire complained that removing John Pickering was a dalliance with the Constitution. "Pickering's removal was desirable," Plumer conceded, "but to make insanity a misdemeanor was to confound all distinctions of law and justice, and to pervert the constitutional provision of impeachment for crime into an unconstitutional mode of removal from office without crime, thus changing the tenor of judicial office from 'good behavior' to that of the good pleasure of Congress." The success the Jeffersonians had in impeaching John Pickering, Plumer believed, was proof "of the ease with which constitutional provisions are made to yield to supposed necessities of the public service, and to the interests, often urgent, of party leaders."[5]

Jefferson was correct in complaining about the difficulty of removing a mentally or physically deficient person from the bench when that person wants to stay. But Plumer was also correct in pointing out that making the process easy and commonplace throws the judges and the judicial system to the political wolves. Plumer's fear was confirmed when he saw that those who had testified against John Pickering were later rewarded with judgeships and other court positions.[6]

To the ardent Federalists there was no question but that the proceedings against John Pickering were politically inspired. Timothy Pickering (not a relative), a Federalist Senator from Massachusetts, witnessed the vote in the Senate finding John Pickering guilty and recorded that the Constitution had been turned into "mere paper—to be folded into any shape to suit the views of the dominant party." Timothy Pickering, who had been Postmaster-General, Secretary of War, and then Secretary of State in the Washington and Adams administrations, had no hesitation in venting his political anger. "Justice should have presided at this trial," he said, "but was not admitted. . . . All who condemned were Jeffersonians, and all who pronounced the accused not guilty were Federalists." He was certain that if the

House impeached any judges, the Senate would find them guilty, "Because there can be no doubt that these measures originate with the administration, are made questions of party, and therefore at all events [are] to be carried into effect, according to the wishes of the prime mover." The "prime mover" was, of course, Thomas Jefferson, the President of the United States.[7]

It was against this background that the proceedings began against Associate Justice Samuel Chase of the United States Supreme Court.

There were doubts even among the Jeffersonians. Nathaniel Macon, a House member from North Carolina and a leader there of the Jeffersonian faction, raised some questions with Nicholson. (Nicholson is the House member to whom Jefferson had first suggested that action be taken against Chase.) Macon asked whether Chase should be impeached for making charges to a grand jury beyond the jury's responsibility, for a charge that was political rather than legal, for a charge containing "political opinions which every man may fully enjoy and freely express," for stating opinions in the charge "which any member of Congress might deliver to the House of which he is a member," and because the charge contained "monarchical opinions." Macon then asked: "Is error of opinion to be dreaded when inquiry is free?" and he added: "Change the scene, and suppose Chase had stretched as far on the other side, and praised where no praise was deserving would it be proper to impeach . . . ?"

Whatever was to be done about the possible impeachment, Macon's "firm conviction" was that Nicholson should not be the leader. Also a Marylander, Nicholson wanted Chase's seat on the Supreme Court.[8] Nicholson ignored Macon's advice.

On Thursday, January 5, 1804, John Randolph stood in the House of Representatives to speak of Chase's conduct. This is the Randolph of the Glenlyvar scandal who would delight over the years in torturing the emotions of Nancy Randolph in his search for satisfaction that his body could not offer him. Randolph also was the leader in the House of the Jefferson forces; when he spoke on political matters, it was assumed he was speaking for the President. He offered a resolution that the House appoint a committee to inquire into Chase's conduct and to report to the House whether Chase "hath so acted in his judicial capacity as to require the interposition of the Constitutional power of this House."[9] It had been almost eight months since Jefferson had first brought the Chase situation to the attention of Nicholson, five months since Macon had expressed his doubts to Nicholson. The movement against Chase had sufficient time to germinate and to be planned. Perhaps Jefferson was staying out of the fight, as his biographers suggest; the evidence, however, indicates he was aware of the move against Chase, was interested in it, and had encouraged it.[10]

On January 7, a Saturday, the House approved by an 81–40 vote the resolution after it had been broadened to include Richard Peters, who had been sitting on the bench with Chase. Peters' name later was dropped. Randolph and Nicholson had led in the debate, and were among the seven men appointed to the committee of inquiry. Of those seven committee members, five were chosen from among those who had voted for the inquiry and only two were from the ranks of those opposed.[11]

The committee's inquiry, not surprisingly, found Chase guilty "of high crimes and misdemeanors" and the House then appointed the five committee members, who had shown their opposition to Chase by their January 7 vote, to draw up articles of impeachment against him. These were reported to the House on Monday, March 26. This report and the subsequent changes made in it are interesting for what they say about Chase's accusers more than for what they charge to Chase.

There are seven articles in the report coming from Randolph's committee on March 26, all directed at the tenor of Chase's conduct while presiding on the bench. Not one charged a crime, although several charged acts that appear to have made a mistrial declaration a responsible reaction, if that procedure had been available. Also, not one would have had significance other than as an attack upon Chase personally; there was nothing in any of the articles which—if the charges had been established as precedents—could be used against any other Justice on the Supreme Court.

The report was put off while Congress was away and taken up again when it returned for its second session later in 1804. On Monday, December 3, Randolph rose to present a changed report, with new articles of impeachment which the House accepted. In most instances the articles were identical with those presented earlier in the year, but there was one major change. Article 6 accused Chase of violating the legal requirement that federal judges follow the rules of the courts of the states in which they were sitting. The understanding had been, previous to the publication of the article, that the requirement applied only to cases in which the contending parties were from different states. If it were true in all cases, as Randolph suddenly claimed, then all Justices of the Supreme Court could be so attacked because not one believed that the federal courts were bound by the state procedures and had so acted. This change made clear that the attack was not against Samuel Chase but against all the Justices of the Supreme Court.[12]

Well aware that the Court was under fire and also concerned that the Jeffersonians would win, John Marshall toyed with the idea of a retreat. It was only briefly, but it again showed that he continued uncertain of the power of the judiciary when it was pitted against the executive and legislative branches. Chase had written to Marshall for information about the Callender trial in Richmond; Marshall had been a spectator there and his brother William was clerk of the court. Chase apparently had asked the Marshalls to provide information for his defense. Marshall answered that he had spoken with his brother William and also with John Wickham about Chase's exclusion of testimony by Colonel Taylor, one of the points in the impeachment. Marshall reported that they remembered the incident "very imperfectly" but that they would try to refresh their memories and commit the incident to writing.

"Admitting it to be true that on legal principles Col. Taylor's testimony was admissible," Marshall continued, "it certainly constitutes a very extraordinary ground for an impeachment." But with Marshall's political sensitivity, he knew that the cause was faked in an atttempt to frighten and control the entire Court. He commented bitterly that "according to ancient doctrine," a jury finding a verdict contrary to law was liable to be charged itself but "the present doctrine seems to be that a judge giving a legal opinion contrary to the opinion of the legislature is liable to impeachment." He then observed that the remedy of a new trial was available to anyone who believed he had been wronged in court.

It was at this point that he unexpectedly said: "I think the modern doctrine of impeachment should yield to an appellate jurisdiction in the legislature. A reversal of those legal opinions deemed unsound by the legislature would certainly better comport with the mildness of our character than a removal of the judge—who has rendered them unknowing of his fault. . . ."[13] The whole point of the judiciary, of course, is to be a check on the legislature. The Supreme Court can be overruled, although that may not have been apparent at the time; in later years the Court's decisions were overturned in the Dred Scott case (by the Civil War), in the legal tender cases (by President U. S. Grant's packing of the Court), in the income tax case (by a constitutional amendment), and in the New Deal era (by assault from a powerful and popular President).[14] But overruling the Court is a difficult process, and it is intentionally so. If it were easy, as it would be under Marshall's plan of building in a system that would obligate the legislature to review Supreme Court decisions, then the Court would be a check on nothing. Marshall's unsteadiness in response to this assault on the Court through Chase would show again when he would be asked to testify in Chase's trial.

And the assault was real. Spurred by Jefferson in the House, it then moved to the Senate for the actual trial and there it was under the guidance of William Branch Giles. An ardent Jeffersonian as well as an old acquaintance of Marshall's, Giles could not accept an independent judiciary as a valid part of the American government structure. Nor could he abide Federalists in office. Shortly after Thomas Jefferson was inaugurated, Giles wrote to the President suggesting that the only way to put any check on the judiciary was to cleanse the courts of all Federalists "indiscriminately." Giles charged that the federal judges had been "the most unblushing violators of constitutional restrictions . . . to retain them in office would be to sanction the pollution of the very fountain of justice. . . ."[15]

Giles' problem if he wished to remove the Federalists from office was that the Constitution says that federal judges shall hold office "during good behaviour" (Art. III, Sec. 1), which means for life, unless impeached and convicted of "Treason, Bribery, or other high Crimes and Misdemeanors" (Art. II, Sec. 4). This requirement of criminal conduct was waived by the Congress in the case of John Pickering because there seemed no other way to rid the system of a man who was both a drunkard and insane. The Jeffersonian Republicans hoped that Congress would also waive it in the case of Samuel Chase because of his extreme partisanship which went beyond judicial bounds. But Giles was after much more. He wished to establish the precedent that impeachment was not a criminal proceeding but a device which the legislature was allowed to use against a judge with whom it disagreed.

He made no secret of this intention. As early as 1802 the Federalists in the House, where Giles then was, heard from him a denunciation of an independent judiciary and the claim that he "was able to prove the inconsistency and danger of such an independence."[16] After the Chase impeachment by the House, Giles saw an opportunity to demonstrate the theory that the judges should not be independent. He was by this time in the Senate and was a leader of the Jeffersonian faction there. As the Senators readied for the trial,* Giles explained his intentions. "We are to

_____

* The Constitution authorizes federal officers and the Senate to the House to impeach, or charge, try them.

sit in this case as a Senate," he told William Plumer, "not as a court, and to use the same discretion in the trial, as we do in legislation. We have authority to remove a judge, if he is disagreeable in his office, or wrongheaded, and opposed to the administration though not corrupt in conduct." Giles insisted that "Judges ought not to be independent of the coordinate branches of the government; but should be so far subservient, as to harmonize with them in all the great measures of the administration."[17] The courts, in other words, were to be an arm of the party which controlled the executive and legislative branches, and so the concept of a government with control balanced between three branches would disappear.

Giles argued his point on the Senate floor and in the cloakrooms. John Quincy Adams wrote in his diary of one day when the Senate business being light, adjournment was early. He was sitting by the fireside where he overheard a conversation between Giles and Israel Smith, a Democratic Senator from Vermont, in which John Randolph later joined. "Giles labored with excessive earnestness to convince Smith of certain principles," Adams reported, "upon which not only Mr. Chase, but all the other judges of the Supreme Court, excepting the one last appointed, must be impeached and removed." The "one last appointed" was William Johnson of South Carolina, named to the Court in 1804 by Thomas Jefferson.

Giles treated the concept of an independent judiciary with contempt. He denied there was any constitutional authority for such a court system, and argued that the judges' "pretensions to it were nothing more or less than an attempt to establish an aristocratic despotism in themselves." He argued to Smith that the House had the power of impeachment without limitation, as the Senate had an unlimited right to try persons impeached. "If the judges of the Supreme Court should dare," he said, his voice growing louder, "as they had done, to declare an act of Congress unconstitutional, or to send a mandamus to the Secretary of State, as they had done, it was the undoubted right of the House of Representatives to impeach them, and of the Senate to remove them, for giving such opinions. . . ."

Giles insisted that impeachment was not a criminal prosecution, that it was no prosecution at all. "The Senate sitting for the trial of impeachments was not a court, and ought to discard and reject all process of analogy to a court of justice," he said to Smith, adding that "A trial of a judge upon impeachment need not imply any criminality or corruption in him. Congress had no power over the person, but only over the office." Next came the point which was the crux of the case against Chase.

Giles told Smith: "[A] removal by impeachment was nothing more than a declaration by Congress to this effect: You hold dangerous opinions, and if you are suffered to carry them into effect you will work the destruction of the nation. *We want your offices*, for the purpose of giving them to men who will fill them better."

Israel Smith, however, had been a judge himself, chief justice of his state's supreme court, and he did not believe that the independence of the judiciary should be played with so freely. Honest error of opinion, he countered, could not be a basis for impeachment. The position Giles and Randolph were taking, he said, would ultimately establish tyranny over opinions.

John Quincy Adams had been quiet throughout the conversation to this point when he said he could not agree with Giles' definition of impeachment. But Giles paid Quincy Adams little attention. A Federalist, Adams would not be expected to vote against Chase. Israel Smith was the important one, and Giles and Randolph worked industriously to secure his vote.

To Quincy Adams, the argument was, in effect, a trial of Chase "over the fireside." Chase was not accused of any crime, and if Giles' definition of impeachment were correct, then he could be convicted; but if Smith's definition were correct, then he could not be convicted. After Giles, Randolph, and Smith had left, the Senate's sergeant at arms, James Mathers, sidled over to Quincy Adams. Mathers had heard the argument and understood its significance perfectly. "If all were of Mr. Giles's opinion," he said, "they never need trouble themselves to bring Judge Chase here."

That Giles, who as a member of the Senate was a juror in the trial of Samuel Chase, was working closely with John Randolph, who as a member of the House committee which drew up the charge was an accuser of Chase, was obvious in Washington during the next few months. Quincy Adams, who recorded this in his diary, concluded that the relationship between Giles and Randolph was "not very consistent with my ideas of impartial justice."[18]

Again, it is difficult to accept that these two men—Jefferson's chief lieutenants in the Congress—were acting without the President's knowledge and approval. This is particularly so because the Chase proceedings appear to have begun with Jefferson's letter to Nicholson.

In the upcoming trial of Samuel Chase, nothing would be left to chance. Particularly Aaron Burr would not. As Vice President of the United States, Burr was the presiding officer of the Senate and would, therefore, preside at the Chase trial. He had earlier that year slain Alexander Hamilton in a duel at Wee-hawken, New Jersey. Much has been written about that event in efforts to elevate both men to positions they probably did not deserve. Dueling was at the time an accepted, if not very common, way of settling arguments. Burr was not conscience-stricken, nor did many Americans of the time believe he should have been. He returned to the Senate when it reconvened in November of 1804 ready to resume his duties without embarrassment. Much of the Jeffersonians' success depended on Aaron Burr and his method of presiding. He had been considered a fair and impartial presiding officer in the earlier 1804 trial in which John Pickering had been removed from office. His possible bias would not, in this second trial, be ignored.

William Plumer, a Federalist and one obviously distressed by Burr's killing of Hamilton, accused the Jeffersonians of "caressing [Hamilton's] murderer." Once Burr returned to Washington, Jefferson showed him more attention than he ever had previously. Gallatin, the Secretary of the Treasury, also paid him attention as did James Madison, the Secretary of State. Dumas Malone charges that these allegations are not true, or at least cannot be proven. He further suggests that Plumer's comments must be suspect because Plumer "afterward suffered from a guilty conscience because of his connection with the [New England] secession plot." Still, Plumer's suspicions were written by him at the time and cannot be ignored completely, particularly because they are supported by others. Uriah Tracy, a Federalist Senator from Connecticut, wrote that "Col. Burr is taken by the hand, with much seeming cordiality by all the Democrats. . . . There is a manifest partiality shown to Burr by the administration, and Duane [publisher then of the *Aurora*, the Jeffersonian newspaper] is no doubt impelled by the higher powers to publish his defense. . . . [Burr] orders all our [the Senate's] printing into Duane's hands, and Duane publishes his defense."

Giles particularly tried to win Burr's favor by circulating a petition in his behalf. Burr had been indicted in New Jersey in connection with Hamilton's death, and the indictment hung over his head, making him liable for arrest.* Giles secured a number

---

* An account in Buell, *Jackson*, vol. I, p. 184, has John Marshall sitting in the Senate chamber during the Chase impeachment when Rufus King turns to him and says: "It is hardly conceivable, Marshall, that the hand wielding that gavel is the same hand that murdered Hamilton a few months ago." To which Marshall supposedly replies: "Well, King, what has that to do with the trial? Isn't he presiding fairly and ruling impartially?" The story is a good one but probably untrue. King's *Life and Letters* indicates he was not in Washington during any part of the Chase trial.

of senatorial signatures asking the governor of New Jersey to drop the indictment. One of Burr's biographers reported that also at about this time many of Burr's relatives and friends quite unexpectedly received prominent appointments.[19]

Burr's favor was important because the outlook for the vote was so close. There were thirty-four Senators, and with two-thirds needed to convict, the votes of twenty-three were needed by Giles. There were twenty-five Jeffersonian Republicans and nine Federalists. The Jeffersonians had to remain almost solid against Chase, and many of them were wavering. Some of those waverers were considered close to Burr.

Whatever Burr's bias and whether he was bought by the Jeffersonians, the Federalists ultimately came to believe that he had been less than honest in his conduct of the Chase trial. John Quincy Adams recorded that Burr allowed Giles to speak "three times without checking him" as Burr had done one of the speakers for Chase previously. "Indeed," continued Quincy Adams, "his partialities to Giles have been frequent and obvious this session."[20]

At noon on Wednesday, January 2, 1805, the members of the United States Senate filed into the chamber to begin the trial of Samuel Chase. James Mathers, the sergeant at arms, began the formal proceedings by announcing that he had delivered a copy of the summons and the specific charges in the impeachment to Samuel Chase the previous December 12. Chase then was called, and Burr informed him that "the Senate were ready to receive any answer he had to make to them." According to the minutes of the trial, "Mr. Chase requested the indulgence of a chair, which was immediately furnished." A footnote in the record explains that a chair had not been provided because the Senate was following the English parliamentary practice of impeachment, in which the accused stands, but that Chase had been informed that if he wished a chair, he could have one. Actually a chair had been provided for Chase, who would be sixty-four years old in less than four months, but Burr ordered it removed a few moments before the Senators entered the chamber. Courtesy toward Chase was not going to be a hallmark of Burr's conduct.[21]

Chase denied having committed any crime or misdemeanor "for which I am subject to impeachment according to the Constitution of the United States." He stressed that all his acts were legal and denied any improper intentions "with which the acts charged are alleged to have been done." Chase's answer, in effect, summed up his defense. He would not countenance in any way Giles' theory of impeachment, that a judge could be removed because he was in disagreement with the legislative and executive branches. He had committed no crime, he was saying; therefore he could not be removed.

Chase said he planned to answer all the charges made against him but that he needed additional time to prepare his defense. He referred specifically to the charge that he had violated Virginia state procedures—"A principle which was not brought into view until a few weeks ago, and the explanation of which will require a careful consideration, of the conduct and proceedings of the supreme and circuit courts of the United States, from the first establishment of our federal system." This was the charge which Giles, Randolph, and Nicholson hoped to use against all members of the Supreme Court, and Chase was informing them they would have a fight on their hands. Samuel Chase understood that more than his own future was at stake.

Chase closed his presentation with a request that his trial be postponed until the first day of the next session—March 5— to allow him time to prepare his defense.[22]

The members of the Senate then met privately in a committee room to argue about how long a delay to give Chase. The argument lasted four hours and was a heated one, with Giles insisting upon a date being set for the trial without any regard to Chase's wishes. He again argued his theory of impeachment and said it did not require any defense; either the Senate agreed or disagreed with the judge, was pleased or displeased by him, and could or could not oust him. No arguments were needed, Giles insisted, only a vote. Finally a compromise was reached, and the date set for Chase's answer was February 4, almost midway between Chase's request for a two-month delay and Giles' insistence upon an immediate vote. Giles apparently was embarrassed by the vindictiveness he had shown in the Senate's private session. As the Senators filed into the chamber the next day, he asked Israel Smith to make the motion setting the date. Smith, however, declined, and Giles ultimately did make the motion himself.[23]

In the month between that motion and the actual opening of the trial, Burr made clear his understanding that he was dealing with a historic event. He directed the Senate chamber be fixed properly for it. The Senate moved its proceedings to a committee room while the chamber was "fitted up in a style beyond anything which has ever appeared in this country," Senator Uriah Tracy reported. A new gallery encircled the room. It was covered with green cloth and the rows of seats rose in steps so all spectators would have a good view of the proceedings. For himself Burr had a large chair placed against one wall and on either side of him benches covered in crimson extended out for the thirty-four Senators. In front of Burr would sit the accused and his accusers. Male spectators were expected to stand in the rear of the chamber while ladies were admitted to the new gallery, but that separation did not last more than a few days.

Tracy continued that the chamber had been transformed into a "Roman amphitheatre, as it respects the seats of the spectators." He correctly analyzed the happening as "a great, interesting and super spectacle." He believed the people were motivated by the same emotions that bring "a group to see a man whipped at this post, or hung upon a gallows. I should feel some excuse for their congregation; but I fear that this same people will soon meet with as much avidity to see gladiators fight, or a mob massacre all who are good or great or worthy." Tracy was right. It did promise to be a good show. The Supreme Court, one of the three branches of the United States government, was under attack.[24]

On February 4, at one o'clock, the trial resumed, with Randolph and Nicholson leading a team of prosecutors from the House, and Chase represented by Luther Martin, Robert Goodloe Harper, Philip Barton Key, and Joseph Hopkinson. For Key, the case had a personal touch. He had been a federal judge, on a circuit court, until his court was abolished. Hopkinson was a brilliant young lawyer from Philadelphia. Harper was a Federalist from South Carolina who had practiced law in Baltimore after his congressional service had finished. Luther Martin was also of Baltimore and probably the greatest trial lawyer in the history of American law. In this case, later in the Burr conspiracy trial, and still later in *McCulloch v. Maryland*, he demonstrated an ability to hold a court enthralled for hours and sometimes for days, not only with appeals to emotion but also with an appeal to law. He would stand for hours, often drunk, and discourse on theory and cite precedents with an ability that amazed all listeners —and impressed them. Luther Martin was a passionate person, a great actor, but above all he was a brilliant lawyer.

Chase's answer to the charges cover forty-nine columns of closely packed type in transcript. More than three and one-half hours were needed to read it, with Chase doing most of the reading but assisted sometimes by Martin and Hopkinson. In his answer Chase attempted to justify all his actions and continued to insist that he had done nothing illegal. In discussing the sixth article of the accusation, the one alleging that Chase had not granted Callender the benefit of Virginia's laws, Chase answered that he was unaware of the law in question and had continued unaware of it until it was included in the impeachment the previous December. He pointed out that neither Callender's lawyers, nor Judge Cyrus Griffin, the local judge who sat with him, ever mentioned the law. Chase continued:

> A judge is certainly bound to use all proper and reasonable means of obtaining a knowledge of the laws which he is appointed to administer; but, after the use of such means, to overlook, misunderstand, or remain ignorant of some particular law, is at all times a very pardonable error. It is much more so in the case of a Judge of the Supreme Court of the United States, holding a circuit court in a particular State, with which he is a stranger, and with the local laws of which he can have enjoyed but very imperfect opportunities of becoming acquainted.

Chase insisted that if he had committed a wrong in this instance, "it is an honest error" and he claimed that he was "not guilty of any high crime or misdemeanor." This was the same claim he made in reference to all the charges. Whatever misconduct he might have engaged in, whatever "honest errors" he might have made, he continued to insist that he could not be removed from office because the Constitution permits removal only for a crime.

The trial was recessed to allow the House managers to draft a response to Chase's answer, and it resumed February 8. Once resumed, it quickly was delayed another day until February 9—an action taken by Burr at the request of John Randolph without the Senate being asked to concur. Quincy Adams thought the action unusual and asked Burr for an explanation. Burr said it was simply because the House managers were not ready, and the business could therefore not proceed. He made the same explanation to the Senate the next morning. Burr was growing more and more "testy" (William Plumer's word). He did not like the criticism he was receiving in the newspapers and from some of the Senators because of his conduct of the trial; his tawdry handling of the matter of a chair for Judge Chase in January rankled many persons in Washington. "He acts more of the tyrant," Plumer said, "is impatient and passionate—scolds. He is in a rage because we do not sit longer."[25]

Randolph delivered the House's reply on Saturday, February 9. He was definitely outclassed. John Randolph of Roanoke was not a lawyer. He was a tempestuous man who believed that he was competent enough to walk into a legislative debate and take command of it without preparing himself. In the House that often had worked, and it sometimes worked even in the Senate. But in this instance the members of the Senate believed themselves to be jurors and they were interested in law. From Randolph they received rambling discourses, remarks offensive to many of them, and generally an inept performance. Simeon Baldwin, a Federalist Representative from Connecticut, attended the session and wrote to his wife the next day that "Mr. Randolph on the part of the managers addressed the Court in a speech of about one hour, but it is generally conceded not much to his Honor or that of the House—he exhibited much of the bitterness and abuse of the Judge, from which the prosecutions originated." Manasseh Cutler of Massachusetts, another Federalist Representative, characterized Randolph's speech as "nothing great." And William Plumer best summed up Randolph's answer: "This speech is the most feeble, the most incorrect that I ever heard him make," wrote Plumer. ". . . He traduced the accused—He vilified other judges—He insulted one of the Judges of this Court [John Quincy Adams] by unnecessarily abusing his father—& he grated the ears of Mr. Burr by a dissertation on murder." Randolph's speech runs twelve columns in the trial record, and it clearly shows that the impeachment cause was in trouble because it did not have a qualified prosecutor.[26]

But then a qualified prosecutor would have been someone versed in the law, and the Jeffersonians did not have a legal case against Chase. Whatever his conduct, the case against him was based on his being a member of a political body—the Supreme Court—which the Jeffersonians opposed.

This became apparent in the following weeks as the prosecutors brought witnesses before the Senate to testify against Chase. This testimony showed the feebleness of the case against Chase. The Federalists, who had believed they were going to see their judges swept from the benches, began to feel optimistic. Timothy Pickering believed by Friday of the second week that "they will not find twenty-three senators hardy enough to condemn him." Simeon Baldwin the next day was writing to his wife that he was growing more doubtful whether Chase would be found guilty. "In quiet times," he told his wife, "I am sure they would not—and if they do, posterity will wonder how and why they did it."[27]

One of the incidents in the Chase impeachment revolved around his conduct during the trial in Richmond in 1800 of James Thomson Callender, the Jeffersonian propagandist, who was charged with sedition. The trial was heavily weighted politically. Callender was known as "Jefferson's man" and had been financed by him. The charge, sedition, was one of the devices that the Federalists had created in the wake of the XYZ Affair. Chase apparently had let his own political prejudices control his conduct as presiding officer. As a witness to these proceedings, the House prosecutors called a man who had been a prominent lawyer in Richmond at the time and who, although not a party to the proceedings, had observed most of the trial. This lawyer was John Marshall.

Marshall was in a difficult position. He as well as anyone realized the attack against Chase was the opening of an attack against himself. He was worried and concerned for the safety of the Supreme Court under assault by the other branches. It was this concern which had prompted him a year earlier to suggest, in his letter to Chase, that the legislature perhaps should have a veto over Supreme Court decisions. This concern now would lead him to compromises in the manner of his testimony. "The Chief Justice really discovered too much caution—too much fear—too much cunning," William Plumer recorded when Marshall's testimony was finished. "He ought to have been more bold—frank and explicit than he was. There was in his manner an evident disposition to accommodate the managers. The dignified frankness which his high office required did not appear." Plumer added: "A cunning man ought never to discover the arts of the trimmer in his testimony."[28]

Randolph asked Marshall whether Judge Chase had interrupted Callender's lawyers more than the usual number of times. Marshall answered that the lawyer was trying to make the point that the Sedition Laws were unconstitutional and Chase refused to accept that point as a valid one for the jury, "and whenever any attempt was made to bring that point before the jury, the counsel for the traverser were stopped. . . . Mr. Hay [Callender's lawyer] still went on, and made some political observations; Judge Chase stopped him again, and the collision ended by Mr. Hay sitting down, and folding up his papers as if he intended to retire."

Randolph then asked if Chase had interrupted only when the lawyers raised the point about the constitutionality of the Sedition Law. Marshall replied: "I believe that it was only at those times, but I do not recollect precisely. I do not remember correctly what passed between the bench and the bar; but it appeared to me that whenever Judge Chase thought the counsel incorrect in their points, he immediately told them so, and stopped them short; but what were the particular expressions that he used, my recollection is too indistinct to enable me to state precisely; what I do state is merely from a general impression which remains on my mind."

Chase had insisted in the Callender trial that the defense lawyers submit certain questions to him in writing. Randolph

ohn Marshall's father, Thomas Marshall [1], as a prominent Virginian, a soldier, and a iend of George Washington. His mother, Mary Randolph Keith Marshall [2], was a reat-granddaughter of William Randolph, hose descendants also included Thomas Jefferson, Edmund Randolph, and the Lees of Virginia. Thomas Marshall built Oak Hill [3] for his family in Fauquier County; the original part appears to the right in the photograph. After John Marshall inherited the estate, he built the larger extension on the left side of the picture. The house still stands and is owned privately.

I

1   LIBRARY OF CONGRESS

2   NATIONAL ARCHIVES

3   NATIONAL ARCHIVES

George III [1] insisted on preserving the powers of his throne and those of Parliament. Americans' demands to govern themselves as Englishmen led to the war known as the American Revolution. The conflict was encouraged by able orators on the American side such as Patrick Henry, who exhorted his fellow Virginians in the House of Burgesses to "Give me liberty or give me death!" [2]. An equally adept propagandist in Boston was Paul Revere, who used his pen rather than his tongue. Shown is a cartoon he did for the *Royal American Magazine* in which America is swallowing British tea—"the bitter draught" [3].

1

2

The formal study of law in the young American nation was at best a casual affair. For a few weeks, Marshall attended the College of William and Mary (shown here in an eighteenth-century engraving [1]), picked up a few rudiments of law, made some valuable friends, including Bushrod Washington, and came under the tutelage of George Wythe [2]. Wythe's professorship of "Law and Police" was the first chair of law in an American college. He saw his role as helping to produce not only lawyers but also leaders. John Marshall and Thomas Jefferson are the finest examples of his vision coming to fruition.

3

THE CULPEPPER MINUTE MEN

LIBERTY OR DEATH.

DONT TREAD ON ME

John Marshall was a hero of the American Revolution, serving four years. He originally was a member of the Culpeper Minutemen; their flag is shown here with the county name spelled incorrectly [1]. He was at Valley Forge [2] when Baron von Steuben began to train the Americans into an army [3] and at Monmouth when they proved themselves and where George Washington's courage earned him the respect of all who were with him that

![Head Quarters White Marsh Novr. 20 1777 order book page](handwritten manuscript)

> 124
> Head Qrs. White Marsh Novr. 20. 177[7]
> Parole Burlington   C Sign { Bristol
> Major Genl. for to morrow Lord Sterling   { Trenton
> Brigadier Maxwell ——
> Lt. Coll. Richardson
> Major of ye 5. N. Carolina Regt. } Field Offrs. of ye day
> Brigade Major McGowen ——
> Lt. John Marshall is ~~appointed~~
> by the Iudge Advocate Genl. appointed
> Depty. Iudge Advocate in the Army of the
> United States & is to be respected as such
> James Munro Esqr. formerly appointed
> an additional Aid de Camp to Major Genl.
> Lord Sterling is now appointed Aid de Camp
> to his Lordship in the room of Major Wilcox
> who resigned on the 20. of Oct. last & is to be
> respected as such.
> Mr Wm. Mountioy is appointed Pay
> Master to the 3. Virginia Regt. & is to be respected
> as such. —— The Clothier has received about
> 400 more Blankets the several Brigades are
> to send for their Quotas of them ——

5   NATIONAL ARCHIVES

6   LIBRARY OF CONGRESS

day [4]. The outcome—shown in the engraving "The Horse America, throwing his Master" [6]—was then inevitable. During the war Marshall received his first legal position—deputy judge advocate—on the same day his friend James Monroe (spelled incorrectly on the order), also received an appointment, as the page of General Heath's Order Book shows [5].

1

2

The most notorious case in which Marshall served as a lawyer was the Randolph scandal. The scene was Glenlyvar, an estate in southern Virginia [1]. It was charged that the beautiful Nancy Randolph [2] gave birth to an illegitimate child and that her cousin, Richard Randolph, was responsible for its death and secret burial. Patrick Henry [3] and Marshall served as defense lawyers and brilliantly succeeded in demonstrating that the

3

4

5

evidence against Nancy and Richard appeared to be built on gossip and misunderstandings. Years later, after Nancy Randolph married Gouverneur Morris [4], John Randolph [5] resurrected the scandal. Nancy acknowledged that she had given birth to an illegitimate child but said that it had been born dead. Rather than upsetting her husband, the revelation made Morris love her all the more.

A.P.V.A.

John Marshall married Polly Ambler and settled down in Richmond to earn his living. He soon became an active lawyer, drawing much of his business from fellow veterans. He built an attractive house in Richmond which still stands and includes much of the original furniture and a Marshall museum. It is operated as a tourist attraction by the Association for the Preservation of Virginia Antiquities (A.P.V.A.). The house was the site of Marshall's famous lawyers' dinners at which he entertained the most prominent men of the community.

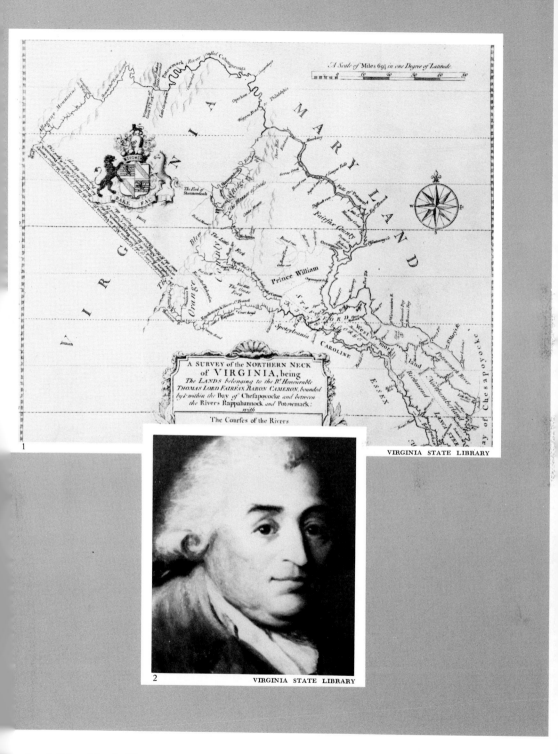

A SURVEY of the NORTHERN NECK
of VIRGINIA, being
The LANDS belonging to the R.t Honourable
THOMAS LORD FAIRFAX BARON CAMERON, bounded
by & within the Bay of Chefapoyocke and between
the Rivers Rappahannock and Potowmack:
with
The Courfes of the Rivers

1   VIRGINIA STATE LIBRARY

2   VIRGINIA STATE LIBRARY

uch of John Marshall's time in the 1790s
as taken up with plans and litigation sur-
unding the purchase of a large tract of
nd from Lord Fairfax [2]. The Fairfax grant,
it was called, comprised most of northern

Virginia [1]. Thomas Jefferson accused Marshall of accepting the XYZ mission because
he needed funds for the Fairfax purchase, but
actually Marshall accepted the appointment
only after financing was assured.

9

1	VIRGINIA STATE LIBRARY
2	NATIONAL ARCHIVES
3	LIBRARY OF CONGRESS
4	LIBRARY OF CONGRESS
5	LIBRARY OF CONGRESS
6	LIBRARY OF CONGRESS
7	LIBRARY OF CONGRESS
8	LIBRARY OF CONGRESS
9	VIRGINIA STATE LIBRARY

War with France threatened in the 1790s. President Adams sent John Marshall [1], Charles Cotesworth Pinckney [2], and Elbridge Gerry [3] to France to negotiate. Waiting for them was the most skillful, and venal, of European diplomats, Talleyrand [4]. When three men—known in history as X, Y, and Z —sought to persuade the Americans to bri the French government to avoid war, Pinckn gave the answer: "It is no. No. Not a S pence." For John Marshall there was perha another adventure in Paris—the beauti Madame Villette [5], at whose house he a Gerry were boarders.

eorge Washington [6] hoped in vain that
olitics would be absent from the nation, as
e cartoons "The Present State of our Coun-
y" [10] and "A Peep into the Antifederal
ub" [11] show. Washington, John Adams
, and Alexander Hamilton [8], Washington's
cretary of the Treasury, were the leaders
of the Federalist party, or "faction"; Jefferson [9], was the leader of the democratic
societies which became the Jeffersonian Republican party. Marshall, because of his devotion to George Washington and his belief
in a strong Union, became a staunch Federalist.

1   LIBRARY OF CONGRESS   2   NATIONAL ARCHIVES

United States of America.

In Senate, January the 27ᵗʰ 1801.

The Senate proceeded to consider the message of the President of the United States of the 20ᵗʰ instant, and the nomination, contained therein, of,

John Marshall, Secretary of State; to be Chief Justice of the United States, in the place of John Jay, who has declined his appointment.

Whereupon,

Resolved, that they do advise and consent to the appointment agreeably to the nomination.

Attest,

Sam. A. Otis Secretary

3   LIBRARY OF CONGRESS

Marshall returned from Paris determined to lead a private life, but George Washington persuaded him to run for Congress. He disavowed his own party's Alien and Sedition Laws, but won anyway, by a scant margin of 108 votes. The Federalist leader Theodore Sedgwick [1] predicted that he "may and probably will give a tone to the federal politics south of the Susquehannah." When Marshall defended President Adams in the famous Nash/Robbins case, the Jeffersonian Republicans asked their leader Albert Gallatin [2] to answer it. "Gentlemen, answer it yourself," said Gallatin, "for my part I think it is answerable."

arshall was appointed Secretary of War and
en Secretary of State, and dealt with the
estions of the British war debts, the possi-
ity of war with France, and the Barbary
ates. President Adams named him Chief
stice of the United States [3] after John
y turned down a reappointment and Adams

declined to nominate Associate Justice William Paterson. Washington, the new capital,
was not as attractive as the two views [4, 5]
and the drawing of the Capitol [6] indicate,
being primarily a few government buildings,
boardinghouses, and mud roads between them.

1   LIBRARY OF CONGRESS   2   LIBRARY OF CONGRESS   3   LIBRARY OF CONGRESS

4   LIBRARY OF CONGRESS   5   LIBRARY OF CONGRESS   6   NATIONAL ARCHIVES

7   LIBRARY OF CONGRESS   8   KARL GRUPPE

JUSTICES OF THE MARSHALL COURT

[1] William Cushing 1790–1810
[2] William Paterson 1793–1806
[3] Samuel Chase 1796–1811
[4] Bushrod Washington 1799–1829

[5] Alfred Moore 1800–1804
[6] William Johnson 1804–1834
[7] Henry Brockholst Livingston 1807–182
[8] Marshall at about the time of his appoi
    ment in 1801

14

[9] Thomas Todd 1807–1826
[10] Gabriel Duval 1811–1835
[11] Joseph Story 1812–1845
[12] Smith Thompson 1823–1834
[13] Robert Trimble 1826–1828

[14] John McLean 1830–1861
[15] Henry Baldwin 1830–1844
[16] James M. Wayne 1835–1867
[17] Marshall in 1832, three years before his death

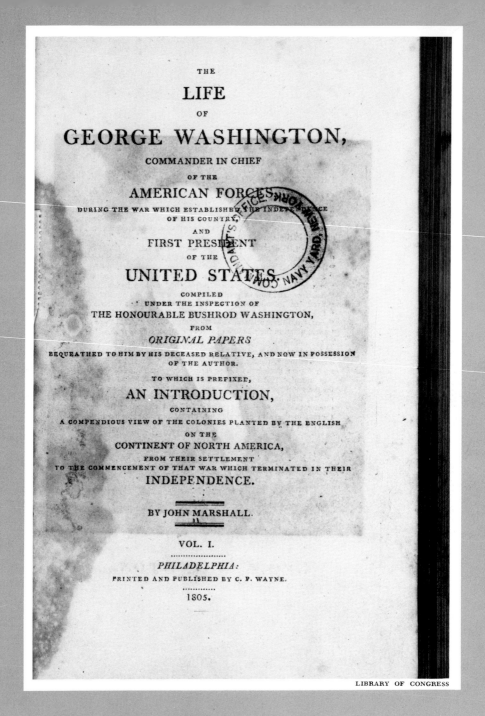

THE

LIFE

OF

GEORGE WASHINGTON,

COMMANDER IN CHIEF

OF THE

AMERICAN FORCES

DURING THE WAR WHICH ESTABLISHED THE INDEPENDENCE
OF HIS COUNTRY,

AND

FIRST PRESIDENT

OF THE

UNITED STATES

COMPILED

UNDER THE INSPECTION OF

THE HONOURABLE BUSHROD WASHINGTON,

FROM

ORIGINAL PAPERS

BEQUEATHED TO HIM BY HIS DECEASED RELATIVE, AND NOW IN POSSESSION
OF THE AUTHOR.

TO WHICH IS PREFIXED,

AN INTRODUCTION,

CONTAINING

A COMPENDIOUS VIEW OF THE COLONIES PLANTED BY THE ENGLISH

ON THE

CONTINENT OF NORTH AMERICA,

FROM THEIR SETTLEMENT
TO THE COMMENCEMENT OF THAT WAR WHICH TERMINATED IN THEIR

INDEPENDENCE.

BY JOHN MARSHALL.

VOL. I.

PHILADELPHIA:
PRINTED AND PUBLISHED BY C. P. WAYNE.

1805.

Marshall's monumental five-volume biography of George Washington was published in 1805, and was intended to confirm Washington as a national hero. Marshall used some of the techniques of modern oral history, seeking eyewitness accounts from persons who knew Washington. He believed the first edition had many errors, and revised it for a second edition in the 1820s, but there are few differences between the two. He tried to have his name deleted from the title page of the first edition, shown here, and refused to allow his title of Chief Justice to appear.

1e view of Richmond in 1812 [1] shows its ntinued growth. The State Capitol [2] was aled by the Monumental Church [3]. Mar- all contributed heavily to the construction the church and often prayed there, kneel- g in the aisle because there was not room ough in the pew for his lanky frame. He was not a communicant, however. Various explanations are offered: that he believed himself unworthy; that he planned to become a communicant but died before being able to do so; or that the corruption of the church in his youth made him doubt its integrity later.

17

Certainly the most famous trial ever held in Richmond, and one of the most exciting in the nation's history, was the treason trial of Aaron Burr [1]. Marshall was the presiding justice and President Jefferson, his old enemy, was industriously working to assure Burr's conviction, pinning his hopes on testimony James Wilkinson [2], who was himself a tr tor. Burr had two brilliant defense lawye Luther Martin [4] and John Wickham [who demanded that the prosecution establ Burr's guilt in strict accordance with

Constitution. Marshall upheld their argument, and Burr was freed. The drama the trial produced is typified by a diorama painted many years later [3]. Inaccurate historically—it places Marshall on a thronelike chair, ignores the second presiding judge, and includes a woman who was not present at the trial—the painting does suggest the emotion of the moment, as the accused, Burr, stands across from Marshall, the only man who can save him from a death sentence.

1

2

The War of 1812, in which the President's House in Washington was destroyed by the British [1], produced more opposition in the nation than any other war in which the United States has fought [2]. Marshall had avoided open political involvement since his appoint ment to the Supreme Court. He flirted wit the idea of becoming a peace candidate fo the Presidency in 1812, but could not rais enough support at the Federalist convention

1

2   3

4   5   6

Marshall administered the oath of office nine times to five occupants of the President's House [1] from 1801 to 1833: Thomas Jefferson [2], James Madison [3], James Monroe [4], John Quincy Adams [5], and Andrew Jackson [6]. Monroe was his old friend from school and the Revolution. Adams was the son of the man who had appointed him to the Supreme Court. He and Madison had fought together in Virginia for that state's ratification of the Constitution. He disliked Jackson and said so publicly, and his hatred for Jefferson never subsided, although he did not speak ill of Jefferson publicly.

21

Marshall's decisions, particularly in *McCulloch v. Maryland* and *Cohens v. Virginia*, strengthened federal power at the expense of state power. Two of his strongest opponents on this issue were the Virginia judge Spencer Roane [1] and the political philosopher John Taylor of Caroline [2], who were disciples of Jefferson and suspicious of federal power. When they spoke of their country, they meant Virginia, not the United States. Their arguments on the supremacy of the state governments were used in the 1950s to justify southern defiance of Supreme Court orders to desegregate public schools.

22

1 DARTMOUTH COLLEGE

2 LIBRARY OF CONGRESS

The likeness of Dartmouth College [1] was made in 1803, a few years before the legal proceedings began that culminated in the 1819 Supreme Court decision affecting the college. At issue was whether a grant by a government unit was a contract and, if so, whether it could be altered by one party. The first point had been decided in the affirmative in an earlier decision by Justice Story. Marshall's negative decision on the second point contributed to the growth of the United States as a commercial entity. Daniel Webster [2] argued the case for the college and held the justices spellbound.

This detail from Samuel F. B. Morse's 1822 painting "The Old House of Representatives" shows from left to right Hugh Nelson of Virginia, Associate Justices Bushrod Washington and Henry Brockholst Livingston, Marshall, and Associate Justice Story. This is the only known painting in which Marshall, Story, and Washington, who often joined in their decisions, are shown together. Story is perhaps the only Justice in the first half of the nineteenth century whose contribution to American judicial history is as significant as Marshall's.

24

he slavery cases that came before Marshall s Chief Justice did not include the question f the legitimacy of the institution, but he sed them as opportunities to criticize slavery. outhern fiction portrayed slaves as happy at eir work and contented with their lot [1], ut "Live Stock, Virginia 1830" [2] is a truer presentation. Thomas Jefferson is shown watching over one of his slaves [3]. That decent men like Jefferson accepted and lived off slavery is one of the greatest and saddest contradictions of American history. Marshall owned slaves too, though a small number.

25

1 VIRGINIA STATE LIBRARY

2 VIRGINIA STATE LIBRARY

In 1829 Marshall was a delegate to the Virginia Constitutional Convention. Once again he defended an independent judiciary, and once again his opponent was William Branch Giles [2]. The Convention had many distinguished members. In the painting by George Catlin [1], Monroe is seated on the left as the presiding officer, and Madison is addressing him. Marshall is seated to the right of Madison. Giles is to the right of Monroe. John Randolph's head appears directly over his. In the third row, the third person going clockwise is Hugh Grigsby, whose account of the convention is considered authoritative.

1 the early 1830s the Supreme Court was aced with two cases involving the Cherokee ndians and the state of Georgia. The Indians ppeared to have the law on their side, but resident Jackson had threatened not to enrce any decision the Court handed down storing the Indians' land against the state's takeover. In the first case the Court appeared to back down, but in the second case involving a missionary named Samuel Worcester [1], the Court decided for the Indians. William Wirt [2] was the lawyer for the Cherokees, and his arguments brilliantly capped an outstanding career as a lawyer.

1

2

Two silhouettes of Marshall in old age show he was gaining weight [1, 2]. He still kept in excellent physical condition by taking lon walks each day and by playing quoits.

The only known portrait of Polly Marshall was made when she was in her advanced years. Though she was an invalid during the last decades of her life, John Marshall's love for her never ceased.

2

Marshall was an active Mason in his youth, rising to the post of Grandmaster [1], though he denied membership in later years, when Masonry had fallen into disrepute. The second portrait is by Alonzo Chappel [2].

KARL GRUPPE

Marshall in 1801, the year he joined the Supreme Court, painted by Ferre de Saint Memin.

Chief Justice of the United States John Marshall in the full robes of his office, painted by Chester Harding.

asked Marshall if this were usual, and Marshall answered that it was not but that it depended on the circumstances. Then Randolph asked whether in these particular circumstances it was the practice to demand the question in writing before or after having heard it (Chase had demanded it in writing before having heard it). Marshall answered: "I never knew it requested that a question should be reduced to writing in the first instance in the whole course of my practice."

Randolph then warned that his next question was delicate and that "nothing but duty" could persuade him to ask it. So persuaded, he continued by asking if Marshall had considered Chase's conduct during the trial as "mild and conciliatory." Marshall juggled the question for a few seconds, and then finally said that "in the progress of the trial, there appeared some . . ." Before he could finish, however, a Senator interrupted with the claim that the charge was an improper one. Randolph offered to withdraw it, but Robert Goodloe Harper said that Chase's counsel had no objection to the question. "We are willing to abide in this trial by the opinion of the Chief Justice," he said.

Still, Randolph dropped the question. He then asked Marshall:

> Did you ever, sir, in a criminal prosecution, know a witness deemed inadmissible, because he could not go a particular length in his testimony—because he could not narrate all the circumstances of the crime charged in an indictment, or in the case of a libel; and could only prove a part of a particular charge and not the whole of it?

The question was a paraphrase of a charge against Samuel Chase, and Marshall replied: "I never did hear that objection made by the court except in this particular case."

At that point in the questioning Aaron Burr interrupted to ask Marshall whether he considered Chase's conduct during the Callender trial as "tyrannical, overbearing, and oppressive?"

"I will state the facts," began Marshall's answer. "The counsel for the traverser persisted in arguing the question of the constitutionality of the sedition law, in which they were constantly repressed by Judge Chase. Judge Chase checked Mr. Hay whenever he came to that point, and after having resisted repeated checks, Mr. Hay appeared to be determined to abandon the cause, when he was desired by the judge to proceed with his argument, and informed that he should not be interrupted thereafter." Marshall concluded: "If this is not considered tyrannical, oppressive, and overbearing, I know nothing else that was so."[29]

Marshall's performance that day was less than exemplary.

His answers do indicate, as Plumer charged, a desire to please the prosecution. He could have been accurate and still less cooperative, particularly considering that he was next on the list once Chase was convicted. The performance can only be understood in the context of John Marshall's unwillingness to join battle outside the courtroom. There he had the resources—the persuasiveness of his decisions—to win or at least to put up a good fight. Outside the courtroom he believed himself powerless.

Among the Federalist judges the trial was naturally a disturbing spectacle. The next night at dinner Bushrod Washington grumbled that the District of Columbia never would grow into a large community because, he said emphatically, "The present government could not exist for any considerable length of time." Even if it survived, he continued, the seat of government would be moved. He did not indicate where he thought it would go, but apparently he was thinking of its moving South to follow the political inclinations of the Jeffersonians. John Marshall was at that dinner also but was not reported to have engaged in the talk to any considerable degree, although he did listen to Robert Goodloe Harper expound on the need for establishing a modified monarchy—a man becomes Vice President at age twenty, President at forty, and retired at sixty.[30]

The judges should not have been so pessimistic because the charges against Chase were falling apart. Testimony such as Marshall's may have confirmed the accusation of poor judgment on Chase's part and other personal failings but could not be used by honest men to remove him from the bench, and this was the point of his defense. On Thursday, February 21, when Joseph Hopkinson began a three-and-one-half-hour speech for the defense, he opened by saying that much more than the fate of Samuel Chase was involved. "There is yet another dread tribunal to which we should not be inattentive," he told the Senators. "We should look to it with solemn impressions of respect. It is posterity . . . the faithful, the scrutinizing historian, who, without fear or favor, will record the transaction. . . ."[31] Perhaps for the first time in its career, but certainly not the last, the Senate was being asked to rise above partisan politics to aspire to a level of statesmanship which every government must reach on occasion if it is to survive and achieve greatness. There was precedent for such aspirations. The Jeffersonians had before them the memory of Patrick Henry at the Virginia ratification convention of 1788. He had lost, but he had taken his loss in good grace and had thus assured the continued growth of the United States.

Thursday had been Hopkinson's day; Friday was Key's; and

Saturday was Luther Martin's. He was to speak five hours that day and three hours on Monday. His appearance when he rose was undistinguished. A short man with thinning hair, his dress casual, even slovenly. His voice was occasionally too low to be heard, his grammar often incorrect, but his passion was real and his knowledge of law, based on a quarter of a century's practice, was spectacular. He not only would captivate in the eight hours he would speak during those two days, he would also inform.

"Mr. President," he began his address, "did I *only* appear in defence of a friend, with whom I have been in habits of intimacy for nearly thirty years, I should feel less anxiety on the present occasion, though that circumstance would be a sufficient inducement; but I am, at this time, actuated by superior motives." In his next sentence he announced that he was not going to allow the Jeffersonian Republicans to escape without the onus of trying to destroy the Supreme Court as an independent body. "I consider this cause not only of importance to the respondent and his accusers," he said, "but to my fellow-citizens in general—whose eyes are now fixed upon us—and to their posterity, for the decision at this time will establish a most important precedent as to future cases of impeachment."[32]

Martin's speech covers seventy-three columns in the formal record. Witty, passionate, scholarly, it revealed that Luther Martin knew more law, more precedents, more history than any of Chase's accusers. Whatever legal basis that Randolph, Nicholson, and Giles had claimed prior to Martin's standing up that Saturday, it no longer existed when he sat down. Chase always remembered the service his old friend had performed. Some years after this impeachment trial he was asked to sign a formal commitment for contempt against Martin because Martin had been drunk and abusive in a court. Chase lifted his pen to make his signature but then threw it down. "Whatever may be my duties as a judge," Chase is reputed to have said, "Samuel Chase can never sign a commitment against Luther Martin."[33]

By this time the Federalists in Congress knew that the attack on Chase was dissipating. Timothy Pickering reported to Rufus King that Giles and Nicholson would do poorly against the likes of Martin, Hopkinson, and Harper even if they had a good case; "with so paltry a one, you may rely upon it, they make a very shabby figure."[34] Chase realized the case against him was crumbling and he believed that ultimately it would do more harm to his opponents than to him. He mentioned this in a conversation with Plumer. The two men had met accidentally one day, and Chase volunteered that he would have considered the attack on himself the most fortunate event of his life if it had happened twenty years earlier. He claimed that it would have made him President of the United States because of the sympathy it would have aroused for him. As it was, he was discouraged because of his health. He feared the prosecution might break him; he did, in fact, leave the trial in the middle because of an attack of gout.[35]

The trial attracted a great deal of attention—Aaron Burr's new galleries were filled every day—and the Senators who were sitting as jurors were impressed with the seriousness of what they would be called upon to do when the time came to vote; they rarely spoke with each other about the merits of the trial during the proceedings, each apparently attempting to make up his own mind.

The vote came on March 1.

With a two-thirds vote necessary to convict it was probable as the Senators filed in that morning that that total would not be reached on any of the counts. All thirty-four Senators were present; Uriah Tracy, sixty years old and ill, was carried in on a stretcher for the two-hour procedure. The Senators and spectators were almost silent as the process began with Aaron Burr's saying, "Gentlemen: You have heard the evidence and arguments adduced on the trial of Samuel Chase, impeached for high crimes and misdemeanors: You will now proceed to pronounce distinctly your judgment on each article."

On the first charge, that in the trial of John Fries in Philadelphia, he had conducted himself in "a manner highly arbitrary, oppressive, and unjust," only sixteen Senators voted guilty and eighteen voted not guilty—not even a majority was obtained. And so it proceeded for the remaining articles. On none of the articles was there the two-thirds vote necessary to convict. On only two counts, the fourth and the eighth, was there even a majority vote against Chase. The fourth count dealt with Chase's conduct during the Callender trial and charged him with "manifest injustice, partiality, and intemperance"; the vote was 18–16 and reflected disapproval of his attitudes toward the defense. The eighth count dealt with Chase's charge to the grand jury in Baltimore in which he had castigated the Jeffersonians. The vote was 19–15 against him, and again was a reflection of disapproval of his personal conduct.

On the two key counts, numbers five and six dealing with a federal judge's responsibility to follow state laws, Chase was almost completely exonerated. The vote on count five was 34–0 in his favor and the vote on the sixth count was 30–4 in his favor. Not only did those two votes destroy the case against Samuel Chase, they also were an affirmation by the Senate of the United States of the integrity and independence of the Supreme Court.

"It, therefore, becomes my duty," Burr announced, "to declare that Samuel Chase, Esquire, stands acquitted of all the articles exhibited by the House of Representatives against him."[36]

The reactions were as could be anticipated. Samuel Latham Mitchill, a Senator from New York who was considered a Democrat, voted with the Federalists on this issue: "We did so on full conviction that the evidence, our oaths, the Constitution, and our consequences required us to act as we have done." He concluded in a letter written the day of the vote that "I suppose we shall be libelled and abused at a great rate for our judgment given this day." John Randolph and Joseph Nicholson ran back to the House of Representatives, their desire for revenge overwhelming. Randolph proposed and the House immediately approved in a 68–33 vote a proposal to amend the Constitution to have federal judges removed by a vote of both the House and the Senate. Nicholson wanted to give the states power to recall their Senators, and the House approved this proposed constitutional amendment also, by a 53–46 vote.[37] Neither proposal became law.

Of course the happiest man probably was Samuel Chase himself. William Plumer visited him in Baltimore three days after the vote and reported that the Senate vote had made the Chase family "as happy as such an event can render those who prize reputation above life."[38]

But more than the fate of Samuel Chase had been at stake. The attempt to unseat him, rather the failure to unseat him, established three points. The first is that federal judges should not be impeached for frivolous reasons, as Giles and the others had wanted to do; that the nation, through its Senators, would not tolerate an abuse of the Constitution was proven. "I do not imagine they will soon attempt to ply it again," John Quincy Adams wrote to his father about the vote. Plumer also was certain that "We shall not hear of another very soon."[39] And they were quite correct. The second point it established is that federal judges should not use their positions on the bench for partisan purposes as Chase had done. That the Jeffersonians had chosen Chase for their attack and that the attack had gone as far as it had was evidence that political dalliance is dangerous for a judge. The third point is the establishment of the Senate of the United States as a body that can rise on occasion to the heights of nonpartisanship. Even William Branch Giles supported Chase on some of the counts; all Jeffersonian Republicans did on one count or another. The Chase impeachment had been a traumatic event for the young United States, one which it survived, and considering the circumstances surrounding the event, one could even say that the survival was a graceful one.

John Marshall's reactions to the votes are unrecorded but he was obviously relieved. He himself was free from attack, the Federalists' positions in the judiciary were saved, and the Supreme Court was free to expound the Constitution in the manner in which Marshall considered proper. No doubt but that series of votes on March 1 was of tremendous significance to Marshall.

At this time Marshall had been Chief Justice for four years. The Court met in February in Washington for a few weeks, and then the Circuit Courts met in the spring and winter in Richmond and Raleigh for a few weeks each time, or only days on some occasions, so that being a judge did not require all of his time. He did not feel that he should practice law while sitting on the bench, and so he began to look around for other activities. He developed a farm outside of Richmond. There were his land speculations; the Fairfax land purchase ultimately would be turned over to his sons who made their homes there, but Marshall was concerned with raising the money to pay off the loans used to buy it. There were other land speculations also; gambling on land was the major sport of the time, and Marshall engaged in it with zest. He wrote long letters to his friends which were a kind of postal gossip column as the men talked back and forth of their politics, their likes and dislikes, and their concerns for the country.

The activity which occupied the major part of Marshall's time during these first four years was the writing of the mammoth biography of George Washington which he undertook at the urging of Bushrod Washington and Martha Washington. The papers of the first President had been left to Bushrod, and when he received them he determined that he should use them as a basis for a biography of his uncle. He did not want to undertake the project himself because of weak eyes, a lack of confidence in his own writing abilities, and a shortage of time. He then decided to find someone whom he could trust with the venture.[40]

John Marshall was a natural choice. He had known George Washington personally, had lived through and participated in many of the events which would be part of any such biography, and his reverence for Washington was such that any biography he undertook would be respectful and probably laudatory. Though Marshall had no professional experience as a writer, he had demonstrated a faculty for compelling exposition in the few Court decisions he had written to this point and in his reports from Paris in the XYZ Affair. Finally, he and Bushrod Washington were good friends, assuring that any necessary collaboration would be carried on without rancor.

The discussions between Bushrod Washington and Marshall about the projected biography began early in 1800, before Marshall had been named to the Supreme Court, and Marshall readily consented. In April of that year, Bushrod Washington wrote to his publisher of "Genl Marshall who is to write the history" and a few months later he again referred to Marshall as "the gentleman who will assist me in the business." Marshall worked industriously on the project, considering the limits on his time. By November of 1802 he was sufficiently familiar with the Washington letters to know what was lacking and what was needed. He began sending letters to his friends from Revolutionary War days and of the postwar period asking them for additional information about specific events and for their general reminiscences of Washington. "This I do not wish to be known," Marshall confided to Charles Cotesworth Pinckney of the projected Washington biography, "but I have no difficulty in communicating it to you." Then followed a long series of questions about the southern campaigns and a request for Pinckney to answer them as comprehensively as possible. During the next several years Marshall constantly was badgering his friends for information. The letters are filled with contemporary gossip, some expected Federalist fumings, and, most important, requests for details. In this respect Marshall created a valuable historical resource. His biography of George Washington, when completed, would contain a mass of firsthand experiences both interesting and valuable to all future biographers of the first President.[41]

Marshall's letter to Pinckney, written in November 1802, reveals that he hoped to keep his project secret for a while, at least while he was doing his research, but Thomas Jefferson became aware of it the previous May. Not only aware of it, but worried by it. Jefferson believed the book would be published just prior to the 1804 election and would be a campaign attack against him. He tried to enlist Joel Barlow to write a history of the United States from "the close of the war downwards." He said that he and Madison were "rich ourselves in materials, and can open all the public archives to you." Jefferson then mentioned the projected Marshall work. "It is written therefore principally with a view to electioneering purposes," he told Barlow. But the Marshall work would be out before Barlow's, Jefferson said, and would aid Barlow "with information as well as point out the perversions of truth necessary to be rectified."[42] Barlow ultimately did agree to write the book but had not finished it when

President Madison sent him to Europe on a special diplomatic mission. Barlow died there in 1812.

Jefferson's concern that Marshall's biography of George Washington would become a political diatribe to be used against him in the election was typical of the worries that elected officials have. The same year another man was similarly worried about the Marshall book but for different reasons. Books then were sold primarily by advance men going through a community selling subscriptions—advance orders. One of the most energetic was a man named Mason Locke Weems, or as history came to know him, Parson Weems. Weems also considered George Washington a good biographical subject and himself later wrote a biography in which he concocted the more fanciful stories about the cherry tree and the like. But as for now he was a salesman, and he was a worried salesman. "The people are very fearful that it will be prostituted to party purposes," he told Marshall's publisher, C. P. Wayne. "I mean, of course, the Life of Washington. For Heaven's sake drop now and then a cautionary hint to John Marshall Esqr. Your all is at stake, with respect to this work. If it be done in a generally acceptable manner, you will make your fortune otherwise the work will fall an Abortion from the press. . . ."[43]

Wayne also used postmasters as salesmen. "These people," he reported to Marshall, ". . . all hold proposals and receive subscribers and although as yet I have heard from but few, yet nine out of ten of them sent me some subscribers and advance money. One of them has sent 130—another 100—a third 50—a fourth 25, etc." Marshall took a strong interest in the selling procedures of the book; money was important to him. He reported to Wayne, for example, hints of "unfaithful collectors" and introduced Weems, via letter, to prominent persons in the South who could help him sell the book.[44]

Marshall was reluctant to have his name appear as author of the book. His reluctance may have been shyness, but more likely it was influenced by what he came to consider the many errors in the book and his anticipation of Jeffersonian attacks against any volume bearing his name. When the volumes finally appeared, the title page was an interesting one. Marshall's name appears at the bottom in type one-eighth inch high, which is the same size type as that used for the name of Bushrod Washington, who is credited with supervising the biography. And Marshall's name carries no title. He had specifically directed that his title of Chief Justice not be included.[45]

A fourteen-page preface by Marshall is almost an apology for the work, indicating his great dissatisfaction with it. The closing of the preface indicates why: "The impatience since discovered by many of the subscribers has carried the following sheets to the press much more precipitately than the judgment of the author would have permitted him to part with them, and he dare not flatter himself that they do not abound with defects so obvious as on a re-perusal to attract even his own observations."[46]

In his private correspondence Marshall was even more blunt. "I . . . am mortified beyond measure to find that [the first volume] has been so carelessly written," he lamented to his publisher. "Its inelegancies are more numerous than I had supposed could have appeared in it. I have thought it necessary to reconstruct very many of the sentences. . . ." When he sent in the fifth and final volume of the work, he confessed that there was "a total inattention to capitals and small letters . . . [and] there are also many words which are misspelled."[47]

The ambition associated with the work is impressive. The first volume is a history of the American colonies through the French and Indian Wars. Drawing on published sources, it is still a readable and comprehensive account. Washington himself does not become a character until the second volume. His personal life is treated in a sketchy fashion, with Marshall beginning Washington's story with the defeat of the British general Edward Braddock by the French and Indians in 1755, a battle in which the young Washington acquitted himself well although he was on the losing side. Then begins an account of the origins of the American Revolution, the military campaigns of that war, and the peace that followed. The volumes describe the troubles after the war in securing a viable government, the adoption of the Constitution, Washington's presidency, and finally his death. It is a broad-stroked history of the young nation through the eighteenth century. Because of Marshall's own involvement in many of the events and because of his efforts to secure firsthand accounts, the book can be compared favorably to modern accounts drawn from oral histories. Despite Marshall's concern at the inelegant writing and errors, the book was not as bad as he feared it was. His writing is at times graphic and moving. The account of the winter at Valley Forge, for example, may be the best description ever written of the Americans' ordeal there. Marshall did revise the work in the 1820s, but the differences between the two editions are not major. The fact is that he wrote a significant biography which has been published in many nations around the world and is constantly reprinted (a new edition appeared as late as 1969). His writer's nervousness, however, caused him to fear the worst.

His work is political biography, a Federalist history. In it Marshall justified the Revolution and the movement toward union. The work also is party propaganda at its most sophisticated. One student of the work, W. R. Smith, has pointed out how Marshall consistently referred to the Federalists in positive terms and to the followers of Thomas Jefferson in negative ones. The differentiation is subtle, and one would not find it without careful examination of the kind that Smith made.[48] But the impact is obvious, and a modern student of the arts of influencing an electorate could examine the Marshall biography of Washington with substantial profit. Despite its political implications, however, in defense of John Marshall it must also be said that he never mentioned Thomas Jefferson's name in the text in a derogatory fashion. Nor did he ever mention himself or his father in the text, although both had played significant roles in parts of the story. Even when discussing the XYZ Affair, Marshall did not mention himself, and in describing the House of Representatives' reaction to Washington's death he was careful to point out that the resolutions approved by the House lauding Washington were written by Henry Lee who "placed them in the hands of the member who moved them"[49]—Marshall himself.

Perhaps the most significant point about the Washington biography, however, is not its partisanship or its eyewitness immediacy. Rather, it fixed firmly in the mind of America a reverence and a respect for George Washington, a citizen of the nation who deserved that reverence and respect perhaps more than any other American. All subsequent biographies of Washington must begin with Marshall's as a source, and all analysis of Washington must begin with Marshall's also. Of Washington as a soldier, Marshall said:

> He could not have been more enterprising without endangering the cause he defended, nor have put more to hazard without incurring justly the imputation of rashness. Not relying upon those chances which sometimes give a favourable issue to attempts apparently desperate, his conduct was regulated by calculations made upon the capacities of his army, and the real situation of his country.

Of Washington as a President, Marshall said:

> Respecting, as the first magistrate in a free government must ever do, the real and deliberate sentiments of the people, their gusts of passion passed over without ruffling the smooth surface of his mind. Trusting to the reflecting

good sense of the nation for approbation and support, he had the magnanimity to pursue its real interests in opposition to its temporary prejudices; and, though far from being regardless of popular favour, he could never stoop to retain by deserving to lose it.

And of Washington as a man, he said:

> No man has ever appeared upon the theatre of public action whose integrity was more incorruptible, or whose principles were more perfectly free from the contamination of those selfish and unworthy passions which find their nourishment in the conflicts of party. Having no views which required concealment, his real and avowed motives were the same; and his whole correspondence does not furnish a single case from which even an enemy would infer that he was capable, under any circumstances, of stooping to the employment of duplicity.[50]

Much has been written about George Washington since John Marshall wrote those lines, but nothing has been written that is more accurate or better said. There is no reason for Marshall to have been apologetic about his biographical tribute to his friend and benefactor and to his nation's hero.

As with any controversial work about a major figure, the immediate reaction was mixed. Marshall determined not to be flustered by his critics. "I remain silent," he insisted to Wayne, explaining that "Perhaps a free expression of my thoughts respecting the inaccuracies of the present edition may add to the current which seems set against it and may therefore be for the present indiscreet." John Quincy Adams once discussed the controversy over the book with Marshall. This was in 1805 and by this time the book had been both widely praised and damned. Marshall told Adams that he was ashamed of the book because "there were so many errors and imperfections." When the final volume came out in 1806, the one detailing the political controversy between the Federalists and the Jeffersonian Republicans, Marshall steeled himself for the onslaught, "for charges which are untrue and abuse."[51]

Most of the criticism came from the Jeffersonians. Jefferson himself considered the volumes "libels" and was certain that the truth ultimately would survive Marshall's attack on him. Even John Adams, late in his life, became critical of Marshall's work, referring to it as "a mausolaeum, 100 feet square at the base, and 200 feet high" which had been written to make money.[52]

That it had been written to make money is, of course, true.

That was one motivating factor, but considering the substantial effort Marshall had put into it, that purpose is not sordid. He needed money to meet additional payments on the Fairfax land and to meet the needs of his growing family; Polly gave birth to their tenth and last child, Edward Carrington Marshall, on January 13, 1805. Marshall took an interest in the promotion of the book. "Genl. Marshall says that you ought by *no means* to send out the 1st vol. unaccompanied by the 2d," salesman Weems reported to the publisher following a talk with Marshall. The two volumes should go out together, Weems quoted Marshall as saying, because "the 1st vol. has not a word about Washington in it. . . ."[53]

Marshall's share of the royalties on this first edition amounted to $19,500. The contract he and Bushrod Washington had with the publisher gave them one dollar for every book subscribed for. Seven thousand sets of five volumes each were subscribed for, giving Bushrod Washington and John Marshall a total of $35,000. In addition there were sales over the original subscription, and for those books the two authors received a total of $4,000 as a compromise, giving them a total of $39,000 to split. Also, there was a small amount realized from sales in England. Although there were indications that Marshall and Washington at one time had fanciful notions of making a considerably larger amount, $40,000 then was a substantial profit for an author. The book was a commercial success.[54]

In Richmond John Marshall continued as a prominent citizen. In 1803 an act of the Virginia legislature named him along with George Wythe, St. George Tucker, Edmond Randolph, and other prominent citizens as a trustee of the Richmond Academy.[55] Marshall had no difficulties in Richmond because of his Federalist leanings. The city actually was a stronghold for members of that party in a state which, otherwise, was inclined to support Jefferson. Most of the city's leading citizens had been officers in the Revolutionary War and were strong supporters, first of Washington, then of Hamilton, and finally of John Marshall. Also there was an unwritten rule, perhaps a carryover from the Barbecue Club's injunction against political discussions, that political opponents would keep their disputes out of their social life. A prominent Richmond resident in the early decades of the 1800s was Thomas Ritchie, an editor of a Jeffersonian newspaper. Ritchie and Marshall reputedly never engaged in a political discussion before 1820 although they saw each other frequently. "The leaders did not hesitate to attack each other through the columns of the press and upon the hustings," said

Ritchie's biographer, "but all was forgotten when they approached a common punch bowl."[56]

To his personal friends Marshall had no hesitation in unburdening himself of his complaints and concerns over the nation's future. The administration of Thomas Jefferson, he came more and more to believe, was threatening the nation's existence. "We have fallen upon evil times," he wrote to Oliver Wolcott, "and I do not clearly perceive a prospect of better." Jefferson was, of course, demonstrating himself to be a strong and effective President. Rather than ruining the nation, he more than doubled its size with the Louisiana Purchase. He made mistakes such as the Embargo Act in his second administration, but his presidency surely did not deserve the fears of it harbored by John Marshall. But then Marshall was not rational in his private comments about the man he considered the traducer of Washington, just as Jefferson lost his own rationality when discussing Marshall, whom he considered to be the traducer of Jefferson. It is a tribute to both men that the animosity they felt toward each other was allowed by neither to show in their public and official duties. When Jefferson was inaugurated for a second term in 1805, he asked Marshall to administer the oath and Marshall did so. Even when they moved against each other, as Jefferson had done in the Chase impeachment and as Marshall moved against Jefferson in the Aaron Burr trial in 1807, each made certain his case was built on something more solid than personal dislike.[57]

An incident reportedly involving Marshall about the time he joined the Court made real for him the danger of slavery. He always had had great respect and admiration for George Washington's wife Martha, and this admiration increased after Washington's death because of the dignity with which Martha conducted herself. Washington in his will had directed his slaves be freed after Martha's death. The tradition growing up is that the slaves hastened Martha's death to hasten their own freedom. The incident involving Marshall had the slaves attempting to set the manor house at Mount Vernon on fire, and Bushrod Washington and John Marshall galloping to Martha's rescue. The house had not been set on fire and Martha was not harmed, but Marshall and Washington advised her to free the slaves early to avoid any similar attacks. Whether or not the specific story about Marshall and Bushrod Washington galloping to the rescue is true, Martha Washington did free the slaves before her death and certainly the emotions illustrated by the story—the eagerness of the blacks for their freedom and the fear of the masters of the lengths to which the blacks would go in securing that freedom—were very real and known to every thoughtful Virginian. As the years went by, John Marshall became increasingly concerned about slavery and was one of the few prominent southerners to recognize early the danger it meant to the Union.[58]

As always, Marshall's gregariousness made him a well-liked person. In Raleigh where he presided over the Circuit Court, he was popular with the lawyers "as well on account of his talents and uprightness as for that sociability and ease of manner which render all happy and pleased when in his company." This correspondent added that Marshall "is certainly remarkably learned and clever. . . ."[59]

Although he had become a prominent member of the government and was presumably receiving a comfortable if not lavish income from his salary as a judge, his landholdings, and his other investments, his style of living did not become more ostentatious. According to the Richmond personal property tax books, in 1801 John Marshall owned eight adult slaves, three horses and mules, and four coaches. In 1805 he owned nine slaves, four horses and mules, and still four coaches.[60] His manner of dress apparently never improved, and the red brick house he had built for his Polly and himself and their growing family almost two decades earlier continued to be their home.

A young Massachusetts Congressman named Joseph Story, soon himself to sit on the Supreme Court and to become a commanding figure in the history of American law, offered a picture of Marshall at this point, after the Virginian had been sitting on the bench for several years. Story enjoyed the Supreme Court— "the scene of my greatest amusement, as well as instruction"— and usually spent several hours there each day if he could leave the House chamber; he often took his meals with the Justices. He wrote that Marshall was a tall, slender man, "not graceful nor imposing, but erect and steady." At this point Marshall was entering his fifties, but, Story's account said, his hair was still black, "his eyes small and twinkling, his forehead rather low, but his features are in general harmonious." Story considered Marshall's manners plain but dignified and said "an unaffected modesty diffuses itself through all his actions." That was always true of Marshall; in his personal conduct he remained unaffected by his position and the praise of others.

Story said that Marshall's manner of dressing was very simple "yet neat" (in later years Story would change his mind about the neatness of Marshall's tailoring). Story also offered a vivid description of John Marshall as a speaker, a description that points out how fortunate Marshall was that he could rely on writing his opinions in advance:

His language chaste, but hardly elegant; it does not flow rapidly, but it seldom wants precision. In conversation he is quite familiar, but is occasionally embarrassed by a hesitancy and drawling. His thoughts are always clear and ingenious, sometimes striking, and not often inconclusive; he possesses great subtilty of mind, but it is only occasionally exhibited. I love his laugh—it is too hearty for an intriguer—and his good temper and unwearied patience are equally agreeable on the bench and in the study.

Story, at this point not yet a personal friend of Marshall's or his co-worker on the Supreme Court, also well analyzed Marshall's ability as a judge. He said:

His genius is, in my opinion, vigorous and powerful, less rapid than discriminating, and less vivid than uniform in its light. He examines the intricacies of a subject with calm and persevering circumspection, and unravels the mysteries with irresistible acuteness. He has not the majesty and compactness of thought of Dr. Johnson; but in subtle logic he is no unworthy disciple of David Hume.[61]

To be Chief Justice, however, more than genius and subtlety is required, more than knowledge and a facility with a written opinion. Being Chief Justice requires courage to stand against the personal and perhaps physical attacks of society in defense of what one considers morally proper. John Marshall was called upon to exhibit this kind of courage in 1807 in the trial of Aaron Burr, who was charged with conspiring to commit treason against the United States. Involved would be not only Marshall and his position in the society of his time and in the history of his nation, but also the independence of the judiciary and the validity of the American political ethic. If that ethic has any meaning, it is that the individual has worth and his rights must not be abused. Even if all seem to turn against him, he must be able to find some element in his government willing to protect his rights and willing to defend him against all other segments in society that might attack him.

This is what happened to Aaron Burr. Charged with a crime—a crime he may very well have committed—he was entitled to the protection of the law. It was the obligation of the American government to make certain that even a person who had appeared to have fallen so far, from Vice President of the United States to traitor, had that protection. Beginning with the President of the United States, however, no one in the government seemed willing to assure Burr of that protection. The military and the legal departments of the administration were turned against Burr as well as the persuasive powers of the presidency. They were not interested in fulfilling the law, which was not only Burr's right but the nation's need, but they were interested in vengeance. John Marshall, however, was interested not in vengeance but in the law.

4

AARON BURR IS ONE of the most interesting figures in American history. A promising young man in the country during its formative years, he could achieve, or so it seemed, any public office he wanted. Burr became Vice President and perhaps could have reached the presidency, but his ambition appeared too great for such aspirations. After his duel with Alexander Hamilton and his subsequent disgrace—and in retrospect it seems he almost courted that disgrace in an attempt to deliberately sever himself from his political base—he cast around for new worlds, literally, to conquer. Not for him was the traditional path of politics, leading to success. He would become an explorer, a swashbuckler, an adventurer!

From the moment of his leaving the vice presidency in 1805 until his 1807 trial he was involved in a great deal of activity, all of it curious. Of the stories that have since been told about this period, many are undoubtedly fact, some are fiction. None, however, tell the real story of Aaron Burr's intentions. Was he a traitor? Did he really intend to sever the western part of the United States? Was his threat to kill President Jefferson ever made seriously, or was the charge only the cry of a braggart named William Eaton who was looking for a favor from his government? Why did Burr seek money from the British government? Was he telling the truth when he spoke of leading an expedition against his own country? Or was he the ultimate in confidence men, bilking a great nation of funds in a scheme for which he never could be charged?

In reality all that can be said about Aaron Burr is that there are witnesses to his activities, some records of his transactions, but few clues to his intentions. He remains an enigmatic figure.

He did, certainly, capitalize on European fears of the United States expanding its influence to the South and the West.

These were areas still important for European trade, and Spain and England looked with suspicion and concern on the United States' movement into them. Matthew Davis, Burr's friend, biographer, and confidant, reported that at this period there was danger of war with Spain over the Mississippi and New Orleans. "Such a war would have been popular with the western people," he wrote in his biography of Burr some years after the event. "Of these opinions and these feelings, Burr took advantage, and undoubtedly, by innuendoes or otherwise, induced some to believe that his arrangements for the invasion of Mexico were with the knowledge, if not the approbation of the government."[1]

Innuendoes or otherwise, Davis said. To almost everyone Burr spoke with, he gave a different story. He wrote his old friend Charles Biddle of Philadelphia—one of the few men to stand with him in the furor after the duel with Hamilton—that he wished to speak with him of "some business of importance." He arrived a few days later and after some casual conversation, said that a "number of gentlemen of the first respectability in every part of the Union" wanted Burr to establish a settlement on the Mississippi River. The settlers would be military men and their purpose would be to become involved in, perhaps to provoke and lead, a revolt against the Spanish who controlled Mexico—"it would make the fortunes of all those concerned in revolutionizing that country."

Biddle later wrote: "I told him [Burr] that such a plan, if carried into effect, would probably involve us in a war with Spain, and I would therefore have nothing to do with it. He said whether we invaded the country or not, we should have a war with Spain. . . . Finding I would not listen to his plans, and that no arguments he could use would have any weight with me, he expressed great regret. . . ."[2]

For Thomas Truxton, an American naval hero of both the Revolution and the hostilities with France, Burr had a somewhat different story: "Mr. Burr did tell me that, in case of a war between the United States and Spain, which he considered inevitable, he intended to attack Vera Cruz and Mexico, give liberty to an enslaved world, and establish an independent government in Mexico." Burr then asked Truxton to command the sea expedition. "I at once declined it," Truxton said, "on asking if the Executive of the United States was privy to, or concerned in, the project and being answered that he was not."[3]

And then there was William Eaton's version. Eaton was a soldier, diplomat, adventurer, and a man frustrated by not receiving the praise and rewards he considered proper for his exploits against the Tripoli pirates. In the taverns and boardinghouses of Washington—after Burr's arrest—Eaton claimed that Burr had repeatedly pressed him to join with him. Eaton continued that "Burr offered to make him [Eaton] second in command—That Burr said that Congress should either declare themselves for his measures or he would expel them from the Capitol —That Burr said he would kill Tom. Jefferson." Eaton added, however, and without explanation, that he had never disclosed any of this to anyone "till this week" and had just then (in January, months after the death threat against the President had allegedly been made) informed Jefferson of it.[4]

And then, of course, there was the British version. This is certainly the most damning charge against Burr, but the most irrelevant in the story of John Marshall and the trial of Burr. The British version was not available at the time of the trial; it was not discovered until near the end of the nineteenth century by the American historian Henry Adams. The documents he found appear to make absolute the case that Burr was seeking British financial and military support in an effort to sever the western lands from the United States, that he was in fact a traitor. "I have just received an offer from Mr. Burr," Anthony Merry, British minister to the United States, reported to the Foreign Office in a dispatch dated August 6, 1804, "to lend his assistance to his Majesty's government in any manner in which they may think fit to employ him, particularly in endeavouring to effect a separation of the western part of the United States. . . ." Burr then was still Vice President of the United States.

Merry himself may have had some doubts, however, for he added in that letter that "if after what is generally known of the profligacy of Mr. Burr's character, his Majesty's ministers should think proper to listen to his offer, his present situation in this country, where he is now cast off as much by the democratic as by the Federal party, and where he still preserves connections with some people of influence, added to his great ambition and spirit of revenge against the present Administration, may possibly induce him to exert the talents and activity which he possesses with fidelity to his employers."[5] The British then, according to the Merry report, were faced with the prospect of dealing with a man who only "may possibly" do as he promised.

The British never did go along with the Burr scheme, or apparent scheme, but they were interested. The next year, on March 29, Merry wrote another report, saying that Burr had talked to him about the desire of the people in Louisiana "to render themselves independent of the United States, and that the execution of their design is only delayed by the difficulty of obtaining . . . assurance of protection and assistance from some

Foreign power, and of concerting . . . their independence with that of the inhabitants of the western parts of the United States. . . . It is clear that Mr. Burr . . . means to endeavour to be the instrument of effecting such a connection." Burr wanted a British squadron at the mouth of the Mississippi plus a loan of "about one hundred thousand pounds."[6]

Burr a traitor? It appears so.

For some years Britain had been interested in driving Spain out of the New World. Spain was often an enemy, and if it could be defeated in America, then it would lose a valuable source of trade. And Britain, of course, could fill that vacuum in commerce caused by Spain's defeat. During the first decade of the 1800s Britain made numerous attempts to spark revolutionary movements in Latin America. Burr certainly must have been aware of that; certainly also he must have been aware that if the British government bought the scheme he had proposed to Merry, it could never declare it nor bring him to account if he seemed to repudiate it. And again, Burr must have known that Anthony Merry was the perfect diplomat to propose such a scheme to. Pompous, accustomed to Europe's refined society, Merry was revolted by the city of Washington with its muddy streets and pale society, and by Thomas Jefferson who formally received him in slippers and dressed in a manner "indicative of utter slovenliness and indifference to appearances." Nothing would please Merry more than to be the instrument to dismember President Jefferson's disgusting little country.[7]

Burr then only a sly confidence man? It could be so.

Edward Channing, the American historian, has drawn a picture of Burr as a hopeless opportunist clutching at any chance that came his way. Channing believed that at first Burr was willing to lead a movement to sever the United States. When that didn't work out, he considered leading a revolution in Mexico. Finally, when that seemed hopeless, Burr envisioned himself as the leader of a great western colonizing expedition.[8]

Those are the three explanations of Burr: traitor, confidence man, and loser. History does not reveal which is correct.

Whatever Burr's motivations and intentions, by late 1806 he had collected men and supplies on an island owned by Harman Blennerhassett* and located in the Ohio River near Marietta. This Blennerhassett was a man of cultivated tastes who chose to live privately on his island with his attractive wife. In later years historians tracked down a scandal about the Blenner-

---

* Blennerhassett's name was sometimes spelled Blannerhassett. Blennerhassett is correct, and I am using that spelling throughout.

hassetts' marriage—Mrs. Blennerhassett apparently was her husband's niece, which explains their desire for privacy. Burr had visited them on several occasions, and they had made their island available for his expedition, as they said later, with the understanding that it was a legitimate one for purposes of colonizing western lands.

Thomas Jefferson, President of the United States, tells the next part of the story. "Some time in the latter part of September [1806] I received intimations that designs were in agitation in the western country, unlawful and unfriendly to peace of the Union; and that the prime mover in these was Aaron Burr, heretofore distinguished by the favor of his country." The evidence was vague, and it was only by the end of October "that the objects of the conspiracy began to be perceived."

Jefferson then said he sent an agent to check out the "intimations" and also wrote to General James Wilkinson, who was the American military commandant in the Mississippi Territory. Wilkinson responded in a letter dated October 21 and received by Jefferson on November 25. From the letter, Jefferson said, "We learn that a confidential agent of Aaron Burr had been deputed to [Wilkinson] with communications partly written in cipher and partly oral, explaining his designs, exaggerating his resources, and making such offers of emolument and command, to engage him and the army in his unlawful enterprise, as he had flattered himself would be successful. The general, with the honor of a soldier and fidelity of a good citizen, immediately despatched a trusty officer to me with information of what had passed, proceeding to establish such an understanding with the Spanish commandant on the Sabine as permitted him to withdraw his force across the Mississippi, and to enter on measures for opposing the projected enterprise. . . ."

Jefferson said he had learned from Wilkinson's report that Burr had two objects. "One of these," he continued, "was the severance of the Union of these States by the Alleghany mountains; the other, an attack on Mexico. A third object was provided, merely ostensible, to wit: the settlement of a pretended purchase of a tract of country on the Washita, claimed by Baron Bastrop." But, Jefferson charged, "this was to serve as the pretext for all his preparations, an allurement for such followers as really wished to acquire settlements in that country, and a cover under which to retreat in the event of final discomfiture of both branches of his real design."

Jefferson then claimed that Burr had to give up his plan to separate the western lands because the settlers there were too loyal to the United States, and because Burr did not have sufficient men to take the country by force. "He took his course then at once," Jefferson continued, "determined to seize on New Orleans, plunder the bank there, possess himself of the military and naval stores, and proceed on his expedition to Mexico. . . ."⁹

Jefferson then said the plot was thwarted because two days after receiving Wilkinson's letter he had issued an order for Burr's arrest. That description by Jefferson of the alleged plot is from a special presidential message to the Congress on January 22, 1807—this was before Aaron Burr was tried. One of the most bizarre events in the Burr saga was that the President, himself a distinguished lawyer, publicly accused a man of a crime and pronounced him guilty without waiting for a trial. The need to alert the public cannot be offered as an excuse. By January 22 the plot, if it existed at any time, no longer did.

Jefferson's case, as outlined in his message to Congress, is based primarily on evidence from Wilkinson. The general possessed, Jefferson said, "the honor of a soldier and fidelity of a good citizen." Actually Wilkinson was a Spanish agent; he had been in the pay of that nation for years. This could not have been known to Jefferson. Still, there were signs to be detected if one wished to detect. Even in retrospect, Wilkinson's delay in reporting the alleged plot until contacted by Jefferson is inexplicable, if a plot against the country did exist. William Eaton also had delayed speaking about the supposed threat against Jefferson's life until there was a public outcry against Burr. These two incidents are by no means proof that Burr's plot was a fiction, but they are "intimations" of the same quality that were available to Jefferson about Burr. Also, the Jefferson administration did have information available that raised questions about Wilkinson.

In the absence of the governor of the Mississippi Territory, Cowles Meade, the acting governor, wrote a letter to James Madison, Jefferson's confidant and Secretary of State, who had jurisdiction over the territory. "The perusal of the instructions of the Secretary of War to Genl. Wilkinson," Meade wrote, "have when contrasted with his conduct very much astonished me— they are directly at variance—they go to confirm my opinion that the General is not faithful to his duty, but is operating to the aid of an association designed to sever this country from the United States." Meade's analysis, although it could not have been proven at the time, was mostly correct (Meade believed Wilkinson was working with Burr when actually Wilkinson was working with the Spaniards). Meade then explained specifically what it was that Wilkinson was doing that had aroused his suspicions. "The Secy. of war," he wrote to Madison, "directs that the convention between General W. and the Spanish commandant be reduced to writing—this has not been done. Genl. Wil. is then ordered even in a case of a pacific issue to leave three companies at Nacka-tochy—this he has not done—but one company remains at that post."

Meade continued: "General W— is ordered in case of a specific issue to repair to Fort Adams with the remainder of the army of the United States—this he has not done; but taken away the whole force, all the army ammunition and even dismantled the fort—all is gone to Orleans—where, he has ordered the troops from Mobile likewise—." Meade's charges against Wilkin-son cannot be ascribed to friendship for Burr; he considered Burr a villain. They appear to stem from Meade's anxiety in being in charge of a territory that was stripped of its defenses while the enemy was approaching. Meade's letter to Madison continued:

> Sir, when I add to these measures [Wilkinson's] requisi-tion of five hundred militia from the territory I am com-pelled to believe that he acts in aid of the views of a cer-tain association, of which you are now informed—and equivocal conduct of the General brings me to the conclu-sion; that if Burr can reach Orleans with the force which he has promised, that the General will meet him with his best services—but if Col. Burr fails, the Genl. will claim the merit of his communication to the general govern-ment—and all this will be decided before the Government can take steps from his information, to defeat the plot. . . .
>
> I will again state that the General has left the territory in a very defenceless state—not a single piece of ord-nance—musket, pound of powder, or other means of de-fence—of this policy you may form some opinion.[10]

Wilkinson's liaison with the Spanish was widely rumored at the time. An account of the affair by Erick Bollman,* a Burr associate, stated that Wilkinson "found it even in agreement with his duties to secure without knowledge of his government the enjoyment of a considerable annual salary from the Spanish."[11] This was published years before the records were found in Spain to substantiate the charge.

If there was an opinion formed of Wilkinson's treason, how-ever, there was no sign of it in Washington. Wilkinson became the chief witness against Burr, and the Jefferson administration did nothing to weaken his credibility.

---

* The name is spelled Erick Bollman in 4 Cranch 75, and I am adhering to that spelling to avoid confusion. His correct name was Justus Erich Bollmann.

There can be no question but that Jefferson believed Burr guilty of treason. To his dinner companions and friends, he spoke and wrote of Burr's guilt as an accepted fact. Almost there is a frenzy about Jefferson's comments, as he tells of Burr's reported dealings with the Spanish ambassador and other Spanish officials, of Burr's thirst to "place himself on the throne of Montezuma," of the extravagance of his plans.[12] Jefferson came to consider the alleged conspiracy as the litmus test identifying the "traitors" and the "good Americans." He wrote Lafayette, for example, that a proclamation informing the people of the alleged conspiracy was sufficient to produce "an instantaneous levee en masse of our citizens wherever there appeared anything to lay hold of and the whole was crushed in one instant." Jefferson wrote that he was confident Burr ultimately would be convicted "unless his federal patrons give him an opportunity of ·running away."[13] There had been, of course, no rising up of American citizens against Burr; more and more the Burr conspiracy was becoming part of Thomas Jefferson's imagination.

History has a habit of enshrining its heroes. Justifiably it has done so regarding Jefferson. The man who authored the Declaration of Independence, who presided over history's first peaceful transfer of power between factions, who gave his nation a dignity and an elegance that it so much needed, cannot be considered less. But Thomas Jefferson was also a human being. In the case of Aaron Burr he allowed his good judgment to be destroyed by his compulsion to justify his actions.

Perhaps the Aaron Burr incident would have been of little consequence except that Burr, after his capture in the Mississippi Territory, was brought to Richmond to be tried there before the Circuit Court of the United States. The presiding justice of that court was John Marshall.

For John Marshall the coming months would be ones of turmoil and conflicting emotions. The man charged, Aaron Burr, was also the man who had killed Alexander Hamilton, one of the public figures whom Marshall most admired. Burr's alleged crime was attempting to dismember the nation, a charge which a nationalist like Marshall must have considered heinous. His accuser was a political figure Marshall had little respect for. Still, the identity of the accuser cannot wipe away a crime if one has been committed. Marshall knew, as everyone knew, that if Burr were found guilty, Thomas Jefferson would be vindicated for having publicly declared Burr a traitor and the public would be satisfied. Marshall also knew, as everyone also knew, that if Burr were found innocent or if the court appeared friendlier toward him than the law allowed, then the public's wrath would turn on Marshall. Either way in the months ahead it appeared that John Marshall could not win. As it turned out, however, the question was not Marshall's victory, nor Burr's guilt or innocence, nor Jefferson's vindication. Rather, the question was whether the nation would win, whether it would emerge from this episode strengthened in its legal protections; or if it would lose, and allow the beginning of the destruction of the rights it had promised in the blood spilled in the American Revolution and in the words written in the Constitution.

For John Marshall the first act of the Burr affair began in Washington with the motion by Erick Bollman and Samuel Swartwout for the Supreme Court to issue a writ of habeas corpus. Bollman and Swartwout were supposedly two conspirators with Burr. Bollman was the "confidential agent of Aaron Burr" who, Jefferson said in his January 22 message, had delivered a cipher letter from Burr to Wilkinson outlining the plot. They were arrested in New Orleans by Wilkinson, who conceded that his actions may not have been legal but insisted that he had the right to act "in the name of national security" and that "to save a whole body, one has to cut off a limb." Wilkinson's intention was to get the arrested men to Washington as quickly as possible. When Bollman and Swartwout were brought before a judge in New Orleans, the judge insisted that Wilkinson substantiate his charges. Wilkinson promised to return to the court the next day with both his prisoners and the substantiation for the charges against them. Instead, however, he sent the prisoners to Washington and ignored the demand for substantiation.[14] When Bollman and Swartwout arrived in Washington, they claimed before the Supreme Court that they were not accused of having committed any crime in the District of Columbia and therefore could not be held there for the crime of treason.

The first question the Supreme Court faced was whether it could issue such a writ. Marshall handed down the decision on February 13, and it is a model of careful phrasing.[15] "As preliminary to any investigation of the merits of this motion," Marshall began, "the court deems it proper to declare that it disclaims all jurisdictions not given by the constitution, or by the laws of the United States." After having claimed that he would do nothing beyond what the most conservative judge would do, Marshall then produced a definition of the power of courts under a written law. "Courts which originate in the common law possess a jurisdiction which must be regulated by common law, until some statute shall change their established principles," he said, and then added: "but courts which are created by written law, and whose jurisdiction is defined by written law, cannot transcend that jurisdiction. . . ." Marshall was enunciating, as he had done before, his belief that common law did not apply to the Supreme Court and that any power the Court exercised must have its origin in the federal Constitution. "To enable the court to decide on such question," he said, "the power to determine it must be given by written law."

After concluding that Congress had indeed given the Supreme Court such power, Marshall explained that he could see no reason why it should not be utilized. "If at any time the public safety should require the suspension of the powers vested by this act in the courts of the United States," he said, "it is for the legislature to say so." As he had done in *Marbury v. Madison*, when he gave Jefferson the victory by refusing Marbury the commission but won the war by establishing a power for the Court, Marshall here was acknowledging that the Court could not overstep its bounds—even when to do so would please its enemies. "That the question depends on political considerations," he continued, "on which the legislature is to decide. Until the legislative will be expressed, this court can only see its duty, and must obey the laws."

The decision that the Court had the power to grant such a writ was not unanimous. One Justice, Cushing, was absent because of illness. Bushrod Washington and Henry Brockholst Livingston, who had joined the Court that term (replacing William Paterson), joined with Marshall. William Johnson, Jefferson's first appointee, dissented, with Chase joining him.* Johnson's argument was the same, interestingly, as the one in Marshall's opinion which expressed the opposite view. Johnson also argued that the Court had only such power as was granted to it specifically in legislation and claimed that no legislation authorized the writ. He also argued that granting the writ was a slap by the judiciary at the executive.

The next question Marshall and the Justices faced was whether the two men, Bollman and Swartwout, should indeed be released on a writ of habeas corpus. The decision was handed down on February 21 by Marshall. Cushing and Chase were absent, and this time Johnson joined with Marshall.[16] First Marshall pointed out that the men were charged specifically with

---

* There has been some dispute over whether Cushing or Chase was the absent judge and over which of the two men joined with Johnson in his dissent. A letter from Henry Clay to T. M. Prentiss, February 18, 1807, in Colton, *Clay*, vol. IV, pp. 14–15, settles the matter.

having committed treason "in levying war against the United States." Immediately he made clear he understood the extreme seriousness of the decision he was about to hand down. "As there is no crime which can more excite and agitate the passions of men than treason," he said, "no charge demands more from the tribunal before which it is made, a deliberate and temperate inquiry. Whether this inquiry be directed to the fact or to the law, none can be more solemn, none more important to the citizen or to the government; none can more affect the safety of both. . . ."

When Marshall spoke of the need for a "deliberate and temperate inquiry," he was not engaging merely in rhetoric. The Americans knew that the charge of treason had been used traditionally as a device against political opposition. If the courts served any purpose in the United States, it was to protect the citizen against a government in which passion had overruled rationality and prejudice had overcome the law. This was the challenge John Marshall now faced.

To demonstrate that the crime of treason had been committed, Marshall said, "war must be actually levied against the United States." No matter how flagitious the crime of *conspiring* to commit treason may be, he said, "such conspiracy is not treason. To conspire to levy war, and actually to levy war, are distinct offenses. The first must be brought into open action, by the assemblage of men for a purpose treasonable in itself, or the fact of levying war cannot have been committed. . . ."

The next paragraph is the one most often used against Marshall both in the Burr trial and in the commentaries on it. "It is not the intention of the court to say, that no individual can be guilty of this crime, who has not appeared in arms against his country," he said. He continued:

> On the contrary, if war be actually levied, that is, if a body of men be actually assembled, for the purpose of effecting by force a treasonable purpose, all those who perform any part, however minute, or however remote from the scene of action, and who are actually leagued in the general conspiracy, are to be considered as traitors. But there must be an actual assemblying of men, for the treasonable purpose, to constitute a levying of war. . . .

Marshall's next point left no doubt that the judiciary with him at its head would, indeed, protect the individual from his government. The man would not be sacrificed for the safety of the government; the man would not serve the government. The government would serve the man, and the laws would protect them both. Marshall spoke of "the framers of our constitution, who not only defined and limited the crime, but with jealous circumspection attempted to protect their limitation" by providing that no person shall be convicted of treason without the testimony of two witnesses to the same act, or without a confession in open court. Marshall argued that the authors of the Constitution, knowing how the treason laws had been abused, particularly in England, "must have conceived it more safe, that punishment, in such cases, should be ordained by general laws, formed upon deliberation, under the influence of no resentments, and without knowing on whom they were to operate, than that it should be inflicted under the influence of those passions which the occasion seldom fails to excite, and which a flexible definition of the crime, or a construction which would render it more flexible, might bring into operation." He then concluded this point with the claim that "It is, therefore, more safe, as well as more consonant to the principles of our constitution, that the crime of treason should not be extended by construction to doubtful cases; and that crimes not clearly within the constitutional definition, should receive such punishment as the legislature in its wisdom may provide."

The impact of Marshall's words can never be as great at a later time as they were in the early years of the Union. The United States was the first large power organized voluntarily by its citizens. Each of those citizens surrendered certain of his rights, accepted restrictions upon his liberties, with the understanding that the government he had formed would protect him if necessary from his neighbors, from his enemies abroad, and from itself. Each had understood that government often was the enemy, and had struggled for a government that would be his servant. The Americans had written a document that said that it was, and the question was, Would the courts in fact insist that the government be the servant? In the trial of these two men, Erick Bollman and Samuel Swartwout, two otherwise inconspicuous figures in the history of man, John Marshall was saying, Yes, the courts of the United States would insist that this new government not oppress its citizens. He was saying that it was better that a man go free, even if he might be guilty, rather than allow the government to destroy itself by becoming an oppressor. Supreme Court Justices have made that same point on many occasions since; the tendency of governments toward tyranny is never absent.

As for the specific case against Bollman and Swartwout, the prosecution produced two letters: one by General Wilkinson and the other by William Eaton which allegedly substantiated the claim that the two men planned to wage war against the United

States. Marshall said that this evidence did not warrant such a charge. The letters did suggest that the two men were involved in a plot to attack a foreign nation, apparently the Spanish possessions, but indicated nothing about an attack against the possessions of the United States. "There certainly is not in the letter delivered [by Bollman] to General Wilkinson [and written by Burr], so far as the letter is laid before the court, one syllable which has a necessary or a natural reference to an enterprise against any territory of the United States. . . . That both of the prisoners were engaged in a most culpable enterprise against the dominions of a power at peace with the United States, those who admit the affidavit of General Wilkinson cannot doubt. But that no part of this crime was committed in the district of Columbia, is apparent. It is, therefore, the unanimous opinion of the court that they cannot be tried in this district. . . ." Bollman and Swartwout went free. Perhaps one could argue that two guilty men went free. Against that, however, one must recognize that the law was upheld.

Thomas Jefferson was furious. He had become deeply involved in the Burr affair, without intending it perhaps; his reputation seemed balanced on the outcome of the Burr trial. And the Marshall opinion in the case of Bollman and Swartwout indicated to him that convicting Burr would not be easy. He grumbled to visitors at the President's House that he feared Aaron Burr would be found innocent because the courts were inclined to construe the law too favorably for the accused and too rigidly against the government. In making these comments, Jefferson referred specifically to John Marshall's decision in the Bollman-Swartwout case as an example of what he meant.[17]

Bringing Aaron Burr to the physical site of the trial was an adventure in itself. In the fall of 1806, when Thomas Jefferson had first learned of the alleged plot, he had sent agents out to arrest the plotters. A gathering of men on Blennerhassett's island was broken up and its members arrested. Controversy existed over whether the government agents did only what the arrest required or whether they deliberately destroyed the beautiful Blennerhassett home. Burr was not on the island. He surrendered himself in the Mississippi Territory, was freed when a grand jury refused to indict him, and then was apprehended again in West Florida, and finally sent overland to Richmond. Because the alleged crime—the organizing of men to make war on the United States—was supposed to have taken place on Blennerhassett's island, the trial must take place in Virginia, the island being within the geographical jurisdiction of the Circuit Court there.

Burr maintained he was innocent of the charge of treason. "I have no design," he wrote to Henry Clay on December 1, 1806, "nor have I taken any measure to promote a dissolution of the Union, or a separation of any one or more States from the residue." He continued that "My views have been fully explained to, and approved by, several of the principal officers of Government, and, I believe, are well understood by the administration and seen by it with complacency. They are such as every man of honor and every good citizen must approve." Who these "principal officers of Government" were, Burr never explained. Burr's letter was convincing to Clay in Frankfort, Kentucky. But when Clay, a United States Senator, arrived in Washington a few weeks later, he became caught up in the emotions generated there by the Burr affair and quickly changed his mind. "Having left Kentucky under a belief that [Burr] was innocent," he said, "it was with no little surprise upon my arrival here that I found I had been deceived."[18]

Burr's denials were to be expected. If he was guilty, he certainly was too intelligent to concede it. If he was not, then it was only natural that he pronounce the charges "utterly false . . . and are the inventions of wicked men." As for the evidence against him offered by Wilkinson, Burr told Cowles Meade to have "some better foundation than the suggestion of rumor, or the vile fabrications of a man notoriously the pensioner of a foreign government."[19] If that last reference to Wilkinson accepting funds from a foreign government—a charge which later was shown to be true—was noticed at the time, there is no record of it.

Aaron Burr was brought to Richmond at the end of March. He was dirty, dressed in the clothes he had worn when first apprehended weeks earlier; the former Vice President had been treated as the worst felon. His reputation had preceded him to Richmond, including accounts of his ability as a lawyer and politician, his supposed amorous escapades, and his adventures in the West. The people of Richmond, like people all over, had an interest in the bizarre and sensational. After Aaron Burr had killed Alexander Hamilton in a duel, for example, a traveling showman had exhibited a model of the duel at fifty cents a head, and it apparently was very popular.[20] But whatever Burr's other failings, he would not permit himself to be seen as distressed by his circumstances. Whether one considers Burr innocent or guilty, moral or immoral, one must admire his bearing over the next few months. He undoubtedly was a great scoundrel and carried it off well.

He came to the city the evening of March 26 accompanied

by—as he phrased it—his "military escort" and was placed in the Eagle Tavern under guard until his future could be determined. "Here the business is to be tried and concluded," he wrote to his daughter Theodosia the next day without giving any indication of his emotions or of his fears for the future.[21]

At noon March 30 the marshal of the court, a Major Scott, and two assistants arrived at Burr's room at the Eagle Tavern. The local newspaper reported that "with perfect civility" they informed him that they had a warrant with them for his appearance before a federal court. They secured him from his military guard and took him to another room where John Marshall waited in his capacity as judge. This hearing was only to determine whether Burr should be released on bail, but even that was a matter of dispute. The government lawyer, George Hay (son-in-law of James Monroe), had objected to the hearing in the Eagle Tavern, saying there was no room there large enough for the crowd of spectators expected. Marshall said he didn't care, and suggested they could avoid the problem by holding the hearing in private. Hay consented to this with the understanding that if there were any dispute between the two sides, the hearing would be moved to a larger room at the state capitol, which could accommodate spectators.

When the hearing began, Hay said it was his duty to charge Burr with treason and also with having prepared a military expedition against the Spanish lands. This last was a misdemeanor. Hay wanted Burr held without bail and, for his evidence, submitted the same material that had been submitted to the Supreme Court in February in the case of Bollman and Swartwout. This was the letters and other evidence of Wilkinson and Eaton. Since Marshall already had said in that earlier case that he did not believe they provided sufficient evidence to constitute a charge of treason, there seemed little doubt that he would rule so again in the matter of Burr's possible bail. That actually had been the feeling all along. William Wirt, a prominent lawyer in Richmond then and within a few weeks one of the prosecution lawyers, had predicted that Burr would be "discharged on a petition to the judge, or let to bail, and make his escape again."[22]

Marshall recessed the court until the next day, March 31, when he scheduled a public hearing in the capitol because there was a dispute between the two sides over the matter of bail. Burr was released on $5,000 bail and directed to return the next morning at ten o'clock. At the correct time John Marshall was seated on the bench, the lawyers for both sides were present, and a large number of local citizens attended as spectators. Aaron Burr, however, was not present. There is no record of what transpired during the next few minutes. Many there had felt, like William Wirt, that Burr, released on bail, would flee. Others, who were Burr's devoted friends, believed otherwise. John Marshall, sitting on the bench, certainly understood that he was about to engage in conflict with Thomas Jefferson, and wondered about the man Burr who had killed Hamilton, wondered perhaps even if he would appear. The records indicate Marshall revealed no emotion, nor in any way showed his feelings. He was being the impartial judge, an impartiality he would demonstrate throughout the trial—with several exceptions.

At ten-thirty Aaron Burr bustled into the courtroom, all apologies to the court. According to the newspaper account. Burr "with some degree of emotion apologized for the apparent delay, declaring he had misapprehended the hour at which he was bound to appear." Marshall, apparently aware of the grumbling in the city over the private hearing the previous day, then moved the session from the capitol's courtroom to the delegate hall so that even more spectators could be accommodated.

Again the question was bail. Hay repeated his request that Burr be committed on the treason and misdemeanor charge. John Wickham, the leading lawyer for the defense, answered that "there was not a shadow of evidence to support the charge of treason." As for the misdemeanor charge, he insisted, the evidence was "trivial." This charge was bailable, Wickham said, and then requested that the bail not be set too high, "as, unfortunately for colonel Burr, he was brought to the place where he had fewer friends or acquaintances, than in almost any other part of the United States, it would be cruelty in counsel to insist on his giving bail in a considerable sum."

Marshall now was faced with making the first of many judicial interpretations that would bring him in conflict with Jefferson and would influence his place in history. His intention, he said, was to give his opinion regarding bail the next day, April 1. It would be in writing, he explained, "to prevent any misrepresentations of expressions which might fall from him." It was indeed important that nothing he said be misrepresented or misunderstood.[23]

While he would be cautious, John Marshall would not evade any issue, not the one specifically before him that April 1 nor any others in the coming months. He began with an explanation of the standards a judge should use in determining whether a person should or should not be allowed bail. "On an application of this kind," he said, "I certainly should not require that proof which would be necessary to convict the person to be committed, on a trial in chief; nor should I even require that which should absolutely convince my own mind of the guilt of the accused: but I ought to require, and I should require, that probable cause be shown; and I understand probable cause to be a case made out by proof furnishing good reason to believe that the crime alleged has been committed by the person charged with having committed it."

Marshall said he considered his definition reconcilable with that of Blackstone, who had said that a person should be committed to jail or released on bond unless the charges against him be groundless. Then Marshall, in the opinion he had written out so there would be no misunderstandings, said:

> I do not understand him [Blackstone] as meaning to say that the hand of malignity may grasp any individual against whom its hate may be directed, or whom it may capriciously seize, charge him with some secret crime, and put him on the proof of his innocence.

According to a footnote in the official transcript, "The Chief Justice explicitly stated to the reporters that, in making the above observations, he had no allusion to the conduct of the government in the case before him, but only meant an elucidation of the general doctrine laid down by Blackstone. He was induced, he said, to make these remarks, because it had been suggested to him by a friend, after he had delivered his opinion that his meaning in the above expressions might possibly be misapprehended." Whatever his intention, Marshall's explanation only served to underscore the remark and to further suggest that the "hand of malignity" was, in fact, Thomas Jefferson's.

In his written decision Marshall then went on to examine whether probable cause existed against Burr. The evidence in the testimony by Eaton—introduced by reference; Eaton had not personally appeared yet—proved that Burr "meditated" an expedition against Mexico, Marshall said. This was a reference to the first charge against Burr, the misdemeanor, that he planned a military expedition against a nation friendly to the United States. As for the evidence of Wilkinson—also by reference; Wilkinson also had not yet appeared—Marshall said if the cipher letter were eliminated, there would be no case against Burr. Marshall said he regretted that the cipher letter he had before him was only a copy, not sworn to, and that Wilkinson was not yet present to testify to the circumstances under which he had received it. Still, Marshall said, he could not discredit the letter at the bail hearing, and "there is probable cause for committing the prisoner on this charge." This again was the misdemeanor.

Marshall then turned to the treason charge. Faced with the same evidence in the Bollman and Swartwout case a few weeks earlier, he had said then he did not believe it constituted a basis for a treason charge. In considering the same evidence against Burr, he would be consistent. The value of his comments, however, lies in what he said about the use of the treason charge as a political weapon. Here was speaking not only the jurist, but the historian who had studied and written much on the American colonists' aspirations for political freedom. Here was writing the soldier who had fought to obtain those freedoms, the American who understood that political freedoms, once gained, must always be protected:

> As this is the most atrocious offence which can be committed against the political body, so is it the charge which is most capable of being employed as the instrument of those malignant and vindictive passions which may rage in the bosoms of contending parties struggling for power. It is that, of which the people of America have been most jealous, and therefore, while other crimes are unnoticed, they have refused to trust the national legislature with the definition of this, but have themselves declared in their constitution that "it shall consist only in levying war against the United States, or in adhering to their enemies giving them aid and comfort." This high crime consists of overt acts which must be proved by two witnesses or by the confession of the party in open court.
>
> Under the control of this constitutional regulation, I am to inquire whether the testimony laid before me furnishes probable cause in support of this charge. The charge is, that the fact itself has been committed, and the testimony to support it must furnish probable cause for believing that it has been actually committed, or it is insufficient for the purpose for which it is adduced.

Marshall was accused then and has been accused since of adhering to the law too closely. Certainly adhering closely to the law is exactly what he intended, as he demonstrated in those two paragraphs. No court over which he presided would allow the laws of the United States to be perverted for political purposes. With his background he could do no less.

Then examining the Eaton and Wilkinson testimony for evidence of treason, Marshall said he could find none. He acknowledged that there was evidence of a conspiracy to commit treason but not of treason itself. The two, the conspiracy and the act, are separate crimes. At this point Marshall scolded the Jefferson administration. If it was so anxious to prove treason, he said, why didn't it produce some evidence? "More than five weeks have elapsed, since the opinion of the Supreme Court [in the Bollman and Swartwout case] has declared the necessity of proving the fact, if it exists. Why is it not proved?" In what must be acknowledged as a snide comment, Marshall said that he could not doubt "that means to obtain information have been taken on the part of the prosecution." And if the proof existed, Marshall continued, he could not doubt that it would have been produced. The fact that it had not been produced, he said, persuaded him not to hold Burr for treason, only for the misdemeanor charge. Bail was set at $10,000, and Burr was scheduled to appear before a federal grand jury on May 22. The amount was high, but at least he could be released. Burr, of course, could still be indicted for treason. But the prosecution knew it had a fight on its hands.[24]

Thomas Jefferson was very aware of the fight he faced. Naturally he was angry at Marshall's suggestion that the prosecution either had been derelict in not producing the evidence of Burr's guilt or had no such evidence. "A moment's calculation will shew that his evidence cannot be collected under 4 months, probably 5, from the moment of deciding when and where the trial shall be," Jefferson wrote to William Branch Giles. Jefferson said he had asked Caesar A. Rodney, the United States Attorney-General, to tell Marshall this informally. There is no record that Rodney did so inform Marshall. If he did, however, Marshall either considered the claim unacceptable or wished deliberately to insult Jefferson. Jefferson continued of Marshall's demand for evidence: "In what terms of decency can we speak of this? As if an express could go to Natchez, or the mouth of Cumberland, and return in 5 weeks, to do which has never taken less than twelve." Jefferson also claimed that the government did not know in which city the hearing was going to be held until March 26, making it impossible to direct the information there in time even if it were available.

Jefferson had no doubt that the outcome of the Burr affair would be decided by politics and not by law: "What loophole Marshall will find in it, when it comes to trial we cannot foresee." He charged that "all the principles of law are to be perverted which would bear on the favorite offenders." And as for there not being probable cause to hold Burr on the treason charge, Jefferson asked, "Is there a candid man in the United States who does not believe some one, if not all, of these overt acts to have taken place?"

But all was not lost for Jefferson even if Burr should be found innocent. "The nation," he said, "will judge both the offender and judges for themselves." The result of that judgment, he said, would be a constitutional amendment authorizing the removal of federal judges. An amendment was needed, he explained, remembering the Chase trial, "for impeachment is a farce which will not be tried again." If such an amendment emerges from the affair, Jefferson said, "it will do more good than his condemnation."[25] The difference between Jefferson and Marshall at this point was that the President saw the Burr trial in terms of politics—"The fact is that the Federalists make Burr's cause their own," he said[26]—while the Chief Justice saw it in terms of law—the protection of the individual against an aggressive state.

A few days after Burr was released on bail on the misdemeanor charge, an incident occurred which gave credence to Jefferson's suspicions. The lawyers in Richmond were a small elite band who were genuinely fond of one another and intimately acquainted. John Marshall and John Wickham had been friends for years, their relationship dating from their years together as young lawyers in the Barbecue Club and in the active social life the Richmond lawyers led. Marshall often had been to Wickham's house, and Wickham frequently attended the lawyers' dinners at Marshall's home. The relationship continued after Marshall became Chief Justice. There was nothing particularly unusual about this. Friendships between judges and lawyers were common in all cities in the young United States, and the judges, particularly when riding circuit, dined often with the lawyers who appeared before them. Even the fact that Wickham was arguing a case before Marshall in Richmond probably would not have prevented the two men from seeing each other socially outside of the courtroom, or that would have been true in most cases.

It was not true in the case of Aaron Burr. Wickham had been Burr's chief counsel in the bail hearing and was personally espousing his cause. Certainly he was well enough aware of the political aspects of the case, and certainly Marshall was well enough aware of them, to understand the need for a greater degree of discretion than usually was evidenced between judges and lawyers. However, a few days after Burr was ordered released on bail by Marshall, Marshall went to a dinner party at Wickham's house. Burr also was a guest at that same party, and the nation was treated to the spectacle of the presiding justice and the defendant sitting at the same table.

There is no explanation for Wickham's having committed such a *faux pas.* The generally accepted story of Marshall's behavior is that at first he did not know that Burr would also be a dinner guest, and when he later learned of Burr's expected presence, he determined to attend the dinner rather than be accused of being overly fastidious or of censuring his friend Wickham. According to the same story, his wife Polly advised him not to attend but he went against her wishes. Polly apparently was aware people might find evil where her husband believed there was only innocence.[27]

This story came originally from St. George Tucker, who was at the dinner and later wrote a friendly biography of Jefferson. He said that he had learned from "an authentic source" that Marshall had accepted the dinner invitation without knowing of Burr's anticipated presence. As for Marshall's relationship with Burr at the dinner, Tucker said his "own distinct recollection" was that Marshall "had no communication whatever with Burr; sat at the opposite end of the table; and withdrew at an early hour after dinner." Tucker conceded that there was "an evident impropriety" in Marshall's having attended the dinner "and no one was afterwards more sensible of it than the chief justice himself, but it was not an act of deliberation, but merely inconsiderate." Tucker believed, however, that it was considered in Richmond as "an undue desire to predispose the public to Burr's favour"—why else would the Chief Justice attend a dinner with Burr unless he believed Burr completely innocent? This, said Tucker, "no doubt contributed to increase the apprehension and alarm of Mr. Jefferson, always sufficiently disposed to judge the federal party with the same harshness that they judged him."[28]

The Chief Justice had his supporters. William Boylan, the editor of the *Minerva*, a pro-Federalist newspaper in Raleigh, North Carolina, said that Marshall was to blame if he had attended the dinner knowing that Burr would be there also. "I am glad however to learn," he continued, "that the Judge says he knew not until the time of entering Mr. Wickham's house that Burr was to be there and that as soon as he had dined he rose from the table and left the house." Boylan said he had heard that version from "the friends of the Judge."[29]

Most of the comments were critical and unsigned. A letter in the *Richmond Enquirer*, identified only as coming from a Richmond Hill resident, granted that Marshall was not motivated by "any corrupt motive" but considered that he was "surely guilty of an unpardonable breach of prudence and decorum, in not preferring the spotless purity of his office." This correspondent also had heard that Marshall had been unaware of Burr's attending the dinner until actually arriving at Wickham's house, but "this I presume could not have deprived him of his faculty of locomotion." The tenor of the criticism is exemplified by another letter in the *Enquirer* signed only by "A Stranger From the Country." "Let me inform the conscience of the chief justice," the stranger wrote, "that the public do not view his dining with Burr, as a circumstance so trivial as he himself may incline to consider it. It is impossible to separate the judge from the man. We regard such conduct as a willful prostration of the dignity of his own character, and a wanton insult he might have spared his country."[30]

In retrospect, one regrets that Marshall did not exercise more care and avoid any possible charge of bias toward Aaron Burr. The grand jury hearing, beginning less than two months after the dinner, was important enough—not only for Marshall, Burr, and Jefferson but also for the nation—for it to be free of any such taint.

Aaron Burr would be brought before the grand jury on May 22, and the weeks between his being released on bail and the start of that procedure were lengthy ones for him. His daughter, Theodosia Alston, was worried about him, and he tried to reassure her. "Such things," he wrote to her, "happen in all democratic governments." He suggested that she amuse herself "by collecting and collating all the instances to be found in ancient history, which you may connect together, if you please, in an essay." He proposed the essay at the end of April and said he hoped to receive it by the day he was scheduled to appear before the grand jury. As that day approached, he began to lose some of his calm. "The grand jury is composed of twenty democrats and four federalists," he wrote Theodosia. "Among the former is W. C. Nicholas, my vindictive and avowed personal enemy—the most so that could be found in this state." He complained that the government was working as industriously as possible to find evidence against him and was spending money "without stint." If he had the same resources, he said, "I could not only foil the prosecutors, but render them ridiculous and infamous." The newspapers were attacking him, his lawyers, and Chief Justice Marshall. "Nothing is left undone or unsaid which can tend to prejudice the public mind, and produce a conviction without evidence. The machinations of this description when used against Moreau in France were treated in this country with indignation. They are practised against me in a still more impudent degree, not only with impunity, but with applause; and the authors and abettors suppose, with reason, that they are acquiring favour with the administration."[31]

In the coming proceedings Burr would be, as one spectator commented, "the great central figure below the bench. There he stood, in the hands of power, on the brink of danger, as composed, as immovable" as a marble statue.[32] While that picture of him was accurate, so was the description of his danger. He was a lone citizen with the entire weight of the federal government against him. He had friends, more than most persons in such a position, and funds available to him, again more than most such persons, but his resources could not equal those of the federal government. Only John Marshall, in his capacity as presiding justice, could assure that the individual had as much importance in the court of law as did the government.

Marshall presided over the Circuit Court with a local judge, Cyrus Griffin. Griffin had been the last president of the Continental Congress, the first federal District Court judge in Virginia, and the man who, on Tuesday, December 17, 1789, had admitted a young lawyer named John Marshall to practice. Almost sixty years old when the Burr trial began, Griffin had the distinction of not uttering one word during the weeks of testimony. He simply enjoyed the oratory. That there would be plenty of. For the prosecution there was George Hay, an intimate friend of Jefferson's as well as the son-in-law of James Monroe. He was assisted by William Wirt, who was one of Richmond's most prominent young lawyers. The third member of the prosecution team was Alexander McRae, who then also was the lieutenant-governor of the state. It was a formidable trio.

Burr had an equally talented list of lawyers on his side. The leader was Edmund Randolph. Randolph had been governor of Virginia, an opponent of the Constitution when he attended the Philadelphia Convention in 1787 and its supporter at the Virginia ratification convention the following year. At the federal level he had served as George Washington's Attorney General and Secretary of State. When the Burr trial began May 22, he was less than three months shy of his fifty-fourth birthday. He was one of the most prominent and brilliant lawyers in the state. The first assistant was John Wickham, who had led the defense in the bail hearing. He had been a Tory during the American Revolution and in the decades following the war became, once Marshall gave up his own practice, the leading lawyer in Richmond. There were three other assistants—Benjamin Botts, John Baker, and Charles Lee—who played lesser roles in the trial but who were considered first-rate lawyers. The final lawyer on Burr's list was Luther Martin, the same Luther Martin who had so ably defended Samuel Chase when Chase was impeached. For him the trial was especially welcome because of Thomas Jefferson's involvement. An old family dispute had convinced Martin that Jefferson was the personification of malevolence. The worst thing Luther Martin could say of any man was that he was "as great a

scoundrel as Thomas Jefferson." Of course, Burr was a participant in his own defense. As a lawyer he was a brilliant tactician,
sensing his opponent's weak points and thrusting at them with
all the skill of a fencer driving for the heart. He often spoke in
his own behalf during the proceedings and disproved that the
lawyer who defends himself has a fool for a client.[33]

The Court of the United States for the Fifth Circuit and
District of Virginia convened at twelve-thirty the afternoon of
May 22 with Justices Marshall and Griffin presiding. Immediately John Marshall had to make a determination, the beginning
of a long series of decisions that would make the Burr trial a
fascinating source of study for lawyers and judges in future years.
Perhaps no justice ever issued so many rulings so rapidly as did
Marshall in this trial. A grand jury of sixteen was to be chosen
from the panel of twenty-four. Apparently two of the original
twenty-four had indicated they did not wish to serve on the grand
jury, and the United States marshal had simply crossed out their
names and substituted two others. Wickham explained to the
court that they were challenging the marshal's action, not because
of the marshal's motives, "But in the present case, where such
important interests are at stake, and where such unjustifiable
means have been used to prejudice the public mind against colonel Burr, it is [Burr's] right to take every advantage which the
law gives him." Wickham also pointed out that if the marshal
"were permitted to alter the panel as he pleased, the life of every
citizen in this state would be held at his pleasure."

Wickham's point was crucial. If a jury can be altered by
one man, no matter what that man's intentions, then that man
can control the justice dispensed in the state. The problem had
not been faced previously by the state courts, so Marshall had to
decide the issue. He began by pointing out that the law authorizes
the marshal to summon twenty-four jurymen "but he is not to
summon a twenty-fifth." Actually, Marshall continued, a twenty-
fifth juror could not be summoned legally unless the marshal
"has the power to discharge a person already summoned." Marshall continued: "He has no such power, unless the jury be composed of bystanders. The twenty-four first summoned must
compose the jury, sixteen of whom constitute a quorum. It follows, therefore, that no one can be in the grand jury, unless he
be one of the twenty-four first summoned, or one who has been
selected from the bystanders by the direction of the court." The
law allowed the judge, not the marshal, to fill out the grand jury
if a quorum of sixteen could not be achieved from the panel
provided by the marshal. Marshall then concluded that "a person
substituted in the place of one actually summoned, cannot be

considered as being on the panel.”[34] The message of Marshall's decision in this instance was that the law would be strictly adhered to. He believed that the law established certain procedural safeguards for the protection of the individual, and he would not allow those safeguards to be tampered with.

As a result of that decision, two persons substituted by the United States marshal were excused from the panel. Then Burr began exercising his other exceptions. The first person he challenged was William Branch Giles because Giles, in Congress, had already declared his belief in Burr's guilt. Giles countered that he could judge fairly, but he did agree to step down. Marshall commented that "if any gentleman has made up and declared his mind, it would be best for him to withdraw." His point was that Giles should not have talked as if he had a right to stay on the jury. The next person Burr challenged was Wilson Cary Nicholas because Nicholas "has entertained a bitter personal animosity against me." Nicholas said he had wished to be excused and stepped down.

Joseph Eggleston then asked to be excused because he also had made strong statements to the effect that he considered Burr guilty. While he believed he could give a fair verdict, he could not say so positively. At this point Burr showed the intelligence which made him such an outstanding lawyer. "Under different circumstances, I might think and act differently," he said, "but the industry which has been used through this country to prejudice my cause, leaves me very little chance that I can expect a better man to try my causes. [Eggleston's] desire to be excused, and his opinion that his mind is not entirely free upon the case, are good reasons why he should be excused; but the candour of the gentleman, in excepting to himself, leaves me ground to hope, that he will endeavour to be impartial." Eggleston stayed on the jury. Burr's polite little speech undoubtedly did much to transform an enemy into a friend.

When the exceptions were done, there were fourteen men on the grand jury, two shy of the sixteen needed for a quorum. Under the law, the court was allowed to name two bystanders, and Marshall named John Randolph and William Foushee, with Randolph to act as the foreman of the grand jury. Randolph asked to be excused, saying he had already formed an opinion. This is the same John Randolph who had been involved in the Randolph scandal, had become Jefferson's lieutenant in the Congress, and led the impeachment proceedings against Samuel Chase. He finally had broken with Jefferson. Although his animosity to the President at this point was well known, his belief in Burr's guilt also was well known, and so those two served to make him objective. At least that was the belief. "The rule is," said the Chief Justice, "that a man must not only have formed, but declared an opinion, in order to exclude him from serving on the jury." When Randolph said he could not remember publicly declaring his attitude toward Burr's guilt or innocence, he was allowed to stay on the jury. Foushee, however, was excused, and was replaced by James Barbour. When Barbour accepted, the grand jury was complete and the proceedings could begin.[35]

The proceedings were a *tour de force* for the lawyers. One could not help but be enthralled by their oratory. On Saturday, May 23, for example, William Wirt for the prosecution accused the defense of attempting to place Thomas Jefferson on trial. "These remarks [critical of Jefferson] were not intended for your ear, sir," said Wirt, addressing John Marshall, "they were intended for the people who surround us; they can have no effect upon the mind of the court. I am too well acquainted with the dignity, the firmness, the illumination of this bench, to apprehend any such consequence."

On Monday, May 25, Edmund Randolph spoke for the defense. The shock is evident in his words. "Colonel Burr was arrested in the Mississippi Territory. Was there no court there? Was there no judge of integrity to try him?" Randolph then carried on about Burr's treatment, "dragged by eight musquetteers . . . ready to shoot him at a moment's warning," denied access to a court, not permitted to write to his daughter. "What is all this, sir," he demanded, "but oppressive and bitter inhumanity?"

John Wickham also spoke for the defense. "The crime is treason," he cried, ". . . and where is the proof of it?" But it was Burr himself, speaking that Monday, who made the most effective comments in his defense. "Our president," he said of Thomas Jefferson, "is a lawyer, and a great one too. He certainly ought to know what it is, that constitutes a war. Six months ago, he proclaimed that there was a civil war. And yet, for six months they have been hunting for it, and still cannot find one spot where it existed. There was, to be sure, a most terrible war in the newspapers; but no where else." Burr pointed out that when he appeared before a grand jury in Kentucky, he was dismissed because "they had no charge to bring against me"; and when he appeared before a grand jury a second time, in the Mississippi Territory, "there was nothing to appear against me." Burr then concluded that "if there was a war, certainly no man can pretend to say, that the government is able to find it out. The scene to which they have now hunted it, is only 300 miles distant, and still there is no evidence to prove this war."[36] It was an effective performance.

It was, however, a performance of oratory and showmanship rather than of law. Burr and his defense lawyers were not hesitating to turn the proceedings into an attack on Jefferson if at all possible. The entire process had become a political one. Jefferson had instituted the legal actions against Burr precipitously, without adequate evidence, and then simply refused to back down. Cornered, he decided to fight viciously, bringing all the power of the federal government against Burr. Burr, in turn, understood that his exoneration might very well depend upon his convincing the public that he was being prosecuted for political purposes rather than for treasonous conduct. Both sides were playing with the law, and John Marshall was the man in the middle.

Even before the grand jury became deeply involved in whether Burr should be indicted on the misdemeanor and treason charges, Marshall was forced to decide whether Burr could be held on bail for the treason charge. This had been denied at the hearing at the end of March but was brought up again by George Hay of the prosecution, who wanted Burr held on bail on the treason charge while the grand jury was meeting. First, Marshall had to decide whether he would entertain the motion. He acknowledged regret that the motion was being made, his point being that the argument on the motion itself might produce evidence which would prejudice the results against Burr. "No man," he said, "feeling a correct sense of the importance which ought to be attached by all to a fair and impartial administration of justice, especially in criminal prosecutions, can view, without extreme solicitude, any attempt which may be made to prejudice the public judgment, and to try any person, not by the laws of his country, and the testimony exhibited against him, but by public feelings, which may be and often are artificially excited against the innocent, as well as the guilty." But the remedy, he argued, is not to refuse to hear a motion that was allowed. Here again, as he would through the entire proceedings, Marshall insisted upon proper procedure. He understood—as a later Supreme Court Justice, Felix Frankfurter, phrased it—that "The history of liberty has largely been the observance of procedural safeguards."[37]

In that instance proper procedure had been of assistance to the prosecution. The next day it aided Aaron Burr. Once Marshall decided to entertain the motion, the arguments began. To make its case for bail, the prosecution had to prove that a crime had been committed and that there was reason to believe that Burr had been involved. After a spat over whether the prosecution could attempt to make these points by presenting evidence in chronological order, the proceedings got down to the basic point. Marshall would not relax proper procedure. The trial records include this account:

> The Chief Justice said, that he was of opinion, that unless there be a fact to be proved, no testimony ought to be produced. The question before the court was not whether there had been a treasonable intent, but an overt act. The fact itself must be proved, before there can be any treason, or any commitment for treason.

Burr finally solved the dispute by voluntarily submitting to bail, "provided it should be understood, that no opinion on the question even of probable cause was pronounced by the court, by the circumstance of his giving bail." A relieved John Marshall set the bail at $10,000, which immediately was produced by four men. One of them was Luther Martin, who obviously considered Aaron Burr not only his client but his cause.

In retrospect, the question of bail may seem to be more furor and folly than vital necessity. It was, however, a significant discussion. The Burr trial, as everyone involved in it was becoming aware, was developing into a major criminal proceeding. What was allowed in that trial, what rules were followed or violated there, would be followed or violated in subsequent trials of other persons accused of crimes. Law is an edifice in the form of an inverted pyramid: it constantly expands, resting on everything that happened before. In this issue, as with other issues of procedure in the Burr trial, Aaron Burr assumed a role of only minor importance. What was really important were the protections being established for every other individual haled before a federal court in later years.

The grand jury then was ready to hear evidence against Burr, but General Wilkinson had not yet arrived from the South, though he had been expected for weeks, and without him there was no case against Burr. It was to him that Burr had written the letter in cipher allegedly plotting to make war against the United States. It was Wilkinson's report to Thomas Jefferson the previous winter which had provided Jefferson's ammunition against Burr. Without Wilkinson there was nothing. So the grand jury recessed for a few days to await his arrival.[38]

A young writer in town to observe the proceedings had his attitudes jaundiced by the whole business. "You can little conceive the talents for procrastination that have been exhibited at this affair," Washington Irving wrote to a friend. "Day after day have we been disappointed by the non-arrival of the magnanimous Wilkinson." Irving then said that the members of the grand jury had taken a few days off so that they could go home, "see their wives, get their clothes washed, and flog their negroes." The great concern, Irving said, was that "if the great hero of the South does not arrive," there might be a request by the prosecution that the trial be postponed. "The Government will be again subjected to immense expense," Irving reported, "and Col. Burr, besides being harassed and detained for an additional space of time, will have to repeat the enormous expenditures which this trial has already caused him." Irving believed that the "most underhand and ungenerous measures" had been used toward Burr but that he "retains his serenity and self-possession."[39]

Burr was not quite as serene as Irving believed. The previous day he had written his daughter a letter that betrayed the rawness of his emotions. "Still waiting for Wilkinson," he began, "and no certain accounts of his approach. The grand jury, the witnesses, and the country grow impatient. It is an ungracious thing, and so deemed, after having for six months been branded as a traitor; after directing that Burr and his followers should be attacked, put to death, and their property seized; after all the violations of law and constitution which have been practised, that government should now say it has not proof!"

Aaron Burr had an interesting relationship with his daughter. Since the death of his wife she had taken on the role of his confidante, the one who shared his secrets and his ambitions. It was a mature role for a young daughter, and it indicates something about Aaron Burr, brilliant lawyer, intriguer, adventurer, great lover: that he sorely missed the woman who had been his wife and would allow no one to take her place in his affections except her daughter. And so he ended that letter to Theodosia with an attempt to show her he could still control his emotions: "Busy, busy, busy from morning till night—from night till morning, yet there are daily amusing incidents; things at which you will laugh, also things at which you will pout and scold."[40]

The grand jury proceedings resumed on June 9, a Tuesday. Wilkinson still had not arrived, and Chief Justice Marshall was preparing to adjourn the court until the next morning at ten o'clock when unexpectedly Aaron Burr rose to make his most daring move. His action sent shock waves between Richmond and Washington, and, more important, between John Marshall and Thomas Jefferson, and still even more important, between subsequent Presidents and subsequent federal justices.

Burr said he had a "proposition" he wished to make to the court. He referred to Jefferson's message to Congress in January in which he had cited Wilkinson's letter. "Circumstances had now rendered it material," Burr continued, "that the whole of this letter should be produced in court." He also insisted that it was necessary that certain other papers, having to do with the military's orders to capture him, also be brought to the court. "The instructions in this order were," Burr insisted, "to destroy my person and my property in descending the Mississippi." Burr said he had attempted to locate these papers and had made overtures in Washington to have them produced, and while he had been promised cooperation, the papers had not been produced. "Hence I feel it necessary," Aaron Burr told John Marshall, "to resort to the authority of this court, to call upon them to issue a subpoena to the president of the United States, with a clause, requiring him to produce certain papers; or in other words, to issue the subpoena *duces tecum*." Burr quickly added that the entire matter could be settled if the United States Attorney would voluntarily produce the papers.

What Aaron Burr had succeeded in doing was transforming the indirect confrontation between John Marshall and Thomas Jefferson into a direct one. If Jefferson would not voluntarily produce the papers, then Marshall was being asked to subpoena him to do so. Who was more powerful? The President or the Chief Justice? Who could command the other's presence? Since 1801 when Thomas Jefferson had become President and John Marshall had become Chief Justice, they had been heading toward this confrontation.

Marshall believed in exercising his power as a judge to its fullest. But he did not believe in wasting that power by engaging in battles that he could not win and that could result only in the weakening of his position. He obviously was uncomfortable at Burr's request. He agreed with Burr's remark that issuing such a subpoena was usual, but he quickly added the condition that it was usual "where there was no great inconvenience to the party summoned." He also said that the situation did not arise often, and where inconvenience would result to the summoned party, "the materiality of his testimony should be fully shown."

Luther Martin commented that he could not understand how there could be any inconvenience whatever. All that Jefferson had to do, he said, was send the papers by mail.[41]

There has developed a belief that John Marshall was asked and subsequently did direct a subpoena be issued commanding that the President of the United States personally appear in the Richmond courtroom.[42] This was not the case, whatever the wording of the directive. Jefferson's presence was not sought; the papers were sought. Edmund Randolph made this clear. "If any arrangement can be made to obtain these papers," he said, "we would rather that it should be a voluntary act on the part of the government."[43]

This was stressed the next day by John Wickham, who said that "Mr. Hay had promised the appearance of these papers; and that was all they wanted. The object was not to bring the president here, but to obtain certain papers which he had in his possession." Still, it was the judiciary directing the executive, and particularly, it was the judiciary directing the executive to do something—deliver the papers—that the executive might not want to do.

The arguments between the attorneys for both sides became heavy and acrimonious. As a judge, Marshall always was patient with the lawyers. He knew most of those who appeared before him, admired them; and the style of the time was such as to allow lawyers to be as florid and dramatic as they wished—Daniel Webster's arguments would be the culmination of these practices. But the arguments this hot June day in Richmond became too much even for Marshall. He scolded the lawyers. He had ignored the discussions which had taken place "in the heat of the debate of which the court did not approve," but now, Marshall said, "the court thought it proper to declare that the gentlemen on both sides had acted improperly in the style and spirit of their remarks; that they had been to blame in endeavouring to excite the prejudices of the people; and had repeatedly accused each other of doing what they forget they have done themselves." He then directed counsel for both sides to stick to the point "really before the court." He said that "their own good sense and regard for their characters required them to follow such a course; and it was hoped that they would not hereafter deviate from it." He then adjourned the court until the next morning, Thursday, at eleven o'clock.[44]

The next morning George Hay began with indications that he had not learned very much from Marshall's admonition. "Many strange positions have been laid down," he said of the defense demand for the subpoena, "but this is monstrous. Mr. [Luther] Martin will excuse me for saying, that I expected sounder doctrine from his age and experience. These principles were not learnt by him in Maryland, nor are they the doctrine of this place."

Edmund Randolph spoke next, for the defense, and his argument is the basic justification for Burr seeking the papers. Because of what was suspected of Wilkinson at the time and what became known of him later, it is difficult to fault Randolph's argument. He said:

What is the nature of the evidence we do ask? We ask for that sort of evidence which may enable us to confront James Wilkinson with himself. There is not an idea beyond this. We wish to show, that James Wilkinson in his official capacity, as commander of the army of the United States at New Orleans, is not the same with James Wilkinson the correspondent of the president. We wish to prove, that James Wilkinson has varied with himself, and that he has varied in most essential points in the greatest degree. Mr. Hay tells us, that every thing depends upon this same James Wilkinson; that he is in reality the *Alpha* and *Omega* of the present prosecution. He is, in short, to supply by his deposition the *sing-song* and the ballads of treason and conspiracy, which we have heard delivered from one extremity of the continent to the other. The funeral pile of the prosecution is already prepared by the hands of the public attorney, and nothing is wanting to kindle the fatal blaze but the torch of James Wilkinson. He is to exhibit himself in a most conspicuous point of view in the tragedy which is fancied will take place. He, James Wilkinson, is to officiate as the high priest of this human sacrifice. . . .

Upon the conviction of colonel Burr, upon the guilt I say of colonel Burr, depends the innocence of general Wilkinson. If colonel Burr be proved guilty, then indeed general Wilkinson may stand acquitted with many of his countrymen; but if colonel Burr be not found guilty, the character, the reputation, in short, every thing that deserves the name of integrity, will be gone for ever from general Wilkinson. Sir, in that event, I say, in the event of Burr's acquittal, as sure as man is man, storms and tempests will cover the western glory of general Wilkinson, and gather darkness all around him. We have therefore the justest cause to scrutinize this gentleman's deposition. We have the strongest reasons to examine this gentleman's character, and to trace him in his most confidential walks.

Randolph concluded:

From his letters we have already had some glimpse of him; but I should wish, as I have said, to have him confronted with himself; I mean, to have his correspondence with the president of the United States opposed to whatever statement he may deliver here. . . .[45]

If a man is going to be attacked in court, it does not seem unreasonable that the credibility of his attacker be established.

Marshall gave his decision on Saturday, June 13. It runs a dozen pages in the trial record and it obviously had been prepared in advance, again to prevent any misinterpretations, although there would be some.[46] The first question Marshall directed himself to was whether Aaron Burr was entitled to have a subpoena issued in his behalf. "So far back as any knowledge of our jurisprudence is possessed," said Marshall, "the uniform practice of this country has been, to permit any individual, who was charged with any crime, to prepare for his defence, and to obtain the process of the court, for the purpose of enabling him so to do." Marshall added: "This practice is as convenient, and as consonant to justice, as it is to humanity." He saw no reason to limit that right, certainly not in the United States where the judicial process has incumbent upon it the obligation of protecting the individual. "Upon immemorial usage, then, and upon what is deemed a sound construction of the constitution and the law of the land," he said, "the court is of opinion, that any person, charged with a crime in the courts of the United States, has a right, before, as well as after indictment, to the process of the court to compel the attendance of his witnesses."

After the acceptance of Burr's right to the use of the subpoena process, the question still remained whether the court could issue one to the President of the United States. Does the judiciary have the power to compel either the President or his papers to be presented in court?

In answering this question, Marshall demonstrated the ability to develop an argument so logically that there seemed little opportunity of challenging it. First he asserted that neither in the Constitution nor in the statutes was there any provision excepting any individual from the power of the court's subpoena. "The obligation, therefore of those provisions is general," he said, "and it would seem, that no person could claim an exemption from them, but one who would not be a witness. At any rate, if an exception to the general principle exist, it must be looked for in the law of evidence." Marshall then made clear he had studied the precedents very carefully and found that the only exceptions are persons who, for some reason, could not give testimony in court. There was one reservation, he said, in the case of the king. "Although he may, perhaps, give testimony," he said, "it is said to be incompatible with his dignity to appear under the process of the court." Could the same claim be made for the President of the United States? Marshall answered:

> Of the many points of difference which exist between the first magistrate in England and the first magistrate of the United States, in respect to the personal dignity conferred on them, by the constitutions of their respective nations,

the court will only select and mention two. It is a principle
of the English constitution, that the king can do no wrong,
that no blame can be imputed to him, that he cannot be
named in debate.

By the constitution of the United States, the president,
as well as every other officer of the government, may
be impeached, and may be removed from office on high
crimes and misdemeanors.

By the constitution of Great Britain, the crown is hereditary, and the monarch can never be a subject.

By that of the United States, the president is elected
from the mass of the people, and, on the expiration of
the time for which he is selected, returns to the mass of
the people again.

Because of these differences, the question of the dignity of
the chief magistrate in each country must be answered differently. Marshall thought that the point "will be perceived by every
person." His next sentence certainly must have angered President Jefferson. "In this respect," said Marshall, "the first magistrate of the Union may more properly be likened to the first
magistrate of a state; at any rate, under the former confederation;
it is not known ever to have been doubted, but that the chief
magistrate of a state might be served with a subpoena *ad testifi-
candum.*" Marshall also asserted that no court previously had
decided that a subpoena could not be issued to the President.

Then he conceded that when Burr had first made his
motion, he had some doubts about the propriety of directing a
subpoena to the President and of requiring "any paper in his
possession, not public in its nature, to be exhibited in court." The
questions which might arise had been considered and rejected:
"The court can perceive no legal objection to issuing a subpoena
duces tecum to any person whatever, provided, the case be such
as to justify the process."

Certainly aware that what he had just said would be considered as another event in the long dispute between himself and
Jefferson, Marshall quickly added that he was acting by direction
of the law rather than by personal pique. "This is said to be a
motion to the *discretion* of the court. This is true," he said. "But
a motion to its *discretion* is a motion, not to its *inclination*, but to
its *judgment*; and its judgment is to be guided by sound legal
principles." What he said was true; still, he must have enjoyed
what he was doing to Thomas Jefferson.

The remainder of the decision includes further justifica-
tions for issuing the subpoena. If the papers sought really were
important to the defense, "would it not be a blot in the page,

which records the judicial proceedings of this country, if, in a case of such serious import as this, the accused should be denied the use of them?" Marshall noted that one objection is that disclosure of the material might be injurious to the nation. He countered that the court would not require such disclosure, "but that, in a capital case, the accused ought, in some form, to have the benefit of it, if it were really essential to his defence." He also stated that nothing had been said in court to indicate that disclosure of the material would be harmful to the national interest.

He spoke again about the possibility of disrespect or indignity to the President. "These observations will be very truly answered by the declaration, that this court feels many, perhaps, peculiar motives, for manifesting as guarded a respect for the chief magistrate of the Union as is compatible with its official duties," he said, adding: "To go beyond these would exhibit a conduct which would deserve some other appellation than the term respect." It is difficult to read those two sentences without understanding that John Marshall was saying that the federal judiciary, as long as he headed it, never would assume anything less than a role equal to that of the presidency.

Marshall closed with the comment that if Burr were found guilty and papers necessary for his defense had been denied him, it would not be the reputation of the government which would be tarnished but, rather, the reputation of the court. "Might I be permitted to utter one sentiment, with respect to myself," he said, "it would be to deplore, most earnestly, the occasion which should compel me to look back on any part of my official conduct with so much self-reproach as I should feel, could I declare, on the information now possessed, that the accused is not entitled to the letter in question, if it should be really important to him."

The point of Marshall's decision, and its genius, was the affirmation of the court's role as the protector of the individual. In those twelve pages he insisted that no matter how high the government official, the courts always must choose for the individual who is charged rather than the official placing the charge; no matter how serious the crime, again the court must rule for the accused. It would have been easy for John Marshall to have skipped these points; Burr's crime was treason and Marshall would have been cheered if he had bent the court's rulings against the suspected traitor—just as he ultimately would be abused for his rulings constantly in the defendant's behalf.

And this was another point of this decision as it would be of all of Marshall's conduct in the entire Burr trial: that the judge is to be above any momentary clamor or passion. In this trial of a former Vice President accused of treason, one of the most emotionally charged moments in the nation's history, John Marshall's example is a guide for every judge. Between the awesome power of the state and the accused individual, that example proclaims, the judge and his court are the only barrier.

During the Burr proceedings so far, Marshall had been concerned by the general public attitude which assumed Burr's guilt. This had begun with Jefferson's message to Congress on January 22, and was reflected in the difficulty surrounding the choosing of an impartial grand jury. It was natural, if impolitic, that in the decision on the subpoena he referred to this public outcry led by the President. "Should it [the case] terminate as is expected on the part of the United States" is the phrase he used, which the prosecution quickly seized on. Alexander McRae, one of the government lawyers, rose when Marshall's decision on the subpoena was finished. "I hope, sir, that I have misunderstood an expression, which has just escaped from your honour," he said. (Actually, he had misunderstood it, as he quoted it incorrectly as: "if the present prosecution terminate as is wished on the part of the United States." Marshall had used "expected" and not "wished.") McRae continued: "I hope, sir, that nothing has appeared in my conduct, nothing in the conduct of the gentlemen who are associated with me on the present occasion, and nothing in the conduct of the government, to produce such a conviction in the breast of the court." McRae then said he wanted to assure the court that the prosecution was more interested in the doing of justice than in having Burr found guilty, and that they would only accept the latter if the former were adhered to. Considering what Jefferson had said publicly and privately about Burr's alleged guilt, McRae's comment can only be considered as charming.

Marshall treated it as such. The transcript does not reveal in what tone he spoke the next words, but certainly a dryness is indicated. "Gentlemen had so often, and so uniformly asserted, that colonel Burr was guilty, and they had so often repeated it before the testimony was perceived, on which that guilt could alone be substantiated," he said, "that it appeared to him probable, that they were not indifferent on the subject."

If Marshall's decision had determined that the court would offer the presidency only respect but not obeisance, it also had put the President of the United States in the position of either violating the law or else bowing to the demands of what had been considered an equal but not superior branch of the government.

Jefferson personally believed that the courts had the right to order the President to do whatever the courts considered proper. But he also believed that the President had the right to determine whether or not he would obey those orders. The Constitution, he had argued several years before the Burr trial, "meant that its coordinate branches should be checks on each other; but to give one a right to control the other, not only in its own sphere of action, but in their respective spheres, would make it despotic."[47]

That was the attitude he took in reacting to the demand first for the Wilkinson letter and then to the subpoena. Jefferson had learned from George Hay that the defense wanted the Wilkinson letter. On June 12, the day before Marshall handed down his decision on the subpoena request, Jefferson wrote Hay from Washington that he would be ready to furnish voluntarily whatever the courts might need, "reserving the necessary right of the president of the United States, to decide, independently of all other authority, what papers coming to him as president, the public interest permits to be communicated." He then said that he considered furnishing the material Burr sought as falling into the category of being contrary to the public interest.

Burr had wanted the letter of General Wilkinson to Jefferson dated October 21, 1806. Jefferson said he believed that Hay actually had the letter or could have access to it, and instructed him to make it public only after excising those sections which "are not directly material for the purposes of justice." As for the other material Burr wanted—the correspondence between the government in Washington and officials in New Orleans regarding Burr's escapades—Jefferson said that so much correspondence was involved "as would amount to the laying open the whole executive books," and should not be turned over to the defense. He said that the Secretary of War was examining the records to determine whether there were any specific letters which the administration might be willing to turn over to the court, but that was as far as he was willing to go. He would respond to the request in a manner befitting his standards, not someone else's.[48]

Henry Adams, in his history of this period, has charged that Jefferson was forced to keep this material private because its publication would demonstrate his own negligence. Despite warnings to the contrary, Adams wrote, Jefferson had left the entire western lands at Wilkinson's "mercy." Adams further claimed that "Disobedience of the subpoena was necessary for the support of Wilkinson; support of Wilkinson was more than ever necessary after refusing to obey the subpoena. The President accepted his full share in the labor."[49] Part of Jefferson's rationale may have been what Adams charged, for the President had become so personally identified as the chief accuser of Burr that he obviously would have been reluctant to produce any documents which Burr could use for his defense. As the prime source of evidence against Burr was turning out to be Wilkinson, if he ever appeared in Richmond, anything that attacked his credibility would also reflect on Jefferson's. But Jefferson must be given more credit than that. As Marshall was right to insist that the material could be subpoenaed, Jefferson was right to refuse to hand it over. The United States government succeeds when each branch watches the others, reprimands them, attacks them, refuses them; and not when one bows to the others. One branch toppling the other is not a checks-and-balance arrangement but a destructive one.

On Friday, June 19, Aaron Burr announced that so far he had received no response to his subpoena. "I now rise to give notice that, unless I receive a satisfactory intimation on this subject before the meeting of the court, I shall, tomorrow, move the court to enforce its process."[50]

The next morning George Hay rose with a letter from Jefferson in which the President explained why he could not comply with the subpoena, either by appearing personally or by sending the papers: "I am persuaded the court is sensible, that paramount duties to the nation at large, control the obligation of compliance with its summons in this case." His point was that the President could not respond to such a summons in various parts of the United States and still be free to exercise his responsibilities in Washington. "To comply with such calls," he said, "would leave the nation without an executive branch." As for delivering the papers, Jefferson argued that the presidency was both a public and a private office. As part of his private duties there were "mere executive proceedings." He then said that "All nations have found it necessary, that, for the advantageous conduct of their affairs, some of these proceedings at least, should remain known to their executive functionary only. He, of course, from the nature of the case, must be the sole judge of which of them the public interest will permit publication."

Although Jefferson had not yet read John Marshall's decision in which the Chief Justice had vowed that the judiciary would extend to the President the respect due to an equal and no more, the President's concluding phrases speak to such an attitude: "The respect mutually due between the dispositions to do for every one what is just will always insure from the executive, in exercising the duty of discrimination confided to him the same candour and integrity, to which the nation has in like manner trusted in the disposal of its judiciary authorities." The conflict between the two men, between the two branches of government, was stalemated. They would be equal; one would not be supreme.[51]

That letter was written by Jefferson to be submitted as part of the trial records, as his formal response to the request for his delivering the papers. It was politely phrased as befitting a document written by the President of the United States. A few days later, however, Jefferson wrote another letter to Hay, a personal one. By this time Jefferson had read Marshall's decision, though he insisted that "I did not read his argument with much attention." Still, he said he saw "readily enough, that, as is usual where an opinion is to be supported, right or wrong, he dwells much on smaller objections, and passes over those which are solid." Jefferson then repeated his objections to answering the court's demand, but this time his tone was not nearly as polite and his animosity toward Marshall was apparent. "Would the executive be independent of the judiciary, if he were subject to the *commands* of the latter, and to imprisonment for disobedience," demanded Jefferson, "if the several courts could bandy him from pillar to post, keep him constantly trudging from north to south and east to west, and withdraw him entirely from his constitutional duties?"[52]

The subpoena question was never really answered, but was allowed to fade. Jefferson, however, continued to fear the possibility of the Chief Justice directing a United States marshal to arrest the President himself and bring him by force if necessary to the Burr trial in Richmond. Some weeks later Jefferson, at Monticello, drafted another letter to George Hay. He said he wanted to conciliate matters and "to avoid conflicts of authority between the high branches of the government which would discredit equally at home and abroad." He then repeated his belief that Burr wished to convert the trial into "a contest between the judiciary and executive branches." While that was to be expected, said Jefferson, "that the Chief Justice should lend himself to it, and take the first step to bring it on, was not expected." Jefferson continued that he did not believe that Marshall would overstep the bounds of prudence and good sense to press the issue, "But should he, contrary to expectation, proceed to issue any process which should involve any act of force to be committed on the persons of the Executive or heads of departments, I must desire you to give me instant notice, by express if you find that can be quicker done than by post." Jefferson also directed Hay to advise the United States marshal on the conduct he would pursue "as he will be critically placed" between the President and the Chief Justice. Jefferson thought the safest course for the marshal in such a situation "will be to take no part in the exercise of any act of force ordered in this case."

Jefferson's next few lines suggest the depth of his feelings against Marshall. "The powers given to the Executive by the Constitution are sufficient to protect the other branches from judiciary usurpation of preeminence, and every individual also from judiciary vengeance, and the marshal may be assured of its effective exercise to cover him." The section is revealing in that it shows Jefferson believed he was dealing not with law but with judicial vengeance. He closed with the hope that Marshall would not press the question, and perhaps Congress at its next session might resolve the conflict or perhaps some Associate Justices might "divide his court and procure a truce."[53]

Marshall never tried to enforce the subpoena. He was not so foolish as to attempt to arrest the President. Jefferson's fear was not born of reality but of the suspicion he had had from the time of his election that the Federalists would not relinquish power voluntarily. Although his fears were baseless, they were natural. The concept of America, of individuals freely choosing their government and of the defeated peacefully surrendering their authority, was still too new to be taken for granted.

While the hassle over the subpoena was going on, General Wilkinson at last arrived in Richmond. His date of arrival was June 13, a Saturday, and he was questioned along with William Eaton, who had come from Washington, much of the following week. Although the grand jury supposedly was stacked in favor of Jefferson, its members did not forget their responsibilities to the law in dealing with these two witnesses. Aaron Burr reported with satisfaction that Eaton "came out of the jury-room in such rage and agitation that he shed tears, and complained bitterly that he had been questioned as if he were a villain." Burr's added comment was: "How else could he have been questioned with any propriety?"[54] As for Wilkinson, who was questioned for several days, the members of the grand jury regretted that a technicality in the law prevented them from indicting him. John Randolph, who was foreman of the jury, said some months later of Wilkinson that "I did not hear a single member of the grand jury express any other opinion than that which I myself expressed of the moral—not of the legal—guilt of the party."[55]

The first meeting between Burr and Wilkinson was, according to Washington Irving, "highly interesting." Burr was seated in the courtroom, his back to the door, talking with one of his lawyers. Wilkinson "strutted" into the courtroom and took a position directly to Burr's left. Irving continued: "Here he stood for a moment swelling like a turkey cock, and bracing himself up for the encounter of Burr's eye." And well he might have braced himself, for it was on his statements primarily that Burr was being attacked in court. And if some, like Burr, charged he was in the pay of the Spanish government, and others believed it, Wilkinson himself knew it was true.

Burr did not take any notice of Wilkinson until Marshall directed that the general be sworn in as a witness. His reaction then was the epitome of magnificent disdain. At the mention of Wilkinson's name, Burr turned and stared at the army officer "full in the face with one of his piercing regards," Irving reported, "swept his eye over the whole person from head to foot, as if to scan its dimensions, and then coolly resumed his former position, and went on conversing with his counsel as tranquilly as ever." Irving summed up the moment:

> The whole look was over in an instant; but it was an admirable one. There was no appearance of study or constraint in it; no affectation of disdain or defiance; a slight expression of contempt played over his countenance, such as you would show on regarding any person to whom you were indifferent, but whom you considered mean and contemptible.[56]

Wilkinson's appearance before the grand jury gave Marshall another of his frequent opportunities to hand down a decision, one that would again draw a line in favor of the individual being challenged by the state, and one that again would become a major part of the standard criminal law of the United States. The grand jury was considering the cipher letter that Burr had sent to Wilkinson, which allegedly outlined a plot to dismember the nation. Wilkinson was asked if, when he received the letter, he understood it. His answer would have many implications. Obviously, if he had understood the letter to be part of such a plot and had not taken immediate action to frustrate it then he had not fulfilled his duties as an American officer and may also have been involved in the plot. Wilkinson declined to answer the question, on the grounds that the answer might tend to incriminate him. Marshall then had to determine whether Wilkinson could be compelled to answer.

Marshall pointed out that two principles were involved. The first is that no person can be compelled to testify against himself, and the second is that a court can compel testimony from anyone it believes has information of value to the issue before the court. Wilkinson argued that only he could determine whether his answer would tend to incriminate him and that, therefore, "he is consequently at liberty to refuse to answer any question." Marshall expressed skepticism of that point. "There may be questions, no direct answer to which, could, in any degree, affect him," said the Chief Justice of Wilkinson, "and there is no case which goes so far as to say, that he is not bound to answer such questions."

Marshall then went on to say that "When two principles come in conflict with each other, the court must give them both a reasonable construction so as to preserve them both to a reasonable extent." Marshall's point deserves study. The entire system of American government, the way it is administered, the manner in which it dispenses justice, is built upon strong principles, many of which conflict with each other. How does one resolve these conflicts, choose which principle reigns supreme? Can a witness be compelled to testify, or can he refuse to incriminate himself? Is the dispute insoluble, or can the two principles be satisfied? The point raised by Wilkinson has been constantly raised in the operations of the American government. In the specific case before him Marshall solved the conflict by a strict adherence to the intentions of the two principles.

"To know and conceal the treason of another is misprision of treason, and is punishable by law. No witness, therefore, is compellable by law," said Marshall, "to disclose a fact which would form a necessary and essential part of this crime." He then said that if the letter were evidence of treason and if Wilkinson was acquainted with the letter's contents, "he may probably be guilty of misprision of treason; and, therefore, the court ought not to compel him to answer any question, the answer to which might disclose his former knowledge of the contents of that letter."

Before Wilkinson could enjoy a sigh of relief, however, Marshall hurried on. If the letter only related to the misdemeanor rather than to the treason, he said, then Wilkinson could not be involved in a crime. On considering the question propounded to Wilkinson, hearing it "more particularly and precisely stated, and finding that it refers only to the present knowledge of the cypher," it appeared to Marshall that the general could answer the question without danger of incriminating himself, "because, his present knowledge would not, it is believed, in a criminal prosecution, justify the inference, that his knowledge was acquired previous to this trial, or afford the means of proving that fact." In other words, if Wilkinson could understand the cipher in June of 1807, that was not proof he had understood it the previous fall. The answer then could not incriminate him, and he must answer the question. There was, of course, no question but that Wilkinson understood the cipher when he received the letter. He and Burr had been using it as early as 1800, according to Wilkinson, "to seek only legitimate objects of gratification."[57]

The point about Marshall's decision on this issue is that he was attempting to uphold both principles involved by refusing to allow either one to be interpreted loosely. If the phrase "strict construction" has any meaning when applied to the judiciary, it was exemplified by that decision. The court would not cheapen any principles that clashed before it; nor would it allow anyone invoking such principles to abuse them.

On June 25 the grand jury presented two bills, charging Burr and Blennerhassett with treason and with the misdemeanor; the members obviously were convinced of the truth of Thomas Jefferson's original charges. Naturally, Aaron Burr and his defense lawyers took the position that the indictments were based on trumped-up evidence. Their comments, however, have a ring of more than necessity about them. Luther Martin spoke at the end of the day, saying: "Persons have been tried for treason before in the United States." But in such cases, he asked, "Was the treasury of the United States thrown open and lavished to employ other counsel, in addition to the attorney for the United States, to prosecute?" He continued: "No persons were then employed to forestal the truth, by taking ex parte affidavits. But such trials," said Martin, his sarcasm and anger growing, "took place 'in the days of terror,' under that old dotard John Adams. Let us contrast it with the proceedings under the enlightened reign of philosophy and philanthropy." He then charged that "Money has been taken out of the treasury to employ two eminent lawyers to aid in the prosecution; compulsive affidavits have been taken; affidavit-men employed to take them, and witnesses brought by force, without relying on the process of the court as sufficient."[58]

Burr did not express his reaction to the indictments in the courtroom, but that night he wrote a letter to his daughter Theodosia. His analysis of the indictment, allowing for his bitterness, is reasonably accurate, and shows the basis of his upcoming defense:

> These indictments for treason are founded on the following allegations: that Colonel Tyler, with twenty or thirty men, stopped at Blennerhassett's Island on their way down the Ohio; that though these men were not armed, and had no military array or organization, and though they did neither use force nor threaten it, yet, having set out with a view of taking temporary possession of New Orleans on their way to Mexico, that such intent was

treasonable, and therefore a war was levied on Blennerhassett's Island by *construction;* and that, though Colonel
Burr was then at Frankfort on his way to Tennessee, yet,
having advised the measure, he was, *by construction of
law,* present at the island, and levied war there. In fact,
the indictment charges that Aaron Burr was on that day
present at the island, though not a man of the jury supposed this to be true.

Burr also charged that of the fifty witnesses who had
appeared before the grand jury, "it may be safely alleged that
thirty at least have been purjured." He closed that letter to his
daughter, the woman who had become his beloved confidante,
with a plea: "I beg and expect it of you that you will conduct
yourself as becomes my daughter, and that you manifest no signs
of weakness or alarm."[59]

There was a subsequent argument over whether Burr
should be held in the penitentiary or allowed to stay in private
but secured lodgings. The prosecution won and Burr was committed to the penitentiary on June 30 to await his trial beginning
August 3. More than three months had passed since Burr had
arrived in Richmond accompanied, as he phrased it, by his "military escort." Already the proceedings could be described as
lengthy, costly, and enervating. Still, his guilt or innocence had
not yet been determined before a court of law. All that had been
determined as the hot summer of 1807 began in Richmond was
that he should be tried. But this is not a failing of the American
legal system. Rather, it is its genius: that no man can be tried for
a serious crime without the most intense deliberation. The individual can rarely be abused under such a system, and when he is,
he has the opportunity to state his case before the public, as Burr
did.

The effectiveness of his presentation is evidenced by the
fact that despite his having been indicted by a grand jury of
Virginia's most eminent citizens and having been branded a
traitor by the President of the United States, Aaron Burr still
had many supporters who believed him innocent. Andrew Jackson, a soldier from the West, had been called to Richmond to give
testimony before the grand jury against Burr. But his belief in
Burr's innocence was so strong and his anger at what he considered Wilkinson's duplicity was so obvious that he was never
called to testify. "I am more convinced than ever that treason
never was intended by Burr," said Jackson.[60]

There were outcries against the indicted Burr, of course,
by persons who did not understand that an indictment is not a
conviction and should not be considered as such. At a July 4th

celebration in Maryland, for example, toasts were drunk to the members of the grand jury which had indicted Burr, congratulating them on their "zeal and patriotism in the cause of liberty" and hoping that they would have "a crown of immortal glory" and that their efforts would be "a death-wound to all conspirators." The same celebrants castigated Luther Martin, a former attorney general of their state, as "the mutual and highly respected friend of a convicted traitor." They urged for him "an honorable coat of tar, and a plumage of feathers." In Richmond also there were many who were reluctant to show friendship for Burr. Washington Irving reported: "It has almost been considered as culpable to evince towards him the least sympathy or support; and many a hollow hearted caitiff have I seen, who basked in the sunshine of his bounty, when in power, who now skulked from his side, and even mingled among the most clamorous of his enemies." Even in this atmosphere, Irving continued, there were many—particularly among the Richmond ladies—who were not afraid to express their sympathy for Burr and their hope for his acquittal. So many of Burr's friends, of both sexes, came to see him at the penitentiary that he confided to Theodosia that "It is well that I have an antechamber, or I should often be gêné with visitors."[61]

Even Thomas Jefferson believed that Burr ultimately would be acquitted. A few days after the indictment, Jefferson wrote to Du Pont de Nemours a revealing letter. In it, the President described Burr's alleged crime as "one of the most flagitious of which history will ever furnish an example." Jefferson then recounted the conspiracy as he understood it—an attempt to enlist men to separate the western lands. He also expressed his belief that the outcome—so few people joining Burr—was a reaffirmation "of the innate strength of the form of our government." More and more, Jefferson had come to view Burr's supposed conspiracy not only as a specific crime but also as a threat to the very existence and continuation of the United States, a threat blocked by Jefferson. Then Jefferson wrote: "Yet altho' there is not a man in the U.S. who is not satisfied of the depth of his guilt, such are the jealous provisions of our laws in favor of the accused, and against the accuser, that I question if he can be convicted. Out of 48 jurors who are to be summoned, he has a right to choose the 12 who are to try him, and if any one of the 12 refuses to concur in finding him guilty, he escapes."[62] Jefferson's description of the upcoming proceedings was accurate, and his phraseology—"jealous provisions . . . in favor of the accused" —is perfect. His obvious disdain for those provisions in this particular case shows that anyone can forget the purpose of the

American legal system. It is service to the individual, to protect him from the state. It is not service to the state, to protect it from the individual.

Burr was given three rooms on the third floor of the penitentiary, a spacious area, and he tried to make light of his situation to Theodosia. "My jailer is quite a polite and civil man," he wrote, "altogether unlike the idea one would form of a jailer. You would have laughed to have heard our compliments the first evening." He then reported this conversation:

JAILER: I hope, sir, it would not be disagreeable to you if I should lock this door after dark.

BURR: By no means, sir; I should prefer it, to keep out intruders.

JAILER: It is our custom, sir, to extinguish all lights at nine o'clock; I hope, sir, you will have no objection to conform to that.

BURR: That, sir, I am sorry to say, is impossible; for I never go to bed till twelve, and always burn two candles.

JAILER: Very well, sir, just as you please. I should have been glad if it had been otherwise; but, as you please, sir.

Burr added that even while he was writing, various servants had brought him messages as well as "oranges, lemons, pineapples, raspberries, apricots, cream, butter, ice and some ordinary articles."[63]

But Burr's incarceration was not as pleasant as he tried to make it appear to his daughter. The prison was about one and one-half miles from town, which meant that his lawyers would be unable to visit him as frequently as they could if he were in town. Washington Irving reported that the only reason Burr had been placed "in this abode of thieves, cutthroats, and incendiaries, was that it would save the United States a couple of hundred dollars," the cost of guarding him at lodgings in the city. Although Burr had written to Theodosia that he had many guests and his guards were most civil, Irving found gaining admission to Burr's cell extremely difficult, even for only a few moments. "The keeper had orders to admit none but his counsel and his witnesses —strange measure these!" he said. When Irving was allowed to enter for a few moments, he found that "Burr seemed in lower spirits than formerly; he was composed and collected as usual; but there was not the same cheerfulness that I have hitherto remarked." Burr told Irving that his servant could come to see him on occasion but only "with difficulty." He had a bad cold, "a result of the dampness of his cell." When Irving left, it was, he said, with a "heavy heart . . . and I never felt in a more melancholy mood than when I rode from his solitary prison."[64]

On Saturday, August 1, Aaron Burr was removed from the penitentiary outside of Richmond and brought to heavily guarded rooms in the city in preparation for the trial. On Monday, August 3, Chief Justice John Marshall called the court to order at twelve o'clock to begin the trial of Aaron Burr. The courtroom itself was packed and the streets were crowded with spectators, all shoving to see the participants in what promised to be a great historical event. The business of the trial began quickly, and then as quickly disintegrated into trifles. The names of one hundred witnesses were called as well as a long list of potential jurors. Then the lawyers fell into lengthy discussions of procedures, discussions that droned on for the entire first week.

A concern arising during this week was whether an impartial jury could be obtained. This concern had also existed during the selection of the grand jury, and it had become a more severe problem as the publicity about Burr's situation had grown. The arguments between defense and prosecution lawyers had gone on for some time when Marshall, on Monday, August 10, interrupted to say that "it might save some altercation, if the court were to deliver its opinion at the present time." His comments during the next two days have become a model for a judge's attitude toward the jury selection process. "That a juryman should come to a trial of a man for life, with a perfect freedom from previous impression," Marshall said, ". . . was certainly one of the clearest principles of natural justice." Also, it was the court's duty, if possible, to obtain men free from bias. Marshall then asked if anyone could be an impartial juror who has declared he believes the accused guilty "but has not heard the testimony." This, Marshall said, is unacceptable because "it manifests a bias that completely disqualified himself from the functions of a juryman."

But then Marshall pointed out that it was "too general" to ask whether a prospective juror has "impressions" about Burr. "The impressions may be so light," said Marshall, "that they do not amount to an opinion of guilt; nor do they go to the extent of believing, that the prisoner deserves capital punishment." The Chief Justice then summed up this day's arguments: "If a juryman were to declare that the attempt to achieve the dismemberment of the union, was treason, it would not be a complete objection or disqualification; but it would be the application of that crime to a particular individual; it would be fixing it on Aaron Burr that would disable him from serving in this case."[65]

The next day, Tuesday, August 11, Marshall returned to this subject. "The jury should enter upon the trial," he said, "with minds open to those impressions, which the testimony and the law of the case ought to make, not with those preconceived opinions, which will resist those impressions." Why refuse to seat a person with personal prejudices? "The law will not trust him," said Marshall, because the law cannot accept that he can be impartial. Marshall then asked, "Is there less reason to suspect him who has prejudged the case, and had deliberately formed and delivered an opinion upon it?" Marshall acknowledged that the individual may believe he will be responsive only to the testimony, "but the law suspects him, and certainly not without reason." The person who has prejudged the case, said Marshall, will listen "with more favour to that testimony which confirms, than to that which would change his opinion: it is not to be expected that he will weigh evidence or argument as fairly as a man whose judgment is not made up in the case." But what of a situation in which a prospective juror had formed an opinion "not upon the full case, but upon an essential part of it, not that the prisoner is absolutely guilty of the whole crime charged in the indictment, but that he is guilty in some of those great points, which constitute it." The answer to this, Marshall concluded, must "always depend, on the strength and nature of the opinion which has been formed."[66]

The next Monday, August 17, the jury finally was selected, two weeks after the trial had begun. The clerk of the court then read the indictment, about how Aaron Burr, "being moved and seduced by the instigation of the devil," worked to create an insurrection by organizing a group of men on Blennerhassett's island with the intention of moving down the Mississippi and capturing New Orleans. When the indictment was done, George Hay, the prosecution's chief attorney, rose and said that the actual gathering of men to make war was in fact a levying of war. "I trust," he said, "that I have shewn, that the reason is completed the very instant that they assemble together with a treasonable design."[67] Hay was quoting the decision John Marshall had handed down months earlier in the case of Bollman and Swartwout. "If war be actually levied," Marshall had said then, ". . . if a body of men be actually assembled, for the purpose of affecting by force a treasonable purpose, all those who perform any part, however minute, or however remote from the scene of action, and who are actually leagued in the general conspiracy, are to be considered as traitors." The prosecution was on an eminently sound basis in using Marshall's own words as the basis for their arguments.

The next day, Tuesday, August 18, the court finally would be able to hear testimony on the alleged conspiracy. Of course, events outside the courtroom had been leading up to this moment for weeks. William Eaton was in Richmond, dressed in "a tremendous hat, with a Turkish sash over colored clothes." To Blennerhassett, languishing in a Richmond jail, Eaton had become "a ridiculous mountebank" who strutted about the streets of Richmond when he was not drinking in the taverns. Eaton still was slated to be one of the chief witnesses against Burr, Blennerhassett, and the alleged conspiracy. Blennerhassett was having difficulty keeping up his spirits. In addition to appearing to be at the mercy of braggarts like Eaton, he heard other disturbing reports. One came from a friend, a Colonel de Pestre. The colonel, who had a relative in the office of the American Secretary of War, reported unpleasant stories of an administration attempt to purchase support in the Burr trial by making handsome provision in the army for soldiers. Nor could Blennerhassett be sanguine of success at the trial. He was naturally counting on Burr's adroitness as a lawyer, but less hopefully after a visit by Edmund Randolph, one of the defense lawyers. Randolph could not understand how Burr allowed a juror named Richard E. Parker to go unchallenged. At the interrogation of prospective jurors, Parker had said that if the newspaper accounts he had read were true, then Burr was guilty, and Burr had said he had no objection to Parker's being on the jury. Randolph told Blennerhassett that Parker was known as "a violent Jeffersonian partisan."

But most disturbing to Blennerhassett was a visit on Sunday, August 16, two days before witnesses were first to be heard in the trial, by General Edward Tupper. Tupper was the army officer who had led the arrest party on Blennerhassett's island, and Blennerhassett at first was concerned that Tupper had come as an enemy. "The news of his arrival in town . . . must have caused some little mental uneasiness last night and this morning, of which I was unable to render an account to myself. This intelligence could not reach my ears without arriving in the same instant at my heart." But when Tupper visited him, it was apparent that the former enemy had been converted into a friend. This is Blennerhassett's account of what Tupper told him:

> It seems much of the artifice of intrigue, on the part of the government or their runners, has been but in requisition to endeavor to mold the General's disposition in the temper of the present prosecutions. He has next encountered attempts upon his honor indirectly, to induce him in some degree to countenance the testimonies of Taylor

and Albright to the facts of his having arrested me, with my rescue and escape from him . . . [and] outrages upon his character and feelings, which he has repelled with that disgust and contempt suggested by his honor, but not without thereby incurring, what, until then, the conservators of Jeffersonian fame never thought of, insinuations of his concern, and threats to involve him in the pains and penalties of the conspiracy. Either before or after this analysis of the stuff, which would not take the dye, proposed, it was politely signified to him, that although he had been recognized as a witness, on the part of the United States, the prosecutors, in kind consideration of the inconvenience another journey might do to him, would dispense with his further attendance. He said, however, he would return were he obliged to travel on his hands and knees.[68]

Tupper, in fact, was not called to testify at the trial although he was in Richmond during the entire time.

On Tuesday, August 18, General William Eaton took the stand. Eaton was a curious man. He was now forty-three years old and would die in another four years from the excesses of his lifestyle. He had been a soldier of fortune, a member of the military, a diplomat, a man both honored and disgraced. Desperate for funds, he was seeking payment for his services in the Mediterranean area, and the payment would come but with both the government and Eaton denying that it had anything to do with his testimony against Burr. Even as he was called, there was a dispute over whether he could take the stand because his testimony went to the intentions of Burr rather than to any act. Marshall ruled that the court must "permit the counsel for the United States to proceed to shew the intention of the act, in order to enable the jury to decide upon the fact, coupled with his intention."

When Eaton took the stand, he began in a blunt manner. "Concerning any overt act . . . I know nothing," he said. "Concerning certain transactions which are said to have happened at Blennerhassett's Island . . . I know nothing." Before anyone thought he might be appearing for the defense, Eaton hurried on: But concerning Colonel Burr's expressions of treasonable intentions, I know much, and it is to these, that my evidence relates. . . ."

Eaton then explained that Burr had approached him about an expedition into Mexico. Eaton explained that he had become suspicious and attempted to learn more about Burr's plans. "Colonel Burr now laid open his project of revolutionizing the territory west of the Allegany," said Eaton, "establishing an independent empire there; New Orleans to be the capital, and he himself to be the chief organizing a military force on the waters of the Mississippi, and carrying conquest to Mexico." Eaton testified that when he suggested obstacles to such a grandiose plan, Burr merely scoffed at them, saying he had traveled the territory and had obtained local support from most of the most prominent persons there.

Burr's lawyers made no secret of their attempt to undermine Eaton's testimony by attacking his credibility. Luther Martin inquired about Eaton's bill for his services in the Mediterranean, a bill which had gone unpaid for months until after Eaton had spoken out against Burr. "What balance did you receive?" Martin wanted to know. Eaton refused to answer and when Martin insisted, Eaton turned to Marshall to ask: "Is that a proper question?" Burr, replacing Martin, quickly explained that he wished to show that "bias" existed on Eaton's part. Marshall allowed the question.

"I cannot say to a cent or a dollar," Eaton answered, "but I have received about $10,000."

"When was the money received?" Burr continued.

"About March 1st."

Burr then dropped the point, allowing the jury to determine for itself whether Eaton's testimony might have been influenced by that payment. He then asked about Eaton's charge that Burr claimed to have a command. Eaton's answer was a heated one. "You stated," he said to Burr, "what I have already mentioned, that you were assured, from the arrangements which you had made, that an army would be ready to appear, when you went to the waters of the western country. I recollect particularly the name of Ephraim Kirby, who had been a ranger in general Wayne's army. You asked me about his spirit. You gave me to understand that his brigade was ready to join you, and that the people also in that country were ready to engage with you in the enterprise. You spoke of *your* riflemen, *your* infantry, *your* cavalry. It was with the same view, you mentioned to me that that man . . ."—at this point Eaton pointed to Wilkinson who was seated in the courtroom behind Burr—"was to have been the first to aid you . . ." Eaton paused, then apologized to the court for the emotion of his remarks. The outburst had been an effective one.

But Burr was an adroit attorney, a brilliant courtroom dramatist. After the heat of the Eaton outburst had subsided, Burr recalled that Eaton had testified to recommending him for a diplomatic post. "Was it after all this that you recommended me to the president, for an embassy?" The implication of the question is clear: how could Eaton recommend such a traitor for an important diplomatic post?

Eaton conceded that he had made the recommendation to Jefferson after having heard the details of the alleged plot, and said to Burr that he did so "to remove you, as you were a dangerous man, because I thought it the only way to avert a civil war."

The Burr-Eaton confrontation trailed off after that, but Burr had succeeded in raising for the jury the question which has since hung over Eaton's role in the conspiracy, for Eaton claimed to have heard Burr threaten to kill the President and to lead a revolt in the western lands, and yet he acknowledged never reporting this. Burr had sown doubt among the jurors.[69]

Blennerhassett wrote in his journal two days later that the Jeffersonian newspapers in Richmond, the *Argus* and the *Inquirer*, praised Eaton's testimony and his appearance as a witness. But Blennerhassett wrote that more objective witnesses said that Eaton "strutted more in buskin than usual on that occasion, and the effect was as diverting to the whole court as it probably was beneficial to the defense."[70]

The next witness that day was Thomas Truxton, the American naval hero whose testimony was similar to his earlier statements and whose account buttressed Burr's explanations of the alleged conspiracy. According to the account Truxton gave the court, Burr contemplated an attack on Mexico (the misdemeanor) but not an effort to separate the western lands from the United States (the treason charge). Burr never said that the President of the United States was privy to the scheme, and the entire plan was predicated on the United States being involved in a war with Spain. If the war did not materialize, then Burr's plan was to settle some western lands.

When Truxton finished his account, Burr asked him: "Were we not in terms of intimacy? Was there any reserve on my part, in our frequent conversations; and did you ever hear me express any intention or sentiment respecting a division of the union?"

Truxton replied: "We were very intimate. There seemed to be no reserve on your part. I never heard you speak of a division of the union."[71] If Truxton had in fact been involved in a treasonable scheme with Burr, the testimony he gave was then improper and self-serving; but there is no reason to believe that this man who had fought brilliantly for his country was giving false testimony that day. His appearance was a point for the defense.

The next witness, however, was not quite as kind to Burr. This was a General John Morgan, who told of being visited by Burr almost a year earlier. Morgan testified:

> After a few words of general conversation, colonel Burr observed to me, that the union of the states could not possibly last; and that a separation of the states must ensue as a natural consequence, in four or five years. Colonel Burr made many inquiries of me, relative to the county of Washington; particularly the state of its militia; its strength,. arms accoutrements, and the character of its officers. These conversations continued some time, besides other things, which I cannot recollect, because I did not expect to be called upon in this way. After travelling some miles, we met one of my workmen, a well-looking young man. Colonel Burr said, he wished he had ten thousand such fellows. At my father's table, during dinner, colonel Burr again observed, that the separation of the union must take place inevitably, in less than five years. . . . Colonel Burr in the course of the conversation at the dinner table, observed, that with two hundred men, he could drive the president and congress into the Potowmac; and with four or five hundred he could take possession of the city of New York.

In his cross-examination Burr did not challenge the details of Morgan's testimony but tried to suggest that it should not be taken seriously. "Do you remember the manner in which I introduced the subject you allude to?" Burr asked. "Was it in the course of a lively conversation? Was there any thing very serious in it?"

Morgan answered: "You only mentioned it in a lively or careless manner."[72]

The next witness was Jacob Allbright, a workman on Blennerhassett's island, who was one of the most important witnesses the prosecution had. "Our object is to prove by his testimony," said George Hay, "the actual assemblage of men on Blennerhassett's island, and it goes of course to prove directly the overt act."

Allbright then testified that he had worked on the island, building a kiln for corn, and "after working some time, Mrs. Blennerhassett told me, that Mr. Blennerhassett and colonel Burr were going to lay in provisions for an army for a year." Allbright then testified that Blennerhassett "asked me first and foremost, whether I would not join with him and go down the river." He quoted Blennerhassett as saying: "Mr. Allbright, we are going to settle a new country." To this point, Allbright's testimony was

meaningless, demonstrating only that the Blennerhassetts anticipated a large number of people congregating on the island and
that the probable object of these people was "to settle" undeveloped lands. There was nothing either treasonable or remotely
illegal in such a possibility. Even his comment that Burr had at
one time been present on the island did not suffice as proof of an
illegal act. The next section of his testimony, however, was different.

"A man by the name of Tupper, laid his hands upon Blennerhassett, and said, 'Your body is in my hands, in the name of
the commonwealth.' Some *such words* as that he mentioned," Allbright testified. This was the General Edward Tupper who had
visited Blennerhassett a few days earlier in jail and who would
not be called as a prosecution witness. Allbright continued that
when Tupper issued that arrest order, "there were seven or eight
muskets leveled at him." Against this show of force, Tupper
backed down—as Allbright told the story—and said, "Gentlemen,
I hope you will not do the like." When one of the men holding a
musket said that he was as mind to shoot Tupper as not, Tupper
said he had no hesitation about allowing Blennerhassett to escape
downriver.

Allbright's testimony was important because it perhaps
established an overt act of treason—men pointing muskets at an
officer come to arrest them. The Constitution, however, requires
two witnesses to an act of treason for conviction. If the incident
were true, there was a corroborative witness, Tupper himself.
The fact that Tupper never was called is the most credible argument against the prosecution's case.

Tupper had filed a deposition in Ohio on his role in the
events on Blennerhassett's island, a deposition that was discovered and reported some years later by a pair of Burr's biographers.
In it Tupper said he had gone to the island by invitation and not
to arrest anyone, that he had not been molested by anyone, nor
had anyone leveled a musket or pointed any other weapon at him.
Tupper's version is that he arrived on the island late in the evening to collect some money Blennerhassett owed him. All the
weapons he saw were two pairs of pistols, "a coarse sword," and
some daggers possessed by a few of the men. When Tupper
arrived, Blennerhassett was anticipating the arrival of the militia
to arrest him. In his deposition Tupper said he urged Blennerhassett to stay and surrender himself to the militia, but Blennerhassett replied that he was afraid of physical harm by
uncontrollable militiamen. Tupper then said he watched as Blennerhassett and the men left the island, and Tupper quoted Blennerhassett as saying that "we shall surrender ourselves to the civil

authority whenever it shall present itself; our object is both lawful and honorable as respects the United States."[73] That deposition, of course, tears the prosecution's case apart. Whether the government lawyers knew Tupper would refute their case or whether they had another reason for not calling him is not known. All that is known is that he was not called.

The first day's testimony had not been slow. There had been Eaton with his rumblings about a sinister plot, Truxton with his denials of a treasonous plan, Morgan with his report on alleged conversations a year old, and Allbright with his unconfirmed story of muskets being levied to block an arrest. Also it was evident that Burr was conducting his own defense. He not only was discussing his case with his lawyers but was actually managing their whole presentation as well as handling most of the cross-examination himself.[74] He was facing the prosecution strategy of tailoring the case to Marshall's decision in the Bolman-Swartwout case. If the prosecution could prove that a treasonable act had taken place, then Burr would be guilty because he had been involved in the adventure although he was not actually on the island at the time. "All those who perform any part . . . however remote from the scene of action" are guilty, Marshall had said then.

The next day, Thursday, John Wickham rose for the defense to counter the prosecution's assertion that Aaron Burr could be guilty of engaging in an act of treason although he was hundreds of miles away at the time the act took place. His argument lasted three days, and is a brilliant *tour de force*. Whatever the politics involved in the Burr case, in this presentation the subject was law only. In his first paragraph Wickham asserted that it was "distinctly admitted" that Burr was "hundreds of miles distant from the scene of action" when the "war is said to have been levied against the United States"—this was the gathering at Blennerhassett's island the previous December.

"The first position I shall lay down," said Wickham, apparently in a bold and calculated attack on the Chief Justice's decision in the Bollman-Swartwout case, "is that no person can be convicted of treason in levying war, who was not personally present at the commission of the act." Wickham then charged that "artificial rules of construction, drawn from the common law and the usages of courts in construing statutes" were being used to give the words of the Constitution "an artificial meaning, drawn from the statute and common law of England." In this argument Wickham underlined the importance of the Burr case, the importance not for Burr but for the nation. The English theory of constructive treason allowed a person to be tried and convicted although he had not participated in the act. It had been used against political opponents, and Wickham was insisting here that to allow the transporting of that English system to the United States would permit the use of the treason law against political opposition.

He argued that the English system could not be relied on in an American federal court. "Under the federal constitution," he said, "I presume, it will hardly be contended by the counsel for the prosecution, that we have any common law, belonging to the United States at large." The Jeffersonians, of course, long had argued that the federal judiciary did not incorporate the common law but had only such authority as the judges could find in the Constitution, a position which John Marshall also had taken. Nor would Wickham accept that, because the federal courts operating in one state had adopted the laws of that state as their rules of procedure, the treason laws of that state applied to federal offenses. "With respect to crimes and offences against the United States, which must be punished in a uniform manner, throughout the Union, it seems clear . . . that none can exist at common law," he said. He continued: "Unquestionably the gentlemen will not deny this uniformity; they will not contend that what is treason in Maryland is not treason in Virginia, or vice versa. If it exist at all, it must be uniform, embracing the whole of the United States."

Wickham said that an act of treason against the United States could not be punished without there being a statutory act "extending throughout the United States." Wickham then referred to the Marshall opinion in the Bollman-Swartwout case as attempting to settle the matter contrary to what he had just said. Rarely has a lawyer appearing before a particular judge argued against that judge's previous decisions, as Wickham did at this moment. "I deny the legislative effect of a decision of the Supreme Court," he said. He called the Marshall ruling "a mere *dictum* or an expression thrown out in argument without consideration" and said it should not be accepted as authority.

Citing the Bollman-Swartwout case specifically, Wickham acknowledged that there "is reported to have fallen from the chief justice" a *dictum* which was in opposition to Wickham's point. He then argued that the decision did not rest on that point, "a determination of that question, one way or the other, would have no effect on the judgment: it was therefore extrajudicial." Wickham now turned boldly to Marshall. "Your honour," he said, "can set me right if I be mistaken; but I believe the point now relied on by the prosecution, either did not come before the court, or was very slightly touched on by the bar."

Wickham then went on to another point, also important in the struggle to prevent treason laws from being used to silence political opposition. "I lay it down as a rule that cannot be controverted," said Wickham, who obviously did not believe in being apologetic, "that even if aiders and abettors in treason be considered as principals, yet their guilt is derivative, and can only be established by legal proof, that the persons whose acts they are answerable for, have committed treason." The point does seem obvious. To prove Burr guilty of treason, the prosecution should first establish that Blennerhassett and the others on the island were guilty; it seemed silly to charge Burr with aiding men involved in treason without their having been convicted of the treasonable act. Wickham summed up this argument with this paragraph, and in doing so, articulated a reasonable rule of law:

> Unless the record of the condemnation of some persons who are proved to be traitors be produced, and the connexion between them and colonel Burr be proved, no other proof is admissible or can be received. That this is the rule in all felonies is beyond all question; the accessory never can be convicted until the principal be found guilty; and a record of the conviction of the principal must be produced on the trial of the accessory.

On the next day Wickham attacked the prosecution's failure to call Tupper. He began by challenging the veracity of Allbright. "It is impossible," he said, "that this man's testimony can be true." Even if it were, he said, the testimony of one man was not sufficient under the Constitution to prove an overt act of treason; testimony by two witnesses was needed. And why didn't the prosecution call Tupper? Wickham's answer: "They would have examined him, if they had believed that he would have confirmed Allbright's evidence. Their not doing it, proves that they thought he would have contradicted Allbright."

Wickham also pointed out that even if the Allbright story were true, there was nothing to suggest that Tupper produced a warrant when he supposedly attempted to arrest Blennerhassett. Wickham argued that "Blennerhassett had a right to resist, if Tupper had no warrant; and this evidence of his arresting a man is without the production of any authority whatever; and yet this is called resistance to law." And if that were not enough, Wickham also said that resistance to arrest—if that is what happened—may be "a great offence" but "is not treason."[75]

John Marshall was, of course, aware that the issues coming before him for decision would become part of the law of the land for generations to come, and he apparently sought the advice of the other Supreme Court Justices. At least, his appeal to William Cushing has survived. "It has been my fate to be engaged in the trial of a person whose case presents many real intrinsic difficulties which are infinitely multiplied by extrinsic circumstances." The first question Marshall wished to discuss with his fellow Justices was whether the testimony of two witnesses was necessary to indict for treason. He conceded in his letter to Cushing that he had waited too long to ask the question, as Burr and the others had already been indicted. But there were other questions "on which I most anxiously desire the aid of all the Judges."

One was how far the doctrine of constructive treason should be applied in the United States; this was the crux of the Burr case. "If a body of men assemble for a treasonable purpose," asked Marshall, "does this implicate all those who are concerned in the conspiracy whether acquainted with the assembly or not? Does it implicate those who advised, directed or approved of it? Or does it implicate those only who were present or within the district?"

He acknowledged that his own opinion in the Bollman and Swartwout case "certainly adopts the doctrine of constructive treason. . . . Ought the expressions in that opinion to be revised?"

After raising several other points brought up by the Burr trial, Marshall said that he was aware of the unwillingness of a judge to commit himself by an opinion on a case not before him. "Could this case be readily carried into the Supreme Court," Marshall said, "I would not ask an opinion in its present stage. But these questions must be decided by the Judges separately on their respective circuits, and I am sure there would be a strong and general repugnance to giving contradictory decisions on the same points."[76]

The significance of that letter is twofold. First it challenges the picture of John Marshall as an arrogant leader of the federal judiciary who sought to impose his predilections on his brethren. The letter is an obvious attempt to solicit advice by one in need of assistance. The second point is that Marshall was protective of the judiciary. He did not believe it would be good practice for the Supreme Court judges on their circuits to handle similar issues in different manners. That would provide ammunition to the Court's critics and also be destructive of the relationship between judges. Thomas Jefferson may have thought of John Marshall as a political opponent, but John Marshall at this time obviously thought of himself as a judge.

The last week of the trial began Monday, August 24, and

was marked more by oratory than by further elucidation of the issues. Alexander McRae began the verbal flourishes with: "The prisoner has never been regarded as an accessory before the fact. He is the first mover of the plot; he planned it, he matured it; he contrived the doing of the overt acts which others have done. He was the *Alpha* and *Omega* of this treasonable scheme, the very body and soul, the very life of this treason."[77] The next day Benjamin Botts, a defense lawyer, decided to have some fun with the imagery the prosecution had been using in its attacks on Burr. Botts' speech is interesting not so much for its insight into law as for its insight into the practice of law in the early 1800s. This is an excerpt:

> I cannot promise you, sir, a speech manufactured out of tropes and figures. Instead of the magnificent image of Bonaparte ascending to quench the stars, so fitted for the dry law question in debate, my humble efforts will be altogether below the clouds. Instead of the introduction of a sleeping Venus with all the luxury of voluptuous and wanton nakedness to charm the reason through the refined medium of sensuality, and to convince us that the law of treason is with the prosecution by leading our imagination to the fascinating richness and symmetry of a heaving bosom and luscious waist, I am compelled to plod heavily and meekly on through the dull doctrines of Hale and Foster. So far though from reproving the gentleman's excitement of the boiling blood of such of us are in the heyday of youth, without the previous caution of clearing the hall of those whose once panting desires have been chilled by age, and upon whom the forced ecstasy sat unnaturally and uneasily, I only lament my utter incapacity to elicit topics of legal science by an imitation of so novel and tempting an example. Nothing but the impossibility of success would prevent me also from grasping at the fame and glory on this grave occasion, and at this time of pleasure, of enriching the leering lasciviousness of a like bewildering thought, to transport anew the old and the young.[78]

There is a tradition in Richmond that the Botts speech produced gales of laughter in the courtroom, and that even John Marshall relaxed his dignity and showed his amusement. Although there is no documentary proof, it is a safe assumption that the tradition is accurate.

As in any trial, at times the arguments between lawyers became heated. At one point Benjamin Botts and William Wirt got into a dispute over Wirt's statement that the men on Blenner-hassett's island were Burr's men because he had enlisted them and they called him their leader while he called them his followers. According to the transcript of the trial, "Here a desultory conversation ensued between Mr. Botts and Mr. Wirt, in which some warm and animated observations were made respecting the evidence and Mr. Wirt's comments thereon. The Chief Justice observed, that the evidence was such that different gentlemen might draw different inferences from it. Their warmth then subsided, and their former amity and good humour returned."[79]

On Friday, August 28, Luther Martin rose to speak for the defense. He spoke for two days and his speech covers 118 pages, or almost one-tenth of the entire Richmond proceedings. His points were cogent, well organized, and effective. His presentation was one of the great courtroom speeches by a lawyer in the history of American law.

The prosecution had sought English precedents for establishing its claim that there was a doctrine known as "constructive treason." Said Luther Martin: "It has been repeatedly declared in our courts that the decisions in Great Britain, however entitled to respect, are not binding authority in this country; and I thank God that this is the case. The principles laid down in Great Britain respecting treason, as appears from the history of their jurisprudence, have been such, that their judges have in the most arbitrary manner carried into execution the most wicked wishes of the persons who held the crown. Even after the revolution of the year 1688, this has been the case, though not so much as formerly; they have extended the rules of evidence, with respect to treason, so as to shock humane judges."

To the prosecution's claim that the act of levying war could have happened without the Burr forces firing a shot, Martin said: "I mean to say that actual force must be used by them, to make them guilty of the treason of levying war against the government. . . . This is my opinion of the law. But admit that it is doubtful; if there be a doubt the court is bound to decide in favour of life. But as to the necessity of force to constitute levying war, I defy the gentlemen to say the contrary, whatever may be jumbled together in the books. But I call on gentlemen to shew or find a single case where a person indicted for levying war, in Great Britain was convicted without proof of his having committed actual violence."

In addition to precedents, Martin used sarcasm in his approach. "We have had two insurrections in Pennsylvania: the one named the *whiskey insurrection*, and the other the *hot* water insurrection. If I were to name this," he told the court, "I would call it the *will o' the wisp* treason. For though it is said to be here and there and every where, *yet it is no where.* It exists only in the newspapers and in the mouths of the enemies of the gentlemen for whom I appear, who get it put into the newspapers."

Martin acknowledged that there had been witnesses claiming to speak of Burr's intentions but he pointed out that such testimony should not be considered as convincing evidence under the Constitution because of that document's requirement that such intentions must be admitted in open court by the person accused. "They can be easily feigned against him by an enemy to gratify his resentment," said Martin, continuing: "If a thousand persons were to come forward and prove such confessions or acknowledgments on the part of the accused, they ought not to be admitted as evidence against him; because however contrary to the truth they might be, they are in their nature incapable of being disproved."

Then Martin specified the points he was making to John Marshall as the presiding justice. Restating that the charge was levying war against the United States while on Blennerhassett's island, Martin asked Marshall to rule that testimony pertaining to any events off the island be excluded; that such testimony already given be ruled insufficient; and that such testimony scheduled to be given be ruled irrelevant. Martin was, in effect, asking that the Chief Justice construe the law as narrowly as possible in favor of the accused. The public climate was, of course, against construing the law in Burr's favor.

Martin alluded to this as he closed his marathon presentation. "We are unfortunately situated," he said. "We labour against great prejudices against my client, which tend to prevent him from having a fair trial." Part of what he was saying was obviously for dramatic effect, but part accurately reflected the fears and prejudices of the moment:

> I have with pain heard it said that such are the public prejudices against colonel Burr, that a jury, even should it be satisfied with his innocence, must have considerable firmness of mind to pronounce him not guilty. I have heard it not without horror. God of heaven! have we already under our form of government—which we have so often been told is best calculated of all governments to secure all our rights—arrived at a period when a trial in a court of justice, where life is at stake, shall be but a solemn mockery, a mere idle form and ceremony to transfer innocence from the gaol to the gibbet, to gratify popular indignation excited by bloodthirsty enemies!

Martin, as well as John Marshall and everyone else in the courtroom, knew that as much of a problem as the jury had, the presiding justice also had; perhaps he had an even greater one.

In his closing paragraph Martin again addressed both the
jury members and Marshall. Although this paragraph amuses
because of its florid language, it still serves as a reminder to those
charged with dispensing justice that they serve a cause nobler
than public clamor. Said Luther Martin:

> When the sun mildly shines upon us, when the gentle
> zephyrs play around us, we can easily proceed forward in
> the straight path of our duty; but when bleak clouds en-
> shroud the sky with darkness, when the tempest rages,
> the winds howl and the waves break over us—when the
> thunders awfully roar over our heads and the lightnings of
> heaven blaze around us—it is *then* that all the energies of
> the human soul are called into action. It is *then* that the
> truly brave man stands firm at his post. It is *then* that by
> unshaken performance of his duty, man approaches the
> nearest possible to the divinity. Nor is there any object
> in the creation on which the supreme Being can look down
> with more delight and approbation than on a human being
> in such a situation and thus acting. May that God who
> now looks down upon us, who has in his infinite wisdom
> called you into existence and placed you in that seat to
> dispense justice to your fellow citizens, to preserve and
> protect innocence against persecution—may that God so
> illuminate your understandings that you may *know* what
> is right; and may he nerve your souls with firmness and
> fortitude to *act* according to that knowledge.[80]

Martin's speech had made it impossible for John Marshall
to ignore the moral implications of his decision, whatever it
might be. Martin's speech had also underscored that the basis of
law is morality. Law is demanding and men must be courageous
to enforce it. But when the demands are met and the men are
brave, the rewards are permanent. The law now was demanding
and the question was whether John Marshall would be brave.

Because of the politics of the situation the difficulties were
enormous. Nathaniel Macon, Speaker of the House of Representatives and a friend of Jefferson's, had commented a few weeks
earlier that "The court begins to be talked about in pretty harsh
terms, so much new law or old new law has been discovered...."[81]

The Sunday following Martin's speech most persons in
Richmond speculated on what Marshall would say the next day
when the court reconvened. As Blennerhassett described a con-

versation between himself and some friends, there was "no other object so natural to engage our interest as a comparison of the foundation of different conjectures respecting decision the Chief Justice will deliver tomorrow on those points which have so long balanced this town between law and faction."[82] How Marshall decided would, of course, greatly influence the outcome of the trial. The jury would be influenced by his description of the testimony given and his limitation, if any, on future testimony, and also by any other comments he made. There also was speculation on how Marshall would deal with his earlier decision in the Bollman-Swartwout case. The defense lawyers had described it as pure dicta, but Marshall could not easily dismiss his own words and still retain respect for himself and his court.

The specific questions before John Marshall were the relevancy of testimony already given or to be given, but the essence of the point was how narrowly Marshall would construe the law. Luther Martin had made everyone understand there could be no evasion.

Marshall wrote his decision over the weekend; he had no more than Saturday evening, all day Sunday, and perhaps some time Monday morning. It is approximately twenty-five thousand words long, and like all Marshall decisions is in some instances repetitious. (In those days of the quill pen, the first draft usually was the last draft.)

He began reading it to the courtroom that Monday, August 31, with the utmost courtesy in his manner. "The question now to be decided has been argued in a manner worthy of its importance," said Marshall, "and with an earnestness evincing the strong conviction felt by the counsel on each side that the law is with them." He praised the counselors for "a degree of eloquence" seldom seen and "a depth of research" which greatly aided the court in forming its opinion. Marshall then stated the motion by the defense, that any testimony connecting Burr with those who committed the alleged act of treason on Blennerhassett's island be dismissed as irrelevant because Burr's absence from the island at the time of the alleged act was acknowledged.

Marshall went on to define treason as "levying war," but found some difference between the American constitutional and English traditional views. In England, he said, a person could be indicted either for levying war or for assisting to levy war, for being either the principal or the accessory. But in the United States, "the terms of the constitution comprise no question respecting principal and accessory," he said. The logical conclusion to draw from those remarks—and this decision like all Marshall decisions grew logically from step to step—was "that those who perform a part in the prosecution of the war may correctly be said to levy war and to commit treason under the constitution." Marshall quickly added that he was excluding "the case of a person who performs no act in the prosecution of the war—who counsels and advises it—or who, being engaged in the conspiracy, fails to perform his part." His addition made quite clear he was talking about the committing of an act, not the conspiracy to commit such an act or sympathy with such an act.

He then turned to his comments in the Bollman and Swartwout decision, that "all those who perform any part, however minute, or however remote from the scene of action, and who are actually leagued in the general conspiracy, are to be considered as traitors." Marshall conceded this was dicta, but he attempted to justify it by saying that the judges might have to act on similar cases while on their circuits, and that "it was not surprising then that they should have made some attempt to settle principles which would probably occur." One feels Marshall stretching here for justification; usually judges refrain from enunciating basic principles of law until such time as they have heard the issue argued before them and a decision cannot be avoided. He then acknowledged that the defense had suggested that the Bollman-Swartwout dicta be ignored. "For myself," said Marshall, "I can say that I could not lightly be prevailed on to disobey it, were I even convinced that it was erroneous." His alternative, Marshall said, was to allow the issue to go before the Supreme Court again if that were possible.

To this point, Marshall's comments appeared to incline toward the prosecution. That there was no difference between an accessory and a principal and that the accused did not have to be present at the moment of the treason—the principles he had just enunciated—were the basis of the prosecution's case. Then, however, Marshall drew the line. "Those only who perform a part and who are leagued in the conspiracy are declared to be traitors," he said. "To complete the definition both circumstances must concur. They must 'perform a part,' which will furnish the overt act; and they must be 'leagued in the conspiracy.' The person who comes within this description in the opinion of the court levies war." This understanding, Marshall then insisted, did not affect the defense motion: "if [Burr] did perform any part, the court could not stop the testimony in its present stage." There was the first clue to Marshall's thinking, that he was going to suggest that it had not been demonstrated that Burr, despite any testimony linking him with vague intention and plans, had been tied to the specific acts which made up the alleged conspiracy.

Marshall insisted that force must be part of the levying

war process. "War is an appeal from reason to the sword," he said, "and he who makes the appeal evidences the fact by the use of the means. His intention to go to war may be proved by words; but the actual going to war is a fact which is to be proved by open deed. The end is to be effected by force; and it would seem that in cases where no declaration is to be made, the state of actual war could only be created by the employment of force or being in a condition to employ it." Marshall next argued that the dicta in the Bollman-Swartwout decision did not refute that basic thesis, that force must either be used or be ready for use.

Marshall came to his crucial point: if an act of treason on the island cannot be proved, then it cannot be proved that a person connected with the events on the island had committed treason. "Admitting such an indictment could be supported by some evidence," he said, "the previous conviction of some person, who committed the act which is said to amount to levying war, is indispensable to the conviction of a person who advised or procured that act." He restated that point for emphasis: "In point of law then, the man, who incites, aids or procures a treasonable act, is not merely in consequence of that incitement, aid or procurement, legally present when that act is committed." Either Burr was present "actually or constructively" when the alleged act took place or else "he who procures an act" may be indicted as if he had performed such act.

It was obvious, Marshall said, that Burr was not present on the island, neither in fact nor constructively. A constructive presence was the one defined by Marshall in the Bollman-Swartwout decision—"all those who perform any part . . . and who are actually leagued in the general conspiracy." Instead, Marshall said, Burr was charged with conspiring to produce the act of treason which allegedly took place.

Two kinds of crime had been discussed in the Burr trial. Planning an act of treason that had never taken place is the crime of conspiracy. Contributing to an act of treason that did take place is the crime of treason. Burr was charged with treason because, Marshall said, he was alleged to have conspired in an action that took place and which was said to be treasonable—and if the act could be proved then the accessory was as guilty as the participants.

"It is a settled principle in the law," Marshall hastily added, "that the accessory cannot be guilty of a greater offence than his principal." Was there some reason in the present case, Marshall asked, to violate that settled principle? He thought not. Several times he repeated the assertion that the accessory could be found guilty only after the principal had been. He cited numerous precedents from English law that "the conviction of some one who has committed the treason must precede the trial of him who has advised or procured it."

As for the motion, Marshall restated that the Constitution mandated that the act of treason be testified to by two witnesses. "It is not proved," he asserted, "by a single witness." Article III, Section 3, of the Constitution directed that "No Person shall be convicted of Treason unless on the Testimony of two Witnesses to the same overt Act, or on Confession in Open Court." The prosecution was as aware of this provision as was John Marshall, and yet it had failed to produce the required two witnesses to the overt act, relying instead on the testimony of Jacob Allbright and on statements by a number of witnesses regarding Burr's intentions, plans, or perhaps only his dreams, or their own faulty memories. The United States government had not made a case against Aaron Burr as the Constitution required.

"It is of necessity the peculiar province of the court to judge of the admissibility of testimony," said Marshall. "If the court admit improper or reject proper testimony, it is an error of judgment; but it is an error committed in the direct exercise of their judicial function." With those words Marshall had defined his role. Now he fulfilled it. "The presence of the accused at that assemblage being no where alleged except in the indictment, the overt act is not proved by a single witness," Marshall said, "and of consequence all other testimony must be irrelevant." The Eaton, the Wilkinson, and the Morgan testimony was irrelevant, all of it. John Marshall had just destroyed Thomas Jefferson's case against Aaron Burr.

The Chief Justice could have stopped there, but he did not. The passions surrounding this case, the conflicts between the major characters, the probable repercussions were too great. He repeated again that testimony which did not prove the overt act of treason was inadmissible. If there was testimony by a second person to the overt act, said Marshall, "let it be offered." (The prosecution already had said it would not offer a second witness.) Then John Marshall spoke of the role of the judge. Although he spoke at this moment of himself, his words can be read with value by any judge, by any person who seeks to approach a problem fairly and with deference to just procedures. "Much has been said in the course of the argument on points on which the court feels no inclination to comment particularly," said Marshall, "but which may, perhaps not improperly, receive some notice." He continued:

[513]

That this court dares not usurp power is most true.

That this court dares not shrink from its duty is not less true.

No man is desirous of placing himself in a disagreeable situation. No man is desirous of becoming the peculiar subject of calumny. No man, might he let the bitter cup pass from him without self reproach, would drain it to the bottom. But if he have no choice in the case, if there be no alternative presented to him but a dereliction of duty or the opprobrium of those who are denominated in the world, he merits the contempt as well as the indignation of his country who can hesitate which to embrace.

He asserted then, for the final time, that evidence regarding Burr's conduct or comments regarding the events on Blennerhassett's island were irrelevant until the treasonous act itself could be established by two witnesses. He again called on the prosecution to offer such testimony by two witnesses—"let it be offered; and the court will decide upon it." Marshall closed: "The jury have now heard the opinion of the court on the law of the case. They will apply that law to the facts, and will find a verdict of guilty or not guilty as their own consciences may direct."[83]

There was no disputing the impact of Marshall's decision on Aaron Burr. As William Wirt phrased it the next day, "Marshall has stepped in between Burr and death." Since the prosecution could not prove the overt act through testimony of two witnesses as ordered by the Constitution, and because, as a result, its evidence linking Burr to the unproven act was inadmissible, it had no case. The next day, Tuesday, September 1, George Hay informed the jury that he had nothing to offer "of evidence or argument; that he had examined the opinion of the court, and must leave the case with the jury."[84]

The jury retired to deliberate, although everyone in the courtroom realized that it must present a verdict of not guilty because Marshall had ruled out all evidence against Burr. The animosity toward Burr in that jury room was so great, however, that the members could not bring themselves to pronounce him above suspicion. When they emerged from their deliberations it was to announce that "We of the jury say that Aaron Burr is not proved to be guilty under this indictment by any evidence submitted to us. We therefore find him not guilty."

The courtroom exploded in an uproar. Burr and his lawyers stammered that the verdict was unusual, informal, and irregular. "The jury can not be indulged," charged Burr. "They have defaced a paper belonging to the court, by writing upon it words which they have no right to write. They ought to be sent back."

The traditional verdict by a jury was either "guilty" or "not guilty," rather than the qualified answer given by the jury foreman, Edward Carrington.* George Hay, the chief prosecution attorney, said the verdict should be recorded as offered by the jury, "which," he said, "was substantially a verdict of acquittal." It was the implication of that word "substantially" which so disturbed the Burr people; Hay was correct in implying that the verdict was not a complete exoneration, that the shadow of that verdict would hang over Aaron Burr for the rest of his life and over his name through history.

The argument seesawed back and forth between the lawyers for the two sides for a few minutes, and then Carrington, the jury foreman, said that the jury members had agreed that if the verdict was considered too informal, "they would alter it; that it was in fact a verdict of acquittal." The Chief Justice tried to compromise the issue by saying that the verdict was the same as an acquittal, and "that it might stand on the bill as it was if the jury wished it; and an entry should be made on the record of 'not guilty.' "

Parker, the jury member who had been so opposed to Aaron Burr, then spoke out, saying that he would produce the same verdict if called upon to decide a second time. He said that every member of the jury knew that the verdict was not phrased in the usual form but that they all had wanted it that way. He insisted that he for one would not agree to its alteration.[85]

And so the original Burr verdict entered the record: an announcement by the jury that, in effect, it considered him a guilty man but was unable to pronounce him so because of the rulings by the Chief Justice. There was much circumstantial evidence against Burr, there was much public opinion against him, there ultimately would be the British papers with their accounts of his conversations, but there was little solid evidence to meet the demands of the Constitution. Certainly there was not and is not sufficient evidence to warrant a guilty verdict, despite the animosity expressed by the members of the jury.

Lawyers perhaps have paid more attention to the subtleties of the decision than have the historians. The historians saw the Burr trial as a clash of two giant figures—Thomas Jefferson and John Marshall—over a man both despised. The trial was indeed such a clash. But it is more important as a study in law, for the confrontation was not between personalities but between a very strict construction of the law and its requirements, and a loose

---

* Carrington was John Marshall's brother-in-law, the second husband of Polly's sister Betsy.

[515]

one. John Marshall, who has mistakenly been accused of expanding the power of the federal judiciary when in reality he only utilized that power to its allowed limits, demanded in the trial of Aaron Burr that the law be construed as strictly as possible. In this trial the federal judiciary declared that it was sincere in its intention to protect the individual against the rampaging state. The *Marbury v. Madison* decision was an announcement that the Supreme Court was a powerful institution. John Marshall's conduct in the Aaron Burr trial was an announcement that the federal judiciary was a noble institution.

Did a traitor escape? No evidence then or now establishes Burr's guilt.

Was Marshall's conduct basically an attempt to embarrass or attack Thomas Jefferson? The charge that Marshall used his power as a judge in this instance against a political enemy cannot be accepted. If Marshall were intent on undermining Jefferson's political position, he would not have used the Burr trial as his vehicle. Defending a man whom the public believes to be a traitor is not an effective means of currying favor with the public.

Only by realizing that John Marshall was interested in forging the judicial process into a means of protecting the individual can the proceedings of the Aaron Burr case be understood. "Courts will always apply the rules of evidence to criminal prosecutions so as to treat the defence with as much liberality and tenderness as the case will admit," said Marshall during those proceedings.[86] If no one believed that before the Burr trial, all believed it after the trial. And the value of that attitude to the United States has continued to manifest itself. In the United States, as in other nations, prosecutions have been brought in the courts as political devices, to resolve unpleasant situations for the existing government or to quiet opposition to that government. But in the United States, unlike in many other nations, the courts have stopped such proceedings. The government can be arrogant but the law is a powerful master. That is the meaning of the Aaron Burr trial, that is its significance in American history, why it will always be studied.

The Burr affair was not finished with the trial. Burr still had to face the misdemeanor charge and then respond to the prosecution's request that he be held for treason again, this time for a trial in the Ohio district. He ultimately was held in $3,000 bond on the misdemeanor charge of preparing a war against Spain. But this trial never was prosecuted; even as George Hay sought the setting of bail, he did not intend for the trial to take place. The great treason trial had, by the end of October 1807, degenerated into pettiness.

President Jefferson naturally was infuriated by the outcome. "I expected that instead of invoking the forms of the law
to cover traitors," he said in a private letter about a year after
the Burr trial ended, "all good citizens would have concurred in
securing them. . . . There are extreme cases where the laws become inadequate even to their own preservation. . . ." Jefferson
sent a message to Congress which can only be read as an invitation to that body to initiate impeachment proceedings against
Marshall. With the message he sent the trial record, "together
with some evidence not there heard." He told the members of
Congress:

> From the whole you will be enabled to judge whether
> the defect was in the testimony, in the law, or in the ad-
> ministration of the law; and wherever it shall be found,
> the legislature alone can apply or originate the remedy.
> The framers of our constitution certainly supposed they
> had guarded, as well their government against destruction
> by treason, as their citizens against oppression under pre-
> tence of it: and if these ends are not obtained, it is of im-
> portance to enquire by what means, more effectual, they
> may be secured.

In response to that appeal some members of Congress attacked
the Chief Justice and the federal judiciary in speeches, but the
Congress as such did not act. Its refusal to respond, its refusal
to seek vengeance, is a tribute to the viability of the democratic
system.[87]

For John Marshall, the trial closing did not end his involvement in the Aaron Burr episode. He was burned in effigy, denounced in newspaper columns, criticized in speeches. About a
month after the trial had ended, Marshall wrote to his friend
Richard Peters in Philadelphia (by now he had relaxed sufficiently so that he could write about the experience): "I received
it [a book Peters had sent him] while fatigued and occupied with
the most unpleasant case which has ever been brought before a
Judge in this or perhaps in any other country which affected to
be governed by law." In the month since the case had ended, he
had not even been home: "The day after the commitment of Colo.
Burr for a misdemeanor, I galloped to the mountains whence I
only returned in time to perform my North Carolina circuit."

Marshall then acknowledged the outcry against him, "about
the attentions paid me in Baltimore and elsewhere." He wrote
that he wished he could laugh about the situation, "but it was
most deplorably serious and I could not give the subject a different aspect by treating it in any manner which was in my power."

He concluded that perhaps "I might have made it less serious to my self by obeying the public will instead of the public law and throwing a little more of the sombre upon others."[88]

But John Marshall never could surrender the public law to the public will.

5

JOHN MARSHALL was not constantly involved on the Supreme Court with constitutional issues, nor in disputes with Thomas Jefferson. Only a handful of the cases that came before him during that first decade dealt with questions of such significance. Most of the cases involved prizes at sea (a reflection of the lawlessness between nations). There were a few involving slavery and some procedural questions, but land disputes occupied much of the time of the federal courts. This last was a reflection of the vagueness of the early land grants.

One of these cases, *Adams v. Woods*,[1] reflected Marshall's common-sense attitude toward the law. The question in the 1804 case was whether an action for a debt could be brought after two years although the law appeared to bar such actions if not brought before that time period had elapsed. Marshall ruled that the law did in fact say what it appeared to say. If it had not, Marshall said, actions for debts could be brought "at any distance of time." He did not accept that the law had intended to be without a statute of limitations—"This," he said, "would be utterly repugnant to the genius of our laws." He pointed out that even treason had a three-year statute of limitations, and said that "it could scarcely be supposed that an individual would remain for ever liable to a pecuniary forfeiture."[2]

Another case that same year is of more significance to a later period in American history when the military assumed a greater importance than it had at the time. In 1799, when the United States was in the midst of its difficulties with France, difficulties that have been described as a quasi-war, Congress authorized the stopping of American ships on the high seas that seemed to be engaged in commercial intercourse with France. The actual effect of the law was that the owner of such a ship did not have redress in American civil courts if it could be proven that his ship was engaged in such commerce. The fifth section of the act by Congress instructed the President to order commanders of American armed vessels "to stop and examine any ship or vessels of the United States on the high seas" if there was any reason to believe the ship was engaged in commerce with France. The presidential order pursuant to the act instructed commanders not only to stop American ships but also "to be vigilant that vessels or cargoes really American, but covered by Danish or other foreign papers, and bound to or from French ports, do not escape you." Such an extensive order was not authorized by the 1799 act and was illegal. Under those instructions a Danish ship, the *Flying Fish*, was stopped by an American ship commanded by a Captain Little. The *Flying Fish* was then brought into Boston harbor. The owner not only sought the return of his ship and its cargo but also sued for damages against Captain Little. In the case known as *Little v. Bareme*[3] the issue was whether the presidential order excused what was obviously an illegal act by Little, the stopping of a neutral ship.

Marshall summed up the question with: "Is the officer who obeys them liable for damages sustained by this misconstruction of the act, or will his orders excuse him?" Society has never quite understood how to deal with this question. The beginning of a war is the beginning of an evil; does that evil have no limits? The Supreme Court declared then that it did. "I confess," Marshall said in his decision, "the first bias of my mind was very strong in favor of the opinion that though the instructions of the executive could not give a right, they might yet excuse from damages." He referred to "That implicit obedience which military men usually pay to the orders of their superiors, which indeed is indispensably necessary to every military system" as strongly influencing him to state that orders from a superior officer, although illegal, should absolve the inferior officer of the consequences of acts performed under those orders.

The other Justices on the Court, however, persuaded Marshall to take a contrary position, "that the instructions cannot change the nature of the transaction, or legalize an act which, without those instructions, would have been a plain trespass." The individual member of the military is responsible for his own acts and cannot transfer that responsibility to a superior authority.[4]

During this period the Court was shunted around in the Capitol. First the Justices met in a small room adjacent to the Senate chamber, and then the basement was fitted up for them at their request, after they had been holding some of their meetings in a nearby tavern. When they met in the basement room, directly under the Senate chamber, they sat beneath a vaulted ceiling whose arches supported the floor of the Senate chamber. The judges sat behind a curved table with the lawyers before them and the spectators in two rows of seats that encircled the room somewhat like the seats in a Roman amphitheater. Court sessions always were crowded; ladies particularly enjoyed attending the sessions to watch their favorite lawyers in forensic battles.[5]

The judges themselves lived together at one boardinghouse, where they had their meetings, their arguments, their consultations, and reached their decisions. Living together each year for four to six weeks could be difficult, but they did it, according to one of them, "with perfect harmony, and as agreeably as absence from friends and from families could make our residence." The talk was uninhibited, with each Justice expressing his opinions fully and without fear of offending. When they were done with their law, their conversation became "gay and frank." At one time two of the Justices were bachelors, and their fellows worked very hard at matchmaking. "We have already ensnared one of the Judges," gleefully reported one of the matchmakers, "and he is now—at the age of forty-seven—violently affected with the tender passion."[6]

The friendship among the Justices was necessary because Washington still was a dull town, a dreadful place to visit and a city even worse to live in. The roads were an outstanding example of inattention to public works, dusty during dry spells and rutted after rain. There were few accouterments of civilization such as sidewalks or gas lamps on the streets. The boardinghouse remained the center of governmental society, with members of different political parties or cliques rooming together. One time, some years later, Daniel Webster was driving through the streets of Washington in a coach when he suddenly ordered the driver to stop. He pointed to an old, decaying mansion and told his companion: "That large white house, with dilapidated walls and broken fences, was the hotel where I boarded when I first entered Congress from New Hampshire. It was then the Federalist headquarters. Governor Gore, Rufus King, and John Marshall were fellow-boarders. Governor Gore used to drive out of that gate in a coach drawn by four horses, and attended by servants in livery."[7]

To John and Polly Marshall, a ninth child, Charles William Marshall, was born February 11, 1803, but he died later that year, the fourth child of theirs to die in infancy. When their tenth child, Edward Carrington Marshall, was born in 1805, Polly was thirty-eight and he was her last child. Polly was becoming more and more ill, drawing more and more into the life of a recluse, a style of life that would be hers for the next quarter of a century. John Marshall's mother also died in this period, on September 19, 1809, near Lexington, Kentucky.

Marshall went out in society in Richmond occasionally by himself. He was a popular person, charming if ungainly. According to one account, even as he was entering his fifties he still had trouble with social accomplishments. "Judge Marshall was not a graceful man in society," goes this report. "He was abrupt and nervous in his movements and could not hand a lady a chair except most awkwardly with both hands, or a cup of tea without spilling it." This same account, written by a young belle of the time, adds, however, that Marshall was also "tall [and] handsome."[8]

At about the time he was finishing his first decade on the Court, Marshall became involved in what was for him obviously a fascinating adventure. He had a great interest in the linking of the east coast with the western lands. This was not only a matter of economics but also of politics. If the western settlers could be oriented to the East for their markets, rather than to the South (via the Mississippi River), then cities like Richmond and Philadelphia would enjoy the fruits of a rich commerce and the two peoples, the easterners and westerners, would be drawn more closely together. Otherwise, the fear was that the westerners would become oriented toward New Orleans and the southern areas which were dominated first by the French and then by the Spanish.

In his study of George Washington's life published in the early 1800s, Marshall had reported the arguments for closer economic ties between the East and the West. He wrote that George Washington had become convinced "that the rivers of Virginia afforded a more convenient, and a more direct course than could be found elsewhere, for that rich and increasing commerce . . . [but] the light in which this subject would be viewed with most interest, and which gave to it most importance, was its political influence on the union." Marshall then quoted a letter by Washington which pointed out that the United States had "other powers" on its borders "and formidable ones too" and that it was therefore important to use the "cement of interest to bind all parts of the union together by indissoluble bonds." Washington concluded that letter with the fear that if the people of the West should have their trade "flow through the Mississippi or the St. Lawrence; if the inhabitants thereof should form commercial connexions, which we know lead to intercourses of other kinds, they would in a few years be as unconnected with us, as are those of South America."[9]

These concerns of Washington and of Marshall were typical of thoughtful men of the period. Leading Virginians, emulating Washington, often had considered canals or river passages between their ports on or near the Atlantic and the settlements in Kentucky. The Virginia legislature, early in 1812, authorized a commission of twenty-two members to set out from Lynchburg to explore the rivers cutting through to the western lands and to report whether they could be made navigable. John Marshall was named to head the commission. There are reasons to consider him a strange choice. He had not been involved in the western lands for some years, and had become more known in the previous ten years as a judicial figure than as an outdoorsman. He may have done some surveying when he was a young boy traveling with his father, but that had been forty years earlier. Still, there were other reasons in favor of his being named to head the commission. He was fifty-six years old at the time, and apparently in excellent health. His spirits and leadership ability were such that the other men probably would be willing to follow him. Also, while men might argue with him as a judge, no one would question his integrity or his judgments on a nonpolitical issue such as opening the West.

A history of that expedition has the twenty-two men leaving Lynchburg on September 1, 1812. By boat they went up the James River to Dunlop's Creek, taking river soundings, and then marking out the most practicable route for a turnpike. Construction would not be difficult, the commissioners said in their report, "since the materials for a turnpike are everywhere convenient, and not more leveling will be necessary than must be expected in passing through a mountainous country." Again by boat, they went down Howard's Creek and the Greenbrier, constantly hampered by the shallowness of the streams. They reported of the Greenbrier that "On an attentive consideration of the obstacles, which were found by your commissioners to be great . . . they are unanimously and decidedly of the opinion that its navigation may be rendered as safe." By boat and horse the men continued on to the Great Kanawha Falls, which they concluded could be circumvented by building a canal to the Ohio River. The final report was impressive. It included a detailed description of how and where to dredge the rivers, build a road, and also a canal. Such a route would be of great value, the commissioners concluded, because "For the want of it, in the course of the last autumn, government was reduced to the necessity of transporting arms in wagons from Richmond to the falls of the Great Kanawha. A similar necessity may often recur." The report was accepted with great praise but work was not begun until the 1820s and never finished, because the need for water transportation was superseded by the need for rail transportation.[10]

For Marshall the need to draw the East and West together was an important fact in his remaining years. In 1828, when he was almost seventy-three, he accepted an appointment to a state convention to consider internal improvements, understood at the time to refer to greater links between the East and the West. That convention was interesting because it destroys the notion that only the aging Federalists were interested in greater ties to the West. The six-day session at Charlottesville, which began July 14, 1828, was chaired by ex-President Madison and included James Monroe, two staunch Jeffersonian Republicans, and a number of other prominent Virginians as well as Marshall. The convention agreed that greater improvements should be undertaken along the lines suggested after Marshall's foray to the West in 1812, but apparently, because of the costs involved, the plans were never brought to fruition.

Still later, in 1832, John Marshall was named chairman of a fourteen-member commission to sell stock in the James River and Kanawha Company, which had as its purpose building a canal to the West. When the books were closed in Richmond, after twelve days, Marshall and his committee had received subscriptions for more than ten thousand shares, worth more than $1 million; the goal, however, was $3 million. The trouble was that while Richmond and Charleston were meeting their quotas, the country between them was not. In August 1832 a message, signed "A Subscriber," went out to the residents of these lands urging them to subscribe. That John Marshall was the author was well known. The words that came then from the seventy-seven-year-old Chief Justice were an appeal to reason—he argued strongly that the economic benefits from the increased trade could not be ignored—and also an appeal to men to live up to their responsibilities. "You are now to decide whether it shall raise us to our former rank among our sister states," Marshall wrote his fellow Virginians, "or add one to the examples already given of the ruinous apathy with which we neglect our natural advantages which Providence has bestowed on our country with so profuse a hand, while they are seized by others." After saying that the city residents were doing their share, Marshall continued that "Richmond and Charleston cannot, of themselves, accomplish this great work. The intermediate country must put forth its strength, or it must fail. The numerous and wealthy inhabitants on the proposed line of communication, must shew that they are willing to participate in its burthens as well as its advantages." In this tract he was espousing what was a basic tenet of his political faith, that men must contribute to their land as well as take from it.[11]

Part of the canal ultimately was built, but it was never maintained properly. Its towpath became the bed, in the 1880s, of the Richmond and Allegheny Railroad. That Marshall was correct about the necessity of uniting the western and eastern lands to give them a common interest was bluntly demonstrated in the Civil War, long after his death, when the men in the western part of Virginia refused to secede with their brethren to the east and formed the separate state of West Virginia.

But Marshall's interest in the western lands and his personal life were but background to his stewardship of the federal judiciary and the animosity between him and Thomas Jefferson. This animosity would continue until both men were dead, and even in the years following, as their followers repeated the charges made by the two men. While Jefferson was President, however, it was a constant part of the relationship between the President and the Chief Justice and continued for many years, after James Madison came to the presidency as Jefferson's successor and disciple. Marshall became angry at Jefferson and Madison for the events that led to the War of 1812 and for the war itself. For one time, and apparently the only time, Marshall considered leaving the bench to run for President—so angered was he by that war.

Jefferson had never forgiven Marshall for the Burr proceedings. Others would talk of law; Jefferson spoke only of politics of the worst kind. In 1810, with Jefferson at Monticello and James Madison in the President's House, Cyrus Griffin was ready to retire from the Circuit Court and a successor would have to be named to sit with Marshall. Jefferson recommended a possible appointee to Madison. That a strong man be named was important, said Jefferson, because "the state has suffered long enough by having such a cypher [Griffin] in so important an office and infinitely the more from the want of any counterpoint to the rancourous hatred which Marshall bears to the government of his country, and from the cunning and sophistry with which he is able to enshroud himself. It will be difficult to find a character of firmness enough to preserve his independence on the same bench with Marshall."[12] Jefferson's image of Marshall, a Machiavelli who could twist the other judges on the bench to his way of thinking, paid no honor to the other Justices, most of whom were intelligent, strong-willed, and not susceptible to any but the strongest arguments.

Jefferson was particularly incensed at Marshall's "cunning and sophistry" in a case that came before the Circuit Court in Richmond in December of 1811. Edward Livingston, a former supporter and then opponent of Jefferson, sued the ex-President for an act Jefferson had performed while President—the ordering of the seizure of property in New Orleans purportedly belonging to Livingston. Livingston sought $100,000 in damages, enough to bankrupt the already financially embarrassed Jefferson. The ex-President grumbled that Livingston had arranged for the case to come before the Circuit Court over which Marshall presided because Livingston believed Marshall would decide in his favor— a reasonable guess on Jefferson's part.

Marshall, however, went along with an argument by Jefferson's lawyers that the Circuit Court did not have jurisdiction because the alleged trespass on Livingston's property had taken place outside of Virginia. Marshall's acquiescence in this point is usually described as grudging, and he did not allow the case to go by without some unpleasant comments about Thomas Jefferson. While accepting Jefferson's point, Marshall did believe, apparently sincerely, that the law should have been changed by Congress to allow such cases to be tried. He made this observation in his decision and in later years.[13] However, as far as the point of the law existing at the time of the trial, there seemed nothing grudging about Marshall's decision. That the case should be tried in the area where the trespass occurred, Marshall said, was a principle of common law—"which is really human reason applied by the courts, not capriciously, but in a regular train of decisions, to human affairs, for the promotion of the ends of justice." Virginia had adopted this common law, Marshall continued, and added: "Had it not been adopted, I should have thought it in force. When our ancestors migrated to America, they brought with them the common law of their native country . . . and I do not conceive that the Revolution would, in any degree, have changed the relations of man to man, or the law which regulated those relations." This had always been Marshall's opinion, that the common law was controlling at the state level, and there was never anything grudging about his attitude toward that concept.[14]

But Marshall did not find cause to improve his opinion of Thomas Jefferson. His attitude toward the President, already one of deep distrust and dislike in 1801, had been further exacerbated in the closing years of Jefferson's tenure as President. The specific issue was the embargo which Jefferson pushed through Congress in 1807. The Embargo Act was perhaps the most misunderstood act of Jefferson's career as President, perhaps one of the most misunderstood of any President's acts, and certainly one of the noblest endeavors of an American President—as well as among the most ineffectual. The United States was being whipsawed between the English and the French, who once again were at each other with reckless abandon. England, in November of 1807, had made neutral ships fair game for attack if they traded with the European continent, which was under French control. Against this background, Jefferson sought a new device to thwart the military thrust of England and France. He wanted to use economic sanctions—an embargo on goods leaving the United States—as a means of pressuring the two warring nations to come to terms.

Economic sanctions were not new then and have been tried since, but rarely on such a grand scale: an entire nation closed its ports to the major trading nations of the world. But economic sanctions never have worked against militarists, and they did not this time. Nor did they have support in the United States. The American people generally will follow their President if he takes them into his confidence, but this Jefferson, who was nearing the end of his eight years as chief executive and a public career that spanned some four decades, did not do. He expected to be followed; he did not lead. The result was that he was charged with waging an economic war against England at the behest of Napoleon in France. Although the Embargo Act applied equally to trade with both nations, the island nation, England, was more affected than was France, which could trade with other continental nations. Typical of the criticism of the time was this letter from John Marshall to Timothy Pickering, about one year after the embargo had first gone into effect:

> If sound argument and correct reason could save our country it would be saved. Nothing can be more completely demonstrated than the inefficacy of the embargo, yet that demonstration seems to be of no avail. I fear most seriously that the same spirit which so tenaciously maintains this measure will impel us to a war with the only power which protects any part of the civilized world from the despotism of that tyrant with whom we shall then be arranged.

Marshall concluded that letter with the amusing statement: "I abstain from remarks on this question."[15] Characteristically, his denial of interest in a current political event came at the end of a long exposition on that event.

After the embargo went into effect, Jefferson's administration was constantly harassed by details of enforcement and administration that it obviously had not anticipated. This, too, led to the failure of the policy. It also became evident that Jefferson did not understand how the United States as an economic entity was developing. He saw it as a collection of independent units. Monticello, after all, was self-sufficient; weren't all family farms and estates? But in the cities a great depression began as sailors, first, were put out of work; and then the workers in the industries and on the farms which produced the goods sold abroad and the workers who serviced them also became unemployed. The American people saw their economy being destroyed for a policy they did not understand and which many of them found highly suspect.

The Federalists naturally seized on the embargo issue in 1808 as a possible means of springing back to power. Charles Cotesworth Pinckney, Marshall's companion from the XYZ Affair, became the Federalist candidate for the presidency, running for the second time. In a series of letters to Pinckney Marshall demonstrated an astute grasp of the political situation and also revealed how deep was his animosity toward the Jefferson administration. "Indeed my dear Sir," he wrote in one of those letters, "I never have known a time which I believed to be more perilous than the present. The internal changes which have been already made & those further changes which are contemplated by a party always hostile to our constitution & which has for some time ruled our country despotically, must give serious alarm to every attentive & intelligent observer." These dangers, created by "despotic" rulers, said Marshall, were insignificant compared to the dangers from outside the United States' borders. "Unless that system which has for some time guided our councils with respect to foreign powers can be changed," he wrote, "the independence of the United States will soon become an empty name & the name itself I fear will not long survive the substance." Marshall insisted that his concern was not the dollar losses from the depression caused by the embargo, "but the political objects which produced it & to which it tends I cannot contemplate without extreme anxiety."

In another letter to Pinckney, Marshall indicated that he did not consider himself above the political battle. "The federalists of Virginia constitute, you know, a small & oppressed minority of our state. Between the rival democratic candidates for the Presidency they were divided, about them few were anxious." Marshall said he considered himself one of the abused Federalists: "We found ourselves abused, insulted, and maltreated by all, and perceived no assurance on which we could confidently rely that the political system which has been adopted would be changed by any of them." In that letter Marshall explained that the Virginia Federalists were supporting James Monroe rather than James Madison, who was Jefferson's choice as a successor. The Federalists' strategy was obvious. They were not numerous enough in that state to swing the state behind a Federalist candidate and hoped, instead, to swing it behind Monroe so, with some dissident Republicans, they could defeat Madison.

The elections did not go well for the Federalists and for other opponents of Jefferson. "I have just returned from North Carolina where the elections are more favorable to the administration than was expected," Marshall reported to his brother. "The federalists counted confidently on four elections and expected five. They can have but four, fear they will not exceed that and may be reduced to two. The democrats say they can have but two." Marshall added that in the southern states, "the embargo is most powerfully supported and a great portion of the people seem madly for a war with England."[16] The Federalists ended up with three presidential electors out of fourteen in North Carolina. Pinckney did badly across the nation, winning only 47 electoral votes to James Madison's 122.

Part of the difficulty as Jefferson's tenure in the presidency ended and Madison's began was the suspicion still lingering from the 1790s when the Jeffersonians were accused of being too friendly with France and the Federalists were accused of being too friendly with England. Undoubtedly that was part of the politics of the time, but it was more than traditional animosity. Jefferson's embargo policy, whatever its potential, was destructive and he had failed to lead the American people to sacrifice. While the Federalists certainly would have attacked Jefferson no matter how much he had attempted to sell his policy to the public, in fact it was Jefferson's own men who thwarted his policies.

The first instance involved William Johnson, whom Jefferson had appointed to the Supreme Court in 1804 as part of his plan to democratize the judiciary by placing some Jeffersonian Republicans on the bench. In 1808, while Johnson was sitting on the Circuit Court in South Carolina, he faced a case growing out of the embargo. A man named Gilchrist wanted permission from the collector of customs of the Charleston port to sail his ship. The collector read the Embargo Law to mean that he could not grant such permission, even if he had no reason to believe the ship might be destined for France or England. The case went to Johnson, who ordered the collector to release the ship.[17] The decision demonstrated that once a man dons the robes of a Justice, no one can predict his future actions by his past politics. Jefferson was furious at the decision by his old friend, for it not only freed Gilchrist's ship to sail but also meant that collectors in other ports would be subject to similar suits.

The second instance in which Jefferson was harassed by his own party involved the congressional repeal of the Embargo Act. The leader in this movement was a young Jeffersonian Republican from Salem, Massachusetts, named Joseph Story. Story, despite his party loyalties, could not stand by and watch the destruction of his native state's commerce and economy. Jefferson was well aware of who his enemy was in this situation and never forgave Story, objecting when later James Madison named him as an Associate Justice of the Supreme Court.[18]

Even after the embargo ended and Jefferson had left the presidency to be replaced by Madison, the national political picture continued to disintegrate as far as John Marshall was concerned. In March of 1810 Elbridge Gerry was elected governor of Massachusetts. As part of his campaign he recalled the XYZ Affair and portrayed himself as the hero and Marshall and Pinckney as the skulking villains. This was too much for Marshall. He wrote to his friend Josiah Quincy in Boston that "The federalists of the south participate with their brethren of the north in the gloomy anticipations which your late elections must inspire." Marshall referred to some attacks on American shipping by the French, and said that he had supposed that when those incidents were added to "previous burnings, ransoms and confiscations [it] would have exhausted to the dregs our cup of servility and degradation." He then added contemptuously that "these measures appear to make no impression on those to whom the people of the United States confide their destinies."[19]

The politics of the time led to the War of 1812, the second conflict between England and the United States. Even more than the Revolution, this war divided the American people. Thirty-seven years earlier when a young John Marshall had met with the Culpeper Minutemen to teach them the manual of arms, the political entity that was to become the United States had not yet been formed and it was to be expected that many Americans would continue to be loyal to the English Crown. But by 1812 many of the young soldiers of the Revolution were well into their middle years—John Marshall became fifty-seven that year—and others had died. The United States was a fact and loyalty to its leaders in time of war was expected. It was a hero of this war, Stephen Decatur, who framed the slogan that politicians ever since have loved. "Our country!" he said. "In her intercourse with foreign nations may she always be in the right; but our country, right or wrong."

The United States in 1812 was John Marshall's country. He

had fought for it. He had worked for it. He had helped, and was helping, to create it. He and many other Federalists believed the war to be a dreadful mistake. While the cause of the conflict was supposedly British harassment of American commerce and impressment of American seamen, Marshall and the other Federalists believed that the real cause was the desire by the western "war hawks" to gain control of the fur trade in the western lands by ridding them of British troops stationed there, as well as to capture Canada. Also, the Federalists believed the war leagued the United States with France, which they regarded as the ultimate imperialistic militaristic nation. The war was destroying the ties between the United States and England, the only nation with which the United States could develop a viable commercial relationship. Also, they believed—and in this respect the Federalists were nearly correct—that the United States could not win what would be primarily a sea war with England. Finally, the Federalists believed that the war might have been avoided by better diplomacy. "Stop this war!" they shouted.

There was one other point that disturbed the Federalists. When war was declared in 1812 Elbridge Gerry wrote to President Madison: "War is declared, God be praised, our country is safe."[20] Since Gerry already had been designated as Madison's running mate, it is reasonable to assume the attitude he expressed was not untypical among the Jeffersonian Republicans. But God should never be praised for a declaration of war, and no country is safe when the war comes. This was something John Marshall understood. War may be a necessity at times, but it is never desirable. The Federalists could have accepted a necessary war if its necessity could have been demonstrated to them, but they could never accept the idea of a desirable war.

Whether the Federalists were right or wrong to oppose the war, to oppose the nation's elected leadership, they had no hesitation about speaking their piece. Bravery is not only demonstrated on a battlefield but also in the public arena by challenging leaders at a time when such a challenge may be misunderstood and even branded as traitorous. In this respect the Federalists exhibited courage and they began a tradition of forceful opposition. Such a tradition serves to warn those in power that their conduct will always be scrutinized and subject to criticism. In a democracy such a tradition is of the utmost value.

There was no question of where Marshall stood. To his friends, knowing full well that they would broadcast his views, he wrote long letters criticizing the administration. France never would have been so bold in its European conquests, except that she was convinced that "from the resentment of the United States, nothing was to be apprehended." He doubted that the Madison administration included "the friends of peace, and I will add, of the real honor and real independence of our country." He was alarmed at efforts made to quiet the administration's critics, and concluded:

> I know very little of what is passing—much less of what is in reserve for us—but the caution incident to age approaches timidity, and I cannot help fearing that real genuine liberty has as much to apprehend from its clamorous votaries as from quarters that are more suspected. In popular government it is I fear possible for a majority to exercise power tyrannically.[21]

Although the lettter was a private one, there could be no question but that its sentiments would become widely known—it was sent to John Randolph, then one of the most vociferous critics of the war. Never has a Chief Justice so taken on a President, never so bluntly and with such calculation.

James Monroe, who was Madison's Secretary of State when war broke out, sent Marshall a copy of the war declaration. Marshall replied politely, saying he hoped that the war declaration "may, in its operation in the interest and honor of our country, disappoint only its enemies." But he also felt he had to make clear to his former friend and political antagonist that he opposed the declaration. "Whether my prayer be heard or not, I shall remain with respectful esteem" is how he signed the letter.[22]

The only apparent way of ending the war and stopping the growing alliance with France was to defeat James Madison in his bid for a second term. As a political party, however, the Federalists were tired. They had not won a presidential election for sixteen years. They did not really have a party policy except, for this election, to be against the war. When a dissident group of Jeffersonian Republicans in New York determined that they would support DeWitt Clinton for the presidency as a peace candidate, it appeared that the Federalists would fall into line behind him for lack of any other candidate to support. Not all Federalists were willing to accept that proposition. Some began scouting around for a prominent Federalist who enjoyed nationwide respect, who was from Virginia preferably so he could perhaps take that state's electoral votes away from Madison, and who definitely was a peace candidate. Timothy Pickering, the

Secretary of State during the XYZ Affair, expressed this opinion early in July: "I am far enough from desiring Clinton for President of the United States. I would infinitely prefer another Virginian—if Judge Marshall could be the man." Pickering added that he would vote for any man other than Madison, so deep was the former Secretary of State's resentment of the war.[23]

John Marshall, of course, had always been attuned to national politics. From the days when he was a young lawyer in Richmond acting as Alexander Hamilton's agent, he was a political being. He was a participant in politics in its noblest sense, as a process by which people of different viewpoints and backgrounds could come together to solve their problems. He had campaigned for office, for the state legislature and for the House of Representatives, but after joining the Supreme Court he had refrained from active politics. He did not even vote in presidential elections. Still, he could not cut himself free from his background. In 1812 he knew that the Federalists were seeking an antiwar candidate, someone who could take Virginia's votes away from James Madison, someone who could perhaps breathe new life into the tattered rags of the Federalist party. Although he could not campaign openly for the nomination, he determined to make clear his availability.

The occasion came in July. Robert Smith, who had been Secretary of State in Madison's administration for a time and then was dismissed, wrote Marshall a letter. Smith, a disgruntled former Madison man, was critical of the President's war policies. John Marshall wrote Smith a long letter in reply. While Marshall believed in the nonpolitical nature of the Chief Justiceship sufficiently to refrain from openly declaring his availability, there can be no other way of reading his letter to Smith except as a declaration of his readiness to become a presidential candidate. Marshall wrote:

> Although I have for several years forborn to intermingle with those questions which agitate and excite the feelings of party, it is impossible that I could be inattentive to passing events, or an unconcerned observer of them. As they have increased in their importance, the interest, which as an American I must take in them, has also increased; and the declaration of war has appeared to me, as it has to you, to be one of those portentous acts which ought to concentrate on itself the efforts of all those who can take an active part in rescuing their country from the ruin it threatens.

He then made clear that he believed the position he held should not be considered a drawback:

> All minor considerations should be waived; the lines of subdivision between parties, if not absolutely effaced, should at least be convened for a time; and the great division between the friends of peace and the advocates of war ought alone to remain. It is an object of such magnitude as to give to almost every other, comparative insignificance; and all who wish peace ought to unite in the means which may facilitate its attainment, whatever may have been their differences of opinion on other points.

Marshall continued with a detailed criticism of administration policies. No one could accuse him of not being knowledgeable about the foreign affairs which had brought the nation to the point where it was deeply divided by the war. He said he could not think of the situation "without excessive mortification," and then added, as he usually did in such letters, a disclaimer of political interest. "It is not however for me to indulge these feelings," he said, "though I cannot so entirely suppress them as not sometimes, though rarely, to allow them a place in a private letter."[24] Because of Smith's political proclivities, that the "private" letter—or at least its sentiments—would be widely circulated was a reasonable assumption.

Marshall's possible candidacy began to attract interest. In August a group of Philadelphians sent out several letters to prominent Federalists around the country saying they would support DeWitt Clinton if necessary, but before committing themselves they wanted to know what other Federalists were doing. William Gaston, a lawyer who frequently practiced before the Circuit Court in North Carolina where Marshall presided, drafted a reply saying that the Federalists in his state would support John Marshall more than "any other man in the Union."[25]

That Marshall would be considered a candidate by the Federalists was natural. Through what now was becoming a long career in national affairs, he was well known to all the prominent leaders of the party but still had managed to stay above the local squabbles of the past several years. His refusal to support the Alien and Sedition Laws years earlier was virtually forgotten. Also, it was believed that he could bring in some additional votes because of his nonpolitical public stance over the past several years. Benjamin Stoddert, who had been Secretary of the Navy during the Adams administration, had known Marshall then, liked him, and followed his career since. In 1812 Stoddert was ready to play a behind-the-scenes kingmaker. "You must see with me, and all men who can see," he wrote to his influential friends, "that without a change of Administration—our Country is ruined." The only way to bring about such a change, he continued, was "setting up" Marshall as a presidential candidate. Stoddert had his strategy. He had been assured by Oliver Wolcott of Massachusetts, who had been Washington's and Adams' Secretary of the Treasury, that the New England state with their eighty-eight electoral votes would be united against Madison, either for DeWitt Clinton or for a Federalist candidate. Wolcott also claimed, so Stoddert reported, that "the existence of the Federalist party and the safety of the Country depend upon the election of a Southern Federalist—Judge [Bushrod] Washington or Marshall."

In addition to the 88 New England votes, the peace candidate also would pick up about 7 votes in Delaware and Maryland, for a total of 95. This would be 15 less than the majority of 110 needed to become President. Where could the opponents of the war find those last 15 votes? "Not one will be had from the West," said Stoddert, "and none is expected south of North Carolina." By elimination then, the votes had to come from either Virginia or North Carolina. Stoddert then wrote:

> In Virginia efforts are making, which I have labored hard and long to produce, to form an opposition ticket to Madison. If formed—and if the meeting at New York nominates Marshall, I verily believe he will get the votes of Virginia—but in this expectation I stand almost alone.

If Virginia didn't produce, then North Carolina would have to give the necessary votes to defeat Madison. "If with honor the whole vote of North Carolina can be given to the opponent of Madison, agreed upon by the meeting at New York, he will be elected if the vote of Massachusetts should not be lost," Stoddert continued in this particular letter which was addressed to a prominent North Carolinian.

Stoddert was anxious to push Marshall because he did not believe that Clinton could be elected; he doubted that Clinton's own state of New York would support him. "My advice to the persons who compose the meeting at New York," Stoddert continued, "has been, and will be, to nominate Marshall President— Clinton or [Rufus] King, Vice President." Stoddert believed Marshall far superior to Clinton—"the difference is as wide as the poles are asunder." Still, however, he would support Clinton if necessary because "the first object is to save the country from the ruin of Madison." Stoddert felt that the Federalists would vote for Clinton if he were the only alternative to Madison, but reluctantly—"It will be on the same kind of principle that a naked man would rush out of a house on fire above his ears, altho he was sure of meeting a mad dog at the door."[26]

When the Federalists came to New York in September sentiment existed for Marshall's nomination but it ran into difficulties. Harrison Gray Otis, a leading Massachusetts Federalist, had locked up that state's delegates for Clinton. To those who continued to press for Marshall's nomination, the answer was that he was needed on the Supreme Court—a more accurate assumption than people realized at the time.[27] Also, the Federalists may have had enough of Presidents from Virginia: with the exception of the four years that John Adams was President, the presidency had been held by a Virginian since 1789.

Clinton then became the peace candidate of the dissident and dovish Republicans and ran with the tacit support of the Federalists. The campaign was a desultory one, but still Clinton and his running mate Jared Ingersoll made a respectable showing against James Madison and Elbridge Gerry. The electoral college vote was 128–89 in Madison's favor. Virginia, with twenty-five electoral votes, and North Carolina, with fifteen, went for Madison. If Marshall had been nominated and taken the North Carolina vote, which seemed likely, plus a few of the Virginia votes, which also seemed likely, as Stoddert had suggested, a candidate might have been elected who would have ended the war before it divided the nation and resulted in the British invasion of the Middle Atlantic states and the burning of the Capitol, the President's House, and the near-capture of the President himself—not to say caused the deaths of many young Americans and British.

Marshall's near-brush with presidential politics was not the end of his involvement in the War of 1812. In 1813 and 1814, when he was fifty-seven and fifty-eight years of age, he was on a Vigilance Committee directed to prepare Richmond against British attack. As a former militia general, it was expected that he would become involved in military preparations. The threat to the state capital was not mere rhetoric. The British were in Virginia and did come dangerously close to Richmond. This war was not a game.[28]

Whether it would have been better for the country if Marshall had given up the Court to become President is impossible to estimate. In any event, he had other challenges before him on the Court. With the *Marbury v. Madison* decision and then with the Aaron Burr trial, he had proven that the federal judiciary he headed was both independent and powerful. As he entered the second decade of his tenure on the Supreme Court his task was to use those tools—independence and power—to engrave in the law that Americans were not residents of separate states but were, instead, one people.

Part II

The Struggle for the Supremacy of the Union

6

IN THE SUMMER OF 1814 the British attacked Washington, ravaged it, and burned the President's House and the Capitol. Although the room the Supreme Court used for its chamber was not destroyed, it was badly damaged and the Court had to use nearby houses to hold its sessions for several years, not returning to the Capitol until 1817. Even then the Court met in a room "temporarily fitted up for their occupation," according to Henry Wheaton, who was keeping the Court records.[1]

But in its temporary chambers the Court in this second decade of John Marshall's stewardship was undertaking work of a permanent nature. When the Constitution had been written, its authors understood that they must make a decision about the supremacy of the federal Union; either it was controlling over the separate states or it was not. They had taken the position that it was supreme, or so it was generally supposed. But that supposition had to be weighed, tested, and accepted. And so it would be in John Marshall's second decade, by the Supreme Court he headed. When that decade was done, the federal Union would be the stronger.

When John Marshall was appointed Chief Justice at the end of John Adams' term as President, the Justices of the Supreme Court were all strong Federalists who had been appointed by Federalist Presidents. Under Jefferson, however, the Supreme Court changed, and it continued to change after 1809 when James Madison became President. In 1804 Alfred Moore resigned from the bench, pleading ill health, and was replaced by William Johnson of South Carolina. Several years after Johnson came to the bench, Joseph Story observed that he had "a strong mathematical head, and considerable soundness of erudition . . . [with] less of metaphysics, and more of logic."[2] Jefferson had hoped that mathematical head and that tendency toward logic would be used to thwart the leadership role of John Marshall. Although Johnson did exercise increasing independence during the years he was on the Supreme Court with Marshall, he never directed a serious challenge to Marshall's leadership. As his own decisions made clear, Johnson came to agree basically with Marshall—notwithstanding Jefferson's imploring him to do otherwise.

In 1806 William Paterson of New Jersey died. His death meant that the Court lost one of its strongest members and the nation one of its founding fathers. Paterson was a true gentleman; he had been gracious to Marshall when the Virginian was appointed Chief Justice although Paterson obviously knew that many Federalists had supported him rather than Marshall. Fortunately, he was replaced by another gentleman, Brockholst Livingston of New York. Joseph Story described Livingston in 1808, after the New Yorker had sat on the bench for two terms: "Livingston has a fine Roman face; an aquiline nose, high forehead, bald head, and projecting chin, indicate deep research, strength, and quickness of mind. He evidently thinks with great solidity, and seizes on the strong points of an argument. He is luminous, decisive, earnest and impressive on the bench. In private society he is accessible and easy, and enjoys with great good humor the vivacities, if I may coin a word of the wit and the moralist." A modern scholar, Gerald T. Dunne, has found Livingston's record on the Supreme Court disappointing, lacking "a juristic or constitutional dimension." But Dunne praised Livingston's "genial and ebullient personality and his concern for the tribunal" which helped make the Marshall Court a close-knit group "and thus assisted in the Court's institutional evolution at a critical period of its history."[3]

In 1807 the Supreme Court was enlarged from six to seven members and the new Justice was Thomas Todd of Kentucky. When he first took his seat on the Court, Joseph Story wrote that he was "a modest, retired man." While he could not "delineate" him, Story said, Todd did not appear "to want talents."[4] Todd did not develop into a forceful member of the Court. His appointment was the last of Jefferson's selections. The three appointees were not distinguished by any serious opposition to Marshall's leadership of the Supreme Court—the prime purpose for which they had been put on the Court. Since none had come to the Court with second-rate credentials, one must conclude that ultimately they came to adopt Marshall's view of an independent judiciary and a supreme Union.

Marshall's control of the direction of the Supreme Court continued after 1812 when Gabriel Duvall and Joseph Story, appointed by James Madison, took their seats. At this point the lineup of the Court included two firm Federalists—John Marshall and his friend and judicial ally, Bushrod Washington—and five men appointed by either Jefferson or his disciple Madison. And yet the course Marshall had mapped out for himself—"Of the importance of the judiciary at all times but more especially the present I am very fully impressed and I shall endeavor in the new office to which I am called not to disappoint my friends," he had written years earlier to Charles Cotesworth Pinckney—was not altered although the majority of the Supreme Court were of a different political persuasion.

Of the two Madison appointees, Duvall later became distinguished for holding on to his seat for many years after he had become aged and infirm because he was fearful of who would replace him, thus inaugurating what has become a popular tradition for subsequent Supreme Court Justices. The second appointee, Joseph Story, served on the Court thirty-three years and became one of America's most influential legal figures—the only Justice in the nineteenth century who can be considered to rank near or perhaps even equal to Marshall. His own opinions from the bench, his demeanor as a judge, his teaching at the Harvard Law School, and his *Commentaries on the Constitution* combine to make him a major figure in the development of American law.

Story, like Marshall, had not been a first choice of the President who appointed him. When William Cushing died, Madison asked Levi Lincoln, who had been Jefferson's first Attorney General, to take the position. When Lincoln declined, Madison nominated Alexander Wolcott, but the Senate rejected him. The President then asked John Quincy Adams, the son of the second President and then the minister to Russia, who also turned it down. Madison finally offered the position to Story. The offer was made against the wishes of Thomas Jefferson, who, although retired to Monticello, still anxiously gave advice to his successor. Jefferson had never forgiven Story's desertion of the embargo cause, but Madison became more and more desperate for an appointee and Story became his choice. Actually Story was making more money as a practicing lawyer in his native Massachusetts than he would make on the Court: $5,000 to $6,000 in fees compared to the $3,500 which the Justices received. He accepted because there were other considerations. He wrote to a friend:

> Notwithstanding the emoluments of my present business exceed the salary, I have determined to accept the office. The high honor attached to it, the permanence of the tenure, the respectability, if I may so say, of the salary, and the opportunity it will allow me to pursue, what of all things I admire, juridical studies, have combined to urge me to this result. It is also no unpleasant thing to be able

to look out upon the political world without being engaged
in it. . . .

The opportunity also . . . of meeting with the great men
of the nation, will be, I am persuaded, of great benefit to
my social feelings, as well as to my intellectual improvement. . . .[5]

Most of Story's expectations would be realized. He pursued
his study of the law, met the great men of the nation, enjoyed
himself socially, and improved himself intellectually. In only one
aspiration was he disappointed during the coming decades; his
desire to look out upon the political world without participating
in it proved a hopeless vision. The Supreme Court then as always
was taking on some of the most difficult political questions the
nation faced, and its members could not fail to be affected by
the political situation; nor could they refrain from participating
in it on occasion.

After the appointments of Duvall and Story the membership of the Supreme Court did not change again until 1823, an
unbroken eleven years. During this period, as the Court developed more and more into a unity, Marshall's style as a judge
become apparent. Again, as he was entering his later years—he
would be sixty in 1815—he was not noted for his ability as an
orator. His decisions read better than they must have sounded.
But he was influential because he wrote his decisions to appeal to
the mind rather than to the beating bosom. A writer of the time
contrasted John Marshall's rhetoric with that of John Randolph,
who had been Jefferson's agent in the House during the early
1800s: "The power of these two gentlemen are strikingly contrasted by nature. In Mr. Marshall's speeches all is reasoning; in
Mr. Randolph's every thing is declamation. The former scarcely
uses a figure; the latter, hardly an abstraction. One is awkward;
the other graceful. One is indifferent as to words, and slovenly
in his pronounciation; the other adapts his phrases to the sense
with poetick felicity; his voice to the sound with musical exactness. There is no breach in the train of Mr. Marshall's thoughts;
little connexion between Mr. Randolph's. Each has his separate
excellence, but either is far from being a finished orator."[6]

The Supreme Court over which John Marshall presided has
often been misconstrued to be John Marshall, as if this one man
was able, by some mysterious alchemy of intelligence and persuasion, to impose his will on his six brethren. It was, in reality,
the Marshall Court—a group of seven judges whom he led but
did not control. How did they arrive at their decisions? Joseph
Story, in his first term on the bench, explained the procedure in
a letter to a friend:

I find myself considerably more at ease than I expected. My brethren are very interesting men, with whom I live in the most frank and unaffected intimacy. Indeed we are all united as one, with a mutual esteem which makes even the labors of jurisprudence light. The mode of arguing causes in the Supreme Court is excessively prolix and tedious; but generally the subject is exhausted, and it is not very difficult to perceive at the close of the cause, in many cases, where the press of the argument and of the law lies. We moot every question as we proceed, and my familiar conferences at our lodgings often come to a very quick, and I trust, a very accurate opinion, in a few hours. On the whole, therefore, I begin to feel the weight of depression with which I came here insensibly wearing away, and a calm but ambitious self-possession gradually succeeding in its place.

Many of the cases argued before the Court were complicated, "long chancery bills, with overloaded documents, and long common law records, with a score of bills of exception attached to them," Story explained. He cited one case, with a printed brief of 230 pages and which required five days of argument: "It was my first cause, and though excessively complex, I had the pleasure to find that my own views were those which ultimately obtained the sanction of the whole Court."[7]

A simple explanation of how the Court operated: The members discussed the details of the case and the law as they understood it and, being reasonable men, eventually came to an agreement. There were, in some instances, variations on that explanation, but basically it held fast during the years Marshall was Chief Justice. That explanation can be too simple, however. Certainly Marshall used his position as Chief Justice, relied on his experience going back to the Revolution, and leaned on the prestige he had gained as he presided over the Court for three decades to influence his brethren. He was not one among equals. He was Chief Justice John Marshall, and no Associate Justice on the Supreme Court could forget that, even if he sometimes might not like it. Also, Marshall read almost all decisions rendered by the Court. The practice gave the Court a unity, the sense of being an institution, and Marshall nurtured this aura to good effect. When he joined the Court, it was an arm of government believed insignificant. When he left the Court more than three decades later, it had attained the rank promised in the Constitution—equal with the executive and legislative branches.

The Justices did at times disagree, and no persuasion or compromise by Marshall could effect a solution. This led to dissents. Justice Johnson, Thomas Jefferson's first appointee, was more than the other Justices a dissenter. The case of *United States v. Palmer*[8] in 1818 is an example of the differences between Marshall and Johnson in reading the law. The defendant had been arrested for robbery on the high seas and the question was whether he could be executed when the death penalty was not allowed as punishment for the same crime committed on land. The law read that "if any person or persons shall commit, upon the high seas, or in any river, haven, basin, or bay, out of the jurisdiction of any particular state, murder or robbery, or any other offence, which, if committed within the body of a county, would by the laws of the United States, be punishable with death . . . such offender shall be deemed, taken, and adjudged to be, a pirate and a felon, and being thereof convicted, shall suffer death."

As a judge, Marshall saw no recourse except to follow the dictates of the law and allow the death penalty. "The legislature having specified murder and robbery particularly," he said for the Court, "are understood to indicate clearly the intention that those offences shall amount to piracy; there could be no other motive for specifying them." Johnson, however, in balancing a strict reading of the law with the value of an individual's life, arrived at a different result. "The crime of robbery," he said in his dissent, "is the offence charged in this indictment, and the question is, whether it must not be shown that it must have been made punishable with death, if committed on land, in order to subject the offender to that punishment, if committed on the high seas." Johnson argued that Marshall was assuming that all the commas and other grammatical constructions were completely accurate. Johnson believed that the phrase "be punishable with death" in the law referred only to "any other offences" and not to robbery. "Upon such a question I here solemnly declare," he said, "that I never will consent to take the life of any man in obedience to any court; and if ever forced to choose between obeying this court, on such a point, or resigning my commission, I would not hesitate adopting the latter alternative."[9]

However one reacts to that specific case and Marshall's insistence on what he considered proper procedure even if the result was an execution, he did use proper procedure—as he had demonstrated in the Burr trial—as a defense for the accused wherever he considered it possible. An 1806 case, *Ex parte Burford*,[10] is an example. John A. Burford of Alexandria, Virginia, had been imprisoned because he was "not of good name and fame, nor of honest conversation, but an evil doer and disturber of the peace." The imprisonment was on the order of local justices of the peace and was upheld by the Circuit Court, but Marshall would not go along with the lower courts. He pointed out that both the Virginia bill of rights and the federal Bill of Rights required that no man be imprisoned unless probable cause existed that a crime had been committed, but the warrant for Burford's imprisonment "states no offense. It does not allege that he was convicted of any crime. . . . The prisoner is discharged."

Another example is in the 1813 case of the *Schooner Hoppet and Cargo v. the United States*, where the question revolved around the confiscation of a ship's cargo because it was illegally imported under the Embargo Act of 1809. In his decision Marshall pointed out that the only part of the 1809 act allowing a ship's cargo to be confiscated required that the illicit cargo be imported with the knowledge of the owner or master. "In the information under consideration," he continued, "neither of these offences is charged." Marshall then declared that the government could not claim that a crime had been committed and then not expect to prove "that the law has been violated." He said: "The rule that a man shall not be charged with one crime and convicted of another, may sometimes cover real guilt, but its observance is essential to the preservation of innocence." This meant, Marshall insisted, that the prosecution must "state the crime which is to be proved, and state such a crime as will justify the judgment to be pronounced." Why? Marshall cited two reasons. First was "That the party accused may know against what charge to direct his defence" and second was "That the Court may see with judicial eyes that the fact, alleged to have been committed, is an offense against the laws, and may also discern the punishment annexed by the law to the specific offense." This case, as the earlier Burr case, obviously involved careless preparation by the government. The result was that the Court did not permit the confiscation of most of the ship's cargo.[11]

In another case the following year, *Clementson v. Williams*, the issue was whether a man's acknowledgment that he had once incurred a debt and that to his knowledge it had not been repaid could nullify the statute of limitations. Marshall said that the statute of limitations "is entitled to the same respect with other statutes, and ought not to be explained away." He admitted that the defendant's acknowledgment that the debt had once existed "goes to the original justice of the account," but then insisted that "this is not enough." The statute of limitations, he pointed out, was not enacted to deal with the validity of claims but to protect persons "from ancient claims, whether well or ill founded." That the debtor had admitted the debt once existed, Marshall said, does not mean that the debt had not been repaid—it may well have been paid by the debtor's partner—and such an admission cannot "take the case out of the statute of limitations."[12]

In *United States v. Wiltberger* Marshall spoke of "the tenderness of the law for the rights of individuals." A man had been charged with manslaughter while on board ship in the China seas. Could he be tried in an American court? Marshall ruled that he could not because the instance was not specified in the law. "It would be dangerous, indeed," he said, "to carry the principle, that a case which is within the reason or mischief of a statute, is within its provisions, so far as to punish a crime not enumerated in the statute. . . ." He acknowledged there was no reason why such crimes should go unpunished, "But Congress has not made them punishable, and this Court cannot enlarge the statute."[13]

Marshall insisted upon proper procedures even to the point of acknowledging that the Supreme Court itself had been in error in the 1817 case involving the ship *Argo* and efforts to claim restitution when she did not arrive at her destination. The United States produced a number of depositions which it attempted to offer in evidence. But Daniel Webster, for the other side, objected, arguing that the laws did not permit the Supreme Court to accept testimony in writing without "a commission issuing from this court." The laws allowed the lower courts to accept written testimony without a specific commission having been issued "but *here* it may not," Webster said of the Supreme Court. The rule's intention was to serve the ends of justice. Webster argued that the Supreme Court "is the tribunal of last resort" and that prohibition against *ex parte* testimony was to prevent the other party from being "surprised by the production of such proof to his irretrievable injury."

Marshall, in a brief decision, agreed with Webster. "A practice has hitherto prevailed to take depositions *de bene esse* in causes pending here, and, as no objection has been made at the bar, it has passed *sub silentio*," Marshall conceded. "Under such circumstances we cannot say that the United States are in default in taking depositions according to the usual practice," he said. Although the United States was not at fault, Marshall continued the case until the next term and told the prosecution if it wished to bring in any depositions then, it had better seek special commissions, as Webster had declared was proper.[14]

Marshall was such a stickler for proper procedure and for following the letter of the law that he inconvenienced himself personally. Bishop Meade, the Episcopal clergyman who became one of Marshall's close friends in his later years, once described Marshall as "a most conscientious man in regard to some things which others might regard as too trivial to be observed." The bishop told of once traveling between Fauquier County and Frederick with Marshall, "the roads being in their worst condition." They came to one road that was almost impassable. But there was a better route through a plantation. "The fence being down, or very low, I proceeded to pass over," recounted the man of God, but the man of the law suggested that they had better go around, by the muddy road which was public, rather than cross over private property. Marshall explained that "it was his duty as one in office to be very particular in regard to such things," said the bishop.[15]

He also was as decent a man as the law would permit him to be, believing that the law did not demand the impossible. He demonstrated this decency in many cases, beginning perhaps in 1805 with *Hallet v. Jenks*.[16] In 1799 an American ship stopped at a French port, landed her cargo, and took on board another cargo in an apparent violation of the federal law of June 13, 1798, prohibiting commercial relations between France and the United States. But the ship had not landed voluntarily. Rather, she had been driven to the port because of bad weather and forced by the French authorities there to deposit her cargo and allowed to pick up produce in return. Marshall ruled that the ship's crew were not in violation of the 1798 act because that law seemed "to imply an intentional offense on the part of the owners."

A somewhat similar case, involving the ship *Venus*, produced a similar reaction from Marshall in 1814. The issue was confiscation of a cargo by an American privateer. The *Venus* had sailed from England in 1812 before the news of the outbreak of the War of 1812 had reached England. It had been captured by an American privateer and its cargo confiscated as being that of an enemy ship. The owners of the *Venus*, however, were American citizens, born in England and naturalized in the United States; one had been living in England at the time the war began.

The majority opinion, written by Bushrod Washington and concurred in by Joseph Story—two judges who often have been charged with adhering entirely to Marshall's viewpoint—upheld the cargo confiscation on the basis of one of the owners being an English resident. Marshall, however, wrote a stinging dissent. It is lengthy (twenty-nine pages in the official reports) and is an appeal to men's consciences as well as to their law. He began by saying that he agreed with the majority when it was critical of an American citizen who would remain in England and conduct business there after learning that the United States and England were at war. But, he said, "I feel myself compelled to dissent" in the case of a citizen residing in England and engaging in trade there before the war began or before the citizen knew the war had begun. Marshall said the question was "undoubtedly complex and intricate," adding that although it was "difficult to draw a line of discrimination which shall be at the same time precise and equitable," he believed that "The difficulty does not appear to me to be sufficient to deter Courts from making the attempt. . . ."

Throughout the argument of the case there had been the suggestion that the owners of the ships were subject to having their cargoes confiscated because they were naturalized American citizens rather than native-born citizens. Marshall could see no justification for two classes of citizenship. "I think it is not for the United States, in such a case as this," he said, "to discriminate between them." He continued that "in a contest between the United States and the naturalized citizen, in a claim set up by the United States to confiscate his property, he may, I think, protect himself by any defence which would protect a native American. In the prosecution of such a claim, the United States are, I think, if I may be excused for borrowing from the common law a term peculiarly appropriate, *estopped* from saying that they have not placed this adopted son on a level with those born in their family."[17]

That Marshall dissent is intriguing from several aspects. First is his dividing with Washington and Story. The break was sharp enough and the language strong enough to dispel the charge that the three men could work only in unison with Marshall leading the way. More important was Marshall's claim that the law could not expect the impossible from people. There was no way the ship's owners in England could have known of the war declaration when the ship sailed. The third point was Marshall's refusal to draw a line between different kinds of citizens. In a new country where the law of citizenship was untested and attitudes had not yet hardened, his insistence that a naturalized citizen had the same rights as a native-born one was a significant commentary.

Several years later, in 1819, Marshall had to wrestle again with the question of citizenship while sitting on the Circuit Court in Virginia. In this instance the question was how to determine in which state a person was a citizen. "The Constitution, as well as the law, clearly contemplates a distinction between citizens of different states," said Marshall. He continued that the determination was not where the person was born, but "A citizen living in a state, with all the privileges and immunities of a citizen of that state, ought to share its burthens also, and will be considered, to every purpose, as a citizen. . . . Otherwise, a citizen by statute could never belong to any state, and could never maintain a suit in the courts of the United States. . . ." Again, in a land where the law of citizenship was still vague, Marshall's opinion that the person was a citizen of the state where he resided rather than where he was born went far to clarify the status of Americans.[18]

In 1815 there was another case in which Marshall demonstrated he was willing to push his basic sense of decency as far as the law and procedural safeguards would allow. The case, known as *Meade v. Deputy Marshal*, arose in the Virginia Circuit Court. A man had been imprisoned by the state court because he declined to pay a fine which had been imposed upon him when he refused to enter the militia. He sought a writ of habeas corpus from the Circuit Court, claiming that only federal courts had authority over questions involving the militia and that the court-martial which had convicted him was improper. Marshall agreed. "It is a principle of natural justice," the Chief Justice said, "which courts are never at liberty to dispense with, unless under the mandate of positive law, that no person shall be condemned unheard, or without an opportunity of being heard. There is no law authorizing courts martial to proceed against any person, without notice. Consequently, such proceeding is entirely unlawful." Marshall also argued that the federal laws establishing the militia had preempted any state authority. This Marshall opinion on the Circuit Court was overturned by the Supreme Court five years later in an opinion by Justice Johnson on a similar case. Johnson argued that the federal laws had not preempted the local laws in this instance, but this reversal does not override the thrust of Marshall's earlier opinion—that no person can be condemned unheard, and that the court-martial proceeding which did so was "entirely unlawful."[19]

As he was loath in the *Meade* case to see any federal power slip away, Marshall also was reluctant to see any improper imposition made on the position of a judge, whether by another branch of government or by a judge himself. In 1813, for example, when a District Court judge in Virginia named Tyler died, Marshall was asked "in several cases, said to be of great urgency, to perform the duties of a District Judge." In writing to the Secretary of State, James Monroe, Marshall explained that he felt compelled to refuse, "being of opinion that the act of Congress which enables a circuit judge to hold district courts during the disability of a district judge, does not confer the same authority after the death of that Judge." Marshall actually was raising a very significant point. If a Circuit Court judge could substitute for a deceased judge in a District Court, Presidents might be persuaded in certain instances not to fill vacancies caused by death, in this way contracting the size of the federal judiciary and making the responsibilities of its members onerous. That was a trifling with the judiciary which Marshall could not allow.

He had the same attitude toward trifling by judges. In 1820 the case known as *United States v. Lancaster* came before the supreme Court. It appeared to be a relatively simple one. It was an action for debt brought originally in a District Court in Pennsylvania, then appealed to the Circuit Court on a writ of error, and finally to the Supreme Court on the certification that the Circuit Court judges were divided on the case. In a brief opinion Marshall pointed out that the District Court judge whose decision was being appealed also had sat on the Circuit Court determining whether the appeal should be granted. This was not allowed, Marshall said. (Supreme Court Justices, in contrast, were allowed to hear appeals from Circuit Court rulings in which they had participated; this had been one of the problems of the job which Marshall hoped would be corrected by the Judiciary Act of 1801. As a matter of practice, however, they did not participate in hearing appeals from their own Circuit Court decisions.) "Consequently," said Marshall, "there could be no division of opinion to be certified to this Court" because the Circuit Court's division was not allowable.[20]

What was developing, of course, was Marshall's style as a judge. Procedure must be enforced. The powers of the court and the role of the judge must not be cheapened. If he was not always certain of the proper course, he decided as much as possible on the basis of the defendant, believing as he did that the judiciary's role was to be protective of individual innocence rather than only of society. Marshall did not hesitate to confess his uncertainty. In the 1820 case of *Conn v. Penn* the Supreme Court was considering an opinion of the Pennsylvania Circuit Court. The Marshall decision reversed the Pennsylvania court action because all the testimony which had been presented before the lower court was not available to the Supreme Court. "The Court has felt considerable doubts on this subject," Marshall confessed, "but thinks it the safe course to require that all the testimony on which the judge found his opinion, should, in cases, within the jurisdiction of this Court, appear in the record." He conceded that the two parties to the suit could consent to waive testimony if they wished, "but if this consent does not appear," he declared, "it cannot be presumed."[21] Through many of his decisions there are declarations like that, that the courts could not presume. It was always important to him that the courts not presume a right to violate procedural safeguards. The law protected the individual from the state, and procedural safeguards protected the individual from the court.

If the safeguards were to be truly effective, it was necessary that there be a universal understanding of the law. Marshall argued that point when his comments were asked on a bill to have the government pay the costs of printing the Supreme Court decisions. That the cases be reported "with accuracy and promptness is essential to correctness and uniformity of decision in all the courts of the United States." It is from the Court's decisions, Marshall said, that the public learns of interpretations of constitutional law and treaties and "It is obviously important that a knowledge of this exposition should be attainable by all." He continued: "It is certainly to be wished that independent tribunals having concurrent jurisdiction over the same subject, should concur in the principles on which they determine the causes coming before them. This concurrence can be obtained only by communicating to each the judgments of the others, and by that mutual respect which will probably be inspired by a knowledge of the grounds on which their judgments respectively stand."[22]

He consistently argued for a law library for the Supreme Court and supported the codification of state laws. In 1824, for example, Marshall and the six Associate Justices seized on some friendly words from President Monroe to formally seek his support for a law library because "the cases brought before the Supreme Court are frequently of such a character as to require extensive research." His friends in the lower courts often wrote him regarding plans to codify the laws in their states, knowing that he would respond favorably and they could then use his letters as endorsements of their plans.[23]

Part of Marshall's style as a judge was not to hesitate to assume for the judiciary the role of interpreting legislative acts. Although a half-century would pass before another act of Congress would be declared unconstitutional as had happened in *Marbury v. Madison*, there were many times when the Marshall Court sought to reaffirm its position as the arbitrator, beginning at least in 1804. The case was known as *Pennington v. Coxe* and involved a complicated taxing provision. The tax problem is long and deservedly forgotten, but Marshall's words regarding judicial interpretation of congressional acts are well remembered: "That a law is the best expositor of itself, that every part of an act is to be taken into view for the purpose of discovering the mind of the legislature; and that the details of one part may contain regulations restricting the extent of general expressions used in another part of the same act, are among those plain rules laid down by common sense for the exposition of statutes which have been uniformly acknowledged."

He used almost identical words eight years later in the 1812 case of *Schooner* Paulina's *Cargo v. United States.* A ship docked at Warwick Bay, Rhode Island, was being loaded with cargo when the cargo was seized on the basis of a violation of the Embargo Act. The Court unanimously decided against the government and allowed the release of the cargo saying that intent to ship the goods across the Atlantic was not proven, as the *Paulina* often had carried goods between American ports. "In construing these laws," said the Marshall opinion, "it has been truly stated to be the duty of the court to effect the intention of the legislature." Where was the intention to be discovered? "In the words which the legislature has employed to convey it," answered Marshall. He continued that while the legislature had the right to restrain a citizen, "it is the province of the court to apply the rule to the case thus explicitly described—not to some other case which judges may conjecture to be equally dangerous." Again, he was assuming for the judiciary all the power it had within its limits as a court—the court had the power to determine the intention of the legislature—but was making clear that the judiciary could not cross from behind the protective wall of its powers to penalize someone it believes dangerous but who was within the law.[24]

Whenever he had the opportunity Marshall asserted the power of the federal judiciary. In the 1817 case of *Slocum v. Mayberry*, involving another seizure of a ship's cargo in Rhode Island, Marshall's opinion shows him almost angry with the state for apparently trying to nibble away at the federal jurisdiction. A federal official had seized a cargo, and a state authority had taken it from him. Marshall would not allow the state's action to stand. "The judiciary act," he declared, "gives to the federal courts exclusive cognizance of all seizures made on land or water." If there was any question about that seizure, Marshall insisted, it "belongs exclusively to the federal courts, and cannot be drawn to another forum; and it depends upon the final decree of such [federal] courts whether such seizure is to be deemed rightful or tortious."[25] Marshall was telling the state courts that he was watching every move they made and that he was ready to pounce on them if they moved into the federal jurisdiction.

But while Marshall would not permit local jurisdictions to seize unauthorized power, he had an equally strong attitude toward such seizures by the federal judiciary. He used power available to him but did not grasp for power that was not his. In 1805 the Court had before it the case of Benjamin More,[26] who had been a justice of the peace in the District of Columbia and who was charged with accepting a fee after the law establishing his judgeship had been repealed. There were several aspects to the case, not the least important being whether Congress could diminish a judge's salary during his term (by repealing the act which authorized his judgeship). But to John Marshall the question was whether Congress had specifically given the Supreme Court appellate jurisdiction over criminal cases. He found that it had not and ruled that the Court was without jurisdiction. "This court," he said, " . . . will only review those judgments of the circuit court of Columbia, a power to re-examine which is expressly given by law."[27]

In an 1809 case, *Hodgson and Thompson v. Bowerbank and Others*, Marshall ruled expressly on the question of whether Congress can broaden the Constitution by legislation.[28] The case involved two aliens, and Congress had given the Circuit Courts jurisdiction over cases involving aliens. Did the Constitution authorize such a grant? "Turn to the article of the constitution of the United States," directed Marshall, "for the statute cannot extend the jurisdiction beyond the limits of the constitution." Asserting that the Constitution did not authorize such jurisdiction, he declared that "the objection was fatal."

Another such case came before the Virginia Circuit Court in 1822. Known as *Coate's Executrix v. Muse's Administrators*, it involved a complicated debtor-creditor relationship and the validity of a state law. The question before John Marshall, sitting as a federal judge on the Circuit Court, was whether the state act could be interpreted to apply to the specific situation. "The question, as I understand," he said, "is now, for the first time, raised in a court of justice." Marshall would have preferred to avoid having to make the interpretation, particularly because the language allowed "different constructions among intelligent gentlemen of the profession." Under those conditions, Marshall said, a judge "will be particularly anxious to avoid giving a first construction; and avoid it, if the case can be otherwise decided." But it was not only his hesitancy to dispute with other lawyers that deterred him. "It is always with much reluctance," he said, "that I break the way, in expounding the statute of a state; for the exposition of the acts of every legislature is, I think, the peculiar and appropriate duty of the tribunals, created by that legislature." However, in this instance Marshall believed himself forced to weigh the state act and did, in fact, uphold it.[29] He did, of course, in his more than three decades on the Supreme Court, challenge many state laws and rulings by state courts, but as this case showed, he did not anxiously seek power over the states.

Another facet of John Marshall's style as a judge was his use of precedents. In the great constitutional decisions which he wrote there are few citations of previous cases—actually this is true for many of his opinions on the Supreme Court. A criticism that has followed Marshall is that he cited so few precedents because he knew so few. That is not so. Before coming to the Supreme Court he had been one of the ablest lawyers in Richmond, a city renowned for its bar. He knew his law. His lack of citations can be attributed to another cause: there were not very many to cite. The creation of the Constitution had done more than set up a new source of law. It had established a new type of law. Previously the judges and the lawyers had to search through the musty records of English history to find the origins and guides for the rules of procedures that they called law. With the establishment of the Constitution, in areas in which it was particularly involved, men had to rely on their own wisdom to understand what the constitutional intention had been and how it could be applied. This did not require precedents so much as it did logic and intelligence. Joseph Story, after he had been on the Court for some years, spelled this out in a letter to an English friend, Sir William Scott. In this letter Story was speaking of admiralty law, but his comments are equally applicable to many of the different kinds of law which came before the Supreme Court. He wrote:

> The predicament, indeed, in which the Courts of this country found themselves at the beginning of the late war [of 1812], affords some apology for the minute discussions occasionally indulged in on mere points of practice, and also for the errors which are probably to be found here and there in the adjudications. We had not the benefit of a long-established and well-settled jurisdiction, and of an ancient customary law, regulating the practice of the Court.
>
> The traditions of former times and the modes of proceeding, were not familiarly preserved by a body of regular practitioners in the Court. The Admiralty Law was in a great measure a new system to us; and we had to grope our way as well as we could by the feeble and indistinct lights which glimmered through allusions incidentally made to the known rules and proceedings of an ancient court. Under these circumstances, every case, whether of practice or principle, was required to be reasoned out, and it

was scarcely allowable to promulgate a rule without at the same time expounding its conformity to the usages of Admiralty tribunals. I hope that a foundation has now been laid, upon which my successors in America may be able to build with more ease and security than fell my lot.[30]

As Herbert Johnson, the editor of the Marshall papers, has pointed out, Marshall and his fellow judges could not impose English public law upon the United States, nor could they select the common law in one state above that in other states. "Decision upon the basis of natural law, right reason, and constitutional intent was the only true course," said Johnson. "In taking the latter alternative, Marshall set forth, not precise rules of constitutional law, but rather the broad general outlines upon which future generations would evolve more explicit constitutional doctrines."[31]

Although he had to go far beyond precedents for the origins of his constitutional decisions, Marshall could use precedents, and did, when they were needed. As a young lawyer in Virginia in the 1780s, he had served on several committees of the Assembly, drawing up compilations of the state laws. He had helped organize them, understood them, and had a grasp of legal scholarship equal to that of any man in the nation. This was particularly evident when he held Circuit Court in Richmond and Raleigh. Then he was more involved with state laws, local business matters which came under common law, and less with the broad strokes of constitutional law. Decisions there required a thorough knowledge of the previous law and an ability to apply it. A case in point is *Black v. Scott*, a complicated suit involving the use of real estate in the payment of debts; Marshall's heavy reliance on precedents and citations showed a comprehensive knowledge of local law.[32]

And so on the Supreme Court when the question of precedents or citations did arise, Marshall demonstrated himself as complete a master as any of the lawyers arguing before him. An example of this mastery is in the 1804 case of *Murray v. Charming Betsy*, in which there are two interesting footnotes. The case revolved around the seizure of a ship which once had been American-owned and whether the seizure could be justified as an effort to regain it for the American owner. One of the lawyers had referred to a case that had been decided against allowing probable cause as a justification for seizure. The first footnote reads: "The Chief Justice observed, that this case was overruled two years afterwards, in a case cited in a note to Gwillim's edition of Bac. Abr." The second footnote reads: "The Chief Justice mentioned the case of the Sally, Captain Joy, in 2 Rob. 185. (Amer. edit.) where a court of vice-admiralty had decreed, in a revenue case, that there was no probable cause of seizure."[33]

Marshall himself once explained his approach to the use of precedents. The explanation came in an 1821 decision, after Marshall had been on the bench for two decades and was therefore speaking from practical experience. He began by saying that "a maxim not to be disregarded" is that "general expressions, in every opinion, are to be taken in connection with the case in which those expressions are used." If such expressions go beyond a particular case, he continued, "They may be respected, but ought not to control the judgment in a subsequent case" even though the questions before the Court may be similar. Why should the comments from one case not be controlling in another? "The reason of this axiom is obvious," Marshall answered. "The question actually before the court is investigated with care and considered in its full extent. Other principles which may serve to illustrate it, are considered in their relation to the case decided," he explained, "but their possible bearing on all other cases is seldom completely investigated."[34]

Marshall was saying that the past cannot be ignored—"general expressions . . . may be respected"—but that the past cannot control the future—"ought not to control the judgment in a subsequent case." The past is a guide and an aid but not a dictator. He seemed to be saying that men must understand that the law develops, builds, and even changes—building upon the principle of decency between men, it absorbs the temporal passion of its time to leave, at the end, only the decency remaining.

This second decade of Marshall's leadership was marked by a number of decisions in the field of international law that went beyond ownership of captured ships and cargoes. Marshall had a profound respect for international law, calling it "a law which contributes more to the happiness of the human race than all the statues which will come from the hands of the sculptor, or all the paintings that were ever placed on canvass."[35]

One of his first major cases was that of the *Schooner Exchange v. M'Faddon*.[36] The ship *Exchange*, owned by two Americans, was captured on the Atlantic Ocean by French ships, given a French name, and sailed as a French ship. Bad weather, however, forced her into the port of Philadelphia where her original owners obtained a court order for her seizure. The question before the Supreme Court was whether it could order the ship returned to its original American owners. Marshall said that the ship could not be returned to the Americans. His decision is a model explanation of the need for what has come to be called diplomatic immunity. "The case involves the very delicate and important inquiry," said Marshall at the beginning of the decision, "whether an American citizen can assert, in an American court, a title to an armed national vessel, found within the waters of the United States."

The jurisdiction of the Supreme Court, he continued, could not extend beyond the jurisdiction of the American nation, and any limits upon that nation within its own territories "must be traced up to the consent of the nation itself." He then said that nations, including the United States, had consented to surrender jurisdiction over sovereigns of other nations who come onto their territory as friends. "The perfect equality and absolute independence of sovereigns," he said, "and this common interest impelling them to mutual intercourse, and an interchange of good offices with each other, have given rise to a class of cases in which every sovereign is understood to waive the exercise of a part of that complete exclusive territorial jurisdiction, which has been stated to be the attribute of every nation." The entire world, Marshall said, had accepted that understanding because a foreign sovereign cannot subject himself "to a jurisdiction incompatible with his dignity, and the dignity of his nation." This extended to the sovereign's ministers and to his ships, and Marshall said it extended to the *Exchange* because she was "commissioned by, and in the service of the Emperor of France. The evidence of this fact is not controverted."[37] In addition to explaining diplomatic immunity, the Marshall decision may have averted a war or at least hostilities because Napoleon certainly would never have permitted the seizure of one of his ships in the port of Philadelphia without some kind of forceful reaction.

Another major case arose out of the War of 1812: *Brown v. United States*.[38] An English-chartered ship had sailed from Savannah to England in 1812, and then was redirected to New Bedford, Massachusetts, because of the Embargo Act of April 4, 1812. When war was declared in November of 1812, the English cargo was sold; but then the United States sued for the proceeds of the sale claiming that the act of war against England had the effect of confiscating English property found within the United States. Marshall acknowledged that "no doubt is entertained" that war allowed full confiscation of "the property of the enemy wherever found." But while it allows it, it does not necessarily direct it; he asked, "Does it vest only a right the assertion of which depends on the will of the sovereign power?" He concluded that it confers the right but that right must be asserted specifically, which was not done in this instance. "The modern rule then would seem to be," Marshall wrote, "that tangible property belonging to an enemy and found in the country at the commencement of war, ought not to be immediately confiscated." He described that rule as "introduced by commerce in favor of moderation and humanity" and received "throughout the civilized world." In expounding the American Constitution, he continued, "a construction ought not lightly to be admitted which would give to a declaration of war an effect in this country it does not possess elsewhere, and which would fetter that exercise of entire discretion respecting enemy property, which may enable the government to apply to the enemy the rule that he applies to us." The United States could not claim the proceeds of the sale.[39] Story disagreed with Marshall in this decision, writing a lengthy and harsh dissent.

Marshall's decisions in cases of international law, as in other types of cases, are models of law being applied to the necessities of life. If the *Exchange* had been returned by the American court to her original owners, then no American ship stopping at a French port would have been safe. If English property could have been confiscated at the beginning of the War of 1812, then any American possessions in England or in other countries also would have been under siege. Marshall recognized that law was a system for society's existence. But he would not surrender American sovereignty under international law, saying that "The decisions of the Courts of every country, so far as they are founded upon a law common to every country, will be received, not as authority, but with respect."[40]

Most cases argued before the Supreme Court during this period lacked the drama and the impact of great constitutional or treaty questions. The dramatic cases bracketed weeks and sometimes years of dry and often dull examinations of fact. Usually the seats in the spectators' sections of the Court chamber were filled, less because of the intellectual contests that might take place than because Washington women enjoyed watching the young lawyers perform. The lawyers were greater dramatists than the actors of the time, and they often could brighten a bored wife's day with a stirring oration. Mrs. Margaret Bayard Smith in her account of Washington society at this point told of how the ladies had their special favorites and often came to the Court chamber to cheer the particular hero of the moment. One favorite during the decade 1810–1820 was William Pinkney of Maryland, who was Attorney General under Madison. Although Mrs. Smith assured her readers that she personally did not believe the Supreme Court was an appropriate place for women, "curiosity" one day compelled her "to join the female crowd who throng the court room." Regarding Pinkney's performance she wrote:

> The effect of the female admiration and attention has been very obvious, but it is a doubt to me whether it has been beneficial, indeed I believe otherwise. A member told me he doubted now, there had been much more speaking on this account, and another gentleman told me, that one day Mr. Pinkney had finished his argument and was just about seating himself when Mrs. Madison and a train of ladies enter'd—he recommenced, went over the same ground, using fewer arguments, but scattering more flowers. And the day I was there I am certain he thought more of the female part of his audience than of the court, and on concluding, he recognized their presence, when he said, "He would not weary the court, by going into a long list of cases to prove his argument, as it would not only be fatiguing to them, but inimical to the laws of good taste, which on the present occasion, (bowing low) he wished to obey." The court was crowded while he spoke; the moment he sat down, the whole audience rose, and broke up, as if the court had adjourned.[41]

But exciting performances were not customary. William Wirt, the Richmond lawyer who had been a member of the prosecution in the Aaron Burr trial and later was United States Attorney General, argued his second case before the Supreme Court in 1817. It involved a ship seizure, and the question was whether the ship and her cargo were neutral or hostile property. Wirt represented the privateers and therefore had to prove that the ship was hostile—i.e., British. His opponents claimed the ship was neutral—i.e., Russian. "This issue of fact," wrote Wirt, "was to be decided by the analysis and synthesis of about five hundred dry, deranged ship documents, which were to be read and commented on." The case disappointed Wirt. "You perceive the utter impossibility of clothing such a subject either with ornament or interest," he said in a letter, "and when you are farther told, that there was not one principle of dubious law involved in the case, you will as readily see that there was no opportunity for the display of any cogency or argument." As dull as the arguments were, the women in the audience stayed in the courtroom until dinnertime, to Wirt's surprise—indicating either that the arguments were not as dull as Wirt reported or that he gave a more attractive performance than the materials at hand indicated was possible.[42]

The work of the Court was increasing. In 1818 Joseph Story lamented that since being appointed in 1812 he had heard and decided four times as many arguments as had his predecessor, who sat on the Court from 1789 until 1811. Story complained that the Justices had not received a salary increase since the first Congress had set their salaries at $3,500 a year in 1789. At that time, the salary was equal to that given the heads of the Treasury and State departments. In 1799 the department heads' salaries were raised to $5,000 a year but the Supreme Court Justices received no increase. In December of 1818 Story was not optimistic about an increase. "Unfortunately," he wrote, "no one seems heartily to exert himself to save the present Judges from starving in splendid poverty." But the next year, despite Story's pessimism, the Justices did receive a $1,000 increase. Marshall's salary as Chief Justice was $500 more than that paid to the other Justices. He received $4,000 a year when he was first appointed, and that was increased to $5,000 in 1819. This, of course, was far below the potential available to him if he had remained a lawyer in private practice and indicates why he felt compelled to write the Washington biography and also why he speculated so much in land development.

The Supreme Court Justices continued to find riding circuit a burden. Each year John Marshall, even in his sixties and seventies, rode from Richmond to Raleigh, North Carolina, to hold Circuit Court there. The roads were bad, and travel was dangerous and debilitating, but it was required of the Justices. In December of 1816 President James Madison included in his message to Congress a request that the Justices be relieved of riding circuit. "The time seems to have arrived," he said, "which claims for members of the Supreme Court a relief from itinerary fatigues, incompatible as well with the age which a portion of them will always have attained as with the researches and preparations which are due to their stations and to the juridical reputation of their country." Congress, however, failed to act, and Justices of the Supreme Court continued to ride circuit throughout most of the nineteenth century.[43]

One aspect of being on the Supreme Court was the entree it offered the judges into Washington's social life. Although the capital of the United States would continue for many decades as a provincial city when compared to the European capitals, it still had its moments—and its places. The House of Representatives was the meeting place of the sexes. "There are here peculiar facilities for forming acquaintances," Mrs. Smith reported, "for a stranger cannot be long here, before it is generally known. The house of representatives is the lounging place of both sexes, where acquaintance is as easily made as at public amusements." The members of the House seemed to enjoy taking time off from the business of government to entertain and mix with the ladies who came to the galleries to ogle them in their oratorical magnificence. Once in 1819, during a speech by John C. Calhoun, Mrs. Smith reported:

> The gentlemen are grown very gallant and attentive and as it was impossible to reach the ladies through the gallery, a new mode was invented of supplying them with oranges, etc. They tied them up in handkerchiefs, to which was fixed a note indicating for whom it was designed and then fastened to a long pole. This was taken on the floor of the house and handed up to the ladies who sat in front of the gallery. I imagine there were near a hundred ladies there, so that these presentations were frequent and quite amusing, even in the midst of Mr. Calhoun's speech. I, and the ladies near me, were more accessible and were more than supplied with oranges, cakes, etc. We divided what was brought us with each other and were as social as if acquainted.[44]

Social life in Washington was generally more refined than that, and meetings took place not over oranges at the tops of poles but at dinner parties. John Marshall, the few weeks he was in Washington each year for the meeting of the Court, was often invited to such parties. He was convivial, well liked, knew everyone, and was a welcome addition. John Quincy Adams in 1818, when he was Secretary of State, remarked about a dinner party attended by Marshall and several other Justices, that "We had a very pleasant and convivial party, and had occasion to repeat a remark made in former years, that there is more social ease and enjoyment in these companies, when all the guests are familiarly acquainted with one another, than at our usual dinners during the session of Congress, when we have from fifteen to twenty members assembled from various parts of the Union, and scarcely acquainted together." Marshall frequently was invited to dine at the White House, and answered "yes" to the invitations with alacrity.

John Marshall and several of the other Justices were such charming and pleasant gadabouts that a contemporary newspaper account classifies them as leaders of the social scene: "The city begins to be gay, but the season of the greatest festivity is after the Supreme Court commences its session. The arrival of the Judges, counsellors, parties, etc., connected with the High Court creates a great stir in the Metropolis. There are now tea and dining parties daily. The President gives two superb dinners a week, and sees gentlemen on business and etiquette every Wednesday. Every other Wednesday evening Mrs. Monroe holds a drawing room."[45]

Although he enjoyed the social life in Washington, Joseph Story sometimes found it a little too much. Occasionally, in fact, he seemed to find Washington a little too much—and in this respect he has been imitated by many subsequent visitors to the city. In 1818 he complained that Court business was so heavy that he had little time to attend "any place of pleasure or fashion." And then he complained that there was "a great deal of gayety, splendor, and as I think, extravagance in the manners and habits of the city." He was neither the first nor the last to lament that "the old notions of republican simplicity are fast wearing away, and the public taste becomes more and more gratified with public amusements and parade." Story liked James Monroe, then President, but he believed that the House of Representatives was becoming too powerful "under its lofty pretensions to be the guardians of the people and its rights." The good men—"of real talent, and real virtue, and real patriotism"—had few differences of opinion. Rather, Story was concerned by "a new race of men . . . springing up to govern the nation; they are the hunters after popularity, men ambitious, not of the honor, so much as of the profits of office—the demagogues whose principles hang laxly upon them, and who follow not so much what is right, as what leads to a temporary vulgar applause." Story was afraid these men would succeed to power "and if so, we may yet live to see many of our best institutions crumble in the dust."[46]

Washington, in short, was becoming what it always would be—a beacon for men who sought power, for the ambitious, and for those who sought to accomplish what they considered worthy goals; and a home for those who had power and who were reluctant to surrender it to those grasping for it. It was the site of the conceited, those who believed themselves to be right and who acknowledged only that others were wrong. It was a city which transformed the wildest maverick to the most conservative establishmentarian. And the wonder of the city, and of the government it houses, is not that these ambitions and conceits exist, but that on the occasions when talent is required, men can overcome their baser instincts and accomplish what must be done.

During his second decade as Chief Justice John Marshall passed from his fifties to his sixties. Like any man in that period of life, he was interested and concerned with the development of his children. As with many children born to famous fathers, there were problems. There seems to be a kind of rule in life that men who succeed in public life cannot succeed with their families.

He had one daughter, Mary, and he apparently doted on

her. Once when she was about sixteen and living with an uncle while attending school, she complained at length about her uncle and said she could not wait to return home. She said she would not ask her uncle for a "cent" no matter how much she might need it. "Thank gracious my father is not like him," she added, "he does not grudge every half cent that he is obliged to spend." She married Jacquelin Burwell Harvie the day after her eighteenth birthday and lived in Richmond. According to a family history, she continued to be close to her father, making her home near his and seeing him daily.[47]

Years later Mary wrote a brief account of her father. Her first recollection of him "was not a very agreeable one." She could not have been more than three years old and, after crying for some time, she heard her father's footsteps on the stairs. "I hoped when everything was quiet that he would return to the dining room, vain hope," she wrote, "he came up the stairs into the nursery and slapped me once or twice. This circumstance with his dignity of deportment and the uniform deference and respect paid him by every one gave me a salutary *awe* of him, which I do not believe I ever entirely lost." She continued:

> Altho he very rarely spoke to [his children] in an excited tone and always gave them his attention when they addressed him, and never exhibited even impatience when interrupted whatever his occupation might be—whether engaged in writing or reading—there was a nursery in the room below his office in which there was frequently a great deal of noise, yet I never knew him to complain or at any time even to request less noise. There was but little variation in his manner toward individuals. He was uniformly polite, kind, attentive and unassuming towards every one; he listened attentively to the humblest individual as to the highest and never failed to understand thoroughly the drift of the speaker and to do full justice to his remarks. His sons were all settled in the county of Fauquier and he was in the habit of visiting them for many years in the spring and summer never attended by a servant, in the spring he traveled on horseback and in a stick gig in the summer. . . . His arrival at the home of either of his sons was always hailed with great pleasure by every member of the family young and old. The servants all evinced their pleasure at seeing him. To each one of them he would speak a kind word and make inquiries as to the condition of their families. . . .[48]

Marshall's eldest son, Thomas, born in 1784, attended Princeton, graduated at the age of nineteen, and practiced law in

Richmond for a time, but became ill and retired to the family property at Oak Hill. He was a well-educated, sophisticated man who brought science to farming and transformed what had become the barren land of his family into a fertile and successful farm. He served in the state legislature and of the Marshall children was the only one who showed the potential to match or at least approach his father's attainments. However, his choice of living in the country and a relatively early death (in 1835) made impossible any substantial achievement.[49]

The next son was Jaquelin Ambler Marshall,* who became a medical doctor and dabbled in theology. He too retired to Fauquier County, to a home called Prospect Hill, where he lived a life of ease made possible by the land that came from his father and the labor that came from slaves. A family history said of him that "With very little ambition, he was satisfied to superintend his farm and to entertain his select friends."[50]

The third son was John, who attended Harvard and should have graduated with the class of 1817. He was dismissed from the school, however, for "immoral and dissolute conduct" in March 1815. Marshall was extremely pained at his son's behavior and spoke of "my culpable son." The Chief Justice said he could not "entirely excuse myself for the unlimited confidence I placed in him. I think myself in some measure accessory to his disgrace." The father wished to help the son "retrieve his reputation and to restore himself to the affection and good opinion of his friends and connexions." But in all honesty he had to concede that he could perceive in his son "no mark of sincere penitence, no deep conviction of his faults, no resolute determination to correct them." Marshall believed that everything depended upon his son's willingness to take himself in hand and straighten himself out. "He may rest assured that it will not be in his power to practice imposition on me," said Marshall to a friend. "In the wounded feelings of a father anxious for the welfare of a son of whose unworthiness he is unwilling to be convinced, your goodness will I trust find an apology for the trouble given you by this letter."

John ultimately returned to Fauquier County, to a home called Mt. Blanc. He married adequately for his family's station. He served in the state legislature on occasion and his spirits were such that he was extremely popular and could have been a successful Virginia politician. His problems from his Harvard days

---

* Polly's father's name was spelled Jacquelin but her son's name was spelled Jaquelin.

followed him, however, and he drank too much. He died in 1833, at the age of thirty-five.[51]

The fourth son, James Keith, was a Harvard student also, a member of the class of 1818. He also left in 1815, but apparently not under the disgrace that the young John had earned. This son was placed with a business firm in Philadelphia and went there directly from Harvard. Marshall wrote to the owners of the firm that he was "extremely anxious respecting the conduct and morals of my son" and hoped that his new employers would watch him closely. "I flatter myself I may say that the more you exercise the authority of a father and guardian and a master the more shall I be indebted to you and the more grateful shall I be for your goodness. . . . His first sliding into bad company, should it happen, will I trust be firmly and sternly corrected." James Keith apparently had no trouble at the business house, staying there several years. In 1821 he married into the prominent Burwell family and, like his brothers, retired to a family home in Fauquier County. His particular estate was known as Leeds Manor. There is a suggestion that in later years James Keith did not find the life of a country gentleman entirely suitable to his tastes. "I wish your speculation may be successful," John Marshall wrote to him in the 1830s. "I have my doubts whenever farmers become merchants. The danger is that they will create bad debts. It is easy to lay out money but difficult to call it in when it is wanted."[52]

The last child was Edward Carrington Marshall. He seems to have been thoroughly spoiled. When he was sixteen he was attending a school in Fauquier County and received this letter from his father: "Had you expressed to your mother a month or two past your wants of shirts, she would have got them ready to send up by Mr. Page or Miss Pickett, but they are gone and it is not probable that another opportunity will offer till I come up in August. You ought to recollect that making of shirts like everything else required some thing more than a mere order for their production." Two years later Edward Carrington enrolled at Harvard, and Marshall asked Joseph Story to watch out for him. Story did so, and the first thing he had to do was advance Edward some money. This greatly embarrassed Marshall, and he made a point of sending his son's allowance to an intermediary, usually Story. "I could have remitted this draft or a bill directly to my son," said Marshall in one account to Story, "but I sent him a bill in August for $100, and my sons, in the North, have such an aptitude for spending money, that I am unwilling to tempt Edward by placing too much in his hands."

[563]

At Harvard Edward was the typical child of a well-to-do family who did not anticipate having to work too hard to subsidize his lifestyle. "I am daily resolving to do better," he announced to his mother, "but cannot become diligent. My whole history can be summed up to you in a few words. I am very hearty, with perhaps too much amusements, and by no means so studious as my beloved mother would wish me." He also returned to Fauquier County, to the estate known as Carrington, and "engaged in agriculture," according to the family history. In the Virginia of the first half of the nineteenth century, that usually meant doing very little.[53]

As an eldest son himself and with both his parents dead, John Marshall became the head of an immense family. His fourteen brothers and sisters had numerous progeny, and he was keeping after them, helping them and keeping track of them. For one nephew there was a letter to the Secretary of the Navy seeking a midshipman's appointment. For another nephew Marshall wrote a letter to his brother Louis in Kentucky, asking him to watch over the nephew's education. "His father when dying," John Marshall wrote, "requested me to supply his place as far as should be in my power and I accepted the trust with an earnest wish to fulfill the engagement. Had the state of my family allowed of my taking him into my own home I should still have preferred his being brought up in the country under your eye. This town is a dangerous place for youth and our seminaries are far from being respectable." And to a sister Marshall had the painful task of reporting that her son had died in an epidemic in Kentucky. "I attempted to prepare her for the event," he said, "and to break it gradually to her; but the instant I mentioned Kentucky, and an epidemic, the whole dreadful truth flashed upon her at once; and I was under the necessity of telling her that her son was dead. Afflicting as is, under any circumstances, the loss of a child, deeply as I have felt it, and often as I have witnessed its effect on others, I could scarcely anticipate the depth of woes, the intensity of grief which was inflicted by this communication."[54]

Marshall still had his own personal problems. His wife Polly, whom he loved devotedly, became increasingly ill. A friendly family account reports that by 1816, to Polly's "extreme nervousness was added an ailment which seems to have been a form of anemia, causing spells of severe weakness. At the age of 51 she had assumed the privileges of an old lady, while the Chief Justice at 62 was eager for life as ever." In that year Marshall confided to his brother Louis that "My wife continues in wretched health. Her nervous system is so affected that she cannot sit in a room while a person walks across the floor. I am now preparing to convey her out of town in order to escape the noisy rejoicing of the [Christmas] season which is approaching." A year later he wrote again to his brother that Polly's health continued to fail: "I am entirely excluded from society by her situation." While the next year there was some improvement in Polly, she never did regain her health and she lived out the remainder of her years as an invalid cared for with love and tenderness by her husband. Although John Marshall was a relatively vigorous man—"as eager for life as ever"—the stories of concubines and of illicit relations with black women slaves which have followed the memories of other prominent Virginians were never circulated about him. He had been captivated by the young woman he had met in Williamsburg years earlier, and he always was her prisoner.[55]*

For Marshall there were other concerns also. In 1811 his interest in farming—besides the land he owned in Fauquier County, he also owned a farm near Richmond—led him to become president of the "First Society for Promoting Agriculture." In 1816 this group was reorganized into the Richmond chapter of the Agricultural Society of Virginia with Marshall as one of the members of its committee of correspondence. The man who succeeded him as president was John Taylor of Caroline. Taylor was an old Jeffersonian who soon would become famous as the author of several studies purporting to show that states had the right to secede from the Union, or at least to refuse to obey laws they disagreed with. His thesis was an extension of the approach Jefferson and Madison had taken in the late 1790s in the Virginia and Kentucky Resolutions. Taylor would use his treatises against the extension of federal authority by the Supreme Court under John Marshall.[56]

Marshall still continued his interest in land; even his home in Richmond was growing. The insurance policy on his property in 1810 shows four units: the house, a laundry, a kitchen, and an office, with a total insured value of $7,600. According to the Fauquier County records, during the period from 1810 to 1820 John Marshall sold almost three dozen parcels of property in the county. And the Marshalls still thought in terms of large tracts

---

* This author has met in Fauquier County an elderly black man whose family tradition has it that John Marshall fathered his grandmother in approximately 1820. There is no documentary evidence to support that tradition, as there would not be. But the timing and other factors involved lead me to believe that it was one of Marshall's sons who fathered this man's grandmother and not Marshall himself. I mention this because the story is well known in that area and may spread beyond the county lines.

of land. A note to a nephew in 1816 includes a list of landholdings in Kentucky which the Marshall brothers had an interest in.
The items were of twelve thousand, five thousand, three thousand, and some for one thousand and two thousand acres.[57]

Through these family concerns and his land investments,
and his watchfulness over the Court, Marshall succeeded in avoiding becoming either pompous or a bore. One of his friends, Joseph
Hopkinson, spoke of Marshall in a relaxed mood: "He was as
playful as a boy. He was not afraid that his dignity would suffer,
by the indulgence of a natural gaiety of temper. He was a hearty
laugher, and caught and enjoyed a joke, beyond any other man
I have known."[58]

Such was the man who would lead the Supreme Court
during his second decade as Chief Justice to a brilliant declaration of the supremacy of the federal government.

7

THE MOST ACTIVE commercial enterprise in the young United
States was land speculation. The states had vast tracts of
unmapped and unmeasured lands which they could not use.
These were sold and the buyers resold them at a profit, and they
were again resold—the price continually rising as one speculator after another tried to share in "a good thing." In some of
these speculations the developers made money; in others they
did not do so well. John Marshall himself is an example of a
cautious speculator who did well with his land investments while
Robert Morris is an example of one who speculated himself into
bankruptcy and jail. Most of this speculation, while financially
dangerous, was legitimate. Then there was the Yazoo land fraud.

The lands along the Yazoo River in what was then Georgia
seemed ripe for speculation; the level of corruption involved is
difficult to comprehend, even in modern times. Georgia was willing to unload the lands because both the Indians and the Spaniards were nibbling at the territory and protecting the lands was
a nuisance. Also, their only value lay in the projected opening of
the Mississippi River to navigation so that products from the
lands could be taken and sold in New Orleans. However, in the
1790s neither Georgia nor the United States had any authority
over the Mississippi River (Spain controlled it). Georgia, in short,
was willing to sell the lands because it believed it was giving
away nothing for whatever was the going price.

This would not have been too bad, perhaps, except that the state government sold very cheaply. The residents of the state were indignant. Why had the legislators set the price so low, they demanded. They seemed to have a point; between one cent and a cent and one-half an acre was very cheap even for land under Indian and Spanish attack. The answer became obvious. Almost every member of the state legislature benefited from the land sale, either as a purchaser or by being affiliated with companies involved in the purchases. By some accounts every member of the legislature except one stood to gain financially from his vote to sell the Yazoo lands cheaply. The people of Georgia then went to the polls in a mood to "throw the rascals out." Millions of acres were involved and, because of the low price, millions of dollars had been lost. The Yazoo land deal was the only issue in the Georgia campaign, and when the people spoke the state government was turned out. The next legislature voted to rescind the sale, and then later, ceded the disputed land to the United States.[1]

There were few people who disagreed with the act of the legislature rescinding the original sale, and that might have been the happy end of a troublesome story except for one factor. The original purchasers, whatever their intention and whatever their morality, had in many cases resold parts of their tracts. This re-selling had gone on while the original arrangement with the state of Georgia was in effect. The second and third and subsequent purchasers thought they were engaging in legitimate land deals. When the legislature rescinded the land sale, they were left with no land although they had paid for it in good faith. While this happened to many people, two men named John Peck and Robert Fletcher brought their case to the Supreme Court. Peck had sold Fletcher fifteen thousand acres of the Yazoo lands for $3,000. The sale had been consummated apparently in good faith by both parties, and only later did Fletcher discover that the original sale of land had been rescinded by the Georgia state legislature, and he was without land as well as being out $3,000. He sued, and the question that confronted the Supreme Court was whether the Constitution restricted the rights of states: Could the Supreme Court of the United States nullify the act of the Georgia legislature rescinding the original sale?

A decade after the original trouble, in 1809, the case was argued before the Supreme Court. (There was a pause in the deliberations so John Marshall could go to another part of the Capitol and swear in James Madison as President of the United States, succeeding Thomas Jefferson.) The disputants in the case were well represented: John Quincy Adams and Robert Goodloe Harper for Peck, who had sold the land, and Luther Martin of

Maryland for Fletcher, the purchaser. The Supreme Court Justices were reluctant to decide the case—which goes contrary to the opinion that under Marshall's leadership the Justices were anxious for opportunities to assert federal authority. Undoubtedly they knew the consequences of taking on a popular cause and perhaps rendering an opinion that would be unpopular. The night of Madison's inaugural there was a ball for him at Long's Hotel. All of Washington society was there, and apparently everyone else in town also—"The crowd was excessive; the heat oppressive, and the entertainment bad," summed up John Quincy Adams. Associate Justice Brockholst Livingston was at the ball and told Quincy Adams that the Court objected to having the case thrust upon it. For some years Congress had been trying to resolve the conflicting Yazoo land claims but had been unable to do so because of political considerations. The Justices believed that *Fletcher v. Peck* was a rigged case, designed to throw the entire matter into the hands of the Supreme Court to solve what the Congress had been unable to. John Marshall also had said much the same thing, Quincy Adams heard. All in all, Adams was not very confident when he returned to the Court chamber a few days later to hear the Court's decision. What he heard was not a decision but a postponement. Marshall read a written announcement stating that the Supreme Court would not hand down an opinion that year because there had been a defect in the pleadings. The controversy over the Yazoo lands already had dragged on for more than a decade. It would continue for another year.[2]

Marshall's decision the next year is one of his most controversial.[3] Dumas Malone has written that Marshall "rendered disservice to his country" with the decision.[4] In it Marshall seemed to countenance fraud and to protect the land speculators. This decision may very well have represented Federalist politics at their worst. There were, however, other factors.

The Chief Justice began his decision, as he often did, with a positive statement that seemed as solid as the rocks in the Blue Ridge Mountains he loved so well: "That the legislature of Georgia, unless restrained by its own Constitution, possesses the power of disposing of the unappropriated lands within its limits, in such manner as its own judgment shall dictate, is a proposition not to be controverted." No one could argue with that. Then, as far as Marshall was concerned, the only question before the Supreme Court was whether there was something in the state constitution which prohibited the disposal of the lands. He answered the question quickly, and his comments are a model of judicial restraint. He said:

The question, whether a law be void for its repugnancy
to the constitution, is, at all times, a question of much
delicacy, which ought seldom, if ever, to be decided in
the affirmative, in a doubtful case. The court, when impelled by duty to render such a judgment, would be unworthy of its station, could it be unmindful of the solemn
obligations which that station imposes. But it is not on
slight implication and vague conjecture that the legislature
is to be pronounced to have transcended its powers, and
its acts to be considered as void. The opposition between
the constitution and the law should be such that the judge
feels a clear and strong conviction of this incompatibil-
ity with each other.

In this case the court can perceive no such opposition.
. . . The Court cannot say that, in passing that act, the legislature has transcended its powers, and violated the constitution. . . .

That by itself was not sufficient. The Yazoo land sale had
been rescinded not because of "slight implication and vague conjecture" but because the members of the legislature which had
authorized the original sale had all been bought. Marshall turned
to that point.

He did not deny the existence of the corruption, and
described its presence in the Yazoo land scheme as "circumstances most deeply to be deplored." But he then raised the question of the third parties, those who had acquired land in good
faith from the original purchasers. "How far a court of justice
would, in any case, be competent, on proceedings instituted by
the state itself, to vacate a contract thus formed, and to annul
rights acquired, under that contract, by third persons having no
notice of the improper means by which it was obtained, is a question which the court would approach with much circumspection,"
he cautioned. If the Court went too far, Marshall seemed to be
asking, could it subsequently be controlled? He continued:

It may well be doubted how far the validity of a law
depends upon the motives of its framers, and how far the
particular inducements, operating on members of the supreme sovereign power of a state, to the formation on
members of the supreme sovereign power of a state, to the
formation of a contract by that power, are examinable in
a court of justice. If the principle be conceded, that an act
of the supreme sovereign power might be declared null by
a court, in consequence of the means which procured it,
still would there be much difficulty in saying to what extent those means must be applied to produce this effect.

Must it be direct corruption, or would interest or undue influence of any kind be sufficient? Must the vitiating cause operate on a majority, or on what number of the members? Would the act be null, whatever might be the wish of the nation, or would its obligation or nullity depend upon the public sentiment?

If the majority of the legislature be corrupted, it may well be doubted, whether it be within the province of the judiciary to control their conduct, and, if less than a majority act from impure motives, the principle by which judicial interference would be regulated, is not clearly discerned.

Considering John Marshall's reputation as an activist jurist, anxious to impose the power of the federal judiciary on the states, those paragraphs are an interesting argument for judicial restraint.

Marshall then pointed out, however, that the suit did not directly involve the state legislature of Georgia but, rather, two individuals, one of whom was caught in a claim that the sale of the land was fraudulent and was faced with the probability that his contract could not be upheld in a court of law. Marshall conceded in his decision that "the conveyance will be set aside" if it were obtained by fraud and the fraud was clearly proven. "But," he quickly added, "the rights of third persons, who are purchasers without notice, for a valuable consideration, cannot be disregarded." He then launched into a plea for justice for the innocent party, a plea which more than a century and a half later still rings with the theme of the law as a recourse, a haven for all, a concept that provides justice:

> Titles, which, according to every legal test, are perfect, are acquired with that confidence which is inspired by the opinion that the purchaser is safe. If there be any concealed defect, arising from the conduct of those who had held the property long before he acquired it, of which he had no notice, that concealed defect cannot be set up against him. He has paid his money for a title good at law, he is innocent, whatever may be the guilt of others, and equity will not subject him to the penalties attached to that guilt. All titles would be insecure, and the intercourse between man and man would be very seriously obstructed, if this principle be overturned.

His message was clear: A person who enters a contract in good faith, fulfills his responsibilities, and possesses a legal title should not be stripped of that title by some action which happened prior to his entering into the contract and for which he had no responsibility and of which he was unaware. The "intercourse between man and man," the ability of society to have business arrangements, to sell and buy products, to develop lands, would be destroyed under such terms. A court of chancery, Marshall said, "would have been bound, by its own rules, and by the clearest principles of equity, to leave unmolested those who were purchasers, without notice, for a valuable consideration."

To this point Marshall's decision is a commentary on contract law, not on constitutional law. And it had seemed from the facts of the case that only the contract issue had been involved. But John Marshall had seen a deeper issue; he had seen that the Constitution itself was under attack. He and the Court he led would come to its defense. He paid his homage to the state legislators—"It is not intended to speak with disrespect of the legislature of Georgia, or of its acts. Far from it." He then acknowledged that the specific issue in *Fletcher v. Peck*, the corruption of the legislators, would not exist in another case, "yet the principle, on which alone this rescinding act is to be supported, may be applied to every case to which it shall be the will of any legislature to apply it."

He was raising a point which had not been raised previously. The original sales had been authorized by an act of one legislature. A second legislature had authorized that those sales be rescinded. Marshall now referred to the actions of that second legislature as the principle which so concerned him. "The principle is this," he said, "that a legislature may, by its own act, devest the vested estate of any man whatever, for reasons which shall, by itself, be deemed sufficient." He did not dispute that one legislature could repeal a law of a previous legislature, but, he insisted, "if an act be done under a law, a succeeding legislature cannot undo it. The past cannot be recalled by the most absolute power."

Absolute power was a concept which concerned him. To give absolute power to any element in government is to corrupt that element, is to say that the people whom government serves can be attacked by that element of government. "It may well be doubted whether the nature of society and of government does not prescribe some limits to the legislative power," said Marshall, "and, if any be prescribed, where are they to be found, if the property of an individual, fairly and honestly acquired, may be seized without compensation." Those lines shine with the spirit that says the law should not be abused. The purchasers of the land had done no wrong; the state could not penalize them by taking their property without paying them. The law protects everyone; it does not favor the state.

Marshall then raised the case to a constitutional level. He referred to the provision in the Constitution that forbids a state from passing any law impairing a contractual obligation. "Does this case now under consideration come within this prohibitory section of the constitution?" he asked and had no difficulty finding that it did:

> Whatever respect might have been felt for the state sovereignties, it is not to be disguised that the framers of the constitution viewed, with some apprehension, the violent acts which might grow out of the feelings of the moment; and that the people of the United States, in adopting this instrument, have manifested a determination to shield themselves and their property from the effects of those sudden and strong passions to which men are exposed. The restrictions on the legislative power of the states are obviously founded in this sentiment; and the constitution of the United States contains what may be deemed a bill of rights for the people of each state.

There was only one dissent to Marshall's opinion, by Justice Johnson, Jefferson's first appointee. Johnson went along with the impact of the majority's decision which, in effect, ruled invalid the repeal of the Yazoo land sales because "I do not hesitate to declare that a state does not possess the power of revoking its own grants." But he could not concede Marshall's interpretation of the applicability of the Contract Clause—"where to draw the line, or how to define or limit the words, 'obligation of contracts,' will be found a subject of extreme difficulty."

The Marshall decision in *Fletcher v. Peck* should almost be read for its sheer verve. In it Marshall spoke to the points of contract law, the arrogance of absolute power, and the supremacy of the Constitution over the state legislatures. The decision shows clearly that he understood that what he and the Court were doing was not enunciating decisions as much as establishing precedents for the guidance of future generations of lawyers and judges. He could not be narrow in his opinion, he believed, because it was necessary from the very beginning to identify the United States as a nation where the rule of law rather than "sudden and strong passions" was controlling, where no institution held absolute power, and where the supreme law could not be interpreted in as many ways as there were states.

The right of a state to revoke a land grant came up also in an 1812 case, *New Jersey v. Wilson.** The state in 1758 had

---

* That is the title as listed in Cranch, but apparently it should have been Wilson against the state, as he was bringing the action.

granted some property to the Delaware Indians in exchange for which the Indians released their claims to other lands. The legislature had agreed to the proposition and specified that the Indians would not sell or lease the land and also that the land would "not hereafter be subject to any tax, any law usage or custom to the contrary thereof, in any wise notwithstanding." In 1801 the Indians wanted to move to New York. At their request, the New Jersey legislature passed a special act giving them the right to sell the land, but this 1801 act made no reference to a change in the land's tax-exempt status. The Indians sold the land, and in 1804 —after the sale—the legislature passed a law lifting the tax-exempt status. Marshall would not allow this 1804 law to stand. He pointed out that the state could have insisted upon lifting the tax exemption as a condition of sale, "But this condition has not been insisted on. The land has been sold, with the assent of the state, with all its privileges and immunities." The purchaser succeeded not only to the land but to all the rights of the Indians. "He stands with respect to this land, in their place and claims the benefit of their contract."[5]

Quite obviously the state legislatures would have to perform at a much higher level of competence if they wished to avoid being charged with usurping rights granted to citizens by the Constitution.

The struggle for federal supremacy was a natural dispute. No one was quite certain he understood how much of their power the states had given to the federal government; or if certain, he often was reluctant to acknowledge it. There were differences between the Federalist approach of Marshall and George Washington and that of Thomas Jefferson, still an influential figure in his Monticello retirement, and his followers; and none of these men could be dismissed casually by the Americans. Perhaps more important, the question was how much power did the federal government require in order to fulfill its responsibilities. It was to the latter question that the Supreme Court addressed itself in the series of cases launched by *Fletcher v. Peck*.

The second major case was built around John Marshall's own purchase of the Fairfax land. In the 1790s David Hunter had begun litigation challenging Denny Martin Fairfax's title to the land, a challenge which, if successful, could have destroyed the right to the land which Marshall had acquired by purchase. The case had come to the Supreme Court then, but was postponed at Hunter's request and he did not seek to bring it before the Court again. Then in 1809 Hunter brought the suit before the Virginia Court of Appeals. This court was headed by Spencer Roane: brilliant jurist, leading politician in Virginia, and Jeffersonian

Republican of impeccable credentials. There was a widespread belief in Virginia that one reason Thomas Jefferson was so angry at the appointment by John Adams of Marshall as Chief Justice in 1801 was that Jefferson had planned to appoint Roane to the position.

In addition to heading the state Court of Appeals, Roane also headed the political machine which Jefferson and James Madison had built. He founded the *Richmond Enquirer* and placed a relative in charge of it. According to a study of his career by William E. Dodd, "Roane was the most powerful politician in the state. He nominated members of the legislature and caused them to be elected, he drew bills and resolutions which the lawmakers passed without amendment."[6] Roane's machine controlled every Virginia politician except one—John Marshall.

It was before the court headed by Spencer Roane that David Hunter resurrected his challenge to the Fairfax landholdings. Not surprisingly, perhaps, Hunter won his case there. John Marshall watched this proceeding with some misgiving. If the issue were left there, then many of his own landholdings and those of others would be questioned. "As this case will probably try the question in which we are all interested would it not be advisable to carry it to the supreme court?" he asked Charles Lee, who would represent him. "I am myself," said Marshall, "of opinion that it is." If Lee agreed with Marshall, then Marshall said he would rush the appeal so that perhaps the case could be argued in the February 1811 term.[7]

The Court did not meet that year, and the case was not argued until 1812 (without Marshall participating). As always in the land cases, the issues were complex. In 1789 the Commonwealth of Virginia had granted a tract of land to Hunter. This tract, however, had been part of the Fairfax estate which may or may not have been in existence then, but which appeared to be protected by the Treaty of 1794 acknowledging the property rights of British citizens in the United States. On the Hunter side, it was argued that Virginia's title to the land was complete before the Treaty of 1794, and that Denny Martin Fairfax, rather than having title through inheritance from his uncle, Lord Fairfax, was only a trustee of an estate.

The Court did not hand down a decision that term but waited until 1813. Neither John Marshall nor Bushrod Washington were present when the decision was read by Joseph Story— both were too closely tied to the Virginia land ownership problems to participate; and Thomas Todd also was absent because of illness. Concurring with Story were Gabriel Duvall and Brockholst Livingston, with William Johnson dissenting. Story's first point was that Lord Fairfax, the original grantee, had been given the proprietorship of the lands. He then insisted that Denny Martin Fairfax had inherited complete title. "At the time of the commencement of this suit—in 1791," said Story, "[Denny Fairfax] was in complete possession and seizin of the land. That possession and seizin continued up to and after the treaty of 1794, which being the supreme law of the land, confirmed the title to him, his heirs and assigns, and protected him from any forfeiture by reason of alienage." Story conceded that prior to the Treaty of 1794 Virginia could have seized the property for itself, but he observed that the state had not done so. Therefore, any title the state claimed to the land as well as any title it granted became "ineffectual and void." Marshall had won his case—or so it seemed.

Justice Johnson's dissent argued that the 1794 treaty was not involved in the case, claiming that the treaty referred to land confiscated by Virginia from British citizens after 1794—a claim contrary to the understanding at the time the treaty was negotiated. He then asserted that Virginia had an unquestioned right to the land as well as a right to assign some of it to David Hunter because the "disability of an alien [Denny Fairfax] to hold real estate is the result of a general principle of the common law, and was in no wise attached to the individual on account of his conduct in the revolutionary struggle."[8]

To this point the *Hunter v. Fairfax* case is of more interest for the impact it might have had on landholdings of the time rather than for its role in the development of constitutional law. However, when the decision reached Virginia and the judges read that they were directed to deny David Hunter the land they had granted him in their 1810 decision, they refused. Spencer Roane decreed that the highest court in the Commonwealth of Virginia was not obligated to obey the highest court of the United States. Section 25 of the Judiciary Act of 1789 had given the federal courts authority over the state courts in any issue involving the Constitution, an act of the federal legislature, or a treaty. There had been no serious dispute with this provision. As Edward S. Corwin has pointed out, "The defenders of State Rights at first applauded this arrangement because it left to the local courts the privilege of sharing a jurisdiction which could have been claimed exclusively by the Federal courts."[9] While the jurisdiction was shared, however, there was no question as to which had the final authority; that belonged to the federal courts and it had not been seriously challenged until Spencer Roane and his fellow judges sought to do so.

Just why they did is a matter of conjecture. Perhaps the

advocates of states' rights felt the time had come to make a stand. William Dodd was inclined to that explanation, writing that "Roane's paper was a political manifesto designed to advance the cause of state sovereignty and to arouse hostility towards Marshall." Perhaps they could no longer control their hatred of Marshall. Edward Corwin acknowledged that possibility, saying that Roane's "opinion in *Hunter v. Martin* disclosed personal animus in every line and was written with a vehemence which was more likely to discomfit a grammarian than its designed victims." Probably it was a combination of both factors, jealousy of the federal courts and hostility toward Marshall, the Virginian who was successfully leading the federal judiciary to new pinnacles of power.[10]

The statements of the judges of the Virginia court were printed in the *Richmond Enquirer*. Judge William H. Cabell's statement said that to follow the orders of the federal court would be conceding the superiority of that jurisdiction. "But one court cannot be correctly said to be superior to another, unless both of them belong to the same sovereignty. . . . The courts of the United States, therefore, belonging to one sovereignty, cannot be appellate courts in relation to the state courts, which belong to a different sovereignty." He acknowledged that there would be cases in which concurrent jurisdiction between the state and federal courts would exist, but once the site of the legal battle had been chosen—either the state or the federal courts— it could not be changed, no matter what the Judiciary Act of 1789 said to the contrary. The second and third judges took the same position, that the act of the federal court was unconstitutional.

Spencer Roane was more elaborate in his oratorical flourishes. "There is a Charybdis to be avoided, as well as a Scylla," he warned, ". . . a centripetal, as well as a centrifugal principle exists in the government, and that no calamity would be more to be deplored by the American people, than a vortex in the general government, which should engulf and sweep away every vestige of the state constitutions." He demanded to know "what is this implication . . . by which a power is to be taken from the state governments, and vested in that of the Union, and the courts of the former taken into the service of the latter? There is no iota of expression in the Constitution, which either takes it from the states, or gives it to the United States." The powers of the state courts in such cases as *Fletcher v. Peck*, he maintained, did not stem from any concession by the federal government but belonged to them inherently. Judge Roane would not concede any inferiority on the part of the states to the federal Union.[11]

The fallacy in Roane's reasoning, as well as in that of the other judges on his court, was that they were allowing the state courts to determine which laws the separate states had to follow. This was the same failing inherent in the Virginia and Kentucky Resolutions, written by Jefferson and Madison. Under the approach of the judges on the Virginia court, there could be no federal Union, no United States of America.

The refusal of the Virginia court to obey the order of the Supreme Court was then taken to the Supreme Court and argued in 1816. The arguments were restatements of the dispute between the exponents of states' rights and those of federal supremacy. "The government is not a mere confederacy, like the Grecian leagues, or the Germanic constitution, or the old continental confederation. In its legislative, executive, and judicial authorities, it is a national government, to every purpose, within the scope of the objects enumerated in the constitution. . . . The state judicatures are essentially incompetent to pronounce what is the law; not in the limited sphere of their territorial jurisdiction, but throughout the union and the world," ran the arguments on the side of federal supremacy. On the other side the arguments also were, by this time, the traditional ones: "The whole scheme of the constitution aims at acting on the citizens of the United States at large, and not on the state authorities. . . . [By attempting to assert federal supremacy, the federal courts] will begin a conflict between the national and state authorities that may ultimately involve both in one common ruin. The taper of judicial discord may become the torch of civil war, and though the breath of a judge can extinguish the first, the wisdom of the statesmen may not quench the latter."[12]

Because of Marshall's personal involvement in the case as an affected landowner, he did not participate in the decision, and it fell to Joseph Story to deliver the opinion of the Court. Story had been, originally, a Jeffersonian Republican but one of an independent mind—his opposition to the embargo had demonstrated that. According to his son, Story had come to the Supreme Court having "given little study" to constitutional law. Once on the Court in 1812, however, Story "devoted himself to this branch of the law," and the result was that he found himself in agreement with the Federalist John Marshall. To the charge that Story allowed himself to fall under the influence of Marshall, his son said that Story did not change his own views so much as actually form them for the first time.[13]

Whatever the cause, Joseph Story leading a Court that consisted entirely of Republicans with the single exception of Bushrod Washington announced a decision that is a strong demand for federal sovereignty. At the beginning of his opinion Story described the questions involved as "of great importance and delicacy," declaring that "Perhaps it is not too much to affirm, that, upon their right decision, rest some of the most solid principles which have hitherto been supposed to sustain and protect the constitution itself." No one since has disagreed with that estimate.

His decision, as it proceeds in the logic of its construction, does in fact read as if it could have been written by Marshall. He began by saying that the Constitution was not a creation of the states but of the people and "there can be no doubt that it was competent to the people to invest the general government with all the powers which they might deem proper and necessary . . . and to give them a paramount and supreme authority." He then explained, as Marshall would have done, and did in fact do three years later, that the federal government can claim "no powers which are not granted to it by the constitution . . . [but] where a power is expressly given in general terms, it is not to be restrained to particular cases." This is the doctrine of implied powers. Story then examined the power of the appellate jurisdiction of the Supreme Court—"in all cases where it has not original jurisdiction; subject, however, to such exceptions and regulations as congress may prescribe." He then went on for six pages to argue that "all" obviously meant all cases and not only some of them. One must wonder as Story dwelled on the obvious if he were not being somewhat sarcastic. For example, he wrote:

> How otherwise could the jurisdiction extend to *all* cases arising under the constitution, laws, and treaties of the United States, or *to all cases* of admiralty and maritime jurisdiction? If some of these cases might be entertained by state tribunals, and no appellate jurisdiction as to them should exist, then the appellate power would not extend to *all*, but to *some* cases.

Nor did Story have much respect for the argument that the independence of state judges might be impaired by their having to follow orders of the federal courts. To assume they could be oblivious to such orders, he said, is to assume their side of the argument—"the very ground in controversy." Story continued that "In respect to the powers granted to the United States, they are not independent; they are expressly bound to obedience by the letter of the Constitution." Story here was, of course, lecturing the state judges on their responsibilities under the law—all men must obey it, he was saying; even judges could not choose which laws they wished to obey and which to ignore.

As for the argument that federal judges may abuse their power in commanding state judges, Story is equally scathing. "From the very nature of things," he argued, "the absolute right of decision, in the last resort, must rest somewhere—wherever it may be vested it is susceptible of abuse. In all questions of jurisdiction the inferior, or appellate court, must pronounce the final judgment; and common sense, as well as legal reasoning, has conferred it upon the latter." What is that legal reasoning? Story offered two answers. The first was "the necessity of *uniformity* of decisions throughout the whole United States, upon all subjects within the purview of the constitution." He pointed out that judges in different states could interpret laws differently, meaning that the laws could then mean different things in different states. "The public mischiefs that would attend such a state of things would be truly deplorable," said Story, "and it cannot be believed that they could have escaped the enlightened convention which formed the constitution . . . the appellate jurisdiction must continue to be the only adequate remedy for such evils." The second reason is that plaintiff, in bringing a suit, could be tempted to originate the suit in the state where he believed the courts most amenable to his arguments. Without a federal appellate jurisdiction, Story continued, "it will follow, that as the plaintiff may always elect the state court, the defendant may be deprived of all the security which the constitution intended in aid of his rights. Such a state of things can, in no respect, be considered as giving equal rights."

The strength of Joseph Story's decision is in its logic. When he was done, there was no disputing that the federal Union could not exist if state courts were able to defy it. The question of federal supremacy had been lifted from the realm of political philosophy to that of political necessity. If the United States is to exist, Story was saying, it must have the powers of a government. The Federalists—and Story by this time certainly was philosophically aligned with people like George Washington and John Marshall—have been charged with wanting a too-powerful government. Certainly they were not afraid of government. They believed that the system constructed would produce good men to govern and that those good men needed the tools to administer the affairs of the nation properly. They were wise enough to realize that not always would the best man come forth to lead, but that failing, they believed, would be true in any system. They had faith that people, when given the tools such as the American government offered, would rise to the occasion and administer their nation justly and honorably. They had to have that faith. The alternative was chaos and anarchy, as history had proven.

The validity of Story's object was so apparent that even William Johnson was obliged to agree with the Story opinion. The case, he said in a concurring opinion, "presents an instance of collision between the judicial powers of the union, and one of the greatest states in the union, on the point the most delicate and difficult to be adjusted." Johnson pointed out that the federal government "must cease to exist" whenever it lost the power of protecting itself or of exercising its constitutional powers. And the only means which government had to exercise their powers, Johnson continued, were force and judicial process. He said: "The former is happily unknown to the genius of our constitution, except as far as it shall be sanctioned by the latter; but let the latter be obstructed in its progress by an opposition which it cannot overcome or put by, and the resort must be to the former, or government is no more."

As a proper Jeffersonian Republican, William Johnson praised the state government and declared that the Americans could not be free if the state governments had to prostrate themselves before the federal. But by this time he had been a Justice of the Supreme Court for thirteen years and had wrestled with the problem of making government work. Slogans and clichés were not sufficient. In the next section of his concurring opinion Johnson seemed to be lecturing Judge Spencer Roane of the Virginia court: "Are then the judgments of this [federal] court to be reviewed in every court of the Union? and is every recovery of money, every change of property, that has taken place under our process, to be considered as null, void, and tortious?" He continued: "We are constituted by the voice of the union, and when decisions take place . . . ours is the superior claim upon the comity of the state tribunals."[14]

In addition to affirming the supremacy of the federal judiciary over that of the states, the decisions in *Martin v. Hunter's Lessee*, both Story's opinion and Johnson's concurrence, demonstrate the value of lifetime appointments for Justices. Story and Johnson were affirming a policy which they believed necessary, and which experience has since proven necessary, even though it was contrary to their political backgrounds and the philosophy of the organizations that had placed them on the bench. They had the strength to do what they considered right, however, because their lifetime appointments had made them secure. They did not have to consider bowing to the political pressures of their time or to any political pressures which might exist when their reappointments would be considered, if reappointments had been required. And that is the purpose of the Supreme Court in American life, to be competent through its security to look beyond the momentary politics, the passions of the times, to determine what America needs, what its purpose requires it to have. The Supreme Court is, of course, fallible like any other institution. It also is capable of correcting itself—it has on numerous occasions. Its fallibility should not detract from its ultimate purpose—to examine the American political experience with perspective. Reading the Story and Johnson opinions in that context, they emerge as brilliant state papers.

The relationship between the federal and state governments was not settled by one decision. Many other decisions would be required, and even a Civil War almost a half-century later would not resolve the issue. But the broad outlines were being formed in the second decade of the Marshall Court. The decisions by John Marshall in the 1819 case of *McCulloch v. Maryland* and the 1821 case of *Cohens v. Virginia* would be the culmination of this outlining process. Before they came, however, there were two other decisions by Marshall which delved into the relationship between the two units, the state and federal governments, and illustrate the development of his approach to defining this relationship.

The first, in 1818, is known as *United States v. William Bevans* and it revolved around the case of a sailor on an American navy ship who murdered a cook's mate. The killing took place aboard the *Independence* when it was tied up in Boston harbor.[15] Although the crime had taken place in Boston harbor, the federal courts took jurisdiction, claiming the federal government had authority over certain crimes "committed on the high seas, or in any river, haven, basin, or bay, out of the jurisdiction of any particular state."

Marshall's consideration of this point is an adroit use of the law. "Whatever may be the constitutional powers of congress," he said, "it is clear that this power has not been so exercised, in this section of the act, as to confer on its courts jurisdiction over any offense committed in a river, haven, basin, or bay; which river, haven, basin, or bay, is within the jurisdiction of any particular state." Having the authority is one thing, Marshall was saying; using it, another. But even if the federal government had not exercised its authority, did Massachusetts still have authority of its own? "We answer, without hesitation," he declared, "the jurisdiction of a state is co-extensive with its territory; co-extensive with its legislative power." This meant, he continued, that the crime took place within the state unless Massachusetts had ceded power over the area to the federal government.

The federal government had claimed its authority under the constitutional provision that extended federal judicial power "to all cases of admiralty and maritime jurisdiction" and also had claimed that this power was exclusive, and that the state government had no authority. But Marshall could not accept this. Because Congress never had exercised its power, said Marshall, "No jurisdiction is given to the courts of the United States, of any crime committed in a ship of war, wherever it may be stationed." Marshall then held for Bevans.

The impact of this Marshall decision is a willingness to defend the rights of states against federal encroachment. Whatever powers the federal government had, he said, must be exercised according to the procedures established by the Constitution: they could not be assumed arbitrarily. Everyone must obey the law—even the federal government.

Where the government had obeyed the law, however, Marshall would not permit a diminution of federal authority. This was apparent in the 1819 case of *Sturges v. Crowninshield*.[16] The case involved two promissory notes which the defendant had not paid, claiming that he had been relieved of any obligation by New York State's 1812 Insolvency Act. The question was, could a state pass a bankruptcy law or had that power been given to the federal government exclusively by the Constitution? In considering that question, Marshall's opinion declared, one must remember that prior to the Constitution the separate states had pretty much the right to do as they wished. The states were "united for some purposes but, in most respects, [were] sovereign." These separate states could exercise any legislative power, including the enactment of bankruptcy laws. He continued:

> When the American people created a national legislature, with certain enumerated powers, it was neither necessary nor proper to define the powers retained by the States. These powers proceed, not from the people of America, but from the people of the several States; and remain, after the adoption of the constitution, what they were before, except so far as they may be abridged by that instrument.

That section sounds as if Marshall were ready to uphold the New York law. But he was a master at seeming to say one thing while pointing out another. The states' rights people would nod in agreement as they read that paragraph and only realize later that the phrase "except so far as they may be abridged by that instrument" was the key one. Marshall acknowledged that the state and federal governments could have concurrent powers where authority had not been expressly denied to the state, as in the situation with William Bevans, but, he insisted, not in every case. "The confusion resulting from such a practice would be endless," he said. He then stated the doctrine of exclusive powers. "Whenever the terms in which a power is granted to Congress, or the nature of the power," he said, "require that it should be exercised exclusively by Congress, the subject is as completely taken from the State Legislatures, as if they had been expressly forbidden to act on it."

This was an audacious strengthening of federal power for the time, one, however, that only added to the conflict between the states and the federal government. The conflict existed because of the confusion over concurrent powers and exclusive powers. When did the federal government and the states share certain powers, and when did the federal government possess those powers exclusively? Marshall would try to answer that question a few years later in *Gibbons v. Ogden*. In developing his answer he was guided by the belief that the Constitution never had been intended to detail every specific action the federal government was allowed to undertake nor to list every specific action forbidden to the state governments. If that had been the intention, then the Constitution would have been a monstrous document instead of a concise statement of fundamental principles. Against this guide, his developing doctrine of exclusive powers for the federal government can be understood as a practical determination as well as an exercise in audacity.

In the *Sturges v. Crowninshield* decision Marshall then turned to whether the power of enacting bankruptcy laws had been taken from the states. He now would say the same thing he had held the previous year in the *Bevans* case. "It is not the mere existence of power, but its exercise, which is incompatible with the exercise of the same power by the States," he said, stressing: "It is not the right to establish these uniform laws, but their actual establishment, which is inconsistent with the partial acts of the States." His next few lines also served—or could be interpreted—to strengthen the states. He denied that because Congress may have exercised the power, that the states' concurrent power had been extinguished. "It can only be suspended," he said, "by the enactment of a general bankrupt law. The repeal of that law cannot, it is true, confer the power on the States; but it removes a disability to its exercise, which was created by the act of Congress." Again, Marshall was saying that the federal government can be neither arrogant nor presumptuous in claiming power; it too must adhere strictly to the law.

This concept of the federal government only being able to

claim the power it specifically had exercised would be challenged in *Gibbons v. Ogden* by Daniel Webster, and his argument then would persuade John Marshall to change his position.

However, he had not yet come to the basic issue of whether the bankruptcy law of New York had been prohibited by the Constitution. To this point his remarks had been dicta, advice to future generations of lawyers and judges. But now he was finished with dicta. "We proceed to the great question on which the cause must depend," he announced. "Does the law of New York, which is pleaded in this case, impair the obligation of contracts, within the meaning of the constitution of the United States?" If it did, then there was no question how John Marshall would decide. He had written twenty years earlier in his biography of Washington that the Constitution "was understood to prohibit all laws impairing the obligation of contracts." This constitutional prohibition, he had said, "had in great measure restored the confidence which is essential to the internal prosperity of nations."[17]

In proceeding to the "great question," Marshall had passed over what was then the secondary question of a conflict between laws enacted by a state legislature and by the federal Congress to deal, instead, with a basic constitutional issue. The Constitution did not anywhere prohibit a state from passing its own bankruptcy law. It did, however, prohibit a state from passing any law impairing the fulfillment of a contract.

> It would seem difficult [said Marshall] to substitute words which are more intelligible, or less liable to misconception, than those which are to be explained. A contract is an agreement in which a party undertakes to do, or not to do, a particular thing. The law binds him to perform his undertaking, and this is, of course, the obligation of his contract.

There was much of John Marshall's background in the paragraph. He had lived almost sixty-four years. In his early years on the frontier he had learned the necessity for contractual arrangements in connection with the ownership of land and the protection of title by courts of law. He had learned then that a role of law is to insure that men accomplish what they promise. The law of contracts would grow, exploding with precedents and interpretations, but Marshall's basic definition learned as a young man and reinforced throughout most of his life cannot be improved upon—an agreement "in which a party undertakes to do, or not to do, a particular thing." The role of law in upholding those agreements also was something that had been instilled in him much earlier. He had seen the anarchy in France because courts there declined to exercise their authority. He had known the uncertainty of law in the wilderness. His life was dedicated to men and governments fulfilling their obligations.

He then reduced the case before the Court to its simplest form: "The defendant has given his promissory note to pay the plaintiff a sum of money on or before a certain day. The contract binds him to pay that sum on this day; and this is its obligation." Any law which relieved the defendant of that obligation impaired the contract and is therefore contrary to the Constitution. "The words of the constitution, then, are express, and incapable of being misunderstood," he declared. "They admit of no variety of construction, and are acknowledged to apply to that species of contract, an engagement between man and man for the payment of money, which has been entered into by these parties."

The argument had been made that bankruptcy laws did not come under the constitutional restriction because states had been enacting similar laws for years without objection and also because the Constitution did not specifically mention either bankruptcy or insolvency. To the first contention Marshall replied that he did not agree that the states had been passing laws similar to New York's for decades. "The insolvent laws of many, indeed, of by far the greatest number of States, do not contain this principle. They discharge the person of the debtor, but leave his obligation to pay in full force. To this the constitution is not opposed," he pointed out. That argument, he was maintaining, was confusing the ending of debtors' prisons with the erasure of debts, as the 1812 New York law provided for.

To the second contention—that insolvency and bankruptcy were not specifically mentioned in the Constitution—Marshall's answer is an insistence that the Constitution implies powers to the federal government beyond those specifically mentioned. "The plain and simple declaration, that no State shall pass any law impairing the obligation of contracts," he said, "includes insolvent laws and all other laws, so far as they infringe the principle the Convention intended to hold sacred, and no farther." The Court held that the debt had not been relieved, that the contract had not been negatived, by the state action.

Sturges v. Crowninshield was one of the three significant cases decided by the Supreme Court during the 1819 term. The other two were the *McCulloch* case and the *Dartmouth College* case. Like the *Dartmouth* case, the *Sturges* decision is much concerned with the law of contracts and goes far to define that term. But the *Sturges* case also contributes to the broadening of federal powers, which makes it part of the struggle for the supremacy of the Union. That the three cases were decided in one term is indicative of how the two problems, the supremacy of the Union and the law of contracts, were coming to the fore. The Supreme Court usually deals with a problem when there seems to be no alternative, either at the state level or federal level, for solution. Before the 1819 term began, Story commented that it "will probably be the most interesting ever known," and he was correct.[18]

Marshall as the presiding officer continued an impressive figure, if one with a sense of humor. A story of him about this time has a lawyer standing before the bench trying to win his case by praising the Chief Justice, praise culminating in telling Marshall that he had reached "the acme of judicial distinction." Marshall replied icily: "Let me tell what that means, young man . . . the ability to look a lawyer straight in the face for two hours with closed ears."[19]

Most descriptions of Marshall, however, were more sincere. "Enter but that hall," said Joseph Story, "and you saw him listening with a quiet, easy dignity to the discussions at the bar; silent, serious, searching; with a keenness of thought, which sophistry could not mislead, or error confuse, or ingenuity delude." With the seriousness, however, there was "a benignity of aspect which invited the modest to move on with confidence," and there also was "a conscious firmness of purpose, which repressed arrogance, and overawed declamation." The opinions were delivered by Marshall "in a low but modulated voice, unfolding in luminous order every topic of argument, trying its strength, and measuring its value, until you felt yourself in the presence of the very oracle of the law."

In the conference room, Story said, "you would observe the same presiding genius, the same kindness, attentiveness, and deference; and yet, when the occasion required, the same power of illustration, the same minuteness of research, the same severity of logic, and the same untiring accuracy of facts and principles." Story compared Marshall's statement of the facts of a case to the statements of the famed English jurist Lord Mansfield: "If it did not at once lead the hearer to the proper conclusion, it prepared him to assent to it as soon as it was announced. Nay, more; it persuaded him that it must be right, however repugnant it might be to his preconceived notions." Story then produced an interesting description of Marshall's technique of building his decisions to a climax: "Perhaps no judge ever excelled him in the capacity to hold a legal proposition before the eyes of others in such various forms and colors. It seemed a pleasure to him to cast the darkest shades of objection over it, that he might show how they could be dissipated by a single glance of light. He would by the most subtle analysis resolve every argument into its ultimate principles, and then with a marvelous facility apply them to the decision of the cause."

Story found that while Marshall had "an uncommon share" of learning in the law, he had to state that Marshall's "learning was not equal to that of many of the great masters of the profession, living or dead, at home or abroad." Story did not consider this a criticism, however, because Marshall was always willing to learn. "He adopted the notion of Lord Bacon," said Story, "that 'studies serve for delight, for ornament, and for ability—in the judgment and disposition of business.' The latter was his favorite object. Hence he 'read not to contradict, and confute; nor to believe and take for granted; nor to find talk and discourse; but to weigh and consider.'" Story said that Marshall also followed another suggestion of Lord Bacon's, that "judges ought to be more learned than witty; more revered than plausible; and more advised than confident."

The Story description of Marshall revealed a man reveling in the law:

> The original bias, as well as the choice, of his mind was to general principles and comprehensive views, rather than to technical or recondite learning. He loved to expatiate upon the theory of equity; to gather up the expansive doctrine of commercial jurisprudence; and to give a rational cast even to the most subtle dogmas of the common law. He was solicitous to hear arguments; and not to decide causes without them. And no judge ever profited more by them. No matter whether the subject was new or old, familiar to his thoughts, or remote from them; buried under a mass of obsolete learning, or developed for the first time yesterday; whatever was its nature, he courted argument, nay he demanded it. It was a matter of surprise to see how easily he grasped the leading principles of a case, and cleared it of all its accidental encumbrances; how readily he evolved the true points of the controversy, even when it was manifest that he never before had caught even a glimpse of the learning upon which it depended. He seized, as it were, by intuition, the very spirit of juridical doctrines, though cased up in the armor of centuries; and he discussed authorities as if the very minds of the judges themselves stood disembodied before them.
>
> But his peculiar triumph was in the exposition of constitutional law. It was here that he stood confessedly with-

out a rival, whether we regard his thorough knowledge of our civil and political history, his admirable powers of illustration and generalization, his scrupulous integrity and exactness in interpretation, or his consummate skill in moulding his own genius into its elements as if they had constituted the exclusive study of his life.[20]

Story's description of John Marshall is, of course, elaborate. But then only an elaborate man could have produced the opinion that John Marshall did in *McCulloch v. Maryland*.

8

WHEN CONGRESS FIRST PASSED an act establishing a national bank, during Washington's administration, the members contended "that incidental as well as express powers must necessarily belong to every government; and that, when a power is delegated to effect particular objects, all the known and usual means of effecting them must pass as incidental to it. To remove all doubt on this subject, the constitution of the United States had recognized the principle, by enabling congress to make all laws which may be necessary and proper for carrying into execution the powers vested in the government."

That explanation of the congressional rationale and statement of implied powers is by John Marshall. It was written in the early 1800s and is part of his biography of George Washington. The words are almost identical to those he used some fifteen years later in the *McCulloch v. Maryland* decision upholding the validity of the national bank. Researchers have found much material relating to the origins of Marshall's decision in that case, but it had its basic roots in Marshall's understanding of the Constitution and its powers, an understanding he had articulated years before he wrote the opinion.

That the national bank was a cause of political differences was evident even when the Congress first acted. Marshall wrote in his Washington biography that Thomas Jefferson, Secretary of State at the time, believed that "Congress had clearly transcended their powers." The bill establishing the original bank "made a deep impression on many members of the legislature, and contributed not inconsiderably to the complete organization of those distinct and visible parties, which in their long and dubious conflict for power, have since shaken the United States to their centre."[1]

That the control of the nation's finances would be a major cause of party difficulties in the young country is not surprising. Who controlled the purse, interest rates, the availability of money, credit, all the tools by which society had commerce, possessed power. The Jeffersonians, representing the farmers, the landholders, those who were not intimately involved with great commercial transactions as were the coastal city businessmen, naturally were reluctant to surrender that power to any group. The national bank was allowed to expire, in fact, because of the opposition. But it was resurrected by Congress again in 1816 as a device to bring some order out of the economic chaos into which the nation was sinking. But all did not go well for the bank, and the hoped-for order was not quick to rise from the disorder. The nation was struggling out of the depression that marked the years after the War of 1812. Everyone was angry and the national bank was the target. Efforts were made in Congress to destroy it. Although those efforts were unsuccessful, still they underscored the growing resentment toward the institution.

Against this background, the state of Maryland claimed that the Second Bank of the United States owed it $15,000 in state taxes. James McCulloch, the cashier of the Baltimore branch of the bank, refused to pay the tax. The demand by the state and the refusal by the cashier turned the politically and economically controversial issue of the national bank into a legally controversial one; the future of the national bank would be determined neither by the legislative leaders nor by the President, but by the Supreme Court of the United States.

The case appeared similar to one which had come before the Supreme Court about ten years earlier, *Bank of the United States v. Deveaux*. Georgia had attempted to tax the first United States Bank, and state officials forcibly entered the bank at Savannah and carried away $2,004 in payment of the tax. Georgia claimed that the federal courts did not have jurisdiction because the suit did not involve citizens of different states. Peter Deveaux, one of the officials who entered the bank premises and made off with the money, was a citizen of Georgia as were most of the stockholders of the Bank of the United States. The bank claimed that at least some of its stockholders were from Pennsylvania. Marshall held for the state and the issue was determined not on the question of whether a federal installation could be taxed by a state government but on the residences of the stockholders. That would not happen in *McCulloch v. Maryland*.[2]

This case caused one of the few charges of improper conduct made against John Marshall. He had owned seventeen shares of stock in the bank in 1817 and 1818, valued at between

$1,500 and $1,700. After Marshall's death it was charged that he still held those shares when the case was argued before him and when he handed down his decision. Actually, he sold his shares prior to hearing the arguments in the case even though he had been advised to hold on to them because they were a good investment. But Marshall said "that he did not choose to remain a stockholder, as questions might be brought before the Supreme Court in which the bank might be concerned."[3]*

At the same time that John Marshall was selling his shares in the United States Bank, Spencer Roane was advising his son William to buy some shares. This is the Spencer Roane who still was head of the Virginia Court of Appeals and whose anger at the Marshall decision upholding the bank would stimulate him to launch a series of newspaper articles attacking the Chief Justice. He did not permit his philosophy to stand in the way of earning a profit. On February 16, 1819, he wrote his son: "I have today deposited in the vaults of the Virga. bank a certificate in your name for 50 shares U.S. bank stock, as per memo., by Mr. Dandridge Enclosed. The shares cost, as you will see, $98 each."[4] The arguments in *McCulloch v. Maryland* opened in Washington three days later.[5]

Daniel Webster led off the arguments for the bank. Congress, he argued first, had the right to establish the bank although there was no provision in the Constitution stating that power explicitly. Even without using the General Welfare Clause, he said, "the grant of powers itself necessarily implies the grant of all usual and suitable means for the execution of the powers granted." He pointed out that "Congress may declare war; it may consequently carry on war, by armies and navies, and other suitable means and methods of warfare. So it has power to raise a revenue, and to apply it in the support of the government, and defence of the country. It may, of course, use all proper and suitable means, not specially prohibited, in the raising and disbursement of the revenue." In using language before Chief Justice Marshall similar to that which Marshall himself had used in his biography of Washington, Webster was doing more than merely

---

* By modern standards, Marshall was only being prudent. By the standards of his time, however, he was being unusually ethical. A few years later, during the Jackson administration. Joseph Story "supplied material for Webster's pro-bank Senate speeches on an issue which might come before him as a judge. And on a lesser note, he intervened to keep government funds in the bank of which he served as president." G. T. Dunne, "Joseph Story," in Friedman and Israel, vol. I, p. 445.

currying favor by imitation. The argument was the basic one for an effective federal government.

"It is not enough to say, that it does not appear that a bank was in the contemplation of the framers of the constitution. It was not their intention, in these cases," insisted Webster, "to enumerate particulars. The true view of the subject is, that if it be a fit instrument to an authorized purpose, it may be used, not being specially prohibited." This explanation was almost identical to the one Marshall had written earlier in his Washington biography—"when a power is delegated to effect particular objects, all the known and usual means of effecting them must pass as incidental to it"—and was similar to words that Marshall would use later to describe the same power.

After making the point that the Congress had the right to establish the bank, Webster then argued that the state of Maryland could not tax the federal installation. "If the States may tax the bank," he asked, "to what extent shall they tax it, and where shall they stop? An unlimited power to tax involves, necessarily, a power to destroy; because there is a limit beyond which no institution and no property can bear taxation." He added that "A question of constitutional power can hardly be made to depend on a question of more or less." A federal installation should not be dependent upon the discretionary power of a state government. "The consequence is inevitable," said Webster. "The object in laying this tax, may have been revenue to the State. In the next case, the object may be to expel the bank from the State." Whatever may have been the failing of the national bank, attacking it by handing the states a device that would destroy federal facilities was destroying the house to patch a crack.

Another lawyer for the bank was William Wirt. When Wirt had first appeared before John Marshall as a prosecution lawyer in the Aaron Burr trial a dozen years earlier, he had impressed spectators as a young man with potential for success and he was living up to that impression; he now was Attorney General of the United States. He elaborated on the same argument that Webster had made, that the Constitution had given the government all necessary and proper powers to fulfill its functions. "The power to establish such a corporation is implied," he said, "and involved in the grant of specific powers in the constitution; because the end involves the means necessary to carry it into effect. A power without the means to use it, is a nullity."

He continued that it was not necessary for the Constitution to have spelled out every action allowed to the government. An interpretation "so strict and literal," Wirt argued, "would render every law which could be passed by Congress unconstitutional" because the authors of the Constitution could never have visualized the specific actions that might have to be taken at a future time. In words which appear to outline the philosophy that underlay Marshall's ultimate decision, Wirt told the Supreme Court that in determining whether the national bank was constitutional, it must "compare the law in question with the powers it is intended to carry into execution; not in order to ascertain whether other or better means might have been selected, for that is the legislative province, but to see whether those which have been chosen have a natural connection with any specific power; whether they are adapted to give it effect; whether they are appropriate means to an end." Wirt insisted that "It cannot be denied, that this is the character of the Bank of the United States."

The paragraph is interesting for its definition of judicial powers. Wirt insisted that the Court had no right to determine whether the legislative act was "good" or "bad," the "most" or "least" efficient means of achieving an end. That is the people's prerogative, through the democratic process. The single task facing the Supreme Court was to determine whether Congress had transcended the authority granted to it by the Constitution. That is, of course, what a "strong" Court does. It does not judge the quality of legislation but does not hesitate to judge the constitutionality of legislation.

That definition of judicial responsibility which Wirt had just enunciated to the Court was also John Marshall's. Wirt really was reminding the Chief Justice in that paragraph that he could not be true to his own philosophy and decide against the bank—something which John Marshall undoubtedly knew.

The case for the state of Maryland was presented by Luther Martin, a veteran of the Aaron Burr trial as well as the Chase impeachment trial. He now was attorney general for the state of Maryland and this would be the last great case he argued; a stroke would incapacitate him the next year. His argument in the bank case showed that he still was the greatest trial lawyer of his time, despite his drinking and other personal problems. The federal government's interest in the bank, Martin conceded, is "not subjected to direct taxation by the law of Maryland." The tax which the state had tried to collect, he insisted, was "a stamp tax upon the notes issued by a banking house within the state of Maryland." Because the United States government has an interest in the bank, Martin argued, is no reason to prohibit the state from levying a tax as it would against any other bank or commercial house.

As for the right to tax being the right to destroy, Martin dismissed the point. "We answer," he said, "that the same objection would equally apply to the right of Congress to tax the State banks." He continued:

> The debates in the State conventions show that the power of State taxation was understood to be absolutely unlimited, except as to imposts and tonnage duties. The States would not have adopted the constitution upon any other understanding.

Realizing he may have gone too far with that statement, Martin amended it by adding that the state could not impose a stamp tax on judicial or customs proceedings:

> As to judicial proceedings, and the custom house papers of the United States, they are not property, by their very nature; they are not the subjects of taxation; they are the proper instruments of national sovereignty, essential to the exercise of its powers, and in legal contemplation altogether extra-territorial as to State authority.

Despite the persuasiveness of Luther Martin's arguments, augmented by his passionate and sincere belief that federal power was usurping states' rights in this case, there was no question but that the Supreme Court had to decide in favor of the bank. To allow the states the right to tax a federal facility was to concede that state power was supreme over the federal power. That could not be allowed if one wished to have a federal Union. The real question was whether the Supreme Court headed by John Marshall would hand down a decision that was persuasive enough to overcome the suspicions of the advocates of states' rights as well as stand the test of history. Because of the sharp conflict of powers, the decision must be a significant statement of the extent of federal powers and an argument for those powers, perhaps the most significant statement and argument in American history. The law was not the point in this case; the explanation was.

A week after the arguments were finished, on March 6, the Supreme Court handed down its decision in the case of *McCulloch v. Maryland*. John Marshall began by summing up the essentials of the case and its importance in a manner that could not be contested:

> In the case now to be determined, the defendant, a sovereign State, denies the obligation of a law enacted by the legislature of the Union, and the plaintiff, on his part,

contests the validity of an act which has been passed by the legislature of that State. The constitution of our country, in its most interesting and vital parts, is to be considered; the conflicting powers of the government of the Union and of its members, as marked in that constitution, are to be discussed; and an opinion given, which may essentially influence the great operations of the government. No tribunal can approach such a question without a deep sense of its importance, and of the awful responsibility involved in its decision.

Marshall cautioned that the decision must be reached peacefully, "or remain a source of hostile legislation, perhaps of hostility of a still more serious nature." The only site where such a peaceful decision could be made, he said, was the Court over which he presided. "On the Supreme Court of the United States," he declared, "has the constitution of our country devolved this important duty."

The first question the Marshall opinion addressed was whether Congress can authorize a national bank. He pointed out that the first bank was authorized by the first Congress after arguments of "zeal and ability" and then established by the President after opposition within his cabinet marked by as much "persevering talent as any measure has ever experienced." This first bank was allowed to die, but a brief experience without a central bank, Marshall said, "convinced those who were most prejudiced against the measure" of the need for the bank. This was a reference to the second national bank, founded during the administration of James Madison, a disciple of Jefferson's. Marshall continued: "It would require no ordinary share of intrepidity to assert that a measure adopted under these circumstances was a bold and plain usurpation, to which the constitution gave no countenance." Then, however, he acknowledged that merely because the bank had been established openly was not sufficient to say that it had been established constitutionally. That question he then turned to.

The first problem was whether the Constitution stemmed from the people of America or from the states. There was more than a semantic difference. If the Constitution was the creation of the states, then the states perhaps could control what was done in the name of the Constitution; that was a basic argument of the Jeffersonian Republicans and the other advocates of states' rights. If, however, the Constitution emanated from the people, then what was done in the name of the Constitution could not be challenged by the state powers.

In dealing with this question, Marshall was not even kind

to the advocates of states' rights. "It would be difficult to sustain this proposition," he said of the claim that the Constitution was a product of the states. He then spoke of the process which led to the ratification of the Constitution, a process with which he was intimately acquainted because he had been a part of it, first as a member of the Virginia legislature which called a special convention for ratification in that state and then as a member of the special convention. The draft of the Constitution had been drawn up by a convention authorized and staffed by vote of the state legislatures, but the resulting document, Marshall declared, "when it came from their hands, was a mere proposal, without obligation, or pretensions to it." The proposed Constitution then went back to the Continental Congress "with a request that it might 'be submitted to a Convention of Delegates, chosen in each State by the people thereof, under the recommendation of its Legislature, for their assent and ratification.'" Congress agreed with this, and "the instrument was submitted to the people." It was ratified by the people, Marshall continued, "in the only manner in which they can act safely, effectively, and wisely, on such a subject, by assembling in Convention." That the conventions were held in the separate states was explained by Marshall as a fact of geographical necessity rather than as a significant political influence. When the people act, the Chief Justice said, they act within their states, "But the measures they adopt do not, on that account, cease to be the measures of the people themselves, or become the measures of the State governments."

This question of the authority behind the Constitution had troubled the American people since the adoption of the document, and Marshall would not leave the subject until he believed he had thoroughly examined every nuance and exhausted every argument. He said: "The assent of the States, in their sovereign capacity is implied in calling a Convention, and thus submitting that instrument to the people. But the people were at perfect liberty to accept or reject it; and their act was final. It required not the affirmance, and could not be negatived, by the State governments. The constitution, when thus adopted, was of complete obligation, and bound the State sovereignties."

One suggestion made was that when the people had granted certain political powers to the state governments, they had no more political powers in reserve to surrender to a federal Union. "Surely," said Marshall, "the question whether they may resume and modify the powers granted to government does not remain to be settled in this country. Much more might the legitimacy of the general government be doubted, had it been created by the States. The powers delegated to the State sovereignties were to be exercised by themselves, not by a distinct and independent sovereignty, created by themselves. To the formation of a league, such as was the confederation, the State sovereignties were certainly competent. But when, 'in order to form a more perfect union,' it was deemed necessary to change this alliance into an effective government, possessing great and sovereign powers, and acting directly on the people, the necessity of referring it to the people, and of deriving its powers directly from them, was felt and acknowledged by all." Under the Articles of Confederation, the federal government had been unable to command compliance because it acted only on the states, and it could apply no power to a state. Under the Constitution, the federal government was able to command compliance because it acted upon individuals. The difference was between an ineffective and an effective government.

In one respect this part of the decision failed. It did not convince the adamant advocates of states' rights of the supremacy of the federal Union. Particularly because many of them soon realized that the institution of slavery would be challenged by such a concept of supremacy, they stood solid against such an understanding. Not even a Civil War fought some forty years later could convince some of these advocates that their cause was both incorrect and improper. Perhaps no exercise in logic, no appeal to man's intellect could overcome such self-serving bias. What can be said of John Marshall's examination of this question is that when he concluded there could be no persuasive argument against his conclusion; emotional appeals, yes, but no rational refutation of his statement that the federal government "is, emphatically, and truly, a government of the people. In form and in substance it emanates from them. Its powers are granted by them, and are to be exercised directly on them, and for their benefit."

After making the point that the Constitution is supreme over state laws, Marshall then turned to the question of what powers the Constitution actually gave to the federal legislature. If anything commanded "the universal assent of mankind," Marshall declared, it was that "the government of the Union, though limited in its powers, is supreme within its sphere of action . . . its powers are delegated by all; it represents all, and acts for all." In the next line he pointed out that "though any one State may be willing to control its operations, no State is willing to allow others to control them." He continued that "The nation, on those subjects on which it can act, must necessarily bind its component parts." Marshall insisted that this was not mere conjecture. "The people," he argued, "have, in express terms, decided it, by saying, 'this constitution, and the laws of the United States, which shall be made in pursuance thereof,' 'shall be the supreme law of the land.'"

In its sphere, then, the Constitution was supreme. Did this sphere include the power to establish a bank? Without any kind of reference to a bank or a national monetary system, could it be assumed that the power was intended? Marshall took care of that point quickly. "A constitution," he said, "to contain an accurate detail of all the subdivisions of which its great powers will admit, and of all the means by which they may be carried into execution, would partake of the prolixity of a legal code, and could scarcely be embraced by the human mind." And to crown its faults, "It would probably never be understood by the public." He continued:

> Its nature, therefore, requires, that only its great outlines should be marked, its important objects designated, and the minor ingredients which compose those objects be deduced from the nature of the objects themselves. That this idea was entertained by the framers of the American constitution, is not only to be inferred from the nature of the instrument, but from the language. Why else were some of the limitations, found in the ninth section of the 1st article, introduced? It is also, in some degree warranted by their having omitted to use any restrictive term which might prevent its receiving a fair and just interpretation. In considering this question, then, we must never forget that it is a constitution we are expounding.

In thirty-four years as Chief Justice of the United States John Marshall never forgot that it was the Constitution he was expounding, a political system by which men and women lived in peace, that allowed all men and women to fulfill themselves to the limit of their abilities if they chose. He never forgot that it was an arrangement by which men and women practice self-restraint and integrity so that while they fulfilled themselves, they did not prohibit others from fulfilling themselves. He never wavered from a belief that it was the achievement of civilization for men to voluntarily agree to live—as their religions have told them since recorded time—by law rather than by their brute strength.

Although neither the words "bank" nor "incorporation" were mentioned in the Constitution, Marshall declared that great powers were listed—to impose and collect taxes, to borrow money, to regulate commerce, to declare and conduct war, and to raise and support an army and navy. "The sword and the purse, all the external relations," said Marshall, "and no inconsiderable portion of the industry of the nation, are entrusted to its government." He criticized as an idea which "can never be advanced" that such powers "draw after them others of inferior importance." He then continued, however, that "it may with great reason be contended, that a government, entrusted with such ample powers, on the due execution of which the happiness and prosperity of the nation so vitally depends, must also be entrusted with ample means for their execution." This was the clue to how John Marshall and his fellow Justices would decide the case. If the bank was a proper means of facilitating a federally entrusted power, then it was legitimate and the Court would uphold it. "The power being given," read Marshall from the opinion, "it is the interest of the nation to facilitate its execution."

Marshall would not accept that the people had intended or would allow the hampering of the execution of delegated powers "by withholding the most appropriate means." He continued that "Throughout this vast republic, from the St. Croix to the Gulph of Mexico, from the Atlantic to the Pacific, revenue is to be collected and expended, armies are to be marched and supported. The exigencies of the nation may require that the treasure raised in the north should be transported to the south, that raised in the east conveyed to the west, or that this order should be reversed." He asked: "Is that construction of the constitution to be preferred which would render these operations difficult, hazardous, and expensive? Can we adopt that construction—unless the words imperiously require it—which would impute to the framers of that instrument, when granting these powers for the public good, the intention of impeding their exercise by withholding a choice of means?" If that were the order of the founding fathers, Marshall said, "we have only to obey." But, he pointed out, the Constitution did not restrict the means by which the powers it confers may be executed "nor does it prohibit the creation of a corporation" if a corporation is necessary to the exercise of constitutional powers. "It is, then, the subject of fair inquiry," he said, "how far such means may be employed."

How far may the government go? Marshall answered: The government which has a right to do an act, and has imposed on it the duty of performing that act, must, according to the dictates of reason, be allowed to select the means; and those who contend that it may not select any appropriate means, that one particular mode of effecting the object is excepted, take upon themselves the burden of establishing that exception." This was a daring pronouncement. Marshall was saying that the federal government had the right to exercise its powers as it saw fit unless its opponents could prove otherwise. All necessary power, he claimed in that paragraph, belonged to the federal government. He would restate this theme in a few moments, in words more enduring.

Was the establishment of a corporation a proper means to effect federal powers? Marshall applied to it the standard he had just enunciated, that the opponents must make a convincing case that establishing a corporation was not allowed. He described creating a corporation not as a power but as "a means by which other objects are accomplished." He explained: "No contributions are made to charity for the sake of an incorporation, but a corporation is created to administer the charity; no seminary of learning is instituted in order to be incorporated, but the corporate character is conferred to subserve the purposes of education. No city was ever built with the sole object of being incorporated, but is incorporated as affording the best means of being well governed. The power of creating a corporation is never used for its own sake, but for the purpose of effecting something else." He had answered his question. "No sufficient reason is, therefore, perceived, why it may not pass as incidental to those powers which are expressly given, if it be a direct mode of executing them."

Marshall had been answering a specific point raised by Maryland. The state had claimed that a national bank could not be chartered by the federal government because such a specific power was not listed in the Constitution. A second argument Maryland had made was that the bank could not be chartered because the Constitution granted the federal government only those powers "necessary and proper" for executing the government's business. The state was interpreting the word "necessary" in a restricted sense—using Marshall's description, "as limiting the right to pass laws for the execution of the granted powers, to such as are indispensable, and without which the power would be nugatory . . . only which is most direct and simple." Marshall actually had already disposed of that point when he had spoken, earlier in the decision, about government being allowed to select the means it wished to enforce its powers. He would repeat that theme of the federal government having expanded and expanding powers. First he went into a long definition of the word "necessary," arguing that it did not have a limited meaning but "is generally understood as employing any means calculated to produce the end." He then insisted the word was to be construed according to the intention of the authors. The authors in this case were the men who had written the federal Constitution, and Marshall was well qualified to interpret their intent. He had lived through that period, joined in the debates, fought for the ratification of the Constitution in Virginia, and worked closely with James Madison, who was one of the principal authors of the document. Certainly Marshall must have studied *The Federalist Papers*, particularly number forty-four which discusses the powers of the federal government and which includes this sentence: "No axiom is more clearly established in law, or in reason, than that wherever the end is required, the means are authorized; wherever a general power to do a thing is given, every particular power necessary for doing it is included." He had seen the application of that axiom turn the young United States from a toddling child into a powerful youth capable of achieving that promise. That axiom had been accepted in the life of America to that point. In 1798 the minority report of the Virginia legislature written in defense of the Alien and Sedition Laws had said that while the federal government "is indubitably limited as to its objects," the means of obtaining those objects are not subject to such limitations. John Marshall is believed to have written that section of the report. In an 1804 case before the Supreme Court, Alexander J. Dallas, an avid Jeffersonian, had said: "Congress have duties and powers expressly given, and a right to make all laws necessary to enable them to perform those duties, and to exercise those powers."[6] John Marshall now would enunciate that axiom of expanding powers, already accepted by the United States, in a manner that would make impossible for the United States to forget it. "We admit, as all must admit," he began, "that the powers of the government are limited, and that its limits are not to be transcended. But we think the sound construction of the constitution must allow to the national legislature that discretion, with respect to the means by which the powers it confers are to be carried into execution, which will enable that body to perform the high duties assigned to it, in the manner most beneficial to the people." He said:

> Let the end be legitimate, let it be within the scope of the constitution, and all means which are appropriate, which are plainly adapted to that end, which are not prohibited, but consist with the letter and spirit of the constitution, are constitutional.

In an effort to blunt criticism of such a bold declaration, Marshall said that the Supreme Court would have to declare unconstitutional a congressional act prohibited by the Constitution, as he had done sixteen years earlier in *Marbury v. Madison.* "But where the law is not prohibited," he said, "and is really calculated to effect any of the objects entrusted to the government, to undertake here to inquire into the degree of its necessity,

would be to pass the line which circumscribes the judicial department, and to tread on legislative ground. This court disclaims all
pretensions to such a power." Marshall not only had asserted a
liberal definition of the federal government's powers, he had done
it in the name of judicial restraint. Whatever one thinks of John
Marshall, whether one be a defender or a critic, one must admire
his agility.

He concluded what was the first half of the decision with
the statement that the "unanimous and decided" opinion of the
Supreme Court was that the act incorporating the United States
Bank was constitutional. The unanimity of the Court is signifi-
cant, of course, because, except for John Marshall and Bushrod
Washington, all members had been appointed by either Thomas
Jefferson or James Madison.

The second half of the decision, now that it had been
determined by the Supreme Court that the bank was constitutional, involved the question of whether Maryland could impose
a tax on the bank.

Marshall began this half of the decision by stating that
the power to tax "is one of vital importance." He conceded that it
was retained by the states and not limited by the constitutional
grant of the same power to the federal Union. The two authorities, the federal and the state, were to exercise the power of taxation concurrently. "But," Marshall continued, "such is the
paramount character of the constitution, that its capacity to withdraw any subject from the action of even this power, is admitted." He pointed out that the states were expressly forbidden from
placing taxes on imports and exports, and said if that prohibition
were conceded, "the same paramount character would seem to
restrain, as it certainly may restrain, a State from such other exercise of this power, as is in its nature incompatible with, and
repugnant to, the constitutional laws of the Union. A law, absolutely repugnant to another, as entirely repeals that other as if
express terms of repeal were used." Continuing on this theme, he
restated the supremacy of laws made by the federal government
under a constitutional mandate, "that they control the . . . laws of
the respective States, and cannot be controlled by them." From
this statement, which, Marshall said, "may be almost termed an
axiom, other propositions are deduced as corollaries." He listed
them: "That a power to create implies a power to preserve. . . .
That a power to destroy, if wielded by a different hand, is hostile
to, and incompatible with these powers to create and preserve. . . .
That where this repugnancy exists, that authority which is
supreme must control, not yield to that over which it is supreme."
The Chief Justice here was showing that he accepted the argu-

ment made by Daniel Webster that to give the state of Maryland the power to tax a federal installation was to give it the power to destroy that installation. "Too obvious to be denied" is how Marshall described the assertion that the power to tax is the power to destroy.

However, the point had been raised that the state's power to tax was an absolute power that could not be restricted beyond the specific limits in the Constitution. Marshall plunged into that issue in his decision. The people of a state give to that state the right to tax them, he said, but that is not the case when the states attempt to tax federal installations. "They," he said of these installations, "are given by all, for the benefit of all—and upon theory, should be subjected to that government only which belongs to all." He acknowledged an objection to that theory was that a state's taxing power was not limited to only people and property but covered "every object brought within its jurisdiction." He did not dispute that, but asked the source of that broad taxing power. He answered that it was part of the sovereign power of the state. Then: "All subjects over which the sovereign power of a State extends, are objects of taxation; but those over which it does not extend, are, upon the soundest principles, exempt from taxation. This proposition may almost be pronounced self-evident." This "self-evident" proposition excluded any federal installations.

He recommended that the limits of the power to tax go no further than the limits of sovereignty because this rule offered "an intelligible standard." He continued: "We are relieved, as we ought to be, from clashing sovereignty; from interfering powers; from a repugnancy between a right in one government to destroy what there is a right in another to preserve. We are not driven to the perplexing inquiry, so unfit for the judicial department, what degree of taxation is the legitimate use, and what degree may amount to the abuse of the power."

Marshall was nearing the end of his decision, a decision that covers thirty-six pages in the official reports. In his eagerness to defend the federal Union from onslaughts that would weaken it, he became more passionate. His love and devotion to the federal Union showed clearly now. "If we apply the principle for which the State of Maryland contends to the constitution generally," he said, "we shall find it capable of changing totally the character of that instrument. We shall find it capable of arresting all the measures of the government, and of prostrating it at the foot of the States. . . . If the States may tax one instrument, employed by the government in the execution of its powers, they may tax any and every other instrument. They may tax the mail;

they may tax the mint; they may tax patent rights; they may tax the papers of the customhouse; they may tax judicial process; they may tax all the means employed by the government." John Marshall declared emphatically: "This was not intended by the American people. They did not design to make their government dependent on the States."

And if the states could tax the federal government, why could they not exercise sovereignty in other ways? Taxation is not the only means by which that sovereignty could be exercised. John Marshall was indeed expounding a Constitution for future generations as well as those Americans of his time. "The question is, in truth," he said, "a question of supremacy; and if the right of the States to tax the means employed by the general government be conceded, the declaration that the constitution, and the laws made in pursuance thereof, shall be the supreme law of the land, is empty and unmeaning declamation."

He closed with a less passionate declaration, perhaps, but one still firm: "The Court has bestowed on this subject its most deliberate consideration. The result is a conviction that the States have no power, by taxation or otherwise, to retard, impede, burden, or in any manner control, the operations of the constitutional laws enacted by Congress to carry into execution the powers vested in the general government. This is, we think, the unavoidable consequence of that supremacy which the constitution has declared."

He stressed the unanimity of the judges in declaring the Maryland tax "unconstitutional and void." Anticipating a howl of complaints from the states, Marshall insisted that the Court's opinion did not deprive the states of any rights "they originally possessed." He said the decision was a narrow one—"It does not extend to a tax paid by the real property of the bank, in common with the other real property within the State, nor to a tax imposed on the interest which the citizens of Maryland may hold in this institution, in common with other property of the same description throughout the State." The decision, rather, he argued in his closing paragraph, was against "a tax on the operations of the bank" which is "consequently, a tax on the operation of an instrument employed by the government of the Union to carry its powers into execution. Such a tax must be unconstitutional."

In that thirty-six-page decision John Marshall had cemented to the federal Union its power to be a government. The young soldier at Valley Forge who had seen the American army floundering because the states would not honor their commitments had developed into the jurist who now made certain that the states never again could successfully subvert the central authority. The states would attempt to do so; the Civil War was only 42 years away. But all challenges subsequent to that decision were doomed to failure, largely because of that decision and what it represented. Marshall had set out to produce not law but a justification of the supremacy of the federal government, a justification reasonable enough to persuade men through the coming decades of its appropriateness. In this, he succeeded.

His success is demonstrated not only in that the other members of the Court agreed with him in this decision but in that they accepted his premise as their own. Two years after *McCulloch v. Maryland* William Johnson said in a decision that every constitutional power includes others "vital to its exercise; not substantive and independent, indeed, but auxiliary and subordinate."[7]

The triumph of John Marshall's reasoning, however, did not deter passionate critics of the decision. The cry of states' rights was becoming boisterous. The doctrine of states' rights was tied to the preservation of slavery, and the South was becoming increasingly suspicious of northern intentions toward that institution. "States' rights" also was a slogan under which a number of well-meaning and intelligent men had developed politically, who were no more capable of rising above their catchwords than are most other politicians. And finally the triumph of John Marshall's reasoning could not still the critics because it should not have. "This decision excites great interest," commented Joseph Story, "and in a political view is of the deepest consequence to the nation."[8] Issues which are so significant should be debated, challenged, and defended many times until the correctness of the solutions offered is accepted beyond doubt. This would happen eventually with the Marshall decision in *McCulloch v. Maryland*.

The furor was anticipated. A few weeks after the decision was handed down, Marshall wrote to his fellow Justice Bushrod Washington that Virginia politicians were much dissatisfied with the Court's decision. "They have no objection to a decision in favor of the bank," said Marshall, "since the good patriots who administer the government wished it, and would probably have been seriously offended with us had we dared to have decided otherwise, but they required an obsequious, silent opinion without reason. That would have been satisfactory, but our heretical reasoning is pronounced most damnable." Marshall knew what was coming. "We shall be denounced bitterly in the papers," he told Washington, "and as not a word will be said on the other side we shall be undoubtedly condemned as a pack of consolidating aristocratics. The legislature and executive who have enacted the law but who have power and places to bestow will escape with impunity, while the poor court who have nothing to give and of whom nobody is afraid, bears all the obloquy of the measure."⁹ Marshall's apparent cynicism may have been, actually, a wry comment by him that the Court's critics could have been bought off with a little patronage if the Court had any to give. Also Marshall's fear that "not a word will be said on the other side" was groundless; he himself would be the defender. As far as is known, John Marshall was not in the habit of attempting to defend his decisions outside of the courtroom. But the *McCulloch v. Maryland* decision would be an exception. Rather than permit the Supreme Court and the principle of a strong federal Union to be attacked without answer, Marshall himself came to their defense in two series of newspaper articles.

The critics of the Supreme Court were angry. Thomas Jefferson, living in retirement at Monticello, fumed that the decision demonstrated the error of lifetime appointments for Justices. He told a visiting young lawyer named Martin Van Buren that he believed annual appointments the best cure for the kind of political heresy found in the decision.¹⁰ There was no help from William Johnson, the strongest Jeffersonian on the bench. He not only went along with Marshall but endorsed the decision in his private correspondence. Since his appointment in 1804 Johnson had become more and more a federalist. "The development was one of growth rather than of substitution," wrote his biographer, Donald G. Morgan. "The appointee of 1804 had in time emerged a nationalist."¹¹ Johnson was allying himself with the nationalistic philosophy that would pull the nation together into a powerful whole rather than allow it to disintegrate into a number of parts.

The vocal opposition would come from other of Thomas Jefferson's disciples, principally William Brockenbrough and Spencer Roane. Brockenbrough was a Richmond judge and Roane was still a leading Virginia politician and the chief judge of the Virginia Court of Appeals. Their opposition would be powerful. "Our opinion in the bank case," said John Marshall, "has roused the sleeping spirit of Virginia if indeed it ever sleeps." Marshall was concerned that the decision "will remain undefended and of course be considered as damnably heretical." He obviously was persuading himself of the wisdom and necessity of undertaking the series of articles in the newspapers defending the decision.¹²

Marshall's concern was more than personal. In Virginia an effort was being made to persuade the state legislature to denounce the decision by resolution when it met in December. "Whether this effort will be successful or not may perhaps depend in some measure on the sentiments of our sister states," said

Marshall in another report to Story. To gain support in other states, he continued, the decision was "grossly misrepresented" or confronted with arguments "too palpably absurd for intelligent men." If the opponents had their way, said Marshall, "the Constitution would be converted into the old confederation." Story had referred to a defense of the decision, but Marshall reported that the defense had not been published in Virginia. "Our patriotic papers admit no such political heresies," he remarked.[13]

Articles attacking the Court's decision began appearing in the *Richmond Enquirer*, which was run by Thomas Ritchie, a cousin of Spencer Roane. The newspaper was considered the chief organ of the local political group known as the Richmond Junto which was led by Roane and which controlled almost all political appointments and elections in the state; it was a model of what a later generation would term "political bossism." Dedicated to the states' rights theory of government, the Junto made certain that all prominent politicians in the state were adherents of that theory.

That Spencer Roane, the man who was buying stock in the United States Bank while John Marshall was selling his, would attack the decision upholding the bank is not as surprising as it appears. As Marshall had pointed out, the critics had no complaint about the extension of the life of the bank. Their concern was caused by the significance of the decision: "they required an obsequious, silent opinion without reason." Marshall's chief points —that the Constitution was authorized by the people rather than by the states, that the federal Union had expanding powers to accomplish by legitimate means the general goals listed in the Constitution, and that the states could do nothing to weaken the power of the federal government—were totally unacceptable to the states' rights advocates. These points must be refuted.

The process of refutation began in a letter signed by "Amphictyon" appearing in the *Richmond Enquirer* of March 30, 1819. The tradition has grown up that "Amphictyon" was Spencer Roane; he did write a series of critiques a few weeks later under the name of "Hampden," but there is no reason to doubt that William Brockenbrough was "Amphictyon," as John Marshall so identified him.[14] This letter of March 30 and a subsequent one on April 2 are brilliant analyses of the *McCulloch* decision, as well as masterpieces of sly attack.

The first letter begins, for example, by praising Marshall's decision as "very able" but then goes on: "This was to have been expected, proceeding as it does from a man of the most profound legal attainments, and upon a subject which has employed his thoughts, his tongue, and his pen, as a politician, and an historian for more than thirty years." The letter proceeded to point out that the subject of the decision has "drawn a broad line of distinction between the two great parties" and said that "on which line no one has taken a more distinguished and decided rank" than Marshall. So much for law!

This first letter attacked two themes in the Marshall opinion: that the power of the federal government comes from the people rather than from the states and that the Necessary and Proper Clause should be interpreted liberally rather than narrowly. The letter correctly stated that "Both of these principles tend directly to consolidation of the States, and to strip them of some of the most important attributes of their sovereignty." First, "Amphictyon" challenged whether it was necessary to determine the source of the federal government's power in determining whether the bank was constitutional. Saying that it was not, "Amphictyon" charged that "the court traveled out of the record . . . the decision of that point is, therefore, obiter, extra-judicial, and not more binding or obligatory than the opinion of any other six intelligent members of the community."

"Amphictyon" then denied that the people had authorized the Constitution and asserted that the states had done so "in their highest political and sovereign authority." "Amphictyon's" strongest argument is also his weakest. It reads:

> The States then being the parties to the constitutional compact, and in their sovereign capacity, it follows of necessity, that there can be no tribunal above their authority to decide in the last resort, whether the compact made by them be violated; and consequently that as the parties to it they must themselves decide, in the last resort, such questions as may be of sufficient magnitude to receive their interposition.

"Amphictyon" was taking the position that the states were sovereign bodies which admitted no authority greater than each of them. As it had been the theme of Jefferson's and Madison's Virginia and Kentucky Resolutions, this would be the theme of the writings a year later by John Taylor which would influence southerners for decades, ultimately contributing to the Civil War and subsequent strife. It would be the theme advanced on occasions when the Supreme Court pronounced a decision objectionable to any particular state or community. In reality the theme is a rejection of law. If each member of a society can determine for himself or herself which laws he or she wishes to obey, then there is no law; there is only personal predilection. The whole point of the Constitution and the American experiment is the acceptance by the individual of a democratically created law.

The second letter, appearing in the *Richmond Enquirer* on April 2, challenged the liberal interpretation of the Necessary and Proper Clause. This challenge, interestingly, used arguments similar to those used by Marshall to interpret the clause liberally. *The Federalist Papers* were quoted to the effect that every general power implies the specific powers needed to carry it out. Ancient English law and the more recent pronouncements of Lord Coke were quoted to support the thesis that when the law gives a responsibility to a person, it gives him the power to fulfill that obligation. But then the letter went on to say that all this meant that the Necessary and Proper Clause "conveys no grant of powers; it was inserted from abundant caution." If the clause had not been inserted, "Amphictyon" said, "Congress then would have had a right to use the means necessary to effectuate their granted powers, and no more; they could only have used those means *sine quo* their express powers could not have been carried into execution. The insertion of the clause has no greater effect: it confers no new powers."

But if the federal government is not strong, then how is the safety of its members protected? "Amphictyon" answered: "The safety of the States will be found in their own firmness, their own vigilance, and their own wisdom."

There is one line in that letter which apparently was not well noticed at the time but which foreshadowed much of the strife that would envelop the nation within a few decades. Considering that the *Enquirer* was the voice of the Richmond Junto, the ruling power in Virginia, and that "Amphictyon" was a prominent member of that group and was obviously speaking for it, as well as being a judge and a person of acknowledged brilliance, the line cannot be considered an accident. Speaking of Virginia, "Amphictyon" wrote that the state had not favored the bank, its Senators and Representatives in Congress had opposed it, yet Virginia had imposed no tax on the national bank. Virginia, "Amphictyon" continued, adopted a wiser course, passing resolutions condemning what it considered unconstitutional laws and attempting to educate the public to its philosophy. "She endeavors to unite and combine the moral force of the States against usurpation," "Amphictyon" wrote, "and she never will employ a force to support her doctrines till other measures have failed." Because people like William Brockenbrough, Spencer Roane, and John Taylor—all responsible men—enunciated the philosophy that force could be used as a last resort by a state which disagreed with federal doctrine, the tragedy of the Civil War became inevitable.

John Marshall was aware of the attacks in the press and concerned by the attack on the decision; his letters to fellow Justices Joseph Story and Bushrod Washington made that clear. At first he lamented that the attacks would go unanswered. But as he thought more about it, apparently he saw no reason why he should not answer them. In his earlier days as a Federalist politician in Richmond he had played the same game—writing political tracts under pseudonyms—and he was fairly skilled at it. He had no trouble returning to his old trade. The first of his letters, signed by "A Friend to the Union," appeared in the *Philadelphia Union* April 24. There is bitterness in it.

Marshall pointed out that the bill establishing the bank had originally become law without "exciting a single murmur." The reason, he said, was obvious. The members of the Congress and the President "are elected by the people, and are of course popular." In addition, Marshall continued, "they possess great power and patronage." If they had been attacked, he said, defenders would have risen immediately. The next part of his public letter reflected the comments he had made earlier in a private letter to Bushrod Washington. "The judges of the Supreme Court, separated from the people by the tenure of office, by age, and by the nature of their duties, are viewed with respect, unmingled with affection, or interest. They possess neither power nor patronage. They have no sops to give; and every coffee house furnishes a Cerberus, hoping some reward for that watchfulness which his bark proclaims; and restrained by no apprehension that any can be stimulated by personal considerations to expose the injustice of his attacks." Marshall then said that no one should be surprised when the Supreme Court is, therefore, singled out for attack. "Hostility to the Union," he wrote, "must cease to be guided by its usual skill, when it fails to select the weakest department as that through which a breach may be effected." Brockenbrough was not alone in the ability to write sly innuendo.

"A Friend to the Union" then pointed out that the decision was in the name of the Supreme Court and not in the name of the Chief Justice or any other individual. "I appeal to Amphictyon himself," said Marshall, "I appeal to every man accustomed to judicial proceedings, to determine whether the judges of the Supreme Court, men of high and respectable character, would sit by in silence, while great constitutional principles of which they disapproved, were advanced in their name, and as their principles." This was a reference to all of the judges, except

Marshall and Washington, having been appointed either by Thomas Jefferson or James Madison. Dissents were not unknown on the Court. From the time William Johnson joined the Court to the time of the *McCulloch v. Maryland* decision in 1819, he was responsible for a dozen dissents. Gabriel Duvall, who had joined the Court in 1812 with Story, had written one dissent and Story had written four; Brockholst Livingston had written two since joining the Court in 1808.[15] The Justices of the Supreme Court could not be accused of reluctance to speak out if they disagreed with the Chief Justice or the Court majority.

Since Marshall had already advanced his arguments in the opinion, he repeated them only briefly in the letters to the Philadelphia paper and devoted more space to ridiculing "Amphictyon." He expressed concern that "a man of Amphictyon's intelligence should have advanced" the opinions in the letters to the Richmond paper, and said that it "only proves that he is too little accustomed to political opposition, and is too confident of the prejudices he addresses, to be very attentive to the correctness of his positions, or the accuracy of his reasoning. . . . His eagerness to censure must be much stronger than his sense of justice."

In a second letter, dated April 28, also in the *Philadelphia Union*, Marshall took specific issue with "Amphictyon's" criticism of the Supreme Court's interpretation of federal powers. "Amphictyon" had said that the Constitution had given the federal government only "the power of resorting to such means as are incidental to the express powers; to such means as directly and necessarily tend to produce the desired effect." In answering this, Marshall commented on what is perhaps the best-known line in all of his decisions. "How much more, let me ask, has been said by the Supreme Court?" he asked. "That court has said: 'Let the end be legitimate, let it be within the scope of the constitution, and all means which are appropriate, which are plainly adapted to that end, which are not prohibited . . . are constitutional.' The word 'appropriate' . . . means 'peculiar,' 'consigned to some particular use or person,'—'belonging peculiarly.' "[16]

Marshall's letters had been written with the knowledge of Bushrod Washington, who encouraged him and also wished the letters to have a wide circulation. Marshall, however, seemed disenchanted with his effort as an anonymous polemicist. When Washington wrote him to ask if the letters defending the Court had been correctly reprinted in the Alexandria newspaper, Marshall replied that he had gone to the coffeehouse to read the paper, but the paper had been mislaid. "I cannot therefore say whether they have appeared in an intelligible shape or not," he reported, "and therefore am not desirous that any further effort should be made to get them before the public." He then went on to talk about a case before him at the Richmond Circuit Court and asked for Washington's opinion.[17]

But the polemics of John Marshall were not at an end. While he might have hoped to retreat from the letter-writing fray, he could not. Such letters as those by "Amphictyon" and "A Friend to the Union" were the chief means of propagandizing at the time. Readers, seeing an attack, expected a defense. Marshall knew this, and so when the second attack came, he again felt obliged to write a new series of articles. This second attack came from the pen of Spencer Roane himself. Signed "Hampden," the letters appeared in the *Richmond Enquirer* in the month of June. They are strident in tone but persuasive in their arguments.

John Marshall and Spencer Roane had similar backgrounds. They both learned their basic law from George Wythe and served, often together, in the Virginia legislature. They obviously knew each other well in Richmond; in the later years of their lives—about the time they were coming so much into conflict over the power of the Supreme Court and the federal Union—they lived near each other. They both were admirers of Patrick Henry; Roane's first wife was Henry's daughter. And both were considered brilliant judges. Roane was appointed to the state Court of Appeals in 1794 and served until his death in 1822. His reputation was distinguished. If Thomas Jefferson had had the opportunity to name a Chief Justice of the United States, the appointment of Roane would have been cheered.

Yet these two men, so much alike in background, were so different in their understanding of the Union and the role of the government. Perhaps because Marshall had been a soldier in the Revolution, had experienced Valley Forge, been an associate of George Washington, who more than anyone dreamed of a strong federal Union; perhaps because he had been to France and seen the disintegration of a society which allowed its members to determine which laws they would obey; perhaps only because John Marshall sat on a federal bench while Spencer Roane sat on a state bench—whatever the factors, John Marshall envisioned men's rights being protected by a system which allowed its law to be devised in democratic fashion and then insisted that all its members adhere to it, while Spencer Roane disputed the universality of the law. That dispute would be the subject of their remarkable exchange of letters.

Roane as "Hampden" began them in the *Enquirer* on June 11. His first letter opened in an exaggerated tone of despair. "I address you, Mr. Editor, on this great subject with no sanguine presage of success," is the opening sentence. "I must say to my fellow citizens that they are sunk in apathy, and that a torpor has fallen upon them. Instead of that noble and magnanimous spirit which achieved our independence, and has often preserved us since, we are sodden in the luxuries of banking. A money-loving, funding, stock-jobbing spirit has taken foothold among us. We are almost prepared to sell our liberties for a 'mess of pottage.' If Mason or Henry could lift their patriot heads from the grave, while they mourned the complete fulfillment of their prophecies, they would almost exclaim with Jugurtha, 'Venal people! you will soon perish if you can find a purchaser.'"

Picking up Marshall's line from the opinion that it was a Constitution they were expounding, Roane went back to the argument that federal powers under the Constitution were limited and specified ones. If more powers were needed, he argued, the Constitution should be amended to include them. "The States have also constitutions," he continued, "and their people rights, which ought also to be respected." Other "Hampden" letters appeared on June 15 and June 18. While they were repetitious of the arguments made in the case and of those listed in the letters by "Amphictyon," they were nonetheless powerful in their emotional appeal to the states' rights people of Virginia.

Marshall read them all and found himself "more stimulated on this subject than on any other." He believed the intent of the letters by "Hampden" was an attack on the Supreme Court and on the Constitution. He expressed his feelings in a letter to Bushrod Washington. While he did not say so, Marshall probably was angry at the stridency and perhaps personal tone he detected in "Hampden's" attacks. "I have therefore thought of answering these essays," he told Washington. The articles Marshall wrote were sent by him to Washington for publication in the *Alexandria Gazette* under the *nom de plume* of "A Friend of the Constitution." Marshall did not believe that the attacks by "Amphictyon" and "Hampden" had made any significant impact in Richmond, "but they were designed for the country and have had considerable influence there. . . ."[18]

The first letter by "A Friend of the Constitution" appeared in the *Gazette* on June 30. Marshall did not hesitate to accuse his opponents of seeking to undermine the Court. He began by saying:

> If it be true that no rational friend of the constitution
> can wish to expunge from it the judicial department, it
> must be difficult for those who believe the prosperity of
> the American people to be inseparable from the preserva-
> tion of this government, to view with indifference the sys-

tematic efforts which restless politicians of Virginia have been for some time making, to degrade that department in the estimation of the public. It is not easy to resist the conviction that those efforts must have other and more dangerous objects, than merely to impair the confidence of the nation in the present judges.

Marshall then charged that those "more dangerous objects" were to strip the federal government of its needed powers and to reinstate the "miserable confederation."

The Chief Justice was particularly angry at "the injust and insidious insinuation" that the Supreme Court had pushed itself into the controversy between the state and the bank. The "Hampden" letters claimed that "The judiciary has also deemed its interference necessary in our country." This charge, that the Supreme Court was a meddler in the affairs of the nation, is one frequently thrown at the Court by its enemies, and Marshall's answer to Spencer Roane has been repeated many times by later Justices of the Supreme Court, if not in identical, certainly in similar words. Marshall said:

> If Hampden does not know that the court proceeded in this business, not because "it deemed its interference necessary," but because the question was brought regularly before it by those who had a right to demand, and did demand, its decision he would do well to suspend his censures until he acquires the information which belongs to the subject; if he does know it, I leave it to himself to assign the motives for this insinuation.

Next Marshall took up the argument that the Court had produced needless dicta when all it had to do was state whether the bank was or was not constitutional. "And how, let me ask, was the court to decide this question?" demanded Marshall. He insisted that an examination of the Constitution was required for the words that were used and what they did or did not allow. "Yet if the judges examine the meaning of the words," said Marshall, "they are stopped by Hampden, and accused of traveling out of the record." Marshall then said that the Court's interpretation of the law may be erroneous—"This is open to argument." But to say that in making that interpretation, the judges are spouting unnecessary dicta "may indeed show the spirit in which these strictures originate; but can impose on no intelligent men. . . ." As for the charge that the Supreme Court was amending the Constitution by judicial interpretation, Marshall threw it back at his accusers. "Is it not less possible that . . . a new mode of amendment, by way of reports of committees of a state legislature and resolutions thereon, may pluck from [the Constitution] power after power in detail, or may sweep off the whole at once by declaring that it shall execute its acknowledged powers by those scanty and inconvenient means only which the states shall prescribe, and without which the power cannot exist. . . ."

The second letter appeared in the *Gazette* on July 1. In this letter "A Friend of the Constitution" examined the powers of the government. "The power to do a thing, and the power to carry that thing into execution, are, I humbly conceive, the same power, and the one cannot be termed with propriety 'additional' or 'incidental' to the other." He attacked "Hampden's" argument that government's power was most limited, citing precedent for precedent, legal argument for legal argument. Taking Roane's and Marshall's arguments together on this facet of the debate, they seem like two champion wrestlers, scoring point after point against each other, with citations, devastating witticisms, and circuitous legal arguments. Despite the fact that this was a lawyer's debate—and the only occasion in which the two great legal minds of Virginia in that period grappled with each other on a point-by-point basis—the argument continues a fascinating one. It is a tribute to both men that no debate over the powers of the federal government has gone beyond theirs. All that had to be said, they managed to say. From the pages of the lengthy newspaper articles emerged the particulars of a debate which continues to convulse the United States. Marshall's letters read like his decision, a logical demand for an understanding that there can be no Union without power going to that Union. History has so far demonstrated that the majority of the American people are willing to struggle and die for the understanding enunciated by John Marshall.

On July 2 Marshall turned to the Roane argument that the power to establish the bank was nonexistent because it was not specified. He repeated, from his Court decision, the explanation that a constitution cannot be burdened with multitudinous details. He described a constitution as "the act of a people, creating a government, without which they cannot exist as a people. The powers of this government are conferred for their own benefit, are essential to their own prosperity, and are to be exercised for their own good, by persons chosen for that purpose by themselves." Inherent in that description is faith in the people's ability to voluntarily devise a workable government rather than have an unworkable one forced upon them.

The Marshall-Roane debate, the conflict between the Federalists and Jeffersonians, the variations of it through American history, all must be viewed against the origins of the United States. The voluntary acceptance of restraints implicit in the

American system was seen by Marshall and the Federalists as the only way to construct a democratic government. To turn away from restraint, to allow the individual or the state to determine when and where he shall exercise restraint, is to permit anarchy, is to say that the weak and powerless, unable to find redress in the courts or the other branches of government, must turn to violence as a means of securing their rights. This had been the course of societies until the development of the United States; it also had been the cause of the United States. Marshall as a federal judge was obliged to insist on the states exercising restraint or else face up to the ultimate decay of a society, as he witnessed in France. The unanimity of the Justices in this decision demonstrated that no person with the responsibilities of a Justice of the Supreme Court could escape that obligation.

Letters from "A Friend of the Constitution" appeared on July 3, 5, and 6. In the last Marshall asked if "Hampden" would deny that the American people have a national existence. "We were charged by the late emperor of France with having no national character, or actual existence as a nation," wrote Marshall, "but not even he denied our theoretical or constitutional existence. If congress declares war, are we not at war as a nation? Are not war and peace national acts? . . . The United States is a nation; but a nation composed of states in many, though not in all, respects, sovereign. The people of these states are also the people of the United States." Marshall insisted "we are all citizens, not only of our particular states, but also of this great republic." That was a more daring statement than it now appears. His opponents were disciples of Thomas Jefferson, who spoke of Virginia as his country, the land of his birth. Marshall in that statement was urging men to break out of this tradition forged prior to the founding of the United States and to recognize that they belonged to an entity greater than a single state.

In the letters which appeared July 9 and 14 Marshall again spoke of the need for a strong Union if the nation were to avoid becoming a government with the failings of the Confederation. In the final letter, July 15, he made a plea for judicial determination of conflicts. Thirty years earlier a young lawyer had stood up before his fellow delegates at the Virginia convention called to ratify the Constitution and asked them: "To what quarter will you look for protection from an infringement on the Constitution, if you will not give the power to the judiciary? There is no other body that can afford such a protection."[19] Now, as a much older man, John Marshall asked the same question; his ideas had changed little, even his words are similar. He wrote:

To whom more safely than to the judges are judicial questions to be referred? They are selected from the great body of the people for the purpose of deciding them. To secure impartiality, they are made perfectly independent. They have no personal interest in aggrandizing the legislative power. Their paramount interest is the public prosperity, in which is involved their own and that of their families.—*No* tribunal can be less liable to be swayed by unworthy motives from a conscientious performance of duty. It is not then the party sitting in his own cause. It is the application to individuals by one department of the acts of another department of government. The people are the authors of all; the departments are their agents; and if the judge be personally disinterested, he is as exempt from any political interest that might influence his opinion, as imperfect human institutions can make him.

The closing paragraph of this series of letters reads more like a plea for a workable government than a defense of a legal opinion:

I have been induced to review these essays the more in detail, because they are intended to produce a very serious effect; and because they advance principles which go, in my judgment, to the utter subversion of the constitution. Let Hampden succeed, and that instrument will be radically changed. The government of the whole will be prostrated at the feet of its members; and that grand effort of wisdom, virtue, and patriotism, which produced it, will be totally defeated.

The debate begun by the *McCulloch v. Maryland* decision and the subsequent newspaper essays—or rather, continued, for it had begun with the proposing of the Constitution three decades earlier—produced considerable animosity between the two sides. Marshall's letters indicated that he was more than philosophically and theoretically disturbed, that he was personally angry with his neighbor Spencer Roane. At Monticello the aging Jefferson, living in his splendid isolation, became increasingly bitter over the Court's action: "We find the judiciary on every occasion still driving us into consolidation." If the Court could declare state laws invalid, he wrote to Spencer Roane, then the Constitution "is a mere thing of wag in the hands of the judiciary, which they may twist and shape into any form they please." Jefferson argued that to give the Court an independent power is to give it an absolute power. That, he said, was "an axiom of eternal truth in politics." He insisted that "Independence can be trusted nowhere but with the people in mass. They are inherently independent of all but moral law. . . ."[20] In examining Jefferson's comments, one can see there is no conflict between what he and John Marshall were saying. Marshall also believed in power to the people, but he understood that the people must use that power to design an effective system of exercising their democratic rights. Such a system is termed government. Even when Thomas Jefferson was President, he worked that system to its limit to effect good government. Once freed from power and responsibility in his later years, however, Jefferson best served his nation by espousing a political philosophy that was a necessary counterbalance to the philosophy of a strong central government. Marshall and Jefferson are portrayed in history as enemies, and that they were, but their philosophies are not in opposition; rather, they are complementary to each other. A strong government can tend to lose sight of its purpose of allowing the fulfillment of democratic rights. The Jeffersonians, fearing that absolute power, would always watch that government did not lose its purpose. The danger in Jefferson's philosophy was that it could result in an ineffective government; the disciples of John Marshall always would watch that it did not.

As a result of the *McCulloch* decision, John Taylor of Caroline wrote a book entitled *Construction Construed* which is considered one of the best defenses of states' rights ever written, being used as late as the 1950s and 1960s as the basis for arguments against desegregation decisions. Almost four decades earlier two young lawyers named John Marshall and John Taylor had disputed each other in the case of *John Bracken v. William and Mary*. In that case Marshall had argued that an institution had the right to do all it considered proper so long as its actions did not specifically transgress the bounds of its charter or constitution. Taylor had disputed that assertion, saying an institution could do only what it was specifically allowed to do by its charter. Neither man had altered his views radically.

Taylor, facing the *McCulloch* decision, was moved by his personal passion and also by the need to codify the arguments against *McCulloch*. The opponents of the decision were as aware as the advocates that a Constitution was being expounded by the Supreme Court for later generations, and that if their arguments were not printed in permanent form, then future generations would have only one side.

Construction Construed is largely repetitious of the arguments used by the lawyers for Maryland before the Court on the case and also of the letters by "Amphictyon" and "Hampden" in the *Richmond Enquirer*. Taylor well stated the philosophy of the states' rights people: that they were citizens of their states rather than of the United States. "No people," he wrote, "or community has ever been composed in the United States, except by the inhabitants of each state, associating distinctly from every other state, by their own separate consent." He also spoke to a point which has become known as the Nullification Doctrine, the right of states to declare null and void those federal laws or programs they find unacceptable. They had such a right under the old Articles of Confederation through a simple refusal: the states did not pay assessments they did not wish to, nor did they honor any other request from the Confederation they wished to ignore. Taylor would have them possess the same right under the Constitution. "These state sovereignties made, may revoke, or can alter the constitution itself," he declared, although a major purpose of the Constitution had been to take that right from the states. As for federal judges denying the constitutionality of state laws, Taylor claimed they had no such power. "The constitutionality of state laws cannot legitimately be decided by the federal courts," he wrote, "because they are not a constituent part of the state governments, nor have the people of the state confided to them any such authority." Taylor employed some flowery oratory to pull men's political hearts from the federal concept that John Marshall had enunciated. An example:

> Veneration of our constitution is the best security for the endurance of our free form of government, and the best infusion for elevating the national character. But, how can a nation love an embryo litter of fluctuating precedents, concealed in the womb of time, each of which as it grows, hustles some principle out of the constitution, as the cuckoo does the sparrow out of its own nest? Had Pygmalion's beautiful statue, after it was animated, been seduced to produce bastards, would he have loved her the better for it? What should we say to a husband, who should surrender the custody of his wife to a set of professed rakes? That which ought to be said of a nation which entrusts its constitution to the care of precedents. They are only the projects or opinions of successive legislators, presidents, judges, generals or statesmen, none of whom will acknowledge that their laws, actions, decisions, orders or schemes are unconstitutional, though they will be forever as various and contradictory as the characters from which they proceed.

Taylor had another point to make which is interesting because it could have been written by John Marshall himself. Marshall did, in fact, say much the same thing in later decisions.

The passage demonstrates how two honorable, educated, and intelligent men can see the same thing by looking in different directions. "The right of each man to his own labour, by which only his life can be preserved, is as much a natural right, as a right to life itself; nor was there any more need to stipulate in actual social compacts for its safety, than for the safety of life." Taylor continued with a statement that expressed a theme that many students of the period ascribe to John Marshall. "The freedom of property," said John Taylor of Caroline, "is the object intended to be vindicated by this treatise."[21] The difference between the two men, of course, was that Marshall insisted upon a universal law to bind all men while Taylor believed that the people of Virginia should be bound by the federal Constitution only when they chose to be.

Marshall realized his decision had created problems for the states and acknowledged this in an 1829 case, *Weston v. City Council of Charleston*. The issue was whether stock issued for loans made to the United States government could be taxed by local governments. Marshall did not allow the local government to tax the federal property, citing the *McCulloch v. Maryland* decision as his precedent. He conceded that "In a society formed like ours, with one supreme government for national purposes, and numerous state governments for other purposes; in many respects independent, and in the uncontrolled exercise of many important powers, occasional interferences ought not to surprise us. The power of taxation is one of the most essential to a state, and one of the most extensive in its operation."[22]

The *McCulloch v. Maryland* decision and the commentaries after it served to define the debate between the advocates of states' rights and those of federalism. The arguments on both sides never have been presented better; each is a call to a cause, a crusade. And this is why the case is a significant one in American history and why the Marshall decision is a major state paper. He seized the opportunity to use an incident to make a statement regarding the sanctity of and need for the federal Union. His decision is the more powerful because he persuaded his fellow Justices to join him despite their political beliefs at the time they had joined the Court. And his decision is, ultimately, significant because of its quality. His arguments remain as forceful today as they were in 1819. "We must never forget that it is a constitution we are expounding," he had said, and everyone understood that John Marshall and his fellow Justices were using the bank case to demonstrate just how they believed that Constitution should be expounded. "Let the end be legitimate, let it be within the scope of the constitution, and all means which are appropriate, which are plainly adapted to that end, which are not prohibited, but consist with the letter and spirit of the constitution, are constitutional," he had said, and no one since has been able to say better and more forcefully that government has the right to use all legal means to achieve the ends entrusted to it.

9

THE DISPUTE BETWEEN John Marshall and Spencer Roane would have done well to have ended there. The arguments, brilliantly articulated, became tedious when repeated over and over again. But the Virginia political machine could not abide the continued assertion of federal power. Joseph Story had made such an assertion in *Martin v. Hunter's Lessee*. John Marshall had made an even more forceful statement in *McCulloch v. Maryland*. In 1821 the Virginia political powers had another opportunity to stab at the federal power, and they seized it—again to their regret. The case is known as *Cohens v. Virginia*,[1] and is considered by many to be the most significant of the Supreme Court cases conferring authority upon that Court to maintain the supremacy of the federal Union.

On Saturday, September 1, 1820, the case of the state of Virginia against P. J. and M. J. Cohen opened at the Norfolk, Virginia, courthouse before the mayor, recorder, and aldermen of the borough. The two Cohens were charged with selling two halves and four quarter tickets of a national lottery, authorized by the federal Congress, with a drawing to be held in Washington. They had made the sale to William H. Jennings, who testified against them. Lotteries were illegal in Virginia, and the two Cohens were quickly found guilty of violating the local law. They were fined $100 for "the use of the president and directors of the literary fund," plus $31.50 for court costs. Counsel for the Cohens asked to take the case to the next highest state court on appeal but the request was denied "inasmuch as cases of this sort are not subject to revision by any other court of the commonwealth."

Those eighteen words were more significant than first study indicated. The Virginia legislature had determined what cases were or were not appealable. If that position held, then a state legislature could determine what cases could or could not be appealed to the state's highest court and from there to a federal court. If that approach held, then the state legislature could decide the limits of the federal courts.

The Cohens claimed there was a federal question involved in their case. Because the lottery for which they admittedly had been selling tickets had been authorized by the federal Congress, they argued that the federal law authorizing the lottery overruled the state law prohibiting any lotteries. On that basis they appealed to the United States Supreme Court. There were two issues involved in the appeal. One was whether the Supreme Court could take cognizance of an action by a state court—to the extent of considering overruling it—if that court was not the highest in the state (the Cohens had not been allowed to take their case to Virginia's highest court). Put another way, would the Supreme Court tolerate any chipping away of its powers by state legislatures? The second point was the relatively simple one of whether the Congress, by authorizing the lottery for the District of Columbia, had superseded all state laws prohibiting such lotteries.

The counsel for Virginia, Philip Barbour, argued that whether the Virginia law was or was not in conflict with federal law was irrelevant. A state could not be sued in a federal court unless the state allowed itself to be sued. If a state legislature enacted a law stating that a certain type of case could not be appealed to the state's highest courts nor to the federal courts, that was the end of it. John Marshall would not allow this. He was sixty-five when this case was decided early in 1821, and he had lost none of his vigor. He might even have gained some. He began, as he usually did, slowly and softly. The case, he said, presented points "of great magnitude, and may be truly said vitally to affect the Union." He summed up Virginia's position: "admitting such violation, it is not in the power of the government to seek a corrective." All his adult life Marshall had believed in the ability of government to seek and apply "a corrective." He could not tolerate the Virginia claim. He continued:

> They [the lawyers for Virginia] maintain that the nation does not possess a department capable of restraining peaceably, and by authority of law, any attempts which may be made, by a part, against the legitimate powers of the whole; and that the government is reduced to the alternative of submitting to such attempts, or of resisting them by force. They maintain that the Constitution of the United States has provided no tribunal for the final construction of itself, or of the laws or treaties of the nation; but that this power may be exercised in the last resort by the courts of every state of the Union. That the constitution, laws, and treaties, may receive as many constructions as there are states, and that this is not a mischief, or, if a mischief is irremediable.

[621]

Marshall continued that if this were a true interpretation of the Constitution, "it is the duty of the court to bow with respectful submission to its provisions." But "if such be not the constitution, it is equally the duty of this court to say so; and to perform that task which the American people have assigned to the judicial department." Marshall being who he was, of course, there was no question how he would decide. He had framed the question in such a manner that there could be no real choice. Either the nation did have the power "of restraining peaceably" or else must use force, he had declared, and he would choose the peaceable course. The manner in which he had framed the question demonstrated his genius. He had seen that the issue involved in the sale of the lottery tickets had become, by the state's actions, a question of government by law or government by force. It was the same problem he had wrestled with all his adult life. Men must devise a means to govern themselves; there could be no society without rules. If one element in that society, whether it be the President, an individual, or a state, can choose to violate those rules and escape punishment, then the rules, the laws, the government, have no meaning. If Virginia, through its legislature, could determine what it would or would not allow the federal government to have jurisdiction over, then the United States would revert to a pack of snarling entities, each one jealous of the others and unwilling to contribute to the welfare of the whole. Marshall understood that and had stated it. He had managed to cut through all the peripheral issues, to eliminate the excess verbiage. The issue, he had said, was whether men would be governed by law or by force.[2]

The issue was not new. In 1809, in a case known as *United States v. Judge Peters*, the Pennsylvania legislature attempted to thwart a federal court order by enacting a law that appeared to overrule the order. John Marshall and the Supreme Court could not tolerate such an action. "If the legislatures of the several states may, at will, annul the judgments of the courts of the United States, and destroy the rights acquired under those judgments," Marshall said, "the constitution itself becomes a mockery, and the nation is deprived of the means of enforcing its laws by the instrumentality of its own tribunals. So fatal a result must be deprecated by all."[3] The same issue had been central to Joseph Story's decision in *Martin v. Hunter's Lessee* and also to Marshall's decision in *McCulloch v. Maryland*. It also was the issue central to the American experience. The point of the Revolution was that men no longer would accept a government imposed upon them. "Taxation without representation" was more than a slogan; it was a declaration against the past. If that war had any value, the Americans must then demonstrate that they could fashion a government to which men would submit voluntarily, which would respect their individuality and encourage their talents and ambitions. But it must be a government. It could not be a discussion society.

Marshall then turned to the question of whether a state could be sued in a federal court. He pointed out in this *Cohens v. Virginia* decision that the Constitution said that the laws of the United States were supreme, binding all judges in the states. "This is the authoritative language of the American people," said Marshall, "and, if gentlemen please, of the American States. It marks, with lines too strong to be mistaken, the characteristic distinction between the government of the Union and those of the states." His next sentence stated a theme that he had presented many times: "The general government, though limited as to its objects, is supreme with respect to those objects. This principle is a part of the constitution; and if there be any who deny its necessity, none can deny its authority." He then concluded that section of the decision:

> When we consider the situation of the government of the Union and of a state, in relation to each other; the nature of our constitution; the subordination of the state governments to that constitution; the great purpose for which jurisdiction over all cases arising under the constitution and laws of the United States is confided to the judicial department, are we at liberty to insert in this general grant, an exception of those cases in which a state may be a party? Will the spirit of the constitution justify this attempt to control its words? We think it will not.[4]

After saying that there could be no exception to the Constitution's claim over all cases, Marshall then went on to the question of whether a decision by a state court could be appealed to the Supreme Court. As Marshall read this section of the Court's decision, the only intriguing point was how—not if—he would deny that the states could limit the Supreme Court's power to hear cases. "When we observe the importance which that constitution attaches to the independence of judges," he said, "we are the less inclined to suppose that it can have intended to leave these constitutional questions to tribunals where this independence may not exist, in all cases where a state shall prosecute an individual who claims the protection of an act of congress." Such a situation as he was implying—a constitutional case being determined by a judge forced to be biased because of his lack of independence—"may take place in times of no extraordinary commotion," he said. "But a constitution is framed for ages to come, and is designed to approach immortality as nearly as human institutions can approach it."

As he continued, Marshall became even less courteous to the states. "There is certainly nothing in the circumstances under which our constitution was formed; nothing in the history of the times, which would justify the opinion that the confidence reposed in the states was so implicit as to leave in them and their tribunals the power of resisting or defeating, in the form of law, the legitimate measures of the Union." He conceded that the government created by the Americans could be disbanded, but, he insisted, only by the people and not by the states. "It is very true that, whenever hostility to the existing system shall become universal, it will be also irresistible. The people made the constitution, and the people can unmake it." He continued that the authors of the Constitution were "unable to make any provisions which should protect the instrument against a general combination of the states, or of the people, for its destruction; and, conscious of this inability, they have not made the attempt. But they were able to provide against the operation of measures adopted in any one state, whose tendency might be to arrest the execution of the laws, and this it was the part of true wisdom to attempt." He concluded this section with: "We think they have attempted it."[5]

During the arguments the Virginia lawyers had tried to discover earlier words of Marshall's to buttress their case. They looked at the *Marbury v. Madison* decision, in which Marshall had ruled invalid a congressional act extending appellate jurisdiction to the Supreme Court. Marshall had ruled then that the Constitution gave only original jurisdiction in certain cases and that, therefore, appeals in such cases could not be heard by the Supreme Court. On this basis, the lawyers for Virginia argued, the Court should not hear an appeal from the state court in the *Cohens* case. This argument has been repeated in more recent times;[6] in effect, it is a charge that Marshall said one thing in *Marbury v. Madison* and the complete opposite in the *Cohens* case. Marshall addressed himself to the charge in his decision. "In the case of Marbury v. Madison," he said, "the single question before the court, so far as that case can be applied to this, was, whether the legislature could give this court original jurisdiction in a case in which the constitution had clearly not given it, and in which no doubt respecting the construction of the article could possibly be raised. The court decided and we think very properly, that the legislature could not give original jurisdiction in such a case." Marshall, however, drew a line of difference between an attempt by the federal legislature to extend the Court's appellate power and an attempt by a state to restrict appellate power on an issue in which the Court clearly had jurisdiction.[7]

Marshall then wrote a paragraph into his decision which, although repetitious of things he had said previously, continues as the ultimate definition of the role of the judiciary:

> It is most true that this court will not take jurisdiction if it should not; but it is equally true, that it must take jurisdiction if it should. The judiciary cannot, as the legislature may, avoid a measure because it approaches the confines of the constitution. We cannot pass it by because it is doubtful. With whatever doubts, with whatever difficulties, a case may be attended, we must decide it if it be brought before us. We have no more right to decline the exercise of jurisdiction which is given, than to usurp that which is not given. The one or the other would be treason to the constitution. Questions may occur which we would gladly avoid, but we cannot avoid them. All we can do, is to exercise our best judgment, and conscientiously to perform our duty. In doing this, on the present occasion, we find this tribunal invested with appellate jurisdiction in all cases arising under the constitution and laws of the United States.
>
> We find no exception to this grant, and we cannot insert one.[8]

Marshall argued that it was not unreasonable that the federal judiciary be considered competent to judge the constitutionality of an action by a state tribunal. "That the United States form, for many, and for most important purposes, a single nation, has not yet been denied," he said in justification of that position. "In war, we are one people. In making peace, we are one people. In all commercial regulations, we are one and the same people. In many other respects, the American people are one; and the government which is alone capable of controlling and managing their interests in all these respects, is the government of the Union." As for the states, Marshall said that "The constitution and laws of a state, so far as they are repugnant to the constitution and laws of the United States, are absolutely void. These states are constituent parts of the United States. They are members of one great empire—for some purposes sovereign, for some purposes subordinate."[9]

Marshall had effectively placed the federal Constitution at the top of the sources of law in the United States. Men could resist that placement, as they would, but never with a chance of victory. The Supreme Court with John Marshall at its head had demonstrated its independence and then used that independence to assert that the Constitution and the federal Union could not be attacked—legally, at least—by those parts and persons over which and whom it had authority. The Constitution was indeed a supreme document. Society had fashioned it. Individuals or states could not destroy it against the wishes of the whole society.

After Marshall had ruled that the Supreme Court could hear an appeal from the Virginia court in the *Cohens* case, he then ruled, and the other Justices backed him unanimously, that Virginia had been correct in arresting the Cohens for violating a state law forbidding the sale of lottery tickets. The Court said that Congress could not authorize the sale of the lottery tickets in this instance outside the District of Columbia.[10]

Marshall had done the same thing in *Marbury v. Madison* —given the case to the Jeffersonians but stated the principle in favor of federalism. In 1803 his adroitness went basically unnoticed because the power of judicial review, the principle taken then for the Court, was not then a controversial one. He would not get off so easily with the *Cohens v. Virginia* decision. The political leaders of the state were not as interested in the $100 for the literary fund as they were in the loss of their right to place a barrier between governmental actions in their state and a review of those actions by the Supreme Court.

Marshall explained what he had done the next year in a letter to his brother James. The letter concerned a legal hassle growing out of the Fairfax land purchase, but Marshall's description of the powers of the federal and state courts, while not directed specifically to the *Cohens v. Virginia* situation, is applicable to it. In these comments he sounds almost as much of a states'-righter as Spencer Roane. He wrote:

> . . . The exposition of any state law by the courts of that state are considered in the courts of all the other states, and in those of the United States as a correct exposition, not to be reexamined. The only exception to this rule is where the statute of a state is supposed to violate the constitution of the United States, in which case the courts of the union claim a controlling and supervising power. . . . The principle is that the courts of every government are the proper tribunals for construing the legislative acts of that government.[11]

Even James Madison, still politically tied to Thomas Jefferson, could not deny the soundness of Marshall's position in the *Cohens* case. In 1823 he wrote Jefferson that he could not accept the Jeffersonian approach, then being espoused by John Taylor of Caroline in *Construction Construed*, that the states could not be judged by the federal courts. Madison, whose activities in the writing of the federal Constitution have earned him the title of Father of the Constitution, said he believed that the Constitutional Convention had considered as "essential to an adequate system of government" a provision for deciding "in a peaceable and regular mode all cases arising in the course of its operation." It was for that purpose, Madison continued in his 1823 letter to Jefferson, that the Constitution and the laws made pursuant to it were considered to be the supreme law of the land. "Even at this time," he said, "an appeal to a national decision would prove that no general change has taken place."

"I am not unaware," Madison added, "that the Judiciary career has not corresponded with what was anticipated. At one period the Judges perverted the Bench of Justice into a rostrum for partisan harangues. And latterly the Court, by some of its decisions, still more by extrajudicial reasonings and dicta, has manifested a propensity to enlarge the general authority in derogation of the local, and to amplify its own jurisdiction, which has justly incurred the public censure." In what almost sounded like a lecture of the venerable Jefferson, Madison said: "But the abuse of a trust does not disprove its existence. And if no remedy of the abuse be practicable under the forms of the Constitution, I should prefer a resort to the Nation for an amendment of the Tribunal itself, to continued appeals from its controverted decisions to that Ultimate Arbiter."[12]

These background discussions, however, were not the significant ones for Marshall and the Supreme Court. The public debates were. The *Richmond Enquirer*, the mouthpiece for Spencer Roane's political organization, began calling for the destruction of the Supreme Court and its replacement by an elected tribunal of elder statesmen such as Thomas Jefferson, James Madison, and other right-thinkers.[13] Roane himself was writing, under the pen name of Algernon Sidney, a series of attacks on the Court, which would be published in the *Enquirer*. Roane was now ill—he would die the next year—but his passion was not diminished. Martin Van Buren, then a young New York lawyer and politician, visited him in Richmond about this time. "I found him to my great regret on a bed of sickness," said Van Buren, "from which, although he lived some time, he never rose." But Roane, although bedridden, continued, so Van Buren reported, "a root and branch Democrat, clear headed, honest hearted, and always able and ready to defend the right regardless of personal consequences." That last phrase must be considered amusing in light of the fact that Roane, as the acknowledged political leader of the Jeffersonians in Richmond, could suffer no consequences for leading that party in the path it already had chosen. When Van Buren visited him, Roane sat up in bed and talked with the New Yorker for several hours, although his family advised him to rest. "Mr. Roane referred, with much earnestness," recorded Van Buren, "to the course of the Supreme Court, under the lead of Chief Justice Marshall. . . ." He gave Van Buren a copy of the Algernon Sidney articles.[14]

Roane began his articles in a tone that he maintained through all five. This was at the beginning of the first article, which appeared in the *Richmond Enquirer* May 25, 1821:

> My appeal to you, I trust, will not be made in vain. You are the same American people who, twenty years ago, put down an infamous sedition-law, by the mere force of public opinion. Yes! and you also put down, therewith, the equally infamous judgments of the federal courts, by which that statute was enforced. You put down, with indignation, and with scorn, those unjust judgments, which had fined and imprisoned divers of our citizens for exercising the sacred rights of speaking and writing guaranteed to them by the constitution. Where is now that act and where are now those judgments? Crucified, dead and buried. They have descended together, to the tomb of the Capulets, and peace be to their names. I am sure that my appeal to you will not be heard with indifference.

Roane pointed out that the fact of Virginia's seeming victory in the case was insignificant—"that great and opulent state is, indeed, permitted to retain the paltry sum of one hundred dollars." The "victory" for Virginia, he continued, was at a cost "of destroying the state governments altogether and establishing on their ruins, one great, national, and consolidated government." Roane argued that if the executive or legislative branches of government violate the Constitution, the public can act to correct this at the voting booth, but this was not true of the Supreme Court. "It is not elected by, nor is amenable to [the people]. Having been appointed in one generation, it claims to make laws and constitutions for another." In a footnote, Roane reminded his readers that Bushrod Washington had been appointed an Associate Justice in the previous century, and that Marshall had been appointed Chief Justice in the first year of the present century. The court "acts always upon the foundation of its own precedents," Roane charged, "and progresses, 'with a noiseless foot and unalarming advance' until it reaches the zenith of despotic power."

In another letter on May 29 Roane described the United States as a "confederation of free states." Then on June 1 he hit at a development that must have galled him as well as Thomas Jefferson: the fact that the men appointed by Jefferson were going along with John Marshall—"the ultra-federal leader." Roane conceded that Marshall was true to the political beliefs he had espoused before joining the Court, although he "has even pushed them to an extreme never until now anticipated," said Roane. "He must be equally delighted and surprised to find his Republican brothers going with him. How is it, but from these prejudices, that they go with him, not only as to the results of his opinions, but as to all the points and positions contained in the most lengthy, artful and alarming opinions?"

On June 4 Roane stated that he "boldly" denied that the judiciary could compel the states to any action. "A federal compact between two parties is a nonentity," he charged, "if it is whatever one of those parties chooses to make it."

Roane's arguments as Algernon Sidney have a note of the ridiculous about them. All of it had been said before, by the lawyers before the Supreme Court and by Spencer Roane himself in his various diatribes. And the arguments were to no point. The American people did not have a "compact." Rather, they had a government, and they understood this. Forty years later, when the South seceded because it would not surrender its notion of a compact, the people of the United States entered one of the bloodiest wars in man's history to demonstrate that it was a government indeed which was at stake.

That the Roane commentaries were to no point, other than to keep alive a fast-weakening argument, could not be understood at the time. John Marshall was disturbed at the attacks on the Court—"a virulence transcending what has appeared on many former occasions" is how he described them. He wrote to Joseph Story that "for coarseness and malignity of invective Algernon Sidney surpasses all party writers who have ever made pretensions to any decency of character." Marshall probably felt moved to say that because of the attacks on the Jefferson and Madison appointees to the Court. Marshall added regarding Roane that "He will be supposed to be the champion of states rights instead of being what he really is, the champion of dismemberment."[15]

Joseph Story wrote Marshall that he should not be so disturbed. What may have been the reactions in Virginia were not the reactions throughout the other states, he said. In his own state of Massachusetts Marshall's decision in the *Cohens* case was considered as "a most masterly and convincing argument, and as the greatest of your judgments." Story continued: "Allow me to say that no where is your reputation more sincerely cherished than here; and however strange it may sound in Virginia, if you were known here only by this last opinion, you could not wish for more unequivocal fame." Story perhaps sensed that Marshall, being the object of so much criticism for so many years from his contemporaries and neighbors in Virginia, was beginning to have doubts about himself. "Will you excuse me for saying that your appointment to the Bench," Story continued in an effort to dispel any such doubts, "has in my judgment more contributed under providence to the preservation of the true principles of the constitution than any other circumstances in our domestic history." Story then said he was compelled to add that because he had recently read a letter by Thomas Jefferson critical of the federal judiciary: "I must say that [Jefferson's letter's] obvious design is, as far as his influence extends, to prostrate the judicial authority and annihilate all public reference of its dignity." Story said that "There never was a period of my life when these opinions would not have shocked me; but *at his age* and in these critical times they fill me alternately with indignation and melancholy. Can he wish yet to have influence enough to destroy the government of his country?"[16]

Marshall answered Story with appreciation for his comments and an expression of concern at what Jefferson had written because Jefferson continued to be so popular that "many—very many" would abide by his opinions. Marshall wrote a paragraph about Thomas Jefferson then which is among the harshest he ever wrote about anyone. It reads:

> For Mr. Jefferson's opinion as respects this department it is not difficult to assign the cause. He is among the most ambitious and I suspect among the most unforgiving of men. His great power is over the mass of the people and this power is chiefly guided by professions of democracy. Every check on the wild impulse of the moment is a check on his own power, and he is unfriendly to the sound from which it flows. He looks, of course, with ill will at an independent judiciary.

Marshall believed that Jefferson was behind "a deep design to convert our government into a mere league of states." The attack was begun through the judiciary, Marshall believed, "because it is without patronage and of course without power and it is equally well understood that every subtraction from its jurisdiction is a vital wound to the government itself."[17]

John Marshall did not understand Thomas Jefferson in the same way that Thomas Jefferson did not understand John Marshall. Jefferson believed in a government of law but was concerned that such a government might eventually trample on the freedoms of the individuals it had been established to protect, which was why he wanted power assigned to the states, the body of government closest to the people. Marshall was very concerned about the freedoms of individuals, but he also understood that individuals must guarantee each other some form of redress, some form of protection—no man should have the freedom to destroy another.

Also, neither man understood that the battle they had been fighting for so many years actually had ended. Through his decisions Marshall had established the supremacy of the federal Union. Jefferson's words had made that Union aware that it must not abuse its power, but the power to govern was there. Both men were victors in that they had contributed to a government that had as its professed aim the freedom of the individual in his society.

There was one final footnote to the *Cohens v. Virginia* case, a piece of doggerel by an unknown author which, if it does not illuminate the legal arguments further, gives insight into the sentiments of the time:

Old Johnny Marshall what's got in ye.
To side with Cohens against Virginny.
To call in Court this "Old Dominion."
To insult her with your foul opinion!
I'll tell you that it will not do
To call old Spencer in review.
He knows the law as well as you.
And once for all, it will not do.
Alas! Alas! that you should be
So much against State Sovereignty!
You've thrown the whole state in a terror,
By this infernal "Writ of Error."
Whence comes this . . . by which of late
You make a subject sue his State?
This "writ of error" is an action,
And no where mentioned in the Paction.
And the Constitution's clear and plain,
That "what we give not, we retain."
But words are things with various meanings,
And Judges too have various leanings.
Then if the words *stand in your way,*
You bring the Spirit *into play,*
And there is nothing you can't do
By stretching "words" and "spirit" too.
What's the use of our appeals?

We may as well give you our seals.
Our state decisions held as naught,
And you *are now* dernier resort!
To cite a state before your Judgeship
You've brought your mind to one conviction—
That you have always *jurisdiction.*
Old Johnny Marshall mend your ways
And let the States alone sir,
Or else before there are many days,
You'll yield your place to Roane Sir.[18]

Part III
The Sanctity of Contracts

10

IN 1824 THE MARQUIS DE LAFAYETTE returned to the United States for a triumphal visit. More than forty years had passed since he had sacrificed the pleasures of Europe for the battlefields of America, and the American people he had befriended looked forward to his visit as an extraordinary event. It had been Lafayette who had led the noblemen of Europe to the American cause. It had been Lafayette who had become the symbol of Europe's contribution to the cause of American independence. To the Americans he was a genuine hero and they intended to treat him as such.

In Virginia particularly the warmth toward Lafayette was keenly felt. Many of the soldiers who had gone to war with George Washington had come to know and admire the Frenchman. As he traveled through the state during the summer and fall of 1824, he was feted in each community he visited, escorted by his old comrades, toasted at dinners, and honored by the venerable men whom Virginia had given to the American nation.

Three former Revolutionary War soldiers who were asked by the state to escort Lafayette were Philip Slaughter, Gabriel Long, and Chief Justice John Marshall.[1] The Lafayette they met had changed much in the four decades since they had last seen him. "His complexion, originally clear and white, is now sunburnt; his forehead, which is very high, is covered very low with a wig," a contemporary account said, continuing: "He appeared in the ordinary dress of a citizen, black coat and pantaloons, and white vest, five feet ten inches high, and limps a little as he walks."[2] But of course all the men had changed. When John Marshall greeted Lafayette that summer he was a few weeks shy of his seventieth birthday; it had been almost fifty years since Marshall had met with the Culpeper Minutemen to tell them about the battles of Lexington and Concord, to teach them the manual of arms, and to offer to race any one of them. He still was tall, his stance erect, but his figure was becoming more rotund, his face lined. His hair, although full, was gray. His voice, as he would reluctantly confess in a few years, was beginning to grow feeble. His eyes, however, remained marvelously alive. In the course of a public life that would span six decades, from the young soldier on the battlefield to the venerable Chief Justice of the United States, people always commented about Marshall's eyes—their depth, that they indicated an extraordinary intellect, and that they seemed to stare directly into a person.

Lafayette's tour of Virginia—Warrenton in Fauquier County, the site of the Cornwallis surrender at Yorktown, Petersburg, Richmond, a meeting with the aged Jefferson at the University of Virginia in Charlottesville—had the air of a festive reunion. In each community the old soldiers came out in their old uniforms, not only to meet Lafayette but to greet former comrades they had not seen for many years, and to honor them. In Warrenton the old soldiers sat down to "a sumptuous and elegant dinner" served to them "under a handsome arbour in the beautiful green" in front of Mrs. Norris' tavern. James Monroe was there and was honored by a toast for "his exalted merit and spotless integrity." Lafayette toasted "The old Virginia line, the militia of 1781, and the present generation of Fauquier—may the Revolutionary services of the fathers find an everlasting reward in the republican prosperity and happiness of their children," which was greeted with many "huzzahs."

Then a toast was offered to John Marshall, "the soldier, the statesman, the jurist—our country with exultation points to her son." He rose to acknowledge his appreciation. "It would not be easy, gentlemen," he began, "to express my thanks for the kindness which I have experienced today, in terms which would do justice to the emotions it has excited." To be associated with the men at this table, he said, "cannot fail to be highly gratifying of my feelings." Among them he saw a soldier who was the oldest surviving officer of the Revolutionary army. He saw Lafayette as "one who relinquished all the pleasures and enjoyments which Europe could furnish to encounter the dangers and share the toils and privations which were the lot of all those who engaged in our struggle for independence." Marshall continued that Lafayette "has since devoted himself to that glorious cause which brought him to our country, and who, through all the vicissitudes of his eventful life, has been its steadfast champion— neither subdued by adversity, nor too much elevated by prosperity."

Marshall then turned to James Monroe. Almost six decades earlier Monroe and Marshall had attended school at Mr. Campbell's academy. They had been soldiers together in the Revolution and young men enjoying the pleasures of growing up in postwar Richmond. Although their political opposition had come between them in later years, it had never lessened their respect for each other. Monroe now was finishing his eighth year as President of the United States. Like his friend the Chief Justice, he had lived well and decently and had received his due honors. Marshall recalled that relationship this August afternoon in front of Mrs. Norris' tavern. "In him," said Marshall of his old friend, "I am proud to recognize one of my earliest associates; one with whom I have frequently acted in the most trying scenes; for whom I have felt, and still retain, the most affectionate and respected esteem, without a taint of that bitter spirit which has been too long the scourge of our country."

The Chief Justice then turned to the people of Fauquier County who also sat at the table. It was particularly gratifying to him, he said, to be honored in Fauquier. "I can never forget," he told them, "that this county was the residence of the revered author of my being, who continued to be your representative, until his military character first, and his removal afterwards, rendered him ineligible; that in this county I first breathed the vital air; that in it my infancy was cradled and my youth reared up and encouraged; that in the first dawn of manhood I marched from it with the gallant young men of the day to that glorious conflict which gave independence to these states, and birth to this mighty nation; that immediately on my return, I was chosen unanimously to represent them in the Legislature, and that they did not cease to support me till I ceased to reside among them." He told them that "Here my affections as well as my interest still remain, and all my sons are planted among you. With so many motives for receiving the kindness of today with peculiar gratitude, allow me, gentlemen, to indulge the feelings it excites. . . ." And here he raised his glass to toast: "The people of Fauquier— Brave soldiers in time of war, good citizens in time of peace, and intelligent patriots at all times."[3]

The reception accorded Lafayette in Richmond was the most elaborate of the festivities in Virginia, with a welcoming ceremony at the dock when his boat from Petersburg landed, a parade, dinners, and a grand ball. Marshall was particularly prominent among the participants in these activities. His name was listed as one of the twenty-two managers of the October 15 ball at the Eagle Hotel; he was on the muster roll of Revolutionary War Officers to formally greet the Frenchman; he presided at a Masonic dinner honoring Lafayette; and he was asked to prepare and deliver a formal address when Lafayette arrived in the city.

The welcoming address was made in front of the state capitol with Lafayette being escorted by an honor guard of old soldiers. In his address Marshall repeated much of what he had said at Warrenton and then continued to make the tribute to the Frenchman even more gracious: "We delight to consider this visit, as furnishing additional evidence that the sentiments we felt, and manifested towards you, sunk deep into your heart, and were greeted by kindred feelings, that as America has always regarded you as one of the best and bravest of her sons, so you have never ceased to regard her as a second country, ranking in your affections next to that which gave you birth. . . ." Marshall told Lafayette that "the distinguished part you bore in the last and glorious scene is indelibly impressed in the memory of all Virginians. In the bosoms of none is it more deeply engraved than in those of the men who stand before you. Some of us served under you in that memorable campaign; many in the course of the war. While duty required obedience, your conduct inspired confidence and love." Marshall continued: "Time, which has thinned our ranks, and enfeebled our bodies, has not impaired those feelings. They retain their original vigor."[4]

The night of Lafayette's arrival in Richmond there was a large dinner in his honor with many toasts—to George Washington, to Lafayette, to Virginia, to the city of Richmond; then it was Chief Justice Marshall's turn to offer one. The sixty-nine-year-old Virginian rose and raised his glass. His words were the sum of his public philosophy, a philosophy that he understood to mean that for each right accorded to a man an obligation was exacted of that man; for each freedom and right given to him, there was an accompanying responsibility to the freedoms and rights of other men. If men could not accept that, then society could exist only by rules imposed by force.

"Rational liberty—the cause of mankind," said Marshall to the heroes of the Revolution, to the people of Virginia, to the generations which would come after him, "its friends cannot despair when they behold its companions."[5]

Lafayette paid a visit to Jefferson a few days later. They met at the rotunda of the University of Virginia, the school being a contribution to the enlightenment of mankind which Jefferson considered one of his proudest achievements. Thomas Jefferson now was eighty-one years old and two years from death. "My friends," he began his comments beneath the university rotunda, "I am old; long in the disuse of making speeches, and without voice to utter them. . . ." For his nation, Jefferson said, he left "the aspirations of a heart warm with the love of country; whose invocations to heaven for its indissoluble union will be fervent and unremitting, while the pulse of life continues to beat, and when that ceases, it will expire in prayers for the eternal duration of its freedom and prosperity." When Jefferson's speech was finished, according to a contemporary account, the soldier Lafayette burst into tears and grasped the hand of the author of the Declaration of Independence.[6]

Richmond had been Marshall's home for more than forty years and he loved its streets and its people, and its citizens were proud of him. He continued his membership in the Barbecue Club, usually appearing at its meetings with his coat slung over his shoulder, and his eagerness for the afternoon's activities showing on his face. He would begin by downing a mint julep, smacking his lips, then getting down to the business of the day—a game of quoits. He still threw the iron quoits, heavier than those used by the other players, and still let out a shout of triumph when his quoit was the winning one. Many foreign visitors to the United States as well as prominent Americans from the North came to the Barbecue Club meetings and were impressed by what they saw. One called it the "real beauty of republicanism," to see one of America's most exalted figures in his shirtsleeves, mingling freely with his fellow Americans. And, after being impressed by Marshall at the Barbecue Club, foreign visitors would be even more impressed a day or two later to see the Chief Justice of the United States strolling through the markets doing the family shopping. The custom of the time in Richmond was that the men did the shopping, and Marshall saw no reason why he should be an exception.[7]

Marshall continued his famous lawyers' dinner parties which he had begun in the 1790s when he was a young attorney and politician. As then, the more prominent and interesting members of the Richmond bar and community came to the red brick house for a fine meal and conversation. The talk had changed, however. When Marshall was a young man, he and the other Richmond citizens would thrash out the topics of their time. Now they were much older, and their talk had much of a reminiscent quality about it. One visitor to the United States in the early 1820s stopped in Richmond and was invited to Marshall's for dinner. "He invited me to dine with him at three o'clock," said John Finch. "On going to his house at that time, I was introduced to several gentlemen residing in Richmond, most of whom were members of the bar. At dinner, I had the pleasure of sitting next to the Chief Judge [sic] of the United States, and he conversed with much affability. After dinner, Judge Marshall related to us the impressions which had been made on his mind by the various orators to whom, during the course of his life, it had been his fortune to listen. Patrick Henry, Pinckney, Fisher Ames,

Wirt, Webster, Clay, and many others, were passed in review, and their merits appreciated. Anecdotes of the olden time were related, and our venerable host became quite animated." Finch concluded that the evening "was the most delightful dinner party at which I have been present in America."[8]

Every summer Marshall went to Fauquier County to spend some time away from the heat and confines of the city. In his earlier years he made the trip on horseback, but by the 1820s he was using his stick gig—a single seat suspended between two wheels and pulled by a horse—for the journey. His children were in Fauquier, Thomas at Oak Hill and the others nearby, and he enjoyed them and the numerous grandchildren they were producing. When in the country, he became part of its social life also. He prayed at the small church there and attended the barbecues which were a favorite outing of the time. And when he went on an outing, he expected to play his favorite game of quoits. Once, finding there were no quoits to be had, the Chief Justice of the United States went searching along the side of a stream for flat stones. He returned later with the stones stretching from his arms to his chin. "There!" he cried, dropping them to the ground. "Here are enough quoits for us all!"[9]

In Washington, too, Marshall was an active participant in society. Although entering his seventies and one of America's most experienced politicians, its leading judicial figure, and one of its more sophisticated leaders, Marshall retained the wonder of the country boy from Fauquier County in the big city. "Since my being in this place I have been more in company than I wish," he wrote Polly from Washington in 1817, "and more than is consistent with the mass of business we have to go through. I have been invited to dine with the President, with our own secretaries, and with the minister of France, and tomorrow I dine with the British minister." Polly, her illness growing worse, did not come to Washington—actually few of the Justices' wives did in those days—and sometimes Marshall felt obliged to assure her that the society in the District of Columbia was not all that attractive to him. "I was in a very great crowd the other evening at Mrs. Adams' drawing room," he wrote Polly in 1826 when Mrs. John Quincy Adams was the First Lady, "but I see very few persons there whom I know and fewer still in whom I take any interest." He assured her that "A person as old as I am [he had just turned seventy] feels that his home is his place of most comfort, and his old wife the companion in the world in whose society he is most happy."

Despite these protestations, however, Marshall obviously enjoyed the amenities that went with being head of the federal judiciary. In 1829 he sounded almost like an excited schoolboy when he wrote to Polly that "I dine tomorrow with the British minister and the next day again with the President. I have never before dined twice with the President [this would be John Quincy Adams, who was retiring in March] during the same session of the court. That on Friday was an official dinner. The invitation for Tuesday is not for all the other judges and I consider it as a personal civility."[10] Perhaps because of the sociability of John Marshall and the other Justices, Washington society never seemed to come alive until the Supreme Court went into session. Whatever the reason, the social season in Washington ever since is considered to begin with the January dinner at the White House honoring the Justices of the Supreme Court.

Although the city of Washington had been the nation's capital for almost a quarter of a century, it was still a dreadful place to live or visit. John Finch was there during his tour of the United States and found the rents high and the cost of living extravagant. "The Potomac River flows at the distance of a mile from the Capitol," he wrote, "an extensive marsh intervenes; the exhalations which it produces in autumn are noxious. The senators assembled at Washington breathe an atmosphere similar to that inhaled by the ancient senators of imperial Rome." Finch stayed at a hotel for a few days but found it too crowded and unpleasant. He moved then to a private boardinghouse "where there were several members of Congress, and every thing was conducted in an agreeable manner."[11] When Congress was not in session, Washington was a city without an excuse for existence. "I reached Washington city," one traveler wrote at the time, "now emptied of the wise men, and which, after quitting Philadelphia, seems mean, indeed, both morally and physically. All the bogs and swamps, in and round the city, are now full of melody from the big, bellowing bull frog, down to the little singing mosquito, while rotting carcasses and other nuisances perfume the warm southern breezes."[12]

The city already had the problems that would later characterize it. "There is not a spot on the globe containing the same number of people that is oppressed with more indigence and human distress, and more cursed with dissipation than Washington City, and yet no one seeks the cause, much less to remove it," grumbled a disgruntled resident. People who live in the Capitol Hill area were plagued by young children throwing rocks at their windows or frightening their horses. "This they learn by going to Sunday school, doubtless, as they attend it constantly," said the same resident.

The Capitol had not yet achieved much in the way of dignity. One woman writer went to the Senate gallery to watch the legislators at work and found it "dark and crowded by vulgar men and boys. It was a most abominable place either to see or hear."[13]

One of the problems that the District of Columbia faced, then as later, was that it was subject to control by nonresidents —the members of Congress. In an 1820 decision, *Loughborough v. Blake*,[14] Marshall upheld that nonresident control and perhaps did much to perpetuate the capital city's difficulties. The case involved the question of whether the Congress had the power to impose direct taxes on the residents of the city although the city was not represented in Congress. This was, after all, the principle on which the American Revolution had been fought— taxation without representation. This is Marshall's response:

> The difference between requiring a continent, with an immense population, to submit to be taxed by a government having no common interest with it, separated from it by a vast ocean, restrained by no principle of apportionment, and associated with it by no common feelings; and permitting the representatives of the American people, under the restrictions of our constitution, to tax a part of the society, which is either in a state of infancy advancing to manhood, looking forward to complete equality so soon as that state of manhood shall be attained, as in the case with the territories; or which has voluntarily relinquished the right of representation, and has adopted the whole body of Congress for its legitimate government, as in the case with the district, is too obvious not to present itself to the minds of all.

As for allowing the District of Columbia to have representation in Congress, Marshall did not believe that would have much significance. "It may be doubted whether, in fact," he said, "its interests would be rendered thereby the more secure; and certainly the constitution does not consider their want of a representative in Congress as exempting it from equal taxation."[15]

In his daily life John Marshall believed strongly in regular exercise. This was one of the reasons why he so enjoyed quoits. In his later years his exercise was in the form of a brisk three-mile walk each day. These daily walks were well known for the speed with which the Chief Justice traveled. One person once tried desperately to overtake Marshall "in his march to the Capitol" and, finally reaching him, asked how he had acquired such a strong and quick step. Marshall answered that he assumed it was a result of his experience as an infantryman in the Revolution.[16]

His great relaxation was reading fiction, and he often read aloud to his invalid wife in the second-floor bedroom of their Richmond home. Joseph Story reported that "While the common publications of the day fell from his hands with a cold indifference, [Marshall] kindled with enthusiasm at the names of the great novelists and poets of the age, and discussed their relative powers and merits with a nice and discriminating skill, as if he were but yesterday fresh from the perusal of them." Jane Austen was a favorite, and another was Catharine Sedgwick, who was becoming famous in the 1820s. "I have seen—who do you think I have seen? Guess—I am sure you will not guess the person," he gushed in a letter to Polly, "and I will therefore tell you without keeping you longer in delightful suspense. I have seen Mrs. [sic] Sedgwick, the author of *Hope Leslie*." This was in 1831, and Marshall had paid a call on the great lady—"a compliment I pay very few ladies, and she thanked me for it." Marshall was not hesitant in confiding his opinions to Polly. He had found Miss Sedgwick "an agreeable, unaffected, not very handsome lady, but not the reverse, of about thirty. I was surprised, though I should not tell her so, at her remaining unmarried. I am sure she would have no objection to a respectable good tempered husband, and I heartily wish her one."[17]

Every year also, when the Supreme Court session was done, Marshall went to White Sulphur Springs in Fauquier, there to rest and restore himself. "According to analysis," goes a description of these springs at approximately the time Marshall was using them, "the water is impregnated with sulphate of magnesia, phosphate of soda, and sulphurated hydrogen." On first arrival, a person would drink three glasses of this water "with some reluctance and . . . a few wry faces." But "This disagreeable taste, however, is soon changed to the most impatient longings; and even a strong appetite for the water, till anon, five or six tumblers full before breakfast, or twenty glasses during the day are not considered an immoderate dose." Supposedly the body, after taking in this quantity of the water for about ten days, "if formerly considered impaired, becomes sensibly renovated." The water operated "purgatively and diuretically; the cuticular pores being opened, perspiration—especially if the mercury stands at ninety degrees—flows easily and copiously." Supposedly, and this was attributed only to anonymous "reports," a man using the springs for three weeks can, "by rubbing his nose against a stone wall, immediately light his cigar thereat; or any lady or pretty miss, having staid the same time, can light her candle by the action of her forefinger on a pine table, so fully impregnated with sulphur does the free drinker of these waters in a short time become!" The account acknowledged that "this may be scandal." Apparently his stay at the springs refreshed Marshall and gave him a period of relaxation after the trying sessions of the Court. He occupied a small cottage on the grounds and ate his meals with the guests in the community dining room. A clergyman who visited there at the same time remembered that Marshall stood patiently by his chair in the dining room until all persons had arrived and then waited quietly until grace was said.[18]

In 1821, when he was sixty-five, John Marshall remarked to his friend Richard Rush that "Time however is marking on some of us more advances than we would be willing to acknowledge." He was exaggerating as far as that statement indicated that he was not in good health for a man his age.[19]

The situation was not the same for his wife. Polly's health was a constant concern of Marshall's and he was as considerate of her as was humanly possible. Constantly he admonished her to take care of herself. "The weather has been so very cold as to fill me with apprehensions for you," he told her. "Indeed my dearest Polly as we grow older we suffer more from the cold and ought to use more precautions against it. Your fears of being too warm push you into the other extreme and you expose yourself to more cold than is consistent with your health or safety. Let me entreat you to be more careful in this particular."

A devoted husband, Marshall went to great lengths so that Polly would not be annoyed. In the summer he took her out of the city so that she would not be harassed by the noisy celebrations of the Fourth of July. In Richmond a familiar sight was the Chief Justice of the United States out in the middle of the night chasing away a stray animal that had been annoying Polly with its bleatings. The grandchildren were frequent visitors in the house, but they rarely saw their grandmother. When they did, she was in bed and they came into her presence on tiptoes, ushered in by their grandfather with his finger to his lips admonishing them to be quiet. One grandson recalled that when John Marshall entered the house, he would take off his shoes at the door and put on his slippers to avoid making any noise to disturb Polly, "who was in weak health and nervous—so much so that the least sound would disturb her and bring on an attack of sickness." One of the stories about Marshall's concern for his wife has him purchasing a horse from a miller at an inflated price so that the miller would no longer disturb Polly by riding past the Marshall house at an early morning hour. On one occasion he begged a neighbor to quiet his dog whose barking kept Polly awake. "Her situation is deplorable," said Marshall, "and if this state of things continues she cannot live." Marshall said he had considered abandoning his house, but his farm in nearby Henrico County included only "a confined and hot chamber in which [Polly] thinks she cannot live" and his wife could not travel to their children's homes in Fauquier County.[20]

Despite her illness and invalid condition, Polly Marshall remained the woman her husband loved. Always a sentimentalist, John Marshall never was restrained in expressing his emotions. In 1824, while in Washington, he was injured in a fall. He assured Polly in a letter that the injury to his arm was not serious, "the swelling has gone entirely down, and I have not the slightest appearance of fever." He was confined to his rooms and acknowledged being pleased at the attentions he was receiving from his friends, and from President Monroe, and from the ladies who "have brought me more jelly than I can eat." Despite those attentions, Marshall told his wife, "I have plenty of time on my hands in the night as well as in the day. How do you think I beguile it? I am almost tempted to leave you to guess till I write again. But, as I suppose you will have rather more curiosity in my absence than you usually show to hear my stories when I am present, I will tell you without waiting to be asked."

How did he beguile his time? It was with the story of a young army officer and a pretty young lady who set her cap for him when she first heard he was coming to Williamsburg many years earlier. "You must know that I begin with the ball at York," he wrote Polly, "and with the dinner on the first at your home next day. I then retrace my visit to York, our splendid assembly at the Palace in Williamsburg, my visit to Richmond, where I acted Pa for a fortnight. . . ." He continued on, recalling "our little tiffs and makings up, my feelings while Major Dick was courting you." He remembered the lock of hair that had sent him racing back to her side after he believed she had rejected him, "and all the thousand indescribable but deeply affecting instances of your attention or coolness which contributed for a time the happiness or misery of my life and will always be recollected with a degree of interest which can never be lost while recollection remains." It was thus, he said forty-one years after he and Polly had exchanged their marriage vows, that he found amusement "for those hours which I pass without company or books."[21]

In all his letters to his wife there is that quality of fondness, that touch of warmth designed to bring life to the quiet body of an ill woman. "I have seldom gone counter to your advice without repenting it," he told her in one letter. In another he begged to hear from her for "In spite of my firm resolution always to hope for the best, I can not suppress my uneasiness about you." In another letter from Washington he told her that his life followed a pattern, with him taking his walk in the morning, working hard all day, eating a hearty dinner and sleeping soundly all night. Sometimes he combed his hair before going to bed, and "while this operation is performing, I always think with tenderness of my sweet barber in Richmond. It is the most delightful sentiment I have."[22]

By the 1820s Marshall was the head of a rapidly multiplying family. In his lifetime his six children would produce forty grandchildren, and there were more than sixty nieces and nephews, many of whom came to look upon him as the center of the Marshall family, the one they could turn to when they needed assistance. If he could, Marshall obliged. To Henry Clay he wrote asking for assistance in securing an appointment for his nephew Thomas Marshall as a federal attorney in Kentucky.[23] To his brother Louis, Marshall offered requested advice on a son's plans to go into politics. "However seductive may be the splendor of political life to a distinguished politician and statesman," was the Chief Justice's comment to his brother's son, "it can afford no compensation to a gentleman not possessing an independent fortune. . . . To a distinguished lawyer who is a member of Congress, the practice in the supreme court may be some thing; but it cannot justify the abandonment of the courts of his state."[24] Like most large families, the Marshalls had their black sheep. A nephew had killed a man in Richmond in a duel, which forced him "to fly from Virginia and from very flattering professional prospects." He then had visited Canada and Texas, and finally planned to settle in New Orleans. His uncle wrote to Henry Clay asking Clay to write letters of introduction for the nephew to people in that city. "I have the most entire confidence in his honor, integrity, and amiable qualities," said John Marshall of his nephew.[25]

In the 1830s, when Congress and the state legislatures approved a number of programs of benefits to veterans of the American Revolution, John Marshall was the one who organized the claims for his family. In 1833 he collected $10,623.43 from the state auditor's office in half-pay payments to his father from February 6, 1782, to December 1, 1802, as allowed by the state Assembly. Marshall's letter filing for the money shows he was acting for himself, his brothers, and also the other heirs of his father in Kentucky. "I took out letters of administration in the General Court where I gave bond with ample security," he explained.[26]

He enjoyed his relatives, followed their activities closely,

and gave them what support he could. He was particularly proud
of his son Thomas, who was becoming involved in Virginia politics as a member of the state legislature from Fauquier County.
"From what I can learn the election will be close and is very
doubtful, more doubtful than I had supposed it to be from what I
heard in Richmond," John Marshall reported to his wife from
Warrenton when their son was a candidate for the legislature.
"Tom will lose some Federal votes who had engaged themselves
before his being known as a candidate." Thomas Marshall did go
to the legislature and had a distinguished career there, a career
in which he became famous for his stand against slavery. That
did not hurt him in Fauquier County; his problems there came
from other votes he had cast. In 1832 John Marshall reported to
his daughter from Fauquier County that "The families are all well
except your brother Tom who complains a good deal, and is probably the worse from an apprehension that he will lose his election, of which there is no little danger. A great cry is raised
against him in consequence of his vote for raising the clerks
fees. . . ."27

John Marshall also was helpful to his sons. "Your hogs
arrived on Wednesday evening," he reported to James Keith
Marshall from Richmond. "I had twelve of them killed on Friday
morning. They weighed 1891. The remaining thirteen will be
killed as soon as the weather will permit, perhaps tomorrow, but
the weather I fear is too hot. I fear you will be disappointed in
the price. It is four dollars only. An immense quantity has come
in from the West. I shall give you four and a quarter, and take
myself what I cannot sell at that price."28

John Marshall never lost his interest in dealing in land and
often called upon his sons in Fauquier to handle transactions for
him. One transaction reveals much about him. Involved was the
purchase of a tract of land owned by a man named Swan; Marshall intended to buy it for his son Edward Carrington, but Swan
apparently was an early-nineteenth-century version of the
wheeler-dealer. Marshall angrily wrote to his son that "I suggested to you the propriety of having no farther communication
with Mr. Swan. He has no idea of that frank dealing to which I
am accustomed. He cannot conceive that the offer I make is all
I mean to give. Should he say any thing farther to you on the subject, let him know that my offer having been rejected I consider
it withdrawn. . . ." But Edward Carrington wanted the land, and
the father was unable to resist the son. In his next letter to
Edward, Marshall said he would borrow $1,000 to pay Swan for
the land. He made no reference to his previous disagreement, but

he cautioned his son: "The sooner you receive the title the better. It will be advisable to look into the clerks office for any deed Swan may have made, for the title ought to be safe and previous examination may save much further trouble and perhaps loss."[29]

Marshall continued to be an active farmer in his later years, usually walking from his red brick house in Richmond to his farm in nearby Henrico County. This was not a plantation cared for by slaves and supervised by overseers, but a working farm in which he took a considerable amount of interest and to which he devoted a great deal of his time and energy. His letters are frequently filled with references to the farm. "I finished cutting my wheat and rye last week. The grain is fine, but the crop not very abundant. . . . I never saw young clover more promising till lately. . . ." "I am much gratified at your prospects for a good crop of wheat. The prospect for price is not a bad one though it has fallen in Richmond. . . . The cold weather and rains have injured my corn and ruined my cotton crop. . . ." After a flood of the James River: "I have lost a large portion of my best land forever. A considerable part could not be planted. Several planted acres were entirely drowned, and several acres so injured as not to be more than four feet high."[30]

During the 1820s he also undertook a project he had wanted to do for some years: the second edition of his five-volume biography of George Washington. "It is one of the most desirable objects I have in this life to publish a corrected edition of that work," he told Bushrod Washington in 1821. ". . . I have gone through the corrections and have only to copy them over so as to make them intelligible to the printer. I can have them ready for the press faster than they will be required." More work than Marshall anticipated was required before the second edition was brought out in 1826; the correspondence between Marshall and Bushrod Washington shows much planning and additional research before the second edition appeared.[31]

At about this time also Jared Sparks planned to bring out an edition of George Washington's papers, the first collection of the First President's works. He asked and received the cooperation of both John Marshall and Bushrod Washington. Sparks in 1826 visited Marshall in Richmond, and his account of that visit is an interesting picture of John Marshall in his early seventies. It reads:

> Called on Chief Justice Marshall; entered his yard through a broken wooden gate, fastened by a leather strap and opened with some difficulty, rang, and an old lady came to the door. I asked if Judge Marshall was at home.

"No," said she, "he is not in the house; he may be in the office," and pointed to a small brick building in one corner of the yard.

I knocked at the door, and it was opened by a tall, venerable-looking man, dressed with extreme plainness, and having an air of affability in his manners. I introduced myself as the person who had just received a letter from him concerning General Washington's letters, and he immediately entered into conversation on that subject. He appeared to think favorably of my project, but intimated that all the papers were entirely at the disposal of Judge Washington. He said that he had read with care all General Washington's letters in the copies left by him, and intimated that a selection only could with propriety be printed, as there was in many of them a repetition, not only of ideas, but of language. This was a necessary consequence of his writing to so many persons on the same subjects, and nearly at the same time.

He spoke to me of the history of Virginia; said Stith's History and Beverly's were of the highest authority, and might be relied on. Of Burk he only remarked that the author was fond of indulging his imagination, "but," he added in a good-natured way, "there is no harm in a little ornament, I suppose." He neither censured nor commended the work. He conversed some time on what he calls an error in the history of Virginia as generally received. . . . Such and other things were the topics of conversation, till the short hour of a ceremonious visit had run out. I retired much pleased with the urbanity and kindly manners of the Chief Justice. There is consistency in all things about him—his house, grounds, office, himself, bear marks of a primitive simplicity and plainness rarely to be seen combined.[32]

A few years after the second edition was published, Marshall abridged the biography so that it could be issued in a children's version. Again he was concerned about errors; he never seemed to be able to eliminate them all, or enough to satisfy himself. In a letter to the publisher of the children's version, Marshall referred to an error in the second volume of the 1826 edition, and said: "This careless inaccuracy mortifies me the more because it is committed by myself."[33]

He never could be done with the Washington biography. In 1827, for example, he received a letter from Lafayette with corrections, and Marshall promised to include them if he published another revised edition. Others wrote to him also, veterans of the Revolution who remembered details differently from Marshall's account. To all such correspondents Marshall wrote long and polite letters asking them for the version of events as they remembered them, and, if those versions seemed accurate, promising to make the required changes.[34]

One student of Marshall's career, Robert K. Faulkner, has described Marshall's dedication to perfecting this work as stemming from his desire "to impress the character of Washington, and the rest of the Washingtonian political creed, upon the country."[35] Surely it was that. John Marshall had admired George Washington more than any other public figure and his desire to enthrone Washington in what he believed to be his proper place in American history is natural. The desire became even more compelling in the 1820s and 1830s as Marshall came to believe that the Jeffersonian Republicans were maligning the man who had given so much for the American cause. Marshall's biography of Washington is a history of the formation of the United States from the Federalist point of view. Considering Marshall's involvement in the events of the time and his relationship to the leaders of that period, it could not be otherwise. However, while it could not be described as objective, the second edition, like the first, avoided harsh criticism of the anti-Federalists and spoke of all participants in America's early struggles, including Thomas Jefferson, with respect.

As always, Marshall professed himself to be outside of politics and uninformed about what was going on in the political world. And as always, once he had announced his ignorance, he then proceeded to demonstrate how really knowledgeable he was. A letter to Charles Hammond, dated December 28, 1823, is an astute appraisal of the prospects for the presidential election the next year, the sentiments for the various candidates and their chances in Virginia. When John Quincy Adams was elected President by the House of Representatives in February 1825, Marshall—in Washington for a Supreme Court session—wrote his brother James Markham Marshall a detailed analysis of how the cabinet appointments were developing.[36]

On March 4, 1825, Marshall swore in John Quincy Adams as the sixth President of the United States. Adams was the fourth man Marshall had sworn into that office, and this was the seventh time Marshall had administered the oath. "I administered the oath to the President in the presence of an immense concourse of people," he wrote to Polly, "in my suit of domestic manufacture. He too was dressed in the same manner, though his cloth was made at a different establishment. The cloth is very fine and smooth." That comment by Marshall on his involvement in the inaugural is typical of him. In matters of law, politics, and history, he was a sophisticated practitioner and commentator; few could equal him and almost none could best him. But he was still the country boy from Fauquier County in matters of society, quite taken by the fact that he and the President were dressed alike in suits of the same cloth.[37]

Marshall was particularly pleased at the election of John Quincy Adams, his own personal friend as well as the son of the man who had appointed him to the Supreme Court. In the next several years when the parties began their politicking for the 1828 election, Marshall became incensed by the attacks on Quincy Adams and by the growing involvement of presidential politics in the work of Congress. "It is infinitely to be deplored that the contests concerning the election of the President, and the factions they generate," he wrote to Lafayette, "should mingle themselves with the legislation of the country. I fear however it is a disease for which no remedy is attainable." As the debates became more fervid, Marshall's despair grew greater, as befitted a man entering the eighth decade of his life. "I begin to fear that our constitution is not to be so long lived as its real friends have hoped. What may follow sets conjecture at defiance. I shall not live to see and bewail the consequences of these furious passions which are breaking loose upon us."[38]

Because of Marshall's Federalist background, he saw Andrew Jackson as a threat to the nation as Marshall had seen it develop. The Jackson drive for the presidency in 1828 produced a greater involvement of the mass of American people than had previously been seen. The people were aroused and they were vocal; and it was a frightening specter to the older men who feared it was an uprising on the order of the French Revolution and did not understand it was the democratic process achieving its potential. On April 11, 1828, a newspaper, the *New York Statesman*, carried the following item on its front page:

National Politics. The paper called the Marylander, lately published the following paragraph:

"We hear that Judge Marshall, Chief Justice of the Supreme Court, a few days since in conversation with a gentleman, observed—'I have not voted for twenty years; but I shall consider it a solemn duty I owe my country, to go to the polls and vote at the next Presidential election —for,' added he, in his impressive manner—'Should Jackson be elected, I shall look upon the Government as virtually dissolved.'

Judge Marshall, unwilling to lie under the imputation of such an absurdity as the last sentence implies, has addressed the following note to the Richmond Whig:

March 29, 1828.

"Sir—I perceive in your paper of today a quotation from the Marylander of certain expressions ascribed to me respecting the pending election of the Presidency of the United States, which I think it my duty to disavow. Holding the situation I do, under the Government of the United States, I have thought it right to abstain from any public declarations on the election; and were it otherwise, I should abstain from a conviction, that my opinion would have no weight.

"I admit having said in private that, though I had not voted since the establishment of the general ticket system, and had believed that I never should vote during its continuance, I might probably depart from my resolution in this instance, from the strong sense I feel of the injustice of the charge of corruption against the President and Secretary of State. I never did use the other expressions ascribed to me.

"I request you to say that you are authorised to declare that the Marylander has been misinformed. Very respectfully, your obedient.

J. Marshall."

From Marshall's own description of the event the newspaper had not been very misinformed, certainly not as to the Chief Justice's intention to vote in the presidential election (something he had not done since his appointment to a judicial position) because of his opposition to Jackson. In a letter to Joseph Story, Marshall explained that he had attempted to refute the original story not because he objected to anyone knowing he favored the reelection of John Quincy Adams "but because I have great objection to being represented in the character of a furious partisan. Intemperate language does not become my age or office, and is foreign to my disposition."[39]

Jackson was elected. A few days before the inauguration, Marshall and Story attended a ball in Adams' honor, and Story's description of the event is a commentary upon the fate of those who enter national politics:

We found President Adams there, but the company, though highly respectable and brilliant in dresses, was small. There was a marked contrast between the fulness of last year and the thinness of the present. Mr. Adams has no favors to bestow, and he is now passed by with indifference, by all the fair-weather friends. They are all ready to hail the rising sun. Never have I felt so forcibly the emptiness of public honors and public favor; it is too transitory and too conspicuous a glory to justify any ambition to seek it. In our country, political eminence, if it can be obtained without stain, can rarely be held without the most painful sacrifices of feeling, and the silent endurance of the grossest injustice, not to say calumny.[40]

Despite his animosity to the leader of what was already being called "King Mob," John Marshall administered the oath to Andrew Jackson. He did not, however, join when thousands of Americans followed the new President to the President's House to celebrate the triumph of democracy.

The picture of John Marshall as he moves through the 1820s, as he passes from his sixties into his seventies, is that of a man with the major accomplishments of his life behind him. Soldier, diplomat, politician, judge, he had been a founder of his country, one who had nurtured it. He had helped to establish the supremacy of the Union and had declared the Court's power to repulse any attack on that supremacy. He had fathered a family, watched the development of his grandchildren, built up an estate, done what he could to assure the financial well-being of his descendants. He was, in short, a man who could claim he would be leaving his nation and his people better for his having been among them.

His life, however, was not finished. In the last quarter of his life, when many others would choose relaxation and ease, Marshall would face several major battles. He had to establish the sanctity of contracts, again struggle to uphold the concept of an independent judiciary, and deal with the tragedy of the United States. This was slavery.

II

O**N JULY 21, 1816**, the aged Jefferson wrote to Governor William Plumer of New Hampshire regarding a speech Plumer had made to the state legislature. Jefferson said how pleased he was by the speech, as it was "replete with sound principles, and truly Republican." He continued: "The idea that institutions, established for the use of the nation, cannot be touched nor modified, even to make them answer their end, because of rights gratuitously supposed in those employed to manage them in trust for the public, may, perhaps, be a salutary provision against the abuses of a monarch, but it is most absurd against the nation itself. Yet our lawyers and priests inculcate this doctrine; and suppose that preceding generations held the earth more freely than we do; had a right to impose laws on us, unalterable by ourselves; and that we, in like manner, can make laws, and impose burdens on future generations, which they will have no right to alter; in fine, that the earth belongs to the dead, and not to the living . . ."[1]

He was commenting on what was quickly becoming a *cause célèbre* in New Hampshire. Dartmouth College, at Hanover, New Hampshire, originally had received its charter from the English Crown. In 1816 the legislature of the state amended the college charter. William H. Woodward, chief justice of the state Court of Common Pleas, then directed that records of the school be turned over to the new trustees. The old trustees, who had been appointed under the original charter, sued to recover those documents, and the case of *Dartmouth College v. Woodward* had begun. This was another of the "great" cases to come before the Supreme Court while John Marshall was Chief Justice. It was significant in that it involved a basic point of constitutional law that Marshall refused to ignore, and its settlement by him has generally come to be accepted as proper and understood to have contributed to the growth of the United States.

Representing the college—that is, the old trustees—in its action against the state (in the name of Woodward) were two prominent lawyers, Jeremiah Smith and Jeremiah Mason. They believed they needed help, and they sought the assistance of a Dartmouth graduate who, although only in his mid-thirties, was already displaying the abilities that made him one of the great trial lawyers of his time. This was Daniel Webster. Smith wrote to Webster and asked him to contact Mason, but Webster was dubious of the value of his involvement in the case. "I have not thought of the subject, nor made the least preparation," he told Mason. "I am sure I can do no good, and must, therefore, beg that you and he will follow up in your own manner, the blows which have already been so well struck." Webster said he was willing to be considered part of the defense, in a consultant's capacity, "but should do no good by undertaking an argument."[2]

At this juncture in his life Daniel Webster was beginning to show that he was a victim of the good life. Once he had been a slender young man, impressively handsome. But he ate well and he had gained an extraordinary amount of weight in a short period of time. When he argued the *Dartmouth* case he weighed more than two hundred pounds, although he stood only five feet ten inches tall. A friendly description has him exchanging his "earlier vivacity for a slow stateliness which was awesome to strangers."[3] Despite this increased girth, he continued a fiery speaker and a brilliant trial lawyer, as his ultimate involvement in the *Dartmouth* case would demonstrate.

He and John Marshall were strong admirers of each other. In 1813 Webster had made a speech on the floor of the House of Representatives which so impressed Marshall that "I did not hesitate to state that Mr. Webster was a very able man, and would become one of the very first statesmen in America, and perhaps the very first." The next year, after Webster had argued several cases before the Supreme Court—"In one case I charged a New Yorker three hundred dollars, and in two other cases, a hundred dollars each. So much for prize causes"—he commented that "There is no man in the court that strikes me like Marshall. He is a plain man, looking very much like colonel Adams, and about three inches taller. I have never seen a man of whose intellect I had a higher opinion."[4] In the approaching case Webster's arguments and Marshall's decision would complement each other.

Although initially reluctant to become involved in the case, Webster changed his mind after Francis Brown, the president of the college, asked him to represent Dartmouth. Webster appeared at Exeter, New Hampshire, when the case was argued before a local court and then planned to lead the school's case before the Supreme Court in Washington. He requested that Joseph Hopkinson—ten years his senior, an eminent lawyer in his own right, and a member of Congress at the time of the arguments—be his co-counsel. A Federalist from Philadelphia, Hopkinson had demonstrated his prowess as a lawyer fifteen years earlier when he was one of the defense attorneys in the Chase impeachment trial.[5]

The college trustees in their action against Woodward as the representative of the state had failed in the New Hampshire courts to win back the books, records, and corporate seal which had been taken from them on Woodward's order. The issue that would come before the Supreme Court was whether the Constitution of the United States had somehow been violated when the state, through its legislature, had changed the college charter. In a letter to Jeremiah Smith in December of 1817, a few weeks prior to the opening arguments before the Supreme Court, Webster discussed his strategy, and the letter gives some insight into how a brilliant lawyer approaches a case. "My impression has been," he wrote, "that we should insert every thing to show, as far as we can, that the State did not found and endow the college. I should wish it rather to appear what they had not done, than what they had; but probably the one can only be shown, by showing the other. . . ."

He continued that "It is our misfortune that our cause goes to Washington on a single point. I wish we had it in such shape as to raise all the other objections, as well as the repugnancy of these acts to the constitution of the United States." He then outlined a strategy of initiating a suit in the local federal court: "Suppose the corporation of Dartmouth College should lease to some man of Vermont . . . one of their New Hampshire farms, and that the lessee should bring ejectment for it . . . the whole question might get before the court in Washington."[6] Webster was being the careful lawyer, of course, in making certain that the case would not be rejected by the Supreme Court for lack of jurisdiction. He followed through on the idea, but the other points he sought to raise never came before the Supreme Court; there was not sufficient time. Actually, he did not need the insurance. The Supreme Court would not reject his case; it was ready for it.

Enforcement of contractual arrangements had been a concern of the federal courts for years. One of Marshall's first cases as Chief Justice had involved landholdings and the contractual arrangements over who was the actual owner.[7] The issue had developed through the western land disputes, the ships seizure cases, and a number of others. What was evolving was a law of contracts, of property. The theme was that when a man earned something, neither a person nor a government should be able to take it from him. One purpose of government is, in fact, to protect a man from assaults on his property, whether those assaults be by marauders, neighbors, or an arm of government itself. The John Marshall who had grown up on the frontier, who had seen the young America split from England because American property was being confiscated in the form of taxation without representation, the John Marshall who had seen the revolutionaries in France usurp property before not only an impotent but a cooperating government, this John Marshall was well aware that government must protect a man from theft by his government.

Involved in the *Dartmouth* case was the question of whether a contractual arrangement is altered when a state legislature attempts to alter property rights granted by a previous legislature or a previous government. In 1810, when Marshall resolved the Yazoo land scandals with his decision in *Fletcher v. Peck*,[8] he said that such an attempt by a state legislature is an attempt to alter a contract against the constitutional prohibition that states may not make any laws negativing contracts. A case more to the point came before the Supreme Court in 1815, *Terrett v. Taylor*.[9] Prior to the protection of religious freedom in Virginia, the Episcopal Church had been granted large tracts of land. It operated this land, sold it, considered itself as a regular property owner—which it was. After the religious freedom declaration, however, the question arose as to whether the state could withdraw the land from the Episcopal Church.

Joseph Story wrote the opinion of the Supreme Court. While he agreed that religious freedom meant an absence of coercion, he did not believe it forbade a state legislature from incorporating a religious institution to enable it to manage its property. The next question was whether the state could take from the corporate church its possessions. Story said that it could not. "The dissolution of the form of government did not involve in it a dissolution of civil rights," he said in his decision, "or an abolition of the common law under which the inheritance of every man in the state were held." What he was saying was that the church was entitled to all the rights of an individual property owner. "It has been asserted as a principle of the common law," continued Story, "that the division of an empire creates no forfeiture of previously vested rights of property. . . . Nor are we able to perceive any sound reason why the church lands escheated or devolved upon the state by the revolution any more than the property of any other corporation created by the royal bounty or established by the legislature."

Story insisted that the legislature had the right to make the original grant, and "it is very clear to our minds that it vested an indefeasible and irrevocable title. We have no knowledge of any authority or principle which could support the doctrine that a legislative grant is revocable in its own nature, and held only *durante bene placito*." Using words that should have given the state of New Hampshire reason to hesitate before attacking the corporate status of Dartmouth later, Story said in that 1815 case:

> . . . [T]hat the legislature can repeal statutes creating private corporations, or confirming to them property already acquired under the faith of previous laws, and by such repeal can vest the property of such corporations exclusively in the state, or dispose of the same to such purposes, as they may please, without the consent or default of the corporators, we are not prepared to admit; and we think ourselves standing upon the principles of natural justice, upon the fundamental laws of every free government, upon the spirit and the letter of the constitution of the United States, and upon the decisions of most respectable judicial tribunals. . . .[10]

Although the Story decision dealt with tangible property, land owned by the Episcopal Church in Virginia, while the *Dartmouth* case would deal with, basically, an intangible—the reins of power

—the precedent was obvious. An institution which receives its charter from the government cannot have its rights abused by a later government seeking to alter that charter without the consent of the institution. The *Dartmouth College* case had been won before it was argued.

All seven Justices were present when the case was argued in 1818, with Marshall sitting in the center of the bench, his appearance dominating the entire assemblage. The Court then held its sessions in a small chamber on the Senate side of the Capitol, its regular chambers not yet having been rebuilt after the fire set by the British in 1814. The chamber was filled primarily with lawyers; Webster's reputation as an advocate was not yet so great as to attract large public crowds. The state's case was being argued by William Wirt—"Wirt is a man of a good deal of ability," said Webster of his opponent, "he is rather more of a lawyer than I expected."[11]

The *Dartmouth College* case argued before the Supreme Court was a combination of law and dramatics, probably the outstanding example of the joining of the actor and the lawyer. Those who were present for the arguments talked about them for years afterwards, and the accounts competed in their emotionality. Perhaps the first of the descriptions of the drama was by Salma Hale, a Democratic Representative from New Hampshire whose sympathies were with the state and against Webster. He strolled over from the House chamber for the arguments and reported: "The two speeches of Wirt and Webster in the college case were as good as any I have ever heard. Webster was unfair in his statement, for which he deserved and received castigation; but his argument was able and his peroration eloquent. He appeared himself to be much affected; and the audience was silent as death. He observed that in defending the college, he was doing his duty—that it should never accuse him of ingratitude—nor address him in the words of the Roman dictator."

Wirt was Webster's equal, according to Hale. "Wirt, in his peroration," continued the Hale letter, "spoke of the long period during which Wheelock was president—of his many services—of the proof of his talents in the eloquence just displayed by his pupil—of his cruel persecution, dismissal and death of a broken heart. He then introduced his ghost, exclaiming 'Et tu Brute!' " Hale concluded: "From this you will perceive how much the speakers in our highest courts of law are indulged in their flights."[12]

But Webster's argument was more than a flight; it was a beautifully constructed piece of legal craftsmanship. The printed account runs forty-nine pages and is approximately fifteen thousand words. There are sixty-seven citations, from the state courts, from earlier Supreme Court cases, from *The Federalist Papers*, from British parliamentary debates, and from British court cases. Webster not only was arguing a case; he was building a wall around the sanctity of contracts—when two parties agree to an arrangement, one of them cannot arbitrarily dissolve it. Before the *Dartmouth* case was done, it would be resolved that not even the government could be arbitrary.

Webster's argument, as he acknowledged, relied heavily on the approach developed by Smith and Mason in their presentations before the lower courts. (They were not present in Washington and did not engage in the arguments before the Supreme Court.) This does not detract from Webster's own competence but points up that he was intelligent enough to utilize material developed by others when it was offered to him and when its value was obvious.

He argued first that the New Hampshire legislature had seemed almost capricious in its action dissolving the old status of the college and establishing a new corporation. "No funds are given to the college by this [Crown] charter," he said. "A corporate existence and capacity are given to the trustees, with the privileges and immunities, which have been mentioned, to enable the founder and his associates the better to manage the funds which they themselves had contributed, and such others as might afterwards obtain." That section seems tailored to fit Story's decision in *Terrett v. Taylor*. Webster continued: "After the institution, thus created and constituted, had existed uninterruptedly and usefully, nearly fifty years, the legislature of New Hampshire passed the acts in question. . . . If these acts are valid, the old corporation is abolished, and a new one created."[13]

The new corporation had been formed, Webster said, because the state believed it had the power to deal with the old corporation as it saw fit, to abolish it, alter it, or alienate it. "It will be contended by the plaintiffs that these acts are not valid and binding on them without their assent. 1. Because they are against common right, and the constitution of New Hampshire. 2. Because they are repugnant to the constitution of the United States." The Supreme Court, of course, could only consider the last point, whether the alteration of the corporation was a violation of the federal Constitution. Webster acknowledged that. "Yet," he said, "it may assist in forming an opinion of their true nature and character, to compare them with those fundamental principles introduced into the state governments for the purpose of limiting the exercise of the legislative power."[14]

When Webster had agreed to undertake the case, he had

been concerned about the strength of that single point as a basis for action by the Supreme Court, wishing that he had several other arguments which the Supreme Court could properly review. He was left, however, with only the one point, but he would make whatever case he could as part of an emotional appeal as well as a historical record.

In dealing with the first point, that the state legislature's actions were a violation of both common right and state law, Webster summed up with:

> If the [state] constitution be not altogether waste paper, it has restrained the power of the legislature in these particulars. If it has any meaning, it is, that the legislature shall pass no act directly and manifestly impairing private property and private privileges. It shall not judge by act. It shall not decide by act. It shall not deprive by act. But it shall leave all these things to be tried and adjudged by the law of the land.[15]

That statement is a rephrasing of the rule of law—for which men like John Marshall had struggled for decades. Society must be governed by rules which cannot be altered by whim, momentary passion, or political considerations. No individual, and no governmental unit, Webster was pointing out, can assume that power.

Then he turned to the basic issue before the Court, whether the state actions violated the section of the federal Constitution that prohibited a state from passing "any bill of attainder, ex post facto law, or law impairing the obligation of contracts." He cited the *Fletcher v. Peck* decision in the Yazoo land scandal as already deciding "that a grant is a contract, within the meaning of this provision; and that a grant by a state is also a contract as much as the grant of an individual." He then referred to Story's decision in *Terrett v. Taylor* and said that it "seems to leave little to be argued or decided in this."[16]

Webster, of course, was correct. The issue already had been decided, not only in the cases he cited but when the Americans had determined to overthrow the arbitrary rule of King George for the disciplined rule of law. Daniel Webster now said as much to the Supreme Court Justices. The American people, he declared, "have, most wisely, chosen to take the risk of occasional inconvenience from the want of power, in order that there might be a settled limit to its exercise, and a permanent security against its abuse." The American people, he continued, had imposed "prohibitions and restraints" on government "and they have not rendered these altogether vain and nugatory by conferring the power of dispensation." There could be no exceptions. He continued:

> If inconvenience should arise, which the legislature cannot remedy under the power conferred upon it, it is not answerable for such inconvenience. That which it cannot do within the limits prescribed to it, it cannot do at all. No legislature in this country is able—and may the time never come when it shall be able—to apply to itself the memorable expression of a Roman Pontiff: "Licet hoc de jure no possumus, volumus tamen de plentitudine potestatis."*

Webster insisted that the case before the Court was important not only for its impact upon Dartmouth but also for its impact on every college in the nation. "They have all a common principle of existence—the inviolability of their charters." He called it "a dangerous, a most dangerous experiment, to hold these institutions subject to the rise and fall of popular parties, and the fluctuations of political opinions." The result of such an experiment? "Colleges and halls will be deserted by all better spirits, and become a theatre for the contention of politics. Party and faction will be cherished in the places consecrated to piety and learning. These consequences are neither remote nor possible only. They are certain and immediate."

The lawyer said it would have been better if the issue had never come before the Supreme Court; if, instead, the rights of the college had been protected at the state level. "That hope has failed," he said, and then stated what lawyers and the American people have come to realize is the ultimate fact of their political existence: that all great questions come before the members of that Court and that the Justices there are members of the court of last resort for the American people; that is, the last resort except for violence. "It is here," Daniel Webster charged the seven Justices, "that those rights are now to be maintained, or they are prostrated forever."[17]

That, basically, was Daniel Webster's case. He had spoken for four hours, beginning at eleven o'clock in the morning and finishing in mid-afternoon. The audience had been enthralled at this consummate actor. His presentation had been wisely understated for the most part, exploding into emotion only occasionally

---

* "Although I cannot do this according to the letter of the law, nevertheless I requested it from the fullness of your judicial power."

but always effectively. A description of the presentation, believed to have been prepared by Joseph Story in 1830, twelve years after the arguments, described the "earnestness of manner [of Webster's argument], and a depth of research, and a potency of phrase, which at once convinced you that his whole soul was in the cause; and that he had meditated over it in the deep silence of the night and studied it in the broad sunshine of the day." And when Webster used dramatics, according to this account, there was "in his whole air and manner, in the fiery flashings of his eyes, the darkness of his contracted brow, the sudden and flying flushes of his cheeks, the quivering and scarcely manageable movements of his lips, in the deep guttural tones of his voice, in the struggle to suppress his emotions, in the almost conclusive clenchings of his hands without a seeming consciousness of the act, there was in these things what gave to his oratory an almost superhuman influence. . . ."[18]

That description is buttressed by one written in 1852, thirty-four years after the event, by another witness, Chauncy A. Goodrich, to Rufus Choate. Goodrich reported that Webster began his argument "in the calm tone of easy and dignified conversation. His matter was so completely at his command that he scarcely looked at his brief, but went on for more than four hours with a statement so luminous and a chain of reasoning so easy to be understood and yet approaching so nearly to absolute demonstration, that he seemed to carry with him every man of his audience without in the slightest effort or weariness on either side." Goodrich did not believe it was Webster's eloquence that was so persuasive as his "pure reason." He remembered Webster turning dramatic "now and then for a sentence or two" when "his eye flashed and his voice swelled into a bolder note as if he uttered some emphatic thought, but he instantly fell back into the tone of earnest conversation which ran throughout the great body of the speech." Goodrich recalled that Story had been prepared to take notes on Webster's argument, but "Hour after hour I saw him fixed in the same attitude, but not a single note on his paper—the argument closed and *he had not taken a single note.*" Goodrich recalled asking Story about this afterwards, and Story's replying: "Every thing was so clear, so easy to remember, that not a note seemed necessary; in fact I thought nothing about my notes."[19]

How Daniel Webster closed his arguments in the *Dartmouth College* case is a matter of historical controversy. The official Court record has him end with a quotation from Cicero in Latin: "Omnia alia perfugia bonorum, subsidia, consilia, auxilia, jura ceciderunt. Quem enim alium appellem? quem obtestor? quem

implorem? Nisi hoc loco, nisi apud vos, nisi per vos, judices, salu-
tem nostram, quae spe exigua extremaque pendet, termerimus;
nihil est praeterea quo confugere possimus."[20]*

In his 1852 letter Goodrich supplied a different ending.
His account has been challenged, or at least questioned, because
it was written so long after the event. Goodrich, however, was a
minister, a teacher, and an author; it is not unreasonable to
assume that his 1852 account was based on notes he had made
at the time. That he could have fabricated entirely or manufactured the quotations he attributes to Webster is difficult to believe.
He has Webster come to the end of his legal argument and stand
"for some moments silent before the court, while every eye was
fixed intently upon him." Finally, Webster turned to John
Marshall and said:

> This, sir, is my case! It is the case not merely of that
> humble institution, it is the case of every college in our
> land! It is more! It is the case of every eleemosynary
> institution throughout our country—of all those great
> charities founded by the piety of our ancestors to alleviate
> human misery, and scatter blessings along the pathway
> of life! It is more! It is, in some sense, the case of every
> man among us who has property of which he may be
> stripped, for the question is simply this, "Shall our state
> legislatures be allowed to take *that which is not their
> own*, to turn it from its original use, and apply it to such
> ends and purposes as they in their discretion shall see fit!"

To this point Chauncey Goodrich's account is a paraphrase,
a dramatic one of what the official record has Webster actually
saying. And that gives his next paragraph more credence. Goodrich quoted Webster:

---

* "Every other protection for
my material possessions, every other
means of comfort, counsel, and assistance, all my legal rights have
collapsed. Who else can I call
upon? Whom do I beseech? Whom
can I implore? Unless it is in this
place, unless it is from you and
through you, magistrates, that I
obtain protection for my life, which
now hangs by a slender thread, I
shall have no other recourse but to
flee."

I am indebted to the Rev. Neil
J. Twombly, S.J., of Georgetown
University, for identifying the quotation for me as Cicero's *Pro Flacco*
oration, 2.3 and 2.4, and for pointing out to me that the Latin—reprinted here as it appears in 4
Wheaton, 600—is inaccurate. There
are several words omitted, and the
omission is not indicated in Wheaton, and the seventh word from the
end of the quotation, "termerimus,"
is inaccurate—there is, in fact, no
such word. The correct word is
"tenuerimus."

Sir, you may destroy this little institution; it is weak, it is in your hands! I know it is one of the lesser lights in the literary horizon of our country. You may put it out! But if you do so, you must carry through your work! You must extinguish, one after another, all these great lights of science which for more than a century have thrown their radiance over our land!

It is, Sir, as I have said, a small college. And yet *there are those who love it!*

If this account is reasonably accurate, then Webster either was a highly emotional man or else the greatest actor America has ever known, for Goodrich reported that at this point Webster's emotions, "which he had thus far succeeded in keeping down, broke forth." His lips quivered, his cheeks trembled, his eyes filled with tears, his voice choked, "and he seemed struggling to the utmost, simply to gain that mastery over himself which might save him from an unmanly burst of feelings." Goodrich continued that he would not give "the few broken words of tenderness in which he went on to speak of his attachment to the college. It seemed to be mingled throughout with the recollections of father, mother, brothers, and all the trials and preventions through which he had made his way into life."

According to Goodrich, the spectators believed the outburst "was wholly unpremeditated—a pressure on his heart which sought relief in words and tears." Goodrich has Webster recovering control of himself after a few moments, and saying again to John Marshall: "Sir, I know not how others may feel . . ."—here glancing at his opponents who sat near where he stood—"but for myself, when I see my *alma mater* surrounded, like Cesar in the Senate house, by those who are reiterating stab upon stab, I would not for this right hand have her say to me 'Et tu quoque, mi fili.'"

Goodrich reported that when Webster at last sat down, the entire courtroom was in tears. Story, in the account attributed to him, does not offer the same quotations, but does give a similar description of the courtroom when Webster concluded: "There was a painful anxiety towards the close. The whole audience had been wrought up to the highest excitement; many were dissolved in tears; many betrayed the most agitating mental struggles; many were sinking under exhausting efforts to conceal their own emotion. When Mr. Webster ceased to speak, it was some minutes before anyone seemed inclined to break the silence. The whole seemed but an agonizing dream, from which the audience was slowly and almost unconsciously awakening."[21]

One should not charge Webster with artificiality in his emotions, nor accuse the members of the Supreme Court and the spectators in the courtroom of gullibility. Suffice it to say, however, that Webster had made a similar argument, in some instances almost word for word alike, when he participated in the case at a state court level at Exeter a few months earlier. It had appeared to be effective then, and there was no reason for Daniel Webster not to use it again before a new audience.

The other side was still to be heard from, but their arguments would be anticlimactic. One of the lawyers for the state argued that the education of youth is an object of civil government and left entirely to the states, and that the Revolution had destroyed the British Crown's authority over the school but had not negated the state's authority over it, nor taken that state authority and given it to the federal government—a position which Joseph Story had effectively destroyed in *Terrett v. Taylor* three years earlier.

William Wirt at this time was Attorney General of the United States but representing the state of New Hampshire as a private lawyer, a practice then allowed. His case did not appear strong. He argued that the Supreme Court had taken the position that it would not overrule a state action if there was any doubt it should, and he insisted that there was considerable doubt here; his point was that the charter did not constitute a contract, although the *Fletcher v. Peck* and *Terrett v. Taylor* decisions had stated that such a charter had the attributes of a contract.[22]

The arguments lasted three days, finishing March 12, 1818. When they were done, lawyers for the state asked whether the Supreme Court intended to hand down its decision that term. Chief Justice Marshall replied that the Court "could not treat lightly an act of the legislature of a state and the decision of a State court, and that the court would not probably render any judgment at this term." Webster considered that a good omen because he did not believe the Court would delay the decision for a year, until the next term, "if the court saw no difficulty in coming to the conclusion that the decision in New Hampshire was right." He believed he and Hopkinson had made a good case, one that had not been answered effectively.[23]

Two days after the arguments had ended, and one day after the Court had adjourned, Webster estimated that John Marshall, Bushrod Washington, and Joseph Story "in the end" would decide for the college. He also estimated "we have much more than an even chance for one of the others," giving them a majority of the seven-man Court. "I think we shall finally succeed."[24]

During the year that passed between the arguments and the decision, Webster and his friends were active. He had his argument printed and five copies sent to Joseph Story so that Story could distribute them to other Justices of the Supreme Court. "I send you five copies of our argument," said Webster's covering letter. "If you send one of them to each of such of the judges as you think proper, you will of course do it in the manner least likely to lead to a feeling that any indecorum has been committed by the plaintiffs." Other approaches were made through James Kent, the highest judicial officer in New York State and a man believed influential with some of the Supreme Court Justices. Kent had indicated that his inclinations were with the state. Officials from the college visited him, gave him a copy of Webster's argument, and discussed it with him. As a result he changed his position, and then is believed to have discussed the case with Brockholst Livingston of New York and William Johnson. Johnson was a key man because as a member of the Supreme Court in 1810 he had dissented in *Fletcher v. Peck* to the concept that a grant by a state is a contract.[25]

As always in major decisions during Marshall's tenure on the Court, as in later years under other Chief Justices, the decision would be watched with interest for all its political nuances. Would the Supreme Court override an act of a state legislature? To do so would greatly strengthen the federal government not only because of the Court's use of its power but also because of its statement that it had the power to determine when the federal Constitution is supreme over the state. While it was natural that Marshall and Washington would decide for the college, perhaps the Court would split politically with those two, appointed by a Federalist President, in dispute with the other five Justices appointed by either Thomas Jefferson or James Madison. To avoid that kind of political cleavage was one reason why there was politicking behind the scenes and so much anxiety and letter-writing among the Justices themselves. When the Supreme Court convened the next year the political aspect of the case, so far as the Court was concerned, had been eliminated. The decision John Marshall read was agreed to by five members of the Court—Marshall, Washington, Story, Livingston, and Johnson. Only Gabriel Duvall dissented. The seventh Justice, Thomas Todd, was not present.

This 1819 term also included the decisions by the Supreme Court in *McCulloch v. Maryland* and *Sturges v. Crowninshield*, making it one of the most significant sittings in the history of the Supreme Court, indeed, in the history of law. It took Marshall more than an hour to read the decision; Daniel Webster found in it Marshall's "own peculiar way. He reasoned along from step to step."[26]

Marshall began as he often did in such cases, by acknowledging that the Supreme Court was entering a controversy: "This court can be insensible neither to the magnitude nor delicacy of this question. The validity of a legislative act is to be examined; and the opinion of the highest law tribunal of a state to be revised. . . ." He continued that the Court had said on previous occasions that it would not take such action in any doubtful cases. He then cited the constitutional mandate against a state interfering with a contract and the directive that the judicial power extended to all cases in equity arising under the Constitution. "On the judges of this court, then," reasoned Marshall, "is imposed the high and solemn duty of protecting, from even legislative violation, those contracts which the constitution of our country has placed beyond legislative control; and, however irksome the task may be, this is a duty from which we dare not shrink."27

The Supreme Court always has been considered a political institution; commentators frequently report lineups on decisions according to the President who appointed the Justices. "Liberals" and "conservatives" are phrases applied to the Justices, who are often described as being for or against an issue on the basis of their backgrounds prior to their sitting on the high bench. But probably at no time in its history was the Supreme Court considered as political as it was during the Marshall tenure. Partly this was because Marshall saw himself as maintaining a political philosophy when the other branches of government were controlled by advocates of other philosophies, as he had promised Charles Cotesworth Pinckney he would many years earlier. Partly it was because respect for the Supreme Court as an institution was not yet a part of American life and the Court was often attacked vigorously. This perhaps explains why Marshall began so many of his decisions with a statement to the effect that the Court could do no less than what it was now doing; he was trying to say the Supreme Court acted as it did because it was obligated to do so, not because it chose to do so.

In this decision Marshall first turned to whether the corporate charter is a contract. If the answer to that question was negative, then there would be no reason to proceed. If the answer was positive, then the Court could determine if state action changing it violated the Constitution. Marshall had no trouble finding that it was a contract. "It can require no argument to prove that the circumstances of this case constitute a contract," he said. "An application is made to the crown for a charter to incorporate a religious and literary institution. In the application, it is stated that large contributions have been made for the object, which will be conferred on the corporation as soon as it shall be created. The charter is granted, and on its faith the property is conveyed. Surely in this transaction every ingredient of a complete and legitimate contract is to be found."[28]

John Marshall had grown to manhood when the struggle for law was the struggle for the bestowing of society's protection upon a man's possessions. Those, perhaps, who had come to manhood when that concept appeared to be part of American life, and not when it had to be fought for, could not understand the significance of defending it. The Chief Justice seemed to be talking to them as he continued:

> . . . The term "contract" . . . must be understood as intended to guard against a power of at least doubtful utility, the abuse of which had been extensively felt; and to restrain the legislature in future from violating the right to property. That anterior to the formation of the constitution, a course of legislation had prevailed in many, if not in all, of the states, which weakened the confidence of man in man, and embarrassed all transactions between individuals, by dispensing with a faithful performance of engagements. To correct this mischief, by restraining the power which produced it, the state legislatures were forbidden "to pass any law impairing the obligation of contracts." . . .[29]

He then said there was less disagreement among the parties as to that general principle than there was on its application to the specific case. He began the process of applying it to the particular case. First, could Dartmouth College be considered a public institution? Marshall allowed that he did not see how it could. Its funds did not come from public sources; they were not spent for public purposes; the teachers were not considered public employees. Then he asked: "Is it from the act of incorporation? Let this subject be considered."

He considered the subject and found it still wanting. The fact of incorporation does not mean that an institution is public —"nothing can be inferred which changes the character of the institution, or transfers to the government any new power over it." Institutions do not develop from their incorporation "but out of the manner in which they are formed, and the objects for which they are created." Merely because the government incorporated them did not give the government the right to change them.

A few moments later he returned to that theme, that government cannot be frivolous. The Dartmouth charter had been granted by the English Crown before the Revolution. Marshall said:

> . . . Had parliament, immediately after the emanation of this charter, and the execution of those conveyances which followed it, annulled the instrument, so that the living donors would have witnessed the disappointment of their hopes, the perfidy of the transaction would have been universally acknowledged. Yet then, as now, the donors would have had no interest in the property; then, as now, those who might be students would have had no rights to be violated; then, as now, it might be said, that the trustees, in whom the rights of all were combined, possessed no private, individual, beneficial interest in the property confided to their protection. Yet the contract would at that time have been deemed sacred by all. What has since occurred to strip it of its inviolability? In reason, in justice, and in law, it is now what it was in 1769.[30]

The meaning of Marshall's words is that the Constitution protects *from* government. The Americans had learned that there were two threats. One was the ravages of their fellow men and the second was the ravages of government. They constructed a government to protect them from their fellow men and imposed a Constitution on top of it to protect them from that government. John Marshall and the other Justices who sided with him in this decision realized the corrupting nature of power, understood that as men enter government, learn to use its offices, see the results they can achieve, they begin to confuse their original obligations with their new purposes, their role as servants of the people with that of arbiters of the people's needs. This arrogance of government is what in a democracy must constantly be guarded against, and the role of guardians and protectors is the one that John Marshall and the Supreme Court he led were assuming. "To what quarter will you look for protection from an infringement on the Constitution, if you will not give the power to the judiciary?" Marshall had asked his fellow Virginians thirty-one years earlier at the ratifying convention. And with his answer—"There is no other body that can afford such a protection"—there was no disagreement then or since.[31]

Marshall next turned in his decision to whether the Dartmouth contract might be excluded from the protection of the Constitution because it was an eleemosynary institution. He made short work of that question. "There is no exception in the constitution, no sentiment delivered by its contemporaneous expounders, which would justify us in making it," he said. Nor, he continued, was there anything in the nature of the specific arrangement to warrant such an interpretation.[32]

After concluding that the Dartmouth charter was indeed a contract which could not be impaired by government, Marshall then turned to whether the New Hampshire legislature had, in fact, damaged the contract. First, Marshall insisted that "the duties, as well as the powers, of government devolved on the people of New Hampshire. . . . It is too clear to require the support of argument, that all contracts, and rights, respecting property, remained unchanged by the revolution. The obligations, then, which were created by the charter to Dartmouth College, were the same in the new that they had been in the old government."

He pointed out that the state laws changing the charter had increased the number of trustees to twenty-one, allowed the governor to appoint the new members, and created a board of twenty-five overseers, all but four of whom would be appointed by the governor, and which would control "the most important acts of the trustees." Marshall continued: "On the effect of this law, two opinions cannot be entertained. . . . The whole power of governing the college is transferred from trustees appointed according to the will of the founder, expressed in the charter, to the executive of New Hampshire. . . . The will of the state is substituted for the will of the donors, in every essential operation of the college. This is not an immaterial change."

To the argument that the change may actually be of benefit to the college or of benefit to literature, Marshall insisted that "it is not according to the will of the donors, and is subversive of that contract, on the faith of which their property was given." The government of the United States had been established as a government of laws and not of men. This meant that people must understand that their lives could not be altered by those taking unto themselves the power to determine what was their best interests. A democracy cannot operate without that principle which John Marshall had just applied in the *Dartmouth College* case.

His conclusion now was an anticlimax: ". . . The acts of the legislature of New Hampshire . . . are repugnant to the constitution of the United States; and that the judgment on this special verdict ought to have been for the plaintiffs. The judgment of the State Court must therefore be reversed."[33]

Of the seven Justices of the Supreme Court, Thomas Todd, being absent, did not participate in the decision; Gabriel Duvall, the dissenter, did not offer an opinion; and the remaining four Justices—Johnson, Livingston, Story, and Washington—concurred in Marshall's decision that the Dartmouth College charter could not be abused by the state. Johnson, the first Jeffersonian appointed to the Court, "concurred, for the reasons stated by the Chief Justice." Bushrod Washington and Joseph Story wrote separate concurring opinions, and Brockholst Livingston "concurred, for the reasons stated by the Chief Justice, and Justices Washington and Story." The closing paragraph in Story's concurring opinion gives some indication of the trauma that the members of the Supreme Court obviously had felt as they had trampled on this action by a state legislature. Story wrote:

> I entertain great respect for the legislature, whose acts are in question. I entertain no less respect for the enlightened tribunal whose decision we are called upon to review. In the examination, I have endeavored to keep my steps super antiquas vias of the law, under the guidance of authority and principle. It is not for judges to listen to the voice of persuasive eloquence or popular appeal. We have nothing to do but to pronounce the law as we find it; and having done this, our justification must be left to the impartial judgment of our country.[34]

Daniel Webster was elated, naturally. "The opinion goes the whole length, and leaves nothing further to be said," he exclaimed. ". . . I feel a load removed from my own shoulders much heavier than they have been accustomed to bear."[35] His little college that he loved had been saved.

Analyses of Marshall's decision in the *Dartmouth* case emphasize two points: that he used the Contract Clause (as he would later use the Commerce Clause) as a restriction on state action; and that he assured the development of corporations and American commerce by protecting them from the whimsy, corruption, and bias of government officials. But the decision has a deeper meaning when considered in the context of its time and its relationship to the development of American democracy. Peoples and nations are like young children struggling to grow and to learn of the world they must live in, how it will shape them, how they can respond to it. The relationship between the American people and their government was, as it must always be, an uncertain one. How much power would the individual surrender? How much power could the government absorb? People would, of course, surrender as little as possible and government would absorb as much as possible—but the Supreme Court would decide that "possible" did not mean beyond the strict limits allowed by the Constitution.

The decision has sometimes been interpreted critically, as a sign that Marshall favored corporate over individual needs. Had he not conceded in his decision that the state proposal might have been more advantageous both to the school and to the literature it was supposed to promulgate? Such an interpretation overlooks his belief that the law was superior to what one man or a few men might believe proper at one particular time. It also overlooks other decisions by John Marshall which demonstrate that he was interested in upholding the law more than any particular economic group. Herbert A. Johnson has pointed out that the student of Marshall must study his decision in the *Providence Bank v. Billings* case as "a chaser" to the *Dartmouth* decision.[36]

In that 1830 case the issue was whether a state, Rhode Island, could tax a bank which it had chartered. The bank claimed it could not be taxed, and cited John Marshall's own decision in *McCulloch v. Maryland* that the power to tax is the power to destroy. In *McCulloch v. Maryland*, however, Marshall had made that point in connection with a state taxing a federal institution, a lower attacking a superior level of government. He would not accept in the Rhode Island case that a state could not tax one of its own chartered institutions. First, Marshall made the point that a "charter incorporating a bank is a contract" and then asked if that contract was "impaired by taxing the banks of the State?"

He found the answer in the incorporation charter. "It contains no stipulation promising exemption from taxation," he said. "The state, then, has made no express contract which has been impaired by the act of which the plaintiffs complain." Marshall then went on to the point that is revealing of his concern for all people and not for one particular economic group. In discussing the taxing power of the state, the power which the banks claimed had been relinquished, Marshall stressed the importance of that power to the people and their government:

> It would seem that the relinquishment of such a power is never to be assumed. We will not say that a state may not relinquish it; that a consideration sufficiently valuable to induce a partial release of it may not exist; but as the whole community is interested in retaining it undiminished, that community has a right to insist that its abandonment ought not to be presumed, in a case in which the deliberate purpose of the state to abandon it does not appear.

There were other sections in the decision pointing out that if the bank's thesis was correct, then land grant property and other legislative grants could not be taxed. The power of taxation, he argued, "operates on all the persons and property belonging to the body politic." That power "is granted by all, for the benefit of all. . . . However absolute the right of an individual may be, it is still in the nature of that right that it must bear a portion of the public burdens; and that portion must be determined by the legislature." Marshall held then that the state could tax the bank.[37]

Another "chaser" worth consideration is a Marshall decision in an earlier case, *Head v. Providence Insurance Co.* The issue was whether the letters between an insurance company and a man it had insured acted to cancel the insurance policy. Marshall found they did not because "they were negotiations preparatory to an agreement, but not an agreement itself." He continued that "It is a general rule that a corporation can only act in the manner prescribed by law. . . . It appears to the court, that an act not performed according to the requisites of the law cannot be considered as the act of the company."[38]

In the *Dartmouth* case the rights of corporations had been protected. In the Rhode Island case Marshall said that those rights are not a grant for avoiding responsibilities. He had spoken of the "whole community" and that all must "bear a portion of the public burdens." In the insurance company case he had insisted that corporations must obey the law. The maxim that a right does not excuse a business organization from its responsibility is amply demonstrated in those two decisions by John Marshall.

12

THE DECADE OF THE 1820s would be a period in which Marshall would greatly expand the commerce power of the federal Union. He did this by restricting the power of states over contracts, as he had done in *Fletcher v. Peck* and in the *Dartmouth College* case, and then by restricting the power of states over commerce in the case of *Gibbons v. Ogden.* He moved cautiously, however, staking out great power circumspectly. In Felix Frankfurter's phrase, "Marshall's boldness was wary."[1]

The Constitution appears to give the power to regulate commerce to the federal Union. The meaning of that grant may now appear vague, but it probably did not to John Marshall and the other men of his time. He had understood that one purpose of the Constitution was to give the Americans some strength in their commercial dealings with other nations. In his biography of George Washington he had written that those who supported the federal Constitution realized "that so long as the American trade remained subject to the legislation of thirteen distinct sovereignties, no system could be adopted and rendered permanent, which might impose such restraints or burdens on British ships or merchants, as would make it the interest of that nation to relax any of those principles on which its maritime grandeur is supposed, in a great measure, to be founded." Marshall continued that the separate states under the Articles of Confederation, "acting without concert, would be no match for Britain in a war of commercial regulation. . . ."[2]

The point was important to the young United States. The small farmers who were beginning to populate the expanding United States, and of whom Thomas Jefferson was so fond, were producing more than they could consume. They wanted to sell their surpluses. They needed markets. They needed to know they could go to the marketplace with assurance that import and export taxes would not be greater or less at another American port, and that if the British abused them, the United States government could seek redress, something which a state government did not have the stature for. Every man is a merchant, no matter how limited the business he does. The early Americans were particularly cognizant of that fact; few of them had been able to avoid the consequences of the English mercantile system before the Revolution, or the pressures of the English trade monolith and the threat to close the Mississippi in the years following the Revolution. These Americans knew, as John Marshall knew, what had been the intention of the Commerce Clause. In his decisions in *Fletcher v. Peck* and the *Dartmouth College* case Marshall's challenge had been to enunciate that intention in such a manner that later generations would understand it and appreciate its value. He would continue to meet this challenge in *Gibbons v. Ogden*, and in that confrontation he would meet it perhaps more effectively than he had in the previous two cases.

Almost from the first day of the first Congress under the new Constitution Americans had been confused over the specifics in the relationship between the states and the Union as far as navigation was concerned. Back in 1789, for example, Sam Adams had written to Elbridge Gerry a worried note, "hastily" venturing an opinion on whether the federal government could erect a lighthouse on property owned by Massachusetts "for its own use, and at its own expense." The state, Adams insisted to his friend, had not relinquished its sovereignty over the piece of land in question, and therefore retained such sovereignty.[3]

As the years passed, the questions became more serious than where the federal government could locate a lighthouse. If a state could control the export taxes charged at its ports, then a single state could control vast territories of the United States. New Orleans, for example, was an important outlet for the products of the western farmers in the first half of the nineteenth century. If the government of Louisiana could control the duties charged there, then it could charge duties high enough to discourage an expansion of American trade. That kind of situation could not be allowed by the federal government; the Americans had fought the Revolution to eliminate it.

The origins of the *Gibbons* case go back to the end of the eighteenth century when the New York State legislature gave an exclusive right to Robert R. Livingston to run steamboats on state waters. There seemed no difficulty with this grant, as the understanding seemed to be that a state had absolute control over waters within its own borders. The issue stayed dormant until 1812 when the New York courts had to determine a challenge to the legislature's act. The state courts upheld the state legislature, and a commercial war began as other states began to confer monopolies also. What was happening was that a ship carrying goods from New Jersey could not go into a New York port. What the Constitution had tried to eliminate, the river monopolies were promoting—the fracturing of the United States into separate entities.

Through an involved series of business dealings, state actions, and personal disputes, two partners, Thomas Gibbons and Aaron Ogden, split up and Gibbons challenged what was Ogden's apparently exclusive right on a New York steamship run. In the New York courts the question was raised whether Congress, in licensing ships of a certain size, had authorized these ships to trade between ports of different states. If Congress had done so, then the monopolies granted by New York and other states could not be upheld. The New York court said that Congress had done no such thing, and that a state retained the right to grant monopolies over its internal waters. The case then went to the Supreme Court, and the issue squarely was one of the power of Congress to regulate commerce on the nation's waterways.

In 1824, when the case was argued before the Court, a New York newspaperman described the sessions. The Court began at eleven o'clock in the morning and the Justices entered, sometimes together, and sometimes one at a time, through a lobby behind the

bench. They then assumed their robes in full view of the spectators "in the same manner as a farmer puts on his frock, or the
sportsman his hunting shirt." Each Justice had an attendant to
assist him in putting on his black gown, "as a servant assists a
lady in resuming her hat and mantle in an antechamber." The
newspaperman thought "changes of apparel should certainly take
place behind the scene."

The court sat from eleven until four in the afternoon, and
was not only one of the most dignified tribunals in the world but
also "one of the most patient." The newspaperman reported that
the arguing lawyers would be heard for hours without being interrupted—"If a man talks nonsense, he is soon graduated and
passes for what he is worth. If he talks to the point, he will be
properly measured, and his talents, discrimination and industry
reflected in the opinion of the Court." The Justices said nothing
but had no hesitation in showing their boredom or detestation of
the lawyer's ramblings.

Chief Justice Marshall was "a large, thick-set, athletic man,
with a grave, substantial complexion, and with no prominent
features, his hair is of an iron gray, cut short before and tied in a
club behind." The newspaperman thought that Marshall's appearance indicated him "to be what he is, in fact, a solid and substantial man, without an extraordinary share of genius, taste or
elegance." But then John Marshall had been underrated all his
life.

Bushrod Washington, who sat at Marshall's right, had "a
sallow countenance, not very strongly marked, but deeply fur-
rowed by the hand of time and bearing the marks of infirm
health. He wears his dark, unfrosted hair, long and combed back
from his forehead."

Next to Bushrod Washington sat Thomas Todd of Kentucky. Todd was "a dark complexioned, good-looking, substantial
man." Little else could be said about him regarding his years on
the bench. Next the newspaperman described Joseph Story, who
did not look as if he were the youngest man on the bench, "by
reason of his baldness and his glasses . . . below middle-size, of
light, airy form, rapid and sprightly in his motions, and polished
and courtly in his manners; his countenance indicates genius,
affability, versatility of thought, and almost anything but the patient research of the scholar and the gravity and wisdom of the
Judge." Yet Story was known to be a "laborious, indefatigable,
not to say, plodding student, and to be among the first on the
Bench for his legal attainments, his literary acquirements, and
general knowledge."

William Johnson sat at Marshall's left—"large, athletic,

well built man of sixty or upwards, with a full, ruddy and fair countenance, with thin white hair, and partially bald." And Gabriel Duvall, reported the newsman, was "a patriarch in appearance with long, thin, and snowy locks, tall and spare, with a thin visage and prominent features."⁴*

Arguing before the Supreme Court again was Daniel Webster. He had made his fame with the passion of his presentment in the *Dartmouth* case, and he would build upon that fame with his arguments in cases like *Gibbons*, to cement his reputation as the greatest lawyer who ever appeared before the Supreme Court. He knew he had a difficult time ahead of him. The concept of states establishing monopolies for their waters was now twenty-five years old. He acknowledged his problem to the Court as he opened his presentation. "It is admitted," he began, "that there is a very respectable weight of authority in favor of the decision which is sought to be reversed. The laws in question, I am aware, have been deliberately re-enacted by the legislature of New York; and they have also received the sanction, at different times, of all her judicial tribunals, than which there are few, if any, in the country, more justly entitled to respect and deference." It was incumbent upon him, he said, to "make out a clear case; and unless we do so, we cannot hope for a reversal." Often those kinds of remarks are obligatory protestations of modesty and humility, but Webster sounded as though he were more sincere than the usual apologist. Particularly so because he then proceeded to lecture the Court on its role, something lawyers do only when they feel desperate.

"It should be remembered, however," he said, "that the whole of this branch of power, as exercised by this court, was a power of revisions. The question must be decided by the state courts, and decided in a particular manner, before it could be brought here at all. Such decisions alone gave the court jurisdiction; and therefore, while they are to be respected as judgments of the learned judges, they are yet in the condition of all decisions from which the law allows an appeal."

In three paragraphs Webster then summed up the problem of the state laws as they then existed, and also the tragedy for a young nation developing its commerce:

> By the law of New York, no one can navigate the bay
> of New York, the North River, the Sound, the lakes, or
> any of the waters of that state, by steam vessels, without

---

* The seventh member of the Supreme Court in the 1824 term was Smith Thompson, who did not take his seat until February 10, and so did not participate in the *Gibbons v. Ogden* case.

a license from the grantees of New York, under penalty of forfeiture of the vessel.

By the law of the neighboring state of Connecticut, no one can enter her waters with a steam vessel having such license.

By the law of New Jersey, if any citizen of that state shall be restrained, under the New York law, from using steamboats between the ancient shores of New Jersey and New York, he shall be entitled to an action for damages, in New Jersey, with treble costs against the party who thus restrains or impedes him under the law of New York. The act of New Jersey is called an act of retortion against the illegal and oppressive legislation of New York; and seems to be defended on those grounds of public law which justify reprisals between independent states.

Listening to Webster's list of commercial antagonisms between the states, it would be difficult to dispute him that "It would hardly be contended that all these acts were consistent with the laws and constitution of the United States." If the United States government had no power to do something about such a situation, he contended, then "the powers of the government were essentially deficient in a most important and interesting particular."

Webster then made the bold assertion that the "power of Congress to regulate commerce is complete and entire, and, to a certain extent, necessarily exclusive; that the state acts in question are regulations of commerce. . . ." He said he was making that assertion "guardedly" and that he did not mean to imply that a state was forbidden to make any law affecting commerce but rather that "such power as has been exercised in this case does not remain with the States."

He acknowledged that the federal power over such a situation may not be spelled out specifically enough for everyone's satisfaction, but insisted that "It is in vain to look for a precise and exact definition of the powers of Congress on several subjects. The Constitution does not undertake the task of making such exact definitions." His next comments are similar to those in Marshall's biography of Washington explaining the reasons behind the adoption of the Constitution. "The sole purpose for which the delegates assembled at Annapolis was to devise means for the uniform regulation of trade," he said. "They found no means but in a general government; and they recommended a convention to accomplish that purpose." Whatever other benefits the government may offer to its citizens, Webster claimed, "it will always be true, as matter of historical fact, that it had its immediate origin in the necessities, by removing their causes, and by establishing a uniform and steady system."

"We do not find, in the history of the formation and adoption of the constitution," he said, "that any man speaks of a general concurrent power, in the regulation of foreign and domestic trade, as still residing in the states. The very object intended, more than any other, was to take away such power. If it had not so provided, the constitution would not have been worth accepting."

Webster interpreted this to mean that the commercial powers were intended to be exclusively allotted to the federal government. "What is it that is to be regulated?" he asked, answering: "Not the commerce of the several states, respectively, but the commerce of the United States." He dwelt on the concept of concurrent powers, that New York could enact monopolies if Congress had failed to legislate in the field, but he would not accept the concept. If there was a concurrent power, he said, "where is the limit, or who shall fix a boundary for the exercise of the power of the states?" He asked: "Can a state grant a monopoly of trade? Can New York shut her ports to all but her own citizens? Can she refuse admission to ships of particular nations? The argument on the other side is, and must be, that she might do all these things, until Congress should revoke her enactments. And this is called concurrent legislation. What confusion such notions lead to, is obvious enough."

Daniel Webster then boldly challenged the assertion John Marshall had made in 1818 and 1819, in the *Bevans* and *Sturges* decisions, that Congress must actually act, that possession of authority is not sufficient to foreclose the states from action. "This doctrine of a general concurrent power in the states is insidious and dangerous," he said. "If it be admitted, no one can say where it will stop. The states may legislate, it is said, wherever Congress had not made a plenary exercise of its power. But who is to judge whether Congress has made this plenary exercise of power? Congress has acted on this power; it has done all that it deemed wise; and are the states now to do whatever Congress has left undone?" His point was that "Congress makes such rules as, in its judgment, the case requires; and those rules, whatever they are, constitute the system."

John Marshall had said that having the power was not the same as using it. Daniel Webster had just told him that no one could judge whether Congress used that power by not making laws as well as by making them. The decision was that of Congress. If Congress did indeed have an exclusive power, it had that power without any ifs, ands, or buts.

The evils to which the confusion of concurrent powers could lead was a dreadful vision for Daniel Webster. Behind the rhetoric was a picture of the United States at war with itself. In this next section Webster called not only for free commerce between the states but also for the visage of the United States as one country. Men like Thomas Jefferson and Patrick Henry had meant Virginia when they spoke of their country. When Daniel Webster argued the case of *Gibbons v. Ogden* the United States was thirty-seven years old, and he was calling on its people to think not of their separate states but of their nation as their country.

He pointed out that the monopoly given by New York State in this steamboat case was given as an act of sovereign political power, and if New York could exercise such power in this instance it could exercise similar power in other instances. He continued:

> If the state may grant this monopoly, it may also grant another for other descriptions of vessels; for instance, for all sloops.
>
> If it can grant these exclusive privileges to a few, it may grant them to many; that is, it may grant them to all its own citizens, to the exclusion of everybody else.
>
> But the waters of New York are no more the subject of exclusive grants by that state, than the waters of other states are subjects of such grants by those other states. Virginia may well exercise, over the entrance of the Chesapeake, all the power that New York can exercise over the bay of New York, and the waters on the shore. The Chesapeake, therefore, upon the principle of these laws, may be the subject of state monopoly; and so may the bay of Massachusetts. But this is not all. It requires no greater power to grant a monopoly of trade, than a monopoly of navigation. Of course, New York, if these acts can be maintained, may give an exclusive right of entry of vessels into her ports. And the other states may do the same. These are not extreme cases. We have only to suppose that other states should do what New York has already done, and that the power should be carried to its full extent.[5]

The lawyers for New York were Thomas J. Oakley and Thomas Addis Emmet. Oakley argued that two kinds of powers had been given to the federal government, exclusive and concurrent. The exclusive powers were of two kinds: those with constitutional origins and those with "an effect and operation" beyond the limits of a state. Powers not exclusive were concurrent. Citing the Marshall decision in *Sturges v. Crowninshield*, he insisted that "It is perfectly settled that an affirmative grant of power to the United States does not, of itself, devest the states of a like power. The authorities cited settle this question, and it is no longer open for discussion in this Court." He then said, as Marshall had said in the *Bevans* and *Sturges* decisions, that a state could legislate when concurrent powers are involved if it did not come into "any actual collision in practice" with the federal government. This, he argued, was the situation with the steamboat monopolies.

The case for New York was summed up by Emmet when, at the close of his argument, he insisted that "The state of New York, from motives not examinable here, made a contract, which is the foundation of our right; it could only do so by a law. The state had a right to contract, and, so far, it stands on the same footing as if one individual contracted, for a valuable consideration, with another. . . . The waters of the state were the domain and property of the state, subject only to the commercial regulations of Congress." Emmet pleaded: "Why should not the contract of a state, in regard to its domain and property, be as sacred as that of an individual? . . . Who is to judge of that but the state legislatures?"[6]

Emmet, however, had allowed himself to be finessed in the very framework he had erected for the defense—that of a contract. If the act of a state was indeed a contractual arrangement, then certainly the contract that New York had made with the other states when it became part of the federal Union and accepted the Constitution as the supreme law of the land superseded any contracts New York might then make with anyone else. Emmet had begun his case, however, with an approach similar to one that John Marshall had used almost thirty years earlier— that the law being challenged in the case predated the Constitution. In *Ware v. Hylton* Marshall had argued that the Virginia laws sequestering the British debts had been made while Virginia was independent of the federal Union and, therefore, were not nullified by the treaty between the United States and England calling for the repayment of those debts. In the *Gibbons* case Emmet pointed out that the first grant of exclusive rights had been made "On the 19th of March, 1787, a short time before the meeting of the Federal convention. . . ."[7] But the Supreme Court had not allowed John Marshall's argument in 1796, and it gave no more respect to Emmet's in 1824.

The final argument was by William Wirt, appearing with Webster for Gibbons against New York. Wirt, then Attorney General of the United States, appeared as a private lawyer. According to a contemporary account, his "lucid and luminous arguments" astonished the Justices of the Supreme Court "and made old Judge Marshall—then 69—lay down his pen, drop back in his chair, turn his coat cuffs, and stare at the speaker in amazement at his powers."[8] Whether Wirt's arguments were all that impressive is a matter of conjecture, but his closing appeal to the Court certainly cut through to the point of the arguments, and to the point of the Constitution and the concept of its supremacy. He said:

> . . . [I]f the state of things which has already commenced is to go on; if the spirit of hostility, which already exists in three of our states, is to catch by contagion, and spread among the rest, as, from the progress of the human passions, and the unavoidable conflict of interests it will too surely do, what are we to expect? Civil wars have often arisen from far inferior causes, and have desolated some of the fairest provinces of the earth. History is full of the afflicting narratives of such wars, from causes far inferior; and it will continue to be her mournful office to record them, till time shall be no more. It is a momentous decision which this Court is called on to make. Here are three states almost on the eve of war. It is the high province of this Court to interpose its benign and mediatorial influence. The framers of our admirable constitution would have deserved the wreath of immortality which they have acquired, had they done nothing else than to establish this guardian tribunal, to harmonize the jarring elements in our system. But, sir, if you do not interpose your friendly hand, and extirpate the seeds of anarchy which New York has sown, you will have civil war. The war of legislation, which has already commenced, will, according to its usual course, become a war of blows.

Was Wirt exaggerating the potential of the situation? Perhaps. But perhaps not. New York, New Jersey, and Connecticut were at odds with one another, the animosities growing more and more raw. It was a violent time, not long removed from the frontier culture in which men often solved their problems with guns. And if those three states could succeed in exercising a monopoly, then certainly other states would also. "If you do not interpose your friendly hand," Wirt had warned the Supreme Court, ". . . you will have civil war." That he was exaggerating is a claim no one could make with confidence. He continued:

> Your country will be shaken with civil strife. Your republican institutions will perish in the conflict. Your constitution will fall. The last hope of nations will be gone. And what will be the effect upon the rest of the world? Look

abroad at the scenes which are now passing on the globe, and judge of that effect. The friends of free government throughout the earth, who have been heretofore animated by our example, and have held it up before them as their polar star, to guide them through the stormy seas of revolution, will witness our fall with dismay and despair. The arm that is everywhere lifted in the cause of liberty, will drop, unnerved, by the warrior's side. Despotism will have its day of triumph, and will accomplish the purpose at which it too certainly aims. It will cover the earth with the mantle of mourning.[9]

Again William Wirt had underscored an essential point. The United States had to succeed not only for itself but for those abroad who looked upon it as proof that man can establish a democratic government, that a government freely arrived at can succeed, and that force is not the only means by which men can be ruled.

William Wirt had been the last lawyer to speak before the Supreme Court. The problem and the challenge were now that Court's.

When John Marshall handed down the decision he spoke for a unanimous Court (Justice Johnson filed a concurring opinion but gave the Court's decision "my entire approbation").[10] The first point Marshall had to deal with was that the challenge before the Supreme Court was to a decision made by a state court. The Supreme Court was still a young enough institution to be wary of taking on another court in open battle, particularly a prestigious one like New York's. So Marshall began as he usually did in such cases, by acknowledging the temerity of what the Court was about to do but claiming that he and the other Justices had no choice. "The state of New York maintains the constitutionality of these laws; and their legislature, their Council of Revision, and their judges, have repeatedly concurred in this opinion. It is supported by great names—by names which have all the titles to consideration that virtue, intelligence, and office, can bestow." This was a reference to Chancellor Kent, the most prestigious judge in New York and one of the most respected jurists in the United States. He had held in his ruling that New York had the right to grant a monopoly over its waters.

"No tribunal can approach the decision of this question without feeling a just and real respect for that opinion which is sustained by such authority," Marshall continued, "but it is the province of this Court, while it respects, not to bow to it implicitly; and the judges must exercise, in the examination of the subject, that understanding which Providence has bestowed upon them, with that independence which the people of the United States expect from this department of government." That should have been the first clue in the courtroom that day as to how the Supreme Court would decide. Whenever Marshall began with a statement that the Court must fulfill its obligations no matter what pressures were against it, he was about to over-rule—and not lightly, but with a smashing fist.

The fist struck quickly. The Constitution, he said, contained a list of enumerated powers "granted by the people to their government." The argument had been made that those powers "ought to be construed strictly." Marshall asked why they should be so construed. He could not find one sentence in the Constitution, he said, calling for such a construction. He pointed out that "In the last of the enumerated powers, that which grants, expressly, the means of carrying all others into execution, Congress is authorized 'to make all laws which shall be necessary and proper' for the purpose." If "necessary and proper" was the limitation referred to by New York State, Marshall insisted that it was a limitation "on the means which may be used" and not "to the powers which are conferred." Marshall then asked a question which is consistently raised in connection with the Supreme Court and its power to interpret the Constitution: "What do gentlemen mean by a strict construction?" His answer to that question is perhaps one of the best offered. He said:

> If they contend only against that enlarged construction which would extend words beyond their natural and obvious import, we might question the application of the term, but should not controvert the principle. If they contend for that narrow construction which, in support of some theory not to be found in the constitution, would deny to the government those powers which the words of the grant, as usually understood, import, and which are consistent with the general views and objects of the instrument; for that narrow construction, which would cripple the government and render it unequal to the objects for which it is declared to be instituted, and to which the powers given, as fairly understood, render it competent; then we cannot perceive the propriety of this strict construction, nor adopt it as the rule by which the constitution is to be expounded.

Marshall, of course, was repeating the point he had made five years earlier in the *McCulloch v. Maryland* opinion. If the end was legitimate and the means used to achieve that end were within the scope of the Constitution, he had said in 1819, then there was nothing the Supreme Court would do to block the action.

The next question he addressed was whether a constitutional issue was involved. The Constitution says that "Congress shall have power to regulate commerce with foreign nations, and among the several states, and with the Indian tribes." Did this include navigation on the waterways? Answering that question, Marshall said, meant defining the word "commerce." He had no difficulty in assuming that assignment because the Constitution enumerated powers but did not define them, and so "to ascertain the extent of the power it becomes necessary to settle the meaning of the word." The lawyers for Ogden had defined the word narrowly, limiting it "to traffic, to buying and selling, or the interchange of commodities, and do not admit that it comprehends navigation." Marshall said such a definition "would restrict a general term, applicable to many objects, to one of its significations." He acknowledged that commerce was traffic, but insisted that it was more than that also. "It is intercourse," he said. "It describes the commercial intercourse between nations, and parts of nations, in all its branches, and is regulating by prescribing rules for carrying on that intercourse." Marshall continued that the mind "can scarcely conceive" a system for regulating commerce that did not include navigation laws and in which commerce would be limited to actions in buying and selling.

This part of the decision—the inclusion of navigation in the congressional powers over commerce—has been attributed to Marshall's lifting a gem from William Wirt's presentation.[11] Marshall himself indicated in the decision he was reading that the definition of commerce came from his entire background and not from one lawyer's arguments: ". . . This power [over navigation] has been exercised from the commencement of the government, has been exercised with the consent of all, and has been understood by all to be a commercial regulation." He insisted that the authors of the Constitution must have so understood it. "The power over commerce, including navigation, was one of the primary objects for which the people of America adopted their government," he said, "and must have been contemplated in forming it." Marshall reasoned that the convention which produced the Constitution "must have used the word [commerce] in that sense; because all have understood it in that sense, and the attempt to restrict it comes too late."

After establishing that commerce included navigation, Marshall went on to affirm that the federal government has authority over areas in which more than one state is involved. "The subject to which the power is next applied, is to commerce 'among

the several states,'" he said. "The word 'among' means inter-
mingled with. . . . Commerce among the states cannot stop at the
external boundary line of each state, but may be introduced into
the interior."

He quickly sought to make clear that his definition did not
include all commerce. "It is not intended to say that these words
comprehend that commerce which is completely internal, which
is carried on between man and man in a state, or between different parts of the same state, and which does not extend to or affect
other states," he said, adding: "Such a power would be inconvenient, and is certainly unnecessary." He continued: "Comprehensive as the word 'among' is, it may very properly be restricted to
that commerce which concerns more states than one." He was
saying that the federal powers apply not only to the external relations of the states but also "to those internal concerns which
affect the states generally." Later decisions of the Supreme
Court were to interpret that doctrine in an expansionist manner,
bringing under the federal government's control almost anything
that could be construed as commerce. Marshall's intent here was
not to expand federal powers but to limit state powers; he simply
did not believe that the United States could exist if each state
possessed the powers New York was claiming for itself, and he
could not believe that the Constitution intended New York to
have such powers.

And if Congress had the power to regulate commerce, that
power, "like all others vested in Congress, is complete in itself,
may be exercised to its utmost extent, and acknowledges no
limitations, other than are prescribed in the constitution." What
he had just done, in the words of Felix Frankfurter, was to pronounce "an audacious doctrine."[12] The effect of his audacity was
that the federal Congress had exclusive rights over navigable
waters. This had been the point argued by Webster and was the
point claimed by Oakley to have been previously settled. But
Marshall had rejected Oakley's argument and accepted Webster's, that New York had no right to grant such a monopoly
even if there had been no federal laws. The power of Congress is
complete "and acknowledges no limitations." He repeated the
point for emphasis, saying that "when a state proceeds to regulate
commerce with foreign nations, or among the several states, it is
exercising the very power that is granted to Congress, and is
doing the very thing which Congress is authorized to do." This,
John Marshall said, the Constitution does not permit.

He still had to confront the problem that he seemed to be
overruling himself. He did this by examining certain powers and
explaining how they could work concurrently. A state could

enact laws effecting commerce if those laws were part of the state's police and health powers. It could enact tax laws for the purposes of state government, but could not interfere with taxes for federal purposes. And a state could not enact a law that interfered with commerce between the states, as had happened in the New York case. That power remained with Congress, and Congress "may, of consequence, pass the jurisdictional line of New York."

Marshall did not do a very good job of explaining his apparent reversal. If he had applied his *Bevans* and *Sturges* criteria to the 1824 case, then he would have been compelled to have found for New York because the New York law was not in collision with a federal law. Why then the reversal? Marshall in 1818 and 1819 may have been stepping lightly, testing the legal waters to determine whether the doctrine of federal supremacy would take hold. Once he saw that it did, he may have felt obliged to take a stronger step. Perhaps he was influenced by his fellow Justices. Prior to the *Gibbons* case William Johnson, sitting on the Circuit Court, had held that the federal commerce power was "paramount and exclusive," and its words "sweep away the whole subject, and leave nothing for the states to act upon."[13] Marshall in his *Gibbons* decision could have been greatly influenced by the first man Jefferson appointed to the Court. Perhaps also Marshall had come to realize the dangers of permitting the states to act unless specifically blocked from doing so by federal legislation; the *Gibbons* case had pointed out that danger.

Marshall himself acknowledged that what he had just said was dicta, unnecessary to support the final conclusion: ". . . The court will enter upon the inquiry, whether the laws of New York, as expounded by the highest tribunal of that state, have, in their application to this case, come into collision with an act of Congress, and deprived a citizen of a right to which that act entitles him. Should this collision exist, it will be immaterial whether those laws were passed in virtue of a concurrent power . . . or in virtue of a power to regulate their domestic trade and police. In one case and the other, the acts of New York must yield to the law of Congress. . . ."

A modern-day judge would not be prone to utilize dicta as much as Marshall did, and certainly not to the point of enunciating such an audacious doctrine as the exclusive rights of the federal Congress. But John Marshall lived at a time when there were no guidelines, no precedents, no general understanding of how the principles embodied in the Constitution should be applied. He saw his role as educating not only the American public but also the legal community to the correctness of the supremacy of the federal Union. He saw it as a means of helping to build a nation. His dicta were not law, and could and would be challenged. But the value of his arguments is that they were just that, arguments which provoked and challenged and caused men to delve into their understanding of how government could work and what the intentions of the United States were. The wisdom of his arguments is such that they generally have come to be widely adopted not as dicta but as law.

There was not much left to the decision at that point. The New York monopoly did conflict with federal law and was, therefore, struck down. The practical effect of the decision was to assure that the United States turned into a giant prosperous common market. But the long-range political effect was the continued growth of the United States Constitution as a spacious document, sufficiently powerful to guide the American people in their quest for a nation under law. The last two paragraphs of the Court's decision read by Marshall are a reaffirmation of that point. He said:

> The court is aware that, in stating the train of reasoning by which we have been conducted to this result, much time has been consumed in the attempt to demonstrate propositions which may have been thought axioms. It is felt that the tediousness inseparable from the endeavor to prove that which is already clear, is imputable to a considerable part of this opinion. But it was unavoidable. The conclusion to which we have come, depends on a chain of principles which it was necessary to preserve unbroken; and, although some of them were thought nearly self-evident, the magnitude of the question, the weight of character belonging to those from whose judgment we dissent, and the argument at the bar, demanded that we should assume nothing.
>
> Powerful and ingenious minds, taking, as postulates, that the powers expressly granted to the government of the Union are to be contracted, by construction, into the narrowest possible compass, and that the original powers of the states are retained, if any possible construction will retain them, may, by a course of well digested, but refined and metaphysical reasoning, founded on these premises, explain away the constitution of our country, and leave it a magnificent structure indeed, to look at, but totally unfit for use. They may so entangle and perplex the understanding, as to obscure principles which were before thought quite plain, and induce doubts where, if the mind were to pursue its own course, none would be perceived.

In such a case, it is peculiarly necessary to recur to safe and fundamental principles to sustain those principles, and, when sustained, to make them the tests of the arguments to be examined.[14]

Marshall's decision came under criticism from those who saw the United States as a league of nations, or preferred it so, rather than as a Union. Marshall was also criticized for relying too much on Daniel Webster's arguments (and Webster boasted that Marshall had indeed relied on his arguments), and for his dicta. "A judicial opinion should decide nothing and embrace nothing that is not before the court," said John Randolph about the *Gibbons* decision. If Marshall had only knocked down the New York monopoly, said Randolph, "I should have been satisfied." But since Marshall's decision in the case of *Cohens v. Virginia*, said Randolph, "I am done with the supreme court." From Randolph's point of view, he was well to be done with that Court. Under John Marshall's leadership it was forcing the United States to acknowledge that it was one nation, to live up to the goal it had set for itself. John Randolph had been a Virginian; if he had had children, they would have grown up as Americans.[15]

The bitterness was reflected in more than words. During the 1820s there were numerous attempts to curb the independence of the Supreme Court in Congress. Bills were sponsored to increase the size of the Court—to "pack" it, to use the phrase descriptive of a much later attempt—to require that more than a majority of the Court be necessary to determine certain cases, or that specific areas be withdrawn from the Court's jurisdiction. That none of them passed did not negate the seriousness with which they were offered and the seriousness with which they were feared at the time.

"We had the Supreme Court before us yesterday, rather unexpectedly," complained Daniel Webster in 1824, when he was a United States Senator from Massachusetts, "and a debate arose which lasted all day." Webster reported to Joseph Story that many of the Supreme Court's decisions were argued on the Senate floor and while "most of the gentlemen were very temperate and guarded, there were, however, some exceptions, especially Mr. Randolph, whose remarks were not a little extraordinary." But Webster believed that despite the opposition to the Court, a bill then before the Senate calling for the concurrence of five Justices (out of the seven then on the Court) "will not prevail."[16]

The attacks on the Court continued through the decade, always a source of alarm to the Justices. John Marshall did not speak of them too often. He now was in his seventies and had been the object of too much criticism in his long life to worry about any that might be forthcoming in his eighth decade. Also, he was basically a calm man. Occasionally a note of despair crept into a comment to a friend, but more often he retained his faith in his nation and its people.

Joseph Story, however, was different. He viewed with concern all attacks on the Court, even those he knew could not be taken seriously and which would not produce serious results. In 1831, for example, he wrote to his wife from Washington that Congress had before it a bill to repeal the twenty-fifth section of the Judiciary Act. Such an action would have blocked the Supreme Court from reviewing acts of the state courts and legislatures, Story reported. Story was certain the bill would not pass— "indeed, the expectation is that it will fall by a very large vote"— still, for him, the very fact that it was introduced "shows the spirit of the times." He also was concerned by a bill (although the House had decisively defeated it by a 115–62 vote) to restrict Supreme Court appointments to seven years.

Story saw the Supreme Court as a victim of scurrilous attacks by politicians and an unprincipled press. "You may, and probably do think my views in respect to the Union, and the fate of the Constitution too gloomy," he wrote to a friend, and conceded that "It may be so." He continued: "The great difficulty is to make the mass of the people see their true interests, there being so many political demagogues, and so many party presses, that are in league to deceive them. We have long been accustomed to think the press the great security of our liberty, and the great source of knowledge. But it seems to be forgotten that the same instrument which can preserve, may be employed to destroy . . . somehow it is a fact that, upon political questions, men are blind, and deaf, and dumb, when you attempt to disabuse them of their prejudices and mistakes."[17]

John Marshall, however, had a little more respect for the American people than that, a little more faith in the democratic process, and did not react as vehemently and as fearfully as did Story. Instead, Marshall continued to lead the Supreme Court in the constant affirmation of the federal Union in matters dealing with commerce and contracts. A case three years after *Gibbons v. Ogden* is one in point. It was called *Brown v. Maryland*[18] and the decision is almost a continuation of the theme Marshall began in *Gibbons v. Ogden*.

The state of Maryland had enacted a law requiring all importers to purchase a license for $50. The act was challenged on the basis that it violated the federal power to control commerce.

A point about the tax was that it was on the occupation of importers; that is, it was not a tax promulgated by the state in connection with its power to inspect or to maintain good health. It was, as a result, the kind of case John Marshall enjoyed dealing with.

"The cause," he said, "depends entirely on the question, whether the legislature of a state can constitutionally require the importer of foreign articles to take out a license from the state, before he shall be permitted to sell a bale or package so imported." He then went on to dispose of the problem of whether the license fee was on the importer rather than the one who actually brings the merchandise into the port. "There is no difference, in effect, between a power to prohibit the sale of an article and a power to prohibit its introduction into the country. The one would be a necessary consequence of the other. No goods would be imported if none could be sold," he said. Nor was he impressed because the license fee was a relatively small amount—"It is obvious that the same power which imposes a light duty can impose a very heavy one, one which amounts to a prohibition. Questions of power do not depend on the degree to which it may be exercised." The next section of this decision is an explanation of why the Supreme Court believes it must act in certain cases at the risk of taking extreme actions. Marshall said:

> If the tax may be levied in this form by a state, it may be levied to an extent which will defeat the revenue by impost, so far as it is drawn from importations into the particular state. We are told, that such wild and irrational abuse of power is not to be apprehended, and is not to be taken into view when discussing its existence. All power may be abused; and if the fear of its abuse is to constitute an argument against its existence, it might be urged against the existence of that which is universally acknowledged, and which is indispensable to the general safety. The states will never be so mad as to destroy their own commerce, or even to lessen it.
>
> We do not dissent from these general propositions. We do not suppose any state would act so unwisely. But we do not place the question on that ground.

He conceded that no state "would be so blind" as to place taxes, duties, or license fees that would result in damaging that particular state's own trade. "Yet the framers of our constitution have thought this a power which no state ought to exercise." The next sentence sums up the rationale for federalism. John Marshall said: "Conceding to the full extent which is required, that every state would, in its legislation on this subject, provide judiciously for its own interest, it cannot be conceded that each would respect the interest of others." He continued by outlining the possibility that "The great importing states would thus levy a tax on the non-importing states, which would not be less a tax because their interest would afford ample security against its ever being so heavy as to expel commerce from their ports." The result of this would be retaliation by other states. "For this, among other reasons," Marshall said, "the whole power of laying duties on imports was, with a single and slight exception, taken from the states." This was the statement of the exclusive powers of Congress which Marshall had made three years earlier in *Gibbons v. Ogden*, and here again it was made without there being a necessity for it. He could have struck down the licensing fee solely on the basis of its being an interference with the commerce of the United States. He spoke to this point in the decision, and in these words one hears not only the jurist but the historian, as well as the man whose personal experience encompasses the events of which he speaks. He said:

> The oppressed and degraded state of commerce previous to the adoption of the constitution can scarcely be forgotten. It was regulated by foreign nations with a single view to their own interests; and our disunited efforts to counteract their restrictions were rendered impotent by want of combination. Congress, indeed, possessed the power of making treaties; but the inability of the federal government to enforce them had become so apparent as to render that power in a great degree useless. Those who felt the injury arising from this state of things, and those who were capable of estimating the influence of commerce on the prosperity of nations, perceived the necessity of giving the control over this important subject to a single government. It may be doubted whether any of the evils proceeding from the feebleness of the federal government contributed more to that great revolution which introduced the present system, than the deep and general conviction that commerce ought to be regulated by Congress. It is not, therefore, matter of surprise, that the grant should be as extensive as the mischief, and should comprehend all foreign commerce and all commerce among the states. To construe the power so as to impair its efficacy, would tend to defeat an object, in the attainment of which the American public took, and justly took, that strong interest which arose from a full conviction of its necessity.

Marshall then described the relationship between the importer and the foreign producer of the goods as a contractual one which should not be interfered with by a state-imposed license fee. "What can be the use of the contract? what does the importer purchase, if he does not purchase the privilege to sell?" asked Marshall. How could the United States respond to a complaint from a foreign government that the government had sent its goods to an American importer who was blocked from selling them by a state law?

As for the state power to tax, Marshall said: "We admit this power to be sacred; but cannot admit that it may be used so as to obstruct the free course of a power given to Congress." That sentence embodies his constant message to the states. No matter how extensive their powers, they could not use them to thwart the Union. When state and federal powers came into conflict, he continued, "that which is not supreme must yield to that which is supreme."

The cases in this period read, one after the other, as challenges to the doctrine of federal supremacy and the Marshall decisions read as affirmations of it. John Marshall was building power into and for a strong national government, and he would not be deterred. Another example is *Osborn v. Bank of the United States*.[19]

The history of that specific case began in 1819, but the origins of the Marshall opinion go back to the 1790s. The Supreme Court in 1793 agreed to hear a complaint by an individual citizen against a state other than that in which he resided.[20] The furor was great as the states saw themselves being haled before the Supreme Court at the whim of any individual outside their borders. The result was the Eleventh Amendment to the Constitution forbidding a suit against a state. This became an issue in the *Osborn* case because the state of Ohio claimed it could not be taken before the Supreme Court because of the Eleventh Amendment. The year 1819 had produced the *McCulloch v. Maryland* decision in which Marshall had stated that the federal government's power was as broad as it needed to be and as it legally could be. A challenge to this doctrine quickly developed in Ohio where there was a large amount of sentiment against the United States Bank. The people of that state had been hit badly by a depression and considered the bank with its emphasis on steady interest rates and noninflationary money one of their chief enemies. The state therefore enacted a law demanding a $50,000 tax on employees of the federal bank. The state auditor, a man named Osborn, then seized $100,000 of the bank's money. When the bank obtained a Circuit Court order demanding the return of the money, the Ohio officials refused to comply. The bank then seized the money and the state officials were jailed. They appealed to the Supreme Court against the bank. The case was argued in 1824. For Marshall there were two important points raised. Could a federal court issue an order for the return of the money, or did the request first have to go through a state court? And, second, did the Eleventh Amendment forbid an action against a state, the Circuit Court's action against the state official in this particular instance?

There could be little doubt how the first point would be decided. The state had argued that the federal courts had only appellate jurisdiction, but Marshall could not accept that. He conceded that the Constitution "enumerates" cases in which the federal judiciary has appellate and original jurisdiction "but does not insinuate that in any such case the power cannot be exercised in its original form by Courts of original jurisdiction." The Constitution did not direct, he declared, that cases "depending on the character of the cause" must first be brought in state courts— "tribunals over which the government of the Union has no adequate control and which may be closed to any claim asserted under a law of the United States." That is what Virginia had attempted to do in the case of *Cohens v. Virginia:* block an appeal to the federal courts from the state's highest courts by refusing to allow the dispute to go to the state's highest court. Marshall had not permitted it then, and would not permit it in the *Osborn* case.

As to what "character of the cause" gave the federal courts jurisdiction, Marshall answered "that when a question, to which the judicial power of the Union is extended by the constitution, forms an ingredient of the original cause, it is in the power of Congress to give the Circuit Courts jurisdiction of that cause, although other questions of fact or law may be involved in it." One federal element in a suit, he was saying, controls the location of the suit—placing it in federal courts. That was a neat extension of federal authority which was largely overlooked.

The second question, whether the Eleventh Amendment had exempted the state of Ohio from a direct challenge before the federal judiciary, was a more serious challenge. The Amendment was another in the lengthening history of the dispute between the federal government and the states, between the notion of a Union and that of a confederacy. The Union obviously brought strengths to the Americans, in their trade, in their defense, in their geographical expansion. But it also brought obligations, primarily in the form of the surrender of certain economic rights; the cases Marshall and the Court were dealing with in his third decade as Chief Justice were the result of states objecting to the surrender of those economic rights—to tax imports and banks, to grant monopolies, to determine bankruptcy laws. If the Eleventh Amendment were allowed to stand broadly interpreted, then the concept of a strong Union would have been placed in jeopardy. In this particular case, if the Eleventh Amendment had been upheld, then a federal agency—the United States Bank —would have been unable to seek redress in court against a state government which had not obeyed the law. John Marshall had to find a way out of that.

He did not hesitate to say that the state was indeed involved—"The interest of the State is direct and immediate." Although the Circuit Court's action directing the state's officers to repay the money and having them imprisoned was not specifically against the state but against individuals, the action "acts directly upon [Ohio] by restraining its officers," Marshall conceded. He then summed up the question as he saw it:

> The eleventh amendment of the constitution has exempted a State from the suits of citizens of other States, or aliens; and the very difficult question is to be decided, whether, in such a case, the Court may act upon the agents employed by the State, on the property in their hands.

The clue to the answer Marshall would offer is in the question he asked. Quite obviously what he intended to do was differentiate between an action brought against a state and one brought against an official of a state, an action brought against the property of a state and that against the property of a state held by an official of the state. If he could justify such a differentiation, then he would destroy the effectiveness of the Eleventh Amendment and further buttress the authority of the federal Union.

Marshall pointed out that to deny jurisdiction as Ohio wanted the Supreme Court to do would be to say that the agents of a state had the power, by themselves, to announce that a federal law is unconstitutional and "may arrest the execution of any law in the United States," and that if a state fined a federal official, it could do so "by a ministerial officer, without the sanction even of its own Courts." More important, perhaps, is that the federal official, "though he perceives the approaching danger, can obtain no protection from the judicial department of the government." The consequences? "The carrier of the mail, the collector of the revenue, the marshal of the district, the recruiting officer, may all be inhibited, under ruinous penalties. . . . Each member of the Union is capable, at its will, of attacking the nation, of arresting its progress at every step, of acting vigorously and effectually in the execution of its designs; while the nation stands naked, stripped of its defensive armor, and incapable of shielding its agent or executing its laws."

Marshall had cited extreme cases which could result from the Supreme Court denying jurisdiction, and he acknowledged that. But the fact that they were extreme did not make them improbable. What was at stake was the ability of a federal officer to fulfill his duties without being blocked by a state. The question was, as Marshall stated it, "whether the constitution of the United States has provided a tribunal which can peacefully and rightfully protect those who are employed in carrying into execution the laws of the Union from the attempts of a particular State to resist the execution of those laws. . . ."

Marshall went through examples of suits brought against state officials in which he said that actions would be upheld, and then announced grandly that "the principle seems too well established to require that more time should be devoted to it. It may, we think, be laid down as a rule which admits of no exception, that, in all cases where jurisdiction depends on the party, it is the party named in the record." This meant that the Eleventh Amendment was limited only to cases in which the state was the specified party rather than an official of the state as in the *Osborn* case. It was "proper" then for the federal Circuit Court to have issued the order against Osborn.

Again, as with so many Marshall decisions, the importance was not the result. Nobody anticipated that the Supreme Court would—or could—say that the Constitution allowed a state to thwart the lawfully constituted actions of the federal government. The importance, rather, was in its logical development, in the persuasiveness of its theme. At that time in the development of the United States a teacher was needed, someone capable of convincing the American people who lived then and who would live later that men must agree to be governed, that the system they had set up to do that governing must be a fair one, and that it must have the authority to do the job demanded of it. The alternative is anarchy.

In the 1819 *Sturges v. Crowninshield* decision the Supreme Court had held unconstitutional a New York State bankruptcy law. In the specific case before the Court the law had been passed after the debt was incurred and the debtor claimed that it negated his debt, but Marshall had held that the law was a disruption of a contractual arrangement and therefore in violation of the Constitution's prohibition against any interference with a contract. The issue arose again in 1821 with an almost identical set of facts except that the two parties were from the same state rather than from different states, as in the 1819 case. But Marshall said that made no difference: "The constitution of the United States was made for the whole people of the Union, and is equally binding upon all the courts and all the citizens."[21]

In both these cases the bankruptcy laws had been passed after the debts were incurred.* But what of a situation in which the law was passed before the debt was incurred? Then no one could say that the law interfered with a contract because contracts were made according to law—at least that was the rationale advanced. The issue was particularly important in the 1820s because the United States was emerging from a depression in which debtors were being actively pursued by their creditors under the *Sturges* doctrine. Businessmen were reluctant to enter into new agreements unless the states offered some promise of relief from future depressions. For this reason the states passed bankruptcy laws which had the effect of eliminating debts by bankrupt persons if the debt was entered into after the bankruptcy law was enacted.

The issue came before the Court in the 1827 case of *Ogden v. Saunders*.[22] The state laws were upheld in a 4–3 decision written by Associate Justice Robert Trimble. Marshall led the dissenters, Story and Gabriel Duvall. Trimble's point was that a bankruptcy law passed before a debt was entered into did not interfere with the Contract Clause. As a matter of law, his decision is the correct one. A contract is always subject to the procedures and regulations of the locality in which it is made unless they are unconstitutional. In this instance, the bankruptcy law would have been part of the contract.

The Marshall dissent is interesting for several reasons. One, it is the first major dissent he produced on a constitutional issue; in his previous twenty-six years on the Supreme Court his views on the Constitution had prevailed with his brethren. More important, the dissent is interesting for its view of John Marshall's sweeping "one people" concept of America and for his passionate devotion to the principle that men must adhere to their agreements or answer before a court of law.

Marshall conceded that there was a difference between

---

* When the *Sturges* case was decided, a case resolved with it, *M'Millan v. M'Neill*, 4 Wheaton 209, involved a bankruptcy law passed before the debt was incurred, but that point seems not to have been mentioned in the arguments or the decision.

retrospective laws, the issue in *Sturges v. Crowninshield*, and prospective laws, the issue in this *Ogden* case. The first he believed could never be justified but conceded that the second might be allowed. "Yet," he said, "when we consider the nature of our Union; that it is intended to make us, in a great measure, one people, as to commercial objects; that, so far as respects the intercommunication of individuals, the lines of separation between States are, in many respects, obliterated; it would not be a matter of surprise, if, on the delicate subject of contracts once formed, the interference of State legislation should be greatly abridged, or entirely forbidden." He argued that a law passed prior to the entering into of the contract for debt is as much an impairment of that contract as if it were passed at the time of the contract entry or after. "The original obligation," he declared, "whatever that may be, must be preserved by the constitution. Any law which lessens must impair it." He continued with a bleak vision of where the majority decision could lead:

> This idea admits of being pressed still farther. If one law enters into all subsequent contracts, so does every other law which relates to the subject. A legislative act, then, declaring that all contracts should be subject to legislative control, and should be discharged as the legislature might prescribe, would become a component part of every contract, and be one of its conditions. Thus one of the most important features in the constitution of the United States, one which the state of the times most urgently required, one on which the good and the wise reposed confidently for securing the prosperity and harmony of our citizens, would lie prostrate, and be construed into an inanimate, inoperative, unmeaning clause. . . .

He then turned to the sacredness of contracts, for him one of the most important concepts of the young country. The point he was discussing was whether the law could enter into the contractual arrangement. "A great mass of human transactions depends upon implied contracts; upon contracts which are not written, but which grow out of the acts of the parties. In such cases the parties are supposed to have made those stipulations, which, as honest, fair, and just men, they ought to have made. When the law assumes that they have made these stipulations, it does not vary their contract, or introduce new terms into it, but declares that certain acts, unexplained by compact, impose certain duties, and that the parties had stipulated for their performance." He emphasized that "The difference is obvious be-

tween this and the introduction of a new condition into a contract drawn out in writing, in which the parties have expressed
everything that is to be done by either."

Nor could he accept that a law dealing with prospective
bankruptcies could become part of the debt contract. "It is not,
we think, true that contracts are entered into in contemplation of
the insolvency of the obligor. They are framed with the expectation that they will be literally performed." He conceded that
insolvency could happen "but," he argued, it "is never expected."
If it did occur, Marshall insisted, "provision is made for it by taking security against it. . . . We have, then, no hesitation in saying that, however law may act upon contracts, it does not enter
into them and become a part of the agreement."

It had been claimed in the arguments that a contract is a
creation of society, and therefore is subject to control by the legislative acts of that society. This Marshall felt compelled to deny
as vehemently as he could:

> So far back as human research carries us, we find the
> judicial power, as a part of the executive, administering
> justice by the application of remedies to violated rights,
> or broken contracts. We find that power applying these
> remedies on the idea of a pre-existing obligation on every
> man to do what he has promised on consideration to do;
> that the breach of this obligation is an injury for which
> the injured party has a just claim to compensation, and
> that society ought to afford him a remedy for that injury.
> We find allusions to the mode of acquiring property, but
> we find no allusion, from the earliest time, to any sup-
> posed act of the governing power giving obligation to
> contracts. On the contrary, the proceedings respecting
> them, of which we know anything, evince the idea of a
> pre-existing intrinsic obligation which human law en-
> forces. If, on tracing the right to contract, and the obliga-
> tions created by contract, to their source, we find them to
> exist anterior to and independent of society, we may
> reasonably conclude that those original and pre-existing
> principles are, like many other natural rights, brought
> with man into society; and although they may be con-
> trolled are not given by human legislation.

Marshall has often been described, or criticized, as an
economic conservative, placing monetary and business considerations above human rights—as if the right to that which one is
entitled to by a voluntary agreement is less a right than that
which one is entitled to by the grace of being a free man. The
United States had won political freedom in the Revolution, estab-

lished representative democracy with the Constitution, and required the Supreme Court in John Marshall's time to buttress the individual's right to keep what he had earned. The other great question—which again the Supreme Court would have to resolve because the other branches of government refused to—was that of the equality of individuals. John Marshall's next paragraph in his *Ogden* dissent so demonstrated his deep concern for the individual, his respect for each man, his devotion to the concept of the equality of all men before the law, that it is difficult to believe that, if he had been Chief Justice in another time, his decisions would not have been majestic ones in the area of human rights. He said:

> In the rudest state of nature a man governs himself, and labors for his own purposes. That which he acquires is his own, at least while in his possession, and he may transfer it to another. This transfer passes his right to that other. Hence the right to barter. One man may have acquired more skins than are necessary for his protection from the cold; another more food than is necessary for his immediate use. They agree each to supply the wants of the other from his surplus. Is this contract without obligation? If one of them, having received and eaten the food he needed, refuses to deliver the skin, may not the other rightfully compel him to deliver it? Or two persons agree to unite their strength and skill to hunt together for their mutual advantage, engaging to divide the animal they shall master. Can one of them rightfully take the whole? or, should he attempt it, may not the other force him to a division? If the answer to these questions must affirm the duty of keeping faith between these parties, and the right to enforce it if violated, the answer admits the obligation of contracts, because upon that obligation depends the right to enforce them. Superior strength may give the power, but cannot give the right. The rightfulness of coercion must depend on the pre-existing obligation to do that for which compulsion is used. It is no objection to the principle that the injured party may be the weakest. In society, the wrong-doer may be too powerful for the law. He may deride its coercive power, yet his contracts are obligatory; and if society acquire the power of coercion, that power will be applied without previously enacting that his contract is obligatory....

The right of entering into a contract had not been surrendered by the individual when he became a part of society. He brought that right with him, and no one could take it away. What he had surrendered was his right to coerce the other party to live up to the arrangement. "This surrender imposes on government the correlative duty of furnishing a remedy." This, of course, was John Marshall's understanding of the law, that it provided a remedy for wrongs so that men did not have to resort to the sword. "To afford a remedy," he said, "is certainly the high duty of those who govern to those who are governed. A failure in the performance of this duty subjects the government to the just reproach of the world. . . ."

Marshall then underscored the obvious, but it was a point so obvious that it was and is often overlooked. "The constitution," he said, "has not undertaken to enforce its performance. That instrument treats the States with the respect which is due to intelligent beings, understanding their duties and willing to perform them; not as insane beings, who must be compelled to act for self-preservation. Its language is the language of restraint, not of coercion." This was a factor in the American experience frequently ignored. The system of government requires the American people to voluntarily submit to law. The American system is one in which there is respect for the people, an understanding that the people desire the law to succeed. A corollary to this is that when people do not adhere to the rule of law, they are risking the destruction of the system. It was for an understanding of this situation that Marshall seemed to be appealing when he spoke of the Constitution acting on those "understanding their duties and willing to perform them."

He closed his dissent with a section, similar to other sections in decisions he wrote about contracts and commerce, which drew on his experience as a young lawyer in the United States before the adoption of the Constitution. He said the states had used the "power of changing the relative situation of debtor and creditor, of interfering with contracts, a power which comes home to every man, touches the interest of all, and controls the conduct of every individual in those things which he supposes to be proper for his own exclusive management" so excessively as to "break in upon the ordinary intercourse of society, and destroy all confidence between man and man."

The situation had become so bad, impairing commerce, threatening the existence of credit, sapping "the morals of the people," and destroying "the sanctity of private faith," that the Constitutional Convention had created a perpetual instrument and the prohibition against trade infringements also was meant to be perpetual. "But," concluded Marshall's dissent, "if the construction for which the plaintiff's counsel contend be the true one, the constitution will have imposed a restriction, in language indicating perpetuity, which every State in the Union may elude at pleasure."

Marshall's lengthy dissent, while it did not become law and did not stop states from passing prospective bankruptcy laws, argued forcefully the powers of the federal government and served as a warning against future attempts to destroy or erode the supremacy of the federal government. If this was a defeat for John Marshall, he made it a brilliant one by the passion and logic of his dissent.

There were, of course, other decisions during this period. One, in the case of *Sexton v. Wheaton*,[23] underlines Marshall's respect for women and for matrimony. A man named Sexton charged that Joseph Wheaton and Wheaton's wife Sally had engaged in a fraud against him. The specific complaint against Sally was that she was aware that her husband had written a letter to Sexton giving "too flattering a picture of his circumstances." Was she obligated to convey this information to Sexton? Marshall could scarcely believe that anyone would suggest so. "All know and feel, the plaintiff as well as others," he said, "the sacredness of the connection between husband and wife. All know, that the sweetness of social intercourse, the harmony of society, the happiness of families, depend on that mutual partiality which they feel, or that delicate forbearance which they manifest towards each other." Marshall wanted to know whether any man would say "that Mrs. Wheaton, seeing this letter, remonstrating against it, and believing that it would be altered, before sending it, ought to have written to this stranger in New York, to inform him, that her husband had misrepresented his circumstances, and that credit ought not to be given to his letters?" Marshall answered his question with: "No man will say so."

In an 1830 case Marshall and the Supreme Court were told that they were playing a dangerous game in forcing a state to come before them.[24] Marshall and the Court ignored the threats and did not hesitate to knock down a decision by a Missouri court, and in the explanation lectured the lawyers involved and any others who would listen about the responsibility of the judiciary: "If the exercise of that jurisdiction which has been imposed upon us by the constitution and laws of the United States, shall be calculated to bring on those dangers which have been indicated: or if it shall be indispensable to the preservation of the union, and consequently of the independence and liberty of these states: these are considerations which address themselves to those departments which may with perfect propriety be influ-

[700]

enced by them. This department can listen only to the mandates of law; and can tread only that path which is marked out by duty."

The Supreme Court continued in its simple trappings. In 1824 a committee on public buildings reported that the meeting room for the Court needed some improvements, "indispensably necessary for the comfort and accommodation of the court," costing a total of $636.57. In 1830 an architect, Alexander J. Davis, said the faults with the chamber were caused "principally from the *absurd* fixtures." He recommended that the judges' bench should be placed on a platform "on the side furthest removed from the entrance door. [The Justices] would be more retired, as the audience should not pass behind them." In 1833 overtures were made to Marshall to do something about the chamber. He said he would be willing to have any alterations made which would suit the bar. "But," he continued, "I have no recollection of any act of Congress authorizing the Judges to alter the present arrangement, or making any appropriation for such alteration, and whatever charges may be brought against me, I have never been in favor of stretching my own powers."[25]

One visitor in the late 1820s was impressed by the Court's simplicity. The chamber he saw was oblong. The Justices sat at a long table, and the lawyers sat on cushioned chairs; the spectators sat on comfortable sofas. Opposite the Justices was a replica of the Goddess of Justice. The visitor, more familiar with English courts, looked for the wigs which were part of the trappings there, and even for the three-cornered hats that the British justices wore over their wigs. But here were only the black gowns. "I did not exactly know what the gowns were for," commented the spectator, "but I thought the Court looked very solemn." The marshal opened the proceedings with "Yea, yea, yea, yea! the Supreme Court of the United States is now in session. All persons having business before the court will be heard. God save the United States and this honorable court." The visitor was having his first glimpse of John Marshall, now in his seventies. This is his description:

> . . . There he sat before me, aged and venerable. He was above the common height; his features strongly marked; an eye that spoke the high order of his intellect. He wore a short cue, black coat, breeches buckled at the knee, long black silk stockings, and shoes with fine buckles. His manner on the bench was exceedingly kind and courteous to the bar. He heard with the greatest attention the arguments and authorities of counsel.

[701]

The Court began that day with an interesting scene. Counsel in one of the cases—Ogden—was not present, and Marshall asked the opposing counsel what to do. This lawyer asked for a dismissal in his favor. Marshall replied: "I am wholly incapable of taking advantage of the absence of counsel; let the case pass until Mr. Ogden arrives."[26]

Marshall continued to have strong personal relationships with his fellow Justices. Chief among these was Bushrod Washington. Though the letters between the two men do not include much indication of a warm comradeship (Washington was an ascetic and did not encourage overtures of intimacy), the two men had been friends since they were students together briefly at William and Mary. Washington's appointment to the Supreme Court had come about because Marshall had refused an appointment as Associate Justice, responding instead to the plea of Bushrod's uncle, George Washington, to run for Congress. They had worked together on the five-volume biography of George Washington. They were on the Supreme Court together for more than two decades. They were united in sorrow—each had an ailing wife—and united in their devotion to a strong federal Union. When Bushrod Washington died in 1829 John Marshall could truthfully say that "I had few friends whom I valued so highly . . . of whose loss I should regret more sincerely. . . . We have been most intimate friends for more than forty years, and never has our friendship sustained the slightest interruption."[27]

The relationship with Joseph Story was one of greater warmth. They wrote each other personal letters when the Court was not in session and sent each other gifts. "I had yesterday the pleasure of receiving your favor of the 9th. I thank you for your quintal of fish and shall try my possibles to observe your instructions in the cooking department. I hope to succeed; but be this as it may, I promise to feed on the fish with an appetite which would not disgrace a genuine descendant of the Pilgrims." And in 1826, a time when Marshall and Story were both lamenting the dangers of the approaching candidacy of Andrew Jackson, Marshall wrote Story that "I sent you by the General Jackson— because the name must render every part of its cargo valuable in your estimation—a small cask of hams which I hope you will find tolerably good in themselves. . . ."[28]

Joseph Story told one of the best known stories about Marshall, one that speaks not only of his affability but also of the comradeship among the Justices when they held their conferences in the boardinghouses. Josiah Quincy reported Story's account in this way:

The invitation to go to Washington with Judge Story did not imply any promise of attention after we arrived in that city, as he was careful to point out when I received it. "The fact is," said he, "I can do very little for you there, as we judges take no part in the society of the place. We dine once a year with the President and that is all. On other days we take our dinner together, and discuss at table the questions which are argued before us. We are great ascetics, and even deny ourselves wine, except in wet weather." Here the Judge paused, as if thinking that the act of mortification he had mentioned placed too severe a tax upon human credulity, and presently added: "What I say about the wine, sir, gives you our rule; but it does sometimes happen that the Chief Justice will say to me, when the cloth is removed, 'Brother Story, step to the window and see if it does look like rain.' And if I tell him that the sun is shining brightly, Judge Marshall will sometimes reply, 'All the better; for our jurisdiction extends over so large a territory that the doctrine of chances makes it certain that it must be raining somewhere.' You know that the Chief was brought up upon Federalism and Madeira, and he is not the man to outgrow his early prejudices."[29]

The makeup of the Court changed in the 1820s. Brockholst Livingston died in 1823. First rumors were that Nathaniel Macon of North Carolina, a strong advocate of states' rights, would be named his successor. "You alarm me respecting the successor of our much lamented friend," Marshall wrote to Story. "I too heard a rumor which I hoped was impossible." James Kent of New York also had been mentioned. The appointment, however, went to Smith Thompson. Thompson was Secretary of the Navy in Monroe's cabinet. A politically ambitious man, he only accepted the Court appointment after realizing he had no chance for the Republican presidential nomination in 1824. He did run for governor of New York in 1828, while retaining his Supreme Court seat. On the Court he would generally follow a policy of opposing Marshall.

In 1829 John McLean replaced Robert Trimble. Trimble had been appointed to the Court in 1826 when Thomas Todd died, then had died himself two years later. McLean was put on the Court by Andrew Jackson to get him out of the cabinet because he would not play the kind of politics the President was interested in. He was often mentioned as a potential presidential candidate, but scrupulously avoided partisan politics while on the bench. Perhaps his greatest contribution to American law was his dissent in the Dred Scott case in 1857. Bushrod Washington was replaced by Henry Baldwin, a former member of the House and earnest supporter of Andrew Jackson. Baldwin at first supported Marshall on the Court but gradually grew away from his federalism.[30]

The composition of the Court produced some changes in the manner of the Court's operation. For years the Justices had come to Washington *sans* family for the few weeks the Court was in session. They roomed together at a single lodging house, took their meals together, and discussed the cases before them. Their dining table was their conference room. But some of the new Justices did not care for this arrangement. "I regret exceedingly, that the Court separated without agreeing to go to Brown's, or to some other house together," lamented Story when one session was done. "I suppose, that we shall be for the future separated, as—I cannot but believe—has been the design of some of our brethren." Marshall struggled to keep the Court together. There is the picture of the Chief Justice of the United States, past his seventy-fifth birthday, scurrying to find lodgings for his brethren. When one lodging house operator moved from Washington, Marshall fretted: "What is to become of us? What arrangements can be made? . . . I will hold myself in readiness to join you any where." Finally, when arrangements had been made, Marshall's relief was plain. "Your arrangements for the ensuing winter will be entirely agreeable to me. . . . I am more easily pleased than any of my brethren and therefore beg you to remember that I shall be content with a less commodious chamber if some one of us must be a little incommoded. I ask only not to have a fire of Lehigh coal. Give me wood or Richmond coal."[31] Marshall was not being noble in offering the most comfortable room to an Associate Justice. He may have been Chief Justice, but he still was the plain man from Fauquier County who had a modest brick house in Richmond and could be excited by a dinner with the President or meeting a prominent author.

13

THE MAIN TOPIC in politically-conscious Richmond in the late 1820s was the prospect of a convention to write a new state constitution. The state had been dividing, between the large plantation owners in the tidewater region with their slave-oriented society, and the western farmers with their smaller land tracts and lesser dependence on slaves. John Marshall, of course, was a most interested spectator to the events and the planning: "The prevailing opinion seems to be that a convention with limited papers will be recommended," he predicted in 1827. The next year he offered a comprehensive analysis of the debate revolving around the convention planning. "There is so much diversity as well as contrariety of opinion that even those who mingle freely with the members and converse [often] with them can only conjecture what will be the result. . . ." Marshall then predicted that the results of the proposed convention would be determined by the manner in which the delegates were chosen. A committee had recommended that delegates be elected on the basis of congressional districting. This would give the slave-holding counties a greater proportion of representatives at the convention, as they were allowed congressional representation not only on the basis of their white population but also on the basis of three-fifths of their slave population. "The members from the West think very differently," Marshall commented. "In their opinion the free white population is the only legitimate basis of representation, and they consider themselves as having advanced to the extreme limit which can be marked by the spirit of conciliation when they offer to elect the members of the convention from [state] senatorial districts."[1]

The people in the west won, and the delegates were chosen from state senatorial districts rather than from the federal congressional districts; in the end, this was not as significant as had been anticipated. Virginia was not yet ready to take any action against slavery. An account by a convention delegate, Hugh Blair Grigsby, written some years after the event, described the delegate election process in this manner:

> Federal politics were laid aside; and public worth and eminent abilities were the only standards in the selection of its members. Actual residence was overlooked, and the unusual sight was presented of one district selecting its representatives from another and a distant one. What was rare still, the opinions of many of persons voted for were unknown, and in a comparatively few instances did any candidate address the people from the hustings.[2]

That account is obviously fanciful in part; Virginia politics never were that noble. Still the people of that state had some distinguished personages to draw upon. William Branch Giles, one of the most forceful advocates of Jeffersonian Republicanism, had served in the federal Congress and in 1829 was governor of the state. He was available and present, although old and on crutches. There were also James Madison and James Monroe, two former Presidents; both old, but still capable of offering a dignity, an intelligence, and a perspective that could not be equaled by others. Then there was John Marshall.

On March 4, 1829, Marshall was in Washington, D.C., swearing in Andrew Jackson as the seventh man to serve as President of the United States. "A great ball was given at night to celebrate the election," he reported. "I of course did not attend it." However, he did mingle with the thousands who had come to celebrate Jackson's victory, including many persons from Richmond. "I am told by several that I am held up as a candidate for the convention. I have no desire to be in the convention and do not mean to be a candidate."[3]

There is no reason to believe that Marshall was insincere in his protestation. The previous year he had served as a delegate to the state convention in Charlottesville, along with Madison and Monroe, to draw up recommendations for internal improvements for the state. Pulling the state closer together by roads and canals always had been an interest of Marshall's, one nurtured by his assignment years earlier to draw up plans for the Kanawha Canal. The convention did recommend canals and improved navigation along the James, Potomac, and Shenandoah rivers and also recommended turnpikes from Richmond to the southwestern part of the state. Having been a member of a state convention then, he had some idea of the work involved.[4]

What happened to Marshall's resolve not to be a candidate in 1829 was best described by himself in a letter to Joseph Story. "I have acted like a girl addressed by a gentleman she does not positively dislike," he wrote, "but is unwilling to marry. She is sure to yield to the advice and persuasion of her friends." Late in March 1829 Marshall was formally asked by a committee of Richmond citizens, headed by John Rutherfoord, to be a candidate for election as delegate to the convention. Marshall refused. "No man feels the importance of the approaching convention more than I do," he wrote, "or looks forward to its proceedings with more anxious solicitude." He explained his refusal on the grounds "that I do not retain those physical powers which would enable me to take that part of the floor of the convention which my constituents would expect, and which their interests might require." He would be seventy-four when the convention opened and his voice had grown noticeably weaker. But the people of Richmond considered him too important a person to do without. His friends pressed him, and he agreed that if the district should choose him "on this great and last occasion," then "my repugnance to becoming a member of the convention shall yield, and my services, such

as they are, shall be at their command." Marshall then was
nominated and elected. "I am almost ashamed of my weakness
and irresolution when I tell you that I am a member of our convention," he said to Story. He predicted that the convention "will
contain a great deal of eloquence as well as talent, and yet will do
I fear much harm with some good. Our freehold suffrage is I
believe gone past redemption. It is impossible to resist the influence. I had almost said contagion of universal example."[5] Marshall was referring to the movement for universal suffrage (for
whites) that would surface at the convention. This was one of the
two important issues at the convention; the other was an independent judiciary.

The convention to write a new constitution for the state of
Virginia convened at twelve o'clock the afternoon of Monday,
October 5, 1829, in the Hall of Delegates at the state capital.
James Madison called the assemblage together. Fifty-three years
earlier the same James Madison had been a delegate to the Virginia convention which had drawn up the first state constitution;
he was the only man present in 1829 who had been at the 1776
convention. He had fought at the side of Thomas Jefferson for the
doctrine of religious liberty. He had helped write the federal Constitution, and then had served in the office of President created by
that Constitution. Madison nominated James Monroe to be president of this convention. Monroe's public service also went back
many years. He had been soldier, diplomat, governor, President
of the United States. Now old and feeble—he would resign from
the convention two months later because of ill health—he came
to Richmond leaning on the arm of his daughter, to fight one
more battle alongside his old comrade, Madison. The Monroe
nomination was seconded by John Marshall, and then approved
unanimously by the delegates. Perhaps no convention ever held
such veneration for three men as that one did for the two ex-
Presidents and the Chief Justice. The oratorical battles would
come, but at that moment there was an understanding that
greatness was present in that trio, and a pride on the part of Virginians that those three men had come from their state.

Other well-known Virginians were also present. John Randolph was a delegate. He came dressed in black, his hat and arms
bound with black strips. When he was asked whom he was
mourning, he replied: "I go in mourning for the old constitution.
I fear I have come to witness its death and funeral."[6]

Then there was William Branch Giles. Almost four decades
earlier he had gone to Washington with a letter of introduction
from John Marshall to James Madison. He had stayed there to
become the nemesis of the Federalists, urging Thomas Jefferson

to purge them from office and leading the attack against Samuel Chase. Now he was governor of Virginia and still perhaps the greatest debater of his time despite his ravaging illness, and certainly one of the outstanding advocates of the Jeffersonian Republicanism that was his rock. "In all things but in the vigor of his intellect," wrote a delegate about Giles, "he was but the shadow of his former self. He could neither move nor stand without the aid of his crutches," and when he concluded a speech and the members pressed their congratulations upon him, "he seemed to belong rather to the dead than the living. His face was the face of a corpse."[7] Giles had come for one last battle, and his target would be, as it had been almost thirty years earlier at the impeachment of Samuel Chase, an independent judiciary. In the earlier battle John Marshall had been quiet, even equivocal, reluctant to enter a battle he could not be certain of winning. Now John Marshall would not be equivocal. He was ready for William Branch Giles.

A man named Charles Campbell, who attended the convention for a few days, described the city and some of the more prominent delegates. "The Capitol, in which the convention sat," he wrote, "is a fine building, nobly situated, more so than any other I have seen in this country." He found Richmond "a picturesque place; the James looks beautiful there . . . the rocks, and islands, and foaming rapids, and murmuring falls, and floating mists, all light and glorious, under a clear blue sky. . . ." On Madison: "Mr. Madison spoke once for half an hour; but although a pin might have been heard to drop, so low was his tone, that from the gallery I could distinguish only one word, and that was, Constitution. He stood not more than six feet from the speaker. When he rose a great part of the members left their seats, and clustered around the aged statesman, thick as a swarm of bees. Mr. Madison was a small man, of ample forehead, and some obliquity of vision—I thought the effect probably of age—his eyes appearing to be slightly introverted. His dress was plain; his overcoat a faded brown surtout." On Monroe: "Mr. Monroe was very wrinkled and weather-beaten—ungraceful in attitude and gesture, and his speeches only commonplace." On Giles: "Mr. Giles wore a crutch—was then Governor of the State. His style of delivery was perfectly conversational—no gesture, no effort, but in ease, fluency and tact, surely he had not there his equal; his words were like honey pouring from an eastern rock."

On John Marshall: "Judge Marshall, whenever he spoke, which was seldom and only for a short time, attracted great attention. His appearance was revolutionary and patriarchal. Tall, in a long surtout of blue, with a face of genius and an eye of fire, his mind possessed the rare faculty of condensation; he distilled an argument down to its essence."[8]

There was another description of the seventy-four-year-old Chief Justice by Hugh Grigsby who came to the convention as a delegate at the age of twenty-two. Twenty-four years later, in 1853, he produced a narrative of that 1829 convention which is considered a definitive account. But in that narrative he was influenced by a certain Virginia chauvinism and the characters appeared, in 1853, much softer than they did in the notes he wrote in 1829. This is the blunt description of Marshall at the state constitutional convention which Grigsby wrote in 1829:

> [Marshall] still retains that vigor of intellect which has so many years rendered him the ornament of the bench. He is tall in person; lean; antique in his dress, and altogether negligent. His head is small; his eyes black and penetrating. His face nowise indicative of intellectual capacity. His voice is bad; has no compass or variety of intonations. He has a song in speaking to which his right arm harmonises with a most ungracious swing. He leans gently forward in speaking; and pours his whole feelings in his speech. His reasoning, which is mathematically true, and his apparent deep conviction of the importance of the cause which he is advocating, render him a powerful advocate and most formidable opponent. I think that the venerable judge is somewhat alive to those passions which we might be apt to imagine his elevated station, established fame, and above all, his great age, had lulled to perpetual repose in his bosom. He winced on several occasions under the speeches of Mr. [Littleton W.] Tazewell; and manifested some ill feeling in the debate I allude to in which Col. [Philip P.] Barbour also took part. Perhaps I may have erred in my perceptions on the subject; but true it is that on the next day, he took occasion to state to the house that if he said what was reported by the papers that he had said, he did not by no means intend to speak so strongly. [William B.] Giles may have fretted him some what, and I doubt not the old Judge felt a grudge against him.[9]

Although Marshall soon would be embroiled in lengthy and heated debates, his manners outside the debates retained for him the personal affection that was so much a part of the attitude the people of Richmond had toward him personally. "I saw him also in the social circle; and at the dinner table, and in the adjournment to the parlor," Grigsby recalled, "where his kind and cordial demeanor endeared him to us all." Another account of the convention has a visitor to Richmond at the market before sunrise one morning and being surprised at seeing Marshall there in "the blue-mixed woolen stockings and the plain black suit—far from superfine—which he usually wore, striding along between the rows of meat and vegetables, catering for his household; and depositing his purchases in a basket, carried by a servant."[10] Marshall had always done the marketing and would not interrupt the routine because of a convention.

The westerners had wanted greater representation in the Virginia Assembly, and they were successful—but not as much as they would have liked. The question caused so much debate that John Randolph reportedly remarked: "Sir, I have been brought by experience and especially by recent observations to the conclusion to which a man of sense and reflection might have arrived a priori—that of all the mechanics under the sun, constitution makers least understand their trade."[11]

The question of who should vote was closely aligned with the western representative question. Virginia never had had universal suffrage, even for free white men. Like most of the colonies and states, Virginia had a freehold, or property, qualification for voters. This was not an issue between parties. The qualification —ownership of fifty acres of unimproved land or twenty-five acres with a house on it—had been placed in the Virginia constitution of 1776 by a committee headed by Thomas Jefferson. John Marshall also believed in property qualifications, although he was aware that the westerners were pressing for universal suffrage. "We shall have a good deal of division and a good deal of heat, I fear, in our convention," he predicted. He anticipated that the freehold qualification would lose to the advocates of universal suffrage, and Marshall viewed that possibility with regret. He always was the politician, however. Rather than allow the freehold principle to be lost entirely, he supported a compromise, which the convention adopted, "by which a substantial property qualification may be preserved." To fight for the freehold principle "to the last extremity may lead to universal suffrage or to something very near it."[12]

John Marshall's opposition to universal suffrage raises the question of whether he was truly a democrat who believed in man's ability to govern himself. That question is answered by his judicial decisions which have as their unifying theme man's need to democratically arrive at just laws and then to observe them. Whenever he spoke of restraint, or "ordered liberty," it was not a restraint imposed for the benefit of a state, or an oligarchy. Rather, it was a restraint sought for the benefit of individuals. He realized that turnabout is not only fair play but natural when a man infringes upon the freedom of another. When men live together, true freedom and democracy is not one man imposing his will upon the others, but rather all individuals agreeing on rules to guide them. That was John Marshall's definition of democracy, as in the end it must be that of every man who chooses to live in a society.

Democracy at that time, however, was only beginning to include the concept of universal suffrage. It had been alien not only to Virginia, but also to most of the United States. The electoral college, as well as the election of United States Senators by state legislatures, was devised by the authors of the Constitution to keep government in the selected hands of the educated and the men of property. By most estimates, at the time of the Virginia convention of 1829, between 40 and 50 percent of the free white adult males in the state had the franchise. The Marshall compromise is believed to have increased that number, but there are no reliable estimates. If this was not democracy by modern standards, it was neither oligarchy nor despotism by any standard. When Jefferson had first proposed the fifty/twenty-five–acre requirement in 1776, he undoubtedly believed he was being liberal, as he undoubtedly was. The Marshall compromise in 1829 was a further liberalization. In Virginia, after the Marshall compromise, the vote belonged to all white adult males except the indigent. It was a middle-class democracy. To judge it by its time —which is the only fair way to judge it—it was a noble advance.[13]

But it was on the subject of an independent judiciary that John Marshall made his mark at that convention. This part of the convention debates had dragged on into January 1830 and threatened to delay Marshall's arrival in Washington for the opening of the Supreme Court. Marshall's first inclination was to leave the convention and report in Washington; he even had reserved a seat on the stagecoach. But his friends pleaded with him to stay in Richmond a few extra days because of the upcoming debate on the judiciary, and Marshall finally consented.[14] The problem arose over assuring the state judges tenure in office. William Branch Giles attacked this concept, and "he showed that he had not forgotten the excitement of a long time gone by, and gave to his auditors the best specimen which they had yet seen, of those powers of debate for which he was so justly renowned."[15] Giles in the Chase impeachment trial in 1805 had taken the position that judges should serve at the pleasure of the legislature. He had not changed his position. "I am as much in favor of the complete independence of the judiciary as the warmest advocate of that principle," he told the 1829 convention, "but I am in favor of its responsibility also. . . . I would make all the Judges responsible, not to God and their own conscience only, but to a human tribunal."[16]

Marshall answered this point "with a directness and an earnest sincerity," according to one report, which continued that "It is said that one of the most beautiful features of the scene was the reverence manifested for Chief Justice Marshall. The gentleness of his temper, the purity of his motives, the sincerity of his conviction, and his wisdom, were confessed by all." Those who replied to his arguments did so without harshness "or asperity of language."

Another description has Marshall's voice extremely feeble, "so that those who sat far off could not hear him: no sooner therefore did he rise, then the members would press towards him, and strain with outstretched necks and eager ears, to catch his words." Those who heard him apparently found that he had lost none of his intellectual powers. According to this description, when a delegate from Augusta tried to answer one of Marshall's speeches, John Randolph ridiculed the attempt, saying: "The argument of the Chief Justice is unshaken, and unanswerable. It is as strong as the fortress of Gibraltar. Sir, the fortress of Gibraltar would be as much injured by *battering it with a pocket pistol*, as that argument has been affected by the abortive and puny assault of the gentleman from Augusta."[17]

When John Marshall at age seventy-four rose to defend the concept of an independent judiciary, he had been Chief Justice for twenty-eight years. His great decisions, the accomplishment of his life, were almost all behind him. For almost sixty years he had studied the law, practiced it, preached it, lived it. For almost sixty years he had watched the American people use the law to form themselves into a nation, and this meant a society by which all could accomplish the goals of their lives with respect for other men. For almost sixty years he had fervently believed what he was now going to say.

"The independence of all those who try causes between man and man," he said, "and between a man and his Government, can be maintained only by the tenure of their office. Is not their independence preserved under the present system? None can doubt it. Such an idea was never heard of in Virginia, as to remove a Judge from office." Marshall well understood what would have happened to the judiciary if the effort to impeach Samuel Chase had succeeded. Anything was acceptable, he argued, except playing with a judge's independence. "You may impose upon him any duty you please," Marshall told the delegates straining to hear him. "You may say, that the Court of Appeals shall sit every day, from the first of January to the last of

December. The Judge of a County Court may be called on to perform his duty on the bench for a whole year. Yet he holds his office during good behavior. . . . [The judges'] independence is not impaired by their being required to do all they can."

To assure having good men as judges, Marshall said, their independence must not be threatened by attacking their tenure. "Will the gentleman recollect," he said, "that in order to secure the administration of justice, judges of capacity, and of legal knowledge are indispensable? And how is he to get them? How are such men to be drawn off from a lucrative practice? Will any gentleman of the profession, whose practice will secure him a comfortable independence, leave that practice, and come to take an office, which may be taken from him the next day? You may invite them, but they will not come. You may elect them, but they will not accept the appointment. You don't give salaries that will draw respectable men, unless by the certainty of permanence connected with them." He asked, if a judge could be removed "at pleasure," would "any lawyer of distinction come upon your bench?" And he answered: "No, sir."

No one had to strain to hear as Marshall concluded: "I have always thought, from my earliest youth till now, that the greatest scourge an angry Heaven ever inflicted upon an ungrateful and a sinning people, was an ignorant, a corrupt, or a dependent judiciary. Will you draw down this curse upon Virginia?" He said that the ancestors of those men in the convention hall had always believed in an independent judiciary. "We thought so till very lately," he said, "and I trust the vote of this day will show that we think so still."[18]

Perhaps the most important phrase in Marshall's speech came at the beginning—"the independence of all those who try causes between man and man and between a man and his Government." His argument was that society needs authorities independent of politics, independent of economic retaliation, or of threats of bodily harm. A judge's understanding of the law may be incorrect. He may have biases invisible until after his appointment. But these failings cannot be prevented other than by an intelligent choice of men to serve. Placing judges under threats, however, can be prevented by assuring them independence. Could a judge under the threat of political coercion have withstood the demands of Thomas Jefferson for the conviction of Aaron Burr despite the fact that Burr's guilt could not be proven? Could judges have upheld the supremacy of the federal Union over the states if they were subjected to physical violence in their homes? Could judges have lectured corporations on their responsibilities to the community if they were subject to economic threats? The answers were written in the career of John Marshall and in the Supreme Court he had led. The Justices had been independent and they had been judges. They had tried causes between man and man and between man and his government, and whatever else could be said about them, it could not be said that they had acted for personal power, for the hope of monetary reward, or for the advancement of their careers. Their independence had allowed them to determine the law as best they could, from the standpoint of what they understood the law to be. Anything else would have been, in John Marshall's phrase, "the greatest scourge an angry Heaven ever inflicted upon an ungrateful and a sinning people."

The proposal to change the independent status of the judges was defeated by a vote of 56–29. John Marshall had won.

Marshall believed that the final document that emerged from the convention for adoption by the people of Virginia was "not precisely what any of us wished, but it is better than we feared." James Madison, more of an authority perhaps on the mechanics of constitution making, thought it somewhat better: "The peculiar difficulties which will have been overcome ought to render the experiment a new evidence of the capacity of men for self-government, instead of an argument in the hands of those who deny and calumniate it." And in this he was correct. The difficulties the Virginians had with their form of government had been solved to the extent that they could continue as a society.[19]

14

IN RETROSPECT one of the most interesting points about the Virginia constitutional convention of 1829 was the absence of debate or discussion about slavery. Slaves had only been considered as part of the dispute over how the vote would be divided; the eastern plantation owners felt their slaves entitled them to a greater representation in the state government as they entitled them to a greater representation in the federal government. This was part of a southern strategy of ignoring the problem as much as possible, and living off the supposed benefits of slavery without facing up to the growing demand that slavery be ended.

John Marshall was intimately involved in the slavery problem most of his life, as a resident of Virginia, as a politician, as a man concerned about the future of his country, and also as a judge. His deep feelings ultimately would be reflected through his son's efforts to force Virginia to end slavery in 1832, an effort that failed but which served to demonstrate that Virginia's claim of benevolence toward the blacks was without foundation.

Marshall owned slaves from the time of his marriage; his father had given him one as a wedding present and the Richmond tax records show he owned a small number of slaves all his life in that city. However, it is doubtful that he traded in slaves, nor is there any record that he sold slaves to augment his income as Thomas Jefferson did on occasion. A slave he purchased in 1787, for example, was sold by Marshall, but to his father-in-law, Jacquelin Ambler, and not on the open market.[1] The Marshall slaves in Richmond were house servants primarily, and the indications are that they were with the family many years. In Fauquier County the Marshall family held more slaves and used them to work the fields. A man whose grandparents had been slaves for the Marshalls has recalled stories he heard from them. The Marshall family, he said, never had a large number of slaves —he offered the number fourteen—and the whites and the blacks existed amicably alongside each other. There was no recollection of blacks speaking ill of the Marshalls or of any member of the Marshall family maltreating a black. In 1854 Edward Carrington Marshall, John's youngest son, freed his slaves and later gave them twenty-five acres of land in Fauquier County, some of which is still owned by their descendants.[2]

Stories about John Marshall demonstrate that he treated blacks with respect and courtesy. An 1842 letter recalled Chief Justice Marshall raising his hat to every Negro who greeted him, "saying, when he was laughed at for the custom by some proud prig, that he was not going to be outdone in politeness by a servant."[3] In this condescension Marshall failed, along with his society, in not understanding that color does not excuse acceding to what the United States was established to prevent—the subjugation of one man by another. It can be said of John Marshall, however, that in his Court decisions on slavery, there was the beginning of the moral criticism of that institution.

As a militia general in Virginia in the 1790s many of Marshall's problems were taken up with the threat of slave uprisings. While he was not in Richmond during the Gabriel uprising in 1800, he and his family certainly were aware of it, and the threat of revolution was always present in his life just as it was in the lives of all white southerners. A concern in the American Revolution and the War of 1812 was that the British might arouse the slaves to turn on their masters. In December 1811, for example, John Randolph suggested that rather than worry about taking

Canada, the United States government should worry about protecting its citizens against black uprisings. "Some of us are shuddering for our safety at home," he said. "I speak from facts when I say, that the night bell never tolls for fire in Richmond, that the mother does not hug the infant more closely to her bosom. I have been a witness of some of the alarms in the capital of Virginia." When the War of 1812 did break out, the possibility of the slaves combining with the British was a real threat. "As for our enemy at home," reported a Washingtonian, "I have no doubt that they will if possible join the British." In Virginia the slaves did just that. "The Northumberland slaves are every day effecting their escape," said one report, and another: "Our negroes are flocking to the enemy from all quarters, which they convert into troops, vindictive and rapacious. . . ."[4]

Virginia and the other slave states should perhaps have learned from these experiences that the most intelligent approach would have been gradual emancipation. But the cotton gin had come to the South, and large numbers of cheap laborers were required to work in the fields. Virginia was not a cotton state, but it did become a slave-breeding state. One of the most dismal pictures in Virginia during these decades was the long row of young blacks being taken in chains to the states further south for sale, like cattle. Also, the Virginians enjoyed slavery. With the blacks doing the manual labor, the whites were free to gamble, drink, or write learned dissertations on the dignity of man.

In 1820 the United States was faced with a major crisis over slavery, and resolved it by allowing Missouri to enter the Union as a slave state. This permitted the slave states to retain an effective voice in the national government, a voice they would use to protect slavery. Virginia was the leader in effecting this compromise, in insisting on the perpetuation of slavery. "The State of Virginia has gone so far as to throw out hints hostile, should the question be decided otherwise than it has: and in this it is understood she would have been supported by the other Slave States all deeply interested in the event," explained one observer. Joseph Story offered a similar account, but he was more scathing. "We have foolishly suffered ourselves to be wheedled by Southern politicians, until we have almost forgotten that the honors and the Constitution of the Union are as much our birthright and our protection, as of the rest of the United States," he charged. Virginia, he said, had united the South and the West, "while the eastern States were thinned by desertion. . . ."[5]

The Missouri Compromise, it was hoped, would stifle the slavery issue. But it did not; it only postponed the reckoning. In 1823 Supreme Court Justice William Johnson, sitting on the Circuit Court, had to face the issue directly. South Carolina had been threatened with a slave revolt and had countered by attempting to prohibit any free black from entering the state. This prohibition included seamen. If a ship entered Charleston port carrying a sailor who was a free black, the sailor was arrested and thrown in jail, to be released only when his ship was leaving and after his captain had paid his jail expenses. If the captain refused to pay, the black could be sold into slavery. This law played havoc with American commerce. The federal government had hoped that South Carolina would not enforce it, but the law was enforced with the arrest and detention of Henry Elkison, a free Negro and a British citizen. Johnson ordered Elkison freed, asserting that the federal commerce power was supreme over the state's police powers. This 1823 decision was a forerunner of the *Gibbons v. Ogden* decision the next year which also asserted the supremacy of the federal commerce power. John Marshall was relieved apparently that Johnson made the decision rather than him, and concerned also over the sentiment reflected in the trial by the proslavery people "that if this be the constitution, it is better to break that instrument than submit to the principle."[6]

Sectionalism had become a political weapon the South used to protect slavery. Daniel Webster underlined this in an 1826 letter when he talked about the approaching presidential election. "The real truth is," he said, "that Mr. Adams will be opposed by all the Atlantic States south of Maryland; so would any other Northern man. They will never acquiesce in the administration of any President on our side of the Potomac. This may be relied on, and we ought to be aware of it. The perpetual alarm which is kept upon the subject of negro slavery, has its objects. It is to keep the South all united and all jealous of the North. . . ."[7]

This sectionalism led to cries of nullification in the late 1820s and early 1830s. For three decades John Marshall on the Supreme Court had been hammering the point that states could not determine which laws they wished to obey. The nullification advocates, drawing from the Virginia and Kentucky Resolutions of Jefferson and Madison and from the states' rights writings of John Taylor, argued that the states could indeed nullify laws they opposed. Much of Marshall's personal correspondence during this period includes denunciations of the doctrine. "The idea that a state may constitutionally nullify an act of Congress is so extravagant in itself," he said in a typical letter, "and so repugnant to the existence of Union between the States that I could with difficulty bring my self to believe it was seriously entertained by any person. Even yet I scarcely know how to think it possible." When Joseph Story confided his own pessimism regarding the

Nullification Doctrine, Marshall answered him: "If the prospects of our country inspire you with gloom, how do you think a man must be affected who partakes of all your opinions, and whose geographical position enables him to see a great deal that is concealed from you." Marshall then said that "I yield slowly and reluctantly to the conviction that our Constitution cannot last." In his later years Marshall is considered to have grown dour and skeptical of democracy. He had lost his faith in the South's ability to rise above the slavery issue, and in this respect he was correct.[8]

His gloom was evident in an exchange of letters with Timothy Pickering, who had been Secretary of State during the XYZ Affair. Pickering recalled that at about the end of the Revolution he had asked a Virginian what "would be the final result of the Negro population in the slave-holding states." The Virginian answered that the blacks would "mingle their blood with the whites." Pickering concluded: "That event would of course bring slavery to an end. But, as Mr. Jefferson remarks, in his notes on Virginia, there appears to be an utter repugnance in the Whites to form such a union—at least a *permanent* one—with the African races. I can think of no cause of gloomy foreboding so dreadful as the extensive and rapidly increasing population of that race, in a state of slavery." Marshall replied:

> I concur with you in thinking that nothing portends more calamity and mischief to the Southern states than their slave population; yet they seem to cherish the evil and to view with an immovable prejudice and dislike every thing which may tend to diminish it. I do not wonder that they should resist any attempt should one be made to interfere with the rights of property, but they have feverish jealousy of measures which may do good without the hazard of harm that is I think very unwise.[9]

There were various plans in the 1820s for the abolition of slavery. One involved having the federal government pay the slave owners compensation for the slaves they freed. In effect, the government would purchase the slaves, then free them. The plan was not welcomed in the South. In the cotton states the owners knew they could not economically replace slave labor. In Virginia the slave breeders realized that emancipation would foreclose future profits. "The two great objects in Virginia are internal improvement and our coloured population," John Marshall lamented in 1832. "On the first I despair. On the second we might do much if our unfortunate political prejudices did not restrain us from asking the aid of the federal government. As far as I can judge, that aid, if asked, would be freely and liberally given."[10]

Lafayette, when he toured the United States in 1824, had given Marshall a copy of *A Plan for the Gradual Abolition of Slavery in the United States*, which recommended that the slaves be freed on credit, and allowed to pay for their freedom over a five-year period with interest. Marshall wrote Lafayette that he did not believe the plan would succeed. "If the profits of slave labour would in fact double a given capital in five years, their owners ought to grow rich with a rapidity of which we have no example." He also did not believe the plan could operate in the most southern states because there is "such a jealousy on this subject as would prove a great impediment to an experiment." Marshall believed that any emancipation plan would have to begin "in the most northern of the slave holding states before it can be introduced in those of the south." In another letter to Lafayette, Marshall conceded that "the disposition to expel slavery from our bosoms, or even to diminish the evil if practicable, does not I think gain strength in the South." Marshall's opinion was that the slaves, if freed, would have to be moved outside the borders of the United States. "I do not know enough of the interior of Mexico to form any opinion on the possibility of giving our coloured population that direction; but I am persuaded that it cannot be safely located on any lands within the United States. The only secure asylum within our reach—beneficial for them and safe for us—is Africa."[11]

In the years between 1820 and 1830 the hope that the slavery problem could be solved by transporting the Negroes back to Africa became widespread. The African Colonization Society was founded and was supported by many prominent Americans, including Joseph Story, Daniel Webster, Henry Clay, James Madison, and Bushrod Washington. Its purpose was to transport free blacks to Liberia on the West African coast and assist them to establish a new society. How pervasive altruism was in this proposal has always been a matter of conjecture. Jared Sparks, a magazine editor as well as the compiler of George Washington's papers, supported the society and his biographer reported that the Colonization Society had as its prime purpose providing a home for the free blacks "who could never expect in this country to acquire full civil rights. At the same time, there was a strong desire on the part of the slave-owners to get rid of these freemen and freedmen, for they were looked upon as dangerous elements in a slaveholding country." Sparks himself said: "No dream can be more wild than that of emancipating slaves who are still to remain among us free. We unhesitatingly express it as our belief —and we speak from some experience—that the free people of color as a class in the slaveholding states are a greater nuisance to society, more comfortless, tempted to more vices, and actually less qualified to enjoy existence, than the slaves themselves."[12] While some supporters viewed the Colonization Society as a means of assisting the blacks or as the best method of ultimately eliminating the problem in America, others obviously saw the free blacks as a threat to slavery. Their presence encouraged the slaves to seek freedom. They were agitators. And many slaveowners wanted them out of the United States.

In 1823, on November 4, a group of Richmond citizens met in the hall of the House of Delegates at the state capital "to organize a Society in the City of Richmond, auxiliary to the American Society for colonizing the free people of colour on the coast of Africa." John Marshall was elected president.

The Society's purpose was to finance the migration of free blacks to Liberia. The 1825 annual meeting reported that $642 had been raised for "the fitting out and taking to the colony 105 colonists from Virginia." That meeting also learned that in several days "another vessel is expected to sail from James River, with about 75 emigrants" and the Richmond group anticipated putting up one-third of the costs. That year's report added that by sending the blacks to Liberia, "We should be reinstating numerous human beings in those social and individual rights, the enjoyment of which elevates and gives to the human nature its true dignity." Two years later, the Society apparently had a greater realization of the problems it faced, and its report carried an appeal to the federal government for support, although the members were reluctant to describe it as an appeal. Marshall continued as president of the Richmond group until his death.[13]

With the assistance of the United States, the Liberian nation did grow, and its ties to the United States are still acknowledged. As a solution to the problem of slavery, however, it was at best a quixotic project, charming in its naïveté, and incapable of success. It could not persuade any slaveowner to free his slaves; nor could it have absorbed the great numbers of blacks if slavery had been ended.

Marshall, however, continued his support of the movement. "I cannot entertain a doubt that Liberia is the best retreat that can be found for our people of colour," he said in the last year of his life. "The soil is good, and the colonist will receive a sufficient quantity for cultivation. Instruction in all religious and moral duties, is carefully attended to, and the education of children is an object of primary solicitude with the Society."[14]

In 1831 there was an event in Virginia which, as much as any single event could, marked a turning point in the state's attitude toward slavery. It sparked the strongest movement in the history of the state for emancipation, and that movement's failure meant that Virginia would not turn from leading her sister states of the Sc th toward Civil War.

On August 23, 1831, Governor John Floyd of Virginia wrote: "This will be a very noted day in Virginia. At daylight this morning the Mayor of the City put into my hands a notice to the public, written by James Trezevant of Southampton County, stating that an insurrection of the slaves in the county had taken place, that several families had been massacred and that it would take a considerable military force to put them down." This was the revolt led by the slave Nat Turner that resulted in the deaths of sixty-one whites in Southampton County. Men, women, and children were slaughtered. The whites coming to the rescue were equally ferocious. They raced into Southampton County and no black was safe, however innocent he was of complicity in the revolt.[15]

The uprising exacerbated the most dreaded fear of all Virginians and most southerners, that of the blacks rising up and murdering them in their beds. The savagery of the whites' response to the uprising also demonstrated how far away the rural South was from the rule of law for which men like John Marshall had worked so long. But the revolt failed to produce in even the more thoughtful Virginians any understanding of the evil of slavery. That, for them, had not been the cause of the revolt. Rather, there had been a conspiracy, one that had made dupes out of otherwise decent Virginians. Governor Floyd in a letter explained what he considered the origin of the revolt. Because he was a respected citizen, elected to his post by the state legislature, it is reasonable to assume his thoughts were universal ones in Virginia. He wrote:

> I am fully persuaded the spirit of insubordination which has, and still manifests itself in Virginia, had its origin among, and eminated from, the Yankee population, upon their first arrival amongst us, but most especially the Yankee pedlars and traders.
>
> The course has been by no means a direct one. They began first by making them religious; their conversations were of that character, telling the blacks, God was no respecter of persons; the black man was as good as the white; that all men were born free and equal; that they can not serve two masters; that the white people rebelled against England to obtain freedom; so have the blacks a right to do so.

In the meantime, I am sure without any purpose of this kind, the preachers, especially Northern, were very assiduous in operating upon our population. Day and night they were at work and religion became, and is, the fashion of the times. Finally our females and of the most respectable were persuaded that it was piety to teach negroes to read and write, to the end that they might read the Scriptures. Many of them became tutoresses in Sunday schools and pious distributors of tracts from the New York Society.

At this point more active operations commenced; our magistrates and laws became more inactive; large assemblies of negroes were suffered to take place for religious purposes. Then commenced the efforts of the black preachers. Often from the pulpits these pamphlets and papers were read, followed by the incindiary publications of Walker, Garrison and Knapp of Boston; these too with songs and hymns of a similar character were circulated, read and commented upon, we resting in apathetic security until the Southampton affair.

From all that has come to my knowledge during and since this affair, I am fully convinced that every black preacher, in the whole country east of the Blue Ridge, was in the secret, that the plans as published by those northern prints were adopted and acted upon by them, that their congregations, as they were called, knew nothing of this intended rebellion, except a few leading, and intelligent men, who may have been head men in the church. The mass were prepared by making them aspire to an equal station by such conversations as I have related as the first step.

I am informed that they had settled the form of government to be that of the white people, whom they intended to cut off to a man, with this difference that the preachers were to be their governors, generals and judges. I feel fully justified to myself, in believing the northern incendiaries, tracts, Sunday Schools, religion and reading and writing has accomplished this end.

I shall in my annual message recommend that laws be passed to confine the slaves to the estates of their master, prohibit negroes from preaching, absolutely to drive from this state all free negroes, and to substitute the surplus revenue in our treasury annually for slaves, to work for a time upon our railroads, etc., and then sent out of the country, preparatory, or rather as the first step to emancipation. This last point will of course be tenderly and cautiously managed, and will be urged or delayed as your state and Georgia may be disposed to cooperate. . . .[16]

This last was a reference to a proposal to come before the state legislature calling for the gradual emancipation of the state's slaves.

Thomas Marshall, the Chief Justice's son, was a leader in the fight for emancipation. He represented Fauquier County, one of the western counties where slavery was not considered extremely important. There was one slave in the western counties for every eight in the eastern. Still, his speech, delivered January 11, 1832, is more than merely an exercise in safe politics. It is a warning of the danger of slavery, of its destructive impact on the whites. "Wherefore, then, object to slavery?" he began, then answered:

> Because it is ruinous to the whites—retards improvement—roots out an industrious population—banishes the yeoman of the country—deprives the spinner, the weaver, the smith, the shoemaker, the carpenter, of employment and support. The evil admits of no remedy. It is increasing, and will continue to increase, until the whole country will be inundated by one black wave, covering its surface. The master has no capital but what is vested in human flesh; the father, instead of being richer for his sons, is at a loss to provide for them. There is no diversity of occupations, no incentive to enterprise. Labor of every species is disreputable, because performed mostly by slaves. Our towns are stationary, our villages almost everywhere declining; and the general aspect of the country marks the curse of a wasteful, idle, reckless population, who have no interest in the soil, and care not how much it is impoverished. Public improvements are neglected; and the entire continent does not present a region for which nature has done so much, and art so little. If cultivated by free labor, the soil of Virginia is capable of sustaining a dense population, among whom labor would be honorable, and where "the busy hum of men" would tell that all were happy, and that all were free.[17]

Thomas Marshall's speech that day summed up what had come to be recognized by thoughtful people as the evil of slavery for the whites. It degraded labor, encouraged otherwise honorable men to trade in human flesh, and prevented men from improving their society. Since the Civil War the South has often blamed the devastation of that war and the northern politics after the war for fostering a century of squalor. But that is a false charge. The southern white destroyed himself when he embraced slavery, as Thomas Marshall charged; the southern white was not destroyed by outside forces.

By this time, however, the exportation of slaves to the states further south had become too profitable an industry for Virginia to end it: at least too profitable an industry for Virginia to have the courage to end it. Estimates are that between eight thousand and nine thousand slaves were sold south every year, and that a healthy black male could bring about $1,000 on the slave market. By the 1830s the state's income from the sale of slaves would be more than $20 million. This all came out in the 1832 debates. There were some faint calls in those debates for the delegates to remember that there was perhaps a moral question involved, the subjugation of one man by another. But primarily the debate revolved around the position taken by Thomas Marshall, that slavery was destructive of white society, versus the position that the breeding of slaves and their subsequent sale were necessary to the state's economy.

History does not encourage delving into what might have been, but there should be indulgence in this instance. John Marshall believed that if Virginia could lead the way, the states further south might have followed her lead in emancipating their slaves. This, however, was not to be. Economics won in the Virginia legislature, and the delegates voted not to free the slaves.

Watching the proceedings in the state capital from his Richmond home, John Marshall was never very hopeful that the legislature would rise to the occasion. A few weeks before the debates began, he said he looked with "anxious solicitude" on the approaching proceedings and "with much more of fear than hope." His estimate was that "a considerable portion is in favor of a separate confederacy, and that this portion contains the boldest and most active of its members. Consequently it strengthens daily." He made these comments in a letter to a friend, and concluded: "Old men are timid. Pray Heaven that my fears may proceed from the timidity of age rather than from rational calculation founded on the actual state of things." Marshall's prediction of a southern confederacy was not inaccurate; it was only thirty years early.[18]

Against this background—a background of fear of blacks, an awareness that whites were being debased by slavery, and realization that the Union might be severed over the issue—John Marshall handed down a series of decisions involving slavery. Slavery was not a major issue to come before the Supreme Court when he presided as Chief Justice; most of the cases concerned technical matters of ownership. At the beginning of this series of cases Marshall wrote brief decisions having to do with the specifics of the law. Toward the end of his tenure, however, he began to use the same tool he had used in his other decisions, dicta, to stake out a moral claim for the termination of slavery. If he could not produce an end to slavery in his time—and he could not—he would contribute to the development of man's sense of morality on the slavery issue.

The first slave case to come before the Supreme Court when Marshall was Chief Justice was *Scott v. Negro London*. Virginia law required a slaveowner who was bringing in a slave from another state to take an oath within sixty days of bringing the slave into Virginia, saying he was not attempting to evade the law against importation of slaves for sale. In this particular case the slave had been brought into the state not by his owner but by his owner's father. The father never took the oath, but the owner did come into Alexandria and take the oath within the proper time. The slave, the Negro London, sought his freedom on the basis that the man who brought him into the state, the owner's father, had not fulfilled the law. The lower court held for the slave, but the Marshall decision reversed that ruling. Marshall believed that so long as the master had complied with the law, there was no reason to assume the law had been violated. "It seems strange," Marshall remarked in his opinion, "where the letter of a law has not been violated, that such an unimportant circumstance should affect its spirit."[19]

Two years later, in *Spires v. Willison* and in *Ramsay v. Lee*, Marshall said that lower courts had erred by not instructing juries in the two cases of the requirement that deeding of slaves required written records. In both cases Marshall specifically said that the Supreme Court was not commenting upon the validity of the titles.[20]

In 1812 and 1813 there were two cases having to do with slavery, both revolving around technical points of law but beginning to raise questions beyond those of the law. The first was *Hezekiah Wood v. John Davis*.[21] A woman named Susan Davis, considered a slave, had been sold by Hezekiah Wood to Caleb Swann. Susan Davis then brought suit against Swann, claiming she had been born free and could not be held in bondage. When she won that suit, her children, John Davis and others, then sought their freedom from Wood, claiming that if their mother was free, they should be free also. They won their case in the lower courts, and Wood then appealed to the Supreme Court. The issue appeared to revolve around whether the children were freed by the fact of the mother's having been judged to have been born free. During the arguments, Associate Justice Duvall, who very much opposed slavery, offered the opinion that when he had argued such cases as a lawyer, the courts always had held that the mother's condition had determined that of the children, "that the subsequent petitioners who claimed under the same title, were only bound to prove their descent." Francis Scott Key, the lawyer for Wood, offered another argument, however—"That Wood, was not a party, nor privy to any party, to the suit of Susan Davis against Swann, and is, therefore, not concluded by the judgment in that case." On that basis the Supreme Court decided the case for Wood. Marshall said: "There was no privity between Swann and Wood; they were to be considered as perfectly distinct persons. Wood had a right to defend his own title, which he did not derive from Swann." Duvall did not dissent from this opinion.

The following year, however, there was a case which caused more concern and debate, and more important, the first discussions in a Supreme Court decision of the morality of slavery. This was the case of *Mima Queen v. Hepburn*.[22] The specific issue before the Supreme Court was the admissibility of hearsay evidence. But Gabriel Duvall this time insisted the Court acknowledge that involved also was the question of human liberty versus property rights. Mima Queen and her child were slaves who petitioned for their freedom on the basis of being able to trace their parentage to free citizens. They demonstrated their free ancestry by hearsay evidence. The lower courts would not accept that evidence and neither would the Supreme Court.

"However, the feelings of the individual may be interested on the part of a person claiming freedom," said Marshall, and that was the first time the Court had acknowledged sympathy for a slave seeking freedom, "the court cannot perceive any legal distinction between the assertion of this and of any other right, which will justify the application of a rule of evidence to cases of this description which would be inapplicable to general cases in which a right to property may be asserted." He continued that any rule pronounced in that particular case would not be confined only to slavery cases "but will be extended to others where rights may depend on facts which happened many years past."

Marshall continued in a justification of the Court's position, and his lengthy comments on the point indicate a heated discussion in conference, as Duvall's subsequent dissent bears out. Marshall said that hearsay was inadmissible not only because more reliable evidence might be available but also because of "its intrinsic weakness, its incompetency to satisfy the mind of the existence of the fact, and the frauds which might be practiced under its cover." He acknowledged that there were several exceptions, but Marshall said the Court could not "lightly" accept the creation of new exceptions. "If the circumstances that the eye witnesses of any fact be dead should justify the introduction of testimony to establish that fact from hearsay," said Marshall, "no man could feel safe in any property, a claim to which might be supported by proofs so easily obtained."

Duvall could not accept the majority's position, however, and produced the only dissent of his Supreme Court career. The state of Maryland, he argued, had permitted hearsay in such cases. Other courts had permitted hearsay, he said and insisted "the reason for admitting hearsay evidence upon a question of freedom is much stronger than in cases of pedigree or in controversies relative to the boundaries of land." He added: "It will be universally admitted that the right to freedom is more important than the right of property." He stressed that excluding hearsay meant that women like Mima Queen would be "without remedy." He closed:

> And people of color from their helpless condition under the uncontrolled authority of a master, are entitled to all reasonable protection. A decision that hearsay evidence in such cases shall not be admitted, cuts up by the root all claims of the kind, and puts a final end to them, unless the claim should arise from a fact of recent date, and such a case will seldom, perhaps never, occur.

Considering that property rights was a major concern of the Court at the time and that blacks were usually refused most legal rights, Duvall's dissent was a daring pronouncement. He may have been alone then, certainly he was with a small minority, in saying that "people of color" were "entitled to all reasonable protection" of the law.

In none of these cases, nor in the other slave cases that came before the Marshall Court, did the Justices have the opportunity to make a judgment on slavery itself. Slavery had been sanctioned by the Constitution in the clause allowing southerners to have Representatives in the House based on the number "of free Persons . . . [and] three fifths of all other persons." It had been sanctioned by the federal government with the enactment of the Fugitive Slave Law and by its refusal to take any action looking toward the end of slavery. It had been sanctioned by the southern states as they built a legislative wall around their slave societies. The acceptance by the young nation of slavery is a classic example of the twisting of law from its ultimate purpose —to give form to morality—to achieve a political end. The result was that slavery was not legally challengeable before the courts created by the Constitution. Marshall's faint expressions of sympathy for slaves and Duvall's stronger statements were sheer dicta. But they were a lecture to the American people, or rather the beginnings of a lecture. The Justices understood, even if they did not articulate the concept, that no law can exist without a basis in morality. Either it would not be obeyed or it would be rebelled against. Living in Virginia, Marshall was well aware that the reaction by slaves to their condition was the spirit of revolt.

As the years passed, Marshall realized that slavery was causing an even greater threat to his country than he had first anticipated; he also realized that the nation seemed incapable of solving the problem. His dicta took the form of stronger pleas. In an 1829 case, *Robert Boyce v. Paul Anderson*,[23] he legally lifted the black slave from the status of personal property to that of human being. Some slaves with their owner's agent were coming down the Mississippi River on the steamboat *Teche*, when it blew up. The passengers, including the slaves and the agent of their owner, Boyce, escaped and landed on shore. They waited there until another steamboat, the *Washington*, came down the river. A small boat from the *Washington* came ashore to pick them up. This small boat loaded the slaves and headed back for the *Washington*. As it neared the steamboat, it overturned and the slaves were drowned. The owner of the slaves, Boyce, claimed that the drowning was due to mismanagement on the part of the *Washington*, that it was set in motion as the small boat approached and that motion had capsized the boat. The Court held for the defendants, saying they were responsible "only in the event of [the deaths] being caused by the negligence or the unskilfulness of their agents."

But Marshall went far beyond the point of law in his dicta. In the 1820s slaves were property, nothing more than chattel, given no greater consideration in law or in society than an animal and often less. John Marshall, however, denied that. "A slave has volition," he said, "and has feelings which cannot be entirely disregarded," a statement that was out-of-keeping with the morality of southern society which saw nothing wrong, for example, in separating slave families by selling their members to different owners. A slave, Marshall declared, "cannot be stowed away as a common package." But in the South exactly that was done, the slave was considered to have the status of a "common package." John Marshall was preaching to his neighbors now as he declared: "Not only does humanity forbid this proceeding but it might endanger his life or health. . . . The carrier has not, and cannot have, the same absolute control over him that he has over inanimate matter. In the nature of things, and in his character, he resembles a passenger, not a package of goods. It would seem reasonable, therefore, that the responsibility of the carrier should be measured by the law which is applicable to passengers, rather than by that which is applicable to the carriage of common goods." By modern standards, Marshall is condescending. By the standards of the time he lived in, however, he was daring, moralistic, even brave.

The most famous slave case in which Marshall participated was *The Antelope*.[24] An American ship had intercepted a ship carrying 280 Africans who had been taken from Spanish and Portuguese ships and obviously were destined to be sold into slavery. The Spanish and Portuguese consuls came to the Supreme Court demanding the return of their property—the Africans who had been taken from their slave ships and then taken a second time by the American ship. As in the other slave cases, the question of slavery itself was not the issue.

The Marshall decision showed a man caught between the law which permitted immorality and his own conscience which told him the practices of slavery and of trading in slaves were morally wrong and should not be upheld by the law he had sworn to uphold. As for the slave trade, Marshall acknowledged that all "Christian and civilized nations of the world" had engaged in it and that it had been sanctioned by nations which "possess distant colonies," however "abhorrent this traffic may be to a mind whose original feelings are not blunted by familiarity with the practice." After referring to trafficking in slaves as "abhorrent," he went on to describe it as "unnatural" and said "the detestation in which it is held is growing daily."

The United States had not permitted the importation of slaves since 1807, but Marshall had to be aware that trafficking in slaves was a major industry in his state. "It is not wonderful that public feeling should march somewhat in advance of strict law," he said. Do you not understand, he seemed to be saying to his fellow Virginians, that what you do may be allowed by law but is certainly not condoned by other Americans?

The law, however, as Marshall explained, said that "the legality of the capture of a vessel engaged in the slave trade, depends on the law of the country to which the vessel belongs." If that law allowed slave trading, then the slaves would have to be returned. He again was about to say more than he had to. "That [the slave trade] is contrary to the law of nature will scarcely be denied. That every man has a natural right to the fruits of his own labour, is generally admitted; and that no other person can rightfully deprive him of those fruits, and appropriate them against his will, seems to be the necessary result of this situation."

In those two sentences the Supreme Court, one of the three

branches of the American government, had done something which neither the presidency nor the Congress had done. It had publicly made a moral judgment against slavery.

The Supreme Court upheld the right of Portugal and Spain to restitution of the slaves; it was powerless to do otherwise. "Whatever might be the answer of a moralist to this question," said Marshall, "a jurist must search for its legal solution. . . ." While affirming the right of restitution, the Court also demanded proof of the claim. Spain had claimed 150 Africans, but "Their proof is not satisfactory beyond ninety-three." And even those ninety-three "had to be designated to the satisfaction of the Circuit Court." Portugal had claimed 133 slaves, but Marshall said that in the five years since the American ship had intercepted the slaves, the real owner of these slaves had not identified himself nor had he claimed the slaves. This was so unusual, said Marshall, that there was "serious suspicion that the real owner dares not avow himself." He then suggested that the slave trader had, in fact, not been a citizen of Portugal but of the United States and was carrying on "this criminal and unhuman traffic" under the Portuguese flag. Marshall did not allow the return of any of the slaves to Portugal.[25]

A recent study of Marshall's slavery decisions charged him with the "legitimation" of slavery.[26] That he did not do. Slavery was legitimized by the people who formed the United States of America under a Constitution. Through congressional action, constitutional amendment, and actions within the states, slavery could have been ended or ameliorated. What Marshall and his brethren did was speak to the conscience of the nation, and this too is a role of judges. When law and morality do not coincide, the judge must urge his fellow citizens to give him the tools with which to bring them together. The southern states would not listen. They did not listen to Nat Turner's cry of revolt, to Tom Marshall's plea in the Virginia legislature, and they did not listen to John Marshall's plea that "every man has a natural right to the fruits of his own labour . . . and that no other person can rightfully deprive him of those fruits, and appropriate them against his will, seems to be the necessary result of this situation."

Late in his life, John Marshall found some hope for the country in an act of England abolishing slavery in her colonies by an edict of Parliament. He had thought that an institution so important could not be abolished by legislative fiat. But when it was done, according to an account by a friend, "He rejoiced in it. He now saw hope for his beloved Virginia, which he had seen sinking lower and lower among the States. The cause, [Marshall] said, was that work is disreputable in a country where a degraded class is held to enforced labor. He had seen all the young, the power of the State, who were not rich enough to remain at home in idleness, betaking themselves to other regions where they might work without disgrace. Now there was hope, for he considered that in this act of the British, the decree had gone forth against American slavery, and its doom was sealed."[27]

But then John Marshall had always been an optimist.

15

IN UPHOLDING THE RIGHT of individuals to enter into and benefit from contracts, John Marshall had stressed man's natural rights and insisted that the purpose of law was to protect those natural rights. In his decisions on the slavery issue, he had attempted to point out that the laws, rather than protecting the natural rights of the blacks, were challenging them; that was the point of his dicta in the *Antelope* and *Boyce* cases. In dealing with the Indians, however, Marshall was much more political. He was faced with what can be described at best as an unfortunate situation. The settlers from the Old World had come to the New and stolen the lands from the Indians. These lands had been cultivated by the settlers, and passed from generation to generation until finally those who now possessed the land, in many cases, were themselves free of any taint of aggression.

Marshall had grown up on the frontier. While he personally did not know the ravages of Indian raids—the wars had ended there at the time of his birth—he obviously had heard many stories from his family. When his father moved to Kentucky, the threat there of Indian raids was much more of a reality. Towards the end of his life, however, Marshall had come to believe that the United States government was not doing well by the Indians. He expressed it this way to Joseph Story in 1828:

> The conduct of our Fore Fathers in expelling the original occupants of the soil grew out of so many mixed motives that any censure which philanthropy may bestow upon it ought to be qualified. The Indians were a fierce and dangerous enemy, whose love of war made them sometimes the aggressors, whose numbers and habits then made them formidable, and whose cruel system of warfare served to justify every endeavour to remove them to a distance from civilized settlements.

[731]

So far, Marshall had written a justification for oppression of the Indian tribes by the United States government. But then he added:

> It was not until after the adoption of our present government that respect for our own safety permitted us to give full indulgence to those principles of humanity and justice which ought always to govern our conduct towards the aborigines when this course can be pursued without exposing ourselves to the most afflicting calamities. This time however is unquestionably arrived; and every oppression now exercised on a helpless people depending on our magnanimity and justice for the preservation of their existence, impresses a deep stain on the American character. I often think with indignation of our disreputable conduct—as I think it—in the affair of the Creeks of Georgia; and I look with some alarm on the course now pursuing in the northwest.[1]

The letter, although it has a tone of the benevolent white man shouldering the responsibility and burden of the colored races, showed that Marshall did believe strongly that the Indians should not be abused. He repeated this in 1830. Speaking of the possibility that the Indians faced removal from their treaty lands, he said: "The subject has always appeared to me to effect deeply the honor, the faith and the character of our country. The cause of these oppressed people has been most ably though unsuccessfully sustained. 'Defeat in such a cause is far above the triumphs of unrighteous power.' "[2]

The problem was that there seemed no equitable way out of the situation. Individuals were not stealing the Indians' land, nor maltreating them; states and nations were. In an 1823 case, *Johnson and Graham's Lessee v. William M'Intosh*,[3] Marshall attempted to solve this dilemma by giving the settlers legal possession of the land without interfering with the Indians' right to live on it. In effect, the Indian tribes became the wards of the white men, who were expected to watch over them benevolently. This was a political decision made because any decision based on the Indians' natural rights to the land they possessed prior to the settlers' arrival would never have been enforced. The obvious hope behind the decision was that the Indians would receive the best treatment possible. Like most compromises, however, it did not work. Men were not so benevolent as John Marshall believed, or hoped, them to be. And the result would be a challenge to the national morality, to the executive branch of the government, and to the Supreme Court. Marshall would be hesitant at first—

he faced this challenge in the closing years of his eighth decade —but ultimately the Supreme Court would meet the challenge.

The challenge came in the dispute centering around the Cherokee Indian nation located within the state of Georgia. The United States government had promised Georgia that the state would possess the Indians' land. It also had promised the Indians that they would be protected, that they could live on their lands as a nation. The two pressures obviously worked against each other over the years, with the Indians seeming to lose more than they gained. In 1802 the Indians possessed twenty-six million acres of land within Georgia's borders. Two decades later the Cherokee holdings had shrunk to nine million. And Georgia wanted that.

Cotton was becoming a popular crop in that state, and large tracts were needed to grow it. Also the American people wanted to move West, and the Cherokee lands seemed ready and waiting for them. Andrew Jackson won the presidency on a campaign of assisting this westward migration. When he took office, he lived up to his campaign promises. Georgia had enacted laws extending its authority over the Indian lands. This was contrary to the treaties between the United States government and the Cherokees; accordingly, then, the President of the United States should have come to the protection of the Indians. He did not. President Andrew Jackson ordered the withdrawal of federal troops from the state and said he would take no steps to enforce the Indians' rights.

The Cherokees long ago had given up the life of the warrior and hunter. They were farmers, well-educated, peaceable people who had adopted the ways of the white man. They had been told that if they surrendered their Georgia lands, they could have new lands across the Mississippi River. This would have meant giving up their homes and traveling to a wilderness which was not particularly suited for agriculture and in which they would be vulnerable to attacks from other Indians. The Cherokee leaders believed they had a treaty which provided them with certain guarantees. Despite the rebuff from President Jackson, they believed the United States government still would honor its commitments. After all, the Constitution of the United States stated that a treaty between the United States and a foreign nation was supreme law, and the Cherokees understood that was the arrangement they had with the United States government. They decided to take their case to the Supreme Court.

The outstanding lawyer available was William Wirt. As a young man, Wirt had been a member of the team prosecuting Aaron Burr in Richmond. He had appeared in a number of

Supreme Court cases, including the *Dartmouth College* case. He had served as Attorney General under both James Monroe and John Quincy Adams. While his background made him a logical choice, it also made the choice difficult for him. He would have to argue in the Supreme Court against the President of the United States and against the untrammeled movement West by Americans. He would be accused of acting only from political motives; Jackson had ousted him from the Attorney General's office. Wirt would have preferred not being the counsel. He did not relish the position he would be placed in, knowing the pain it would bring him. He also knew that the case would place the Supreme Court "in a delicate and fearful predicament," as he expressed it to James Madison. "Yet, from the beginning," Wirt continued to Madison, "I have not been able to perceive how I could have shrunk from the part thus cast upon me, without admitting myself to have been unworthy of my profession." Wirt's predicament was that facing most lawyers on occasion in their careers, whether to take on an unpopular cause. After he had made his decision to take the case, Wirt was relieved and was able to go on without concern for the calumny being hurled at him by the press. "I have a higher bar to answer at than any in this world," he wrote to a relative, "and if I can secure a judgment there, I care little for what the unworthy may say of me here."[4]

Although Wirt believed that the Cherokees had the law on their side, he was sympathetic enough with their plight not to wish to place them in an untenable position. "If they had no hope from the Supreme Court," he said, the Cherokees would accept the offer to move West, "thinking it the least of evils." He made those comments in a letter to Dabney Carr, a Virginia judge who was a good friend of both Wirt and John Marshall. The letter also included the following:

> . . . tell me, since I have shown you how deeply the Supreme Court may be interested in this subject, whether there would be any impropriety in your conversing with the Chief Justice on this subject, as a brother judge, and giving me his impressions of the political character of this people, in the respect I have mentioned. I would not have you conceal from him that the question may probably come before the Supreme Court.

Dabney Carr showed the letter to Marshall, who declined to indicate how he would decide or how he believed the other Justices would decide, which is what Wirt had asked. He did say in a letter to Carr that "I have followed the debate in both houses of Congress, with profound attention and with deep interest, and have wished, most sincerely, that both the executive and legislative departments had thought differently on the subject. Humanity must bewail the course which is pursued, whatever may be the decision of policy."[5] Wirt's request, conveyed through Carr, was unusual if not improper. It can only be explained by his deep concern for the well-being of the Indians. The request, however, did give Marshall the opportunity to avoid what he knew would be a difficult position for the Supreme Court. If it decided for the Indians, it would be issuing a decree which it could not enforce and which it could not expect President Jackson to enforce. If it decided against the Indians, then it would be accused of ignoring morality. Marshall's refusal to respond to Wirt's request sometimes has been interpreted as meaning he eagerly anticipated having to decide the case.[6] More likely, considering his basically cautious nature and his reluctance to become involved in disputes he could not handle or resolve to his liking, John Marshall probably refused to answer because he believed it was improper for him to predict his decisions.

But as a result of his refusal, the case of the *Cherokee Nation v. Georgia* came before the Supreme Court in 1831. However one considers the pros and cons of this dispute—and there were arguments on Georgia's side—it cannot be disputed that Georgia's arrogance toward the Supreme Court of the United States was supreme. First, the state refused even to send counsel to argue its case before the Court, claiming by its refusal that it considered the Court to be without jurisdiction. Second, it executed a man rather than acknowledge even that the Supreme Court had authority within its borders. The best description of the situation was by Joseph Story in a letter to his wife at the time the case was being argued. He wrote:

> You ask, in your last letter, that I would give you some intelligible account of the Georgia case; it is, in substance, this. The Cherokee Indians reside within the limits of the State of Georgia, and until recently, their territory and persons have been exempted from the operation of the Georgia Laws. So that they tried all cases, civil and criminal, in their own way, before their own tribunals. And they allege that their independence in their territory, possessions, and laws, has been guaranteed to them by the treaties of the United States. About six months ago the State of Georgia passed a law extending jurisdiction over the whole territory and tribe, appropriating their lands, and declaring them subject to a trial in all cases, civil and criminal. One Tassels, a Cherokee, committed a murder in the Cherokee territory; he was arrested and tried before a Georgia court, found guilty, and sentenced

to be hanged. At the trial, he pleaded in his defence, that he was exempted from the jurisdiction of the Courts of Georgia, and could be tried only by his own nation, according to the treaties of the United States. His defence was rejected. He applied for a writ of error, to have the question reexamined as a treaty case, before the Supreme Court. The Chief Justice—Marshall—granted the writ, and issued a citation—that is a notice—to the State of Georgia, to appear and show cause, if they pleased, why there was no error in their proceedings. This is the whole case. Tassels is hanged, and the writ of error is now gone, as he cannot be brought to life again. You will, from this statement, understand the case well enough to judge of the intemperate and indecorous proceedings of Georgia on the question. . . .[7]

So the case of Corn Tassels, the Cherokee Indian, was never heard by the Supreme Court. Georgia executed him immediately rather than acknowledge that the federal courts had any jurisdiction over her territory.

When the Indians' case was argued before the Supreme Court by William Wirt, it was done so on the basis of the supremacy of the treaty between the Indians and the United States government over any laws to govern the Indians made by Georgia. If the state had sent counsel to argue before the Supreme Court, those counsel could have argued that it was untenable for the state to have within its borders a large population over which she had no control. But this presentation was not made, and the case rested on Wirt's arguments.

Wirt believed his chief problem was the Supreme Court's fear that President Andrew Jackson would not enforce any order the Court issued. Wirt addressed the point specifically, saying the Court should not concern itself over whether Jackson would enforce the order. "It will be time enough to meet that question when it shall arise," he said, insisting that worrying about enforcement should come after the order has been issued, because "the presumption is that the decision of the courts will be respected. . . ." His comments became more emotional as he seemed to be appealing not only to the Court, but to the President, and to the entire nation. "What is the value of that government in which the decrees of its courts can be mocked at and defied with impunity? Of that government, did I say? It is no government at all," he said, and: "In pronouncing your decree you will have declared the law: and it is part of the sworn duty of the President of the United States to 'take care that the laws be faithfully executed.' It is not for him, nor for the party defendant, to sit in appeal on your decision. The Constitution confers no such power." Wirt's feelings were strong enough for him to raise the specter of impeachment proceedings against Jackson. The President, Wirt said, is authorized to use federal troops to enforce the law as laid down by the Court. "If he refuses to perform his duty," said Wirt, "the Constitution has provided a remedy." The reference was to Article II, Section 4, of the Constitution saying a President "shall be removed from Office on Impeachment for, and Conviction of . . . high Crimes."

Wirt's concluding paragraph transformed his presentation from an argument in a specific case to an appeal for the rule of law:

> Sir, unless the Government be false to the trust which the people have confided to it, your authority will be sustained. I believe that if the injunction shall be awarded, there is a moral force in the public sentiment of the American community which will, alone, sustain it and constrain obedience. At all events, let us do our duty, and the people of the United States will take care that others do theirs. If they do not, there is an end of the Government, and the Union is dissolved. For, if the judiciary be struck from the system, what is there, of any value, that will remain?[8]

When John Marshall handed down his decision four days later, he declined to accept the challenge outlined by William Wirt. The Court did not issue an order protecting the Indians against Georgia law. As Marshall often did, he began the decision with a summary of the situation. "This bill is brought by the Cherokee Nation, praying an injunction to restrain the state of Georgia from the execution of certain laws of that state," he said, "which, as is alleged, go directly to annihilate the Cherokees as a political society, and to seize, for the use of Georgia, the lands of the nation, which have been assured to them by the United States in solemn treaties repeatedly made and still in force." He said his sympathies were with the Cherokees—"a people once numerous, powerful, and truly independent" who had been subjugated by white men, and who had surrendered their lands by treaty to white men with the promise that what remained would be theirs inviolate.

However, for the treaties to be supreme over state law, in compliance with the Constitution, then the Cherokee nation must be a foreign state. Wirt had argued that the Indians did fit the constitutional definition of a foreign nation and that the United States in dealing with the Cherokees had always considered them so. Marshall conceded that the Cherokee nation made up an independent state, an independent people, but he then asked if the Cherokees could be considered a foreign state "in the sense of the constitution?" Said Marshall: "The counsel have shown conclusively that they are not a state of the union, and have insisted that, individually, they are aliens, not owing allegiance to the United States. An aggregate of aliens composing a state must, they say, be a foreign state. Each individual being foreign, the whole must be foreign. This argument is imposing, but we must examine it more closely before we yield to it." The relationship between the Indians and the United States, Marshall declared, "is marked by peculiar and cardinal distinctions which exist nowhere else."

First, he said, Indian land was within the territorial boundaries of the United States. Also, the Indians acknowledged that they were under the protection of the United States, and that the United States had the authority to regulate their trade. "It may well be doubted whether those tribes which reside within the acknowledged boundaries of the United States can, with strict accuracy, be denominated foreign nations." Marshall described them as, instead, "domestic dependent nations." Marshall suggested that reference to the Indians bringing suit in federal courts had been omitted from the Constitution because at the time that document was created the Indians' "appeal was to the tomahawk." He suggested that the term "foreign nations" did not include Indians when applied to treaties because another section of the Constitution empowered Congress to regulate commerce with foreign nations, between the states, "and with the Indian tribes." This led Marshall to the conclusion that the founding fathers saw foreign nations and Indian tribes as different kinds of entities. The conclusion then was that the Cherokees were not a foreign nation as described in the Constitution "and cannot maintain an action in the courts of the United States."

In addition to the Cherokees not fitting the definition of a foreign nation, Marshall said there were other objections to action by the Supreme Court. One was that the Court was being asked to restrain Georgia from exercising its legislative powers "over a neighboring people asserting their independence," and Marshall declared that the Court could not interfere, "at least in the form in which those matters are presented." As for the question of possession of the land, Marshall said the Court could not decide such a question. Legal title could be decided by the Supreme Court, he said, "but the Court is asked to do more than decide on the title. The bill requires us to control the legislature of Georgia, and to restrain the exertion of its physical force." For the Court to take such action, Marshall insisted, "savors too much of the exercise of political power to be within the proper province of the judicial department." If the Cherokees have been wronged, he said, they must seek redress from another source of government.[9] The difficulty with Marshall's decision, however, is that he did not specify what this source was.

By that ending John Marshall had been most deliberate in denying William Wirt's challenge; he said the Supreme Court would not enter into a political struggle with the President of the United States. Marshall always had been leery of such disputes. In *Marbury v. Madison* he had avoided a confrontation by giving the point to the executive branch and keeping the principle for the Court. In the Burr trial he had seen the dispute created by the subpoena to the President deteriorate into petty squabbling. Even in the decisions he had written upholding the federal Commerce Clause over the states, he had moved cautiously. That "exclusive" power was not as exclusive in *Sturges v. Crowninshield* as it was in *Gibbons v. Ogden*, decided five years later.

Still, there is the suspicion that Marshall was unhappy with his and the Court's performance in the *Cherokee Nation v. Georgia* case. Not that the decision was bad law. He had made a presentation that was within the understanding of the relationship between the Indians and the federal government, and it also was consistent with his earlier decision in *Johnson v. M'Intosh*, in which he had declared the Indians wards of the government. He did, however, later encourage Justice Thompson to write a dissent, with which Story concurred, saying that the Cherokees were entitled to part of the relief they sought. Also, he encouraged Richard Peters, who was then publishing the Court reports, to print a separate volume devoted exclusively to the Cherokee case. "As an individual," Marshall wrote Peters, "I should be glad to see the whole case. It is one in which the public takes a deep interest, and of which a very narrow view has been taken in the opinion which is pronounced by the court." Then Marshall did something he rarely did. He apologized for one of his decisions. In the letter to Peters Marshall said that in writing the decision he did not have time to consider its various ramifications, nor did he believe he should have produced anything but a decision based on "narrow limits." He indicated that the concurring opinions—Baldwin and Johnson had agreed that the Court lacked jurisdiction but for reasons other than those stated by Marshall —"look to our side of the question only." He then mentioned the dissent by Thompson, which he had encouraged but had not yet seen, and said he was sure it presented "with ability the other side of the question."[10]

Marshall here seemed anxious to stir up public feeling, to keep the case alive. In his decision he had suggested the Cherokees seek redress from another arm of government, and perhaps he hoped that continued publicity might goad the administration into action. Or perhaps he believed the case would come again before the Supreme Court in another form, so he would have a second opportunity to consider the issue. If this was his hope, he would not be disappointed.

On September 24, 1831, *Niles' Weekly Register* carried this item:

> High crime and great penalty. On the second Monday of this month the superior court of Gwinnett county, Ga., commenced its session, when ten white men were to be indicted for the crime of residing within the limits of the Georgia charter without taking the oath of allegiance. Penalty—not less than four years hard labor at the penitentiary.[11]

The paper listed the ten names, one of which was "S. A. Worcester." Samuel A. Worcester was a Congregational minister who had given up a comfortable life in Vermont to do missionary work among the Cherokees. Believing fervently in their cause, he was willing to sacrifice his freedom to support it. Georgia had passed a law prohibiting white men from living within the Cherokee territory without a license from the state; Worcester and the others were arrested and convicted of violating that law. All of the men accepted pardons except Worcester and a second missionary, Elizur Butler. These two went to the Supreme Court, challenging Georgia's right to impose any laws within the Indian territory. The Cherokees were being given another day in court, and John Marshall was being given a second opportunity to face up to the challenge of Andrew Jackson's threat of not enforcing a court order.

Again Georgia would ignore the argument that the federal government had authority over anything that transpired within her borders. On November 10, 1831, Associate Justice Baldwin sent the governor of Georgia, Wilson Lumpkin, a formal notice that the case of *Worcester v. Georgia* would be argued at the next term of the Supreme Court. Lumpkin passed the notice on to his state's General Assembly with a message saying he intended to ignore it:

Such a control over our criminal jurisdiction, as these proceedings indicate, it is believed, has not been delegated to the United States, and consequently cannot be acquiesced in or submitted to.

Any attempt to infringe the evident right of a state to govern the entire population within its territorial limits, and to punish all offences committed against its laws, within those limits—due regard being had to the cases expressly excepted by the constitution of the United States —would be the usurpation of a power never granted by the states. Such an attempt, whenever made, will challenge the most determined resistance; and if persevered in, will inevitably eventuate in the annihilation of our beloved union.

In exercising the duties of that department of government, which devolve on me, I will disregard all unconstitutional requisitions, of whatever character or origin they may be; and to the best of my abilities, will protect and defend the rights of the state, and use the means afforded to me, to maintain its laws and constitution.[12]

Lumpkin's position that the state had the right to enact laws for its entire population was not an unreasonable one, and considering that the Supreme Court, in the first *Cherokee* case, had pretty much upheld Georgia's right to watch over its territory, the state probably had a chance of winning the *Worcester* case. Lumpkin's refusal to even consider going before the Supreme Court, then, had to be taken as a direct challenge to the authority of the federal government and of the Court's role to interpret that authority. This time John Marshall was ready for those challenges.

Despite the lust for the Cherokee lands, there was a growing sympathy for the Indians. This was illustrated by a letter from Joseph Story to his wife early in 1832. On his way to Washington for the opening of the Supreme Court, Story stopped in Philadelphia where he met two chiefs of the Cherokee people "so sadly dealt with by the State of Georgia." Story was impressed by the chiefs. He found them educated and thought they "conversed with singular force and propriety of language." They knew the law involved "perfectly," said Story. "I never in my whole life was more affected by the consideration that they and all their race are destined to destruction," the Justice told his wife. "And I feel, as an American, disgraced by our gross violation of the public faith towards them. I fear, and greatly fear, that in the course of Providence there will be dealt to us a heavy retributive justice. . . ."[13]

The arguments presented to the Court in 1832, again by William Wirt chiefly, were basically the same as had been presented the previous year. There was one crucial difference, however. In the previous case, the issue—the legal point—had been whether the Cherokees were a foreign nation as contemplated in the Constitution and thus able to bring a case before the United States Supreme Court. The Court majority had ruled they were not. In this new case the issue was whether the federal law or the state law had authority over an individual who was an American citizen. There was no question but that the citizen, Worcester, had a right to be heard. Story thought Wirt's arguments were "fine" and were "brought before us in a new form."[14]

There were political ramifications in this case. William Wirt was a candidate for the presidency, on the Anti-Masonic ticket. His co-counsel, John Sergeant, was the vice presidential candidate for the National Republican party, which had seized on the Georgia-Cherokee case as a campaign issue. And both were campaigning against President Andrew Jackson, the man most responsible for Georgia's maltreatment of the Indians. Whatever the Supreme Court did in this case, it could not escape the political ramifications.

Two weeks after the arguments, John Marshall read the Court's decision. Harriet Martineau, a writer of the time, described the scene:

> I have watched the assemblage when the C.J. was delivering a judgment . . . judges on either hand, gazing at him more like learners than associates. . . . The Attorney General [Wirt], his fingers playing among his papers, his quick black eyes, and the thin, tremulous lips for once fixed, his small face pale with thought. . . . These men absorbed in what they are listening to, thinking neither of themselves nor each other, while they are watched by the group of idlers and listeners. Among them the newspaper corps. The dark Cherokee chiefs, the stragglers from the far West, the gay ladies in their waving plumes, and the members of either house that have stepped in to listen; all these I have seen constitute the silent assemblage, while the mild voice of the aged C.J. sounded through the court.[15]

Marshall's voice now was very weak; he would be seventy-seven later in the year, and his age had weakened his physical powers. Still, he apparently read the entire decision, which consumes twenty-eight pages in the official reports. He began his decision with the customary summary statement, saying: "This cause . . . is of the deepest interest." He then said: "The legislative power of a state, the controlling power of the constitution and laws of the United States, the rights, if they have any, the political existence of a once numerous and powerful people, the personal liberty of a citizen, are all involved in the subject now to be considered. . . ."

He then reviewed the arguments made by Wirt and Sergeant that the state law under which Worcester had been arrested was unconstitutional because it conflicted with the jurisdiction given the Cherokees by a treaty between them and the United States government, "that the act under which the prosecution was instituted is repugnant to the said treaties, and is, therefore, unconstitutional and void." Marshall then declared that the twenty-fifth section of the Judiciary Act, listing cases under which state court actions could be appealed to the Supreme Court, authorized the federal court to hear Worcester's plea. He next included a protestation that had come to be typical in cases with heavy political overtones. After saying that the Court had the duty to hear the plea, Marshall continued: "This duty, however unpleasant, cannot be avoided. Those who fill the judicial department have no discretion in selecting the subjects to be brought before them."

Marshall then stated that one effect of the Georgia law was to impose state control over the Indians. Had the state this power? Marshall's answer is a lengthy one, giving a detailed history of the relationships between the Indians and the white man in North America. He did not challenge the right of the white man to have conquered the Indians, saying that "power, war, conquest, give rights which, after possession, are conceded by the world; and which can never be controverted by those on whom they descend."

He denied, however, the white man's right to rule the Indians. Some have found in this decision conflicts with Marshall's earlier decision, *Johnson v. M'Intosh*, in which he also had defended the rights of the conquerors and had spoken of the white man's compelling military power. To Marshall, however, the distinction he was making in this 1832 decision was significant. The conquerors, he said, never had attempted to govern whatever Indian affairs had gone on inside the boundaries of the Indian territory. (Marshall did say, however, that "The King purchased [the Indian] lands, when [the Indians] were willing to sell, at a price they were willing to take; but never coerced a surrender of them." This was in contradiction to his statements in the *Johnson* case as well as being dubious history.)

The decision continued that the relationship between the

British King and the Indians had been continued by the Americans, and that Congress had passed many laws, still in force, which "manifestly consider the several Indian nations as distinct political communities, having territorial boundaries, within which their authority is exclusive, and having a right to all the lands within those boundaries, which is not only acknowledged, but guaranteed by the United States."

In a brief piece of dicta Marshall seemed to be announcing publicly his regret at the decision a year earlier in the first *Cherokee* case. Then he had challenged the definition of Indian tribes as foreign nations and also had appeared to question their subsequent right to make treaties with the United States government. If they were foreign nations, they could make treaties. If they were not foreign nations, as Marshall had said in 1831, the corollary would be that they could not make treaties. In 1832 he made clear that had not been the Court's intention. "The constitution," he said, "by declaring treaties already made, as well as those to be made, to be the supreme law of the land, has adopted and sanctioned the previous treaties with the Indian nations, and consequently, admits their rank among those powers who are capable of making treaties." He insisted that Georgia had acknowledged this supremacy of the treaties until 1828, when great interest in acquiring the Indian lands had developed.

The conclusion of the decision was then obvious. The act of Georgia requiring any white man who wished to enter the Cherokee lands to obtain a license from the state was unconstitutional, and the Supreme Court had the right to strike it down. Worcester had entered the Indian territory under the protection of federal law, and the federal government then had the obligation to protect him. The closing two paragraphs of the decision are significant in the story of John Marshall. As a judge he had been basically a cautious man. The judicial review approach he had announced in *Marbury v. Madison* was a common approach by state-level judges at the time. The theory of a Constitution with powers expanding to meet its obligations which he spoke of in *McCulloch v. Maryland* also had origins going back many years. The supremacy of the federal contract law over state incursions had such support from logic that it could not be seriously challenged. When, however, Marshall had been faced with placing the Supreme Court in a direct conflict with another branch of government, he had been reluctant—the first *Cherokee* decision had reflected that caution. The caution had not been based on timidity, but, rather, on the belief that the Court had only certain powers. It could not send legions of soldiers into the field to enforce its orders. For the Court to order more than the executive would command was for the Court to risk its prestige for a dubious outcome. On occasion, however, a risk must be taken. That is as true for the Supreme Court as for anything else. John Marshall understood this. In the first *Cherokee* decision he had attempted to deal with political realities as well as to protect the Indians. It had not worked. Now he must use his power as a moral voice for the nation. He began the last two paragraphs of his decision with a reference to the Georgia laws dealing with the Cherokees:

> [The laws] are in direct hostility with treaties, repeated in a succession of years, which mark out the boundary that separates the Cherokee country from Georgia, guaranty to them all the land within their boundary, solemnly pledge the faith of the United States to restrain their citizens from trespassing on it, and recognize the pre-existing power of the nation to govern itself. . . .
>
> It is the opinion of this court that the judgment of the superior court for the county of Gwinnett, in the state of Georgia, condemning Samuel A. Worcester to hard labor in the penitentiary of the state of Georgia for four years, was pronounced by that court under color of a law which is void, as being repugnant to the constitution, treaties, and laws of the United States, and ought, therefore, to be reversed and annulled.[16]

Of this decision, it usually is reported that President Andrew Jackson said: "John Marshall has made his decision, now let him enforce it." Although a recent study challenges that report, the evidence is that if Jackson did not say that, he certainly meant it.[17] The President was furious at the decision. He charged that the Supreme Court had combined with his enemies "to embarrass me." He insisted that the Court would not be able to get away with attacking him. "I have always relied on the good intelligence and virtue of the people," he said. "They will decide."[18]

As for the Supreme Court, there was no question among its members that they had done their duty and the next step was up to the President. "Thanks be to God," cried Joseph Story, "the court can wash their hands clean of the iniquity of oppressing the Indians and disregarding their rights." And if the President did not enforce the law, Story said, "I, for one, feel quite easy on the subject, be the event what it may. The Court has done its duty. Let the nation now do theirs. If we have a Government, let its command be obeyed; if we have not, it is as well to know it at once, and to look to consequences. . . ."[19]

Georgia did not release Worcester as the Supreme Court had ordered; he was pardoned a year later by the Governor of Georgia. President Jackson made no effort to enforce the Court's decision, and the Indians ultimately were removed from the Georgia territory. Their move West has become known as the "Trail of Tears," and it remains in modern times one of those incidents in American history which shame the nation. Jackson had said the people will decide, and they did. Perhaps not at the moment, but through generations that followed they came to understand that the morality spoken by the Marshall Court in the decision of *Worcester v. Georgia* was a call to the conscience of the American people. Nothing can excuse the ruthlessness of the whites toward the Indians; and the conduct of the state of Georgia, and of Andrew Jackson in refusing to enforce the Court's decision, demonstrates the folly of refusing to obey the law. The people decided, as Jackson had predicted. They have recorded in their histories that Andrew Jackson and the state of Georgia acted to deprive people of their legal rights. In a nation built on law, there can be no greater condemnation.

16

As JOHN MARSHALL ENTERED the second half of his eighth decade of life, he still retained his remarkably good health —partly an inheritance from his parents, partly due to his youth on the frontier, and partly a result of his efforts to take care of himself. His three-mile walks each day had become legendary. A Congressman, Edward Everett, was riding in a hack through the streets of Washington and was "ashamed of myself . . . to see the Chief Justice, who is seventy-five years old, trudging up to Court on foot." Everett thought the example proved too much. "In his youth," he said of Marshall, "he was dissipated: attended horse races and cock fights, gamed, bet, and drank. In my youth, I was a demure lad, indulged in no dissipation, ran the gauntlet of Europe without being betrayed into vice, then I am, at the age of thirty-seven, obliged to drive up to the Capitol, while the Old Chief Justice walks."[1]

But the Chief Justice was aging. A few months after Everett had been embarrassed by the sight of him trudging on foot to Capitol Hill, Marshall began to feel ill. This was in 1831, and Marshall first noticed a problem in May when he returned from Circuit Court in North Carolina. His regular doctor apparently diagnosed the condition correctly, but Marshall would not believe him. Finally, he had to accept the obvious, that he was seriously ill. A journey to Philadelphia and treatment by a doctor there was necessary. His friends in Richmond realized how ill he was and did not anticipate his recovery.[2]

Marshall's difficulty was that stones had developed in his bladder, which made urinating painful, and he also experienced pain whenever he made any quick motion. The cure was a lithotomy, the cutting into the bladder to remove the calculus, or stone. It was a dangerous operation then, and the foremost practitioner was Dr. Philip Syng Physick in Philadelphia, who was called the Father of American Surgery. Marshall journeyed to Philadelphia to see him.

Dr. Physick was by this time sixty-three years old and had not performed any extensive surgery, as this would be, for several years. He suggested that his young assistant, Dr. Jacob Randolph, perform the operation. But Randolph, realizing that this would perhaps be Physick's last operation, insisted that Physick perform it, and he agreed. A room was found for Marshall at a Mrs. Sword's, and the doctor there began his examinations, which were basically to determine the location of the obstruction.

Marshall was impressed by him. "He deliberates very much," he said of the doctor, "is determined to do nothing rashly, and seems anxious to be perfectly master of my case." Marshall wrote Polly that he was hopeful of recovery, for all that a doctor could do, Marshall was certain Physick would do, and: "I anticipate with a pleasure which I know you will share the time when I may sit by your side by our tranquil fireside and enjoy the happiness of your society without inflicting on you the pain of witnessing my suffering. . . ."[3]

While he was under observation by the doctor, the people and the lawyers of the city formally paid him honors. One time he visited a "free trade convention" and, according to a news account, "the delegates rose en masse to receive him—nullificators, anti-25th-section-men, and all!" The bar formally adopted a resolution informing the Chief Justice of the "high respect and profound veneration for your character felt by us all. . . . We cannot but consider the whole nation indebted to one who for so long a series of years has illuminated its jurisprudence, and enforced with equal mildness and firmness its constitutional authority; who has never sought to enlarge the judicial power beyond its proper bounds, nor feared to carry it to the full extent that duty required. . . ." Marshall obviously was pleased by the remarks. "Might I be permitted to claim for myself as well as for my associates," he replied to the bar, "any portion of the liberal consideration your partial favor bestows, it would be, that we 'have never sought to enlarge the judicial power beyond its proper bounds, nor feared to carry it to the full extent that duty required.' . . ." This, of course, had been John Marshall's understanding of judicial responsibility, that judges must fulfill their responsibilities by using their powers to their limits, but must not assume powers that were not theirs.[4]

The examination of Marshall lasted about two weeks. Physick insisted upon the operation, but there was difficulty securing a proper room; hospitals were not considered because of their potential for disease. Finally, "a family which occupied a very convenient room resigns it to me today . . . and it will soon be in a state of readiness." Physick himself was delayed because of rain; he did not go out in the rain because of his poor health. "Today we see the sun," wrote Marshall to Polly on October 12, "and I hope [Physick's] operations will begin. My room is now preparing and he has just left me with directions to take a tablespoonful of castor oil two hours after dinner . . . my own Landlady is extremely attentive to me. She has engaged one of the best male nurses in the city who now attends me altho he is not needed. . . ."[5]

The morning of the operation, Physick's assistant, Dr. Randolph, visited Marshall. He found the Chief Justice in good spirits, eating his breakfast. "Well, Doctor, you find me taking breakfast," said Marshall, "and I assure you I have had a good one. I thought it very probable that this might be my last chance, and therefore I was determined to enjoy it and eat heartily." Randolph commented that he hoped the difficulties "would soon be happily over." Marshall replied he was entering the operation without anxiety. He said he had no desire to live under the pain he had suffered and that he was willing to risk the operation. He said, as Randolph recorded it, "that if he could be relieved by it he was willing to live out his appointed time, but if not, would rather die than hold existence accompanied with the pain and misery which he then endured."

After breakfast, Marshall took some medicine and then asked when the operation was scheduled. Randolph said eleven, and Marshall replied: "Very well; do you wish me now for any other purpose, or may I lie down and go to sleep?" When Randolph said sleep was desirable, Marshall stretched out on his bed and fell into a deep sleep until Randolph woke him for the operation. "He exhibited the same fortitude, scarcely uttering a murmur, throughout the whole procedure, which, from the peculiar nature of his complaint, was necessarily tedious." The operation was performed on October 13, and it was a typical lithotomy of the time. The neck of the bladder was divided with a gorget, Dr. Physick felt the prostate gland with his finger and found it considerably enlarged, with the third lobe projected upwards, forming a tumor about the size of one end of Physick's fingers. Being unable to reach with his finger into the cavity of the bladder through these tumefied parts and feel the stone, he used a forceps to withdraw the stone. To the doctor's surprise, he found that rather than there being one stone, there were a number of small ones. At first he believed them to be the pieces of one large stone, which might have been broken by the forceps taking hold of it. On examining the pieces individually, however, he realized that they were not parts of one stone, but that each was a separate stone with a smooth, polished surface. The operation was completed by removing the stones with forceps, and by injecting barley water into the bladder to wash out any that might escape the forceps. The estimate was that more than one thousand stones were removed, varying in size from that of a large pea to that of a pin's head. They were analyzed and found to be composed of uric acid.[6]

The operation was an incredible success, and the doctors agreed that one reason for its success was Marshall's strength and good health. His recovery was so swift that he astonished even Dr. Physick. After the operation, the doctor had ordered the strictest quiet for his patient, not a muscle was to be moved. The next time he visited the Chief Justice, however, he found him sitting up in bed.[7]

Marshall underwent the operation on October 13 and stayed in bed until November 8. The newspapers carried accounts of his progress, and his friends in Philadelphia passed on the news to the Chief Justice's admirers all over the nation. His illness, because of the danger of death, had become almost a national event.[8]

The first letter he wrote was, of course, to his Polly. "I have at length risen from my bed and am able to hold a pen," he wrote on November 8. "The most delightful use I can make of it is to tell you that I am getting well. . . . Nothing delights me so much as to hear from my friends and especially from you." Polly was unable to write a full letter herself, but she added a few lines to a letter which their daughter Mary had written. "How much was I gratified at the line from your own hand in Mary's letter," he told his dearest but very ailing wife.[9]

Two days after rising from his bed on November 8 Marshall was walking across the room—"This I do with a tottering feeble step," he wrote Joseph Story. He also was planning to leave Philadelphia in time to open the Circuit Court in Richmond on

November 22. Marshall reported on the success of the operation and his hopes for complete recovery: "I am however under the very disagreeable necessity of taking medicine continually to prevent new formations. I must submit too to a severe and most unsociable rejimen. Such are the privations of age. You have before you I trust many, very many years unclouded by such dreary prospects."[10]

Marshall left Philadelphia on Saturday morning, November 19, on the steamboat *William Penn*, and arrived in Richmond on Wednesday morning "after a very tempestuous passage down the bay."[11]

Although his own health was completely restored, his wife's had become increasingly worse. For years she had left the red brick house in Richmond only rarely, usually to attend church on Communion Sunday. Her grandchildren remembered her, according to a family history, "as the thinnest little lady they ever saw, who was often ill; and that it was the law that they must whisper and tiptoe in her presence."[12]

A few weeks after Marshall's return from his operation in Philadelphia, he realized that his Polly was near death. "My poor wife lies dangerously ill and has been so for more than a fortnight," he wrote to his brother James a few days before Christmas. Marshall's fears, he confessed, "are stronger than my hopes."[13] All her married life Mary Willis Ambler—his dearest Polly—had worn around her neck a locket containing some strands of her hair. It was the lock of hair that her cousin John Ambler had snipped from her head that day many years ago when she had told her suitor "no" when she meant "yes." On the day before Christmas 1831, Polly Marshall took the locket from around her own neck and placed it around her husband's. The next day, three months before her sixty-sixth birthday, she died.

John Marshall was inconsolable. A few weeks later, when the Court was meeting in Washington, Story entered Marshall's room at their boardinghouse and found the Chief Justice in tears. Marshall told his friend that rarely did he pass a night without crying over Polly. "She must have been a very extraordinary woman to have attached him," thought Story, "and I think he is the most extraordinary man I ever saw, for the depth and tenderness of his feelings."[14]

On the first anniversary of Polly's death, Marshall wrote a few lines in which he recalled his life with her, described the love he felt for her, her judgment "sound and so safe," and then concluded: "I have lost her! And with her I have lost the solace of my life! Yet she remains still the companion of my retired hours—still occupies my inmost bosom."[15]

In the summer of 1833, his youngest son, Edward Carrington Marshall, and his wife Rebecca had a new baby daughter and wrote the Chief Justice inviting him to name the child. One of their daughters already had been named Mary, after Polly, and John Marshall could not enter into the spirit of the naming. He recommended Rebecca as it would fit aunts of both Edward and Edward's wife. "I barely make these suggestions," Marshall wrote to his son, "but must decline the compliment you pay of giving any definitive name to my grand daughter. My whole preference was concentrated in the single name Mary. I have no other preference and that which most pleases Rebecca and yourself will most please me." They followed his advice and named the child Rebecca.[16]

About this time Marshall, perhaps influenced by his loneliness and grief following Polly's death, came to some reconciliation with religion. Like most men of his time, Marshall was not a communicant of a formal church. The churches in the United States, particularly the Episcopal Church in Virginia, were corrupt; Bishop Meade, one of those who worked in the early 1800s to rebuild the church, described the Virginia institution as "low and hopeless." In the eighteenth century the church had been supported through state taxation, and the clergy—not required to maintain any standards of conduct or effort—sank into lethargy and personal immorality. In the 1780s Jefferson and Madison effectively separated the church from the state. Although their action was denounced at the time as antireligious, it worked to benefit the church. The church's growth and advancement, and its service to the people, dates from this time. Marshall had not supported the separation movement. His understanding as a youth that the vestry is a form of government that holds a community together forced him to be against the bill. There may have been another reason. "The American population is entirely Christian," he wrote in a letter in 1833, "and with us, Christianity and Religion are identified." With that kind of a belief, it is not surprising he had not objected to a proposal that the civil government collect a tax from all citizens of the state for distribution to the various clergymen.

Although Marshall could not become a communicant of a church, he supported the institution with the hope, a very faint one, that eventually it would improve. Bishop Meade told the story of asking Marshall for a contribution to a theological seminary, and, said Meade, though Marshall "gave with his accustomed liberality, he could not refrain from saying, that it was a hopeless undertaking, and that it was almost unkind to induce young Virginians to enter the Episcopal ministry, the Church being too far gone ever to be revived."[17]

When the Monumental Church was built in Richmond in 1814, Marshall was one of the leading fundraisers as well as a generous contributor. He was active in church affairs, for example, serving in 1814 as a delegate to the convention of the Protestant Episcopal Church of Virginia. He had his own pew at the church, number twenty-three, for which he had paid $390. It was off the center aisle and was in the second row back from the altar. He would press his body together so he could fit into the pew and had to kneel in the aisle because his legs were so long. Still, he refused communion. A list of communicants in 1829 included "Mrs. Judge Marshall" but not her husband. Actually only 179 people were listed as communicants, indicating that many others were with Marshall in declining to take communion.[18]

Still, Marshall was a believer in religion and in Christianity. A famous story told of him about this time has him stopping at a hotel in Winchester, and listening as some young men berated religion and God's existence, until one of the young men turned to Marshall, not realizing who he was, and said: "Well, old man, what do you think of these things?" The story continued:

> The old chief said they were very important matters, and he had not thought as much upon them as he ought to have done; but such crude thoughts as he had he would give them. He commenced as he would have done to babes in knowledge, stating that creation must have had a creator; that the creator must also have been omnipotent, to have filled unlimited space with worlds; that he must have been all-wise to have produced universal harmony; that he must have all goodness to have provided the means of happiness for all his creatures.[19]

According to family accounts, Marshall did not accept the divinity of Christ until very late in his life, and then did plan to be baptized and wished to do it publicly. If so, he never fulfilled that ambition.

"Christian" in John Marshall's Virginia meant Protestant, as it did in most of the United States. There was a great deal of anti-Catholicism at the time. Marshall, however, was free of this bias—an unusual achievement in Virginia and in the rest of the United States during the first half of the nineteenth century. In North Carolina in 1833 a lawyer named William Gaston was being considered for an appointment to the state Supreme Court. Gaston was a Roman Catholic and there was a question as to whether the state constitution allowed Catholics to hold appointed office. Marshall was well known to the legal community and it was well known to him; also Gaston was a good friend of his who often had argued cases before the Circuit Court where Marshall presided.

Two of Gaston's friends in North Carolina, Thomas Devereux and George F. Badger, asked Marshall his opinion about the propriety of nominating a Catholic to the state Supreme Court. Marshall's answer was quick in coming, and consisted of three parts. First, he said that as a federal judge he would have no hesitation in upholding Gaston's right to a judgeship if the question came before him in that capacity. Then he said that he did not believe he should publicly comment in an unofficial capacity—he was a resident of Virginia, not of North Carolina, and feared any such statement might be considered "as an officious interference." But in case there was any doubt, he concluded that if he were a member of the North Carolina legislature, he would not hesitate to vote for Gaston, adding that the religious question "was a matter addressed solely to the mind of the candidate himself and which could in its nature be determined by no other person." Marshall must have known that his comments had been sought so they could be widely broadcast in North Carolina to assist in securing the appointment for Gaston.[20]

As an old man, Marshall enjoyed playing the role of elder statesman and was fond of giving advice and comments to whosoever sought them. With his friends he engaged in discussions of political philosophy. The "true and substantial dividing line between parties in the United States" is the argument over whether the Constitution created "a league and not a government."[21] Although he had favored the electoral college device of choosing the President when the Constitution was first proposed, by the 1830s he believed that system had become so mired in politics as to threaten "the most serious danger to the public happiness." Conceding that he might have grown timid because of his age, he announced that "certain it is that I now dread consequences which I once thought imaginary." He then said he favored a plan under which the people would elect a group equal in number to one-third the Senate and the President would be chosen by lot from this group.[22]

As for the possibility of legislation affecting working conditions, Marshall wondered whether such laws are not "a branch of the more general question of demand and supply?" He asked: "Does not [such laws'] practicability depend on the abundance of labor and the demand for laborers?" In 1832 when Marshall was sent a proposal for "A Congress of Nations for the amicable adjustment of national differences," he replied that he thought "the human race would be eminently benefitted by the principle you advance." Yet Marshall, who had had some experience with the Congress of Nations concept when he was Secretary of State dealing with the Barbary pirates, allowed that "I must avow my belief that it is impracticable."[23]

Marshall became a strong advocate of public education, not a universal practice then. He believed a public education system "among the most meritorious efforts of patriotism" and considered it "more indispensable in governments entirely popular than in any other that the mass of the people should receive that degree of instruction which will enable them to perform with some intelligence the duties which devolve on them." He was constantly urging his grandchildren to tend to their studies. "I am very glad to hear of your progress in arithmetic, and to see that you improve your handwriting," he wrote to one, continuing: "If you have been unable to go to school, the time, I am sure has not been lost. Nothing is more precious than time, especially to the young, and yet nothing slips from us less regarded or less valued." To another grandson: "Proficiency in Greek and Latin is indispensable to an accomplished scholar. . . . There is no exercise of the mind from which more valuable improvement is to be drawn than from composition. . . . The first step toward writing and speaking clearly is to think clearly. . . ."[24]

His interest in agriculture stemmed from his own farm lands and from a realization that the land must be properly cared for it if is to continue productive. "I have been croaking on this subject when I could get anybody to listen to me these thirty years," he wrote a friend in 1830, "but have made no other progress than to get myself placed among those old men who are always extolling the times that are past at the expense of the present. Yet the evil is of real magnitude and its consequences are continually manifesting themselves. We have scarcely a man in our country who is now opulent that may not look for paupers among his grandchildren."[25]

Marshall never could forgive his old opponent, Thomas Jefferson. To the aged Marshall, Jefferson's greatest sin still was that he had been critical of George Washington. "The sentiment excited by the name of Washington has on more than one occasion, shown itself with great strength," Marshall wrote to a friend in 1833. Marshall then recalled the emotion the name had created during the Revolutionary War, the respect it elicited even from the British, and then said: "It was not until the French revolution maddened the world, and gave efficacy to the machinations of one of our most skilful politicians, that the devotion of his fellow citizens was in any degree impaired. Even then, the affection of the great body of the people remained unshaken. Only the party leaders deserted him."[26]

To the people of Richmond, where he had made his home now for half a century, he was not so much the elder statesman as "the old Chief," and in those words were as much affection as the townspeople could address to John Marshall. He still walked through the city streets, tall and unbent, his step sprightly. On the street people saluted him, and according to one witness, "noisy disputants ceased their clamors on his approach and the very children stopped their amusements to take a look at the venerable old man."[27]

Even in the 1830s it continued the custom for the men to do the marketing, and John Marshall, as always, enjoyed the outing. He shook hands with his friends, chatted with them to pick up the latest gossip, and, with his coat slung over his shoulder in warm weather, laughed heartily at their stories. Marshall was forgetful and often went marketing without his basket. One lawyer enjoyed telling the story of meeting the Chief Justice on the street as Marshall was returning from his marketing. From one of Marshall's long arms hung a huge turkey with its legs tied together and its head hanging down. In his other was a pair of ducks, and in the pockets of his coattails were a beefsteak and chitterlings. This was the man whose Supreme Court decisions had established the principle of judicial review, the supremacy of the Union over the states, and the sanctity of contracts.[28]

The most famous story of John Marshall's marketing has him overhear a young well-dressed man complain that his mother had told him to buy a turkey but that he refused to carry it through the streets like a servant. Marshall then offered to carry the turkey for the young man, as he was going in the direction of the young man's home. The young man accepted the offer, without knowing who his elderly benefactor was. Marshall carried the turkey as far as his own home, at which point he handed the turkey to the young man. "This is where I live," said Marshall. "Your house is not far off; can't you carry the turkey the balance of the way?" The young man recognized the house as that of the Chief Justice and suddenly realized who his benefactor was; he seized the turkey and carried it home. The young man was ashamed of himself and often told the story, apparently as part of his penance.[29]

Drawings of the time show that Marshall's lean figure had begun to grow round despite his long walks. His long hair was tied in a queue, and he dressed—as he always had done—mod-

estly, carelessly, and without regard to style. He wore an un-
brushed long-skirted black coat, a badly fitting waistcoat, and
knee-breeches. A white cravat, rarely clean, black stockings, and
low shoes with silver buckles completed the costume. Joseph
Story wrote about this time that Marshall's body "seemed as ill
as his mind was well compacted." Story said that Marshall was
"without proportion" and that his arms and legs dangled, looking
"half dislocated." The Chief Justice dressed "in the garb—but I
would not dare to say in the mode—of the last century," the
clothes appearing to come "from the wardrobe of some antiquated
slopshop of second-hand raiment."

His family was defensive about his appearance. "He was
extremely neat," reported a granddaughter some years later, "but
careless as to the style of his dress and always looked old-fashioned, I suppose." But the family also conceded that his dress was
beneath his station. Among the various stories about him is one
having him call on a sister-in-law he never before had met. The
woman, the wife of his brother, mistook him for a butcher.[30]

Marshall's casualness about his dress to the very end of his
life was a reflection of his basic humbleness. Although he was
head of a powerful branch of the federal government, he often
answered the door of his red brick Richmond house himself. More
often a visitor could just turn the handle and walk in; the door
was rarely locked. In Raleigh, North Carolina, where he held
Circuit Court, Marshall went out in the morning to collect his
own firewood rather than insist upon his landlord supplying it. "I
suppose it is not convenient for Mr. Cook to keep a servant," he
explained, "so I make my own fires." He made the journey from
Richmond to Raleigh in a stick gig—a wooden chair supported on
two wheels and two shafts pulled by one horse. It was not uncommon for him to nap as he rode along. On one occasion, so the
story goes, the gig ran over a sapling and was tilted, the jolt wak-
ing Marshall who found himself unable to move the gig either to
the right or left. An old Negro came along and rescued Marshall
by suggesting the obvious: that the Chief Justice back up the gig.
The advice was sound, and Marshall more than anyone might
have enjoyed the Negro's description of Marshall as a nice old
gentleman who wasn't too bright.[31]

In his old age Marshall never forgot the men he had marched
with in the Culpeper Militia nearly sixty years earlier. One story
had Marshall meeting an old army comrade who was in desperate financial straits, needing $3,000 immediately if his home
and property were not to be confiscated. Marshall did not say anything but left a check for the amount for him. The man raced
after Marshall to return the check; Marshall appeased the man's

pride by accepting security for the loan but never called for payment of the debt. In the 1830s Marshall was valuable to his old army friends because the government was offering pensions to those who could prove their service affiliation, and Marshall was a reliable witness. A relative of Philip Slaughter, who had been in the Culpeper Minutemen with Marshall, came to the Supreme Court chamber and sent up a note to Marshall asking when he could discuss with him Philip Slaughter's pension claim. Marshall left the bench immediately and came to the young man. "How is Phil?" he asked, and when the young man said Marshall's old friend was seriously ill and not expected to live, Marshall was visibly affected. The Chief Justice provided all the assistance he could in establishing the pension claim.[32]

Not only his old friends but young people and sometimes strangers were moved by his kindness, his graciousness, and the simplicity of his life. A young man named John Randolph Bryan took the steamboat for Washington one day—"She was one of the old-fashioned craft, with her cabin all under deck, abaft of the engine, without any staterooms, open berths, over each other, with a plain calico curtain." They arrived about a mile down the Potomac from Washington at four o'clock in the morning. Bryan arose, planning to walk to the city, and then was joined by the Chief Justice, also an early riser. Another passenger thrust his head out from his berth curtains and called to Marshall: "Why, Judge, what are you getting up this time of morning for? You can't hold court at this hour." Marshall replied: "No, but I am not going to let this young gentleman get ahead of me." He then turned to young Bryan and asked if he could walk with him to the city. "Being myself quite a young man," Bryan recalled later, "I was not only gratified but deeply impressed with the perfect ingenuousness and simplicity of the Chief Justice; free from any conscious superiority, he at once placed himself on a footing with me. . . ."

Perhaps the most famous anecdote about Marshall in Raleigh was told by the editor of the newspaper there shortly after Marshall's death. The Circuit Court in Raleigh had a new crier who was taking his job very seriously except when the moment came for Marshall to deliver his charge to the grand jury. Then the crier slipped into a reverie and forgot to issue the customary caution of silence. Marshall waited a few moments, shrugged, and then began to read his charge. After he had begun, however, the court crier awoke, considered the whole procedure irregular, and stepped up to Marshall. "Stop, sir! Stop, sir!" he said to the Chief Justice of the United States. Marshall stopped, and the crier shouted: "Oyes! oyes! oyes! All manner of persons are required to keep silence, upon pain of imprisonment, while the honorable judge is giving his charge to the grand jury!" The story continued: "When he had finished this proclamation, he turned to the court, with an air of complacency and a wave of the hand, and said to the chief justice—'You may go on, sir.' Everyone expected to see the unfortunate crier sent to jail, as a matter of course, but, without cracking a smile, the chief justice commenced his charge de novo and went through as though nothing had happened."[33]

His kindnesses to children were many. According to one story, Marshall patronized a carriage shop and became friendly with the son of the owner. He was a studious child who was interested in becoming a doctor, but lacked the financial resources to attend medical school. Marshall paid for the boy's medical education. Another young boy, very bashful, arrived at Marshall's home one day on an errand. The Chief Justice, detecting the boy's nervousness, said: "Billy, I believe I can beat you playing marbles; come into the yard, and we will have a game." The engagement was on, and while history does not record its winner, it does record that the game was exciting and that Marshall was indeed a skillful player. History also records that the boy completely lost his bashfulness. Another time, riding his stick gig in Fauquier County, Marshall was struck by a mudball thrown by some children who did not know his identity. The ringleader of the boys was forced by his family to apologize to Marshall, who casually dismissed the whole incident with "Oh, never mind. Boys will be boys!"[34]

It was because of his kindnesses, his decency, his lack of any sign of haughtiness that the people of Virginia were so fond of him although his decisions were so opposed to the general trend of political thought in that state. A congressman named James Buchanan pointed this out in a speech in 1830, saying of Marshall: "His decisions upon constitutional questions have ever been hostile to the opinions of a vast majority of the people of his own State; and yet with what respect and veneration has he been viewed by Virginia? Is there a Virginian, whose heart does not beat with honest pride when the just fame of the Chief Justice is the subject of conversation? They consider him, as he truly is, one of the greatest and best men which this country has ever produced."[35]

It was not only his personal traits that so endeared him to his neighbors. They had plenty of opportunity to see him as a judge when he presided over the Circuit Court in Richmond, and they came to have great respect for him professionally. A lawyer named Gustavus Schmidt was in Richmond during the last half-dozen years Marshall presided as a judge. He left a detailed description of Marshall the man and the jurist. When Marshall entered the courtroom, Schmidt wrote, a few minutes before the court was called to order, his conversation was cheerful and his mind seemed unclouded. He chatted with the lawyers and "no attempt was ever made to claim superiority, either on account of his age or his great acquirements; neither was there any effort to acquire popularity." Instead his conduct "was evidently dictated by a benevolent interest in the ordinary affairs of life, and a relish for social intercourse." These were Marshall's friends, in that courtroom, and he always had enjoyed associating with them, over wine at his popular lawyers' dinners, over a game of billiards, or in just casual talk. He was constitutionally incapable of aloofness.

Schmidt's account of Marshall continued: "The moment, however, he took his seat on the bench his character assumed a striking change. He still continued the same kind and benevolent being as before; but instead of the gay and cheerful expression which distinguished the features while engaged in social conversation, his brow assumed a thoughtfulness and an air of gravity and reflection, which invested his whole appearance with a certain indefinable dignity, which bore, however, not the slightest resemblance to sternness. . . . We do not recollect . . . ever to have seen [Marshall] indicate impatience even by a gesture."

Schmidt saw Marshall always acting "on the principle, that a Court of Justice was a sanctuary, where parties had a right to be heard . . . [that] the law had wisely interposed a special class of agents, called lawyers, to protect the interests of suitors . . . they acted in behalf of the citizens of the community, for those whose benefit the administration of justice was created, and because the highest and lowest member of society was entitled to equal favor in a Court of Justice."[36]

In his later years John Marshall continued his close interest in national politics without allowing himself to become formally involved. His opposition to the Jackson presidency was well known and in September 1831 a group of anti-Jacksonites elected him chairman of their committee; this obviously was an attempt to capitalize on his name, as Marshall was within a few days of being seventy-six years of age and could not provide active leadership. Marshall declined the appointment in a public letter printed in the *Richmond Whig*, citing his age, "my habits, which separate me from all party contests," and "above all, the public office I hold." But he did nothing to disabuse the public of the impression that he opposed the election of Jackson the next year. Later, however, when Jackson came out strongly against the Nullification Doctrine, Joseph Story said that "the Chief Justice and myself have become [Jackson's] warmest supporters."

After Jackson's second inaugural in 1833 politicians in Virginia immediately began thinking of the next presidential election—"her trade of President making" is how Marshall phrased it. He was not above mentioning to a friend in Philadelphia that the Virginians were divided and that, as a result, Pennsylvania could be a key state in the next election. His letters on politics were the usual mixtures for him of skillful analyses and disclaimers. This one in September 1833 to Henry Lee is an example. Marshall wrote:

> Our canvass for the successor of President Jackson has commenced. A strong foundation has been laid for the election of Mr. Van Buren, but he will encounter much opposition. Many counties of Virginia have shown a disposition to bring forward our friend Mr. Leigh. Should he be taken up by the legislature, which is not improbable, he bids fair to be supported by the South. I know very little of what is passing in the political world.[37]

In his later years Marshall continued as an active member of the Barbecue Club. He attended most Saturday sessions and his foremost activities there were downing mint juleps—"very strange to me," reported one young man in 1833 of a gathering of the club, "Judge Marshall was intoxicated"—and playing quoits. John Marshall continued as the undisputed champion in Richmond. But he left nothing to chance. Chester Harding, the artist, told of visiting one of the Barbecue Club's sessions in 1829. "The battleground was about a mile from the city in a beautiful grove," he wrote. "I went early, with a friend, just as the party were beginning to arrive. I watched for the coming of the old chief. He soon approached with his coat on his arm, and his hat in his hand, which he was using as a fan. He walked directly up to a large bowl of mint julep, which had been prepared, and drank off a tumbler full of the liquid, smacked his lips, and then turned to the company, with a cheerful 'how are you, gentlemen?' "

Harding reported that Marshall "was looked upon as the best pitcher of the party, and could throw heavier quoits than any other member of the club." Harding found the game exciting. "There were several ties," he said, "and, before long, I saw the great Chief Justice of the Supreme Court of the United States, down on his knees, measuring the contested distance with a straw, with as much earnestness as if it had been a point of law; and if he proved to be in the right, the woods would ring with his triumphant shout." Harding wondered: "What would the dignitaries of the highest court of England have thought, if they had been present?" A Marshall descendant has said that the Chief Justice was so popular that his friends might sometimes bend things slightly in his favor. "On one occasion," the descendant reported, "an old Scotchman was called on to decide between [Marshall's] quoit and that of another member; after seemingly careful measurements he announced, 'Mister Marshall has it a leattle,' when it was clear that the contrary was the case."[38]

The Barbecue Club was almost the only social organization to which he belonged in his later years. As a young man he had been a very active Mason, but the Masonic movement had fallen into disrepute by the time Marshall was older. Perhaps Marshall's memory failed him as he downplayed his earlier participation in the Masonic movement—"I followed the crowd for a time" is how he described his activities which were actually more of a leader's than of a follower's. However, there is no reason to doubt his comment in 1833 that "though there were several lodges in the city of Richmond, I have not been in one of them for more than forty years, except once on an invitation to accompany General Lafayette."[39]

But there were many honorary associations tendered him, and sometimes Marshall seemed bewildered by the attention. "I am much honoured by being elected a member of the Bunker Hill monument association," he wrote to Edward Everett, "and beg you to make my profound acknowledgements to the institution. As I am entirely uninformed of what it may be proper for me to do, I ask this favour of you to make me such communications as will enable me to do whatever is requisite." When the American Philosophical Society elected him a member, Marshall accepted the notice "with my regrets at my utter inability to make any contributions which may be worthy of acceptance by this institution." In December 1831 the Virginia Historical and Philosophical Society was organized at the state capital, and Marshall was elected president, a title he held until his death; however, the society's minutes indicate that he did not attend meetings and the title was an honorary one.[40]

One organization of which he was elected president was particularly important to him: the Washington Monument Society, formed for the purpose of erecting a monument in the nation's capital to honor George Washington. "I have always wished it, and have always thought that the metropolis of the union was the fit place for the national monument," he responded. "I cannot therefore refuse to take any place which the society may assign me." His devotion to the memory of George Washington, how-

ever, could not overcome the aging process. In 1832 he was asked
by a joint committee of the Senate and House of Representatives
in Washington to deliver an address to a joint session on the centennial birthday of Washington. He turned down the invitation,
citing the pressure of his official duties and then confessed: "I
am physically unable to perform the task I should assume. My
voice has become so weak as to be almost inaudible even in a
room not unusually large. In the open air it could not be heard
by those nearest me. I must therefore decline the honor proposed."[41]

John Marshall, in his late seventies, was a universally loved
man. Joseph Story told of going to the theater in Washington one
night in 1833 with the Chief Justice, "and on the Chief Justice's
entrance into the box, he was cheered in a marked manner. He
behaved as he always does, with extreme modesty, and seemed
not to know that the compliment was designed for him."[42]

17

H E ALSO CONTINUED BEING A JUDGE.
Each session of the Supreme Court presented its own particular problems, its own challenges, and John Marshall never
was willing to escape those challenges, as difficult as they might
appear. "I look with infinite apprehension at the approaching time
of the Supreme Court," he said a few days before the 1833 term.
"It will bring with it much that is peculiarly unpleasant. But its
very unpleasantness furnishes some motives for meeting the difficulties which must be foreseen. I wish it were possible to avoid
them."[1]

When he came to the Court session he was in good health,
although he had turned seventy-seven the previous September.
According to Daniel Webster, Marshall may have been in better
health than most of his brethren. Webster reported that Judge
Baldwin had become insane; Johnson was recuperating from an
illness; Duvall was in good health "tho his ability to *hear* causes
is not so good as formerly"; Thompson was "as well as usual";
and "The Chief Justice is understood to be in exceedingly good
health, both in the inner and the outer man."[2]

An interesting case that year was *Barron v. Baltimore*. Barron claimed that the city had, in effect, confiscated his property
without proper payment, in violation of the Fifth Amendment
to the Constitution of the United States. The question before the

Court was whether the amendment, part of the Bill of Rights, applied to local governmental actions. The Court ruled that the intention of the Bill of Rights had been to place restrictions on the federal government. "These amendments contain no expression indicating an intention to apply them to the state governments," said the Court. "This court cannot so apply them."[3]

This year also, in a letter to Story, Marshall reiterated a point that was essential to him, that the law cannot be ignored by anyone—even judges. He was discussing a limitation upon the issuing of an arrest warrant. "This restraint upon the power is absurd," said Marshall, "and would not I believe have been imposed had the Congress perceived its effect, but it cannot be disregarded."[4]

The 1834 session abounded "with subjects of great excitement," Marshall reported to a friend the next year. "The old federalists see much to deplore and not much to approve. We fear the fabric created for us by our predecessors is about to be tumbled into ruins." Marshall again inserted one of his disclaimers— "I mix so little with politicians that it would be presumption in me to hazard conjectures on the future." He had despaired many times for his country in the past, Marshall said, but "Providence has saved us more than once, and I hope will save us again."[5] He had lived long enough, through so many more trials than most people, that he could evince optimism with confidence.

Although there were no great constitutional cases in these last years of Marshall's chief justiceship, there were decisions in which he could join in the stating of principles he considered important. In one case the Supreme Court was asked to act against a New York State judge who, it was charged, had refused to respond to a Supreme Court order. Marshall and the other Justices doubted that the New York judge had been all that slow. Also, the Supreme Court Justices realized they had restraints upon them: that they could issue orders; but they could not enforce them. "We have only to say, that a judge must exercise his discretion in those intermediate proceedings which take place between the institution and trial of a suit," the Court's opinion said, "and if in the performance of this duty he acts oppressively, it is not to this court that application is to be made." In another case Marshall went along with a decision written by Justice McLean in a complicated copyright case. "It is clear there can be no common law of the United States," said McLean's opinion. "The federal government is composed of twenty-four sovereign and independent States, each of which may have its local usages, customs and common law. There is no principle which pervades the Union and has the authority of law that is not embodied in the Constitution or laws of the Union." This was part of Marshall's creed also, that the Constitution had created a new system, one built on specific law.[6]

For some years John Marshall had been considering retirement. In 1829 he had told Story that after leaving office, he planned "to read nothing but novels and poetry." He delayed thought of quitting the bench until the next presidential election, hoping Jackson would be defeated. "You know how much importance I attach to the character of the person who is to succeed me," Marshall confided to Story, "and calculate the influence which probabilities on that subject would have on my continuance in office." In 1831, when Marshall became ill and went to Philadelphia for surgery, he again considered retiring but determined to postpone any decision until after his recovery. The successful operation restored his health and Andrew Jackson was reelected President, two events which persuaded him to postpone retirement. Also, despite his occasional protestations, he enjoyed the work of the Supreme Court. He enjoyed traveling to Washington every year, meeting with his brother Justices—some, like Story, were intimate friends by now. In a letter to Story at the end of the year 1834 Marshall described the great pleasure with which he anticipated meeting with the other Justices in Washington. Retirement and parting from such friends—"an event which though not intended to be immediate, cannot be very distant"—would be "among the most painful of the emotions."[7]

Despite Marshall's indecision about retirement, or perhaps because of it, there was considerable speculation about the circumstances under which he would leave the Court and about who would replace him. The most popular story was that Marshall had agreed to retire if he could be assured that Daniel Webster would be named Chief Justice. President Jackson was willing, and Webster was inclined to accept if the offer were made to him; but Webster also was unwilling to make a firm commitment, fearing he would appear to be bargaining for the position. The arrangement was never consummated.[8]

Although Marshall was reluctant to choose a time for his retirement, he realized that it had to come and he began to plan for it. His wish was to return to the hills of his birth in Fauquier County; there perhaps to recall his youth and to spend his remaining years with his children and grandchildren. When he confided to a granddaughter that he would come to live with her, she shrieked with childish delight: "Oh, grandpa, I am so glad you are coming to live with us, you shall have turkey and plum-cake every day for your dinner." Marshall laughed and answered:

"Ah, my dear little girl, you will soon kill your poor old grandfather, if you keep him on such a diet as that."

Leeds Manor, the home of his son James Keith Marshall,
was chosen as the retirement site. Plans were made in 1833 to
build an addition to the house at a cost of $900. Marshall sent
his son $500 that September and promised to send the remaining
$400 the following spring. In the discussions over the size of the
addition, Marshall pointed out to his son that "I however can
only occupy it for a few years. It will I hope be of some service
to you long after I shall be deposited by the side of your mother.
It is my wish therefore that in making any reduction you should
be governed entirely by your views for the future." The digging
of the foundation for the extension was begun in October of
1833.[9]

Marshall also prepared his will in 1832, a prudent act for a
man his age. The will includes one interesting provision, suggesting a conceit of a man hoping for the perpetuation of his name.
"I give to each of my grandsons named John one thousand acres,"
this provision reads, "part of my tract of land called Canaan lying
in Randolph County. If at the time of my death either of my sons
should have no son living named John then I give the thousand
acres to any son he may have, named Thomas, in token for my
love for my father and veneration of his memory."[10]

On the second Monday of January 1835 the Supreme Court
opened its session for that year. Only five Justices were present.
William Johnson, who had come to the Supreme Court shortly
after Marshall carrying the hope of Thomas Jefferson to counter
Marshall's Federalism and had stayed on the Court to embrace
Federalism, had died. James M. Wayne of Georgia was appointed
to replace him, and he took his seat two days later. Gabriel Duvall
also had resigned that year, and Marshall wrote him a friendly
note on behalf of the other Justices and himself.[11]

A ten-year-old boy named William Allen Butler, then the
son of the Attorney General of the United States and later a
distinguished lawyer in his own right, sat in on the Supreme
Court sessions that year. "I well remember walking up Pennsylvania Avenue in company with my father . . . ," Butler recalled,
"and going into the old court room, where the library now is, and
looking at the procession of judges, with the Chief Justice at its
head, and being particularly struck with their putting on their
gowns in the courtroom before they went on the bench. I have
seen every Chief Justice since that time and argued cases before
them all, but none of them equaled, in personal interest and
judicial supremacy, their illustrious predecessor. . . ."

Harriet Martineau, the writer, offered another description of Marshall early in 1835. "How delighted we were to see Judge Story bring in the tall, majestic, brighteyed old man! old by chronology, by the lines on his composed face, and by his services to the republic; but so dignified, so fresh, so present to the time, that no feeling of compassionate consideration for age dared to mix with the contemplation of him."[12]

The cases that year were not significant in the history of law, but one did give Marshall an opportunity to speak once again on the role of the judge. The case, *Mitchel v. United States*, had to do with the validity of a land grant, and the specific point to which Marshall spoke was whether the decision should be delayed. He reviewed the history of the case, already seven years old, and asserted that all reasonable information seemed to be available. To the charge that one party might feel aggrieved, Marshall said:

> Though the hope of deciding causes to the mutual satisfaction of parties would be chimerical, that of convincing them that the case has been fully and fairly considered, and that due attention has been given to the arguments of counsel, and that the best judgment of the court has been exercised on the case, may be sometimes indulged. Even this is not always attainable. In the excitement produced by ardent controversy, gentlemen view the same object through such different media that minds not infrequently receive therefrom precisely opposite impressions. The court, however, must see with its own eyes, and exercise its own judgment, guided by its own reason.[13]

There it was again, in the last sentence: judges must act as they believe proper; it was their responsibility, which they could not avoid. The opinion was the last Supreme Court decision in which John Marshall participated.

Marshall's health was visibly declining. As Joseph Story watched him in the Court sessions and in the boardinghouse conferences, he believed that Marshall would resign "after a year or two. . . . What a gloom will spread over the nation." When the Chief Justice returned to Richmond he realized the extent of his decline, but he bore it stoically. "Could I find the mill which would grind old men, and restore youth, I might indulge the hope of recovering my former vigor and taste for the enjoyment of life. But as that is impossible, I must be content with patching myself up and dragging on as well as I can." Story heard of Marshall's further degeneration but was loath to write the Chief Justice to inquire about his health "lest it should give him uneasiness, and perhaps precipitate his quitting the Bench."[14]

Every Sunday afternoon when he was in Richmond, Marshall walked the mile and one-half from his house to the Shockoe Hill cemetery to visit Polly's grave. Early in June 1835 he was making that walk when he collapsed from exhaustion. Two men saw him and carried him home. He then went to Philadelphia and again placed himself in the care of Dr. Physick, who had done so well by him in the 1831 operation. His trouble this time was a diseased liver, which had been enlarged and which contained several tuberculous abscesses. Jacob Randolph, Dr. Physick's associate, reported that the pressure of the enlarged liver "upon the stomach had the effect of dislodging this organ from its natural situation, and compressing it in such a manner, that for some time previous to [Marshall's] death it would not retain the smallest quantity of nutriment."

His son Edward Carrington Marshall was with him in Philadelphia, and when the stay there became longer than expected, his eldest son, Thomas Marshall, planned to replace him. On June 29 Thomas Marshall was passing through Baltimore on his way to visit his father in Philadelphia when there was a sudden thundershower. Thomas retreated into a building, one that had been partially destroyed by fire. The wind from the storm apparently dislodged a chimney which crumbled into the interior of the building, striking and killing him. The Chief Justice was not informed of the death of his eldest son. John Marshall himself died on Monday evening, July 6, at approximately six o'clock. According to the information reaching Richmond, he was "perfectly in his senses to the last and as death approached nearer to him his pain ceased and he went off without a struggle."[15]

One way of gauging John Marshall's impact is to imagine how the United States might have developed without his decisions. One quickly would conclude that there could be no modern United States without a Supreme Court empowered with judicial review; without a Constitution allowing the United States to do what needed to be done to govern; without a central authority holding power over the states; no modern United States without business relationships that would be honored; and no modern United States of value without a defendant's being assured of certain protections against the state. All these were products of John Marshall's tenure on the Supreme Court. He did not create them, but he did insist that they become irrevocably a part of America.

Another way of gauging Marshall's impact is to study what the great men of American law have said about him. For James Bradley Thayer he was "one of the greatest, noblest and most engaging characters in American history." Oliver Wendell Holmes believed "that if American law were to be represented by a single figure, sceptic and worshipper alike would agree without dispute that the figure could be but one alone, and that one John Marshall." And Felix Frankfurter has declared that "the decisive claim to John Marshall's distinction as a great statesman is as a judge. And he is the only judge who has that distinction."[16]

But Marshall's impact must be gauged by more than the sum of his specific accomplishments and the grandeur of the compliments paid him, as valuable as were these accomplishments and as true the compliments. He must be gauged, rather, by his vision of the world and his vision of the relationship of men with one another. He was with Washington and Jefferson in understanding that law is the only way of life for a society if it wishes to exist and thrive. Jefferson's Declaration of Independence is not an appeal to men's hearts but to their minds, to their understanding that the law had been violated by the British King. The phrases are beautifully constructed and have been hallowed by time, but that cannot obscure that the Declaration of Independence essentially is a legal brief written by lawyers and would be appropriate in a courtroom. The Revolution of which that document was a part was a struggle for the rule of law; no man who participated in that war envisioned escaping the responsibility of the law when it was done.

George Washington, as a supporter of the constitutional drafting and ratification process and then as first President, realized that the necessity was to establish this rule of law so firmly and so fairly that no man would ever seriously challenge it. He had cried for the United States to have a government or to know the worst, and then had struggled for that government because he realized how bad the worst could be.

For John Marshall the challenge was to make certain that the law dispensed by that government was, as had been hoped, both firm and fair. He exhorted judges to do their duty no matter what the consequences. He lectured Presidents on their responsibility to obey the law. He would not allow state governments or any level of government to be capricious or arbitrary. He understood that men must have rules to live by, and that if those rules are not democratically arrived at and fairly administered, then men cannot be expected to obey them. The alternative to law is armed might.

And this alternative can no longer be tolerated in a society that wishes to enjoy the benefits of modern civilization. The impact of Thomas Jefferson, George Washington, and John Marshall on modern society is in their vision of the law as a means of solving conflicts. The impact of the United States on modern society is not in her commerce nor in her armed might but in her declaration that law is the force by which people and nations must be governed. No member of society can fail to appreciate the desperate need for the teaching and learning of that lesson.

Such is the true role of America and of the American. The true responsibility each American inherits from those earlier Americans who gave so much of themselves is to be an apostle of that vision of men being governed by law. The Bible tells of God staying Abraham's hand and allowing his son Isaac to live, the lesson being that life is sacred and violence is a violation of man's spirit. Since then civilized man has been trying to develop a world in which neither nation nor man should have to fear either that his neighbor can physically molest him without punishment or that his natural rights to life, liberty, and the pursuit of happiness can be denied by a majority. John Marshall's life in law was part of that attempt, as must be each American's.

But gauging the impact of John Marshall was a matter for the future; at the time of his death, the impact was grief. His remains arrived in Richmond on Thursday, July 9, aboard the steamer *Kentucky*. The body was met by the longest procession the city of Richmond had ever seen, and the most solemn. There were members of the military, judges, the governor and his executive council, Masons, the few remaining of Marshall's Revolutionary War comrades, the white citizens of the city in their carriages, and the black slaves on foot who came to say farewell to the man who had always been such a gentleman to them.

The flags flew at half-staff and the church bells tolled as the procession followed the body of John Marshall to the red brick home that had been his for so many years. Then it was carried to the Shockoe Cemetery where, after a brief service, John Marshall was buried beside his dearest Polly.[17]

John Marshall had written the epitaph for his tombstone, except for the final dates, and it was engraved on the stone as he wished. The soldier, the politician, the diplomat, the judge, the man that was John Marshall asked that he be remembered this way:

[769]

John Marshall
son of Thomas and Mary Marshall
    was born the 24th of September 1755
Intermarried with Mary Willis Ambler
    the 3d of January 1873
Departed this life
    the sixth day of July 1835.[18]

The marker still stands.

Bibliography

MANUSCRIPT SOURCES

American Baptist Historical Society (Rochester, N.Y.)
American Philosophical Society Library (Philadelphia, Pa.)
Boston University Library
Bostonian Society
Bowdoin College, Hawthorne-Longfellow Library
Charleston Library Society
Chicago Historical Society
College of William and Mary, Swem Library, John Marshall Papers
Colorado College, Charles Leaming Tutt Library
Connecticut Historical Society
Connecticut State Library
Cornell University Library, Department of Rare Books
Dartmouth College Library
Duke University
Filson Club (Louisville, Ky.)
Free Library of Philadelphia
Harvard University, Houghton Library, University Archives
Haverford College
Henry E. Huntington Library and Art Gallery (San Marino, Calif.)
Historical Society of Delaware
Historical Society of Pennsylvania
Illinois State Historical Library
Indiana University, Lilly Library
Iowa State Department of History and Archives
Kansas State Historical Society
Keeper of the Public Records, London
Library of Congress, Manuscript Division
Maryland Historical Society
Massachusetts Historical Society
Minneapolis Public Library
Missouri Historical Society
National Archives
New-York Historical Society
New York Public Library, Manuscript Division
New York Society Library
New York State Library
Newberry Library (Chicago, Ill.)
Ohio Historical Society
Pierpont Morgan Library

Princeton University Library
Rosenbach Foundation
Rutgers University, Special Collections Department
Stanford University Libraries, Department of Special Collections,
    Manuscripts Division
State Historical Society of Wisconsin
University of Chicago Library
University of Kansas, Kenneth Spencer Research Library, Depart-
    ment of Special Collections
University of Michigan, William L. Clements Library
University of Minnesota, University Libraries, Special Collections
    Department
University of North Carolina Library, The Southern Historical Col-
    lection
University of Rochester Library
University of South Carolina, South Caroliniana Library
University of Texas at Austin
University of Virginia; the Law Library, the Manuscripts Department
    and the Tracy W. McGregor Library of the University of Vir-
    ginia Library
Valentine Museum (Richmond, Va.)
Virginia Historical Society (Richmond, Va.)
Virginia State Library (Richmond, Va.)
Washington and Lee University
Washington University Libraries
Williams College
Wyoming Historical Society (Wilkes-Barre, Pa.)
Yale University; Beinecke Rare Book and Manuscript Library, Sterling
    Memorial Library

PUBLISHED SOURCES

Adams, Charles Francis (ed.), *Memoirs of John Quincy Adams*,
    Philadelphia, 1874.
Adams, Charles Francis (ed.), *The Works of John Adams*, Boston,
    1853.
Adams, Henry (ed.), *Documents Relating to New England Federal-
    ism*, Boston, 1905.
Adams, Henry, *History of the United States of America*, New York,
    1921 ed.
Adams, Henry, *The Life of Albert Gallatin*, Philadelphia, 1879.
Adams, Herbert B. (ed.), *The Life and Writings of Jared Sparks*,
    Boston, 1893.
Adams, John, *Correspondence Between the Hon. John Adams and the
    Late William Cunningham, Esq.*, Boston, 1823.
Adams, John Stokes (ed.), *An Autobiographical Sketch by John Mar-
    shall*, Ann Arbor, Mich., 1937.

Alden, John R., *A History of the American Revolution*, New York, 1969.

Alden, John R., *Rise of the American Republic*, New York, 1963.

Ambler, Charles H., *The Life and Diary of John Floyd*, Richmond, 1918.

Ambler, Charles H., *Sectionalism in Virginia from 1776 to 1861*, Chicago, 1910.

Ambler, Charles H., *Thomas Ritchie*, Richmond, 1913.

American Colonization Society, *Fifteenth Annual Report*, Washington, D.C., 1832.

American State Papers, Class I, Foreign Relations, Washington, D.C., 1832.

Ames, Seth (ed.), *Works of Fisher Ames*, Boston, 1854.

Ammon, Harry, *James Monroe—The Quest for National Identity*, New York, 1971.

Anderson, Dice Robins, *William Branch Giles: A Biography*, Menasha, Wis., 1915.

Andrews, Matthew Page, *Virginia—The Old Dominion*, Garden City, N.Y., 1937.

Annals of Congress, Washington, D.C., 1851 ed.

Annual Report of the American Historical Association, 1912, Washington, D.C.

Aptheker, Herbert, *American Negro Slave Revolts*, New York, 1963 ed.

Austin, James T., *The Life of Elbridge Gerry*, Boston, 1828–1829.

Autobiography of Martin Van Buren, The, vol. II of the *Annual Report of the American Historical Association for the Year 1918*, Washington, D.C.

Bailyn, Bernard, *The Ideological Origins of the American Revolution*, Cambridge, Mass., 1967.

Baker, Leonard, *Back to Back—The Duel Between FDR and the Supreme Court*, New York, 1967.

Baker, Liva, *Felix Frankfurter*, New York, 1969.

Baldwin, Leland D., *Whiskey Rebels*, Pittsburgh, 1939.

Baldwin, Simeon E., *Life and Letters of Simeon Baldwin*, New Haven, Conn., 1919.

Bancroft, Frederic, *Slave-Trading in the Old South*, Baltimore, 1931.

Barton, William E., *The Paternity of Abraham Lincoln*, New York, 1920.

Bassett, John Spencer (ed.), *Correspondence of Andrew Jackson*, Washington, 1926–1933.

Bassett, John Spencer, *The Life of Andrew Jackson*, New York, 1928 ed.

Beard, Charles A., *An Economic Interpretation of the Constitution of the United States*, New York, 1929 ed.

Beirne, Francis F., *Shout Treason—The Trial of Aaron Burr*, New York, 1959.

Bemis, Samuel Flagg, *Jay's Treaty*, New Haven, Conn., 1962 ed.

Benson, George C. S. (ed.), *Essays in Federalism*, Claremont, Calif., 1961.

Beveridge, Albert J., *The Life of John Marshall*, Boston, 1916–1919.

Bickel, Alexander M., *The Supreme Court and the Idea of Progress*, New York, 1970.

Biddle, Charles, *Autobiography of Charles Biddle*, Philadelphia, 1883 (privately printed).

Bill, Alfred H., *Valley Forge—The Making of an Army*, New York, 1952.

Binney, Horace, *An Eulogy on the Life and Character of John Marshall*, Philadelphia, 1835.

Binney, Horace, *Bushrod Washington*, Philadelphia, 1858.

Bolles, Albert S., *The Financial History of the United States*, New York, 1894 ed.

Boogher, William F., *Gleanings of Virginia History*, Washington, D.C., 1903.

Boudinot, J. J. (ed.), *The Life of Elias Boudinot*, Boston, 1896.

Boyd, Julian P. (ed.), *The Papers of Thomas Jefferson*, Princeton, N.J., 1950–1965.

Bradshaw, Herbert C., *History of Prince Edward County, Virginia*, Richmond, 1955.

Brant, Irving, *James Madison*, Indianapolis, 1941–1961.

Bridenbaugh, Carl, *Seat of Empire*, Williamsburg, Va., 1950.

Brockenbrough, William, *Brockenbrough Reports (Reports of Cases Decided by the Honourable John Marshall in the Circuit Court of the United States)*, Philadelphia, 1837.

Brown, David Paul, *The Forum: or Forty Years Full Practice at the Philadelphia Bar*, Philadelphia, 1856.

Brown, Everett S. (ed.), *William Plumer's Memorandum of Proceedings in the United States Senate*, New York, 1923.

Brown, John Mason, *The Political Beginnings of Kentucky*, Louisville, 1889.

Brown, William G., *The Life of Oliver Ellsworth*, New York, 1905.

Bruce, William Cabell, *John Randolph of Roanoke*, New York, 1922.

Brumbaugh, Gaius Marcus, *Revolutionary War Records*, vol. I, Washington, 1936.

Bryant, James R. M., *Eulogium on Chief Justice Marshall*, Washington, 1835.

Buchanan, James, *Works*, Philadelphia, 1908.

Buchanan, William, *Louis Marshall, M.D.*, 1941 master's thesis at the Washington and Lee University Library.

Buell, Augustus C., *History of Andrew Jackson*, New York, 1904.

Burr, Samuel Engle, Jr., *Napoleon's Dossier on Aaron Burr*, San Antonio, 1969.

Butler, Mann, *A History of the Commonwealth of Kentucky*, Louisville, 1836.

Butterfield, L. H. (ed.), *Diary and Autobiography of John Adams*, Cambridge, Mass., 1961.

Calhoun, Arthur W., *A Social History of the American Family*, New York, 1960 ed.

Callender, James T., *The Prospect Before Us*, Richmond, 1800.

Call, Daniel, *Call's Reports (Reports of Cases Argued and Adjudged in the Court of Appeals, Virginia)*, Richmond, 1824.

Cappon, Lester J. (ed.), *The Adams-Jefferson Letters*, Chapel Hill, N.C., 1959.

Channing, Edward, *A History of the United States*, New York, 1929.

Chapin, Bradley, *The American Law of Treason*, Seattle, 1964.

Chappelear, B. Curtis, *Maps and Notes Pertaining to the Upper Section of Fauquier County, Virginia*, Warrenton, Va., 1954.

Christian, W. Asbury, *Richmond—Her Past and Present*, Richmond, 1912.

Churchill, Winston S., *A History of the English Speaking Peoples*, New York, 1967.

Clark, Allen C., *Greenleaf and Law in the Federal City*, Washington, D.C., 1901.

Clarkson, Paul S., and R. Samuel Jett, *Luther Martin of Maryland*, Baltimore, 1970.

Colt, LeBaron B., *An Address on John Marshall Day*, Providence, R.I., 1901.

Colton, Calvin (ed.), *The Works of Henry Clay*, New York, 1904.

Commager, Henry Steele, and Richard B. Morris, *The Spirit of 'Seventy-Six*, Indianapolis, 1958.

Conway, Moncure D., *Omitted Chapters of History*, New York, 1888.

Corwin, Edward S., *The Doctrine of Judicial Review*, Princeton, N.J., 1914.

Corwin Edward S., *John Marshall and the Constitution*, pt. 2, vol. IX, of The Chronicles of America Series, New Haven, Conn., 1919.

Cotton, Joseph P., Jr. (ed.), *The Constitutional Decisions of John Marshall*, New York, 1969 ed.

Craighill, Robert T., *The Virginia Peerage*, Richmond, 1880.

Craigmyle, Lord, *John Marshall in Diplomacy and Law*, New York, 1933.

Cranch, William, *Cranch Reports (Reports of Cases Argued and Adjudged in the Supreme Court of the United States, 1801–1815)*, Philadelphia.

Crozier, William A. (ed.), *Virginia County Records*, vol. VI, New York, 1909.

Cutler, William P., and Julia Perkins Cutler, *Life, Journals and Correspondence of Rev. Manasseh Cutler, LL.D.*, Cincinnati, 1888.

Dallas, A. J., *Dallas Reports (Reports of the Cases Ruled and Adjudged in the Courts of Pennsylvania, including Supreme Court Reports, 1790–1800)*, Philadelphia.

Davis, Matthew L., *Memoirs of Aaron Burr*, New York, 1836–1837.

Debates and Other Proceedings of the Convention of Virginia (1788), Richmond, 1805.

Dewey, Donald O., *Marshall Versus Jefferson: The Political Background of Marbury v. Madison*, New York, 1970.

Dictionary of American Medical Biography, New York, 1928.

Dillon, John F., *John Marshall—Life, Character and Judicial Services*, Chicago, 1903.

Dodd, Anna Bowman, *Talleyrand*, New York, 1927.

Dodd, William E., *The Life of Nathaniel Macon*, Raleigh, N.C., 1903.

Dodd, William E., *Statesmen of the Old South*, New York, 1911.

Donnan, Elizabeth (ed.), *Papers of James A. Bayard*, vol. II of the *Annual Report of the American Historical Association, 1913*, Washington, D.C.

Dunaway, Wayland Fuller, *History of the James River and Kanawha Company*, New York, 1922.

Dunne, Gerald T., *Justice Joseph Story and the Rise of the Supreme Court*, New York, 1970.

DuPonceau, Peter S., *A Dissertation on the Nature and Extent of the Jurisdiction of the Courts of the United States*, Philadelphia, 1824.

Early, R. H., *By-Ways of Virginia History*, Richmond, 1907.

Eleventh Annual Report, James River and Kanawha Canal, 1844–1845.

Elliot, Jonathan (ed.), *Debates of the Several State Conventions*, Washington, D.C., 1835.

Ellis, Richard E., *The Jeffersonian Crisis*, New York, 1971.

Farrand, Max (ed.), *The Records of the Federal Convention of 1787*, New Haven, Conn., 1911.

Faulkner, Robert K., *The Jurisprudence of John Marshall*, Princeton. N.J., 1968.

Fauquier County (Virginia), Warrenton, Va., 1959.

Finch, John, *Travels in the United States of America*, London, 1833.

Fisher, George D., *History and Reminiscences of the Monumental Church*, Richmond, 1880.

Fitzpatrick, John C. (ed.), *The Diaries of George Washington*, Boston, 1925.

Fitzpatrick, John C. (ed.), *The Writings of George Washington*, Washington, D.C., 1931–1944.

Flanders, Henry, *The Life of John Marshall*, Philadelphia, 1905.

Force, Peter (ed.), *American Archives*, Washington, D.C., 1843.

Ford, Paul Leicester (ed.), *The Works of Thomas Jefferson*, New York, 1904–1905.

Ford, Worthington C. (ed.), *Letters of Joseph Jones*, Washington, D.C., 1889.

Ford, Worthington C. (ed.), *The Writings of George Washington*, New York, 1891.

Ford, Worthington C. (ed.), *Writings of John Quincy Adams*, New York, 1913–1914.

Fortescue, Sir John (ed.), *The Correspondence of King George the Third*, London, 1927.

Fothergill, Augusta B., *Wills of Westmoreland County, Virginia*, 1925.

Frankfurter, Felix, *The Commerce Clause under Marshall, Taney and Waite*, Chapel Hill, N.C., 1937.

Frankfurter, Felix, *Of Law and Men*, Hamden, Conn., 1965 ed.

Freeman, Douglas Southall, *George Washington*, New York, 1948–1957.

Friedman, Leon, and Fred L. Israel (eds.), *The Justices of the United States Supreme Court 1789–1969*, New York, 1969.

Fuess, Claude Moore, *Daniel Webster*, Boston, 1930.

Garland, Hugh A., *The Life of John Randolph*, New York, 1969 ed.

Garnett, James M., *Lectures on Female Education*, Richmond, 1825.

Gilmer, Francis Walker, *Sketches, Essays and Translations*, Baltimore, 1828.

Goddard, Henry P., *Luther Martin: The "Federal Bull Dog,"* Baltimore, 1887.

Goebel, Julius, Jr., *Antecedents and Beginnings to 1801*, vol. I of *The Oliver Wendell Holmes Devise—History of the Supreme Court of the United States*, New York, 1971.

Greene, Jack P., *The Quest for Power*, Chapel Hill, N.C., 1963.

Grigsby, Hugh Blair, *Discourse on the Life and Character of the Hon. Littleton Waller Tazewell*, Norfolk, Va., 1860.

Grigsby, Hugh Blair, *The History of the Virginia Federal Convention of 1788*, Richmond, 1890.

Grigsby, Hugh Blair, *The Virginia Convention of 1829–30*, vol. I of *The Virginia Historical Reporter*, Richmond, 1854.

Groome, H. C., *Fauquier During the Proprietorship*, Baltimore, 1969 ed.

Gunther, Gerald (ed.), *John Marshall's Defense of McCulloch v. Maryland*, Stanford, Calif., 1969.

Gwathmey, John H., *Historical Register of Virginians in the Revolution*, Richmond, 1938.

Hall, Wilmer L. (ed.), *Journals of the Council of the State of Virginia*, vol. III, Richmond, 1952.

Hamilton, J. G. de Roulhac, *The Papers of Thomas Ruffin*, Raleigh, N.C., 1918.

Hamilton, John C. (ed.), *The Works of Alexander Hamilton*, New York, 1850.

Hamilton, Stanislaus Murray (ed.), *The Writings of James Monroe*, New York, 1898–1903.

Hand, Learned, *The Spirit of Liberty*, New York, 1960 ed.

Harding, Chester, *A Sketch of Chester Harding*, Boston, 1929 ed.

Harrell, Isaac Samuel, *Loyalism in Virginia*, Durham, N.C., 1926.

Hart, Freeman H., *The Valley of Virginia in the American Revolution*, Chapel Hill, N.C., 1942.

Heads of Families at the First Census of the United States Taken in the Year 1790, vol. X (Virginia), Washington, D.C., 1908.

Hecht, Marie B., *John Quincy Adams*, New York, 1972.

Hening, William W. (ed.), *The Statutes at Large*, New York, Philadelphia, Richmond, 1820–1823.

Henkle, M. M., *Life of Henry Bidleman Bascom*, Nashville, 1856.

Henry, William Wirt, *Patrick Henry*, New York, 1891.

Hess, Stephen, *America's Political Dynasties*, New York, 1966.

Holdsworth, Sir William, *A History of English Law*, London, 1938.

Hone, Philip, *Diary*, New York, 1889.

Howe, Henry, *Historical Collections of Virginia*, Baltimore, 1969 ed.

Hughes, Charles Evans, *The Supreme Court of the United States*, Garden City, N.Y., 1936.

Hunt, Gaillard, *The Department of State of the United States*, New Haven, Conn., 1914.

Hunt, Gaillard (ed.), *The Writings of James Madison*, New York, 1909–1910.

Hunting, Warren B., *The Obligation of Contracts Clause of the United States Constitution*, Baltimore, 1919.

Hustings Court Order Book No. 1, 1782–1787, Richmond, Va. (On microfilm at the Virginia State Library.)

Irving, Pierre M., *The Life and Letters of Washington Irving*, New York, 1863.

Jackson, Robert H., *The Struggle for Judicial Supremacy*, New York, 1941.

Jensen, Merrill, *The Articles of Confederation*, Madison, Wis., 1940.

Jensen, Merrill, *The New Nation*, New York, 1965.

Johnson, Allen, *Jefferson and His Colleagues*, pt. 1, vol. IV, of The Chronicles of America Series, New Haven, Conn., 1919.

Jones, W. Melville (ed.), *Chief Justice John Marshall, A Reappraisal*, New York, 1971 ed.

Jordan, Winthrop D., *White Over Black*, Chapel Hill, N.C., 1968.

Journals of the Continental Congress, Washington, D.C. 1904–1936.

Journals of the House of Delegates, Virginia. (On microfilm at the Library of Congress.)

Kapp, Friedrich, *Justus Erich Bollmann*, Berlin, 1880.

Kelby, Robert H., *Addenda to Heitman's Historical Register of Officers of the Continental Army During the War of the Revolution*, New York, 1932.

Kennedy, John P., *Memoirs of the Life of William Wirt*, Philadelphia, 1856.

Ketcham, Ralph, *James Madison*, New York, 1971.

King, Charles R. (ed.), *The Life and Correspondence of Rufus King*, New York, 1894–1900.

Konefsky, Samuel J., *John Marshall and Alexander Hamilton*, New York, 1964.

Kurland, Philip B. (ed.), *James Bradley Thayer, Oliver Wendell Holmes, and Felix Frankfurter on John Marshall*, Chicago, 1967.

Kurtz, Stephen G., *The Presidency of John Adams*, Philadelphia, 1957.

BIBLIOGRAPHY

La Rochefoucauld-Liancourt, François, *Voyage dans les Etats-Unis d'Amérique*, Paris, published in the 7th year of the Republic.

The Law and Chief Justice John Marshall, Williamsburg, Va., 1969.

Lee, Richard Henry, *Life of Arthur Lee*, Boston, 1829.

Levy, Leonard W., *Jefferson and Civil Liberties*, Cambridge, Mass., 1963.

Lewis, William D. (ed.), *Great American Lawyers*, Philadelphia, 1907.

Libby, Charles F., *John Marshall—An Address*, Brunswick, Me., 1901.

Lipscomb, Andrew A., and Albert E. Bergh (eds.), *The Writings of Thomas Jefferson*, Washington, D.C. 1903.

Little, Lewis Peyton, *Imprisoned Preachers and Religious Liberty in Virginia*, Lynchburg, Va., 1938.

Lodge, Henry Cabot (ed.), *The Works of Alexander Hamilton*, New York, 1904.

Loth, David, *Chief Justice*, New York, 1949.

Lyman, Theodore, Jr., *The Diplomacy of the United States*, Boston, 1828 (2nd ed.).

McAllister, J. T., *Virginia Militia in the Revolutionary War*, Hot Springs, Va., 1913.

McCabe, Joseph, *Talleyrand*, London, 1906.

McClung, John A., *Sketches of Western Adventure*, Louisville, Ky., 1879 ed.

McDonald, Forrest, *We the People*, Chicago, 1958.

McGrane, Reginald C., *The Correspondence of Nicholas Biddle*, Boston, 1919.

McMaster, John B., *A History of the People of the United States*, New York, 1928.

McRee, Griffith J., *Life and Correspondence of James Iredell*, New York, 1857.

Madison, James, *Letters and Other Writings*, Philadelphia, 1865.

Magruder, Allan B., *John Marshall*, Boston, 1898 ed.

Malone, Dumas, *Jefferson and His Time*, Boston, 1948–1970.

Marshall, Humphrey, *The History of Kentucky*, Frankfurt, Ky., 1824.

Marshall, John, *An Autobiographical Sketch by John Marshall*, edited by John Stokes Adams, Ann Arbor, Mich., 1937 (cited also under Adams).

Marshall, John, *The Life of George Washington*, Philadelphia, 1805–1807. (This work was reprinted in 1826, and the subsequent editions have been based on the 1826 version. There are differences between the first and second editions, but they are not significant, and I have cited the original edition throughout.)

Marshall, John, *Writings upon the Federal Constitution*, Boston, 1839.

Marshall, Maria Newton, *Recollections and Reflections of Fielding Lewis Marshall*, Orange, Va., 1911 (privately printed).

Martineau, Harriet, *Autobiography*, Boston, 1877.

Martineau, Harriet, *Retrospect of Western Travel*, London, 1838.

Mason, Frances Norton, *My Dearest Polly*, Richmond, 1961.

Mason, Jeremiah, *Autobiography*, Kansas City, 1917 ed.

Matthews, Shailer, *The French Revolution 1789–1815*, New York, 1928.

Mathiez, Albert, *The French Revolution*, New York, 1928.

Mayo, Bernard, *Henry Clay*, Boston, 1937.

Mayo, Bernard (ed.), *Instructions to the British Ministers of the United States—1791–1812*, vol. III of the *Annual Report of the American Historical Association*, 1936, Washington, D.C.

Mayo, Robert, *Political Sketches of Eight Years in Washington*, Baltimore, 1839.

Mays, David John, *The Letters and Papers of Edmund Pendleton*, Charlottesville, Va., 1967.

Meade, Robert Douthat, *Patrick Henry—Patriot in the Making*, Philadelphia, 1957.

Meade, Robert Douthat, *Patrick Henry—Practical Revolutionary*, Philadelphia, 1969.

Meade, Bishop (William), *Old Churches, Ministers and Families of Virginia*, Philadelphia, 1857.

Meigs, William M., *The Life of Charles Jared Ingersoll*, Philadelphia, 1897.

Mesick, Jane Louise, *The English Traveller in America*, New York, 1922.

Millis, Walter, *Arms and Men*, New York, 1958 ed.

Mitchell, Broadus, *Alexander Hamilton—The National Adventure 1788–1804*, New York, 1962.

Mitchell, Stewart, *New Letters of Abigail Adams*, Boston, 1947.

Morgan, Donald G., *Justice William Johnson—The First Dissenter*, Columbia, S.C., 1954.

Morison, Samuel Eliot, *Harrison Gray Otis*, Boston, 1913.

Morison, Samuel Eliot, *Harrison Gray Otis—The Urbane Federalist*, Boston, 1969.

Morley, John, *Edmund Burke—A Historical Study*, New York, 1924.

Morris, Richard B., *Fair Trial*, New York, 1967 ed.

Munford, Beverley B., *Virginia's Attitude toward Slavery and Secession*, New York, 1969 ed.

Munford, George Wythe, *The Two Parsons*, Richmond, 1884.

Murray, Charles Augustus, *Travels in North America*, London, 1839.

Naval Documents Related to the Quasi-War Between the United States and France—Naval Operations from June 1800 to November 1800, Washington, D.C., 1938.

Naval Documents Related to the United States Wars with the Barbary Powers, Washington, D.C., 1939.

Niemcewicz, Julian Ursyn, *Under Their Vine and Fig Tree*, Elizabeth, N.J., 1965 (translated and edited by Metchie J. E. Budka).

Oster, John Edward, *The Political and Economic Doctrines of John Marshall*, New York, 1967 ed.

Parkes, Henry Bamford, *The American Experience*, New York, 1959 ed.

Parmet, Herbert S., and Marie B. Hecht, *Aaron Burr*, New York, 1967.

Parton, James, *The Life and Times of Aaron Burr*, Boston, 1872 ed.

Paulding, James K., *A Life of Washington*, New York, 1835.

Paxton, W. M., *The Marshall Family*, Cincinnati, 1885.

Pearson, Drew, and Robert S. Allen, *The Nine Old Men*, Garden City, N.Y., 1937.

Peters, Richard, Jr., *Peters Reports (Reports of Cases Argued and Adjudged in the Supreme Court of the United States, 1828–1835)*, Philadelphia.

Peterson, Merrill D., *Thomas Jefferson and the New Nation*, New York, 1970.

Plumer, William, Jr., *Life of William Plumer*, Boston, 1857.

Poore, Benjamin Perley, *Reminiscences*, Philadelphia, 1886.

Proceedings and Debates of the Virginia State Convention of 1829–30, Richmond, 1830.

Proceedings of the M. W. Grand Lodge of Ancient York Masons of the State of Virginia, vol. I, Richmond, 1874.

Quincy, Edmund, *Life of Josiah Quincy*, Boston, 1874 ed.

Quincy, Josiah, *Figures of the Past*, Boston, 1883.

Randall, Henry S., *The Life of Thomas Jefferson*, New York, 1858.

Randolph, Jacob, *A Memoir on the Life and Character of Philip Syng Physick, M.D.*, Philadelphia, 1839.

Report of the Commissioners Appointed to View Certain Rivers Within the Commonwealth of Virginia, Richmond, 1819.

Rhodes, Irwin S., *The Papers of John Marshall*, Norman, Okla., 1969.

Robertson, David, *Reports of the Trials of Aaron Burr*, Philadelphia, 1808.

Roche, John P. (ed.), *John Marshall—Major Opinions and Other Writings*, Indianapolis, 1967.

Rose, John Holland, *Life of William Pitt*, London, 1923.

Rossiter, Clinton (ed.), *The Federalist Papers*, New York, 1961.

Royall, Anne, *The Black Book*, Washington, D.C., 1829.

Rutland, Robert Allen, *George Mason—Reluctant Statesman*, Williamsburg, Va., 1961.

Safford, William H., *The Blennerhassett Papers*, Cincinnati, 1861.

Samuel, Mordecai, *Richmond in By-Gone Days*, Richmond, 1856.

Schachner, Nathan, *Aaron Burr*, New York, 1937.

Schauinger, J. Herman, *William Gaston—Carolinian*, Milwaukee, 1949.

Schoepf, Johann David, *Travels in the Confederation*, New York, 1968 ed. (translated from the German by Alfred J. Morrison).

Scott, Mary Wingfield, *Old Richmond Neighborhoods*, Richmond, 1950.

Scott, Winfield, *Memoirs of Lieut.-General Scott, LL.D.*, New York, 1864.

Shepherd, Samuel, *The Statutes at Large of Virginia*, Richmond, 1835.

Shirley, John M., *The Dartmouth College Causes*, Chicago, 1895.

Simkins, Francis Butler, *A History of the South*, New York, 1963, 3rd ed.

Simms, Henry H., *Life of John Taylor*, Richmond, 1932.

Skeel, Emily E. F., *Mason Locke Weems*, New York 1929.

Slaughter, Philip, *History of St. Mark's Parish*, printed in Green, Raleigh Travers, *Notes on Culpeper County, Virginia*, Baltimore, 1958.

Slaughter, Philip, *The Virginian History of African Colonization*, Richmond, 1855.

Slaughter, William B., *Reminiscences of Distinguished Men*, Madison, Wis., 1878.

Smith, Margaret Bayard, *The First Forty Years of Washington Society*, New York, 1906.

Smith, Oliver Hampton, *Early Indiana Trials and Sketches*, Cincinnati, 1858.

Smith, Page, *John Adams*, New York, 1962.

Smith, William Henry, *The St. Clair Papers*, Cincinnati, 1882.

Smith, William Raymond, *History as Argument*, The Hague, 1966.

Stanard, Mary Newton, *Richmond—Its People and Its Story*, Philadelphia, 1923.

State Papers and Publick Documents of the United States, Boston, 1819, 3rd ed.

Steiner, Bernard C. (ed.), *The Life and Correspondence of James McHenry*, Cleveland, 1907.

Stern, Jean, *Belle et Bonne*, Paris, 1938.

Story, Joseph, *An Address by Mr. Justice Story on Chief Justice Marshall* (a 1900 reprint of an address delivered in 1835).

Story, William W. (ed.), *Life and Letters of Joseph Story*, Boston, 1851.

Stoudt, John Joseph, *Ordeal at Valley Forge*, Philadelphia, 1963.

Sydnor, Charles S., *Gentlemen Freeholders*, Chapel Hill, N.C., 1952.

Syrett, Harold C., and Jean G. Cooke (eds.), *Interview in Weehawken*, Middleton, Conn., 1960.

Taylor, John, *Construction Construed and Constitutions Vindicated*, Richmond, 1820.

Taylor, John, *Disunion Sentiment in Congress in 1794*, Washington, D.C., 1905.

Taylor, John, *New Views of the Constitution*, Washington, D.C., 1823.

Taylor, John, *Tyranny Unmasked*, Washington, D.C., 1822.

Terhune, Mary, *Some Colonial Homesteads and Their Stories*, New York, 1897.

Thayer, James Bradley, *Cases on Constitutional Law*, Cambridge, Mass., 1895.

Thayer, James Bradley, *John Marshall*, Boston, 1901.

Thompson, John J., *The Letters of Curtius*, Richmond, 1798.

Thwaites, Reuben Gold (ed.), *Early Western Travels 1748–1846*, Cleveland, 1904.

BIBLIOGRAPHY

Tocqueville, Alexis de, *Democracy in America*, New York, 1946 ed.

Toulmin, Harry, *The Western Country in 1793*, San Marino, Calif., 1948 ed.

Trial of Samuel Chase, Washington, D.C., 1805.

Tucker, St. George, *The Life of Thomas Jefferson*, Philadelphia, 1837.

Tyler, Lyon G., *The Letters and Times of the Tylers*, Richmond, 1885.

Tyler, Moses Coit, *Patrick Henry*, Ithaca, N.Y., 1962 ed.

United States Congress, House of Representatives, 58th Congress, 2nd Session, Report No. 646, *Documentary History of the Construction and Development of the United States Capitol Building and Grounds*, Washington, D.C.

United States Department of State, *Documentary History of the Constitution*, Washington, 1894–1905.

Vail, Philip, *The Great American Rascal*, New York, 1972.

Vallee, Leon (ed.), *Memoirs of Talleyrand*, New York, 1903.

Van Santvoord, George, *Sketches of the Lives and Judicial Services of the Chief Justices of the Supreme Court of the United States*, New York, 1854.

Virginia Slavery Debate, Richmond, 1832.

Wagstaff, H. M. (ed.), *The Papers of John Steele*, Raleigh, N.C., 1924.

Walz, Jay, and Audrey Walz, *The Bizarre Sisters*, New York, 1950.

Wandell, Samuel H., and Meade Minnigerode, *Aaron Burr*, New York, 1925.

Ward, Christopher, *The War of the Revolution*, New York, 1952.

Ward, Robert D., *An Account of General La Fayette's Visit to Virginia*, Richmond, 1881.

Warren, Charles, *The Supreme Court in United States History*, Boston, 1928 ed.

Washington, Bushrod, *Washington Reports (Reports of Cases Argued and Determined in the Court of Appeals of Virginia)*, Richmond, 1798–1799.

Webster, Daniel, *Writings and Speeches*, Boston, 1903.

Weedon, George, *Valley Forge Orderly Book*, New York, 1902.

Wentworth, John, *Congressional Reminiscences*, Chicago, 1882.

Wertenbaker, Thomas J., *Patrician and Plebeian in Virginia*, New York, 1959 ed.

Wertenbaker, Thomas J., *Virginia Under the Stuarts*, New York, 1959 ed.

Wheaton, Henry, *Wheaton Reports (Reports of Cases Argued and Adjudged in the Supreme Court of the United States, 1816–1827)*, Philadelphia.

Whitridge, Arnold, *Rochambeau*, New York, 1965.

Wildes, Harry E., *Valley Forge*, New York, 1938.

Wilkinson, James, *Memoirs of My Own Times*, Philadelphia, 1816.

Williams, Charles Richard (ed.), *Diary and Letters of Rutherford Birchard Hayes*, Columbus, Ohio, 1922.

Willison, George F., *Patrick Henry and His World*, New York, 1969.

Wilson, Rufus R., *Washington—The Capital City*, Philadelphia, 1902.

Wilson, Woodrow, *Constitutional Government in the United States*, New York, 1927 ed.

Wingo, Elizabeth, *The Battle of Great Bridge*, Norfolk, Va., 1964.

Wirt, William, *The Letters of the British Spy*, Baltimore, 1803.

Wirt, William, *Sketches of the Life and Character of Patrick Henry*, Philadelphia, 1818, 3rd ed.

Wood, Gertrude S., *William Paterson of New Jersey*, Fair Lawn, N.J., 1933.

Wood, John, *The Suppressed History of the Administration of John Adams (from 1797 to 1801)*, Philadelphia, 1846 ed.

Young, James Sterling, *The Washington Community 1800–1828*, New York, 1966.

NEWSPAPERS AND PERIODICALS

African Repository and Colonial Journal
Alexandria Gazette
American Bar Association Journal
American Heritage
American Historical Review, The
American History Illustrated
American Journal of Legal History, The
American Journal of Medical Sciences, The
American Political Science Review, The
American Quarterly Review, The
Atlantic Monthly, The
Aurora (Philadelphia)
Bulletin of the Historical and Philosophical Society of Ohio
Bulletin of the New York Public Library
Bulletin of the Virginia State Library
Bulletins of the Fauquier County (Va.) *Historical Society*
Calendar of Virginia State Papers
Calumet, The
Century, The (a New York City newspaper)
Century Magazine, The
Columbian Centinel (Boston)
Current Comment and Legal Miscellany
Daily Advertiser, The (New York)
Daughters of the American Revolution Magazine
Federal Gazette & Baltimore Daily Advertiser
Filson Club History Quarterly, The (Louisville, Ky.)
Freemasonry Pamphlets, 1829–1840
Green Bag, The
Harper's Magazine
Historical Magazine
History Today (London)
House Beautiful, The

Independent Chronicle (Boston)
John P. Branch Historical Papers
Journal of Southern History, The
London Gazette, The
Louisiana Law Journal, The
Magazine of American History
Mississippi Valley Historical Review, The
Nation, The
New England Palladium (Boston)
New England Quarterly, The
New-York American
New York Evening Post
New York Review, The
New York Spectator
New York Tribune, The
Niles' Weekly Register
North American Review
Papers of the American Historical Association
Philadelphia Inquirer
Philadelphia Union
Political Science Quarterly
Porcupine's Gazette
Port Folio
Proceedings of the American Antiquarian Society
Proceedings of the Massachusetts Historical Society
Proceedings of the New York State Bar Association
Proceedings of the Virginia Historical Society
Richmond Enquirer
Richmond Examiner
Richmond Whig
South Atlantic Quarterly
South Carolina Historical and Genealogical Magazine, The
Southern Literary Messenger
Stanford Law Review
Tyler's Quarterly Historical and Genealogical Magazine
Virginia Cavalcade
Virginia Gazette (Various newspapers were published under this
    name in Williamsburg, Va. In the citations the name in paren-
    theses identifies the editor of the specific newspaper cited, which
    is how the papers are arranged in most collections.)
Virginia Free Press
Virginia Historical Register
Virginia Magazine of History and Biography, The
Washington Federalist (Georgetown)
Washington Post, The
West Virginia History
William and Mary Quarterly
World's Work, The

Notes

BOOK ONE: SOLDIER

[1]

1. Binney, *Eulogy*, p. 23.
2. Marshall, *Autobiographical*, p. 7.
3. Binney, *Eulogy*, pp. 22–24.
4. W. B. Slaughter, p. 102.
5. Freeman, vol. I, p. 51.
6. Fothergill, p. 133; F. N. Mason, p. 24.
7. Calhoun, p. 286.
8. *Fauquier County Records, Deed Book 1*, pp. 1–2, Virginia State Library.
9. Groome, p. 179.
10. *Fauquier County Records, Deed Book 3*, pp. 70–72, Virginia State Library.
11. *Fauquier County Records, Minute Book 1764–1766*, pp. 213–14, Virginia State Library.
12. Hening, vol. VIII, p. 10.
13. Fitzpatrick, *Diaries*, vol. I, pp. 316, 348, 349; vol. II, p. 186.
14. Bridenbaugh, pp. 10–11.
15. *Fauquier County*, p. 85.
16. M. N. Marshall, p. 65.
17. Little, pp. 197–98.
18. *Fauquier County Records, Minute Book 1764–1766*, p. 137, Virginia State Library; Groome, pp. 166–67, 172.
19. J. Story, p. 8.
20. Sallie E. Marshall Hardy, "John Marshall as Son, Brother, Husband and Friend," *The Green Bag*, Dec. 1896, p. 480.
21. Libby, p. 37.
22. *Bulletins, Fauquier*, July 1924, pp. 430–32.
23. Peterson, pp. 27–28.
24. Ketcham, p. 12.
25. Marshall, *Autobiographical*, pp. 3–4.
26. *Ibid.*
27. *Ibid.*
28. Bishop Meade, vol. II, p. 219; Dillon, vol. I, p. lvii(*n*); W. B. Slaughter, *Reminiscences*, p. 107.
29. Ketcham, pp. 83–84.
30. Marshall, *Autobiographical*, p. 7.
31. *Virginia Gazette* (Hunter & Dixon), Nov. 25, 1775, p. 1.
32. Quoted in Parkes, p. 45.
33. Marshall, *Washington*, vol. II, p. 68.
34. *Ibid.*, p. 70.
35. Fitzpatrick, *Writings*, vol. II, p. 471.
36. Marshall, *Washington*, vol. II, p. 87.
37. Peterson, p. 41.
38. Morley, p. 127.
39. Commager, vol. I, p. 2.
40. *Ibid.*, p. 19.
41. G. Washington to Bryan Fairfax, July 20, 1774, Fitzpatrick, *Writings*, vol. II, pp. 232–33.
42. G. Washington to George William Fairfax, June 10, 1774, Fitzpatrick, *Writings*, vol. III, pp. 223–24.
43. Fortescue, vol. I, p. xiv; vol. II, p. x.
44. King, vol. III, pp. 545–46.
45. Churchill, vol. III, p. 172.
46. *New England Quarterly*, vol. II, no. 1, pp. 156–62.
47. *American Heritage*, June 1960, p. 95.
48. Churchill, vol. III, p. 163.
49. *American Heritage*, June 1960, pp. 97–98.
50. Fortescue, vol. III, pp. 131, 156.
51. *Ibid.*, vol. II, p. 476.
52. *Ibid.*, vol. III, p. 59.
53. Marshall, *Washington*, vol. II, p. 177.

54. Fitzpatrick, *Writings*, vol. III, pp. 24–25.
55. Peterson, p. 79.
56. Marshall, *Washington*, vol. II, p. 71.
57. *London Gazette*, Apr. 8–Apr. 11, 1775.
58. *Bulletins, Fauquier,* July 1922, pp. 137, 138.
59. A stone commemorating these meetings was unveiled in Williamsburg May 26, 1904; *William and Mary Quarterly,* July 1904, pp. 65–66.
60. Commager, vol. I, p. 22.
61. Marshall, *Washington*, vol. II, p. 151.
62. See, for example, Freeman, vol. III, p. 404(*n*).
63. Wirt, *Spy*, pp. 70–71.
64. *Ibid.*
65. From an essay by Edmund Randolph, written in 1809, and printed in *Virginia Magazine of History and Biography,* July 1935, p. 219.
66. Wirt, *Henry*, p. 142.
67. Henry, vol. I, p. 319.
68. JM letter, Feb. 6, 1832, Revolutionary War Pension Files, David Jameson File—S 5607, National Archives.
69. P. Slaughter, *St. Mark's,* pt. 2, pp. 2–3.
70. *Ibid.*, pt. 2, pp. 2–3; pt. 1, p. 47.
71. *Ibid.*
72. Spotswood, Dec. 9, 1775, in Force, p. 224.
73. Woodford to Virginia Convention, Dec. 10, 1775, in Force, p. 227.
74. Marshall, *Washington*, vol. II, p. 196.
75. *Ibid.*
76. C. F. Adams, *John Adams,* vol. II, p. 428.
77. *Virginia Gazette* (Hunter & Dixon), Nov. 25, 1775, p. 3.
78. Marshall, *Washington*, vol. II, p. 342.
79. *Ibid.*, p. 343.
80. JM to Samuel Templeman, Sept. 16, 1832, Samuel Templeman Revolutionary War Records—S 6204, RG 93, National Archives.
81. Scott to Southall, *Virginia Gazette* (Pinkney), Dec. 9, 1775, p. 2.
82. *Ibid.*
83. Woodford to Virginia Convention, Dec. 10, 1775, in Force, p. 227. (Some secondary accounts have the slave's desertion to the British a ruse masterminded by Thomas Marshall. All contemporary evidence, however, points to the Negro's leaving to escape slavery.)
84. Wingo, p. 20.
85. Woodford to Virginia Convention, Dec. 10, 1775, in Force, p. 227.
86. Marshall, *Washington*, vol. II, p. 343.
87. Woodford to Virginia Convention, Dec. 10, 1775, in Force, p. 227.
88. *Virginia Gazette* (Pinkney), Dec. 20, 1775, pp. 2–3.
89. *Ibid.*, Dec. 23, 1775, p. 2.
90. Woodford to Virginia Convention, Dec. 10, 1775, in Force, p. 227.
91. Marshall, *Washington*, vol. II, p. 344.

[2]

1. Marshall, *Autobiographical*, p. 5.
2. *Journals of the Continental Congress,* vol. II, pp. 140–41.
3. Force, vol. II, pp. 1870–71.
4. *Pennsylvania Archives,* 8th series, vol. VIII, pp. 352–53; Commager, vol. I, pp. 281–82.
5. Joseph Hawley to E. Gerry, Feb. 18, 1776, Gerry Papers, Correspondence 1773–1817, New York Public Library.
6. Force, vol. III, pp. 240–41.
7. Marshall, *Washington*, vol. II, p. 365.
8. C. F. Adams, *John Adams,* vol. IX, p. 418.
9. Biddle, p. 86.
10. C. F. Adams, *John Adams,* vol. IX, pp. 420–21.
11. JM to William Stark, June 12, 1832, William Stark Revolutionary War Record—S 7592, RG 93, National Archives.

12. Quoted in C. Ward, p. 335.
13. Capt. John Marshall's Co., 12 muster rolls, Dec. 1778–Nov. 1779, Roll 105, Jacket 201, M246, National Archives.
14. Marshall, *Washington*, vol. III, p. 129.
15. *Ibid.*
16. *Virginia Gazette* (Hunter & Dixon), Jan. 13, 1776, p. 3.
17. *Calendar*, vol. VIII, p. 134.
18. Fitzpatrick, *Writings*, vol. VI, pp. 133–34.
19. *Tyler's*, vol. XII, pp. 118–19, 126, 131.
20. *Virginia Gazette* (Hunter & Dixon), Oct. 3, 1777, p. 3; *Tyler's*, vol. XII, p. 26.
21. Fitzpatrick, *Writings*, vol. IX, pp. 301–02; *Virginia Gazette* (Purdie), Nov. 21, 1777.
22. C. Ward, p. 364.
23. Marshall, *Washington*, vol. III, pp. 162–64.
24. *Ibid.*
25. Lt. Sir Martin Hunter diary, in Commager, vol. I, p. 626.
26. T. Will Heth to Col. John Lamb, Oct. 12, 1777, in Commager, vol. I, p. 630.
27. Marshall, *Washington*, vol. III, p. 341.
28. Surgeon Albigence Waldo diary, in Commager, vol. I, pp. 640–41.
29. *Ibid.*
30. Fitzpatrick, *Writings*, vol. X, pp. 192–98.
31. Marshall, *Washington*, vol. III, pp. 297, 298.
32. Libby, p. 8; J. Story, "John Marshall," *North American Review*, Jan. 1828, p. 8.
33. Flanders, p. 22*n*.
34. P. Slaughter, *St. Mark's*, pt. 2, p. 12.
35. Marshall, *Washington*, vol. II, p. 295.
36. *Ibid.*, vol. III, p. 315.
37. General Johann de Kalb to Count Charles Francis de Broglie, Dec. 25, 1777, in Commager, vol. I, p. 647.
38. P. Slaughter, *St. Mark's*, pt. 2, pp. 3–4.
39. Marshall, *Washington*, vol. III, p. 318.
40. Brig. Gen. James M. Varnum to Nathanael Greene, Feb. 12, 1778, in Commager, vol. I, p. 650.
41. Adams to Gerry, Gerry Papers, French Commission Mss., p. 28, Pierpont Morgan Library.
42. Marshall, *Washington*, vol. III, p. 349.
43. Gen. Heath's Order Book, May 23, 1777–Oct. 20, 1778, p. 124, RG 93, National Archives.
44. JM's combined service record, RG 93, National Archives.
45. Marshall, *Washington*, vol. III, pp. 338–39.
46. *Ibid.*, p. 431.
47. Marshall, *Washington*, vol. I, p. vii.
48. Jackets 289, 290, Roll 110, M246, RG 93, National Archives. These show JM listed as first lieutenant in Aug. 1778 and as captain the next month. Marshall years later said the date of his promotion was May 1777 (*Autobiographical*, p. 6), but his memory obviously had failed him on this minor detail.
49. Sallie E. Marshall Hardy, "John Marshall as Son, Brother, Husband and Friend," *The Green Bag*, Dec. 1896, p. 480.
50. Marshall, *Washington*, vol. III, pp. 246–47.
51. *Ibid.*, vol. IV, p. 69.
52. Mildred Smith to Eliza Ambler, Carrington letters, Library of Congress.
53. JM to Chittenden Lyon, Dec. 24, 1830, in William Bayliss Revolutionary War Pension File—S 12953, RG 15, National Archives; JM affidavit, June 12, 1832, in Humphrey Marshall Revolutionary War Pension File—S 31234, RG 15, National Archives; Marshall, *Autobiographical*, p. 6.
54. Betsy Ambler letter, written between 1810 and 1823, Carrington letters, Library of Congress.
55. *Brockenbrough*, vol. I, p. x.
56. D. P. Brown, vol. I, p. 224.
57. Calhoun, p. 291.
58. Printed in *William and Mary Quarterly*, Jan. 1908, p. 215.

59. Malone, vol. I, p. 51.
60. *William and Mary Quarterly*, July 1900, p. 22; D. R. Anderson, "The Teacher of Jefferson and Marshall," *South Atlantic Quarterly*, Oct. 1916, p. 340.
61. For Wythe biographical material, see D. R. Anderson, "The Teacher of Jefferson and Marshall," *South Atlantic Quarterly*, Oct. 1916, pp. 327–29; Malone, vol. I, pp. 68–71; Calhoun, p. 297.
62. Printed in *William and Mary Quarterly*, Jan. 1922, p. 41.
63. Brown letter, July 6, 1870, in *William and Mary Quarterly*, Oct. 1900, p. 80.
64. D. R. Anderson, "The Teacher of Jefferson and Marshall," *South Atlantic Quarterly*, Oct.
65. F. N. Mason, p. 7.
   1916, p. 329.
66. "Original Records of the Phi Beta Kappa Society," *William and Mary Quarterly*, April 1896, pp. 213, 215, 236.
67. W. F. Swindler, "John Marshall's Preparation for the Bar," *American Journal of Legal History*, 1967, pp. 207–13.
68. A photocopy of the Marshall notebooks is in the Manuscript Division, Library of Congress.
69. County Court Minutes, Fauquier County, Va., 1773–1780, p. 473 (a microfilm

copy is at the Virginia State Library).
70. *Southern Literary Messenger*, Feb. 1836, p. 183.
71. See Beveridge, vol. I, pp. 144–45, for an anti-Jefferson account of this incident; and Malone, vol. I, pp. 354–57, and Peterson, p. 236, for friendlier ones.
72. Peterson, p. 164.
73. JM statement, June 4, 1828, Revolutionary War Pension Files, John Crawford—S 8256, National Archives.
74. Printed in Howe, p. 528.
75. Printed in *The London Gazette*, undated clipping in Pickering Papers, Library of Congress.
76. Fortescue, vol. V, p. 256.
77. Rose, pt. 1, p. 100.
78. Fortescue, vol. VI, p. 416.
79. King, vol. III, p. 202.
80. Marshall, *Autobiographical*, p. 7.
81. P. Slaughter, *St. Mark's*, pt. 1, p. 73; Calhoun, vol. I, pp. 247–48.
82. The lock of hair story was told by Edward Carrington Marshall in *The Green Bag*, Dec. 1896, p. 481. The locket now is in the possession of Mrs. Kenneth Higgins of Richmond, Va., who kindly showed it to the author Aug. 12, 1969.
83. F. N. Mason, p. 20; *Virginia Cavalcade*

BOOK TWO: LAWYER AND POLITICIAN

[1]

1. Howe, p. 266; *Century*, June 4, 1859, p. 1.
2. Marshall, *Autobiographical*, p. 7.
3. "Chief Justice Marshall," *New York Review*, Oct. 1838, p. 333.
4. Quoted in Flanders, p. 25.
5. "Auditor's Certificates 1781," vol. 176, pp. 146, 152, 153, 160, 161, 167, 171, 176, 182, 204, 213, 216, 226, 231, 235,

254, 271, 324, 357, 403, in RG 93, National Archives.
6. "Auditor's Certificates 1781," vol. 176, pp. 49, 51.
7. Military Certificates, No. 1, 1-1805, p. 6; Land Office Military Certificates, Box 122, Bounty Warrants, Box 99, Virginia State Library.
8. Jefferson to Nicholas Biddle, Dec. 26, 1809, Nicholas Biddle Papers, vol. II, #236, Library of Congress.
9. Grants 15, 1787, pp. 393–

97; Warrants 17721, 19450, 19451, 19452, 1783; Land Office Military Certificates, Box 122, Virginia State Library.

10. Schoepf, vol. II, p. 61.
11. Freeman, vol. 1, p. 160; *Virginia Magazine of History & Biography*, July 1952, pp. 420–21; Samuel, pp. 18–46.
12. Schoepf, vol. II, p. 61.
13. Stanard, p. 53.
14. Schoepf, vol. II, pp. 61–63, 94–95; Samuel, pp. 117–19; Calhoun, p. 243; Simkins, p. 69.
15. Mays, vol. II, p. 392.
16. *Bulletins, Fauquier*, July 1922, pp. 139–40; *Fauquier County Records*, Roll 28 (on microfilm at the Virginia State Library).
17. H. Marshall, vol. I, p. 121.
18. *Calendar*, vol. II, p. 672; Hening, vol. XI, p. 283; Executive Letter Book, 1788–1792, p. 10, Virginia State Library.
19. *Calendar*, vol. IV, p. 391.
20. McClung, pp. 184, 216–18. (In F. N. Mason, pp. 58–59, Thomas Marshall is incorrectly identified as John's brother.)
21. Fitzpatrick, *Writings*, vol. XXVIII, p. 209; Fitzpatrick, *Diaries*, vol. III, p. 97.
22. Executive Papers, Box 55, Virginia State Library.
23. Van Santvoord, p. 321.
24. Corwin, *John Marshall*, p. 33.
25. "Life of Judge Marshall," *Port Folio*, Jan. 1815, p. 6.
26. Christian, p. 30.
27. A. Gallatin letter, Feb. 15, 1848, *Virginia Historical Register*, 1848, vol. I, p. 96.
28. JM, Mar. 17, 1785, Gulick Autograph Collection, Princeton.
29. JM to Alexander, Feb. 10, 1787, JM Papers, Library of Congress.
30. Washington Papers, vol. XVI, p. 139, Reel 6, and vol. XVI, p. 184, Reel 7, Library of Congress.
31. Henry E. Huntington Library, RB 39002:8 (p. 436).
32. F. N. Mason, p. 32.

33. JM to Monroe, Feb. 24, 1784, Monroe Papers, New York Public Library.
34. M. N. Marshall, p. 115.
35. Mays, vol. II, p. 429.
36. *Calendar*, vol. III, pp. 375, 386; Journal of Governor's Council, Reel 2, Virginia State Library; Box 27, Executive Papers, Virginia State Library.
37. Hall, pp. 193, 198, 237, 334, 221–22.
38. *Journal of the House of Delegates*, Oct.–Dec. 1782 session.
39. JM to Leven Powell, Dec. 9, 1783, in *John P. Branch Historical Papers*, June 1902, pp. 130–31.
40. JM letter, Feb. 12, 1783, photostat Von Hemert Autograph Collection, Princeton.
41. JM letter, Dec. 12, 1783, Library of Congress.
42. JM to James Monroe, Apr. 17, 1784, Monroe Papers, New York Public Library.
43. JM to Lee, Apr. 17, 1784, Lee Family Papers, Mss. 1-L51a6, vol. II, pp. 251–52, Virginia Historical Society.
44. JM to Monroe, May 15, 1784, Monroe Papers, Series 1, Reel 1, Library of Congress.
45. *Journals of the House of Delegates*, May–June 1784 session.
46. Henry, vol. II, p. 219.
47. See Alden, *A History*, pp. 350, 354; Peterson, pp. 135, 141, 142; Julius F. Prufer, "The Franchise in Virginia," *William and Mary Quarterly*, Oct. 1927, p. 259; Malone, vol. I, p. 279; Hart, p. 137; Hunt, *Madison*, vol. II, p. 183(n); Ketcham, pp. 162–65.
48. Madison, vol. I, pp. 252, 253, 262.
49. Virginia Acts, Oct. 1785, p. 19, Virginia State Library.
50. Executive Communications, Oct. 16, 1786–Jan. 11, 1787, Virginia State Library.
51. Richmond City Records, Hustings Court Order Books 1 and 2, Virginia State Library.
52. Carrington Letters, Library of Congress.

53. JM told that story in June 25, 1831, letter to J. Story, JM Papers, Library of Congress.
54. JM letter, Apr. 3, 1799, Library of Congress.
55. Carrington Letters, Library of Congress.
56. *Calendar*, vol. IV, p. 436.
57. JM letter, Jan. 3, 1785, Manuscripts Division, Department of Special Collections, Stanford; *Calendar*, vol. V, pp. 522–24.
58. *Calendar*, vol. VI, pp. 345, 532.
59. Christian, pp. 28–29.
60. See JM Papers, Henry E. Huntington Library, Cat. No. BR Box 22, A.L.S. Cat. No. BR Box 22, D.S. Cat. No. BR Box 22; *Proceedings . . . Masons*, pp. 139–40, 144.
61. Samuel, pp. 183–90.
62. G. W. Munford, pp. 326–38.

[2]

1. Young, p. 14.
2. Coxe letter, Sept. 13, 1786, Executive Communications, Virginia State Library.
3. Marshall, *Washington*, vol. V, pp. 81, 72.
4. Nathan Dane to Rufus King, Oct. 8, 1785, King, vol. I, p. 68.
5. Marshall, *Washington*, vol. V, pp. 61, 31.
6. *Ibid.*, pp. 89–90.
7. From Massachusetts Legislative Doctrines, vol. XXIII, p. 260, in King, vol. I, p. 58.
8. McRee, vol. II, p. 48.
9. Beard, p. 48.
10. William Plumer to John Hale, Sept. 18, 1786, Plumer Papers, Letters, Container 7, Library of Congress.
11. Marshall, *Washington*, vol. V, pp. 111–12.
12. *Ibid.*, p. 113.
13. *Ibid.*, p. 119.
14. *Ibid.*, p. 114.
15. Madison to Edmund Pendleton, Feb. 24, 1787, printed in U.S. Department of State, *Documentary Hist.*, vol. IV, p. 83; Parkes, p. 109.

16. Marshall, *Washington*, vol. V, pp. 44–46.
17. *Ibid.*, pp. 94–95.
18. JM to James Wilkinson, Jan. 1, 1787, Durrett Collection—Miscellaneous Mss., University of Chicago Library.
19. JM to Arthur Lee, Mar. 5, 1787, Lee Family Papers, Mss. L 51a6, vol. II, pp. 235–37, Virginia Historical Society.
20. Lee, vol. II, p. 320.
21. *Proceedings*, vol. XVII, p. 470.
22. Churchill, vol. III, p. 256.
23. Biddle, pp. 217–18.
24. Monroe to J. Madison, Oct. 13, 1787, in Hamilton, *Monroe*, vol. I, p. 176.
25. *Journal of the House of Delegates*, Oct. 1787, p. 25; Bradshaw, p. 141.
26. Fitzpatrick, *Writings*, vol. XXIX, pp. 357–58.
27. Hunt, *Madison*, vol. V, pp. 121–22.
28. Grigsby, *Convention of 1788*, vol. I, p. 54; St. George Tucker letter, June 29, 1788, printed in Conway, p. 106.
29. Grigsby, *Convention of 1788*, vol. I, pp. 9–12.
30. Gerry Papers, Correspondence 1773–1817, New York Public Library.
31. McRee, vol. II, p. 170.
32. Fitzpatrick, *Writings*, vol. XXIX, pp. 51–52, 302, 323–24.
33. *Ibid.*, pp. 327–28.
34. Hamilton, *Monroe*, vol. I, p. 181.
35. Marshall, *Washington*, vol. V, p. 132.
36. Henry to John Lamb, June 9, 1788, in Henry, vol. II, p. 343.
37. Conway, pp. 100–01; Van Santvoord, p. 315.
38. Marshall, *Autobiographical*, pp. 9–11.
39. Fitzpatrick, *Writings*, vol. XXIX, p. 278, 278(*n*).
40. J. M. Brown, pp. 78, 84, 118; H. Marshall, vol. I, p. 254; JM to George Muter, Feb. 11, 1787, JM Papers, Library of Congress.
41. J. M. Brown, pp. 78–79.

42. W. C. Ford, *Writings of Washington*, vol. X, p. 488.
43. M. C. Tyler, pp. 310–11, 307.
44. Fitzpatrick, *Writings*, vol. XXIX, p. 450.
45. Grigsby, *Convention of 1788*, vol. I, pp. 25–28.
46. Henry, vol. II, p. 399; Fitzpatrick, *Writings*, vol. XXIX, p. 508.
47. Grigsby, *Convention of 1788*, vol. I, pp. 31–32; J. M. Brown, p. 107; Marshall, *Washington*, vol. V, pp. 131–32; see Beveridge, vol. I, p. 320, for a differing view.
48. *Debates*, 1788, p. 13.
49. King, vol. I, p. 330.
50. Grigsby, *Convention of 1788*, vol. I, p. 4.
51. Farrand, vol. III, pp. 124–26.
52. *Ibid.*, pp. 644–45; Randolph letter, Sept. 15, 1787, Executive Communications, Virginia State Library; Grigsby, *Convention of 1788*, vol. I, pp. 84–85; Conway, pp. 92–93; Madison, vol. I, p. 387.
53. Elliot, vol. III, pp. 24–26.
54. William Grayson to Nathan Dane, June 4, 1788, Dane Papers, Library of Congress.
55. *Debates*, 1788, pp. 32–33.
56. *Ibid.*, pp. 51–61.
57. Fitzpatrick, *Writings*, vol. XXIX, p. 512.
58. Elliot, vol. II, pp. 178–79.
59. *Ibid.*, pp. 51–61.
60. F. N. Mason, p. 52.
61. King, vol. I, p. 336.
62. See *Debates*, 1788, Tyler, *Henry*, pp. 331–32.
63. Grigsby, *Convention of 1788*, vol. I, p. 83.
64. *Ibid.*, p. 157(*n*).
65. *Ibid.*, pp. 176–80; F. N. Mason, p. 54.
66. *Debates*, 1788, pp. 163–72.
67. *Ibid.*, pp. 297–99.
68. William Grayson to Nathan Dane, June 18, 1788, Dane Papers, Library of Congress.
69. Grigsby, *Convention of 1788*, vol. I, p. 281.
70. *Debates*, 1788, p. 371.
71. Jackson, p. xi.
72. *Debates*, 1788, pp. 391–95.
73. Ketcham, p. 59.
74. James Madison to Rufus King, June 13, June 22, 1788, in King, vol. I, pp. 332, 336–37.
75. *Debates*, 1788, pp. 467, 468; H. Marshall, vol. I, p. 287; Grigsby, *Convention of 1788*, vol. I, pp. 318–19.
76. B. Mitchell, pp. 2–3.
77. Monroe to T. Jefferson, July 12, 1788, in S. M. Hamilton, vol. I, pp. 185–86.
78. King, vol. I, pp. 337–38.
79. J. Madison to Rufus King, June 22, 1788, King, vol. I, p. 337.
80. Grigsby, *Convention of 1788*, vol. I, p. 318.
81. Elliot, vol. III, p. 652.
82. *Ibid.*
83. Spencer Roane to Philip Aylett, June 26, 1788, Roane Letters, *Bulletin of New York Public Library*, 1906, p. 167.
84. G. Washington to Benjamin Lincoln, June 29, 1788, Fitzpatrick, *Writings*, vol. XXX, p. 12.
85. Printed in Frank I. Schechter, "The Early History of the Tradition of the Constitution," *American Political Science Review*, Nov. 1915, p. 726.
86. W. W. Story, vol. I, pp. 391–92.
87. See Beard, especially pp. 149, 324–25.

[3]

1. The best overall description of the case, and the one on which the above account is drawn, is by John Marshall himself, in the notes he made on the trial and which are at the Virginia Historical Society. For Henry's role, see Henry, vol. II, pp. 491–92; R. D. Meade, *Henry . . . Revolutionary*, pp. 417–20. For the Randolph side, see Bruce, vol. I, pp. 102–12, and vol. II, pp. 282–83, and Garland, vol. I, pp. 12, 61, 63. Jefferson's advice to his daughter is in Randall, vol. II p. 221; his comment on Marshall was told by Rutherford B. Hayes,

who heard it in a Harvard Law School lecture by Joseph Story, and was reported in Williams, vol. I, p. 116. The more recent accounts referred to are Hess, pp. 375–77; Walz; and Francis Biddle, "Scandal at Bizarre," *American Heritage*, Aug. 1961, p. 10. The Dumas Malone description of Randolph is in Malone, vol. IV, p. 444. Copies of the Marshall-Morris letters are among JM Papers, William and Mary College.

2. The case is reported in 3 Call 495–501. See also Simms, pp. 40–43.
3. Peterson, pp. 122–23.
4. 3 Dallas 199.
5. Bemis, pp. 285, 356, 435.
6. McRee, vol. II, p. 395.
7. John Nicholas to John Breckinridge, June 9, 1793, Breckinridge Family Papers, vol. IX, p. 1474, Library of Congress.
8. Supreme Court Records, Microcopy 215; Roll 1; Microcopy 217, Roll 1, National Archives.
9. Van Santvoord, p. 329.
10. Kennedy, vol. II, p. 76.
11. Supreme Court Records, Microcopy 215, Roll 1, National Archives; Warren, vol. I, pp. 144–46.
12. Supreme Court Records, Microcopy 215, Roll 1, National Archives; 3 Dallas 199–285 (JM's arguments, pp. 210–15; Chase opinion, pp. 220–45; Cushing opinion, pp. 281–84.)
13. Copy of JM's account book is in Library of Congress; two letters of JM to John Breckinridge, undated, Breckinridge Family Papers, vol. VII, pp. 1046–48, Library of Congress; JM to James Breckinridge, Oct. 12, 1793, Dartmouth College.
14. JM to Hudson Martin, Nov. 16, 1795, JM Papers, Library of Congress; JM to Jones, Jan. 17, 1787, JM Correspondence, vol. I, Library of Congress; JM letter, Mar. 14,

1796, Historical Society of Pennsylvania; JM to Zachariah Johnston, undated, Duke University; JM to Anthony W. White, Mar. 1789, photostat in Von Hemert Autograph Collection, Princeton University.

15. Grigsby, *Tazewell*, p. 33; See JM to Henry, Aug. 31, 1790, Accession Item 24615b, Virginia State Library; JM to Gallatin, Jan. 3, 1790, New-York Historical Society.
16. JM to Giles, Feb. 9, 1790, New York Public Library; JM to Giles, no date, Blue-Box-Letter Book "M," Virginia Historical Society; JM to Madison, Nov. 29, 1790, Madison Papers, Reel 4, Library of Congress.
17. Morris to JM, Dec. 29, 1795, Morris Papers, Library of Congress.
18. Alexander Smyth letter, May 6, 1796, *Calendar*, vol. VIII, p. 367.
19. La Rochefoucauld-Liancourt, pp. 301–11, 347, 349.
20. Marshall, *Autobiographical*, pp. 11–12.
21. Marshall, *Washington*, vol. V, p. 607.
22. RG 59, Permanent Presidential Commissions, 1789–1802, p. 39, National Archives.
23. JM to Washington, Oct. 14, 1789, Carson Law Collection, additions, Free Library of Philadelphia; Marshall, *Autobiographical*, p. 12.
24. Washington to JM, Aug. 26, 1795, Washington Papers, vol. XIX, Reel 7, p. 126, Library of Congress; JM to Washington, Aug. 31, 1795, RG 59, M-179, Roll 13, National Archives.
25. Fitzpatrick, *Writings*, vol. XXXIV, pp. 333–35, 317, 405.
26. Washington to JM, July 8, 1798, Washington Papers, vol. XIX, Reel 7, p. 193, Library of Congress; JM to Washington, July 11, 1796, Aug. 12, 1796, Washington Papers, Reel 109, Library of Congress.

27. Washington to JM, July 15, 1796, Washington Papers, vol. XXIV, Reel 9, p. 208, Library of Congress.

28. Marshall, *Autobiographical*, p. 13.

29. JM to Monroe, Dec. 2, 1789, Monroe Papers, Series 1, Reel 1, Library of Congress.

30. Virginia Acts, Oct. 1789, p. 227, Virginia State Library.

31. See *Journal of the House of Delegates*, Oct. 1789 session; *Calendar*, vol. V, p. 68.

32. Marshall, *Autobiographical*, p. 13.

33. JM to Gov., Dec. 24, 1786, Box 45, Executive Papers, and JM to Gov., Feb. 4, 1789, Box 58, Executive Papers, Virginia State Library.

34. Robert Brooke to Roger West, Mar. 23, 1795, Executive Letter Books, 1794–1800, p. 57, Virginia State Library, for a statement of JM as Attorney General; for the cases, see *Calendar*, vol. VII, pp. 347–48, 384.

35. Hening, vol. I, p. vii, and Virginia Acts, Nov. 1795, pp. 13–14, Virginia State Library.

36. For Dec. 12, 1796, letter, see Box 98, Executive Papers, Virginia State Library (the letter also is printed in *Calendar*, vol. VIII, pp. 454–55, but with the wrong date); Shepherd, vol. II, p. 69.

37. Hening, vol. XII, p. 598; *North American Review*, Jan. 1828, p. 23.

38. Henry Lee to JM, Oct. 15, 1793, Executive Letter Books, 1792–1794, p. 278, Virginia State Library; JM to Henry Lee, Oct. 15, 1793, Executive Papers, Box 81, Virginia State Library.

39. JM reported the *Unicorn* incident in two lengthy letters to Virginia Governor Henry Lee, July 23, July 28, 1794, *Calendar*, vol. VII, pp. 228–35, 246. See also Henry Lee to JM, July 30, 1794, Executive Letter Books, 1792–1794, p. 474, Virginia State Library.

40. Military Journal of Lt. William Feltman, May 26, 1781, to April 25, 1782, Historical Society of Pennsylvania, quoted in Jordan, p. 159.

41. Niemcewicz, pp. 100–05.

42. Peterson, pp. 153, 91–92.

43. See, for example, C. F. Adams, *John Adams*, vol. II, p. 428; *Calendar*, vol. II, p. 233.

44. F. N. Mason, pp. 172, 250.

45. Box 81, Executive Papers, Virginia State Library.

46. *Calendar*, vol. V, p. 534; Aptheker, p. 213, quoting *Boston Gazette*, Sept. 3, 1792.

47. Aptheker, p. 213, quoting *Boston Gazette*, Sept. 3, 1792.

48. J. T. Callender, Sept. 29, 1800, quoted in Aptheker, p. 218.

49. Marshall, *Washington*, vol. V, p. 368.

50. Stanard, pp. 82–85; Christian, pp. 52–53; Jordan, p. 393.

51. Letter to JM, Aug. 23, 1793, Executive Letter Books, 1792–1794, p. 236, Virginia State Library; JM letters, Sept. 23, 1793, Oct. 3, 1793, Box 81, Executive Papers, Virginia State Library. See also *Calendar*, vol. VII, p. 148; Executive Letter Books, 1792–1794, p. 506; 1794–1800, p. 69; and Henry E. Huntington Library, Cat. No. RB 39006.

52. The narratives are from Ambler, *Ritchie*, pp. 13–16, and Toulmin, pp. 38–42; also see M. W. Scott, pp. 97, 114; B. Mayo, *Clay*, pp. 19–20.

53. Accession Item 26078, Virginia State Library; F. N. Mason, pp. 57–59; and this author's article, "John Marshall's Federalist House," *The Washington Post*, March 28, 1971, p. G–1.

54. See Richmond City Personal Property and Land Book, Virginia State Library, for appropriate year.

55. Record Group 53, National Archives, is filled with records of JM's stock transactions. See Entry 308, vol. 1221, May 26, 1800; Entry

307, vols. 1109, 1111, 1113, 1136, 1138, 1142; Receipts for Interest on Assumed Debt, vols. 1193B, 1193C, 1194C; Entry 286, vol. 1137; Entry 292, vol. 1081; Account Book-Pension Fund, vol. 1107.

56. Malone, vol. IV, p. 115.
57. *Debates*, 1788, p. 76.
58. JM to Archibald Stuart, May 28, 1790, Mar. 27, 1794, *William and Mary Quarterly*, Oct. 1925, pp. 285–88.
59. Marshall, *Washington*, vol. V, pp. 33–34.
60. Fitzpatrick, *Writings*, vol. XXXIII, pp. 464–65.
61. See Henry, vol. II, p. 532; Bailyn, p. 61.
62. Marshall, *Washington*, vol. V, p. 777.

63. Harry Ammon, "The Formation of the Republican Party in Virginia," *Journal of Southern History*, Aug. 1953, p. 303.
64. Jefferson to Madison, June 29, 1792, P. L. Ford, vol. VII, p. 130; see also Hunt, *Madison*, vol. VI, pp. 195–96.
65. In his *Autobiographical Sketch*, pp. 20–22, JM reports winning the battle, and this was picked up by Story for his account of JM's life in *North American Review*, Jan. 1828, pp. 25–26. But the *Journal of the House of Delegates*, session beginning Nov. 8, 1796, clearly shows that the JM forces lost in the protracted debate.

BOOK THREE: DIPLOMAT

[1]

1. Biddle, pp. 252–53.
2. T. Jefferson to Madison, July 7, 1793, P. L. Ford, vol. VI, pp. 338–39.
3. Washington to R. H. Lee, Oct. 24, 1793, Fitzpatrick, *Writings*, vol. XXXIII, p. 138.
4. Marshall, *Washington*, vol. V, pp. 488–89.
5. *Richmond Gazette and General Advertiser*, Aug. 21, p. 3; Harry Ammon, "Agricola Versus Aristedes," *Virginia Magazine of History and Biography*, July 1966, p. 314.
6. *Richmond Gazette and General Advertiser*, Sept. 11, 1793, p. 3.
7. Harry Ammon, James Monroe's most recent and thorough biographer, has found two letters which leads him to conclude that JM was both "Gracchus" and "Aristedes"; see "Agricola Versus Aristedes," *Virginia Magazine of History and Biography*, July 1966, pp. 312–13. I do not consider the evidence substantial enough to be conclu-

sive; nor do I consider the "Aristedes" letters compatible with JM's style.
8. *Richmond Gazette and General Advertiser*, Sept. 4, 1793, p. 3.
9. *Ibid.*, Sept. 11, 1793, p. 2.
10. *Ibid.*, Oct. 9, 1793, p. 2.
11. *Ibid.*, Oct. 16, 1793, p. 2.
12. *Ibid.*, Nov. 13, 1793, pp. 1, 2.
13. *Ibid.*, Nov. 20, p. 2; Dec. 4, 1793, p. 2.
14. Taylor, *Disunion*, pp. 20–23.
15. Morison, *Otis*, vol. I (1913 version), p. 54.
16. Marshall, *Autobiographical*, p. 17.
17. Marshall, *Washington*, vol. V, p. 616(*n*).
18. *Ibid.*, p. 632.
19. S. Mitchell, p. 85.
20. Fauchet's memoir was written Dec. 15, 1795, shortly after he returned to France, and is printed in the *Annual Report of the American Historical Association*, 1936, vol. I, pp. 83–119; the quoted section is from pp. 110–11.
21. Plumer Papers, Diary, Feb. 22, 1807, Library of Congress.
22. Marshall, *Autobiographical*, p. 16.

23. Marshall, *Washington*, vol. V, pp. 625–26.
24. Marshall, *Autobiographical*, pp. 13–16.
25. *Journal of the House of Delegates*, Nov. 10, 1795, session, pp. 27–29.
26. Marshall, *Autobiographical*, pp. 17–19.
27. McRee, vol. II, p. 456.
28. Jefferson to Madison, Nov. 26, 1795, P. L. Ford, vol. VIII, pp. 197–98.
29. Fauchet's memoir, Dec. 15, 1795, printed in *Annual Report of the American Historical Association*, 1936, vol. I, pp. 117–118.
30. W. E. Dodd, *Macon*, pp. 83–84.
31. Marshall, *Washington*, vol. V, pp. 652–54.
32. Simms, p. 63.
33. Edmund Randolph to Madison, Apr. 25, 1796, in Conway, p. 362.
34. JM to Hamilton, Apr. 25, 1796, J. C. Hamilton, vol. VI, pp. 108–09.
35. *Virginia Gazette and General Advertiser*, Apr. 27, 1796, p. 3.
36. JM to King, Apr. 25, 1796, Marshall Collection, New-York Historical Society.
37. JM to King, May 24, 1796, Marshall Collection, New-York Historical Society.
38. McRee, vol. II, p. 496.

[2]

1. W. C. Ford, *J. Q. Adams*, vol. II, p. 25.
2. J. Q. Adams to J. Adams, Jan. 14, 1797, W. C. Ford, *J. Q. Adams*, vol. II, p. 81.
3. *American State Papers*, vol. III, p. 171.
4. In E. W. Lyon, "The Directory and the U.S.," *American Historical Review*, Apr. 1938, pp. 516–17.
5. J. Q. Adams to Abigail Adams, Feb. 8, 1797, in W. C. Ford, *J. Q. Adams*, vol. II, p. 110; Marshall, *Washington*, vol. V, p. 736.

6. Marshall, *Washington*, vol. V, pp. 739–40; C. F. Adams, *John Adams*, vol. IX, pp. 113–14.
7. J. Adams to Senate, May 31, 1797, President's Messages—Executive Nominations, 1st Session, RG 46, National Archives; and see Donnan, p. 41.
8. Abigail Adams, June 3, 1797, S. Mitchell, p. 94; P. L. Ford, vol. VIII, p. 296.
9. Marshall, *Autobiographical*, pp. 21–23.
10. S. E. M. Hardy, "John Marshall," *The Green Bag*, Dec. 1896, p. 480; Tucker, vol. II, p. 23.
11. J. Adams to E. Gerry, June 20, 1797, C. F. Adams, *John Adams*, vol. VIII, p. 546.
12. Steiner, p. 224.
13. H. Adams, *Gallatin*, p. 185.
14. Malone, vol. I, pp. 100, 421.
15. P. L. Ford, vol. VIII, pp. 313–14.
16. J. Adams to E. Gerry, July 8, 1797, C. F. Adams, *John Adams*, vol. VIII, pp. 547–48.
17. S. G. Tucker to J. Page, June 23, 1797, courtesy of Edwin C. Hutten of Buffalo.
18. See Washington letters, Fitzpatrick, *Writings*, vol. XXXV, pp. 477, 471; JM to Polly, June 24, 1797, F. N. Mason, pp. 90–91.
19. JM to Caesar Rodney, June 31, 1797, Carson Law Collection, Box 14, Free Library of Philadelphia; JM to Polly, July 12, 1797, F. N. Mason, p. 99.
20. JM to Polly, July 2, 1797, *William and Mary College Quarterly*, Apr. 1923, pp. 73–74.
21. JM to Polly, July 5, 1797, *William and Mary Quarterly*, Apr. 1923, pp. 74–75.
22. JM to Polly, July 10, 1797, F. N. Mason, pp. 96–97.
23. JM to Polly, July 11, 1797, *William and Mary Quarterly*, Apr. 1923, pp. 75–76.
24. JM to Polly, July 14, 1797, F. N. Mason, pp. 100–01.

25. JM to Polly, July 20, 1797, *William and Mary Quarterly*, Apr. 1923, pp. 76–77.
26. JM to Polly, Aug. 3 and Aug. 29, 1797, F. N. Mason, pp. 107–08; JM to Timothy Pickering, Sept. 2, 1797, M-34, Roll 8, RG 59, National Archives.
27. JM to Timothy Pickering, Sept. 2, 1797, M-34, Roll 8, RG 59, National Archives.
28. JM to Timothy Pickering, Sept. 9, 1797, M-34, Roll 8, RG 59, National Archives.
29. JM to Timothy Pickering, Sept. 15, 1797, M-34, Roll 8, RG 59, National Archives.
30. JM to G. Washington, Sept. 15, 1797, photocopy in JM Papers, Library of Congress.
31. JM to Polly, Sept. 9, 1797, JM Papers, Library of Congress.
32. Pinckney to Pickering, Sept. 24, 1797, M-34, Roll 7, pp. 179–82, RG 59, National Archives.
33. JM to Charles Lee, Sept. 22, 1797, JM Papers, Emmet Collection 2137, New York Public Library.
34. W. Vans Murray to J. Q. Adams, Oct. 1, 1797, in *Annual Report of the American Historical Association*, 1912, pp. 361–63.
35. J. Marshall, "Paris Journal," p. 1, Library of Congress; M-34, Roll 8, RG 59, National Archives.
36. Pickering to Pinckney, JM, Gerry, July 15, 1797, M-28, Roll 4, pp. 89–106, RG 59, National Archives.
37. B. Mayo, *Instructions*, p. 140(*n*).
38. J. A. James, "France and the U.S., 1795–1800," *American Historical Review*, Oct. 1924, pp. 51–52.
39. *Ibid.*, pp. 45–47; E. W. Lyon, "The Directory and the U.S.," *American Historical Review*, Apr. 1938, p. 520.
40. Credences 1789–1906, vol. I, pp. 84–87, RG 59, National Archives.

[3]

1. Vallee, vol. I, pp. 1, iii, viii; Craigmyle, pp. 46–48.
2. A. B. Dodd, pp. 372–74.
3. *Ibid.*, pp. 378, 384; Vallee, vol. I, p. viii.
4. E. Quincy, pp. 49–50.
5. JM, "Paris Journal," p. 2, Library of Congress; Gerry Papers, Letterbook, 1797–1801, New York Public Library; M. Pinckney in letter begun Oct. 5, 1797, Manigault Family Papers, South Caroliniana Library, University of South Carolina.
6. JM, "Paris Journal," pp. 2–4, Library of Congress.
7. *American State Papers*, vol. III, p. 477; JM, "Paris Journal," p. 4, Library of Congress.
8. JM, "Paris Journal," pp. 4–5, Library of Congress.
9. JM, "Paris Journal," pp. 6–10, Library of Congress; *American State Papers*, vol. III, pp. 477–82.
10. Marshall, "Paris Journal," pp. 10–11, Library of Congress; *State Papers*, vol. III, pp. 482–87.
11. W. Vans Murray to J. Q. Adams, Nov. 4, 1797, printed in *Annual Report . . . Historical Association*, 1912, p. 366.
12. JM Papers, Library of Congress.
13. *State Papers*, vol. III, pp. 490–94; Marshall, "Paris Journal," pp. 13–18, Library of Congress. (Marshall's journal and the formal reports are so similar that obviously the journal was the source of the formal reports. Pinckney is not identified as the one who said: "It is no. No. Not a sixpence" in the formal report but is specifically so identified in Marshall's journal.)
14. Marshall, "Paris Journal," p. 11, Library of Congress.
15. W. C. Ford, *J. Q. Adams*, vol. II, pp. 341–42.
16. *State Papers*, vol. III, pp. 495–96; Marshall, "Paris

Journal," pp. 11–12, 18–19, Library of Congress.

17. Gerry to William Vans Murray, Oct. 30, 1797, Gerry Papers, Letterbook 1797–1801, New York Public Library.

18. *State Papers*, vol. III, pp. 497–98; Marshall, "Paris Journal," pp. 20–22, Library of Congress.

19. *State Papers*, vol. IV, pp. 5–10; Marshall, "Paris Journal," pp. 22–29, Library of Congress.

20. *State Papers*, vol. IV, p. 10; Marshall, "Paris Journal," p. 29, Library of Congress.

21. *State Papers*, vol. IV, pp. 10–11; Marshall, "Paris Journal," pp. 29–31; Library of Congress.

22. JM to Lee, Nov. 3, 1797, JM Papers, Library of Congress.

23. J. Q. Adams to William Vans Murray, Nov. 24, 1797, W. C. Ford, *J. Q. Adams*, vol. II, p. 224; J. Q. Adams to Elbridge Gerry, Nov. 26, 1797, Elbridge Gerry Papers, French Commission Mss., p. 27, Pierpont Morgan Library.

24. King, vol. II, p. 245.

25. *State Papers*, vol. IV, pp. 16–17.

26. M. Pinckney letter, Oct. 22, 1797, Manigault Family Papers, South Caroliniana Library, University of South Carolina; JM to Polly Marshall, Nov. 27, 1797, *William and Mary Quarterly*, Apr. 1923, pp. 80–81.

27. M. Pinckney letter, Oct. 5, 1797, Manigault Family Papers, South Caroliniana Library, University of South Carolina.

28. E. Gerry to wife, Nov. 25, 1797, Gerry Papers, Letterbook 1797–1801, New York Public Library.

29. See JM to C. C. Pinckney, Jan. 1798, Middleton Collection of Pinckney Papers, South Carolina Historical Society, typescript in JM Papers, William and Mary College; Mary Pinckney's letters from Paris, particularly

letter of Mar. 9, 1798, Manigault Family Papers, South Caroliniana Library, University of South Carolina. Beveridge wrote that Madame Villette and JM became "especially good friends," vol. II, pp. 290–91.

30. Marshall, "Paris Journal," p. 35, Library of Congress.

31. King, vol. II, p. 248.

32. Quoted in S. E. Morison, "Elbridge Gerry," *New England Quarterly*, Jan. 1929, p. 24.

33. M. Pinckney letter, Dec. 6, 1797, Manigault Family Papers, South Caroliniana Library, University of South Carolina.

34. W. Vans Murray to J. Q. Adams, Apr. 13, 1798, *Annual Report . . . Historical Association*, 1912, pp. 393–94.

35. S. E. Morison, "Elbridge Gerry," *New England Quarterly*, Jan. 1929, p. 24.

36. *State Papers*, vol. IV, pp. 18–19. Beveridge, vol. II, p. 291, stated as fact that "Talleyrand's fair agent" was Madame Villette, who was using her feminine wiles on Pinckney because he lacked Marshall's "penetration and adroitness." The belief that the lady was Madame Villette began apparently with Lyman's account a few years after the event (p. 336(*n*)). He wrote that the lady was "understood to be Madame de Villette" and also charged that "an intimation is given that that part of the affair was not much to the credit of the Americans." In a biography of Gerry written about the same time, Lyman's account is challenged (Austin, vol. II, p. 202(*n*)), the basis for the challenge being that the lady was one acquainted with Pinckney and not with either Gerry or Marshall as was Madame Villette. There is no evidence that the lady was Madame Villette, nor

that Madame Villette was operating at any time as Talleyrand's agent.

37. Washington to JM, Dec. 4, 1797, Washington Papers, vol. XXI, p. 8, Reel 8, Library of Congress.
38. Marshall, "Paris Journal," pp. 36–39, Library of Congress.
39. Rufus King described the bribe offer in a letter to Secretary of State Pickering, Dec. 23, 1797, in King, vol. II, p. 261.
40. JM to Rufus King, Dec. 24, 1797, King Papers, Library of Congress.
41. *State Papers*, vol. IV, p. 17.
42. J. A. Bayard to R. Bassett, Dec. 30, 1797, Donnan, p. 46.
43. Marshall, "Paris Journal," p. 39, Library of Congress.

[4]

1. W. Vans Murray to J. Q. Adams, Jan. 15, 1798, *Annual Report . . . Historical Association*, 1912, p. 371; J. Q. Adams to W. Vans Murray, Jan. 27, 1798, W. C. Ford, *J. Q. Adams*, vol. II, p. 246.
2. Pinckney, JM, Gerry letter, Jan. 17, 1798, JM Papers, Miscellaneous Collection, New York Public Library.
3. *State Papers*, vol. III, pp. 451–52.
4. Marshall, "Paris Journal," p. 39, Library of Congress.
5. *Ibid.*, p. 40.
6. W. Vans Murray to J. Q. Adams, Jan. 17, 1798, *Annual Report . . . Historical Association*, 1912, p. 279.
7. Marshall, "Paris Journal," pp. 40–41, Library of Congress.
8. RG 59, M-34, Reel 8, n.p., National Archives.
9. C. C. Pinckney to E. Gerry, Feb. 2, 1798, Gerry Papers, French Commission Mss., p. 82, Pierpont Morgan Library.
10. Marshall, "Paris Journal," p. 41, Library of Congress; N. Cutting letter, Feb. 17, 1798, Oliver Wolcott Jr. Mss., vol. XII, no. 40, Connecticut Historical Society.

11. Marshall, "Paris Journal," pp. 41–46, Library of Congress.
12. *Ibid.*, pp. 46–48.
13. *Ibid.*, pp. 46, 48–49; undated State Department copy in RG 59, M-34, Roll 8, n.p., National Archives; E. Gerry to J. Adams, July 5, 1799, Gerry Papers, Letterbook 1797–1801, New York Public Library.
14. Marshall, "Paris Journal," pp. 52–67, Library of Congress.
15. E. Gerry to J. Adams, July 5, 1799, Gerry Papers, Letterbook 1797–1801, New York Public Library.
16. Marshall, "Paris Journal," pp. 67–68, Library of Congress.
17. *State Papers*, vol. IV, pp. 83–88; Marshall, "Paris Journal," pp. 68–73, Library of Congress.
18. Marshall, "Paris Journal," pp. 73–75, Library of Congress.
19. *State Papers*, vol. IV, pp. 88–92.
20. J. Adams' message to Congress, Feb. 5, 1798, *State Papers*, vol. III, p. 439; A. Gallatin letter, Jan. 11, 1798, in H. Adams, *Gallatin*, p. 189.
21. Washington letter, Mar. 4, 1798, Fitzpatrick, *Writings*, vol. XXXVI, p. 179; T. Jefferson to J. Madison, Feb. 22, 1798, P. L. Ford, vol. VIII, p. 373.
22. Abigail Adams letter, Mar. 5, 1798, S. Mitchell, pp. 140–41; P. Smith, vol. II, pp. 952–56.
23. R. G. Harper letter, Mar. 9, 1798, Donnan, p. 51.
24. *State Papers*, vol. III, p. 455–56.
25. Jefferson to Monroe, Mar. 21, 1798, P. L. Ford, vol. VIII, pp. 388–89.
26. P. Smith, *Adams*, vol. II, pp. 956–60.
27. Pickering letter, Mar. 23, 1798, RG 59, M-28, Roll 4, pp. 249–52, National Archives.
28. JM to Washington, Mar. 8, 1798, JM Papers, Library of Congress.
29. Marshall, "Paris Journal," pp. 87–93, Library of Congress.

30. E. Gerry memorandum on Pickering report of Jan. 21, 1799, Gerry Papers, Letterbook 1797–1801, unpaged and undated, New York Public Library; Austin, vol. II, p. 241(*n*).

31. Marshall, "Paris Journal," pp. 93–98, Library of Congress.

32. Mrs. Carrington letter, dated 1800, Carrington letters, Library of Congress.

33. Marshall, "Paris Journal," pp. 98–102, Library of Congress.

34. *Ibid.*, pp. 102–07.

35. JM letter, Apr. 9, 1798, JM Papers, Library of Congress.

36. Marshall, "Paris Journal," pp. 107–14, Library of Congress.

37. C. C. Pinckney to Rufus King, Apr. 16, 1798, Pinckney Family Papers, Box 10, Library of Congress.

38. JM to C. C. Pinckney, Apr. 21, 1798, Pinckney Family Papers, Box 10, Library of Congress.

39. JM to Skipworth, Apr. 21, 1798, JM Papers, Historical Society of Pennsylvania.

40. W. Vans Murray to J. Q. Adams, May 4, 1798, in *Annual Report . . . Historical Association*, 1912, p. 404.

41. J. Q. Adams to W. Vans Murray, Apr. 19, Apr. 27, 1798, in W. C. Ford, *J. Q. Adams*, vol. II, pp. 278–79, 282–83.

42. See *State Papers*, vol. IV, pp. 157–58; E. Gerry to wife, Apr. 20, 1798; E. Gerry memorandum to John Adams re Pickering report to Congress, Jan. 21, 1799, Gerry Papers, Letterbook 1797–1801, New York Public Library.

43. A.A.E., Etats-Unis, vol. XLIX, f. 184v, quoted in E. W. Lyon, "The Directory and the United States," *American Historical Review*, Apr. 1938, pp. 522–23.

44. McCabe, p. 159; A. B. Dodd, pp. 385–86.

45. Hunt, *Madison*, vol. VI, pp. 315–16.

46. *State Papers*, vol. IV, pp. 161, 175–76, 179, 247.

47. JM letter, June 18, 1798, JM Collection, New-York Histori-

cal Society; *Porcupine's Gazette*, June 19, 1798, June 20, 1798, p. 3; Boudinot, vol. II, p. 141, Niemcewicz, pp. 121–24.

48. Jefferson to Madison, June 21, 1798, P. L. Ford, vol. VIII, pp. 439–40.

49. Jefferson to JM, JM Papers, Mss 1 M3566a 23, Virginia Historical Society; JM to Jefferson, Jefferson Papers, vol. CII, p. 17542, Library of Congress.

50. *Porcupine's Gazette*, June 22, 1798, p. 2; June 25, 1798, p. 3; *Claypoole's American Daily Advertiser*, June 25, 1798, p. 3. For Pinckney's acknowledgment that Harper originated the "Millions for defence . . ." slogan, see *South Carolina Historical . . . Magazine*, Jan. 1900, pp. 100–03.

51. *Virginia Herald*, July 13, 1798, p. 3.

52. Niemcewicz, pp. 122–24.

53. T. Pickering to E. Gerry, RG 59, M-28, Roll 4, pp. 309–10, National Archives; R. Troup to R. King, July 10, 1798, in King, vol. II, pp. 363–64.

54. See JM to T. Pickering, Sept. 15, 1798; T. Pickering to JM, Oct. 19, 1798; JM to T. Pickering, Oct. 22, 1798; T. Pickering to JM, Nov. 5, 1798; JM to T. Pickering, Nov. 12, 1798; JM to E. Gerry, Nov. 12, 1798; all in JM Correspondence and Papers, vol. I, Library of Congress; Austin, vol. I, p. 283.

55. See E. Gerry to J. Adams, July 15, 1799; E. Gerry to Jefferson, Jan. 15, 1801, and Jan. 20, 1801; E. Gerry's undated memo, Gerry Papers, Letterbook 1797–1801, New York Public Library; *Boston Patriot*, Mar. 28, 1810, pp. 1–2.

56. T. Pickering to JM, July 24, 1798, JM Correspondence and Papers, vol. I, Library of Congress; Washington letter, May 6, 1798, in Fitzpatrick, *Writings*, vol. XXXVI, p. 254; Washington letter, Dec. 25,

57. 1798, in Fitzpatrick, *Writings*, vol. XXXVII, pp. 66–67.

57. Liston to Grenville, May 2, 1798, Crown Copyright, Keeper of the Public Records, London.

58. *State Papers*, vol. IV, p. 137; Abigail Adams letter, June 25, 1798, S. Mitchell, p. 196; W. E. Dodd, *Macon*, p. 128; *Claypoole's American Daily Advertiser*, June 20, 1798, p. 2, June 25, 1798, p. 1, and June 26, 1798, p. 1.

59. See Kurtz, p. 340; P. Smith, p. 971.

60. George Cabot to R. King, Oct. 6, 1798, Feb. 16, 1799, in King, vol. II, pp. 438–39, 542–43.

61. J. Q. Adams to W. Vans Murray, June 19, 1798, W. C. Ford, *J. Q. Adams*, vol. II, p. 310; W. Vans Murray to R. King, June 1, 1798, King Papers, Library of Congress; Grenville to Liston, June 8, 1798, Crown Copyright, Keeper of the Public Records, London.

62. J. A. James, "France and the U.S., 1795–1800," *American Historical Review*, Oct. 1924, pp. 52–54; E. W. Lyon, "The Directory and the U.S.," *American Historical Review*, Apr. 1938, p. 529; W. E. Dodd, *Macon*, p. 131; F. B. Tolles, "Unofficial Ambassador," *William and Mary Quarterly*, Jan. 1950, pp. 3–25.

63. W. Short to E. Gerry, Aug. 27, 1798, Gerry Papers, French Commission Mss., p. 84, Pierpont Morgan Library.

64. J. Adams' message to Congress, Dec. 8, 1798, *State Papers*, vol. IV, pp. 144–46.

65. W. Short to Jefferson, Aug. 2, 1798, Short Papers, vol. XXX, Library of Congress, cited in Channing, vol. IV, p. 188; see also *State Papers*, vol. IV, pp. 244–46, 292–94.

66. Marshall, *Washington*, vol. V, p. 741.

67. JM to Henry Lee, Jan. 29, 1832, JM Papers, Library of Congress.

68. P. L. Ford, vol. I, p. 355; Beveridge, vol. II, p. 211; H. A. Johnson, "John Marshall," Friedman and Israel, vol. I, p. 287; and see I. Brandt in Jones, p. 44.

69. For Monroe's account, see RG 53, Entry 36, Accounts Current of Ministers and Consuls, vol. XCII, National Archives; for Pinckney's account, see same, and Pinckney Family Papers, Folder 11, Library of Congress, and RG 53, Entry 41, Journal of Accounts with the State Department, Nov. 20, 1795–June 23, 1800, vol. XCIX, National Archives; for E. Gerry's accounts, see RG 59, Entry 221, National Archives, and RG 53, Entry 36, Accounts Current of Ministers and Consuls, vol. XCII, National Archives.

70. RG 53, Entry 36, Accounts Current of Ministers and Consuls, vol. XCII, National Archives; RG 53, Entry 41, Journal of Accounts with the State Department, Nov. 20, 1795–June 23, 1800, vol. XCIX, National Archives; RG 59, Entry 223, National Archives.

71. Paxton, p. 69; F. N. Mason, pp. 65, 114; William Buchanan, "Louis Marshall, M.D.," a master's thesis on file in the Washington and Lee Library, see especially pp. 7–13.

72. Groome, pp. 218–27; Elliot, vol. III, p. 559; 3 Dallas 305–06, 306(*n*).

73. JM to Gov. Brooke, Mar. 2, 1795, *Calendar*, vol. VII, p. 446; Gov. Brooke to JM, Mar. 21, 1795, Executive Letter Books, 1794–1800, p. 45, Virginia State Library; Virginia Acts, Nov. 1796, p. 14, Virginia State Library.

74. F. N. Mason, pp. 63–64; JM to R. H. Lee, Jan. 18, 1793, Lee Family Papers, University of Virginia; R. Morris to J. M. Marshall, Nov. 4, 1795, and Mar. 4, 1796, Morris Papers, Library of Congress.

75. R. Morris to J. M. Marshall, Nov. 1, 1796; Morris to JM, Dec. 30, 1796; R. Morris to J. M. Marshall, Feb. 10, 1797, and Apr. 27, 1797, Morris Papers, Library of Congress.

76. J. M. Marshall to D. M. Fairfax, Sept. 6, 1797, Filmer & Wykeham-Martin Papers, Misc. Reel 428, vol. XXIII, C23/23, Virginia State Library; see JM to Edward Carrington, Dec. 28, 1800, Beinecke Library, Yale University, and J. M. Marshall to J. Ambler, Apr. 5, 1806; Elizabeth Cocke Coles Collection, No. 4640, University of Virginia; Groome, pp. 227–35; indenture agreement between JM, J. M. Marshall, and Rawleigh Colston, dated Oct. 5, 1808, Box No. 1106, University of Virginia; agreement between J. M. Marshall, Rawleigh Colston, John Ambler, and JM, dated Sept. 11, 1801; Cornell University; *Fauquier County*, pp. 30–31; R. Church, "James Markham Marshall," *Virginia Cavalcade*, pp. 26–29.

[5]

1. Marshall, *Autobiographical*, pp. 25–26.

2. Marshall, *Washington*, vol. V, pp. 759–60; G. Washington to B. Washington, in Fitzpatrick, *Writings*, vol. XXXVI, p. 420.

3. This story is one of the more frequently told about JM. This version is the family one, printed in M. N. Marshall, p. 153; a different one is in Paulding, vol. II, pp. 191–92.

4. This account is drawn from JM's letter to J. K. Paulding, Apr. 4, 1835, JM Papers, Library of Congress. See also J. Story, "Chief Justice Marshall's Public Life and Services," *North American Review*, Jan. 1828, pp. 28–29; *Bulletin . . . Virginia State Library*, Sept. 1925, pp. 246–47; *Autobiography of Van Buren*, pp. 177–79; and Fitzpatrick, *Diaries*, vol. IV, pp. 283–84.

5. JM to T. Pickering, Oct. 1, 1798, Oct. 15, 1798, copies in JM Correspondence and Papers, vol. I, Library of Congress; J. Adams to T. Pickering, Sept. 26, 1798, in C. F. Adams, *John Adams*, vol. VIII, p. 597. Beveridge reports that JM was offered the Wilson seat prior to Washington asking him to run for Congress (see Beveridge, vol. II, pp. 347, 378). But all contact regarding the Supreme Court offer came late in September, after the meeting with Washington. Beveridge did not have the date of that meeting.

6. Marshall, *Washington*, vol. V, pp. 360–61, 593.

7. *Kentucky Gazette*, Nov. 23, 1793, p. 3; B. Mayo, *Clay*, p. 51; Marshall, *Washington*, vol. V, pp. 575, 586.

8. Jefferson to T. McKean, Feb. 19, 1803, in P. L. Ford, vol. VIII, p. 216.

9. See F. M. Anderson, "The Enforcement of the Alien and Sedition Laws," *Annual Report of the American Historical Association*, 1912, pp. 119–26.

10. *Virginia Magazine of History and Biography*, Apr. 1921, p. 174.

11. Jefferson to S. T. Mason, Oct. 11, 1798, in P. L. Ford, vol. VIII, p. 450; JM to Henry Lee, Oct. 25, 1830, University of Virginia.

12. JM to T. Pickering, Aug. 11, 1798, JM Correspondence and Papers, vol. I, Library of Congress.

13. "A Freeholder" letter published in *Columbian Centinel*, Oct. 20, 1798; JM's answer published in same and *Alexandria Advertiser*, Oct. 11, 1798, p. 3.

14. For discussion of common law issue, see Faulkner, p. 88, Ketcham, pp. 400–01, and *Tyler's Quarterly*, vol. VII, pp. 159–60. For JM's

opinions on common law, see his letter to unknown person, Nov. 27, 1800, JM Papers, Library of Congress.

15. Morison, *Otis*, 1913 ed., vol. I, p. 157; Ames, vol. I, p. 246; T. Pickering to T. Sedgwick, Nov. 6, 1798, Pickering Papers, Library of Congress.

16. Thompson, pp. 3–40.

17. Peterson, p. 615.

18. See Beveridge, vol. II, p. 406.

19. The minority report is reprinted in Roche, pp. 32–48.

20. Washington to JM, Dec. 30, 1798, Washington Papers, vol. XXI, p. 232, Reel 8, Library of Congress; JM to Washington, Jan. 8, 1799, JM Papers, Library of Congress.

21. Henry's letter is in M. C. Tyler, pp. 408–11, and Henry, vol. II, pp. 592–93.

22. Callender, vol. I, pp. 126–27, 135, 140.

23. See, for example, Bridenbaugh, p. 16.

24. The scandal story is told in J. Wood, pp. 186–87, first printed in 1802, reprinted in 1846 and 1968.

25. JM to James Markham Marshall, Apr. 3, 1799, JM Correspondence and Papers, vol. I, Library of Congress; G. W. Munford, pp. 208–11, for the description of the Parsons' votes (one accepts this account for the accuracy of the spirit portrayed rather than for the accuracy of detail; the account has the wrong man elected), and *Virginia Magazine of History and Biography*, Apr. 1921, pp. 176–77.

26. Washington to JM, May 5, 1799, Washington Papers, Reel 114, Library of Congress; T. Sedgwick to R. King, July 26, 1799, in King, vol. III, p. 69.

27. G. Cabot to R. King, Apr. 26, 1799, in King, vol. III, p. 9.

28. *Annals*, 6th Cong., 1st Sess., 185.

29. *Ibid.*, 189–97; P. Smith, vol. II, p. 1020.

30. O. Wolcott to F. Ames, Dec.

29, 1799, in Van Santvoord, p. 341; Morison, *Otis*, 1913 ed., vol. I, p. 178 (a slightly different account is in the 1969 ed., p. 165); T. Sedgwick to King, Dec. 29, 1799, in King, vol. II, p. 163; G. Cabot to R. King, in King, vol. III, p. 184.

31. JM to John Ambler, Dec. 29, 1799, in Oster, p. 184; *Annals*, 6th Cong., 1st Sess., 203–04; Marshall, *Washington*, vol. V, pp. 763–66; JM to C. W. Hansen, Mar. 29, 1832, JM Papers, Myers Collection, New York Public Library.

32. *Annals*, 6th Cong., 1st Sess., 229–45.

33. H. Adams, *Gallatin*, pp. 155–56.

34. *Annals*, 6th Cong., 1st Sess., 532–33.

35. JM to J. M. Marshall, Feb. 28, 1800, JM Correspondence and Papers, vol. I, Library of Congress.

36. *Annals*, 6th Cong., 1st Sess., 596–618; *Journals of the House of Delegates*, Oct. 1784–Jan. 1785, p. 41; H. Adams, *Gallatin*, p. 232.

37. T. Pickering to R. King, March 10, 1800, JM Correspondence and Papers, vol. I, Library of Congress; Joseph Hopkinson eulogy in *Brockenbrough*, vol. I, p. xii; W. B. Slaughter, p. 112; JM to Reuben George, Mar. 16, 1800, Accession Item 24119, Virginia State Library.

38. J. A. Bayard to Richard Bassett, Feb. 1, 1800, in Donnan, p. 95.

39. *Annals*, 6th Cong., 1st Sess., 519–20.

40. T. Sedgwick to R. King, May 11, 1800, in King, vol. III, pp. 236–39.

41. *Annals*, 6th Cong., 1st Sess., 534.

42. *Ibid.*, 251, 395; JM to Charles Dabney, Jan. 20, 1800, Accession No. 24816 (27), Virginia State Library; Manlius critique, Evans Number 37820.

43. *Annals*, 6th Cong., 1st Sess., 404, 419–20, 423.

44. *Ibid.*, 720.
45. T. Sedgwick to R. King, May 11, 1800, in King, vol. III, pp. 236–39.
46. Marshall Family Bible, courtesy of Mrs. Kenneth Higgins.
47. F. N. Mason, pp. 132–33.
48. *Fauquier County Records*, Deed Book 8, pp. 241–42, Virginia State Library.
49. Fitzpatrick, *Writings*, vol. XXXI, p. 239(*n*).
50. Fitzpatrick, *Writings*, vol. XXXI, pp. 211–12; vol. XXXIII, p. 378; vol. XXXIV, pp. 157–58, 415.
51. Thomas Marshall to JM, Sept. 9, 1796, in F. N. Mason, p. 84; F. N. Mason, p. 130.
52. Thomas Marshall to John Adams, Apr. 28, 1797, RG 59, Roll 15, unpaged, National Archives.
53. Marshall, *Autobiographical*, pp. 27–28; Secretary of War nomination is in RG 46, Records of the U.S. Senate, National Archives. A note on the back says it was received May 7 and that the Senate consented May 9.
54. Nomination as Secretary of State is in RG 46, Records of the U.S. Senate; Confirmation is in RG 59, Entry 342, Senate Confirmation and Rejections of Presidential Nominations; Commission is in RG 59, Permanent Presidential Commissions, 1789–1802, p. 365, all in National Archives; Lee to JM, May 13, 1800, in JM Correspondence and Papers, vol. I, Library of Congress.
55. Marshall, *Autobiographical*, pp. 28–29.
56. G. Hunt, *Department of State*, p. 191; *Daily Advertiser*, June 13, 1800; *Naval Documents, France*, vol. VI, pp. 492, 512.
57. John Adams to JM, Aug. 2, 1800, RG 59, M-179, Roll 17, unpaged; JM to William Eaton, Aug. 30, 1800, RG 59, M-28, Roll 5, p. 357, all in National Archives.
58. *Naval Documents, Barbary Powers*, vol. I, p. 365; John Adams to JM, July 11, 1800, RG 59, M-179, Roll 17, unpaged; JM to J. Q. Adams, July 24, 1800, RG 59, M-28, Roll 5, unpaged, both in National Archives; JM to Roger Griswold, Jan. 15, 1801, William Griswold Collection, Sterling Memorial Library, Yale University.
59. JM to D. Humphreys, Sept. 8, 1800, in *Naval Documents, France*, June 1800–Nov. 1800, pp. 326–31.
60. JM letter, Aug. 28, 1800, JM Correspondence and Papers, vol. I, Library of Congress; A. Hamilton to JM, Oct. 2, 1800, JM Papers, William and Mary; JM to J. Adams, Sept. 17, 1800, C. F. Adams, *John Adams*, vol. IX, p. 85(*n*).
61. D. Lenox to State Department, Apr. 1, 1800, RG 59, Entries 863, 862, National Archives; JM to D. Lenox, Dec. 17, 1800, Houghton Library, Harvard University; see also JM letter, Dec. 12, 1800, Henry E. Huntington Library, L.S. Cat. No. HM 4685; JM to D. Lenox, June 26, 1800, RG 59, M-28, Roll 5; Jacob Wagner to William Ellergy, Aug. 19, 1800; JM to Collector of Customs, Boston, Oct. 30, Dec. 12, 1800, both in RG 36, Records of the Bureau of Customs, Letters from the Treasury, vol. VI, pp. 77, 78, all in National Archives.
62. JM to R. King, Sept. 20, 1800, *American State Papers, Foreign Relations*, vol. II, p. 489.
63. Charles D. Wolfe to JM, RG 76, Great Britain, 1794–1824, British Spoliations, Unsorted Papers, Box 4, Folder L; see also there H. A. and J. G. Coster to JM, June 24, 1800, Box 1, Folder C, and Rogers & Owings to JM, Aug. 9, 1800, Box 3, Folder G; see also JM to Samule and Miers Fisher, Sept. 8, 1800, RG 76, Spain Treaty, Feb. 22, 1819, vol. XC, Ship Suxxex; JM to R. King, Sept. 18, 1800, RG 59, M-28, Roll 5, all in National Archives.

64. JM to R. King, Aug. 23, 1800, Rufus King Collection, Henry E. Huntington Library, L.S. Cat. No. RK 538; JM to R. King, Sept. 20, 1800, copy in Marshall Collection, New-York Historical Society; JM to R. King, May 5, 1801, King, vol. II, pp. 116–18 (the letter is misdated in King); see also Malone, vol. IV, p. 92.

65. JM to Treasury Secretary, Mar. 3, 1801, RG 53, Entry 47, vol. CVI, p. 35; JM memorandum, Feb. 2, 1801, RG 59, M-179, Roll 18, both in National Archives.

66. JM to J. M. Marshall, Dec. 16, 1799, JM Papers, Library of Congress.

67. J. Wendell to E. Gerry, Mar. 18, 1800, Gerry Papers, Correspondence 1773–1817, New York Public Library; *Tyler's Quarterly*, vol. VII, p. 155.

68. JM to H. G. Otis, Aug. 8, 1800, JM Correspondence and Papers, vol. I, Library of Congress; JM to R. Peters, Oct. 30, 1800, copy in Dillon, vol. I, p. 96.

69. JM to C. C. Pinckney, Nov. 20, 22, Dec. 6, 18, 1800, Pinckney Family Papers, Box 10, Library of Congress.

70. JM to E. Carrington, Dec. 28, 1800, Beinecke Library, Yale University.

71. A. Hamilton to J. A. Bayard, Dec. 27, 1800; JM to A. Hamilton, Jan. 1, 1801, both in J. C. Hamilton, vol. VI, pp. 499–502.

72. *Richmond Examiner*, Feb. 10, 13, 17, 1801.

73. Jefferson to T. Coxe, Dec. 31, 1800, Jefferson Papers, vol. CVIII, p. 18551, Library of Congress; A. Gallatin letter, Jan. 15, 1801, in H. Adams, *Gallatin*, pp. 253–54; J. Monroe to T. Jefferson, Jan. 6, Jan. 18, Jan. 27, 1801, in S. M. Hamilton, vol. III, pp. 253–57.

74. Washington to Edmund Randolph, Sept. 28, 1789; Washington to John Jay, Oct. 5, 1789, both in Fitzpatrick, *Writings*, vol. XXX, pp. 418–19, 428–29.

75. Jefferson to Monroe, Mar. 2, 1796, P. L. Ford, vol. VII, p. 59.

76. T. Pickering to R. King, Jan. 5, 1801, in King, vol. III, pp. 366–67.

77. J. Adams to John Jay, Dec. 18, 1800, C. F. Adams, *John Adams*, vol. IX, pp. 91–92; Senate confirmation of Jay is in RG 59, Entry 342, Senate Confirmations and Rejections of Presidential Nominations, National Archives; Jay to Adams, printed in Friedman and Israel, vol. I, p. 19. Note: There is a widespread belief that Adams offered Jay the appointment only to salve political difficulties and never anticipated his accepting it. This is a subjective reaction, and my own belief is contrary. Adams' letter to Jay asking him to accept sounds sincere, and there is no reason to doubt Adams' intention.

78. This account of JM's appointment is by JM himself and is found in his *Autobiographical*, pp. 29–31. Apparently it was written in 1827, more than a quarter of a century after the fact. However, while one may question the total accuracy of the quotations, there seems no reason to doubt the essential facts.

79. J. Adams to E. Boudinot, Jan. 26, 1801, C. F. Adams, *John Adams*, vol. IX, pp. 93–94.

80. The downgrading of JM's ability as a lawyer appears to have begun with Beveridge. In vol. II, p. 554, note 3, he described JM's knowledge of the law as "extremely limited," which is not correct. This estimation has frequently been picked up. See, for example, J. A. Garraty, "The Case of the 'Missing' Commissions," *American Heritage*, June 1963, p. 7.

81. J. Adams to JM, Gray-Glines Collection, Connecticut State Library.

82. J. Dayton to W. Paterson, Jan. 20, 28, 1801, Special Collections Department, Rutgers University; Paterson to JM, Jan. 26, 1801, referred to in JM to Paterson, Feb. 2, 1801, Paterson Papers, New York Public Library; Record of Senate Confirmation of JM is in RG 59, Entry 342, Senate Confirmations and Rejections of Presidential Nominations, National Archives.

83. JM to J. Adams, and J. Adams to JM, Feb. 4, 1801, C. F. Adams, *John Adams*, vol. IX, p. 96; Minutes of the Supreme Court, Microcopy 215, Roll 1, National Archives.

84. RG 267, SC-Office of the Clerk, Subject File, Box 1, Folder 7, National Archives; U.S. Congress, *Documentary History of the Capitol*, p. 94.

85. J. A. Bayard to R. Bassett, Jan. 3, 1801, and J. A. Bayard to Andrew Bayard, Jan. 8, 1801, in Donnan, pp. 117, 119.

86. H. Adams, *History*, vol. I, pp. 197–99; *Annals*, 6th Cong., 2nd Sess., 763–66.

87. M. B. Smith, pp. 25–26.

88. JM to R. King, Feb. 26, 1801, Carson Law Collection, Box 14, Free Library of Philadelphia.

89. Monroe to Jefferson, Mar. 3, 1801, in S. M. Hamilton, vol. II, pp. 263–64; see St. George Tucker to John Page, Feb. 27, 1801, no. 3640, University of Virginia; Morison, *Otis*, 1913 ed., vol. I, p. 202.

90. Jefferson to JM, Mar. 2, 1801; JM to Jefferson, Mar. 2, 4, 1801, both in Jefferson Papers, vol. CX, pp. 18821, 18825, 18847, Library of Congress; Jefferson to JM, Mar. 4, 1801, RG 59, M-179, Roll 18, National Archives; see W. E. Dodd, "Chief Justice Marshall and Virginia," *American Historical Review*, vol. XII, p. 776.

91. The quotations from the Jefferson inaugural come from *Annals*, 6th Cong., 2nd Sess., 763–66. There are several versions of this address, differing in minor detail, and some discussion that, rather than the Republican and Federalist parties, Jefferson may have meant people of republican and federalist persuasions. As Marshall's letter to Pinckney indicates, the speech was judged as a conciliatory one and reading any version indicates Jefferson intended it as such, and I am staying out of the other arguments.

The Marshall letter to Pinckney may be one of the most misquoted letters in American historical literature. Beveridge cited it twice (vol. III, pp. 11, 18). He omitted the first paragraph in which Marshall spoke of not trying to disappoint his Federalist friends. Beveridge also dropped a "not" from a subsequent sentence so that it read, "With the latter [absolute terrorists] I am disposed to class Mr. Jefferson." Marshall, of course, had said just the opposite—"I am not disposed to class Mr. Jefferson." Beveridge changed a "his" to a "this" in another sentence so as to make it read that Marshall considered Jefferson's inaugural as "strongly characteristic" of the "violent party declamation" which elected him. Actually, Marshall was saying that Jefferson's conciliatory speech reflected Jefferson's own spirits as opposed to the violent party orations.

The letter is available at the Charleston Library Society, and the complete and accurate text was printed for the first time, I believe, by Richard J. Hooker in *American Historical Review*, vol. LIII, pp. 518–20, and has since been cited accurately by most writers of the period. I make such a point of it, however, because the misquotations so distort Marshall's attitudes at the time and, I believe, his character.

Also the misquotations sometimes are picked up and repeated. See, for example,

F. N. Mason, p. 150; Loth,
pp. 172–77; Beirne, pp. 50–
51.

BOOK FOUR: JUDGE

Part I: The Struggle for an Independent Judiciary

[1]

1. 2 Dallas 419.
2. 1 Cranch 1–45.
3. 1 Cranch 45–103.
4. Brant, vol. III, pp. 357–58.
5. *Ibid.*
6. 1 Cranch 103–10.
7. 3 Dallas 199, 171.
8. D. P. Brown, vol. I, pp. 356–60.
9. Malone, vol. IV, pp. xix–xx.
10. S. T. Mason to John Breckin-ridge, Feb. 12, Feb. 19, 1801, Breckinridge Family Papers, Library of Congress; Jeffer-son to A. Stuart, Apr. 8, 1801, Lipscomb and Bergh, vol. X, p. 257.
11. Warren, vol. I, pp. 195–97; Ellis, p. 40.
12. W. B. Giles to Jefferson, Mar. 16, 1801, in W. S. Carpenter, "Repeal of the Judiciary Act of 1801," *American Political Science Review*, Aug. 1915, p. 521; W. B. Giles to Jeffer-son, June 1, 1801, in Malone, vol. IV, p. 116.
13. John Jay letter, RG 267, SC-Office of the Clerk—Letters to and from Justices, Box 1, Na-tional Archives.
14. John Jay to R. King, Dec. 22, 1793, King, vol. I, p. 509.
15. For a discussion of the im-pact of the land cases on the passage of the Judiciary Act of 1801, see Kathryn Turner, "Federalist Policy and the Judiciary Act of 1801," *Wil-liam and Mary Quarterly*, Jan. 1965, pp. 3–32.
16. J. Adams to JM, Sept. 27, 1800; J. Adams speech text, Nov. 22, 1800, C. F. Adams, *John Adams*, vol. IX, pp. 85, 114.
17. JM to R. King, Jan. 18, 1801,

Naval Documents, France, vol. VII, p. 98; JM to W. Paterson, Feb. 2, 1801, Wil-liam Paterson Papers, New York Public Library.
18. J. A. Bayard letter, Mar. 3, 1802, Donnan, p. 150; A. Hamilton to C. C. Pinckney, Mar. 15, 1802, Lodge, vol. X, pp. 428–29; JM letter, Apr. 5, 1802, Oliver Wolcott, Jr., Mss., vol. XLVIII, no. 30, Connecticut Historical So-ciety.
19. JM to William Cushing, Apr. 19, 1802; R. T. Paine letters, Massachusetts Historical So-ciety; JM to William Pater-son, Apr. 6, 19, May 3, 1802, Paterson Papers, New York Public Library; William Pat-erson to JM, June 11, June 18, 1802, Paterson Papers, New York Public Library; S. Chase to JM, Apr. 24, 1802, Paterson Papers, New York Public Library. See also Ellis, pp. 60–61; W. S. Carpenter, "Repeal of the Judiciary Act of 1801," *American Political Science Review*, Aug. 1915, p. 528.
20. 1 Cranch 299.
21. 1 Cranch 137.
22. Bonham's Case, 8 Coke Rep., 114a (in London, 1826 ed., p. 368).
23. Holdsworth, vol. V, pp. 428–29.
24. A. M. Schlesinger (père), "Colonial Appeals to the Privy Council," *Political Science Quarterly*, vol. XXVIII, pp. 279–97, 433–50.
25. Winthrop v. Lechmore, in J. B. Thayer, *Cases on Constitu-tional Law*, vol. I, p. 34.
26. A. M. Davis, "The Case of Frost v. Leighton," *American*

Historical Review, vol. II, pp. 229–30.

27. Mass. 5, Quincy, 474.

28. Court action of Feb. 8, 1766, printed in Tyler's Quarterly, vol. II, p. 217, quoting Virginia Gazette.

29. J. B. Thayer, Cases on Constitutional Law, vol. I, p. 63.

30. Ibid., pp. 69–70.

31. Ibid., p. 72.

32. Ibid., pp. 72–73(n).

33. A. Scott, "Holmes vs. Walton: The New Jersey Precedent," American Historical Review, vol. IV, pp. 456–60.

34. 1 Cranch 299.

35. Mays, vol. II, p. 422.

36. 4 Call 5.

37. Symsbury Case, Kirby (Conn.), 444, 447.

38. Bayard v. Singleton, 1 Martin 42, in McRee, vol. II, pp. 145–49.

39. Corwin, Marshall and the Constitution, pp. 11–12.

40. Goebel, pp. 205–06.

41. Farrand, vol. I, pp. 97, 109.

42. Ibid., vol. II, pp. 27–28, 76, 78.

43. Ibid., vol. II, pp. 298–99.

44. Elliot, vol. II, p. 196; vol. III, p. 554.

45. Rossiter, pp. 466–67; see also The Federalist Papers, nos. 16, 22, 81, and 84.

46. Jefferson to Wythe, July 1776; Jefferson to Madison, Mar. 15, 1789, in P. L. Ford, vol. II, p. 218; vol. V, p. 461.

47. Annals of Congress, 1st Cong., 1st Sess., 472–608.

48. 3 Dallas 410.

49. 3 Dallas 171.

50. W. Bradford to A. Hamilton, in B. Mitchell, p. 337.

51. Columbian Centinel, Mar. 30, 1799, pp. 1–2.

52. Annals of Congress, 7th Cong., 1st Sess., 178–83.

53. Austin v. University of Pennsylvania, 1 Yeates 260–61.

54. Stidger v. Rogers, 2 Kentucky Reports 52.

55. Whittington v. Polk, 1 Harris and Johnson (Maryland) 236.

56. Ogden v. Witherspoon, 2 Haywood (North Carolina) 227.

[2]

1. JM to J. M. Marshall, Mar. 18, 1801, JM Correspondence and Papers, vol. I, Library of Congress.

2. Malone, vol. IV, pp. 73–74; R. Troup to R. King, Aug. 8, 1801, King, vol. III, p. 495.

3. RG 267, SC-Original Jurisdiction Cases, Box 5, National Archives.

4. 1 Cranch 137–80; see also RG 267, SC-Original Jurisdiction Cases, Box 5, and RG 59, Entry 342, Entry 339, and Minutes of the Supreme Court, Microcopy 215, Roll 1, National Archives. The Marshall description is in Wirt, Spy, pp. 114–24.

5. For Boston see Columbian Centinel, Feb. 28, Mar. 12, Aug. 20, 1803; Independent Chronicle, Mar. 10, 14, June 16, 1803; New England Palladium, Apr. 12, 1803. For New York see Spectator, Mar. 30, Apr. 2, 1803; Evening Post, Mar. 23, 24, 1803. For Philadelphia see Aurora, Mar. 23, 24, 1803. For Baltimore, see Federal Gazette & Baltimore Daily Advertiser, Feb. 28, 1803. For Washington see Federalist, Feb. 25, Apr. 20, 22, 27, May 18, 1803; National Intelligencer, Mar. 16, 26, 1803. For Richmond see Argus, Apr. 16, 23, 1803. For Charleston see Courier, Mar. 11, 30, 31, 1803. For Savannah see Georgia Republican and State Intelligencer, Mar. 17, 1803.

6. Independent Chronicle, Mar. 10, 1803, p. 2. Beveridge, vol. III, pp. 112–13(n), claimed the commentary must have been written before the decision was handed down, but I do not believe even his own explanation justifies the claim.

7. Argus, Apr. 16, 23, 1803; Aurora, Apr. 16, 23, 1803. See also Corwin, Marshall and the Constitution, p. 65; and H. Adams, History, vol. II, p. 146.

8. *Washington Federalist,* Apr. 20–27, 1803.
9. Frankfurter, *Law and Men,* p. 17; Jackson, p. 9.
10. U.S. v. Fisher, 2 Cranch 384.
11. Jefferson to A. Adams, Sept. 11, 1804, Lipscomb and Bergh, vol. XI, pp. 50–51. Note: Warren, vol. I, pp. 259–60, cited Jefferson's letter to Archibald Rowan, Sept. 26, 1798, as proof that Jefferson acknowledged juridical power. A reading of the letter's full text (in P. L. Ford, vol. VII, pp. 280–81) makes clear that Jefferson was talking not about judicial authority but about states' rights—state judges protecting against the alleged evils of the federal government.
12. Jefferson to W. Johnson, June 12, 1823, P. L. Ford, vol. XII, p. 257(*n*).
13. Corwin, *Marshall and the Constitution,* p. 124.
14. Holdsworth, vol. XII, p. 478.
15. 3 Cranch 97, 187.
16. Jefferson to James Pleasants, Dec. 26, 1821, and Jefferson to W. Johnson, Oct. 27, 1822, both in P. L. Ford, vol. XII, pp. 216, 247–50.
17. W. Johnson to Jefferson, Dec. 10, 1822, Jefferson Papers, Library of Congress, quoted in Morgan, pp. 181–82. Morgan, pp. 306–07, has an admirable chart of the number and nature of opinions rendered by the Justices from 1805 to 1833, showing majority, concurring, and dissenting opinions.
18. 3 Cranch 300.
19. Lewis, vol. II, pp. 349–50; D. P. Brown, vol. I, pp. 562–63.

[3]

1. Dec. 5, 1801 letter; Jan. 4, 1802 letter, both in Cutler, vol. II, pp. 47, 62.
2. Jefferson to J. H. Nicholson, May 13, 1803, Lipscomb and Bergh, vol. X, pp. 387–90.
3. D. P. Brown, vol. I, pp. 353–54.

4. P. L. Ford, vol. I, p. 121.
5. Plumer, pp. 272–74.
6. *Ibid.,* p. 274.
7. T. Pickering to T. Lyman, Mar. 14, 1804, Pickering Papers, Library of Congress.
8. N. Macon to J. H. Nicholson, Aug. 6, 1803, printed in W. E. Dodd, *Macon,* pp. 187–88.
9. *Annals of Congress,* 8th Cong., 1st Sess., 805–06.
10. See, for example, Plumer's Papers, Letters, Container 7, W. Plumer to J. Mason, Jan. 14, 1804, and Plumer's Notes of Proceedings, U.S. Congress, for this period, both in Library of Congress. Plumer was a partisan, but his notes were written at the time and cannot be dismissed entirely as only the ravings of a disgruntled Federalist. See also Cutler, vol. II, p. 157.
11. *Annals of Congress,* 8th Cong., 1st Sess., 875–76.
12. *Ibid.,* 1237–40; *Ibid.,* 2nd Sess., 728–31.
13. JM to S. Chase, Jan. 23, 1804, JM Papers, Historical Society of Pennsylvania.
14. See Hughes, *The Supreme Court of the U.S.,* and Leonard Baker, *Back to Back.*
15. W. B. Giles to Jefferson, Mar. 16, 1801, in Anderson, pp. 77–78.
16. Cutler, vol. II, pp. 77–78.
17. Plumer, pp. 320–21.
18. Anderson, pp. 95–96; C. F. Adams, *J. Q. Adams,* vol. I, pp. 322–23, 353. Bruce in *John Randolph,* vol. I, pp. 200–01, claimed that Randolph "was not privy" to any plans for removing JM. Bruce, who had read the Adams diaries, ignored the entries which substantiated a contrary opinion.
19. Plumer Papers, Notes of Proceedings, U.S. Congress, Nov. 26, 1804, Library of Congress; Malone, vol. IV, pp. 432–33; U. Tracy letter, Dec. 10, 1804, Pierpont Morgan Library; Schachner, pp. 262–63; see also Dr. Samuel L. Mitchill letter, Nov. 30, 1804,

in *Harper's*, Apr. 1879, p. 748, and Anderson, p. 97.

20. C. F. Adams, *J. Q. Adams*, vol. I, p. 325.

21. The complete record of the Chase trial is found in *Annals of Congress*, 8th Cong., 2nd Sess., 81–676. For the chair incident, see 92; see also C. F. Adams, *J. Q. Adams*, vol. I, pp. 327–28; and Notes of Proceedings, Plumer Papers, Jan. 2, 1805, Library of Congress.

22. *Annals of Congress*, 8th Cong., 2nd Sess., 92–98.

23. C. F. Adams, *J. Q. Adams*, vol. I, p. 328; Notes of Proceedings, U.S. Congress, Jan. 3, 1805, Plumer Papers, Library of Congress.

24. U. Tracy letter, Feb. 4, 1805, Pierpont Morgan Library; *Annals of Congress*, 8th Cong., 2nd Sess., 100; H. Adams, *History*, vol. II, p. 227; S. E. Baldwin, p. 348; M. L. Davis, vol. II, p. 357.

25. Chase's answer is in *Annals of Congress*, 8th Cong., 2nd Sess., 101–50, and the quotes used are from 140, 142. See also C. F. Adams, *J. Q. Adams*, vol. I, pp. 345–49; Cutler, vol. I, p. 182. For Burr's testiness, see Notes of Proceedings, U.S. Congress, Jan. 8, Feb. 8, 1805, Plumer Papers, Library of Congress.

26. Randolph's speech is in *Annals of Congress*, 8th Cong., 2nd Sess., 153–65; S. E. Baldwin, p. 349; Cutler, vol. II, pp. 182–83; Notes of Proceedings, U.S. Congress, Feb. 9, 1805, Plumer Papers, Library of Congress.

27. T. Pickering to R. King, Feb. 15, 1805, King, p. 439; S. E. Baldwin, p. 350.

28. Notes of Proceedings, U.S. Congress, Feb. 16, 1805, Plumer Papers, Library of Congress.

29. *Annals of Congress*, 8th Cong., 2nd Sess., 262–67.

30. Joseph S. Watson letter, Feb. 19, printed in *Virginia Magazine of History and Biography*, Apr. 1921, pp. 170–71.

31. *Annals of Congress*, 8th Cong., 2nd Sess., 355.

32. *Ibid.*, 429. Cutler, vol. II, p. 184; Notes on Proceedings, U.S. Congress, Feb. 23, 1805, Plumer Papers, Library of Congress.

33. Martin's speeches are in *Annals of Congress*, 8th Cong., 2nd Sess., 425–502; the commitment story is in D. P. Brown, vol. I, p. 355.

34. T. Pickering to R. King, Feb. 24, 1805, King, vol. IV, pp. 441–42.

35. Plumer, pp. 322–24.

36. *Annals of Congress*, 8th Cong., 2nd Sess., 664–69.

37. Samuel L. Mitchill letter, Mar. 1, 1805, in *Harper's*, Apr. 1879, p. 749; *Annals of Congress*, 8th Cong., 2nd Sess., 1213–14.

38. Notes on Proceedings, U.S. Congress, Mar. 4, 1805, Plumer Papers, Library of Congress; Plumer, p. 326.

39. J. Q. Adams letter, Mar. 8, 1805, W. C. Ford, *Writings of J. Q. Adams*, vol. III, p. 117; Plumer letter, Feb. 25, 1805, Plumer Papers, Letters, Container 6, Library of Congress.

40. B. Washington letter, Feb. 18, 1800, in L. B. Custer, "Bushrod Washington and John Marshall: A Preliminary Inquiry," *American Journal of Legal History*, Jan. 1960, p. 48.

41. B. Washington to C. P. Wayne, Apr. 11, Sept. 18, 1800, Historical Society of Pennsylvania; see, for example, JM to C. C. Pinckney, Nov. 21, 1802, in *William and Mary Quarterly*, Oct. 1955, pp. 644–46, in which JM gave the beginning date as March of that year, although other letters indicate he would be the author months before then; and JM to Oliver Wolcott, Jr., 1806, Oliver Wolcott, Jr., Mss., vol. XCVIII, no. 69, Connecticut Historical Society.

42. Jefferson to J. Barlow, May 3, 1802, P. L. Ford, vol. IX, p. 372.

43. M. L. Weems to C. P. Wayne, Feb. 14, 1802, in Skeel, vol. II, p. 256.
44. C. P. Wayne to JM, Feb. 17, 1803, JM Correspondence and Papers, vol. I, Library of Congress; JM letter, undated, JM Papers, Historical Society of Pennsylvania.
45. JM to C. P. Wayne, Jan. 10, 1804, and B. Washington to C. P. Wayne, Jan. 24, 1804, in Flanders, pp. 204–05.
46. Marshall, *Washington*, vol. I, pp. xv–xvi.
47. JM to C. P. Wayne, Aug. 10, 1804, JM Papers, vol. I, Library of Congress; JM to C. P. Wayne, June 28, 1806, JM Papers, Historical Society of Pennsylvania.
48. W. R. Smith, pp. 40–169.
49. Marshall, *Washington*, vol. V, p. 765(*n*).
50. *Ibid.*, pp. 775, 776, 777.
51. JM to C. P. Wayne, Sept. 8, 1804, JM Papers, vol. II, Library of Congress; C. F. Adams, *J. Q. Adams*, vol. I, p. 349; JM to Oliver Wolcott, Jr., June 28, 1806, Wolcott Mss., vol. XLVIII, no. 71, Connecticut Historical Society.
52. Cappon, vol. II, Jefferson to J. Adams, June 15, 1813, pp. 332–33, and J. Adams to Jefferson, July 3, 1813, p. 349.
53. M. L. Weems to C. P. Wayne, Jan. 28, Feb. 15, 1804, Skeel, vol. II, pp. 291, 293.
54. B. Washington to Mrs. Elizabeth Hamilton, Dec. 14, 1819, Papers of Alexander Hamilton, Hamilton-McLane Series, Box 3, Library of Congress; and H. B. Adams, vol. II, p. 44.
55. Virginia Acts, Dec. 1803, pp. 28–29, Virginia State Library.
56. Ambler, *Ritchie*, p. 17.
57. JM letter, Mar. 2, 1803, Oliver Wolcott, Jr., Mss., vol. XVI, no. 75, Connecticut Historical Society; Jefferson to JM, Mar. 1, 1805, Jefferson Papers, vol. CXLVII, p. 25688, Library of Congress.
58. The JM/B. Washington story is told in Binney, *Washington*, p. 26.
59. J. Haywood to J. Steele, undated, in Wagstaff, vol. I, p. 454.
60. Richmond City Personal Property and Land Book, 1801 and 1805, Virginia State Library.
61. J. Story to S. Fay, Feb. 16, Feb. 25, 1808, W. W. Story, vol. I, pp. 162–64, 167.

[4]

1. Davis, vol. II, p. 379.
2. Biddle, pp. 313–14.
3. T. Truxton to J. Alston, Feb. 24, 1807, published in *Richmond Enquirer*, Apr. 14, 1807, pp. 2–3.
4. Diary entry, Jan. 21, 1807, Plumer Papers, Library of Congress.
5. Crown Copyright, London, Keeper of Public Records, FO 5/42.
6. *Ibid.*, FO 5/45.
7. E. Quincy, pp. 92–93. An interesting account of the British involvement in the Burr episode is R. A. Mohl, "Britain and the Aaron Burr Conspiracy," *History Today* (London), June 1971.
8. Channing, vol. IV, pp. 343–44.
9. P. L. Ford, vol. IX, pp. 14–17.
10. C. Meade to J. Madison, Dec. 15, 1806, RG 59, Territorial Papers, Mississippi, 1797–1817, National Archives.
11. Kapp, p. 335.
12. See, for example, Diary entry, Dec. 27, 1806, Plumer Papers, Library of Congress; and Jefferson to H. Clay, Jan. 11, 1807, P. L. Ford, vol. IX, p. 7.
13. Jefferson to Lafayette, May 26, 1807, P. L. Ford, vol. IX, p. 66.
14. Kapp, p. 338.
15. 4 Cranch 93.
16. *Ibid.*, 125–36.
17. E. S. Brown, p. 641.
18. A. Burr to H. Clay, Dec. 1, 1806, H. Clay to T. Prentiss, Feb. 15, 1807, both in Colton, vol. IV, pp. 13–15.

19. A. Burr to C. Meade, Jan. 12, 1807, *Virginia Argus*, Mar. 13, 1807, p. 3.
20. Stanard, p. 99.
21. A. Burr letter, Mar. 27, 1807, in Davis, vol. II, p. 405.
22. The account of the Mar. 30 proceeding is from Robertson, vol. I, pp. 1–3, and the *Richmond Enquirer*, Mar. 31, 1807, p. 3. Wirt quote is from W. Wirt to wife, Mar. 26, 1807, Kennedy, vol. I, pp. 151–52.
23. Robertson, vol. I, pp. 3–10; *Richmond Enquirer*, Apr. 3, 1807, p. 2.
24. Robertson, vol. I, pp. 11–20.
25. Jefferson to W. B. Giles, Apr. 20, 1807, P. L. Ford, vol. X, pp. 385–88.
26. Jefferson to J. Bowdoin, Apr. 2, 1807, P. L. Ford, vol. X, p. 383.
27. See F. N. Mason, p. 179; Thayer, *Marshall*, pp. 80–81. Thayer said he had learned from a JM descendant that JM knew Burr would be present, but Beveridge—overly protective of his subject—disputed that (vol. III, p. 396[n]). Irving Brandt, in *Madison*, vol. IV, p. 511, in turn, disputed Beveridge, saying that "Thayer knew both Marshall and his children personally." Brandt is right to dispute Beveridge, but not for that reason. Thayer, born in 1831, of course did not know JM personally.
28. Tucker, vol. II, pp. 231, 231(n).
29. W. Boylan to J. Steele, Apr. 28, 1807, in Wagstaff, vol. II, p. 510.
30. *Enquirer*, Apr. 28, Apr. 10, 1807.
31. A. Burr to T. Alston, Apr. 26, May 15, 1807, Davis, vol. II, pp. 405, 406.
32. W. Scott, p. 13.
33. Van Santvoord, p. 373; Lewis, vol. II, pp. 27–28; W. Scott, p. 14; Christian, pp. 42, 49.
34. Robertson, vol. I, pp. 31–37.
35. *Ibid.*, pp. 37–46.
36. *Ibid.*, pp. 62, 70–71, 74, 78.
37. *Ibid.*, p. 81; Liva Baker, p. 256.
38. Robertson, vol. I, pp. 82, 96, 105–06.
39. Irving, vol. I, pp. 191–92.
40. A. Burr to T. Alston, June 3, 1807, Davis, vol. II, p. 406.
41. Robertson, vol. I, pp. 113–15.
42. See, for example, I. Brandt in Jones, p. 51.
43. Robertson, vol. I, pp. 116–18.
44. *Ibid.*, pp. 119–47.
45. *Ibid.*, pp. 151–56.
46. *Ibid.*, pp. 177–89.
47. Jefferson to A. Adams, Sept. 11, 1804, in Tucker, vol. II, p. 167.
48. Jefferson to G. Hay, June 12, 1807, in Robertson, vol. I, pp. 210–11.
49. H. Adams, *History*, vol. III, p. 455.
50. Robertson, vol. I, p. 249.
51. *Ibid.*, p. 255.
52. Jefferson to G. Hay, June 20, 1807, in P. L. Ford, vol. IX, pp. 59–60.
53. Jefferson to G. Hay, Aug. 7, 1807, in P. L. Ford, vol. IX, p. 62.
54. A. Burr to T. Alston, June 18, 1808, in Davis, vol. II, pp. 406–07.
55. *Annals of Congress*, 10th Cong., 1st Sess., 1807–08.
56. W. Irving to J. K. Paulding, June 22, 1807, in Irving, vol. I, pp. 194–95.
57. Robertson, vol. I, pp. 242–45; Wilkinson, vol. II, p. 271. For an interesting and pertinent comment on JM's decision on this issue, see Justice Potter Stewart's comments in Hoffa v. U.S., 385 *U.S. Reports* 293 (303–04) (1966).
58. Robertson, vol. I, pp. 349–50.
59. Davis, vol. II, p. 408.
60. Bassett, *Life of Jackson*, p. 52; Bassett, *Correspondence of Jackson*, vol. I, p. 181.
61. Parton, vol. II, p. 127; Irving, vol. I, pp. 201–03; Davis, vol. II, p. 410.
62. Jefferson letter, July 14, 1807, P. L. Ford, vol. IX, pp. 11–12.
63. Davis, vol. II, p. 409.
64. Irving, vol. I, pp. 201–03.
65. Robertson, vol. I, pp. 369–70.

66. *Ibid.*, pp. 415–17.
67. *Ibid.*, pp. 430–32, 440.
68. Safford, pp. 315–16, 328–29, 339, 332–33, 339; Robertson, vol. I, p. 378.
69. Robertson, vol. I, pp. 470, 473–84.
70. Safford, p. 343.
71. Robertson, vol. I, pp. 486–89.
72. *Ibid.*, pp. 497–500.
73. *Ibid.*, pp. 506–10; Wandell and Minnigerode, vol. II, pp. 148–49, 208–09.
74. Safford, pp. 342, 343.
75. Robertson, vol. I, pp. 532–86.
76. JM to W. Cushing, June 29, 1807, R. T. Paine Papers, Massachusetts Historical Society.
77. Robertson, vol. II, p. 39.
78. *Ibid.*, pp. 123–24.
79. *Ibid.*, pp. 176–77.
80. *Ibid.*, pp. 260–378.
81. N. Macon to A. Gallatin, June 30, 1807, New-York Historical Society.
82. Safford, p. 374.
83. Robertson, vol. II, pp. 401–45.
84. *Ibid.*, p. 446.
85. *Ibid.*, pp. 446–47; Safford, p. 299.
86. Robertson, vol. II, p. 534.
87. Jefferson to J. Brown, Oct. 27, 1808, Lipscomb and Bergh, vol. XII, p. 183; Jefferson's message, Oct. 27, 1807, P. L. Ford, vol. IX, pp. 163–64; see also W. W. Story, vol. I, p. 159.
88. JM to R. Peters, Nov. 23, 1807, JM Papers, Historical Society of Pennsylvania.

[5]

1. 2 Cranch 336.
2. *Ibid.* 342.
3. *Ibid.* 170.
4. *Ibid.* 178–80.
5. U.S. Congress, *Documentary History of the Capitol*, pp. 122, 163.
6. J. Story letter, Mar. 8, 1812, in Warren, vol. I, p. 473; J. Story to wife, Mar. 12, 1812, W. W. Story, vol. I, p. 219.
7. Fuess, vol. I, p. 151.
8. F. N. Mason, p. 209.
9. Marshall, *Washington*, vol. V, pp. 12–17.
10. Dunaway, pp. 50–59; Howe, p. 268; "Report of the Commissioners Appointed to View Certain Rivers Within the Commonwealth of Virginia," typescript copy at William and Mary College; Ambler, *Sectionalism*, pp. 97–98.
11. Dunaway, pp. 75–76, 100–01, 104; Christian, pp. 11, 117, 120 *passim;* the Appendix to the *Eleventh Annual Report, James River and Kanawha Canal Co.*, pp. 109–10.
12. P. L. Ford, vol. XI, pp. 139–40.
13. See, for example, JM to R. G. Harper, Apr. 20, 1815, Maryland Historical Society—MS 1349.
14. *Brockenbrough*, vol. I, pp. 206–11.
15. JM to T. Pickering, Dec. 19, 1808, JM Correspondence and Papers, vol. II, Library of Congress.
16. JM to C. C. Pinckney, Sept. 21, Oct. 19, 1808, Pinckney Family Papers, Library of Congress; JM to J. M. Marshall, Nov. 21, 1808, Ambler Family Papers, Mss 1 Am 167a, Virginia Historical Society.
17. The case is Gilchrist v. Collector of Charleston, 10 Federal Cases 355, No. 5420 (Circuit Court for the District of South Carolina 1808); see Peterson, pp. 905–06.
18. Dunne, pp. 68–69.
19. JM to J. Quincy, Apr. 23, 1810, in E. Quincy, p. 204.
20. E. Gerry to J. Madison, July 5, 1812, Gerry Papers, Correspondence 1773–1817, New York Public Library.
21. JM to J. Randolph, June 18, 1812, Houghton Library, Harvard University.
22. JM to J. Monroe, June 25, 1812, Monroe Papers, Series 1, Reel 5, Library of Congress.
23. T. Pickering to E. Pennington, July 12, 1812, in H. Adams, *Federalism*, p. 389.

24. JM to R. Smith, July 27, 1812, Historical Society of Pennsylvania.
25. Philadelphian's letter, Aug. 10, 1812; J. S. Newbern to W. Gaston, Aug. 28, 1812; Gaston letter, undated; all in Gaston Papers, Reel 1, University of North Carolina. See also R. D. Connor, "William Gaston," in *Proceedings*, American Antiquarian Society, 1933, p. 425, although Connor has some of the letters dated incorrectly.
26. B. Stoddert to J. Steele, Sept. 3, 1812, in Wagstaff, vol. II, pp. 682–85.
27. Morison, *Otis* (1913 ed.), vol. I, p. 310.
28. Christian, pp. 86–87; *Virginia Magazine of History and Biography*, Jan. 1900, pp. 225–41.

Part Two: The Struggle for the Supremacy of the Union

[6]

1. Wheaton's notebook for 1817, Pierpont Morgan Library; see also Warren, vol. I, pp. 458–62.
2. A. Moore to J. Madison, Jan. 26, 1804, RG 59, Entry 339, National Archives; J. Story to S. P. P. Fay, Feb. 25, 1808, in W. W. Story, vol. I, p. 168.
3. J. Story to S. P. P. Fay, Feb. 25, 1808, in W. W. Story, vol. I, p. 167; G. T. Dunne, "Brockholst Livingston," in Friedman and Israel, vol. I, p. 394.
4. J. Story to S. P. P. Fay, Feb. 25, 1808, in W. W. Story, vol. I, p. 168.
5. W. W. Story, *Story*, vol. I, pp. 200–01; P. L. Ford, vol. IX, p. 277; Dunne, pp. 69–70.
6. Gilmer, p. 24.
7. J. Story letter, Feb. 24, 1812, printed in Warren, vol. I, pp. 423–24.
8. 3 Wheaton 610.
9. *Ibid.*, 628, 636–37.
10. 3 Cranch 448–53.
11. 7 Cranch 390–95.
12. 8 Cranch 74.
13. 5 Wheaton 95, 96, 104, 105.
14. 2 Wheaton 288–89.
15. M. N. Marshall, p. 154.
16. 3 Cranch 210–19.
17. 8 Cranch 288–317.
18. Prentiss v. Barton's, *Brockenbrough*, vol. I, pp. 390–91.
19. *Brockenbrough*, vol. I, p. 328; the Johnson opinion is in Houston v. Moore, 5 Wheaton 1.
20. JM to J. Monroe, Jan. 18, 1813, in RG 59, M-179, Roll 27, National Archives; 5 Wheaton 434.
21. 5 Wheaton 426.
22. JM to Dudley Chase, Feb. 7, 1817, RG 46-U.S. Senate, Senate 14A-K3, National Archives.
23. Letter signed by JM and Associate Justices, Feb. 4, 1824, RG 59, M-179, Roll 49, National Archives; JM to T. S. Grimke, Aug. 7, 1827, Grimke Papers; JM to H. Wheaton, Mar. 20, 1826, New York State Library.
24. 2 Cranch 33 (52); 7 Cranch 60–61.
25. 2 Wheaton 9–10.
26. 3 Cranch 159.
27. *Ibid.* 173.
28. 5 Cranch 303–04.
29. *Brockenbrough*, vol. I, pp. 542, 549–50.
30. J. Story to W. Scott, Jan. 14, 1819, in W. W. Story, vol. I, p. 319.
31. H. A. Johnson, "John Marshall," in Friedman and Israel, vol. I, p. 298; see also pp. 289–90 for a debunking by Johnson of Beveridge's description of JM as an inadequate lawyer.
32. *Brockenbrough*, vol. II, pp. 325, 327–49.
33. 2 Cranch 73, 74; see also Rose v. Himely, 4 Cranch 268, and Wetzell v. Bussard, 11 Wheaton 310, for other cases before the Supreme

Court where JM made ample use of precedents.

34. Cohens v. Virginia, 6 Wheaton 264 (399).

35. JM to H. Wheaton, Mar. 24, 1821, JM Papers, Pierpont Morgan Library.

36. 7 Cranch 116.

37. 7 Cranch 135, 136, 137, 146–47.

38. 8 Cranch 110.

39. *Ibid.* 121–27.

40. Thirty Hogsheads of Sugar v. Boyle, 9 Cranch 191 (198).

41. M. B. Smith, pp. 95–96.

42. Kennedy, vol. II, p. 18.

43. J. Story to H. Wheaton, Aug. 12, 1818, and Dec. 9, 1818, in W. W. Story, vol. I, pp. 302, 313; Hunt, *Madison*, vol. VIII, p. 381. Marshall received his salary in quarterly payments; see JM to G. Simpson, Mar. 18, 1803, Historical Society of Pennsylvania; and JM to J. Campbell, Treasury Warrant 1174, RG 56, Office of the Secretary of the Treasury, Letters Sent, Series F, Judiciary, pp. 43–48, National Archives.

44. M. B. Smith, pp. 94–95, 146–47.

45. C. F. Adams, *J. Q. Adams*, vol. V, pp. 322–23; JM to President, Carson Law Collection, Box 14, Free Library of Philadelphia; *New York Commercial Advertiser*, Feb. 7, 1818, in Warren, vol. I, p. 471.

46. W. W. Story, vol. I, pp. 310–11.

47. Mary Marshall to Polly Marshall, Feb. 1, 1811, JM Papers, Swem Library, William and Mary College; Paxton, p. 100.

48. Mss. in possession of Mrs. James Green, Fauquier County, Va.

49. Paxton, pp. 90–92; M. N. Marshall, pp. 20–21.

50. Paxton, p. 99.

51. Letter to author from Harley P. Holden, Curator, Harvard University Archives, Aug. 25, 1972; JM letter, Apr. 9, 1815, American Philosophical Society; Paxton, p. 101.

52. Paxton, p. 101; JM letter, May 2, 1815, Historical Society of Pennsylvania; JM letter, Aug. 16, 1816, Duke; JM letter, Nov. 5, 1817, Historical Society of Pennsylvania; JM to J. K. Marshall, Oct. 8, 1832, Mss 1M3566a, Virginia Historical Society.

53. JM to E. C. Marshall, June 24, 1821, Peyton Papers, Mss 1 P468a376, Virginia Historical Society; J. Story to JM, June 22, 1823, *William and Mary Quarterly*, Jan. 1941, p. 16; JM to J. Story, July 2, 1823, Sept. 26, 1823, JM Correspondence and Papers, vol. II, Library of Congress; E. C. Marshall to Polly Marshall, Nov. 8, 1825, Swem Library, William and Mary College; Paxton, p. 103.

54. JM to Secretary of Navy, Feb. 23, 1820, A. L. Butler Autographs, vol. III, no. 4, Connecticut Historical Society; JM to L. Marshall, Dec. 23, 1816, and JM letter, July 1, 1820, and JM to L. Marshall, July 1, 1820, Louis Marshall Papers, Southern Historical Collection, University of North Carolina.

55. F. N. Mason, p. 233; JM to L. Marshall, Dec. 23, 1816, Louis Marshall Papers, Southern Historical Collection, University of North Carolina; JM to L. Marshall, Dec. 7, 1817, copy in JM Papers, William and Mary College; E. Colston letter, Mar. 27, 1818, private collection.

56. *William and Mary Quarterly*, Jan. 1918, p. 169; Accession no. 2 (34), Virginia State Library; Simms, p. 154.

57. Copy of policy in JM Papers, William and Mary College; Fauquier County, Deeds, Index, Virginia Historical Society; JM to M. Marshall, Sept. 10, 1816, Breckinridge-Marshall Papers, Filson Club.

58. From eulogy by J. Hopkinson before American Philosophical Society, Mar. 3, 1837, printed in *Brockenbrough*, vol. I, pp. xv–xvi.

[7]

1. C. H. Haskins, "The Yazoo Land Companies," *Papers of the American Historical Association*, vol. V, pt. 4, Oct. 1891, pp. 84–85, 396–98.
2. C. F. Adams, *J. Q. Adams*, vol. I, pp. 543–47.
3. Fletcher v. Peck, 6 Cranch 128.
4. Malone, vol. IV, p. 456.
5. 7 Cranch 167.
6. W. E. Dodd, "Chief Justice Marshall and Va.," *American Historical Review*, vol. XII, p. 777.
7. JM to C. Lee, May 7, 1810, copy in JM Papers, William and Mary College.
8. 7 Cranch 603.
9. Corwin, *Marshall and the Constitution*, p. 174.
10. W. E. Dodd, "Chief Justice Marshall and Va.," *American Historical Review*, vol. XII, p. 779; Corwin, *Marshall and the Constitution*, p. 175.
11. *Richmond Enquirer*, Jan. 27, 1816, in Simms, pp. 173–77.
12. 1 Wheaton 305–21.
13. W. W. Story, vol. I, pp. 276–77.
14. 1 Wheaton 323–81.
15. 3 Wheaton 386–91.
16. 4 Wheaton 192–203.
17. Marshall, *Washington*, vol. V, p. 178.
18. W. W. Story to H. Wheaton, Dec. 9, 1818, in Story, vol. I, p. 313.
19. William H. Gaines, "Bench, Bar, and Barbecue," *Virginia Cavalcade*, Autumn 1955, p. 10.
20. J. Story, pp. 52–55.

[8]

1. Marshall, *Washington*, vol. V, pp. 296, 297, 299.
2. 5 Cranch 61, 62, 86–87.
3. See correspondence between B. W. Leigh and N. Biddle, in McGrane, pp. 283–88.
4. *John P. Branch Papers*, June 1905, pp. 134, 136.
5. 4 Wheaton 323.
6. U.S. v. Fisher, 2 Cranch 384.

7. Anderson v. Dunn, 6 Wheaton 204.
8. J. Story to wife, Mar. 7, 1819, in W. W. Story, vol. I, p. 325.
9. JM to B. Washington, Mar. 27, 1819, in *Tyler's*, 1922–1923, pp. 69–70.
10. *Autobiography of Van Buren*, pp. 183–84.
11. Morgan, pp. 123–25.
12. JM to J. Story, Mar. 24, 1819, JM Correspondence and Papers, vol. II, Library of Congress.
13. JM to J. Story, May 27, 1819, JM Correspondence and Papers, vol. II, Library of Congress.
14. JM letter, Aug. 3, 1819, JM Papers, Library of Congress.
15. Morgan, pp. 306–07.
16. JM to B. Washington, Apr. 28, 1819, JM Papers, Swem Library, William and Mary College, established that JM wrote the letters in the Philadelphia newspapers.
17. JM to B. Washington, May 31, 1819, University of Kansas.
18. JM to B. Washington, June 17, 1819, New-York Historical Society; JM to B. Washington, undated, JM Papers, Library of Congress. "A Friend of the Constitution" was first identified as John Marshall by Gerald Gunther in a remarkable piece of historical detective work.
19. Elliot, vol. III, p. 554.
20. Jefferson to S. Roane, Sept. 6, 1819, in P. L. Ford, vol. X, pp. 140–41.
21. Taylor, *Construction Construed*, pp. 45, 46, 122, 135, 196, 206–07.
22. 2 Peters 465–67.

[9]

1. 6 Wheaton 264.
2. *Ibid.* 376–77.
3. 5 Cranch 115, 136.
4. 6 Wheaton 379–83.
5. *Ibid.* 387–90.
6. See Corwin, *Judicial Review*, p. 6.
7. 6 Wheaton 399–402.

8. *Ibid.* 404.
9. *Ibid.* 413–14.
10. *Ibid.* 447.
11. JM to J. M. Marshall, July 9, 1822, JM Folder, Misc. Coll., Box 31, Library of Congress.
12. J. Madison to Jefferson, June 27, 1823, in Hunt, *Madison*, vol. IX, pp. 14–15.
13. Ambler, *Ritchie*, pp. 80–81.
14. *Autobiography of Van Buren*, pp. 126–27.
15. JM to J. Story, June 15, 1821,

JM Correspondence and Papers, vol. II, Library of Congress.
16. J. Story to JM, June 27, 1821, Accession Item 21730, Virginia State Library.
17. JM to Story, July 13, Sept. 18, 1821, JM Correspondence and Papers, vol. II, Library of Congress.
18. Carr-Cary Papers (1231), McGregor Library, University of Virginia.

Part Three: The Sanctity of Contracts

[10]

1. W. B. Slaughter, pp. 113–14.
2. R. D. Ward, pp. 26–27.
3. *National Intelligencer*, Sept. 14, 1824; *Fauquier County*, pp. 133–35; R. D. Ward, pp. 114–17.
4. Revolutionary War Pension Files, Churchill Gibbs–S-46002, National Archives; *William and Mary Quarterly*, Oct. 1921, pp. 290–91; R. D. Ward, pp. 67–68, 18–19, 59–61.
5. Christian, p. 103; R. D. Ward, p. 53.
6. R. D. Ward, pp. 93–94.
7. William H. Gaines, "Bench, Bar, and Barbecue," *Virginia Cavalcade*, Autumn 1955, p. 12.
8. Finch, p. 266.
9. William H. Gaines, "Bench, Bar, and Barbecue," *Virginia Cavalcade*, Autumn 1955, pp. 12–13.
10. JM to Polly Marshall, Feb. 24, 1817, Mar. 12, 1826, *William and Mary Quarterly*, Apr. 1923, pp. 84–87; JM to Polly Marshall, Feb. 1, 1829, in F. N. Mason, p. 304.
11. Finch, p. 197.
12. From William Faux's journal of his trip to North America, published in London in 1823, and reprinted in Thwaites, vol. XII, p. 87.
13. Royall, pp. 180–81, 200, 111.
14. 5 Wheaton 317.

15. *Ibid.* 324–25.
16. JM to Polly Marshall, Jan. 31, 1830, McGregor Collection, University of Virginia; T. Pickering to JM, Jan. 2, 1827 (1828), JM Correspondence and Papers, vol. III, Library of Congress; unsigned notes in Harvie Papers, Mss 1 H2636a24, Virginia Historical Society.
17. J. Story, p. 10; F. N. Mason, p. 294; JM to Polly, Feb. 7, 1831, in F. N. Mason, pp. 328–29.
18. *Bulletins*, Fauquier, Aug. 1921, pp. 99–102; F. N. Mason, pp. 246–47.
19. JM to R. Rush, Mar. 16, 1821, Rush Family Papers, Princeton University.
20. JM to Polly Marshall, Feb. 16, 1818, in F. N. Mason, pp. 242–43; JM to B. Washington, July 6, 1822, JM Collection, New-York Historical Society; Sallie E. Marshall Hardy, "John Marshall as Son, Brother, Husband and Friend," *The Green Bag*, Dec. 1896, pp. 484–85; M. N. Marshall, p. 150; D. P. Brown, pp. 367–68; JM to Rawlings, July 28, 1829, in F. N. Mason, pp. 308–09.
21. JM to Polly Marshall, Feb. 23, 1824, *William and Mary Quarterly*, Apr. 1923, pp. 86–88.
22. JM to Polly Marshall, Feb. 8, 1825, in F. N. Mason, pp.

278–79; JM to Polly Marshall, Jan. 31, 1830, McGregor Library, University of Virginia.

23. JM to H. Clay, Jan. 20, 1827, RG 59, M-531, Roll 5, National Archives.

24. JM to L. Marshall, Apr. 5, 1830, Louis Marshall Papers, Southern Historical Collection, University of North Carolina.

25. JM to H. Clay, Mar. 13, 1833, Colton, vol. V, pp. 352–53.

26. JM to J. E. Heath, Feb. 24, 1833; Auditor's Office, Mar. 16, 1833, in *Tyler's*, 1923–1924, pp. 28–29.

27. JM to Polly Marshall, Apr. 11, 1823, in F. N. Mason, p. 245; JM to Mary Harvie, Apr. 22, 1832, JM Papers, Swem Library, William and Mary College.

28. JM to J. K. Marshall, Dec. 14, 1828, in Oster, p. 62.

29. JM to E. C. Marshall, Aug. 29, 1828, Alderman Library, Reel M689, University of Virginia.

30. JM to J. K. Marshall, July 3, 1827, Swem Library, William and Mary College; JM to E. C. Marshall, July 10, 1832, and July 26, 1833, Alderman Library, Reel M689, University of Virginia.

31. JM to B. Washington, Dec. 27, 1821, JM Papers, Library of Congress. See subsequent correspondence between the two men through 1826. See also JM to H. Lee, July 6, 1824, Tucker Family Papers, Southern Historical Collection, University of North Carolina.

32. H. B. Adams, vol. I, pp. 421–22. See also pp. 405, 411; JM to B. Washington, Dec. 27, 1826, JM Papers, Library of Congress.

33. JM to Cary and Lea, June 13, 1833, Miscellaneous Collection, New York Public Library.

34. JM to Lafayette, May 2, 1827, Cornell University. See JM letters to Charles Minor, Feb. 15, June 9, June 25, 1831, Wyoming Historical Society.

35. Faulkner, p. 146.

36. JM to C. Hammond, Dec. 28, 1823, State Museum, Ohio Historical Society; JM to J. M. Marshall, Feb. 14, 1825, Miscellaneous Collection, Box 31, JM folder, Library of Congress.

37. JM to Polly Marshall, Mar. 9, 1825, in F. N. Mason, pp. 282–83.

38. JM to Lafayette, May 2, 1827, Cornell University; JM to J. Story, Dec. 30, 1827, in Marshall, *Autobiographical*, p. 37.

39. JM to J. Story, in F. N. Mason, p. 297.

40. J. Story, Feb. 25, 1829, in W. W. Story, vol. I, p. 562.

[11]

1. Jefferson to W. Plumer, July 21, 1816, Plumer, pp. 440–41.

2. D. Webster to J. Mason, Sept. 4, 1817, Webster, vol. XVII, pp. 265–66.

3. Quoted in Fuess, vol. I, p. 207.

4. *Ibid.*, p. 158; Webster letter, Mar. 28, 1814, Dartmouth College.

5. Webster to J. Mason, Nov. 27, 1817, Webster, vol. XVII, p. 266.

6. D. Webster to J. Smith, Dec. 8, 1817, Webster, vol. XVII, pp. 267–68.

7. Wilson v. Mason, 1 Cranch 45.

8. 6 Cranch 87.

9. 9 Cranch 43.

10. *Ibid.* 48–52.

11. D. Webster to J. Mason, Feb. 22, 1818, in Webster, vol. XVII, p. 271.

12. *Ibid.*, p. 548.

13. 4 Wheaton 553–54.

14. *Ibid.* 557.

15. *Ibid.* 579.

16. *Ibid.* 590–91.

17. *Ibid.* 599–600.

18. Printed in Fuess, vol. I, p. 232(*n*).

19. C. A. Goodrich to R. Choate, Nov. 25, 1852, Dartmouth College.

20. 4 Wheaton 600.

21. C. A. Goodrich to R. Choate,

Nov. 25, 1852, Dartmouth College; Story account in Fuess, vol. I, p. 232(n); see also Webster, vol. I, p. 42, for a third and similar description.

22. 4 Wheaton 601–08.
23. D. Webster to Brown, and to J. Mason, Mar. 13, 1818, Webster, vol. XVII, pp. 275–76.
24. D. Webster to J. Smith, Mar. 14, 1818, Webster, vol. XVII, pp. 276–77.
25. Fuess, vol. I, pp. 235–36; D. Webster to J. Story, Aug. 16, 1818, and Sept. 9, 1818, Webster, vol. XVII, pp. 286, 287.
26. D. Webster to J. Mason, Feb. 4, 1819, Dartmouth College.
27. 4 Wheaton 625.
28. *Ibid.* 627.
29. *Ibid.* 628.
30. *Ibid.* 636, 638, 643.
31. Elliot, vol. III, p. 554.
32. 4 Wheaton 645.
33. *Ibid.* 650, 651, 652, 653–54.
34. *Ibid.* 666, 713.
35. D. Webster to F. Brown, Feb. 2, 1819, Dartmouth College.
36. H. A. Johnson, "John Marshall," in Friedman and Israel, vol. I, p. 299; 4 Peters 514.
37. 4 Peters 560–63.
38. 1 Cranch 127, 165, 167.

[12]

1. Frankfurter, *Commerce*, p. 25.
2. Marshall, *Washington*, vol. V, p. 712.
3. S. Adams to E. Gerry, Aug. 22, 1789, Gerry Papers, Correspondence 1773–1817, New York Public Library.
4. Printed in Warren, vol. I, pp. 466–68.
5. Webster's argument is printed in Webster, vol. XI, pp. 3–23, and in 9 Wheaton 3–32, in slightly different versions.
6. 9 Wheaton 156.
7. *Ibid.* 79.
8. J. Mason, p. 112(n).
9. 9 Wheaton 184–86.
10. *Ibid.* 222.
11. George Dangerfield, "The

Steamboat's Charter of Freedom," *American Heritage*, Oct. 1963, p. 80.
12. Frankfurter, *Commerce*, p. 19.
13. D. G. Morgan, "William Johnson," in Friedman and Israel, vol. I, pp. 367–68.
14. 9 Wheaton 186–222.
15. Quoted in Bruce, vol. I, pp. 487–88.
16. D. Webster to J. Story, May 4, 1824, Webster, vol. XVII, p. 350.
17. J. Story to wife, Jan. 28, 1831; J. Story letter, Feb. 13, 1831, W. W. Story, vol. II, pp. 43–44, 49–50.
18. 12 Wheaton 419.
19. 9 Wheaton 738.
20. Chisholm v. Ga., 2 Dallas 419.
21. Farmers' & Mechanics' Bank of Pa. v. Smith, 6 Wheaton 134.
22. 12 Wheaton 213.
23. 8 Wheaton 239.
24. Craig v. Mo., 4 Peters 410, 419–20, 438.
25. U.S. Congress, *Documentary History of the Capitol*, pp. 258–59; RG-267, SC-Office of the Clerk, Subject File, Box 1, Folder 6, National Archives; JM to R. Peters, May 4, 1833, Library of the Supreme Court of the U.S., copy in JM Papers, William and Mary College.
26. O. H. Smith, pp. 137–39.
27. See, for example, JM to B. Washington, Apr. 15, June 17, 1822; Aug. 19, 1827, May 6, 1829, JM Papers, Library of Congress; and JM to B. Washington, May 28, 1822, JM Papers, New-York Historical Society; and JM to B. Washington, May 31, 1824, Chicago Historical Society. JM to G. Washington, Nov. 29, 1829, JM Papers, in the William Alexander Smith Collection, property of the Metropolitan Museum of Art, on deposit in New York Public Library.
28. JM to J. Story, Sept. 18, 1821, *William and Mary Quarterly*,

Jan. 1941, p. 12; May 30, 1826, JM Correspondence and Papers, vol. II, Library of Congress.

29. J. Quincy, pp. 189–90.
30. JM to J. Story, June 22, 1823, *William and Mary Quarterly*, Jan. 1941, p. 17; JM to B. Washington, Aug. 6, 1823, Morristown National Historical Park, copy in JM Papers, William and Mary College.
31. J. Story to JM, May 29, 1831, *William and Mary Quarterly*, Jan. 1941, p. 23; JM to J. Story, Nov. 16, 1833, JM Correspondence and Papers, vol. III, Library of Congress; JM letter, Dec. 26, 1833, Henry E. Huntington Library.

[13]

1. JM to J. Randolph, Jan. 13, 1827, Accession Item 22479a, Virginia State Library; JM to J. Randolph, Dec. 24, 1828, Cornell.
2. Grigsby, *1829–30*, pp. 16–17.
3. JM to Polly Marshall, Mar. 5, 1829, in F. N. Mason, p. 307.
4. Bradshaw, pp. 325–26.
5. JM to J. Story, June 11, 1829, JM Papers, vol. III, Library of Congress; JM to J. Rutherfoord, Mar. 25, 1829, Houghton Library, Harvard University; Mar. 28, 1829, Duke University Library.
6. Howe, p. 226.
7. Grigsby, *1829–30*, pp. 34–36.
8. Notes by Charles Campbell, *Southern Literary Messenger*, vol. III, pp. 237–38, printed in Christian, p. 113.
9. *Virginia Magazine of History and Biography*, July 1953, pp. 322–23.
10. H. Grigsby to H. Binney, Feb. 22, 1869, JM Misc. Papers, New York Public Library; *Southern Literary Messenger*, Feb. 1836, p. 188.
11. *William and Mary Quarterly*, Apr. 1930, p. 110.
12. Julius F. Prufer, "The Franchise in Virginia," *William and Mary Quarterly*, Oct. 1927, pp. 255–57; JM letter, undated, JM Papers, vol. III, Library of Congress.
13. See Faulkner, p. 123; Julius F. Prufer, "The Franchise in Virginia," *William and Mary Quarterly*, Oct. 1927, pp. 28–29. For a critique of JM's position, see Andrew C. McLaughlin's review of the Beveridge biography in the *American Bar Association Journal*, May 1921, p. 232.
14. JM to J. Story, Jan. 8, 1830, JM Papers, vol. III, Library of Congress.
15. Grigsby, *1829–30*, p. 35.
16. *Proceedings, 1829*, p. 919.
17. W. B. Slaughter, pp. 120–22; *Southern Literary Messenger*, Feb. 1836, p. 188.
18. *Proceedings, 1829*, pp. 618–19.
19. JM to T. W. Griffith, Feb. 7, 1820, Maryland Historical Society; J. Madison to Lafayette, Feb. 1, 1830, Madison, vol. IV, pp. 59–60.

[14]

1. Sale Record, July 3, 1787, Welling Collection, Connecticut Historical Society.
2. Author's interview with Paul Wells, Aug. 9, 1969.
3. J. K. Kasson letter, Dec. 27, 1842, in *Virginia Magazine of History and Biography*, Oct. 1948, p. 420.
4. Aptheker, p. 23; M. B. Smith, p. 90; *Calendar*, vol. X, pp. 338–39, 368.
5. Thwaites, vol. XII, p. 311; W. W. Story, vol. I, pp. 366–67.
6. Morgan, pp. 192–96; JM to J. Story, Sept. 26, 1823, Massachusetts Historical Society.
7. D. Webster to J. Mason, Mar. 27, 1826, in J. Mason, p. 296.
8. Quotes are from JM to E. Everett, Nov. 3, 1830, Everett Papers, Massachusetts Historical Society; JM to J. Story, Sept. 22, 1832, JM Papers, vol. III, Library of Congress. See also JM to J. S. Johnston, May 22, 1830, JM Papers, Historical Society of Pennsyl-

vania; JM to J. C. Calhoun, Aug. 27, 1832, Headly Collection, Box I, Chief Justices, Connecticut Historical Society; JM to T. S. Grimké, Oct. 6, 1832, JM folder, Misc. Mss. Collection, Box 31, Library of Congress; JM to H. Marshall, May 7, 1833, printed in *New York Tribune*, Feb. 7, 1861.

9. T. Pickering to JM, Jan. 17, 1826; JM to T. Pickering, Mar. 20, 1826, JM Papers, vol. II, Library of Congress.

10. JM to E. C. Marshall, Feb. 15, 1832, Alderman Library, Reel M689, University of Virginia, property of Mrs. J. J. Marshall.

11. JM to Lafayette, Aug. 26, 1825, May 2, 1827, Cornell University.

12. H. B. Adams, vol. I, pp. 247–48.

13. "Minutes of the Virginia Branch, American Colonization Society, Nov. 4, 1823–Feb. 5, 1869," American Colonization Society Papers, Mss 3AM353al, Virginia Historical Society. Beveridge has the wrong dates for the organization of the Virginia chapter and for JM's election as president. Beveridge, vol. IV, p. 474.

14. JM letter, Feb. 8, 1835, printed in "Emancipation," *African Repository and Colonial Journal*, 1836, p. 165.

15. Ambler, *Floyd*, p. 155. See pp. 156–68 for excerpts from Gov. Floyd's diary concerning the revolt. For the best modern account of the uprising, see Henry I. Tragle, "Slave Revolt," *American History Illustrated*, Nov. 1971, p. 4 *passim*.

16. Ambler, *Floyd*, pp. 89–91.

17. *Virginia Slavery Debate*, p. 6.

18. JM to W. Gaston, Dec. 20, 1832, Gaston Papers, Reel 5, University of North Carolina.

19. 3 Cranch 330–31.

20. 4 Cranch 400–03.

21. 7 Cranch 271–73.

22. 7 Cranch 290–299.

23. 2 Peters 151–56.

24. 10 Wheaton 66.

25. *Ibid.* 115–32.

26. D. M. Roper, "In Quest of Judicial Objectivity: The Marshall Court and the Legitimation of Slavery," *Stanford Law Review*, Feb. 1969, pp. 532–39.

27. Sallie E. Marshall Hardy, "John Marshall as Son, Brother, Husband and Friend," *The Green Bag*, Dec. 1896, p. 488.

[15]

1. JM to J. Story, Oct. 29, 1828, JM Papers, vol. III, Library of Congress.

2. JM to T. Freylinghuysen, May 22, 1830, copy in JM Papers, William and Mary College.

3. 8 Wheaton 543.

4. In Kennedy, vol. II, pp. 259–60.

5. W. Wirt to D. Carr, June 21, 1830, JM to Carr, undated, in Kennedy, vol. II, pp. 253–58.

6. Joseph C. Burke, "The Cherokee Cases: A Study in Law, Politics and Morality," *Stanford Law Review*, Feb. 1969, p. 510.

7. J. Story letter, Jan. 28, 1831, W. W. Story, vol. II, pp. 44–45.

8. Kennedy, vol. II, pp. 291–93.

9. 5 Peters 15–20.

10. JM to R. Peters, May 18, 1831, JM Papers, Historical Society of Pennsylvania.

11. *Niles'*, Sept. 24, 1831, p. 70.

12. *Ibid.*, Dec. 24, 1831, p. 313.

13. J. Story to wife, Jan. 13, 1832, W. W. Story, vol. II, p. 79.

14. J. Story to wife, Feb. 26, 1832, W. W. Story, vol. II, p. 84.

15. Unsigned notes, Harvie Papers, Mss. 1, H2636a24, Virginia Historical Society.

16. 6 Peters 536, 539, 541, 543, 547, 556, 559, 561–62.

17. Joseph C. Burke, "The Cherokee Cases: A Study in Law, Politics, and Morality," *Stanford Law Review*, Feb. 1969, p. 500 *passim* (525).

18. Bassett, *Correspondence of Jackson*, vol. IV, p. 415.
19. J. Story to wife, Mar. 4, 1832, in Dillon, p. 681; J. Story letter, Mar. 8, 1832, W. W. Story, vol. II, p. 83.

[16]

1. E. Everett to wife, Feb. 25, 1831, Massachusetts Historical Society.
2. Ambler, *Floyd*, p. 162.
3. JM to Polly Marshall, Oct. 6, 1831, *William and Mary Quarterly*, Apr. 1923, pp. 89–90.
4. *Niles'*, Oct. 15, 1831, p. 131; JM Papers, Mss 9:1 M3567:1, Virginia Historical Society.
5. JM to J. K. Marshall, Oct. 12, 1831, JM Papers, William and Mary College; JM to Polly Marshall, Oct. 13, 1831, JM Papers, Swem Library, William and Mary College.
6. Randolph, pp. 38–39, 96–99; *American Journal of the Medical Sciences*, 1831, pp. 263, 537–38; *Dictionary of American Medical Biography*, New York, 1928, pp. 965–66.
7. Thayer, *Marshall*, p. 150(*n*).
8. *Niles'*, Oct. 22, 1831, p. 153; J. Story to R. Peters, Oct. 28, 1831; W. W. Story, vol. II, p. 70.
9. JM to Polly Marshall, Nov. 8, 1831, F. N. Mason, pp. 340–41.
10. JM to J. Story, Nov. 10, 1831, JM Correspondence, vol. III, Library of Congress.
11. *Niles'*, Dec. 3, 1831, p. 259; JM to R. Peters, Nov. 24, 1831, JM Papers, Historical Society of Pennsylvania.
12. F. N. Mason, p. 285.
13. JM to J. M. Marshall, Dec. 19, 1831 (misdated 1832), JM Papers, Library of Congress.
14. W. W. Story, vol. II, pp. 86–87.
15. JM Papers, Mss 1 M3566a 21, Virginia Historical Society.
16. JM to E. C. Marshall, July 26, 1833, JM Mss., No. 4873, University of Virginia, property of E. R. Marshall.

17. Meade, *Old Churches*, vol. I, p. 30; JM to J. Adams, May 9, 1833, Clements Library, University of Michigan.
18. Fisher, pp. 9, 18–19, 29, 31–32, 35, 53–54, 106; Christian, p. 82; author's tour of church with Dr. Glenn H. Pratt, Dec. 10, 1969.
19. This is a well-known JM story. This version is from W. B. Slaughter, pp. 115–16. Slightly different versions are found in F. N. Mason, pp. 324–25; Howe, p. 275; Craighill, pp. 268–69.
20. T. Devereux to W. Gaston, Nov. 14, 1833; G. E. Badger to W. Gaston, Nov. 14, 1833, Gaston Papers, University of North Carolina.
21. JM to T. F. Grimké, Oct. 6, 1832, Virginia State Library.
22. JM to J. Hillhouse, May 26, 1830, Hillhouse Family Papers, Sterling Library, Yale University.
23. JM to R. H. Wilde, Aug. 1, 1832, JM Papers, Montague Collection, New York Public Library; *The Calumet*, Nov.–Dec. 1832, p. 290.
24. JM to R. Mayo, Jan. 26, 1823, in R. Mayo, p. 47; JM to C. F. Mercer, Apr. 7, 1827, Boston Public Library; JM letter, Mar. 11, 1835, Oster, pp. 61–62; JM letter, Dec. 7, 1834, Essex Institute, in JM Papers, William and Mary College.
25. JM to J. M. Garnett, Dec. 17, 1830, Garnett Papers, Mss 1C4855a, Folder 22, Virginia Historical Society.
26. JM to H. Lee, Sept. 21, 1833, JM Papers, Misc. Collection, New York Public Library.
27. *Louisiana Law Journal*, May 1841, p. 98.
28. Terhune, pp. 91–92; *The Century*, June 4, 1859, p. 1.
29. This version of the turkey story is taken from M. N. Marshall, p. 150.
30. Poore, vol. I, p. 85; Murray, vol. I, pp. 158–60; "Anecdotes of John Marshall," *World's Work*, Feb. 1901, p. 394; Sallie Ewing Marshall, "Chief

Justice John Marshall," *Magazine of American History*, July 1884, p. 69; Sallie E. Marshall Hardy, "John Marshall as Son, Brother, Husband and Friend," *The Green Bag*, Dec. 1896, pp. 479–82.

31. Murray, p. 159; S. E. Marshall, "Chief Justice John Marshall," *Magazine of American History*, July 1884, p. 69; *World's Work*, Feb. 1901, p. 395.

32. *The Century*, June 4, 1859, p. 1; W. B. Slaughter, pp. 113–14.

33. John Randolph Papers, pp. 193–94, Mss 2 R 1554–a13, Virginia Historical Society; *Niles'*, Oct. 20, 1838, p. 117.

34. F. N. Mason, p. 286; *The Century*, June 4, 1859, p. 1; *World's Work*, Feb. 1901, pp. 394–95; M. N. Marshall, pp. 151–52; *Fauquier County*, p. 150.

35. J. Buchanan, vol. I, p. 442.

36. *Louisiana Law Journal*, May 1841, pp. 85–90.

37. *Niles'*, Sept. 24, 1831, p. 70; W. W. Story, vol. II, p. 119; JM to J. Hopkinson, Sept. 20, 1833, JM Papers, Library of Congress; JM to H. Lee, Sept. 21, 1833, Robert E. Lee Mss., Duke University.

38. Lewis D. Crenshaw to Winifred C. Crenshaw, July 6, 1833, copy in JM Papers, William and Mary College; Harding, pp. 146–47; Sallie E. Marshall Hardy, "John Marshall as Son, Brother, Husband and Friend," *The Green Bag*, Dec. 1896, p. 482.

39. JM to E. Everett, July 22, 1833, in *Freemasonry*, vol. II, pt. 12, pp. 1–4.

40. JM to E. Everett, May 3, 1825, Kansas Historical Society; JM to J. K. Kane, Mar. 26, 1830, American Philosophical Society; Minutes of the Virginia Historical Society, printed in *Virginia Magazine of History and Biography*, Jan., Apr., July 1959, pp. 5, 12–23, 190, 338.

41. JM to W. Cranch, Nov. 25, 1833, RG 42, Records of the Office of Buildings and Grounds, Washington Historical Monument Society Records, National Archives; JM to H. Clay and P. Thomas, Feb. 10, 1832, RG 128, 22nd Cong., Committee Report on the Centennial Birthday of George Washington, National Archives.

42. J. Story letter, Jan. 20, 1833, W. W. Story, vol. II, pp. 116–17.

[17]

1. JM to R. Peters, Dec. 3, 1832, JM Papers, Historical Society of Pennsylvania.

2. D. Webster to W. Dutton, Jan. 4, 1833, Baker Library, Dartmouth College.

3. 7 Peters 243, 249.

4. JM to J. Story, June 3, 1833, JM Correspondence and Papers, vol. III, Library of Congress.

5. JM to H. Lee, Jan. 18, 1834, JM Papers, Library of Congress.

6. Bradstreet v. Huntington, 8 Peters 588, 590; Wheaton v. Peters, 8 Peters, 591, 658.

7. JM to J. Story, Sept. 30, 1829; June 26, Oct. 12, 1831; Dec. 30, 1834, all in JM Correspondence and Papers, vol. III, Library of Congress.

8. *Niles'*, Feb. 16, 1833, p. 403.

9. Sallie E. Marshall Hardy, "John Marshall as Son, Brother, Husband and Friend," *The Green Bag*, Dec. 1896, p. 489; JM to J. K. Marshall, Sept. 13, Oct. 14, 1833, JM Papers, William and Mary College; Thomas Marshall to JM, Oct. 29, 1833, JM Papers, Swem Library, William and Mary College.

10. JM Papers, Mss 2 M3567 a2, Virginia Historical Society.

11. 9 Peters iii, v; Attorney General's Papers, Letters Received, Supreme Court—1816–1840, RG 60, National Archives; Duvall Papers, Box 1, Library of Congress.

12. Dillon, vol. I, pp. lvi–lvii(*n*); Martineau, *Western Travel*, vol. I, p. 150.

13. 9 Peters 711, 723.

14. J. Story letter, Mar. 2, 1835, W. W. Story, vol. II, p. 193; JM to R. Peters, Apr. 30, 1835, JM Papers, Historical Society of Pennsylvania; J. Story to R. Peters, May 20, 1835, W. W. Story, vol. II, p. 194.

15. Sallie E. Marshall Hardy, "John Marshall as Son, Brother, Husband and Friend," *The Green Bag*, Dec. 1896, pp. 481–82; J. Randolph letter, Mar. 25, 1836, *Southern Literary Messenger*, Apr. 1836, p. 318.

16. Kurland, pp. 125, 133, 136.

17. Thomas Marshall to E. C. Marshall, June 19, 1835, Thomas Marshall Folder, Misc. Mss. Collection, Box 31, Library of Congress; Hone, vol. I, p. 145; E. Anderson to J. P. Preston, July 9, 1835, Accession Item 26078, Virginia State Library.

18. The epitaph in JM's handwriting at Alderman Library, Reel M689, University of Virginia, property of Mrs. J. Jones Marshall, Farmville, Va.

Index

DATE DUE		
MAR 1 5 '95		